# RIGHTS AND CONSTITUTIONALISM

# RIGHTS AND CONSTITUTIONALISM

## THE NEW SOUTH AFRICAN LEGAL ORDER

*edited by*

**Dawid van Wyk**
**John Dugard**
**Bertus de Villiers**
**Dennis Davis**

CLARENDON PRESS · OXFORD

Oxford University Press, Walton Street, Oxford OX2 6DP
Oxford New York
Athens Auckland Bangkok Bogota Bombay
Buenos Aires Calcutta Cape Town Dar es Salaam
Delhi Florence Hong Kong Istanbul Karachi
Kuala Lumpur Madras Madrid Melbourne
Mexico City Nairobi Paris Singapore
Taipei Tokyo Toronto
and associated companies in
Berlin Ibadan

Oxford is a trade mark of Oxford University Press

Published in the United States
by Oxford University Press Inc., New York

© Juta & Company Limited 1995

Published by arrangement with Juta & Company Limited

P O Box 14373
Kenwyn
7790
Cape Town
Republic of South Africa

First published in hardback by Juta and Co, South Africa, 1994
Reprinted by Oxford University Press 1996

All rights reserved. No part of this publication may be reproduced,
stored in a retrieval system, or transmitted, in any form or by any means,
without the prior permission in writing of Oxford University Press.
Within the UK, exceptions are allowed in respect of any fair dealing for the
purpose of research or private study, or criticism or review, as permitted
under the Copyright, Designs and Patents Act, 1988, or in the case of
reprographic reproduction in accordance with the terms of the licences
issued by the Copyright Licensing Agency. Enquiries concerning
reproduction outside these terms and in other countries should be
sent to the Rights Department, Oxford University Press,
at the address above

British Library Cataloguing in Publication Data
Data available

Library of Congress Cataloging in Publication Data

ISBN 0-19-826225-6

Printed in Great Britain by
Biddles Ltd., Guildford and King's Lynn

# PREFACE

When this book was first planned towards the end of 1992 it was hoped that it would be published before the new South African Constitution came into effect. Unfortunately the academicians proved to be slower than the negotiators and this work will now be published after the first constitutional judgments have appeared in the Law Reports.

This book is not intended to be a detailed commentary on Chapter 3 of the South African Constitution. Its objective is to provide an introduction to the new legal order created by the Constitution by examining this order in a comparative and international context. Hence the title, *Rights and Constitutionalism: The New South African Legal Order*. In the preparation of the chapters the authors have drawn on the constitutional experience of other countries, such as Canada, India, Germany, and the United States, which greatly influenced the drafting of Chapter 3.

Although authors had the opportunity to revise their chapters after the Constitution was adopted, the work does not purport to be a detailed constitutional commentary. While it can be expected that much of the current text will find its way into the 'final' Constitution, which is to be drafted within two years, it was decided to concentrate on an analysis of the fundamental principles of the new order rather than describe the details of a transient order. These principles, which are bound to shape the 'final' Constitution, are the supremacy of the Constitution (as opposed to the supremacy of Parliament), the notion of a democratic constitutional state (a 'regstaat'), and the judicial protection of fundamental rights. A clear understanding of these concepts provides the key to the interpretation of the Constitution. Consequently it is the examination of these concepts which constitutes the major theme of the present study.

The work is divided into four parts. The first deals with constitutionalism, democracy, and constitutional interpretation. The theory of constitutional interpretation, which has become a subject of much academic and political controversy, is a prominent feature of this part.

The second part provides an examination of the historical background of the 1993 Constitution and a description of its principal features.

The third part, which contains an analysis of the key fundamental rights, constitutes the main focus of the study. Civil and political rights, social and economic rights, the concepts of equality and administrative justice, and the circumstances in which limitations may be imposed on rights are examined in an international and comparative setting. A separate chapter is devoted to the international protection of human rights as s 35(1) of the Constitution directs that regard should be had to this branch of law in the interpretation of Chapter 3.

The final part comprises a bibliography of the works cited in the text which follows the sequence of the chapters. This provides the reader with an easy reference guide to the most significant literature on each chapter. The full text of Chapter 3 is provided in an appendix for easy reference.

Several institutions contributed to the preparation of this book. The Centre for Applied Legal Studies at the University of the Witwatersrand, the Verloren van Themaat Centre for Public Law Studies (with gratefully acknowledged financial support from the Research and Bursary Fund of its home institution, the University of South Africa), and the Centre for Constitutional Analysis at the Human Sciences Research Council all assisted substantially and we are most grateful to them.

The publishers' patience was tested to the limit by our inability to meet deadlines. However, their enthusiasm for this work never faltered and their constant encouragement and assistance ensured that the project would be completed. The contributions of Richard Cooke and particularly Simon Sephton deserve mention. Lindsay Norman and the script editor, Rod Prodgers, excelled in their professional and expeditious editing and production of the work. The authors would also like to thank Oxford University Press for their assistance in bringing this book to an audience outside South Africa.

We wish also to thank the other contributors to the work, many of whom were drawn into the constitution-making process and consequently completed their chapters under difficult circumstances.

The text was delivered to the publishers at the end of May 1994. Every care had been taken to accommodate South African developments during the first months of 1994, but, given the pace of events of the first democratic election on 27 April 1994, this has not always been possible. It is hoped that this work will grow into a standard and regularly updated commentary on the South African Bill of Rights.

DAWID VAN WYK
JOHN DUGARD
BERTUS DE VILLIERS
DENNIS DAVIS

# CONTENTS

| Chapter | Page |
|---|---|
| Preface | v |
| List of Contributors | ix |
| Table of Cases | xi |
| Table of Statutes | xxvii |

## PART I

DEMOCRACY AND CONSTITUTIONALISM: THE ROLE OF CONSTITUTIONAL INTERPRETATION
Dennis Davis, Matthew Chaskalson & Johan de Waal . . . . . . . . . . 1

## PART II

INTRODUCTION TO THE SOUTH AFRICAN CONSTITUTION
Dawid van Wyk . . . . . . . . . . . . . . . . . 131

## PART III

INTERNATIONAL HUMAN RIGHTS
John Dugard . . . . . . . . . . . . . . . . . . 171

EQUALITY AND EQUAL PROTECTION
Dennis Davis . . . . . . . . . . . . . . . . . . 196

PERSONAL RIGHTS: LIFE, FREEDOM, AND SECURITY OF THE PERSON, PRIVACY, AND FREEDOM OF MOVEMENT
Lourens M du Plessis & Jacques de Ville . . . . . . . . . . . 212

FREEDOM OF EXPRESSION
Johann van der Westhuizen . . . . . . . . . . . . . 264

FREEDOM OF ASSEMBLY: VOTING WITH YOUR FEET
Stuart Woolman & Johan de Waal . . . . . . . . . . . . . 292

FREEDOM OF ASSOCIATION: THE RIGHT TO BE WE
Stuart Woolman & Johan de Waal . . . . . . . . . . . . . 338

ADMINISTRATIVE JUSTICE
Hugh Corder . . . . . . . . . . . . . . . . . . 387

PROCEDURAL RIGHTS
John Milton, Michael Cowling, Graham van der Leeuw, Mathew Francis, PJ Schwikkard & James Lund . . . . . . . . . . . 401

| Chapter | Page |
|---|---|
| CONSTITUTIONALIZATION OF LABOUR RIGHTS<br>Dennis Davis | 439 |
| PROPERTY RIGHTS, LAND RIGHTS, AND ENVIRONMENTAL RIGHTS<br>André van der Walt | 455 |
| FAMILY RIGHTS<br>June Sinclair | 502 |
| CULTURE, EDUCATION, AND RELIGION<br>Charles Dlamini | 573 |
| SOCIAL AND ECONOMIC RIGHTS<br>Bertus de Villiers | 599 |
| LIMITATION AND SUSPENSION<br>Gerhard Erasmus | 629 |

## PART IV

BIBLIOGRAPHY . . . . . . . . . . . . . . . . . . . . . 655

## APPENDIX

CHAPTER 3: FUNDAMENTAL RIGHTS . . . . . . . . . . . . . . . 695

INDEX . . . . . . . . . . . . . . . . . . . . . . . . . . . 701

# LIST OF CONTRIBUTORS

CHASKALSON, M — BA (Hons) LLB (Witwatersrand); Lecturer in Law, University of the Witwatersrand

CORDER, H M — BComm LLB (Cape Town) LLB (Cantab) DPhil (Oxon); Professor of Law and Head of the Department of Public Law, University of Cape Town

COWLING, M G — BA (Rhodes) LLB (Natal) LLM (Cantab); Associate Professor of Law, University of Natal, Pietermaritzburg

DAVIS, D M — BComm LLB (Cape Town) MPhil (Cantab); Director of the Centre for Applied Legal Studies and Professor of Law, University of the Witwatersrand

DE VILLE, J R — BComm LLB (PU vir CHO) LLD (Stell); Senior Lecturer in Law, University of the Western Cape

DE VILLIERS, B — BA LLD (RAU); Head of the Centre for Constitutional Analysis, Human Sciences Research Council, Pretoria

DE WAAL, J — BA LLB (Stell) LLM (Notre Dame); Lecturer in Law, University of the Witwatersrand

DLAMINI, C R M — BProc LLB LLM LLD (Zululand) LLD (Pret) LLD (UWC); Rector and Vice-Chancellor, University of Zululand

DUGARD, C J R — BA LLB (Stell) LLB Dip Int Law LLD (Cantab) Hon LLD (Natal); Professor of Law, University of the Witwatersrand

DU PLESSIS, L M — BIur et Comm BPhil LLD (PU vir CHO); Professor of Law, University of Stellenbosch

ERASMUS, M G — BIur LLB (UOVS) MA (Fletcher) LLD (Leyden); H F Oppenheimer Professor of Human Rights Law, University of Stellenbosch

FRANCIS, M — BA (Hons) (UWC) MA (Natal) LLB (Natal); Senior Lecturer in Law, University of Natal, Pietermaritzburg

LUND, J R — BA LLB (Natal); Professor of Law, University of Natal, Pietermaritzburg

MILTON, J R L — BA LLM PhD (Natal); James Scott Wylie Professor of Law, University of Natal, Pietermaritzburg; Fellow of the University of Natal

SINCLAIR, J D — BA LLB (Witwatersrand); Honorary Professor of Law; Vice-Principal and Deputy Vice-Chancellor, University of the Witwatersrand

SCHWIKKARD, P J — BA (Witwatersrand) LLM (Natal); Senior Lecturer in Law, University of Natal, Pietermaritzburg

VAN DER LEEUW, P G — BComm LLB (Natal) MLitt (Oxon) JD (William Mitchell); Sometime Senior Lecturer in Law, University of Natal, Pietermaritzburg

VAN DER WALT, A J — BIur (Hons) BA LLD (PU vir CHO) LLM (Witwatersrand); Professor of Law, University of South Africa

VAN DER WESTHUIZEN, J V — BA LLD (Pret); Professor of Law and Director of the Centre for Human Rights, University of Pretoria

VAN WYK, D H — BIur et Art (PU vir CHO) LLB (RAU) LLM LLD (Unisa); Professor of Law, University of South Africa

WOOLMAN, S — BA (Wesleyan) JD MA (Columbia); Lecturer in Law, University of the Witwatersrand

# TABLE OF CASES

## SOUTH AFRICA

| | |
|---|---|
| Achterberg v Glinister 1903 TS 326 | 190 |
| Adair Properties, Ex parte 1967 (2) SA 622 (R) | 190 |
| Administrator, Natal v Edouard 1990 (3) SA 581 (A) | 547 |
| Allen v Attorney-General 1936 CPD 302 | 411 |
| ANC (Border Branch) v Chairman, Council of State of Ciskei 1992 (4) SA 434 (Ck) | 194 |
| Archer v Archer 1989 (2) SA 885 (E) | 554 |
| Attorney-General, Namibia, Ex parte: In re Corporal Punishment by Organs of State 1991 (3) SA 76 (NmS) | 117, 193, 194, 195, 241, 433, 434, 435 |
| B v P 1991 (4) SA 113 (T) | 535, 536 |
| B v S 1993 (2) SA 211 (W) | 535, 536 |
| B v V (unreported) case 35144/91 | 535, 536 |
| Bamford v Minister of Community Development and State Auxiliary Services 1981 (3) SA 1054 (C) | 421 |
| Beaumont v Beaumont 1987 (1) SA 967 (A) | 554 |
| Beehari v Attorney-General, Natal 1956 (2) SA 59 (N) | 410 |
| Binga v Cabinet for South West Africa 1988 (3) SA 155 (A) | 190 |
| Boesak v Minister of Home Affairs 1987 (3) SA 665 (C) | 632 |
| Bongopi v Chairman of the Council of State, Ciskei 1992 (3) SA 250 (Ck) | 2 |
| Brandwagpers (Edms) Bpk v Raad van Beheer oor Publikasies 1975 (2) SA 32 (D) | 281 |
| Catholic Commission for Justice and Peace in Zimbabwe v Attorney-General & others 1993 (4) SA 239 (ZS) | 193, 195, 228 |
| Christian League of Southern Africa v Rall 1981 (2) SA 821 (O) | 526 |
| Chunilall v Attorney-General, Natal 1979 (1) SA 236 (D) | 410 |
| Claassens v Claassens 1981 (1) SA 360 (N) | 519, 554 |
| Claassens v Wilkens 1905 ORC 139 | 190 |
| Clarke v Hurst NO & others 1992 (4) SA 630 (D) | 232 |
| Coetzee v Coetzee 1991 (4) SA 702 (C) | 546 |
| Collins v Minister of the Interior 1957 (1) SA 552 (A) | 135 |
| Conjwayo v Minister of Justice, Legal and Parliamentary Affairs 1992 (2) SA 56 (ZS) | 436 |
| D v L 1990 (1) SA 894 (W) | 535 |
| Davids v The Master 1983 (1) SA 458 (C) | 569 |
| De Vos, Ex parte 1953 (2) SA 642 (SR) | 423 |
| Douglas v Mayers 1987 (1) SA 910 (Z) | 535 |
| Duncan v Minister of Law and Order 1984 (3) SA 460 (T) | 409 |
| Edouard v Administrator, Natal 1989 (2) SA 368 (D) | 547 |
| Edwards v Edwards 1960 (2) SA 523 (D) | 556 |
| F v B 1988 (3) SA 948 (D) | 535 |
| F v L 1987 (4) SA 525 (W) | 535 |
| G v Superintendent, Groote Schuur Hospital 1993 (2) SA 255 (C) | 231, 526, 530, 547 |
| Gillingham v Attorney-General 1909 TS 572 | 411 |
| Glazer v Glazer NO 1963 (4) SA 694 (A) | 570 |
| Goldberg v Minister of Prisons 1979 (1) SA 14 (A) | 438 |
| Government of the Republic of Bophuthatswana v Segale 1990 (1) SA 434 (BA) | 2, 122, 123, 125, 126 |
| Grasso v Grasso 1987 (1) SA 48 (C) | 519, 555 |
| Hajaree v Ismail 1905 TS 451 | 190 |
| Harris v Minister of the Interior 1952 (2) SA 428 (A) | 135 |
| Hassim v Officer Commanding, Prison Command, Robben Island 1973 (3) SA 462 (C) | 432, 435, 438 |
| Heimann v Heimann 1948 (4) SA 926 (W) | 556 |
| Human en Rousseau Uitgewers (Edms) Bpk v Snyman NO 1978 (3) SA 836 (T) | 286 |
| Hurter v Hough 1989 (3) SA 545 (C) | 423 |
| Inter-Science Research and Development Services (Pty) Ltd v Republica Popular de Mocambique 1980 (2) SA 111 (T) | 190 |

Ismail v Ismail 1983 (1) SA 1006 (A) . . . . . . . . . . . . . . . . . . . . . . . . . 562, 563, 568
J v O (unreported) case 1407/90 . . . . . . . . . . . . . . . . . . . . . . . . . . . . . . . . . 535
Jacobs en 'n ander v Waks en andere 1992 (1) SA 521 (A) . . . . . . . . . . . . . . . . . 421
K v G (unreported) case 10433/92 . . . . . . . . . . . . . . . . . . . . . . . . . . . . 535, 536
Kaffraria Property Co v Government of the Republic of Zambia 1980 (2) SA 709 (E) . . . . . . 190
Kastan v Kastan 1985 (3) SA 235 (C) . . . . . . . . . . . . . . . . . . . . . . . . . . . . . . 556
Katz v Katz 1989 (3) SA 1 (A) . . . . . . . . . . . . . . . . . . . . . . . . . . . . . . . . . 554
Kroon v Kroon 1986 (4) SA 616 (E) . . . . . . . . . . . . . . . . . . . . . . . . . . . . . . 555
Lewis v Minister of Internal Affairs 1991 (3) SA 628 (BA) . . . . . . . . . . . . . . . . . . . . 2
LSD Ltd v Vachell 1918 WLD 127 . . . . . . . . . . . . . . . . . . . . . . . . . . . . . . . 406
Mandela v Minister of Prisons 1983 (1) SA 938 (A) . . . . . . . . . . . . . . . . . . . . . . 435
Mathabathe v Mathabathe 1987 (3) SA 45 (W) . . . . . . . . . . . . . . . . . . . . . . . . 549
Maynard v The Field Cornet of Pretoria (1894) 1 SAR 214 . . . . . . . . . . . . . . . . . . 190
Metal and Allied Workers Union v Stobar Reinforcing (Pty) Ltd (1983) 4 *ILJ* 84 (IC) . . . . . 191
Milbourn v Milbourn 1987 (3) SA 62 (W) . . . . . . . . . . . . . . . . . . . . . . . . . . . 549
Minister of Defence, Namibia v Mwandinghi 1992 (2) SA 355 (NmS) . . . . . . . . . . . . . 194
Minister of Native Affairs, Ex parte: In re Molefe v Molefe 1946 AD 315 . . . . . . . . . . . 549
Minister of the Interior v Harris 1952 (4) SA 769 (A) . . . . . . . . . . . . . . . . . . . . . 135
Monnakale v Republic of Bophuthatswana 1991 (1) SA 598 (BA) . . . . . . . . . . . . . . . . 2
Nakani v Attorney-General 1989 (3) SA 655 (Ck) . . . . . . . . . . . . . . . . . . . . . . . 191
Natal Bottle Store-Keeping and Off-Sales Licensees' Association, Ex parte 1962 (4) SA 273 (D) 421
Natal Newspapers (Pty) Ltd v State President of the Republic of South Africa 1986 (4) SA 1109
   (N) . . . . . . . . . . . . . . . . . . . . . . . . . . . . . . . . . . . . . . . . . . . . . . 294
National Automobile and Allied Workers Union v Pretoria Precision Castings (Pty) Ltd (1985) 6
   *ILJ* (IC) . . . . . . . . . . . . . . . . . . . . . . . . . . . . . . . . . . . . . . . . . . 191
Ndlwana v Hofmeyr 1937 AD 229 . . . . . . . . . . . . . . . . . . . . . . . . . . . . . . . 135
Nduli v Minister of Justice 1978 (1) SA 893 (A) . . . . . . . . . . . . . . . . . . . . . . . . 190
Neethling v Du Preez & others; Neethling v The Weekly Mail & others 1991 (1) SA 708 (A) . . 288
Noll v Alberton Frames (Pty) Ltd 1989 (1) SA 730 (T) . . . . . . . . . . . . . . . . . . . . 421
Ntenteni v Chairman, Ciskei Council of State 1993 (4) SA 546 (Ck) . . . . . . . . . . . . . . 194
Nyamakazi v President of Bophuthatswana 1992 (4) SA 540 (B) . . . . . . . . . . . . . . . . 194
Pachourie v Additional Magistrate, Ladysmith, & another 1978 (3) SA 986 (N) . . . . . . . . . 412
Pakendorf v De Flamingh 1982 (3) SA 146 (A) . . . . . . . . . . . . . . . . . . . . . . . . 288
Pan American World Airways Incorporated v SA Fire and Accident Insurance Co Ltd 1965 (3) SA
   150 (A) . . . . . . . . . . . . . . . . . . . . . . . . . . . . . . . . . . . . . . . . . . . 190
Pasela v Rondalia Versekeringskorporasie van Suid-Afrika Bpk 1967 (1) SA 339 (W) . . . . . 569
Persad v Persad 1989 (4) SA 685 (D) . . . . . . . . . . . . . . . . . . . . . . . . . . . . . 553
Pommerel v Pommerel 1990 (1) SA 998 (E) . . . . . . . . . . . . . . . . . . . . . . . 519, 555
Publications Control Board v Gallo (Africa) Ltd 1975 (3) SA 665 (A) . . . . . . . . . . . . . 281
Publications Control Board v William Heinemann Ltd 1965 (4) SA 137 (A) . . . . . . . . . . 272
R v Barlin 1926 AD 459 . . . . . . . . . . . . . . . . . . . . . . . . . . . . . . . . . . . . 428
R v Britz 1949 (3) SA 292 (A) . . . . . . . . . . . . . . . . . . . . . . . . . . . . . . . . . 427
R v Camane 1925 AD 570 . . . . . . . . . . . . . . . . . . . . . . . . . . . . . . . . . . . 412
R v Lionda 1944 AD 348 . . . . . . . . . . . . . . . . . . . . . . . . . . . . . . . . . . . . 190
R v Maleleke 1925 TPD 491 . . . . . . . . . . . . . . . . . . . . . . . . . . . . . . . . . . 426
R v Rautenbach 1949 (1) SA 135 (A) . . . . . . . . . . . . . . . . . . . . . . . . . . . . . 432
R v Runyowa 1966 (2) SA 495 (PC) . . . . . . . . . . . . . . . . . . . . . . . . . . . 433, 434
R v Samhando 1943 AD 608 . . . . . . . . . . . . . . . . . . . . . . . . . . . . . . . . . . 429
R v Sisulu 1953 (3) SA 276 (A) . . . . . . . . . . . . . . . . . . . . . . . . . . . . . . . . 377
R v W 1949 (3) SA 772 (A) . . . . . . . . . . . . . . . . . . . . . . . . . . . . . . . . . . 432
R v Webb 1934 AD 493 . . . . . . . . . . . . . . . . . . . . . . . . . . . . . . . . . . . . 280
Rome, In re 1991 (3) SA 291 (A) . . . . . . . . . . . . . . . . . . . . . . . . . . . . . . . . 422
S v A Juvenile 1990 (4) SA 151 (ZS) . . . . . . . . . . . . . . . . . . . . . 193, 194, 241, 251, 435
S v Adams; S v Werner 1981 (1) SA 187 (A) . . . . . . . . . . . . . . . . . . . . . . . . . 190
S v Balhuber 1987 (1) PH H22 (A) . . . . . . . . . . . . . . . . . . . . . . . . . . . . . . 432
S v Budlender & another 1973 (1) SA 264 (C) . . . . . . . . . . . . . . . . . . . . . . . . . 294
S v Chabalala 1986 (3) SA 623 (BA) . . . . . . . . . . . . . . . . . . . . . . . . . 433, 434, 435
S v Colt 1992 (2) SACR 120 (E) . . . . . . . . . . . . . . . . . . . . . . . . . . . . . . . . 429
S v D 1992 (1) SACR (Nm) . . . . . . . . . . . . . . . . . . . . . . . . . . . . . . . . . . 425
S v Daniels 1991 (2) SACR 403 (C) . . . . . . . . . . . . . . . . . . . . . . . . . . . . 191, 652
S v Davids; S v Dladla 1989 (4) SA 172 (N) . . . . . . . . . . . . . . . . . . 191, 412, 414, 415
S v De Bellocq 1975 (3) SA 538 (T) . . . . . . . . . . . . . . . . . . . . . . . . . . . . . . 231
S v Eliasov 1967 (4) SA 583 (A) . . . . . . . . . . . . . . . . . . . . . . . . . . . . . . . . 192
S v F 1989 (3) SA 847 (A) . . . . . . . . . . . . . . . . . . . . . . . . . . . . . . . . . . . 432

# TABLE OF CASES

S v Giannoulis 1975 (4) SA 867 (A) . . . . . . . . . . . . . . . . . . . . . . . . . . . 433
S v Harber & another 1988 (3) SA 396 (A) . . . . . . . . . . . . . . . . . . . . . . 287
S v Hartman 1975 (3) SA 532 (C) . . . . . . . . . . . . . . . . . . . . . . . . . . . . 231
S v Holshausen 1983 (2) SA 699 (D) . . . . . . . . . . . . . . . . . . . . . . . . . 426
S v Jabavu 1969 (2) SA 466 (A) . . . . . . . . . . . . . . . . . . . . . . . . . . . . 432
S v Johardien 1990 (1) SA 1026 (C) . . . . . . . . . . . . . . . . . . . . . . . 570, 571
S v Jordaan 1992 (2) SACR 498 (A) . . . . . . . . . . . . . . . . . . . . . . . . . . 430
S v K 1983 (1) SA 65 (C) . . . . . . . . . . . . . . . . . . . . . . . . . . . . . . . . 282
S v Kantor 1972 (4) SA 683 (O) . . . . . . . . . . . . . . . . . . . . . . . . . . . . 434
S v Kaplan 1967 (1) SA 634 (T) . . . . . . . . . . . . . . . . . . . . . . . . . . . . 410
S v Khanyile 1988 (3) SA 795 (N) . . . . . . . . . . . . . . . . . . . . . . . . 191, 414
S v Khumalo 1992 (2) SACR 411 (N) . . . . . . . . . . . . . . . . . . . . . . 426, 429
S v Koopman 1991 (1) SA 474 (NC) . . . . . . . . . . . . . . . . . . . . . . . . . 422
S v Kumalo 1965 (4) SA 565 (N) . . . . . . . . . . . . . . . . . . . . . . . . . . . 434
S v M 1992 (2) SACR 188 (W) . . . . . . . . . . . . . . . . . . . . . . . . . . . . . 432
S v Machwili 1986 (1) SA 156 (N) . . . . . . . . . . . . . . . . . . . . . . . . . . 434
S v Magwaza 1985 (3) SA 29 (A) . . . . . . . . . . . . . . . . . . . . . . . . . . . 429
S v Maphalele 1982 (4) SA 505 (A) . . . . . . . . . . . . . . . . . . . . . . . . . . 426
S v Marx 1989 (1) SA 222 (A) . . . . . . . . . . . . . . . . . . . . . . . . . . . . . 433
S v Masia 1968 (1) SA 271 (T) . . . . . . . . . . . . . . . . . . . . . . . . . . . . . 434
S v Masondo 1969 (1) PH H58 (N) . . . . . . . . . . . . . . . . . . . . . . . . . . 434
S v Mbatha 1985 (2) SA 26 (D) . . . . . . . . . . . . . . . . . . . . . . . . . . . . 426
S v Minnies 1991 (3) SA 364 (Nm) . . . . . . . . . . . . . . . . . . . . . . . 240, 425
S v Mkhize 1978 (3) SA 1067 (T) . . . . . . . . . . . . . . . . . . . . . . . . . . . 412
S v Mohamed 1977 (2) SA 531 (A) . . . . . . . . . . . . . . . . . . . . . . . . . . 411
S v Motsoesoana 1986 (3) SA 350 (N) . . . . . . . . . . . . . . . . . . . . . 434, 435
S v Mthethwa; S v Khanyile 1978 (2) SA 773 (N) . . . . . . . . . . . . . . . . . 414
S v Mthwana 1989 (4) SA 361 (N) . . . . . . . . . . . . . . . . . . . . . . . . . . 191
S v Mushimba 1977 (2) SA 829 (A) . . . . . . . . . . . . . . . . . . . . . . . . . . 426
S v Ncube 1988 (2) SA 702 (ZS) . . . . . . . . . . . . . . . . 193, 194, 241, 251, 433, 434
S v Ndaba 1987 (1) SA 237 (T) . . . . . . . . . . . . . . . . . . . . . . . . . . . . 434
S v Nel 1987 (4) SA 950 (W) . . . . . . . . . . . . . . . . . . . . . . . . . . . . . 426
S v Nkoana 1985 (2) SA 395 (T) . . . . . . . . . . . . . . . . . . . . . . . . . . . 434
S v Penrose 1966 (1) SA 5 (N) . . . . . . . . . . . . . . . . . . . . . . . . . . . . . 190
S v Petane 1988 (3) SA 51 (C) . . . . . . . . . . . . . . . . . . . . . . . . 173, 190, 194
S v Peters 1992 (1) SACR 292 (E) . . . . . . . . . . . . . . . . . . . . . . . . . . . 428
S v Radebe; S v Mbonani 1988 (1) SA 191 (T) . . . . . . . . . . . . . . . . . 414, 415
S v Ramgobin 1986 (4) SA 117 (N) . . . . . . . . . . . . . . . . . . . . . . . . . . 426
S v Rudman 1989 (3) SA 368 (E) . . . . . . . . . . . . . . . . . . . . 173, 190, 191, 194
S v Rudman; S v Mthwana 1992 (1) SA 343 (A) . . . . . . . . . . . . . . . . 191, 414
S v Ruiters 1975 (3) SA 526 (C) . . . . . . . . . . . . . . . . . . . . . . . . . . . . 434
S v S 1993 (2) SA 200 (W) . . . . . . . . . . . . . . . . . . . . . . . . . . . . 535, 536
S v Sallem 1987 (4) SA 772 (A) . . . . . . . . . . . . . . . . . . . . . . . . . . . . 412
S v Sheehama 1991 (2) SA 860 (A) . . . . . . . . . . . . . . . . . . . . . . . . 426, 429
S v Staggie 1990 (1) SACR 669 (C) . . . . . . . . . . . . . . . . . . . . . . . . 191, 652
S v Tcoeib 1993 (1) SACR 274 (Nm) . . . . . . . . . . . . . . . . . . . . . . . 433, 435
S v Turrel 1973 (1) SA 248 (C) . . . . . . . . . . . . . . . . . . . . . . . . . . . . 294
S v V 1989 (1) SA 532 (A) . . . . . . . . . . . . . . . . . . . . . . . . . . . . . . . 434
S v Van Niekerk 1972 (3) SA 711 (A) . . . . . . . . . . . . . . . . . . . . . . . . 287
S v Vengetsamy 1972 (4) SA 351 (D) . . . . . . . . . . . . . . . . . . . . . . . . . 570
S v W 1975 (3) SA 841 (T) . . . . . . . . . . . . . . . . . . . . . . . . . . . . . . 282
S v Ward 1992 (1) SA 271 (B) . . . . . . . . . . . . . . . . . . . . . . . . . . . . . 422
S v Werner 1980 (2) SA 313 (W) . . . . . . . . . . . . . . . . . . . . . . . . . . . 190
S v Xaba 1983 (3) SA 717 (A) . . . . . . . . . . . . . . . . . . . . . . . . . . . . . 412
S v Yolelo 1981 (3) SA 1002 (A) . . . . . . . . . . . . . . . . . . . . . . . . . . . 428
Sachs v Dönges NO 1950 (2) SA 265 (A) . . . . . . . . . . . . . . . . . . . . . . 632
SANTAM Bpk v Fondo 1960 (2) SA 467 (A) . . . . . . . . . . . . . . . . . . . 569
Schlebusch v Schlebusch 1988 (4) SA 548 (E) . . . . . . . . . . . . . . . . . . . 556
Seedat's Executors v The Master (Natal) 1917 AD 302 . . . . . . . . . . . . . . 562
Shell SA (Edms) Bpk v Voorsitter Dorperaad van die Oranje Vrystaat 1992 (1) SA 906 (O) . . 426
Smith v Attorney-General, Bophuthatswana 1984 (1) SA 196 (B) . . . . . . . . . . . . . 411, 633
South African Defence and Aid Fund v Minister of Justice 1967 (1) SA 31 (C) . . . . . . . . . 377
South African Defence and Aid Fund v Minister of Justice 1967 (1) SA 263 (A) . . . . . . . . 377

South African Optometric Association v Frames Distributors (Pty) Ltd t/a Frames Unlimited 1985
   (3) SA 100 (O) .................................................. 421
South Atlantic Islands Development Corporation v Buchan 1971 (1) SA 234 (C) ........ 190
T v V (unreported) case 2840/91 ........................................ 535, 536
Transvaal Indian Congress v Land Tenure Advisory Board 1954 (2) SA 506 (T) ....... 421
Tregea v Godart 1939 AD 16 ............................................. 423
United African Motor and Allied Workers Union v Fodens SA (Pty) Ltd (1983) 4 *ILJ* 212 (IC) . 191
Van der Westhuizen NO v United Democratic Front 1989 (2) SA 242 (A) ............ 294
Van Erk v Holmer 1992 (2) SA 636 (W) ................................. 535, 536
W v S 1988 (1) SA 475 (N) .............................................. 535
Yorigami v Maritime Construction Co Ltd v Nissho-Iwai Co Ltd 1977 (4) SA 682 (C) ..... 190
Zimbabwe Township Developers (Pvt) Ltd v Lou's Shoes (Pvt) Ltd 1984 (2) SA 778 (ZS) ... 127


FOREIGN JURISDICTIONS

BOTSWANA
S v Petrus (1985) LRC (Const) 699 (Botswana CA) ..................... 433, 434
Unity Dow v A-G, Botswana Civil Appeal 4/91 ........................... 127

CANADA
Act to Amend the Education Act, Reference re an (1986) 25 DLR (4th) 1 ........... 589
AG of Canada v Dupond (1978) 2 SCR 770 ............................... 308
Alex Couture v Canada (1991) 83 DLR (4th) 577 ........................... 357
Andrews v Law Society of British Colombia (1989) 56 DLR (4th) 1   32, 33, 34, 129, 206, 207, 261
Assn of Professional Engineers of Saskatchewan v SGEU (1992) 91 DLR (4th) 694 ....... 357
Attorney-General of Canada v Lavell (1974) 38 DLR (3rd) 481 ............ 205, 206, 207
BCGEU v AG British Columbia (1985) 20 DLR (4th) 339 (BCCA) .................. 307
Binder v Canada (1985) 23 DLR (4th) 481 ................................ 209
Black v Law Society of Alberta (1989) 58 DLR (4th) 317 (SCC) 338 ............ 261, 262
Bliss v A-G, Canada (1979) 92 DLR (3rd) 417 ........................ 205, 206, 207
Borowski v Attorney General for Canada (1989) 1 SCR 342 ..................... 525
Broadway Manor Nursing Home (1984) 4 DLR (4th) 231 ....................... 441
Butler v R (1983) 5 CCC 356 (FCTD) ..................................... 307
Canadian Civil Liberties Association v Canada (1992) 91 DLR (4th) 38 ....... 307, 314, 357
Canadian Newspapers Co and Director of Public Road and Traffic Services of City of Quebec, Re
   (1986) 36 DLR (4th) 641 ............................................ 316
Canadian Newspapers Co v Montreal [1988] RJQ 482 ......................... 316
Canadian Newspapers Co v Victoria (1990) 63 DLR (4th) 1 .................... 316
Cheema v Ross (1991) 82 DLR (4th) 213 ................................... 357
Chiarelli v Minister of Employment & Immigration, Re (1992) 90 DLR (4th) 289 ......... 31
City of Edmonton v Orchard ('Forget (Re)') (1990) 74 DLR (4th) 547 ................ 315
Committee for the Commonwealth of Canada v Canada (1991) 77 DLR (4th) 385  ... 34, 308–9,
                                                                              310, 311, 313
Edwards Books and Art Ltd v R (1986) 2 SCR 713, (1987) 35 DLR (4th) 1 ........ 311, 643
Family Benefits Act, Reference re (Nova Scotia) (1986) 26 CRR 336 ................. 32
Fraser v AG, Nova Scotia (1986) 24 CRR 78 (NSSC) ........................... 307
French Language Rights of Accused, Reference re (Saskatchewan Criminal Proceedings) (1987) 44
   DLR (4th) 16 .................................................... 32
Germany and Rauca, Re (1983) 145 DLR (3rd) 638 (Ont CA) .................... 262
Hunter et al v The Southam Inc (1985) 11 DLR (4th) 641 ........... 122, 125, 126, 443, 633
Irwin Toy Ltd v Quebec (1989) 58 DLR (4th) 577 ........................ 309, 310
Jones v Ontario, Rheaume v Ontario (1992) 89 DLR (4th) 11 .................... 357
Kindler v Canada (CCPR/C/48/D/470/1991; view of 11 November 1993) ............ 195
Lavigne & OPSEU, Re (1985) 29 DLR (4th) 321 ............................. 442
Lavigne v OPSEU (1991) 81 DLR (4th) 545 ......................... 356, 357, 358
Law Society of Upper Canada v Skapinker (1984) 9 DLR (4th) 161 ....... 35, 260, 261, 262
Mahe v The Queen (1988) 42 DLR (4th) 514 ............................... 197
McKinney v University of Guelph (1991) 76 DLR (4th) 545 ................... 32, 206
Morgentaler v The Queen (1988) 44 DLR (4th) 385 (SCC) ...................... 231
Motor Vehicle Act, Reference re Section 94(2) of the, (1988) 24 DLR (4th) 536 .......... 31
New Brunswick Broadcasting Co v Radio, Television & Telecommunications Commission (1984)
   13 DLR (4th) 77 ................................................. 316

# TABLE OF CASES

Osborne v Canada (1991) 82 DLR (4th) 321 . . . . . . . . . . . . . . . . . . . . . . . . 357
PSAC v Canada (1987) 38 DLR (4th) 249 . . . . . . . . . . . . . . . . . . . . . . . . . 356
Public Service Employee Relations Act, Reference re (1985) 16 DLR (4th) 359 . . . . . . 442
Public Service Employee Relations Act, Reference re (1987) 1 SCR 313, 38 DLR (4th) 161
    193, 355, 356
R v Big M Drug Mart Ltd (1985) 18 DLR (4th) 321 . . . . . . . . . . 28, 30, 261, 291, 646, 649
R v Butler (1992) 89 DLR (4th) 449 (SCC) . . . . . . . . . . . . . . . . . . . . . . . 284
R v Chaulk (1990) 62 CCC (3d) 193 . . . . . . . . . . . . . . . . . . . . . . . . . . . 309
R v Collins (1937) 1 SCR 265 . . . . . . . . . . . . . . . . . . . . . . . . . . . . . . 404
R v Ertel (1987) 30 CRR 209 . . . . . . . . . . . . . . . . . . . . . . . . . . . . . . . 32
R v Jones (1984) 10 DLR (4th) 765 . . . . . . . . . . . . . . . . . . . . . . . . . . . 588
R v Keegstra (1990) 3 SCR 697, (1990) 61 CCC (3d) 1, (1991) 2 WWR 1 . 33, 277, 310, 311, 358
R v Morgentaler (1988) 1 SCR 30 . . . . . . . . . . . . . . . . . . . . . . . . . . . . 527
R v Oakes (1986) 26 DLR (4th) 200 . . . . . . . . . . 27, 28, 29, 30, 35, 262, 265, 309, 311, 633,
    642, 643, 646, 649
R v Ontario Labour Relations Board ex parte Trenton Construction Workers Association 1963
    DCR 593 . . . . . . . . . . . . . . . . . . . . . . . . . . . . . . . . . . . . . 596
R v Skead (1984) 4 CNLR 108 (Alta Prov Ct) . . . . . . . . . . . . . . . . . . . . . . 307
R v Turpin (1989) 39 CRR 306 . . . . . . . . . . . . . . . . . . . . . . . . . . . . 33, 35
Retail, Wholesale and Department Store Union v Dolphin Delivery Limited (1986) 33 DLR (4th)
    174 . . . . . . . . . . . . . . . . . . . . . . . . . . . . 269, 357, 442, 443, 450
Retail, Wholesale and Department Store Union v Saskatchewan (1985) 19 DLR (4th) 609 . . . 442
Saskatchewan v RWDSU (1987) 38 DLR (4th) 277 . . . . . . . . . . . . . . . . . . . . . 356
Schmidt v The Queen (1987) 39 DLR (4th) 18 (SCC) . . . . . . . . . . . . . . . . . . . 262
Southam Inc v Hunter (1984) 2 SCR 145 . . . . . . . . . . . . . . . . . . . . . . . . . 403
Thompson Newspapers Limited v Restrictive Trade Practices Commission (1990) 67 DLR (4th)
    161 . . . . . . . . . . . . . . . . . . . . . . . . . . . . . . . . . . . . . 28, 29
Thomson Newspapers v Canada (Director of Investigation and Research, Restrictive Practice
    Commission) (1990) 1 SCR 425 . . . . . . . . . . . . . . . . . . . . . . . . . 633
Tremblay v Daigle (1989) 2 SCR 530 . . . . . . . . . . . . . . . . . . . . . . . . . . 527
United Assn of Journeymen & Apprentices of Plumbing Industry of US and Canada, Local 740 and
    Pitts Atlantic Construction Ltd, Re (1984) 7 DLR (4th) 609 (Nfld CA) . . . . . . . 307
USA v Controni (1989) 48 CCC (3d) 193 . . . . . . . . . . . . . . . . . . . . . . . . 311

## ENGLAND

Blathwayt v Cawley (Baron) & others [1976] AC 397 (HL) . . . . . . . . . . . . . . . . . 191
Bradford Navigation Company, Re (1870) 5 Ch App 600 . . . . . . . . . . . . . . . . . . 55
C v S [1987] 1 All ER 1230 . . . . . . . . . . . . . . . . . . . . . . . . . . . . . . . 547
Council of Civil Service Unions v Minister for the Civil Service [1984] 3 All ER 935 (HL) . . . 632
Kuruma v R [1955] AC 197, [1955] 1 All ER 236 . . . . . . . . . . . . . . . . . . . 424, 426
Learie Collymore v AG [1970] AC 538 (PC) . . . . . . . . . . . . . . . . . . . . . . . 443
Minister of Home Affairs v Fisher [1980] AC 319 . . . . . . . . . . . . . . . . . 126, 174, 193
Paton v British Pregnancy Advisory Service Trustees [1979] 1 QB 276 . . . . . . . . . . . 547
Poyser v Minors (1881) 7 QBD 329 . . . . . . . . . . . . . . . . . . . . . . . . . . . 401
Pratt v Attorney-General for Jamaica [1993] 4 All ER 769 (PC) . . . . . . . . . . . . . . 195
R v Birmingham City Council: Ex parte Equal Opportunities Commission [1989] AC 1155 (HL) 209
R v Sang [1980] AC 402 (HL), [1979] 2 All ER 1222 . . . . . . . . . . . . . . . . . 424, 426
Salomon v Commissioner of Customs and Excise [1966] 3 All ER 871 (CA) . . . . . . . . . 190

## EUROPEAN COURT OF HUMAN RIGHTS

Barford Case 22/2/1989, Series A vol 14 . . . . . . . . . . . . . . . . . . . . . . . . 288
Belgian Linguistics Case (No 2), ECHR, Series A, vol 6, Judgment of 23 July 1968; (1968) EHRR
    252 . . . . . . . . . . . . . . . . . . . . . . . . . . . . . 130, 186, 584, 587
Campbell & Hartley v UK (1991) 12 EUHR 157 . . . . . . . . . . . . . . . . . . . . . . 130
Campbell and Cosans v United Kingdom (1982) 4 EHRR 293 . . . . . . . . . . . . . . . . 435
Cheall v UK [1983] 1 All ER 1130, (1986) 8 EHRR 74 . . . . . . . . . . . . . . . . . . . 448
Dorothea Vogt v Germany, 30/11/1993, Application No 17851/91 . . . . . . . . . . . . . 276
Dudgeon v UK, ECHR, Series A, vol 45, Judgment of 22 October 1981; (1982) 4 EHRR
    149 . . . . . . . . . . . . . . . . . . . . . . . . . . . . . . . . . . . 186, 202
Estrella v Uruguay 2 Selected Decisions HRC (1983) . . . . . . . . . . . . . . . . . . . 176
Ethiopia and Liberia v South Africa 1962 ICJ Rep 319, 1966 ICJ Rep 6 . . . . . . . . . . . 178
Golder Case, ECHR, Series A, vol 18, Judgment of 21 February 1975 . . . . . . . . . . . 186

Grandrath v Federal Republic of Germany Report of 29 June 1967, Yearbook of the European
Convention on Human Rights X (1967) 626 . . . . . . . . . . . . . . . . . . . . . . . . 595
Greek Case (Commission, 1969) . . . . . . . . . . . . . . . . . . . . . . . . . . . . . . . . . . 653
Gudmundsson v Iceland Appeal 511-59 Yearbook of the European Convention of Human Rights III
(1960) 394 . . . . . . . . . . . . . . . . . . . . . . . . . . . . . . . . . . . . . . . . . . . 201
Handyside v United Kingdom, European Commission of Human Rights (EUCM) 5493/72, 30 Sept
1975; ECHR, Series A, vol 24, 7/12/1976 . . . . . . . . . . . . . . . . . . . . . 265, 642
Informationsverein Lentia & others v Austria, 24/11/1993 . . . . . . . . . . . . . . . . . . . 290
Ireland v The United Kingdom, ECHR, Series A, vol 25, Judgment of 18 January 1978 . . . . . 186
Izquierdo v Uruguay 1 Selected Decisions HRC (1980) . . . . . . . . . . . . . . . . . . . . . 176
Johnston Series A 112 (1987) 26 . . . . . . . . . . . . . . . . . . . . . . . . . . . . . . . . 201
Kjeldsen & others v Denmark Series A, vol 23, Judgment of 7 December 1976 . . . . . . . . . 587
Klass v Federal Republic of Germany (5029/71) 2 EHRR 214 . . . . . . . . . . . . . . . . . 645
Lawless Case, ECHR, Series A, vol 3, Judgment of 1 July 1961 . . . . . . . . . . . . 186, 653
Lingers v Austria 8/7/1986, Series A vol 103, (1986) 8 EUHR 407 . . . . . . . . . . . 130, 288
Lovelace v Canada 2 Selected Decisions HRC (1981) . . . . . . . . . . . . . . . . . . . . . . 177
Müller & others, 24/5/1988, Series A vol 130 . . . . . . . . . . . . . . . . . . . . . . . . . 286
National Union of Belgium Police v Belgium (1975) 1 EHRR 578 . . . . . . . . . . . . . . . 448
Neumeister Case, ECHR, Series A, vol 7, Judgment of 27 June 1968 . . . . . . . . . . . . . 186
Nydahl v Sweden, 11/1/1993, Application No 17505/90 . . . . . . . . . . . . . . . . . . . 290
Oberschlick v Austria, 23/5/1991, Series A vol 20 . . . . . . . . . . . . . . . . . . . . . . 288
Otto-Preminger-Institut v Austria 14/1/1993, Application No 13470/87 . . . . . . . . . . . . 281
Paton v UK (1980) 3 EHRR 408 . . . . . . . . . . . . . . . . . . . . . . . . . . . . . . . . 547
Soering v United Kingdom, ECHR Series A, vol 161, Judgment of 7 July 1989 . . . . . . 187, 195
South West Africa Cases, Second Phase 1966 ICJ Reports 6 . . . . . . . . . . . . . . . . . . 173
Sunday Times v United Kingdom 6538/74, 2 EHRR 245; ECHR, Series A, vol 30, Judgment of 26
April 1979 . . . . . . . . . . . . . . . . . . . . . . . . . . . . . . . . . . . . . . 186, 643
Svenska Lokmannaforbunder v Sweden (1976) 1 EHRR 617 . . . . . . . . . . . . . . . . . 448
Tyrer v United Kingdom (1978) 2 EHRR 1; ECHR, Series A, vol 26, Judgment of 25 April 1978
186, 194, 433, 435
Van der Mussele Series A 70 (1983) 22 . . . . . . . . . . . . . . . . . . . . . . . . . . . . 201
Wemhoff Case, ECHR, Series A, vol 7, Judgment of 27 June 1968 . . . . . . . . . . . . . . 186
X v Austria Application 1753/63; Yearbook of the European Convention on Human Rights VIII
(1965) 174 . . . . . . . . . . . . . . . . . . . . . . . . . . . . . . . . . . . . . . . . 595
X v Germany (1985) 7 EHRR 461 . . . . . . . . . . . . . . . . . . . . . . . . . . . . . . . 448
X v United Kingdom Application 6886/75; Decisions and Reports of the European Commission of
Human Rights No 5 (1976) 100 . . . . . . . . . . . . . . . . . . . . . . . . . . . . . 595
X v United Kingdom Application 7992/77; Decisions and Reports of the European Commission of
Human Rights No 14 (1978) 234 . . . . . . . . . . . . . . . . . . . . . . . . . . . . 596
XSA v The Netherlands, 11/1/1994, Application No 21472/33 . . . . . . . . . . . . . . . . . 290
Young, James and Webster v UK (1982) 4 EHRR 38 . . . . . . . . . . . . . . . . . . 443, 448

## GERMANY

*Aufwertungs* case of 1925 . . . . . . . . . . . . . . . . . . . . . . . . . . . . . . . . . . . 112
1 *BVerfGE* 14 . . . . . . . . . . . . . . . . . . . . . . . . . . . . . 70, 71, 81, 85, 87, 72
1 *BVerfGE* 27 . . . . . . . . . . . . . . . . . . . . . . . . . . . . . . . . . . . . . . . . 246
1 *BVerfGE* 39 . . . . . . . . . . . . . . . . . . . . . . . . . . . . . . . . . . . . . . . . 230
1 *BVerfGE* 65 . . . . . . . . . . . . . . . . . . . . . . . . . . . . . . . . . . . . . . . . 246
1 *BVerfGE* 299 . . . . . . . . . . . . . . . . . . . . . . . . . . . . . . . . . . . . . . . 105
2 *BVerfGE* 1 . . . . . . . . . . . . . . . . . . . . . . . . . . . . 70, 109, 373, 374, 376
2 *BVerfGE* 124 . . . . . . . . . . . . . . . . . . . . . . . . . . . . . . . . . . . . . . . . 76
2 *BVerfGE* 151 . . . . . . . . . . . . . . . . . . . . . . . . . . . . . . . . . . . . . . . 259
2 *BVerfGE* 213 . . . . . . . . . . . . . . . . . . . . . . . . . . . . . . . . . . . . . . . 113
2 *BVerfGE* 266 . . . . . . . . . . . . . . . . . . . . . . . . . . . . . 84, 91, 116, 257, 258
2 *BVerfGE* 380 . . . . . . . . . . . . . . . . . . . . . . . . . . . . . . . . . . . . . . . . 80
3 *BVerfGE* 19 . . . . . . . . . . . . . . . . . . . . . . . . . . . . . . . . . . . . . . . . 372
3 *BVerfGE* 58 . . . . . . . . . . . . . . . . . . . . . . . . . . . . . . . . . . . . . . . . 116
3 *BVerfGE* 135 . . . . . . . . . . . . . . . . . . . . . . . . . . . . . . . . . . . . . . . 259
3 *BVerfGE* 225 . . . . . . . . . . . . . . . . . . . . . . . . . . . . . . . 70, 72, 83, 87, 91
3 *BVerfGE* 383 . . . . . . . . . . . . . . . . . . . . . . . . . . . . . . . . . . . . 363, 371
4 *BVerfGE* 7 . . . . . . . . . . . . . . . . . . . . . . . . . . . 84, 87, 124, 361, 363, 365, 366
4 *BVerfGE* 27 . . . . . . . . . . . . . . . . . . . . . . . . . . . . . . . . . . . . . . . . 373

# TABLE OF CASES

|  |  |
|---|---|
| 4 *BVerfGE* 31 | 80, 372 |
| 4 *BVerfGE* 115 | 114 |
| 4 *BVerfGE* 144 | 91, 116 |
| 4 *BVerfGE* 157 | 84, 99 |
| 4 *BVerfGE* 273 | 372 |
| 4 *BVerfGE* 375 | 371, 373 |
| 5 *BVerfGE* 77 | 372 |
| 5 *BVerfGE* 85 | 70, 75, 375, 376 |
| 6 *BVerfGE* 32 | 77, 87 |
| 6 *BVerfGE* 55 | 91 |
| 6 *BVerfGE* 84 | 373 |
| 6 *BVerfGE* 389 | 105 |
| 7 *BVerfGE* 99 | 372, 373 |
| 7 *BVerfGE* 198 | 78, 88, 89, 92, 108, 327 |
| 7 *BVerfGE* 377 | 116 |
| 7 *BVerwGE* 125 | 363 |
| 7 *BVerwGE* 297 | 472 |
| 8 *BVerfGE* 51 | 375 |
| 8 *BVerfGE* 104 | 72 |
| 8 *BVerfGE* 210 | 83, 91 |
| 8 *BVerfGE* 274 | 84, 87, 90, 114 |
| 9 *BVerfGE* 137 | 95 |
| 10 *BVerfGE* 59 | 87 |
| 10 *BVerfGE* 89 | 361, 363, 366 |
| 10 *BVerfGE* 354 | 361, 363, 366 |
| 11 *BVerfGE* 105 | 366 |
| 11 *BVerfGE* 126 | 105 |
| 12 *BVerfGE* 10 | 372 |
| 12 *BVerfGE* 45 | 120 |
| 12 *BVerfGE* 124 | 327 |
| 12 *BVerfGE* 140 | 258 |
| 12 *BVerfGE* 205 | 72, 102, 110, 114 |
| 12 *BVerfGE* 296 | 375 |
| 12 *BVerfGE* 319 | 361, 366 |
| 12 *BVerfGE* 341 | 90 |
| 13 *BVerfGE* 54 | 114 |
| 13 *BVerfGE* 123 | 375 |
| 13 *BVerfGE* 155 | 375 |
| 13 *BVerfGE* 174 | 364 |
| 13 *BVerfGE* 181 | 113 |
| 13 *BVerfGE* 248 | 82 |
| 13 *BVerfGE* 290 | 90 |
| 14 *BVerfGE* 21 | 99 |
| 14 *BVerfGE* 121 | 372 |
| 14 *BVerfGE* 263 | 361, 365 |
| 14 *BVerfGE* 288 | 469, 472 |
| 15 *BVerfGE* 235 | 361 |
| 15 *BVerfGE* 337 | 83 |
| 15 *BVerwGE* 3 | 472 |
| 16 *BVerfGE* 130 | 82, 83 |
| 16 *BVerfGE* 147 | 364 |
| 16 *BVerfGE* 194 | 95 |
| 17 *BVerfGE* 280 | 83, 91 |
| 18 *BVerfGE* 288 | 82 |
| 18 *BVerfGE* 315 | 116 |
| 19 *BVerfGE* 342 | 108, 109 |
| 19 *BVerfGE* 377 | 81 |
| 20 *BVerfGE* 56 | 80, 83 |
| 20 *BVerfGE* 56 | 119 |
| 20 *BVerfGE* 56 | 372, 374 |
| 20 *BVerfGE* 150 | 316 |
| 20 *BVerfGE* 162 | 103, 327 |
| 20 *BVerfGE* 290 | 363 |
| 21 *BVerfGE* 12 | 82 |

| Case | Page |
|---|---|
| 21 *BVerfGE* 73 | 472 |
| 21 *BVerfGE* 329 | 82 |
| 21 *BVerfGE* 362 | 291, 363 |
| 22 *BVerfGE* 349 | 82 |
| 23 *BVerfGE* 98 | 72 |
| 23 *BVerfGE* 242 | 82 |
| 23 *BVerfGE* 353 | 363 |
| 24 *BVerfGE* 260 | 371 |
| 24 *BVerfGE* 299 | 374 |
| 24 *BVerfGE* 300 | 83, 374, 375 |
| 24 *BVerfGE* 367 | 90, 472 |
| 25 *BVerfGE* 1 | 116 |
| 25 *BVerfGE* 101 | 91, 116 |
| 25 *BVerfGE* 112 | 471 |
| 25 *BVerfGE* 167 | 83, 91 |
| 25 *BVerfGE* 198 | 363 |
| 25 *BVerfGE* 256 | 103 |
| 25 *BVerwGE* 272 | 363 |
| 26 *BVerfGE* 228 | 363 |
| 27 *BVerfGE* 12 | 246 |
| 27 *BVerfGE* 253 | 94 |
| 27 *BVerwGE* 228 | 361, 363, 366 |
| 28 *BVerfGE* 243 | 97, 323 |
| 30 *BVerfGE* 1 | 70, 249 |
| 30 *BVerfGE* 173 | 89, 323 |
| 30 *BVerfGE* 227 | 363, 364 |
| 30 *BVerfGE* 292 | 469 |
| 31 *BVerfGE* 58 | 90 |
| 31 *BVerfGE* 229 | 90, 472 |
| 31 *BVerfGE* 297 | 366 |
| 31 *BVerfGE* 315 | 102 |
| 31 *BVerwGE* 368 | 373 |
| 32 *BVerfGE* 54 | 250, 251 |
| 32 *BVerfGE* 98 | 323 |
| 32 *BVerfGE* 145 | 84 |
| 32 *BVerfGE* 288 | 78 |
| 32 *BVerfGE* 373 | 246 |
| 32 *BVerwGE* 308 | 361, 366 |
| 33 *BVerfGE* 1 | 98 |
| 33 *BVerfGE* 52 | 84 |
| 33 *BVerfGE* 303 | 83, 87, 100 |
| 34 *BVerfGE* 9 | 113 |
| 34 *BVerfGE* 160 | 119 |
| 34 *BVerfGE* 238 | 246 |
| 34 *BVerfGE* 269 | 85, 91, 247 |
| 35 *BVerfGE* 79 | 83, 103, 120 |
| 35 *BVerfGE* 202 | 82, 246 |
| 35 *BVerfGE* 257 | 99 |
| 35 *BVerfGE* 263 | 105, 363 |
| 36 *BVerfGE* 1 | 80, 81, 85, 99, 112, 116 |
| 36 *BVerfGE* 193 | 113 |
| 36 *BVerfGE* 281 | 472 |
| 36 *BVerfGE* 314 | 113 |
| 36 *BVerfGE* 342 | 99 |
| 37 *BVerfGE* 132 | 72, 472 |
| 37 *BVerfGE* 363 | 114 |
| 37 *BVerwGE* 344 | 368 |
| 38 *BVerfGE* 281 | 361, 366, 367 |
| 38 *BVerfGE* 348 | 72 |
| 39 *BVerfGE* 1 | 72, 83, 96, 97, 116, 120, 123, 247, 529 |
| 39 *BVerfGE* 169 | 83 |
| 39 *BVerfGE* 210 | 116 |
| 39 *BVerfGE* 302 | 363 |
| 39 *BVerfGE* 334 | 325, 375 |

| Case | Page |
|---|---|
| 39 *BVerwGE* 100 | 366 |
| 40 *BVerfGE* 88 | 84 |
| 40 *BVerfGE* 287 | 375 |
| 40 *BVerfGE* 296 | 83, 85 |
| 41 *BVerfGE* 29 | 106 |
| 41 *BVerfGE* 251 | 95 |
| 41 *BVerfGE* 291 | 105 |
| 41 *BVerfGE* 399 | 372, 374 |
| 42 *BVerfGE* 20 | 77 |
| 42 *BVerfGE* 64 | 472 |
| 42 *BVerfGE* 143 | 327 |
| 42 *BVerfGE* 212 | 259 |
| 42 *BVerfGE* 263 | 472 |
| 43 *BVerfGE* 142 | 119 |
| 43 *BVerfGE* 203 | 257 |
| 44 *BVerfGE* 125 | 119 |
| 45 *BVerfGE* 63 | 363 |
| 45 *BVerfGE* 187 | 96, 116 |
| 46 *BVerfGE* 160 | 96 |
| 47 *BVerfGE* 31 | 250 |
| 47 *BVerfGE* 130 | 375 |
| 47 *BVerfGE* 198 | 80, 119, 371, 372, 375 |
| 47 *BVerfGE* 253 | 119 |
| 47 *BVerfGE* 327 | 323 |
| 48 *BVerfGE* 127 | 83 |
| 48 *BVerfGE* 271 | 372 |
| 49 *BVerfGE* 89 | 87, 88, 89, 97 |
| 49 *BVerfGE* 286 | 246 |
| 50 *BVerfGE* 290 | 87, 93, 94, 97, 102, 116, 120, 360, 361, 363, 364, 365, 366, 469 |
| 50 *BVerfGE* 290 | 79, 97, 102, 110 |
| 51 *BVerfGE* 97 | 250 |
| 52 *BVerfGE* 1 | 76, 82, 469, 471 |
| 52 *BVerfGE* 63 | 83, 372, 375 |
| 53 *BVerfGE* 30 | 96, 97, 103 |
| 53 *BVerfGE* 257 | 469 |
| 54 *BVerfGE* 11 | 82 |
| 54 *BVerfGE* 148 | 247 |
| 54 *BVerfGE* 277 | 84 |
| 54 *BVerwGE* 211 | 364 |
| 55 *BVerfGE* 100 | 81 |
| 55 *BVerwGE* 175 | 368, 369 |
| 56 *BVerfGE* 54 | 97, 116 |
| 56 *BVerfGE* 90 | 77 |
| 56 *BVerfGE* 254 | 257 |
| 56 *BVerwGE* 63 | 317 |
| 57 *BVerfGE* 29 | 325 |
| 57 *BVerfGE* 295 | 102 |
| 58 *BVerfGE* 26 | 367 |
| 58 *BVerfGE* 300 | 94, 469 |
| 59 *BVerfGE* 95 | 250 |
| 60 *BVerfGE* 234 | 327 |
| 60 *BVerfGE* 360 | 77 |
| 61 *BVerfGE* 68 | 89 |
| 61 *BVerfGE* 82 | 363 |
| 61 *BVerfGE* 149 | 82 |
| 61 *BVerwGE* 218 | 368 |
| 62 *BVerfGE* 1 | 71, 81, 84, 105 |
| 62 *BVerfGE* 230 | 327 |
| 62 *BVerfGE* 338 | 89 |
| 65 *BVerfGE* 1 | 77, 82, 83, 90, 247, 251, 325 |
| 65 *BVerfGE* 182 | 94 |
| 65 *BVerfGE* 196 | 90 |
| 66 *BVerfGE* 100 | 82 |
| 67 *BVerfGE* 26 | 76 |

| | |
|---|---|
| 67 *BVerfGE* 157 | 250 |
| 67 *BVerfGE* 213 | 89 |
| 68 *BVerfGE* 1 | 75 |
| 68 *BVerfGE* 155 | 81 |
| 68 *BVerfGE* 193 | 363 |
| 69 *BVerfGE* 92 | 83, 375 |
| 69 *BVerfGE* 112 | 81 |
| 69 *BVerfGE* 315 | 317, 318, 319, 320, 321, 322, 323, 324 |
| 70 *BVerfGE* 35 | 80 |
| 70 *BVerfGE* 297 | 89 |
| 71 *BVerfGE* 162 | 89 |
| 71 *BVerfGE* 224 | 85 |
| 72 *BVerfGE* 200 | 258 |
| 72 *BVerfGE* 330 | 82 |
| 73 *BVerfGE* 1 | 83, 374 |
| 73 *BVerfGE* 40 | 82, 83, 375 |
| 73 *BVerfGE* 118 | 83, 102 |
| 73 *BVerfGE* 206 | 321, 322 |
| 74 *BVerfGE* 297 | 102 |
| 75 *BVerfGE* 40 | 101 |
| 75 *BVerfGE* 318 | 250 |
| 76 *BVerfGE* 1 | 116 |
| 76 *BVerfGE* 143 | 89 |
| 77 *BVerfGE* 84 | 81, 83 |
| 77 *BVerfGE* 84 | 112 |
| 77 *BVerfGE* 103 | 83 |
| 77 *BVerfGE* 170 | 83, 97 |
| 79 *BVerfGE* 174 | 83 |
| 79 *BVerfGE* 311 | 83 |
| 83 *BVerfGE* 238 | 102 |
| 111 *RGZ* 320 322 | 67 |
| 1970 *Juristenzeitung* 283 | 320, 325 |
| 1982 *NJW* 1008 | 324 |
| *BGH* 1954 *NJW* 834 | 365 |
| *BGH* 1958 *NJW* 1867 | 365 |
| *BGH* 1969 *NJW* 1770 | 322 |
| *BGH* 1972 *NJW* 1414 | 259 |
| *BGH* 1982 *NJW* 189 | 322 |
| *BGH* 1988 *NJW* 3201 | 472 |
| *BVerfG* 1979 *NJW* 706 | 364 |
| *BVerfG* 1981 *JZ* 828 | 471 |
| *BVerfG* 1990 *NJW* 3002 | 373 |
| *BVerfG* 1992 *DVBl* 149 | 324 |
| *BVerwG* 1954 *NJW* 1947 | 369 |
| *BVerwG* 1962 *NJW* 1311 | 361, 366 |
| *BVerwG* 1977 *NJW* 945 | 472 |
| *BVerwG* 1981 *NJW* 2137 | 472 |
| *BVerwG* 1982 *NJW* 1008 | 324 |
| *BVerwG* 1986 *NJW* 738 | 320 |
| *BVerwG* 1987 *NJW* 82 | 325 |
| *BVerwG* 1989 *NJW* 2411 | 317 |
| *BVerwG* 1990 *NJW* 135 | 373 |
| *OLG Hamburg Beschl* 1952 *NJW* 943 | 367 |
| *OLG Stuttgart* 1955 *NJW* 833 | 365 |

## INDIA

| | |
|---|---|
| ABSK Sangh (Railway) v Union of India AIR 1981 SC 298 | 47, 58 |
| Addl Distt Magistrate, Jabalpur v Shivkant Shukla AIR 1976 SC 1206 | 40, 45 |
| Ahmedabad St Xavier College Society & others v State of Gujarat AIR 1974 SC 1389 | 577 |
| Ajay Hasia v Khalid Mujib AIR 1981 SC 487 | 204 |
| Akar v Attorney General (1966–67) ALR (SL) 283 | 41 |
| All India Bank Employees' Association v National Industrial Tribunal AIR 1962 SC 171 | 444 |
| Anwar Hossain Chowdhury v Bangladesh [1989] BLD (spl) 1 | 41 |
| Bandhua Mukti Morcha v Union of India AIR 1984 SC 802 | 52, 53, 55 |

## TABLE OF CASES

Bhalchandra Dharmajee Makaji v Alcock Ashdown and Co Ltd (1972) 42 Comp Cas 190 .... 54
Chandra Bhawan Boarding and Lodging Bangalore v The State of Mysore AIR 1970 SC 2042   620
Chetty, R D v International Airport Authority of India 1979 (3) SCC 489 ............. 52
Chhara v Sardarnagar Municipality AIR 1986 Guj 49 ............................ 50
Citizens' Action Committee, Nagpur v Civil Surgeon, Mayo Hospital, Nagpur, & others AIR 1986
    Bom 136 ................................................................ 50
Cooper v Union of India ('Bank Nationalization' case) AIR 1970 SC 564 ......... 38, 39
DAV College Bhatinda v State of Punjab AIR 1971 SC 1731 ..................... 577
Federation of AIC and CE Stenographers v Union of India AIR 1988 SC 1291 ......... 621
Francis Coralie Mullin v Union Territory of Delhi AIR 1981 SC 746 ......... 46, 49, 204
Golak Nath v State of Punjab AIR 1967 SC 1643 ..................... 37, 38, 39, 42
Gupta, S P v Union of India AIR 1982 SC 149 ........................... 44, 46, 55
Hoskot, M O v State of Maharashtra 1979 (1) SCR 192 .......................... 46
Hussainara Khatoon v State of Bihar AIR 1979 SC 1361 .................. 46, 48, 49
Indian Express Newspapers (Bombay) Private Ltd v Union of India AIR 1986 SC 515 ...... 63
Indira Gandhi v Raj Narain AIR 1975 SC 2299 ............................... 40, 44
Kameshwar Singh v Province of Bihar AIR 1950 Pat 392 .......................... 37
Kerala Education Bill, In re AIR 1959 SC 995 ................................ 619
Kesavananda v State of Kerala AIR 1973 SC 1461 ............ 36, 39, 40, 41–5, 47, 58
Kishen v State of Orissa AIR 1989 SC 677 .................................. 50, 60
Krishnaswami v State of Madras AIR 1964 SC 1515 ............................. 37
Kunhikoman v State of Kerala AIR 1962 SC 723 ................................ 37
Madras v Champakam Dorairajan AIR 1951 SC 226 ............................ 619
Maneka Ghandi v Union of India AIR 1978 SC 597, (1978) 1 SCC 248 ........... 46, 620
Mehta, M C v Union of India AIR 1987 SC 965 .............................. 50, 54
Mehta, M C v Union of India AIR 1987 SC 982 ................................ 58
Mehta, M C v Union of India AIR 1987 SC 1086 ................................ 51
Minerva Mills Ltd v Union of India AIR 1980 SC 1843 ........................ 618, 620
Minerva Mills v Union of India AIR 1980 SC 1789 ............................ 44, 48
Mukesh Advani v State of Madya Pradesh AIR 1985 SC 1368 ...................... 56
Nalla Thampy, Dr P v Union of India AIR 1984 SC 74, 1983 (4) SCC 598 ......... 50, 60
National Textile Workers' Union v Ramakrishnan AIR 1983 SC 75 ........ 54, 450, 451, 621
Pandey v State of West Benghal [1988] LRC (Const) 241 (SC) ............. 51, 59, 61
People's Union for Democratic Rights v Union of India AIR 1982 SC 1473 ..... 46, 47, 51, 52,
                                                                           53, 54, 55, 57, 59
Pradeep Jain v Union 1984 AIR SC 1420 ..................................... 204
Quareshi, M H v State of Bihar AIR 1958 SC 731 .............................. 619
Ramana v International Airport Authority of India AIR 1979 SC 1628 ............. 46
Reserve Bank Employers Association v Reserve Bank (1966) 1 SCR 25 ............. 621
Rev Father W Proost v State of Bihar AIR 1969 SC 465 ......................... 577
Royappa, E P v State of Tamil Nadu 1974 AIR SC 555 .......................... 204
Rural Land and Entitlement Kendra, Dehradun v State of Uttar Pradesh AIR 1985 SC 652 50, 54, 58
Sajjan Singh v State of Rajasthan AIR 1965 SC 845 ............................ 620
Sanjiev Coke Mfg Co v M/S Bharat Coking Coal Ltd AIR 1983 SC 239 ............. 620
Sanjit Roy v State of Rajastan AIR 1983 SC 328 ............................... 52
Sharma, M K v Bharat Electronics Ltd AIR 1987 SC 1792 ........................ 51
Sheela Barse v State of Maharashtra AIR 1983 SC 378 .......................... 57
Sheela Barse v Union of India AIR 1983 SC 378 ............................... 49
Som Prakash Rekhi v Union of India 1981 (1) SCC 448 .......................... 52
Sonia Bhalai v State of Andra Pradesh AIR 1981 SC 1274 ....................... 621
State of Bihar v Kameshwar Singh AIR 1952 SC 252 ......................... 37, 619
State of Bombay v Bombay Education Society & others AIR 1954 SC 561 ............ 577
State of Gujarat v Ambica Mills Limited 1974 AIR SC 1300 ...................... 203
State of Himachal Pradesh & another v Umed Ram Sharma & others AIR 1986 SC 847 .... 221
State of Himachal Pradesh v Sharma 1986 (2) SCC 68 ....................... 49, 58, 60
State of Kerala v Thomas AIR 1976 SC 516 .................................. 619
State of Tamil Nadu v Abu Kavier Bai AIR 1984 SC 725 ..................... 474, 620
State of West Bengal v Bela Bannerjee AIR 1954 SC 170 ........................ 38
Suk Das v Union Territory of Arunchal Pradesh 1986 (4) SCC 401 ................ 49
Surinder Singh v The Engineer in Chief, Central Public Works Dept AIR 1986 SC 584 ..... 51
Tellis & others v Bombay Municipal Corporation & others; Kuppusami & others v State of
    Maharashta & others AIR 1987 LRC 351 .......................... 50, 60, 221, 621
Uppendra Baxi v State of Uttar Pradesh 1986 (4) SCC 106 ............. 49, 57, 58, 59

UPSE Board v Hari Shankar (1979) ASC 69 . . . . . . . . . . . . . . . . . . . . . . . 621
Vajravelu v Special Deputy Collector AIR 1965 SC 1017 . . . . . . . . . . . . . . 38

## IRELAND

Buckley v Attorney General IR (1950) 57 . . . . . . . . . . . . . . . . . . . . . . . 616
Byrne v Ireland IR (1972) 241 . . . . . . . . . . . . . . . . . . . . . . . . . . . . . 617
Comyn v Attorney General IR (1950) 142 . . . . . . . . . . . . . . . . . . . . . . . 616
Landers v Attorney General IR (1982) 109 . . . . . . . . . . . . . . . . . . . . . . 617
Murtagh Properties v Cleary IR (1972) 330 . . . . . . . . . . . . . . . . . . . 612, 617
O'Brien v Manufacturing Engineering Co Ltd IR (1973) 334 . . . . . . . . . . . 617
Ryan v Attorney General IR (1965) 294 . . . . . . . . . . . . . . . . . . . . . . . 617
Somjee v Minister of Justice IR (1982) 142 . . . . . . . . . . . . . . . . . . . . . 616

## UNITED STATES OF AMERICA

A & M, In re 61 AD 2d 426, 403 NYS 2d 375 (1978) . . . . . . . . . . . . . . . . 430
Abington School District v Schempp 374 US 203 (1960) . . . . . . . . . . . . . 595
Abood v Detroit Board of Education 431 US 209 (1977) . . . . . . . 344, 357, 441, 442
Abrams v US 250 US 616 (1919) . . . . . . . . . . . . . . . . . . . . . 268, 279, 280
Adair v United States 208 US 161 (1908) . . . . . . . . . . . . . . . . . . . . . . 440
Adderly v Florida 385 US 39 (1966) . . . . . . . . . . . . . . . . . . . . . . 303–4, 305
Adkins v Children' Hospital 261 US 525 (1923) . . . . . . . . . . . . . . . . . . . 440
Allied Structural Steel Co v Spannus 438 US 234 (1978) . . . . . . . . . . . . . . . 8
Amalgamated Food Employers v Logan Valley 391 US 308 (1968) . . . . . . . 306, 307
American Booksellers Assoc Inc v Hudnut 771 F 2nd 323 (7th Cir 1985), 475 US 1001 (1986) . 284
Aptheker v Secretary of State 378 US 500, 84 SCt 1659, 12 LEd 2d 992 . . . . . . . . 256
Arnett v Kennedy 416 US 134 (1974) . . . . . . . . . . . . . . . . . . . . . . . . 330
Bates v Little Rock 361 US 516 (1960) . . . . . . . . . . . . . . . . . . . . . . . 343
Bell v Wolfish 441 US 520, 545, 60 LEd 2d 447 (1979) . . . . . . . . . . . . . 435, 436
Bethel School District v Fraser 478 US 675 (1986) . . . . . . . . . . . . . . . . . 304
Bigelow v Virginia 421 US 809, 44 LEd 2d 600, 95 SCt 2222 . . . . . . . . . . . . 256
Board of Directors of Rotary International v Rotary Club of Duarte 481 US 537 (1987)
 . . . . . . . . . . . . . . . . . . . . . . . . . . . . . . . . . . . . . . 344, 346, 350
Boling v Sharpe 347 US 497 (1954) . . . . . . . . . . . . . . . . . . . . . . . . . 202
Boos v Barry 485 US 312 (1988) . . . . . . . . . . . . . . . . . . . . . . . . . . 301
Bowers v Hardwick 478 US 186, 92 LEd 2d 140, 106 SCt 2481 (1986) . . . . . 10, 125, 203, 243,
 244, 253, 348, 349
Boyle v United Technical Corporation 487 US 500 (1988) . . . . . . . . . . . . . . 25
Brandenburg v Ohio 395 US 444 (1969) . . . . . . . . . . . . . . . . . 275, 277, 280, 346
Breard v City of Alexandria 341 US 622 (1951) . . . . . . . . . . . . . . . . . . . 306
Bridges v California 314 US 252 (1941) . . . . . . . . . . . . . . . . . . . . . 271, 287
Brinegar v US 338 US 160 (1949) . . . . . . . . . . . . . . . . . . . . . . . . . . 403
Brotherhood of Railroad Trainmen v Virginia 377 US 1 (1964) . . . . . . . . . . . . 343
Brown v Board of Education of Topeka 347 US 483 (1954) . . . 9, 10, 18, 25, 581, 585, 586, 587
Brown v Louisiana 383 US 131 (1966) . . . . . . . . . . . . . . . . . . . . . . 302, 305
Brown v The Board of Education 349 US 294 (1954) . . . . . . . . . . . . . . . . . 83
Caban v Mohammed 441 US 380 (1979) . . . . . . . . . . . . . . . . . . . . . . 539
Califano v Aznavorian 439 US 170 (1978) . . . . . . . . . . . . . . . . . . . . . 257
Carey v Population Services International 431 US 678 (1977) . . . . . . . . . . 348, 350
CBS v Democratic National Committee 412 US 94 (1973) . . . . . . . . . . . . 289, 307
CBS, Inc v FCC 453 US 367 (1981) . . . . . . . . . . . . . . . . . . . . . . . . . 307
Central Hudson Gas v Public Service Commission 447 US 557 (1980) . . . . . . . . 290
Chaplinsky v New Hampshire 315 US 568 (1942) . . . . . . . . . . . . . . . . 275, 284
Chapman v California 386 US 18 (1967) . . . . . . . . . . . . . . . . . . . . . . . 23
Chicago Police Department v Mosely 408 US 92 (1972) . . . . . . . . . . . . . . 301
Chicago Teachers Union v Hudson 475 US 292 (1986) . . . . . . . . . . . . . . . 357
Chimento v Stark 414 US 802, 94 SCt 125, 38 LEd 2d 39 . . . . . . . . . . . . . . 256
Citizens Against Rent Control v Berkley 454 US 290 (1981) . . . . . . . . . . . 346, 441
City of Dallas v Stangelin 490 US 19 (1989) . . . . . . . . . . . . . . . . . . . . . 346
City of Richmond v J A Croson 488 US 469 (1989) . . . . . . . . . . . . . . . . . 6, 8
Clark v Community for Creative Non-Violence 468 US 288 (1984) . . . . . . . . 264, 301
Coates v City of Cincinnati 402 US 611 (1971) . . . . . . . . . . . . . . . . . . 302, 353
Coker v Georgia 433 US 584, 53 LEd 2d 982 (1977) . . . . . . . . . . . . . . . 433, 434
Collin v Smith 447 F Supp 676 (ND Ill 1978), 578 F 2d 1197 (7th Cir 1978) . . . . . . . 302, 346

# TABLE OF CASES xxiii

Communications Workers of America v Beck 487 US 735 (1988) . . . . . . . . . . . . . . . . 357
Connally v General Construction 269 US 385 (1926) . . . . . . . . . . . . . . . . . . . . . . . 330
Coppage v Kansas 236 US 1 (1914) . . . . . . . . . . . . . . . . . . . . . . . . . . . . . . . . . 467
Cousins v Wigoda 419 US 477 (1975) . . . . . . . . . . . . . . . . . . . . . . . . . . . . . . . 347
Cox v Louisiana 379 US 536 (1965) . . . . . . . . . . . . . . . . . . . . . . . . . . . . . . . . 303
Cox v Louisiana (Cox I) 379 US 536 (1965) . . . . . . . . . . . . . . . . . . . . . . . . . . . 275
Craig v Harvey 331 US 367 (1947) . . . . . . . . . . . . . . . . . . . . . . . . . . . . . . . . . 287
Crandall v Nevada 73 US 35, 18 LEd 745 . . . . . . . . . . . . . . . . . . . . . . . . . . . . . 255
Crusan v Director, Missouri Department of Health 110 SCt 2841, 58 LW 4916 (1990) . . . . 6, 232
Curtis Pub Co v Butts; Associated Press v Walker 388 US 130 (1967) . . . . . . . . . . . . . 288
Danbury Hatters 208 US 274 (1908) . . . . . . . . . . . . . . . . . . . . . . . . . . . . . . . . 440
Dandrige v Williams 397 US 471 (1970) . . . . . . . . . . . . . . . . . . . . . . . . . . . . . . 612
Davis v Board of School Commissioners of Mobile County 402 US 33 (1970) . . . . . . . . . 586
De Jonge v Oregon 299 US 353 (1937) . . . . . . . . . . . . . . . . . . . . . . . . . . . . . . 300
Debs v US 249 US 211 (1919) . . . . . . . . . . . . . . . . . . . . . . . . . . . . . . . . . . . 279
Democratic Party of the United States v Wisconsin 450 US 107 (1981) . . . . . . . . . . . . 347
Dennis v US 341 US 494 (1951) . . . . . . . . . . . . . . . . . . . . . . . . . . . . . . . . . . 279
Deshaney v Winnebago County Dept of Social Services et al 489 US 189 (1990) . . . . . . . 125
Doe v University of Michigan 721 F Supp 852 (ED Mich 1989) . . . . . . . . . . . . . . . . 275
Dunn v Blumstein 405 US 330, 31 LEd 2d 274, 92 SCt 995 . . . . . . . . . . . . . . . . 255, 256
Edwards v California 314 US 160, 86 LEd 119, 62 SCt 164 . . . . . . . . . . . . . . . . 255, 256
Edwards v South Carolina 372 US 229 (1963) . . . . . . . . . . . . . . . . . . . . . . . . 302, 303
Eisenstadt v Baird 405 US 438 (1972) . . . . . . . . . . . . . . . . . . . . . . . . . . . . . . . 348
Ellis v Brotherhood of Railway, Airline and Steamship Clerks 466 US 435 (1984) . . . . . . 357
Employment Division, Department of Human Resources v Smith 110 SCt 1595 (1990) 6, 594, 595
Enmund v Florida 458 US 782, 73 LEd 2d 1140 (1982) . . . . . . . . . . . . . . . . . . . . . 434
Estelle v Gamble 429 US 97 (1976) . . . . . . . . . . . . . . . . . . . . . . . . . . . . . . . . 125
Evansville-Vanderburgh Airport Authority Dist v Delta Airlines Inc 405 US 707, 31 LEd 2d 620,
    92 SCt 1349 . . . . . . . . . . . . . . . . . . . . . . . . . . . . . . . . . . . . . . . . . . . 256
Everson v Board of Education of Township of Ewing 330 US 1 (1947) . . . . . . . . . . . . 594
Fernandez v Wilkinson 505 F Supp 787 (D Kan 1980) . . . . . . . . . . . . . . . . . . . . . 174
Filartiga v Pena-Irala 630 F 2d 876 (2d Cir 1980) . . . . . . . . . . . . . . . . . . . . . . 173, 174
Frohwerk v US 249 US 204 (1919) . . . . . . . . . . . . . . . . . . . . . . . . . . . . . . . . . 279
Furman v Georgia 408 US 233, 33 LEd 2d 346 (1972) . . . . . . . . . . . . . . . . 432, 433, 434
Garcia v Texas State Board of Medical Examiners 421 US 995 (1975) . . . . . . . . . . . . . 344
Gideon v Wainwright 372 US 335 (1963) . . . . . . . . . . . . . . . . . . . . . . . . 405, 418, 604
Gillette v United States 401 US 437 (1971) . . . . . . . . . . . . . . . . . . . . . . . . . . . . 595
Ginsberg v New York 390 US 629 (1968) . . . . . . . . . . . . . . . . . . . . . . . . . . . . . 284
Gitlow v New York 268 US 652 (1925) . . . . . . . . . . . . . . . . . . . . . . . . . . . . . . 279
Goldberg v Kelly 397 US 254 (1970) . . . . . . . . . . . . . . . . . . . . . . . . . . . . . 124, 612
Graham v Richardson 403 US 365, 29 LEd 2d 534, 91 SCt 1848 . . . . . . . . . . . . . . . . 255
Greer v Spock 424 US 828 (1976) . . . . . . . . . . . . . . . . . . . . . . . . . . . . . . . . . 304
Greg v Georgia 428 US 153, 49 LEd 2d 859 (1976) . . . . . . . . . . . . . . . . . . . . . . . 434
Gregory v Chicago 394 US 111 (1969) . . . . . . . . . . . . . . . . . . . . . . . . . . . . . . 303
Griffin v California 380 US 609 (1965) . . . . . . . . . . . . . . . . . . . . . . . . . . . . . . 405
Griggs v Duke Power Company 401 US 424 (1971) . . . . . . . . . . . . . . . 198, 199, 200, 209
Griswold v Connecticut 381 US 479, 14 LEd 2d 510, 85 SCt 1678 (1965)   7, 20, 21, 243, 244, 348
Hague v CIO 307 US 496 (1939) . . . . . . . . . . . . . . . . . . . . . . . . . . . . . . . . . . 301
Hammer v Dagenhart 247 US 251 (1918) . . . . . . . . . . . . . . . . . . . . . . . . . . . . . 440
Heffron v International Society for Krishna Consciousness 452 US 640 (1981) . . . . . . . . 305
Herndon v Lowry 301 US 242 (1937) . . . . . . . . . . . . . . . . . . . . . . . . . . . . . . . 279
Hobbie v Unemployment Appeals Commission 480 US 136 (1987) . . . . . . . . . . . . . . 594
Holden v Hardy 169 US 366 (1898) . . . . . . . . . . . . . . . . . . . . . . . . . . . . . . . . 439
Hudgens v NLRB 424 US 507 (1976) . . . . . . . . . . . . . . . . . . . . . . . . . . . . . . . 306
Hynes v Mayor 425 US 610 (1976) . . . . . . . . . . . . . . . . . . . . . . . . . . . . . . . . . 272
Illinois ex rel McCollum v Board of Education 333 US 203 (1948) . . . . . . . . . . . . . . . 595
International Associational Machinists v Street 367 US 740 (1961) . . . . . . . . . . . . . . . 357
International Shoe Co v State of Washington, Office of Unemployment Compensation and
    Placement 326 US 310 (1945) . . . . . . . . . . . . . . . . . . . . . . . . . . . . . . . . . 418
Jacobellis v Ohio 378 US 184 (1964) . . . . . . . . . . . . . . . . . . . . . . . . . . . . . . . . 284
Jacobson v Massachusetts 197 US 11, 49 LEd 643, 25 SCt 358 . . . . . . . . . . . . . . . . . 255
Jones v North Carolina Prisoners' Union 433 US 119, 53 LEd 2d 629 (1977) . . . . . . . . . 436
Katz v United States 389 US 347, 19 LEd 2d 576, 88 SCt 507 . . . . . . . . . . . . . . . 243, 245
Kent v Dulles 357 US 116, 2 LEd 2d 1204, 78 SCt 1113 . . . . . . . . . . . . . . . . . . 256, 257

Keystone Bituminous Coal Association v De Benedictus 107 SCt 1232 (1987) . . . . . . . . . 467
Korematsu v US 323 US 214 (1944) . . . . . . . . . . . . . . . . . . . . . . . . . 23, 202, 651
Kurz v US 88 SCt 507 (1967) . . . . . . . . . . . . . . . . . . . . . . . . . . . . . . . . . . 403
Lakewood v Plain Dealer Publishing Co 468 US 750 (1989) . . . . . . . . . . . . . . . . . . 303
Lehnert v Ferris Faculty Association 111 SCt 1950 (1991) . . . . . . . . . . . . . . . . . . . 357
Lehr v Robertson 463 US 248 (1983) . . . . . . . . . . . . . . . . . . . . . . . . . . . . . . 539
Lloyd v Tanner 407 US 551 (1972) . . . . . . . . . . . . . . . . . . . . . . . . . . . . 306, 307
Lochner v New York 198 US 45 (1905) . . . . . . . . . . . . . 9, 10, 439, 449, 450, 466, 467
Lovell v Griffin 303 US 444 (1938) . . . . . . . . . . . . . . . . . . . . . . . . . . . . . . . 303
Loving v Virginia 388 US 1, 18 LEd 2d 1010, 87 SCt 1817 . . . . . . . . . . . . . . . . . . . 244
Mapp v Ohio 367 US 643 (1961) . . . . . . . . . . . . . . . . . . . . . . . . . . . . . . . . 424
Marbury v Madison 5 US 137 (1803), 2 LEd 60 (1803) . . . . . . . . . . . . . . . . . . . 5, 112
March Fong Eu v San Francisco County Democratic Central Committee 489 US 214 (1989) . . 347
Marchioro v Chaney 442 US 191 (1979) . . . . . . . . . . . . . . . . . . . . . . . . . . . . 347
Marsh v Alabama 326 US 501 (1946) . . . . . . . . . . . . . . . . . . . . . . . . . . . . . 306
Maryland v Joseph Munson 467 US 947 (1984) . . . . . . . . . . . . . . . . . . . . . . . . 330
Massachusetts Board of Retirement v Murgia 427 US 307 (1976) . . . . . . . . . . . . . . . 612
Masses Publishing Co v Patten 244 F 535 (SDNY 1917) . . . . . . . . . . . . . . . . . . . . 279
McCarthy v Philadelphia Civil Service Commission 424 US 645, 96 SCt 1154, 47 LEd 2d 366   255
McLaughlin v Florida 379 US 184 (1964) . . . . . . . . . . . . . . . . . . . . . . . . . . . 202
Memorial Hospital v Maricopa County 415 US 250, 94 SCt 1076, 39 LEd 2d 306 (1974) . . . 256
Metromedia, Inc v San Diego 453 US 490 (1981) . . . . . . . . . . . . . . . . . . . . . . . 301
Meyer v Nebraska 262 US 390, 67 LEd 1042, 43 SCt 625, 29 ALR 1446 (1923) . . 236, 243, 351
Miami Herald Pub Co v Tornillo 418 US 241 (1974) . . . . . . . . . . . . . . . . . . . . . 307
Michael H v Gerald D 491 US 110, 109 SCt 2333 (1989) . . . . . . . . . . . . . . . . . 12, 24
Michelet P v Gold, In re 10 AD 2d 68, 419 NYS 2d 704 (1979) . . . . . . . . . . . . . . . . 430
Miller v California 413 US 15 (1973) . . . . . . . . . . . . . . . . . . . . . . . . . . . . . 284
Miranda v Arizona 384 US 436 (1966) . . . . . . . . . . . . . . . . . . . . . . . . . . . . 404
Moore v East Cleveland 431 US 494, 52 LEd 2d 531, 97 SCt 1932 (1977) . . . . 14, 243, 244, 349
Muller v Oregon 208 US 412 (1908) . . . . . . . . . . . . . . . . . . . . . . . . . . . . . . 439
NAACP v Alabama ex R E L Patterson 357 US 449 (1958) . . . . . . . . . . . . . . 342, 343, 441
NAACP v Button 371 US 415 (1963) . . . . . . . . . . . . . . . . . . . . . . . . . . . 270, 343
NLRB v Jones & Laughlin Steel Corporation 301 US 1 (1937) . . . . . . . . . . . . . . . . . 440
New York State Club Association v City of New York 487 US 1 (1988) . . . . . . 344, 346, 350
New York Times Co v Sullivan 376 US 254 . . . . . . . . . . . . . . . . . . . 268, 270, 271, 288
New York v Ferber 458 US 747 (1982) . . . . . . . . . . . . . . . . . . . . . . . . . . . . . 284
Niemotko v Maryland 340 US 268 (1951) . . . . . . . . . . . . . . . . . . . . . . . . . . . 301
Nollan v California Coastal Comm'n 483 US 825 (1987) . . . . . . . . . . . . . . . . . . . . 8
Norwood v Harrison 413 US 455 (1973) . . . . . . . . . . . . . . . . . . . . . . . . . . . . 344
O'Lone v Estate of Shabazz 482 US 342, 96 LEd 2d 282, 290 (1987) . . . . . . . . . . 435, 436
Olmstead v United States 277 US 438, 72 LEd 944, 48 SCt 564, 66 ALR 376 . . . . . . . . . 243
Osborne v Ohio 110 SCt 1691 (1990) . . . . . . . . . . . . . . . . . . . . . . . . . . . . . 244
Palko v Connecticut 302 US 319 (1937) . . . . . . . . . . . . . . . . . . . . . . . . . . . . 349
Paul v Virginia 75 US 168, 19 LEd 357 . . . . . . . . . . . . . . . . . . . . . . . . . . . . 255
Pennel v City of San Jose 485 US 1 (1988) . . . . . . . . . . . . . . . . . . . . . . . . . . . 8
Pennsylvania Coal Co v Mahon 260 US 393 (1922) . . . . . . . . . . . . . . . . . . . . . . 467
People v Fitzgerald 101 Misc 2d 712, 422 NYS 2d 309 . . . . . . . . . . . . . . . . . . . . 430
Personnel Administrator v Feeney 442 US 256 (1979) . . . . . . . . . . . . . . . . . . . . . 35
Pierce v Society of Sisters 268 US 510, 69 LEd 1070, 45 SCt 571, 39 ALR 468 (1925) . . 243, 351
Planned Parenthood of Southeastern Pennsylvania v Casey 112 SCt 931, 112 SCt 2791 (1992) . . .
                                                                                12, 244, 525
Plessy v Ferguson 163 US 537 (1896) . . . . . . . . . . . . . . . . . . . . . . . . . . . . . 585
Poe v Ullman 367 US 497 (1961) . . . . . . . . . . . . . . . . . . . . . . . . . . . . . . . . 26
Posadas de Puerto Rico Association v Tourism Company of Puerto Rico 478 US 328 (1986) . . 290
Pruneyard Shopping Center v Robins 447 US 74 (1979) . . . . . . . . . . . . . . . . . . . 306
R v Wagner (1985) and R v Ross Wise (1990), discussed by Check in Itzin (ed) *Pornography.*
    *Women Violence and Civil Liberties. A Radical New View* (1992) . . . . . . . . . 284, 285
RAV v City of St Paul 112 SCt 2538 (1992) . . . . . . . . . . . . . . . . . . . . . . . 275, 330
Red Lion Broadcasting Co v FCC 395 US 367 (1969) . . . . . . . . . . . . . . . . . . 289, 307
Regents of the University of California v Bakke 438 US 265 (1978) . . . . . . . . . . . . . . 24
Reynolds v Sims 377 US 533 (1964) . . . . . . . . . . . . . . . . . . . . . . . . . . . . . . 18
Reynolds v United States 98 US 145 (1878) . . . . . . . . . . . . . . . . . . . . . . . 593, 594
Rhodes v Chapman 452 US 337, 69 LEd 2d 59 (1981) . . . . . . . . . . . . . . . . . . . . 436

# TABLE OF CASES

Roberts v United States Jaycees 468 US 609 (1984) . . . . . . 344, 345, 346, 347, 348, 350, 351
Roe v Wade 410 US 113, 35 LEd 2d 147, 93 SCt 705 (1973) . . . . . . 10, 25, 231, 243, 244, 348, 525, 527, 528, 529
Rostker v Goldberg 453 US 57 (1981) . . . . . . . . . . . . . . . . . . . . . . . . . . 197
Roth v United States 354 US 476 (1957) . . . . . . . . . . . . . . . . . . . . . . . 270, 284
Ruffin v Commonwealth 62 Va 790 (1871) . . . . . . . . . . . . . . . . . . . . . . . . 435
Runaway Express Agency v New York 336 US 106 (1949) . . . . . . . . . . . . . . . . 200
Rust v Sullivan 111 SCt 1759 (1991) . . . . . . . . . . . . . . . . . . . . . . . . . . . 25
Ryan, In re 123 Misc 2d 854, 474 NYS 2d 931 . . . . . . . . . . . . . . . . . . . . . 430
San Antonio Independent School District v Rodriguez 411 US 1 (1973) . . . . . . 612
Santa Clara Pueblo v Martinez 436 US 49 (1978) . . . . . . . . . . . . . . . . . . . 351
Schenk v US 249 US 47 (1919) . . . . . . . . . . . . . . . . . . . . . . . . . . . . . . 278
Shapiro v Thompson 394 US 618, 22 LEd 2d 600, 89 SCt 1322 (1969) . . . . . . 100, 125, 255, 256
Shelley v Kraemer 334 US 1 (1948) . . . . . . . . . . . . . . . . . . . . . . . . . . . . 92
Shelton v Tucker 364 US 479 (1960) . . . . . . . . . . . . . . . . . . . . . . . . . 353, 441
Sherbert v Verner 374 US 398 (1963) . . . . . . . . . . . . . . . . . . . . . . . . . . 594
Shuttlesworth v Birmingham 394 US 147 (1969) . . . . . . . . . . . . . . . . . . . . 303
Sierra Club v Morton 405 US 727 (1972) . . . . . . . . . . . . . . . . . . . . . . . . 421
Skinner v Oklahoma 316 US 535 (1942) . . . . . . . . . . . . . . . . . . . . . . . . . 348
Smith v Allwright 321 US 649 (1944) . . . . . . . . . . . . . . . . . . . . . . . . . . 346
Smith v Collin 439 US 916 (1978) . . . . . . . . . . . . . . . . . . . . . . . . . . . . 275
Smith v Maryland 442 US 735, 61 LEd 2d 220, 99 SCt 2577 . . . . . . . . . . . . . . 245
Solem v Helm 463 US 277, 77 LEd 2d 637 (1983) . . . . . . . . . . . . . . . . . . . 433
Sosna v Iowa 419 US 393, 95 SCt 553, 42 LEd 2d 532 . . . . . . . . . . . . . . . . 256
Stanley v Georgia 394 US 557 (1969) . . . . . . . . . . . . . . . . . . . . . . . . 244, 284
Stanley v Illinois 405 US 645 (1972) . . . . . . . . . . . . . . . . . . . . . . . . . . 350
Starns v Malkerson 401 US 985, 91 SCt 1231, 28 LEd 2d 527 . . . . . . . . . . . . 256
Strauder v West Virginia 100 US 303 (1880) . . . . . . . . . . . . . . . . . . . . . 198
Street v New York 394 US 576 (1969) . . . . . . . . . . . . . . . . . . . . . . . . . 302
Stromberg v California 283 US 359 . . . . . . . . . . . . . . . . . . . . . . . . . . . 270
Tashjian v Republican Party of Connecticut 479 US 208 (1986) . . . . . . . . . . . 347
Tate v Short 401 US 395, 28 LEd 2d 130 (1971) . . . . . . . . . . . . . . . . . . . . 437
Terminiello v Chicago 337 US 1 (1949) . . . . . . . . . . . . . . . . . . . . . . . . . 302
Terry v Adams 345 US 461 (1953) . . . . . . . . . . . . . . . . . . . . . . . . . . . . 346
Texas v Johnson 491 US 397 (1989) . . . . . . . . . . . . . . . . . . . . . . . . . . . 275
Thomas v Collins 323 US 516 (1945) . . . . . . . . . . . . . . . . . . . . . . . . . . 300
Thomas v Review Board, Employment Division 450 US 707 (1981) . . . . . . . . . . 594
Thornhill v Alabama 310 US 88 (1940) . . . . . . . . . . . . . . . . . . . . . . . . . 330
Tinker v Des Moines School District 393 US 503 (1969) . . . . . . . . . . . . . 264, 275
Trop v Dulles 356 US 86, 2 LEd 2d 630 (1958) . . . . . . . . . . . . . . . . . . . . . 433
Turner v Safley 482 US 78, 96 LEd 2d 64 (1987) . . . . . . . . . . . . . . . . . 435, 436
United Mine Workers v Illinois Bar Ass'n 389 US 217 (1967) . . . . . . . . . . . . 343
United States v Associated Press 52 F Supp 362 . . . . . . . . . . . . . . . . . . . 268
United States v Carolene Products Company 304 US 144 (1938) . 16, 17, 18, 19, 22, 23, 123, 202
United States v Eichman 110 SCt 2404 (1990) . . . . . . . . . . . . . . . . . . . . . 275
United States v Grace 461 US 171 (1983) . . . . . . . . . . . . . . . . . . . . 301, 304, 305
United States v Laub 385 US 475, 17 LEd 2d 526, 87 SCt 574 . . . . . . . . . . . . 256
United States v Lee 455 US 252 (1982) . . . . . . . . . . . . . . . . . . . . . . . . . 594
United States v Little 321 F Supp 388 D Del (1971) . . . . . . . . . . . . . . . . . 244
United States v Miller 425 US 435, 48 LEd 2d 71, 96 SCt 1619 . . . . . . . . . . . 245
United States v O'Brien 391 US 367 (1986) . . . . . . . . . . . . . . . . . . . . 264, 275
United Transportation Union v State Bar of Michigan 401 US 576 (1971) . . . . . 343
Valentine v Christensen 316 US 52 (1942) . . . . . . . . . . . . . . . . . . . . . . . 290
Village of Arlington Heights, The v Metro Housing Development Corporation 429 US 252
 (1977) . . . . . . . . . . . . . . . . . . . . . . . . . . . . . . . . . . . . . . . . . . . 35
Village of Belle Terre v Boraas 416 US 1 (1973) . . . . . . . . . . . . . . . . . 349, 350
Virginia Pharmacy Bd v Virginia Consumer Council 425 US 748 (1976) . . . . . . . 290
Ward v Rock Against Racism 491 US 781 (1989) . . . . . . . . . . . . . . . . . . . . 301
Washington v Davis 426 US 229 (1976) . . . . . . . . . . . . . . . . . . . 23, 35, 199, 200
Webster, Attorney General of Missouri & others v Reproductive Health Services & others
 106 LEd 410 (1989) . . . . . . . . . . . . . . . . . . . . . . . . . . . . . . . . . . . 525
Weeks v United States 232 US 383 (1914) . . . . . . . . . . . . . . . . . . . . . . . 424
Weems v United States 217 US 349, 54 LEd 793 (1910) . . . . . . . . . . . . . . . . 433

West Coast Hotel Company v Parrish 300 US 379 (1937) . . . . . . . . . . . . . . . . . 440
West Virginia Board of Education v Barnette 319 US 624 (1943) . . . . . . . . . . . . 352, 595
Whalen v Roe 429 US 589, 51 LEd 2d 64, 97 SCt 869 . . . . . . . . . . . . . . . . . . 244
Whitney v California 274 US 357 (1927) . . . . . . . . . . . . . . . . . . . 270, 279, 291
Widmar v Vincent 454 US 263 (1981) . . . . . . . . . . . . . . . . . . . . . . . . . 304
Williams v Fears 179 US 270, 45 LEd 186, 21 SCt 128 . . . . . . . . . . . . . . . . . 255
Wisconsin v Yoder 406 US 205 (1972) . . . . . . . . . . . . . . . . . . . . . . . . . 351
Wood v Georgia 370 US 375 (1962) . . . . . . . . . . . . . . . . . . . . . . . . . . 287
Woodson v North Carolina 428 US 280, 49 LEd 2d 944 (1976) . . . . . . . . . . . . 433, 434
Wooley v Manard 430 US 705 (1977) . . . . . . . . . . . . . . . . . . . . . . . . . 353
Yates v US 354 US 298 (1957) . . . . . . . . . . . . . . . . . . . . . . . . . . . . . 279
Young, Ex parte 209 US 123 (1908) . . . . . . . . . . . . . . . . . . . . . . . . . . 124
Youngberg v Romeo 457 US 307 (1982) . . . . . . . . . . . . . . . . . . . . . . . . 125
Zablocki v Redhail 434 US 374, 54 LEd 2d 618, 98 SCt 673 . . . . . . . . . . . . . . 243
Zemel v Rusk 381 US 1, 85 SCt 1271, 14 LEd 2d 179 . . . . . . . . . . . . . . . . . 256

# TABLE OF STATUTES

| No | Year | Short Title | Page |
|---|---|---|---|
| | | **SOUTH AFRICA** | |
| 206 | 1993 | Abolition of Restrictions on Free Political Activity | 274, 377, 378 |
| 2 | 1975 | Abortion and Sterilization | 526, 532, 547 |
| | | s   3 | 530 |
| | | 5 | 530 |
| | | 6 | 530 |
| | | 7 | 530 |
| 41 | 1971 | Abuse of Dependence-producing Substances and Rehabilitation Centres | 413 |
| 66 | 1965 | Administration of Estates | |
| | | s   49(1) | 569 |
| | | 72 | 522 |
| 31 | 1974 | Affected Organizations | 378 |
| 147 | 1993 | Agricultural Labour | 452 |
| 75 | 1969 | Arms and Ammunition | 296, 336 |
| | | s   38A | 296 |
| 57 | 1968 | Armaments Development and Production | 278 |
| 92 | 1992 | Attorney-General | 411 |
| 38 | 1927 | Black Administration | 377, 520, 541 |
| | | s   5 | 254 |
| | | 11(1) | 565 |
| | | 11(3) | 566 |
| | | 11(3)(b) | 521, 544, 567 |
| | | 11A | 566 |
| | | 22 | 564, 569 |
| | | 22(1) | 523, 558, 564 |
| | | 22(2) | 523, 558 |
| | | 22(3) | 564 |
| | | 22(6) | 541, 543, 549, 567 |
| | | 22(7) | 564, 569 |
| | | 25 | 293 |
| | | 27 | 293 |
| | | 29 | 274 |
| | | 35 | 558, 565 |
| 47 | 1953 | Black Education | 589 |
| 27 | 1913 | Black Land | 134, 506 |
| | | s   1 | 254 |
| 76 | 1963 | Black Laws Amendment | |
| | | s   31 | 558, 569, 570 |
| | | 31(2) | 569 |
| 25 | 1945 | Black (Urban Areas) Consolidation | |
| | | s   38(3)(r) | 293 |
| 73 | 1976 | Broadcasting | 288 |
| 74 | 1983 | Child Care | |
| | | s   18(4)(d) | 534, 535 |
| | | 27 | 558 |
| 82 | 1987 | Children's Status | 533 |
| 6 | 1981 | Code of Zulu Law (KwaZulu) | 544, 566 |
| | | s   27(3) | 544 |
| 16 | 1985 | Code of Zulu Law (KwaZulu) | 544, 566 |
| | | s   12 | 566 |
| | | 13 | 567 |
| | | 14 | 566 |
| | | 27 | 567 |

# TABLE OF STATUTES

| No | Year | Short Title | Page |
|---|---|---|---|
| 16 | 1985 | Code of Zulu Law (KwaZulu) *(cont)* | |
| | | s 27(3) | 541, 542, 544, 566, 567 |
| | | 35 | 567 |
| | | 35(1) | 541, 543 |
| | | 36(1) | 568, 569 |
| | | 38 | 565 |
| | | 48 | 568 |
| | 1987 | Code of Zulu Law (Natal) (Proc R151 *GG* 10966 of 9 October 1987) | |
| | | s 12 | 566 |
| | | 13 | 567 |
| | | 14 | 566 |
| | | 27 | 567 |
| | | 27(3) | 566, 567 |
| | | 36(1) | 568, 569 |
| | | 38 | 565 |
| | | 48 | 568 |
| 25 | 1965 | Civil Proceedings Evidence | |
| | | s 10 | 430 |
| | | 10(1) | 571 |
| | | 10(2) | 571 |
| | | 12 | 571 |
| | | 14 | 428 |
| | | 42 | 428 |
| 67 | 1977 | Civil Protection | 297 |
| 200 | 1993 | Constitution of the Republic of South Africa | *passim* |
| | | s 1 | 541, 542 |
| | | 4 | 192, 632 |
| | | 4(1) | 543, 564, 632 |
| | | 4(2) | 523, 631 |
| | | 7 | 210, 264, 421, 523, 538, 560, 564, 647, 657 |
| | | 7(1) | 128, 210, 452, 494, 521, 522, 523, 560, 631, 632 |
| | | 7(2) | 210, 211, 452, 522, 523, 560 |
| | | 7(3) | 212, 252, 290 |
| | | 7(4) | 399, 632, 640, 643, 661 |
| | | 7(4)(*a*) | 426 |
| | | 8 | 206, 207, 210, 211, 264, 420, 518, 524, 525, 526, 538, 544, 565, 571 |
| | | 8(1) | 129, 207, 208, 231, 431, 546 |
| | | 8(2) | 207, 208, 253, 431, 487, 494, 564, 641, 658 |
| | | 8(3) | 207, 208, 209 |
| | | 8(4) | 209 |
| | | 9 | 218, 219, 220, 227, 229, 299, 234, 438, 526, 658 |
| | | 10 | 252, 264, 406, 408, 438, 526, 636, 642, 658 |
| | | 11 | 234, 235, 263, 408, 438, 526, 642, 661 |
| | | 11(1) | 235, 236, 237, 238, 408, 409, 546 |
| | | 11(2) | 228, 235, 239, 437, 438, 658 |
| | | 12 | 642, 658 |
| | | 13 | 242, 251, 252, 253, 264, 269, 406, 407, 526, 538 |
| | | 14 | 264, 269, 280, 281, 528, 559, 592, 507, 641, 658 |
| | | 14(1) | 235, 236, 642 |
| | | 14(3) | 558, 565 |
| | | 15 | 264, 265, 638, 642 |
| | | 15(1) | 235, 237, 264, 285, 286, 287 |
| | | 15(2) | 264, 287, 289, 641 |
| | | 16 | 264, 327, 328, 329, 331, 334, 335, 642 |
| | | 17 | 237, 264, 378, 379–81, 453, 642 |
| | | 18 | 237, 254, 255, 263, 642 |
| | | 19 | 237, 254, 255, 263 |
| | | 20 | 254, 255, 263 |
| | | 21 | 642 |
| | | 22 | 399, 420 |
| | | 23 | 264, 270, 395, 398, 430, 641, 642 |

# TABLE OF STATUTES

| No | Year | Short Title | Page |
|---|---|---|---|
| 200 | 1993 | Constitution of the Republic of South Africa *(cont)* | |

s  23(2)(a) .................................................. 408
   24 ............................. 271, 395, 398, 399, 546, 642
   24(a) ................................................... 399
   24(c) ................................................... 399
   24(d) ................................................... 399
   25 .......................... 237, 263, 409, 420, 427, 430, 438, 660, 661
   25(1) ............................... 237, 410, 415, 421, 432
   25(1)(a) ................................................ 408
   25(1)(b) ................................................ 410
   25(1)(c) ...................................... 410, 415, 641
   25(1)(d) ................................................ 410
   25(1)(e) .......................................... 237, 410
   25(2) ............................................. 408, 415
   25(2)(a) ...................................... 408, 416, 429
   25(2)(b) .......................................... 408, 641
   25(2)(c) ................................................ 428
   25(2)(d) .......................................... 411, 641
   25(3) ............................. 239, 264, 412, 413, 416
   25(3)(a) ................................................ 412
   25(3)(b) ................................................ 412
   25(3)(c) .......................................... 412, 417
   25(3)(d) ..................................... 413, 417, 431
   25(3)(e) .......................................... 413, 415
   25(3)(f) ................................................ 413
   25(3)(g) ................................................ 413
   25(3)(h) ................................................ 413
   25(3)(i) ................................................ 413
   25(3)(j) ................................................ 413
   26 ................................................. 263, 264
   26(1) ............................................. 237, 255
   26(2) ................................................... 641
   27 ................................... 451, 452, 453, 454
   27(1) ................................................... 658
   27(2) ................................................... 658
   27(5) ................................................... 453
   28 ................................................ 193, 487, 627
   28(1) ........................... 487, 493, 494, 495, 499, 500
   28(2) ......................................... 487, 496, 498
   28(3) .................................... 487, 488, 496, 497, 641
   29 ............................................ 222, 421, 501
   30 ............................................ 220, 222, 538, 627
   30(1)(b) .......................................... 538, 557
   30(1)(d) ..................................... 546, 642, 659
   30(1)(e) .......................................... 642, 659
   30(2) ........................................ 238, 642, 659
   31 ...................................................... 579
   32 ...................................................... 591
   32(c) ................................................... 641
   33 ..... 129, 237, 264, 265, 272, 327, 399, 408, 409, 438, 498, 627, 630–50, 659
   33(1) ... 209, 223, 224, 235, 242, 253, 254, 328, 406, 407, 432, 437, 438, 452, 453, 454, 493, 497, 498, 641, 643, 644, 659
   33(1)(a) ................................... 223, 235, 242, 265
   33(1)(a)(i) ............................................. 408
   33(1)(a)(ii) ........................................ 408, 646
   33(1)(b) ......... 223, 227, 228, 229, 235, 265, 277, 408, 637, 659
   33(1)(aa) ..................................... 223, 228, 229, 255, 438
   33(1)(bb) ......................................... 255, 265, 408
   33(2) ........................................ 288, 452, 499, 659
   33(3) ............................................. 494, 641
   33(4) ................................................... 640

| No | Year | Short Title | | Page |
|---|---|---|---|---|
| 200 | 1993 | Constitution of the Republic of South Africa *(cont)* | | |
| | | s | 33(5) | 452, 454 |
| | | | 33(5)*(a)* | 451, 452, 454 |
| | | | 33(5)*(b)* | 451 |
| | | | 34 | 224, 235, 242, 255, 631, 640, 650–3 |
| | | | 34(1) | 652, 653, 654, 655, 656, 657, 659 |
| | | | 34(2) | 655 |
| | | | 34(3) | 656 |
| | | | 34(4) | 235, 242, 410, 657 |
| | | | 34(5) | 657 |
| | | | 34(5)*(a)* | 659 |
| | | | 34(5)*(c)* | 224, 641, 658, 659 |
| | | | 34(6) | 235, 237, 410, 658, 661 |
| | | | 34(6)*(c)* | 661 |
| | | | 34(6)*(c)*(i) | 410 |
| | | | 34(6)*(c)*(ii) | 410 |
| | | | 34(6)*(d)* | 410, 415 |
| | | | 34(6)*(e)* | 410 |
| | | | 34(6)*(f)* | 410 |
| | | | 34(6)*(g)* | 410, 658 |
| | | | 34(7) | 658, 661 |
| | | | 35 | 127, 129, 237, 264, 265, 427, 431, 633, 636 |
| | | | 35(1) | 127, 128, 171, 192, 193, 194, 195, 218, 237, 265, 437, 634, 637, 638, 639, 640, 644, 651 |
| | | | 35(2) | 127, 407, 428, 494 |
| | | | 35(3) | 128, 210, 211, 265, 281, 287, 288, 452, 523, 632, 633, 636 |
| | | | 40(1) | 161 |
| | | | 41 | 161 |
| | | | 43*(b)* | 161 |
| | | | 47 | 161 |
| | | | 48 | 161 |
| | | | 49 | 161 |
| | | | 54 | 161 |
| | | | 55–62 | 161 |
| | | | 55(1) | 161 |
| | | | 57(3) | 161 |
| | | | 58 | 161 |
| | | | 59 | 161 |
| | | | 60 | 161, 167 |
| | | | 61 | 161 |
| | | | 62 | 162 |
| | | | 64(1) | 162 |
| | | | 65(2) | 162 |
| | | | 66 | 162 |
| | | | 68(1) | 160 |
| | | | 71 | 170 |
| | | | 71(1) | 159 |
| | | | 71(2) | 159 |
| | | | 72(2) | 170 |
| | | | 73 | 170 |
| | | | 73(1) | 170 |
| | | | 74(1) | 160 |
| | | | 75 | 162, 632 |
| | | | 77 | 162 |
| | | | 77(4) | 163 |
| | | | 81(1) | 632 |
| | | | 82 | 162, 654, 657 |
| | | | 82(1) | 163 |
| | | | 82(1)*(b)* | 162 |
| | | | 82(1)(i) | 192 |
| | | | 82(2) | 163 |
| | | | 82(3) | 162, 163, 657 |

| No | Year | Short Title | | Page |
|---|---|---|---|---|
| 200 | 1993 | Constitution of the Republic of South Africa *(cont)* | | |
| | | s | 82(4) | 654 |
| | | | 82(4)(*a*) | 163 |
| | | | 82(4)(*b*)(i) | 163, 659 |
| | | | 83(2) | 163 |
| | | | 84 | 163 |
| | | | 84(3) | 163 |
| | | | 85 | 163 |
| | | | 86(2) | 162 |
| | | | 88 | 163 |
| | | | 88(1) | 162, 164 |
| | | | 88(5) | 163 |
| | | | 88(8) | 164 |
| | | | 88(9) | 164 |
| | | | 89(1) | 164 |
| | | | 92 | 163, 164 |
| | | | 92(1) | 164 |
| | | | 93 | 162, 164 |
| | | | 94 | 164 |
| | | | 95 | 164 |
| | | | 96(2) | 420 |
| | | | 96(3) | 264, 287, 420 |
| | | | 97–100 | 160 |
| | | | 98 | 632 |
| | | | 98(1) | 168 |
| | | | 98(2) | 168 |
| | | | 98(2)(*b*) | 632 |
| | | | 98(2)(*c*) | 632, 656 |
| | | | 98(2)(*e*) | 632 |
| | | | 98(4) | 632 |
| | | | 98(5) | 543, 564 |
| | | | 100(2) | 168 |
| | | | 101 | 632 |
| | | | 101(3) | 168 |
| | | | 101(3)(*c*) | 632 |
| | | | 101(3)(*d*) | 632 |
| | | | 101(4) | 168 |
| | | | 101(5) | 168 |
| | | | 102 | 168 |
| | | | 103(2) | 210 |
| | | | 105 | 168 |
| | | | 105(2) | 168 |
| | | | 107 | 420 |
| | | | 110 | 395, 419 |
| | | | 111 | 396 |
| | | | 111(1) | 420 |
| | | | 111(2) | 420 |
| | | | 111(3) | 420 |
| | | | 112 | 396 |
| | | | 112(1) | 160 |
| | | | 113 | 397 |
| | | | 114 | 397, 419 |
| | | | 115 | 193, 420 |
| | | | 115–118 | 571 |
| | | | 116 | 160 |
| | | | 116(2) | 193, 194 |
| | | | 116(3) | 420 |
| | | | 119–120 | 141, 160, 571 |
| | | | 121 | 160, 487 |
| | | | 121(1)–(3) | 487 |
| | | | 121(1)(*a*), (*b*) | 488 |
| | | | 121(3) | 488 |

| No | Year | Short Title | Page |
|---|---|---|---|
| 200 | 1993 | Constitution of the Republic of South Africa *(cont)* | |

    s  121(4) . . . . . . . . . . . . . . . . . . . . . . . . . . . . . . . . . . . . . . . . 487
        121(4)*(a)*, *(b)* . . . . . . . . . . . . . . . . . . . . . . . . . . . . . . . . . 488
        121(5) . . . . . . . . . . . . . . . . . . . . . . . . . . . . . . . . . . . . . . 487
        121(6) . . . . . . . . . . . . . . . . . . . . . . . . . . . . . . . . . . . . . . 487
        122 . . . . . . . . . . . . . . . . . . . . . . . . . . . . . . . . . . . . . 160, 487
        122(1) . . . . . . . . . . . . . . . . . . . . . . . . . . . . . . . . . . . . . . 487
        122(1)*(c)* . . . . . . . . . . . . . . . . . . . . . . . . . . . . . . . . . . . 487
        123 . . . . . . . . . . . . . . . . . . . . . . . . . . . . . . . . . 160, 487, 488
        123(2) . . . . . . . . . . . . . . . . . . . . . . . . . . . . . . . . . . . . . . 488
        123(4) . . . . . . . . . . . . . . . . . . . . . . . . . . . . . . . . . . . . . . 488
        124 . . . . . . . . . . . . . . . . . . . . . . . . . . . . . . . . . . . . 148, 165
        124(1) . . . . . . . . . . . . . . . . . . . . . . . . . . . . . . . . . . . . . . 165
        124(2) . . . . . . . . . . . . . . . . . . . . . . . . . . . . . . . . . . . . . . 165
        124(5) . . . . . . . . . . . . . . . . . . . . . . . . . . . . . . . . . . . . . . 165
        124(6) . . . . . . . . . . . . . . . . . . . . . . . . . . . . . . . . . . . . . . 165
        124(15) . . . . . . . . . . . . . . . . . . . . . . . . . . . . . . . . . . . . . 165
        126 . . . . . . . . . . . . . . . . . . . . . . . . . . . . . . . . . . . . 166, 559
        126(3) . . . . . . . . . . . . . . . . . . . . . . . . . . . . . . . . . . . 166, 559
        126(4) . . . . . . . . . . . . . . . . . . . . . . . . . . . . . . . . . . . 166, 559
        126(5) . . . . . . . . . . . . . . . . . . . . . . . . . . . . . . . . . . . . . . 166
        155–159 . . . . . . . . . . . . . . . . . . . . . . . . . . . . . . . . . . . . . 166
        155 . . . . . . . . . . . . . . . . . . . . . . . . . . . . . . . . . . . . . . . 167
        155(1) . . . . . . . . . . . . . . . . . . . . . . . . . . . . . . . . . . . . . . 166
        155(2) . . . . . . . . . . . . . . . . . . . . . . . . . . . . . . . . . . . . . . 166
        155(2A) . . . . . . . . . . . . . . . . . . . . . . . . . . . . . . . . . . . . . 167
        156 . . . . . . . . . . . . . . . . . . . . . . . . . . . . . . . . . . . . 166, 167
        156(1A) . . . . . . . . . . . . . . . . . . . . . . . . . . . . . . . . . . . . . 167
        156(1B) . . . . . . . . . . . . . . . . . . . . . . . . . . . . . . . . . . . . . 166
        157 . . . . . . . . . . . . . . . . . . . . . . . . . . . . . . . . . . . . 166, 167
        157(1A) . . . . . . . . . . . . . . . . . . . . . . . . . . . . . . . . . . . . . 167
        160 . . . . . . . . . . . . . . . . . . . . . . . . . . . . . . . . . . . . . . . 167
        161(1) . . . . . . . . . . . . . . . . . . . . . . . . . . . . . . . . . . . . . . 167
        164(1) . . . . . . . . . . . . . . . . . . . . . . . . . . . . . . . . . . . . . . 167
        164(2) . . . . . . . . . . . . . . . . . . . . . . . . . . . . . . . . . . . . . . 167
        174–180 . . . . . . . . . . . . . . . . . . . . . . . . . . . . . . . . . . . . . 167
        174(3) . . . . . . . . . . . . . . . . . . . . . . . . . . . . . . . . . . . . . . 167
        175 . . . . . . . . . . . . . . . . . . . . . . . . . . . . . . . . . . . . . . . 167
        179 . . . . . . . . . . . . . . . . . . . . . . . . . . . . . . . . . . . . . . . 167
        180 . . . . . . . . . . . . . . . . . . . . . . . . . . . . . . . . . . . . . . . 167
        181–184 . . . . . . . . . . . . . . . . . . . . . . . . . . . . . . . . . . . . . 168
        183(2) . . . . . . . . . . . . . . . . . . . . . . . . . . . . . . . . . . . . . . 560
        184 . . . . . . . . . . . . . . . . . . . . . . . . . . . . . . . . . . . . . . . 165
        184(5) . . . . . . . . . . . . . . . . . . . . . . . . . . . . . . . . . . . 559, 560
        184A . . . . . . . . . . . . . . . . . . . . . . . . . . . . . . . . . . . . . . 165
        184A(2) . . . . . . . . . . . . . . . . . . . . . . . . . . . . . . . . . . . . . 168
        184B . . . . . . . . . . . . . . . . . . . . . . . . . . . . . . . . . . . . . . 165
        184B(3) . . . . . . . . . . . . . . . . . . . . . . . . . . . . . . . . . . . . . 168
        185–208 . . . . . . . . . . . . . . . . . . . . . . . . . . . . . . . . . . . . . 169
        191–194 . . . . . . . . . . . . . . . . . . . . . . . . . . . . . . . . . . . . . 164
        192A(2) . . . . . . . . . . . . . . . . . . . . . . . . . . . . . . . . . . . . . 192
        195–197 . . . . . . . . . . . . . . . . . . . . . . . . . . . . . . . . . . . . . 164
        198–206 . . . . . . . . . . . . . . . . . . . . . . . . . . . . . . . . . . . . . 165
        200(1) . . . . . . . . . . . . . . . . . . . . . . . . . . . . . . . . . . . . . . 169
        207–208 . . . . . . . . . . . . . . . . . . . . . . . . . . . . . . . . . . . . . 165
        227(2) . . . . . . . . . . . . . . . . . . . . . . . . . . . . . . . . . . . . . . 638
        227(2)*(e)* . . . . . . . . . . . . . . . . . . . . . . . . . . . . . . . . . . . 193
        229 . . . . . . . . . . . . . . . . . . . . . . . 169, 542, 543, 560, 567, 632
        229–251 . . . . . . . . . . . . . . . . . . . . . . . . . . . . . . . . . . . . . 169
        230(1) . . . . . . . . . . . . . . . . . . . . . . . . . . . . . . . . . . . . . . 169
        231 . . . . . . . . . . . . . . . . . . . . . . . . . . . . . . . . . . . . 637, 639
        231(1) . . . . . . . . . . . . . . . . . . . . . . . . . . . . . . . . . . . . . . 169

# TABLE OF STATUTES

| No | Year | Short Title | Page |
|---|---|---|---|
| 200 | 1993 | Constitution of the Republic of South Africa *(cont)* | |
| | | s 231(2) | 192 |
| | | 231(3) | 192, 195 |
| | | 231(4) | 638 |
| | | 232 | 169 |
| | | 232(2)*(b)* | 632 |
| | | 232(4) | 128, 204, 207, 634 |
| | | 232(5) | 148 |
| | | 233 | 169 |
| | | 233(1)(viii) | 159 |
| | | 233(3) | 147 |
| | | 233(4) | 147, 163 |
| | | 234–236 | 169 |
| | | 234(1) | 169, 191 |
| | | 234(2) | 169 |
| | | 236(2) | 169 |
| | | 237 | 169 |
| | | 238–241 | 169 |
| | | 242 | 169 |
| | | 243–246 | 169 |
| | | 245(1) | 156 |
| | | 245(3) | 156 |
| | | 247 | 169, 592 |
| | | 250(4) | 148 |
| | | 251 | 129 |
| | | Schedule 1 | 165, 567 |
| | | Schedule 2 | 161 |
| | | Schedule 4 | 129, 170, 634 |
| | | Schedule 6 | 166, 167, 559 |
| | | Schedule 7 | 541, 542 |
| | | Constitutional Principles (Schedule 4) | |
| | | I | 129, 159, 207 |
| | | II | 634 |
| | | III | 159 |
| | | V | 159, 207 |
| | | VI | 159 |
| | | VII | 159 |
| | | XI | 635 |
| | | XII | 159 |
| | | XIII | 159, 636 |
| | | XVII | 159 |
| | | XXXII | 159 |
| | | XXXIII | 159, 634 |
| | | XXXIV | 160 |
| 2 | 1994 | Constitution of the Republic of South Africa Amendment | 559 |
| | | s 1 | 165 |
| | | 2*(c)* | 166 |
| | | 3 | 166 |
| | | 8*(a)* | 167 |
| | | 9 | 168 |
| | | 13*(b)* | 160 |
| 3 | 1994 | Constitution of the Republic of South Africa Second Amendment | |
| | | s 1 | 167 |
| | | 2 | 159 |
| 53 | 1985 | Control of Access to Public Premises and Vehicles | 297 |
| 8 | 1959 | Correctional Services | 278 |
| | | s 54(2)*(d)* | 191 |
| 8 | 1953 | Criminal Law Amendment | 293 |
| 107 | 1990 | Criminal Law Amendment | 226, 227 |
| 39 | 1989 | Criminal Law and Criminal Procedure Act Amendment | |
| | | s 1 | 521, 545 |

| No | Year | Short Title | Page |
|---|---|---|---|
| 126 | 1992 | Criminal Law Second Amendment | 410, 413 |
| | | s 18 | 416 |
| | | 20 | 417 |
| | | 20(4)(b)(i) | 412 |
| | | 21 | 411 |
| | | 23 | 407, 409 |
| | | 23(1) | 409 |
| | | 23(3)(a) | 409 |
| | | 23(3)(c) | 409 |
| | | 23(4) | 409 |
| 51 | 1977 | Criminal Procedure | 227, 406, 411 |
| | | s 7 | 412 |
| | | 7(1)(a) | 412 |
| | | s 21 | 406 |
| | | 25 | 242, 407 |
| | | 26(1)(g)(ii) | 414 |
| | | 26(1)(g)(iii) | 414 |
| | | 29 | 407 |
| | | 40 | 407 |
| | | 43 | 407 |
| | | 49(2) | 229 |
| | | 50 | 407, 409 |
| | | 60(1) | 410 |
| | | 61 | 411 |
| | | 73 | 414, 415, 430 |
| | | 73(1) | 414 |
| | | 73(2) | 414 |
| | | 115 | 412, 416 |
| | | 115(2) | 417 |
| | | 192 | 430 |
| | | 195 | 570 |
| | | 195(1) | 570 |
| | | 195(2) | 570 |
| | | 198 | 430, 571 |
| | | 198(2) | 571 |
| | | 199 | 571 |
| | | 203 | 428 |
| | | 217 | 416, 428 |
| | | 218 | 416 |
| | | 218(2) | 429 |
| | | 219A | 416, 428 |
| 71 | 1968 | Dangerous Weapons | 296 |
| | | s 2 | 297 |
| 44 | 1957 | Defence | 278 |
| 71 | 1982 | Demonstrations in or near Court Buildings Prohibition | 294, 296 |
| 18 | 1936 | Development Trust and Land | 134, 293, 506 |
| | | s 25 | 254 |
| | | 26 | 254 |
| 26 | 1989 | Disclosure of Foreign Funding | 378 |
| 70 | 1979 | Divorce | 505, 544 |
| | | s 6(3) | 556 |
| | | 7 | 549, 550, 568 |
| | | 7(2) | 544 |
| | | 7(4) | 551 |
| 3 | 1992 | Domicile | 521, 538, 545 |
| 140 | 1992 | Drugs and Drug Trafficking | |
| | | s 12 | 408 |
| 146 | 1993 | Education Labour Relations | 452 |
| 202 | 1993 | Electoral | 145, 148, 150, 155 |
| | | s 1(ix) | 155 |
| | | 2 | 155 |
| | | 3(2) | 153 |

| No | Year | Short Title | Page |
|---|---|---|---|
| 202 | 1993 | Electoral *(cont)* | |
| | | s 4 | 155 |
| | | 15 | 155 |
| | | 21(2) | 155 |
| 63 | 1975 | Expropriation | 488 |
| 103 | 1992 | Gatherings and Demonstrations in or near the Union Buildings | 296 |
| 52 | 1973 | Gatherings and Demonstrations in the Vicinity of Parliament | 293, 296 |
| 132 | 1993 | General Law Fourth Amendment | 180, 511, 520, 521, 538, 542, 543, 544, 567 |
| | | s 11(1) | 542 |
| | | 11(2) | 542 |
| | | 11(3) | 542 |
| | | 11(4) | 542 |
| | | 29 | 510, 520 |
| | | 30 | 510, 520, 544 |
| 92 | 1970 | General Law Further Amendment | |
| | | s 15 | 292 |
| 41 | 1950 | Group Areas | 134, 376, 377 |
| 36 | 1966 | Group Areas | 254, 506 |
| 192 | 1993 | Guardianship | 511, 522, 534, 535, 538, 544, 545 |
| | | s 1 | 521 |
| | | 1(1) | 534 |
| | | 1(2) | 534 |
| | | 2 | 534 |
| 65 | 1983 | Human Tissue | 233 |
| 5 | 1927 | Immorality | 134 |
| 37 | 1967 | Indecent or Obscene Photographic Matter | 282 |
| 153 | 1993 | Independent Broadcasting Authority | 145, 152–5, 288–9 |
| | | s 1(1)(xx) | 155 |
| | | 1(1)(xxi) | 154 |
| | | 1(1)(xxviii) | 154 |
| | | 1(1)(xxix) | 154 |
| | | 2 | 288 |
| | | 2*(a)–(u)* | 152 |
| | | 3–20 | 288 |
| | | 4(1) | 153 |
| | | 4(2) | 153 |
| | | 4(3) | 153 |
| | | 5(1) | 153 |
| | | 6(1) | 153 |
| | | 6(2) | 153 |
| | | 13 | 152 |
| | | 20(1)–(3) | 153 |
| | | 21 | 153 |
| | | 21(1)*(a)* | 153 |
| | | 21(1)*(b)* | 153 |
| | | 21(2) | 153 |
| | | 22 | 153 |
| | | 22(2) | 153 |
| | | 22(3)*(a)* | 153 |
| | | 22(3)*(b)* | 153 |
| | | 23(1) | 153, 154 |
| | | 23(2) | 153, 154 |
| | | 27 | 154 |
| | | 28 | 154 |
| | | 28(2)–(7) | 154 |
| | | 28(8) | 154 |
| | | 30 | 153, 154 |
| | | 45 | 154 |
| | | 49(6) | 155 |
| | | 50 | 154 |
| | | 50(3) | 155 |
| | | 53(3)–(4) | 154 |

| No | Year | Short Title | Page |
|---|---|---|---|
| 153 | 1993 | Independent Broadcasting Authority *(cont)* | |
| | | s 53(7) | 154 |
| | | 56 | 154, 288 |
| | | 56(2) | 154 |
| | | 58–61 | 154 |
| | | 62–65 | 153, 154, 288 |
| | | 80 | 155 |
| | | 82 | 153 |
| | | 83(1)*(a)* | 155 |
| | | 83(1)*(b)* | 153, 155 |
| 150 | 1993 | Independent Electoral Commission | 145, 147, 148–50 |
| | | s 3(2) | 148 |
| | | 5(1) | 148 |
| | | 5(2)*(a)* | 148 |
| | | 5(2)*(b)* | 148 |
| | | 6(1) | 148 |
| | | 6(2) | 148 |
| | | s 7 | 148 |
| | | 8 | 148 |
| | | 9 | 148, 152 |
| | | 13 | 148 |
| | | 13(3) | 149 |
| | | 14 | 149 |
| | | 18 | 149 |
| | | 21(2) | 149 |
| | | 21(3)*(b)* | 149 |
| | | 21(3)*(c)* | 149 |
| | | 21(4) | 149 |
| | | 24(1) | 149 |
| | | 24(1)*(j)* | 149 |
| | | 24(1)*(k)* | 149 |
| | | 24(2) | 149 |
| | | 24(3) | 149 |
| | | 25–27 | 149 |
| | | 28(1) | 150 |
| | | 28(2) | 150 |
| | | 29 | 150 |
| | | 29(2) | 150 |
| | | 30(1) | 150 |
| | | 30(2) | 150 |
| | | 31 | 150 |
| | | 32 | 150 |
| | | 33 | 150 |
| | | 33(1)*(a)* | 150 |
| | | 33(2) | 150 |
| | | 33(4) | 150 |
| | | 33(5) | 150 |
| | | 34 | 148, 152, 155 |
| | | 36 | 150 |
| | | 38 | 148 |
| | | 41(1) | 149 |
| 148 | 1993 | Independent Media Commission | 145, 151–2 |
| | | s 1(xv) | 152 |
| | | 2(2) | 151 |
| | | 3 | 151 |
| | | 4(1) | 151 |
| | | 4(2) | 151 |
| | | 4(2)*(a)* | 151 |
| | | 5(1) | 151 |
| | | 5(2) | 151 |
| | | 5(3) | 151, 153 |
| | | 5(3)*(b)* | 151 |

| No | Year | Short Title | Page |
|---|---|---|---|
| 148 | 1993 | Independent Media Commission *(cont)* | |
| | | s 6 | 151 |
| | | 6(1) | 153 |
| | | 15(1)*(a)* | 151 |
| | | 15(1)*(b)* | 151 |
| | | 15(2) | 151 |
| | | 15(3) | 151 |
| | | 15(4) | 151 |
| | | 16(1) | 151 |
| | | 16(2) | 151 |
| | | 16(3) | 151 |
| | | 17(1) | 152 |
| | | 17(2) | 152 |
| | | 18–22 | 152 |
| | | 23 | 152 |
| | | 23(12) | 152 |
| | | 24(1) | 152 |
| | | 24(2) | 152 |
| | | 24(3) | 152 |
| | | 26 | 152 |
| | | 33 | 152, 155 |
| | | 35(2) | 151 |
| 24 | 1936 | Insolvency | |
| | | s 21(13) | 558 |
| 74 | 1982 | Internal Security | 278, 293, 294, 378, 410, 413 |
| | | s 4(1) | 378 |
| | | 28 | 407 |
| | | 29 | 407, 409 |
| | | 29(3)*(a)*(i) | 409 |
| | | 29(3)*(a)*(ii) | 409 |
| | | 29(3)*(d)*(ii) | 409 |
| | | 29(9) | 409 |
| | | 46(1) | 294, 296 |
| | | 46(2) | 296 |
| | | 46(3) | 294, 296 |
| | | 47 | 296 |
| | | 48 | 296 |
| | | 49 | 296 |
| | | 51 | 296 |
| | | 52 | 293 |
| | | 53 | 292, 296 |
| | | 57 | 296 |
| | | 58 | 293 |
| | | 59 | 293 |
| | | 62 | 274, 277, 296 |
| | | 66 | 430, 431 |
| | | 71 | 242 |
| 79 | 1976 | Internal Security Amendment | 293, 378 |
| 138 | 1991 | Internal Security and Intimidation Amendment | 378 |
| 72 | 1982 | Intimidation | 297 |
| 28 | 1956 | Labour Relations | 452 |
| | | s 65 | 453, 454 |
| | | 79(1) | 453 |
| 45 | 1988 | Law of Evidence Amendment | |
| | | s 3 | 431 |
| | | 3(4) | 431 |
| | | 6 | 570 |
| 91 | 1985 | Laws on Co-operation and Development Amendment | |
| | | s 1 | 544, 566 |
| 209 | 1993 | Local Government Transition | 147, 156 |
| | | s 1(1)(iv) | 156 |
| | | 1(1)(xi) | 156 |

| No | Year | Short Title | Page |
|---|---|---|---|
| 209 | 1993 | Local Government Transition *(cont)* | |
| | | s 1(1)(xv) | 156 |
| | | 1(1)(xvii) | 156 |
| | | 1(1)(xviii) | 156 |
| | | 5(1) | 156 |
| | | 6 | 156 |
| | | 7(1) | 156 |
| | | 8(1) | 156 |
| | | 126(1) | 156 |
| | | 126(3) | 156 |
| | | Schedule 1 | 156 |
| | | Schedule 6 | 156 |
| 27 | 1989 | Liquor | |
| | | s 160*(d)*(i) | 282 |
| 23 | 1963 | Maintenance | 555 |
| | | s 5(6) | 568, 570 |
| 2 | 1991 | Maintenance Amendment | 555 |
| 27 | 1990 | Maintenance of Surviving Spouses | |
| | | s 1 | 570 |
| | | 2(1) | 570 |
| 25 | 1961 | Marriage | |
| | | s 3 | 558 |
| | | 25(4) | 534 |
| 21 | 1978 | Marriage (Transkei) | |
| | | s 3 | 541 |
| | | 37 | 541, 544, 567 |
| | | 39 | 541, 542, 543, 567 |
| | | Schedule | 541, 544 |
| 3 | 1988 | Marriage and Matrimonial Property Law Amendment | 505, 520, 541, 542, 543, 549, 550, 558, 564, 567 |
| | | s 1 | 523, 569 |
| | | 1*(a)*, *(b)* | 558 |
| 37 | 1953 | Matrimonial Affairs | 534 |
| | | s 5 | 522, 534 |
| | | 5(3)*(b)* | 534 |
| | | 5(4) | 534 |
| 88 | 1984 | Matrimonial Property | 505, 542, 550, 552 |
| | | s 2 | 543, 549, 551 |
| | | 4(1)*(b)*(ii) | 551 |
| | | 4(1)*(b)*(iii) | 551 |
| | | 11 | 520, 541, 544, 545 |
| | | 12 | 544 |
| | | 13 | 510, 511, 520, 521, 534, 544, 545 |
| | | 25 | 541 |
| | | 36 | 549, 550 |
| 18 | 1973 | Mental Health | 278 |
| 102 | 1980 | National Key Points | 278 |
| 89 | 1970 | National Supplies Procurement | 278 |
| 21 | 1923 | Native (Urban Areas) | |
| | | s 10 | 505 |
| 92 | 1982 | Nuclear Energy | 278 |
| 120 | 1977 | Petroleum Products | 278 |
| 7 | 1958 | Police | 278 |
| 30 | 1950 | Population Registration | 133, 134, 506 |
| 44 | 1958 | Post Office | 278 |
| | | s 118A | 242 |
| 133 | 1993 | Prevention of Family Violence | 510, 521, 538, 545 |
| | | s 4 | 546 |
| | | 5 | 510, 546 |
| 139 | 1991 | Prevention of Public Violence and Intimidation | 297 |
| 55 | 1949 | Prohibition of Mixed Marriages | 134, 376, 377 |
| 51 | 1968 | Prohibition of Political Interference | 378 |

# TABLE OF STATUTES

| No | Year | Short Title | | Page |
|---|---|---|---|---|
| 84 | 1982 | Protection of Information | | 278 |
| 3 | 1953 | Public Safety | | 294, 297, 631 |
| | | s | 5*(b)* | 631 |
| | | reg | 7(1) | 294 |
| | | | 7(1)*(b*A) | 294 |
| | | | 7(1)*(d)* | 294 |
| 102 | 1993 | Public Service Labour Relations | | 452 |
| 42 | 1974 | Publications | | 135, 271, 273, 286 |
| | | s | 2 | 271 |
| | | | 4 | 271 |
| | | | 35 | 271 |
| | | | 47(2) | 274 |
| | | | 47(2)*(a)* | 282 |
| | | | 47(2)*(b)* | 281 |
| | | | 47(2)*(c)* | 274, 277 |
| | | | 47(2)*(d)* | 274 |
| | | | 47(2)*(e)* | 278, 280 |
| 3 | 1952 | Radio | | 288 |
| 205 | 1993 | Regulation of Gatherings | | 296–9, 336 |
| | | s | 3(2) | 297, 335 |
| | | | 4(2)*(b)* | 297 |
| | | | 4(3) | 297 |
| | | s | 4(4)*(b)* | 297 |
| | | | 6 | 298 |
| | | | 6(5) | 298 |
| | | | 8(5) | 298 |
| | | | 8(6) | 298 |
| | | | 8(7) | 298 |
| | | | 9(1)*(c)* | 297 |
| | | | 9(2)*(d)* | 299 |
| | | | 9(2)*(e)* | 298, 299 |
| | | | 9(3) | 299 |
| | | | 13(1)*(b)* | 299 |
| 32 | 1961 | Republic of South Africa Constitution | | 132 |
| 110 | 1983 | Republic of South Africa Constitution | | 66, 132, 135 376 |
| | | | Preamble | 597 |
| | | s | 2 | 597 |
| | | s | 7 | 163 |
| 27 | 1914 | Riotous Assemblies | | 293 |
| 17 | 1956 | Riotous Assemblies | | 293 |
| | | s | 2(1) | 294 |
| | | | 17 | 293 |
| 30 | 1974 | Riotous Assemblies Amendment | | |
| | | s | 2(1) | 293 |
| 49 | 1953 | Separate Amenities | | 376, 377 |
| 23 | 1957 | Sexual Offences | | |
| | | s | 16 | 242 |
| | | | 19(6) | 282 |
| | 1909 | South Africa | | 131, 132, 134 |
| 89 | 1977 | Status of Bophuthatswana | | 376 |
| 110 | 1981 | Status of Ciskei | | 376 |
| 100 | 1976 | Status of the Transkei | | 376 |
| 107 | 1979 | Status of Venda | | 376 |
| 44 | 1950 | Suppression of Communism | | 135, 377, 378 |
| | | s | 2(2) | 377 |
| | | | 5 | 293 |
| | | | 9 | 293 |
| 151 | 1993 | Transitional Executive Council | | 143–7, 150 |
| | | s | 1 | 144 |
| | | | 2*(a)* | 145 |
| | | | 3 | 143 |
| | | | 4(1) | 144 |

| No | Year | Short Title | Page |
|---|---|---|---|
| 151 | 1993 | Transitional Executive Council *(cont)* | |
| | | s 4(3) | 144 |
| | | 4(5) | 144 |
| | | 4(8) | 144 |
| | | 7 | 145 |
| | | 7(1)*(b)* | 146 |
| | | 7(1)*(f)* | 146 |
| | | 7(2) | 146 |
| | | 7(3) | 146 |
| | | 7(9) | 144 |
| | | 8(1) | 144, 146 |
| | | 8(1)*(f)* | 141 |
| | | 8(2) | 144 |
| | | 9 | 145 |
| | | 9(1) | 145 |
| | | 9(1)*(a)* | 146 |
| | | 9(3) | 145 |
| | | 12 | 145 |
| | | 13–22 | 145 |
| | | 14 | 145, 156 |
| | | 14*(e)* | 146 |
| | | 16(2)*(f)* | 145 |
| | | 16(11) | 147 |
| | | 17(1)*(h)* | 146 |
| | | 18 | 145 |
| | | 19 | 141 |
| | | 23 | 145, 146 |
| | | 23(1) | 147 |
| | | 23(3) | 147 |
| | | 23(5) | 147 |
| | | 23(6) | 147 |
| | | 25 | 144, 146 |
| | | 25(1) | 146 |
| | | 25(2) | 146 |
| | | 25(2)*(a)* | 146 |
| | | 25(2)*(b)* | 146 |
| | | 25(2)*(c)* | 146 |
| | | 28(1) | 147 |
| | | 28(2) | 147 |
| | | 29(1) | 147 |
| 34 | 1960 | Unlawful Organizations | 377 |
| | | s 1(1) | 377 |
| 30 | 1941 | Workmen's Compensation | |
| | | s 4(3) | 558 |

## FOREIGN JURISDICTIONS

### AUSTRIA

| | 1984 | Federal Constitutional Law | 477 |
|---|---|---|---|

### BERMUDA

Constitution .................................................. 193

### BOTSWANA

Constitution .................................................. 127
art 8 ........................................................ 476

### BRAZIL

Constitution
art 5 ........................................................ 477
5.XXII–XXVI ............................................... 477

# TABLE OF STATUTES xli

| No | Year | Short Title | Page |
|---|---|---|---|
| | | Constitution, Brazil *(cont)* | |
| | | art 5.XXX | 477 |
| | | 7 | 606 |

## CANADA

| No | Year | Short Title | Page |
|---|---|---|---|
| | | Barristers' and Solicitors' | |
| | | s 42 | 206 |
| | 1867 | British North America | 261 |
| | 1982 | Charter of Rights and Freedoms | 26–35, 129, 255, 284, 290, 307–16, 342, 355–8, 442, 443, 633 |
| | | s 1 | 27, 30, 31, 33, 41, 260, 262, 277, 309, 310, 311, 312, 313, 314, 315, 356, 358, 442 |
| | | 2 | 314 |
| | | 2*(a)* | 33 |
| | | 2*(b)* | 34, 266, 277, 308, 309, 310, 311, 312, 313, 314, 315, 357 |
| | | 2*(c)* | 307 |
| | | 2*(d)* | 355, 356, 357, 358 |
| | | 6 | 260 |
| | | 6(1) | 262 |
| | | 6(2) | 260, 262 |
| | | 6(2)*(a)* | 261, 262 |
| | | 6(2)*(b)* | 35, 260, 261, 262 |
| | | 6(3) | 260, 261 |
| | | 6(3)*(a)* | 262 |
| | | 6(4) | 260 |
| | | 7 | 29, 31, 233, 235, 236, 405, 473, 527, 588, 589, 633 |
| | | 8 | 403 |
| | | 10*(b)* | 404 |
| | | 11*(c)* | 404 |
| | | 13 | 404 |
| | | 15 | 32, 33, 34, 35, 205, 207, 261 |
| | | 15(1) | 32, 205, 577, 578 |
| | | 15(2) | 32, 33 |
| | | 16–20 | 577, 578 |
| | | 23 | 606 |
| | | 24(2) | 240 |
| | | 25 | 33 |
| | | 27 | 32, 578 |
| | 1970 | Combines Investigation | 29 |
| | 1960 | Constitution | |
| | | s 1*(a)* | 472 |
| | 1982 | Constitution | |
| | | Part I (Charter of Rights and Freedoms, *qv*) | |
| | | s 11 | 473 |
| | | 91 | 473 |
| | | 92(13) | 473 |
| | 1985 | Criminal Code | 284 |
| | | s 219 | 33 |
| | | 319(2) | 277 |
| | 1982 | Inflation Restraint | 441, 442 |
| | 1970 | Indian | 205 |
| | 1986/8 | Institute | 357 |
| | | Law Society | |
| | | s 28*(c)* | 260, 261 |
| | | Motor Vehicle (British Columbia) | |
| | | s 94(1) | 31 |
| | | 94(2) | 31, 32 |
| | 1985 | Security Intelligence Service | 314, 315 |
| | | s 12, 21–26 | 314 |
| | 1978 | Trade Union | 357 |
| | 1971 | Unemployment | 205 |

## CONGO (BRAZZAVILLE)

Constitution
- art 30 .................................................... 476
- 31 .................................................... 476
- 33 .................................................... 476
- 34 .................................................... 476

## GERMANY

1953 Assembly (*VersammlG*) ........................... 316–27
- art 1.1 ................................................. 318
- 2.2 .............................................. 214, 320
- 2.3 .................................................... 323
- 3 ...................................................... 324
- 3.2 .................................................... 324
- 5 ...................................................... 325
- 5.3 .................................................... 321
- 6–12 ................................................... 321
- 13.1.2 ................................................. 321
- 13.2 ................................................... 319
- 14 ..................................................... 324
- 15 ............................................... 322, 324
- 15.1 ................................................... 324
- 15.2 ................................................... 324
- 17a .................................................... 323
- 17a.3.2 ................................................ 322
- 18.3 ................................................... 325
- 19.4 ................................................... 325

1964 Association (*VereinsG*) ............................ 368
- art 1.2 ................................................. 318
- 2.1 .................................................... 360
- 2.2 .................................................... 369
- 3.1 .............................................. 369, 370
- 3.2 .................................................... 369
- 3.2.4 .................................................. 369
- 4–5 .................................................... 369
- 6 ...................................................... 370
- 8 ...................................................... 369
- 10 ..................................................... 370
- 10–13 .................................................. 370
- 12 ..................................................... 370
- 16.1 ................................................... 370
- 20 ..................................................... 370

1949 Basic Law (*GG*) . 64–121, 316–27, 342, 359–76, 418, 419, 614, 633, 635, 650
- art 1 ........................................ 70, 87, 88, 252
- 1.1 ............... 71, 82, 91, 95, 219, 245, 246, 247, 363
- 1.2 ............................................... 71, 219
- 1.3 ......................... 71, 72, 88, 94, 230, 367
- 2.1 .... 77, 82, 87, 89, 91, 92, 95, 100, 107, 245, 247, 257, 258, 316, 317, 318, 319, 320, 321, 322, 325, 326, 360, 363, 364, 366, 371
- 2.2 ....................................... 96, 103, 218, 233
- 2.2.1 .................................................. 97
- 2.2.2 ............................................. 322, 326
- 3 ...................................................... 445
- 3.1 ..................... 90, 91, 95, 100, 107, 258, 372, 373
- 3.2 ..................................................... 91
- 4 ...................................................... 327
- 5 ................................... 108, 119, 266, 327, 376
- 5.1 ............................................... 102, 360
- 5.2 .................................................... 108
- 5.3 ............................................. 103, 326, 360
- 6 ...................................................... 445
- 6.1 ............................................. 91, 445, 521
- 6.1–6.4 ................................................ 102
- 6.2 ..................................................... 92

# TABLE OF STATUTES

xliii

| No | Year | Short Title | | Page |
|---|---|---|---|---|
| | 1949 | Basic Law (*GG*) *(cont)* | | |
| | | art | 6.5 | 83, 91 |
| | | | 7.4.1 | 101 |
| | | | 8 | 119, 317, 319, 321, 322, 326, 327, 360 |
| | | | 8.1 | 317, 319, 320 |
| | | | 8.2 | 322, 323 |
| | | | 9 | 119, 327, 359, 360, 372 |
| | | | 9.1 | 93, 102, 359, 360, 361, 363, 364, 365, 366, 367, 371 |
| | | | 9.2 | 70, 325, 367, 368–71 |
| | | | 9.3 | 91, 93, 102, 326, 366, 444 |
| | | | 10 | 70, 245, 248 |
| | | | 10.1 | 98 |
| | | | 10.2 | 249, 250 |
| | | | 11 | 84, 257, 258, 259 |
| | | | 11.1 | 257, 258 |
| | | | 11.2 | 84, 257, 258, 259, 260 |
| | | | 12 | 116, 258, 360 |
| | | | 12.1 | 100 |
| | | | 12a.1 | 445 |
| | | | 13 | 245 |
| | | | 13.1 | 250 |
| | | | 13.2 | 250 |
| | | | 13.3 | 250, 251 |
| | | | 14 | 83, 360, 365, 469, 470, 471 |
| | | | 14.1 | 468, 469, 470, 471, 482 |
| | | | 14.1.2 | 72, 92, 94 |
| | | | 14.2 | 72, 468, 470, 482 |
| | | | 14.3 | 472 |
| | | | 16.2 | 257 |
| | | | 17a.2 | 250, 257, 259 |
| | | | 18 | 70, 75, 276, 325, 369 |
| | | | 19 | 108 |
| | | | 19.1 | 250, 260, 323 |
| | | | 19.2 | 70, 71, 250, 468 |
| | | | 19.3 | 71, 212, 290, 319, 360, 363, 364 |
| | | | 20 | 70, 72, 87, 445 |
| | | | 20.1 | 89, 276 |
| | | | 20.2 | 81, 276 |
| | | | 20.3 | 71, 72, 87, 90, 95 |
| | | | 21 | 327, 360, 371–6 |
| | | | 21.1 | 364, 375 |
| | | | 21.2 | 70, 325, 326, 369, 374, 375 |
| | | | 21.2.2 | 75 |
| | | | 23 | 73 |
| | | | 26 | 369 |
| | | | 28.1 | 91 |
| | | | 28.1.3 | 320 |
| | | | 33 | 375 |
| | | | 33.1 | 258 |
| | | | 33.5 | 325 |
| | | | 38 | 374 |
| | | | 38.1 | 372 |
| | | | 41 | 75 |
| | | | 59.2 | 75 |
| | | | 61 | 75 |
| | | | 67 | 68, 71 |
| | | | 72.1 | 113 |
| | | | 72.2 | 113 |
| | | | 77.4 | 114 |
| | | | 79 | 81 |
| | | | 79.1 | 81 |
| | | | 79.3 | 68, 70, 71 |

| No | Year | Short Title | Page |
|---|---|---|---|
| | 1949 | Basic Law (*GG*) (*cont*) | |
| | | art 83 | 72 |
| | | 92–103 | 73 |
| | | 93.1 | 75 |
| | | 93.1.2 | 75, 76 |
| | | 93.1.3 | 75 |
| | | 93.1.4 | 75 |
| | | 93.1.4a | 77 |
| | | 93.1.4b | 75 |
| | | 93.2 | 76 |
| | | 94.1.1 | 74 |
| | | 98.2 | 75 |
| | | 99 | 75 |
| | | 100.1 | 76, 84 |
| | | 100.2 | 75 |
| | | 100.3 | 75 |
| | | 101–104 | 95 |
| | | 102 | 218 |
| | | 104 | 258 |
| | | 115.h | 73 |
| | | 116 | 257 |
| | | 117.1 | 91 |
| | | 126 | 76 |
| | | 140 | 359, 360 |
| | | Civil Code (*Bürgerliches Gesetzbuch, BGB*) | |
| | | art 39 | 367 |
| | | 63 | 367 |
| | | 138 | 259 |
| | | 826 | 367 |
| | | 903 | 469 |
| | | 1363ff | 549 |
| | | 1587ff | 549 |
| | 1976 | Co-determination | 93, 105, 361, 365 |
| | | Criminal Code (*Strafgesetzbuch, StGB*) | |
| | | arts 85–86 | 370 |
| | | 123 | 492 |
| | | 130 | 276 |
| | | 131 | 276 |
| | | 136a.i–ii | 425 |
| | | 152 | 405 |
| | | 171–175 | 405 |
| | | 184 | 284 |
| | 1815 | German Confederation (*Deutsche Bundesakte*) | 66 |
| | | art 13 | 64 |
| | 1933 | Enabling | 68 |
| | 1951 | Federal Constitutional Court (*BVerfGG*) | 73, 82 |
| | | art 1 | 73 |
| | | 1.3 | 73 |
| | | 2.3 | 74 |
| | | 3 | 74 |
| | | 4 | 74 |
| | | 5 | 74 |
| | | 7 | 74 |
| | | 13.14 | 76 |
| | | 24 | 78 |
| | | 26 | 78 |
| | | 30.2.1 | 79 |
| | | 31.1 | 80, 81 |
| | | 31.2 | 80, 82, 83 |
| | | 32.2 | 81 |
| | | 34.1 | 78 |
| | | 34.2 | 78 |

| No | Year | Short Title | Page |
|---|---|---|---|
| | 1951 | Federal Constitutional Court (*BVerfGG*) *(cont)* | |
| | | art 34.4 | 78 |
| | | 35 | 81 |
| | | 39.2.2 | 79 |
| | | 43.1 | 70 |
| | | 43–47 | 375 |
| | | 48 | 75 |
| | | 79.1 | 82 |
| | | 80.2 | 76 |
| | | 90.1 | 78 |
| | | 90.2 | 77 |
| | | 93b.1 | 78 |
| | | 93b.2 | 78 |
| | | 93c | 78 |
| | | 105 | 73 |
| | 1990 | Federal Electoral (*Bundeswahlgesetz*) | |
| | | art 21 | 373 |
| | 1908 | German Imperial Associations (*Reichsvereinsgesetz*) | 368 |
| | | art 12 | 318 |
| | 1871 | German Imperial Constitution (*Reichsverfassung*) | 66 |
| | 1849 | Paulskirche Constitution | 65, 359 |
| | | art 1 | 257 |
| | | 7.29 | 317 |
| | | 126 | 66 |
| | 1967 | Political Parties (*PartG*) | |
| | | art 2 | 371 |
| | | 10 | 367 |
| | | 10.4 | 373 |
| | | 18 | 374 |
| | 1919 | Weimar Constitution (*Weimar Reichsverfassung, WRV*) | 67, 68, 69, 90, 359 |
| | | art 11 | 257 |
| | | 13.2 | 67 |
| | | 76 | 68 |
| | | 76.1 | 67 |
| | | 123 | 317 |
| | | 136–139 | 359 |
| | | 141 | 359 |

## GREECE

| | | | |
|---|---|---|---|
| | | Constitution | |
| | | art 16 | 613 |
| | | 21 | 613 |
| | | 22 | 613 |
| | | 24 | 478 |

## HUNGARY

| | | | |
|---|---|---|---|
| | | Constitution | 478 |

## INDIA

| No | Year | Short Title | Page |
|---|---|---|---|
| | | Bihar Land Reforms | 37 |
| 1 | 1956 | Companies | |
| | | s 398(1)(*a*) | 54 |
| | | 433(*f*) | 54 |
| | 1950 | Constitution | 35–64, 89, 124, 618–21 |
| | | Preamble | 55 |
| | | art 12 | 52 |
| | | 13 | 52 |
| | | 14 | 37, 38, 46, 49, 53, 54, 204 |
| | | 15(2) | 53 |
| | | 16 | 606 |
| | | 17 | 52, 53 |
| | | 19 | 37 |

| No | Year | Short Title | Page |
|---|---|---|---|
| | 1950 | Constitution, India *(cont)* | |
| | | art 19(1) | 474 |
| | | 19(1)*(a)* | 63, 267 |
| | | 19(1)*(b)* | 63 |
| | | 19(1)*(c)* | 63 |
| | | 19(1)*(d)* | 63, 222 |
| | | 19(1)*(e)* | 63 |
| | | 19(1)*(f)* | 36, 63, 474 |
| | | 19(1)*(g)* | 63 |
| | | 19(2) | 63 |
| | | 19(5) | 36, 474 |
| | | 19(6) | 63 |
| | | 21 | 46, 48, 49, 50, 51, 53, 54, 63, 220, 221, 222, 224 |
| | | 23 | 51, 52, 53 |
| | | 24 | 52, 53 |
| | | 29 | 577 |
| | | 29(1) | 576, 577 |
| | | 29(2) | 576 |
| | | 30 | 577 |
| | | 31 | 36, 37, 38, 474 |
| | | 31(1) | 37 |
| | | 31(4) | 37 |
| | | 32 | 55, 59 |
| | | 36–51 | 614, 618 |
| | | 37 | 619 |
| | | 38(2) | 222 |
| | | 39 | 474 |
| | | 39*(a)* | 221 |
| | | 39*(b)* | 474 |
| | | 41 | 221 |
| | | 43A | 55, 451 |
| | | 48A | 478 |
| | | 49 | 50, 51 |
| | | 368 | 37, 39, 43 |
| | | Amendments | |
| | | First | 37 |
| | | Fourth | 38 |
| | | Seventh | 37 |
| | | Seventeenth | 37 |
| | | Twenty-fourth | 39 |
| | | Twenty-fifth | 39, 620 |
| | | Thirty-ninth | 40 |
| | | Forty-second | 55, 620 |
| | | Forty-fourth | 474 |
| | 1970 | Contract Labour | 53, 54 |
| | 1976 | Equal Remuneration | 53, 54 |
| | 1979 | Inter State Migrant Workmen | 53, 54 |
| | 1894 | Land Acquisition | 38 |
| | 1948 | Minimum Wage | 620 |

## IRELAND

| No | Year | Short Title | Page |
|---|---|---|---|
| | 1942 | Central Bank | |
| | | s 6.1 | 616 |
| | 1922 | Constitution | 615–18 |
| | | art 40.3.3 | 230 |
| | | 42 | 613 |
| | | 43 | 476 |
| | | 43.1.1 | 476 |
| | | 43.1.2 | 476 |
| | | 43.2.1 | 477 |
| | | 43.2.2 | 477 |
| | | 45 | 614, 615 |

| No | Year | Short Title | Page |
|---|---|---|---|
| | 1922 | Constitution, Ireland *(cont)* | |
| | | art 45.1 | 616 |
| | | 45.2.2 | 617 |

## ITALY

Constitution .................................................. 375
    art    18 ............................................. 445
              39 ............................................. 445
              40 ......................................... 445, 446

| | 1970 | Workers' Statute ................................ | 445, 446 |

## JAPAN

Constitution
    art    25 ............................................. 625

## LESOTHO

Constitution .................................................. 478

## MALAWI

Constitution

| 23 | 1966 | s 2(1)(iv) ................................ | 476 |

## MALAYSIA

| | 1957 | Constitution | |
| | | art 13 .................................... | 477 |
| | | 13(1) ................................... | 477 |
| | | 13(2) ................................... | 477 |

## MAURITIUS

Constitution
    art    8 .............................................. 476

## MOZAMBIQUE

Constitution
    art    12 ............................................. 476
              13 ............................................. 476

## NAMIBIA

Constitution
    art    6 ......................................... 226, 234
              7 ......................................... 234, 405
              8(2)*(b)* ........................... 234, 241, 404, 425
              10 ........................................ 425, 475
              11(1) ........................................... 404
              12 .............................................. 405
              12(1)*(a)* ................................... 405, 418
              12(1)*(d)* ........................................ 405
              12(1)*(e)* ........................................ 405
              12(1)*(f)* ............................... 240, 404, 425
              13 ........................................ 403, 425
              13(1) ........................................... 403
              13(1)*(f)* ....................................... 405
              13(2) ........................................... 403
              14(3) ........................................... 606
              16 .............................................. 475
              16(1) ........................................... 475
              16(2) ........................................... 475
              18 .............................................. 388
              20 .............................................. 613
              21 .............................................. 267

| No | Year | Short Title | Page |
|---|---|---|---|
| | | Constitution, Namibia *(cont)* | |
| | | art 22 | 650 |
| | | 23 | 475, 613 |
| | | 95 | 613 |
| | | 95*(h)* | 419 |
| | | 95–101 | 613, 614 |

### NETHERLANDS, THE

Constitution . . . . . . 473
art 1.18 . . . . . . 613
 1.20 . . . . . . 613
 20.1 . . . . . . 477
 20.2–.3 . . . . . . 477
 21 . . . . . . 477, 478
Criminal Code
art 138 . . . . . . 492

### NEW ZEALAND

| 94 | 1993 | Films, Videos and Publications Classification | 284 |
|---|---|---|---|

### NIGERIA

| | 1960 | Independence Constitution | |
|---|---|---|---|
| | | art 14–22 | 614 |
| | | 40 | 476 |
| | | 42(1) | 475 |
| | | 42(2) | 475 |

### PORTUGAL

Constitution
art 9 . . . . . . 614
 10 . . . . . . 478
 60 . . . . . . 446
 65 . . . . . . 613
 66 . . . . . . 625
 67 . . . . . . 613

### SENEGAL

Constitution
art 12 . . . . . . 476

### SIERRA LEONE

Constitution
art 11 . . . . . . 476

### SOMALIA

Constitution
art 28 . . . . . . 476

### SPAIN

Constitution
art 37 . . . . . . 606
 39–52 . . . . . . 614
 43 . . . . . . 625
 45(1) . . . . . . 478

### SRI LANKA

Constitution
art 27(14) . . . . . . 478

TABLE OF STATUTES                                                                                    xlix

## SWEDEN

|      | Constitution | 445 |
| 1976 | Joint Regulation of Working Rights |  |
|      | s 7 | 445 |

## SWITZERLAND

Constitution
art 24*sept* ................................................. 478
    26 ..................................................... 613

## TANZANIA

Constitution
art 24 ..................................................... 476

## TRINIDAD AND TOBAGO

Constitution ................................................. 444
s 13 ......................................................... 41

## TURKEY

Constitution
art 56 ..................................................... 478

## UGANDA

Constitution
art 13 ..................................................... 476

## UNITED KINGDOM

| 1967 | Abortion | 547 |
| 1982 | Canada |  |
|      | Schedule B | 473 |
| 1989 | Children | 509 |
| 1984 | Matrimonial and Family Proceedings | 507, 549, 553 |
| 1973 | Matrimonial Causes | 549, 554 |
| 1970 | Matrimonial Proceedings and Property | 549 |
| 1959 | Obscene Publications | 284 |
| 1984 | Police and Criminal Evidence |  |
|      | s 78 | 424 |

## UNITED STATES OF AMERICA

| 1964 | Civil Rights | 76 |
|      | Title VII | 198, 440 |
| 1917 | Conscription | 278 |
|      | Constitution | 89, 299–307, 342–55, 478, 529, 612, 633, 648 |
|      | art 1 | 593 |
|      | 4(2) | 258 |

Amendments
First ........ 25, 243, 266, 275, 279, 284, 290, 300–1, 302, 305,
                306, 307, 343, 344, 345, 346, 347, 353, 441, 593,
                                                            594, 595
First–Tenth ............................................... 418
Third ..................................................... 243
Fourth ................................... 243, 245, 403, 404, 424
Fifth .......... 3, 4, 23, 219, 233, 243, 255, 256, 258, 405, 418,
                                                    424, 464, 465, 466
Sixth ................................................. 418, 431
Seventh ................................................... 418
Eighth ................................................ 3, 4, 433
Ninth .................................................. 15, 243
Thirteenth ................................................. 53
Fourteenth ...... 15, 34, 35, 198, 199, 207, 219, 233, 243, 255, 302,
                         333, 343, 349, 405, 418, 464, 465, 527
Fifteenth ............................................. 346, 347

| No | Year | Short Title | Page |
|---|---|---|---|
| | 1776 | Constitution of the State of Virginia | |
| | | art  1 | 601 |
| | 1972 | Equal Employment Opportunity | 440 |
| | 1917 | Espionage | 278 |
| | 1989 | Flag Protection | 275 |
| | 1935 | National Labour Relations | 440 |
| | 1890 | Sherman Anti-Trust | 440 |
| | 1940 | Smith 279 | |

## ZAÏRE

Constitution
art  21 . . . . . . . . . . . . . . . . . . . . . . . . . . . . . . . . . . . 476

## ZAMBIA

Constitution
art  18 . . . . . . . . . . . . . . . . . . . . . . . . . . . . . . . . . . . 476

## ZIMBABWE

1979 Constitution
s  15(1) . . . . . . . . . . . . . . . . . . . . . . . . . . . . . . . 228, 241
  16 . . . . . . . . . . . . . . . . . . . . . . . . . . . . . . . . . 476

## INTERNATIONAL

1981 African Charter on Human and Peoples' Rights (Banjul Charter) . . . 127, 182, 184, 188–9, 238, 242, 532, 651
    art  4 . . . . . . . . . . . . . . . . . . . . . . . . . . . . . . 217, 225, 234
        6 . . . . . . . . . . . . . . . . . . . . . . . . . . . . . . . . . . 234
        9 . . . . . . . . . . . . . . . . . . . . . . . . . . . . . . . . . . 266
        12 . . . . . . . . . . . . . . . . . . . . . . . . . . . . . . . . . 254
        14 . . . . . . . . . . . . . . . . . . . . . . . . . . . . . . . . . 464
        15 . . . . . . . . . . . . . . . . . . . . . . . . . . . . . . . . . 610
        16 . . . . . . . . . . . . . . . . . . . . . . . . . . . . . . . . . 610
        17 . . . . . . . . . . . . . . . . . . . . . . . . . . . . . . . 584, 610
        18 . . . . . . . . . . . . . . . . . . . . . . . . . . . . . . . 521, 610
        20 . . . . . . . . . . . . . . . . . . . . . . . . . . . . . . . . . 189
        27–29 . . . . . . . . . . . . . . . . . . . . . . . . . . . . . . . . 464
        58 . . . . . . . . . . . . . . . . . . . . . . . . . . . . . . . . . 189
1969 American Convention on Human Rights . . . . . . . . . . . . 187–8, 190, 230
    art  4 . . . . . . . . . . . . . . . . . . . . . . . . . . . . . . . . . 234
        4(1) . . . . . . . . . . . . . . . . . . . . . . . . . . . . . 187, 217, 229
        4(2) . . . . . . . . . . . . . . . . . . . . . . . . . . . . . . . . 225
    art  4(3) . . . . . . . . . . . . . . . . . . . . . . . . . . . . . . . . 225
        4(4) . . . . . . . . . . . . . . . . . . . . . . . . . . . . . . . . 225
        5 . . . . . . . . . . . . . . . . . . . . . . . . . . . . . . . 234, 237
        11 . . . . . . . . . . . . . . . . . . . . . . . . . . . . . . . . . 242
        13 . . . . . . . . . . . . . . . . . . . . . . . . . . . . . . . . . 266
        21 . . . . . . . . . . . . . . . . . . . . . . . . . . . . . . . 187, 464
        22 . . . . . . . . . . . . . . . . . . . . . . . . . . . . . . . . . 254
        26 . . . . . . . . . . . . . . . . . . . . . . . . . . . . . . . . . 187
        27 . . . . . . . . . . . . . . . . . . . . . . . . . . . . . . . . . 464
        28 . . . . . . . . . . . . . . . . . . . . . . . . . . . . . . . . . 187
        45 . . . . . . . . . . . . . . . . . . . . . . . . . . . . . . . . . 187
    Protocols
1988     Additional . . . . . . . . . . . . . . . . . . . . . . . . . . . . . 187
1948 American Declaration on the Rights and Duties of Man . . . . . . . . 187, 188
    art  1 . . . . . . . . . . . . . . . . . . . . . . . . . . . . . . . . . 188
        4 . . . . . . . . . . . . . . . . . . . . . . . . . . . . . . . . . 266
        22 . . . . . . . . . . . . . . . . . . . . . . . . . . . . . . . . . 447
        23 . . . . . . . . . . . . . . . . . . . . . . . . . . . . . . . . . 464
1948 Charter of the Organization of American States . . . . . . . . . . . 187, 188

| No | Year | Short Title | Page |
|---|---|---|---|
| | 1984 | Convention against Torture and Other Cruel, Inhuman or Degrading Treatment or Punishment | 181, 189, 195 |
| | | art 1 | 181 |
| | | 1(1) | 239 |
| | | 2(2) | 240 |
| | | 2(3) | 240 |
| | | 20 | 181, 182 |
| | | 28 | 182 |
| | 1962 | Convention on Consent to Marriage, Minimum Age for Marriage and Registration of Marriages | 189 |
| | 1979 | Convention on the Elimination of Discrimination against Women | 127, 179–80, 189, 195 |
| | | art 1 | 179 |
| | | 4(1) | 179 |
| | | 4(2) | 179 |
| | | 16(e) | 546 |
| | 1957 | Convention on the Nationality of Married Women | 189 |
| | 1953 | Convention on the Political Rights of Women | 189 |
| | | Convention on the Prevention and Punishment of the Crime of Genocide | 225 |
| | 1961 | Convention on the Reduction of Statelessness | 183 |
| | 1989 | Convention on the Rights of the Child | 180, 189, 195, 537, 539 |
| | | art 1 | 230 |
| | | 6 | 230 |
| | | 6(1) | 230 |
| | | 6(2) | 230 |
| | | 9 | 537 |
| | | 12 | 537 |
| | 1951 | Convention relating to the Status of Refugees | 183 |
| | 1967 | Protocol | 183 |
| | 1954 | Convention relating to the Status of Stateless Persons | 183 |
| | 1981 | Declaration on the Elimination of All Forms of Intolerance and Discrimination Based on Religion or Belief | 183 |
| | 1986 | Declaration on the Right to Development | 182, 183 |
| | 1959 | Declaration on the Rights of the Child | 229, 230 |
| | 1950 | European Convention for the Protection of Human Rights and Fundamental Freedoms | 127, 184–7, 190, 191, 192, 194, 195, 539, 609, 610, 639, 645, 647, 653 |
| | | art 1 | 184, 263 |
| | | 2 | 234, 584, 585, 587, 588 |
| | | 2(1) | 217, 225 |
| | | 2(2) | 217, 228 |
| | | 3 | 234 |
| | | 4(3)(B) | 596 |
| | | 5 | 234, 237 |
| | | 5(1) | 237 |
| | | 8 | 242 |
| | | 9 | 595, 596 |
| | | 9(2) | 506 |
| | | 10 | 266 |
| | | 11 | 318, 447 |
| | | 11(1) | 443, 448 |
| | | 13 | 185 |
| | | 14 | 201, 202, 207 |
| | | 15 | 652, 654 |
| | | 15(1) | 654, 657, 660, 663 |
| | | 24 | 185, 186 |
| | | 25 | 185, 547 |
| | | 26 | 185 |
| | | 27 | 185 |
| | | Protocols | |
| | | First | 184, 584, 585, 588 |
| | | Fourth | 254 |

| No | Year | Short Title | Page |
|---|---|---|---|
| | 1950 | European Convention for the Protection of Human Rights and Fundamental Freedoms, Protocols *(cont)* | |
| | | Sixth | 184, 217, 225, 226 |
| | 1987 | European Convention on Torture | 181 |
| | | European Economic Community Treaty | |
| | | art  119 | 448 |
| | | Directive 75/117 | 449 |
| | 1961 | European Social Charter | 184, 610, 614 |
| | | art  1 | 609 |
| | |       2 | 609 |
| | |       5 | 447 |
| | |       6 | 447 |
| | |       11 | 609 |
| | |       12 | 609 |
| | |       30(1) | 660 |
| | 1949 | Geneva Conventions on the Laws of War | 660, 661 |
| | | Additional Protocol II | 660 |
| | 1965 | International Convention on the Elimination of All Forms of Racial Discrimination | 178–9, 189, 195 |
| | | Preamble | 268 |
| | | art  1(1) | 178 |
| | |       1(4) | 179 |
| | |       2 | 178 |
| | |       2(1)*(d)* | 178 |
| | |       2(2) | 179 |
| | |       3 | 178 |
| | |       4 | 179, 274 |
| | |       5 | 178, 576 |
| | |       5*(d)*(v) | 463 |
| | |       5*(f)* | 178 |
| | |       6 | 178 |
| | |       14 | 179 |
| | 1973 | International Convention on the Suppression and Punishment of the Crime of Apartheid | 180–1 |
| | | art  1 | 180 |
| | |       2 | 180 |
| | |       3 | 180 |
| | |       4 | 180, 181 |
| | |       5 | 180 |
| | |       11 | 180 |
| | 1966 | International Covenant on Economic, Social and Cultural Rights | 177–8, 447, 606, 608, 614 |
| | | art  2 | 177, 608 |
| | |       2(2) | 177 |
| | |       6 | 177, 608 |
| | |       7 | 177, 608 |
| | |       7*(a)* | 608 |
| | |       8 | 177 |
| | |       9 | 177, 608 |
| | |       10 | 608 |
| | |       11 | 177 |
| | |       12 | 177 |
| | |       13 | 177 |
| | |       13(1) | 583 |
| | |       13(2) | 583 |
| | |       15 | 177, 575 |
| | 1966 | International Covenant on Civil and Political Rights | 174–7, 181, 184, 187, 189, 190, 191, 192, 195, 201, 209, 217, 607, 639, 644, 653 |
| | | art  1 | 174, 226 |
| | |       2 | 226 |
| | |       2(1) | 578 |
| | |       4 | 652, 654 |

# TABLE OF STATUTES

| No | Year | Short Title | Page |
|---|---|---|---|
| | 1966 | International Covenant on Civil and Political Rights *(cont)* | |
| | | art 4(1) | 654, 655, 657, 660, 663 |
| | | 4(2) | 226 |
| | | 6 | 174, 216, 225, 226, 227, 229, 234 |
| | | 6(1) | 216, 217, 223 |
| | | 6(2)–(6) | 216, 218, 224, 225, 434 |
| | | 6(3) | 225 |
| | | 6(4) | 225, 434 |
| | | 6(5) | 225, 229, 434 |
| | | 6(6) | 225 |
| | | 7 | 174, 234, 238, 241 |
| | | 8 | 174 |
| | | 9 | 174, 234, 237 |
| | | 11 | 237 |
| | | 12 | 175, 254 |
| | | 14 | 174, 209 |
| | | 15 | 174 |
| | | 17 | 242 |
| | | 18 | 175, 593 |
| | | 19 | 175, 266 |
| | | 19(2) | 266 |
| | | 19(3) | 266 |
| | | 20 | 175, 266, 274 |
| | | 21 | 175 |
| | | 22 | 175, 447 |
| | | 23 | 175 |
| | | 24 | 175 |
| | | 25 | 175 |
| | | 26 | 175, 578 |
| | | 27 | 175, 177, 576, 578 |
| | | 40(4) | 176 |
| | | 41 | 176 |
| | | Protocols | |
| | | First | 176 |
| | | Second | 174 |
| | 1985 | Inter-American Convention on Torture | 181 |
| | | International Labour Organization | 446–7 |
| | | Convention 87 | 446, 447 |
| | | 98 | 446, 447 |
| | | 135 | 447 |
| | | 141 | 447 |
| | | 151 | 447 |
| | | 153 | 447 |
| | 1926 | Slavery Convention | 183 |
| | 1953 | Protocol Amending | 183 |
| | 1957 | Standard Minimum Rules for the Treatment of Offenders | 183, 191 |
| | | art 31 | 191 |
| | 1945 | Statute of the International Court of Justice | 193 |
| | 1993 | Vienna Declaration on Human Rights and Programme of Action | 183 |
| | 1945 | United Nations Charter | 171–2, 189, 190, 192 |
| | | art 1 | 171 |
| | | 2(4) | 654 |
| | | 2(7) | 172 |
| | | 13 | 172 |
| | | 51 | 654 |
| | | 55 | 172, 178 |
| | | 56 | 172 |
| | 1948 | Universal Declaration of Human Rights | 172–4, 184, 187, 189, 190, 194, 217, 612 |
| | | art 3 | 216, 229, 233, 237 |
| | | 12 | 242 |
| | | 13 | 254 |

| No | Year | Short Title | Page |
|---|---|---|---|
| | 1948 | Universal Declaration of Human Rights *(cont)* | |
| | | art 17 | 175, 463 |
| | | 18 | 593 |
| | | 19 | 266 |
| | | 20 | 447 |
| | | 21(3) | 601 |
| | | 22 | 607 |
| | | 23 | 447, 607 |
| | | 25 | 607 |
| | | 26 | 583, 584 |
| | | 26(1) | 583 |
| | | 26(2) | 583 |
| | | 26(3) | 583 |
| | | 27 | 575 |
| | | 27(1) | 575 |
| | | 29 | 463 |

# DEMOCRACY AND CONSTITUTIONALISM: THE ROLE OF CONSTITUTIONAL INTERPRETATION

DENNIS DAVIS, MATTHEW CHASKALSON & JOHAN DE WAAL

1   INTRODUCTION

Constitutionalism has finally been placed on the South African political agenda. In itself, this could produce a legal revolution. To date South African public law has been dominated by English antecedence, both in its structure and content. The British colonization of the Cape in the eighteenth century resulted in a dominance of English legal tradition such that the South African legal profession, both academic and practising, adopted an almost slavish adherence to Anglocentric legal traditions and concepts. Dicey became the jurisprudential source of South African constitutional law and it was his concept of the rule of law which constituted the yardstick by which to test the democratic nature of the principles and content of South African public law.

Briefly stated, Dicey's concept of the rule of law comprised three fundamental tenets: the regular law of the land was supreme so that individuals should not be subject to arbitrary power; state officials were subject to the jurisdiction of the ordinary courts of the land in the same manner as individual citizens; and the Constitution was the result of the ordinary law of the land so that the courts should determine the position of the executive and the bureaucracy by principles of private law. The equation of the common law, which protects the private sphere of individual autonomy, with the ordinary law of the land prevented the development of adequate legal principles to which the bureaucracy was subject.

South African constitutional law became a mixture of Diceyean constitutionalism and white majoritarianism, in which democratic rights were conflated with the rights of the majority of the white people, or the majority of their parliamentary representatives. It proved to be a fatal brew. With the acceptance of a constitutional democracy the output of the majoritarian legislature and executive is to be filtered by radically different concepts of constitutional law. Whatever its content, the new South African Bill of Rights will accord greater weight to certain rights than to the decisions of Parliament, notwithstanding the latter's ostensible democratic pedigree. In short, South Africans will bind themselves to certain values which trump the output of a transient legislature.

Herein lies the puzzle of constitutionalism: what is the basis for the binding quality of rights and their ability to trump the outcome of democratic decision-making? One contemporary US commentator has suggested that the explanation is to be found in the courts' custodial function of preserving the decisions of 'we the people' against any potential undermining thereof by government. When 'we the people' have formulated a constitutional choice, it binds the more limited authority of government, however constituted. The people are the source of constitutional values, but the government is not 'the people', for a constitutional structure which separates the powers of the legislative and executive arms of government from that of the judiciary with a constitutional power of review prevents one branch of the government from being able authoritatively to represent 'we the people', according to Ackerman.[1]

This argument is vulnerable to the criticism that no clear distinction can easily be drawn between normal and constitutional politics. However, Ackerman's thesis has the benefit that it emphasizes that majoritarianism has no exclusive claim on the meaning of democracy. Constitutionalism proclaims that there are characteristics fundamental to the democratic enterprise which cannot be amended or destroyed even by a majority government. Each citizen must be allowed to participate within the political process and thereby be empowered to make a difference to the character of political decisions. This process of participation cannot be qualified or limited by assumptions of talent, ability, or economic resources. Individuals can only count as members of the political community when the principle of equal concern and respect is safeguarded.

But if 'we the people' set down principles in a constitutional document, the onus is placed upon the judges to preserve these principles against incursions by government. In this role the judiciary does not engage in a simple exercise of interpretation of statutes. Unfortunately South African judges, trained in the ways of Westminster-type constitutional law, have not always grasped this distinction. In cases such as *Government of the Republic of Bophuthatswana v Segale*,[2] *Monnakale v Republic of Bophuthatswana*,[3] and *Lewis v Minister of Internal Affairs*[4] the court interpreted the Bophuthatswana Bill of Rights in terms of adherence to the clear and unambiguous language of statutes encroaching on fundamental rights and not the other way round, particularly where the interests of the state so demanded. A similar approach was adopted by Pickard CJ in *Bongopi v Chairman of the Council of State, Ciskei*,[5] as illustrated in the following passage:

> 'This court has always stated openly that it is not the maker of laws. It will enforce the law as it finds it. To attempt to promote policies that are not to be found in the law itself or to prescribe what it believes to be the current public attitudes or standards in regard to these policies is not its function.'

Unlike ordinary legislation, a Bill of Rights enjoys particular status as a link between the political morality and aspirations of a society and positive law. Consequently a particular set of political convictions gains the imprimatur of positive legal authority. Thus it constrains competing moralities with which it is inconsistent in the name of 'the people', from whom the document draws its sovereign authority. Furthermore, unlike ordinary legislation, a Bill of Rights talks to society and informs

---

[1] Ackerman *We the People* (1991).
[2] 1990 (1) SA 434 (BA).
[3] 1991 (1) SA 598 (BA).
[4] 1991 (3) SA 628 (BA).
[5] 1992 (3) SA 250 (Ck) at 265H–I.

it, not only of what kind of society it is but also of the one which it ought to be. It contains not only constraints but also aspirations.

As custodians of the vision of the society as outlined in the Constitution, judges have a complex task. In particular they have to grapple with the plasticity and ambiguity of language. It is in this area that we confront perhaps the most vigorous and important debate in so far as a Bill of Rights is concerned: the most appropriate theory according to which the Constitution should be read. Surprisingly it was a conservative US Supreme Court judge, William Rehnquist, who in 1976 said:

> 'The framers of the Constitution wisely spoke in general language and left to succeeding generations the task of applying that language to the unceasingly changing environment in which they would live ... Where the framers ... have used general language, they have given latitude to those who would later interpret the instrument to make that language applicable to cases that the framers might not have foreseen.'[6]

Notwithstanding that Rehnquist has subsequently sought to distance himself from these ideas, the point remains valid. The influence of a different historical context and the openness of language do compel judges to make some basic choices in giving the Constitution its content. As another member of the present US Supreme Court, John Paul Stevens, has observed:

> 'If the task of judicial construction began and ended with the grammatical and etymological analysis of legal texts, or even if it were slightly expanded to include an analysis of the original intent of those who drafted and enacted that text into positive law, one would expect an impartial court to reject any claim that the word "liberty", as used in the 1791 Constitution, endorsed the revolutionary idea that all men were created equal. For the text of the 1791 Constitution, before as well as after the ratification of the bill of rights, expressly approved of invidious discrimination. Article IV provided positive protection for the institution of slavery and art I provided for the purpose of apportioning congressional representatives, each slave should be counted as three-fifths of a person ... The framers had constructed a document that, like the fledgling nation itself, could be described as a house divided against itself — an institution that was half slave and half free. A Constitution that expressly tolerated the worst kind of discrimination could not simultaneously condemn all irrational discrimination.'[7]

The judicial role in constitutional interpretation turns on the ability to tease from a series of written clauses a political philosophy upon which society is to be based. This requires an engagement with the text, a task which is succinctly illustrated by Laurence Tribe and Michael Dorf in their recent work as follows:[8] they refer to the Fifth Amendment of the Constitution, which provides that no person shall be deprived of life, liberty, or property without due process of law. Former Chief Justice Berger argued that the authors of the Constitution obviously must have contemplated that with due process of law a person may be deprived of life. Thus capital punishment imposed after due process of law is constitutional. The simplicity of the argument is superficially attractive until consideration is given to the fact that the Fifth Amendment is only part of the Constitution. The Eighth Amendment, which provides that cruel and unusual punishment should not be imposed, is as vital to the consideration of the constitutionality of the death penalty as is the Fifth Amendment.

---

[6] Rehnquist 'The Notion of a Living Constitution' (1976) 54 *Texas LR* 693 at 694.
[7] Stevens 'A Bill of Rights: A Century of Progress' in Stone, Epstein & Sunstein *The Bill of Rights in the Modern State* (1992) 13 at 21.
[8] Tribe & Dorf *On Reading the Constitution* (1992) 21–2.

In 1791 both the Fifth and Eighth Amendments were ratified and capital punishment was clearly not considered to be a cruel and unusual punishment, but today, in an era in which the overwhelming majority of industrialized nations have abolished capital punishment, the result could well be different. Indeed, if reliance is placed only on the Fifth Amendment, the amputation of the hands of thieves could well be constitutional, provided that it was sanctioned by due process of law. As Tribe & Dorf note, 'no one could seriously argue today that bodily mutilation employed on occasions of punishment during colonial times could withstand scrutiny under the Eighth Amendment'.

The fact that the US Constitution is more than 200 years old serves to highlight the need to transcend the limitations of an exclusively textual interpretation. The art of contextualizing history forces value choices upon judges. These constitutional choices cannot be made without recourse to a system of values which is external to the text in the sense that the values emanate from the ideas which underpin the text rather than from the express wording thereof.

The history of comparative constitutionalism reveals a considerable ideological and jurisprudential struggle on the part of the judiciary to develop a coherent set of constitutional values which emanate clearly from a Bill of Rights and which can act as reliable signposts *en route* to a decision. It is to this struggle and the competing treatment within the body of comparative constitutional jurisprudence that we now turn.

To obtain guidance for an enterprise in which South African judges will soon participate we have attempted to analyse four jurisdictions, the precedents of which could well be important in the development of constitutional principles in South Africa. It was the potential influence upon our law that motivated us to examine theories of constitutional interpretation which have dominated in the US, Canada, India, and Germany. From these we hoped to gain greater guidance in an attempt to develop a suitable conceptual apparatus for constitutional jurisprudence in South Africa.

These jurisdictions have also been chosen because of the influence which the Constitutions of these countries had upon the drafting of Chapter 3 of the 1993 Constitution of the Republic of South Africa. In particular several important clauses — including the concept of equal protection, the principle and content of the limitation clause, and the application clause — find their source in the German, US, and Canadian Constitutions.

Given the nature of the previous Constitution, it is not surprising that there is virtually no scholarship on *how* courts in a future South Africa will review legislative and executive acts under a Constitution. The literature that exists discusses more immediate practical concerns such as the actual structure of a Bill of Rights[9] and the nature of the role to be played by the current South African judiciary.[10]

South African judges will be confronted with a further difficulty. The Bill of Rights with which South Africa will commence its constitutional course will not have been derived from 'we the people' nor will it represent the outcome of a

---

[9] See Dugard 'A Bill of Rights for South Africa' (1990) 23 *Cornell Int LJ* 441.

[10] See Forsyth 'Interpreting a Bill of Rights: The Future Task of a Reformed Judiciary?' (1991) 7 *SAJHR* 1; Cameron 'Judicial Accountability in South Africa' (1990) 6 *SAJHR* 251; Bjornlund 'The Devil's Work? Judicial Review under a Bill of Rights in South Africa and Namibia' (1990) 26 *Stan J Int L* 391. For an important contribution see Du Plessis & De Ville 'Bill of Rights Interpretation in the South African Context: Diagnostic Observations' (1993) 4 *Stell LR* 59.

democratic national debate. Consequently the justification for the interim Bill of Rights cannot be found in a set of values considered by society to be inviolable against the programmes of the legislature.

A court will have to seek coherence in a document cobbled together at Kempton Park during a process characterized by a lack of transparency. It will need to view the interim Bill of Rights as an attempt to create the most appropriate conditions for the free exercise of the democratic process, leading to the acceptance of a permanent Constitution. The techniques to be adopted by the courts, however, will not be dissimilar from those employed by the courts under review.

## 2 THE PRECEDENT OF HISTORY: CONSTITUTIONAL REVIEW IN THE UNITED STATES OF AMERICA

### 2.1 Constitutionalism and democracy

In the Federalist Paper No 78 Alexander Hamilton offered the following justification for the introduction of a Bill of Rights and its importance to the democratic enterprise:

'There is no position which depends on clearer principles, than that every act of a delegated authority, contrary to the tenor of the commission under which it is exercised, is void. No legislative act, therefore, contrary to the Constitution, can be valid. To deny this, would be to affirm that the deputy is greater than his principal; that the servant is above his master; that the representatives of the people are superior to the people themselves; that the men acting by virtue of powers, may do not only what their powers do not authorize, but what they forbid.'

This expression of the constitutional idea, notwithstanding the Bill of Rights, did not expressly provide for judicial review of legislation which offended the provisions of the Bill of Rights. Consequently more than a decade elapsed before the courts' power of review was confirmed. In *Marbury v Madison*[11] John Marshall, the Chief Justice, wrote an opinion explicitly asserting the power of judicial review. In it he reasoned as follows:

'So if a law be in opposition to the Constitution; if both the law and the Constitution apply to a particular case, so that the court must either decide that case conformably to the law, disregarding the Constitution; or conformably to the Constitution, disregarding the law; the court must determine which of these conflicting rules governs the case. This is of the very essence of judicial duty.

If then, the courts are to regard the Constitution, and the Constitution is superior to any ordinary act of the legislature, the Constitution, and not such ordinary act, must govern the case to which they both apply.

Those then who controvert the principle that the Constitution is to be considered, in court, as a paramount law, are reduced to the necessity of maintaining that courts must close their eyes on the Constitution, and see only the law. This doctrine would subvert the very foundation of all written constitutions. It would declare that an act which, according to the principles and theory of our government, is entirely void, is yet, in practice, completely obligatory.'

The ambit and scope of the power of judicial review has remained the subject of considerable controversy. For some the Constitution was intended to protect certain freedoms against majoritarian intervention. The Constitution contained a particular political morality which judges are required to enforce. For this reason, non-positive

---

[11] 5 US 137, 2 LEd 60 (1803).

rights are protected by the Constitution, being accorded not only a moral but also a legal status.[12]

By contrast a radically different approach developed in which the Constitution was viewed as protecting the freedom of individuals only when the majority so wills or where a positive constitutional provision so mandates.[13] In recent times Judge Antonio Scalia has best articulated this approach. In *Employment Division v Smith*[14] Scalia J urgently summarizes his position as follows:

> '[A] society that believes in the negative protection accorded to religious belief can be expected to be solicitous of that value in its legislation as well. It is therefore not surprising that a number of states have made an exception to their drug laws for sacramental peyote use . . . But to say that a nondiscriminatory religious-practice exemption is permitted, or even that it is desirable, is not to say that it is constitutionally required, and that the appropriate occasions for its creation can be discerned by the courts. It may fairly be said that leaving accommodation to the political process will place at a relative disadvantage those religious practices that are not widely engaged in; but unavoidable consequence of democratic government must be preferred to a system in which each conscience is a law unto itself or in which judges weigh the social importance of all laws against the centrality of all religious beliefs.'

To a considerable extent this debate turns upon competing concepts of democracy. Must a constitutional instrument be construed as narrowly as possible in order to allow for the expression of majority opinion or does the Constitution contain certain core moral values which trump a transient majority's intention, thereby converting these moral values into legal rights? An examination of this question is an invitation to engage in an analysis of the so-called countermajoritarian dilemma.

## 2.2 The countermajoritarian dilemma

Constitutional scholars in the US have long struggled with what has come to be known as the 'countermajoritarian difficulty'. In 1962 Alexander Bickel described the problem as follows:

> '[W]hen the Supreme Court declares unconstitutional a legislative act . . . it thwarts the will of the . . . people of the here and now; it exercises control, not on behalf of the prevailing majority, but against it.'[15]

In other words, judicial review is undemocratic or, as Bickel wrote, 'judicial review is a deviant institution in American democracy'.[16] It is deviant because it permits unelected judges who are accountable to nobody to nullify the acts of democratically elected legislatures and executives who are accountable to the people.

Over the past thirty years a vast body of literature has developed to resolve this

---

[12] See in general Tribe & Dorf op cit (n 8).
[13] See *Crusan v Director, Missouri Department of Health* 110 SCt 2841 (1990). See also the majority judgment in *City of Richmond v J A Croson* 488 US 469 (1989), in which the majority of the court held that a programme setting aside a percentage of contracts for minorities was unconstitutional. By contrast Brennan and Marshall JJ argued in their dissenting judgments that a state may remedy private discrimination and failure to do so would enmesh the state in those very discriminatory practices.
[14] 110 SCt 1595, 1606 (1990).
[15] Bickel *The Least Dangerous Branch* (1962) 16–17.
[16] At 18.

difficulty.[17] The general approach has been designed either to discount the countermajoritarian difficulty or to identify a workable interpretive theory that judges should use to review the constitutionality of legislation and, despite differing political views, to reach consistent conclusions when faced with similar factual situations.[18] Unfortunately virtually every theory fails to resolve the problem, raising the spectre that the development of constitutional theory in the US is an impossible task.[19]

This section summarizes the major US attempts to resolve the countermajoritarian difficulty, describes the different theories of judicial review that scholars have espoused in an attempt to resolve the problems of majoritarianism as well as some of their critics' responses, and examines the implications for South African jurisprudence.[20]

Recent US experience with judicial review clearly demonstrates why South Africa should be concerned about a Bill of Rights enforced by a largely unaccountable judiciary. For US conservatives the Warren Court's sweeping expansion of constitutional rights, from the rights of criminal defendants to the rights of women, based partly on the court's flexible constitutional theory, was generally unwanted and perceived as unwise.[21] As a result of the Warren Court's liberal activism a generation of US conservatives grew up demanding that judges exercise judicial restraint. By contrast, a generation of US liberals, who supported the Warren Court's adoption of their political agenda, became strong supporters of the flexible theories of constitutional interpretation that the Warren Court frequently used.[22]

During the 1980s the debate changed dramatically. With the appointment of conservative judges by Presidents Reagan and Bush, culminating in the Rehnquist Court, judicial activism began to boomerang on US liberals. Judicial activism was no longer a mechanism for liberal reform. Instead it became a vehicle for

---

[17] In fact, people have wrestled with the countermajoritarian difficulty since the Constitution's inception. As Bickel points out, Alexander Hamilton's response to the problem was to deny it; he argued that the judiciary's power of judicial review did not make it superior to the legislature. Rather, 'the power of the people is superior to both' (at 16).

[18] As Michael Klarman has effectively argued, a theory that successfully solves the countermajoritarian difficulty must pass two tests: first, it must be susceptible to 'objective' implementation — i e it must apply criteria of sufficient determinacy to enable judges of different political predispositions to derive generally consistent results in applying the theory to particular factual settings; secondly, the theory must be normatively attractive — meaning, in essence, that its underlying criteria of constitutional interpretation embody principles of political theory consonant with the views of most living Americans: Klarman 'The Puzzling Resistance to Political Process Theory' (1991) 77 *Va LR* 747 at 768–9.

[19] See Brest 'The Fundamental Rights Controversy: The Essential Contradictions of Normative Constitutional Scholarship' (1981) 90 *Yale LJ* 1063; Tushnet 'Darkness on the Edge of Town: The Contribution of John Hart Ely to Constitutional Theory' (1980) 89 *Yale LJ* 1037.

[20] The brevity of this summary might be somewhat simplistic; quite simply, it is impossible to describe adequately a theory in two or three pages when an individual has written an entire book outlining it. Nevertheless, an attempt is made to canvass the major points and provide an introduction to the debate surrounding judicial review in America.

[21] A good example of conservatives' dislike of the Warren Court's liberal jurisprudence was the 'Impeach Earl Warren' movement in the mid-1960s.

[22] Perhaps the most famous example of this is *Griswold v Connecticut* 381 US 479 (1965), in which the court held a statute that limited access to contraception to be unconstitutional. The court found that the statute violated the right to marital privacy despite the fact that the Constitution does not specify such a right. The court identified this right by arguing (at 484) that 'specific guarantees in the Bill of Rights have penumbras, formed by emanations from those guarantees that help give them life and substance. Various guarantees create zones of privacy.'

conservative activism.²³ Given the possibility that the use of a flexible constitutional theory is as likely to produce a conservative as a liberal jurisprudence, earlier calls for judicial activism in the South African context might prove inappropriate to a transformative political enterprise.²⁴

## 2.3 But does the countermajoritarian difficulty matter?

A number of scholars have argued that the countermajoritarian difficulty is, in fact, not really a 'deviant institution' in US democracy. Their arguments range from Alexander Bickel's belief that judges play a unique and important role in the US democratic system to Stephen Carter's suggestion that judges can only obstruct the will of the majority for a limited amount of time. In essence, while they do not deny the existence of the countermajoritarian difficulty, they argue that we need not get overly upset about it.

### 2.3.1 *The judiciary's unique role*

Alexander Bickel acknowledged that judicial review is a countermajoritarian force in the legal system.²⁵ Stating that society should 'strive to support and maintain enduring general values', Bickel argued that 'courts have certain capacities for dealing with matters of principle that legislators and executives do not possess'.²⁶ He went on to say:

> '[W]hen the pressure for immediate results is strong enough and emotions ride high enough, [legislators] will ordinarily prefer to act on expediency rather than take the long view ... Not merely respect for the rule of established principles but the creative establishment and renewal of a coherent body of principled rules — that is what our legislators have proven themselves ill equipped to give us. Judges have, or should have, the leisure, the training, and the insulation to follow the ways of the scholar in pursuing the ends of government. This is crucial in sorting out the enduring values of a society ... [The court can] appeal to men's better natures, to call forth their aspirations, which may have been forgotten in the moment's hue and cry.'²⁷

Given this characteristic of judges, Bickel states that '[t]he result may be a tolerable accommodation [of judicial review] with the theory and practice of democracy'.²⁸ Bickel appeared to place considerable faith in the judiciary as Platonic philosopher kings of yore who would perceive the universal truth hidden

---

[23] Klarman op cit (n 18) 830n362 collects some examples of the Rehnquist Court's conservative activism: *City of Richmond v J A Croson* (supra) (holding affirmative action presumptively unconstitutional); *Pennel v City of San Jose* 485 US 1 (1988) (arguing that rent control ordinance that takes into account 'hardship' to the tenant is an unconstitutional taking, Scalia J concurring in part and dissenting in part); *Nollan v California Coastal Comm'n* 483 US 825 (1987) (apparently imposing a means–end *nexus* requirement more substantial than minimum rationality review in determining whether government land-use regulation constitutes a taking); *Allied Structural Steel Co v Spannus* 438 US 234 (1978) (reinvigorating the long-defunct contract clause of the Constitution by invalidating a state law imposing pension fund obligations upon large employers). See Maltz 'The Prospects for a Revival of Conservative Activism in Constitutional Jurisprudence' (1990) 24 *Ga LR* 629.

[24] Oddly enough, many US liberals have yet to acknowledge this fact. With the election of Bill Clinton and the certainty that his judicial appointees will be more liberal than those of Reagan and Bush, liberals, at least those who learned the foregoing lesson during the 1980s, may well forget that flexible constitutional theories, such as theories based on fundamental rights, can easily be co-opted by conservatives to produce a distinctly conservative constitutional jurisprudence.

[25] Bickel op cit (n 15) 16.
[26] At 25–7.
[27] At 24–6.
[28] Quoted by Brest op cit (n 19) 1066.

in the Constitution and compel the politicians to yield to the inexorable force of the Constitution. Unfortunately, thirty years after Bickel wrote this passage it appears hopelessly idealistic. Furthermore, is it fair to treat judges as Platonic philosopher kings who would inevitably arrive at the correct decision, the correct decision being defined as the true encapsulation of the *'volksgeist'*? If anything, US judges have demonstrated, in no uncertain terms, that the content of America's 'enduring general values' defies definition.[29] Accordingly, Bickel's response to the countermajoritarian difficulty is unsatisfactory.

### 2.3.2 *Judicial review is a necessary part of a democratic system*

James Madison believed in a democratic system that was not entirely majoritarian. Robert Bork described the Madisonian system as one in which '[t]here are some things a majority should not do to us no matter how democratically it decides to do them'.[30] This view has led some scholars to suggest that while judicial review is incompatible with US democracy, it is absolutely necessary in order to 'protect individual rights which are not adequately represented in the political processes'.[31] Accordingly, the Supreme Court 'constitutes a working part of the democratic political life of the nation because the power of judicial review has been historically exercised to restrain the majority'.[32]

Yet this 'solution' to the countermajoritarian difficulty is inadequate, for it begs the question. As Jesse Choper comments, 'the process of judicial review is not democratic because the Court is not a politically responsible institution ... Although the Supreme Court may play a vital role in the preservation of the American democratic system, the procedure of judicial review is in conflict with the fundamental principle of democracy — majority rule under conditions of political freedom.'[33] Hence the problem is the reconstruction of democracy with judicial supervision of the exercise of the majority will.

### 2.3.3 *Why distrust judges?*

Frederick Schauer has adopted a different approach, attacking the common assumption that unconstrained judicial review is dangerous, or that, as John Hart Ely puts it, we should distrust unaccountable judges.[34] Schauer points out that it is just as likely that a court will exercise its power of judicial review in a positive way[35] as it will do so in a negative way.[36] Just as an unconstrained decision-maker can do bad or good, a constrained decision-maker is prevented from doing bad or good.[37] Thus

---

[29] The debate which has raged over abortion both inside and outside the courtroom provides a good example of the elusive nature of enduring values! For a comprehensive examination of this topic, see Tribe *Abortion: The Clash of Absolutes* (1992).

[30] Bork 'Neutral Principles and Some First Amendment Problems' (1971) 47 *Ind LJ* 1 at 2–3.

[31] Choper *Judicial Review and the National Political Process* (1980) 2.

[32] Bork op cit (n 30) 9, quoting Rostow 'The Supreme Court and the People's Will' (1958) 33 *Notre Dame LR* 573 at 576.

[33] Op cit (n 31) at 9–10.

[34] Schauer 'The Calculus of Distrust' (1991) 77 *Va LR* 653.

[35] See *Brown v Board of Education* 347 US 483 (1954) (striking down the doctrine of 'separate but equal').

[36] See *Lochner v New York* 198 US 45 (1905) (holding that laws that limit the number of hours an employee may work in one week are unconstitutional).

[37] Schauer op cit (n 34) 664.

our desire for constraint reveals a belief that an unconstrained decision-maker will do more harm than good.[38] It also reveals a 'rosy view of the status quo', for leaving our decision-makers without constraints will open the door to change.[39] Accordingly, unconstrained judges may, in the final analysis, benefit society.

These are powerful arguments. It may be that the risk that judges will hand down opinions such as *Brown v Board of Education*[40] is worth the cost of the occasional *Lochner*[41] (assuming no objective interpretation of the Constitution could justify these decisions). However, one must not allow this calculation to be affected by the Supreme Court's past thirty years. Liberals must then take decisions such as *Bowers v Hardwick*[42] and conservatives decisions such as *Roe v Wade*[43] in their stride, for they are the inevitable result of such a flexible, and thus somewhat unpredictable, system. Schauer's analysis may reduce the concern that some people have about an unconstrained judiciary, but it does not resolve the countermajoritarian difficulty. It also begs the question.

### 2.3.4 Majoritarianism will ultimately win

Yet another theory argues that the problems caused by the countermajoritarian difficulty are minor because the Supreme Court's constitutional decisions 'are never for long out of line with the policy views dominant among the law-making majorities of the United States'.[44] In other words, if the Supreme Court hands down an unpopular constitutional decision, public criticism will lead it to reverse its decision before long.[45]

There are major difficulties with this argument. First, it is not a small matter that the Supreme Court has managed to block legislation for 'decades at a time'.[46] For instance, in the early part of this century the court successfully blocked the establishment of national child labour law for approximately twenty-five years despite widespread popular support.[47] Secondly, this argument ignores the role that a constitutional decision has in 'moulding public opinion, and thus in changing the terms of the political debate'.[48] As Klarman argues, 'people are loath to surrender privileges they have come to think of as rights'.[49]

---

[38] Ibid.
[39] At 666.
[40] Supra.
[41] Supra.
[42] 478 US 186 (1986) (holding that a law that criminalized homosexual sodomy was constitutional).
[43] 410 US 113 (1973) (holding that women have a constitutional right to abortion).
[44] Dahl 'Decision-making in a Democracy: The Supreme Court as a National Policy-maker' (1957) 6 *J Pub L* 279 at 285, quoted in Klarman op cit (n 18) 774. See also Carter 'Constitutional Adjudication and the Indeterminate Text: A Preliminary Defense of an Imperfect Muddle' (1985) 94 *Yale LJ* 821 at 851 ('Relatively few judicial decisions cannot be circumvented by a sufficiently clever legislature or an adequately aroused populace').
[45] One possible example of this was the Supreme Court's position on the death penalty. During the course of a single decade the court ruled the death penalty to be unconstitutional and later, following considerable public criticism of the case, ruled it to be constitutional.
[46] Klarman op cit (n 18) 775.
[47] Ibid.
[48] At 774.
[49] Ibid.

## 2.3.5 Conclusion: the countermajoritarian difficulty does matter

These arguments notwithstanding, the countermajoritarian difficulty does matter. Judges have not been able to maintain, let alone identify, enduring general values. A decision to ignore the problem because James Madison might not have perceived it to be a problem begs the question. Trusting judges to exercise their discretion in a 'good' manner has resulted in an inconsistent and often contradictory constitutional jurisprudence. Finally, dependence upon the democratic process to correct judicial excesses has historically proven itself unreliable. Thus scholars have looked elsewhere for a solution to the countermajoritarian difficulty.

The search for a coherent constitutional theory to deal with this problem has produced a rich and diverse literature.

## 2.4 Alternative theories

The bulk of scholarship on judicial review consists of attempts to identify a workable theory that judges can use to review the constitutionality of legislation and, notwithstanding differing political views, reach consistent conclusions when presented with similar factual situations. There appear to be four different theories, each of which identifies a different authority to which judges should look to produce an objective, consistent, and fair body of constitutional jurisprudence: theories relying upon the original text of the Constitution or the original intent of its framers; theories that rely on tradition or consensus; theories that rely on fundamental rights; and political process theory.

### 2.4.1 Originalist theories

It has been argued that courts should interpret a constitutional provision according to its original meaning. They argue that reference by contemporary judges to the 'original' understanding of a particular constitutional provision at the time of its ratification limits the power of judicial review, thereby eliminating the countermajoritarian problem. Particularly influential in this regard was a speech by former Attorney-General Edwin Meese, who in 1985 argued that the court should return to a jurisprudence of original intention by construing the Constitution in line with the intentions of the framers.[50]

#### 2.4.1.1 Strict intentionalism

One group of theorists believe that judges must decide constitutional issues as the framers of the constitutional provision in question would have.[51] For example, a judge should strike down a law that discriminates against women only if the framers of the Fourteenth Amendment's equal protection clause intended for it to protect

---

[50] (1986) 45 *Public Admin LR* 701.
[51] Berger *Government by Judiciary* 1–19, quoted in Brest op cit (n 19) 1090. See also Berger 'Constitutional Interpretation and Activist Fantasies' (1993) 82 *Kentucky LJ* 1 at 28 where he argues:
 'An activist more candid than most, Thomas Grey considers the question whether the Court may "enforce principles of liberty and justice [when they are] . . . not to be found within the four corners" of the Constitution as "perhaps the most fundamental question we can ask about our fundamental law". For me it is the most fundamental proposition, because any judicial arrogation of undelegated power invades the right of the people to control their own destiny.'

women. The justification for strict intentionalism is that the Constitution, being the supreme law of the land, manifests the will of the citizens of the US. Consequently the objective of the judicial process of interpretation is to ascertain this will. Adherence to the text as well as to an original understanding constrains the discretion of the judiciary and provides the best guarantee that the Constitution will be interpreted consistently over its history to accord with the will of the people.[52] Joined by Rehnquist CJ, White J, and Thomas J, Scalia J succinctly summarized this approach in *Planned Parenthood v Casey*[53] as follows:

> 'The issue is whether [abortion] is a liberty protected by the Constitution of the United States. I am sure it is not. I reach that conclusion ... because of two simple facts: One that the Constitution says absolutely nothing about it and two the longstanding traditions of American society have permitted it to be legally proscribed.'

The attempt to balance the objectives of the Constitution with the discretion of unaccountable judges obviously holds the key to the constitutional conundrum. However, the theory of strict intentionalism fails to achieve this objective for a number of reasons.

First, it is usually impossible to ascertain exactly what the framers of a particular clause intended it to protect. For instance, did the framers intend the equal protection clause to protect only blacks or any group facing irrational discrimination? An inability to produce a clear answer indicates that the theory lacks the necessary precision to resolve the countermajoritarian difficulty.[54] Secondly, if fortuitously the framer's intent is clear, it can prove problematic for contemporary society to be restrained by the values and beliefs of people who lived as much as 200 years ago. Furthermore, adoption of such a theory within the US context would require the court to reverse many of its recent decisions, throwing constitutional jurisprudence into even more serious disarray.

### 2.4.1.2 Borkean originalism

Robert Bork's theory of originalism is based on the proposition that judges must 'accept any value choice the legislature makes unless it runs clearly contrary to a choice made in the framing of the Constitution'.[55]

Bork argues as follows:

> 'The requirement that the Court be principled arises from the resolution of the seeming anomaly of judicial supremacy in a democratic society. If the judiciary really is supreme, able to rule as it sees fit, the society is not democratic. The anomaly is dissipated, however, by the model of government embodied in the structure of the Constitution, the model upon which popular consent to a limited government by the Supreme Court also rests.'

---

[52] Brest 'The Misconceived Quest for the Original Understanding' (1980) 60 *Buffalo U LR* 20420.
[53] 112 SCt 2791, 2874 (1992).
[54] Scalia J responded to this 'level of generality problem' by relying on 'the most specific level at which a relevant tradition protecting, or denying protection to, the asserted right can be identified': *Michael H v Gerald D* 491 US 110n6 (1989). This response, however, is problematic. As Christopher Wolfe commented:
> '[H]ow do we measure "specificity"? Take a case like *Roe v Wade*. If there is no dispositive tradition regarding the right of women to control their reproductive freedom when it results in the destruction of a fetus (as the Court argued) then what is the next most specific tradition? A tradition regarding women's reproductive freedom in general? A tradition regarding the rights of the fetus ...? One must simply choose, because specificity cannot be measured here.'

Wolfe 'The Result-Orientated Adjudicator's Guide to Constitutional Law' (1992) 70 *Texas LR* 1325 at 1329.
[55] Bork op cit (n 30) 10–11.

Bork is quick to recognize the dilemma of countermajoritarianism. He notes that 'majority tyranny occurs if legislation invades the areas properly left to individual freedom. Minority tyranny occurs if the majority is prevented from ruling where its power is legitimate.' Furthermore,

> '[t]his dilemma is resolved in constitutional theory, and in popular understanding, by the Supreme Court's power to define both majority and minority freedom through the interpretation of the Constitution. Society consents to be ruled undemocratically within defined areas by certain enduring principles believed to be stated in, and placed beyond the reach of majorities by the Constitution.
>
> But this resolution of the dilemma imposes severe requirements upon the Court. For it follows that the Court's power is legitimate only if it has, and can demonstrate in reasoned opinions that it has, a valid theory, derived from the Constitution, of the respective spheres of majority and minority freedom. If it does not have such a theory but merely imposes its own value choices, or worse if it pretends to have a theory but actually follows its own predilections, the Court violates the postulates of the Madisonian model that alone justifies its power. It then necessarily abets the tyranny either of the majority or of the minority.'[56]

If one were to take this theory at face value, it would resolve the counter-majoritarian difficulty, albeit in a controversial manner.[57]

Hence it appears that Bork would have judges engage in interpretation that requires knowledge of uncertain historical attitudes and beliefs. This process is to be made less uncertain by the method advocated to ascertain the meaning of the text.

Bork argues that the content of a choice made in the framing of the Constitution is to be determined by the public understanding of the provision at the time of its ratification rather than the framer's private understanding.[58] In other words, what did the average enfranchised person on the street understand the provision to mean when it was ratified? The obvious problem with this approach is that the content of this original 'public understanding' is usually unclear. Just like the strict intent theory, Borkean originalism faces the level of generality problem: did the public understand the equal protection clause to protect just blacks or any group subject to irrational discrimination?[59] Bork attempts to alleviate this problem by arguing:

> '[A]ll that a judge committed to original understanding requires is that the text, structure and history of the Constitution provide him not with a conclusion but with a major premise. The major premise is a principle or ... value that the ratifiers wanted to protect against hostile legislation or executive action. The judge must then see whether that principle or value is threatened by the statute or action challenged in the case before him.'[60]

Thus Borkean originalism can be extremely flexible, and therein lies its flaw. Isolating a principle or value based on original understanding is an extremely imprecise exercise for '[b]oth the historical inquiry and the interpretive inquiry constitutive of the originalist approach to constitutional adjudication are often indeterminate'.[61] Indeed, Bork concedes that this is a difficult task,[62] but argues that

---

[56] At 11.
[57] See below, 17 for a complete explanation as to why this would be unattractive.
[58] Bork *The Tempting of America: The Political Seduction of the Law* (1990) 144.
[59] Perry 'The Legitimacy of Particular Conceptions of Constitutional Interpretation' (1991) 77 *Va LR* 669.
[60] Bork op cit (n 58) 162.
[61] Perry op cit (n 59) 696–8, 711.
[62] Macedo 'Originalism and the Inescapability of Politics' (1990) 84 *Northwestern U LR* 1203 at 1205.

'an acceptable range of meanings can usually be discerned'.[63] This, however, lacks the precision necessary to guarantee the objective adjudication of constitutional issues. Accordingly, Bork's view of original intent fails to pass muster.[64] The dilemma is resolved for Bork by the Supreme Court's power to define both majority and minority freedoms when it interprets the Constitution. As society has consented to be ruled by a Constitution which is to be interpreted by an unaccountable judiciary, it has consented 'to be ruled undemocratically within defined areas by certain enduring principles, believed to be stated in, and placed beyond the reach of the majority by the Constitution'.[65]

### 2.4.1.3 Consensus and tradition

A number of scholars have proposed constitutional theories based on tradition or consensus. In *Moore v East Cleveland* [66] Powell J argued that the fact that the 'extended family is deeply rooted in this Nation's history and tradition' meant that a housing ordinance that limited occupancy to members of a narrowly defined 'family' was unconstitutional. In a related vein, Harry Wellington argued for a consensus approach when he stated that 'the Supreme Court is . . . well positioned to translate conventional morality into legal principle'.[67]

There are clear problems inherent in both these approaches. First, '[t]radition . . . is problematic both because of the level of generality, time frame, and relevant community from which one infers a constitutional tradition is susceptible to almost infinite manipulation, and because it is unclear why today's generation should be shackled by the standards of yesteryear'.[68] Similarly, 'meaningful consensus [is] unlikely to exist on pressing policy debates . . . but even if consensus did exist one might reasonably question why the judiciary is comparatively advantaged vis-à-vis the legislature at discerning it'.[69] Since neither theory can provide judges with an objective system of judicial review, the dilemma remains unresolved.

### 2.4.1.4 Fundamental rights theories

One popular approach argues that the 'Constitution is an essentially open text inviting interpretation, rather than mandating obedience to original intent or legislative will'.[70] In other words, the Constitution is open and 'possibilistic', and the judges may, in the extreme, use it as a 'vehicle for progressive social change'.[71] Yet these theorists do not contend that the Constitution is an empty shell. Instead it provides judges with some general guiding principles and leaves them to fill in the gaps as they arise.

The justification for this general approach to constitutional interpretation rests

---

[63] Ibid.
[64] For an interesting criticism of Bork's work, see Nichol 'Bork's Dilemma' (1990) 76 *Va LR* 337.
[65] Op cit (n 30) 11.
[66] 431 US 494, 503 (1977).
[67] Wellington 'Common Law Rules and Constitutional Double Standards: Some Notes on Adjudication' (1973) 83 *Yale LJ* 221 at 267.
[68] Klarman op cit (n 18) 771.
[69] Ibid.
[70] West 'Progressive and Conservative Constitutionalism' (1990) 88 *Mich LR* 641 at 707.
[71] At 708–9.

with the intent of the framers. Indeed it is well established, though rarely acknowledged, that the framers' 'interpretive intentions appear to have been to cede to succeeding generations the task of supplying content to the Constitution's open-ended phrases'.[72] The Ninth Amendment[73] and the Fourteenth Amendment's privileges and immunities clause[74] are frequently cited as evidence for this proposition.

But where do judges look to find fundamental rights? Scholars have suggested a number of possible sources ranging from 'neutral principles'[75] to conventional morality to natural law. Harry Wellington, for example, advocates the use of conventional morality. In doing so he argues that '[j]udicial reasoning in concrete cases must proceed from society's set of moral principles and ideals ... And that is why we must be concerned with conventional morality, for it is there that society's set of moral principles and ideals are located.'[76] Wellington goes on to define 'conventional morality' as 'standards of conduct which are widely shared in a particular society'.[77] Unfortunately Wellington's theory leaves it to judges to identify such widely shared standards. Since it is often impossible, and inevitably extremely imprecise, to identify widely shared standards with accuracy, reliance on Wellington's conventional morality cannot produce an objective system of judicial review. One need not look beyond the abortion debate in the US to find support for this conclusion!

Similarly, reliance on natural law is problematic. First, as Geoffrey Hazard asked, 'who is the authoritative expounder of natural law in any of its formulations? It used to be God, but He is now dead, or perhaps living in the Sun Belt.'[78] Secondly, as Ely pointed out, 'all the many attempts to build a moral and political doctrine upon the conception of a universal human nature have failed. Either the allegedly universal ends are too few and abstract to give content to the idea of the good, or they are too numerous and concrete to be truly universal ... Our society does not ... accept the notion of a discoverable and objectively valid set of moral principles.'[79] Thus natural law also provides judges with unconstrained licence to interpret vague constitutional provisions as they see fit.

Accordingly, the fundamental rights approach to constitutional adjudication cannot resolve the countermajoritarian difficulty. As Klarman states, 'To the extent that fundamental rights exist only in the eye of the beholder, such a constitutional theory represents not so much an attempt to cope with the countermajoritarian

---

[72] Klarman op cit (n 18) 770. In a more extreme version this view is propounded by Tribe & Dorf: 'Fundamentally, the Constitution is, rather, a text to be interpreted and reinterpreted in an unending search for understanding' (op cit (n 8) 32–3, quoted in Wolfe op cit (n 54) 1332–3).

[73] The Ninth Amendment states that '[t]he enumeration in the Constitution of certain rights shall not be construed to deny or disparage others retained by the people': US Constitution Amendment IX.

[74] This clause states that '[n]o state shall make or enforce any law which shall abridge the privileges and immunities of citizens of the United States ...': US Constitution Amendment XIV s 1.

[75] Wechsler 'Towards Neutral Principles of Constitutional Law' (1959) 73 *Harvard LR* 1 (arguing that courts have the power and duty to decide constitutional cases and that their reasoning and analysis must transcend the immediate result). Wechsler argues that judicial review obliges the courts to adopt a principled approach. For him,
'a principled decision ... is one that rests on the reasons with respect to all the issues in the case, reasons that in their generality and their neutrality transcend any immediate result that is involved. When no sufficient reasons of this kind can be assigned for overturning value choices of the other branches of the government or the state, these choices must, of course, survive.'

[76] Wellington op cit (n 67) 244.

[77] Ibid.

[78] Hazard 'Commentary on the "Fundamental Values" Controversy' (1981) 90 *Yale LJ* 1110.

[79] Ely *Democracy and Distrust: A Theory of Judicial Review* (1980) 51–4.

problem as a surrender to it.'⁸⁰ It is somewhat curious that many liberal constitutional scholars, such as Laurence Tribe, have espoused this view, for a general acceptance of such an imprecise and flexible standard could easily become a vehicle for the type of conservative judicial activism that has marked many recent decisions by the Rehnquist Court.⁸¹

### 2.4.1.5 Political process theory: John Hart Ely

John Hart Ely's *Democracy and Distrust*, published in 1980, introduced new life into the ongoing debate over constitutional theory. In this book Ely argued for what is now known as the political process theory of judicial review, an attempt to justify a role for the courts in constitutional adjudication that was most consistent with the generally democratic nature of the US political system.⁸² Thus political process theory avoids the countermajoritarian problem by aligning judicial review with democracy. Ely 'allows courts to strike down legislative actions but only when the legislature has acted undemocratically, not when the courts merely disagree with the legislative outcome'.⁸³ The democratic role for the courts is to combine the licence held by the courts to invalidate some laws with a set of constraints to curb abuse of that licence. Ely argues that judicial review is justified when

> '(1) the ins are choking off the channels of political change to ensure that they will stay in and the outs will stay out, or (2) though no one is actually denied a voice or a vote, representatives beholden to an effective majority are systematically disadvantaging some minority out of simple hostility or a prejudiced refusal to recognize commonalities of interest, and thereby denying that minority the protection afforded other groups by a representative system.'⁸⁴

Ely bases this theory on Judge Harlan Stone's famous footnote 4 of *United States v Carolene Products Company*, which articulated three different bases for legitimate judicial review.⁸⁵ In the footnote's first paragraph the court states that it may invoke

---

⁸⁰ Klarman op cit (n 18) 772.
⁸¹ A reasonable person, for instance, could easily argue that abortion violates certain 'fundamental rights'. See Tribe & Dorf op cit (n 8), particularly at 116, where the authors submit:
'The basic choice to be made — the choice that neither the Constitution's text, nor its structure, nor its history can make for us — is a choice between emphasizing "conservative" functions of both the liberty and equality clauses (as well as others) and emphasizing their potential as generated from critique and change. The choice one makes must be justified extra-textually, but may and should be implemented in ways that draw as much guidance as possible from the text itself.'
⁸² Ely op cit (n 79) 1–4.
⁸³ Ortiz 'Pursuing a Perfect Politics: The Allure and Failure of Process Theory' (1991) 77 *Va LR* 721 at 725.
⁸⁴ Ely op cit (n 70) 103.
⁸⁵ 304 US 144 (1938). At 152 Stone J stated:
'[E]ven in the absence of such aids the existence of facts supporting a legislative judgment is presumed, for regulatory legislation affecting ordinary commercial transactions is not to be pronounced unconstitutional unless in the light of the facts made known or generally assumed it is of such a character as to preclude the assumption that it rests upon some rational basis other than the knowledge and experience of the legislators.'
At the end of the word 'legislators' Judge Stone added footnote 4, in which he said:
'[T]here may be narrow scope for operation of the presumption of constitutionality when legislation appears on its face to be within a specific prohibition of the Constitution such as those of the first ten amendments, which are deemed equally specific when held to be embraced within the Fourteenth . . . .
It is unnecessary to consider now whether legislation which restricts those political processes which can ordinarily be expected to bring about the repeal of undesirable legislation, is to be subjected to more exacting judicial scrutiny under the general prohibitions of the Fourteenth Amendment on most other types of legislation . . . .
Nor need we inquire whether similar considerations enter into the review of statutes directed at particular religious . . . or national . . . or racial minorities . . . [W]hether prejudice against discrete and insular minorities

originalism when it voids legislative actions that contravene a 'specific prohibition of the Constitution'.[86] In the second paragraph the court argues that it may legitimately review 'legislation which restricts those political processes which can ordinarily be expected to bring about repeal of undesirable legislation'.[87] In the third paragraph the court suggests that it may legitimately review legislation that burdens certain religious, ethnic, or racial minorities or when 'prejudice against discrete and insular minorities . . . curtail[s] the operation of those political processes ordinarily to be relied upon to protect minorities'.[88]

Thus, according to paragraph two of footnote 4, a court could legitimately review legislative or executive acts in which the enacting government officials cannot be trusted 'neutrally to weigh the costs and benefits'.[89] This means that a court could review a law that limited people's freedom of political speech because we should not trust legislators to protect our ability openly to criticize their performance.[90] But a court could not review legislation that limited people's freedom of speech in non-political areas.[91] Similarly, a court could review legislation regarding apportionment because we cannot trust legislators to apportion themselves out of their jobs.[92]

Yet Ely did not believe that judicial review as contemplated by paragraph two of the *Carolene Products* footnote 4 alone would provide sufficient protection.[93] Accordingly, he argued that the prejudice addressed by paragraph three of the footnote also provided adequate grounds for judicial review. This part of the political process theory, however, has been severely and successfully criticized. To justify the use of paragraph three as a ground for judicial review Ely tries to identify a non-substantive theory of prejudice — one that every type of judge, regardless of political beliefs, could use and reach the same result.

Laurence Tribe has provided a cogent critique of Ely's use of paragraph three. For instance, Tribe argues, burglars are subject to widespread hostility.[94] Nevertheless, we would never characterize them as a suspect class because of the 'substantive

---

may be a special condition, which tends seriously to curtail the operation of those political processes ordinarily to be relied upon to protect minorities and which may call for a correspondingly more searching judicial inquiry.'
[86] Ibid.
[87] Ibid.
[88] Quoted by Ortiz op cit (n 83) 727.
[89] At 772.
[90] Klarman op cit (n 18) 753–4.
[91] At 754–5.
[92] At 757–8.
[93] Ely op cit (n 79) 135; see Ortiz op cit (n 83) 729–30 ('To get anywhere interesting, process theory must invoke paragraph three'); but see Klarman op cit (n 18) 788–832. Ely has suggested that his theory would account for and justify the central decisions of the Warren Court being the quintessential representation of a reforming court. See Ely op cit (n 79) 73–104.
[94] Tribe 'The Puzzling Persistence of Process-Based Constitutional Theories' (1980) 89 *Yale LJ* 1063 at 1075. In more general terms Tribe has argued, together with Dorf (*On Reading the Constitution* (1991)), that Ely's theory is 'deeply flawed' because of its attempt to read the entire Constitution as having a central non-substantive aim of perfecting democracy by reinforcing the effective workings of representative government. They argue that from that perspective there turn out to be particularly problematic clauses in the Constitution, such as that no state shall 'abridge the privileges or immunities of citizens of the United States'. They note of course that Ely does not argue that the text of this clause or its history is concerned only with representative government, but rather that since the general point of the Constitution as a whole is to preserve representative government and since judicial activism is most readily defended when it reinforces rather than undermines representation, we must attempt to squeeze our interpretation to fit this clause into the vision. As the authors note, 'reading things out of the Constitution in order to bring the document into line with the theory seems no more defensible than reading things into the Constitution for the same reason' (at 27).

value we attach to personal security and its rules of transfer'.[95] Thus the determination of who is the victim of prejudice is a substantive decision. Furthermore, it is often impossible to determine whether a group's interests were ignored because of prejudice or rejected on account of insufficient numerical support.[96]

Given the problems inherent in the use of paragraph three of the *Carolene Products* footnote 4, Klarman has modified Ely's theory.[97] Klarman rids the theory of the prejudice prong and constructs a constitutional theory based on only paragraphs one and two of footnote 4. Klarman argues that Ely and Ortiz were wrong in their belief that political process theory without paragraph three fails to provide sufficient protection. In doing so Klarman tries to show, using compelling historical evidence, that blacks, had they been fully and fairly enfranchised since the Civil War's end, would have been able to protect themselves through the political process without the protection of the courts.[98] For instance, in Mississippi, South Carolina, and Louisiana, three states infamous for their racial intolerance, blacks comprised a majority of the total population after the Civil War.[99] The voting power of these blacks during Reconstruction led each of these states to enact statutory or constitutional bans on racial segregation of schools or places of public accommodation.[100] Thus, had the courts protected blacks' ability to vote, as required under paragraph two of footnote 4, blacks would have been able to protect themselves.

Klarman does not argue that an effective black vote would have been 'a panacea' for America's racial problems.[101] Rather he argues that, given black majorities in three southern states and hundreds of black belt counties, and near majority in several other southern states, 'blacks would have been well-positioned to defend their interests politically had their voting rights been adequately defended'.[102] Ultimately he concludes that the historical evidence strongly suggests that had blacks been enfranchised, *Brown v Board of Education* might well have been unnecessary.[103]

Klarman's revision of the political process theory is, however, not without difficulty. First, '[t]here is no reason to suppose that . . . [the] rules defining the basic structure of political and legal relations . . . can or should be essentially neutral on matters of substantive value'.[104] The Constitution, for instance, does not articulate the details of people's ability to participate in the political process. Accordingly, even the Supreme Court's decision to use the one person one vote rule for legislative district apportionment is substantive.[105] Secondly, as Richard Posner points out, one's ability to cast a vote freely and fairly is not the only calculation necessary to ensure that one has a political voice:

---

[95] Tribe op cit (n 94).
[96] Klarman op cit (n 18) 786.
[97] At 748.
[98] At 788–832.
[99] At 790.
[100] Ibid.
[101] At 803.
[102] At 804.
[103] At 805–19.
[104] Tribe op cit (n 94) 1068.
[105] See *Reynolds v Sims* 377 US 533 (1964).

'Voting power is ... only one element of political power; the others include money, education, age, membership in or good access to a constitutionally privileged class, such as the press, and membership in a politically effective interest group. So various is the allocation of political power wholly apart from whether state legislatures are malapportioned that it is impossible to predict whether reapportionment will have any systematic impact on policy outcomes.'[106]

The major difficulties raised by Tribe and Posner can perhaps be rebutted. The 'substantive' choices involved in setting the rules by which Americans vote are minor; the one person one vote rule, for instance, is completely uncontroversial. Arguably, and within the context of US history, Klarman's detailed historical argument concerning the power of an unfettered black franchise not only largely refutes Posner's argument but also provides a basis on which to tackle the counter-majoritarian problem.

Within the South African context Klarman's arguments provide little guarantee that the legacies of apartheid would be terminated and that a democratic enterprise could be forged. Klarman's thesis is an invitation to restrict constitutionalism in the probably vain hope that majoritarianism is able to replace the need for entrenched rights. Given the need to promote a core set of values which are essential to a participative political process, the court will need to go further than Klarman's limited vision if it wants to be consistent with the purpose of the Bill of Rights.

## 2.5 Conclusion

The US experience of judicial review allows for the elimination of three constitutional theories: those that rely upon tradition, consensus, or natural-law-based fundamental rights. The reason for this is simple: what constitutes 'tradition', when does one have 'consensus', and what is a 'fundamental right'? These terms defy meaningful definition. Accordingly, save where there is express provision to the contrary, a constitutional jurisprudence that relies on any of these three sources inevitably requires substantive input by judges.

The US experience with judicial review, however, is not simply a road filled with potholes that South Africa should avoid; it is an experience from which South Africa can build an objective form of judicial review that avoids the potholes into which US courts have fallen. There are some guidelines which can be teased out of the jurisprudence described above.

### 2.5.1 *If in doubt, defer to legislative determinations*

The first prong of a system of judicial review must engage the problem of uncertainty in the text. If there is any uncertainty in the meaning of a constitutional provision, as there inevitably will be, however diligent the framers are and however detailed the language is, the courts must defer to the legislature.[107] The benefit of such a system is clear, for it would assist in ensuring that judicial review would not be countermajoritarian. In the US, however, this theory is normatively unattractive for three reasons, each of which South Africa can easily avoid or does not face.

---

[106] Posner 'Democracy and Distrust Revisited' (1991) 77 *Va LR* 641 at 648.
[107] See footnote 4 of the *Carolene Products* case.

First, since so many of the US Constitution's provisions are vague, this form of judicial review would, if strictly applied, tend to water down the precommitments made by the framers in the Constitution. Strictly speaking, it may require courts to defer decisions about the equal protection clause to the legislature.[108]

By contrast, if an equality clause follows the standard formulation, namely that everyone shall be equal before the law,[109] and if there is a further provision that there shall be no discrimination, coupled with the list of specific grounds, including race, gender, sexual orientation, and creed, on the basis of which discrimination is prohibited, it will be more difficult for judicial deference to legislative value choices to be able to circumvent prior constitutional commitments.

The judgment of Douglas J in *Griswold v Connecticut*[110] is particularly illustrative. The case dealt with the question of Connecticut's birth control law, which had been challenged twice before *Griswold's* case, and in each instance the Supreme Court did not deal with the major issues, for it relied upon the question of standing. Connecticut had not generally enforced laws against individual doctors or married couples. The main impact of the legislation was to prohibit the poor from receiving the same birth control information as was available to the middle class. After birth control became part of the statute the state sought to enforce laws against the doctors and their patients. The matter reached the Supreme Court. In setting aside the legislation Douglas J enunciated a clear approach to the interpretation of the Bill of Rights. He said that specific guarantees in the Bill of Rights

> 'have penumbras, formed by emanations from those guarantees that help give them life and substance . . . [V]arious guarantees create zones of privacy. The right of association can be contained in the penumbra of the First Amendment as one, . . . the Third Amendment's prohibition against the quartering of soldiers, in any house, in times of peace without the consent of the owner, is another facet of threat to privacy . . . .
> 
> The present case then concerns the relationship lying within the zone of privacy created by several fundamental constitutional guarantees. It concerns the law which, in forbidding the use of contraceptives rather than regulating their manufacture or sale, seeks to achieve its goals by means of having a maximum destructive impact upon the relationship.'

Robert Bork had the following to say about this judgment:

> 'The *Griswold* opinion fails every test of neutrality. A derivation of the principles utterly specious, and so was the definition. In fact, we are left with no idea of what the principle really forbids. Derivation and definition are interrelated here. Just as Douglas calls the amendments and their penumbras "zones of privacy" though of course they are not that at all. They protect both private and public behaviour and so would more properly be labelled "zones of freedom". If we follow Justice Douglas in his next step, these zones would then add up to an independent right to freedom which is to say a constitutional right to be free of legal coercion, a manifest impossibility in any society. *Griswold* is an unprincipled decision, both from the way in which it derives a new constitutional right and in the way it defines a right, or rather fails to find it. We are left with no idea of the sweep of the right to privacy and hence no notion of the cases to which it may or may not be applied in the future. The truth is that the court could not reach its result in *Griswold* through principle.'

---

[108] See Klarman op cit (n 18) 769: 'It is simply impossible, I submit, to elicit from the phrase "equal protection of the laws" determinate answers to questions such as the permissibility of race-conscious legislation . . ..'

[109] An attempt could be made to blend substantive equality with formal equality by the inclusion of equal benefit. This would invite a more international stance because the court could be required to evaluate budgetary priorities.

[110] Supra.

What the court did in *Griswold*, as far as Bork was concerned, was to adopt its own value preferences and to impose them upon a majority. Later in his critique, however, Bork makes an important concession when he asserts that since 'the Constitution does not embody the moral, ethical choice, the judge has no basis other than his own values upon which to set aside the . . . judgment embodied in the statute. That, by definition, is an inadequate basis for judicial supremacy.'

If a Bill of Rights makes clear its underlying moral and ethical choices, then, Bork's supporters notwithstanding, the court is obliged to follow this approach, an approach which would approximate in methodology that adopted by Douglas J in the *Griswold* case,[111] who sought to articulate the premise upon which the Constitution was predicated before dealing with the validity of the Connecticut statute.

The second major problem is that this theory is unattractive in the US because it would require of the Supreme Court to overturn much of modern civil rights law, as much of this law cannot be justified under Bork's theory. For instance, it would throw into question the analytical framework developed for modern equal protection analysis including cases that prohibit 'various types of discrimination against women, aliens, illegitimates, nonresidents and poor Americans'.[112]

Finally, this theory requires that the legislative system be truly responsive to its constituents, or, in other words, that those constituents may reasonably expect to enact constitutional amendments. Both of these factors may not be present in the US today. As Ely has written recently, 'there has developed something approaching a consensus among political scientists and other observers that Congress has essentially lost the ability to function as a policy-making alternative to the executive . . . Congress can act negatively, to disrupt the policy the President pursues, but it cannot act affirmatively to carry out a comprehensive substitute policy of its own.'[113] If this is in fact true, then it will be dangerous for those who need constitutional protection if courts in the US are required to defer to an ineffective Congress.

The alternative, of course, is to pass a constitutional amendment. History has shown, however, that this is an extremely difficult process in the US despite the presence of a sufficient majority which supports the content of an amendment. As Ely wrote about the failure to pass a constitutional amendment that banned the burning of US flags, 'if Old Glory can't do it, what can?'[114] While the reason for the inability to pass constitutional amendments is elusive, it may well have

---

[111] Reference should be made to the powerful critiques which have been directed against Bork's theory to the effect that any reading of the text involves a value judgment. For example, Fish *Is there a Text in this Class* (1980) 327 has argued that interpretation is 'not the art of construing but the art of constructing'. For Fish a search for the objectivity of a text is illusory, for interpreters do not so much interpret a text but rather make it. In similar vein, Levinson 'Law as Literature' (1982) 60 *Texas LR* 373 at 387 notes: 'One no longer would say, for example, that *Dred Scott* or *Lochner v New York* or any other case was "wrongly" decided for that use of language presupposes belief in the knowability of constitutional essence. One could obviously show that constitutional tastes and styles shift over time, but this retreat into historicism has nothing to do with the legal science so desperately sought by Landell and his successors.'

[112] Nichol op cit (n 64) 340–1.

[113] Ely 'Another Such Victory: Constitutional Theory and Practice in a World Where Courts are No Different from Legislatures' (1991) 77 *Va LR* 833 at 855–63.

[114] At 868–9.

something to do with the reverence with which most Americans seem to view their Constitution and the 'founding fathers'.[115]

It is not inevitable that a Constitution cannot solve these difficulties. Framers can make it clear that the Constitution they draft is not a document of unquestionable wisdom, but one that is inevitably flawed and will require periodic adjustments and repairs.[116] In this manner a Constitution can be viewed as a living document so that groups unidentified at the time of drafting the document are not left without constitutional protection and heretofore unpredictable circumstances do not go without a constitutional resolution. Accordingly, the textual theory, strictly interpreted, needs to be carefully evaluated because it could be suggested that it provides South Africa with the first prong of a workable solution to the countermajoritarian difficulty.

### 2.5.2 *Protection of political access*

As Ely and Klarman have aptly pointed out, the judiciary cannot and must not defer to the legislature when the 'legislation [at issue] . . . restricts those political processes which can ordinarily be expected to bring about repeal of undesirable legislation'.[117]

A court may legitimately review legislative or executive acts without reference to the legislature's values when those acts interfere with the possibility of equal participation in the affairs of society, such as political speech and assembly, the franchise, all reapportionment decisions, the right to travel, as well as any areas expressly delegated in the Constitution to the judiciary.[118] In short, 'groups disabled from competing on equal terms in the political marketplace are entitled to special judicial solicitude'.[119]

If the Bill of Rights expresses a commitment to equality, as it does in South Africa, the court could respond in a similar fashion and insist that legislation exhibit a similar commitment to equality.

The two-pronged approach outlined above attempts to reconcile the majoritarian difficulty with that of the entrenchment and protection of core values by means of judicial review. There is a possible danger that South African lawyers, versed in the traditions of the Westminster parliamentary system and cognizant of the historical inability of a judiciary to promote the core values of a liberal legal tradition, have

---

[115] The US, for instance, has overturned by constitutional amendment a constitutional decision by the Supreme Court only four times in its 200-year history, only one of which was in this century (at 868).

[116] Indeed, Thomas Jefferson believed this so strongly that he argued for an 'intergenerational Constitution'. Such a Constitution would automatically expire after a designated period, leaving the next generation to construct its own Constitution. As Jefferson wrote, 'no society can make a perpetual Constitution . . . The earth belongs to the living generation . . . They are masters . . . of their own persons, and consequently may govern them as they please' (letter from Thomas Jefferson to James Madison (6 September 1789), reprinted in Kock & Peden (eds) *The Life and Selected Writings of Thomas Jefferson* (1944) 488 at 491). Given the enormous difficulties involved in negotiating America's first Constitution (as well as the force used by the American framers to get the Constitution ratified), Jefferson's 'intergenerational Constitution' probably does not make sense for South Africa. Nevertheless, Jefferson's point serves to underline the need for a nation to update on a continual basis its Constitution through amendments. If the US were better able to do this, perhaps discrimination in public accommodations would be unconstitutional under the equal protection clause, which it logically should be, rather than the committee clause.

[117] *United States v Carolene Products* (supra).

[118] Klarman op cit (n 18) 750–68. As Klarman points out, criminal procedure in the US is one example of an area in which the legislature has delegated all authority to the judiciary.

[119] At 753.

generally tended to advocate a far more aggressive form of judicial approach to legislation. Some might adopt the same approach to a process of judicial review within the context of an entrenched Constitution. This approach would, in the words of James Madison, as quoted by Black J, see 'independent tribunals of justice [as] . . . an impenetrable bulwark against the very encroachment upon rights expressly stipulated for in the Constitution'.[120]

The US experience illustrates that the task of extracting core values does not easily admit of a 'right' answer. One answer which has been viewed with some favour during the process of South Africa's constitutional negotiations has been to adopt the scrutiny theory developed during the course of US constitutional jurisprudence. Compliance with the three levels of scrutiny first outlined in *Carolene Products* is equally fraught with interpretive difficulties. Superficially the system appears to admit of easy implementation, as Black J noted in *Korematsu v US*:[121]

> 'All legal restrictions which curtail the civil rights of a single racial group are immediately suspect. That is not to say that all such restrictions are unconstitutional. It is to say that courts must subject them to more rigid scrutiny.'

However, the application has proved far more complex. An example from the jurisprudence relating to racial discrimination should suffice. In *Washington v Davis*[122] several African Americans filed suit in the District of Columbia, attacking the constitutionality under the Fifth Amendment as well as the legality under civil rights statutes of the hiring practices for police in the District. To be accepted for the police training programme an applicant had to receive a grade of at least 40 out of 80 on 'Test 21', an examination used throughout the federal civil service to gauge verbal ability, reading, and comprehension. Plaintiffs claimed that Test 21 excluded a far larger proportion of African Americans than whites and bore no relationship to job performance, and asked for a summary judgment on the constitutional issue. The district court found the test was a valid instrument, but the Court of Appeal reversed the decision. The District of Columbia sought and obtained *certiorari*.

In reversing the decision of the Court of Appeal, White J, on behalf of the Supreme Court, noted:

> 'The central purpose of the Equal Protection Clause of the Fourteenth Amendment is the prevention of official conduct discriminating on the basis of race. It is also true that the Due Process of the Fifth Amendment contains an equal protection component prohibiting the United States from invidiously discriminating between individuals or groups. But our cases have not embraced the proposition that a law or other official act, without regard to whether it reflects a racially discriminatory purpose, is unconstitutional *solely* because it has a racially disproportionate impact . . . .'[123]

White J went on to conclude:

> '[W]e have difficulty understanding how a law establishing a racially neutral qualification for employment is nevertheless racially discriminatory and denies "any person . . . equal protection of

---

[120] *Chapman v California* 386 US 18, 21 (1967).
[121] 323 US 214, 216 (1944).
[122] 426 US 229 (1976).
[123] At 234.

the laws" simply because a greater proportion of Negroes fails to qualify than members of other racial or ethnic groups.'[124]

In *Regents of the University of California v Bakke*[125] the difficulties inherent in the scrutiny approach were even more pronounced. The university had argued that discrimination against members of the 'white' majority could not be reviewed if its purpose was 'benign'. Powell J said:

> '[B]y hitching the meaning of the equal protection clause to these transitory considerations, we would be holding as a constitutional principle, that judicial scrutiny of classifications touching on racial and ethnic background may vary with the ebb and flow of political forces . . ..'[126]

He went on to conclude:

> '[W]hen a state's distribution of benefits or imposition of burdens hinges on the colour of a person's skin or ancestry, that individual is entitled to a demonstration that the challenged classification is necessary to promote a substantial state interest.'[127]

By contrast Brennan J found:

> '[R]acial classifications are not *per se* invalid under the Fourteenth Amendment . . . Unquestionably we have held that a government practice or statute which restricts "fundamental rights" or which contains "suspect classifications" is to be subject to "strict scrutiny" and can be justified only if it furthers a compelling government purpose and even then, only if no less restrictive alternative is available . . . But no fundamental right is involved here. Nor do whites as a class have any of the "traditional indicia of suspectness: the class is not saddled with such disabilities, or subjected to such a history of purposeful unequal treatment, or relegated to such a position of political powerlessness as to command extraordinary protection from the majoritarian political process".'[128]

Both Powell and Brennan JJ concede the existence of strict scrutiny. The difference between their approaches is to be found in Brennan J's conclusion as to the purpose of the affirmative action policy of the university. Whereas Powell J treats a doctrine of strict scrutiny as a monolith, Brennan is prepared to link the doctrine to the purpose of protecting fundamental rights and the intrinsic quality of the latter in order to uphold the university's programme.

Furthermore, the doctrine of strict scrutiny appears to have developed in US constitutional law as a result of an absence of a limitation clause in the US Bill of Rights which would have served to curtail the scope of certain rights contained therein in order to reconcile the Bill of Rights with the political process. In other words, the concept of strict scrutiny was a judicial creation in which the courts created a judicial form of limitation clause where none had previously existed.

The purposive approach itself is not free of problems. Its adoption can also produce unexpected consequences. In a footnote which might be considered to be the conservative equivalent of Stone J's famous footnote 4, Scalia J appended a footnote 6 to his judgment in *Michael H v Gerald D*.[129] In reply to the dissenting judgment of Brennan J against the decision of the court to uphold the Californian

---

[124] At 245.
[125] 438 US 265 (1978).
[126] At 298.
[127] At 320.
[128] At 356–7.
[129] 109 SCt 2333 (1989).

law denying parental rights to a man claiming to be the biological father of a child born to a woman married to another man, Scalia J said:

> '[W]e do not understand why, having rejected our focus upon the societal tradition regarding a natural father's rights vis-à-vis a child whose mother is married to another man, Justice Brennan would choose to focus instead on "parenthood". Why should the relevant category not be even more general — perhaps "family" relationships; or "personal relationships", or even "emotional attachments in general"? Though the dissent has no basis for the level of generality to select, we do; we refer to the most specific of all which are relevant traditions protecting, or denying protection to, and the assertive right can be protected.'

Scalia J attempted in footnote 6 to extract fundamental rights from societal tradition. However, this approach is no more value-neutral than the extraction of fundamental rights from legal precedent. In addition there is no universal test of specificity against which to measure a right.[130]

As Calebresi has observed,[131] 'the irony of today's great American debate between former Judge Robert Bork and other recent judicial appointees on one side and Justice William Brennan and much of the academic constitutional law establishment on the other, is that both sides share the same approach to judicial review'. In short, Calebresi argues that both sides advocate the Madisonian notion of review. But, he notes, it is here that the two groups differ because of 'Robert Bork and his fellow travellers' understandable fear of abuse of judicial power if courts grant constitutional protection to every value that judges believe to be fundamental. As a result, they retreat into a narrow originalism that is impossible in theory and produces outrageous results in practice. Justice Brennan and others, seeing the foolish results of the Bork position, cheerfully find and enforce rights whenever and wherever they desire.' Calebresi points to a danger of extended judicial review whenever either a libertarian or communitarian approach dominates, for given the nature of language and the re-creation of a text by the interpreter, judicial review often involves the enforcement by judges of their own views rather than the citizenry's notion of the ambit of good government.

Calebresi refers to the difference between the Warren and Rehnquist Courts and suggests that their contrasting records can be explained less by reference to judicial restraint or lack thereof and more by an analysis of a particular ideological approach. For example, he argues that the disfavour with which the Supreme Court has viewed litigation involving products liability represents a particular political view. In *Boyle v United Technical Corporation*[132] the court held that a federal common law supposed not to exist overruled the laws of the state and immunized those who had contracted with the government from products liability claims, notwithstanding Congress's failure to grant such immunity. The ideological commitment of the court influenced its aggressive approach to this area of law. The Warren Court, adopting a different political ideology, would doubtless have been equally active, but in the opposite direction.[133]

---

[130] See Tribe & Dorf op cit (n 8) 98.
[131] 'The Supreme Court — Forward' (1991) 105 *Harvard LR* 80 at 109.
[132] 487 US 500 (1988).
[133] Cf, for example, the criticism which was levelled against the court in *Brown v Board of Education* and *Roe v Wade* with a recent example of the Rehnquist Court's approach in *Rust v Sullivan* 111 SCt 1759 (1991), in which Rehnquist CJ used the opportunity to curtail the ambit of the First Amendment and to impose upon the court an anti-rights approach to this crucial clause in the Bill of Rights.

The introduction of a Bill of Rights into the South African legal system will compel lawyers to engage with competing conceptions of democracy, thereby enjoining them to fashion a democratic model which accommodates both the will of a political majority, albeit of a transient nature, and those core values established in the Constitution which can on occasion trump such will.

An acceptable theory of democracy must attempt to reconcile these two processes. The US experience provides some hope for the ascertainment of appropriate guidelines for judicial review in the context of such a democracy. A jurisprudence of judicial review should provide judges with a theory of justification upon which they might ground their constitutional decisions, thereby restricting the introduction of personal choice in the process of constitutional decision-making. Constitutional theory needs to develop a means of justification which should explain the constitutional enterprise and its relationship to popular democracy. To do so it must extract those values which make the most sense of the Constitution, i e the interpretation which justifies the existence of the very document itself as a contributor to the promotion of democracy.

The dissent of Harlan J in *Poe v Ullman*[134] provides such an illustration. In his judgment he wrote:

> '[T]he full scope of the liberty guaranteed by the Due Process Clause . . . is not a series of isolated points pricked out in terms of the taking of property; the freedom of speech, press and religion; the right to keep and bear arms; the freedom of unreasonable searches and seizures; and so on. It is a rational continuum which, broadly speaking, includes a freedom from all substantial arbitrary impositions and purposeless restraints and which also recognizes what a reasonable and sensible judgement must, that certain interests require particularly careful scrutiny of the state needs asserted to justify their abridgement.'

In short, having ascertained a specific set of liberties contained in the Bill of Rights, Harlan J inferred therefrom the existence of a set of unifying principles which together promote the most coherent meaning.

Judicial review safeguards this set of unifying principles which emanate from the Constitution and which are designed to create conditions for democracy. Judges, however, must be careful not to impose their conception of the political process on the society, but to balance the protection and promotion of these values with the legitimate activity of the political process.

However, subjective choice can never be eliminated from any process of interpretation. Judicial review should attempt to safeguard the set of core values which emanate from the Constitution and which are designed to provide democratic definition to a future South African society. Outside the zone of these core values, judges must be particularly careful not to impose their conception of the values contained in a Constitution upon the programmes introduced by a democratically elected legislature.

## 3 CANADA: FROM A WESTMINSTER CONSTITUTION TO A CHARTER

On 17 April 1982 the Canadian Charter of Rights and Freedoms became law, thereby ushering in a new era in Canadian constitutional history. For the first time the

---

[134] 367 US 497, 543 (1961).

Canadian judiciary was required to operate outside the framework of a Westminster model of parliamentary sovereignty, to confront fundamental issues of rights which had been entrenched in the Charter, and to develop appropriate remedies for infringements thereof. Unlike the US Bill of Rights, the Canadian Charter is a modern document which expressly provides for the protection of fundamental freedoms of conscience and religion, thought, belief, opinion, and expression, of the press and other media communications, of peaceful assembly, and of association, as well as containing a limitation clause.

The judicial interpretation section (s 1) of the Charter contains arguably the most important provision of the Charter. It guarantees the rights and freedoms set out in the Charter, subject only to such reasonable limits described by law as can demonstrably be justified in a free and democratic society. By implication the Charter invites litigants to provide evidence concerning those reasonable limitations to be imposed by a court on the freedoms enshrined in the Charter and further provides that fundamental freedoms can be overridden where the circumstances dictate.[135]

Judicial approach to s 1 has held the key to the theory of interpretation underlying the Canadian Charter and more generally to the scope and ambit of judicial review. In *R v Oakes*[136] Dickson CJ laid down an approach to s 1 which has been considered by some commentators to represent the appropriate democratic approach to interpretation of the Constitution.[137] Dickson CJ considered that s 1 fulfilled two functions: it constitutionally guaranteed the rights and freedoms contained in the Charter, and stated explicitly that there exist justificatory criteria against which limitations on those rights and freedoms must be measured. The onus of proof that a limit on a right or freedom was reasonable and demonstrably justified in a free and democratic society rested upon the party seeking to uphold the limitation. While the standard approved is a civil standard, i e on a balance of probabilities, the test must be applied rigorously, and where evidence is required to prove the constituent elements of a s 1 inquiry, such evidence should be cogent and persuasive, and make clear the consequences of the imposition of any limitation. The court would also be required to know what alternative measures would be available for the implementation of the objective of the legislator.

Dickson CJ went on to add:

> 'There may be cases where certain elements of the section 1 analysis are obviously self evident. To establish where the limit is reasonable and demonstrably justified in a free and democratic society, two central criteria must be satisfied. First the objective which the measures responsible for a limit on a Charter Right or Freedom are designed to serve must be of "sufficient importance to warrant overriding a constitutionally protected right of freedom". The standard must be high in order to ensure that objectives which are trivial or discordant with the principles integral to the free and democratic society do not gain section 1 protection... Secondly, once a sufficiently significant objective is recognized, then the party invoking section 1 must show that the means chosen are reasonable and demonstrably justified. This involves a form of proportionality test. Although the nature of the proportionality test will vary depending on the circumstances, in each case the courts will be required to balance the interests of society with those of individuals and groups. There

---

[135] Ritter 'Charter of Rights and Freedoms' in Blaustein (ed) *Constitutions of the World* (Permanent Volume) (1991).
[136] (1986) 26 DLR (4th) 200.
[137] See in particular Beatty *Talking Heads and the Supremes: The Canadian Production of Constitutional Review* (1990).

are ... three important components of a proportionality test[:] first the measures adopted must be carefully designed to achieve the objective in question ... [S]econdly, the means, even if rationally connected to the objective in this first sentence should impair "as little as possible" the right or freedom in question ... Thirdly there must be proportionality between the effects of the measures which are responsible for limiting the Charter, right or freedom and the objective which has been identified as of "sufficient importance".'[138]

Beatty[139] has suggested that the *Oakes* approach should be followed by the courts in attempting to strike a balance in the reconciliation of a potential tension between democracy and the protection of human rights, i e between the output of a legislature elected by a majority and an interpretation of a Constitution by a judiciary which has been appointed rather than elected. In terms of this approach judges should approach constitutional review with two fundamental questions in mind: first, has there been an infringement of a right protected by the Bill of Rights? Secondly, is the policy underlying the actual omission which caused the infringement demonstrably justifiable in a free and open democracy and has an acceptable method been used in its implementation?

As far as the first question is concerned, a violation will have to be established as a matter of law and fact, i e an applicant will need to demonstrate that the interest or activity sought to be protected falls within the protected ambit of a Bill of Rights and the impugned measure violates such protection.

With regard to the second question, the objectives and means of the impugned law or action will be evaluated and ought to establish that the limit on freedom is reasonable and demonstrably justified in a free and open democracy. The onus of proof that the restriction on a guarantee is so reasonable and demonstrably justified will rest on the respondent. To answer the second question inquiries will need to be initiated: first, whether the objective which the measure is designed to serve is of sufficient importance to warrant trumping the protection and, secondly, whether the means adopted were proportional to the stated objective.

Beatty's application of the *Oakes* theory has not gone uncriticized. It has proved to be a controversial proposal and some commentators have suggested that this form of constitutional review can well subvert the democratic process. For example, Alan Hutchinson[140] has referred to the ambivalent consequence of an application of the Beatty test as exemplified in *Thompson Newspapers Limited v Restrictive Trade Practices Commission*,[141] where the majority of the court held that a power granted to the Restrictive Trade Practices Commission to compel production of documents and order testimony under oath to further inquests into protecting pricing contrary to the Combined Investigation Act was not consistent with the provisions of the Charter, particularly ss 7 and 8 thereof.

---

[138] *R v Oakes* (supra) at 227. See *R v Big M Drug Mart Ltd* (1985) 18 DLR (4th) 321 at 366, where Dickson CJ said:
'At the outset it should be noted that not every government interest or policy objective is entitled to s 1 consideration. Principles will have to be developed for recognizing which government objectives are of sufficient importance to warrant overriding the constitutionally protected right or freedom. Once a sufficiently significant government interest is recognized then it must be decided if the means chosen to achieve this interest are reasonable — a form of proportionality test. The court may wish to ask whether the means adopted to achieve the end sought do so by impairing as little as possible the right or freedom in question.'
[139] Op cit (n 137) 128.
[140] 'Waiting for Coraf' (1991) 41 *U Toronto LJ* 350.
[141] (1990) 67 DLR (4th) 161.

In adopting the *Oakes* approach Wilson J characterized the criminal nature and held that although corporations were not entitled to protection under s 7, corporate officers' rights were infringed. Moreover, she found such investigatory powers could not be justified under s 7, although in furtherance of important social objectives they did not amount to the least drastic measure available.

As Hutchinson notes, 'even assuming that the correct resort to *Oakes* would have led to the whole court's concurring with Wilson's judgment, such a decision cannot count as progressive. It not only fails to help the disadvantaged and dispossessed, but scuttles the future possibility of important measures to improve their lot.'[142] Hutchinson observes that the purpose of the Combined Investigation Act was to regulate anti-competitive practices by large corporations that work to the disadvantage of the community at large, and particularly poorer consumers: it was 'an unabashed effort at state intervention for progressive ends'.

In upholding the legislation La Forest J wrote:

> 'The degree of privacy the citizen can reasonably expect may vary significantly depending upon the activity that brings him or her into contact with the state. In a modern industrial society, it is generally accepted that many activities in which individuals can engage must nevertheless to a greater or lesser extent be regulated by the state to ensure that the individual's pursuit of his or her self-interest is compatible with the community's interest in the realization of collective goals and aspirations. In many cases this regulation must necessarily involve the inspection of private premises or documents by agents of the state.'[143]

Given that a company acts as an individual, the legislation must concern itself with the conduct of individuals who happen to be the corporate officials of the company. Thus, although a corporation cannot claim the protection of s 7, the officials or individuals can so claim rights. As L'Heureux-Dube J noted, to allow company officials to invoke Charter protection would be to grant corporations rights which they cannot enjoy.[144]

Hutchinson's critique of the Beatty position represents a warning that the consequences of judicial interpretation are not inevitable and that it is incorrect to characterize, as Beatty has done, judicial review as a dialogue or debate between citizens and state about the reasonableness of government action. Hutchinson notes:

> 'If there is any debate it is between different branches of government: citizens' complaints merely provide an occasion for a discussion in which those citizens can listen hopefully and can only speak episodically in high priced words of an arcane legal vocabulary.'[145]

For this reason the implication of the US constitutional experience, namely that judicial review should be given a carefully constructed ambit in order to harmonize the principles of accountability and democracy, should be taken carefully into account in evaluating the Canadian experience.

The countermajoritarian argument is well illustrated in an analysis of the Canadian Supreme Court's first hundred Charter decisions.[146] Morton et al note that from

---

[142] Op cit (n 140) 350.
[143] *Thompson Newspapers* (supra) at 220.
[144] At 271.
[145] Op cit (n 140) 356.
[146] Morton, Russell & Withey 'The Supreme Court's First Hundred Charter of Rights Decisions: Statistical Analysis' (1992) 30 *Osgoode Hall LJ* 1. As Morton et al note (at 15), the usage of liberal and conservative synonyms for judicial activism and judicial conservatism when discussing the Charter are misleading, for this
  'reflects simplistic attitudes of "the more rights the better", an attitude that fails to grasp either the complexity

1984 to 1987 the court rejected all but one of the eleven s 1 defences presented by the Crown. By contrast, in 1988 and 1989 it accepted eight of the fourteen. As the authors comment, '[t]he Charter confirms what was already an open secret: the Court has become value divided on how to handle the Section 1 issues'.[147] The authors also note that the explanation of the change in the court's approach cannot simply be attributed to a conservative series of Mulroney appointments to the court. The better explanation is that the change reflected 'a working out of the tension between the activist behaviour and the legalistic pretence in the Court's earlier decisions'. In a similar way to the debates in America between judicial review of constitutional rights and parliamentary democracy, disagreements amongst the justices were exacerbated as more cases came before the court. In the final analysis the way in which the Canadian Supreme Court has attempted to deal with the interpretation of the Charter can be located in the resolution of a conflict between two doctrines, the first of which was articulated in *R v Big M Drug Mart Ltd*.[148] In this case the court suggested that guaranteed rights should be given a generous interpretation. The second doctrine, that articulated in *R v Oakes*,[149] suggested that a stringent ambit of justification of s 1 is required before a right guaranteed under the Charter can be eroded.

Peter Hogg[150] has attempted to reconcile these two cases by posing the question of how the scope of the Charter of Rights can be restricted without abandoning or undermining the civil liberty values protected by the Charter. He suggests that the Supreme Court has answered the question in its insistence on a purposive interpretation of Charter rights. Thus in the *Big M Drug Mart* case the court attempted to ascertain the purpose of each Charter right and then to interpret such rights to include the activity that comes within the purpose thereof and to exclude activity that does not. Guidance for finding the purpose of a section can be obtained from the language in which the right is expressed, the implications to be drawn from the context in which the right is to be found and its relationship to other sections of the Charter, and the pre-Charter history of the right as appears from the legislative history of the Charter. In the *Big M Drug Mart* case Dickson CJ warned against 'over-shooting' the purpose of a right.[151] For this reason Hogg is probably correct to suggest that the adaptation of the purposive approach can narrow the scope of the right and for this reason this approach accommodates the stringent standard of justification set out in s 1 of the Charter.

The approach of the court in the *Big M Drug Mart* case was that when s 1 was applicable the court was required to adopt a standard of proportionality: a balancing of the character of the protected right, the degree of infringement, and the importance of the public policy or purpose to be achieved. However, the standard of

---

or ambiguity of rights. The wrongheadedness of this common practice can be illustrated by comparing judges with legislators. It is simply perverse to describe a politician who supports state intervention to regulate or redistribute private power as a liberal, and to simultaneously describe a judge who strikes down such laws as a liberal. Similarly it is hardly clear why a politician who votes against interventionist, statist projects should be described as a conservative while a self-restrained judge who votes to uphold the same laws is described as a conservative.'

[147] At 14.
[148] Supra.
[149] Supra.
[150] Hogg 'Interpreting the Charter of Rights' (1990) 28 *Osgoode Hall LJ* 817 at 820.
[151] Supra at 360.

# THE ROLE OF CONSTITUTIONAL INTERPRETATION

proportionality followed upon an analysis of the rights protected in the Charter. By employing a purposive approach to such rights the court took a more restrictive view of rights than would have been the case had it adopted a generous interpretation of the Charter, but considered it more appropriate in reconciling the restrictions imposed by s 1 with those rights, the scope and meaning of which had been amplified by the use of the purposive approach to interpretation.

The applicability of original intent was canvassed by the court in *Reference Re Section 94(2) of the Motor Vehicle Act*.[152] Section 94(1) of the Motor Vehicle Act of British Columbia provided that

> 'a person who drives a motor vehicle while he is prohibited from driving or while his driver's licence is suspended commits an offence and is liable on first conviction to a fine and to imprisonment for not less than seven days and not more than six months'.

Section 94(2) provides that the offence created by s 94(1)

> 'creates an absolute liability offence in which guilt is established by proof of driving, whether or not the defendant knew of the prohibition or suspension'.

The question arose as to whether s 94(2) was consistent with s 7 of the Charter of Rights and Freedoms. The government argued that the concept of fundamental justice contained in s 7 applies only to procedural justice and hence s 94(2) does not conflict with s 7.

The government relied upon speeches made in the legislature at the time of the enactment of the Charter as well as the minutes of the Select Committee of Parliament, which had a responsibility for the drafting of the Charter, in order to support its submission. On behalf of the court Lamer J admitted this evidence, but went on to say:

> '[T]he simple fact remains that the Charter is not the product of a few individual public servants, however distinguished, but of a multiplicity of individuals who played major roles in the negotiating, drafting and adoption of the Charter. How can one say with any confidence that within this enormous multiplicity of actors, without forgetting the role of the provinces, the comments of a few federal civil servants can in any way be determinative?
>
> Were this Court to accord any significant weight to this testimony, it would in effect be assuming a fact which is nearly impossible of proof, i e the intention of the legislative bodies which adopted the Charter. In view of the indeterminate nature of the data, it would in my view be erroneous to give these materials anything but minimal weight.
>
> Another danger with casting the interpretation of s 7 in terms of the comments made by those heard at the joint committee proceedings is that, in so doing, the rights, freedoms and values embodied in the Charter in effect become frozen in time to the moment of adoption with little or no possibility of growth, development and adjustment to changing societal needs. Obviously, in the present case, given the proximity in time of the Charter debates, such a problem is relatively minor, even though it must be noted that even at this early stage in the life of the Charter, a host of issues and questions have been raised which were largely unforeseen at the time of such proceedings. If the newly planted "living tree" which is the Charter is to have the possibility of growth and adjustment over time, care must be taken to ensure that historical materials, such as the Minutes of Proceedings and Evidence of the Special Joint Committee, do not stunt its growth.'[153]

The court held that a purposive analysis of s 7 in general and the concept of

---

[152] (1988) 24 DLR (4th) 536.
[153] At 554–5. See also *Re Chiarelli v Minister of Employment & Immigration* (1992) 90 DLR (4th) 289.

fundamental justice in particular clearly meant that fundamental justice was not synonymous with natural but with wider principles of substantive justice. Thus s 94(2), which imposed an absolute liability, violated the principles of fundamental justice as it had the potential of depriving a person of his or her liberty or security.

## 3.1 The purposive approach and the *Andrews* case

The approach of the court in *Andrews v Law Society, British Columbia*[154] is perhaps most illustrative of the purposive approach. In this case the Supreme Court was required to interpret equality rights guaranteed by s 15 of the Charter. Section 15(1) of the Charter provides that every individual is equal before and under the law and has the right to equal protection and an equal benefit of the law without discrimination and, in particular, without discrimination based on race, national ethnic origin, colour, religion, sex, age, or mental or physical disability. Section 15(2) provides that subsec (1) does not preclude any law, programme, or activity that has as its object the amelioration of conditions of disadvantaged individuals or groups including those that are disadvantaged because of race, national ethnic origin, colour, religion, sex, age, or mental or physical disability.

Prior to the *Andrews* case, which was the first s 15 decision of the Supreme Court, the most widely held view in so far as equality was concerned involved a test termed the 'similarly situated test', which was a modification of the Aristotelian principle of formal equality, namely that 'things that are alike should be treated as alike and things that are unalike should be treated as unalike in proportion to their unlikeness'.[155]

The *Andrews* court rejected the 'similarly situated test' and adopted a different approach which flowed from the identification by the court of the purpose of Charter equality rights as provided in s 15. The court found that the purpose of s 15 was related to the purpose of human rights legislation and civil rights statutes, i e to prevent discrimination and prejudice against groups who historically are disadvantaged and who have been identified by personal characteristics such as those outlined in s 15(2) of the Charter. The court found that the number of possible equality claims which fell within the meaning of s 15 were limited to claims based on grounds listed in the section. The court did, however, confirm that as long as an analogous ground to one specified in s 15 involving discrimination could be found to exist, either through a direct provision in the law or through the intended or unintended consequence of a law on a particular group, the section would be applicable.[156]

In setting out the principles upon which the judgment was based, McIntyre J said:

'The promotion of equality entails the promotion of a society which all are secure in the knowledge that they are recognized at law as human beings, equally deserving of concern, respect and consideration ... It must be recognized, however, ... that the promotion of equality under s 15 has a much more specific goal than the mere elimination of discrimination. If the Charter was intended to eliminate all distinctions then there would be no place for sections such as 27 (multicultural

---

[154] (1989) 56 DLR (4th) 1.
[155] See, for example, *Reference re Family Benefits Act* (Nova Scotia) (1986) 26 CRR 336; *Reference re French Language Rights of Accused* (Saskatchewan Criminal Proceedings) (1987) 44 DLR (4th) 16; *R v Ertel* (1987) 30 CRR 209.
[156] See this approach confirmed in *McKinney v University of Guelph* (1991) 76 DLR (4th) 545 at 647.

heritage); 2(a) (freedom of conscience and religion); 25 (aboriginal rights and freedoms); and other such provisions designed to safeguard certain distinctions. Moreover, the fact that identical treatment may frequently produce serious inequality is recognized in s 15(2).'[157]

In dealing with the question of which groups could be considered to be analogous to those enumerated in s 15, Wilson J said that the determination 'is not to be made only in the context of the law which is subject to challenge, but rather in the context of the place of the group in the entire social, political and legal fabric of our society'.[158]

The *Andrews* case confirmed that the court had leaned towards an acceptance of a purposive interpretation of the Charter. It examined the purpose of s 15 and found that it was connected with the promotion of a society in which all would be secure in the knowledge that they were recognized at law as human beings 'equally deserving of concern, respect and consideration'. This section was to be read as one whole, and from the purpose of the section together with the context of the Charter an interpretation of this section and its ambit can be reached.

Subsequent courts[159] have interpreted the *Andrews* judgment as comprising a three-stage inquiry in terms of s 15:

*(a)* Was there a denial of equality before or under the law or of the equal protection or equal benefit of the law to an individual?
*(b)* If so, did the denial relate to discrimination?
*(c)* If there is denial of equality with discrimination, is the provision nevertheless a reasonable limit demonstrably justified in a free and democratic society?

The *Andrews* case adopts a purposive interpretation of the section in question and then, having established the ambit and scope of a particular section of the Charter, moves to apply s 1 in so far as examining whether the proponents of the relevant legislation have discharged the onus that it is justifiable. Many of the members of the court appeared willing to relax the standard of review. For example, social and economic legislation appears to be regarded as calling for a greater degree of judicial deference.[160] It is interesting to note that when the *Andrews* case was heard by the Court of Appeal the court held that, to a considerable extent, the limitations on equality rights were to be determined at the stage of deciding whether there was a violation of s 15, which thus left a very limited role for s 1.[161]

A theory of constitutional interpretation must be harmonized with the nature and content of the limitations clause. In particular the question arises as to whether the clause providing for a substantive right should be given a wider meaning, with the curtailment of its constitutional protection taking place at the stage of interpreting the limitation clause, or whether a restrictive approach is permissible at the first

---

[157] *Andrews v Law Society, British Columbia* (supra) at 171.
[158] At 152.
[159] *R v Turpin* (1989) 39 CRR 306.
[160] See Gold 'Comment: *Andrews v Law Society of BC*' (1989) 34 *McGill LJ* 1063 at 1076; Wilson J at 194 and La Forest J at 185 of the *Andrews* case (supra).
[161] A number of cases have followed the approach contained therein, the most notable being *R v Keegstra* (1991) 2 WWR 1, which upholds s 219 of the Canadian Criminal Code, which prohibited the wilful promotion of hatred against identifiable groups distinguished by colour, race, religion, and the like against the challenge based on freedom of expression.

stage. Although the *Andrews* case appeared to clarify this issue, some manner of uncertainty has continued to exist as a result of subsequent judgments.

In *Committee for Commonwealth v Canada*[162] Lamer CJC appeared to adopt an overtly restricted approach to s *2(b)*, which protects freedom of thought, belief, opinion, and expression, including freedom of the press and other media of communication. In this case the plaintiffs wanted to disseminate their political ideas by carrying placards and distributing pamphlets in the public terminal concourse of an airport. The airport management prohibited such activity whether it was political, religious, or otherwise. The plaintiffs brought an action against the Crown seeking declarations that the airport management had not observed the fundamental freedoms of the plaintiffs and that the areas of the airport open to the public constituted a public forum where fundamental freedoms could be exercised.

Lamer CJC concluded that s *2(b)* cannot be interpreted so as to consider only the interests of the person wishing to communicate. Thus:

> 'I come to the conclusion that s *2(b)* of the Charter cannot be interpreted so as to consider only the interests of the person wishing to communicate. As the Attorney-General of Ontario properly points out, s *2(b)* of the Charter does not protect "expression" itself, but freedom of expression. In my opinion, the "freedom" which an individual may have to communicate in a place owned by the government must necessarily be circumscribed by the interests of the latter and of the citizens as a whole: the individual will only be free to communicate in a place owned by the state if the form of expression he uses is compatible with the principal function or intended purpose of that place.'[163]

In this manner Lamer CJC sought to balance individual interests and governmental interests within the freedom of expression clause, rather than in terms of the limitation clause.

By contrast L'Heureux-Dube J appears to follow the *Andrews* approach in giving s *2(b)* a wider ambit of protection. L'Heureux-Dube J acknowledged the existence of the two approaches. As she observed:

> 'Should [s *2(b)*] be construed narrowly, thus avoiding the need to resort to s 1 as fewer Charter violations will be established; or should it be read broadly, thus requiring that most limitations must be anchored within s 1, with the burden of proof resting upon the government?'[164]

Although not drawing a clear distinction between a generous and purposive approach, L'Heureux Dube J gave a 'larger and liberal application'[165] to s *2(b)* and then proceeded to curtail the effect thereof when examining the consequences of the limitation clause. While her judgment can be criticized for its approach to the limitation clause, the conceptual understanding of the two-stage approach is to be supported.[166]

It has been suggested[167] that the Canadian treatment of s 15 is far superior to the equality jurisprudence developed by the US Supreme Court under the Fourteenth Amendment to its Constitution. This submission has been made not only because of the court's departure from the principle of formal equality but also owing to its

---

[162] (1991) 77 DLR (4th) 385. For a trenchant analysis of this case, see Woolman & De Waal 'Freedom of Assembly: Voting with Your Feet' below, 308–14.
[163] At 394–5.
[164] At 415.
[165] Ibid.
[166] See Woolman & De Waal below, 312.
[167] Smith 'The Charter, Equality Rights since Andrews' (Unpublished paper, 1992).

conclusion that s 15 guarantees equality with respect to unintended effects of apparently neutral provisions and that greater protection is afforded to aggrieved persons. As Wilson J said in the *Turpin* case,

> 'if the larger context is not examined, the s 15 analysis may become a mechanical and sterile categorization process conducted entirely within the four corners of the impugned legislation. A determination as to whether or not discrimination has taken place, if based exclusively on an analysis of the law under challenge, is likely, in my view, to result in the same kind of circularity which characterized the "similarly situated test" clearly rejected by this court in *Andrews*.'[168]

It could well be that the limitations of the US equality jurisprudence can be located in the text of the US Constitution and that the formulation contained in s 15 proves to be more amenable to an enlightened jurisprudence. It is indicative that the purposive approach to the Charter as a whole and the particular section under analysis can promote important democratic concepts which are contained within the spirit of the Charter.[169]

Once a right is confined to its purpose the government ought to comply with the stringent standard of justification to uphold legislation which may well erode such a right. In this manner the purposive approach to the contents of the Charter can be reconciled with the *Oakes* approach, i e that a stringent standard of justification be proved before any legislation limiting a right is justified. Hogg suggests that the purposive approach to the definition of Charter rights will gradually supplant the 'generous' approach.[170] This conclusion appears to be supported by the empirical research of Morton et al, which reveals that the generous approach which was initially adopted by the court has been replaced by a more careful purposive approach to the ambit of such rights.

## 4 INDIAN CONSTITUTIONAL LAW: A CLASH BETWEEN THE STATUS QUO AND SOCIAL TRANSFORMATION

### 4.1 Introduction

This part is divided into two broad sections: the first deals with the history of post-colonial constitutional law in India, the second with the rise of public interest law in India and the developments in constitutional law upon which this was premised. The first section is primarily historical and contains very little legal comment. This is because the case law over this period was not particularly

---

[168] *R v Turpin* (supra) at 336.

[169] See by contrast the US Supreme Court's interpretation of a constitutional guarantee of equal protection of the law under the Fourteenth Amendment, which has been held not to extend to unintended effects in the cases, for example, of *Washington v Davis* 426 US 229 (1976); *The Village of Arlington Heights v Metro Housing Development Corporation* 429 US 252 (1977); and *Personnel Administrator v Feeney* 442 US 256 (1979).

[170] There were earlier precedents in which the court adopted a generous interpretation of the Charter, meaning an approach whereby the courts avoided a narrow interpretation of a kind that might be appropriate in construing a detailed statute or a statute in derogation of individual rights. Thus in *Law Society of Upper Canada v Skapinker* (1984) 9 DLR (4th) 61 the Supreme Court rejected the Ontario Court of Appeal's interpretation of one of the mobility rights in s 6 of the Charter. The Ontario Court of Appeal held that s 6(2)(*b*), which confers on the citizen or permanent resident the right to pursue the gaining of a livelihood in any province, was an absolute ban on the requirement of citizenship as a qualification for the practice of law. The Supreme Court found that the language of s 6(2)(*b*) could bear this meaning, but, in the context of the section and having regard to the heading of mobility rights which preceded s 6, the guaranteed right protected only persons who were discriminated against because they came from another province. While this was a less generous interpretation than that followed by the Ontario Court of Appeal, it probably reflected the purpose of the section, and indeed of the Charter, more accurately.

interesting. The history remains of crucial importance because it illustrates some of the problems which judicial review of legislation can produce. A basic knowledge of this history is also essential to an understanding of the emergence of public interest law in India in the post-Emergency period. The second section contains a discussion of some of the major features of this public interest law as well as the conceptions of judicial review, constitutionalism, and democracy which underpin it. We have also tried to illustrate the thematic points with some summaries of a few major public interest cases. These summaries, and the extensive use of direct quotations from the judges, are included because they help to describe the nature of Indian public interest law, which is seemingly without precedent in an English-speaking jurisdiction.

## 4.2 History

### 4.2.1 *Struggles over property*

Nehru regarded poverty and inequality as the most important issues facing the independent India. He warned in the Constituent Assembly Debates: 'If we cannot solve this problem soon, all our paper Constitutions will become useless and purposeless.'[171] Nevertheless, in a political compromise with the conservative wing of the Congress Party he conceded the inclusion of two property protection clauses, arts 19(1)*(f)* and 31, in the Constitution. Article 19(1)*(f)* provided that 'all citizens shall have the right . . . to acquire, hold and dispose of property'. It had to be read with art 19(5), which authorized the state to impose reasonable restrictions on the right to property. Article 31 read:

> '(1) No person shall be deprived of his property save by authority of law.
> (2) No property movable or immovable, including any interest in, or in any company owning, any commercial or industrial undertaking, shall be taken possession of or acquired for public purposes under any law authorizing the taking of such possession or such acquisition, unless the law provides for compensation for the property taken possession of or acquired and either fixes the amount of compensation, or specifies the principles on which the compensation is to be payable.'

Nehru actually piloted these two articles through the Constituent Assembly and his speech to the Assembly shows that he envisaged that the clauses would provide an extremely limited protection to property. He said that the state should provide compensation for petty acquisitions of property, but that large-scale social engineering schemes affecting millions of poor people could not be subordinated to the property rights of a few individual landowners. In cases of social engineering compensation should be equitable when viewed from the perspective of society rather than the individual. The judiciary would not be able to question amounts of compensation unless there was gross abuse of law.[172]

The judiciary were to prove Nehru wrong. The Indian judges treated social engineering schemes as falling clearly within the scope of their review power to

---

[171] Quoted by Khanna J in *Kesavananda v State of Kerala* AIR 1973 SC 1461 at 1880.
[172] Austin *The Indian Constitution: Cornerstone of a Nation* (1974); Seervai *Constitutional Law of India* (1984) vol 2 1097; Ghouse 'The Right to Property and Planned Development in India' in Dhavan & Jacob (eds) *Indian Constitution: Trends and Issues* (1978) 80; Murphy 'Insulating Land Reform from Constitutional Impugnment: An Indian Case Study' (1992) 8 *SAJHR* 362 at 363.

protect property rights, and the first twenty-five years of the Indian Constitution were dominated by a struggle between Parliament and the courts over property rights. This period saw a sequence of judgments invalidating legislation aimed at social reform, followed by constitutional amendments to overrule the judgments.[173] In this process the Supreme Court lost most of its popular support, and constitutional democracy under judicial review was discredited to the point that the legislature was prepared to abolish the institution of independent judicial review altogether.[174]

Conflict between the court and Parliament over property rights began almost immediately in *Kameshwar Singh v Province of Bihar*.[175] Article 31(4) protected legislation aimed at the abolition of the *zamindar* system from the scope of art 31(1). The Patna High Court invoked the equality clause in art 14 to invalidate legislation providing for a graded system of compensation for land expropriated from the *zamindars*.[176] This reliance on equality to protect privilege provoked the passage of the First Amendment, in which Parliament expressly excluded *zamindari* abolition and state acquisition of agricultural estates from the protection of arts 14, 19, and 31.

Nevertheless, in *State of Bihar v Kameshwar Singh*[177] the Supreme Court still managed to reject the constitutionality of the Bihar Land Reforms Act, characterizing it as an Act which authorized confiscation under the guise of acquisition of property. Parliament responded by passing the Seventh Amendment to overrule this judgment. The court then set back land reform again in *Kunhikoman v State of Kerala*[178] and *Krishnaswami v State of Madras*.[179] These cases invalidated legislation setting a ceiling on agricultural landholdings. The court achieved this by giving an extremely restricted meaning to 'estate' in the First Amendment. Parliament responded by passing the Seventeenth Amendment to extend the operation of the First Amendment to all agricultural landholdings whether or not they constituted 'estates'.

The court's response to Parliament's repeated amendments of the Constitution to circumvent decisions on property rights was *Golak Nath v State of Punjab*.[180] A majority of six judges to five in *Golak Nath* held that the fundamental rights, including the right to property, were absolutely sovereign. Not even a two-thirds majority of Parliament, exercising its power to amend the Constitution under art 368, had the authority to infringe the fundamental rights. Thus any constitutional amendment which purported to repeal or even to restrict a fundamental right was invalid. The court conceded that it would be impossible to undo all the amendments

---

[173] There was no attempt to conceal this conflict. Thus the string of constitutional amendments passed by Parliament would each usually be prefaced by a statement of objects and reasons in which the offending Supreme Court judgment that was the object of the amendment would be named.

[174] The following account of this process is taken from Ghouse op cit (n 172) 79–98, Murphy op cit (n 172) 362–88, and Rudolph & Rudolph *In Pursuit of Lakshmi: The Political Economy of the Indian State* (1987).

[175] AIR 1950 Pat 392. The *zamindars* were intermediaries between the colonial authorities and the Indian population who had been granted massive landholdings by the authorities in return for supervising the collection of tax from the people occupying the granted land.

[176] The Bihar Land Reforms Act provided that compensation was to be paid on a sliding scale — the greater the extent of the landholding expropriated, the smaller the amount of compensation per acre.

[177] AIR 1952 SC 252.

[178] AIR 1962 SC 723.

[179] AIR 1964 SC 1515.

[180] AIR 1967 SC 1643.

to the Constitution already passed which fell foul of this rule of sovereignty of the fundamental rights, but it insisted that any future amendments which did not satisfy the rule would be invalidated.

While the court and the state had been fighting over the constitutionality of land reform legislation, they were also engaged in a battle over the meaning of compensation under the Constitution. Nehru and the Congress Party in the Constituent Assembly had deliberately chosen not to qualify 'compensation' in the Constitution with 'just' or 'adequate', and they clearly believed that in appropriate circumstances the Constitution allowed expropriation with compensation which did not amount to market value. Once again the courts took a different view.

In *State of West Bengal v Bela Bannerjee*[181] the Supreme Court read into art 31 the notion of just compensation and held that the Constitution demanded payment of compensation at market value. The Fourth Amendment was passed to overturn this judgment. It stated explicitly that the adequacy of compensation was non-justiciable under the Constitution. The court simply ignored the obvious meaning of this Amendment. In *Vajravelu v Special Deputy Collector*[182] Subba Rao CJ ruled that although the adequacy of compensation was non-justiciable, the court retained the power to inquire into the relevancy of the principles according to which the legislation provided for compensation. If the legislature had been motivated by irrelevant considerations, its legislation was unconstitutional. As the court considered market value the only consideration relevant to the *quantum* of compensation, this judgment had the effect of reinstating market value as the measure of compensation demanded by the Constitution. In fact, the court in *Vajravelu* went even further. Noting that the Land Acquisition Act of 1894[183] provided for compensation at market value plus 15 %, the court held that the availability of two different modes of calculating payment of compensation on expropriation infringed the equality provision in art 14 and thus any legislative provision less favourable to the landowner than the Land Acquisition Act was held to be unconstitutional. The principles of *Vajravelu* were confirmed in *Cooper v Union of India*.[184] This is generally referred to as the *Bank Nationalization* case because it concerned the Ghandi government's attempt to nationalize the fourteen largest commercial banks in India.

The judgment of Subba Rao CJ in *Golak Nath* illustrates the attitude of the court to constitutionalism and democracy during these struggles over property rights:

'No authority created under the Constitution is supreme and all the authorities function under the supreme law of the land. The rule of law under the Constitution has a glorious content . . . Having regard to the past history of our country, [the Constitution] could not implicitly believe the representatives of the people, for uncontrolled and unrestricted power might lead to an authoritarian state. It, therefore, preserves the natural rights against state encroachment and constitutes the higher judiciary of the state as the sentinel of the said rights . . . .'[185]

The Hobbesian fear of the elected representatives coupled with an appeal to

---

[181] AIR 1954 SC 170.
[182] AIR 1965 SC 1017.
[183] This was a piece of colonial legislation designed to protect the property of English settlers in India from expropriation by the colonial government.
[184] AIR 1970 SC 564.
[185] *Golak Nath v State of Punjab* (supra) at 1655 para 15.

natural law are recurrent features of the Supreme Court judgments of this period. The fact that the court chose to confront the potentially authoritarian state by protecting property rights against social reform legislation is significant. Many commentators attribute this to the hostility of privileged and conservative judges to redistribution of wealth.[186] If this is not the case, there is tremendous irony in the fact that when the authoritarian state actually did rear its head, the court did nothing to confront it. During the Ghandi government State of Emergency from 1975 to 1977 the court was totally compliant towards the state. The irony is compounded by the fact that even if the court had had the will to confront the state during the Emergency, it lacked the political authority to do so, primarily because it had been totally discredited by the attitude it had taken in the struggles over property rights.

To return to those struggles: soon after the *Bank Nationalization* judgment the Congress Party won a two-thirds majority in both Houses in the February 1971 elections, which were fought, in part, on a platform of social reform. The Congress election campaign had been characterized by strong anti-judicial rhetoric, and soon after the election victory it struck back at the judges with the Twenty-fourth and Twenty-fifth Amendments. The Twenty-fourth Amendment overrode *Golak Nath* by making the fundamental rights subject to Parliament's amending power under art 368. The Twenty-fifth Amendment was aimed at the *Bank Nationalization* judgment by attempting, once more, to make the question of compensation for takings of property non-justiciable. The constitutionality of these two amendments was raised in *Kesavananda v State of Kerala*.[187] The struggle between courts and state over property rights thus came to a head in *Kesavananda*, which had also to consider the broader issue of the constituent power of Parliament to amend the Constitution. *Kesavananda* was heard by a Full Bench of thirteen judges. The outcome of the case can be summarized as follows: on the amending power of Parliament, a majority of seven judges (Sikri, Shelat, Grover, Hegde, Mukherjea, Reddy, and Khanna) held that art 368 did not allow Parliament to abrogate the basic features of the Constitution; the minority of six (Chandrachud, Ray, Mathew, Dwivemi, Palekar, and Beg) rejected the distinction between essential and non-essential features of the Constitution altogether and suggested that art 368 extended to the entire Constitution. However, Khanna J differed from his fellow majority judges by holding that no single fundamental right, least of all the right to property, could be considered an essential feature of the Constitution. Thus the validity of the Twenty-fourth and Twenty-fifth Amendments was upheld.

*Kesavananda* marks a watershed in the history of Indian constitutional law. The majority judgments in the case reflect much of the attitude to constitutionalism that informed the court in its confrontations with the state over the previous two decades; the minority judgments prefigure some of the new directions that the court was to take in the 1980s. The legal significance of the case is discussed in detail below. In political terms it represented a compromise between court and state. The court recognized the validity of the Twenty-fourth and Twenty-fifth Amendments and

---

[186] See, for example, Ghouse & Dhavan *The Supreme Court: A Socio-legal Critique of its Juristic Techniques* (1977).
[187] Supra.

conceded that the right to property was not a fundamental feature of the Constitution, but it retained its right to review all amendments in terms of their compatibility with the essential core of the Constitution.

### 4.2.2 *The Emergency*

The compromise, however, did not end the political confrontations. The day after judgment was handed down in *Kesavananda* Ghandi appointed A N Ray as Chief Justice. Ray's primary qualification for this job seemed to be that his judgments had consistently favoured the state. This was not the only reason his appointment was controversial — it was a break from established convention in that he was appointed over the heads of three more senior judges, all of whom promptly resigned in protest.

By the following year the authoritarian state which had repeatedly concerned the courts was finally rearing its head. Although the Ghandi administration continued to accuse the court of being an enemy of 'progressive' forces in India, 'progressive' had now become a euphemism for the partisan interests of the Congress government. The free-enterprise and anti-left convictions of Sanjay Ghandi had dominated the Congress Party since the death of Mohan Kumaramangalam in May 1973, and political repression was being used by the central government on a scale unprecedented in post-colonial India. By June 1975 Indira Ghandi's political survival looked unlikely. The Congress Party had been humiliated in state elections in Gujarat and she had been convicted of corrupt electoral practices by the Allahabad High Court. Pending her appeal to the Supreme Court, she was prevented from sitting in Parliament under Indian law.

Ghandi's response to this situation was to declare a State of Emergency on 26 June 1975. Thousands of political leaders, including many of her opponents within the Congress Party, were detained and rigid press censorship was introduced. The rump Parliament retrospectively repealed the legislation under which Ghandi had been convicted. It also passed the Thirty-ninth Amendment, which removed the jurisdiction of the Supreme Court to deal with complaints of electoral offences against the Prime Minister and the Speaker. The Supreme Court unanimously upheld Ghandi's appeal by relying on the repeal of the legislation.[188] It would not, however, accept the Thirty-ninth Amendment, which it found to be in violation of the fundamental features of the Constitution in that it impaired free elections. This show of defiance by the court prompted the circulation of government proposals to introduce a new Constitution in which the institution of independent judicial review would not be recognized.[189] The court, suitably chastised, responded with a series of executive-minded judgments in *habeas corpus* cases brought by or on behalf of emergency detainees.[190]

When Ghandi lifted the Emergency and allowed elections in March 1977 her party was overwhelmingly rejected by the electorate in favour of the Janata Party.

---

[188] *Indira Gandhi v Raj Narain* AIR 1975 SC 2299.

[189] For a full discussion of these proposals and the effect they had on the court, see Baxi *The Indian Supreme Court and Politics* (1980).

[190] The most significant of these was the *Habeas Corpus* case, *Addl Distt Magistrate, Jabalpur v Shivkant Shukla* AIR 1976 SC 1206. Khanna J delivered a dissenting judgment in this case, publication of which was banned by the Emergency censorship authorities.

Janata was a loose coalition of anti-Ghandi forces with a platform based on a commitment to citizens' rights, the rule of law, and (ironically enough) the abolition of constitutional protection of property rights. The end of the Emergency and the Janata election victory were accompanied by an explosion of popular democratic activity.[191] Local-level political organizations and action groups sprung up around the country and the liberal press emerged as a powerful institution in India for the first time, publishing a series of exposés of the abuse of state power at local and national level.[192] The court sought to align itself actively with these developments, and the development of Indian public interest law must be seen in this context. Before considering the question of public interest law, however, there is a need to return to the *Kesavananda* case, which is possibly the most important case in modern Indian constitutional law.

### 4.2.3 *Kesavananda*

The *Kesavananda* judgments are crucial in two respects: they illustrate the central debates around judicial review and democracy which took place in the first twenty-five years of Indian constitutional law;[193] and they prefigure the shifts in interpretation which took the Indian Supreme Court into public interest law. Both the majority and minority groups of judges sought to legitimate their position in terms of the doctrine of original intent. Original intent was deployed in familiar fashion by both sets of judges and there is no need to discuss this in detail. However, two factors which gave the doctrine of original intent added strength in India need to be considered. These were the relative youth of the Constitution and the tremendous moral authority retained by the drafters by virtue of the fact that they had led the struggle for independence against Britain.[194] These issues serve to distinguish the Indian constitutional experience from that of many developed countries and

---

[191] For a discussion of this period in the history of India, see Frankel *India's Political Economy, 1947–1977: The Gradual Revolution* (1978).

[192] On the importance of investigative journalism to the development of public interest litigation in India, see Bhagwati 'Judicial Activism and Public Interest Litigation' (1985) 23 *Columbia J of Transnational L* 561 at 573–4.

[193] That these debates focused on the power of Parliament to amend the Constitution is a function of the flexibility of the Indian Constitution. The difficulties entailed in amending the US Constitution mean that judicial decisions reviewing legislation are in almost all cases irreversible. Most sections of the Indian Constitution are amendable by a two-thirds majority of Parliament. Thus Parliament has the power to circumvent judicial decisions with which it is sufficiently dissatisfied. Conversely, unlike many Commonwealth Constitutions, the Indian Constitution does not provide a mechanism for Parliament to circumvent the chapter on fundamental rights. (Cf the general derogation clause in s 1 of the Canadian Charter or the provision in s 13 of the Trinidad and Tobago Constitution for legislation which infringes fundamental rights to be passed with special majorities.) Thus the amending power is frequently exercised by the Indian Parliament. In the first forty years of the Indian Constitution it was amended on sixty-one separate occasions. (See Bakshi (ed) *The Constitution of India: Comments and Subject Index* (1990).) This goes some of the way towards explaining the Indian court's willingness to overturn ordinary parliamentary legislation without being unduly concerned about the implications for democracy. It also explains why the court was prepared to read into the Constitution a tacit prevention of amendments which attacked its basic structure. If the Constitution is repeatedly amended, it may be necessary to scrutinize the substantive content of amendments, irrespective of their formal validity. In India this scrutiny has been exercised with extreme caution. Nevertheless, the notion that a court has substantive review powers over constitutional amendment remains controversial. Baxi *Courage, Craft and Contention: The Indian Supreme Court in the Eighties* (1985) speculates that '[t]he Indian Supreme Court is probably the only court in the history of humankind to have asserted the power of judicial review over amendments to the Constitution'. Cottrell points out that the courts of Sierra Leone and Bangladesh have also claimed this power. (See *Akar v Attorney General* (1966–67) ALR (SL) 283 and *Anwar Hossain Chowdhury v Bangladesh* [1989] BLD (spl) 1, both cited in Cottrell 'Indian Judicial Activism, the Company and the Worker: A Note on *National Textile Workers' Union v Ramakrishnan*' (1990) 39 *ICLQ* 433 at 438n28.)

[194] The passage quoted below, n 197 illustrates this point.

they are obviously going to be of crucial importance in South African constitutional law.

In addition to their reliance on original intent, both the majority and minority judgments share an appeal to populism. However, the different conceptions of democracy which inform the majority and minority judges produce significantly different versions of populism. The populism of the majority judgments presents itself in a curious form. The judges invoke the people as the font of constitutional sovereignty, yet simultaneously echo *Golak Nath* in their Hobbesian fear of what the people's representatives in Parliament are capable of doing with power. The judgments are replete with worst-case scenarios of what might happen if Parliament is given unfettered power of amendment over the Constitution. We are told that Parliament might destroy the sovereignty of the country, institute authoritarian government, break up the unity of country, destroy the secular character of the country, abrogate all fundamental rights, revoke the welfare state mandate, and extend its own life indefinitely.[195] The appeal to the people is sustained in this context by the drawing of a distinction between Parliament and the people. The judges stress that even a two-thirds majority of Parliament need not represent a majority of the people and that Parliament cannot therefore wield constituent sovereignty which vests solely in the people.[196]

If 'the people' are not to be found in Parliament, the majority judgments do not explain where they are to be found, nor how they are to exercise their constituent authority. Instead they present us with a theory of democracy based on judicial paternalism. The people, exercising their constitutional sovereignty through the Constituent Assembly, have given themselves the Constitution. The task of the judge is now to protect this Constitution from the depredations of Parliament.[197] This can only be done if the basic features of the Constitution are held to be unamendable, for the people themselves are no political match for Parliament:

'[The respondents] tried to tone down the effect of their claim by saying that, though legally there is no limitation on the amending power, there are bound to be political compulsions which make it impermissible for Parliament to exercise its amending power in a manner unacceptable to the people at large. The strength of political reaction is uncertain. It depends upon various factors such as the political consciousness of the people, their level of education, strength of the various political organizations in the country, the manner in which the mass media is used and finally the capacity of the government to suppress agitations. Hence the peoples' will to resist an unwanted amendment cannot be taken into consideration in interpreting the ambit of the amending power. Extralegal forces work in a different plane altogether.'[198]

The judge restraining parliamentary power is not preventing social change, nor

---

[195] See, for example, Sikri CJ at paras 292–302, and Hegde and Mukherjea JJ at paras 663–9.
[196] See Shelat and Grover JJ at para 557, Hegde and Mukherjea JJ at paras 669–80.
[197] This argument cannot account for the fact that the Indian Parliament is considerably more representative of the people than the Constituent Assembly was. The attempt of Hegde and Mukherjea JJ at para 668 is extraordinary:
'The statement in the preamble that the people of the country conferred the Constitution on themselves is not open to challenge before this Court. Its factual correctness cannot be gone into by this Court which again is a creature of the Constitution. The facts set out in the preamble have to be accepted by this Court as correct. Anyone who knows the composition of the Constituent Assembly can hardly dispute the claim of the members of that Assembly that their voice was the voice of the people. They were truly the representatives of the people, even though they had been elected under a narrow franchise.'
[198] Hegde and Mukherjea JJ at 1623–4 para 666.

acting undemocratically; rather he is controlling the pace of change in the interests of the democratic freedoms which the people have given to themselves in the Constitution. Thus Sikri CJ states:

> '[I]f the meaning I have suggested is accepted, a social and economic revolution can gradually take place while preserving the freedom and dignity of the individual ... It would enable Parliament to adjust fundamental rights in order to secure what the directive principles direct to be accomplished, while maintaining the freedom and dignity of every citizen.'[199]

This conception of judicial review is not based on the usual concerns of anti-majoritarianism which have motivated much of US constitutional law.[200] With their distinction between Parliament and the people, the courts are reluctant even to concede that Parliament represents a majoritarian position. They appear to be driven by a fear that those wielding political power will inevitably tend towards authoritarianism at the expense not only of minorities but also of their own supporters. In this regard the unimpressive history of post-colonial democracy is clearly a factor which influences them.[201] Thus Hegde and Mukherjea JJ warn:

> 'Human freedoms are lost gradually and imperceptibly and their destruction is generally followed by authoritarian rule. That is what history has taught us. Struggle between liberty and power is eternal. Vigilance is the price that we like every other democratic society have to pay to safeguard the democratic values enshrined in our Constitution.'[202]

It is a clear premise of the majority judgments that the people are incapable of exercising this vigilance, so it is up to the judiciary to do so on their behalf.

The judgment of Khanna J is the one majority judgment which does not share the general fear of parliamentary power. Khanna J regards a two-thirds majority of Parliament as an adequate check on unfettered amendment. He points out that no generation has a monopoly on knowledge which entitles it to bind future generations irreversibly, and warns that a Constitution which denies people the right of amendment invites attempts at extralegal revolutionary change.[203] He criticizes the anti-Parliament argument of his fellow majority judges as 'essentially an argument of fear and distrust in the majority of representatives of the people',[204] and states that the 'best safeguard against abuse of power is public opinion and the good sense of the majority of the members of Parliament'.[205] Nevertheless, he accepts the majority position that the amending power in art 368 cannot extend to the essential structure of the Constitution. The basic institutional character of the state must remain intact. Parliament cannot change its democratic, secular nature, and it cannot end constitutional government.[206] Such changes would amount to more than an amendment —

---

[199] At 1535 paras 296 and 299.

[200] In 300 pages of majority judgments there are only fleeting mentions of anti-majoritarianism. Hegde and Mukherjea JJ point out that the representatives of tribal minorities in the Constituent Assembly gave up demands for special protection in return for the fundamental rights and that it would thus be unacceptable to allow these rights to be destroyed. See 1624 para 669. Sikri CJ hints at this point at 1515 para 182.

[201] Once again this is a feature of Indian constitutional law which will probably present itself in South Africa.

[202] At 1629 para 682.

[203] See 1849, 1850 paras 1401–2, 1406.

[204] At 1855 para 1427.

[205] At 1903 para 1550.

[206] See 1859–61 paras 1437–44. His stress on the inability of Parliament to interfere with the democratic character of the Constitution bears some similarities to US political process theorists (see, for example, John Hart Ely *Democracy and Distrust: a Theory of Judicial Review* (1980)). However, he sees a broader role for judicial review than that proposed by the political process theorists. It is clear from his judgment that some of the core features of the Constitution cannot be reduced to democracy-enhancing devices.

they would constitute an abrogation of the Constitution and a replacement of it by a new Constitution.

Khanna J hovers between the majority and the minority. His faith in parliamentary sovereignty as the basis of democracy is a crucial principle which he shares with the minority judges. Nevertheless, he is unwilling to extend this principle to an extreme which would entirely subordinate constitutional government to a two-thirds majority of both Houses of Parliament. Rather he sees certain core features of the Indian Constitution which cannot be attacked by Parliament. These core features derogate from democracy because they are absolutely immune from parliamentary revision. Thus the identification of core features must be approached with caution. Only those values which are absolutely essential to the Constitution can be said to be core values.[207] The right to property is not one of these. The foremost objective of the Constitution is the provision of social, economic, and political justice to all citizens of India and 'there is nothing in it which gives primacy to the claims of individual right to property over the claims of social, economic and political justice'.[208]

The minority judges share much common ground with Khanna J, but they are unwilling to recognize any core features of the Constitution which are immune from parliamentary amendment. The judicial paternalism of the six majority judgments and, to a lesser degree, the judgment of Khanna J are seen as a threat to democracy. Government by the people through Parliament is set up as the democratic alternative to government by the courts on the basis of a Constitution drawn up by a Constituent Assembly that was less representative of the people than Parliament is.[209]

> 'Democracy proceeds on the basic assumption that the representatives of the people in Parliament will reflect the will of the people and that they will not exercise their powers to betray the people or abuse the trust and confidence reposed in them by the people.'[210]

> 'Trust in the elected representatives is the corner-stone of democracy. When that trust fails, everything fails.'[211]

> 'True democracy and true republicanism postulate the settlement of social, economic and political issues by public discussion and by the vote of the people's elected representatives, and not by judicial opinion. The Constitution is not intended to be the arena of legal quibbling for men with long purses.'[212]

> 'The Constitution has not set up a Government of Judges in this country. It has confided the duty of determining paramount norms to Parliament alone. Courts are permitted to make limited value choices within the parameters of the Constitutional value choices.'[213]

As far as the minority judges were concerned, the people are perfectly capable of looking after their own interests; they do not need the judiciary to protect them

---

[207] Subsequent courts have echoed the cautious approach of Khanna J to the core features doctrine. In fact the restrained manner in which the doctrine has been invoked by the Indian Supreme Court to invalidate constitutional amendments is fully consistent with a political process theory of judicial review. The relevant cases involved constitutional amendments which interfered with electoral democracy (*Indira Gandhi v Raj Narain* (supra)) and independent judicial review (*Minerva Mills v Union of India* AIR 1980 SC 1789; *S P Gupta v Union of India* AIR 1982 SC 149).

[208] At 1878 para 1492. See also 1877–81 paras 1486–96.

[209] See the passages quoted below and Ray J at 1681–2 paras 914–17, Palekar J at 1809 para 1301, Beg J at 1976 para 1837.

[210] Matthew J at 1937–8 para 1679.

[211] Chandrachud J at 2042 para 2102.

[212] Dwivedi J at 2009 para 1960.

[213] Dwivedi J at 2008 para 1957.

against Parliament. Public opinion and the threat of popular revolt will serve to keep Parliament in tune with the needs of the people.[214] The worst-case scenarios presented by the majority are no basis on which to make judicial decisions.

Where the majority judges were concerned to avoid radical change, the minority were concerned to avoid stasis. Notions of what is essential change over time and the views of one generation of Constitution-makers cannot be allowed to fetter future generations:

> 'A fundamental right may be regarded as fundamental by one generation. It may be considered to be inconvenient limitation upon legislative power by another generation. Popular sovereignty means that the interest which prevails must be the interest of the mass of men.'[215]

> 'The fundamental rights themselves have no fixed content; most of them are mere empty vessels into which each generation must pour its contents in the light of its experience. Restrictions, abridgment, curtailment, and even abrogation of these rights in circumstances not visualized by the Constitution-makers might become necessary.'[216]

The attitude of the minority towards constitutional change is premised on a belief that the main aim of the Constitution is social revolution and that all interpretation of the Constitution must take place in this light.[217] Thus the fundamental rights must be read subject to the directive principles, and the amending power of Parliament in pursuit of social and economic justice cannot be fettered at all. This stress on interpreting the Constitution as a programme for social and economic justice, which the minority judges share with Khanna J, was later to form the basis of the development of Indian public interest litigation.

### 4.2.4 The post-Emergency attempt to re-establish legitimacy of the court

The legitimacy of the Supreme Court had reached a low point during the Emergency years. The post-Emergency court was crucially aware of this and deliberately set about trying to recreate legitimacy for itself and for the rule of law. There seems to have been a conscious decision taken to adopt an activist role in protection of citizens' rights coupled with an attempt to champion the rights of the poor and the underprivileged. These two projects were now easily compatible because the right to property had been removed by the Janata government.[218]

The post-Emergency period of Indian constitutional law is dominated by the figure of Judge P N Bhagwati. He sat on the Supreme Court Bench for ten years from 1976,[219] the last two of which were as Chief Justice. He was the architect of Indian public interest litigation, which involved the most creative judicial developments of constitutional law in Indian legal history. Bhagwati's judgments were explicitly motivated by the need for the court to re-establish itself as a legitimate institution of Indian society. The court 'had become a sentinel of the interests of the propertied classes rather than a protector of the rights of the poor and the under-

---

[214] See, for example, Beg J at 1982 para 1860.
[215] Ray J at 1707 para 1031.
[216] Mathew J at 1952–3 para 1728.
[217] See, for example, Ray J at 1707 para 1029, Mathew J at 1714–21, Palekar J at 1802–4 paras 1288–9.
[218] See Baxi 'The Post-Emergency Supreme Court: A Populist Quest for Legitimation' in *The Indian Supreme Court and Politics: Mehr Chand Memorial Law Lectures* (1980).
[219] He was actually one of the majority judges in the *Habeas Corpus* case, an early low point in his Supreme Court career.

privileged'.[220] The judge's task was to change this. Transforming the judicial system was the only way to save it:

> 'The time has now come when the courts must become the courts for the poor and struggling masses of this country. They must shed their character as upholders of the established order and the status quo. They must be sensitized to the need of doing justice to the large masses of people to whom justice has been denied by a cruel and heartless society for generations. The realization must come to them that social justice is the signature tune of our Constitution and it is their solemn duty under the Constitution to enforce the basic human rights of the poor and vulnerable sections of the community and actively help in the realization of the constitutional goals. This new change has to come if the judicial system is to become an effective instrument of social justice, for without it, it cannot survive for long.'[221]

Judicial activism was demanded by the circumstances:

> '[O]ur Constitution is not a non-aligned rational charter. It is a document of social revolution which casts an obligation on every instrumentality including the judiciary . . . to transform the status quo ante into a new human order in which justice, social, economic and political, will inform all institutions of national life and there will be equality of status and opportunity for all. The judiciary has therefore a socio-economic destination and a creative function . . ..
> 
> Now [the British] approach to the judicial function may be all right for a stable and static society but not for a society pulsating with urges of gender justice, worker justice, minorities justice, *dalit* justices and equal justice between chronic unequals. Where the contest is between those who are socially or economically unequal, the judicial process may prove disastrous from the point of view of social justice, if the judge adopts a merely passive or negative role and does not adopt a positive or creative approach. The judiciary cannot remain a mere bystander or spectator but must become an active participant in the judicial process ready to use law in the service of social justice through a pro-active goal-oriented approach.'[222]

The first expression of the new judicial activism came in *Maneka Ghandi v Union of India*,[223] a case dealing with the withdrawal by the Janata government of the passport of Indira Ghandi's sister-in-law. Article 21 of the Constitution gives protection against deprivation of life and liberty 'except according to procedure established by law'. This wording had been deliberately chosen by B N Rao, an advisor to the Constituent Assembly who had been warned by Felix Frankfurter of the problems created by 'due process of law' in the US Constitution. The court in *Maneka* was aware of the origin of art 21, but chose nevertheless to read substantive due process into the clause 'with a view to forging greater protection for the citizen in respect of his life and personal liberty'. The court thus invokes the general character of the Constitution to override the specific intention of the drafters in respect of one clause. In cases building on *Maneka* the expanded art 21 was then read together with the equality clause in art 14 to require that all state action be reasonable, non-arbitrary, and in the public interest.[224] Public interest can be

---

[220] Bhagwati 'Public Interest Litigation' (1986) 2 *The Commonwealth Lawyer* 61 at 65.
[221] *People's Union for Democratic Rights v Union of India* AIR 1982 SC 1473 at 1478 para 3.
[222] *S P Gupta v Union of India* (supra) at 196–7.
[223] AIR 1978 SC 597.
[224] See, for example, *Ramana v International Airport Authority of India* AIR 1979 SC 1628; *Francis Coralie Mullin v Union Territory of Delhi* AIR 1981 SC 746; *M O Hoskot v State of Maharashtra* 1979 (1) SCR 192; and *Hussainara Khatoon v State of Bihar* 1980 (1) SCC 81.

## 4.2.5 Social justice interpretation

This focus on the preamble and the directive principles is closely related to another hallmark of the post-Emergency court — its social-justice-based interpretation. The court adopted as its starting point the fact that the Indian Constitution is designed to create a democratic welfare state and that all constitutional interpretation has to be consistent with this primary goal. The judgments of Khanna J and the minority judges in *Kesavananda* laid the basis for this approach to interpretation. Since 1978 it has become the dominant approach to constitutional interpretation of the Indian court and the judgments reflect this explicitly:

> 'A Constitution like ours, born of an anti-imperialist struggle, influenced by constitutional instruments, events and revolutions elsewhere, in search of a better world and wedded to the idea of justice, economic, social and political, to all, must receive a generous interpretation so as to give all its citizens the full measure of justice so proclaimed . . . And so when the constitutional instrument to be expounded is a Constitution like the Indian Constitution, the expositors are to concern themselves not with words and mere words only, but, as much, with the philosophy or what we may call the "spirit and the sense" of the Constitution.'[226]

> 'The Constitution-makers have given us one of the most remarkable documents in history for ushering in a new socio-economic order and the Constitution which they have forged for us has a social purpose and an economic mission and therefore every word or phrase in the Constitution must be interpreted in a manner which would advance the socio-economic objective of the Constitution.'[227]

Social justice interpretation has a particular understanding of the relationship between fundamental rights and directive principles. It rejects the traditional way of treating fundamental rights as superior to directive principles. Fundamental rights serve to protect political democracy and are of no value unless they can be enforced in court. Directive principles serve to advance social and economic democracy. The Constitution provides that they are unenforceable, but this does not make them any less important than the fundamental rights. In a country like India with limited resources the legislature must decide on the allocation of these resources. If the court were able to control this allocation in the name of enforcement of directive principles, parliamentary democracy would be reduced 'to an oligarchy of judges'.[228] However, the Constitution instructs all organs of the state to treat the directive principles as fundamental in the governance of the country. Thus the court itself is bound to apply the directive principles in interpreting the Constitution, even those sections of it which relate to the fundamental rights. The directive principles should serve the courts as a code of interpretation and should be read into the fundamental rights wherever possible. The court should be extremely reluctant to invalidate state action which is performed in pursuance of the directive principles

---

[225] See Bhagwati 'Human Rights as Evolved by the Jurisprudence of the Supreme Court of India' *Commonwealth Law Bulletin* (January 1987) 236 at 239–42.
[226] Chinappa Reddy J in *ABSK Sangh (Railway) v Union of India* AIR 1981 SC 298 at 335 para 123.
[227] Bhagwati J in *People's Union for Democratic Rights* (supra) at 1490.
[228] Chinappa Reddy J in *ABSK Sangh (Railway) v Union of India* (supra) at para 124.

but which infringes fundamental rights.[229] Bhagwati J dwelt at length on the reasons for this approach in his dissenting judgment in *Minerva Mills Ltd v Union of India*:[230]

> 'The fundamental rights are no doubt important and valuable in a democracy, but there can be no real democracy without social and economic justice to the common man and to create socio-economic justice to everyone, is the theme of the directive principles. It is the directive principles which nourish the roots of our democracy, provide strength and vigour to it and attempt to make it a real participatory democracy which does not remain merely a political democracy but also becomes social and economic democracy with fundamental rights available to all irrespective of their power, position or wealth ... Under the present socio-economic system, it is the liberty of the few which is in conflict with the liberty of the many. The directive principles, therefore, impose an obligation on the state to take positive action for creating socio-economic conditions in which there will be an egalitarian social order with social and economic justice to all so that individual liberty will become a cherished value and the dignity of the individual a living reality, not only for a few privileged citizens. It will thus be seen that the directive principles enjoy a very high place in the constitutional scheme and it is only in the framework of the socio-economic structure envisaged in the directive principles that the fundamental rights ... can become meaningful and significant for the millions of our poor and deprived people who do not have even the bare necessities of life and who are living below the poverty level.'[231]

Social justice interpretation thus approaches constitutional law in a way that differs from the approach advocated by most US scholars. Rights are not seen as a protected domain of individual autonomy into which the state cannot encroach. In fact the collective action/individual autonomy dichotomy around which most of US constitutional law is structured is substantially broken down.

### 4.3 Public interest law

Social justice interpretation provided the constitutional framework for the most ambitious project of public interest law ever undertaken by a Supreme Court. In India the 1980s witnessed an explosion of class action litigation around social issues as the Supreme Court relaxed rules of procedure and standing, transformed the relationship between rights and remedies, and creatively extended the scope of the fundamental freedoms entrenched in the Constitution.

#### 4.3.1 *Public interest law and social justice interpretation*

A striking feature of Indian public interest litigation is the way the court has recognized that rights involve relationships between state and individual. In so doing it has been able to expand the range of fundamental rights so that they serve a social, rather than an individual, function. The right to life and liberty in art 21 is the right which has been most expansively interpreted in this fashion. In *Hussainara Khatoon v State of Bihar*[232] the court dealt with a writ petition based on newspaper reports about backlogs in criminal trials and the problems of the prevailing bail system which led to people being held in custody for up to ten years before trial. Bhagwati J

---

[229] Ibid.
[230] Supra.
[231] At 1847.
[232] AIR 1979 SC 1361.

ruled that the current monetary bail system offended art 14 in that it discriminated against the poor. It also infringed art 21 because the right to life and liberty included the right to a speedy trial. It was thus unconstitutional. The reasoning of the court was firmly grounded in social justice interpretation:

> 'Ours is a socialist republic with social justice as the signature tune of our Constitution and Parliament would do well to consider whether it would not be more consonant with the ethos of our Constitution that instead of risk of financial loss, other relevant considerations such as family ties, roots in the community, job security, membership of stable organizations, etc should be the determinative factors in grant of bail and the accused should in appropriate cases be released on his personal bond without monetary obligation.'[233]

Subsequent judgments in this case established the right to counsel as an incident of the right to liberty protected by art 21.[234]

Article 21 was extended further in *Francis Coralie Mullen v Union of Territory of Delhi*:[235]

> 'We think that the right to life includes the right to live with human dignity and all that goes along with it, namely, the bare necessaries of life such as adequate nutrition, clothing and shelter over the head and facilities for reading, writing and expressing oneself in diverse forms, freely moving about and mixing and commingling with fellow human beings.
>
> Of course the magnitude and content of the components of this right would depend upon the extent of the economic development of the country ... [but] every act which offends against or impairs human dignity would constitute deprivation *pro tanto* of this right to live and it would have to be in accordance with reasonable, fair and just procedure established by law which stands the test of other fundamental rights.'[236]

The petitioner was a detainee who had been denied visits from her family. The court accepted that the deprivation of liberty of a detainee or prisoner was authorized by the Constitution. However, the actions of the authorities in preventing her from receiving family visits amounted to an unconstitutional deprivation of her right to human dignity encompassed by her right to life. The court adopted a similar line of reasoning in *Uppendra Baxi v State of Uttar Pradesh*[237] to order the improvement of conditions in a state-run protective home for women in Agra.

In *State of Himachal Pradesh v Sharma*[238] the applicant was a resident of Bukho, an isolated village in Himachal Pradesh. He had initiated proceedings by writing to the president of the Himachal Pradesh High Court complaining that the villagers' only access to the rest of India was by a 4–5-mile descent down a steep mountain on foot and that under these circumstances democracy was meaningless to them. In 1972 the state government had authorized the construction of a road to Bukho, but for various reasons the road had never been constructed. The applicant asked the court to order the state to construct the road. The Supreme Court obliged:[239]

---

[233] Bhagwati J in *Hussainara Khatoon v State of Bihar* (supra) at 1363 para 4.
[234] See *Sheela Barse v Union of India* AIR 1983 SC 378 and *Suk Das v Union Territory of Arunchal Pradesh* 1986 (4) SCC 401.
[235] Supra.
[236] At 753.
[237] 1986 (4) SCC 106.
[238] 1986 (2) SCC 68.
[239] The judgment dealt extensively with the issues of separation of powers and the limits of the Supreme Court to interfere with state expenditure. These aspects of the judgment are discussed in the section below on public interest litigation and the separation of powers.

'[The applicant] has also the right under art 21 to his life and that right under art 21 embraces not only physical existence of life but the quality of life and for residents of hilly areas, access to a road is access to life itself . . . We accept the proposition that there should be a road for communication in reasonable conditions in view of our constitutional imperatives and denial of that right would be denial of life as understood in its richness and fullness by the ambit of the Constitution. To the residents of the hilly areas as far as feasible and possible society has [a] constitutional obligation to provide roads for communication.'[240]

*Tellis v Bombay Municipal Corporation*[241] adopted a similarly broad approach to the right to life to hold that the eviction of pavement dwellers by the Bombay municipality in the absence of suitable alternative accommodation constituted a deprivation of their right to life. Other cases extending the ambit of art 21 include *Kishen v State of Orissa*[242] and *Dr P Nalla Thampy v Union of India*.[243] *Kishen* dealt with 400 000 of the worst-off Indians who were trapped in rural poverty in Kalahandi and Koraput and forced to sell labour and rice cheaply to large landowners and occasionally even to sell children. *Thampy* concerned railway accidents which were allegedly the product of maladministration of the national railway system. *Tellis*, *Kishen*, and *Thampy* also illustrate the limits of public interest litigation. Although the court found that there was a violation of the right to life in all three these cases, it was not prepared to make any order against the administration primarily because it was reluctant to become too deeply involved in questions of allocation of public expenditure.[244]

The court has also used the right to life to give strength to art 49 of the Constitution, directing the state to provide its citizens with a clean and healthy environment. In *Chhara v Sardarnagar Municipality*[245] and *Citizens' Action Committee, Nagpur v Civil Surgeon, Mayo Hospital, Nagpur, & others*[246] the court responded to complaints from urban residents about the collapse of municipal roads and sanitation systems, which prejudiced public health. *Rural Land and Entitlement Kendra, Dehradun v State of Uttar Pradesh*[247] involved limestone quarries which represented an environmental hazard. The quarries were on land owned by the state, but let to private limestone companies. After appointing various committees to investigate allegations of environmental damage caused by the quarries, the court shut down certain quarries and ordered others to take specified conservation measures on pain of being shut down. The state was ordered to implement afforestation and soil conservation programmes. Soon after the Bhopal disaster there was a leak of oleum gas from a factory in Delhi, causing at least one death. After a public interest petition in *M C Mehta v Union of India*[248] the factory was closed pending resolution of the litigation. The court had to balance environmental considerations against the fact that permanent closure of the plant would put 4 000 workers out of their jobs. It ultimately allowed the plant to reopen subject to stringent safety

---

[240] At 75 11.
[241] [1987] LRC (Const) 351 (SC).
[242] AIR 1989 SC 677.
[243] 1983 (4) SCC 598.
[244] See above, n 239 and below, 60.
[245] AIR 1986 Guj 49.
[246] AIR 1986 Bom 136.
[247] AIR 1985 SC 652.
[248] AIR 1987 SC 965.

measures which were to be monitored on a continuing basis by the state and by an expert committee appointed by the court. The court also recommended that the Government of India should set up a standing committee to look into hazardous industries and an Ecological Sciences Research Group so that the court could obtain independent advice in environmental cases of this nature.[249]

In all of these environmental cases the court based its orders on existing environmental or municipal health legislation which imposed public duties on the state. In defining the extent of these duties and the degree to which the court had jurisdiction to compel their implementation, however, the approach of the court was influenced by art 49 and by the extended interpretation of the right to life in art 21. This was made explicit in *Pandey v State of West Benghal*,[250] a case involving an attempt to prevent the construction of a luxury hotel on land currently used by the Calcutta zoo:

> 'When the court is called upon to give effect to the directive principle and the fundamental duty, the court is not to shrug its shoulders and say that priorities are a matter of policy and so it is a matter for the policy-making authority. The least that the court may do is to examine whether appropriate considerations are borne in mind and irrelevancies excluded. In appropriate cases, the court may go further, but how much further must depend on the circumstances of the case. The court may always give necessary directions.'[251]

Labour law has been a major focus of public interest litigation and social justice interpretation. The court held in *Surinder Singh v The Engineer in Chief, Central Public Works Dept*[252] that the equality clause placed the state under a constitutional duty to pay the same wages to daily labourers as it did to permanent workers for the same work done. The state argued that the distinction between permanent and daily status was a reasonable basis on which to differentiate in the payment of wages. The court rejected this argument summarily, stating that it lay 'ill in the mouth of the Central Government for it is an all too familiar argument with the exploiting class and a welfare state committed to a socialist pattern of society cannot be permitted to advance such an argument'.[253]

In *People's Union for Democratic Rights v Union of India*[254] Bhagwati J used social justice interpretation to broaden the scope of art 23, which prohibits forced labour. The petitioners complained about the widescale employment of workers on construction projects for the Asian Games at wages below the legal minimum. Bhagwati J ruled that art 23 must be read in an extended form — it must cover all forms of compulsion, even economic duress where there appears to be consent in the form of a contract. This was clearly the case when there was payment below the legal minimum, which was thus unconstitutional as well as illegal.[255] *People's*

---

[249] See also *M K Sharma v Bharat Electronics Ltd* AIR 1987 SC 1792 and *M C Mehta v Union of India* AIR 1987 SC 1086, which were art 21 petitions against radiation hazards at a public-sector factory and the Jawaharlal Nehru University respectively.
[250] [1988] LRC (Const) 241 (SC).
[251] Chinnappa Reddy J in *Pandey v State of West Benghal* (supra) at 247d.
[252] AIR 1986 SC 584.
[253] At 584–5.
[254] Supra.
[255] This was not just legal overkill. The finding that the payment of subminimum wages was unconstitutional had important procedural consequences. It meant that the petitioners were entitled to apply to the Supreme Court for immediate relief under art 32 and did not have to rely on statutory rights and the state courts. It also meant that the court was more easily able to entertain a public interest petition.

*Union* has been followed by a series of cases which have developed the protection offered by art 23 even further.[256]

### 4.3.2 Public interest law, the Constitution, and private law

The environmental and labour law cases discussed above illustrate some of the ways in which public interest litigation has brought the fundamental rights into play in private law. The chapter of the Indian Constitution dealing with the fundamental rights is introduced by art 13, which provides that '[t]he state shall not make any law which takes away or abridges the rights conferred by this Part and any law made in contravention of this clause shall, to the extent of the contravention, be void.' Apart from art 13, there is no general provision dealing with the effect of the fundamental rights. Some of the specific provisions dealing with the fundamental rights seem to limit the rights to protection from state action; others seem to be of general application.[257] Initially Indian judges sought to draw an inflexible distinction between private and public law in respect of the fundamental rights. Fundamental rights were held to relate exclusively to public law. Thus disputes between private individuals were held not to be subject to review in terms of the Bill of Rights, nor were disputes between individuals and the state where the state was acting in its private capacity.[258] This rigid distinction between state infringement of rights and private infringement of rights was broken down significantly in *People's Union for Democratic Rights v Union of India*.[259] Bhagwati J's judgment in *People's Union* is significant in two respects: it emphasizes that certain fundamental rights are automatically enforceable against private individuals and it also suggests a way of importing constitutional law into the private law where the fundamental right is not automatically protected from private infringement.

*People's Union* dealt with infringements of arts 23 (bonded labour) and 24 (employment of children) by contractors employed by the Union of India, Delhi Administration, and the Delhi Development Authority on construction projects linked to the Asian Games. The contractors argued that the petitioners were not entitled to constitutional relief because the Constitution could not be relied upon in disputes between private individuals. The court rejected this argument, relying on the general prohibitive wording of the articles in question[260] and the nature of the right which they sought to protect:

'So far as art 24 of the Constitution is concerned, it embodies a fundamental right which is plainly

---

[256] See, for example, *Sanjit Roy v State of Rajastan* AIR 1983 SC 328 and *Bandhua Mukti Morcha v Union of India* AIR 1984 SC 802.

[257] An example of the former would be the equality provision in art 14, which reads as follows: 'The state shall not deny to any person equality before the law or the equal protection of the laws within the territory of India.' Article 17, dealing with untouchability, seems to have a broader scope: 'Untouchability is abolished and its practice in any form is forbidden. The enforcement of any disability arising out of untouchability shall be an offence punishable in accordance with law.'

[258] Article 12 defines 'state' to include 'the Government and Parliament of India and the Government and the Legislatures of each of the States and all local or other authorities within the territory of India or under the control of the Government of India'. There is a substantial body of case law around this definition of state and, in particular, the meaning of 'other authorities'. We do not propose to deal with this case law here. Much of it relates to the constitutional reviewability of decisions of nationalized industries and parastatals. The general approach of the court is set out in *R D Chetty v International Airport Authority of India* 1979 (3) SCC 489 and *Som Prakash Rekhi v Union of India* 1981 (1) SCC 448.

[259] Supra.

[260] Article 23: 'Traffic in human beings and *begar* and other similar forms of forced labour are prohibited and any contravention of this provision shall be an offence punishable in accordance with law.'

and indubitably enforceable against everyone and by reason of its compulsive mandate no one can employ a child below the age of 14 years in a hazardous employment . . . .'[261]

'Now many of the fundamental rights enacted in Part III operate as limitations on the power of the state and impose negative obligations on the state not to encroach on individual liberty and they are enforceable only against the state. But there are certain fundamental rights conferred by the Constitution which are enforceable against the whole world and they are to be found inter alia in arts 17,[262] 23 and 24[263] . . . The Constitution-makers . . . decided to give teeth to their resolve to obliterate and wipe out this evil practice [of forced labour] by enacting constitutional prohibition against it in the chapter on fundamental rights, so that the abolition of such practice may become enforceable and effective as soon as the Constitution came into force. This is the reason why the provision enacted in art 23 was included in the chapter on fundamental rights. The prohibition against "traffic in human beings and *begar* and other forms of forced labour" is clearly intended to be a general prohibition,[264] total in its effect and all-pervasive in its range and it is enforceable not only against the state but also against any other person indulging in such practice.'[265]

The court held that there was a constitutional duty on the state to ensure that private individuals did not infringe arts 23 and 24. If infringement took place, the rights protected by arts 23 and 24 could be enforced either against the state or directly against the offending private individual on application for constitutional relief by the victim.[266]

The discussion of *People's Union* thus far covers only a few specifically worded rights in Chapter III. However, the judgment also suggests a way in which all the fundamental rights can affect private-law relationships. The argument proceeds as follows: where the state enacts legislation to protect fundamental rights in private-law relationships, it is placed under a constitutional duty to ensure that the legislation is complied with; the private-law victim of a violation of this legislation has a constitutional-law action against the state to ensure that there is general compliance with the legislation. The court held that the contractors' failure to observe certain provisions of the Equal Remuneration Act, the Contract Labour Act, and the Inter State Migrant Workmen Act allowed the petitioners to bring a constitutional writ against the state in terms of arts 14 and 21:

'It is the principle of equality embodied in art 14 of the Constitution which finds expression in the provisions of the Equal Remuneration Act 1976 . . . If any particular contractor is committing a breach of the provisions of the Equal Remuneration Act 1976 and thus denying equality before the law to the workmen, the Union of India, the Delhi Administration and the Delhi Development Authority as the case may be, would be under an obligation to ensure that the contractor observes

---

Article 24: 'No child below the age of fourteen years shall be employed to work in any factory or mine or engaged in any other hazardous employment.'
[261] At 1483 para 10.
[262] The wording of art 17 is set out in above, n 257.
[263] At least one right which should also appear in this list is that protected by art 15(2): 'No citizen shall, on grounds only of religion, race, caste, sex, place of birth or any of them, be subject to any disability, liability, restriction or condition with regard to *(a)* access to shops, public restaurants, hotels and places of public entertainment; or *(b)* the use of wells, tanks, bathing *ghats*, roads and places of public resort maintained wholly or partly out of state funds or dedicated to the use of the general public.'
[264] The stress on the general nature of the prohibition seems to be an obvious basis on which to recognize an exception to the state action doctrine. It is interesting that the exception has not been recognized in the US in respect of the Thirteenth Amendment, which is framed in similarly general terms: 'Neither slavery nor involuntary servitude . . . shall exist within the United States or any place subject to their jurisdiction.'
[265] At 1486–7 para 12.
[266] This was later confirmed in the similar case of *Bandhua Mukti Morcha v Union of India* (supra).

the provisions of the Equal Remuneration Act 1976 and does not breach the equality clause enacted in art 14.'[267]

'Now the rights and benefits conferred on the workmen employed by a contractor under the provisions of the Contract Labour Act 1970 and the Inter State Migrant Workmen Act 1979 are clearly intended to ensure basic human dignity to the workmen and if the workmen are deprived of any of these rights and benefits to which they are entitled under the provisions of these two pieces of social welfare legislation, that would clearly be a violation of art 21 by the Union of India, the Delhi Administration and the Delhi Development Authority *which, as principal employers, are made statutorily responsible for securing such rights and benefits to the workmen.*'[268]

The stressed portion of the latter quotation shows that the judgment is premised on the fact that the state was principal employer of the petitioners. Thus *People's Union* does not of itself amount to a major departure from the state action doctrine. However, later judgments of the Supreme Court, particularly those on environmental issues, have implicitly extended the argument of *People's Union* into situations where the state has no direct relationship with the private party who infringes another's constitutional right which has been expressed in legislation. Thus in *M C Mehta v Union of India*[269] and *Rural Land and Entitlement Kendra Dehradun v State of Uttar Pradesh*[270] the court upheld writ petitions against the state based on the violation of the right to life in art 21 by contravention of certain environmental legislation by private parties with no links to the state.[271]

The determination of questions of public interest and public policy has afforded the Indian courts another means of bringing constitutional-law issues into private-law cases. Relying on the preamble to the Constitution and the Directives of State Policy, the post-Emergency Supreme Court judges have taken a much more robust approach to these questions than that taken by their predecessors. *National Textile Workers' Union v Ramakrishnan*[272] is illustrative.[273] The Companies Act in India allows members who complain that the affairs of the company are being conducted in a manner prejudicial to the public interest to apply for a winding-up order.[274] The Act also provides for winding up on application by creditors or shareholders on the familiar 'just and equitable' grounds.[275] In *Ramakrishnan* the Supreme Court relied on these provisions to hold that judges cannot exercise their discretion to wind up a company without taking into account the needs of the workers of the company. Moreover, the court held that it was impossible to take these needs properly into account unless the workers were given a right to be heard.[276] In reaching this

---

[267] At 1484 para 10.
[268] At 1485 para 11.
[269] AIR 1987 SC 965.
[270] Supra.
[271] The facts of both of these cases are set out above, 50.
[272] AIR 1983 SC 75.
[273] Much of the discussion of the case which follows is based on Cottrell 'Indian Judicial Activism, the Company and Worker: A Note on *National Textile Workers' Union v Ramakrishnan*' (1990) 39 *ICLQ* 451.
[274] Section 398(1)(a) of Act 1 of 1956.
[275] Section 433(f) of Act 1 of 1956.
[276] An Indian court had previously recognized that the workers' interests were relevant in an application for winding-up, but there was no authority for the workers' right to be heard. See *Bhalchandra Dharmajee Makaji v Alcock Ashdown and Co Ltd* (1972) 42 Comp Cas 190, quoted in *Ramakrishnan* (supra) at 86.

conclusion the court emphasized the particular interest which workers have in the continued existence of a company:

> 'Unlike the shareholders, to most of whom the shares they hold represent mere investments and to some of whom, the means to control the affairs of the company, to the workers, the life of the company is their own and its welfare is theirs. They are so intimately tied up that their interest in the survival and well-being of the company is much more than any shareholder.'[277]

The court also stressed that the Constitution offered guidance on questions of justice, equity, and public interest. Here the preamble and art 43A were of particular importance. The preamble states that India should be a 'sovereign *socialist* secular democratic republic'.[278] Article 43A provides as follows:

> 'The state shall take steps, by suitable legislation or in any other way, to secure the participation of workers in the management of undertakings, establishments or other organizations engaged in any industry.'

In the light of these provisions of the Constitution Bhagwati J concluded that it was 'idle to contend . . . that the workers should have no voice in the determination of the question whether the enterprise should continue to run or be shut down under an order of the Court'.[279] Thus an established private-law rule adopted from English company law[280] had to yield to the imperatives of the Constitution.

### 4.3.3 *Public interest law and procedural flexibility*

Public interest law always has to confront problems of procedure and standing. In India the Supreme Court adopted an extremely radical approach to these issues in the name of the rule of law, arguably in reponse to the traditional Anglo-American approach to procedure and standing, which effectively denied justice to the vast majority of Indian society. Bhagwati J explained:

> 'It must be remembered that the problems of the poor which are now coming before the Court are qualitatively different from those which have hitherto occupied the attention of the Court and they need a different kind of lawyering skill and a different kind of judicial approach. If we blindly follow the adversarial procedure in their case, they would never be able to enforce their fundamental rights and the result would be nothing but a mockery of the Constitution.'[281]

At the start of the expansion of public interest law in India Bhagwati J was Chairperson of the National Committee for the Implementation of Legal Aid Schemes. Many letters were addressed to him in this capacity, complaining of various abuses of power by state authorities. He took it upon himself to treat some of these letters as writ petitions under art 32 of the Constitution,[282] which he then disposed of in his Constitutional Court 2. From this starting point the 'epistolary jurisdiction' exploded so that thousands of public interest cases have now been

---

[277] *Per* Chinnappa Reddy J at 89.
[278] The emphasis is added. The word 'socialist' was inserted into the preamble by the Forty-second Amendment in 1976. See Bakshi *The Constitution of India: Comments and Subject Index* (1990) 1–2.
[279] At 83–4.
[280] The principle that no one other than members and creditors have a right to be heard in applications for winding-up seems to have been accepted in English law since *Re Bradford Navigation Company* (1870) 5 Ch App 600.
[281] *Bandhua Mukti Morcha v Union of India* (supra) at 815 para 13.
[282] This is the article which allows any citizen to apply to the Supreme Court for protection of his/her constitutional rights.

initiated by letter. The court has been so eager to entertain public interest litigation that, unsolicited, it has even treated a letter to a newspaper editor about bonded labour as a petition to initiate proceedings.[283]

The court's approach to fact-finding shows a similar flexibility with respect to procedure. Much of public interest litigation depends on Brandeis briefs. The cost of preparing this sort of evidence is beyond the means of most public interest litigants. Thus the court takes on the fact-gathering function itself.[284] It appoints fact-finding commissions to investigate the issues alleged by the petitioner and report to the court with specific findings and recommendations which the parties are free to challenge. The commissions are given extensive powers to compel discovery of official documents and to subpoena relevant witnesses.[285] The commissions are frequently kept in place to monitor the ultimate implementation of the court's order.

The purpose of public interest litigation is to make justice popularly accessible. So the court is particularly accommodating on issues of *locus standi*. Where the victim of a legal wrong is unable to approach the court directly because of poverty, ignorance, or any other reason related to a social or economic handicap, the court will allow any *bona fide* person to bring litigation based on that wrong. The capacity of the public interest litigant is not clear. Some cases treat such persons as suing in a representative capacity on behalf of the actual victims while others refer to a vindication of a direct interest in the rule of law:

> 'Public interest litigation is brought before the court not for the purpose of enforcing the right of one individual against another as happens in the case of ordinary litigation, but it is intended to promote and vindicate public interest which demands that violations of constitutional or legal rights of large numbers of people who are poor, ignorant or in a socially or economically disadvantaged position should not go unnoticed and unredressed. That would be destructive of the rule of law which forms one of the essential elements of public interest in any democratic form of government. The rule of law does not mean that the protection of the law must be available only to a fortunate few or that the law should be allowed to be prostituted by the vested interests for protecting and upholding the status quo under the guise of enforcement of their civil and political rights. The poor too have civil and political rights and the rule of law is meant for them also, though today it exists only on paper and not in reality.'[286]

Craig calls this approach 'citizen standing'. It illustrates a shift in the court's role from protecting individual rights to guarding against any violation of the rule of law.[287] This shift is reflected in the court's attitude to the relationship between rights and remedies. One of the features of Indian public interest law is that extensive relief is granted in preliminary orders, which are made before there is a determination of rights on the facts or even an investigation of the likelihood of success on the merits. This may not sound like a significant change from traditional approaches to preliminary relief, but because of the fact-finding and conciliatory procedures

---

[283] *Mukesh Advani v State of Madya Pradesh* AIR 1985 SC 1368.

[284] See Bhagwati's explanation of the necessity of court-appointed commissions of inquiry in 'Judicial Activisim and Public Interest Litigation' (1985) 23 *Columbia J of Transnational L* 561 at 574.

[285] There is a discussion of the powers of court-appointed commissions in Peiris 'Public Interest Litigation in the Indian Subcontinent: Current Dimensions' (1991) 40 *ICLQ* 65 at 77–81.

[286] *People's Union for Democratic Rights v Union of India* (supra) at 1476–7. See also *S P Gupta v Union of India* (supra) at 190.

[287] Craig 'Public Interest Litigation' (1987) 29 *J of the Indian Law Institute* 502.

adopted in public interest litigation (see below), interim orders often are in effect for several years.

The departure from tradition is even more marked in respect of final relief. Public interest orders frequently take the form of a directive to the state authorities to establish a prescribed system for the implementation of the public duties they are alleged to have abused. The prescribed system will be made available to all citizens, irrespective of whether they actually were victims of abuse under the previous system. In fact, once the general potential for abuse has been shown the court does not even demand proof of any actual abuse as a prerequisite for relief. Thus in *Sheela Barse v State of Maharashtra*[288] the court prefaced its final order with the following remarks:

> 'It is not necessary for the purpose of this writ petition to go into the various allegations in regard to the ill-treatment meted out to the women prisoners in the police lock-up ... because we do not propose to investigate the correctness of these allegations which have been disputed by the State of Maharashtra.'[289]

Instead of ordering a remedy for the particular abuses alleged in *Sheela Barse*, the court handed down detailed guidelines for the treatment of all pre-trial prisoners in the State of Maharashtra. Similarly, in *Peoples Union for Democratic Rights* Bhagwati J instituted a system for the payment of all workers engaged on construction projects for the Asian Games after saying that it was unnecessary to investigate whether particular employers were paying wages below the legal minimum because the purpose of the public interest litigation was not to punish individual employers but to ensure that all workers' rights were not violated in the future.[290]

The court's departure from traditional approaches to rights and remedies and its reluctance to assign blame are features of its attempt to present public interest litigation as non-adversarial litigation:

> 'Public interest litigation, as we conceive it, is essentially a co-operative or collaborative effort on the part of the petitioner, the state or public authority and the court to secure observance of the constitutional or legal rights, benefits and privileges conferred upon the vulnerable sections of the community and to reach social justice to them. The state or public authority against whom public interest litigation is brought should be as much interested in ensuring basic human rights, constitutional as well as legal, to those who are in a socially and economically disadvantaged position, as the petitioner who brings the public interest litigation before the court.'[291]

Cunningham shows how this conception of public interest litigation as alternative dispute resolution between state and citizen results in a change in the role of the court, which takes on new functions. It acts as ombudsman, receiving complaints from citizens, and bringing the more serious complaints to the attention of the authorities; it provides a forum for the airing of issues of pressing public concern; and it performs a mediating role between state and public interest litigant, suggesting compromises and pushing the parties towards agreement.[292]

---

[288] Supra.
[289] At 379.
[290] Supra at 1479 para 4.
[291] *People's Union for Democratic Rights v Union of India* (supra) at 1477–8. See also Bhagwati 'Public Interest Litigation' (1986) 2 *The Commonwealth Lawyer* 61 at 76 and *Uppendra Baxi v State of Uttar Pradesh* (supra) at 117.
[292] Cunningham 'Public Interest Litigation in The Indian Supreme Court: A Study in the Light of American Experience' (1987) 29 *J of the Indian Law Institute* 504–5.

### 4.3.4 *Public interest litigation and separation of powers*

From the discussion thus far it will be clear that public interest litigation has involved the courts in a range of activities which are conventionally considered to be those of other branches of the state. The court has been careful not to invade the province of the legislature. It has repeatedly stressed that it has no authority to order the legislature to pass laws or to allocate state revenue to a particular purpose.[293] There has probably been less parliamentary legislation set aside on judicial review in the post-Emergency period than in any other period since independence.

The court has not been so restrained when it comes to the traditional province of the executive. Much of public interest litigation has involved the court in taking over control of the administration of a particular issue from the executive by what Uppendra Baxi has called the 'creeping jurisdiction' of the Supreme Court in public interest cases — the process of issuing a series of interim orders to monitor and to rectify administration pending final relief.[294] Most public interest cases involve some degree of creeping jurisdiction. An example would be *Uppendra Baxi v State of Uttar Pradesh*,[295] where the court sought to control the administration of the Agra protective home for women by issuing directives over a period of more than five years. Five years of creeping jurisdiction is not unusual for public interest cases. In fact, final orders are rarely made in public interest cases. Even when a resolution to the problem appears to have been reached through the courts the last order issued usually leaves open the possibility of future intervention.[296]

The difference in the court's approach to legislature and executive in public interest matters is linked to a notion of the relationship between judicial review and democracy which underpinned the judgments of Khanna J and the minority in *Kesavananda*. As we saw above, these judges regarded parliamentary accountability to the public as the cornerstone of democracy and were reluctant to restrict Parliament's legislative and constituent powers. They also saw the function of judicial review under the Indian Constitution as being the encouragement of social justice. Successive parliamentary governments have shared a public commitment to social democracy which has been reflected in their legislative programmes. So the court has seen no reason to interfere with the exercise of legislative power. However, the exercise of executive power presents a different situation. The Indian public service is dominated by competing privileged groups (primarily wealthy farmers, traditional authorities, and industrial and commercial capitalists) who have been able to appropriate the resources of the public sector as a source of wealth, patronage, and political power. There have been numerous parliamentary statutes passed with the intention of altering the existing social conditions, but these are frequently frustrated by an autonomous bureaucracy antagonistic to social

---

[293] See, for example, *State of Himachal Pradesh v Sharma* (supra) at 79–82 and *ABSK Sangh (Railway) v Union of India* (supra) at 335 para 124.

[294] 'Taking Suffering Seriously: Social Action Litigation in the Supreme Court of India' *The Review* No 29, December 1982, 37 at 42.

[295] Supra.

[296] See, for example, *Rural Land and Entitlement Kendra, Dehradun v State of Uttar Pradesh* (supra) and *M C Mehta v Union of India* (supra).

change.[297] Under these circumstances it is natural that the court should have made the executive the focus of its attempts to regulate state power by judicial review.[298]

The court's attitude towards extending its powers into the conventional domain of the executive has predictably been criticized as an undemocratic infringement of the doctrine of separation of powers by conservatives within the Indian legal system. Questions have also been raised about the court's capacity to enforce its orders, which involves the exercise of substantial administrative powers.[299] Some judges have reacted defensively to this criticism, but their responses do not justify their position in terms of a conception of democracy. The closest we get to this are vague statements such as those of Chinnappa Reddy J in *Pandey v State of West Benghal*[300] and Bhagwati J in *People's Union for Democratic Rights v Union of India*:[301]

> 'Of course, the task of restructuring the social and economic order so that the social and economic rights become a meaningful reality for the poor and lowly sections of the community is one which legitimately belongs to the legislature and the executive, but mere initiation of social and economic rescue programmes by the executive and the legislature would not be enough and it is only through multi-dimensional strategies including public interest litigation that these social and economic rescue programmes can be made effective.'[302]

Bhagwati clearly felt that the overlap of the powers of the court and the executive presented no significant problems of enforcement. He believed that the court could enforce its orders by the appointment of commissions to monitor compliance.[303] However, the limits of this procedure were exposed in *Uppendra Baxi v State of Uttar Pradesh*.[304] After the court had spent five years supervising improvements to the Agra protective home for women the state, without notice to the court, moved the home to another location which was every bit as bad as the original home ever was. The judgment reveals the frustration of the court when the state does not co-operate with it:

> 'It is obvious that what has been done has the effect of subverting the authority of this court and unless proper and adequate expression of regret is forthcoming from the concerned officials, we may have to consider whether we should adopt appropriate proceedings against the erring officials . . . Despite our anguish at shifting of the Protective Home from the old building to the new building, we cannot do anything about it . . . and the best that can be done is to start the process

---

[297] For a detailed discussion of the reactionary role of the Indian bureaucracy, see the articles in Kohli (ed) *India's Democracy* (1988). See also Frankel op cit (n 191).

[298] See Cassels 'Judicial Activism and Public Interest Litigation in India: Attempting the Impossible' (1989) 37 *Am J Comp L* 495 at 510–12. Here the Indian experience is directly relevant to us in South Africa. At least for the foreseeable future the post-apartheid South African bureaucracy is likely to remain dominated by people who are hostile to a democratic government. So a Constitutional Court in South Africa might have to emulate the Indian court by taking a more robust attitude to constitutional review of administrative acts than to review of legislation.

[299] The Indian Bar was particularly hostile to public interest litigation. Although much of the Bar's criticism of PIL has been presented in arguments about democracy, the indignation was at least partially linked to the fact that the high volume of public interest litigation which the court entertained on an urgent basis under art 32 substantially increased the delay in getting before the court in conventional cases. The complaints of the advocates have also been voiced by some judges. See, for example, Tulzapurkar 'Judiciary: Attacks and Survivals' AIR 1982 Journ 9.

[300] Supra. The passage is quoted above, 51.

[301] Supra.

[302] At 1477–8.

[303] See Bhagwati 'Public Interest Litigation' (1986) 2 *The Commonwealth Lawyer* 61 at 76.

[304] Supra.

all over again and commence giving directions for improving the living conditions in the new building.'[305]

As public interest litigation developed, courts increasingly resigned themselves to the fact that their orders could not be enforced. From the mid-1980s many judgments reveal an acceptance that orders in public interest matters cannot be of more than persuasive value. Thus in a writ petition based on the right to life, complaining of frequent railway accidents in Kerala, the court listed a number of measures which required attention and then stated:

> 'Giving directions in a matter like this where availability of resources has a material bearing, policy regarding priorities is involved, [and] expertise is very much in issue, it is not prudent and we do not, therefore, propose to issue directions. We, however, do hope and believe that early steps shall be taken to implement in a phased manner the improvements referred to in the counter-affidavit and in our decision.'[306]

Similarly, in *State of Himachal Pradesh v Sharma*[307] the court rebuked the High Court of Himachal Pradesh for intervening too much:

> '[T]he High Court may not take any further action and [must] leave it to the judgment of the priorities and initiative both of the executive and the legislature to pursue this matter. The High Court has served its high purpose of drawing attention to a public need and indicated a feasible course of action. No further need be done by the High Court in this matter.'

An acceptance of the limits of the court's power in public interest matters is necessary. The court has neither the resources nor the expertise to take over the administration of every branch of the executive in respect of which there has been a public interest complaint filed. Nevertheless, public interest litigation and social justice interpretation remain important. The development of the range of fundamental rights through social justice interpretation has been an important legal achievement. The Indian Supreme Court has identified certain issues which the Constitution invests with particular importance and has emphasized that state action or inaction in respect of these issues will be subjected to added scrutiny. The precise nature of this scrutiny has not been settled. Some of the more grandiose ambitions of early public interest litigation judgments have not been realized and it may be that all that can come of public interest litigation is an extended form of rationality review.[308] This would remain an important achievement. Courts are traditionally hostile to rationality review because they do not want to hear a potentially limitless number of cases from the people disappointed with administrative decisions. Social justice interpretation has offered a way of filtering the broad mass of administrative decisions so that constitutionally significant decisions are subjected to extended rationality review while others are not. Moreover, the procedural devices developed in public interest litigation have provided the Indian court with the tools to test the rationality of administrative decisions in a comprehensive fashion. The enforcement of public interest orders remains a real problem, but the popular legitimacy of the court has served to prompt the executive into more accountable behaviour. Even if

---

[305] At 111–12.

[306] *P Nalla Thampy Thera v Union of India* AIR 1984 SC 74 at 80 para 24.

[307] Supra at 82. This was the roadbuilding case discussed above.

[308] This is the practical conclusion which we draw from a reading of the judgments in *P Nalla Thampy Thera v Union of India* (supra), *State of Himachal Pradesh v Umed Ram Sharma* (supra), *Tellis v Bombay Municipality* (supra), and *Kishen v State of Orissa* (supra).

the court has exercised no ultimate sanction, there have been few Indian administrators with the temerity flagrantly to defy an order of the post-Emergency court.

### 4.3.5 The future of public interest litigation

An acceptance by judges of the limits of their power over executive matters need not undermine the importance of public interest litigation. In India, however, this acceptance seems to have been linked to a growing uneasiness of judges with public interest law. In part this was related to the retirement of Bhagwati and Krishna Iyer JJ, the two Supreme Court judges with whom public interest law had been most closely associated. In part it was due to the very success of the public interest litigation movement, which left the judges feeling totally overwhelmed. Public interest litigation put unprecedented strains on the resources of the court. Between January 1987 and March 1988 the court received 23 772 letters requesting the initiation of public interest proceedings and by the end of 1987 the court estimated that it would take fifteen years simply to clear the already existing backlog of cases.[309] Judicial despair with the strains of public interest litigation was expressed in *Pandey v State of West Benghal*:[310]

> 'Public interest litigation has now come to stay. But one is led to think that it poses a threat to courts and public alike. Such cases are now filed without any rhyme or reason. It is therefore necessary to lay down clear guidelines and to outline the correct parameters for entertainment of such petitions. If courts do not restrict the free flow of such cases in the name of public interest litigations, the traditional litigation will suffer and the courts of law, instead of dispensing justice, will have to take upon themselves administrative and executive functions.'[311]

It seems likely that this judicial exasperation will lead to some reappraisal of the Indian court's attitude to public interest litigation. The courts will have to devise some system of sorting public interest petitions.[312] Additional institutions for the resolution of public interest disputes are also necessary. Whether the Indian court and state are able to meet this challenge remains to be seen. If they cannot, the court may be tempted simply to retreat from public interest litigation and social justice interpretation.[313] This temptation should be avoided. The flood of public interest petitions reflected a real social need rather than an abundance of vexatious litigants in India.[314]

---

[309] Cassels 'Judicial Activism and Public Interest Litigation in India: Attempting the Impossible' (1989) 37 *Am J Comp L* 495 at 508.
[310] Supra.
[311] Khalid J at 275a–b.
[312] Because of problems in gaining access to sources we have not been able to follow the history of Indian constitutional law into the 1990s, but we have been informed that the epistolary jurisdiction has now been tempered by the establishment of a screening committee which examines all requests for judicial review and selects cases which it considers important, giving directions for the drawing up of affidavits where appropriate.
[313] The 1989 *Annual Survey of Indian Law* reported increasing judicial reluctance to entertain public interest litigation. See Singh 'Public Interest Law' in Jacob (ed) *Annual Survey of Indian Law* vol XXV (1991). Nevertheless, we have been informed by Indian practitioners that Indian public interest litigation has, for the most part, survived the judicial backlash of the late 1980s.
[314] *Pandey v State of West Benghal* (supra) is one of the few cases in which there is a suggestion from the court that the litigation should not have been initiated.

## 4.4 Conclusion: constitutional democracy in South Africa and the Indian experience

What does this survey of Indian constitutional law suggest for South Africa? There are obvious lessons to be drawn by our courts from the history of post-independence India. Our courts, like their Indian counterparts, will feel a need to assert their institutional autonomy from other branches of government and to scrutinize the activities of the legislature and executive for hints of unconstitutionalism. The Indian experience suggests that the courts should approach this exercise with extreme care. Given the cost of litigation, we can anticipate that much of the constitutional litigation that will come before South African courts will be brought by the wealthy and the powerful in an attempt to protect their wealth and power. A court which in the name of constitutionalism and the rule of law appears to protect existing distributions of wealth and power from state interference can do untold damage to the very principles which it purports to espouse. The Indian property rights conflicts between court and state left the Indian Supreme Court a politically discredited institution and the rule of law in ruins. The Ghandi government's plan to remove the institution of constitutional review was only viable because the Supreme Court had been totally discredited in the eyes of the public by its role in protecting property rights. Similarly, the inability of the court to protect the rule of law during the State of Emergency was a function of its institutional weakness caused by the conflicts over property rights. Our courts must learn from the Indian history because our country cannot afford to repeat it.

The countermajoritarian problem cannot be ignored by a South African Constitutional Court. It is an unfortunate, if not wholly accidental, fact of South African history that we have received a sovereign Bill of Rights at the same time as we elected a democratic government. Under these circumstances the recently enfranchised majority of the South African population is likely to regard a Bill of Rights as an instrument designed to protect privilege and will not easily be won over to the notion of government subject to a Bill of Rights. If the rule of law is to gain popular legitimacy, our judges will have to approach constitutional rights adjudication with sensitivity and creativity. In this connection the Indian experience offers more than warnings of pitfalls to avoid. There is much positive that can be drawn from the post-Emergency Indian case law.

The post-Emergency Supreme Court developed a purposive rights jurisprudence based on a set of values which are central to the Indian Constitution. The values of social and political justice, substantive equality, and human dignity were identified from an overall reading of the Indian Constitution, with a particular focus on the preamble and the directive principles of state policy. The court then re-examined and redefined rights in the light of these central values. The result was a body of constitutional law which differs significantly from the US constitutional law, which developed under a Bill of Rights structured around the core values of liberty and property.[315]

---

[315] For a discussion of the extent to which a concern for property has shaped US constitutional law, see Nedelsky *Private Property and the Limits of American Constitutionalism: The Madisonian Framework and its Legacy* (1990) and 'Reconceiving Rights as Relationship' (Paper delivered at the Gender and Law Conference, Centre for Applied Legal Studies, University of the Witwatersrand, Johannesburg, 20 March 1993).

'This approach shifts the focus from protection against others to structuring relationships so that they foster autonomy. Some of the most basic presuppositions about autonomy shift: dependence is no longer the antithesis of autonomy, but a precondition in the relationships — between parent and child, student and teacher, state and citizen — which provide the security, education, nurturing, and support that make the development of autonomy possible. And autonomy is not a static quality that is simply achieved one day. It is a capacity that requires ongoing relationships that help it flourish; it can wither or thrive throughout one's adult life. Interdependence becomes the central fact of political life, not an issue to be shunted to the periphery in the basic question of how to ensure individual autonomy in the inevitable face of collective power. The human interactions to be governed are not seen primarily in terms of the clashing of rights and interests, but in terms of the way patterns of relationship can develop and sustain both an enriching collective life and the scope for genuine individual autonomy. The whole conception of the relation between the individual and the collective shifts: we recognize that the collective is a source of autonomy as well as a threat to it.

The constitutional protection of autonomy is then no longer an effort to carve out a sphere into which the collective cannot intrude, but a means of structuring the relations between individuals and the sources of collective power so that autonomy is fostered rather than undermined.'[316]

In keeping with this approach and with its concern not to perform an anti-democratic function the Indian court has often been willing to defer to the legislature over the infringement of fundamental rights.[317] It has, however, been extremely harsh on administrative interference with fundamental rights and on administrative failures to implement legislation that furthers the directive principles of state policy. In all of these situations the court has taken an overtly purposive approach to the rights. The identification of the purpose of a right proceeds from an examination of its context in the Constitution. So state action (or inaction) is assessed against the backdrop of the entire Constitution and not against the standard of any decontextualized absolute right.[318]

This, it seems, is the crucial lesson to be drawn from the Indian experience. The post-Emergency Indian cases provide a fascinating example of the products of a purposive approach to constitutional review. Some might be attracted to these decisions; others might find them horrifying, but this is not the point. A South African court should not follow any individual Indian decision because our Constitution will differ significantly from the Indian Constitution. Values crucial to Indian constitutional law may turn out to be relatively unimportant to our constitutional arrangements. Thus the purpose of a right in the context of the South African

---

[316] Nedelsky 'Reconceiving Rights as Relationship' 7. Although Nedelsky's work is not in any way based on Indian constitutional law, the notion of rights as relationship captures much of the theoretically unarticulated practice of the post-Emergency Indian Supreme Court. This is related to the fact that the core values around which Nedelsky would structure her theory of judicial review are very close to the values identified by the Indian court as being at the core of the Indian Constitution.

[317] The Constitution frequently makes provision for legislative interference with fundamental rights. Thus in distinguishing US judgments on freedom of speech, the court stated: 'The pattern of art 19(1)(*a*) and of art 19(1)(*g*) of our Constitution is different from the pattern of the First Amendment to the American Constitution which is almost absolute in its terms. The rights guaranteed under art 19(1)(*a*) and art 19(1)(*g*) of the Constitution are to be read along with Clauses (2) and (6) of art 19 which carve out areas in respect of which valid legislation can be made' (*Indian Express Newspapers (Bombay) Private Ltd v Union of India* AIR 1986 SC 515 at 531 para 42). Other rights which are recognized by the Constitution to be subject to reasonable limits are the right of assembly (art 19(1)(*b*)), the right of association (art 19(1)(*c*)), freedom of movement and settlement (art 19(1)(*d*) and (*e*)), and the right to life and liberty (art 21).

[318] The Canadian contrast between a purposive approach and a 'generous' approach to rights is not always replicated in Indian constitutional law. Thus the purposive approach to the right to life adopted by the Indian court produces an extremely 'generous' construction of the right.

Constitution will, in all likelihood, differ significantly from the purpose of the 'same' right in the Indian Constitution. By adopting the underlying approach to judicial review of the post-Emergency Indian Supreme Court we can accept this fact and be free to develop our own creative constitutional jurisprudence which will at once address the countermajoritarian problem and give effect to the values at the core of our Constitution.

## 5 GERMANY: FROM NAZI RULE TO CONSTITUTIONALISM

### 5.1 An historical overview[319]

In Germany a distinction is made between constitutional and judicial review.[320] Constitutional review refers to the resolution of disputes between the primary organs of government. Judicial review involves the measurement of acts of government against the provisions of the Constitution. The origins of constitutional review can be traced to the days of the Holy Roman Empire when Maximillian I created, in 1495, the *Reichskammergericht* for the resolution of disputes between the princes of the Empire.[321] Mainstream German jurisprudence remained adverse to judicial review until after World War I. This antagonism is reflected in the Constitutions of nineteenth-century Germany. These Constitutions either accepted the sovereignty of the monarch or organized the co-operation between the major social powers — the monarchy, the nobility, and the citizenry — by facilitating compromises and consensus, particularly through the legislative process.[322] In the first case no judicial review was possible, in the second only the process of achieving the social compromise, the legislative procedure, was subjected to the control of the judiciary.[323] Substantive judicial review was not possible until the twentieth century.[324]

*Grundrechte* (fundamental human rights) appeared for the first time in *Länder* (provincial) Constitutions of the early nineteenth century, approximately at the time when representative Parliaments were given a share in the exercise of legislative power.[325] These *Länder* Constitutions were prompted by art 13 of the *Deutsche Bundesakte* of 1815 in terms of which each *Land* had to realize the *Bundesakte*'s

---

[319] The history is included as a Constitution necessarily includes more than the text: past experiences, traditions, cultural streams, and the hopes and dreams of people all form part of the Constitution. See Häberle *Verfassung als öffentlicher Prozess. Materialien zu einer Verfassungstheorie der offenen Gesellschaft* (1978) 199. Also, even though the founders of the Basic Law reacted primarily to the kinds of abuses of power by and in the Nazi state, their reaction was informed by more than 100 years of pre-World War I constitutional history. English readers may be less familiar with this part of German constitutional history and a summary thereof is therefore included.

[320] See in general Kommers *The Constitutional Jurisprudence of the Federal Republic of Germany* (1989) 4; Kommers *Judicial Politics in Western Germany: A Study of the Federal Constitutional Court* (1976) 27.

[321] Kommers *Constitutional Jurisprudence* 5.

[322] Gusy *Parlamentarischer Gesetzgeber und Bundesverfassungsgericht* (1985) 20.

[323] Gusy *Richterliches Prüfungsrecht* (1985) 72 states that, as a matter of constitutional theory, judicial review remained impossible as long as the origin of state (monarchial) power was seen as coming from outside of the Constitution. Once it was recognized that the Constitution produced state power the door for judicial review was opened. For the prospect of substantive judicial review to become realized, two further vital principles — the primacy of the Constitution and the doctrine of separation of powers — had to be recognized.

[324] Gusy op cit (n 322) 25 sees the acceptance of democracy as the political event which lead to the acceptance of judicial review. After democracy emerged the legislative process suddenly proved incapable of integrating the diverse interests and the institution of judicial review became necessary to protect minorities.

[325] The earlier constitutionalization of civil liberties was merely an encouragement to the legislator to make the intricate transition from feudal to modern society. See Lübbe-Wolff 'Safeguards of Civil and Constitutional Rights — The Debate on the Role of the *Reichsgericht*' in Wellenreuther (ed) *German and American Constitutional Thought: Contexts, Interaction and Historical Realities* (1990) 353.

rudimentary provisions relating to human rights through the adoption of legislation.[326] As there was no time constraint on *Länder* legislatures and neither substantive nor procedural judicial review was possible, little protection of human rights resulted.[327] Moreover, the two great powers of the *Bund* — Prussia and Austria — never took their obligations seriously and exercised enough influence on the weaker states to effect the suspension of those laws which sought to implement the freedoms. It is therefore no surprise that the *Bundesakte*'s provision for freedom of the press, for example, in practice meant that *Länder* governments were obliged to censor and supervise the press.[328]

Nationally, the relationship between civil rights and political freedom was recognized for the first time in the Paulskirche Constitution of 1848. This Constitution also represents the high point for liberal constitutional development in nineteenth-century Germany. Its drafters placed heavy reliance on the US Constitution, which was seen as an ingenious framework within which one could bring about national unity, individual freedom, economic success, and independence from foreign domination: precisely the goals for which Germans strove.[329]

The calls for unity — for the formation of a national German state — along with the demand for civil political rights mobilized the grassroots support which the 1848 revolution enjoyed.[330] This explains why the Paulskirche Constitution also included 'rights of the state'.[331] Given the time, the inclusion of social rights was even more extraordinary. Their enumeration should, however, be contextualized. Ultimately the Paulskirche Constitution was the product of an uprising lead by the propertied and academic bourgeoisie. No social revolution took place.[332] A proposal on suffrage which would have excluded women along with servants, day-labourers, journeymen, and factory workers was, despite the equality provision in the Constitution, narrowly defeated.[333] One should therefore be careful not to attach too much significance to the Paulskirche Constitution's commitment to social rights.

The *Reichsgericht*[334] (Imperial Constitutional Court) of the Paulskirche Constitution was modelled after the US Supreme Court.[335] The federal guarantee, rather than the judicial review of legislative acts, was at the centre of the court's inception, but the individual constitutional complaints to the *Reichsgericht* (*Verfas-*

---

[326] Stern *Das Staatsrecht der Bundesrepublik Deutschland* III/1 (1988) 109.

[327] During this era the 'monarchial principle', in terms of which all state power rested in the hands of the monarch, stood in the way of any form of judicial review. Some of the Constitutions adopted after 1830, however, recognized review of administrative action in terms of enabling legislation. See Gusy op cit (n 323) 23, 40.

[328] Kühne 'Civil Rights and German Constitutional Thought 1848–1871' in Wellenreuther op cit (n 325) 211.

[329] Pieroth '*Amerikanischer Verfassungsexport nach Deutschland*' (1989) 42 *NJW* 1333; Steinberger 'America and German Constitutional Development' in Henkin & Rosenthal (eds) *Constitutionalism and Rights: The Influence of the American Constitution Abroad* (1990) 201.

[330] Kühne op cit (n 328) 210.

[331] At 206.

[332] Hucko *Von der Paulskirche zum Museum Koenig Vier Deutsche Verfassungen* (1984) 13.

[333] At 20. The principle of a universal and equal direct secret ballot for men was finally accepted by the delegates. This acceptance was in itself quite progressive for mid-nineteenth-century Europe.

[334] See in general Von Beyme 'The Genesis of Constitutional Review in Parliamentary Systems' in Landfried (ed) *Constitutional Review and Legislation* (1988) 27. All the imperial institutions were subject to the court's jurisdiction.

[335] Kommers op cit (n 320) 32; for a comparison see Wieland '*Der Zugang des Bürgers zum Bundesverfassungsgericht und zum US Supreme Court*' (1990) 29 *Der Staat* 351; Pieroth op cit (n 329) 1334. The *Reichsgericht* was, for example, under no duty to decide cases, but could, as the US Supreme Court, choose which cases it wanted to hear.

*sungsbeschwerde*) were also recognized.[336] In the other sections of the Constitution vertical and horizontal divisions of power were combined in such a manner that the traditional monarchial bases of the power in the states were preserved. The executive apparatus therefore remained in the hands of the state monarchies.[337]

Efforts to please the monarchies were in vain. The Paulskirche Constitution was never implemented. The rivalry between Prussia and Austria resulted in a split. The King of Prussia then refused to accept the crown of the (now smaller) North German Empire, and unity and the Constitution were doomed. An expensive lesson was learned: in nineteenth-century Germany Constitutions at best represented a compromise between the prince and the people; at worst the monarch adopted the Constitution unilaterally.[338]

With the collapse of the Paulskirche Constitution the liberal human rights movement lost steam.[339] Intellectually, historicism and romantic-religious ideas of the state were erected as barriers to libertarianism.[340] The liberal movement was also divided between those working for a unified Germany and those who fought for individual freedom. Neither group saw *Grundrechte* as inalienable human rights, but rather as concessions from rulers which were conferred on citizens and subject to revocation.[341] Constitutionally the *Deutsche Bundesakte* of 1815 came into effect again. Socially the full impact of the Industrial Revolution hit Germany comparatively late and unification became increasingly imperative for Germany to compete with France and Britain.[342]

After the 1866 war against Austria Prussia became the recognized power in central Europe.[343] Under Bismarck's personal influence unity was formally sealed with the adoption of the 1871 Constitution. This Constitution did not contain a list of basic rights.[344] Priority was given to the political organization of unity.[345] As with the *Bundesakte*, the protection of *Grundrechte* was left to *Länder* Constitutions and *Länder* legislatures. In cases such as the *Kulturkampf* against political Catholicism and the proscription of the Socialists, civil political liberties were infringed — rather than protected — by *Länder* legislation.[346] Bismarck's empire was, however, no

---

[336] Article 126, Paulskirche Constitution. The scope and the procedure of the constitutional complaint mechanism was left for legislative definition. Judicial review was not expressly recognized in the Constitution, but most delegates accepted during the deliberations that governmental acts could be measured against the provisions of the Constitution. See Gusy op cit (n 323) 53. Compare Steinberger op cit (n 329) 205. He argues that the fundamental rights of Paulskirche were not directly applicable law, but they needed legislative implementation.

[337] Bolt 'Federalism as an Issue in the German Constitutions of 1849 and 1871' in Wellenreuther op cit (n 325) 259, 268. The *Länder*, right up to the present, execute Federal laws as their own.

[338] Kühne op cit (n 328) 216.

[339] At 212.

[340] At 220.

[341] Steinberger op cit (n 329) 202; Stern op cit (n 326) 109.

[342] Hucko op cit (n 332) 31.

[343] Bolt op cit (n 337) 280.

[344] Stern 'A Society Based on the Rule of Law and Social Justice' 1981 *TSAR* 241 labels the 1871 Constitution in Germany and the 1983 South African Constitution as 'organizational statutes' because of the absence of basic rights. Stern proposed that basic rights should be protected via ordinary legislation in the South African case. Sadly, nothing of this nature has happened during the ten-year existence of the 1983 Constitution.

[345] Bismarck felt that a Bill of Rights might disturb the precariously balanced federal structure of the Constitution. In other words, the delicate nature of the unification process precluded the inclusion of fundamental rights in the 1871 Constitution. See Steinberger op cit (n 329) 206; Hucko op cit (n 332) 41.

[346] Hucko op cit (n 332) 42.

more authoritarian than the other European states. Bismarck, after all, installed a — for his time — rather progressive, if paternalistic, social security system.[347]

In the 1871 Constitution the courts were trusted with the review of state legislation for compatibility with Federal law, but the resolution of conflicts of 'non-private-law nature' between the *Länder* was left to a political organ: the *Bundesrat*.[348] Judicial review of Federal statutes was restricted to the verification of proper promulgation and publication and no substantive judicial review was possible.[349] The consequences of an exercise of substantive judicial review would have been severe: the *Reichsgericht* itself was the product of an unconstitutional exercise of power by the Federation.[350] In conclusion: the 1871 Constitution was merely an organizational norm. It defined the roles of the social powers in the making of legislation, and little more than formal judicial review was therefore possible.[351]

With the acceptance of the Weimar Constitution the constitutional monarchy was replaced with a republican Constitution based on the sovereignty of the people. Constitutional review was accepted by the drafters of the Weimar Constitution.[352] The question of judicial review was left open.[353] Nevertheless, the *Reichsgericht* held in 1925 that statutes which conflicted with the Constitution could not be applied to the extent of their deviation.[354] According to this decision, legislation which conflicted with the Constitution were considered futile attempts to amend the Constitution and they could consequently be overturned by the judiciary on this 'procedural' ground. Rights were therefore not seen as natural and inalienable, but they were as vulnerable to amendment as any other part of the Constitution.[355]

Some argue that the formal reasoning of the court masks the judges' deep distrust of the democratic legislature and their allegiance to the interests of the propertied and educated middle class.[356] Others do not see the exercise of judicial review in Weimar as anti-democratic: Radbruch's warning that judicial review undermines

---

[347] Steinberger op cit (n 329) 207; Benda 'The Constitutional and Legal Situation of German Industrial Society and the Historical Development of Social Change' in Wellenreuther op cit (n 325) 478.

[348] Article 76.1 *WRV*; Säcker *Das Bundesverfassungsgericht* (1989) 18; Gusy op cit (n 323) 24.

[349] According to Steinberger op cit (n 329) 207, reality in some states was even bleaker: judgments which overturned legislation on grounds of a defective enactment procedure were ignored and some governments even acted against such 'activist' judges. Regulations could be reviewed for compatibility with enabling legislation. See Kommers *Judicial Politics* 36; Gusy op cit (n 323) 27. The restriction of judicial review to formal procedural review was most consistently (but by no means only) advocated by legal positivists (Gusy op cit (n 323) 71).

[350] Lübbe-Wolff op cit (n 325) 359. At approximately the same time the South African Republic was facing a constitutional crisis of even greater proportions. The procedure for making legislation in the Republic was so cumbersome and the majorities required so high that the Constitution was almost consistently ignored. See Dugard *Human Rights and the South African Legal Order* (1978) 19 for a discussion of Kotze CJ's attempt to exercise judicial review after a long period of consistent irreverence for the procedural requirements of the Constitution of the South African Republic.

[351] Ipsen 'Constitutional Review' in Stark (ed) *Main Principles of the German Basic Law* (1983) 108.

[352] Most constitutional conflicts were entrusted to the *Staatsgerichtshof*, but the *Reichsgericht* had the power (conferred by ordinary legislation) to decide on the compatibility of *Länder* law with Federal law in terms of art 13.2 *WRV*.

[353] Steinberger op cit (n 329) 209; Kommers *Judicial Politics* 38.

[354] 111 *RGZ* 320 322 (*Aufwertungs* case).

[355] Steinberger op cit (n 329) 211. The decision of the *Reichsgericht* was by no means consistently followed. On the contrary, the status of rights was unclear and most commentators conclude that they could be limited by ordinary legislation. See below, nn 361–3.

[356] In other words, it is argued that the values of a particular segment of society, and not the values expressed in the Constitution, served as the real limitation of the will of the majority. Gusy op cit (n 323) 88 mentions the use of the constitutional rights to equality and property and the rights of the bureaucracy by the judiciary to restrain the legislator while, at the same time, the judiciary showed deference to the emergency regulations. See also Lübbe-Wolff op cit (n 325) 368; Schlaich *Das Bundesverfassungsgericht: Stellung, Verfahren und Entscheidungen*

the legitimacy of the legislature was coldly answered by Ernst von Hippel: the authority of the legislature was as vulnerable as that of the judiciary and the latter's control over the former may even be necessary for the survival of both.[357] Another less cynical explanation for the *Reichsgericht*'s assumption of judicial review relies on the rise of the Free Law School, which felt that judges are not bound to enforce the letter of the law, but may follow its spirit.[358] Finally, the existence of a small yet powerful minority of Weimar parliamentarians, who accepted the idea of judicial review, is often mentioned.[359]

The Weimar Constitution contained not only traditional liberal rights but also social and economic provisions. The inclusion of the latter contributed to the unclear status of all fundamental rights.[360] The judiciary by no means protected the fundamental rights consistently against infringing state action. In fact most commentators conclude that rights in the Weimar Constitution could be limited by statutory law.[361] The Weimar Constitution is also often described as being 'value relative' as no effective control existed over the will of the majority as long as that will was properly formed.[362]

In many ways the founders of the Basic Law reacted to the problems experienced in Weimar: *Verfassungsdurchbrechung*;[363] the weak political parties and coalitions;[364] the consequently weak Chancellor and governments;[365] and the strong emergency powers of the President.[366]

---

(1991) 72. Judicial training was further of such a nature that only the rich could qualify. See Zimmermann 'Judges shall be Independent and Subject only to the Law' (1985) 48 *THRHR* 291 at 300. One of the arguments in favour of centralized review during the drafting of the Basic Law was that it would preclude another attempt by the professional judiciary to frustrate the wishes of legislative majorities. See Asmal 'Constitutional Courts — A Comparative Survey' (1991) XXIV *CILSA* 315 at 317.

[357] Quoted in Lübbe-Wolff op cit (n 325) 368. For a discussion of theoretical approaches to judicial review in Weimar, especially the work of Heller, Schmitt and Kelsen, see Gusy op cit (n 323) 90.

[358] Kommers *Judicial Politics* 37. In general, positivism prevailed under the members of the judiciary and legal academics, but one cannot simply associate the denial of judicial review with positivism. One obvious refutation of such an oversimplification is the work and life of Hans Kelsen. See Schenke '*Vierzig Jahre Grundgesetz*' (1989) 14 *Juristenzeitung* 653 at 655; Zimmermann op cit (n 356) 300.

[359] Kommers *Judicial Politics* 38.

[360] The words *recht* and *freiheit* were not associated with the social and economic clauses. Carl Schmitt, one of the most influential legal scholars of the time, described *Grundrechte* as 'in the proper sense, only individual freedom rights and not social demands' (Schmitt *Verfassungslehre* (1928) 163–70, quoted from Currie '*Positive und Negative Grundrechte*' (1986) 111 *Archiv des Öffentlichen Recht* 230 at 235).

[361] See Von Bismarck & Partsch 'Revolution and Continuity: Constitutional Developments in the Five New States of the Federal Republic of Germany and their Influence on the Amendment of the Constitution of the Federal Republic, the Basic Law' (1992) XXV *CILSA* 156 at 158; Blaauw 'The *Rechtsstaat* Idea Compared with the Rule of Law as a Paradigm for Protecting Rights' (1990) 107 *SALJ* 80. It is argued that Weimar was therefore a formal, but not a material, *Rechtsstaat*. The rights are then described as of 'residual nature'.

[362] The lack of effective judicial review, especially in its function of protecting individual human rights, rather than the biases of the judiciary, is therefore seen as a central shortcoming of the Weimar Constitution. See Grimm '*Vierzig Jahre Grundgesetz*' (1989) 42 *NJW* 1305 at 1306; Gusy op cit (n 322) 29.

[363] The Constitution could be changed, without amending the text, by legislation adopted by two-thirds of the members of Parliament *present* (art 76 *WRV*). Hitler used this procedure, known as *Verfassungsdurchbrechung*, to supplement the Weimar Constitution with the Enabling Act of 1933. Article 79.3 *GG*, which prohibits the amendment of the most important principles of the Basic Law and the extensive power entrusted to the Constitutional Court in the Basic Law, must be seen in this context.

[364] Small, weak political parties destabilized the Weimar democracy. The Basic Law's 5 % hurdle for *Bundestag* (lower chamber of Parliament) representation, the requirement for intra-party democracy, and party privileges should be seen in this light.

[365] Weimar experienced twenty governments over fourteen years. The Basic Law's answer to this problem is the constructive vote of no confidence (art 67 *GG*).

[366] Owing to the fact that the Weimar Republic faced emergencies from beginning to end, the democratically elected, but supposedly impartial, figure-head President became the most powerful executive figure. The Chancellor and the Cabinet were reduced to mediators between the coalition parties and the President.

Even if one assumes that the *Reichsgericht*'s motive for asserting the right to exercise judicial review was to serve as a check for the 'general consciousness' on the democratic legislature,367 one must keep in mind that nothing similar to the battle between Roosevelt and the US Supreme Court developed.368 Courts and the institution of judicial review never played such an important role in the Weimar Republic.369 One can therefore only conclude that the first German experience with judicial review was a short-lived and confused one.

Hitler suspended the civil liberties guaranteed by the Constitution.370 Individual liberties could have no place in a scheme where judges had to interpret the law in the spirit and for the furtherance of the Nazi goals.371 Even the role of defence lawyers declined as the judges' interpretation of the interests of the state and the community became the main focus of the trial.372

## 5.2 The Basic Law (*Grundgesetz* or *GG*)

Constitutional experts — mostly academics — from the new West German *Länder* met at the *Herrenchiemsee* in 1948 and formulated a first draft of the new Constitution in two weeks.373 The *Länder* then sent delegates to form a parliamentary council which adopted the Basic Law eight months later.374

It is sometimes said that the Basic Law represents a revolution from the outside: this is certainly a gross oversimplification. The Allied Forces demanded a federal and democratic Constitution.375 There is little evidence that the Allies renounced a veto right because the Germans accepted judicial review of legislation.376 The drafters of the Basic Law were influenced to a greater extent by pre-Bismarck traditions and the abuses which occurred under the Nazi regime.377 In settling for a

---

367 Schlaich, '*Die Verfassungsgerichtsbarkeit im Gefüge der Staatsfunktionen*' (1981) *VVDStRL* 98 at 103.

368 Lübbe-Wolff op cit (n 325) 368.

369 Säcker op cit (n 348) 19, but cf Gusy op cit (n 323) 119. Gusy argues that the inability of the Weimar Parliament to operate positively and constructively in the public interest left a vacuum, which was then filled by the second (President) and third (courts) powers. The normativity of the *WRV* — which placed Parliament at the centre of state power — and democracy was weakened in this process.

370 See Fernandez 'The Law, Lawyers and the Courts in Nazi Germany' (1985) 1 *SAJHR* 124 at 125.

371 At 126. Nazi ideology has nothing in common with legal positivism. Nevertheless, legal positivism, exemplified by the '*Reine Rechtslehre*' of Kelsen, suffered a set-back in Germany after World War II. Whether this set-back can be justified remains controversial. Some argue that positivism is partly to blame for the Nazi human rights abuses in that the purification of constitutional law from historical, political, and philosophical considerations enabled the preservation of a static conception of the constitutional order despite a changing reality. See Müller 'The Judge and Unjust Law: A German Perspective' (1985) 10 *TVR* 152 at 155; Schenke op cit (n 358) 653.

372 See Reifner 'The Bar in the Third Reich: Anti-Semitism and the Decline of Liberal Advocacy' (1986) 32 *McGill LJ* 97. The defence of individual liberty was associated with 'Jewish liberalism'. Jewish lawyers did indeed constitute a progressive force both at the bar and among academia. Their contributions were initially discredited by the likes of Carl Schmitt and eventually Jewish lawyers were prevented from exercising their profession, and in many instances killed, by the Nazi regime. The judiciary offered little resistance. On the contrary, Reifner (at 104) argues that the judges became a useful ally to the regime as their co-operation with the Nazis legitimized the legal system in the eyes of ordinary German citizens. Reifner (at 103) states that German courts condemned at least 30 000 people to death between 1942 and 1945.

373 Kommers *Judicial Politics* 70.

374 The three biggest political parties: FDP (Liberal Democrats), CDU (Christian Democrats), and SPD (Social Democrats) voted for the new Constitution and the rest against (result: 52–12). See Hucko op cit (n 332) 75.

375 Kröger '*Die Entstehung des Grundgesetzes*' (1989) 42 *NJW* 1318 at 1319.

376 Von Beyme op cit (n 334) 31; but cf Pieroth op cit (n 329) 1336.

377 Von Beyme op cit (n 334) 32; Kröger op cit (n 375) 1319.

system of centralized judicial review in the form of a Federal Constitutional Court (FCC), the founders were influenced by the work of Hans Kelsen.[378]

The outstanding feature of the Basic Law is the attempt to secure democratic rule in Germany by binding the democratic process to the values and principles expressed in the Constitution. The Basic Law establishes a democratic, but not a value-free, order. Several provisions in the Constitution seek to protect this value-bound order.

First, the core values of the Constitution may under no circumstances be amended by the people.[379] Article 79.3 *GG* bars any amendment to art 1 *GG*, which proclaims that the 'dignity of man is inviolable',[380] and to art 20 *GG*, which describes Germany as a 'democratic, social and federal *Rechtsstaat*'. Clearly some constitutional amendments can therefore be unconstitutional.[381] In addition art 21.2 *GG* gives the FCC, on request of the Federal government, the *Bundestag*, or *Bundesrat*,[382] the power to ban political parties which seek either to impair or destroy the basic democratic order, or to endanger the existence of the Federal Republic of Germany.[383] Article 9.2 *GG* (allowing the banning of certain associations by the government) and art 18 *GG* (forfeiture of individual rights when abused) complete the protection of the value-bound 'fighting democracy'.[384]

A second significant attempt to strengthen the effectiveness of the rights is provided in the special enumerated limitation order. No general limitation clause exists in Germany, but specific limitations are attached to most of the *Grundrechte*.[385]

---

[378] Kommers *Judicial Politics* 71. In this respect the delegates to the parliamentary council accepted the proposals of the *Herrenchiemsee* experts. Some delegates felt that the 'purely legal' jurisdiction of the ordinary courts should not be 'tainted' with 'political matters'. See Kröger op cit (n 375) 1323; Schlaich op cit (n 367) 101.

[379] See Stern 'The Genesis and the Evolution of European-American Constitutionalism: Some Comments on the Fundamental Aspects' (1985) XVII *CILSA* 187 at 195.

[380] Zajadlo '*Überwindung des Rechtspositivismus als Grundwert des Grundgesetzes. Die verfassungsrechtliche Aktualität des Naturrechtsproblems*' (1987) 26 *Der Staat* 207 at 227 goes as far as describing the dignity clause as the *Grundnorm* of the Basic Law, the difference to Kelsen's *Grundnorm* being that human dignity has real content. Zimmermann 'Self-determination, Paternalism or Human Care? Suicide and Criminal Responsibility in South African and German Law' 1979 *TSAR* 183 at 186 describes this clause as meaning, at least, that the state exists for the sake of man and not man for the sake of the state. The dignity clause forms the basis of the objective value order and therefore of the doctrine of indirect *Drittwirkung* of the *Grundrechte*.

[381] In 1 *BVerfGE* 14 32 the FCC said that constitutional amendments which conflict with 'the elementary constitutional principles and those principles which express the pre-constitutional nature of the *Grundrechte*' in the Basic Law are invalid. Further, 'every constitutional provision must be interpreted to conform with these elementary constitutional principles and fundamental decisions' of the Basic Law. In 30 *BVerfGE* 1 the court had to decide on the constitutionality of an amendment to art 10 *GG*, which protects the privacy of post and telecommunication. The amendment makes it possible for the state to invade the individual's privacy of mail and communication without informing him/her if the purpose of the state action is to protect the free, democratic basic order. The court held (at 24) that the elementary constitutional principles of art 79.3 *GG* are protected from amendment, but that this provision is analogous to art 19.2 *GG*: the essence of the elementary principles may, in other words, not be amended. Nothing prevents the constitutional legislator from modifying the elementary principles in a '*systemimmanent*' way. The constitutional amendment was then interpreted in conformity with the Constitution and found to be compatible with art 79.3 *GG*. See also 3 *BVerfGE* 225 231; Robbers '*Die Änderungen des Grundgesetzes*' (1989) 42 *NJW* 1325 at 1326.

[382] The *Bundestag* and *Bundesrat* are respectively the lower and upper chambers of Parliament. See also art 43.1 *BVerfGG* (Federal Constitutional Court Act).

[383] See below, 376 in connection with the banning of the Socialist Reich (2 *BVerfGE* 1) and Communist (5 *BVerfGE* 85) Parties in the 1950s.

[384] Kommers *Constitutional Jurisprudence* 43.

[385] The difference between the jurisprudence of courts in the US, Canada, and Germany concerning the limitation of rights are often overestimated. Naturally, the existence of a general limitation clause in the Canadian Constitution led to a greater emphasis on the principle of proportionality as the sole limiting device of fundamental rights. In the US the absence of any enumerated limitations resulted in a jurisprudence which emphasizes balancing of all relevant interests within the individual rights with the help of 'levels of scrutiny'. In Germany the enumeration of specific limitations led to a shift in emphasis to the content of the right and the scope of its limitation, but the

Thirdly, the influence of natural law in the debates surrounding the drafting of the Basic Law is reflected in several of its provisions.[386] The Basic Law recognizes the *Grundrechte* as inviolable and inalienable and as forming the basis of peace and justice in every human society.[387]

Finally, art 1.3 *GG* binds the legislature, the executive, and the judiciary as directly enforceable law. Every citizen, and in the case of some *Grundrechte* every person, may therefore claim his/her rights against the state.[388]

The other main features of the Basic Law are:

- **Separation of powers**  The parliamentary system of government entails that the Chancellor is elected by and is dependent on a *Bundestag* majority.[389] The Chancellor may be replaced only by a constructive vote of no confidence. In other words, a new Chancellor has to be elected before the incumbent can be dismissed.[390]

---

principle of proportionality proved to be crucial to determine the constitutionality of state actions in individual cases. Moreover, since the enumerated limitations do not constitute the only permissible limitation of fundamental rights and some *Grundrechte* are protected without specific enumerated limitations, the FCC has resorted to balancing of constitutional interests in order to develop further limitations to the *Grundrechte*. The results of the decisions show remarkable similarities. The specific enumerated limitations in Germany can therefore almost be seen as guidelines to the FCC — and indeed any other court — to determine the weight to attach to the different interests at stake. Comparative constitutional analysis cannot be restricted to the decisions of courts, but must also take cognizance of the provisions of the Constitution and the legislation which seek to concretize and implement those provisions.

[386] See arts 1.1 *GG*; 19.2 *GG*; 20.3 *GG*; 79.3 *GG*.

[387] Article 1.2 *GG*. For Luhmann *Grundrechte als Institution: ein Beitrag zur politische Soziologie* (1965) 40, the mere characterization of rights as pre-constitutional (cf 1 *BVerfGE* 14 18, 32, 61) and natural does not really strengthen them normatively. On the contrary, it looks like an attempt by the founders to try and isolate rights from legitimate objections. A court which overturns the will of the majority, not on the basis of critical argumentation, but with an authoritative claim to the objective correctness of its decisions which has, in fact, no justification other than the mystical natural law, is a dangerous institution. The decisions of such a court are isolated from rational criticism and become everlasting truths. See also Häberle op cit (n 319) 93; Karpen '*Grundgesetz, Konsens und Wertewandel*' (1987) 8 *Juristische Schulung* 593 at 594; Robinson 'Die Ouer–Kind Verhouding in die Lig van 'n Menseregteakte — 'n Beknopte Oorsig oor die Posisie in Duitsland' (1992) 7 *SAPR/PL* 228 at 237 argues that there is a 'special relationship' between the German Constitution and natural law. If this relationship is of an historical nature, one can agree because the value of natural law for the process of constitutional interpretation lies precisely in the guidance it provides for the determination of the historical meaning of a *Grundrecht*.

Zajadlo op cit (n 380) 210f argues that modern conceptions of natural law have little in common with its classical formulation. Just as positivism nowadays does not mean that only positive law is law and that all positive law is law, natural law does not necessarily mean that eternal and absolute principles of law are derived from the nature of humans or from God, but may merely mean that legitimacy of law and the legal system may be judged critically against some external standard. Zajadlo (at 226) then argues that the FCC never rejected natural law, but followed the logical development from natural law as a normative system to natural law as a critical way of thinking. Zajadlo (at 224) also defends the 'pre-constitutional nature' of the *Grundrechte* with reference to a 'consensus-based legitimacy'. The consensus is analogous to the *volonté générale* of Rousseau. Further, because the Basic Law confers legitimacy with varying degrees of intensity on its different parts, an objective value order and the unconstitutional constitutional norm become possibilities. Contrast Häberle op cit (n 319) 143. He dismisses the *volonté générale* as fiction, along with all other theories which claim absolute validity for the *Grundrechte*.

[388] The distinction is further made between the ability to be the subject of *Grundrechte* (*Grundrechtsfähigkeit*) and the ability to exercise *Grundrechte* (*Grundrechtsmündigkeit*). All Germans are the subjects of the *Grundrechte* and are therefore protected by the rights against the state, but the ability to exercise and rely on the *Grundrecht* independently accrues to the individual at a certain age and that age has to be determined by the court on a case-by-case basis. Juristic persons have *Grundrechte* in so far as the nature of the *Grundrechte* makes them applicable (art 19.3 *GG*); public corporations and state organs do not have any *Grundrechte*. See Schlaich op cit (n 367) 122.

[389] Traditionally separation of powers on the continent is aimed at preventing interference between the branches and is therefore not so much geared towards control or 'checks and balances', but the vote of no confidence and the doctrine of ministerial responsibility are, of course, important 'checks' on the power of the executive. See Cappelletti 'Judicial Review of the Constitutionality of State Action: Its Expansion and Legitimacy' 1992 *TSAR* 256 at 262.

[390] Article 67 *GG*; 62 *BVerfGE* 1; Dürig 'An Introduction to the Basic Law of the Federal Republic of Germany' in Karpen (ed) *The Constitution of the Federal Republic of Germany* (1988) 20.

- **Federalism**[391] The *Bundesrat* is made up of representatives of the *Länder* governments. These representatives vote *en bloc* in the *Bundesrat*. Federal laws are usually executed by the *Länder* governments.[392] The *Länder* may include new rights in their own Constitutions, but the basic tenets of the Basic Law must be followed.[393] A complicated system of tax apportionment between *Bund* and *Länder* is constantly being revised.

- **Social state** No socio-economic rights were included, but the right to property was specifically limited[394] and the German state is described in art 20 *GG* as a social one.

- **Rechtsstaat** According to art 20.3 *GG*, legislation is subject to the constitutional order and the executive and the judiciary are bound by law and justice.[395] In addition to art 20.3 *GG*, art 1.3 *GG* clearly establishes the Basic Law as higher law.[396]

---

[391] See in general Blair *Federalism and Judicial Review in West Germany* (1981). Blair (at 48) divides the disputes between the *Länder* governments and the *Bund* into the following categories:
1. *Pure federal disputes* Sometimes this kind of dispute will be carried forward by a successor *Land* government from a different political party, or solidarity will be shown by *Länder* governments of different political persuasion. Example: *South West* case (1 *BVerfGE* 14).
2. *Federal disputes with party-political implications* In these cases the powers or obligations of *Land* and *Bund* are still the issue, but there are party-political undertones. Examples: *Atomic Weapons Referendum* case (8 *BVerfGE* 104) and the *Television* case (12 *BVerfGE* 205).
3. *Disputes about non-federal issues* The *Land* government petitions the FCC for abstract judicial review of Federal legislation either because they provide a better platform of attack than one-third of the *Bundestag*; or the *Land* government feels less prepared to compromise than the political party representatives in the *Bundestag*. Example: Abortion reform law (39 *BVerfGE* 1 — Bavaria challenge).

[392] Article 83 *GG*.

[393] See Von Bismarck & Partsch op cit (n 361) 166. Socio-economic rights have found their way into some of the *Länder* Constitutions.

[394] In terms of art 14.1.2 *GG* the legislator should determine the content and limitations of the right to property. Article 14.2 *GG* states 'Property imposes duties. It should also be used in the public interest.' The first provision demands legislative definition and the last enables legislative restriction of property in the public interest (see 37 *BVerfGE* 132 140; 38 *BVerfGE* 348 370). Property is, however, protected institutionally and the legislator may therefore not rescind the institution of private property.

[395] Müller op cit (n 371) 159 argues that the last part of art 20.3 *GG* means that judges will have to refer to a 'meta-positive system of law' when the 'contradiction between legislation and justice reaches such untenable proportions that the law has to yield to justice as not being law at all'. Müller makes it clear that law and justice, though not the same, are not 'fixed and immutable entities, but living structures, in which dynamic change is inherent'. Justice is informed by the supreme constitutional principles, especially the provisions which protect the dignity of persons. Rules which conflict with justice to this 'unbearable extent' are rare. In 23 *BVerfGE* 98 106 the court declared a 1941 rule which deprived German Jews, domiciled in a foreign country, of their citizenship to be invalid on this ground. The ordinary courts may not apply such rules; they never became law and are *ab initio* void. See also 3 *BVerfGE* 225; Mischke 'The Inseparability of Powers: Judge-made Law in the German Legal System' (1992) 7 *SAPR/PL* 253 at 254.

[396] The 'supremacy clause' in Germany means that rules are ranked abstractly and that constitutional rules have the highest rank. See Denninger 'Judicial Review Revisited: The German Experience' (1984–5) 59 *Tulane LR* 1013 at 1016. The Basic Law is therefore not only a formal *Rechtsstaat* but also a material *Rechtsstaat*. See in this regard Blaauw op cit (n 361) 76. The *Rechtsstaat* principle also entails that legal rules must be clear and consistently enforced. Concerns have been expressed that the *Rechtsstaat* is in danger, especially by the non-enforcement of legislation in the politically controversial areas of illegal labour (*Schwarzarbeit*) and environmental protection. The clarity of the codes is also under suspicion. See Sendler '*Vierzig Jahre Rechtsstaat des Grundgesetzes: Mehr Schatten als Licht?*' (1989) 42 *Die Öffentliche Verwaltung* 482 at 488. Sendler, writing as President of the Federal Administrative Court, argues that the situation is so bad that litigants often feel that they play roulette by going to court. According to him, the nebulous character of the codes opens the door for litigants to exploit the judicial process in order to win time or pursue political motives. Müller op cit (n 371) 152 argues that the administration of the welfare state penetrates most areas of social and economic life and it addresses specific problems of classes of people with specific measures. No legal rules of fixed and general condition can be used to rule such a diverse and ever-changing society. The danger of an encroachment of constitutional rights, however, becomes acute and it is increasingly up to judges to achieve a fair balance of conflicting interests and to realize justice in particular cases (at 163).

- **Party state** The institution of political parties is recognized as essential for the formation of the political will of the people. The Basic Law founded a republican democracy.[397] The political parties, as associations with their roots in both state and society, are called upon to regulate the influence and the interdependence between state and society.[398]

## 5.3 The Federal Constitutional Court (FCC, *Bundesverfassungsgericht*, or *BVerfG*)

### 5.3.1 *Autonomy*

Although the Basic Law contains a complete section[399] dealing with the administration of justice in general and the FCC in particular, much of the important fine-tuning concerning the structure, powers, and jurisdiction of the court was only finalized in the Federal Constitutional Court Act (*BVerfGG*), which was promulgated in 1951.[400] Vital decisions concerning the court were therefore made by ordinary majorities of Parliament and can consequently be changed by such majorities. This possibility of manipulation has not been exploited.[401] On the contrary, the judges' demands for status equal to that of the *Bundestag*, *Bundesrat*, the Chancellor, and the President were conceded.[402] Moreover, budgetary autonomy — the court nowadays bargains directly with Parliament and the Minister of Finance — and full autonomy over the internal administration and procedures of the FCC were added to the powers of the court by the FCC Act.[403] An FCC judge may further be dismissed only by the Federal President, and then pursuant to a motion filed by the court itself.[404] Even during a constitutional state of emergency the court's functions may not be impaired unless a request for suspension is made by two-thirds of the judges of the court.[405] It is therefore no wonder that the judges of the court do not consider themselves to be civil servants, as the rest of the German judiciary are, but rather see the court as an independent constitutional organ of the state.[406]

---

[397] Scepticism existed about plebiscites in reaction to the Nazi era, but some elements of direct democracy are protected through the freedoms of assembly and speech. These *Grundrechte* are seen as essential complimenters to representative democracy. See Kröger op cit (n 375) 1320; Karpen op cit (n 387) 594. See Calliess '*Strafzwecke und Strafrecht*' (1989) 42 *NJW* 1338 at 1342. After the re-unification in 1990 the new states, incorporated under art 23 *GG*, all included elements of direct democracy in their Constitutions. See Von Bismarck & Partsch op cit (n 361) 171 and below, the chapters on freedom of assembly and freedom of association, passim.
[398] Kirchhof '*Gegenwartsfragen an das Grundgesetz*' (1989) 10 *Juristenzeitung* 453 at 455. Badura '*Der Sozialstaat*' (1989) 42 *Die Öffentliche Verwaltung* 482 at 497 argues that the calls for the democratization of business organizations express, besides a socialist orientation, a scepticism in political parties and representative democracy. This conflicts with the clear commitment of the Basic Law to a parliamentary democracy and legislation as the vehicle for social reform. It can, however, also be argued that co-determination does not conflict with, but merely supplements, the 'party state'.
[399] Articles 92–103 *GG*.
[400] Kommers *Constitutional Jurisprudence* 17; Kommers *Judicial Politics* 78.
[401] The CDU/CSU coalition in 1956 and the SPD/FDP in 1971 planned to change the selection procedure, but their plans were thwarted by an unyielding *Bundesrat*. See Kommers *Judicial Politics* 141.
[402] See in particular the *Status-Denkschrift* written by the judges themselves in 1952, printed in Häberle *Verfassungsgerichtbarkeit* (1976) 224; Kommers *Judicial Politics* 84.
[403] Article 1.3 *BVerfGG*; Kommers *Constitutional Jurisprudence* 18.
[404] Article 105 *BVerfGG*.
[405] Article 115.h *GG*.
[406] Article 1 *BVerfGG*; Kommers *Judicial Politics* 84.

## 5.3.2 Selection[407]

Judges are elected for a single term of twelve years.[408] Judges must be at least 40 years of age[409] and must retire at the age of 68.[410] Half of the judges are elected by a two-thirds majority of a special committee of the *Bundestag* — the Judicial Selection Committee — and the other half by a two-thirds majority of the *Bundesrat*.[411] The selection process is one of intensive political bargaining, but smaller opposition parties, such as the Green Party, which are incapable of upsetting the outcome of the vote, are overlooked.[412] Judges are elected on the basis of their party affiliations, despite the lack of public discussion of the candidates in the press, in Parliament, or even within the parties.[413]

The jurisdiction of the court is divided between two senates.[414] Eight judges serve in each senate. Three judges of each senate must be selected from the Federal courts.[415] The rest of the judges are selected from the ranks of active politicians, civil servants, and academia.[416] All the judges must have official legal training.[417] Judges have generally not been representative of Germany's geographical regions,[418] but the religious groups are more equally represented.[419]

## 5.3.3 Powers

More power was afforded to the German Federal Constitutional Court than to any

---

[407] See in general Asmal op cit (n 356) 320; Olivier 'Die Duitse Konstitusionele Hof: 'n Riglyn vir 'n Nuwe Suid-Afrikaanse Bestel?' 1992 *TSAR* 667; Clark 'The Selection and Accountability of Judges in West Germany: Implementation of a *Rechtsstaat*' (1988) 61 *Southern California LR* 1795 at 1826–9 for other summaries of the selection, composition, and the jurisdiction of the court. The importance of the selection process for the 'efficacy and integrity of the constitutional Bill of Rights' is stressed by Beatty 'The Rule (and Role) of Law in a New South Africa: Some Lessons from Abroad' (1990) 109 *SALJ* 408 at 424. As will become clear below, the selection process, the procedural rules adopted by the court, and the effect of the court's decisions form an integral part of constitutional interpretation.

[408] Article 4 *BVerfGG*.

[409] Article 3 *BVerfGG*.

[410] Article 4 *BVerfGG*.

[411] See art 5 *BVerfGG*, art 7 *BVerfGG*. Selection by Parliament confirms the political nature of judicial review in Constitutional Court systems. See Motala 'Independence of the Judiciary, Prospects and Limitations of Judicial Review in terms of the United States Model in a New South African Order: Towards an Alternative Judicial Structure' (1991) XXIV *CILSA* 285 at 310. Motala, whilst recognizing the political nature of constitutional interpretation, wants to see judges on the Constitutional Court isolated from political pressure.

[412] Kommers *Constitutional Jurisprudence* 25. The seats on the court seem to be divided between the two major political parties. The CDU and SPD each gave the FDP a seat. Despite this arrangement, the two-thirds requirement for selection still encourages the selection of compromise candidates. See Schlaich op cit (n 356) 32.

[413] Von Brünneck 'Constitutional Review and Legislation in Western Democracies' in Landfried (ed) *Constitutional Review and Legislation* (1988) 225. Not all the judges are members of a political party. The horse-trading between the parties is not continued within the parties as the leadership of the political parties has succeeded in isolating itself from the rest of the party structure in this area of political decision-making. See Kommers *Judicial Politics* 114.

[414] See Kommers *Constitutional Jurisprudence* 19.

[415] Article 94.1.1 *GG*; art 2.3 *BVerfGG*.

[416] Kommers *Judicial Politics* 143.

[417] Article 3 *BVerfGG*; Clark op cit (n 407) 1802–6; Schlaich op cit (n 356) 29. Landfried 'Constitutional Review in the Federal Republic of Germany' in Landfried op cit (n 413) 149 argues that judges with experience in the legislature have shown themselves to be less activistic than the professional judiciary and, especially, less activistic than legal academics.

[418] See Blair op cit (n 391) 19. The high mobility of German people after World War II renders statistics relating to the representation of the regions on the court senseless.

[419] Kommers *Judicial Politics* 150. The strong value-orientated approach of the court in its early years is sometimes linked to the relatively stronger representation of Catholics on the court during that time.

previous court[420] and the court has not hesitated to utilize its powers to the fullest extent, even when this has meant confrontation with the other branches of government.[421] The powers of the court are normally divided into the following categories:

1   **Protection of the politico-constitutional order embodied in the Constitution**   The FCC decides on the constitutionality of political parties[422] and the exercise of individual rights.[423] The FCC further plays a most important role in impeachment procedures against the Federal President and Federal judges.[424]

2   **Supervision over elections and political representation**   The validity of election results are determined by the *Bundestag* itself. The FCC may, however, review the *Bundestag*'s decisions.[425]

3   **Resolution of conflicts relating to the horizontal and vertical distribution of state power**   Vertically, the public-law disputes among and within the Federation, *Länder*, and local government may be resolved by the FCC at the request by one of the parties to such disputes.[426] Horizontally, conflicts about the constitutional rights and duties of the highest Federal organs — the *Bundestag*, the *Bundesrat*, the President of the Federation, the Permanent Commissions of the *Bundestag*, and political parties[427] — can be dealt with by the FCC if requested to do so.[428]

4   **The place of international law in German law and whether rights and duties for German individuals are created by international law**[429]   This concrete review procedure differs from the abstract review of the legislation necessary to implement treaties. Implementing legislation needs to be reviewed before the ratification of treaties.[430] The latter procedure is aimed at preventing the embarrassment which would result if implementing legislation is declared unconstitutional after the ratification of treaties.

---

[420] See in general Olivier op cit (n 407) 670; Schenke '*Der Umfang der bundesverfassungsgerichtlichen Überprüfung*' (1979) 32 *NJW* 1321; Schlaich op cit (n 356) 1; Brewer-Carias *Judicial Review in Comparative Law* (1989) 203.

[421] The court must decide on all cases presented to it (Von Beyme op cit (n 334) 35; Wieland op cit (n 335) 349), but the court is not bound to specific time constraints. In the early 1950s the first senate of the court 'slept' on a request of the Adenauer government to consider the constitutionality of the Communist Party. The court clearly hoped that Adenauer would withdraw a complaint which was considered either as not justiciable or as politically unwise. In the process the court developed its own version of the 'political question doctrine'. As the second senate was more sympathetic to the Adenauer government, Adenauer threatened to remove jurisdiction for the case from the first to the second senate. This left the first senate of the court with little choice but to decide the matter and the Communist Party was declared unconstitutional in 1956. See 5 *BVerfGE* 85.

[422] Article 21.2.2 *GG*.

[423] Article 18 *GG*.

[424] Article 61 *GG* and art 98.2 *GG* respectively.

[425] Article 41 *GG* with art 48 *BVerfGG*.

[426] Article 93.1 *GG*. The FCC may decide on the compatibility of *Land* law with Federal law (art 93.1.2 *GG*) and disputes about the constitutional rights and duties of *Bund* and *Länder* (art 93.1.3 *GG*); public-law disputes within a *Land*, between *Länder*, and between *Länder* and the *Bund* may be referred to the FCC if recourse to another court does not exist (art 93.1.4 *GG*); *Land* law may even determine that all constitutional disputes have to be handled by the FCC (art 99 *GG*); *Länder* Constitutional Courts may only diverge from the opinions of the FCC or other *Länder* Constitutional Courts with FCC approval (art 100.3 *GG*); local governments may lodge a direct constitutional complaint if their right to self-government has been infringed (art 93.1.4b *GG*).

[427] Political parties may use this procedure only to the extent that they are claiming an infringement or imminent danger of their special constitutional status (68 *BVerfGE* 1 65).

[428] Article 93.1 *GG* (*Organstreit*); Schlaich op cit (n 356) 51.

[429] Article 100.2 *GG*.

[430] Article 59.2 *GG*. Indirectly the norms of the treaty are reviewed. See Schlaich op cit (n 356) 79.

5   **Concrete judicial review (*konkrete Normenkontrolle*)**   The FCC is the only court to decide on the constitutionality of the statutes of the Federal and *Länder* Parliaments.[431] A lower-court judge has to certify that s/he is convinced that the statute is unconstitutional and that the constitutionality of the legislative norm is material to the outcome of the decision.[432] The proceedings before the lower court are then stayed and the issue is referred to the Constitutional Court. The importance of concrete judicial review is that the legal and factual consequences of statutes often become clear only once the statute has been applied. In these proceedings the FCC reviews the constitutionality of only the norm referred to it by the ordinary judge, and not the whole statute. The particular norm is, however, reviewed against the whole of the Basic Law.[433] The FCC does not decide the original case, but only whether the specific statutory norm brought before it is constitutional.[434]

6   **Abstract review (*abstrakte Normenkontrolle*) of legislation**[435]   Federal and *Länder* legislation and regulations may be reviewed abstractly, i e without a real case having arisen, for compatibility with the Basic Law.[436] Applicants are limited to the Federal government, the *Länder* governments, or a third of the members of the *Bundestag*. The compatibility of *Land* law with Federal law may also be the subject of abstract review, but as potential conflict is mostly resolved through negotiation between *Bund* and *Länder*, this procedure is seldom used.[437] Once the request for abstract review has been made the FCC

---

[431] Article 100.1 *GG*. The separate treatment of constitutional and ordinary legal issues is of course the hallmark of the centralized Austrian or Constitutional Court system of review. This separate treatment should not be exaggerated. The ordinary courts must apply the Constitution, according to the doctrine of 'the radiating effect' of the Basic Law, in their specialized areas of jurisdiction, but ordinary judges may not declare legislation of any Parliament invalid. Ordinary judges may declare subordinate legislation and executive action invalid. Normal courts may also review all legislation which came into force before 1949 for constitutionality (art 100.1 *GG*; 2 *BVerfGE* 124 128). The problem with this arrangement was that only the FCC has the power to declare statutes invalid with binding affect on all other state organs (*ergo omnes* effect) and in the absence of the principle of *stare decisis* the decisions of the normal judges were only binding on parties to the disputes. The FCC later ruled (52 *BVerfGE* 1 17) that pre-constitutional statutes which had been confirmed (promulgated anew or considerably altered after the coming into existence of the Basic Law) by the post-constitutional legislature had to be submitted to the FCC in accordance with art 100.1 *GG*: normal concrete judicial review, in other words.

Schlaich op cit (n 356) 15 comes to the conclusion that there is little relief that the FCC can offer parties beyond that which ordinary judges offered them. A final and generally binding interpretation of the Basic Law further remains the prerogative of the FCC. Matters accepted by the FCC are matters which require a binding decision for reasons of legal certainty. See also art 126 *GG*; art 13.14 *BVerfGG*; Ipsen op cit (n 351) 112.

[432] The Constitutional Court has applied the requirements for access strictly. See Schlaich op cit (n 356) 93. In 67 *BVerfGE* 26 37 the court made clear that it will not tolerate the use of the mechanism for concrete review by interest groups or individuals who seek the abstract review of legislation but lack the standing to institute such proceedings.

[433] Article 80.2 *BVerfGG*; Schlaich op cit (n 356) 102; Geiger '*Das Bundesverfassungsgericht im Spannungsfeld zwischen Recht und Politik*' (1985) *EuGRZ* 404 regrets this development as it enables the FCC to determine other legal questions than the one(s) raised by the lower court.

[434] Müller '*Zur sogenannten subjektif- und objektiv- rechtlichen Bedeutung der Grundrechte Rechtsvergleichende Bemerkungen aus schweizer Sicht*' (1990) 29 *Der Staat* 33 at 36 suggests that the separate treatment of constitutional and ordinary legal issues may be counterproductive, especially when dealing with social problems of the magnitude of racial and gender discrimination. Müller argues that the effectiveness of the Civil Rights Act and the Equal Protection Clause in the US is partly due to the fact that one court can apply both to the same problem.

[435] Articles 76–79 *BVerfGG*. See generally Ipsen op cit (n 351) 107; Schlaich op cit (n 356) 115–25.

[436] Article 93.1.2 *GG*.

[437] Ipsen op cit (n 351) 118; Zeidler 'The Federal Constitutional Court of the Federal Republic of Germany: Decisions on the Constitutionality of Legal Norms' (1987) 62 *Notre Dame LR* 504 at 505.

must consider the issue,⁴³⁸ and, if it is in the public interest, may even continue to do so after the request for review is withdrawn.⁴³⁹

**7     Individual complaints (*Verfassungsbeschwerde*)**    Anyone is entitled to submit a complaint to the FCC alleging violation of their *Grundrechte* by public authorities.⁴⁴⁰ The complaint may be directed against administrative action, judicial decisions, and, if the requirements are met, also against statutes of the legislatures.⁴⁴¹ Complaints will only be considered if the infringement affects the complainant personally and if it is the direct and immediate consequence of a governmental act.⁴⁴² If a statute requires an executive act to impose direct injury to the complainant and this act has not yet been carried out (in other words, the statute is not self-executing), the FCC will not consider the complaint.⁴⁴³ Individual complaints against executive action will only be heard if the applicant has exhausted all alternatives, save where the issue is one of general importance, or where the applicant will suffer serious harm if s/he were to exhaust the alternative remedies.⁴⁴⁴

The consistent practice of the FCC to interpret the free realization of the individual's personality⁴⁴⁵ as amounting to a general freedom to act, and therefore as constituting personal liberty to be protected from all unlawful state interference, has expanded the scope of judicial review and the constitutional complaint mechanism considerably.⁴⁴⁶ This practice is tempered by the requirement that the complainant must assert the specific infringement of a *Grundrecht* before the FCC

---

⁴³⁸ The possibility to take unresolved political disputes on abstract review resulted in many controversial decisions of the court. As no principle of subsidiarity or political question doctrine applies, the court has little choice but to decide on the disputes referred to it for abstract review.

⁴³⁹ Brewer-Carias op cit (n 420) 210.

⁴⁴⁰ Article 93.1.4a *GG*; Cappelletti op cit (n 389) 261.

⁴⁴¹ This will, for example, be case if the statute forces the individual to make decisions resulting in consequences which would be difficult to rectify later (60 *BVerfGE* 360 372) or when a compelling state interest relating to legal certainty exists (65 *BVerfGE* 1 37). See also Ipsen op cit (n 351) 125; Asmal's observation (op cit (n 356) 317) that statutes most often are attacked with the constitutional complaint procedure is not correct in the German context — 95 % of constitutional complaints are directed against judicial decisions. See Kommers *Constitutional Jurisprudence* 32; Schlaich op cit (n 356) 125.

⁴⁴² Wieland op cit (n 335) 336; Schlaich op cit (n 356) 135.

⁴⁴³ This requirement explains why such a high proportion of the FCC's decisions are concerned with the constitutionality of judicial decisions. The constitutionality of the executive action in terms of the statute are often the real reason for the case before the ordinary judge. The constitutional complaint mechanism is then used to 'appeal' against the outcome of the original case on the basis that the ordinary judge's decision infringed a *Grundrecht* of the complainant. The constitutionality of the statute is then reviewed indirectly by the FCC.

⁴⁴⁴ Article 90.2 *BVerfGG*. The principle of subsidiarity, which essentially means that the FCC is a last and extraordinary alternative to existing relief available, is used increasingly to limit access to the court. See Schlaich op cit (n 356) 146f; Schenke *Verfassungsgerichtsbarkeit und Fachgerichtsbarkeit* (1987) 15.

⁴⁴⁵ Article 2.1 *GG* has been interpreted as a general catch-all freedom. See Rautenbach & Watney 'Oorsig van die Reg op Vrye Vergadering in die Federale Republiek van Duitsland' 1990 *TSAR* 641 at 642; Giesen 'From Paternalism to Self-determination to shared Decision-making' 1988 *Acta Juridica* 107 at 108 for an explanation in the context of the patient's right to be informed of the consequences of medical treatment; Zimmermann op cit (n 380) 186 argues that art 2.1 *GG* protects the decision to commit suicide.

⁴⁴⁶ Since 6 *BVerfGE* 32 36; Ipsen op cit (n 351) 128. See Schlaich op cit (n 356) 11. The constitutional complaint became a mechanism for the control of the application of norms, because all unlawful state action is an infringement of the free development of the individual's personality because of the *lack of due process*. Moreover, *legislation* which is merely procedurally (or materially) defective can be considered an infringement of art 2.1 *GG* (42 *BVerfGE* 20 27). Such legislation remains the exception, and because of the difficulties associated with showing direct and personal injury resulting from legislation the majority of complaints are not directed against statutes but against judicial decisions. According to the FCC (56 *BVerfGE* 90 107), every *judicial* infringement of a right without legal basis infringes art 2.1 *GG*. Every incorrect application of ordinary law is potentially such an infringement, but the FCC only admits complaints which assert an infringement of 'specific constitutional law' or a 'specific *Grundrecht*'. See Schlaich op cit (n 356) 13, 126, 166f.

will review unlawful actions of the administration or the judiciary under the individual complaint procedure.[447] The criteria for accepting cases remain vague and leave room for manipulation by the court.[448]

Constitutional complaints come mostly from rank-and-file citizens and in principle the constitutional complaint is free of charge.[449] The complainants have no right to legal assistance and most approach the court themselves.[450] Individual complaints are screened by a committee of three judges and, if passed, the complaint is entertained by the full senate.[451] The senate accepts the complaint only when it raises a constitutional point which needs clarification or when the complainant stands to suffer unavoidable and serious harm if consideration is refused.[452] The decisions of the committee and the senate concerning admissibility are taken without hearing and the reasons for the refusal to consider the complaint need not be given.[453] The applicant is in practice always informed of the legal point which led to the rejection of his/her complaint.[454]

### 5.3.4 *Procedure and evidence*

The court's procedure has a nature of its own.[455] The court may determine facts by any means it finds appropriate.[456] The court has on occasion gathered empirical evidence — mostly by requesting expert reports (*Gutachten*) — and has engaged in rational prognosis. And, although there are rules relating to the formal joining of third parties to the process, the court will, as a matter of course, solicit the opinions of all the relevant political players in the matter.[457] The court will therefore not

---

[447] Article 90.1 *BVerfGG*.

[448] Extensive interpretation of the *Grundrechte* led to more access to the court, which was tempered with restrictive interpretation in the area of standing. The court disclaims supervision (7 *BVerfGE* 198 207) over the interpretation and application of ordinary law, but the effect of its decisions contradicts the disclaimer. See Schlaich op cit (n 356) 168; Wieland op cit (n 335) 338; Von Brünneck op cit (n 413) 232.

[449] Article 34.1 *BVerfGG*. If the complaint is not accepted, a fee of DM1 000 (R2 000) — or by abuse of the constitutional complaint system a fine of up to DM5 000 (R10 000) — may be levied (arts 34.2 and 4 *BVerfGG*). See Säcker op cit (n 348) 75.

[450] Kommers *Constitutional Jurisprudence* 17; Häberle op cit (n 319) 71 sees a popularization of rights and the Constitution in this development. The constitutional complaint in the Constitutional Court system seeks to achieve the ideal that every citizen knows and is able to enforce his/her rights and therefore takes part in the development of the Constitution. See Blaauw 'Alternatives to Military Service' (1989) 5 *SAJHR* 240 at 242.

[451] Article 93b.1 *BVerfGG*. According to Kommers *Constitutional Jurisprudence* 16, only 3 % of complaints survive the scrutiny before the committee. The committee may also sustain complaints which are either clearly valid, or concern matters already decided by the FCC (art 93b.2 *BVerfGG*).

[452] Article 93c *BVerfGG*.

[453] Most complaints are denied on the basis that they are clearly unjustified or inadmissible (art 24 *BVerfGG*). See Kommers *Constitutional Jurisprudence* 22.

[454] See Wieland op cit (n 335) 339; Olivier op cit (n 407) 670. The access to the FCC had to be restricted for the court to deal with the roughly 3 000 individual complaints and the fifty other briefs it gets each year. The US Supreme Court deals with its 4 000 briefs (10 % appeals and the rest cert-petitions) in a slightly different way: the court may refuse to entertain a *certiorari* petition on the ground that it is not important enough to consider (Gusy op cit (n 322) 54). Whereas the Supreme Court, therefore, decides primarily on issues which should be cleared up in the public interest, the FCC, as the only constitutional tribunal, tries to fulfil the function as the primary protector of individual rights as well. This function has become an increasing headache for the court. The introduction of the objective and subjective importance of the complaint by art 93c *BVerfGG* (see above, n 452) should be seen in this context. According to Korinek '*Verfassungsgerichtsbarkeit im Gefüge der Staatsfunktionen*' (1981) *VVDStRL* 34, the FCC nowadays sees its role similar to that of the US Supreme Court in that its decisions set general guidelines for the legal system; in contrast the Austrian court concentrates strictly on the individual case. Schlaich op cit (n 356) 163 welcomes this development.

[455] 32 *BVerfGE* 288 291.

[456] Article 26 *BVerfGG*.

[457] See Schlaich op cit (n 356) 42.

necessarily base its reasoning on the arguments presented by the parties. The court has shown a tendency to evaluate all the relevant arguments, including all the methods of interpreting the Basic Law.[458] Oral argument is seldom entertained by the FCC.[459]

The court does not have to defer to the facts as determined by the legislature. This second-guessing of legislative facts by the court has, of course, clear implications for the doctrine of separation of powers and the relationship between democracy and judicial review.[460]

Before a matter is considered by the full senate a detailed opinion (the *votum*) is prepared by one of the judges — the reporter. The *votum* is then used as the basis for the decision.[461] The reporter can, depending on his/her ability and credibility in the court, exercise considerable influence via the *votum*.[462] This is especially so since a strong feeling still prevails among the judges that one can arrive at the 'right' decision (in the sense of the 'best' and not the lowest common denominator type of consensus) through extensive deliberation.[463] Persuasion is therefore more important than voting. The process of decision-making and the selection process further encourage moderation as extreme viewpoints cannot be advocated if a judge hopes to gain consistent approval of his/her *vota*.[464]

Dissenting opinions were allowed for the first time in 1970 and they remain the exception to the rule.[465] The civil-law tradition that judges should only apply and not make law plays no role in the Constitutional Court and therefore cannot explain

---

[458] Cf the US Supreme Court, which tends to rely more on the arguments presented to it by the parties. See Bungert *'Zeitgenössische Strömungen in der amerikanischen Verfassungsinterpretation'* (1992) 117 *Archiv des Öffentlichen Recht* 71 at 94.

[459] Kommers *Constitutional Jurisprudence* 29. Mahrenholz *'Verfassungsinterpretation aus praktischer Sicht'* in Schneider & Steinberg (eds) *Verfassungsrecht zwischen Wissenschaft und Richterkunst* (1990) 53 at 55 claims that oral argument has had great significance despite being allowed in only a few instances.

[460] In an interesting study Philippi *Tatsachenfestellung des Bundesverfassungsgerichts* (1971) argues that the court's fact-finding has in no way been inferior to that of the legislator. Moreover, the court does not necessarily have less time to spend on considering issues than the legislator. The advantage of judicial fact-finding has been the firm grounding of opinions in reality. The disadvantage is that the court may duplicate work already done by the legislator. A more mainstream view is that of Scheuner *'Der Umfang der bundesverfassungsgerichtlichen Überprufung'* (1974) 27 *NJW* 1321 at 1326. He argues that the FCC must only control legislative facts and prognosis where the essence of *Grundrechte* is endangered (otherwise the intensity of control should vary in accordance with the principle of proportionality), where the legislation is irreversible, and where Parliament itself is affected by such legislation (e g public finance of the political parties). Vogel *Das Bundesverfassungsgericht und die übrigen Verfassungsorgane* (1988) 182 states that the real facts, on which legislation rests, are thoroughly reviewed by the FCC, but the intensity with which legislative balancing and prognosis are reviewed varies according to the criteria developed in the *Co-determination* case (50 *BVerfGE* 290 333). Von Brünneck op cit (n 413) 230 claims that the court has been reluctant to the consider natural and social science data and will only entertain these data when presented to it by the parties. In South Africa judicial fact-finding was welcomed by Bila, Maleka, Mnisi, Molatedi & Mukhari 'A Rare Example of Sociological Jurisprudence and Judicial Realism in South Africa' (1989) 106 *SALJ* 595.

The gathering of empirical evidence and the making of prognosis can clearly be manipulated. The problem is neither avoided nor resolved by an extensive reliance on the principle of proportionality, which require the suitability, necessity and proportionality (in the narrow sense) of state action. Suitability requires extensive empirical research, necessity requires a prognosis as to whether the state has employed the 'mildest' means available, and proportionality (in the narrow sense) a determination as to whether the means are proportional to the ends achieved.

[461] Kommers *Constitutional Jurisprudence* 29.

[462] At 30.

[463] At 52.

[464] Von Brünneck op cit (n 413) 229.

[465] Article 30.2.1 *BVerfGG*. The dissenting opinion should be distinguished from the publication of the outcome of a vote on a decision or the reasoning in terms of art 30.2.2 *BVerfGG*; 90 % of the court's decisions remain unanimous. See Kommers *Constitutional Jurisprudence* 31.

the lack of dissenting opinions.[466] The belief in an objective 'right' decision by the judges is more illuminating: judges on the Constitutional Court distinguish between the process of constitutional interpretation, which they regarded as objective and capable of arriving at a 'right' decision, and the effects of the court's decisions, which they acknowledge to be of a political nature.[467]

### 5.3.5 *Effect of decisions*

The decisions of the FCC bind all the state organs of the *Bund* and the *Länder*.[468] In addition to binding the parties to the dispute and organs of the state, the decisions of the FCC also become law.[469] This provision is necessary — in the absence of the principle of *stare decisis*[470] — to ensure legal certainty and uniformity of interpretation and application of the Constitution by all levels and branches of government.[471]

Critics have argued that the preoccupation with certainty has caused inflexibility: the decisions of the court become almost impossible to change unless the court is prepared to correct itself. The FCC is not bound by its own decisions,[472] but a constitutional tribunal can obviously not ignore its previous decisions as easily as a normal court. Sudden and drastic changes may endanger the continuity of the whole political system.

The problem is that every time the court interprets the Basic Law the discretionary powers of state organs are necessarily limited.[473] Some writers have even expressed concern that the *erga omnes* effect of the court's decisions might be in breach of

---

[466] Professional German judges also accept the idea of judicial law-making, but their opinions remain very formal and abstract, and they display little doubts on the part of the judges. See H Köts 'The Role of the Judge in the Court-room: The Common Law and Civil Law Compared' 1987 *TSAR* 41; Cappelletti op cit (n 389) 263; Zimmermann op cit (n 356) 302; Clark op cit (n 407) 1835.

[467] Kommers *Constitutional Jurisprudence* 50. The problem is that the judges do foresee not only the legal but also the socio-political consequences of their judgments, and these consequences are taken into account when judges make decisions. See Korinek op cit (n 454) 38. Alternatively, the reason for unanimous decisions may be a perception that unanimous decisions will be accepted more readily by the public, precisely because the court is showing a united front. Häberle op cit (n 319) 25 welcomes dissenting opinions and argues that they can only increase the credibility of the court in the public's eyes. Dissenting opinions show that the arguments of the losing party were at least taken seriously and that the arguments of the minority, though rejected, may be accepted in the future. In this way the court contributes to the stability of the democratic process.

[468] Article 31.1 *BVerfGG*.

[469] Article 31.2 *BVerfGG*. See 47 *BVerfGE* 198 (the effect of the decision on the allocation of television time to political parties is binding on all political parties and all television stations). Decisions of the court will therefore also be binding on private persons and organizations.

[470] *Stare decisis* is sometimes seen in Germany as incompatible with the teleological method of interpretation which looks forward (hardly ever backwards) towards discovering the truth. For this reason the original intent of the framers is also less important than in the US. In the US the teleological argument is used less frequently (the 'structural argument' in the US context is a combination of the systematic and the teleological arguments). See Bungert op cit (n 458) 93. Cappelletti op cit (n 389) 263 argues that the absence of the principle of *stare decisis* explains why a system of diffuse judicial review would have been difficult to implement on the European continent: no mechanisms exist whereby the highest court has the final word.

[471] In one early case (36 *BVerfGE* 1 36) the court made all the grounds for its decision binding on the state. In general only the arguments which form the basis for the decision become binding. The distinction remains problematic. See Schlaich op cit (n 356) 255; Korioth '*Die Bindungswirkung normverwerfender Entscheidungen des Bundesverfassungsgericht für den Gesetzgeber*' (1991) 30 *Der Staat* 549 at 558.

[472] See 4 *BVerfGE* 31 38; 20 *BVerfGE* 56 86; 70 *BVerfGE* 35 53. In 2 *BVerfGE* 380 401 the court said that constitutional norms may undergo a change of meaning if new facts emerge or if known facts appear in a different context or with different significance.

[473] Korioth op cit (n 471) 552.

separation of powers.[474] The court responded and, in a radical departure from its prior decisions,[475] it declared in an *obiter dictum* in 1987 that the legislature is not bound by FCC decisions, but is only bound by the Constitution itself.[476] Nothing therefore prevents the legislature from re-enacting the same or a similar provision after it has been found unconstitutional by the court. In such a case the legislature obviously carries the responsibility of justifying its dissent from the court's decision, and the court will then reconsider the matter. The advantage of this ruling is that it spreads the potential for innovation to the legislative branch and it stops the Constitution from stagnating. The *obiter dictum* has had little impact and in the immediate future the status and the persuasive power of the court will probably still ensure adherence to its decisions.[477]

Formally, a finding of unconstitutionality means the norm is void *ex tunc*,[478] but the court has avoided the drastic consequences of such decisions by creating a variety of alternatives.[479] All of these initially looked like efforts at judicial restraint, but all show potential for increased court manipulation over the legislature. These alternatives are:

- Nothing prevents the court from enumerating the legal consequences of its decision and the manner of their execution in detail.[480]
- The FCC rarely declares a whole statute unconstitutional and void. The unconstitutional provisions can normally be separated from the rest of the statute

---

[474] See Wischermann *Rechtskraft und Bindungswirkung verfassunggerichtlicher Entscheidungen* (1979) 38. Wischermann argues that art 31.1 *BVerfGG* must be interpreted restrictively to mean that the decisions of the FCC is binding only on the parties to the dispute. He further argues that the structure and the procedures adopted by the FCC are not suited for the function of law-making. Häberle op cit (n 319) 100 argues that separation of powers (art 20.2 *GG*) is a dynamic concept which shifts with the function of the court. The internal organization of the court is in turn dependent on and determined by its functions. According to Häberle, the court has adapted its internal structures extremely well to its functions.

[475] 1 *BVerfGE* 14 37; 19 *BVerfGE* 377 392; 36 *BVerfGE* 1 36.

[476] 77 *BVerfGE* 84 103. All organs of the state are, in other words, interpreters of the Constitution (see also 62 *BVerfGE* 1 39). The decisions of the FCC take precedence only in relation to the determination of the constitutionality of completed state action.

[477] In 69 *BVerfGE* 112 115 the Second Senate of the FCC committed itself to the traditional position which makes the reasons for the court's decisions binding on the legislator and the latter is therefore prevented from re-enacting invalidated norms (*Normwiederholungsverbot*). Cf Heun *Funktionell-rechtliche Schranken der Verfassungsgerichtsbarkeit: Reichweite und Grenzen einer dogmatischen Argumentationsfigur* (1992) 58–60, who argues that the decisions of the court do not have constitutional rank themselves. The court cannot amend the Constitution by its decisions. The *Rechtsstaat* principle and art 79.1 *GG* disallow any change to the Constitution other than by the prescribed procedure. This means that the court may only void legislation with reference to the Constitution and not, as the constitutional legislator, on the basis of 'political' grounds. Moreover, the court may always change its decision, but it may never change the text of the Constitution. Heun therefore supports the First Senate's decision and argues that although reasons for a decision need to be given for *Rechtsstaat* considerations and to ensure control over the court, these reasons have no higher status than ordinary judge-made law. The French Constitutional Court seems to avert the problem by giving very brief explanations for its decisions.

[478] The operation of art 79 *BVerfGG* drastically reduced the *ex tunc* effects of a declaration of unconstitutionality. This provision saves most legal acts, based on the unconstitutional provision, from being void themselves. Article 79 *BVerfGG* therefore tends to resolve the conflict between legal certainty and substantive justice in favour of the former. See Schlaich op cit (n 356) 206–8.

[479] See in general Vogel op cit (n 460) 214–57; Gusy op cit (n 322) 182–222.

[480] Article 35 *BVerfGG*. The court has either given instructions to the legislator or has spelled out the consequences of the invalidation itself. See 55 *BVerfGE* 100 113; 68 *BVerfGE* 155 173. There is clearly less of a separation of powers problem in these cases, as the court determines how the legislator should handle the *consequences* of unconstitutional state action. It seems more fair that the court and not the legislator should address the consequences of the latter's unconstitutional effort. See Zeidler op cit (n 437) 519. The court may give a preliminary judgment in cases of pressing public interest (art 32.2 *BVerfGG*).

without forfeiting the meaning of the statute. In such cases partial unconstitutionality is ordered.[481]

- The court has on occasion declared legislation constitutional, and yet appealed to the legislature to address a threat to the constitutionality of the legislation. Mostly this decision is used when legislation may become unconstitutional because of changing circumstances.[482]

- Since the change in the Federal Constitutional Court Act in 1970 the FCC may declare legislation unconstitutional (*Verfassungswidrig*) without declaring it null and void.[483] In these cases the legislative norm is not voided, but the legislature is called on to rectify or supplement the (unconstitutional) legislation. In principle such legislation may not be applied, but the court may, for reasons of legal certainty, decide to allow the continued operation of the unconstitutional provision[484] or it may put an interim regulation of its own in place until a new legislative regulation is promulgated. This kind of decision, which is mostly the result of the court's desire to preserve the discretion of the legislature, may be prompted by a variety of circumstances: when crucially important legislation (e g tax laws) would be rendered illegal if the court was to decide that the legislation was void;[485] when nullification of the legislation would restrict the legislative discretion to such an extent that it would become difficult for the legislature to deal with a complex situation or fulfil its constitutional duties;[486] and when benefits are conferred in an unequal way because of the exclusion of particular group(s).[487]

---

[481] The potential for ignoring the intention of the legislator is as great with a declaration of partial unconstitutionality as it is with interpretation in conformity. See in general 61 *BVerfGE* 149 206. In 65 *BVerfGE* 1 the court partly voided a census statute for infringing the right to 'informational self-determination'. The right is derived from art 2.1 *GG* with art 1.1 *GG* and it forms part of the personality rights of the individual. The right to informational self-determination does not imply a right of control over or a property interest in personal data, but data processing must be organized by the state in a way which respects personal autonomy. This means that the individual must know who, what, when, and how data about him/her will be used. See also 35 *BVerfGE* 202 (court prohibited the showing of a television drama about a notorious crime on the grounds that it infringed a convict's personality rights and the public's interests in the resocialization of criminals). See in this regard Schwartz 'The Computer in German and American Constitutional Law: Towards an American Right of Informational Self-determination' (1989) 37 *Am J Comp L* 675; Zeidler op cit (n 437) 508; Pieters 'Social Fundamental Rights in National Constitutions' (1987) 2 *SAPR/PL* 68 at 76; Gerber '*Die Rechtssetzungsdirektiven des Bundesverfassungsgerichts*' (1989) 16 *Die Öffentliche Verwaltung* 698 at 702.

[482] See 16 *BVerfGE* 130 (population shifts led to a constitutional challenge of election laws on the ground that they did not reflect the population properly; the court decided that the situation was still tolerable as far as the previous election was concerned, but had to be addressed by the legislator before the next election; in this case the court had no choice as the elections laws could only be rectified by the 'unconstitutionally' elected legislator); 52 *BVerfGE* 1 39 (small gardens in cities, used during the war to produce food, were rented by tenants at a nominal rate; as the function of the '*Kleingarten*' became one of leisure for their tenants, existing restrictions overburdened the property of owners in unconstitutional way); 54 *BVerfGE* 11 36 (inequalities regarding taxation of civil servants' pensions resulted because of the gradual increase of their benefits). If one accepts that a constitutional situation can become unconstitutional, then such decisions do not present problems, but the truth of the matter is that the reason for future unconstitutionality is almost always already there at the time of the decision.

[483] Articles 31.2 and 79.1 *BVerfGG*.

[484] Cf 72 *BVerfGE* 330 422.

[485] See 21 *BVerfGE* 12 42 (the court found that sales tax legislation was unconstitutional since it had a discriminatory effect on smaller businesses which did not have the ability to combine production and distribution; Parliament was given time to rectify the situation); 23 *BVerfGE* 242 257 (discriminatory valuation of taxable assets).

[486] See 73 *BVerfGE* 40 101 (the statute was not voided in order to keep the legislator's discretion intact). Heun op cit (n 477) 26 do not see these decisions as presenting problems as, he argues, they are instances where both the court and the legislator lack the sufficient factual basis to determine the consequences and effects of the regulation. A declaration which would void the statute *ex tunc* is inappropriate as the consequences, which might lead to the declaration of unconstitutionality, have yet to materialize.

[487] See 13 *BVerfGE* 248 260; 18 *BVerfGE* 288 301; 66 *BVerfGE* 100; 21 *BVerfGE* 329 (discrimination against widowers regarding social security benefits); 22 *BVerfGE* 349 359 (court held that voiding the legislation is of no

A declaration of unconstitutionality has been combined with appeals to the legislature, and the court sometimes added ultimata and detailed instructions to the legislature.[488] On occasion the court devised interim regulations[489] and threatened judicial handling of the situation in the event of legislative inaction.[490] These decisions have become increasingly controversial as it is argued that they interfere with the legislature's discretion to rectify the unconstitutional situation itself.[491]

- Interpretation in conformity with the Constitution (*verfassungskonforme Auslegung*) is frequently practised by the court. This entails that if more than one interpretation of legislation is possible, the court should choose the constitutional alternative(s).[492] Interpretation in conformity grew from the presumption in favour of the constitutionality of legislation into a tool which expanded, at least potentially, the powers of the court. The danger is that the

---

assistance to the complainant, as it would merely mean that the benefit is now unavailable to everyone and not just to the complainant). Schlaich op cit (n 356) 210 argues that these cases are the only legitimate application of art 31.2 *BVerfGG* because the constitutional norm *is not void per se*, but only unconstitutional due to the absence of further norms which would eradicate the inequality. Schlaich argues that in cases outside the area of equality the court has to decide whether the existing unconstitutional legislation is preferable (more constitutional) to no legislation. If so, the court will have to allow the unconstitutional situation to continue for the interim period until a new statutory regulation is promulgated. See, for example, 33 *BVerfGE* 303 347. The court found that admission of students to university without any legislative basis would be even more unconstitutional than the (existing) unconstitutional legislative regulation.

[488] 15 *BVerfGE* 337; 16 *BVerfGE* 130; 35 *BVerfGE* 79; 39 *BVerfGE* 169 194; 40 *BVerfGE* 296 329; 65 *BVerfGE* 1; 73 *BVerfGE* 118.

[489] See 39 *BVerfGE* 1 2 (abortion); 48 *BVerfGE* 127 184 (conscientious objection); 73 *BVerfGE* 40 102 (finance of political parties). An interim regulation was handed down on 28 May 1993 with the court's decision to invalidate the existing abortion regulation.

[490] The Basic Law commands that the same legal regulations should apply to legitimate and illegitimate children (art 6.5 *GG*) and equality between the spouses in the marriage should be achieved. In both instances the court first reminded the legislator and gave it time to fulfil the constitutional commands (illegitimate children: 8 *BVerfGE* 210; 17 *BVerfGE* 280; 25 *BVerfGE* 167 173; equality between the spouses: 3 *BVerfGE* 225). On both occasions the FCC threatened to instruct lower courts to implement equal treatment directly. Lower courts did exactly that with regard to equality between the spouses between 1953 and 1958. Thus, although the court is seldom in the position to implement its own decisions, especially in a civil-law system, in the field of equality between the spouses the court seemed to have done exactly this. Cf the similar tactics of the Indian Supreme Court and the US Supreme Court in the second *Brown v The Board of Education* (349 US 294 (1954)) decision. See Zeidler op cit (n 437) 513.

[491] The court seems to be far less worried about legislative compliance with its decisions than it was before. Cf the court's earlier response to slow or inadequate legislative compliance — for example, 25 *BVerfGE* 167 173 in connection with the position of illegitimate children — to the strong emphasis on legislative discretion in 77 *BVerfGE* 84 103 (also 77 *BVerfGE* 170 214; 79 *BVerfGE* 174 202; 79 *BVerfGE* 311 343). The *obiter dictum* in 77 *BVerfGE* 103 could even be interpreted as an invitation to the legislator to disagree with the reasoning of the court. This means that the court will engage in little more than a serious 'conversation' with the legislator when it uses this kind of admonitory decisions. This 'conversation' might be in conflict with the *Rechtsstaat* provision. The court's non-confrontational attitude is probably the result of concerns about court interference with the legislator's function as well as the enhanced status of the court. Generally speaking, legislative compliance with the decisions of the court has not been a problem (but cf the compliance problems with the court's rulings on state funding to political parties: 20 *BVerfGE* 56; 24 *BVerfGE* 300; 52 *BVerfGE* 63; 69 *BVerfGE* 92; 73 *BVerfGE* 1; 73 *BVerfGE* 40). It should further be remembered that lower courts can also refuse to co-operate with the FCC: they may refuse to implement the decisions of the court, but they may also refuse to refer cases to the FCC. Such divergences appear to exist concerning the interpretation of art 14 *GG* (property guarantee) where the ordinary courts seem to be more protective of property than the FCC. See Schneider '*Verfassungsinterpretation aus theoretischer Sicht*' in Schneider & Steinberg (eds) *Verfassungsrecht zwischen Wissenschaft und Richterkunst* (1990) 52. The constitutional complaint mechanism has proved helpful to overcome resistance of the ordinary courts since individuals may directly approach the Constitutional Court when the lower courts infringe a fundamental right by an incorrect interpretation or application of the Constitution. The principle of *Verfassungsorgantreue* (comity towards other constitutional organs of the state) could also be helpful in this regard. See in general Schenke *Die Verfassungsorgantreue* (1977).

[492] See in general Müller *Die Rechtsprechung des Bundesgerichts zum Grundsatz der verfassungskonformen Auslegung* (1980); Betterman *Die verfassungskonforme Auslegung: Grenzen und Gefahren* (1986); Ebsen *Das Bundesverfassungsgericht als Element gesellschaftlicher Selbstregulierung: eine pluralistische Theorie der Verfassungsgerichtsbarkeit im demokratischen Verfassungsstaat* (1985) 90; Schlaich op cit (n 356) 229

court may diverge from the intention of the legislature in its effort to save the statute from unconstitutionality.[493] For this reason the court has became increasingly careful not to reshape the normative content of legislation.[494] Problems are exacerbated when the effect of the court's decision is not only to provide a constitutional interpretation but also when its interpretation becomes binding on all those who apply the law.[495] Alternatively, the court may declare a particular interpretation of the law to be unconstitutional and therefore prohibit lower courts from interpreting the legislation in such an unconstitutional way.[496]

- Related to *verfassungskonforme Auslegung* are two techniques employed by the court. In the *Saarland* judgment the court said that even if the statute in question did not completely conform with the Basic Law, under the circumstances it was acceptably in comformity and the statute should therefore be upheld.[497] The court has also considered the unchallenged exercise of power as having given a constitutional norm a specific content and purpose. The exercise of power would thus become constitutional over time even though there might have been serious doubts about the original exercise of the power.[498]

---

distinguishes *verfassungskonforme* interpretation from Constitution-orientated interpretation. The latter entails that the court interpret legislation by taking the norms of the Constitution into account. The rationale is: if the needs of the legal community, the nature of the case, and legal-ethical considerations may be taken into account for interpreting legislation, why should the Constitution itself not be considered?

[493] In 2 *BVerfGE* 266 a German, who left the Soviet-occupied zone, was refused residence in West Germany by a West German official in terms of a discretion conferred to the latter by art 1 of the Act (*Notaufnahmegesetze*). According to art 1 of the Act, the discretion of the administration was almost unlimited, but the provision was re-interpreted by the FCC into a right to entry which could be limited only in terms of art 11.2 *GG* (the limitations of freedom of movement in the Basic Law). The court found (at 272) that 'all Germans, including those living in the Soviet-occupied zones, enjoy freedom of movement' (art 11 *GG*). See also 4 *BVerfGE* 7 22; 8 *BVerfGE* 274 324; 33 *BVerfGE* 52 83; which appear to be transgressing the limits of interpretation in conformity as well.

[494] 54 *BVerfGE* 277 299: interpretation in conformity must stay within the framework of the text of the legislation and the fundamental decisions, values, and goals of the legislator may not be changed. Gerber op cit (n 481) 705 argues that every decision — also the invalidation of legislation — gives some normative direction and therefore shapes the legislative will.

[495] Gusy op cit (n 322) 217. Cf Zeidler (an ex-President of the Constitutional Court) op cit (n 437) 509 and Geiger op cit (n 433) 403, who feel that the FCC provides only a (constitutional) interpretation and nothing prevents ordinary courts from applying other (constitutional) alternatives.

[496] 40 *BVerfGE* 88 94; Schlaich op cit (n 356) 231 states that a *verfassungskonforme* interpretation has the same binding effect as the rest of the FCC's decisions. It is difficult to imagine a lower court diverging from an interpretation proposed by the FCC. Again, the potential for undermining the system of separation of powers is inherent in the method of interpretation. *Verfassungskonforme* interpretation is even more controversial when it is employed by the lower courts to avoid referring matters to the FCC in terms of art 100.1 *GG* (concrete review). The danger of qualifying or even negating the intention of the legislator becomes manifestly clear. On the other hand, the ordinary courts are required, in accordance with the doctrine of the 'radiating effect' of the Constitution, to take the Constitution into account when interpreting ordinary law. Indeed, some constitutional principles such as proportionality and legality are so important for areas such as administrative law that every interpretation seems like one in conformity with the Constitution. See Müller *Der Positivität der Grundrechte: Fragen einer praktischen Grundrechtsdogmatik* (1990) 143. Heun op cit (n 477) 29–30 argues that interpretation in conformity is not problematical as long as the wording or meaning of the norm is not changed. A slight divergence from the normative content might be preferable to nullification of the statute since the legislator retains the power, if it is unsatisfied with the court's interpretation, to repeal the legislation and promulgate something else. The objection to Heun's reasoning has been that it might be politically impossible for the legislator to repromulgate legislation.

[497] 4 *BVerfGE* 157 168f (the government tried to implement a treaty and the terms of the treaty were obviously not in the sole discretion of the government). See Blair op cit (n 391) 37.

[498] See 32 *BVerfGE* 145 155; 62 *BVerfGE* 1 39 (1983 adjournment of Parliament); Blair op cit (n 391) 39; Schneider op cit (n 491) 47.

- The exact status of the *obiter dicta* of the FCC remains unclear. They may in reality be as binding as the *ratio decidendi* of the decided case, and *obiter dicta* therefore present a further mechanism for the court to control the political process.[499]

## 5.4 Theories of *Grundrechte*

The literalist approach to the interpretation of rights was rejected in the early years of the court in favour of a value-orientated approach. As was stated above, some commentators blamed legal positivism for the lack of resistance to the abuses which occurred in the Nazi era.[500] The recourse to a value-orientated approach to constitutional interpretation immediately after World War II must be seen in this context.[501] Proceeding from the 'unity of the Constitution'[502] and the paramount importance of the principle of 'human dignity',[503] the FCC tried to develop an objective value order. The *Soraya* decision exemplifies this approach.[504] According to this decision, the judiciary has to uncover and realize the values which are inherent in the constitutional legal order. The act of recognition has some volitive elements, but is primarily value-orientated.[505]

Recognizing rights as embodying values in itself gave little guidance to judicial decision-making or the democratic process. The objective value order did, however, serve as a springboard for the development of functions for the *Grundrechte* beyond the negative state-directed protective function. An objective value-deciding dimension to each fundamental right has been recognized. The objective dimension of the right in turn formed the basis for the development of the doctrine of indirect *Drittwirkung* and the influence of the Constitution on ordinary law, the development of duties on the state to protect extra-textual limitations of rights, and the functional and institutional methods of interpretating rights.

An overextension of the Constitution and the process of judicial review can be observed in this development. As a result the emphasis in constitutional theory shifted from the meaning of the Constitution to the functions of judicial review.

In this section theories of interpreting fundamental rights will be discussed. The

---

[499] Gusy op cit (n 322) 255 refers to them as '*urbiter et orbiter apodicta*'. The court may note that new regulation of the subject-matter is needed (71 *BVerfGE* 224 229) or may indicate which changes need to be effected in detail (40 *BVerfGE* 296 329). See further Mahrenholz in Landfried op cit (n 413) 173. Schenke op cit (n 420) 1329 argues that the danger is that the FCC resorts to positive action with *obiter dicta*. Therefore, instead of reacting to action of other branches, the court prescribes to the other branches how to deal with situations over and above the one under consideration. Especially dangerous is the situation where the court (36 *BVerfGE* 1 36) determines which parts of its decision are *rationes decidendi* and consequently binding on the other branches.

[500] Zimmerman op cit (n 356) 299; Häberle op cit (n 319) 94. Denninger op cit (n 396) 1013 states that the traditional German respect for the '*Staat*' was shattered and legal positivism did not influence governmental action (including the courts) till the end of the 1950s.

[501] Zajadlo op cit (n 380) 209; Hiemstra 'Suid-Afrika Terug in die Wêreld langs die Weg van die Regsstaatbeginsel' 1985 *TSAR* 3.

[502] 1 *BVerfGE* 14 32.

[503] Häberle 'Menseregte as Tema van 'n Demokratiese Staatsregteorie' (1982) 7 *TVR* 5 at 7.

[504] 34 *BVerfGE* 269.

[505] At 287. At the same page the court goes on to say that 'the court must close gaps in the legal order with reference to practical reasoning and the consolidated and general conceptions of justice in the community'. This sentence should be seen in the context of the court's development of a new right: a 'personality' right in the case. See Mischke op cit (n 395) 255; Denninger op cit (n 396) 1019.

theories of *Grundrechte* are systematic beliefs about the general character, the normative aims, and the substantive reach of the *Grundrechte*.[506] The danger inherent in these theories is that if a commitment to a certain theory precedes the process of interpretation, the process of interpretation takes place abstractly and therefore without reference to the specific facts of the case under consideration. *Grundrechte* could in this way become legal philosophical niceties rather than the basis for judicial decision-making. The discussion of the theories will be followed in the next section by of an analysis of the theories of constitutional intepretation. The emphasis will then shift to the consequences of a particular theory of interpretation for the democratic process.

### 5.4.1 *Grundrechte as negative defensive rights (Abwehrrechte)*

In the classical liberal tradition rights were seen as pre-state natural zones of freedom for the individual.[507] Within his or her rights the freedom of the individual was unlimited and the power of the state to interfere with the liberty of the individual was, in principle, limited.[508] The consequences of this theory for the interpretation of rights are as follows. First, the state does not have the responsibility to make the exercise of rights possible. Individuals in society have the liberty to make use of their rights if they can and choose to do so.[509] Secondly, *Grundrecht* freedom is guaranteed freedom without any specific purpose. The motivations or the objectives of users are not relevant for defining the content and the limitations of the rights.[510] Thirdly, legal institutions created by the state, ordinary law, and other human rights do not bear any relation to the content of a *Grundrecht* and are merely complementary insurance for the general and legally undefined freedoms.[511] Fourthly, rights are guarantees of freedom from *state* interference.[512] The horizontal operation of rights is excluded. The theory therefore rests on a public–private (state–society) dichotomy. Finally, rights are subjective guarantees and not objective state goals. Individuals must therefore at all times be able to enforce their rights through independent courts against the state.

In nineteenth-century Germany the concept of the formal *Rechtsstaat* became the constitutional expression of this theory of rights and the *Rechtsstaat* principle still forms the constitutional basis for the theory underpinning the Basic Law.[513] The classical theory of rights continues to inform much of the FCC's jurisprudence. In

---

[506] Böckenförde '*Grundrechtstheorie und Grundrechtsinterpretation*' (1974) 27 *NJW* 1529; Starck '*Über Auslegung und Wirkungen der Grundrechte*' in Heyde & Starck (eds) *Vierzig Jahre Grundrechte in ihrer Verwirklichung durch die Gerichte* (1990) 10.

[507] See in general Ossenbühl '*Die Interpretation der Grundrechte in der Rechtsprechung des Bundesverfassungsgerichts*' (1976) 29 *NJW* 2100.

[508] At 2101; Böckenförde op cit (n 506) 1531.

[509] Böckenförde op cit (n 506) 1531.

[510] At 1530.

[511] At 1531.

[512] Ossenbühl op cit (n 507) 2101.

[513] The formal *Rechtsstaat* developed in reaction to the absolutist state. In contrast to the rule of law, the *Rechtsstaat* principle did not seek to limit state power through the democratic process, but rather subjected the ruler to the law. See Blaauw op cit (n 361) 89f; Van Wyk 'Suid-Afrika en die Regstaatsidee' 1980 *TSAR* 152 at 155; Stern op cit (n 344) 246; Luhmann op cit (n 387) 29. After World War II the formal *Rechtsstaat* principle was supplemented by the material *Rechtsstaat* principle. The latter implies that the state is bound to higher values and that individual freedom may only be realized within the value system founded by the Constitution. The material *Rechtsstaat* principle goes further than the formal *Rechtsstaat* and encapsulates the essence of modern constitutionalism. See Van Eikema Hommes '*De Materiële Rechtsstaatidee*' 1978 *TSAR* 42; Corder & Davis 'The Constitutional Guidelines of the African National Congress: A Preliminary Assessment' (1989) 106 *SALJ* 633; Van Wyk op cit

the *Co-determination* case the court made it clear that *Grundrechte* are first and foremost individual rights and that the function of *Grundrechte* as objective principles lies in the strengthening of their consequences for the individual.[514] The court stressed that in the development of functions for rights over and above the protection of individual freedom sight may not be lost of the original meaning of rights.[515]

The danger of an exclusive reliance on the classical theory has not been ignored. The twentieth century witnessed individuals becoming increasingly dependent on the state and power constellations in society itself for the realization of their freedom.[516] The classical theory provides no answers to these dependencies. On the contrary, the imbalances of power within society are to an extent the product of the theory itself: different use was made of freedom.[517]

### 5.4.2 *Grundrechte as value-deciding norms*

The value-orientated approach views rights not only as subjective protection for individuals[518] but also as objective norms which express values.[519] The Basic Law erected an objective value order.[520] This *Grundrecht* order forms the underlying framework for the state and society — for the political and the legal order.[521]

---

(this note) 156; Blaauw op cit (n 361) 85. Most importantly, individual freedom is guaranteed in the material *Rechtsstaat* subject to art 20.3 *GG*: *Grundrecht* freedom is guaranteed for all Germans in an equal way. Individual freedom is thus limited by the equal freedom of others. See also art 2.1 *GG*; Kirchhof op cit (n 398) 459. In general it can be said that the dichotomy between freedom and equality is handled in German constitutional law by equating freedom with proportional limitations on freedom and equality with the prohibition of irrational differentiation by the state. See Kirchhof op cit (n 398) 462.

[514] 50 *BVerfGE* 290 337 ('*in erste Linie individuelle Rechte*'); cf 33 *BVerfGE* 303 329 ('*wesentlicher Teilaspekt*' of *Grundrecht* protection).

[515] See also 49 *BVerfGE* 89 (construction of nuclear plants). The court is obviously concerned that the negative, subjective, freedom dimension of rights has became meaningless owing to the recognition of the objective dimension of rights. At the bottom of the court's concern is a conception of constitutionalism which sees rights as freedom zones of individuals which are so important that their protection may not be left to the whims of parliamentary majorities.

[516] Calliess op cit (n 397) 1338.

[517] See 4 *BVerfGE* 7 15; 8 *BVerfGE* 274 329 ('individual is tied in the community'); Böckenförde op cit (n 506) 1532; Kirchhof op cit (n 398) 459; Habermas *Strukturwandel der Öffentlichkeit* (1990) 326 illustrates how the re-thinking of rights was necessitated by new social conditions existing under the social welfare state.

[518] The objective dimension of *Grundrechte* has, despite the *dictum* of the FCC in the *Co-determination* case (supra), independent operation. The separate objective character of rights, which is in no way connected to a strengthening of the subjective defensive aspect of rights, made it possible for the court to developed functions for *Grundrechte* over and above the negative defensive, but also created considerable uncertainty as to the content and reach of the individual rights. See Jarass 'Grundrechte als Wertentscheidungen bzw objektivrechtliche Prinzipien in der Rechtsprechung des Bundesverfassungsgerichts' (1985) 110 *Archiv des Öffentlichen Recht* 363 at 366.

[519] The FCC describes the objective dimension of rights as 'value-deciding norms' or 'objective principles'.

[520] Schenke op cit (n 358) 655 sees the roots of the value order in the integration theory of Smend. Others see the influence of natural law in the value order. See Diestelkamp '*Die Verfassungsentwicklung in den Westzonen bis zum Zusammentreten des parlamentarischen Rates (1945–1948)*' (1989) 42 *NJW* 1312 at 1318; Venter 'The Western Concept of Rights and Liberties in the South African Constitution' (1986) XIX *CILSA* 99 at 102. Häberle op cit (n 319) 94n10 argues that there is a difference between the value-order and natural-rights theories. The court is as closed to natural-rights arguments as it is open to value-order arguments. Cf 1 *BVerfGE* 14 61; 3 *BVerfGE* 225 232; 10 *BVerfGE* 59 81. The value order does not rank constitutional principles abstractly, constitutional values all having, in principle, the same weight (3 *BVerfGE* 225 231), but balancing in individual cases may lead to a ranking order of values. See Richter & Schuppert *Casebook Verfassungsrecht* 2 ed (1991) 5, who differ from Gusy op cit (n 322) 61, who sees, at least from the *Elfes* decision (6 *BVerfGE* 32), a recognition by the court of a ranked value order in the Basic Law itself, with arts 1 and 20 *GG* at the top.

[521] The framework set up by the Constitution binds the organs of the state formally and substantively and the Constitutional Court has to determine the content of the framework: Korinek op cit (n 454) 41. The question is whether the Constitution also, as Häberle op cit (n 319) 123 states, sets the framework for *society*. Jarass op cit (n 518) 373 argues that the foundational nature and meaning of the *Grundrechte* for the whole of state and society has been clear ever since the inception of the idea of rights, but positivism prevented the judicial recognition of rights as objective principles.

The basic formulation of this approach is the *Lüth* decision, where the court stated:

> '[T]he Basic Law has erected, by the inclusion of a section on fundamental rights, an objective value order and has strengthened the effect of the *Grundrechte* in this way. The central meaning of the value order lies in the free development of the human personality and its dignity in the social community. The value order, as a fundamental decision of the Constitution, is valid for all areas of the law; the legislature, the executive and the judiciary are informed by the directives and impulses of the value order.'[522]

Not only is an objective value order founded but also each individual *Grundrecht* has an objective dimension which operates in all areas of law.[523] Every right therefore contains both a subjective defensive freedom dimension against the state and an objective normative value decision valid for all areas of law.[524]

The consequences of the acceptance of the theory of rights as objective values by the FCC are far-reaching. The objective working of the *Grundrechte* forms the basis for every *Grundrecht* theory which goes beyond the purely negative defensive theory of rights.[525] The recognition of an objective dimension of rights is not necessarily a radical departure from the ideas underlying the classical conception of rights, but can be seen as the extension thereof. The classical approach sees rights as the protection of those historically vulnerable areas of individual and societal freedom against state interference. The individual's dependence on the state for the realization of his/her rights and the individual's need for protection from societal infringements of his/her rights is addressed by the objective dimension.[526]

The court has recognized that the objective dimension is dependent on legislative realization and has therefore been careful not to overturn legislation which seeks to realize the objective guarantees,[527] in some instances even where such legislation has resulted in the infringement of individual rights in the process.[528] Whereas the Constitution guarantees the negative subjective dimension clearly and extensively, the bare minimum of the objective dimension is justiciable. The complications for the democratic process resulting from the recognition of the objective dimension in the courts are obvious: individuals will now be able to force the state, more particularly the legislature, into taking positive action by relying on their

---

[522] 7 *BVerfGE* 198 205; and see 49 *BVerfGE* 89 141.

[523] The extent to which the court has recognized an objective dimension varies considerably from *Grundrecht* to *Grundrecht*. Whereas the objective elements of such rights as human dignity, corporal integrity, family and marriage, and freedom of information, press, art, and conscience have been well developed, the objective dimensions of freedom of association, assembly, equality, and self-realization have hardly featured in the jurisprudence of the court. To a certain extent the discrepancies can be attributed to textual differences: art 1 *GG* requires not only that the state refrain from infringing human dignity but also that the state protect human dignity. See Jarass op cit (n 518) 369; Currie op cit (n 360) 237.

[524] The distinction between the objective and subjective dimensions of rights is, in itself, not satisfactory. *Grundrechte*, as defensive rights, are not always merely protective of individual freedom, but may at the same time be functional to a whole range of institutions of state and society and the objective dimension of the *Grundrechte* may, in some circumstances, be enforced subjectively. See Jarass op cit (n 518) 368.

[525] Alexy '*Grundrechte als subjektive Rechte und als objektive Normen*' (1990) 29 *Der Staat* 49; Jarass op cit (n 518) 367.

[526] Generally speaking, duties to protect and indirect *Drittwirkung* were developed to protect the individual from societal infringement of his/her rights. Rights to participation and institutional guarantees were developed to address the increasing dependence on the state. See below and Häberle op cit (n 319) 66.

[527] Known as *Ausgestaltung* in Germany.

[528] Jarass op cit (n 518) 394.

*Grundrechte*.[529] The FCC has therefore shown restraint in recognizing subjective claims of individuals in respect of their objective guarantee.[530]

The following areas of *Grundrecht* operation are all the direct result of their objective working:

### 5.4.2.1 The 'radiating' effect (or *Drittwirkung*[531])

This effect of the *Grundrechte* derives from the objective working of the *Grundrechte*. As the Constitution is law of a higher order, ordinary law may be reviewed for possible unconstitutionality.[532] Not only may rules of ordinary law not conflict with the *Grundrechte* and other constitutional norms but all rules of ordinary law must be interpreted and applied in the light of the Basic Law.[533]

The FCC tried to give greater clarity to the intensity and the extent of the radiating effect. The court has emphasized the discretion of the *legislature* (*Gestaltungsspielraum*) in shaping the ordinary law, a discretion which is limited by the Constitution, especially by the *Grundrechte* and the constitutional principles of art 20.1 *GG*. The *executive* is bound to the Constitution and legislation, but an essence of administrative discretion is protected from legislative interference.[534] In reviewing the decisions of the *ordinary courts* the FCC has emphasized that it is not an institution of 'super review'.[535] Initially it stated that it will not interfere with the interpretation of ordinary law (in other words, law other than the specific constitutional law over which the court has exclusive jurisdiction) as long as the interpretation is not informed by a misconception of the meaning of a *Grundrecht* or where the interpretation itself infringes a *Grundrecht*.[536] The test has been substantially modified and the intensity of judicial scrutiny now seems to be proportional to the degree to which the lower-court decision has affected *Grundrecht* protection.[537]

---

[529] See Böckenförde '*Grundrechte als Grundsatznormen. Zur gegenwartigen Lage der Grundrechtsdogmatik*' (1990) 29 *Der Staat* 1 at 16. Rights may be used to undermine the system of separation of powers and democratic governance if individuals are allowed to use their rights to procure state action. Problems are exacerbated by an extensive interpretation of the objective value order, which transforms all state tasks into *Grundrecht* realization. See Müller op cit (n 434) 42. Alexy op cit (n 525) 68 argues that the subjective claims to procure positive state action are valid as long as there is a clear connection with a subjective *Grundrecht* of the complainant. The proper organization of the media may therefore be enforced subjectively as long as the individual's freedom of speech and freedom to information is at stake. It is again interesting to compare the German position with that in the US. According to Currie op cit (n 360) 252 the US Constitution, as interpreted by the Supreme Court, recognizes only negative defensive rights, while the FCC talks explicitly of positive duties on the state. Yet the effects of the two courts' decisions do not differ radically. This conclusion led Currie to doubt the effectiveness of 'positive *Grundrechte*' for the creation of a social welfare state.

[530] Jarass op cit (n 518) 394. It is not entirely inappropriate therefore to draw an analogy between the objective dimension of rights in Germany and the use of directive principles of state policy in the Indian Constitution.

[531] According to Böckenförde op cit (n 529) 10, the doctrines of direct and indirect *Drittwirkung* are no more than an attempt to come to grips with the radiating effect of the *Grundrechte*.

[532] Article 1.3 *GG*.

[533] 7 *BVerfGE* 198 205.

[534] 49 *BVerfGE* 89 125; Richter & Schuppert op cit (n 520) 6.

[535] 7 *BVerfGE* 198 207.

[536] 30 *BVerfGE* 173 188 (Mephisto formula). Examples of FCC interference: where the ordinary judge did not recognize that a *Grundrecht* was relevant for the interpretation or application of the ordinary law (71 *BVerfGE* 162 178) or had a wrong conception of the meaning, especially the extent or significance of *Grundrecht* protection (70 *BVerfGE* 297 317); objectively untenable and therefore irrational decisions of ordinary courts conflicting with art 3.1 *GG* will be reviewed (62 *BVerfGE* 338 347); distortions of the intention of the legislator conflicting with the *Rechtsstaat* principle and therefore art 2.1 *GG* (61 *BVerfGE* 68 73). See Schlaich op cit (n 356) 173; Schneider op cit (n 491) 48.

[537] 67 *BVerfGE* 213 223; 76 *BVerfGE* 143 161; Schlaich op cit (n 356) 179; Böckenförde op cit (n 529) 9; Ossenbühl op cit (n 507) 2102. See in general Schenke op cit (n 444) for an analysis of the relationship between the Constitutional Court and the ordinary courts.

The problematical relationship between the interpretation and the application of ordinary law and the interpretation of the Constitution is the inevitable result of the system of centralized judicial review. In order to elucidate upon that relationship the influence of the court's interpretation of the Basic Law in five areas of ordinary law is now discussed.

- Private law

The private-law codes were to some extent influenced by the same values which later found constitutional expression in the Weimar Constitution and the Basic Law.[538] The introduction of the Basic Law nevertheless led to meaningful changes in private law.

Although the starting point is that private law should conform to the Basic Law,[539] the meaning thereof is not entirely clear. Four levels of influence can be distinguished. First, the Constitution guarantees certain institutions of ordinary law such as marriage and property. Secondly, the Constitution, especially the *Grundrechte*, has inspired ordinary law reform. Thirdly, the state should take the *Grundrechte* into consideration when balancing positions of individuals in private law. Fourthly, there is the direct and indirect *Drittwirkung* of the *Grundrechte*.[540] These four levels will now be separately discussed.

First, the essence of the right to property is protected from state interference.[541] The legislature may therefore not destroy the institution of private property. Under the Basic Law nothing of this sort happened and litigation revolved around the definition and limitation of property by the legislature. So, for example, an amendment to copyright legislation which allowed the inclusion of small extracts from already published literary and musical works in collections to be used for educational purposes was struck down by the court as no compensation was paid to the authors and this infringed their property rights.[542]

Secondly, despite private law having developed its own equality order and prohibitions against abuse of rights,[543] the general equality provision has been the

---

[538] In Germany a pattern roughly similar to that of France was followed: a civil code was followed by a code on criminal procedure which was then completed by the administrative law code. See Hesse *Verfassungsrecht und Privatrecht* (1988) 8. In nineteenth-century Germany constitutional law never influenced private law. Private-law principles of fairness and justice were, however, developed to realize values which would find constitutional expression only much later. In this way, lawyers argued, what is known today as constitutional-law matters, developed via private law. This argument is sometimes used to deny the necessity of the horizontal operation of the *Grundrechte*. See Ossenbühl op cit (n 507) 2102; Gotz '*Die Verwirklichung der Grundrechte durch die Gerichte im Zivilrecht*' in Heyde & Starck op cit (n 506) 39. The influence of the constitutional law should not be overstated. See, for example, the article by Zimmermann & Du Plessis 'Grondtrekke en Kernprobleme van die Duitse Verrykingsreg' 1992 *Acta Juridica* 57. The law of enrichment has not been 'constitutionalized' at all and balancing remains entirely of private-law nature.

[539] Article 20.3 *GG*.

[540] The levels of influence are set out by Gotz op cit (n 538) 41.

[541] 24 *BVerfGE* 367 389.

[542] 31 *BVerfGE* 229. The essence of marriage (31 *BVerfGE* 58 69), personality (65 *BVerfGE* 1 41), and freedom to contract (8 *BVerfGE* 274 328; 12 *BVerfGE* 341 347; 65 *BVerfGE* 196 211) are protected. In the *Joint Income Tax* case (13 *BVerfGE* 290) a heavier tax burden on married couples — compared with two individuals filing separately — was declared unconstitutional. The FCC said that this form of taxation was not only discriminatory against women but also detrimental to the institution of marriage.

[543] Gotz op cit (n 538) 66 argues that art 3.1 *GG* (general equality provision) influenced and stabilized a parallel development in private law.

most important inspiration for law reform.[544] The position of illegitimate children was found to be in need of reform.[545] After the period (set by art 117.1 *GG*) laid down for the legislature to abolish legal discrimination against women expired the court took the initiative[546] and used the special equality provision[547] in conjunction with the special protection for the marriage[548] to bring about substantial reforms in family law.[549] After this period of judicial activism (1953–8) the legislature intervened and promulgated new regulations in the field.[550]

Few private-law norms were found to be repugnant to the Basic Law and the Basic Law contains few provisions which demand private-law reform with such clarity that the court could implement the reforms itself. The third level of influence is therefore of paramount importance. Normally the legislature does not intervene in private-law areas to infringe upon the liberties of subjects, but rather it interferes to balance the rights and freedoms of subjects. This balancing remains of a private-law nature, albeit private law as transformed by the Basic Law. Two models of balancing are used: the legislative demarcation of freedom spheres, and the judicial demarcation of those spheres.[551] The judicial model controls the law of delict. More specifically, conflicts between personality rights and the right to exercise occupation and freedom of speech, the press, and art are handled by the court.[552] Where property had to be weighed against other freedoms, legislation is the only way to strike the

---

[544] The Basic Law's demands to the legislator to reform private law remain mostly too vague to be justiciable. Equality — knowing no degree of realization — constitutes the exception and has therefore been influential. The general equality clause (art 3.1 *GG*) is supplemented by special equality provisions: art 3.2 *GG* (gender), art 6.5 *GG* (illegitimate children), art 9.3 *GG* (unions) and art 28.1 *GG* (equality of the vote at *Länder* and local levels). Judicial scrutiny becomes much stricter when legal consequences are attached to personal characteristics. This explains the courts' activism in the field of illegitimate children and equality between the spouses. Outside the area of personal characteristics the equality clause operates less effectively: the state merely has to show that its differentiation does not rest upon irrational (*Willkürverbot*) grounds. The general equality clause has therefore had a broad influence, but with fluctuating intensity. Concerning the general equality clause see 2 *BVerfGE* 266 281 ('factually and clearly inappropriate statutory measures in relation to the actual situations which they are supposed to regulate'); 4 *BVerfGE* 144 155 ('what is essentially equal should not arbitrarily be treated unequally, nor should essentially unequals arbitrarily be treated equally'); 25 *BVerfGE* 101 105 ('where there is no clearly relevant ground for statutory differentiation'). See Kirchhof op cit (n 398) 461.

[545] See 8 *BVerfGE* 210; 17 *BVerfGE* 280; 25 *BVerfGE* 167 173. In the last case the court clarified that art 6.5 *GG* is a binding constitutional command on the legislator to rectify the existing (legal) inequalities of illegitimate children.

[546] In 3 *BVerfGE* 225 the FCC held that equality was one of the characteristics (the others being heterosexuality, monogamy, consensus, living together, maintenance duties) which defines the essence of marriage.

[547] Article 3.2 *GG*.

[548] Article 6.1 *GG*.

[549] See, for example, 6 *BVerfGE* 55 81 and Hübner 'Basic Problems of Codification and Modern Tendencies in the German Civil Law' 1977 *TSAR* 22 at 25; Van Wyk 'Matrimonial Property Systems in Comparative Perspective' 1983 *Acta Juridica* 53 at 55.

[550] Some say that the court's handling was in some ways superior to that of the legislator. See Hübner op cit (n 549) 25.

[551] Gotz op cit (n 538) 78. It should, however, be noted that the legislator remains bound to the *Grundrechte* and the Basic Law as a whole when it legislates in private-law areas and the FCC may of course review such legislation. Heun op cit (n 477) 61–6 acknowledges that this means that the FCC's control does extend to all areas of law, but this does not necessarily give the court's control a different quality. In other words, no greater degree of interference by the court over legislative decision-making results from indirect *Drittwirkung* than the degree of interference presupposed by the classical function of the court.

[552] It was decided in the *Soraya* decision (34 *BVerfGE* 269) that the general personality right — art 1.1 *GG* with art 2.1 *GG* — is a fixed part of the private legal order. The personality rights are absolute 'subjective' rights — along with others such as copyright, patent rights, and property — which are protected against intrusion, not only from the state but from everyone. See Venter 'Die Publieke Subjektiewe Reg — 'n Voorraadopname' (1991) 54 *THRHR* 349 at 356. The difference between personality rights and the other absolute 'subjective' rights is that the content and the limitations of the latter rights have been defined by the legislator. As no legislation regulates, an

balance.⁵⁵³ When the legislature intervenes it should be remembered that it has a wide discretion when balancing *Grundrecht*-protected positions in private-law areas, and judicial control over such legislation is reduced to considerations of proportionality and equality.⁵⁵⁴ In general it must be said that the FCC is reluctant to control private-law norms directly. It appears to prefer to infuse general private-law clauses with the meaning of *Grundrechte* relevant to the particular situation (in other words, indirect *Drittwirkung*).

Fourthly, direct *Drittwirkung* means that the *Grundrecht* operation is extended to cover the relationships between private legal subjects. The *Grundrechte* themselves then form the basis for the rights and duties of individuals in private law and other areas of ordinary law.⁵⁵⁵ The dominant opinion in German law rejects direct *Drittwirkung*. It is argued that the well-refined private-law principles, developed over a long time and based upon fairness, should not be abrogated in favour of the vague norms of the Constitution.⁵⁵⁶ Indirect *Drittwirkung* is accepted. According to this doctrine, the subject of *Grundrechte* has the legitimate expectations not only that *all law* conforms to the Constitution but also that *all law* will be interpreted in the light of the *Grundrechte*. A court which refuses to interpret private-law norms, for example, in this light infringes not only the objective value norm but also, as an organ of the state, the court infringes the *Grundrecht* of the individual by the improper interpretation of private law.⁵⁵⁷ The emphasis naturally shifts to the interpretation and application of general clauses of the codes such as 'undue hardship', '*boni mores*' and 'the public order'.⁵⁵⁸ It is further accepted that judges may use the *Grundrechte* to fill gaps in areas of ordinary law.⁵⁵⁹

---

infringement of a personality right will become clear only once all the interests are weighed against one another. An infinite extension of personality rights is therefore feared by Hübner op cit (n 549) 278.

For another example of judicial demarcation of freedom spheres in private law, see Robinson op cit (n 387) 249: the *Grundrecht* of the parents to care for their children (art 6.2 *GG*) is, according to the dominant opinion, not in conflict with the right of the child to realize him/herself (art 2.1 *GG*). The parents may decide for the child because, and for as long as, the latter cannot decide for him/herself.

⁵⁵³ Article 14.1.2 *GG* demands legislative definition and limitation of property. So, for example, in the area of lease property was balanced against the social state principle.

⁵⁵⁴ Gotz op cit (n 538) 79.

⁵⁵⁵ Müller op cit (n 496) 37 argues that the question of *Drittwirkung* must be distinguished from a situation where the court is the organ of public power which infringes the *Grundrecht*. Therefore, in the case of a painter who is sued in delict for insulting somebody by his/her work, the court infringes the freedom of the artist (*Kunstlerfreiheit*) with a money fine; *Drittwirkung* doesn't come into the picture. In the case of the eviction of a tenant for putting up election posters on the landlord's property, the infringement comes essentially from the landlord and the issue should be resolved by private law. In the latter case the court is asked only to confirm an infringement which already took place.

It is interesting to compare *Shelley v Kraemer* 334 US 1 (1948), where 'state action' was located in the decision of the court to enforce a restrictive covenant. This approach potentially implies that all legal relationships between individuals will be made subject to the principles of the Constitution. It has consequently not been followed in the US.

⁵⁵⁶ Implicit in the argument is that private-law norms are not as open — and therefore capable of being loaded with political content — as are constitutional norms. Hübner op cit (n 549) 27; Schenke op cit (n 358) 657; Hesse *Grundzüge des Verfassungsrechts der Bundesrepublik Deutschland* 18 ed (1991) 25.

⁵⁵⁷ 7 *BVerfGE* 198 206; cf Robinson op cit (n 387) 234. Earlier in his article (at 231) Robinson seems to be saying that *Grundrechte*, as value-deciding norms, do not provide any basis for individual claims.

⁵⁵⁸ Ossenbühl op cit (n 507) 2102. So, for example, a restrictive covenant will not be enforceable in Germany because the principle of equality infuses the *contra bones mores* requirement with meaning.

⁵⁵⁹ This, Böckenförde op cit (n 529) 10 argues, implicitly recognizes direct *Drittwirkung*. He further argues that where *Grundrecht* influence cannot be achieved via the interpretation and the application of the general clauses (indirect *Drittwirkung*), direct *Drittwirkung* becomes imperative. Direct *Drittwirkung* has been affirmed in Switzerland for a range of rights: see Müller op cit (n 434) 40. The acceptance of direct *Drittwirkung* by the Swiss court should be seen in the context of the system of diffuse/ordinary judicial review in Switzerland.

- Labour law

The freedom to form unions and employer associations (*Koalitionsfreiheit* — art 9.3 *GG*) is protected separately from the general right of association (*Vereinigungsfreiheit* — art 9.1 *GG*). *Koalitionsfreiheit* is the only *Grundrecht* which expressly orders *Drittwirkung*. Moreover, unions and employer associations (*Koalitionen*) are *institutionally* protected — from state interference and from each other — for the fulfilment of public functions. The state must therefore create a system wherein collective bargaining can fulfil the function of regulating labour relations. The *Koalitionen* must be able to regulate at least the essence of the collective agreement — the compensation of the worker — autonomously.[560]

The institutional nature and direct *Drittwirkung* of *Koalitionsfreiheit* should be distinguished from the operation of other *Grundrechte* in the employee–employer relationship.

The general principles underlying the decisions in the latter area are:

(i) Limitations of the *Grundrechte* of the worker are only permissible in the interest of fulfilling his/her obligations under the contract of service.
(ii) Limitations of the rights of workers may not extend further than necessary for the achievement of a work-related goal.
(iii) The essence of the worker's rights may not be denied, but must be seen in the context of the long-term relationship between the worker and the employer. The health of the worker is protected absolutely, but single infringements of some of the other rights may have to be tolerated by the worker.[561]

The consequences of an unconstitutional infringement of the worker's rights differ: the act of the employer can be declared invalid, equal treatment may be ordered, or the employer may be ordered to make compensation payments.[562]

The claims of workers to co-determination are necessarily in conflict with that of the owners of the business enterprise to undisturbed use of their property.[563] In 1976 the FCC was confronted by the problem when the Co-determination Act was promulgated.[564] On the constitutional level the tension was reflected in the ostensible dichotomy between property and the social state principle. In its decision the

---

[560] The court recognized that labour unions, without sufficient power to exercise pressure on the employer, have the *Koalitionsfreiheit*, but as they have no bargaining power, they cannot be trusted to make binding agreements (laws) on behalf of their members. The court compared the position of these trade unions with political parties which, because they did not pass the 5 % hurdle, cannot move into Parliament. See Ebsen 'The *Bundesverfassungsgericht* and Industrial Democracy after the Second World War' in Wellenreuther op cit (n 325) 462. Collective agreements can only become binding on outsiders to the bargaining process when the state ratifies them. *Koalitionsfreiheit* and democracy are balanced in this way.

[561] Gamillscheg '*Die Verwirklichung der Grundrechte durch die Gerichte in Arbeits- und Sozialrecht*' in Heyde & Starck op cit (n 506) 90.

[562] At 104.

[563] For background see O'Regan 'Possibilities for Worker Participation in Corporate Decision-making' 1990 *Acta Juridica* 113 at 125; Verloren van Themaat 'Property Rights, Workers' Rights and Economic Regulation — Constitutional Protection for Property Rights in the United States of America and the Federal Republic of Germany: Possible Lessons for South Africa' (1990) XXIII *CILSA* 53 at 58; Ebsen op cit (n 560) 453; Schuppert 'The Right to Property' in Karpen op cit (n 390) 108.

[564] 50 *BVerfGE* 290. Politically, the statute was an effort to democratize and legitimize the exercise of power in the private sphere. Shareholders tried to use their property rights and their rights of association to isolate themselves from having to account for their decisions. See Grimm op cit (n 362) 1310; Reese 'The Need for Democratic Consent for Private Property' (1976) IX *CILSA* 81; Verloren van Themaat op cit (n 563) 60.

court said that the Basic Law does not prescribe a particular economic system.[565] The court also accepted that the strength of constitutional protection of property is relative to the use of property. The greater the social connection and the function of the property, the greater the freedom of the legislature to limit property rights.[566] The court was not requested to decide whether equal representation on the controlling supervisory board is an unconstitutional infringement of the property rights of the shareholders, as no parity in representation was achieved by the 1976 Act. The chairperson of the supervisory board, with a deciding vote in the case of a deadlock, was elected by the shareholders and one of the workers' representatives on the supervisory board had to be a white-collar worker. This compromise was reached in Parliament and the outcome of the case was therefore no surprise: the Act was declared to be constitutional.[567]

- Social law

Social law has been influenced by the objective working of the social state principle. The standard definition of this principle is that the state is obligated to guarantee a dignified existence for all, to minimize the gap between the haves and the have-nots, and to control or eliminate relationships of dependence in society.[568] The social state clause incorporates the social welfare philosophy into constitutional law and sets limits to liberal aspirations of an autonomous society.[569]

The social state principle operates only objectively; it cannot form the basis of subjective claims by individuals.[570] The social state principle serves as an inspiration to the legislature and the government; judicial control is practically non-existent in so far as the principle operates *on its own* as a directive to the judiciary.[571] The social state principle is mainly concretized through legislation and the principle is consequently more dependent on the political process than any other.[572]

- Administrative law

There is no doubt that administrative law and action must comply with the Constitution and the *Grundrechte*.[573]

---

[565] 50 *BVerfGE* 290 337. Badura op cit (n 398) 494 distinguishes between the content and judicial enforceability of the social state clause and argues that the Basic Law founded a social welfare state, but that its realization is left to the legislator. It is in this sense that the Basic Law is economically neutral. Schneider op cit (n 491) 44 sees the economic neutrality in the lack of relevant concrete standards of the Constitution in this area.

[566] 50 *BVerfGE* 290 340. In general the court has been hesitant to interfere with legislative definition of the limitations on property in terms of art 14.1.2 *GG* (58 *BVerfGE* 300 336); Schuppert op cit (n 563) 110.

[567] See Klein 'The Parliamentary Democracy' in Karpen op cit (n 390) 164. The Act was adopted with no significant dissent. Häberle op cit (n 319) 143 feels that the degree of consensus amongst the political parties must have influenced the court's decision. Häberle argues that less scrutiny should be applied in cases where issues were thoroughly debated in Parliament and consensus was achieved.

[568] Kunig 'The Principle of Social Justice' in Karpen op cit (n 390) 189.

[569] Badura op cit (n 398) 492.

[570] 27 *BVerfGE* 253 283.

[571] See Mischke op cit (n 395) 255; Kunig op cit (n 568) 198. The decisive influence of the social state principle has been its use as a tool for interpreting and limiting *Grundrechte*.

[572] See 65 *BVerfGE* 182 193; Badura op cit (n 398) 494. It can be argued that legislation which implements the social state principle is constitutionally entrenched against changes by simple parliamentary majorities (see Kunig op cit (n 568) 194), but this would necessarily mean the end to legislative freedom to give content to social justice. Inadequate or out-dated legislative realization of the principle will be 'frozen' in the legal order. See Stern op cit (n 344) 248.

[573] Article 1.3 *GG*. See in general Schulze 'Notes on Judicial Review of Administrative Action in the Federal Republic of Germany' (1992) 7 *SAPR/PL* 290; Frowein 'Administrative Structures for the Protection of Human Rights' (1990) 53 *THRHR* 250. The 'radiating effect' of the *Grundrechte* is stronger in public than private law. See Schlaich op cit (n 356) 188.

In a democratic society the administration may place limitations on the use of *Grundrechte* only when it is authorized to do so by the legislature.[574] The *Rechtsstaat* principle implies that statutes have to define administrative powers clearly. At worst, vague legal terms should be interpreted by the administrative courts and not by the administration itself. The administration may, however, be given the discretion whether to use their powers or not. This discretion was found to be constitutional as it protects the individual from unnecessary interferences by the administration.[575]

- Criminal law and procedure

Criminal procedure has been shaped by the special constitutional procedural guarantees (arts 101–104 *GG*) and the *Rechtsstaat* principle.[576] The special guarantees are: recourse to impartial judges, the right to be heard, *nulla poena sine lege*, no double jeopardy,[577] and the right to a speedy trial.[578]

The *Rechtsstaat* principle, as the social state principle, is no basis *in itself* to substantiate individual claims.[579] The *Rechtsstaat* principle nevertheless formed the basis for the development of fair procedure. It has, for example, been decided that a functionally capable penal system tries to establish the truth, but not at the cost of treating the accused as the object of the criminal trial.[580] The effort has therefore been made to equalize the weapons of the accused (right to legal representation) and the state.[581]

Criminal law has been influenced by the development of duties to protect from art 1.1 *GG*. The state is under a duty to protect human dignity and, if necessary, it should employ the strongest means at its disposal — the criminal sanction — to this

---

[574] The greater the invasion of the individual's rights, the greater the need for legislative authority. See 41 *BVerfGE* 251 (*Länder* legislators should make all decisions regarding education); De Jager 'Geweld by Inhegtenisneming in die Duitse Reg' 1989 *TSAR* 24; Schuppert 'Self-restraint *der Rechtsprechung. Überlegungen zur Kontrolldichte in der Verfassungs- und Verwaltungsgerichtsbarkeit*' (1988) 24 *DVBl* 1191 at 1194.

[575] 9 *BVerfGE* 137 146; Sattler '*Die Verwirklichung der Grundrechte durch die Gerichte im Verwaltungsrecht*' in Heyde & Starck op cit (n 506) 127 at 132; Kirchhof op cit (n 398) 464 argues that legislators may delegate a discretion to the administration on grounds as vague as 'in the public interest' or 'on important grounds'. Kirchhof argues that a case-by-case application by an expert bureaucracy can be more advantageous to individual freedom than detailed legislation. Legislation should be geared towards the future and should therefore be as open and general as possible. The resulting wide discretion to the administration is the unavoidable result of the social welfare state where the administration must be able to react to constantly changing conditions. See Grimm op cit (n 362) 1309; Häberle op cit (n 319) 53.

[576] See in general Nehm '*Die Verwirklichung der Grundrechte im Prozessrecht und Strafrecht*' in Heyde & Starck op cit (n 506) 173; for the influence on civil procedure, see Schumann *Bundesverfassungsgericht, Grundgesetz und Zivilprosess* (1983).

[577] See De Jager 'Dubbele Blootstelling in die Duitse Reg' 1985 *TSAR* 161 at 246.

[578] A large proportion of constitutional complaints assert infringement of these '*Justizgrundrechte*'. See Schlaich op cit (n 356) 185.

[579] The *Rechtsstaat* and social state principles form the basis of the Basic Law's vision of the function of the state. Article 20.3 *GG* created a '*sozialer Rechtsstaat*' — a state which not only serves the freedom of the individual but also his/her welfare. See Stern op cit (n 344) 241 for a discussion of the interaction between the two concepts. The *Rechtsstaat* is often used with art 2.1 *GG* (free development of the personality) and social state with art 3.1 *GG* (general equality) to form the basis for individual claims.

[580] See 16 *BVerfGE* 194 (court-ordered puncture of a person's vertebral canal for the purpose of determining ability to stand trail invalidated).

[581] The state also provides legal representation in the US. The reasoning is, however, different: in the US the state may not deprive the subject of his/her liberty without due process of law.

purpose.[582] Duties were found on the state to prevent abortion[583] and to guard against terrorism.[584]

The constitutionality of lifelong imprisonment was also judged against the objective working of the right to life and human dignity.[585] The court held that such imprisonment can only be compatible with human dignity if the prisoner retained a realizable expectation of eventual release.[586]

The 'radiating effect' of *Grundrechte* has influenced ordinary law substantially, but it has by no means been the only consequence of the objective working of fundamental rights.

### 5.4.2.2 Duties on the state

The second consequence of the objective working of the *Grundrechte* has been the development of duties on the state to protect the individual from infringements of his/her rights. Some examples have been discussed above. The state is required 'to protect and promote the legal goods mentioned by the right and, in particular, to safeguard them against the unlawful infringement by others'.[587] Duties to protect developed primarily in connection with the rights to life and corporal integrity.[588] In the first *Abortion* case[589] the FCC decided that the measures employed to fulfil the state's obligation to protect life should be commensurate with the importance of the legal interest to be safeguarded. Under the circumstances it was found that, unless special eugenic, ethical, or social reasons exist (*Indikationen*) for the termination of the pregnancy, the criminal sanction remains the only effective deterrent which could relieve the state of its duty under the Basic Law to protect developing life.[590] The principle of proportionality was in effect applied by the court to find the means of protection inadequate, given the importance of the object to be protected.[591]

---

[582] See in general Herrmann 'Development and Reform of Criminal Procedure in the Federal Republic of Germany' (1978) XI *CILSA* 183.
[583] 39 *BVerfGE* 1.
[584] 46 *BVerfGE* 160. Because of the unpredictability of the threat the court could not order any specific state action in a case where the petitioner wanted to force the state to meet the terrorists' demands in order to secure the release of his father. The court held that the government has the responsibility to decide which steps should be taken.
[585] 45 *BVerfGE* 187.
[586] At 245. The decision led to the amendment of the Penal Code. The code now allows the court to suspend the remainder of a life sentence if: the offender has served 15 years, the gravity of the offence does not require that s/he stays in prison, and circumstances indicate that the attempt to find out whether the offender will lead a law-abiding life outside of prison is justified. Statistics indicate that the new regulation has not produced a significant increase in 'early' releases. See Van Zyl Smit 'Is Life Imprisonment Constitutional? The German Experience' 1992 *Public L* 263 at 273–4.
[587] 53 *BVerfGE* 30 57; Rautenbach & Watney op cit (n 445) 647.
[588] Article 2.2 *GG*; Böckenförde op cit (n 529) 12.
[589] 39 *BVerfGE* 1. See in general Kommers 'Abortion and the Constitution: The United States and West Germany' (1977) 25 *Am J Comp L* 255; Fabricius 'Aspects of the Abortion Reform in West Germany' (1976) 39 *THRHR* 72.
[590] The exceptions have virtually eroded the prohibition. Moreover, after re-unification a new bill was passed which legalizes abortion in the first three months after mandatory counselling. The operative part of this statute, para 218, was declared invalid and unconstitutional by the FCC on 28 May 1993. The court stated that abortion is in principle unlawful, but the state does not necessarily have to criminalize the decision of the mother to abort the foetus. The state's measures (mandatory counselling) were nevertheless found to be inadequate. One of the major consequences of the decision is that pregnant women will not be able to get financial assistance from medical insurance schemes for abortions as abortion was declared unlawful. A new law was passed by the German Parliament in May 1994 in response to this judgment.
[591] Starck op cit (n 506) 19; Böckenförde op cit (n 529) 13.

The jurisprudential effects of the *Abortion* case were tempered by the 'air traffic noise case'.[592] Although the duty to protect the individual from air noise was recognized as flowing from the right to corporal integrity, the court held that the other organs of the state, and not the court, have the primary responsibility to determine the manner in which this duty should be fulfilled.[593] In principle the FCC has recognized the subjective enforcement of duties to protect the individual.[594]

### 5.4.2.3 Extra-textual limitations

Duties to protect form the basis for the development of the third consequence of the objective working of fundamental rights: extra-textual limitations of *Grundrechte*. Once a duty to protect is recognized the legislature must limit the actions of third parties if they, in the exercise of their rights, infringe the objectively protected content of the *Grundrecht*.[595] In a value-bound order limitless rights are unthinkable.[596] Without legislative intervention the *general and abstract* limiting effect of the objective working of the *Grundrechte per se* — immanent or inherent limitations — is restricted to cases of existing duties to protect. So, for example, in the *Co-determination* case the court held that the workers' rights do not directly limit the property rights of the shareholders as there is no duty on the legislature to institute a system of co-determination.[597] In any event, the general rules relating to *Grundrecht* collisions also apply in these cases.[598]

The social state principle has further served as an important limitation on the *Grundrechte*, but it may not be recognized by courts without legislative intervention.[599] Legislative demarcation of *Grundrecht*-protected areas has therefore become imperative.

---

[592] 56 *BVerfGE* 54 (constitutional complaint against air traffic noise as being an infringement of the right to corporal integrity: art 2.2.1 *GG*).

[593] See 56 *BVerfGE* 54 80 (the court will only interfere in cases of manifest legislative neglect to fulfil the duty to protect, unless legal goods of the highest order are at stake); 53 *BVerfGE* 30 (state's duty to protect citizens against potential danger from nuclear plants); 49 *BVerfGE* 89 142 (the court held that the state's duty to protect depends on the nature, the immediacy of and the extent of the danger to, as well as the nature and rank of, the constitutionally protected goods). Heun op cit (n 477) 68–9 argues that as the court may only prohibit state action — and may not require the state to protect the *Grundrechte* of third parties in a positive way — the development of duties to protect cannot be accepted.

[594] 77 *BVerfGE* 170 214.

[595] Jarass op cit (n 518) 384.

[596] 28 *BVerfGE* 243 261; Häberle op cit (n 503) 8. The objective working of a *Grundrecht* may limit the freedom of individuals protected by another, or the same, *Grundrecht*. In these cases balancing needs to be undertaken in accordance with the principle of proportionality. This in turn has expanded the power of the court considerably. See Heun op cit (n 477) 10.

[597] 50 *BVerfGE* 290 349.

[598] 28 *BVerfGE* 243 261. The rules have been developed for concrete cases. *Grundrechte* do of course limit each other in concrete cases, but in such cases the court expresses a preference only within the context of the specific case. The weaker norm is forced into the background only to the extent logically and systematically necessary and the essence (*sächliche Grundwertgehalt*) of the weaker norm may under no circumstance be violated. See Bethge *Zur Problematik von Grundrechtskollisionen* (1986).

[599] In the social medical insurance scheme the socially weak are forced to join and to contribute according to their income, but they may then claim according to their needs. See Goerlich 'Fundamental Constitutional Rights: Content, Meaning and General Doctrines' in Karpen op cit (n 390) 64; Gamillscheg op cit (n 561) 118; Badura op cit (n 398) 494; Kunig op cit (n 568) 201.

### 5.4.2.4 Special relationships

Finally, the objective working of the *Grundrechte* makes them applicable to the so-called 'special relationships'.[600] The FCC decided that the *Grundrechte*, in principle at least, apply fully to these status relationships and that there cannot be any prior abstract limitation because of the nature of the relationship.[601] The *Grundrechte* of prisoners or students may therefore only be limited with specific legislation and in so far as is necessary to achieve the object of the special relationship in an orderly fashion.[602] The rights of civil servants are limited in a similar way.[603]

The impact of a recognition of the objective working of fundamental rights has been tremendous. The concern has been expressed that the value order is the first step in a process of interpretation which could mean that the *Grundrechte* would lose their subjective enforceability completely.[604] Critics have also argued that the objective guarantees mean that *Grundrechte* are protected according to predetermined criteria and may be exercised only in accordance with those criteria.[605] These criteria, it is argued, will to a large extent be determined by the cultural consciousness of the time and, more specifically, by the preferences of the deciding authority. This process relativizes rights with potentially disastrous implications for individuals and outsider groups.[606] With the acceptance of the value order it has also been argued that the legislature lost its ability to mould the legal order, as the task of the legislature became the execution of the Constitution under the supervision of the Constitutional Court.[607]

On a methodological level it has been suggested that the value order has remained so abstract and indeterminate that it has been hermeneutically unproductive.[608] Luhmann argues that the belief in *Grundrechte* as setting up a natural hierarchical order stops short of the vital question: the function of rights.[609] But, as will become clear in the discussion of approaches to constitutional interpretation, even a functional interpretation of rights leaves open several alternatives to the deciding

---

[600] The term 'special power relationships' was coined roughly a hundred years ago in administrative law to describe relationships of increased dependence of citizens on the state. The special relationship implies less freedom for the citizen as his/her freedom is determined with reference to the objective of the special relationship. See Stern op cit (n 326) 1377.

[601] 33 *BVerfGE* 1 9.

[602] Huber 'Safeguarding of Prisoner's Rights under the New West German Prison Act' (1978) 2 *SACC* 229 at 232. In 33 *BVerfGE* 1 4 the court found that free contact with the outside world was potentially dangerous for the object of the status relationship: the enforcement of the sentence. In this case letters of a prisoner were intercepted on the basis of a *regulation*. The court found that any encroachment on the *Grundrechte* of prisoners by the prison authorities needed *legislative* authorization, but no infringement of art 10.1 *GG* (privacy of mail) ensued as Parliament needed time to fulfil its obligations created by the *GG*'s objective value order. The 1976 Act resulted.

[603] Other special relationships include those between school authorities and pupils, and defence force and soldiers.

[604] Scheuner op cit (n 460) 1327.

[605] Böckenförde op cit (n 506) 1534.

[606] See below, 5.3.4.1.

[607] Not only is the legislator undermined but the burdening of the court with day-to-day political problems also undermines the court. See Gusy op cit (n 322) 69, 83.

[608] Ossenbühl op cit (n 507) 2107; Alexy op cit (n 525) 50.

[609] Luhmann says that constitutional interpretation will remain Aristotelian in nature as long as the essence of rights forms the main enquiry rather than the function of rights. See Luhmann op cit (n 387) 57–60 and the comment of Dieter Grimm in Landfried op cit (n 413) 169.

authority.[610] This realization led to the shift in emphasis from the functions of rights to the development of functions for judicial review.[611]

### 5.4.3 Functional approaches to the Grundrechte

The functional approaches to *Grundrechte* were also developed from an objective dimension of rights. These approaches try to tie the content of the *Grundrecht* to the function which the right is intended to fulfil.

#### 5.4.3.1 Democratic-functional

According to this theory, political rights, especially the communication freedoms, are given an elevated status when they are used with political motives. More protection is therefore afforded to politically relevant actions than to politically indifferent behaviour.[612] Political associations will receive more protection than private associations[613] and assemblies held with political motives will receive more protection than other assemblies.[614]

According to this theory, the democratic political process rather than individual freedom becomes the subject of *Grundrecht* protection.[615] The sense of the *Grundrechte* lies in their being constituent factors of democracy which shape the state.[616] The *Grundrecht* guarantees make the formation of the democratic will possible. *Grundrechte* belong to citizens in their capacity as members of the community and must be used as such.[617] The public function of rights legitimizes them and determines their content.[618]

The problem with the democratic-functional theory is that the freedom of the individual becomes relative and depends on the purpose of the individual's actions. The distinctions between political/non-political and public/private are further essential to this theory.[619] This raises the question whether these distinctions can and/or should be made.

#### 5.4.3.2 Social state-functional

The objective value order opened the door for seeing rights as directives or commands to the legislature. This in turn led to a re-interpretation of rights as demands imposed on the state. The point of departure is the acknowledgement that the social presuppositions for the exercise of freedom rights do not exist for the vast majority of the population and that the freedom rights are therefore merely empty shells.[620] Moreover, the real threat to individual liberty does not come from the state,

---

[610] Häberle op cit (n 319) 165.
[611] See 4 *BVerfGE* 157 168; 35 *BVerfGE* 257 261; 36 *BVerfGE* 1 14; 36 *BVerfGE* 342 356 (relationship with the *Länder* Constitutional Courts) and Schuppert op cit (n 574) 1191.
[612] Ossenbühl op cit (n 507) 2103; Böckenförde op cit (n 506) 1535.
[613] Political parties do receive more protection in the Basic Law than normal associations. See below, 371ff.
[614] Rautenbach & Watney op cit (n 445) 643; Klein *Die Grundrechte im demokratischen Staat* (1972).
[615] Böckenförde op cit (n 506) 1535.
[616] At 1534.
[617] See 14 *BVerfGE* 21 25.
[618] Böckenförde op cit (n 506) 1535.
[619] Ibid.
[620] Ibid.

but from society itself. The slogan 'from legal to real freedom' describes the motivation behind the theory. The individual is increasingly dependent on government performances and those performances are the actual presuppositions for the exercise of his/her rights.[621] The state must therefore establish the necessary social preconditions for the exercise of *Grundrechte*. *Grundrechte* are then called rights to state performances (*Leistungsrechte*).[622]

Two contexts in which the FCC has recognized the social state-functional theory will be discussed:

- In the *Numerus clausus* decision[623] the FCC said that the freedom dimension of *Grundrechte* is complemented by a guarantee of equal participation in government performances to the degree that the state advances culture or provides for social security.[624] The more the modern state provides for the social security and cultural advancement of its citizens, the more claims of citizens will be directed towards participation in such benefits.[625] In this case a student claimed, on the basis of art 3.1 *GG* read with art 12.1 *GG* and the social state clause, that a study place be made available for him in a particular area of study. The court refused to decide whether an individual may force the state to create a study place for him/her, as the court held that the assignment of existing study places was done in a fair manner. The individual's claim to participation can be rejected if existing facilities are utilized to the maximum. The court added that the individual's claim to participation was in any event limited to what the individual can reasonably expect from the community.[626] What does emerge from the *Numerus clausus* case is that once the state makes benefits available it has to distribute the benefits in an equal and fair manner. Challenges on the basis of equality have therefore been combined with rights to participate in state benefits. The *Grundrechte* therefore mediate participation in state performances (*Teilhaberechte*).[627]

---

[621] At 1536.

[622] Naturally the social state principle featured strongly in this re-interpretation of the *Grundrechte*. Unfortunately this development appears to have reduced the scope for the independent development of the principle, i e other than within the context of the specific individual rights. See Kunig op cit (n 568) 196. Some see the creation of surrogates for the lack of social and environmental rights in the Basic Law in this method of interpretation. See Badura op cit (n 398) 495; Häberle op cit (n 503). No constitutional right to environmental integrity has been recognized. Kunig 'German Constitutional Law and the Environment' (1982–3) 8 *Adelaide LR* 318–22 argues that it might be attempted to derive such a right from the interpretation of the Basic Law as a whole, but it could be more fruitful to seek the protection of particular environmental concerns by relying on rights to life and physical integrity and property or to stop damage to the environment by arguing that the free development of the personality is infringed (art 2.1 *GG*). See further in general Rabie 'A Constitutional Right to Environmental Integrity: A German Perspective' (1991) 7 *SAJHR* 208; Huber 'The Protection of the Environment in German Criminal Law' (1990) XXIII *CILSA* 84. The major political parties seem to be in agreement that the state's obligation to protect the environment should be included as a directive of state policy, but this approach is rejected as ineffective and even dangerous by academics.

[623] 33 *BVerfGE* 303.

[624] At 330.

[625] At 331.

[626] At 333. Schuppert *Funktionell-rechtliche Grenzen der Verfassungsinterpretation* (1980) 16 argues that the decision is a theoretical translation of the realization that social security in the industrialized state does not depend on the disposition over private property, but rather on the public distribution of rights of access to the job market — here entry being presupposed by the necessary education.

[627] The present social security system is not constitutionally protected from change because the social state clause and the equality clause guarantee participation only in *existing* benefits. The social state principle has been associated to a greater degree with the equality clause than with the other *Grundrechte*. This is no surprise as the eradication of inequality of opportunity lies at the heart of the principle. See Schenke op cit (n 358) 659; Badura op cit (n 398) 483, 495; Pieters op cit (n 481) 75. Cf the US Supreme Court in *Shapiro v Thompson* 394 US 618 (1969).

- The extent to which the right to private education constitutes a right to state performance was examined in the *Financial help* case of 1987, where government assistance to a private school was demanded.[628] In a careful judgment the court proceeded in three steps: it first asked whether a guaranteed norm existed; it then examined whether there was a duty on the state to intervene; and it finally determined the nature and the extent of that duty. The right to form private schools is constitutionally protected.[629] The existence of the right is threatened because of the financial difficulties facing the private education system.[630] In principle the legislature has a duty to intervene, but also has the discretion to decide — taking other community interests and the economic realities into account — on the extent and nature of support. The claim to support is limited to what could reasonably be expected from the community.[631]

Critics of the social state-functional theory have argued that if the theory is accepted, the state will only be able to fulfil its obligations to a certain unspecified degree.[632] The status of the *Grundrechte* therefore is reduced to mere guidelines and the individual will lose the ability to make direct claims against the state.[633] In reality the extension of potential claims leads to diminished *Grundrecht* protection.

The theory further implies that the court may force the legislature into positive action. Critics have argued that the democratically elected legislature should decide on which alternative(s) to employ to realize a particular state objective. In other words, the discretion on how to spend the limited funds available to the state should always rest with Parliament and not with the court.[634] The full consequences of this theory may result in the priorities for the distribution of state funds becoming part of the process of interpretation.

### 5.4.4 *Grundrechte as institutional guarantees*

The institutional theory of interpretation is distinguished from Carl Schmitt's *Institutsgarantie* and *Institutionsgarantie*. Schmitt's enterprise concerned those constructs of public, state, political, religious, and private lives which are so important for the Constitution that their character-determining nucleus is protected against legislative change.[635] Constructs of ordinary law were protected in this way. Examples are the self-administration of the communities,[636] the bureaucracy, political parties, marriage and family, and property.[637]

---

[628] 75 *BVerfGE* 40.
[629] Article 7.4.1 *GG*.
[630] 75 *BVerfGE* 40 63.
[631] At 68.
[632] Böckenförde op cit (n 506) 1536.
[633] Ibid.
[634] Parliament has complete control over the budget. It seems that the court is suggesting that the right to participation and to state performance is limited to what is possible in the existing budget. The planning of the budget can therefore not be influenced by individual claims to performance and remains geared towards the interests of the nation as a whole. See Kirchhof op cit (n 398) 456; Heun op cit (n 477) 66–8.
[635] Ossenbühl op cit (n 507) 2103.
[636] See Thomashausen 'Local and Regional Autonomy: The Comparative Law Approach to Residential and Spatial Conflicts' (1985) XVIII *CILSA* 297 at 314.
[637] See Bekker 'Interaction between Constitutional Reform and Family Law' 1991 *Acta Juridica* 1 at 6; Robinson 'Die Ouer–Kind Verhouding in die Lig van 'n Menseregteakte — 'n Beknopte Oorsig oor die Posisie in Duitsland' (1992) 7 *SAPR/PL* 228 at 229–30.

The institutional theory sees *Grundrechte* as demanding the construction of certain institutions for the fulfilment of particular functions in society.[638] The legislature is called upon to realize the institutions legally and factually.[639] The institutional theory therefore leaves much more room for legislative intervention in the constellation (*Ausgestaltung*) of the protected areas, but also limits the legislative intervention to the functions of the *Grundrecht*.[640] According to this theory, legislation builds institutional freedom. Whole normative complexes emerge around the *Grundrecht* institutions which give the use of the *Grundrechte* direction, certainty, content, and order.[641] This process of *Ausgestaltung* (or regulating and content-giving) is distinguished from the infringement of the subjective freedom dimension of *Grundrechte*. It is argued that the infringement of the subjective dimension of *Grundrechte* is not brought about by the institutional approach to the interpretation of *Grundrechte*.

It cannot be denied that the social effectiveness of *Grundrecht* use depends on legislative and executive support. In this way most *Grundrechte* presuppose some legislative constellation. Articles 6.1–4 *GG*, 9.1 *GG*, and 9.3 *GG* presuppose respectively: the family and marriage, law of associations (*Vereinsrecht*), and labour relations legislation (*Tarifvertragsrecht*). Legislation is, in other words, necessary for these *Grundrechte* to be socially workable. In the *Co-determination* case the FCC said that 'freedom of association is dependent on legislation which incorporates the free associations and their life into the general legal order, guarantee legal certainty, protect the interests of members and third parties as well as the public interest. This necessity belongs to the content of freedom of association.'[642]

The institutional approach, however, entails much more legislative construction than the extract from the *Co-determination* case suggests. This is best illustrated by the institutional character of the broadcasting industry.[643] Originally an institutional approach to broadcasting was justified with reference to the limited frequencies available and the high costs involved in the setting up and operation of transmitters (12 *BVerfGE* 205 at 261), but nowadays the necessity of pluralism in the media of a democratic society seems to provide the justification. *Länder* legislatures are required to make rules which ensure that programmes are independent from government control and balanced and that every significant social, cultural, and political group has access to the media and is represented on their supervisory bodies.[644]

Freedom of the press is a separate and independent freedom[645] and it is also

---

[638] Böckenförde op cit (n 506) 1532.

[639] Ibid.

[640] The legislator does not have complete freedom on how it defines and puts the rights into operation. The essential core elements of the *Grundrecht* guarantees set limits to the legislative prerogative to realize them. See Nierhaus '*Grundrechte aus der Hand des Gesetzgebers? —Ein Beitrag zur Dogmatik des Art 1 Abs 3 GG*' (1991) 116 *Archiv des Öffentlichen Recht* 111.

[641] Nierhaus op cit (n 640) 111.

[642] 50 *BVerfGE* 290 354.

[643] See Barendt 'The Influence of the German and Italian Constitutional Courts on their National Broadcasting Systems' 1991 *Public L* 93; Karpen 'Freedom of Expression' in Karpen op cit (n 390) 102.

[644] See the *Television* cases: 12 *BVerfGE* 205; 31 *BVerfGE* 315; 57 *BVerfGE* 295; 73 *BVerfGE* 118; 74 *BVerfGE* 297; 83 *BVerfGE* 238. Both public and private stations carry the responsibility to ensure plurality in the broadcasting industry, but the dependence of the latter on income derived from advertising is taken into account when the diversity of programmes in this 'dual' system is judged.

[645] Article 5.1 *GG*.

protected institutionally. In other words, the freedom is protected as a discrete area of life vital to society, and not only as the right of the individual to start up a newspaper, for example.[646] The court has recognized that the press is essential to the democratic process. The press must therefore be structured in such a way so as to assure the formation, the preservation, and the encouragement of open and free public discourse.[647] The court has nevertheless trusted the market to a much greater extent as the regulator in the area of the press than in broadcasting.[648]

The institutional approach has also led to successful challenges to the organizational and procedural structures of public institutions.[649] The court held that the objective dimension of the freedom to scientific research not only entails the duty of the state to create functionally capable research institutions but also implies a right for the individual to those organizational measures which are necessary for the protection and exercise of his/her *Grundrecht* to engage in scientific research.[650]

Critics of the institutional theory have argued that if legislation concretizes rights, such legislation obtains constitutional status.[651] The status quo is protected in this way against change.[652] Another criticism has been that, despite the proponents' claims to the contrary, the institutional theory realizes the objective dimension of freedom through limiting the subjective dimension.[653]

## 5.5 Theories of interpretation

The adoption of a particular *Grundrecht* theory as the basis for a judicial decision inevitably has consequences for the division of functions between the different organs of the state. The recognition of an objective dimension of rights and the use of functional and institutional theories of interpretation in some *Grundrechte* have increased the discretionary powers of the Constitutional Court dramatically. The court has become, at least potentially, a threat to the balance of power in Germany.

Every method of interpretation affects the relationship between the different powers and '[t]he Basic Law applies, in practice, as it is interpreted by the *Bundesverfassungsgericht*'.[654] The relationship between theories of constitutional interpretation and the division of powers will now be examined in more detail. The focus of the first three approaches (classical, concretizing, pluralistic) remains normative, in that the meaning of the Constitution is the central inquiry. The focus of the last two approaches (restrictive, functional) shifts to the relationship between

---

[646] In 25 *BVerfGE* 256 the boycott of a small newspaper — forced by pressure from a big newspaper company — was held to be constitutionally unprotected, in circumstances where the boycott amounted to unfair competition.

[647] See in general 20 *BVerfGE* 162 (*Der Spiegel*).

[648] Ossenbühl op cit (n 507) 2104. The press and broadcasting are moving closer together as technology improves and more — and cheaper — channels for broadcasting become available. The court's differentiation between the press and the broadcasting industry is therefore in need of an alternative justification.

[649] See Jarass op cit (n 518) 388. The unsuccessful challenge in the *Numerus clausus* case was also primarily a procedural one. Compare 53 *BVerfGE* 30 65: the state has to ensure that life (art 2.2 *GG*) is protected, which entails enforcing certain procedural rules relating to the installation and operation of nuclear power reactors.

[650] 35 *BVerfGE* 79 130. Article 5.3 *GG* was therefore interpreted to mean that academics (and not students) had to remain in control over decisions concerning scientific research.

[651] Böckenförde op cit (n 506) 1533; Müller op cit (n 434) 42.

[652] Böckenförde op cit (n 506) 1533; Schenke op cit (n 358) 658.

[653] Böckenförde op cit (n 506) 1533.

[654] Smend *Das Bundesverfassungsgericht* (1963) 24.

the powers, and consequences for the process of interpretation are drawn from there.[655]

### 5.5.1 Classical hermeneutical approach

The Constitution is interpreted as any other piece of legislation: the objective meaning of the Constitution should be determined with the help of the grammatical, teleological, historical, and systematic methods of interpretation.[656] The uniqueness of the Constitution can be accommodated within the classical methods of interpretation.[657]

The following arguments are levelled against the classical methods as a model for constitutional interpretation:

- The classical methods presuppose a high level of clarity in the content and meaning of the text to be interpreted. The text of the Constitution, especially the *Grundrechte*, is far less specific than legislation. The Constitution sets parameters and goals, but it does not specify the means for or intensity of the realization of its objectives.[658] The classical methods are therefore in themselves insufficient guidelines for constitutional interpretation.[659]

- The Constitution stands alone and cannot be contextualized with reference to the legal order as a whole. The manner in which the meaning of legislation is concretized does not apply to the interpretation of the Constitution. On the contrary, the Constitution is supposed to give direction to the legal order and therefore cannot be concretized with reference to the latter.[660]

- Historical intent is not as rich a source for constitutional interpretation as it is for statutory interpretation. First, it is difficult to distinguish between the opinions of individuals partaking and the intention of the parliamentary council, which was responsible for drawing up the Constitution. Secondly, the real reasons for accepting a certain formulation over another were in most cases raised in informal or private, even secret, negotiations.[661] The general feeling seems to have been to leave the *Grundrechte* open-ended.[662]

---

[655] This is not to say that proponents of the classical, concretizing, and pluralistic approaches merely accept the consequences of their approach for the separation of powers. A mere shift in emphasis is indicated.

[656] See in Böckenförde '*Die Methoden der Verfassungsinterpretation — Bestandaufnahme und Kritik*' (1976) 29 *NJW* 2089 at 2090.

[657] Ulrich Karpen argues that although the FCC may rectify minor divergences between the law and reality by the interpretation of the Constitution, more serious gaps need to be filled by constitutional amendment. The court's method of interpretation is, according to Karpen, not all that different from the ordinary court's interpretation of statutes. Karpen then, however, goes on to say that both the ordinary courts and the FCC use, among other principles of interpretation, the unity of the law ('constitution as one law') and must look at the historical, social, and political context within which the law was promulgated. See Karpen 'The Rule of Law' in Karpen op cit (n 390) 169 at 180.

[658] Böckenförde op cit (n 656) 2091; Sendler op cit (n 396) 489 argues that 'almost anything can be proved with constitutional arguments' and that the political parties therefore resort to the courts as a matter of course once they have lost the battle in Parliament. This results in the overextension of the Constitution and the demise of the *Rechtsstaat*. Compare Schlaich op cit (n 367) 103.

[659] Hesse op cit (n 556) 22.

[660] Böckenförde op cit (n 656) 2091. Von Savigny developed the classical methods for the interpretation of the private-law codes which had, according to the historical school, to be interpreted with reference to the historical-dogmatic whole of the legal order. He never had his theory in mind for constitutional interpretation.

[661] Ebsen op cit (n 492) 55; Mahrenholz op cit (n 459) 57 attributes less significance to the historical intent behind a specific textual formulation because that formulation of *Grundrechte* is, for him, trapped within a particular historical moment in time. The history of the *Grundrecht*, rather than that of the text, is therefore of importance. Such an historical interpretation provides scope for comparative analysis in the interpretation of *Grundrechte*.

[662] The search for the subjective intent therefore becomes futile. See Hesse op cit (n 556) 22.

- Constitutional provisions are often of a principled nature[663] and their weight depends on the particular context within which they are applied.[664]

- The ideological content of some of the *Grundrechte* makes dogmatic consensus (one of the prerequisites for legal determination in the classical sense) between the judges and among academics an impossibility.[665]

- Some constitutional provisions reflect historical compromises and some decisions were therefore deliberately postponed.[666] The task of constitutional interpretation then becomes the constant rekindling of the compromises.[667]

- The Constitution fulfils what Rudolf Smend called an 'integrative function'. It is necessary to keep the text open, through interpretation, to enable the Constitution to fulfil the integrative function.[668]

- The classical methods of interpretation do not take account of the techniques developed by the court to retain and expand the flexibility of the Constitution.[669] Furthermore, the court's efforts to expand its own powers of discretion are ignored.

The court has stated that the objective will of the framers remains a central inquiry.[670] The FCC has also expressed its commitment to the other classical modes of interpretation,[671] but the court's reliance on doctrines such as the division of functions between legislature and judiciary, the desirability of the consequences of a mode of interpretation, and the political, sociological, and historical cohesiveness of arguments have cast serious doubt on that commitment.[672]

---

[663] Principles are used here in the Dworkinian sense: principles as opposed to legal rules.

[664] Ebsen op cit (n 492) 57.

[665] At 63.

[666] See Murphy & Tanenhaus *Comparative Constitutional Law: Cases and Comments* (1977) 27. The authors' suggestion that law, as a compromise between different interest groups, is an 'American notion' and 'alien to the German idea of law that triumphed in the codes' cannot be accepted. The Co-determination Act is a clear example of a compromise, not to mention the many provisions of the Basic Law which are themselves the product of historical compromises (e g education, socio-economic rights, and aspects of federalism) and, as will be argued below, these compromises are recognized and kept alive by the FCC. See also Mischke op cit (n 395) 261; Stern op cit (n 344) 247; Kröger op cit (n 375) 1321.

[667] Constitutional interpretation can be seen as the constant adaptation of an historical consensus to changing conditions. The constant adjustments ensure that the Constitution remains normatively effective because only a changing Constitution can preserve the consensus within society. A change of society's values will therefore result in a change in the Constitution. See Karpen op cit (n 387) 595.

[668] Häberle op cit (n 319) 72 states that the classical methods of interpretation are poor equipment for achieving a fair balance of interests in specific cases, while at the same time keeping the process of interpretation and the Constitution open in order to enable it to serve as the decision-making mechanism in future cases. Häberle describes the classical methods of interpretation as 'the rings in the trunk of the living Constitution'.

[669] Scheuner op cit (n 460) 1322.

[670] 1 *BVerfGE* 299 312.

[671] 11 *BVerfGE* 126 130; 35 *BVerfGE* 263 278. The subjective intentions of the founding fathers are irrelevant in German constitutional interpretation. The history of the Basic Law's inception may be of supportive value for a particular interpretation or cast doubt on another, but has little significance on its own, as the historical intent was effectively neutralized by the acceptance of the objective value order. Historical developments before the existence of the Basic Law can be relevant, as well as the debates of the Parliamentary Council (printed in JÖR, 1951). See Scheuner op cit (n 460) 1327; 6 *BVerfGE* 389 431; 41 *BVerfGE* 291 309; 62 *BVerfGE* 1 45; Bungert op cit (n 458) 90. Cf Corder 'Lessons from North America' (1992) 109 *SALJ* 204 at 206 for the situation in North America. Kanner's comment ('Citizenship and Scholarship' (1990) 90 *Columbia LR* 2017 at 2025, quoted in Bungert op cit (n 458) 99), that the jurisprudence of Robert Bork is not only outside the mainstream, but outside the entire river basin, will not find unconditional support in Germany. Few will, however, disagree that the FCC has on several occasions expressly departed from the text of the Constitution to give better effect to the value decisions and the principles of the Constitution (see Hesse op cit (n 556) 23 and the cases quoted there) and that systematic interpretation has received a special meaning through the development of the doctrine of 'unity of the Constitution'.

[672] See Hesse op cit (n 556) 23.

## 5.5.2 Interpretation as the concretizing of norms through rational arguments

Most commentators see constitutional interpretation as the 'concretization of norms', but no consensus exists as to the exact meaning of this term. In general, concretization means that the court is bound by the normative standards of the Constitution. More specifically the task of the court lies in concretizing the material standards for application in each individual case and the boundaries of constitutional interpretation are derived in this process of problem-solving.[673] The work of three prominent German jurists, Konrad Hesse, Friedrich Müller, and Robert Alexy, will be used to illustrate 'concretization' as being the approach followed by most German jurists.

Konrad Hesse sees the task of constitutional interpretation as finding the 'correct result' through a rational and controllable process of interpretation. This process must contribute to legal certainty and predictability.[674] The classical methods of interpretation must be supplemented with an analysis of the legal and factual domain to which the norm refers, because the process of interpretation is not only bound to the norm to be concretized but also to the presuppositions associated with the interpreter(s) and the problem to be solved.[675]

Hesse suggests that the following guidelines be used for problem-solving in individual cases: the *unity of the Constitution* refers to the cohesiveness and the interdependence of the individual elements of the Constitution; *practical concordance* means optimizing colliding constitutionally protected legal goods by placing proportional limitations on both rather than to resort to balancing;[676] *functionally correct* are decisions which respect the division of functions in the Constitution; the *integrating function* of the Constitution entails that solutions which contribute to political unity are to be preferred over others; arguments which optimize the *normative effect* of the Constitution are to be preferred over other arguments.[677] For Hesse the text of the Constitution remains the ultimate limitation on the use of these constitutional principles: they may therefore not be employed without sensible textual support and they may never be employed to contradict the text.[678]

Friedrich Müller is another proponent of concretization. Arguing in the context of the interpretation of *Grundrechte*, Müller agrees with Hesse that balancing must be avoided at all cost, especially when the objective value order forms part of the balancing process.[679] A totality such as the value order is not only normatively

---

[673] Schlaich op cit (n 356) 268; Compare Schuppert op cit (n 574) 1191.
[674] Hesse op cit (n 556) 20.
[675] At 25.
[676] Practical concordance was first formulated by Hesse, but has also been employed by the FCC (see 41 *BVerfGE* 29 51).
[677] Hesse op cit (n 556) 28.
[678] At 29. Gusy op cit (n 322) 139, 148 binds the competence to interpret and concretize strictly to the ability of the Basic Law to give sufficient and clear direction to the process of concretization. The legislator may therefore, for example, be compelled to act only if its *omissio* is clearly unconstitutional. Contrast Stein *Reihe Alternativkommentare, Kommentar zum Grundgesetz für die Bundesrepublik Deutschland* II (1989) r 97. For Stein concretization supplements the traditional methods of interpretation when the latter proves insufficient for the resolution of conflicts. The objective of concretization is the development of a new rule to decide the individual case. An analysis of the conflicting interests and a comparison of other (similar) situations of conflict form the basis for designing possible solutions. The consequences of the different solutions should then be evaluated against the constitutional standards applicable to the case, and the solution which gives best effect to the values of the Constitution should be chosen.
[679] Müller op cit (n 496); also critical of balancing is Geiger op cit (n 433) 404.

senseless, but when it forms the basis for the balancing of goods it becomes positively dangerous as principles and objectives not mentioned in the Constitution may infiltrate and influence the balancing process.[680] Balancing in this abstract sense is in any event nothing but the weighing of a word without any value, factual, or conceptual meaning against another such word. The decision then merely confirms that the value preferred by the interpreter gains preference.

Müller believes that the starting point of interpretation should be the acknowledgement of the independent protection afforded by each of the individual *Grundrechte*.[681] A stabilizing dogma can only be developed by first determining the factual reach of the *Grundrechte*. *Grundrechte* are not general proscriptions, but they are rich in content; they have a practical function which should be concretized in the particular case under discussion.[682] These qualities of *Grundrechte* contain their ultimate limitation and definition of their content.[683] And, while the distinction between *Grundrechte* and ordinary law may not be blurred, the essence (*Wesensgehalt*) of the rights must be determined from the social, factual, and action domains within which the rights operate. Ordinary law therefore recognizes, receives, adapts, and normatively informs the *Grundrechte*.[684]

Once the reach of the *Grundrecht* has been determined the limitation of the *Grundrecht* is examined.[685] The *Grundrechte* are not limited inherently (by implication) and nothing prevents their use even if danger to the stability and continuity of society result.[686] Inherent limitations are neither written nor unwritten constitutional law. The limitations of art 2.1 *GG* may not be transplanted to the other *Grundrechte*.[687] Limitations of *Grundrechte* may further not be derived from the 'whole of the constitutional value system'. The latter has no normative value in itself and lacks sufficient clarity to satisfy *Rechtsstaat* considerations.[688] According to Müller, the criteria for limiting the *Grundrechte* must come from the Constitution itself. A differentiation in the intensity of protection by the individual *Grundrechte* is caused by the Basic Law's enumeration of specific limitations to the individual *Grundrechte*. The rank and the weight of every *Grundrecht* in the Basic Law's system of protection must therefore be determined separately.[689]

Müller argues that where *Grundrechte* are guaranteed without reservation they may not be limited by the legislature or any of the other branches of government. The general laws cannot serve as the limitation of such *Grundrechte* because

---

[680] Müller op cit (n 496) 18.
[681] Müller op cit (n 496) 41.
[682] Müller op cit (n 496) 43.
[683] At 40. Articles 2.1 *GG* (free development of the personality) and 3.1 *GG* (equality) are general clauses which cannot be compared with the other rights. They do not have the same limited reach as the other *Grundrechte*. They became general norms (through FCC interpretation) and all legislation is tested against them to a greater or lesser degree.
[684] Müller argues that the constitutional norms are only the nucleus of the normative order. In order to be applicable to practical cases constitutional norms need to be concretized to decision norms. This happens by the reciprocal concretizing and precisioning of norms to facts and facts to norms.
[685] See Starck op cit (n 506) 13.
[686] Ibid.
[687] At 11. The right to free development of the personality (art 2.1 *GG*) is limited by the rights of others, the constitutional order, and the community's morality (*boni mores*).
[688] At 18.
[689] At 19. Cf Trengove 'Judicial Ideologies in the Interpretation of a Bill of Rights in South Africa' (1992) 6 *Responsa Meridiana* 118 at 131, who propagates a holistic approach to interpretation: all rights 'should enjoy equal protection'.

ordinary law cannot replace the preferences expressed in the Constitution. The normative reach of the *Grundrechte* remains their ultimate limitation.[690]

*Grundrechte* with reservations also have a certain normative factual reach, but their reach may further be limited by legislation which exploits the elements of the reservation.[691] In the context of free speech, which is specifically limited by the general laws,[692] the FCC determined that only laws which do not direct themselves specifically against speech may qualify as general laws.[693] According to Müller, it is only possible to assess whether legislation directs itself against speech once the content of free speech has been determined.[694]

Müller's next step is to determine the impact of the legislation under consideration. The objective meaning of the legislation and not the subjective intention of the legislature is of importance. If the objective meaning of the legislation infringes upon the normative reach of the right, the constitutionality of the legislation is determined according to the principle of proportionality and art 19 *GG*.[695] Proportional state action means that the means chosen by the state must be suitable, necessary, and proportional (in the narrow sense) to the ends. These three principles are collectively known as proportionality in the wide sense and are usually derived from the *Rechtsstaat* principle.[696] However, according to a 1965 FCC decision, the principle of proportionality follows directly from the *Grundrechte* themselves. The reasoning behind this deduction is that the *Grundrechte* are the expression of the freedom of the citizens and they may be limited only when absolutely necessary in the public interest.[697] The extensive use of the principle of proportionality has not been uncontroversial as judgments (especially in cases of abstract review) concerning the causal connection between goals and means are often necessary. Hypothetical projections such as these, it is argued, must be left to the legislature. The principle further endangers the generality of legislation.[698]

Müller recognizes the possibility of a collision between two rights in a concrete case. Constitutional norms then do limit each other, but before there can be resort to practical concordance consideration should be given to the reach of each right and therefore whether the *Grundrechte* in fact collide. Practical concordance, reciprocal interaction, and the unity of the Constitution, as principles of constitutional interpretation, must be used only in actual cases of conflict as the norms of decision-making. Practical concordance does not mean that colliding *Grundrechte* are limited to the same degree, i e until they 'fit'. The limitation of a right in the practical case should rather be determined by the intensity with which the right

---

[690] Müller op cit (n 496) 55; the copying of somebody's work of art is not protected by art 5 *GG* (artistic freedom) as copying is not part of the factual normative reach of art 5 *GG*.

[691] Müller op cit (n 496) 59.

[692] Article 5.2 *GG*. See in general Karpen 'Freedom of Expression' in Karpen op cit (n 390) 97.

[693] 7 *BVerfGE* 198 209.

[694] Müller op cit (n 496) 69.

[695] At 73. Article 19 *GG* requires that legislation which seeks to limit rights must be general and mention the *Grundrecht* to be limited, and such legislation may not infringe the essence of the *Grundrecht*. The principle of proportionality normally renders much more protection of the *Grundrechte* than art 19 *GG*. Cf 19 *BVerfGE* 342 348.

[696] Starck op cit (n 506) 15.

[697] See Grimm op cit (n 362) 1309. Müller op cit (n 371) 152 says that a pluralistic democracy must have a concept of the public interest and that judges help to define this concept over time.

[698] Starck op cit (n 506) 30.

protects the specific freedom in question and the intensity of the infringement by the legislature. If practical concordance is any better than balancing, it must recognize not only that different *Grundrechte* protect with different intensity but also that a difference in the intensity of protection exists within the reach of the same *Grundrecht*.[699]

The Müller method of interpretation, which is roughly the same as that of the FCC, will lead to a ranking of the *Grundrechte* because of the different intensities with which the rights work in different contexts, but this order is the by-product of the process of interpretation and not its starting point.[700]

Robert Alexy sees the justification of legal decisions in the rationality of legal argumentation. Legal argumentation is considered a special case of practical discourse.[701] Alexy further distinguishes between legal rules and principles.[702] He describes principles (*Optimierungsgebote*) as norms to be realized to the highest degree possible, given the factual and legal alternatives.[703] *Grundrechte* are legal principles. When, in a concrete case, a principle is to be realized only by curtailing another principle, balancing should take place in accordance with the principle of proportionality.[704] The degree of non-realization of the latter must, in other words, be proportional to the importance of the realization of the first.[705]

Alexy, unlike Hesse and Müller, considers balancing unavoidable when dealing with principles. Theories which seek optimization of all the rights affected, or practical concordance of rights, cannot work until the metrification of the principles has been achieved to such an extent that the decision which will maximize all the principles affected can be found.[706] Balancing does produce the correct result if all the factors are taken into account for the particular historical moment in time, but rigid rule-making should be avoided as it makes future constitutional interpretation less flexible.

The FCC has employed both balancing and practical concordance. Other variants of these doctrines include:

- Under 'relations of tension' the FCC understands tension which is built into the Constitution. Principles therefore collide, abstractly, in the Constitution. In such cases the FCC will not express a preference for one or the other principle abstractly. The possibility of either principle getting preference is left open until a concrete case arises. A preference is then expressed within the facts of the concrete case.[707]

- Under reciprocal interaction (*Wechselwirkung*) the FCC understands the

---

[699] Starck op cit (n 506) 89. The distribution of the work of art also belongs to the protected (artistic) freedom, but is protected with a different intensity than the making of the work. In principle the artist may only resort to the ways of distribution which are sanctioned by the general legal order.

[700] Müller op cit (n 496) 54.

[701] See in general Alexy *A Theory of Legal Argumentation* (1989).

[702] Alexy *Theorie der Grundrechte* (1985) 71.

[703] At 75.

[704] According to Alexy op cit (n 702) 100 the FCC has recognized the principled character of the *Grundrechte* by declaring the principle of proportionality to be part of the nature of rights (19 *BVerfGE* 342 348). See also Thomashausen 'Savings Clauses and the Meaning of the Phrase "Acceptable in a Democratic Society" — A Comparative Study' (October 1989) XXX *Codicillus* 56 at 57.

[705] See Alexy op cit (n 525) 55.

[706] Alexy op cit (n 702) 142.

[707] See the *Socialist Reich Party* decision (2 *BVerfGE* 1).

relationship between the *Grundrechte* and the legislation which limits the *Grundrechte*. The latter may limit rights, but should in turn be interpreted in the light of the rights, and the limiting legislation is therefore narrowly construed.[708]

### 5.5.3 *Pluralistic approach*

In terms of this approach the process of interpretation is open and consideration is given to a wider range of arguments than those allowed in terms of the other methods of interpretation. The vague normative content of the Constitution may be used, along with or besides norms of ordinary law, if they are useful, for solving the problem under consideration.[709] Normally the vague provisions of the Constitution are concretized by means of connecting formulas (*topoi*), such as the unity of the Constitution, practical concordance, balancing, and the integrating function of the Constitution, before they are applied to the problem.[710] The classical methods of statutory interpretation, the consequences of different interpretations, the consensus between the parties,[711] or, according to some, the consensus of the *res publica* further help to determine the constitutional persuasiveness of the arguments.[712]

Peter Häberle has democratized and radicalized this method in three steps. First, interpretation is connected to the democratic process through the normative power of the public sphere.[713] Secondly, constitutional interpretation should further seek the common good.[714] Thirdly, the participants in the process of interpretation are extended to include all the organs of the state and all citizens and interest groups.[715] Häberle proposes that the process of interpretation should be public and not merely open. The Constitution need not only mirror reality and the public sphere; the

---

[708] Ossenbühl op cit (n 507) 2107 argues that reciprocal interaction enables ordinary-law norms to infiltrate the process of constitutional balancing.

[709] Böckenförde op cit (n 656) 2092.

[710] At 2093. These connecting formulae tend to gain a life of their own. See Scheuner op cit (n 460) 1323. One of the problems with the formulae is that do not have any rank or range of application.

[711] The pluralistic approach suggests that a court look not only at the legislation itself but also at the legislative process. The greater the consensus among the political parties, the less likely the court will be to interfere (e g the *Co-determination* case 50 *BVerfGE* 290). Schlaich op cit (n 367) 107 emphasizes the conventional viewpoint: it is the result of the legislative process, the statute, which must be tested for formal and material constitutionality. The consistency of arguments in favour of the legislation, the legislative process, or the behaviour of the legislators are irrelevant. Compare the first *Television* case (12 *BVerfGE* 205), where the style of negotiations of the Adenauer government was found to be in conflict with the Constitution. Schlaich argues further that if the process and not the result is to be controlled, then parliamentary representatives would be wise to keep quiet in Parliament and refer matters to expert commissions.

[712] It is argued that the intensity of review depends on the interpreter of first instance (less scrutiny for legislation than executive action, in other words); whether the issue has been properly and publicly debated; the degree to which there is consensus/dissensus between the parties; and whether the interests of out-groups and not representable interests are at stake. See Häberle op cit (n 319) 175. Scheuner op cit (n 460) 1326 rejects these distinctions for threatening the independence of the judiciary.

[713] Häberle op cit (n 319) 74; Cappelletti op cit (n 389) 265 argues that judicial review is not necessarily anti-democratic as it ensures the participation of the citizens most directly involved in the dispute. Courts may in many instances be more accessible than the political organs. In the latter regard Cappelletti seems to refer to the way in which political parties have, instead of facilitating access to the state, isolated the state from societal influence.

[714] By stressing, for example, the public function of the press. See Häberle op cit (n 319) 132.

[715] Häberle op cit (n 319) 123 argues that constitutional interpretation must be by and for an 'open society of constitutional interpreters'. The press, the churches, the trade unions and employers, the scientists, and the artists are producing valuable self-interpretations of their freedoms. He further (at 155) states that theorists traditionally concentrate on the purposes and methods of constitutional interpretation and have neglected the participants. Häberle op cit (n 319) 166 criticizes Luhmann's concentration on legitimization through procedure alone; real legitimization can only be achieved through participation and influence in the decision-making process.

Constitution should be the public process itself.[716] In other words, the Constitution not only mirrors reality but is also a reflective source of light because the Constitution helps to constitute reality.[717] The most important task of constitutional theory is to create the conditions for uninhibited communication and public discourse.[718]

In order for communications from outside to achieve the necessary effect Häberle stresses the relativity of the FCC's autonomy. The selection procedure of the judges, public discussion of judges' backgrounds, opinions, and judgments, and the dependence of the court on the co-operation of the other branches of the state and the lower courts ensure that the FCC's autonomy remains relative.[719]

Häberle further connects constitutional theory with a pluralistic theory of society.[720] Plurality in society is constitutionally made possible by keeping constitutional norms such as human dignity, free speech, association, art, democracy, and the social and cultural state workable. These consensus-based provisions facilitate agreement and dissent at the same time.[721] At the same time constitutional interpretation must actively seek the compromise: this presupposes sound knowledge of political realities and possibilities in the process of interpretation.[722]

Häberle has been criticized for reducing judicial review to nothing more than the sanctioning and the legitimization of political consensus.[723] The further problem with his theory is that the democratization of the judicial process conflicts with the independence of the judiciary. Häberle implicitly denies that the parliamentary process — representative democracy, in other words — is any better than the judicial process for reaching societal compromises and solutions.[724] Häberle's theory has therefore received almost no recognition in the courts.

### 5.5.4 *Restrictive interpretation*

The judicialization of politics and the politicization of justice are the main concerns of those propagating a restrictive attitude towards constitutional interpretation.[725]

---

[716] According to Häberle op cit (n 319) 89, the question is not so much what changes the Constitution allows for, but rather what changes the Constitution demands.

[717] Häberle op cit (n 319) 168.

[718] The court's procedural rules must also ensure maximum possibility for communication. See Häberle op cit (n 319) 108, 115.

[719] The intensity of the other pressures on the court depends on how open the court's procedures are.

[720] Häberle op cit (n 319) 146. Cf the comments of Hiemstra 'Constitutions of Liberty' (1971) 88 *SALJ* 45 to the effect that a Bill of Rights is the translation of the moral tradition of the nation in words and democracy can only flourish in a homogeneous or nearly homogenous society; see Schmitt *Der Hüter der Verfassung* (1931). See the discussion of Post 'Jurisdictional Unity, Cultural Hegemony, and the Impetus for Human Rights' in Wellenreuther (ed) *German and American Constitutional Thought* (1990) 244 and Heyns ' "Reasonableness" in a Divided Society' (1990) 107 *SALJ* 279 at 283 of similar ideas of ties between rights and culture.

[721] Häberle op cit (n 319) 143.

[722] Häberle op cit (n 319) 42.

[723] Böckenförde op cit (n 656) 2094 criticizes Häberle's theory for forfeiting the normativity of the Constitution. The Constitution becomes as open to change as the general consensus. Häberle's response (op cit (n 319) 106) is simple: the Constitution does not know absolute truths.

[724] Ebsen op cit (n 492) 255 argues that the issue at stake is not the relative independence of the judiciary, but the relative autonomy of the institution of judicial review. The fears are inspired by doubts about whether an autonomous institution of judicial review will be capable of preserving the necessary consensus when faced with societal crises.

[725] See in general Corder op cit (n 671) 204 for a discussion of the terminology and similar problems in North America. Cf Landfried op cit (n 413) 161; Von Beyme op cit (n 334) 22 for a political overview of the German situation. It is argued that judicial review is more readily accepted in countries with a weak parliamentary tradition than in countries with a strong tradition of democracy. In Germany the constitutionally legalized state, the *Rechtsstaat*, preceded parliamentary democracy for quite a period of time and was even used to compensate the rising political bourgeoisie for their lack of parliamentary rights. The democratic process, more than the institution

Both the judiciary and parliamentarians contribute to the juridification of politics. It is argued that German parliamentarians have displayed too much obedience to the court. The legislature nowadays seems more concerned about the constitutionality of bills than their wisdom.[726] The FCC became the final arbiter of too many of these 'constitutional' parliamentary debates via the abstract review procedure. The mesh of decisions, resulting from the frequency of appeals to the court, is slowly beginning to undermine the function of the legislature.[727] Insecure parliamentarians and overconfident judges caused judicial review to become a danger to democracy.[728] Political alternatives for future generations are reduced in the process.[729]

These problems are unfortunately not addressed very imaginatively by the proponents of restrictive interpretation. Instead of limiting the effect of the court's decisions,[730] some writers suggest that the court *should avoid making* some decisions. In other words, the FCC should adopt something like the political question doctrine.[731] Such an approach presupposes the content of legal principles which can be found purely by cognition, and the content of those which require a legal-political decision.[732] It is then argued that the Constitution, as the higher form of *law*, only prevails over all lower forms of *law*.[733]

One problem with the restrictive position is that the Constitution, as a social contract and compromise, is a rigid document and its amendment is therefore subject to qualified majorities. The protection for the minority lies in the qualified majority; this protection is undermined if an ordinary majority of Parliament could 'amend' the Constitution through its re-interpretation.[734] A second problem is that the court's

---

of judicial review, needs stabilizations. Vague constitutional principles such as freedom, equality, fairness, and morality should therefore not be used as mechanisms of constitutional control, but their content should be left to the legislator — being the democratically elected branch of government — to interpret.

[726] This problem is labelled, quite appropriately, 'Karlsruhe astrology'. See Schlaich op cit (n 367) 117; Landfried 'Introduction' in Landfried (ed) *Constitutional Review and Legislation* (1988) 12.

[727] Eventually the legislator may not be able to fulfil its function to adapt the law to the changing social conditions. Such stagnation of the law cannot be compatible with a social democratic *Rechtsstaat*. See 77 *BVerfGE* 84 104.

[728] The Austrian court is, on the other hand, accused of practising too much restraint. The procedural rules of the Austrian court are correspondingly tighter and they reduce access to the court. See Korinek op cit (n 454) 32. The Swiss court seems to be even more active than the FCC. See Häberle op cit (n 319) 212; Schlaich op cit (n 356) 3.

[729] Landfried op cit (n 726) 16.

[730] See above, 80.

[731] In 36 *BVerfGE* 1 14 the court used the expression 'judicial self-restraint' explicitly, but nevertheless (at 36) made each of the court's reasoning part of the *ratio decidendi* and therefore binding on all other organs of the state. Ipsen op cit (n 351) 133 argues that the principle of self restraint indicates an attitude of the court and it does not mean that the court will not entertain the matter at all.

[732] The call for restraint has not been accompanied (until recently) by clear guidelines as to what the court should be restricted to. The distinction between legal and political arguments in constitutional law, exemplified by the '*reine Rechtskontrolle*' of Kelsen, is highly problematic today. See Scheuner op cit (n 460) 1322; Gusy op cit (n 322) 41; Vogel op cit (n 460) 20. Geiger op cit (n 433) 401 argues that the judge's political power lies in finding and applying the law and not in changing the political relationship to his/her own liking. Ebsen argues that all law is political law, but, in contrast to the other areas of law, constitutional law stands in a reciprocal relationship with politics: not only is constitutional law the object and the product of the political process, but the political process is also the object and the product of constitutional law. Some proponents of restrictive interpretation argue that politics, economics, language, and the law all change at different speeds. Friction is caused by the processes of change and the law can be used as a mediator only if it is more stable, more conservative, than the other disciplines.

[733] Ebsen op cit (n 492) 169 claims the original formulation of this approach must be Hamilton's justification for judicial review as 'neither force nor will but merely judgment'. *Marbury v Madison* 5 US 137 (1803) and the *Aufwertungs* case of 1925 are examples of such 'naïve' justifications for judicial review.

[734] Ossenbühl op cit (n 507) 2107; Korinek op cit (n 454) 45 argues that the democratic legislator is bound to the value framework of the Constitution because the Constitution has higher democratic legitimacy than the legislator itself. Parliament may therefore not re-interpret the Constitution, because Parliament lacks the democratic legitimacy to do so. Häberle op cit (n 319) 64 identifies the clear problem with Korinek's argument: the democratic legitimacy of the Constitution is tied to a particular historical moment. Korinek is, however, also a proponent of

refusal to decide, despite having jurisdiction, is as much a transgression of the court's competence as is a decision without the necessary jurisdiction.[735]

The fears of those propagating a restrictive mode of interpretation are not valid for all areas of constitutional interpretation. In areas outside the scope of the *Grundrechte*, as will be illustrated below with reference to developments in the area of federalism, the court seems to be more reluctant to interfere with the political process.

Federalism was chosen to illustrate the reluctance of the FCC to interfere with the political process — outside the area of *Grundrechte* — as the strong commitment of the Basic Law to a federal system of government was met with an equally strong drive for centralism in post-World War II German society. The idea of nationhood and union, the smallness of the country, the mobility of the people, the striving for equal living conditions, and the social state's vast range of activities, not to mention the *Grundrecht* part of the Basic Law, are all strong centralizing factors in Germany.[736]

Most of the legislative powers in the Basic Law belong to the concurrent category; both the *Bund* and the *Länder* therefore have the power to legislate. The Basic Law states that the *Bund* shall have the right to legislate, in areas of concurrent jurisdiction, to the extent that the matter cannot be effectively regulated by the legislation of the individual *Länder*.[737] From the start this has been interpreted as a non-justiciable guideline which should be left to the interpretation of the Federal legislature.[738] According to the principle of Federal pre-eminence, *Land* legislation becomes inoperative to the extent that the Federal legislature occupies the field.[739] In earlier cases the court did not readily accept that Federal activity automatically excluded *Land* activity,[740] but later the FCC made it clear that *Länder* could not see the principle of Federal pre-eminence as one which allowed them to improve on Federal legislation which they perceived to be inadequate.[741] The concurrent powers of the *Länder* were limited even further after it was decided that the *Bund* could occupy the field through several successive and complementary laws in accordance with a general strategy, and that this would debar the *Länder* from any action in the field whatsoever.[742]

The *Länder*'s loss in the area of concurrent power was compensated for by the court's restricted interpretation of the power of the *Bund* to enact framework legislation and an extensive interpretation of the powers of the *Bundesrat*. The FCC

---

judicial restraint. If Parliament may not 'amend' the Constitution via its own interpretation, then Korinek's justification for judicial restraint must rest on the ability of Parliament to amend the Constitution formally. See Korinek op cit (n 454) 48. This rather mechanical approach to constitutionalism does not solve the problem because, as Häberle op cit (n 319) 217 points out, constitutional interpretation and amendment are parts of the same process, and one cannot analyse them separately. Schlaich op cit (n 367) 119 points to the little attention which is paid to the workings of Parliament in constitutional law. Parliament is, after all, the most important institution of the Basic Law.

[735] Heun op cit (n 477) 12.
[736] The fundamental rights section of the Basic Law sets limits to the ability of *Länder* to go their own way. See Karpen 'Federalism' in Karpen op cit (n 390) 219.
[737] Article 72.2 *GG*.
[738] 2 *BVerfGE* 213 224; Blair op cit (n 391) 79.
[739] Article 72.1 *GG*.
[740] 13 *BVerfGE* 181 196.
[741] 36 *BVerfGE* 193 202; 36 *BVerfGE* 314 320. See Blair op cit (n 391) 75.
[742] 34 *BVerfGE* 9 28.

decided that framework legislation presupposes *Land* legislation. *Bund* frameworks cannot stand on their own — they must be capable of being completed by the *Länder* and may not confine the latter to predetermined legal alternatives.[743] According to the Basic Law, the *Bundesrat* always has the power to delay legislation, but its veto can be overridden by an equivalent majority of the *Bundestag*.[744] However, bills which affect the legal status of the *Länder* or the relationship between the *Länder* and the *Bund* require the consent of the *Bundesrat*. Almost half of all legislation belongs to this category since most of the *Bund*'s legislation is executed by the *Länder*. In effect this means that the administrative nature of a single clause in a bill will give the *Bundesrat* a veto over the entire bill.[745] These veto powers of the *Bundesrat* have presented problems in cases where political parties have exploited their majorities in the *Bundesrat* to block the reforms of their opponents in the *Bundestag*. Realizing the dangers that such stalemates might provide for the democratic process, the court changed its approach.[746] Amendments of legislation which initially required *Bundesrat* consent require renewed *Bundesrat* consent only when they seek a 'systemic shift' in the power relations between *Bund* and *Länder*.[747] The court also found the practice of the *Bundestag* of presenting provisions relating to the execution of the legislation by the *Länder* in a separate bill to Parliament to be quite legitimate.[748]

The doctrine of federal comity (*Bundestreue*) was initially used by the court to resolve problems of federalism. The doctrine was applied in the first *Television* judgment, when the court found that the style of negotiations of the Adenauer government with the *Länder* conflicted with federal comity.[749] Adenauer's (central) government employed a strategy of divide and rule to establish a second television station under joint *Bund* and *Länder* control.[750] This decision was considered to be a drastic interference with the political process. Again, the court responded. Nowadays a concrete constitutional relationship between *Bund* and *Länder* has to exist before comity is required. The principle of comity then governs the way in which rights, arising from the constitutional relationship, should be exercised.[751] The FCC has placed more emphasis on the resolution of political problems through the political institutions (*Bundesrat* and *Bundestag*) and stressed that the wisdom of Federal or *Länder* legislation may not be challenged with the doctrine of federal comity. This shift in attitude was brought about by severe criticism from academics who argued that comity to the *Bund* boiled down to nothing but comity to the government of the day.[752]

---

[743] The legislation must leave the *Länder* to decide on matters of 'substantial weight' so that the *Länder* can regulate the matter in accordance with any special conditions which might exist in their region (4 *BVerfGE* 115 129).

[744] Article 77.4 *GG*: majority veto must be overturned by another majority in the *Bundestag*; a two-thirds majority requires a two-thirds majority to override.

[745] 8 *BVerfGE* 274 294; see Blair op cit (n 391) 93.

[746] The FCC acted to save the political process as, over time, more and more bills became amendments of existing legislation and if the absolute veto were extended to all of these amendments, the government would not have been able to govern without the consent of the opposition (unless the same coalition controls both the *Bundesrat* and the *Bundestag*). The whole democratic political process would have been frustrated.

[747] 37 *BVerfGE* 363 379.

[748] Ibid; see also Blair op cit (n 391) 103.

[749] 12 *BVerfGE* 205 255.

[750] See Blair op cit (n 391) 177.

[751] 13 *BVerfGE* 54 75.

[752] See Blair op cit (n 391) 204.

The changing nature of the modern administrative state forced most of the changes in the court's handling of federalism: the doctrine of federal comity was in some way the legal response to the challenge; the doctrine of co-operative federalism is the political response.[753] Co-operative federalism made the principle of comity almost unnecessary. Federal comity requires the parties in the Federal system to have some consideration for the legitimate interests of other parties in the system; co-operative federalism goes beyond this and deals with the changes of governments' functions in the modern state. The development of co-operative federalism was largely uninfluenced and uncontrolled by the FCC.[754]

Nothwithstanding the doubtful validity of the concerns — at least for some areas of constitutional interpretation — the call for judicial restraint has gained in strength as well as content and definition over the last years.[755] It seems unlikely that these calls will have no influence on the FCC.

### 5.5.5 Functional/process approaches to judicial review

Proponents of a functional approach to judicial review argue that state functions are awarded to organs with appropriate structures to deal with them; these structures should in turn be orientated to the fulfilment of the tasks awarded. Some proponents try to identify or develop different levels of scrutiny based on the nature of disputes coming to the court. The level of scrutiny depends on the court's function in the state and society.[756] Generally, proponents of a functional approach first determine the function of the court and thereafter develop a method of constitutional interpretation. Proponents of the other theories of interpretation tend to accept the consequences — not uncritically — of their theory of interpretation for the court's function. But functional approaches are diverse: some are merely descriptive and no standard for judicial review or 'method of constitutional interpretation' is developed.[757] The court's function is, moreover, not always derived from the Constitution itself. The functional approach has therefore also been subjected to increasing criticism.[758]

---

[753] At 209.
[754] At 254.
[755] Most persuasive are the calls for restraint which are combined with propositions of a functional nature. See Schneider 'Verfassungsinterpretation aus theoretischer Sicht' in Schneider & Steinberg (eds) Verfassungsrecht zwischen Wissenschaft und Richterkunst (1990) 39 at 44, who does not see judicial restraint as an act of voluntary deference, but rather as the methodological consequence of the 'oneness' of the Constitution. He distinguishes between structural oneness (historical, constitutional compromises), material oneness (vague, abstract norms), and functional oneness (contradictory principles which could be differently concretized and accentuated — e g social Rechtsstaat). Judicial restraint merely means respecting this oneness. See also Mahrenholz op cit (n 459) 64, who sees judicial restraint as sticking to facts of the case. Only then, he argues, is adjudication normative and not political. Gusy op cit (n 322) 17 acknowledges that the calls for restraint have not been concretely defined in the past. In order to solve the problem he suggests that material law must be brought in contact with constitutional directives and, in this way, be determinative of the division of competencies. It is not enough that the constitutional goals are achieved in some way; *they should rather be achieved via the prescribed procedures.* Gusy then (at 98–137) contrasts the procedures of the court with that of the legislator. The legitimacy of legislative decisions rests on democratic election, that of the FCC on the *Rechtsstaat*, social state and democratic commands of the Constitution. It is not the desirability of the outcome of decisions, but the difference in procedure and legitimacy which forms the basis for the determination of the division of competencies. Besides the directives of the Constitution, the ability of a procedure to be practical and guarantee legal certainty are determinative of the division of competencies.
[756] The work of Schneider 'Verfassungsgerichtsbarkeit und Gewaltenteilung' (1980) 33 *NJW* 2103 could therefore be described as proposing a functional rather than a restrictive mode of interpretation.
[757] Schneider op cit (n 491) 40.
[758] Schlaich op cit (n 356) 228.

The FCC distinguishes between three levels of review:[759] mere control of manifest (*Evidenz*) infringements;[760] control of the justifiability (*Vertretbarkeit*)[761] of state action; and intensive control of the content of the regulation.[762] The FCC determined that the intensity of judicial scrutiny depends on the nature of the material regulated by the legislation,[763] the intensity of the legislative invasion,[764] the importance of the legal goods in question, and the possibility (or impossibility) of making clear and straightforward decisions.[765] The principle of proportionality has therefore not been the only yardstick to determine the constitutionality of *Grundrecht* limitations.[766] The results of the levels of review approach have been criticized as giving almost no protection to some *Grundrechte*, and too much to others, such as the freedom of expression and demonstration. According to critics, the result has been a general weakening of the *Rechtsstaat* principle.[767] The different levels of scrutiny outlined by the court in the *Co-determination* case and in the area of equality[768] are often seen as proof of the FCC's acceptance of a functional theory of review.[769]

---

[759] 50 *BVerfGE* 290 333 (*Mitbestimmung*).

[760] This level of scrutiny requires a manifest infringement of a right without a rational justification before the court will invalidate the legislation. See 36 *BVerfGE* 1 17 (*Ostpolitik*, '*offensichtlich*'); 56 *BVerfGE* 54 82 ('evident').

[761] The court reviews whether the legislative decision is objectively justifiable (25 *BVerfGE* 1 12, 17; 39 *BVerfGE* 210 225 — both cases deal with the free exercise of a profession — art 12 *GG*). In these instances the court does not review the content of the legislation in detail, but rather considers whether the legislature has 'applied its mind properly'.

[762] The court will determine the facts and make a prognosis for itself. In matters concerning life or the elementary freedoms of the individual the state is not allowed to experiment. See 7 *BVerfGE* 377 415 (pharmacies and national health), 39 *BVerfGE* 1 46, 51 (abortion); 45 *BVerfGE* 187 238 (lifelong imprisonment); Zeidler op cit (n 437) 523; Philippi op cit (n 460) 188; Schuppert op cit (n 574) 1197. The more intense the scrutiny, the less room for the legislature to manoeuvre. Vogel op cit (n 460) 210 rejects these levels of scrutiny as unhelpful.

[763] With regard to economic legislation the court will exercise even more restraint than its normal minimum rationality scrutiny (39 *BVerfGE* 210 230 — legislation must be 'clearly missing its purpose'); 18 *BVerfGE* 315 331; cf the US Supreme Court's deferential attitude in the area of economic regulations.

[764] The greater the legislative invasion, the more compelling justifying grounds are required (7 *BVerfGE* 377 405; 50 *BVerfGE* 290 332).

[765] So, for example, the court stressed the importance that the Basic Law attaches to marriage and the family (76 *BVerfGE* 1, (1988) 41 *NJW* 626).

[766] Proportionality remains the most important tool to control state, especially administrative, action. So, for example, the administration has to show — in order to justify banning an assembly — that the prohibition of the demonstration is necessary to protect legal interests as important as the right of assembly. In practice the state normally passes this hurdle easily, but the difficulty lies in showing that the threat to the other legal interests is immediate enough to warrant the limitation of the right of assembly. See Rautenbach & Watney op cit (n 445) 651.

[767] Ipsen '*Über das Grundgesetz — nach 25 Jahren*' (1974) 27 *Die Öffentliche Verwaltung* 289; Sendler op cit (n 396) 484.

[768] The court emphasizes the discretion of the legislator when applying the general equality clause (3 *BVerfGE* 58 135; 2 *BVerfGE* 266 281; 4 *BVerfGE* 144 155; 25 *BVerfGE* 101 105), but is much stricter when the special equality provisions are affected. The provisions of the general equality provision has been watered down to review for irrationality (*Willkürverbot*). This development has been seen as proof that the court distinguishes between norms to act (*Handlungsnorm*) and norms of control (*Kontrollnorm*). The general equality provision demands that the legislature creates material conditions of equality as a *Handlungsnorm*, but as a *Kontrollnorm* it means only that equals may not be treated unequally without a rational basis for the distinction. See Heun op cit (n 477) 46–53, who mentions several objections to the distinction between *Handlungs-* and *Kontrollnorm*. Heun (at 50) argues that, in the absence of FCC control, a *Handlungsnorm* can mean very little but a utopian goal for the legislature which lacks any enforceability.

[769] See Schuppert op cit (n 626) 26, who distinguishes between one- and multi-dimensional freedom problems. While the former concerns the control of state infringement of individual freedom zones, the latter is about the balancing and reconciliation of interest, freedom, and value conflicts. Review must necessarily be less intense when dealing with multi-dimensional balancing problems as the Constitution contains a more legitimate process — the legislative process — for solving multi-dimensional freedom problems. In this regard Schuppert's argument relies on Luhmann *Legitimation durch Verfahren* (1969).

An interesting version of the functional approach is proposed by Ingwer Ebsen, which will now be discussed in some detail. Ebsen criticizes the dominant approach which, while it recognizes the political nature of constitutional law, still expects the court to defer to the other, especially the legislative, branches of government when the court deals with 'political' issues.[770] These commentators are forced into what Ebsen calls the *'aporetische'* approach.[771] For example, the judge may not invent but only discover constitutional principles by cognition (with legal scientific methods);[772] judges should take the political consequences of their decisions into account, but may only decide on disputes which can be resolved through the legal process;[773] the judge concretizes the vague norms of the Constitution, but develops and adapts the Constitution to changing realities at the same time;[774] general constitutional principles, such as the equality clause and the *Rechtsstaat* principle, must be concretized, taking meaningful intellectual, economic, sociological, and political realities into account, but the Constitution still normatively ties the hands of the judge;[775] or, as Mohamed J stated within the context of the Namibian Constitution: 'It is, however, a value judgment which requires objectively to be articulated and identified, regard being had to the contemporary norms, aspirations, expectations and sensitivities of the people as expressed in its national institutions and its Constitution . . ..'[776]

Ebsen argues that these contradictions result because of the belief that constitutional norms — and not the institution of judicial review — mediate between opposing ideas and interests.[777] As the Constitution cannot have the ability to change and control its own change and changes in society at the same time, contradictions are inevitably within the *'aporetische'* position.[778]

According to Ebsen, the FCC, as an autonomous integrator of interests, needs a theory of society which explains the relationship between the court, the political parties, other state institutions, and social interest groups. Such a theory about society is imperative to defend the court against the accusations about the accountability and the personal preferences of judges.[779] Society is a self-governing system geared towards consensual system goals. The FCC's role can only be justified if it helps to steer society towards these goals. Balance and survival are the keywords with which to describe the goals of society. Survival refers to the preservation of the democratic constitutional state. Balance means that interest groups should

---

[770] Ebsen *Das Bundesverfassungsgericht als Element gesellschaftlicher Selbstregulierung: eine pluralistische Theorie der Verfassungsgerichtsbarkeit im demokratischen Verfassungsstaat* (1985).
[771] At 142.
[772] Ebsen op cit (n 770) 160 describes Otto Bachof.
[773] Ebsen op cit (n 770) 143, 154 contributes this to the jurisprudence of Gerhard Leibholz.
[774] Ebsen op cit (n 770) 169 in connection with Detlef Merten.
[775] Justice Wintrich, member of the FCC, quoted from Ebsen op cit (n 770) 171.
[776] *Ex parte Attorney-General, Namibia: In re Corporal Punishment by Organs of State* 1991 (3) SA 76 (NmS) at 86. Whether corporal punishment is inhuman clearly needs to be answered with reference to the Constitution, but it is not clear how the contemporary norms, expressed in the Constitution, can serve to concretize the Constitution and inform a value judgment.
[777] Ebsen's argument (op cit (n 770) 192) that the justification for judicial review cannot be found in an archimedial point outside the political process (such as the normativity of the Constitution) is rejected by Schlaich. Schlaich op cit (n 356) 26 argues that the court's regulation of the political process is merely a side-effect of its legal activities.
[778] Ebsen sees the institution of judicial review as the substantive check on majority rule.
[779] In short, a defence against, among others, the de-constructionalist or CLS objection that interpretation must necessarily be subjective in time and person. See Van der Merwe 'A Moral Case for Lawyer's Law' (1992) 109 *SALJ* 619 at 640ff; Van Doren 'Critical Legal Studies and South Africa' (1989) 106 *SALJ* 648.

remain committed to the Constitution despite the existence of conflict over aspects of the legal order and over the legitimacy of the elected government officials.[780]

The court contributes towards the resolution of conflict in society and in this way it contributes to steering society towards its goals. Three types of conflict exist within society: conflict between social interests; conflict over political power positions; and conflict of opinion.[781] The court's decisions are the result of both strategic acts (power struggles with the aim of achieving a result) and relating discourse arguments (both parties believe subjectively in a correct solution to the problem).[782] Discourse arguments are practical or legal. In the latter instance, only those arguments which are based on rules acknowledged by the law as relevant to the case are allowed.[783]

- *Conflict of social interests* The crux of this battle — in the constitutional political sense — lies in the struggle over the legitimacy of all existing socio-economic distribution structures.[784] In these decisions the judge looks for the universal justification. The decision must appear to be impartial. A unanimous decision of the court is ideal, but irreconcilable arguments can of course only be resolved through the vote. The tendency to compromise decisions in this area is caused by the pressure to reach consensus and the background and training of most of the judges.[785]

- *Conflict over political power positions* This category of conflict exists over the competencies of organs of the state (especially the constitutional organs), and the battle of minorities not be disadvantaged in the political process.[786]

- *Conflict of opinion* Conflict over the proportionality of state action is a good example of such conflict. The result cannot be identified with the interests of social and political groups. Discursive arguments dominate the proceedings before the court. Conflicts of opinion form by far the bulk of the work of the court.[787]

The historical context, the constitutional principles and text of the Basic Law, the selection and autonomy of the judges, procedures adopted by the court, the decision-making process itself, the powers of the judges, and the effect of the court's decisions are all structural influences[788] within which the court seeks to resolve conflict and steer society towards its goals. In particular the court contributes by fulfilling the functions of securing individual liberty, maintaining an open political process, and integrating competing interests.[789] In trying to fulfil each of the

---

[780] Ebsen op cit (n 770) 226.

[781] At 294. These conflicts are taking place in and outside of court all the time. The FCC itself is the subject of the conflict over political positions when selection of judges takes place.

[782] At 233.

[783] At 249. See Alexy *A Theory of Legal Argumentation* (1989) 177.

[784] Socio-economic distribution mechanisms refers to those institutions of the state and society which affect the individual's material well-being. First and foremost are the structures at the work-place (See *Co-determination* case). Connected conflicts are those about the press, television, and education. The third group of conflicting social interests concerns treaties and re-armament; the relationship to the distribution mechanism is less clear, but the conflict is clearly that of interests groups.

[785] Ebsen op cit (n 770) 294; Clark op cit (n 407) 1846.

[786] Ebsen op cit (n 770) 299.

[787] At 302.

[788] At 255.

[789] See Ebsen op cit (n 770) 320.

functions the court is confronted with all three types of conflict to a greater or a lesser extent, and in its endeavours to resolve a particular conflict the court may fulfil more than one of its functions.

The first function of the court is to protect the individual against the state's power and stabilize the constitutional system of government despite rapid and constant changes in circumstances.[790] Freedom does not only mean freedom from state interference but also entails that the citizen must be able to influence the security of his/her freedom. The state organizes and distributes the factual preconditions for the enjoyment of freedom: for beneficiaries the distribution process has the same character as the freedom guarantees.

Both the negative and the positive (social state) dimensions of securing individual liberty are, to an extent, based upon consensus. Both dimensions of securing individual liberty can be the goal of judicial review only to the extent that it embodies consensus. The consensus about freedom in the negative sense is presently much broader and better defined in Germany than freedom in the positive (social state) sense.[791] Most questions concerning freedom in the positive sense deal with conflicts of social interests and are therefore more about the preservation of the Constitution as a social compromise. The function of judicial review in these areas is more concerned with integration than the security of individual liberty. The review of the existing law against consensual conceptions of freedom — in the negative sense — has reached a high degree of intensity. The battles of yesterday can not be renegotiated in the FCC today. In fact, in the context of freedom in the negative sense the FCC has been given the status of a petition committee or ombud-type institution,[792] and in all these cases the FCC has been very thorough and sensitive. Parliament, on the other hand, has shown the tendency to make vague legislation and to delegate more and more discretionary power to the executive. The court tries to ensure that Parliament makes all the vital decisions.

The second function of the court is that of a 'referee' who ensures that the democratic process remains open.[793] Minorities accept majority rule partly because the possibility of becoming the majority exists.[794] The court has to mediate between different opinions in the community,[795] supervise the institutionalized party struggle,[796] and control the formation of will within organs of the state.[797]

---

[790] At 321.
[791] At 324.
[792] At 332.
[793] At 340.
[794] Cf the more sceptical (pluralist) approach of Von Arnim. For Von Arnim the adversarial battle of interests stands at the centre of democracy. Because of the inequality of influence and the difference in organizationability and conflictability of the different interests, democracy does not always operate in the general interest. Keeping the political process open is therefore inadequate to ensure that consistent losers will 'stick to the political game'. On the contrary, an open political process ensures their defeat. These imbalances need to be brought in line by the FCC. The FCC 'talks' to the legislative majority over the correctness of their goals and means and then allows public opinion to umpire the outcome. See Von Arnim *Staatslehre der Bundesrepublik Deutschland* (1984) 383; and cf Ely *Democracy and Distrust: A Theory of Judicial Review* (1980); Ossenbühl op cit (n 507) 2106.
[795] Here the communication freedoms and institutions (arts 5 *GG*; 8 *GG*; 9 *GG*) are important. See 34 *BVerfGE* 160 (broadcasting time for political parties); 47 *BVerfGE* 198 (political advertising).
[796] Examples: the right to vote and equality of the vote; equality of chances for the political parties (47 *BVerfGE* 253); legitimacy of government propaganda (44 *BVerfGE* 125); state financial support to political parties (20 *BVerfGE* 56).
[797] Examples: protection of the opposition (43 *BVerfGE* 142); qualified majorities for amendment of the Constitution.

Conflicts over the formation of the public opinion are conflicts of social interests; those over the disadvantages faced by the minorities are conflicts over political power positions; and election disputes are conflicts of opinion. In general the court endeavours to protect minorities, but not political radicalism. The court has exercised a high degree of scrutiny to ensure the equality of chances of political parties.[798]

The third function of the court is that of integration. The constitutional principles which entrenched social compromises assist the court in its third function.[799]

For Rudolf Smend it was immaterial whether the process of integration is called a value system, cultural system, or integration system.[800] The meaning of the Constitution is that it is the legal order of a process of integration. This process of integration continuously re-creates the state and this gives the state a real life and gives orientation to the process of interpretation. *Grundrechte* are the expressions of the cultural (value) beliefs of the nation, but constitutional interpretation incorporates both value constellations and streams of the *Zeitgeist* (consciousness of the time).[801]

For Ebsen integration refers to the Constitution as a social compromise. The Constitution circumscribed the ability of the majority of Parliament to change the content of the compromise. The process of judicial review seeks to give meaning and to realize the social compromise by carrying the debate over constitutional compromises into the realm of practical discourse.[802] It is the opportunity to resort to constitutional litigation about social compromises — not the existence of the compromise in the Constitution — which persuades social interest groups to maintain the compromise. By using the court parties to the conflict consent to respect the decision of the court, while knowing that the decision of the court may be reversed in time.[803]

In practice the FCC tries to find a solution that will accommodate all the relevant powers. Another compromise, rather than a decision, is often the outcome.[804] The court emphasizes that arguments must strive towards universality and correctness, but different solutions must remain possible. In this regard the court contributes to Luhmann's understanding of democracy: 'keeping complexity intact despite continuous decision-making'.[805] This should be no surprise as both Luhmann and Ebsen see the rationality and the humanity of democracy in the temporary character of its decisions.

## 5.6 Conclusion

Four years after the Nazi regime capitulated the drafters of the Basic Law were confronted with the consequences of Hitler's holocaust; the response was no longer

---

[798] Ebsen op cit (n 770) 344.
[799] At 346.
[800] The objective value order is just such a framework. In this sense the integration theory of Smend has been accepted by the FCC. See Schenke op cit (n 358) 656; Böckenförde op cit (n 656) 2094.
[801] Böckenförde op cit (n 656) 2094 sets out the integration theory of Smend.
[802] Ebsen op cit (n 770) 346f.
[803] Abortion (39 *BVerfGE* 1), co-determination (50 *BVerfGE* 290), the structure of the universities (35 *BVerfGE* 79), and decisions concerning conscientious objection (12 *BVerfGE* 45) are all examples of the integrating function of the court.
[804] Ebsen op cit (n 770) 357.
[805] Quoted from Häberle op cit (n 319) 23.

to the war, but upon the reflection it had cast on German attitudes to human dignity, equality, and democracy. The drafters responded by tying the new democracy tightly to a set of values and by giving extensive powers to a Constitutional Court to guard over the democratic process.

The court responded by quickly establishing itself as a major player on the German political scene. Its value-orientated approach to the interpretation of fundamental rights, especially when combined with extensive use of the principle of proportionality, enables the court to set the parameters for political discourse in Germany. Its influence has expanded tremendously. More importantly, the recognition of a value order, either derived abstractly from the Constitution itself or as the product of balancing in individual cases, opened the door for the court to determine, at least potentially, the outcome of all political controversies. Furthermore, the court developed its own procedural rules which give it the discretion over to whom, for what, and when access to the court will be granted. Finally, a vast array of alternatives to straight invalidation of state action were devised to enable the court to manipulate the consequences of its decisions.

It is arguable that no other *Constitutional Court* has achieved the status and has had the impact on society comparable to the German Federal Constitutional Court. The jurisprudence of the FCC shows that with some imagination a Constitutional Court can transform a legal system. Serious challenges to the court's new role in the political process emerged only in the 1970s when political parties started to exploit the possibilities provided by the combination of the abstract review procedure and the court's value-orientated approach to constitutional interpretation. The court became another forum to which losers in the political process habitually turned. And, as democracy in Germany settled, the debate about judicial review became more robust. Some commentators feel that the network of the decisions of the court have not only established a framework for state and society, but have demoted the other branches of government to mere executors of the court's vision of Basic Law demands. The so-called *Kompetenz-Kompetenz* (the court's ability to determine its own competence) became an issue which generated increasingly heated exchanges among academic lawyers. The debate spread to encompass the entire relationship between the democratic processes and the court and the search for an appropriate justification for judicial review became as much of a focal point in German constitutional law as it has been in the other jurisdictions (India, US, and Canada) discussed.

The focus of the debate in Germany seems to have moved from the meaning of rights to the function of judicial review. The main reason for the shift in focus is the realization that it is not the Basic Law, but the institution of judicial review, which lies at the heart of constitutionalism. The extent to which one can learn from the elaborate and sophisticated precedents of the German Federal Constitutional Court on moral, social, and political questions may be as debatable as whether one should follow all the intricate solutions Germans have developed to deal with the unique problems presented by the adoption of a Constitutional Court system of judicial review. What does seem clear is that the problematical relationship between judicial review and democracy will have to be addressed in any system committed to the notion of constitutionalism.

## 6 CONCLUSION: TOWARDS A PURPOSIVE APPROACH

'The task of expounding a Constitution is crucially different from that of construing a statute. A statute defines present rights and obligations. It is easily enacted and easily repealed. A Constitution, by contrast, is drafted with an eye to the future. Its function is to provide a continuing framework for the legitimate exercise of governmental power and, when joined by a Charter of Rights, *for the unlimiting protection of individual rights and liberties*. Once enacted, its provisions can't easily be repealed or amended. It must, therefore, be capable of growth and development over time to meet new social, political and historical realities often unimagined by its framers. *The judiciary is the guardian of the Constitution* and must, in interpreting its provisions, bear these conditions in mind.'[806]

'That court was not concerned with a Bill of Rights. Nevertheless, the *dicta* are applicable when interpreting the relevant provisions of the Constitution and also when interpreting s 31. What appears from all the above authorities is clear. *The task of the courts is to ascertain from the words of the statute in the context thereof what the intention of the Legislature is*. If the wording of the statute is clear and unambiguous they state what that intention is. It is not for the court to invent fancied ambiguities and usurp the functions of the Legislature.'[807]

The portents for a rigorous constitutional jurisprudence in South Africa are not particularly promising. In the past South African courts, when confronted with constitutional legislation, have failed to recognize the fundamental dissimilarity between an interpretive process relating to a Constitution and that relating to ordinary legislation. South African jurisprudence has been dominated by an adherence to literalism in which interpretation is viewed as a mechanistic enterprise. Each text is thus interpreted in the same manner and no concession is given to the influence of text upon the process of interpretation.[808]

This chapter has attempted to draw on the rich experience of four different jurisdictions — the United States of America, Canada, India, and Germany — in an attempt to develop a coherent approach to constitutional interpretation which is based upon an understanding of the purpose of a Constitution and not simply on the literal meaning of the words of the text. Unfortunately a sterile literalist approach to constitutional interpretation has been evident in the judgments delivered by South African courts, although this approach is not confined to South Africa, as our comparative analysis reveals.

Two approaches to constitutional interpretation have dominated the literature. The first argues in favour of the development of a set of fundamental principles which government should respect in its treatment of all citizens. A Bill of Rights comprises general comprehensive moral standards that must be respected by government. According to this approach, government is not legally free to disregard fundamental principles of liberty, justice, and equality in terms of which each individual citizen must be treated with equal concern. Adherents to this approach argue that 'a constitutional principle, enforced by independent judges is not undemocratic. On the contrary it is a precondition of legitimate democracy that government is required to treat individual citizens as equals and to respect their fundamental liberties and dignity.'[809] This approach argues that, should these conditions not be

---

[806] *Hunter et al v The Southam Inc* (1984) 11 DLR (4th) 641 at 649.
[807] *Government of the Republic of Bophuthatswana v Segale* 1990 (1) SA 434 (BA) at 448.
[808] See in general Du Plessis & De Ville 'The Bill of Rights: Interpretation in the South African Context: Diagnostic Observations' (1993) 4 *Stell LR* 59 at 86.
[809] Dworkin *Life's Dominion* (1993) 123.

met, there can be no genuine democracy because the majority has no legitimate moral title to govern.

An alternative approach to constitutional jurisprudence is one which the court in *Segale's* case appeared to adopt enthusiastically. A Bill of Rights represents the requirements for a democratic society as articulated by the politicians who drafted and originally endorsed its contents. Accordingly the clauses of a Bill of Rights can only be interpreted to support the outcome which the drafters would have expected.

This approach renders a constitutional enterprise extremely problematic. Why, for example, should a South African government democratically elected fifty years after the acceptance of a Bill of Rights be restricted by the social vision of negotiators at Kempton Park?

A further problem inherent in the original intentionalist approach is its failure to fulfil its proclaimed aim, i e to eradicate judicial choice from the process of judicial decision-making. It has been shown, particularly in the examination of the record of the US Supreme Court, that the narrow originalist approach to a Bill of Rights does not provide a meaningful restraint on the discretion of a judge in imposing his or her values upon a constitutional text. In all four jurisdictions analysed in this chapter the courts tended to develop away from original intent and towards a purposive approach in terms of which the adjudicating court attempts to develop a theory as to the nature of the fundamental principles contained in a Bill of Rights, which in turn makes the most sense of the purpose of a Bill of Rights within the context of a society proclaiming democratic aspirations.

These principles contain the basis for the democratic vision enshrined in the Constitution and they, rather than the concrete convictions of the original authors, constitute the guidelines which a court seeks to discover and apply in the context of a particular case.

The comparative record reveals that the development of these guidelines presents a continuing challenge for courts. In this connection the doctrine of scrutiny employed by US jurisprudence is illustrative. After the celebrated footnote 4 in *United States v Carolene Products Company*[810] many US constitutionalists argued that there should be stricter judicial protection for some liberties rather than for others by showing how the former possessed intrinsically deeper civic values than remaining liberties. There is, however, no general consensus as to what constitutes the fundamental principles without which there can be no freedom. For example, can one say that freedom of expression is more essential to personal fulfilment than proprietary security or freedom of choice in productive endeavours?[811]

The debate surrounding the doctrine of strict scrutiny points to an even more significant question: whether a Bill of Rights poses affirmative duties upon government. Some courts have interpreted a Bill of Rights in this manner. The German Constitutional Court, for example, has declared:

> 'The state's duty to protect [life] is extensive. Not only is the state obliged to refrain from directly infringing upon developing life, but the state should protect and foster developing life and this means, above all, to protect it from the unlawful interference from others.'[812]

---

[810] 304 US 144, 152–3 (1938).
[811] Michaelman *Constitutional Method* (1992) 59 *U Chicago LR* 91 at 96.
[812] 39 *BVerfGE* 1 42; see also Currie 'Positive and Negative Rights' (1986) 53 *U Chicago LR* 864 at 870.

The German court has viewed the Basic Law as incorporating a vision of citizenship which emphasizes both the personal and the communal elements of citizenship. While attempting to protect the individual's personal search for self-fulfilment, the individual is viewed in the context of these social attachments and commitments.[813] Ernst Böckenförde, a judge of the Federal Constitutional Court, has summarized the German court's approach in this regard as follows:

> '[A] particular liberty enshrined in the basic right is qualified in a special way by relating all basic rights to values. As a result of this value dimension it is aimed at realizing and fulfilling the value expressed in and through such rights. This makes possible and justifies the drawing of a legally relevant distinction between uses of liberty that realize and uses that jeopardize that value. A particular liberty is thus qualified and is made subject to the logic of fluctuating values.'[814]

The Indian Supreme Court has arguably been the most activist Constitutional Court amongst the jurisdictions under review. The Indian judiciary, perhaps conscious of the shortcomings of the legislative process, have carried out constitutional mandates within an increasing sphere of activity, causing Chinnapa Reddy J to observe extrajudicially, 'it is not the Judiciary but the Parliament and the Executive that have failed the people'.[815]

As noted earlier in this chapter, the post-Emergency Indian Supreme Court developed a purposive approach to the Indian Constitution by seeking a set of values which it considered to be central to the Constitution. These values comprise social and political justice, substantive equality, and human dignity, which the court identified from a reading of the complete text, including the preamble and the directive principles of state policy. The rights contained in Part III of the Indian Constitution were then redefined and extended in accordance with these values. In this manner the Indian courts assessed state action or inaction against a touchstone of the entire Constitution as opposed to examining such action by applying a decontextualized analysis of a particular right.

Notwithstanding the negatively phrased nature of their Bill of Rights, the US courts have not confined their constitutional activity to the defence of negative rights. The court has been aware that the enforcement of a negative right could include the continuation of a financial obligation. In *Goldberg v Kelly*[816] the court held that the due process clause forbade the termination of welfare benefits under state- and Federal-assisted welfare programmes prior to welfare recipients being afforded an evidentiary hearing. As Currie notes, 'here is arguably an affirmative obligation of sorts: that the state may not stop paying means it must pay'.[817] In *Ex parte Young*[818] the court held that a provision imposing a fine so high as to discourage violating a law in order to test its validity constituted a deprivation of

---

[813] In an early decision, 4 *BVerfGE* 7 15, the court laid the foundation for this approach: It said 'The Basic Law does not view the individual as isolated and sovereign; it rather resolved the individual–society tension by recognizing that a person is part of and tied to a community, but this bond may not relinquish the self-worth of the individual ... This means that the individual must accept the reasonable limits drawn by the legislator in particular circumstances upon her/his freedom to act when those limits are drawn to nurse and promote a social existence for people together. This presupposes that individual autonomy is preserved.'

[814] As quoted in Kommers 'German Constitutionalism: A Prolegomenon' (1991) 40 *Emory LJ* 837 at 860.

[815] Chinnapa Reddy 'Socialism, Constitution and the Country Today' 1983 *AIR J* 33 at 39. See also Cottrell 'Indian Judicial Activism in Company Law' (1990) 39 *ICLQ* 433 at 451.

[816] 397 US 254 (1970).

[817] Currie op cit (n 812) 872.

[818] 209 US 123 (1908).

property without due process of law. In *Shapiro v Thompson*[819] the court held that it was unconstitutional to exclude individuals from participating in welfare programmes on the grounds that they had not lived in the state for a year. The judgment was grounded on the principle of equal protection as there was not sufficient justification for distinguishing between old and new residents.

However, the far more individualistic nature of the US Bill of Rights demands that a *caveat* be inserted in this submission. The need for this caution is succinctly illustrated in *Deshaney v Winnebago County Dept of Social Services et al*.[820] In his judgment Rehnquist CJ said:

> 'But nothing in the language of the Due Process Clause itself requires the state to protect the life, liberty and property of its citizens against invasion by private actors. The Clause is phrased as a limitation on the state's power to act, not as the guarantee of certain minimal levels of safety and security . . . [I]ts language cannot fairly be extended to impose an affirmative obligation on the state to ensure that those interests do not come to harm through other means.'

In short, as Rehnquist CJ notes, the courts view the purpose of the Constitution as being 'to protect the people from the state, not to ensure that the state protected them from each other. The framers were content to leave the extent of governmental obligation in the latter area to the democratic political processes.'[821]

The debate surrounding the appropriate means of interpreting a Bill of Rights gives rise to a further critical distinction between enumerated and unenumerated rights. If the Bill of Rights enumerates only certain rights, leaving others unmentioned, some would argue that judges have the power to enforce only those rights actually enumerated. Thus judges should not be allowed to operate beyond the strict parameters of the Constitution for this will prevent any significant limitation with judicial power. It was this concern of White J which formed the premise upon which he found in *Bowers v Hardwick*[822] that the Supreme Court should not uphold that the constitutional right of privacy did not prohibit states from prescribing private, consensual sexual conduct between homosexuals. White J noted that judge-made constitutional law was suspect when it had 'little or no cognizable roots in the language or design of the Constitution'.[823] It follows, however, from the purposive approach outlined that, if a Bill of Rights is grounded upon broad principles of political morality, a specific right should have constitutional force irrespective of whether it is expressly enumerated in the Constitution, provided the unenumerated right can be brought within the dimension of political morality that is immanent within the Bill of Rights read as a complete text. In this connection certain judgments of the US Supreme Court, the Indian Supreme Court, and the German Constitutional Court which have been analysed are significant.[824]

The extracts from the *Hunter* and *Segale* judgments are illustrative of the differences in approach which have been the subject of heated debate among

---

[819] 394 US 618 (1969).

[820] 489 US 189, 195 (1990).

[821] At 196. See by contrast Brennan J's dissent, in which he stated (at 205): 'Because of the Court's initial fixation on the general principle that the Constitution does not establish positive rights, it is unable to appreciate our recognition in *Estelle* and *Youngberg* [*Estelle v Gamble* 429 US 97 (1976) and *Youngberg v Romeo* 457 US 307 (1982)] that this principle does not hold true in all circumstances.'

[822] 478 US 186 (1986).

[823] At 193.

[824] See Dworkin 'Unenumerated Rights: Whether and How *Roe* should be Overruled' (1992) 54 *U Chicago LR* 381.

constitutional lawyers. In our view neither is satisfactory. *Segale's* case reflects a sterile literalism whereas the Canadian Supreme Court in *Hunter's* case emphasizes the unqualified supremacy of individual rights without attempting to reconcile the protection of individual rights with the promotion of social equality. Given the limitation clause in the Canadian Charter and its imitation in the South African Bill of Rights, the pronouncement that individual rights are an all-powerful trump would appear to be out of harmony with the overall text.

The test for a constitutional enterprise cannot be reduced to the simple proposition that the state should not encroach on the liberty of the individual, thereby reducing all constitutional protection to a defence of negative rights. Whilst the German and Indian courts have been the most aggressive in the development of positive rights, the Canadian, and in certain cases US, jurisprudence cannot be reduced simply to the protection against state intrusions of constitutional entitlements. As Sunstein has noted in the context of freedom of expression,

'for those who believe either that the judiciary should play a limited role in the US government or that the Constitution's meaning is fixed by the original understanding of the ratifiers, the First Amendment is a particular embarrassment. The current state of free speech in America owes a great deal to extremely aggressive interpretations by the Supreme Court.'[825]

The fundamental premise for constitutional interpretation must be to approach the Bill of Rights in a different manner to ordinary legislation, a point acknowledged by even courts schooled in the system of Westminster parliamentary sovereignty. For example, in an oft-quoted passage Lord Wilberforce said in *Minister of Home Affairs v Fisher*,[826] after noting that there were two approaches to construing a Constitution:

'The first would be to say that, recognizing the status of the Constitution as, in effect, an Act of Parliament, there is room for interpreting it with less rigidity, and greater generosity, than other Acts . . . The second would be more radical: it would be to treat a Constitution instrument such as this sui generis, calling for principles of interpretation of its own, suitable to its character as already described, without necessary acceptance of all the presumptions that are relevant to legislation of private law . . . A Constitution is a legal instrument giving rise, amongst other things, to individual rights capable of enforcement in a court of law. Respect must be paid to the language which is being used and to the traditions and usages which have given meaning to that language. It is quite consistent with this, and with the recognition that rules of interpretation may apply, to take to the point of departure for the process of interpretation a recognition of the character and origin of the instrument, and to be guided by the principle of giving full recognition and effect to those fundamental rights and freedoms with a statement of which the Constitution commences.'

A Constitution must be viewed as being of a different legal genus to ordinary legislation. Hence the courts' task is to ascertain the set of core principles which justify the constitutional enterprise as contained in the text. In this manner the entire document can be viewed as one integrated text, its justification being found in a set of principles immanent in the text itself. Having achieved this task, the court is able to protect encroachments against liberties and, where appropriate, to develop positive rights to ensure that all South Africans may participate equally in the shaping of their political destiny.

---

[825] Sunstein 'Free Speech Now' (1992) 59 *U Chicago LR* 255 at 256.
[826] [1980] AC 320 at 329.

## 7 CHAPTER 3 OF THE NEW CONSTITUTION AND INTERPRETIVE THEORY

Chapter 3 contains express provisions which support the arguments set out in this chapter. In particular s 35 of the new Constitution contains a set of principles to be employed by courts in interpreting the Bill of Rights. The section provides as follows:

> '(1) In interpreting the provisions of this chapter a court of law shall promote the values which underlie an open and democratic society based on freedom and equality and shall, where applicable, have regard to public international law applicable to the protection of the rights entrenched in this Chapter, and may have regard to comparable foreign case law.
>
> (2) No law which limits any of the rights entrenched in this chapter, shall be constitutionally invalid solely by reason of the fact that the wording used *prima facie* exceeds the limits imposed in this chapter, provided such a law is reasonably capable of a more restricted interpretation which does not exceed such limits, in which event such law shall be construed as having a meaning in accordance with the said more restricted interpretation.
>
> (3) In the interpretation of any law and the application and development of the common law and customary law, a court shall have due regard to the spirit, purport and objects of this chapter.'

Section 35(1) provides statutory support for the purposive approach. It summarizes the purpose of the Constitution as the promotion of the values which underlie an open and democratic society based on freedom and equality. In short, the aim of Chapter 3 is the development of a society based upon these values. For this reason, when a court is confronted with a problem of unenumerated rights it should seek to answer the question as to whether the development of a right which is unenumerated in the Constitution would foster or promote those values which underlie an open and democratic society based on freedom and equality.

The section also enjoins the court to have regard to public international law where applicable. The question of using public international law as authority was canvassed recently by the Botswana Court of Appeal in *Unity Dow v A-G, Botswana*.[827] The court *a quo* had relied upon the international obligations of Botswana in support of its decision that sex-based discrimination was prohibited by the Constitution. The appellant objected to the respondent's use of the African Charter on Human and Peoples' Rights, the European Convention for the Protection of Human Rights and Fundamental Freedoms, and the Convention on the Elimination of Discrimination against Women in order to give interpretive content to the applicable provisions in the Botswana Constitution. Aguda JA set out the court's approach as follows:

> 'Even if it is accepted that those treaties and conventions do not confer enforceable rights on individuals within the state until Parliament has legislated its provisions into the law of the land in so far as such relevant international treaties and conventions may be referred to as an aid to construction of enactments, including the Constitution, I find myself at a loss to understand the complaint made against their use in that manner in interpretation of what no doubt are some difficult provisions of the Constitution. The reference made by the learned judge *a quo* to these materials amounts to nothing more than that.'

Section 35(2) contains a presumption of constitutionality used by many Constitutional Courts. As Georges CJ stated in *Zimbabwe Township Developers (Pvt) Ltd v Lou's Shoes (Pvt) Ltd*:[828]

---

[827] Civil Appeal 4/91. For a more detailed discussion, see below, 171ff and 629ff.
[828] 1984 (2) SA 778 (ZS) at 783.

'If one possible interpretation falls within the meaning of the Constitution and others do not, then the judicial body will presume that the law-makers intended to act constitutionally and uphold the piece of legislation so interpreted. This is one of the senses in which a presumption of constitutionality can be said to arise. One does not interpret the Constitution in the restricted manner in order to accommodate the challenged legislation. The Constitution must be properly interpreted, adopting the approach accepted above. Thereafter the challenge to legislation is examined to discover whether it can be interpreted to fit into the framework of the Constitution.'

Given the debate about the horizontal application of Chapter 3,[829] s 35(3) is of particular interest. It provides that in the interpretation of legislation, common law, or customary law recourse must be had to Chapter 3. Should any such law fall foul of the spirit, purport, and object of Chapter 3, it may be struck down as invalid. In other words, s 35(3) is an invitation to our courts to ensure that the principles contained in the chapter, i e the values which promote an open and democratic society based on freedom and equality, should be the touchstone of the development of our common law. In many ways these principles will replace the old Roman-Dutch law as an authority when our courts are confronted with penumbral situations. While sympathetic commentators may argue that writers such as Grotius and Voet represented a *laissez faire* model of society in which freedom was important, it can hardly be argued that the concept held equal sway.

The location of egalitarian philosophy might well be found in debates surrounding the American and French Revolutions and the development of socialism and the responses thereto. But whatever the genesis of such philosophy, the idea that liberty and equality were inextricably linked does not reflect the philosophical substructure on which the works of our old authorities are predicated. For this reason s 35(3) is an invitation to a creative engagement with a new set of jurisprudential principles which will test the further application of old authorities to the limit. It has been suggested that s 35(3) can be used to counter the argument in favour of horizontal application of Chapter 3. This argument can be summarized as follows: if the Bill of Rights had applied horizontally, there would be no need for s 35(3). As the drafters appeared to be concerned to ensure a measure of generous application of the rights contained in the chapter, they expressly inserted s 35(3) to meet some of these concerns. There might well be merit in this approach. However, without evaluating the merits of the general argument relating to horizontality, it would appear that s 35(3) recognizes that a Bill of Rights is merely a minimum set of societal standards for grievances which have been placed beyond the reach of a transient legislature. Whether such minimum standards apply vertically or horizontally is one issue. That the principles contained in these minimum standards should be used to enrich the very content of the greater body of the law would appear to represent the express purpose of s 35(3). For this reason s 35(3) should be used to transform our law in accordance with the Chapter's express objectives and not be employed in a disingenuous way to restrict the minimum content of the Chapter to a mere vertical operation.

The basic purpose of Chapter 3 is not only set out in one phrase of s 35(1). In terms of s 232(4) of the Constitution the various schedules to the Constitution as

---

[829] See in particular the attempt to restrict the ambit of Chapter 3 to an exclusively vertical application as a result of the omission of the word 'judiciary' in s 7(1), which provides that this chapter shall bind all legislative and executive organs of state at all levels of government.

well as the section which is contained directly after the last express provision of the Constitution (s 251), and which is headed 'National Unity and Reconciliation', are expressly given the same weight as other constitutional provisions. Consequently Schedule 4, i e the Constitutional Principles, and the 'after-amble' provide further textual support for the adoption of the theme which makes the most sense of Chapter 3, i e those values which promote an open and democratic society based upon freedom and equality. Indeed, Constitutional Principle I provides that the Constitution shall provide for the establishment of one sovereign state, common South African citizenship, and a democratic system of government committed to achieving *equality* in men and women and people of all races.[830]

These principles will provide significant guidance to a court in the interpretation of the substantive clauses. Take the equality provision. Section 8(1) provides that every person shall have the right to equality before the law and to equal protection of the law. Will a South African court interpret equality in terms of the Aristotelian concept, i e that justice considers that 'persons who are equal should have assigned to them equal things' and that 'there is no inequality when unequals are treated in proportion to the inequality existing between them'?[831] The adoption of this approach to equality will doubtless entrench a commitment to formal equality in our law. The court will ensure fair and equal treatment for all individuals as all are subject to a clear rule of law. Judges might then correct formal injustice, but ignore the distributive consequences of these judgments.

Hence the question arises as to whether equality in s 8(1) can be given a similar meaning to that traditionally adopted by the US Supreme Court or in many of the earlier Canadian cases. A commitment to the spirit, object, and purpose of Chapter 3 outlined in s 35, the 'after-amble', and the preamble must steer the court in a different direction. These tests, which emphasize the need for reconciliation and the reconstruction of South African society along the lines of freedom and equality, provide ample textual guidance for a court which seeks to ascertain the dominant purpose of the chapter and to use this as the touchstone in the interpretive process.

Accordingly the equality provision should be formulated to promote the ability of all to participate in the political and economic life of the country and hence prevent the reinforcement of inequality of the status of millions of South Africans by protecting those who stand to benefit from an exclusive commitment to a formal concept of equality and the consequent monopoly by a jurisprudence of negative rights.

The limitation clause contained in s 33 of the Constitution reflects the powerful influence of the Canadian Charter of Rights and Freedoms. Accordingly the relationship between the ambit of a substantive right and the limitation clause will doubtless vex the Constitutional Court as it has the Canadian Supreme Court. In particular the question arises as to whether the interpretation of the substantive right can be subject to careful scrutiny prior to the application of the limitation clause.

In *Andrews v Law Society of BC*[832] McIntyre J approved of a separation of the

---

[830] Our emphasis. The legal system shall ensure the equality of all before the law and an equitable legal process. Equality before the law includes laws, programmes, or activities that have as their object the amelioration of the conditions of the disadvantaged, including those disadvantaged on the grounds of race, colour, or gender.
[831] *The Politics of Aristotle* (translated by E Barker) (1966) Book III, XII, 1282b.
[832] (1989) 56 DLR (4th) 1.

two inquiries: whether an infringement of a governmental right has occurred and, thereafter, whether a justification for such infringement could be constitutionally established, for

> '[i]t is important to keep them analytically distinct if for no other reason than the different attribution of the burden of proof. It is for the citizen to establish that his or her Charter right has been infringed and for the state to justify the infringement.'[833]

The court is required to establish the meaning, ambit, and scope of a substantive right before it engages in an inquiry into a possible limitation thereof. This is best illustrated by the nature of the limitation inquiry. First, a court must examine whether a law which seeks to override a right guaranteed in Chapter 3 has an objective which relates to concerns which are 'pressing and substantial' in a free and democratic society. Secondly, the court must balance the nature of the right against the extent of its infringement and the degree to which the limitation furthers the attainment of the legitimate goal as reflected in the infringing legislation. To implement this inquiry the starting point must be to establish the meaning and range of the constitutional right. The entire inquiry is predicated upon the scope of this right. Accordingly a purposive approach is essential as a first stage in the constitutional inquiry. To attempt to restrict the constitutional right and thereafter to apply a limitation clause would be to distort the inquiry and to curtail the constitutional enterprise of promoting an open and democratic society based upon freedom and equality. The more limiting approach adopted by early European cases and certain judgments of the US Supreme Court should be considered in the context of the particular wording of the constitutional instruments which these courts were required to interpret. Hopefully South African constitutional jurisprudence will build upon this experience rather than subjecting the country to the conceptual confusion of the earlier comparative precedents.

---

[833] At 21. See also the contrasting approach of the European Court of Human Rights, which appears to adopt a restrictive approach to the interpretation of the substantive right before addressing the question of the limitation: *Belgium Linguistic Case (No 2)* (1968) EHRR 252 at 284. Several more recent cases appear to have adopted the advocated approach including *Lingers v Austria* (1986) 8 EUHR 407 and *Campbell & Hartley v UK* (1991) 12 EUHR 157.

# INTRODUCTION TO THE SOUTH AFRICAN CONSTITUTION

DAWID VAN WYK

## 1 INTRODUCTION

Modern South Africa was born at the beginning of the twentieth century when the four British colonies, Cape of Good Hope, Natal, Orange River, and Transvaal, merged and became the Union of South Africa. From its inception the South African constitutional system was in peril. The looming danger stemmed from the failure of the early fathers — they were all men — of the British-based, Westminster-oriented South Africa Act of 1909 to provide for an inclusive democracy. Instead, the Union of South Africa would be governed by whites, even then a minority of the overall population.[1] The writing was on the wall. Over decades the differences hardened into bitter and violent confrontation, played out not only on the South African stage but also, after World War II, increasingly in the council chambers of the world, where the terms of reference were also confrontation, Cold War, East versus West.

The global political changes of the late 1980s and, closer to home, the resolution of the Namibian question[2] paved the way in South Africa for the long-overdue acknowledgement of the ignored protests of generations of blacks. It started on 2 February 1990.

It is hardly necessary to recall the events at that annual opening of Parliament. The effect of State President F W de Klerk's speech was irreversibly to change the face of South African politics.[3] It was not so much his commitment to a negotiated political settlement and his explicit acceptance of a bill of fundamental rights, but the practical steps he announced which made the difference: the African National Congress (ANC), Pan-Africanist Congress (PAC), South African Communist Party (SACP), and other organizations were to be unbanned; political prisoners would be released, Mr Nelson Mandela first of all and without delay; the stringent emergency regulations would either be lifted or ameliorated; and the restrictions on a number of organizations, mostly sympathetic to the liberation movements, would be removed.

The events following this announcement, hailed throughout the world as dramatic in any sense of the word, are a matter of history. However, early expectations of a swift settlement of the South African constitutional question gradually withered

---

[1] For a modern account of the formation of the Union and the political forces at play, see Davenport *South Africa: A Modern History* 4 ed (1991) ch 9. At 202 he ventures the opinion that pro-Boer agitation during the war years had so affected British opinion in respect of injustice done to the Afrikaners that the British were prepared to compensate them at the expense of others. On the National Conventions that drafted the Union of South Africa Act, see Walton *The Inner History of the National Convention of South Africa* (1912; reprinted 1970); Brand *The Union of South Africa* (1909) chs III and IV; Thompson *The Unification of South Africa 1902–1910* (1969) chs IV and V; Davenport op cit 220–5.
[2] See Van Wyk, Wiechers & Hill (eds) *Namibia Constitutional and International Law Issues* (1991).
[3] For the full text of the speech see 1990 *Debates of Parliament* col 1ff.

away as the political leaders moved with greater or lesser ease to overcome one impasse after the other. Apart from purely constitutional questions, three issues dominated the agenda: first, the release of political prisoners; secondly, increasing violence and lawlessness; and, finally, the need for an inclusive negotiation body.

The political prisoner question was resolved with relative ease. The other two remained thorny throughout the negotiations. Violence continued unabated, even at times increased, posing a constant threat to the brittle constitutional negotiating process. The Multi-Party Negotiating Process (MPNP)[4] specifically, and the political negotiations in general, remained subject to the whims of political leaders and groups, with progress slower than anticipated. Despite all attempts to make it so, the process never became all-inclusive, with several political groupings, such as the Azanian People's Organization (AZAPO) and a number of white rightwing organizations, either refusing to participate or leaving the process. The Conservative Party (CP), the KwaZulu government, and the Inkatha Freedom Party (IFP) withdrew after the first and only meeting of the Negotiating Forum, with the governments of Ciskei and Bophuthatswana following them towards the end of the negotiations. This did not herald the end of their involvement, though. During the ensuing months, and right up to the election in April 1994, active and often successful negotiations involving the ANC, the South African government, and groups of parties or individual parties continued.

For a better perspective on the Constitution two issues require brief discussion: the constitutional and political situation in South Africa before 2 February 1990, and the most important events after that date, including the negotiating process and transitional measures.

## 2   THE PERIOD BEFORE 2 FEBRUARY 1990

Pre-1990 South African political and constitutional history is well documented and hardly bears repetition.[5] Suffice it to say that the 1993 Constitution of the Republic of South Africa[6] has eliminated the core notions and latter-day practices of its three predecessors:[7] parliamentary sovereignty, a dominant executive, indiscernible separation of powers, underdeveloped political accountability, no Bill of Rights, and finally, a racist base. Some remarks about the old regime are necessary, however, for three reasons: first, constitutional continuity has formally been maintained, with the transition to democracy taking place in terms of laws made by the existing 'tricameral' Parliament under the Republic of South Africa Constitution Act 110 of 1983.[8] Secondly, the new Constitution is in essence the product of an interaction

---

[4] The official designation of the negotiations that took place at the World Trade Centre in Kempton Park between March and December 1993.

[5] A recent broad-brush overview was given by Carpenter 'The Changing Face of South African Public Law' 1993 *SAPR/PL* 1. For more detailed discussions, see Carpenter *Introduction to South African Constitutional Law* (1987); Boulle, Harris & Hoexter *Constitutional and Administrative Law* (1989); Boulle *South Africa and the Consociational Option* (1984); Wiechers *VerLoren van Themaat Staatsreg* 2 ed (1981); Dugard *Human Rights and the South African Legal Order* (1978); Dugard 'The South African Constitution 1910–1980' in Mellett et al (eds) *Our Legal Heritage* (1982) 105.

[6] Act 200 of 1993 as amended.

[7] The South Africa Act 1909, the Republic of South Africa Constitution Act 32 of 1961, and the Republic of South Africa Constitution Act 110 of 1983.

[8] For an interesting mid-stream analysis of the transition, with special reference to CODESA, see Davis *South Africa and Transition: From Autocracy to What? A Preliminary Analysis about a Tentative Process* Centre for Applied Legal Studies Working Paper 18 (June 1992).

between constitutional and political forces deeply rooted in South African history, but largely wished away, ignored, denied, and ultimately suppressed by the ruling establishment. At this point it is worth noting that in recent years a number of thorough studies on 'protest politics' have been published, shedding valuable light on this other mainstream of South African politics.[9] Finally, the debate about South Africa's constitutional future has for decades been waged in many forms and fora. The result was a considerable body of literature, a substantial volume of which will retain its reference value under a new constitutional order.

Between 1910 and 1990 the main features of the formal South African constitutional regime were the following:

- The evolving scheme of apartheid, typified by the constitutional entrenchment of white rule, and its attendant platform for Afrikaner domination of the political system[10] resulted in more emphasis on 'power' than on 'rights'.

- There was formal classification and territorial and spatial separation of what came to be known as 'population groups'. The key law in this respect was the Population Registration Act,[11] although a myriad other laws also contained provisions distinguishing and discriminating between persons on the basis of race.[12]

- Related to this, especially in the later years, central executive control of government functions in respect of 'white' areas increased, culminating during the closing years of the apartheid era in the abolition of the representative ('white') provincial authorities.[13]

- Hand in hand with centralization politics in respect of whites went various attempts at greater decentralization and devolution for blacks, evidenced by the four nominally independent TBVC (Transkei, Bophuthatswana, Venda, Ciskei) states and six 'self-governing' territories.

- Reliance on security laws and practices increased as a result of escalating confrontation between the South African authorities, on the one hand, and the 'underground' liberation movements and sympathetic support organizations[14] on the other.

---

[9] Examples are: Lodge *Black Politics in South Africa since 1945* (1983); Odendaal *Vukani Bantu! The Beginnings of Black Protest Politics in South Africa to 1912* (1984); Motlhabi *Black Resistance to Apartheid* (1984); Maylam *A History of the African People of South Africa: From the Early Iron Age to the 1970s* (1986); Ansprenger *Der African National Congress — ANC. Geschichte und Aktuelle Politik einer Befreiungsbewegung* (1987); Frederikse *The Unbreakable Thread. Non-racialism in South Africa* (1990); Davenport op cit (n 1) passim; Lodge *All Here and Now: Black South African Politics in the 1980s* (1992). An earlier classic is Ballinger *From Union to Apartheid. A Trek to Isolation* (1969). Asmal *Victims, Survivors and Citizens — Human Rights, Reparations and Reconciliation* (inaugural lecture, UWC, 1992) 6 sums it up by saying that 'throughout the history of the resistance movement, the emphasis has been on the golden thread of non-racialism . . .'.

[10] The ideological underpinnings of Afrikaner domination — in certain political circles probably articulated and experienced as 'self-determination' and nationalism — found expression in e g the establishment, in 1948, of the South African Bureau of Racial Affairs, better known as SABRA, and its mouthpiece, *Journal of Racial Affairs* (*JRA*), which had as its primary aim the systematic and scientific elaboration and propagation of apartheid and 'separate development'. Typical contributions that appeared in this mainly Afrikaans journal, included De Wet Nel 'Waarom die Beleid van Apartheid?' (1960) 11 *JRA* 167 and Hugo 'Separate Development: Outside Criticism and South Africa's Reaction Thereto' (1969) 20 *JRA* 180.

[11] Act 30 of 1950.

[12] For a summary and further references, see Van Wyk in Joubert (ed) *LAWSA* vol 21 'Race' 386ff; Rycroft, Boulle, Robertson & Spiller (eds) *Race and the Law* (1987).

[13] See Carpenter *Introduction* (n 5) at 426, in particular 428ff.

[14] Notably at the time the National Education Crisis Committee (NECC), the United Democratic Front (UDF), the Congress of South African Trade Unions (COSATU), and the South African National Students Congress (SANSCO).

- The rule of law was undermined through undue pressure on the courts, subject to the sovereignty of Parliament, to apply and enforce laws which violated the most basic of human rights. This led to tension and mistrust in the administration of justice, to greater or lesser degrees of subservience on the part of the judiciary, and ultimately to a questioning of the legitimacy of the legal system.[15]
- Despite undertakings to the contrary following the Information scandal of the late 1970s, secrecy in government increased,[16] the bureaucracy became bloated, more and more power rested in the hands of ministers and officials responsible for security, and corruption and swindling of public moneys grew.[17]
- Political accountability and parliamentary government dissipated, evidenced by a number of commissions of inquiry which uncovered irregularities in government at different levels.
- The philosophy of 'total onslaught' developed, following growing isolation from the mainstream of global developments, especially in the field of human rights.

In more concrete terms, a dominant feature of this period was the growing body of laws which impaired the status of persons who were not white, or 'European', in terms of earlier terminology. As an almost axiomatic corollary a growing web of security measures developed to contain the rather restive situation. Some of these laws, especially those in regard to restrictions on blacks, predated Union in 1910. Yet the South Africa Act 1909 with its qualified franchise for certain blacks in the Cape Province and Natal heralded the beginning of a new era of deterioration in the legal position of 'non-whites': the removal of their limited right to vote in the thirties (in the case of blacks), and in the fifties (for 'coloureds'); the Land Acts of 1913 and 1936; the Native Representative Council;[18] the Group Areas Acts, the Immorality Act, and its predecessors; the Prohibition of Mixed Marriages Act; the Population Registration Act; the various influx control measures; discriminatory labour laws; the laws underpinning the system of 'homelands' and dual 'citizenship' for blacks. Many of these laws stretched out tentacles into a labyrinth of subordinate legislation, ranging from proclamations by the State President to local-government by-laws.

Politically speaking, one of the gravest results of the way in which the policy of 'separate development', or apartheid, was pursued was that black opposition groups, in particular the ANC and the PAC, were forced 'underground' in the early 1960s. The ensuing armed stuggle for liberation, as it was called by these organizations, was ruthlessly suppressed under legal nomenclature such as 'terrorism', 'sabotage', 'subversion', and 'treason'. 'Communism' was defined widely enough to include

---

[15] See, for example, Dugard *Human Rights*; Cameron 'Legal Chauvinism, Executive-mindedness and Justice — L C Steyn's impact upon South African Law' (1982) 99 *SALJ* 38; Wacks 'Judges and Injustice' (1984) 101 *SALJ* 266; Forsyth *In Danger for their Talents* (1985); Cameron 'Nude Monarchy: The Case of the South African Judges' (1987) 3 *SAJHR* 338; Dlamini 'The Influence of Race on the Administration of Justice in South Africa' (1988) 4 *SAJHR* 37; Mathews *Freedom, State Security and the Rule of Law: Dilemmas of the Apartheid Society* (1986); Suttner 'The Ideological Role of the Judiciary in South Africa' in Hund (ed) *Law and Justice in South Africa* (1986) 81; Nicolson 'Ideology and the South African Judicial Process — Lessons from the Past' (1992) 8 *SAJHR* 50.

[16] For an analysis of the level of official secrecy and confidentiality at the end of the 1970s, cf Mathews' seminal work *The Darker Reaches of Government* (1978).

[17] See in general Du Plessis 'Korrupsie en Meeluistering: Magsbeperking of Magsbehoud' 1992 *SAPR/PL* 238.

[18] For an extensive account of the history and meaning of this institution, see Ballinger op cit (n 9).

virtually any doctrine or ideology considered undesirable by the state. Information on the 'struggle' became increasingly sparse. In terms of the Suppression of Communism Act of 1950 'listed' persons might not be quoted, and later the *Goverment Gazette* contained long weekly inventories of publications, national and international, banned, under the Publications Control Act, for their political content. Constitutional and political development in South Africa became unilateral and lopsided, with little room for legitimate democratic opposition.

It is within this context that the failure of the 1983 Constitution should be seen. Towards the end of the 1970s even the South African government realized that fundamental constitutional change was inevitable. The search for a new South African order began. It started as a doomed unilateral exercise, with a draft Constitution being published by the government in 1979.[19] The result was a Commission of Inquiry and, in 1983, the 'tricameral' Constitution.[20] While hailed as a 'step in the right direction' by the majority of whites in an all-white plebiscite in 1983, black leaders foresaw its violent consequences. Much of the anger and resentment fanned by this event, and followed by five years of emergency measures, spilled over into the post-1990 period.

On the positive side, also with a view to the future, a solid body of constitutional literature from an ever-growing number of constitutional lawyers has been produced over the years. Earlier literature, such as the textbooks by Kennedy & Schlosberg,[21] May,[22] and VerLoren van Themaat,[23] reflected formal South African constitutional law. South Africa's status as a dominium, its increasing independence from the UK, and the assertion of its domestic sovereignty formed key elements of the period. Well-known South African judgments originated in these years, all tellingly related to political rights: *Ndlwana v Hofmeyr*,[24] the two *Harris* cases,[25] and, finally, *Collins v Minister of the Interior*.[26]

Since 1950 public-law writing picked up in volume, mirroring a variety of approaches to the fundamentals of the South African constitutional order. Banned, however, were the views of the 'struggle', including the *Freedom Charter* of 1955. Even so, with certain exceptions and with time, legal literature in South Africa became unequivocally critical and intolerant of the existing constitutional set-up, and started gearing itself for the introduction of a different Constitution with a Bill

---

[19] Cf Jacobs (ed) *'n Nuwe Grondwetlike Bedeling vir Suid-Afrika: Enkele Regsaspekte* (1981); Vorster & Viljoen 'Die Nuwe Grondwetlike Bedeling' 1979 *TSAR* 201.

[20] The Republic of South Africa Constitution Act 110 of 1983: referred to as 'sham consociation' by Boulle 'The Likely Direction of Constitutional Change in South Africa over the Next Five Years' in Dean & Van Zyl Smit *Constitutional Change in South Africa* (1983) 70. Works covering the 1983 Constitution include Booysen & Van Wyk *Die '83-Grondwet* (1984); Van der Vyver *Die Grondwet van die Republiek van Suid-Afrika: Wet 110 van 1983* (1984); Carpenter *Introduction*; Basson & Viljoen *Suid-Afrikaanse Staatsreg* 2 ed (1988); Boulle, Harris & Baxter op cit (n 5); Rautenbach & Malherbe *Staatsreg* (1993).

[21] *The Law and Custom of the South African Constitution* (1935).

[22] *The South African Constitution* 2 ed (1949) (a revision of Kennedy & Schlosberg op cit (n 21), 3 ed (1955).

[23] *Staatsreg* (1956), 2 ed (1967) with Wiechers; Wiechers *VerLoren van Themaat Staatsreg* 3 ed (1981).

[24] 1937 AD 229.

[25] *Harris v Minister of the Interior* 1952 (2) SA 428 (A) and *Minister of the Interior v Harris* 1952 (4) SA 769 (A).

[26] 1957 (1) SA 552 (A). See Wiechers' visionary discussion of this judgment: 'The Fundamental Laws Behind our Constitution' in Kahn (ed) *Fiat Iustitia: Essays in Memory of Oliver Deneys Schreiner* (1983).

of Rights. Specialized law journals[27] in this field joined an array of established journals, and the Human Sciences Research Council and others produced impressive tomes on political, constitutional, and economic models and alternatives for a 'new' South Africa.[28] A large number of more popular works on change and a future South African Constitution and political system also began to appear, here and abroad.[29]

The South African government and other political organizations also came alive in this field. In 1986 the government instructed the South African Law Commission to launch an investigation into group and human rights,[30] despite the fact that the very minister who commissioned the investigation a scant two years earlier had put up a staunch defence against a Bill of Rights.[31] The ANC in 1988 produced its *Constitutional Guidelines for a Democratic South Africa*,[32] based on the Freedom Charter.[33]

A new era dawned in 1987 when, for the first time, a number of 'internal' South Africans formally met with representatives of the still banned ANC in Dakar, Senegal. The result was a series of meetings and conferences at different levels in various places outside South Africa. One that may be singled out took place in Harare, Zimbabwe, in February 1989. This was less than six months after the release of the ANC's *Guidelines for a Democratic South Africa*. A group of 'internal' South African academic lawyers and prominent members of the ANC, including the chairperson and members of its Constitutional Committee, attended a conference on constitutional issues and fundamental rights. The communiqué issued after the conference contained the following telling line: 'The high point of the conference was the consensus reached on the need for a new constitutional order, a justiciable Bill of Rights and an independent judiciary.'[34]

---

[27] Notably *SAJHR* (1985–) and *SAPR/PL* (1986–). A useful source of information on constitutional development in South Africa is the chapter on Constitutional Law in the regular editions of *Annual Survey of South African Law*.

[28] See, as typical examples, Van Vuuren & Kriek *Political Alternatives for South Africa. Principles and Perspectives* (1983); Van Vuuren, Wiehahn, Rhoodie & Wiechers *South Africa: The Challenge of Reform* (1988); Faure et al (eds) *Suid-Afrika en die Demokrasie* (1988); Berger & Godsell *A Future South Africa. Visions, Strategies and Realities* (1988); Schrire (ed) *Critical Choices for South Africa. An Agenda for the 1990s* (1990). The momentum picked up after 1990 with works such as Giliomee & Schlemmer *From Apartheid to Nation-building. Contemporary South African Debates* (1990); Maasdorp & Whiteside *Towards a Post-apartheid Future. Political and Economic Relations in Southern Africa* (1992); Friedman *Options for the Future. Government Reform Strategy and Prospects for Structural Change* (1990); Van Zyl Slabbert *The Quest for Democracy. South Africa in Transition* (1992); Motimele & Semenya *Constitution for a Democratic South Africa* (1993).

[29] To mention but a few random examples: Kendall & Louw *South Africa: the Solution* (1986); Kendall *Let the People Govern* (1990); Sethi (ed) *The South African Quagmire. In Search of a Peaceful Path to Democratic Pluralism* (1987); Kitchen (ed) *South Africa: In Transition to What?* (1988); Fourie (ed) *Strategies for Change* (1989). This trend perpetuated itself after 1990 with works such as Kendall *The Heart of the Nation. Regional and Community Government in the New South Africa* (1991); Godsell (ed) *Shaping a Future South Africa. A Citizen's Guide to Constitution-making* (1990); Nurnberger et al (eds) *A Democratic Vision for South Africa* (1991).

[30] Its *Project 58: Group and Human Rights* Working Paper 25 (1989) became quite well known, as did its author, Mr Justice P J J Olivier. On the Working Paper, see Wiechers ' 'n Monument in die Suid-Afrikaanse Regsontwikkeling: Die Werkstuk van die Suid-Afrikaanse Regskommissie oor Groeps- en Minderheidsregte' 1989 *THRHR* 311; Du Plessis 'Glosses to the Working Paper of the South African Law Commission on Group and Human Rights (with Particular Reference to the Issue of Group Rights)' 1989 *THRHR* 421.

[31] Coetsee 'Hoekom nie 'n Verklaring van Menseregte nie?' 1984 *TRW* 5.

[32] The *Guidelines* were reprinted in (1989) 5 *SAJHR* 129. For comments, see Van der Vyver 'Comments on the Constitutional Guidelines of the African National Congress' (1989) 5 *SAJHR* 133; Corder & Davis 'The Constitutional Guidelines of the African National Congress: A Preliminary Assessment' (1989) 106 *SALJ* 633.

[33] On the Freedom Charter, see Suttner & Cronin *The Freedom Charter in the Eighties* (1986); Sanders 'The South African Freedom Charter' in Hund op cit (n 15) 222ff; Polley (ed) *The Freedom Charter and the Future* (1988); Steytler (ed) *The Freedom Charter and Beyond. Founding Principles for a Democratic South African Legal Order* (1992).

[34] Cf Feb 1989 *Democracy in Action* 11.

## 3 THE PERIOD AFTER 2 FEBRUARY 1990

### 3.1 General

The process set in motion on 2 February 1990 was essentially aimed at normalizing the political situation in South Africa. Reactions were mixed, ranging from exhilaration and overjoy, on the one hand, to anger and resentment on the other, with resignation to reality another strong emotion. The four years spanning the gap between 2 February 1990 and 27 April 1994, when the first negotiated Constitution came into operation, can broadly be divided into three periods: from 2 February 1990 to the start of the Convention for a Democratic South Africa (CODESA) in December 1991;[35] from CODESA to the beginning of the MPNP in March 1993;[36] and finally from the MPNP to 27 April 1994.

A number of formal steps had to be taken to prepare the table for negotiations. Apart from the release of a large number of political prisoners, arrangements had to be made for the return of persons who had fled the country on account of their political views. A further sensitive issue arising from the unbanning of the liberation movements was the position of the latters' so-called armed wings.

Progress was complicated by the fact that the ANC was the only one of all the previously prohibited organizations to engage in open contact with the government. While the ANC was widely accepted as the most influential and representative of all the liberation movements, the others, notably the PAC and AZAPO, could not be left out in the cold with any comfort.

The first formal meeting between representatives of the South African government and the leadership of the ANC took place at Groote Schuur, Cape Town, on 4 May 1990. The resulting Groote Schuur Minute was the first in a line of documents embodying various agreements and understandings which became the landmarks of the process leading to the eventual adoption of the 'interim' Constitution at the end of 1993.

### 3.2 Landmarks of the negotiating process[37]

The key points of the Groote Schuur Minute, which were fine-tuned in a number of subsequent agreements and which became the centrepieces of all subsequent political developments, were the resolution of the climate of violence in the country and a commitment to stability and peaceful negotiations. The Groote Schuur Minute itself identified the following aspects for achieving these overriding objectives:

- the definition of political offences and matters relating to the release of political prisoners;
- immunity for political offences;
- review by the government of existing security measures, the lifting of the

---

[35] For a wide-ranging survey of this period see Moss & Obery (eds) *South African Review 6. From 'Red Friday' to Codesa* (1992).

[36] A good account and analysis of the Codesa process can be found in Friedman (ed) *The Long Journey. South Africa's Quest for a Negotiated Settlement* (1993). See also Klug 1992 *Annual Survey of South African Law* 693–8.

[37] For a chronological account of events during this period, see Beukes 'Southern African Events of International Significance' in successive numbers of *SAYIL*; for topical treatment of events, see Levine (ed) 'Human Rights Index' in intermittent numbers of *SAJHR*.

prevailing state of emergency and the creation of effective channels of communication between the government and the ANC, especially with a view to the curbing of violence and intimidation.

In respect of exiles, an understanding was reached with the United Nations High Commissioner for Refugees. Provision was further made for indemnity for returnees who would, on their arrival, be technically subject to arrest for offences committed in terms of existing laws. The High Commissioner established a presence in South Africa and, according to all accounts, the repatriation scheme ran smoothly.

The Groote Schuur Minute was followed by two further agreements, the Pretoria Minute of 6 August 1990 and the D F Malan Agreement of February 1991. The former reiterated the commitment to the Groote Schuur Minute and some of the issues addressed in that Minute were taken further (political prisoners, violence, the state of emergency which still existed in Natal, and security measures). Two new items were the ANC's renunciation of the armed struggle and the creation of effective channels of communication at national, regional, and local level, especially to address what were called 'public grievances'. The Minute concluded by stating that the way was clear for negotiations on a new Constitution, and that 'exploratory talks' would be held soon.

The D F Malan Agreement, named after the airport in Cape Town where it was concluded, specifically clarified uncertainties arising from para 3 of the Pretoria Minute relating to the ANC's suspension of armed action. As in the case of the Groote Schuur and Pretoria Minutes, the dark thread of the violence in South Africa ran through this document as well.

In order to address this problem a National Peace Accord was signed amidst great publicity by a large number of political organizations on 14 September 1991.[38] This elaborate document contained a rather detailed framework for procedures and mechanisms to bring an end to the 'scourge of political violence which has afflicted our country', as it was stated in the opening paragraph.[39] The ten chapters of the Accord dealt with: principles, centering mostly on democracy, fundamental rights, reconstruction, and socio-economic development, and the commitment to terminate violence and intimidation; a code of conduct for political parties and organizations, with specific reference to the need for a climate of democratic tolerance; general provisions relating to the security forces, in particular the police; a police code of conduct; measures for socio-economic reconstruction and upliftment; the Commission of Inquiry regarding the Prevention of Public Violence and Intimidation;[40] peace structures, specifically the National Peace Secretariat, and regional and local dispute resolution committees; the National Peace Committee; enforcement mechanisms; and special criminal courts.

Political negotiations gathered momentum, bolstered by the positive effect of the Peace Accord. Shortly before Christmas 1991, almost two years after the watershed speech of February 1990, a sufficiently large number of political organizations had reached a point where they were ready to start negotiating a Constitution.

---

[38] See Levine (1992) 8 *SAJHR* 146–7.
[39] *National Peace Accord* 3.
[40] This Commission, established in terms of the Prevention of Public Violence and Intimidation Act 139 of 1991, is better known under its popular name, the Goldstone Commission, after its chairperson, Richard Goldstone JA.

## 4 CONVENTION FOR A DEMOCRATIC SOUTH AFRICA (CODESA)

This first round of negotiations, CODESA, took place at the World Trade Centre in Kempton Park, east of Johannesburg. It was not to be the final round. With hindsight it is clear that agreement at CODESA was not near, that as an opening round it was an exercise in preparation for what was to follow.[41]

Various reasons could be adduced for the fact that CODESA was not to be the ultimate constitution-maker. First, political factors played a role. A snap plebiscite had to be called among whites on 17 March 1992 to counter growing signs that a substantial number of white voters had misgivings about the course political events were taking. While the outcome was a resounding victory in favour of negotiations, it had a double-edged effect on the negotiations: on the one hand, it hardened opposition to the process, while on the other it gave at least some government negotiators a false sense of power.[42]

Another critical factor was the structure of CODESA. After the plenary meeting on 21 December 1991, which in itself was an achievement as the first formal public meeting from 'the broadest ever cross-section of the country's political leaders',[43] five working groups were set up. Each working group had two delegates and two advisers from every participating party or organization. With nineteen parties present, each group consisted of almost a hundred persons. Despite the confidentiality of the working group sessions, the very size of the groups hampered negotiations. Some groups set up subcommittees; another, Working Group 3, appointed its own technical committee to prepare a draft report.

The briefs of the working groups also caused problems, given the relatively short period of time before the next plenary session, scheduled for mid-May 1992. Working Group 1 was saddled with conditions for ensuring free and equal participation in the political process. Its terms of reference covered two pages of fine print.[44] Working Group 2 was assigned Constitutional Principles, Working Group 3 had to look at transitional measures, Working Group 4 had to deal with the TBVC states, and Working Group 5 dealt with time frames.

The degree of success — if not frustration — of the Working Groups could be seen from the reports submitted to the second plenary of CODESA, officially known as CODESA 2.[45] Working Group 1 reported some progress, but listed a number of outstanding matters. Working Group 2 did not submit a formal report for lack of time; deadlocks in this Working Group caused a delay of the plenary session. Working Group 3 produced a rather comprehensive structure and set of principles for the first phase of the transition to democracy, i e until the first elections.[46] Working Group 4 had a brief report, outlining difficulties, while Working Group 5 lamented the fact that its progress depended on movement in the other groups, which had been slow and limited.

---

[41] Friedman op cit (n 36) 171–2.
[42] At 40.
[43] At 22.
[44] The terms of reference of all the Working Groups were reprinted in (1992) 8 *SAJHR* 126–34.
[45] See *Working Documents for CODESA 2. 15 & 16 May 1992* vols 1 and 2.
[46] This was the only report from the CODESA negotiations which had a significant effect on the subsequent MPNP. The Working Group proposed a Transitional Executive Council (TEC), the main task of which would be to ensure that the country was governed in such a way until the first election that no party or organization was prejudiced or advantaged, or, as the colloquial phraseology had it, that the 'playing field would be level'.

CODESA had its own rules of procedure. A fundamental but controversial aspect, which predictably spilled over to the MPNP and which caused tension, was the requirement for agreement. Decisions would be taken by consensus, failing which 'sufficient consensus', as it was termed, would be acceptable. In terms of para 3(3) of the Standing Rules of Procedure for Plenary Sessions 'sufficient consensus' would have been achieved 'when consensus is of such a nature that the work of the Convention can move forward effectively'. It was known that especially the IFP had serious misgivings about the notion of sufficient consensus all along.

The political impact of the failure of CODESA was almost disastrous, with recriminations flying in all directions. A tenuous link was maintained between the ANC and the South African government, with their chief negotiators exploring avenues to bridge the gaps. After a 'bosberaad'[47] between the ANC and the government, State President De Klerk and ANC president Nelson Mandela held a meeting at the World Trade Centre in Kempton Park and issued a document entitled 'Record of Understanding', dated 26 September 1992. Despite denials on both sides, it was clear that the 'understandings' in the document were in effect agreements between the government/National Party (NP) and the ANC aimed at getting the negotiating process back on track.

The Record of Understanding covered a number of persisting bones of contention, such as violence, the release of political prisoners, and so on. Most important, however, was the agreement that the new Constitution should be drafted by an elected constitution-making body, that there would be constitutional continuity, and that, in view of this, the constitution-making body would also serve as an interim or transitional Parliament.

While the Record of Understanding eventually succeeded in its purpose of revitalizing constitutional negotiations, it had the negative effect of further alienating the IFP. This effect reverberated through the ensuing negotiating process and up to the elections in April 1994. One of the results of the Record of Understanding was the formation of the Concerned South Africans Group (COSAG), with the IFP, the KwaZulu government, the governments of Ciskei and Bophuthatswana, and the CP as the leading members. It also precipitated the eventual withdrawal of these parties and organizations from the MPNP nine months later.

A further consequence of the Record of Understanding was the Multi-Party Negotiating Process, which produced the interim Constitution and other legislation aimed at facilitating the transition to democracy.

## 5  THE MULTI-PARTY NEGOTIATING PROCESS (MPNP)

### 5.1  Introduction

Like CODESA, the MPNP took place at the World Trade Centre, Kempton Park. While the MPNP was not formally seen as the successor to CODESA, the reports of the latter were accepted as sources of reference. Some lessons learnt at CODESA

---

[47] The South African political vernacular has been enriched during the negotiation process by the addition of expressions such as 'bosberaad' (a retreat to some unknown place in the 'bush' for consultations), 'bilaterals', 'multilaterals' (discussions between two or more specific parties/organizations on specific aspects of the process) and others: see also Haysom 'Negotiating a Political Settlement in South Africa' in Moss & Obery op cit (n 35) 26.

were applied to the MPNP with good effect. To begin with, the structure differed. Instead of the flat two-level design of CODESA — plenary and working groups — the MPNP had a pyramid formation, with a plenary at the top, followed by a Negotiating Forum, the Negotiating Council, and a Planning Committee. In the plenary every participant had ten representatives, in the Negotiating Forum two delegates and four advisers, and in the Negotiating Council two delegates and two advisers. The Planning Committee consisted of a fluctuating but smaller number of persons appointed from its own ranks by the Negotiating Council. It is worth mentioning that the Negotiating Forum met once, in July 1993. The most significant result of that meeting was that 27 April 1994 was set as the date for the first inclusive election. At the same time the Forum recognized in so many words that there was such a slight difference between itself and the Negotiating Council, where all the formal negotiations took place, that there was little point in meeting again.

With twenty-six participants, the MPNP started on a more representative basis than CODESA. However, in the course of time the CP, the IFP, the KwaZulu government, the Ciskei government, and the government of Bophuthatswana withdrew.

A special feature of the MPNP was the way in which the position of women was addressed from the outset. This was a momentum carried forward from CODESA, where a Gender Advisory Committee had been established. The effect was not only seen in the structures of the MPNP but in its results as well. Examples are the Subcouncil on the Status of Women of the Transitional Executive Council[48] (TEC) and the Commission on Gender Equality established in terms of the Constitution.[49]

The Negotiating Council and the Planning Committee were the heart of the MPNP. The proceedings in the Council were public; those in the Planning Committee confidential. A practice soon developed that sensitive issues which would delay the work of the Council or which would benefit from further confidential consideration would be referred to the Planning Committee. The Planning Committee would return to the Council with one or more proposals, and more often than not, after debate, the Council would take a decision on the matter.

## 5.2 Decisions

As in the case of CODESA, decisions were taken by consensus, or sufficient consensus. Although it is fair to say that sufficient consensus was not readily declared if either of the large parties, the ANC or the government, objected to a resolution, it was not a hard-and-fast rule. Soon after the meeting of the Negotiating Forum in July 1993 the IFP and the KwaZulu government applied to the Supreme Court in Pretoria to have the proceedings of the Negotiating Forum and the Negotiating Council set aside for not observing what they thought was sufficient consensus. The motion failed, the court holding that the MPNP had no basis in law and that it was a political forum where a political question such as that before the court should be addressed.

---

[48] Section 8(1)(f) read with s 19 of the Transitional Executive Council Act 151 of 1993.
[49] Sections 119–120.

## 5.3 The technical committees

At one of its first sessions the Negotiating Council appointed seven technical committees to deal with the following: violence; fundamental rights during the transition; the repeal or amendment of legislation impeding free political activity and discriminatory legislation; constitutional affairs; the Transitional Executive Council (TEC); an Independent Broadcasting Authority (IBA) and an Independent Media Commission (IMC); and the Independent Electoral Commission (IEC). Members of the technical committees were mostly academic and practising lawyers, joined by a number of state legal advisers and others. The committees commenced work in May 1993.

Following as it did in the footsteps of CODESA, the need for such a range of committees might have been obvious. However, as it turned out, the committees could not deal with their briefs equally effectively. The Technical Committee on Violence, for instance, had to slot into a network of existing bodies created primarily with a view to addressing violence, particularly the various structures of the National Peace Accord and the Goldstone Commission. It was not surprising that this committee did not feature prominently in the workings of the MPNP.

The Committee on the Repeal or Amendment of Legislation Impeding Free Political Activity and Discriminatory Legislation was faced with an almost impossible task if it was expected to submit a list of all laws that had to be repealed. In its first report of 13 May 1993 it advised against this approach and recommended the adoption of a higher code against which laws could be tested and declared invalid. The Negotiating Council decided to combine the approaches and instructed the committee to produce a list of inhibiting and discriminatory legislation and to draft a higher code. This the committee did in its second and final report. The committee then effectively dissolved. Months later, the Negotiating Council appointed another *ad hoc* committee to investigate the matter afresh.

Although the negotiations did not proceed as swiftly as anticipated, the five other committees eventually produced legislation to govern the transitional period. Predictably, the less contentious measures were completed first and passed by Parliament during a short session in September 1993. The Committee on the IMC and the IBA drafted the Independent Media Commission Bill and the Independent Broadcasting Authority Bill; the Committee on the IEC was responsible for the Independent Electoral Commission Bill; while the Committee on the TEC produced the Transitional Executive Council Bill.

The Constitution and the Electoral Bill took longer, and required another session of Parliament in November 1993. Even then the Constitution was not finalized. Another session took place at the end of February 1994 to accommodate demands of certain parties, while a final session was held on 25 April 1994, two days before the election, to amend the Constitution yet again in order to ensure the IFP's participation in the election.

## 6 THE TRANSITION

### 6.1 Introduction

Two related questions dominated the early stages of the negotiating process: first, who was going to write the Constitution? and, secondly, how were all the various existing governments in South Africa going to be prevented from benefiting in the political process from their access to public funding? The legitimate fear existed that especially the South African government, as a dominant party in the process, would have an unfair advantage as 'player and referee', as it was called.

The need for transitional mechanisms was obvious. The ANC-led alliance saw the transition in two stages, the first being the period leading to the election of a constitution-making body, followed by the writing of the Constitution. All this was to take just over a year.[50] The South African government, supported by the IFP, favoured a single-stage transition. CODESA would draft the Constitution, after which elections would be held.

Even during CODESA it became clear that the single-stage model would not be feasible. During the course of the negotiations, particularly in Working Group 3, a two-stage process was accepted, with the Working Group confining itself in its recommendations to CODESA 2 to the first stage of the transition.[51] The Working Group report had the support of all the participants.

After CODESA the IFP and the KwaZulu government reverted to their initial position of a single-stage process and remained committed to it until it finally agreed, on 19 April 1994, to participate in the elections. The government's acceptance of the two-stage model was confirmed by the Record of Understanding of 26 September 1992, para 2 of which stated the principle of a democratically elected constitution-making body.

By the time the MPNP commenced in March 1993 the two-stage model was a firm point of departure. Apart from the drafting of a transitional Constitution for the second stage, the focus during the first stage would be to ensure that the political 'playing field was level' for the holding of a fair and free election. To this end the TEC and other institutions were to be established. However, it was agreed by the Negotiating Council that none of these bodies would start functioning before agreement had been reached on the Constitution. Contrary to most hopes, this did not happen before 17 November 1993, with the result that an inordinate amount of pressure was put on the transitional structures to accomplish their task by 27 April 1994 and before.

## 6.2 The Transitional Executive Council (TEC)

### 6.2.1 *Introduction*

The TEC was the strongest direct link between CODESA and the MPNP, its gist being rooted in the report of Working Group 3 to CODESA. The main object of the TEC and its subcouncils was to ensure that during the period leading to the first democratic elections a climate for free political participation, conducive to the holding of fair and free elections, was created and maintained.[52]

---

[50] Cf, for example, 'Negotiations step-by-step Draft Proposals' February 1992 *Mayibuye* 11.
[51] Paragraph 9 of the *Report of Working Group 3 to Codesa 2*:
 'As will appear from the agreements set out below, the Working Group was of the opinion that the transition to democracy involves two preliminary stages. The first stage is one during which preparations will be made for the holding of free and fair elections for an elected parliament under an interim constitution with the power to draft in terms of agreed procedures a new constitution and to act as an interim legislature . . .'.
[52] TEC Act 151 of 1993 s 3. The long title of the Act refers to 'the preparation for and transition to a democratic order in South Africa'. The following exposition is not intended to do full justice to the TEC. For a more detailed account, see Heunis 'Transitional Executive Council' in De Villiers (ed) *The Birth of a Constitution* (1994).

As the primary political institution bridging the old and new orders, the TEC and its powers had to be described in careful and often inventive terms. Given the varied composition of the Negotiating Council of the MPNP and its direct link to the TEC, 'participants' — the generic term used by the Act — had to be circumscribed with sufficient clarity and inclusiveness. This was done by distinguishing between 'governments', 'political parties', and 'organizations'. Another challenge was to define the 'military forces' (again the generic term) of a number of participants in an embracing way without negating obvious differences. This led to a distinction between an 'armed' and a 'defence' force. The former was non-statutory, such as Umkhonto we Sizwe (MK) and the Azanian People's Liberation Army (APLA), the latter was under the control of a government and established in terms of law.

The nominally independent TBVC states had to be accommodated as well. Provision was made in both the definition of 'government' in s 1 and in other sections for their participation on condition that the provisions of the TEC Act had been incorporated into their law.

Finally, decision-making in terms of the Act showed signs of a typical political compromise in so far as different levels of majority were required depending on the sensitivity of the matter under discussion.[53]

### 6.2.2 *Composition*

#### 6.2.2.1 The TEC

The TEC consisted of all participants in the Negotiating Council that had committed themselves to adhere to the Act and decisions made in terms of the Act and had renounced violence for political purposes.[54] Provision was made for new members at the discretion of the TEC, subject to the same conditions of being bound by the Act and decisions thereunder and the renunciation of violence.[55] Section 4(8) contained disciplinary measures. The TEC could direct a participant that persistently breached its undertakings in terms of the Act to cease such behaviour, failing which the participant could be suspended from the TEC. The sting in the tail was that in terms of s 7(9) such a participant remained bound by its obligations under the Act.

Every participant could nominate one person to represent it. Officially the members were appointed by the State President.[56]

#### 6.2.2.2 The subcouncils

The Act provided for seven subcouncils:[57] on regional and local government, including traditional authorities; finance; foreign affairs; the status of women; law, order, and stability; defence; and intelligence. This was two more than the subcouncils proposed by Working Group 3 of CODESA, the newcomers being the Subcouncils on the Status of Women and Intelligence. In terms of s 8(2) room was left for the establishment of additional subcouncils.

---

[53] Section 25.
[54] Section 4(1).
[55] Section 4(5). Ciskei, who had withdrawn from the MPNP and stated its intention not to participate in the TEC, was subsequently admitted as a participant.
[56] Section 4(3).
[57] Section 8(1).

Subcouncils varied in size, again depending on the political sensitivity of their area of activity. The Subcouncils on Regional and Local Government, the Status of Women, Finance, and Defence were limited to six members each. The Subcouncils on Defence, Law, Order, and Stability, and Intelligence each had eight members.[58] While the Act left it to the TEC to decide whether members of the TEC would serve in a full-time or part-time capacity, s 9(1) was explicit in its direction that members of subcouncils would be full-time. No participant in the TEC was allowed more than one representative per subcouncil.[59] Appointment was by the TEC itself.[60]

### 6.2.2.3  Powers

Both the TEC and the subcouncils had a number of general powers assigned to them.[61] Of greater importance, however, were the specific powers allocated in terms of ss 13–22, the bulk of the Act.

Section 13 enjoined governments, administrations, and other participants in the TEC to provide the TEC with information about intended legislation and actions. If the TEC was of the opinion that such legislation or other action would impact negatively on the attainment of the objects of the TEC, it could direct such government or body not to proceed with the legislation or other action. Any dispute in this regard could be resolved in terms of s 23.

Sections 14–20 listed the powers of the TEC and the subcouncils on the basis of the areas for which subcouncils had been established. Except for foreign affairs[62] and local and regional government and traditional authorities,[63] the lists for the other subcouncils were rather extensive, reflecting the sensitive political nature of those other areas. Each section started with a standard introductory paragraph, stating that the TEC would have certain powers in regard to the specific issue, and that such powers would be exercised through the subcouncil concerned.

In addition to the powers conferred by the Act, the TEC was also given powers in terms of the other transitional measures, specifically the Independent Electoral Commission Act, the Independent Media Commission Act, the Independent Broadcasting Authority Act, and the Electoral Act, and even the Constitution.

A question drawing different answers was whether the TEC and the subcouncils had effective powers of government, or whether they were in effect advisory bodies. It would appear that in terms of the purpose of the Act and its provisions the truth lay somewhere in between. The Act itself[64] granted the TEC executive powers. Section 13 further authorized the TEC to order governments, administrations, political parties, and other organizations to refrain from doing certain things. The powers and duties of the TEC and subcouncils, on the other hand, contained a substantial number of 'non-executive' items, such as research,[65] making proposals

---

[58] See s 9.
[59] Section 9(3).
[60] Section 9(1).
[61] Sections 7 and 12.
[62] Section 18.
[63] Section 14.
[64] Section 2*(a)*.
[65] See s 16(2)*(f)*.

for budgets,[66] and making recommendations.[67] It was clear that the TEC was not supposed to be a direct or 'hands-on' executive body. It is equally clear that it was intended to have sufficient effective power to achieve its objectives and to prevent any government or other participant in the transition to democracy from using its power in an adverse way. The best examples of the TEC using its powers and influence are the loss of their independence by Bophuthatswana and Ciskei in March 1994 and the declaration of a state of emergency in KwaZulu/Natal in April 1994.

#### 6.2.2.4 Relationship between the TEC and the subcouncils

Despite the fact that the TEC exercised most of its powers through the subcouncils, the TEC had final authority. This was clear from the general power of the TEC to issue directions to a subcouncil,[68] to make rules for the meetings of subcouncils,[69] to delegate powers to subcouncils without relinquishing such powers,[70] and to appoint the members of a subcouncil.[71] Ultimately, ss 7(3) and 8(1) stated in direct terms that the TEC exercised full control over subcouncils.

#### 6.2.2.5 Decisions and deadlocks

The final and most difficult compromise that Working Group 3 of CODESA had to reach before the completion of its report related to the decision-making mechanism of the TEC. History repeated itself at the MPNP. The proposal inherited from CODESA was that decisions should be taken by consensus, in the absence of which 80 per cent would suffice. Section 25 of the TEC Act contained the eventual agreement. In terms of subsec (1) all decisions of the TEC or a subcouncil had as far as possible to be made by consensus. If, in the words of s 25(2), 'total consensus' could not be reached, the required majority depended on whether the decision was taken by the TEC itself or by a subcouncil. In the case of the TEC, 75 per cent of all the members of the TEC could pass a valid resolution.[72] In the case of a subcouncil, it depended on the nature of the issue under decision. In the event of local and regional government and traditional authorities, finance, the status of women and foreign affairs, two-thirds of the members could take a decision.[73] Since the subcouncils responsible for these matters consisted of six members each, this requirement was similar to a bare majority. The Subcouncils on law, order, and stability, defence, and intelligence required 75 per cent of their members to be in favour of a decision, i e six out of eight.[74]

Section 23 of the Act provided for the resolution of disputes, with the emphasis on expeditiousness. The Special Electoral Court established in terms of the

---

[66] See s 14(e).
[67] See s 17(1)(h).
[68] Section 7(1)(b).
[69] Section 7(1)(f).
[70] Section 7(2).
[71] Section 9(1)(a).
[72] Section 25(2)(a). This requirement was subject to two exceptions: s 15(2)(b) required 80 per cent of the Council to vote for the termination of a state of emergency; the same level of support was required in terms of s 22(4)(b) for the members of the Access to Information Committee established in terms of s 22(4)(a).
[73] Section 25(2)(c).
[74] Section 25(2)(b).

Independent Electoral Commission Act[75] was appointed sole arbiter of disputes.[76] Any dispute about the interpretation of the objects of the TEC, or whether legislation or any other action would have an adverse impact on the objects of the TEC, or whether a direction of the TEC should be followed, could be referred to the court by the affected government or other organization. The court had to deal with the matter as soon as it could and its order was final.[77] To prevent disputes from being used either to stall or to obstruct the process of transition, s 23(6) provided that unless a government or other organization referred a dispute to the court within three days after its being notified of a direction of the TEC, the direction would be final.

### 6.2.2.6  Duration of the Act

In view of its transitional nature, the TEC Act provided for its own termination when the first Cabinet in terms of the interim Constitution assumed office.[78] This would result in all structures established in terms of the Act being undone, including the National Peacekeeping Force envisaged by s 16(11). It was open to doubt whether the life of the Peacekeeping Force, for example, could be extended by the Council by amending the Act in terms of s 28(1) because s 28(2) provided expressly that any change to the Act could only be effected to facilitate the 'pursuance of the objects' of the Act.

### 6.2.2.7  Concluding remarks on the TEC

In a nutshell, the importance of the TEC lay in its political significance, on the one hand, and its constitutional importance as a broadly supported instrument for bridging the transition from one constitutional order to a fundamentally different one, on the other.

Unfortunately the TEC Act did not completely avoid a syndrome not uncommon to law, and in particular South African law: the use of legalese. This Act, and the other transitional measures, abound with the expression 'in consultation with'. To the initiated the meaning may be clear, and also distinguishable from 'after consultation with' or 'on the advice of'. On most others it would be lost. This may explain why the drafters of the Constitution[79] saw fit to explain that 'in consultation with' means 'in agreement with', and that 'after consultation with' means taking a decision in good faith after serious consideration of the views of those to be consulted. The question remains: why not simply say 'with the concurrence of', when that is what is meant?[80]

---

[75] Act 150 of 1993 ch VIII.
[76] Section 23(1) of the TEC Act.
[77] Section 23(3) and (5).
[78] Section 29(1).
[79] Constitution of the Republic of South Africa 200 of 1993 s 233(3) and (4).
[80] The words used in s 4(1) of the Local Government Transition Act 209 of 1993 (Afrikaans: 'met die instemming van').

## 6.3 The Independent Electoral Commission (IEC)

### 6.3.1 *Introduction*

According to its long title, the IEC Act[81] had a twofold purpose: to ensure that the election in South Africa was fair and free, and to provide for certain referenda. A wide-ranging structure was established by the Act for the achievement of these objects. The overarching body was the IEC, supplemented by an Election Administration Directorate, Election Monitoring Directorate, Election Adjudication Secretariat, Electoral Tribunals, Electoral Appeal Tribunals, and a Special Electoral Court.

Provision was made in the Act for the IEC, unlike the TEC, to have its life extended well into the transitional period. While s 9 provided for the IEC to be dissolved by the President 'upon the completion of its mandate', ss 124 and 232(5) of the Constitution contain express provisions for the IEC to oversee referenda and elections regarding the provinces. The IEC would also continue to function in terms of s 250(4) of the Constitution if it was unable to certify that the first elections were free and fair.

Section 34 provided that in the event of a conflict the provisions of the Act took precedence over any other law in respect of the conduct and supervision of elections.

### 6.3.2 *The IEC*

The seven to eleven South African and, at the most, five international members of the IEC were appointed by the State President 'upon the advice' of the TEC.[82] To qualify as a South African member a person had to be impartial, respected, suitably qualified, without a high political profile, had to be a voter, and represent a broad cross-section of the population. An international member could not vote in the IEC, nor would he or she form part of any quorum.[83]

A high premium was placed on the impartiality, good faith, and independence of members.[84] The same applied to the IEC itself, which was enjoined by s 8 to act without bias and interference, and with independence. Members of the IEC, the directorates, and the Election Adjudicating Secretariat were bound to secrecy in respect of their official duties.[85]

### 6.3.3 *Powers of the IEC*

Section 13 listed the powers of the IEC. These included the organization, conduct, administration, and supervision of any election; the prevention of intimidation; and

---

[81] Act 150 of 1993. For a discussion of the Act, see Murphy 'The Independent Electoral Commission Act 1993' (1993) 8 *SAPR/PL* 283. The Act was amended by the Independent Electoral Commission Amendment Act 209 of 1993 to bring it in line with provisions of the Electoral Act 202 of 1993 and to be more specific concerning certain aspects of electoral adjudication.

[82] Section 5(1) and (2)*(a)*. In terms of s 3(2) the State President is obliged to follow the advice, giving the expression 'upon the advice of' a meaning very similar to 'in consultation with' as used in the Constitution and the TEC Act (cf above, 6.2.2.7 'Concluding remarks on the TEC'). Kriegler JA was appointed chairperson, with Mr Dikgang Moseneke SC deputy chairperson.

[83] Section 5(2)*(b)*. One of the better-known international commissioners was Prof Walter Kamba, erstwhile Vice-chancellor of the University of Zimbabwe.

[84] Section 6(1). See further ss 6(2) and 7.

[85] Section 38.

voter education. Monthly reports had to be submitted to the TEC and the State President. In addition, in terms of s 41(1) the IEC had a wide field within which it could make regulations.

The most important part of the IEC's brief was to certify the results between two and ten days after the poll and declare that the election was either substantially free and fair, or that it was not.[86]

### 6.3.4 *The international advisory committee*

The extent to which the search for a South African constitutional solution had become the affair of the international community, and the degree to which South Africa had accepted that the involvement of the international community could have had positive effects on that process, were further reflected in the provisions of s 14. On the advice of the TEC, the State President could appoint an advisory committee of international experts to assist the IEC. No limitation was placed on the number of members, and the committee would be the master of its own procedure.

### 6.3.5 *The directorates*

The Act provided for two directorates, the Election Administration Directorate and the Election Monitoring Directorate.[87] Both were headed by a Chief Director, a key function of whom would be to hear appeals against decisions or actions of the directorate concerned.[88] Both directorates operated under the direct supervision and instruction of the IEC.[89]

As far as the Election Administration Directorate was concerned, the Act did not contain much in terms of functions, although it was fair to assume that the directorate was responsible for the administrative support for an election. The bulk of its specific activities were contained in the Electoral Act.

The powers, duties, and functions of the Chief Director: Election Monitoring were listed in the Act.[90] They included the appointment and co-ordination of monitors, registration of observers, investigation of infringements of the Electoral Code of Conduct, and mediation between parties participating in the election.

Both Chief Directors had extensive powers of delegation.[91]

### 6.3.6 *Electoral adjudication*

#### 6.3.6.1 The Election Adjudicating Secretariat

The Election Adjudicating Secretariat[92] operated under the instruction and supervision of the IEC, independently of the two directorates, and provided the administrative infrastructure for the system of electoral adjudication.

---

[86] Section 18.
[87] Chapters III and IV respectively.
[88] Sections 21(2) and 24(2).
[89] Cf ss 13(3), 21(3)*(b)* and *(c)*, and 24(1)*(j)* and *(k)*.
[90] Section 24(1).
[91] Sections 21(4) and 24(3).
[92] Sections 25–27.

### 6.3.6.2 The tribunals

Two types of electoral tribunal were established in terms of the Act: the Electoral Tribunals and the Electoral Appeal Tribunals.[93] The exact scope of the tribunals' functions was left to regulation,[94] but essentially their task was to hear cases of alleged irregularities and misconduct during the electoral process.

An Electoral Tribunal operated in a determined area, and consisted of one legally trained person.[95] It could impose appropriate penalties prescribed by or in terms of the Act or the Electoral Act.[96]

An Electoral Appeal Tribunal heard appeals from the Electoral Tribunals and could review their decisions.[97] It consisted of three persons appointed by the IEC with a judge as chairperson and one other lawyer. The third member had to be suitably qualified without being a lawyer.[98]

### 6.3.6.3 The Special Electoral Court (SEC)

The Special Electoral Court was the highest in the hierarchy of electoral adjudication. It consisted of five members appointed by the TEC. Three of the members were judges of the Supreme Court (the chairperson being a Judge of Appeal), while one of the remaining two also had to be a suitably qualified lawyer. As in the case of the Electoral Appeal Tribunals, one of the members did not need to be a legally trained person.[99]

Section 33 made it obvious that the SEC was designed to perform its functions on an urgent basis. Such functions included reviewing decisions of the IEC,[100] hearing appeals against decisions of the IEC and Appeal Tribunals,[101] and the resolution of disputes in terms of the Transitional Executive Council Act.

The SEC was master of its own procedure.[102] Section 36 contained detailed provisions governing appeal and review.

### 6.3.7 *Concluding remarks about the IEC*

Given the fact that the IEC, like the other transitional institutions, was put into operation rather late because of slow progress with the Constitution, it had to perform its mammoth task under extreme pressure. Under the circumstances and from all accounts it had performed remarkably well, despite a number of hiccups during the election itself.

---

[93] Chapters VI and VII respectively.
[94] Sections 28(1), 29, and 31.
[95] Section 28(1) and (2).
[96] Section 29(2).
[97] Section 30(1).
[98] Section 30(2).
[99] Section 32.
[100] Section 33(1)*(a)*.
[101] Section 33(2) and (4): appeals against decisions of the IEC were confined to the interpretation of laws and other matters provided for in the Electoral Act — s 33(2).
[102] Section 33(5).

## 6.4 The Independent Media Commission (IMC)

### 6.4.1 *Introduction*

The Independent Media Commission Act was the third in the package of transitional measures aimed at insuring that the the 'playing field' for the first democratic elections was 'level'. In particular, it was aimed at electronic media, state-financed publications, and state information services.[103] The controlling body established in terms of the Act was the Independent Media Commission (IMC). Like the IEC, its existence was directed at the first election, but the Act could be extended into the 'new' South Africa with minor amendments.

### 6.4.2 *The IMC*

The State President, acting on the advice of the TEC, appointed the members of the IMC.[104] Not more than seven persons, including the chairperson, could be appointed.[105] All the commissioners had to be able to act independently and without bias,[106] had to represent a broad cross-section of the population, had to be committed to free speech[107] and the principles of the Act, and had to be of high standing, merit, qualifications, experience, and expertise.[108] Section 6 contained a list of disqualifications for membership of the IMC, most of which were aimed at ensuring that persons of unquestionable integrity were appointed.

The chairperson had to be a judge, retired judge, or other senior lawyer, while at least two of the commissioners had to be experienced in the broadcasting world and at least one in the printed media.[109]

### 6.4.3 *Committees and experts*

The IMC had to establish two committees: a broadcasting committee, and a state-financed publication and state information services committee.[110] The IMC could also appoint other committees to assist it with the performance of its functions.[111] Chairpersons for the committees had to be drawn from the membership of the IMC,[112] but the two or more additional members could be from outside the IMC, provided they would have qualified for membership of the IMC.[113]

The IMC could appoint experts, including foreign experts, on a contract basis to assist it. Such experts had to report to the IMC.[114]

---

[103] See the long title and s 3.
[104] Section 4(2). As in the case of the IEC, 'on the advice' was described as a duty to obey: s 35(2).
[105] Section 4(1).
[106] Section 4(2)(*a*) read with s 2(2).
[107] The specific wording of s 5(3)(*b*) is instructive: '. . . persons who are committed to fairness, freedom of expression, the right of the public to be informed and openness and accountability on the part of those holding public office . . .'.
[108] Section 5(3).
[109] Section 5(1) and (2).
[110] Section 15(1)(*a*) and (*b*) respectively.
[111] Section 15(2).
[112] Section 15(3) and (4).
[113] Section 16(1) and (2).
[114] Section 16(3).

### 6.4.4 *Powers and functions of the IMC*

The IMC had to monitor broadcasts and state-financed publications and state information services to ensure that nothing was published that would have a negative effect on a climate for free political participation and the holding of fair and free elections. The IMC had to report any irregularity in this regard to the TEC and the IEC.[115]

Sections 18–22 contained the heart of the Act by providing for the regulation of political broadcasting and advertising during the election period,[116] by ensuring the equitable treatment of political parties, and by preventing state-financed publications and information services from advancing the cause of any political party.

In terms of s 23 a political party could lodge a written complaint with the IMC, which had to conduct a public hearing in adjudicating the complaint and before giving its ruling. The IMC could also of its own accord investigate suspected infringements of the Act.[117]

Competent orders for contraventions of the Act ranged from directing broadcasting licensees to make specific broadcasts, to the payment of a fine or the temporary termination of a broadcasting service.[118] Where the order was against a broadcaster the IMC had to inform the Independent Broadcasting Authority,[119] and in the case of a state-financed publication or a state information service the TEC had to be informed of the ruling.[120]

Section 26 of the Act required the IMC to report on a quarterly basis to the TEC. Finally, s 33 of the Independent Media Commission Act provided, like s 34 of the Independent Electoral Commission Act, that its provisions would take precedence over any other law in the event of conflict.

### 6.4.5 *Concluding remarks about the IMC*

The IMC did not assume the high profile of the IEC during the run-up to the first election. Its presence was nevertheless seen and heard in the way in which especially the electronic media handled the election campaigns of the various parties.

### 6.5 **The Independent Broadcasting Authority (IBA)**

### 6.5.1 *Introduction*

The IBA was established in terms of the Independent Broadcasting Authority Act,[121] which is at the same time the longest of the four transitional measures negotiated at the MPNP and the most technical. From its objects clause it is clear that it was aimed at regulating the broadcast industry in South Africa in consonance with the constitutional and political transformation taking place in the country.[122] The vehicle

---

[115] Section 17(1) and (2).
[116] Defined in s 1(xv) as the time between the commencement of the Act and the dissolution of the IEC in terms of s 9 of the Independent Electoral Commission Act.
[117] Section 23(12).
[118] Section 24(1).
[119] Section 24(2). As to the IBA, see below.
[120] Section 24(3).
[121] Act 153 of 1993.
[122] Cf s 2*(a)–(u)*, read with s 13.

designed for this purpose is the Independent Broadcasting Authority. Unlike the TEC, the IEC, and the IMC, the IBA was not intended as a purely transitional institution.[123] The governing body of the IBA is simply referred to as 'the Council'.

### 6.5.2 *The Council*

The composition of and qualifications for membership of the Council follow a pattern similar to that of the IMC; in other words, not more than seven appropriately respected and qualified persons, appointed by the State President on the advice[124] of the TEC. The IBA Act goes further, though, by requiring that the appointments are subject to public participation in the nominations, transparency and openness, and the publication of a shortlist of candidates.[125] Two 'co-chairpersons' may be appointed instead of one.[126]

The chairperson serves for five years and other councillors for four, with half of the latter vacating their seats after two years to introduce a rotational system, and hence continuity.[127]

The Council submits an annual report to the Minister responsible for the administration of the Act. The report has to be tabled in the National Assembly.[128]

### 6.5.3 *Committees, experts, and inquiries*

The Council may establish standing committees, special committees, and regional broadcasting committees.[129] Standing committees have to include a Broadcasting Technical Committee and a Broadcasting Monitoring and Complaints Committee.[130] The chairperson of each of these committees has to be a judge, retired judge, or senior lawyer.[131] At least one member of every standing committee has to be a member of the Council and, except in the case of the Broadcasting Technical Committee and the Monitoring and Complaints Committee, the councillor will also be the chairperson of the committee concerned.[132] Two or four additional members, all suitably qualified, make up the rest of a standing committee.[133] Standing committees assist the Council in the effective performance of its functions.[134]

Special committees are appointed on an *ad hoc* basis to assist the Council, and

---

[123] Cf, for example, ss 4(1) and 83(1)*(b)*.

[124] The wording of s 82, which provides for the State President to be bound by the Act 'in so far as he or she is required by this Act to act on the advice of' the TEC or the National Assembly, is less clear than in the case of the IEC Act (see above, n 82). It presumably means that the President has to follow the advice, but this construction is arguable. The Electoral Act 202 of 1993 s 3(2) is clearer where it stipulates that the President is 'obliged' to follow the advice.

[125] Section 4(1). Cf s 4(2) for qualifications similar to those in s 5(3) of the IMC Act; and s 5(1) for disqualifications similar to those contained in s 6(1) of the IMC Act.

[126] Section 4(3).

[127] Cf s 6(1) and (2).

[128] Section 20(1)–(3).

[129] Sections 21, 22 and 23(1) and (2).

[130] Section 21(1)*(a)* and *(b)*. The responsibilities of the former are listed in s 30. Sections 62–65 set out the functions of the Monitoring and Complaints Committee.

[131] Section 22(3)*(a)*.

[132] Section 22(3)*(b)*.

[133] Section 22(2).

[134] Section 21(2).

regional broadcasting committees are set up after consultation[135] with the regional government concerned.[136]

In terms of s 27, and like the IMC, the Council may appoint experts on contract to assist it.

Section 28 empowers the IBA to hold inquiries. An important feature in this regard is the procedure for public participation, openness, and transparency.[137] In terms of s 28(8) the IBA is enjoined to hold inquiries soon after its establishment into existing public broadcasting licences, cross-media control of private broadcasting licences, and certain other aspects of television and other broadcasting services.[138]

### 6.5.4 Functions

The IBA takes control of the airwaves in South Africa. In terms of Chapter IV of the Act it is entrusted with the administration, management, planning, and use of broadcasting services frequency bands. The Broadcasting Technical Committee plays an important role in this respect.[139] Chapters V and VI place the issuing of broadcasting signal distribution licences and broadcasting licences respectively in the hands of the IBA.

### 6.5.5 Code of conduct

Section 56 provides for a Code of Conduct for Broadcasting Services. The code itself is contained in the first schedule to the Act. In terms of s 56(2) a broadcasting licensee may be exempt from the code if it can satisfy the IBA that it and/or its members are bound by a code acceptable to the IBA.

### 6.5.6 Party election broadcasts and political advertisements

Sections 58–61 govern political broadcasts and advertisements. Section 61 lays down that a party election broadcast[140] and a political advertisement[141] may only be broadcast during an election period as defined in s 1(1)(xxi), and subject to the provisions of ss 59 and 60.

The latter two sections each contains a list of guidelines ensuring fair and equitable treatment of political parties should a broadcaster decide to allow party election broadcasts and political advertising. Section 61 reinforces the requirement of equitable treatment of political parties during an election period.

The Broadcasting Monitoring and Complaints Committee is the main instrument for the enforcement of these provisions of the Act.[142] The IBA is given wide-ranging

---

[135] Meaning that the Council is not bound by the input of the body consulted; to be distinguished from 'in' consultation with, which means 'with the agreement of': see above, 6.2.2.7 'Concluding remarks on the TEC'.
[136] Section 23(1) and (2).
[137] Section 28(2)–(7).
[138] Sections 45, 50, and 53(7) read with s 53(2)–(4).
[139] See s 30.
[140] Defined in s 1(1)(xxviii) as 'a direct address or message broadcast free of charge on a broadcasting service and which is intended or calculated to advance the interests of any particular political party'.
[141] Defined in s 1(1)(xxix) as 'an advertisement broadcast . . . intended or calculated to advance the interest of any particular political party' which is directly or indirectly being paid for.
[142] Cf ss 62–65.

powers to make orders following the findings of the Monitoring and Complaints Committee.

### 6.5.7 *Miscellaneous provisions*

The commencement of the Act was in the hands of the TEC.[143] After much wrangling the Act came into operation only in March 1994. Two provisions, ss 49(6) and 50(3), will come into operation on only 1 January 1996.[144]

Like s 33 of the IMC Act and s 34 of the IEC Act, s 80 provides that the provisions of this Act will take precedence over any other law in the event of conflict. For the future this is clearly subject to the overriding force of the Constitution.

### 6.5.8 *Concluding remarks about the IBA*

Strictly speaking the IBA is not a transitional body in the class of the TEC, the IEC, and the IMC. In fact, the definition of 'election' in s 1(1)(xx) expressly excludes the first election from its jurisdiction. This may be the main reason for its late introduction. Given the history and perceived political overtones of airwave control in South Africa, it was a matter that was best dealt with as part of the package of transitional measures.

## 6.6 The Electoral Act 202 of 1993

The Electoral Act is more than a transitional measure. It is designed to govern all elections for the National Assembly and provincial legislatures in terms of the Constitution.[145] However, it is clear that the Act was specifically tailored for the first election of April 1994 as well. There is ample evidence in support of this contention, notably the way in which the Act refers to various transitional structures such as the IEC and the TEC. In fact, the administration of the Act was entrusted to the IEC.[146]

An interesting provision of the Act is s 15, in terms of which citizens and permanent residents were entitled to vote in the first election. Section 21(2) of the Constitution gives every citizen the fundamental right to vote. Section 6 allows Parliament to extend the vote to non-citizens as well. The clear difference is that this 'right' of non-citizens can be revoked by ordinary law of Parliament, unlike the fundamental citizens' right in s 15.

## 6.7 Local government

A critical aspect of the political transition in South Africa is local government. However, during all the negotiations at CODESA and the MPNP it did not receive much attention. One of the reasons may be that in many political and constitutional minds the so-called third level of government is perceived to be less important than

---

[143] Section 83(1)*(a)*.
[144] Section 83(1)*(b)*. Both deal with exemption from certain limitations.
[145] Section 2.
[146] Section 4, read with the definition of 'Commission' in s 1(ix).

the national and regional levels.[147] Furthermore, it was difficult enough — with limited time and the surrounding problems of drawing in a broader spectrum of participants, violence, and the complexity of the issues — to negotiate a suitable Constitution for the national and provincial levels. Traditionally at the coalface of apartheid, immersed in group areas and influx control and with people living their daily lives close together, local government was in itself a sufficiently hard nut to crack. The result was a separate negotiating process, initially less formal and structured than the 'main' process, but eventually running side by side and ultimately dovetailing with it.

A major agent in the process was the Local Government Negotiating Forum (LGNF), a wide-ranging and increasingly influential non-statutory collection of bodies with a direct interest in local and metropolitan government. Its critical role in the transitional process was recognized in s 14 of the TEC Act, which contained the mandate of the Subcouncil on Regional and Local Government.

The centrepiece of the LGNF's work was the Local Government Transition Act,[148] which has to be read in conjunction with Chapter 10 of the Constitution. Broadly speaking, the Act provides for a two-phase transformation of local government to make it 'non-racial and inclusive', in the words of s 5(1). The first phase is the pre-interim phase, defined in s 1(1)(xi) as the period between the commencement of the Act and the next phase, predictably known as the interim phase.

During the pre-interim phase negotiating forums were to be established and recognized in terms of Part IV of the Act.[149] The main purpose of a forum would be to negotiate the creation of nominated 'transitional councils'[150] and a host of related matters.[151]

The interim phase is characterized by elected transitional councils, respectively known as transitional local councils for metropolitan areas and transitional metropolitan councils for metropolitan areas.[152] This phase lasts until the 'implementation of final arrangements to be enacted by a competent legislative authority'.[153] Being entrusted with local government by the Constitution, this will invariably be a provincial legislature, subject to s 126(3), which provides for instances where parliamentary legislation may override provincial laws.[154] Obviously any final arrangement will have to be reconcilable with the Constitution, in particular Chapter 10, which contains the framework provisions for local government, and the relevant provisions of Chapter 11 on traditional authorities.[155]

---

[147] This is evidenced by the rarity of contributions on local government in law journals: even a specialized public law journal, *SAPR/PL*, carried only three articles on local government during the last four years: Van Wyk & Van Wyk 'The Observance by a Local Authority of a Town Planning Scheme' (1990) 5 *SAPR/PL* 256; Barrie & Carpenter 'The Legal Framework within which Local Government Functions' (1993) 8 *SAPR/PL* 269 and 'Ethics and Insider Trading in Local Government: Or a Case of the Law and the Profits' (1994) 9 *SAPR/PL*.

[148] Act 209 of 1993, in operation since 2 Feb 1994.

[149] Section 6. Schedule 1 contains detailed directions on the composition, area, membership, and other matters relating to a forum, while the annexure to the schedule provides a full set of standard rules of procedure.

[150] Defined in s 1(1)(xv), read with paras (xvii) and (xviii).

[151] Section 7(1).

[152] Section 8(1).

[153] Definition of 'interim phase' in s 1(1)(iv).

[154] Section 126(1), read with sched 6. In terms of s 245(1) of the Constitution, all restructuring of local government has to take place in terms of the Local Government Transition Act until elections have been held during the interim phase.

[155] Cf s 245(3) of the Constitution.

## 7 THE CONSTITUTION
### 7.1 Introduction

It is beyond the scope of this work to assess the full extent to which the proposals of the various political actors had affected the shaping of the Constitution of 1993.[156] In the context of the Bill of Rights, Lourens du Plessis singled out two overriding influences, a libertarian and a liberationist, which led to an optimalist and a minimimalist approach in terms of the number of rights claimed to be included.[157] The ANC and the other participants from the 'struggle' clearly belonged to the liberationist camp, the 'establishment' parties, including the NP as 'newcomers', to the libertarian. In respect of the issue of power, this classification is too narrow, though. There were at least four approaches, not always clearly distinguishable. First, there were the convinced centralists, who for a number of reasons maintained that the history of South Africa, in particular apartheid, required a strong central government to initiate and direct a vigorous programme of reconstruction on the basis of equality. The ANC was the main proponent of this line of reasoning. On the other side of the spectrum were the complete decentralists who, from a variety of premises, argued for very weak central government, with the bulk of power in the hands of smaller units. The models advocated covered secession, confederation, and extreme federalism, often under the umbrella term of 'self-determination'. The IFP, with its *Constitution for the State of KwaZulu/Natal* (1992), the CP, other rightwing organizations,[158] and outspoken libertarian movements (such as Frances Kendall's Groundswell), fell into this category. In between were the proponents of liberal democracy and federalism, with the Democratic Party (DP) as the strongest voice, and the South African government/NP falling into this category. The latter, accustomed to power and historically and at heart centralist, advocated decentralization, but more with a view to retaining some power through 'power-sharing', it seemed, than as a matter of principle.

The political balance between these approaches may explain why, unlike the Namibian constitution-making process,[159] no party at the MPNP in Kempton Park submitted anything resembling a draft Constitution that could be used as a working document. Intentionally, it would appear, the driving political forces were content with a process of unfolding the constitutional text, having agreed on a set of

---

[156] Apart from the massive input by the SA Law Commission (*Group and Human Rights* Interim Report (1991) and *Report on Constitutional Models* (1991)), especially the ANC produced a number of discussion documents following various workshops, conferences, and research efforts by its Constitutional Committee. See, for example, *Constitutional Guidelines for a Democratic South Africa* (1988); *What is a Constitution?* (1990); *ANC Discussion Document on the Structure of a Constitution for a Free South Africa* (1991); *A Bill of Rights for a New South Africa* (1990); *A Bill of Rights for a Democratic South Africa* (1992); *ANC Draft Bill of Rights. Preliminary Revised Version 1.1* (1992); *ANC Draft Bill of Rights. Preliminary Revised Version February 1993* (1993); *Ten Proposed Regions for a United South Africa* (1992); *ANC Regional Policy* (1992); *Ready to Govern* (1993) particularly at 3–12. The National Party's constitutional principles were published in a booklet entitled *Constitutional Rule in a Participatory Democracy* (1991), followed by the government's proposal for a Bill of Rights, entitled *A Bill of Rights for South Africa* (1993). The Democratic Party also issued a number of discussion documents. For a description of the development of the Constitution, see De Villiers op cit (n 52).

[157] 'The Genesis of the Chapter on Fundamental Rights in South Africa's Transitional Constitution' (1994) 9 *SAPR/PL* 1.

[158] The IFP, the governments of Bophuthatswana and Ciskei, the CP, and a number of other organizations first formed the Concerned South Africans Group (COSAG) during the MPNP, later dissolving into the Freedom Alliance (FA), which essentially conducted negotiations from outside the formal structures of the MPNP.

[159] Cf Van Wyk 'The Making of the Namibian Constitution: Lessons for Africa' (1991) XXIV *CILSA* 341.

Constitutional Principles that would also bind the constitution-making body charged with the drafting of the 'final' Constitution. As it turned out, the transitional constitution-making process did not end until two days before the election on 27 April 1994.[160]

Long before the drafting of the Constitution started it was clear that two main issues, each with its own set of subissues, would dominate the debate: the so-called 'form of state', and fundamental rights. That the latter was handled in a far more comfortable way than the former may be due to the fact that the fundamental rights debate had gathered steam in the mid-eighties with all the important political actors expressing a positive sentiment. The result was numerous conferences, books, reports, and working documents[161] and, if not a 'rights culture', at least a culture of debate and accommodation and an acceptance that Chapter 3 of the Constitution can be used as a basis for further development.[162] 'Affirmative action' and restitution have been part of this agenda all along.

The form of state and the concomitant questions of checks and balances, the relationship between the 'central' and regional/local levels of government, were identified as thorny issues years ago.[163] Yet even with the commencement of the 1993 Constitution they have not been finally resolved.

## 7.2 General features of the Constitution

The Constitution is a hefty document, numbering 227 pages of print in its English and Afrikaans versions. Its 251 sections, in fifteen chapters, and seven schedules[164] must rank it amongst the longest in the world. A specifically peculiar feature in a South African context is the concluding part in ordinary prose under the title 'National Unity and Reconciliation'. With the preamble, in which emphasis is placed on South Africa as a democratic constitutional state and on equality, fundamental rights, national unity, and 'restructuring', it captures the essence of the 1993 Constitution: first and foremost it is the symbol of a new, apartheid-free South Africa; at the same time it forms the governmental bridge between the past and the future, and the constitutional basis for the writing of a 'final' Constitution. It is clearly a transitional document, as is evident from a number of other explicit

---

[160] On 25 April 1994 the tricameral Parliament had its final sitting in Cape Town to amend the Constitution of 1993 for the second time to accommodate the position of the Zulu king in the future dispensation (in order to ensure the participation of the IFP in the election).

[161] See literature referred to above, nn 30, 32, 33, 155, as well as Van der Westhuizen & Viljoen *A Bill of Rights for South Africa. 'n Menseregtehandves vir Suid-Afrika* (1988); Sachs *Protecting Human Rights in a New South Africa* (1990); Corder et al *A Charter for Social Justice. A Contribution to the South African Bill of Rights Debate* (1992); and the seminal collection of papers in Forsyth & Schiller *Human Rights: The Cape Town Conference* (1979).

[162] Cf Du Plessis op cit (n 156).

[163] Cf Dugard 'The Quest for Liberal Democracy in South Africa' 1987 *Acta Juridica* 237 at 239ff; 'Towards a Liberal Democratic Order for South Africa' (1990) 2 *Revue Africain de Droit International et Comparé* 361 at 365ff. See also Erasmus 'Towards a New Constitution: What are the Issues?' 1991 *De Rebus* 665.

[164] The chapters are entitled 'Constituent and Formal Provisions' (1); 'Citizenship and Franchise' (2); 'Fundamental Rights' (3); 'Parliament' (4); 'The Adoption of the New Constitution' (5); 'The National Executive' (6); 'The Judicial Authority and the Administration of Justice' (7); 'The Public Protector, Human Rights Commission, Commission on Gender Equality and Restitution of Land Rights' (8); 'Provincial Government' (9); 'Local Government' (10); 'Traditional Authorities' (11); 'Finance' (12); 'Public Service Commission and Public Service' (13); 'Police and Defence' (14); and 'General and Transitional Provisions' (15). The schedules are: 'Definitions of Provinces' including 'Contentious Areas' (1); 'System for Election of National Assembly and Provincial Legislatures' (2); 'Oaths and Affirmations of Office' (3); 'Constitutional Principles' (4); 'Procedure for Election of President' (5); 'Legislative Competences of Provinces' (6); and 'Repeal of Laws' (7).

references: the prohibition in terms of Constitutional Principles XXXII and XXXIII on the recomposition of the Cabinet and a general election before 30 April 1999; the role of Parliament as constitution-making body; and the regular references to the new or final constitutional text.

An unattractive feature of the Constitution, which it is hoped will be avoided in drafting the 'new' text, is its stylistic deference to the old order. On the purely formal level it is understandable: the Constitution is, after all, an Act of Parliament under the old system, and as such it fulfils the crucially important requirement of constitutional continuity. On the other hand, however, it also represents a fundamental break with the old order of parliamentary sovereignty and its peculiar way of legislative drafting. As the supreme law, the *Grundnorm* of the 'new' South Africa, the Constitution is one law that does not need to be cast in the typical stilted linguistic mode of days gone by.

The Constitution turns around seven critical areas: the Constitutional Principles, fundamental rights and their enforcement, structures of government, intergovernmental relations, finance, the transitional provisions, and the adoption of the new Constitution.

### 7.2.1 *The Constitutional Principles*

Given their fundamental importance to the constitution-making process since the days of the MPNP and under the 1993 Constitution, one can only speculate about the reasons for tucking the Constitutional Principles away in a schedule to the Act. It might have had something to do with the South African style of legal drafting; there might have been other reasons as well. The fact remains that no next constitutional text, called 'final' in the preamble and 'new' in the definitions,[165] will be of any force unless it has been certified by the Constitutional Court to be in compliance with the Constitutional Principles.[166]

On 27 April 1994, the day when the Constitution came into operation, there were thirty-four Constitutional Principles. The preamble to the Constitution describes them as a solemn pact. While most of the Principles reflect proven democratic notions and values such as equality and no discrimination,[167] separation of powers,[168] and an independent judiciary,[169] several have a particular South African, even African, ring. The requirement of democratic representation at all levels of government is tempered by a provision on 'traditional leadership'.[170] In order to accommodate the IFP, this principle was amended days before the first election to stipulate that the Constitution has to recognize and protect provincial provisions on the 'institution, role, authority and status of a traditional monarch'.[171] Principle XII refers to 'collective rights of self-determination'; in a subsequent attempt, by and large successful, to involve a part of the electorate with strong nationalist propensities in the first election, this principle was expanded to include self-

---

[165] Section 233(1)(viii).
[166] Section 71(1) and (2).
[167] Principles I, III, and V.
[168] Principle VI.
[169] Principle VII.
[170] Principle XVII, read with Principle XIII.
[171] Section 2 of the Constitution of the Republic of South Africa Second Amendment Act 3 of 1994.

determination 'in a territorial entity within the Republic or in any other recognized way'.[172]

The scurrying to amend the Constitutional Principles before 27 April 1994 is explained, on the one hand, by s 74(1), which precludes the new legislature from amending the Principles, and the requirement that the new Constitution has to be certified by the Constitutional Court, on the other.

### 7.2.2 *Fundamental rights and their enforcement*

The bulk of this work deals with the fundamental rights contained in Chapter 3 of the Constitution, their interpretation, and their enforcement. Hardly enough emphasis can be placed on the network of institutions created in terms of the Constitution for the promotion and protection of fundamental rights. Apart from the formal judicial system and the Constitutional Court, with its ultimate jurisdiction in all matters constitutional,[173] the Public Protector and provincial public protectors,[174] the Human Rights Commission,[175] the Commission on Gender Equality,[176] and the Commission on Restitution of Land Rights[177] are all entitled and empowered to develop and strengthen the fundamental rights regime of the Constitution.

### 7.2.3 *Structures of government*

In a nutshell, the Constitution provides for democratic and representative institutions of government at the three usual levels: national, provincial, and local. In terms of Chapter 11 traditional authorities form an integral part of provincial and local government. Like its predecessor, the 1993 Constitution is closer to a parliamentary system of government than to anything else.

#### 7.2.3.1 The national level

Government at the national level is in the hands of Parliament, the President,[178] and the Cabinet. In terms of Chapter 5, Parliament also sits as the Constitutional Assembly. As such it embodies the transitional nature of the Constitution: it replaces the legislature of the 1983 Constitution; as constitution-maker it becomes the constitutionalized, legitimized, and democratically elected extension of the MPNP.

❑ Parliament

Parliament consists of the National Assembly and the Senate. The 400 members of the former were elected by proportional representation, based on a provincial and

---

[172] Principle XXXIV, inserted by s 13*(b)* of the Constitution of the Republic of South Africa Amendment Act 2 of 1994.

[173] Chapter 7, in particular ss 97–100. Unfortunately, the provisions determining the jurisdiction of the court, especially in relation to other courts, are anything but clear and would require the careful attention of the Constitutional Assembly (cf s 68(1)).

[174] Especially in terms of s 112(1).

[175] See s 116 for its powers and functions.

[176] Sections 119 and 120 provide the basis, an Act of Parliament will have to furnish the details of this commission.

[177] Section 122, read with ss 121 and 123.

[178] The change in nomenclature should be noted: since 1961, when the Republic of South Africa was established, the somewhat awkward form of 'State President' has been used. Under the new Constitution it is simply 'President'.

national list system and a restricted mandate.[179] The National Assembly is presided over by the Speaker or Deputy Speaker, elected from its own ranks.[180] It is master of its own procedure, except for ordinary business where one-third, and for legislative business where half, of its total membership is required for a quorum.[181]

The Senate is composed of ten members per province, nominated by provincial legislatures on the basis of proportional representation.[182] Its business is presided over by a President and Deputy President, elected from the ranks of the Senate. As in the case of the National Assembly, the Senate makes its own rules, subject to the requirement that one-third of all the Senators, and in the case of legislation, one-half, has to be present to constitute a quorum.[183]

Sections 55–62 contain essential procedural provisions, ranging from parliamentary privilege to public access to Parliament. The more pertinent of these provisions are the following:

- Section 57(3), which permits the President to request a joint sitting of the National Assembly and the Senate to be convened.
- The passing of legislation, of which four categories are distinguished by the Constitution itself:

  — *Ordinary bills*, which may be introduced in either House of Parliament, and are required to be passed by both. In the event of a dispute between the Houses, an ordinary bill is referred to a joint committee of both Houses, and thereafter passed by an ordinary majority of the total membership of both Houses. All bills are ordinary bills, except the new constitutional text and those dealing with money, with certain provincial matters, and with constitutional amendments.[184]

  — *Money bills*, which deal with the appropriation of revenue and taxation, may only be introduced in the National Assembly and by the Minister responsible for national finance. Such a bill has to be considered by a joint parliamentary committee first and, if required, by the Financial and Fiscal Commission established in terms of Chapter 12. If a money bill is rejected by the Senate, it becomes law after it has been passed by the National Assembly for a second time.[185]

  — *Bills affecting the boundaries and powers of provinces* may only be passed separately by the National Assembly and the Senate and with the approval of the majority of Senators from the province or provinces concerned. This does not derogate from the requirements for constitutional amendment.[186]

  — *Constitutional amendments* can only be effected by a joint sitting of

---

[179] Section 40(1) read with the provisions of sched 2. Section 43*(b)* provides that a member who changes political allegiance loses his or her seat.

[180] Section 41. An historical achievement was the election of a woman, Frene Ginwala, as the first Speaker of the new Parliament.

[181] Sections 55(1), 58, and 47 respectively.

[182] Section 48.

[183] Sections 49 and 54.

[184] Section 59.

[185] Section 60.

[186] Section 61.

Parliament at which at least two-thirds of all the members of both Houses pass the amendment. However, when an amendment relates to the legislative and executive powers of a province, the two Houses should sit separately and pass the bill with at least two-third majorities, while the consent of the provincial legislatures concerned will also have to be obtained.[187]

- The President's assent to bills, which has to be given unless there appear to be procedural shortcomings.[188]
- Section 65(2), which provides that in the event of a linguistic conflict between the copies of an Act the one signed by the President will prevail.
- Section 66, in terms of which the President, the Executive Deputy Presidents, Ministers, and Deputy Ministers may sit and speak in a House of which they are not members, but without having the vote.

☐ The National Executive

Despite the wording of s 75, which professes to put executive authority at the national level in the hands of the President, real executive authority vests in the Cabinet, consisting of the President, the Executive Deputy Presidents, and not more than twenty-seven Ministers. While the Constitution itself, following in the footsteps of its predecessor, singles out the President for separate treatment, it is clear from all the provisions of Chapter 6 that the President can do very little on his or her own. In fact, in the ordinary course of events the President will always be dependent on the concurrence of the rest of the Cabinet.

In its attempt to treat the President separately the Constitution runs into structural difficulties. On the one hand, s 88(1) defines the Cabinet as consisting of the President, the Executive Deputy Presidents, and the Ministers. Section 82(3), on the other hand, requires the President to exercise the vast majority of his or her powers 'in consultation with' the 'Cabinet'. The definition of 'in consultation with'[189] suggests that the Cabinet has an existence separate from the President. This impression is reinforced by s 93, which refers to a motion of no confidence in the Cabinet, 'including' or 'excluding' the President. It is suggested that the deference shown to the President by the Constitution is out of place in a constitutional state where the executive is effectively a collective one, and the system essentially parliamentarian. This criticism would further seem to be warranted by the emphasis placed by the Constitution, as is done for instance in s 86(2), on the notion of the 'spirit underlying the concept of a government of national unity'.

The President is elected by the members of the National Assembly in terms of the procedure contained in s 77.[190] Under normal cicumstances he or she will hold office for the duration of the 1993 Constitution.

Section 82 governs the powers and functions of the President. Three categories are foreseen: a number of specific powers, some of which the President may exercise

---

[187] Section 62.
[188] Section 64(1), read with s 82(1)(b).
[189] See above, text to nn 79 and 80.
[190] Mr Nelson Mandela was elected President in terms of s 77 on 9 May 1994.

on his or her own; those in respect of which the Executive Deputy Presidents have to be consulted; and, finally, those which have to be performed in consultation with the Cabinet. The first category includes the assent to bills passed by Parliament, convening of meetings of the Cabinet, conferment of honours, appointment of ambassadors, and so on.[191] Unlike s 7 of the 1983 Constitution, no reference is made to prerogative powers. It is not inconceivable, in view of the superior nature of the Constitution, that these common-law powers have finally been put out to pasture.

The President has to consult the Executive Deputy Presidents on five issues: policies of the national government; the management of the Cabinet and the performance of its business; the assignment of powers and functions to Executive Deputy Presidents; the appointment of foreign representatives; and a number of matters contained in s 82(1).[192]

All other powers have to be exercised in consultation with the Cabinet.[193] Any act performed in this mode has to be countersigned by a Minister.[194] By a separate subsection the President is proclaimed Commander-in-Chief of the National Defence Force and empowered to declare a state of national defence with the approval of Parliament.[195]

Sections 84 and 85 govern the office of Executive Deputy President. Every party with 20 per cent of the votes would qualify for one Executive Deputy President. If no party or only one party achieved 20 per cent, provision is made for the appointment of two Executive Deputy Presidents, one each by the two largest parties. As things turned out, two parties achieved more than 20 per cent, with the resultant two Executive Deputy Presidents.

Unlike the President, who automatically upon election vacates his or her seat, an Executive Deputy President has the choice of retaining his or hers.[196] The office was obviously designed to give effect, at the highest level, to the idea of national unity.

The third component of the executive at the national level, besides the President and the Executive Deputy Presidents, are the ministers of the Cabinet. Their position is primarily governed by ss 88 and 92. The former governs the allocation of portfolios and the appointment of ministers; the latter deals with ministerial and Cabinet responsibility, or accountability, as it is called in the Constitution.

Section 88 is comprehensive in its directions for the appointment of not more than twenty-seven Ministers. Briefly, every party with at least 5 per cent of the vote and which has decided to participate in the government of national unity is entitled to representation in the Cabinet on a proportional basis. The President, 'after consultation with'[197] the Executive Deputy Presidents and the leaders of the participating parties, decides on portfolios and appoints the ministers to administer them. Subsection (5) is important in so far as it requires the appointment of ministers and the allocation of portfolios to take place in the 'spirit underlying the concept of

---

[191] Section 82(1).
[192] Section 82(2).
[193] Section 82(3).
[194] Section 83(2).
[195] Section 82(4)(*a*) and (*b*)(i).
[196] See ss 77(4) and 84(3).
[197] See s 233(4) and above, text to nn 79 and 80.

a government of national unity', and hence with consensus at all times. However, when such consensus cannot be achieved the President will have the final word over the portfolios and the nominees of his or her party, while the leaders of the other parties will decide on the candidates from their respective parties. In practice, 'consensus at all times' in this area could mean an agreement from the outset that the President and the leaders of the parties will have the first and final say as far as their own party appointments are concerned.

Subsections (8) and (9) expressly direct a minister not to engage in activities which may lead to a conflict of official and personal interests, or to personal enrichment or the enrichment of any other person.

Section 92, on ministerial and Cabinet accountability, is not perfectly clear. Subsection (1) leaves no doubt that Ministers are individually responsible to the President and to Parliament for their departments. It goes further to state that 'all members of the Cabinet shall correspondingly be accountable collectively' for the actions of the national government. All members of the Cabinet can hardly be responsible to the President, with the President being a member of the Cabinet him- or herself in terms of s 88(1). It is assumed that all members of the Cabinet, including the President, are collectively responsible to Parliament. Apart from a ring of authoritarianism reminiscent of the first years of the 1983 Constitution, it would hardly make sense to require the Executive Deputy Presidents and all the ministers to be collectively responsible to the President as well.

Responsibility to Parliament is reinforced by s 93, which governs events where a vote of no confidence is passed. Depending on whether it is a vote of no confidence in the whole Cabinet, or only in the President, or only in the other members of the Cabinet, the President is allowed a number of possibilities, including compulsory resignation, voluntary resignation, and a dissolution of Parliament.

Cabinet meetings are chaired by the President or the Executive Deputy Presidents on a rotational basis.[198] Again emphasis is placed on the notion of 'the consensus-seeking spirit underlying the concept of a government of national unity', this time amplified by the 'exigencies of government' and 'the need for effective government'.

In s 94 the Constitution provides for deputy ministers, to be appointed by the President along the same lines as ministers. Deputy ministers do not form part of the Cabinet, however.

Section 95 casts a safety net in case all parties, except that of the President, declined to participate in the government of national unity. In such an event the President's party would form the government.

☐ Other institutions at the national level

The Constitution provides for a number of other institutions of government appointed at the national level, often, however, not limited in their actions to the national level. These are the Public Protector, the Human Rights Commission, the Commission on Gender Equality, and the Commission on Restitution of Land Rights of Chapter 8; the Auditor-General;[199] the South African Reserve Bank;[200] the

---

[198] Section 89(1).
[199] Sections 191–194.
[200] Section 195–197.

Financial and Fiscal Commission;[201] the Commission on Remuneration of Representatives;[202] the Public Service Commission in terms of Chapter 13; and the South African Police Service and the National Defence Force provided for in Chapter 14.

Two institutions deserving separate attention are the Council of Traditional leaders and the Volkstaat Council. The former, established in terms of s 184, enjoys advisory powers and is also entitled to comment on any bill which affects 'traditional authorities, indigenous law or the traditions and customs of traditional communities', to use the words of s 184. The Volkstaat Council was a late insertion in the Constitution and resulted from hard negotations between the erstwhile government, the ANC, and certain rightwing organizations. In terms of ss 184A and 184B the twenty-member Council, elected by members of Parliament who support the idea, is a constitutional instrument for the pursuit of the Volkstaat notion.

### 7.2.3.2 The provincial level

❐ General

While it would be fair to say that the form and nature of institutions at the national level are not altogether foreign to South African constitutional law, the provincial dispensation resembles the most striking deviation from what used to be the South African Constitution.

First, instead of four provinces and ten nominally independent or self-governing 'homelands', South Africa has nine new provinces, each with an elected provincial legislature and a provincial executive of national unity. The pattern is virtually the same as that of the national government. Secondly, a provincial legislature enjoys wider legislative powers than the erstwhile provincial councils, and is entitled to enact its own provincial Constitution.

The transitional nature of the 1993 Constitution is clearly mirrored by many of the provisions relating to provincial government. Insufficient time during the negotiating process, vested regional interests that had to be taken into account, disputes over boundaries in certain areas, and sharp differences over the constitutional status of regional government left provincial government somewhat in the lurch and pregnant with impending change.

Section 124 is the example *par excellence.* In subsec (1) the nine provinces are established and named, with the proviso that if a provincial legislature so requests, Parliament has to change the name of the province in accordance with the wish of the province concerned.[203] Subsection (2) refers to the boundaries of the provinces, to be found in sched 1, identifying at least fourteen[204] disputed areas. The rest of the section contains detailed directions for the final determination of provincial boundaries. Petitions from residents and referenda are the cornerstone of the procedure. Subsection (15) is interesting to the extent that it allows laws to be passed by Parliament by ordinary majority if 'consequential amendments' to the Constitution were required to give effect to boundary changes. It should also be noted that

---

[201] Sections 198–206.
[202] Sections 207–208.
[203] The name of the province of Natal had already been changed to KwaZulu/Natal before the commencement of the Constitution: Constitution of the Republic of South Africa Amendment Act 2 of 1994 s 1.
[204] See s 124(2), (5) and (6).

the Independent Electoral Commission is given a prominent role in the redrawing of provincial boundaries.

Two further specific areas of provincial controversy are the legislative powers of provinces and finance.[205] In its original form, s 126 granted provinces 'concurrent' powers with Parliament in respect of a number of matters listed in sched 6. After stiff resistance from certain political organizations, and in an attempt to include them in the electoral process, the word 'concurrent' was removed from the section and the list of matters in sched 6 increased.

As things stand, provincial legislatures have overriding powers in respect of the matters in sched 6, subject to five exceptions:[206]

(i) where the province cannot deal with the matter effectively;
(ii) where uniform norms or standards throughout the Republic are required for the effective performance of a function;
(iii) where minimum standards are required across the Republic for the rendering of public services;
(iv) where the maintenance of economic unity, environmental protection, the promotion and protection of various aspects of interprovincial relations, and national security require parliamentary regulation; and
(v) where a provincial law has a materially negative effect on economic, health, or security interests of another province or the country as a whole, or if it obstructs the implementation of economic policies on a national scale.

Further safeguards to provincial autonomy are contained in subsecs (4) and (5). The former provides that an Act of Parliament will only override a provincial law if such Act applies uniformly throughout the Republic, while in terms of the latter, parliamentary and provincial laws have to be construed in harmony with each other, unless and only in so far as they are inconsistent with each other.

The other bone of contention, fiscal matters, saw changes to all five sections on provincial finance in the Constitution even before they came into operation. The principle is laid down in s 155(1): every province is entitled to an equitable share of national income. The controversy surrounded the sources of the equitable share. Initially, individual and value-added tax collected in the province concerned, with the addition of other allocations from national revenue, would form the basis of the 'equitable share'.[207] This was changed, however, in three respects: first, the personal and value-added tax components were extended to the national level; secondly, by the allocation of a fixed percentage of any national fuel levy; and, thirdly, by allowing a province any transfer duty collected at the national level on property in that province.[208]

Restrictions on provincial powers of taxation in terms of s 156 and provincial loan competence under s 157 were also reduced. In addition provinces were given the exclusive power to impose tax and levies on casinos, gambling, wagering, lotteries, and betting.[209]

---

[205] Sections 126 and 155–159 respectively.
[206] Section 126(3) as amended by s 2*(c)* of Act 2 of 1994.
[207] Section 155(2).
[208] Amendments effected by s 3 of Act 2 of 1994.
[209] Section 156(1B).

Provincial immunity from ready parliamentary intervention was strengthened by the insertion in ss 155, 156, and 157 of a new subsection in terms of which bills before Parliament dealing with provincial finances will not be seen as financial bills subject to the procedures prescribed by s 60 of the Constitution.[210]

☐ **The development of a system of provincial government**

Reference has been made in the preceding section to the fact that Chapter 9 contains little more than a tentative framework for provincial government. This observation is confirmed in so many words by ss 161(1) and 164(1). In s 161(1) the Constitutional Assembly is expressly enjoined to give 'priority attention' to the development of a system of provincial government. Section 164(1) contains the purpose of the Commission on Provincial Government, namely to 'facilitate the establishment of provincial government'. In order to achieve its object the Commission is given wide-ranging powers to advise the Constitutional Assembly, the national government, and provincial governments.[211]

A number of factors will play a crucial role in the direction the development of provincial government will take. One of these is the attitude of the provinces themselves, particularly the Western Cape and KwaZulu/Natal, where the ANC did not achieve majorities in the April 1994 election. The IFP, the majority party in KwaZulu/Natal, has outspoken federal preferences, and it was largely at their insistence that s 160 of the Constitution was amended twice before its inception — first to entitle a province to create constitutional structures differing from those of the 1993 Constitution[212] and subsequently to provide for express recognition of traditional monarchs, in particular the Zulu king.[213]

### 7.2.3.3   Local government

Chapter 10 of the Constitution deals with local government in seven sections.[214] It is hardly more than a bare and broad framework, which should be understood in view of the separate negotiations that took place on local government during the negotiating process.[215] The key constitutional provisions relating to local government are ss 174(3) and 175, which guarantee local government autonomy. Local government is further a provincial function, provided that the provisions of Chapter 10 are observed.[216] Local governments must have a democratic base,[217] while s 180 determines that a code of conduct for members and officials of local government has to be provided by law.

### 7.2.3.4   Traditional authorities

Traditional authorities fall under provincial jurisdiction,[218] subject to the provisions

---

[210] See ss 155(2A), 156(1A), and 157(1A).
[211] See s 164(1) and (2).
[212] Section 8(*a*) of Act 2 of 1994.
[213] Section 1 of the Constitution of the Republic of South Africa Second Amendment Act 3 of 1994.
[214] Sections 174–180.
[215] See above, 6.7 'Local government'.
[216] Schedule 6 of the Constitution.
[217] Section 179.
[218] Schedule 6 of the Constitution.

of the Constitution. The latter expressly recognizes the existence of both traditional authorities and indigenous law, links traditional leaders to local government, makes provision for a provincial House of Traditional Leaders, and also creates a national Council of Traditional Leaders.[219] The way in which traditional authorities and indigenous law have been accommodated in the Constitution is an encouraging symbol of the realism of the negotiators.

### 7.2.3.5 The Volkstaat Council

A result of the negotiations which followed the adoption of the Constitution by Parliament in 1993 was Chapter 11A on a Volkstaat Council.[220] Section 184B(3) foresees an Act of Parliament to provide for the procedures to be followed by the council in the pursuit of its objective, which is to promote a Volkstaat for those who want it.[221]

### 7.2.4 *The judiciary*

The major change to the South African judicial system is the establishment of the Constitutional Court in terms of s 98(1) of the Constitution. As the court of final instance over any matter in connection with the 'interpretation, protection and enforcement of the provisions'[222] of the Constitution, it will have a material effect on the administration of justice in South Africa.

The existing court structure remains intact, with the Appellate Division and other divisions of the Supreme Court and lower courts continuing their work.

A possible complication arises from the fact that the Constitutional Court and the Appellate Division are treated on an equal footing, with the Appellate Division being expressly precluded from adjudicating any matter within the jurisdiction of the Constitutional Court.[223] Other divisions of the Supreme Court, however, have first-instance constitutional jurisdiction in addition to their 'ordinary' jurisdiction.[224] The extent and complexity of s 102, entitled 'Procedural matters', bears testimony to the care with which the jurisdictional issue was handled.

The Judicial Service Commission established by s 105 is another novelty, with precedents in neighbouring countries, though.[225] It is widely representative of the legal profession and has a three-pronged mandate:[226] to make recommendations on the appointment of judges to the Constitutional Court and the Supreme Court, and to advise the national and provincial governments on all matters pertaining to the judiciary and the administration of justice.

---

[219] Chapter 11 (ss 181–184).
[220] Inserted by s 9 of Act 2 of 1994. See also above, 164 'Other institutions at the national level'.
[221] See s 184A(2).
[222] The wording used in s 98(2). Direct access to the court may be allowed in terms of the rules of the court if it is in the interests of justice to do so: s 100(2).
[223] Section 101(5).
[224] See especially s 101(3) and (4).
[225] Namibia and Zimbabwe, for example, also have Judicial Service Commissions.
[226] Section 105(2).

## 7.2.5 *Finance*

Chapter 12[227] of the Constitution deals with 'general financial affairs'. Apart from provisions relating to the National Revenue Fund, the annual budget, special pensions for persons who have contributed in any way to the establishment of a democratic order, and so on, it also contains specific sections on the Auditor-General, the South African Reserve Bank, the new Financial and Fiscal Commission, and the Commission on Remuneration of Representatives. Of these, the Financial and Fiscal Commission deserves special mention for its pivotal role in intergovernmental financial relations. Provincial funding will be a burning issue, a fact which is reflected in the composition of the commission: each of the nine provincial Executive Councils is entitled to nominate one member to the eighteen-member commission.[228]

## 7.2.6 *Transitional provisions*

Even the transitional provisions, bundled together in Chapter 15 and entitled 'General and transitional provisions',[229] bear the mark of the interim nature of the Constitution. A few are ordinary transitional measures, such as the continuation of existing laws and international agreements.[230] The chapter also contains an interpretation clause and a number of definitions.[231]

The bulk of the chapter is made up of carefully crafted provisions to ensure that the transition does not create unwanted upsets. Sections 230(1) and 234(1), for instance, secure existing pensions and pension rights, while ss 234(2) and 236(2) safeguard the positions of public servants and others. The other areas covered are also telling. There are transitional arrangements for legislative authorities, for executive authorities, for public administration, for public service commissions, for assets and liabilities, for the State Revenue Fund, for the judiciary, for the Ombudsman, for the Auditor-General, for local government, and for the pensions of political office-bearers.[232] There are rather extensive provisions regarding the rationalization of the public service and court structures,[233] while s 247 precludes the new government under the Constitution from changing educational structures without *bona fide* negotiation.

It can safely be said that these transitional provisions reflect the remarkable spirit in which the changeover in South Africa was negotiated and effected.

## 7.2.7 *The new Constitution*

The elation and importance of the first election and the ensuing introduction of the 1993 Constitution can easily obscure the fact that these events were designed, first and foremost, to provide a platform for the writing of the 'real' Constitution. Hence Chapter 5 of the 1993 Constitution, in terms of which the National Assembly and

---

[227] Sections 185–208.
[228] See s 200(1).
[229] Sections 229–251, one of the longer chapters in the Constitution.
[230] Sections 229 and 231(1).
[231] Sections 232 and 233.
[232] Sections 234–236, 238–241, and 243–246.
[233] Sections 237 and 242.

the Senate, sitting together, form the Constitutional Assembly. The Assembly has to pass the new Constitution within two years after the first sitting of the National Assembly.[234] Section 73 contains a series of steps in the event of the Constitutional Assembly failing to pass the new Constitution with the required majorities. These include referral of the text to the panel of experts established in terms of s 72(2) and ultimately a referendum in which at least 60 per cent of the voters should give their approval.

The critical requirement to be met in the creation of the new Constitution, arising from the evolutionary transition from apartheid to a democratic order, is certification by the Constitutional Court that the Constitution conforms in all respects to the Constitutional Principles contained in sched 4.[235] The rule is simple: no compliance, no Constitution.

---

[234] Section 73(1).
[235] See s 71.

# INTERNATIONAL HUMAN RIGHTS

### JOHN DUGARD

Human rights have played a prominent role in international law since the conclusion of World War II and the creation of the United Nations. South Africa has taken no positive part in the development of international human rights jurisprudence on account of its policy of apartheid. From a negative perspective, however, South Africa's contribution has been considerable as United Nations action against apartheid, taken in defence of human rights, succeeded in generating many new norms which have added substantially to the corpus of international human rights law.

The confrontation between the international community and South Africa over human rights had a severe impact on South African law and legal practice. The courts and the legal profession were largely isolated from the international community's new law of human rights and took little, if any, interest in the norms and treaties that comprised this body of law. Consequently arguments based on international human rights law were seldom raised in South Africa's courts and, when they were, received little serious attention.

The Bill of Rights contained in Chapter 3 of the 1993 Constitution, which is inspired by and based on international human rights conventions, will radically alter the situation as South African courts are specifically required by s 35(1) to draw on international human rights jurisprudence in their interpretation of this instrument. In order to assist South African lawyers to meet this challenge, the present chapter sets out to accomplish two goals: first, to describe the international and regional treaties that comprise the corpus of international human rights law (both the substance of the treaties and the methods of enforcement are described in order to provide a comprehensive picture of the current state of the law); secondly, to examine the role of international human rights law under the 1993 Constitution.

## 1 INTERNATIONAL HUMAN RIGHTS LAW*

### 1.1 The United Nations Charter

The commitment of the United Nations to human rights is made clear in the Preamble to the Charter, which reaffirms 'faith in fundamental human rights, in the dignity and worth of the human person, in the equal rights of men and women'. Ironically the Preamble was in large measure drafted by South Africa's Prime Minister, General Smuts, who as President of the Commission on the General Assembly played a leading part in the formation of the United Nations. The Charter itself contains a number of references to human rights. Article 1 includes among the purposes of the United Nations the promotion and encouragement of human rights,

---

* This section of the present chapter is substantially similar to the author's description of international human rights norms in *International Law: A South African Perspective* (1994) ch 13.

while art 13 obliges the General Assembly to initiate studies and make recommendations for promoting human rights. Most important are arts 55 and 56. Article 55 obliges the United Nations to promote 'universal respect for, and observance of human rights and fundamental freedoms for all without distinction as to race, sex, language, or religion'; and in art 56 '[a]ll members pledge themselves to take joint and separate action in co-operation with the Organization for the achievement of the purposes set forth in Article 55'.

The human rights clauses of the Charter suffer from several defects. First, they are vague and give no indication of the rights protected, apart from that of non-discrimination. Secondly, no enforcement machinery is provided for, unless the denial of human rights assumes such egregious proportions that it constitutes a threat to international peace under Chapter VII of the Charter. Thirdly, it is not clear that the clauses create any legal obligations for states, although the pledge to co-operate in promoting human rights in art 56 'at least implies a negative obligation not so to act as to undermine human rights'.[1] Fourthly, there is a conflict between the human rights clauses and art 2(7) of the Charter which provides:

'Nothing contained in the present Charter shall authorize the United Nations to intervene in matters which are essentially within the domestic jurisdiction of any state or shall require the members to submit such matters to settlement under the present Charter, but this principle shall not prejudice the application of enforcement measures under Chapter VII.'

These weaknesses in the legal status of the human rights clauses were vigorously exploited by South Africa as it sought to exclude debate, and later action, by the United Nations on its racial policies.[2]

## 1.2 Universal Declaration of Human Rights[3]

In 1946 the Economic and Social Council of the United Nations established a Commission on Human Rights, whose first task was to draft an International Bill of Rights, comprising a declaration and a multilateral treaty. The first step in this direction was the drafting of the Universal Declaration of Human Rights, which was approved by the General Assembly[4] on 10 December 1948, by forty-eight votes in favour, none against, and eight abstentions. South Africa, now under a National Party government, abstained, together with the Byelorussian SSR, Czechoslavakia, Poland, Saudi Arabia, the Ukrainian SSR, the USSR, and Yugoslavia.

The Universal Declaration proclaims both first-generation rights (civil and political rights) and second-generation rights (economic, social, and cultural rights) in the language of aspiration. For the Declaration is not a treaty but a

---

[1] Brierly *The Law of Nations* 6 ed by Waldock (ed) (1963) 293. For this reason, wrote Waldock, 'South Africa's racial segregation policies appear to be out of harmony with her obligations under the Charter'.
[2] See on South Africa's arguments, Fincham *Domestic Jurisdiction* (1948); Biermann (ed) *The Case for South Africa, As Put Forth in the Public Statements of Eric Louw, Foreign Minister of South Africa* (1963); Heunis *United Nations versus South Africa* (1986); Booysen *Volkereg* 2 ed (1989) 428–32. *Sed contra* see Dugard 'The Legal Effect of United Nations Resolutions on Apartheid' (1966) 83 *SALJ* 44 and 'Apartheid: A Case Study in the Response of the International Community to Gross Violations of Human Rights' in Cotler & Eliadis (eds) *International Human Rights Law Theory and Practice* (1992) 301; Özgur *Apartheid, the United Nations and Peaceful Change in South Africa* (1982).
[3] See Lauterpacht 'The Universal Declaration of Human Rights' (1948) 25 *BYIL* 354; Humphrey 'The Universal Declaration of Human Rights: Its History, Impact and Judicial Character' in Ramcharan (ed) *Human Rights: Thirty Years After the Universal Declaration* (1984).
[4] Resolution 217A(111).

recommendatory resolution of the General Assembly and is therefore not legally binding on states. According to its Preamble, it is to serve 'as a common standard of achievement for all peoples and all nations'. Although not binding, the Universal Declaration has undoubtedly guided the political organs of the United Nations in their interpretation and application of the human rights clauses in the Charter.[5]

The impact of the Universal Declaration on the development of human rights has been immense. It has inspired the International Covenant on Civil and Political Rights, the International Covenant on Economic, Social and Cultural Rights, and several regional human rights conventions; it has served as a model for national Bills of Rights; it has been used by the organs of the United Nations as a standard by which to measure the conduct of states; and it is invoked by the 1975 Final Act of the Conference on Security and Co-operation in Europe (the 'Helsinki Accord').[6] Consequently it is argued that the Universal Declaration now forms part of customary international law. In 1968, at an International Conference on Human Rights in Teheran, called by the United Nations to review the progress made since the adoption of the Universal Declaration, a Proclamation of Teheran was adopted by eighty-four states which declared:

> 'The Universal Declaration of Human Rights states a common understanding of the peoples of the world concerning the inalienable and inviolable rights of all members of the human family and constitutes an obligation for the members of the international community.'

The Proclamation of Teheran goes too far if it suggests that *all* the rights contained in the Universal Declaration have acquired the status of customary international law. On the other hand, Conradie J goes too far in the other direction in *S v Petane*, where he states:

> '. . . [I]t is dangerous to denaturate the practice-oriented character of customary law by making it comprise methods of law-making which are not practice-based at all. This undermines the certainty and clarity which the sources of international law have to provide. The Universal Declaration on Human Rights may be taken as an example in this respect. It has been asserted that in the course of time its provisions have grown into rules of customary international law. This view is often substantiated by citing abstract statements by states supporting the Declaration or references to the Declaration in subsequent resolutions or treaties. Sometimes it is pointed out that its provisions have been incorporated in national constitutions. But what if states making statements like these or drawing up their constitutions in conformity with the Universal Declaration at the same time treat their nationals in a manner which constitutes a flagrant violation of its very provisions, for instance, by not combating large-scale disappearances, by practising torture or by imprisoning people for long periods of time without a fair trial? Even if abstract statements or formal provisions in a constitution are considered a state practice, they have at any rate to be weighed against concrete acts like the ones mentioned.'[7]

The truth lies closer to the centre of the spectrum. Some of the more basic principles of the Universal Declaration — such as that of non-discrimination, the right to be tried, and the prohibition on torture,[8] cruel, and inhuman or degrading treatment — undoubtedly belong to the corpus of customary law today despite the

---

[5] See the dissenting opinion of Judge Tanaka in the *The South West Africa Cases, Second Phase* 1966 ICJ Reports 6 at 293.
[6] The text appears in (1975) 14 *ILM* 1293.
[7] 1988 (3) SA 51 (C) at 58G–J. See too *S v Rudman* 1989 (3) SA 368 (E) at 376A–B.
[8] *Filartiga v Pena-Irala* 630 F 2d 876 (2d Cir 1980); (1980) 19 *ILM* 966.

fact that they may not always be observed. Their status as custom is assured by both *opinio juris* and *usus*.

During the apartheid era both governmental and non-governmental organizations frequently judged South Africa by the standards of the Universal Declaration.[9] Now that the laws of apartheid have been repealed the Declaration is destined to play a more constructive role as a guide to municipal courts in their interpretation of laws affecting human rights. As an authoritative statement of the international community, several of whose provisions have acquired force of customary law, it is eminently suited for such a role. Courts in other jurisdictions have not hesitated to invoke the Universal Declaration for this purpose.[10] If South African courts are serious about their commitment to human rights, they should do likewise.

## 1.3 The international Covenants

Ideological differences between East and West made it impossible to produce a single multilateral treaty giving legal effect to the Universal Declaration. Instead two Covenants were drafted, one dealing with civil and political rights and the other with social, economic and cultural rights. They were adopted by the General Assembly in 1966, but came into force only in 1976, following the required thirty-fifth ratification. Today both are widely accepted, each with some one hundred ratifications. In 1992 the US ratified the International Covenant on Civil and Political Rights. South Africa is not a party to either Covenant.

### 1.3.1 *The International Covenant on Civil and Political Rights (ICCPR)*[11]

The ICCPR, like the International Covenant on Economic, Social and Cultural Rights, commences with the recognition of the right of self-determination (art 1). Unlike other UN instruments which recognize this right in the context of decolonization, the ICCPR asserts the right of self-determination in general.

Although it proclaims the right to life (art 6), the death penalty is not prohibited except in respect of persons below the age of 18 and pregnant women. In 1989 a Second Optional Protocol was adopted which outlaws the death penalty completely. To date this Protocol has attracted only a small number of states.

Torture, cruel, inhuman, or degrading treatment (art 7), and slavery (art 8) are prohibited. The right to liberty and security of person is recognized (art 9) and everyone is entitled to a fair and public trial with due regard to a number of minimum guarantees (art 14). The principle of *nulla poena sine lege* is recognized, except in respect of 'any act or omission which at the time when it was committed, was criminal according to the general principles of law recognized by civilized nations' (art 15) — i e war crimes, crimes against humanity, and, possibly, the crime of apartheid.[12]

---

[9] See Robertson (ed) *Human Rights for South Africans* (1991).

[10] Courts of the US have invoked the Universal Declaration in a number of cases: *Filartiga v Pena-Irala* (supra); *Fernandez v Wilkinson* 505 F Supp 787 (D Kan 1980). See further Burke et al 'Application of International Human Rights Law in State and Federal Courts' (1953) 18 *Texas J of Int L* 291 at 305. The influence of the Universal Declaration was recognized by Lord Wilberforce in *Minister of Home Affairs v Fisher* [1980] AC 319 at 328–9.

[11] For an examination of the *travaux préparatoires* of this Covenant, see Bossuyt *Guide to the* 'Travaux Préparatoires' *of the International Covenant on Civil and Political Rights* (1987). See too Henkin (ed) *The International Bill of Rights* (1981).

[12] See below, 180f.

The Covenant recognizes the freedoms of movement (art 12), thought, conscience and religion (art 18), expression (art 19), assembly (art 21), and association (art 22), but accepts that these rights may be restricted where this is necessary to protect national security, public order, public health or morals, or the rights and freedom of others. Article 20 qualifies the freedom of expression by prohibiting war propaganda and 'any advocacy of national racial or religious hatred that constitutes incitement to discrimination, hostility or violence'.

Every citizen is to have the right to vote in periodic elections and to participate in public life (art 25). Privacy (art 12), family life (art 23), and the protection of children (art 24) are recognized.

All persons are to enjoy equality before the law and 'are entitled without any discrimination to the equal protection of the law'. Discrimination on grounds of 'race, colour, sex, language, religion, political or other opinion, national or social origin, property, birth or other status' is prohibited (art 26). Of particular importance for an ethnically diverse society such as South Africa is art 27 which provides:

> 'In those states in which ethnic, religious or linguistic minorities exist, persons belonging to such minorities shall not be denied the right, in community with other members of their group, to enjoy their own culture, to profess and practice their own religion, or to use their own language.'

In times of public emergency threatening the life of the nation, states may derogate from their obligations under the Covenant 'to the extent strictly required by the exigencies of the situation'. No derogation is permitted, however, from a number of absolute provisions, such as the right to life, and the freedom from torture and cruel, inhuman, or degrading treatment or punishment.

Unlike the Universal Declaration,[13] the ICCPR is silent on the right to property.

States are obliged to ensure that their legal systems provide effective remedies against violations of the Covenant, including violations committed by government officials.

### 1.3.1.1 Human Rights Committee[14]

International supervision of the ICCPR is entrusted to the Human Rights Committee, a body of eighteen experts (mainly lawyers) elected by the contracting states for four-year terms, which may be renewed. In the election of the committee consideration is to be given to equitable geographical distribution of membership and to the representation of the different forms of civilization and of the principal legal systems. The committee is not a full-time body and holds three sessions per year. It supervises the Covenant in three ways.

❐ Reports[15]

All contracting states are required to submit reports on the measures they have adopted to give effect to the Covenant. The initial report must be submitted within

---

[13] Article 17 of the Universal Declaration provides: '(1) Everyone has the right to own property alone as well as in association with others; (2) No one shall be arbitrarily deprived of his property.'

[14] For a comprehensive study on the work of this committee, see Goldrick *The Human Rights Committee. Its Role in the Development of the International Covenant on Civil and Political Rights* (1991).

[15] See Fischer 'Reporting under the Covenant on Civil and Political rights: The First Five Years of the Human Rights Committee' (1982) 76 *Am J Int L* 142.

one year of becoming a contracting state. Thereafter reports are submitted every five years. The Human Rights Committee considers each report together with any information submitted to it by other sources (for instance by non-governmental organizations such as Amnesty International). The committee discusses the report with the representative of the reporting state. Article 40(4) permits the committee to submit appropriate 'general comments' only to the contracting states, which has been interpreted by an ideologically divided committee determined to reach consensus as denying the power of the committee to report on whether a particular state has fulfilled its obligations. Clearly this is not an onerous method of enforcement. To make matters worse, some states are seriously out of time in their submission of reports.

❒ Inter-state disputes

Article 41 provides for an optional system of inter-state disputes. According to this, one contracting state may, on condition of reciprocity, accuse another contracting state of a violation of the Covenant. The Human Rights Committee is then empowered to seek to settle the dispute amicably and, if this fails, to submit the dispute to an *ad hoc* conciliation commission. If this body is unable to settle the dispute, it may make a non-binding report on its findings. Although some thirty states have made declarations accepting this procedure, to date it has not been invoked.

❒ Individual petitions[16]

The First Protocol to the ICCPR, known as the Optional Protocol, permits contracting states to recognize the competence of the committee to receive and consider petitions from individuals who claim to be victims of a violation of the Covenant by a contracting state. The individual must have exhausted all available domestic remedies first and the same matter must not be the subject of any other international investigation (for example, by the European Commission on Human Rights acting under the European Convention on Human Rights). The complaint is considered on the basis of written submissions without an oral hearing. The committee then formulates its 'views', which are forwarded to the defendant state and the complainant. These 'views' are not legally binding and there is no provision for a court to take a binding decision on the matter (as under the European Convention on Human Rights). The 'views' of the Human Rights Committee are therefore substantially similar to the report of the European Commission on Human Rights, which is described below.

Today some fifty states have accepted the Optional Protocol and the committee has considered a substantial number of complaints. In its early years the committee was busily occupied with complaints of torture, murder, disappearance, and illegal detention from Uruguay after the government which had ratified the Optional Protocol was overthrown by a revolutionary regime. In all these cases the committee found against Uruguay.[17] An interesting case to be considered by the committee is

---

[16] De Zayas, Moller & Opsahl 'Application of the International Covenant on Civil and Political Rights under the Optional Protocol by the Human Rights Committee' (1985) 28 *GYIL* 9.
[17] See, for example, *Estrella v Uruguay* 2 *Selected Decisions HRC* (1983); *Izquierdo v Uruguay* 1 *Selected Decisions HRC* (1980).

that of *Lovelace v Canada*, in which it found that Canada had violated art 27, dealing with the rights of ethnic minorities, by denying Mrs Lovelace, a Canadian Indian, the right to return to her reserve following the dissolution of her marriage to a non-Indian.[18]

The effectiveness of the 'views' of the committee depends largely on the credibility of the committee and the sensitivity of the defendant state. In the past differing ideological attitudes towards human rights have hampered the work of the committee. Changes in Eastern Europe have removed some of these obstacles and there is some prospect that the committee will play a more activist role in the future.

### 1.3.2 *The International Covenant on Economic, Social and Cultural Rights (ICESCR)*[19]

The ICESCR deals with second-generation rights, such as the right to work (art 6), to the enjoyment of just and favourable conditions of work — including fair wages and safe and healthy working conditions (art 7), to form and join trade unions (art 8), to social security (art 9), to an adequate standard of living (art 11), to the enjoyment of the highest attainable standard of physical and mental health (art 12), to education — including free and compulsory primary education (art 13), and to participate in cultural life (art 15).

Civil and political rights are capable of immediate implementation in the sense that they do not require material resources for their implementation. Also they are negative in that they prohibit certain forms of conduct, which renders them open to judicial determination — i e they are justiciable. Economic, social, and cultural rights differ in these respects. First, they depend on the availability of resources for their implementation. Hence art 2 of the ICESCR provides that each party to the Covenant undertakes, not to implement the Covenant immediately as is the case with the ICCPR (art 2), but instead 'to take steps . . . to the maximum of its available resources, with a view to achieving progressively the full realization of the rights recognized in the present Covenant by all appropriate means'. Secondly, the rights protected require positive implementation in accordance with the availability of resources, which renders them less capable of judicial determination.[20] For this reason no provision is made for inter-state claims or individual complaints, as with the ICCPR. Instead a supervisory body, the Committee on Economic, Social and Cultural Rights (CESCR), which in structure resembles that of the ICCPR Human Rights Committee, receives national reports and considers them in much the same way as that body.[21] Unfortunately many states have failed to submit such reports and there is little that the committee can do to enforce compliance. These national

---

[18] 2 *Selected Decisions HRC* (1981).

[19] See Alston 'Out of the Abyss: The Challenges Confronting the New UN Committee on Economic, Social and Cultural Rights' (1987) 9 *Human Rights Quarterly* 332.

[20] The justiciability of economic, social, and cultural rights is a subject of controversy. It is not necessarily correct to say that all these rights are incapable of enforcement in the same way as civil and political rights. For instance the right to join a trade union and the prohibition on non-discrimination (art 2(2)) are clearly justiciable.

[21] Initially the ICESCR was monitored by the Economic and Social Council (ECOSOC) through a working committee. This proved inadequate and in 1985 (ESC Res 1985/17) CESCR was established. See Alston & Simma 'First Session of the UN Committee on Economic, Social and Cultural Rights' (1987) 81 *Am J Int L* 747, and 'Second Session of the UN Committee on Economic, Social and Cultural Rights (1988) 82 *Am J Int L* 603.

reports constitute the only method of 'enforcement' (if it can be so termed) under the ICESCR.

## 1.4 Non-discrimination[22]

In the 1960–6 proceedings over South West Africa before the International Court of Justice (*Ethiopia and Liberia v South Africa*)[23] one of the most controversial issues was whether the international law recognized a norm of non-discrimination which rendered South Africa's policy of apartheid, as pursued in South West Africa, contrary to the obligation in the Mandate for South West Africa to 'promote to the utmost' the well-being of the inhabitants. As the court found that the applicant states lacked the necessary *locus standi*, it avoided pronouncing on this issue.

Today the existence of such a norm derived from custom, general principles of law, and convention is beyond doubt. As far as conventional law is concerned the affirmation of the principle of non-discrimination on grounds of race and sex contained in art 55 of the UN Charter has been confirmed by several conventions.

### 1.4.1 International Convention on the Elimination of All Forms of Racial Discrimination[24]

This Convention, which was opened for signature in 1966 and came into force in 1969, has been ratified by some 130 states.

The Convention defines racial discrimination in art 1(1) as

'any distinction, exclusion, restriction or preference based on race, colour, descent, or national or ethnic origin which has the purpose or effect of nullifying or impairing the recognition, enjoyment or exercise, on an equal footing, of human rights and fundamental freedoms in the political, economic, social, cultural or any other field of public life'.

Contracting states condemn racial discrimination and undertake to eliminate it by all appropriate means (art 2). Apartheid receives particular condemnation (art 3). In pursuance of the undertaking to eliminate racial discrimination states agree to guarantee civil and political rights and economic, social, and cultural rights in a non-discriminatory manner (art 5). Furthermore, states undertake to assure to everyone within their jurisdiction effective protection and remedies against acts of racial discrimination (art 6).

The more controversial features of the Convention are those concerning private or non-governmental discrimination, restrictions on freedom of speech, and affirmative action. Although art 1(1) defines racial discrimination as comprising certain distinctions 'in the political, economic, social, cultural or any other field of *public life*' (italics added), art 2(1)(*d*) obliges states 'to bring to an end, by all appropriate means, including legislation as required by circumstances, racial discrimination by any persons, group or organization' and art 5(*f*) guarantees equality before the law

---

[22] McKean *Equality and Discrimination under International Law* (1983); Greenberg 'Race, Sex and Religious Discrimination in International Law' in Meron (ed) *Human Rights in International Law. Legal and Policy Issues* (1984) 307.

[23] See Dugard *The South West Africa/Namibia Dispute* (1973) 239–375.

[24] Lerner *The UN Convention on the Elimination of All Forms of Racial Discrimination* 2 ed (1980); Schwelb 'The International Convention on the Elimination of All Forms of Racial Discrimination' (1966) 15 *ICLQ* 966; Meron 'The Meaning and Reach of the International Convention on the Elimination of All Forms of Racial Discrimination' (1985) 79 *Am J Int L* 283.

in '[t]he right of access to any place or service intended for use by the general public, such as transport, hotels, restaurants, cafés, theatres and parks'. All of this indicates that discriminatory action by non-governmental parties is prohibited by the Convention.[25] Racist speech is clearly outlawed. Article 4 obliges states to criminalize 'all dissemination of ideas based on racial superiority' and 'incitement to racial discrimination' and to prohibit organizations which 'promote and incite racial discrimination'. Affirmative action is recognized in two ways. First, art 1(4) excludes affirmative action from the ambit of racial discrimination provided 'such measures do not, as a consequence, lead to the maintenance of separate rights for different racial groups and that they shall not be continued after the objectives for which they were taken have been achieved'. On the other hand, art 2(2) actually obliges states to take affirmative action 'when the circumstances so warrant'.

Enforcement of the Convention is entrusted to the Committee for the Elimination of Racial Discrimination (CERD), which is substantially similar to the ICCPR Human Rights Committee both in its composition and powers. The principal method of supervision is the submission and consideration of national reports. Provision is made for a *compulsory* system of inter-state claims (as compared with the ICCPR's system of optional inter-state claims), but so far no use has been made of this procedure. An *optional* system of individual complaints is also provided for (art 14).

### 1.4.2 *Convention on the Elimination of Discrimination against Women (CEDAW)*[26]

This Convention was opened for signature in 1979 and came into force in 1981. Over one hundred states have ratified or acceded to the Convention. For the purpose of the Convention discrimination means any distinction made on the basis of sex which 'has the effect or purpose of impairing or nullifying the recognition, enjoyment or exercise by women, irrespective of their marital status, on a basis of equality of men and women, of human rights' in any field (art 1). The Convention condemns discrimination against women and obliges states to ensure that their legal systems guarantee equal rights to women in all spheres of life. Affirmative action is recognized in art 4(1), which permits states to adopt 'temporary special measures aimed at accelerating *de facto* equality between men and women'. Article 4(2) provides that special measures aimed at protecting maternity 'shall not be considered discriminatory'.

Although 'reservations incompatible with the object and purpose' of the Convention are prohibited, no criteria are given for the determination of incompatibility. Consequently a number of reservations have been made, particularly those that preserve the Islamic Sharia, which seem to defeat the purpose of the Convention.[27] Compliance with the Convention is also weakened by its enforcement system.[28]

---

[25] Meron op cit (n 24) 291–5.

[26] (1980) 19 *ILM* 33. See Greenberg op cit (n 22). For a critique of the Convention and male dominance in the international legal order, see Charlesworth, Chinkin & Wright 'Feminist Approaches to International Law' (1991) 85 *Am J Int L* 613. For a guide to the literature, see Cook 'Bibliography: The International Right to Non-discrimination on the Basis of Sex' (1989) 14 *Yale J of Int L* 161. See also Evatt 'Eliminating Discrimination against Women' (1991) 18 *Melbourne U LR* 435.

[27] Clark 'The Vienna Convention Reservations Regime and the Convention on Discrimination against Women' (1991) 85 *Am J Int L* 281.

[28] Meron 'Enhancing the Effectiveness of the Prohibition on Discrimination against Women' (1990) 84 *Am J Int L* 213.

Unlike other conventions, no provision is made for inter-state claims or individual petitions. Instead enforcement is left to a twenty-three person Committee on the Elimination of Discrimination against Women which receives and considers national reports.

South Africa signed the Convention on the Elimination of All Forms of Discrimination against Women on 29 January 1993, but has yet to ratify it. In October 1993 Parliament adopted the General Law Fourth Amendment Act 132 of 1993 which paves the way for ratification of CEDAW by removing all traces of legislative discrimination against women.

### 1.4.3 Convention on the Rights of the Child[29]

In 1989 the General Assembly adopted the Convention on the Rights of the Child, which came into force in 1990. The Convention protects children against discrimination and asserts their civil, political, economic, social, and cultural rights. Like CEDAW, the Convention is to be monitored by a committee without any provision for state or individual petitions. South Africa signed the Convention on 29 January 1993, but has yet to ratify it.

### 1.4.4 International Convention on the Suppression and Punishment of the Crime of Apartheid [30]

This Convention was approved by General Assembly Resolution 3068 (XXVIII) of 30 November 1973, which was adopted by ninety-one votes in favour, twenty-six abstentions, and four negative votes (Portugal, South Africa, the UK, and the US). Although some ninety states have ratified the Convention, no Western European state has done so.

The Convention denounces apartheid as a crime against humanity in violation of international law (art 1). Apartheid is not limited to South Africa, but includes similar practices in other countries. It is defined (in art 2) as covering the denial and suppression of basic rights 'committed for the purpose of establishing and maintaining domination by one racial group of persons over any other racial group of persons and systematically oppressing them'.

This Convention is principally to be enforced through the procedures of international criminal law. International criminal responsibility is attached 'irrespective of the motive involved, to individuals, members of organizations and institutions and representatives of the states' guilty of committing the crime of apartheid (art 3). Contracting states are required either to try or extradite such persons. In considering extradition states agree not to consider the crime of apartheid as a 'political crime' (art 11). States agree to enact the necessary legislation for the purpose of trying offenders (art 4). Article 5 provides that suspected offenders 'may be tried by a competent tribunal of any State Party to the Convention which may acquire jurisdiction over the person of the accused or by an international penal tribunal having jurisdiction with respect to those States Parties which have accepted its

---

[29] (1989) 28 *ILM* 1448.
[30] (1974) 13 *ILM* 50. For criticisms of this Convention, see Booysen 'Convention on the Crime of Apartheid' (1976) 2 *SAYIL* 56 and *Volkereg* 2 ed (1989) 178; Barrie 'The Apartheid Convention after Five Years' 1981 *TSAR* 280; Heunis *United Nations versus South Africa* (1986) 281.

jurisdiction'. As no such international tribunal has been established, it is envisaged that any contracting state may try an offender over whom it happens to acquire jurisdiction in its own domestic courts. The UN Commission on Human Rights is empowered to prepare a list of individuals, organizations, and representatives of states alleged to be guilty of the crime of apartheid.

No prosecutions have been instituted under this Convention. In practice its effect has therefore been entirely symbolic.

The model for the Apartheid Convention is the Genocide Convention, which was adopted by the General Assembly in 1948,[31] but came into force only in 1961. This Convention likewise attaches criminal responsibility to those guilty of genocide 'whether they are constitutionally responsible rulers, public officials or private individuals' (art 4) and employs the principle of *aut dedere aut judicare* for its enforcement. Contracting states agree to extradite offenders and not to treat genocide as a political crime. It is also agreed that states will make provision in their domestic law for the prosecution of offenders. Alternatively they may be tried by an international penal tribunal.

## 1.5 Torture[32]

Torture and other cruel, inhuman, or degrading treatment is prohibited by the International Covenant on Civil and Political Rights, the European, American, and African regional human rights conventions, the 1985 Inter-American Convention on Torture,[33] the 1987 European Convention on Torture,[34] and the 1984 Convention against Torture and Other Cruel, Inhuman or Degrading Treatment or Punishment.[35]

The principal anti-torture convention, the 1984 Convention against Torture, came into force in 1987 and has been ratified by over sixty states. South Africa signed the Convention on 29 January 1993, but has yet to ratify it. It defines torture, in art 1, as

'any act by which severe pain or suffering, whether physical or mental, is intentionally inflicted on a person for such purposes as obtaining from him or a third person information or a confession, punishing him for an act he or a third person has committed or is suspected of having committed, or intimidating or coercing him or a third person, or for any reason based on discrimination of any kind, when such pain or suffering is inflicted by or at the instigation of or with the consent or acquiescence of a public official or other person acting in an official capacity. It does not include pain or suffering arising only from, inherent in or incidental to lawful sanctions.'

The ban on torture is to be enforced by both municipal criminal sanctions and international supervision. First, states undertake either to try or extradite torturers. Secondly, a ten-person Committee on Torture is established with powers similar to those of other supervisory committees. The committee receives and considers national reports, and there is provision for optional state and individual petition procedures. An innovation, contained in art 20, allows the committee to examine

---

[31] 78 UNTS 277. Robinson *The Genocide Convention* (1960); Kuper *Genocide* (1982).
[32] See generally Sieghart *International Law of Human Rights* (1983) 149; Cassese (ed) *The International Fight against Torture* (1991); Burgers & Danelius *The United Nations Convention against Torture* (1988).
[33] (1986) 25 *ILM* 519.
[34] (1988) 27 *ILM* 1152. See further Cassese 'A New Approach to Human Rights: The European Convention for the Prevention of Torture' (1989) 83 *Am J Int L* 128; Evans & Morgan 'The European Convention for the Prevention of Torture: Operational Practice' (1992) 41 *ICLQ* 590.
[35] (1985) 24 *ILM* 535.

allegations of systematic torture in a state, if necessary by an inspection *in loco*, provided the host state consents. States may, however, exclude the operation of art 20 by a special declaration (art 28).

## 1.6 Third-generation rights

In recent years 'third-generation' people's, group, or collective rights have been asserted, particularly by developing countries.[36] The right to self-determination is the most widely recognized of these rights. Others are the right to the environment and the right to development. The latter controversial right was proclaimed by the General Assembly in 1986 in the Declaration on the Right to Development.[37] Third-generation rights feature prominently in the African Charter on Human and Peoples' Rights.

## 1.7 The UN Commission on Human Rights[38]

A key organ in the promotion of human rights is the Commission on Human Rights, created in 1946 to draft the International Bill of Rights. A subsidiary body of the Economic and Social Council (ECOSOC), it comprises forty-three state representatives. It is assisted by a Sub-Commission on Prevention of Discrimination and Protection of Minorities, which consists of twenty-six experts who serve in their individual capacities.[39] Initially the Commission confined itself to the preparation of human rights instruments and the promotion of human rights, and declined to consider complaints concerning violations. In 1967, however, ECOSOC in Resolution 1235 (XLII) authorized the Commission and the Sub-Commission to examine information relating to gross violations of human rights contained in communications and to consider situations which revealed a consistent pattern of human rights violations (such as apartheid in South Africa), and to make recommendations to ECOSOC. This power was extended by ECOSOC in Resolution 1503 (XLVIII) of 1970, which authorizes the Sub-Commission to investigate situations 'which appear to reveal a consistent pattern of gross and reliably attested violations of human rights'.[40] The requirement that such investigations be undertaken only with the consent of the state in question and the insistence on confidentiality until a report is made to ECOSOC have deprived this procedure of real effectiveness.

## 1.8 Conventions, declarations, and standards

The multilateral treaties described above constitute the principal universal, as

---

[36] See Crawford (ed) *The Rights of Peoples* (1988). Cf the position of minorities in Strydom 'Views on International Measures for the Protection of Minorities' (1992/3) 18 *SAYIL* 134.

[37] Resolution 41/128. See on this right, Rich 'The Right to Development: A Right of Peoples' in Crawford op cit (n 36) 39; Alston 'Making Space for New Human Rights: The Case of the Right to Development' (1988) 1 *Harvard Human Rights Yearbook* 3; Forsythe (ed) *Human Rights and Development. International Views* (1989).

[38] See Tolley *The UN Commission on Human Rights* (1987). For a critical examination of the Commission, see Guest *Behind the Disappearances: Argentina's Dirty War Against Human Rights and the United Nations* (1990).

[39] For a picture of the work of the Sub-Commission, see Garber & O'Connor 'The 1984 UN Sub-Commission on Prevention of Discrimination and Protection of Minorities' (1985) 79 *Am J Int L* 168; Reierson & Weissbrodt 'The Forty-Third Session of the UN Sub-Commission on Prevention of Discrimination and Protection of Minorities: The Sub-Commission under Scrutiny' (1992) 14 *Human Rights Quarterly* 232.

[40] See on these procedures, Zuijdwijk *Petitioning the United Nations* (1982); Bossuyt 'The Development of Special Procedures of the United Nations Commission on Human Rights' (1985) 6 *Human Rights LJ* 179.

opposed to regional, human rights treaties. There are, however, many other treaties dealing with specific human rights issues. For instance, there are several treaties aimed at the suppression of slavery[41] which date back to the League of Nations period. Indeed these are the only human rights treaties to which South Africa was a party during the apartheid era. The conventions aimed at the protection of refugees[42] and stateless persons[43] are also an important branch of international human rights law.

The corpus of international human rights law extends beyond treaties to include declarations[44] of the General Assembly and other political organs of the United Nations or its specialized agencies and standards formulated by such bodies. On 25 June 1993 a World Conference on Human Rights, sponsored by the United Nations, adopted the Vienna Declaration on Human Rights and Programme of Action, which proclaims the universality of human rights. This Declaration, which led to the appointment of a United Nations High Commissioner for Human Rights, is likely to play an important role in the promotion of human rights in the future.

Of particular importance are the standards laid down by the International Labour Organization and the Standard Minimum Rules for the Treatment of Prisoners.

### 1.8.1  *ILO Standards*

The International Labour Organization (ILO) has adopted several hundred conventions and recommendations enunciating standards in the field of industrial relations.[45] Conventions are adopted by the General Conference and submitted to member states for ratification. If ratified, such a convention has the same effect as a treaty. Recommendations, on the other hand, are designed to provide guidelines to states. Conventions and recommendations have laid down standards on matters such as freedom of association, conditions of work, social security, health and safety, working hours, etc.

### 1.8.2  *Standard Minimum Rules for the Treatment of Offenders*[46]

In 1955 the First United Nations Congress on the Prevention of Crime and the Treatment of Offenders adopted a set of Standard Minimum Rules for the Treatment of Offenders, which was subsequently approved by the UN Economic and Social Council in 1957.[47] The Rules have been widely accepted by governments and have influenced judicial decisions in many countries. The South African government, which was represented at the 1956 Congress which adopted the Rules, has sought

---

[41] Slavery Convention of 1926, 134 BFSP 355; 1953 Protocol Amending the 1926 Convention, 183 UNTS 378.

[42] Convention relating to the Status of Refugees of 1951, 189 UNTS 137; Protocol relating to the Status of Refugees of 1967, 606 UNTS 267 and (1967) 6 *ILM* 78.

[43] Convention relating to the Status of Stateless Persons of 1954, 360 UNTS 117; Convention on the Reduction of Statelessness of 1961, UN Doc A/Conf 915 (1961).

[44] For example, the Declaration on the Right to Development op cit (n 37) and the Declaration on the Elimination of All Forms of Intolerance and Discrimination Based on Religion or Belief, Resolution 36/55 (1981).

[45] The texts appear in *International Labour Conventions and Recommendations 1919–1981* (1982). A selected number of conventions is to be found in Brownlie *Basic Documents on Human Rights* 2 ed (1981) 171ff.

[46] See Van Zyl Smit *South African Prison Law and Practice* (1992) 80–1; Rodley *The Treatment of Prisoners under International Law* (1987).

[47] Resolution 663C (XXIV) of 31 July 1957. The text of the Rules appears in *Human Rights: A Compilation of International Instruments* UN publication: Sales No E88 XIV 1 section G (1988).

to incorporate them into its law and practice. In 1990 the General Assembly of the United Nations gave its support to the Standard Minimum Rules.[48]

## 1.9 Regional human rights conventions

Europe, the Americas, and Africa have adopted regional human rights conventions which complement and reinforce universal human rights conventions. These conventions are likely to be more successful than their universal counterparts because the closer political and cultural homogeneity and shared judicial traditions and institutions within a region provide the basis for confidence in the system, which is necessary for effective implementation.[49] The experience of both the European and American Conventions bear this out. The African Charter on Human and Peoples' Rights, which came into force only in 1986, is still too young to judge in this respect.

## 1.10 The European Convention on Human Rights[50]

The European Convention for the Protection of Human Rights and Fundamental Freedoms ('the European Convention'), which was adopted by the Council of Europe in 1950, came into force in 1953. Today it is an essential component of the political order of Europe with over twenty members which include all historically 'Western European' states, Turkey, and erstwhile 'Eastern European' states such as Hungary, the Czech Republic, and Slovakia. The European Convention is confined to civil and political rights. Economic, social, and cultural rights are protected in a separate convention, the European Social Charter of 1961.[51]

The European Convention and the International Covenant on Civil and Political Rights share a common source of inspiration, the Universal Declaration of Human Rights, and consequently follow the same pattern. There is no protection for property rights in the European Convention, but this right was later guaranteed in the First Protocol to the Convention.[52] The death penalty is not outlawed in the Convention, but this was later done in the Sixth Protocol of 1983,[53] which has been ratified by most states. Today the death penalty has been abolished *de facto* or *de jure* by all parties to the Convention.

The Convention has succeeded in extending human rights to millions of Europeans, largely as a result of the effectiveness of its methods of enforcement, through both domestic law and international machinery.

Contracting states are required to 'secure to everyone within their jurisdiction' the rights contained in the Convention (art 1) and to ensure that their municipal law

---

[48] Resolution 45/111 of 14 December 1990.
[49] Weston, Lukes & Hnatt 'Regional Human Rights Regimes: A Comparison and Appraisal' (1987) 20 *Vanderbilt J of Transnational L* 585.
[50] 213 UNTS 221. There is a wealth of literature on this Convention. See, for example, Fawcett *The Application of the European Convention on Human Rights* 2 ed (1987); Castberg *The European Convention on Human Rights* (1987); Weston et al op cit (n 49); Robertson & Merrils *Human Rights in Europe* 3 ed (1993); Higgins 'The European Convention on Human Rights' in Meron (ed) *Human Rights in International Law. Legal and Policy Issues* (1984) 495; Van Dijk & Van Hoof *Theory and Practice of the European Convention on Human Rights* 2 ed (1990); Macdonald, Matscher & Petzold *The European System for the Protection of Human Rights* (1993); Stavros *The Guarantees for Accused Persons under Article 6 of the European Convention on Human Rights* (1993); Delmas-Marty *The European Convention for the Protection of Human Rights* (1991).
[51] 529 UNTS 89. This Charter entered into force in 1965. See Harris *The European Social Charter* (1984).
[52] 213 UNTS 262.
[53] Text in Fawcett op cit (n 50) 428.

provides 'an effective remedy' (art 13). As treaties form part of the municipal law of most European countries without the need for any act of legislative incorporation, the Convention is part of the local law of most of Europe. Consequently it is considered and enforced by domestic courts of these countries in the first instance.[54] The UK,[55] Ireland, and the Scandinavian countries, which follow a dualist approach to treaties, are in a different position as they have failed to incorporate the Convention into municipal law with the result that it may not be applied directly by municipal courts. In order to ensure their compliance with the Convention they have, however, sought to amend their legislation where appropriate. Furthermore, their courts have used the Convention as an interpretive guide in human rights cases.

The international machinery for the enforcement of the Convention comprises three tiers: the European Commission of Human Rights, the European Court of Human Rights, and the Committee of Ministers of the Council of Europe. Both the court and Commission are based in Strasbourg.

The Commission, which consists of a number of members equal to that of the contracting parties, is elected by the Committee of Ministers. Although not required by the Convention, in practice members of the Commission are lawyers. The jurisdiction of the Commission covers inter-state applications (art 24) and petitions submitted by individuals, groups, or non-governmental organizations claiming to be victims of a violation of the Convention by one of the contracting states (art 25). The inter-state complaint procedure is binding automatically on all states, whereas the petition procedure is optional. (Today, however, only very few states fail to accept the petition system.) The role of the Commission is to decide whether the complaint is admissible,[56] to investigate and ascertain the facts, and to attempt to secure a friendly settlement between the parties. If a friendly settlement is not reached, the Commission compiles a report in which it states whether it finds that there has been a breach of the Convention or not. This report is forwarded to the Committee of Ministers. It may, however, also be submitted to the Court of Human Rights if the states involved have accepted the jurisdiction of the court.

The European Court, elected by the Consultative Assembly of the Council of Europe, consists of a number of judges equal to that of the members of the Council of Europe, who hold office for nine-year terms. Although the court's jurisdiction is optional, it has been accepted by almost all states. Only states and the Commission may bring complaints to the court, but the Commission may (and frequently does) refer individual complaints to the court, in which case the individual is permitted to participate in both the preparation and presentation of the case before the court. The judgment of the court is both final and binding. In practice most judgments of the court are declaratory, but on occasion it has made compensatory awards.

The execution of the court's judgment is the responsibility of the Committee of Ministers, a political body. To date all judgments have been followed without the need for enforcement. The Committee of Ministers is also responsible for enforcing

---

[54] Drzemczewski *European Human Rights Convention in Domestic Law. A Comparative Study* (1983).

[55] See Dugard 'International Human Rights Norms in Domestic Courts: Can South Africa Learn from Britain and the United States?' in Kahn (ed) *Fiat Justitia. Essays in Memory of Oliver Deneys Schreiner* (1983) 220 at 223–8.

[56] Articles 26 and 27. The Commission will not, for example, consider a complaint where local remedies have not first been exhausted.

reports of the Commission where the matter is not referred to the court. In the final resort the Committee has the power to exclude a delinquent state from the Council of Europe, a measure with serious political and economic implications for a state. Although this power has not been exercised, Greece did withdraw from the Council of Europe in 1970 when it faced expulsion following a finding of serious human rights violations by the military junta and returned only in 1973 after the restoration of democracy.[57]

The inter-state complaint procedure under art 24 has been sparingly used by states as they are generally reluctant to disturb relations with their fellow European states by taking up the case of the victims of human rights violations against their own states. In most cases in which this procedure has been employed the complainant state has had close cultural or ethnic ties with the victims, which has resulted in political sympathy for the victims within the complainant state. Thus Ireland brought a complaint against the UK in 1971 arising out of the internment and 'in-depth interrogation' of IRA suspects in Northern Ireland.[58]

The majority of cases before both the Commission and the court are today brought by individuals. (Between 1973 and 1986 34 015 individual applications were received by the Commission, of which only some 4 per cent were found to be admissible.[59]) In large measure this may be ascribed to the fact that the European Convention is so well known to the European people that both individuals and their lawyers see the right of individual petition as a basic legal remedy.

In recent times there have been few instances of patterns of serious human rights violations in Western Europe. Consequently the machinery of the Convention has increasingly come to resemble the judicial system of states with the Commission playing the role of a court of first instance and the court that of an appellate court. The court has grown considerably in stature and its judgments are now referred to by human rights lawyers with the deference accorded the US Supreme Court under Chief Justice Earl Warren. Important decisions have been delivered by the court on matters such as interrogation as a form of inhuman and degrading treatment,[60] the circumstances in which a state may derogate from its obligations in time of national emergency,[61] contempt of court proceedings as a violation of freedom of expression,[62] the punishment of homosexual conduct between consenting adults in private as an invasion of privacy,[63] corporal punishment as degrading treatment,[64] failure to bring an accused to court within a reasonable time,[65] the right of a prisoner to communicate with his lawyer,[66] separate language schools and the principle of non-discrimination,[67] and the obligation of European States not to extradite persons

---

[57] Buergenthal 'Proceedings against Greece under the European Convention on Human Rights' (1968) 62 *Am J Int L* 441.
[58] European Court of Human Rights (ECHR), Series A, vol 25, Judgment of 18 January 1978.
[59] Op cit (n 49) 616, 633–4.
[60] Op cit (n 58).
[61] *Lawless Case*, ECHR, Series A, vol 3, Judgment of 1 July 1961.
[62] *Sunday Times Case*, ECHR, Series A, vol 30, Judgment of 26 April 1979.
[63] *Dudgeon Case*, ECHR, Series A, vol 45, Judgment of 22 October 1981.
[64] *Tyrer Case*, ECHR, Series A, vol 26, Judgment of 25 April 1978.
[65] *Wemhoff Case*, ECHR, Series A, vol 7, Judgment of 27 June 1968; *Neumeister Case*, ECHR, Series A, vol 7, Judgment of 27 June 1968.
[66] *Golder Case*, ECHR, Series A, vol 18, Judgment of 21 February 1975.
[67] *Belgian Linguistics Case*, ECHR, Series A, vol 6, Judgment of 23 July 1968.

to the US for capital crimes where they may be subjected to the 'death-row phenomenon'.[68]

## 1.11 The inter-American system[69]

The inter-American system for the protection of human rights has two sources: the Charter of the Organization of American States (OAS), and the American Convention on Human Rights of 1969. The two overlap and supplement each other. Indeed one of the principal organs, the Inter-American Commission on Human Rights, is shared by both regimes.

In 1948, at the time of the founding of the OAS, and seven months before the adoption of the Universal Declaration of Human Rights, the American states adopted the American Declaration on the Rights and Duties of Man,[70] a non-binding resolution. In 1959 the Inter-American Commission on Human Rights was established,[71] which has evolved into an effective human rights investigative body.

The American Convention on Human Rights (ACHR)[72] was adopted in 1969 by an inter-governmental conference convened by the OAS and came into force in 1978. Over twenty of the thirty-three OAS member states have ratified the Convention, but several of the more powerful states, such as the US and Brazil, have yet to do so.

The American Convention is devoted almost entirely to civil and political rights. However, art 26 obliges states progressively to realize second-generation rights, a matter which is dealt with more fully in a 1988 Additional Protocol. Although the Convention follows broadly the same pattern as the European Convention and the International Covenant on Civil and Political Rights, there is a number of important differences. The right to life commences 'from the moment of conception' (art 4(1)); property is protected (art 21); and special provision is made for the limited application of the Convention in federal states (art 28).[73]

Like the European Convention, the American Convention provides for a three-tier enforcement system, by means of the Inter-American Commission on Human Rights, the Inter-American Court of Human Rights, and the General Assembly of the OAS (which plays the same role as the European Committee of Ministers).

The Inter-American Commission, comprising seven experts, has, under the ACHR, compulsory jurisdiction over individual petitions (art 44) and optional jurisdiction over inter-state complaints (art 45) (i e the reverse of the position under the European Convention). No use has been made of the inter-state procedure and the system of individual petitions has not been successful, partly due to the

---

[68] *Soering Case*, ECHR, Series A, vol 161, Judgment of 7 July 1989; (1989) 28 *ILM* 1063.

[69] Buergenthal, Norris & Shelton *Protecting Human Rights in the Americas* (1986); Buergenthal 'The Inter-American System for the Protection of Human Rights' in Meron (ed) *Human Rights in International Law. Legal and Policy Issues* (1984) 439; Weston op cit (n 49).

[70] Resolution XXX, Final Act of the Ninth International Conference of American States, Bogotá, Colombia; 30 March–2 May 1948. The text is reprinted in Brownlie *Basic Documents on Human Rights* 2 ed (1981) 381.

[71] The Inter-American Commission was incorporated into the OAS Charter system only in 1970. See Buergenthal in Meron op cit (n 69) 470ff.

[72] 1144 UNTS 123; (1970) 9 *ILM* 673. Sometimes this Convention is described as the 'Pact of San Jose, Costa Rica' — where it was approved.

[73] See further on this subject Buergenthal in Meron op cit (n 69) 445.

Commission itself and partly due to the general ignorance about the Convention among the peoples of the Americas.[74]

The American Court of Human Rights[75] comprises seven judges and sits in Costa Rica. As under the European Convention, only states and the Commission may refer cases to the court — provided that the states in question have accepted the jurisdiction of the court (art 62). In addition to these proceedings in contentious cases, the court has an advisory jurisdiction to give opinions on the interpretation of the ACHR or any other treaty concerning the protection of human rights in the Americas — at the instance of any member state of the OAS.

The Inter-American Commission operates under the Charter of the OAS and not the ACHR when it considers complaints relating to the violation of the American Declaration on the Rights and Duties of Man by member states of the OAS, whether or not such a state has ratified the ACHR. Thus the Commission was able to investigate the compatibility of the imposition of the death penalty on juveniles in the US with the guarantee of the right to life contained in art 1 of the American Declaration.[76] The Commission, acting under the OAS Charter, has the power to conduct inspections *in loco*, with the consent of the defendant state, into human rights violations. This power, which is appropriate for large-scale human rights violations, has been used with some success in states in which there was a consistent pattern of human rights violations.[77] Unlike the European Commission, the Inter-American Commission has a promotional role, which it fulfils by means of national reports, and studies on subjects such as disappearances, torture, and refugees.

## 1.12 The African Charter on Human and Peoples' Rights[78]

The African Charter on Human and Peoples' Rights, also known as the Banjul Charter,[79] was approved by the Organization of African Unity (OAU) in 1981 and came into force in 1986. Over forty of the OAU's fifty-one members are parties to the Charter.

Although inspired by other human rights conventions, it has a distinctly African character. Like other conventions, it recognizes the basic civil and political and social, economic, and cultural rights. In addition recognition is accorded to third-generation collective rights such as the rights to development, self-determination, and a satisfactory environment. The meaning of the term 'peoples' in the Charter is not clear.[80] In the light of the OAU's commitment to the preservation of colonial borders it would be wrong to interpret the right of a people to self-determination to

---

[74] Weston op cit (n 49) 617, 635.

[75] See Frost 'The Evolution of the Inter-American Court of Human Rights: Reflections of Present and Former Judges' (1992) 14 *Human Rights Quarterly* 171.

[76] See Fox 'Inter-American Commission on Human Rights Finds United States in Violation' (1988) 82 *Am J Int L* 601.

[77] Weston op cit (n 49) 618–20.

[78] Umozurike 'The African Charter on Human and Peoples' Rights' (1983) 77 *Am J Int L* 902; Kiwanuka 'The Meaning of "People" in the African Charter on Human and Peoples' Rights' (1988) 82 *Am J Int L* 80; Dlamini 'Towards a Regional Protection of Human Rights in Africa: The African Charter on Human and Peoples' Rights' (1991) XXIV *CILSA* 189; Welch 'The African Commission on Human and Peoples' Rights: A Five Year Report and Assessment' (1992) 14 *Human Rights Quarterly* 43; Motshekga 'The African Charter on Human Rights and Peoples' Rights — Its Importance to Human Rights Thinking in South Africa' (1987) 30 *Codicillus* 31.

[79] The Charter was drafted in Banjul in the Gambia. The African Commission of Human and Peoples' Rights is based in Banjul.

[80] See Kiwanuka op cit (n 78).

include a right to secession — despite the fact that a literal reading of the Charter's art 20 permits such an interpretation. Unlike other conventions it recognizes the duties of the individual — towards family, society, and state.

The Charter contains no derogation clause for emergency situations. On the other hand, the proclaimed rights are undermined by 'claw back clauses' that confine the Charter's protection to rights as defined in national law. For example, art 6 provides that 'no one may be deprived of his freedom *except for reasons and conditions previously laid down by law*' (italics added).

The supervisory organ is the African Commission on Human and Peoples' Rights, comprising eleven persons who serve in their personal capacities. Unlike the European and US systems, there is no provision for a court to monitor the Charter. The Commission meets twice a year in fortnightly sessions. Its principal function is to promote human rights in Africa by means of public education. Some of the enforcement mechanisms of other conventions also appear in the Charter. The Commission may consider both inter-state complaints and individual petitions. The Commission may only act on individual petitions at the request of the Assembly of Heads of State and Government of the OAU when they 'relate to special cases which reveal the existence of a series of serious or massive violations of human and peoples' rights' (art 58). Measures taken shall, however, remain confidential unless the Assembly of Heads of State and Government decides otherwise. Member states undertake to submit reports every two years on their compliance with the Charter.

It is too early to judge the success of the African Charter. To date no inter-state complaint has been brought and few individual petitions considered, while the reporting record of states is disappointing.[81]

## 2 INTERNATIONAL HUMAN RIGHTS AND SOUTH AFRICAN LAW[82]

South Africa is not a party to any human rights convention, apart from those dealing with the suppression of slavery. It is a party to the United Nations Charter, but has refrained from incorporating its provisions into municipal law by legislation. It abstained from voting on the Universal Declaration of Human Rights. South Africa is now set upon a new course. In January 1993 it signed the Torture Convention of 1984, the Convention on the Rights of the Child of 1989, the Convention on the Political Rights of Women of 1953, the Convention on the Nationality of Married Women of 1957, and the Convention on the Elimination of All Forms of Discrimination against Women of 1979. It also acceded to the Convention on Consent to Marriage, Minimum Age for Marriage and Registration of Marriages of 1962. Ratification of these conventions is expected shortly. Moreover, it is confidently anticipated that South Africa will become a party to other human rights conventions — such as the International Covenant on Civil and Political Rights and the International Convention on the Elimination of All Forms of Racial Discrimination — in the near future.

---

[81] See Welch op cit (n 78).
[82] See Titus *The Applicability of the International Human Rights Norms to the South African Legal System — with Specific Reference to the Role of the Judiciary* (LLD, Leiden 1993); Dugard op cit (n 55); Keightley 'International Human Rights Norms in a New South Africa' (1992) 8 *SAJHR* 171.

## 2.1 International human rights norms in South African courts before 1993

Before the 1993 Constitution came into force it was possible for South African courts to apply international human rights norms in a number of ways.

*(a)* Customary international law has always been part of our common law,[83] with the result that it was open to courts to apply those norms of human rights law that had acquired the status of custom — unless they were in conflict with legislation. As the apartheid legislative order violated almost every right recognized in the Universal Declaration of Human Rights, there was little scope for the application of customary norms. Where legislation was silent our courts showed no inclination to invoke customary rules. In *S v Petane* the court rejected the argument that the rights contained in the Universal Declaration of Human Rights had acquired the status of customary law,[84] while in *S v Rudman* Cooper J, with no attempt to examine legal authority outside South Africa, dismissed the Universal Declaration of Human Rights, the International Covenant on Civil and Political Rights, and the European and American Conventions as instruments inspired by 'laudable ideals' which 'do not form part of customary international law'.[85]

*(b)* Although South Africa has signed and ratified the Charter of the United Nations, it has not been incorporated into municipal law by statute. Consequently the human rights clauses in the Charter may not be directly invoked by a South African court.[86] The clauses, which assert the principle of non-discrimination, may, however, be invoked to interpret an ambiguous statute in accordance with the presumption that the legislature does not intend to violate international law.[87] In *S v Werner*[88] the Appellate Division declined to apply this reasoning to its interpretation of the Group Areas Act. Moreover, the presumption in favour of compliance with international treaty obligations was seriously undermined by an *obiter dictum* of Van Heerden JA in *Binga v Cabinet for South West Africa*[89] in which he found that the presumption in favour of compliance with international treaty obligations applies only where the statute seeks to give effect to the treaty in question. This *obiter dictum*, based on the *dictum* of Diplock LJ in *Salomon v Commissioner of Customs and Excise*,[90] is contradicted by a wealth of subsequent English decisions

---

[83] *South Atlantic Islands Development Corporation v Buchan* 1971 (1) SA 234 (C) at 238C–D; *Inter-Science Research and Development Services (Pty) Ltd v Republica Popular de Mocambique* 1980 (2) SA 111 (T) at 124H; *Kaffraria Property Co v Government of the Republic of Zambia* 1980 (2) SA 709 (E) at 712E–G, 715A; *Yorigami v Maritime Construction Co Ltd v Nissho-Iwai Co Ltd* 1977 (4) SA 682 (C) at 696E; *Nduli v Minister of Justice* 1978 (1) SA 893 (A) at 906B. See further Dugard *International Law: A South African Perspective* (1994) ch 4.

[84] Supra at 58G–J.

[85] Supra at 376A–B.

[86] *Pan American World Airways Incorporated v SA Fire and Accident Insurance Co Ltd* 1965 (3) SA 150 (A) at 161C–D; Dugard *International Law: A South African Perspective* 51–2.

[87] Devenish *Interpretation of Statutes* (1992) 212; Hahlo & Kahn *The South African Legal System and its Background* (1968) 114, 211; Cockram *Interpretation of Statutes* 3 ed (1987) 131; *Maynard v The Field Cornet of Pretoria* (1894) 1 SAR 214; *S v Penrose* 1966 (1) SA 5 (N) at 11E–F; *Achterberg v Glinister* 1903 TS 326 at 334; *Claassens v Wilkens* 1905 ORC 139 at 141; *R v Lionda* 1944 AD 348 at 352; *Hajaree v Ismail* 1905 TS 451 at 456; *Ex parte Adair Properties* 1967 (2) SA 622 (R) at 627B–F.

[88] The case is reported in *S v Adams; S v Werner* 1981 (1) SA 187 (A) at 113. See too *S v Werner* 1980 (2) SA 313 (W) at 328C.

[89] 1988 (3) SA 155 (A) at 184–5.

[90] [1966] 3 All ER 871 (CA) at 875–6.

invoking the European Convention on Human Rights (which Britain has signed but not incorporated) as a guide to statutory interpretation.[91]

(c) International human rights conventions and declarations not binding on South Africa either as custom or treaty might be invoked by courts as a guide to judicial policy in the formulation of a rule of law.[92] In *S v Khanyile*[93] Didcott J invoked the International Covenant on Civil and Political Rights and the European Convention on Human Rights to support a finding that an indigent person might not be sentenced to a substantial jail term without counsel, but this reasoning was rejected by the Eastern Cape Division,[94] another Natal court,[95] and the Appellate Division.[96]

In a number of decisions the industrial court has relied on unincorporated conventions and recommendations of the ILO in giving substance to the term 'unfair labour practice'.[97]

The United Nations Standard Minimum Rules (SMR) have been invoked as a guide to the interpretation of the laws governing the treatment of prisoners.[98]

The failure of South African courts to use the limited opportunities available to them to apply international human rights norms can be ascribed to a number of factors, including an unfamiliarity with international law, a lack of awareness of the importance attached to international human rights norms in other jurisdictions, and an antipathy to the international human rights movement, which had succeeded in isolating South Africa from the international community. Whatever the reasons, the South African courts' negative attitude towards international human rights norms discouraged counsel (themselves largely unfamiliar with this branch of law) from raising arguments premised on international human rights norms in municipal courts.

## 2.2 The 1993 Constitution

The 1993 Constitution makes it clear that international law is to play a major role in the new South African legal order, particularly in the fields of human rights and humanitarian law.

Section 231(4) provides that '[t]he rules of customary international law binding on the Republic, shall, unless inconsistent with this Constitution or an Act of

---

[91] Duffy 'English Law and the European Convention on Human Rights' (1980) 29 *ICLQ* 585 at 589; Dugard op cit (n 55) 234–6.

[92] *Blathwayt v Cawley (Baron) & others* [1976] AC 397 (HL) at 426; Mann *Studies in International Law* (1973) 340.

[93] 1988 (3) SA 795 (N) at 801A–D. Followed in *S v Davids; S v Dladla* 1989 (4) SA 172 (N).

[94] *S v Rudman* (supra) at 375–6. Cf *Nakani v Attorney-General* 1989 (3) SA 655 (Ck).

[95] *S v Mthwana* 1989 (4) SA 361 (N).

[96] *S v Rudman; S v Mthwana* 1992 (1) SA 343 (A). Criticized in 'Focus on *Rudman*' (1992) 8 *SAJHR* 90.

[97] See *Metal and Allied Workers Union v Stobar Reinforcing (Pty) Ltd* (1983) 4 *ILJ* 84 (IC); *United African Motor and Allied Workers Union v Fodens SA (Pty) Ltd* (1983) 4 *ILJ* 212 (IC); *National Automobile and Allied Workers Union v Pretoria Precision Castings (Pty) Ltd* (1985) 6 *ILJ* (IC). See further Woolfrey 'The Application of International Labour Norms to South African Law' (1986–7) 12 *SAYIL* 135; Brassey, Cameron, Cheadle & Olivier *The New Labour Law* (1987) 169–71.

[98] In 1990 in *S v Staggie* 1990 (1) SACR 669 (C) Conradie J applied art 31 of the SMR, which declares that corporal punishment is 'completely prohibited' as a punishment for disciplinary offences in prisons, to the interpretation of s 54(2)(d) of the Correctional Services Act 7 of 1959. This case was reaffirmed in *S v Daniels* 1991 (2) SACR 403 (C) at 405F–I. See further Van Zyl Smit *South African Prison Law and Practice* (1992) 73–85.

Parliament, form part of the law of the Republic'. Although this provision merely confirms the common-law position,[99] there is little doubt that its inclusion in the Constitution, which is the 'supreme law of the Republic',[100] gives customary international law a more elevated status.

The role of treaties in the new legal order is less certain. Under the previous system treaties signed and ratified by the executive became part of municipal law only if incorporated by Act of Parliament.[101] In practice treaties were not so incorporated unless domestic implementation was essential for compliance with South Africa's international obligations. Consequently even the United Nations Charter has not been incorporated by statute into municipal law. Under the 1993 Constitution treaties are to be negotiated and signed by the executive,[102] but will not become binding on the Republic unless ratified by Parliament under s 231(2).[103] Although the Negotiating Council of the Multi-Party Negotiating Process envisaged that a treaty ratified by Parliament would form part of South African law unless it was expressly excluded by Act of Parliament,[104] the final draft approved by Parliament reversed the position so that a treaty ratified by Parliament will only become part of our law 'provided Parliament expressly so provides'.[105] While Parliament is not required to incorporate a ratified treaty by Act of Parliament for it to become part of domestic law, it is not clear how the incorporation will take place in practice. Probably an endorsement of incorporation attached to the act of parliamentary ratification will suffice. If this becomes the general rule, as was envisaged by the Negotiating Council, the number of treaties incorporated into municipal law will multiply; and any human rights convention ratified by Parliament will immediately become part of municipal law. If, on the other hand, Parliament requires an additional and separate process for the incorporation of treaties ratified by Parliament for international purposes under s 231(2), the 1993 Constitution will probably bring little change to existing practice and few treaties will be incorporated into municipal law. This could result in South Africa becoming a party to the major human rights conventions, without incorporating them into municipal law — as is the case with Britain, which has refused to incorporate the European Convention on Human Rights and the International Covenant on Civil and Political Rights into municipal law.[106]

International law is to play an important role in the interpretation of the Bill of Rights contained in Chapter 3 of Act 200 of 1993. According to s 35(1):

> 'In interpreting the provisions of this Chapter a court of law shall promote the values which underlie an open and democratic society based on freedom and equality and *shall*, where applicable, have regard to public international law applicable to the protection of the rights entrenched in this Chapter, and *may* have regard to comparable foreign case law.'

(Italics added).

---

[99] See above, n 83.
[100] Section 4 of Act 200 of 1993.
[101] Above, n 86.
[102] Section 82(1)(i).
[103] Unfortunately the Constitution takes no account of the fact that some treaties come into effect on signature by the executive, without the need for ratification. See *S v Eliasov* 1967 (4) SA 583 (A). See Dugard op cit (n 86) 344.
[104] Section 192A(2) of the Final Draft. See further Dugard op cit (n 86) 343.
[105] Section 231(3) of Act 200 of 1993.
[106] Australia has likewise declined to incorporate the International Covenant on Civil and Political Rights into municipal law.

In addition the Human Rights Commission, provided for in s 115 of the Constitution, is required to measure any proposed legislation against the Bill of Rights or 'norms of international human rights law which form part of South African law' or 'other relevant norms of international law' and to report any conflict between such norms and the proposed legislation to the relevant legislature.[107] Provision is also made for the recognition of humanitarian law governing armed conflict.[108]

The Bill of Rights is clearly inspired by international human rights conventions. Moreover, it draws heavily on the language and structure of these conventions. In these circumstances there can be little doubt that had there been no reference to international law in the Bill of Rights, South African courts would have been obliged to turn to international human rights law for guidance. The courts of Canada,[109] Zimbabwe,[110] and Namibia,[111] whose Bills of Rights contain no express direction to apply international law, have not hesitated to draw on international human rights treaties, customary law, and the decisions of the European Court of Human Rights to assist them in interpreting their Bills of Rights, relying on the presumption in favour of compliance with international law,[112] the similarity of the domestic provisions to those in international human rights conventions,[113] or the legislative history of the Bill of Rights.[114] Section 35(1) further strengthens the role of international law in the interpretive process as it obliges courts to apply international law where it is 'applicable'. As virtually every provision in the South African Bill of Rights has some counterpart in an international human rights convention or is governed by general principles of international law (for example, s 28 dealing with property rights), it is difficult to imagine situations where public international law will not be applicable under s 35(1).

Section 35(1) does not limit a court's inquiry to treaties to which South Africa is a party or to customary rules that have been accepted by South African courts. (The phrase 'where applicable' is clearly not capable of such a meaning.) That it was the intention of the founding fathers of Kempton Park not to qualify the applicable rules of international law in this way is confirmed by s 116(2), which directs the Human Rights Commission to judge South African legislation by the 'norms of international human rights law which form part of South African law' *or 'other relevant norms of international law'*. This means that South African courts will be required to consult all the sources of international law recognized by art 38(1) of the Statute of the International Court of Justice, i e:

'*(a)* international conventions, whether general or particular, establishing rules expressly recognized by the contesting states;

*(b)* international custom, as evidence of a general practice accepted as law;

---

[107] Section 116(2).

[108] According to s 227(2)*(e)*, the National Defence Force shall 'in armed conflict comply with its obligations under international customary law and treaties binding on the Republic'.

[109] See Schabas *International Human Rights Law and the Canadian Charter* (1991) 32.

[110] *S v Ncube* 1988 (2) SA 702 (ZS) at 714–15, 719–21; *S v A Juvenile* 1990 (4) SA 151 (ZS) at 156, 161, 167, 168, 170–3; *Catholic Commission for Justice and Peace in Zimbabwe v Attorney-General & others* 1993 (4) SA 239 (ZS) at 261–4.

[111] *Ex parte Attorney-General, Namibia: In re Corporal Punishment by Organs of State* 1991 (3) SA 76 (NmS) at 87–8, 90.

[112] *Reference Re Public Service Employee Relations Act* [1987] 1 SCR 313, 38 DLR (4th) 161.

[113] *S v A Juvenile* (supra) at 155G–I, 159I; *Ex parte Attorney-General, Namibia: In re Corporal Punishment by Organs of State* (supra) at 87B–C.

[114] In *Minister of Home Affairs v Fisher* [1980] AC 319 at 328–9 Lord Wilberforce held that in interpreting the Bermuda Constitution Act it was necessary to recall that it was influenced by the European Convention on Human

(c) the general principles of law recognized by civilized nations;
(d) ... judicial decisions and the teachings of the most highly qualified publicists of the various nations, as subsidiary means for the determination of rules of law.'

Although a court is normally obliged only to apply treaties to which South Africa is a party, it is apparently required to consider all relevant general or multilateral treaties, whether South Africa is a party to the multilateral treaty in question or not. Such a conclusion follows logically from the use of the term 'public international law' without qualification in s 35(1) and the language of s 116(2). In any event it would be ridiculous to limit multilateral treaties to those to which South Africa is a party (or may become a party) as this would prevent a court from considering the jurisprudence of the European Commission and Court of Human Rights, which provides the most valuable source of international human rights law. The guidance which non-European courts may obtain from the decisions of the European Court of Human Rights is illustrated by the judgments of the courts of Canada,[115] Zimbabwe,[116] Namibia,[117] and Ciskei[118] on human rights matters. Indeed it is highly likely that the drafters of s 35(1) had the jurisprudence of the European Convention in mind when they directed courts to apply 'public international law' in their interpretation of the Bill of Rights.

The main advantage of the approach adopted by s 35(1) is that courts will not be required to conduct an inquiry into the question whether a particular principle contained in one or more human rights conventions is backed by sufficient practice (*usus*) and *opinio juris* to qualify as a customary rule binding on South Africa.[119] Instead they may simply seek guidance in the language employed in multilateral human rights conventions and the decisions of the bodies charged with the task of interpreting such conventions. The manner in which this exercise is to be carried out is well illustrated by the decisions of the courts of Zimbabwe and Namibia on the question whether corporal punishment constitutes a form of 'inhuman or degrading treatment or punishment'. In *S v Ncube*[120] and *S v A Juvenile*[121] the Zimbabwe Supreme Court invoked the decision of the European Court of Human Rights in *Tyrer v United Kingdom*[122] to support its finding on the unconstitionality of corporal punishment. A similar approach was adopted by the Namibia Supreme

---

Rights and the Universal Declaration of Human Rights, and that 'these antecedents . . . call for a generous interpretation, avoiding what has been called the "austerity of legalism", suitable to give to individuals the full measure of the fundamental rights and freedoms' contained in the constitution. This *dictum* was approved in *Minister of Defence, Namibia v Mwandinghi* 1992 (2) SA 355 (NmS) at 362–3; and *ANC (Border Branch) v Chairman, Council of State of Ciskei* 1992 (4) SA 434 (Ck) at 447. Canadian courts have also adopted this approach: see Schabas op cit (n 109) 32. See too the *dictum* of Friedman J in *Nyamakazi v President of Bophuthatswana* 1992 (4) SA 540 (B) at 570H.

[115] Schabas op cit (n 109) 55–8.
[116] *S v Ncube* (supra) at 714–15, 719–21; *S v A Juvenile* (supra) at 156, 161, 167, 168, 170, 171, 172–3.
[117] *Ex parte Attorney-General, Namibia: In re Corporal Punishment by Organs of State* (supra) at 87–8, 90.
[118] *ANC (Border Branch) v Chairman, Council of State of Ciskei* (supra) at 447, 449, 450; *Ntenteni v Chairman, Ciskei Council of State* 1993 (4) SA 546 (Ck) at 554–5.
[119] Courts will therefore not be required to embark on the type of inquiry made by Conradie J in *S v Petane* (supra) at 58G–J and Cooper J in *S v Rudman* (supra) at 375–6. See further on the process of proving a customary rule, Dugard op cit (n 86) 24–32.
[120] Supra at 714–15, 719–21.
[121] Supra at 156, 161, 167, 170, 171–3.
[122] Supra.

Court in *Ex parte Attorney-General, Namibia: In re Corporal Punishment by Organs of State*.[123] Another illustrative Zimbabwean decision is that of *Catholic Commission for Justice and Peace, Zimbabwe v Attorney-General, Zimbabwe*,[124] in which the Supreme Court held that a prolonged period on death row constituted inhuman or degrading treatment or punishment in violation of the Bill of Rights. In setting aside the death sentences imposed on four prisoners who had spent between 52 and 72 months on death row and substituting sentences of life imprisonment, the court relied on the judgment of the European Court of Human Rights in *Soering v United Kingdom*[125] and dissenting opinions in the Human Rights Committee on the death-row phenomenon.[126]

The European Convention on Human Rights forms part of the municipal law of many European states (the UK, Ireland, and the Scandanavian countries being the most notable exceptions).[127] Consequently it is applied directly by the municipal courts of many states. These decisions, too, appear to be relevant to the inquiry to be conducted under s 35(1) as they constitute a source of public international law.[128] (Alternatively, they qualify as foreign case law under s 35(1).) In interpreting the Bill of Rights South African courts are therefore required to have regard to international law contained in general treaties, custom, general principles of law, the writings of jurists, and the decisions of international and municipal courts.

Section 35(1) does not compel courts to apply international-law norms. It does, however, oblige them to 'have regard' to such norms, 'where applicable', in their search for an interpretation of the Bill of Rights that will 'promote the values which underlie an open and democratic society based on freedom and equality'. These norms will be elevated to a higher statutory status if — when? — South Africa becomes a party to the various international human rights conventions. The Convention on the Elimination of All Forms of Discrimination against Women, the Convention on the Rights of the Child, and the Convention against Torture have already been signed and will no doubt soon be ratified. South Africa will also, in all probability, become a party to the International Convention on the Elimination of All Forms of Racial Discrimination and the International Covenant on Civil and Political Rights. When these treaties are incorporated into municipal law in terms of s 231(3) courts will be obliged to apply them as they would an ordinary statute. International human rights norms will then have a double statutory basis in municipal law. International human rights law which has hitherto been ignored by our courts and repudiated by the legislature and executive is therefore destined to play a central role in constitutional litigation.

---

[123] Supra at 87–8, 90.
[124] Supra at 261–4. This decision is endorsed by the Privy Council in *Pratt v Attorney-General for Jamaica* [1993] 4 All ER 769 (PC).
[125] Supra.
[126] See the decisions referred to in the *Catholic Commission* case at 264. See too the dissenting opinions in *Kindler v Canada* (CCPR/C/48/D/470/1991; view of 11 November 1993).
[127] Drzemczewski *European Human Rights Convention in Domestic Law* (1983).
[128] Jennings & Watts (eds) *Oppenheim's International Law* 9 ed (1992) vol 1 41–2.

# EQUALITY AND EQUAL PROTECTION

DENNIS DAVIS

Most constitutions seek to promote both liberty and equality as their guiding principles. Taken together they appear to represent a commitment to improve the life chances of individual citizens. Some might argue that liberty is valuable for its own sake and that it places such a fundamental metaphysical claim upon us that it must be constitutionally protected no matter what the consequences. However, if this claim is correct, it cannot simply be asserted. It must be proved, which in itself raises a host of controversial philosophical problems.

The more understandable view, because it offers a justification, is that we want liberty because a society which commits itself to that principle is one in which we would prefer to live rather than in one that does not. It is a better society because it affords an opportunity to all the citizens to contribute to the shaping thereof.

That is of course but one justification for liberty. There are others. Take freedom of speech, for example. Its justification could be based upon the search for truth, or as a necessary prerequisite for the democratic enterprise, or as necessary for individual self-expression. Utilitarians rely on policy considerations while rights-based claims rely on the intrinsic quality of rights as necessary for the protection and promotion of the dignity and self-worth of each citizen. Whatever the view, an argument for liberty requires justification.

A society committed to equality attempts to make the lives of all its citizens better by insisting that each person must be shown equal concern and respect. Without such an enterprise members of society who have a compelling interest in developing and exploiting their own capacity for autonomy, in promoting their own conceptions of the good life, and analysing and criticizing other conceptions will find their ability dependent upon an initial arbitrary distribution of resources. Equality thus is inextricably linked to the conception of liberty if society is to allow the promotion of competing interests.

Where equality is different, however, to liberty is that it depends upon a comparator. It is here that equality becomes an enigmatic concept. In confronting the question of equality a court will have to examine A's claims against those of B. A will be entitled to protection only in so far as B is similarly protected. A will now be entitled to as much protection as B if a court decides that it was obliged to extend protection to A at all. In this it would have to require that A's treatment be made equal to that of B. This simple example reveals the major difficulty: that equality is not a principle which lives in abstraction. It depends upon comparison. The problem is compounded if it is accepted that difference is relational rather than intrinsic and that there exists no single, coherent perspective which asserts an objective truth.[1]

---

[1] See Minow 'Justice Endangered' (1987) 101 *Harvard LR* 10 at 33.

Constitutional lawyers are engaged in practical exercises. They require a comparator to measure equality. Invariably the starting point for much of this comparison is located in Aristotle's view:

> 'Equality in morals means this: those things that are alike should be treated alike, while things that are unalike should be treated unalike in proportion to their unlikeness! Equality and justice are synonymous: to be just is to be equal, to be unjust is to be unequal.'[2]

The difficulty with this proposition is that it provides no guidance as to the determination of which things are equal for the purposes of determining equality. The claim that equals shall be treated equally does not define who equals are. In short, the Aristotlean conception of equality turns on a prior question, namely the establishment of which persons are in fact equal for the purposes of the enquiry.[3]

To this end a number of cases within US jurisprudence have adopted the so-called 'similarly situated' test. In *Rostker v Goldberg*,[4] in which the constitutionality of the registration of males but not females for military conscription was upheld, Rehnquist CJ held that women are differently situated for the purposes of the draft from men, for women as a group, unlike men, are not eligible for combat. The difficulty with determining which criteria are appropriate for the decision as to who is similarly situated was illustrated in the dissenting judgment of Marshall J in the *Rostker* case. Marshall J considered that women conscripts perform equally well as male conscripts in certain positions. As he observed of the evidence, 'nothing ... supports the Court's intimation that women must be excluded from registration because combat eligibility is a prerequisite for all the positions that would need to be filled in the event of a draft'.[5] He considered that the classification adopted by Rehnquist CJ gave rise to unequal treatment of persons who indeed were equal in the relevant legal sense, that the two groups were similarly situated in that women were not ineligible for all military positions. Taken from this perspective, the government had breached the equality provision.

The 'similarly situated' test has been correctly criticized by the Canadian courts in *Mahe v The Queen*[6] as follows:

> 'The test accepts an idea of equality which is almost mechanical, with no scope for considering the reason for the distinction. In consequence, subtleties are found to justify a finding of similarity which reduces the test to a categorization game. Moreover the test is not helpful. After all, most laws are enacted for the specific purpose of offering a benefit or imposing a burden on some persons and not on others. The test catches every conceivable difference in legal treatment.'

In short, the concept of equality cannot be used to deny to the law the ability to prescribe differentiated treatment to different individuals. There are rich comparative sources which South African lawyers can tap in order to find authority for this approach.

---

[2] Aristotle *Nichomachean Ethics* (Ross (ed) 1925) vol III 1131.
[3] See Westen 'The Empty Idea of Equality' (1982) 95 *Harvard LR* 537, particularly at 543 et seq. See also Kamenka & Tay (eds) *Justice* (1979) at 97 et seq.
[4] 453 US 57 (1981).
[5] At 97.
[6] (1988) 42 DLR (4th) 514 at 546.

## 1 AMERICAN PRECEDENT

Given that the US Bill of Rights has been in operation for two centuries, it is understandable that there exists far more jurisprudence to be examined from the law reports of the US Supreme Court than from any other comparative jurisdiction. In the US the constitutional right to equality derives from the Fourteenth Amendment to the Constitution, which provides that no state shall deny to any person within its jurisdiction the equal protection of the law. It has been suggested that three different meanings have been given to the equal protection clause by the US Supreme Court.[7]

The first approach regards the clause as nothing more than an opportunity for a judicial attack on legislative mistakes. Accordingly the courts exist to articulate permissible levels of overinclusion or underinclusion in legislative classifications and to remit to the legislature statutes that have exceeded these limits. This approach effectively represents a negative concept of equal protection, the courts being more concerned to check upon the legislature than to develop a jurisprudence which might remedy conditions associated with inequality.

The second approach is the concept of equal protection in terms of the rationale of fundamental rights.[8] If a fundamental right is considered to exist, the court must use the equal protection jurisprudence to set aside legislation which impinges upon this right. At a point in its history the Warren Court appeared to use the doctrine of fundamental rights to promote the principles of distributive justice as part of its constitutional enterprise.

The third meaning of equal protection was outlined by the US Supreme Court in *Strauder v West Virginia* more than a hundred years ago:[9]

> 'The words of the amendment... contain the necessary implication of a positive immunity or right, most valuable to the coloured race; the right to exemption from unfriendly legislation against them distinctively as coloured, exemption from legal discriminations, implying inferiority in civil society, lessening the security of their employment from the rights which others enjoy, and discriminations which are steps towards reducing men to the condition of a subject race.'

Here the court was concerned with the concept of substantive equal protection, focusing on the end or the purpose of the clause: to reduce a position of inequality or conversely to attempt to produce some sense of equality in society.

There have been few cases in US constitutional history which have attempted to develop this concept of substantive equal protection. However, the case of *Griggs v Duke Power Company*,[10] although dealing with Title VII of the Civil Rights Act of 1964, is widely interpreted as representing an attempt in this direction.[11] The issue in *Griggs* was whether an employer is prohibited by Title VII of the Civil Rights Act of 1964 from requiring a high-school education or passing of a standardized general intelligence test as a condition of employment in or transfer to jobs where *(a)* either standard is shown to be significantly related to successful job performance, *(b)* both requirements operate to disqualify blacks at a substantially higher rate than white applicants, and *(c)* the jobs in question formerly had been filled by white

---

[7] Freeman 'Legitimizing Racial Discrimination through Anti-Discrimination Law: A Critical Review of the Supreme Court Doctrine' (1978) 62 *Minnesota LR* 1049 at 1058 et seq.
[8] Freeman op cit (n 7) 1059.
[9] 100 US 303, 307–8 (1880).
[10] 401 US 424 (1971).
[11] See Freeman op cit (n 7) 1093 et seq.

employees as part of a long-standing practice of preferring whites to blacks. The court unanimously found that the employer was so prohibited. The court reasoned that

> 'what is required by Congress is the removal of artificial, arbitrary and unnecessary barriers to employment when the barriers operate invidiously to discriminate on the basis of racial or other impermissible classifications'.[12]

The court went on to hold:

> 'The Act proscribes not only overt discrimination but also practices which are fair in form, but discriminatory in operation. The touchstone is business necessity. If an employment practice which operates to exclude negroes cannot be shown to be related to job performance, the practice is prohibited.'

For the first time the Supreme Court held that a neutral practice which does not purposively discriminate, but nevertheless failed to admit blacks to jobs, had to be justified or be declared invalid. The court found:

> 'Good intent or absence of discriminatory intent does not redeem employment procedures or testing mechanisms but operates as built-in head winds for minority groups ... Congress directed the thrust of the Act to the consequences of employment practices, not simply the motivation.'[13]

Perhaps the most important aspect of the *Griggs* case is that it indirectly introduces a positive component to the interpretation of Title VII. An employer who wishes to avoid litigation or avoid the adoption of one or more difficult procedures would either have to make the system of merit seem to operate fairly on its own terms or 'make up for its flaws through affirmative action'.[14] In its interpretation of Title VII the court in *Griggs* had given a positive connotation to the notion of equal protection.

*Griggs* unfortunately was restricted to an interpretation of Title VII, and later the Supreme Court declined to apply its jurisprudence to the interpretation of equal protection as contained in the Fourteenth Amendment.

The formal approach to equality jurisprudence was revealed in the case of *Washington v Davis*.[15] This involved a test which attempted to measure verbal ability, vocabulary, reading, and comprehension. The test was challenged in court and in the context of its role as a means for permitting applicants to a training programme for police officers. The failure rate was four times as high for blacks as for whites. Consequently the plaintiff submitted that the test was *prima facie* unconstitutional. The court held that without direct or even indirect proof that the test was employed with the objective of producing racially disproportionate results the difference in failure rate was not in itself significant enough to create a *prima facie* case of discrimination. Furthermore, there was no requirement that the test demonstrate its inner rationality. The court rejected the view that it should adopt a similar approach to the Fourteenth Amendment as it had done to racial discriminatory practices in terms of Title VII. White J stated (at 239):

---

[12] At 430–1.
[13] At 432.
[14] See Freeman op cit (n 7) 1099.
[15] 426 US 229 (1976).

'[W]e have never held that the constitutional standard of adjudicating claims of invidious racial discrimination is identical to the standards applicable under Title VII and we decline to do so today.'

The court revealed its underlying thinking in this passage of the judgment:

'[A] contrary rule would raise serious questions about, and perhaps invalidate, a whole range of tax, welfare, public service, regulatory, and licensing statutes that may be more burdensome to the poor and to the average black than to the affluent white.'[16]

The conservatism of the Supreme Court in *Washington v Davis* apart, it would appear that the differing approach to the *Griggs* case reveals two different meanings of equality: first, equality before the law; and, secondly, equality in the law.[17]

John Stuart Mill has suggested that equality before the law affords 'equal protection to the rights of all'.[18] Equality before the law reflects a fundamental commitment to the rule of law, that all should be treated according to one and the same rule. It is in other words a fundamental principle of legality, namely that all should be equal before the law, that the law should apply universal standards to each member of the society.[19]

Equality in the law appears to represent a wider concept and is not restricted simply to a formal guarantee. It invites a commitment which is separate from and wider than the concept of the rule of law. As Jackson J stated in *Runaway Express Agency v New York*:[20]

'There is no more effective practical guarantee against arbitrary and unreasonable government than to require that the principles of law which officials would impose upon a minority must be imposed generally.'

By contrast to the concept of equality before the law, the principle of equality in law does not shy away from differentiated treatment. Equality in the law rejects the idea that once a law confers rights or imposes duties upon a certain group it should confer the same right or impose the same duties upon all citizens who were subject to that particular legal system.

These concepts of equality have received rarer treatment than has the concept of discrimination. It would appear that problems have turned mainly on distinguishing between discriminatory and benign forms of differentiation. In itself the determination of this distinction rests on a value judgment. As Sadurski notes:

'The reasonableness of the choice of certain criteria for classification of people by legal rules rests upon value judgments which are not derived from the value of equality: for instance, that it is just, or useful, or wise to admit people to the universities on the basis of merit only. Any other practical solution would be considered "unequal" for the same observer because he would judge it unjust. This valuation is based on a hierarchy of values which cannot be reduced to the value of equality.'[21]

It is in the attempt to distinguish between discriminatory and benign forms of differentiation that equality jurisprudence leads to the conceptual problem of anti-discriminatory law.

---

[16] At 248.
[17] See in general Sadurski 'Equality Before the Law: A Conceptual Analysis' (1986) 60 *Australian LJ* 131.
[18] Mill *Utilitarianism, On Liberty: Essay on Bentham* (1962) 301.
[19] See Kelsen *What is Justice?* (1971) 15.
[20] 336 US 106, 112 (1949).
[21] Sadurski op cit (n 17) 134.

## 2 ANTI-DISCRIMINATION LAW: COMPARATIVE JURISPRUDENCE

In its General Comment 18 the Human Rights Committee established under the International Covenant on Civil and Political Rights noted:

> 'The term "discrimination" is used in the Covenant and should be understood to imply any distinction, exclusion, restriction or reference which is based on any ground such as race, colour, sex, language, religion, political or other opinion, national or social origin, property, birth or other status, which has the purpose or effect of nullifying or impairing the recognition, enjoyment or exercise by all persons and an equal footing of all rights and freedoms. Not every differentiation or treatment will constitute discrimination. If the criteria for such differentiation are reasonable and objective and if their aim is to achieve a purpose which is legitimate under the Covenant.'[22]

Article 14 of the European Convention on Human Rights provides:

> 'The enjoyment of the rights and freedoms set forth in this Convention shall be secured without discrimination on any ground such as sex, race, colour, religion, political or other opinion, national or social origin, association with a national minority, property, birth or other status.'

In general the European Court of Human Rights has found that a violation of art 14 arises if there is differential treatment in circumstances where there is no objective and reasonable justification or, in the event that there is such justification, proportionality is lacking between the aims sought and the means employed.

In examining the question of differential treatment the European Court and the European Commission of Human Rights have not shied away from an examination of substantive inequality, namely where there is differentiation in treatment, particularly with the objective of eliminating existing inequality. These institutions have held that a progressive income tax system is not discriminatory, provided the system is proportional and can contribute to a fairer distribution of income. For this reason the complaint concerning the difference in treatment under fiscal legislation was declared to be 'manifestly ill founded' by the European Commission of Human Rights on the basis that 'it is a common incident of taxation laws that they apply different degrees to different entities in the community'.[23] The court has attempted to use the comparability test in order to ascertain equality.

In the case of *Johnston*[24] the applicant alleged that there had been a violation of art 14 on the grounds that he was unable to obtain a divorce in order subsequently to remarry whereas other persons resident in Ireland, having the necessary means, could obtain a divorce abroad which would be recognized in Ireland. The court noted that in terms of the general rule of Irish conflict of laws foreign divorces were recognized only if they had been obtained by persons domiciled abroad. Consequently the situation of such persons and of the applicant could be regarded as analogous.

Similarly in the *Van der Mussele*[25] case it was alleged that Belgium avocats, unlike medical practitioners, veterinary surgeons, pharmacists, or dentists are required to provide their services free of charge to indigent persons and that such a difference in treatment constituted arbitrary inequality. The court found that there

---

[22] General Comment 18 (37) (United Nations, New York 1989) para 7.
[23] *Gudmundsson v Iceland* Appeal 511-59 *Yearbook of the European Convention of Human Rights* III (1960) 394 at 424.
[24] Series A 112 (1987) 26.
[25] Series A 70 (1983) 22.

was a difference between the Bar and other professions, particularly with regard to legal status, conditions for entry into the profession, the nature of the functions involved, and the exercise of such functions. The court held that there was no similarity between the disparate situations in question because each one was characterized by a body of different rights and obligations.

To a considerable extent, however, anti-discrimination cases have turned upon the justification for such differentiation. In *Dudgeon v UK*[26] the court was required to examine the Northern Ireland legal provisions which prohibited certain homosexual acts, irrespective of the circumstances in which these took place and of the age of the persons involved. The applicant was a 35-year-old man who alleged that the provision constituted a violation of art 14 because the legislation prevented him from having sexual relations with young men under 21, even in private and with their consent. By comparison the minimum age for heterosexual and lesbian relations was 17. The court recognized

> 'the legitimate necessity in a democratic society for some degree of control over homosexual conduct, notably to provide safeguards against exploitation and corruption of those who were specially vulnerable by reason, for example, of their youth'.[27]

The court consequently decided that the determination of appropriate safeguards, including the age of consent to protect the morals of a society, fell within the competence of the national authority. This case is of particular interest as it turned not on the use of a comparability test but rather on the justification for the differentiation.

The justification for differentiation has also been fundamental to anti-discrimination jurisprudence in the US. Classifications based upon racial criteria are considered to be suspect and the doctrine of strict scrutiny has been applied to them. In such cases it is not sufficient to justify a differentiation on the basis of a rational relationship between the classification and a state interest. The classification must be shown to be a necessary means to the promotion of a 'compelling' and 'overriding' state interest.[28]

The doctrine of strict scrutiny essentially entails that the challenge of classification is strictly relevant to the purpose of the legislation, that it be the least restrictive alternative available for the defined purpose, and that the purpose claimed by the state as the basis for the justification of the classification be 'compelling' or 'overriding' and not simply amount to a legitimate state purpose.

Obviously the adoption of the strict scrutiny test increases the possibility of the invalidation of the statute which introduces differentiated treatment. Accordingly the Supreme Court has adopted an intermediate level of scrutiny which requires that

---

[26] (1982) 4 EHRR 149.
[27] At 168.
[28] See *Boling v Sharpe* 347 US 497, 499 (1954) and *McLaughlin v Florida* 379 US 184, 191 (1964). The origin of the doctrine can be traced to *US v Carolene Products* 304 US 144, 152 (1938) where Stone J in his famous footnote 4 suggested 'prejudice against discreet and insular minorities may be a special condition which tends seriously to curtail the operation of those political processes ordinarily to be relied upon to protect minorities and which may call for a correspondingly more searching judicial enquiry'. Although testimony to judicial moral expediency, the court did pay lip service to this doctrine in *Korematsu v US* 323 US 214 (1944), in which the US government sought to justify its policy of interning US citizens of Japanese origin. Significantly Black J wrote:
> 'All legal restrictions which could curtail the civil rights of a single racial group are immediately suspect ... [T]he courts must subject them to the most rigid scrutiny. Pressing public necessity may sometimes justify the existence of such restrictions; racial antagonism never can.'

classifications which serve important government objectives must be substantially related to the achievement of those objectives.[29] The intermediate level of scrutiny stands between the strict scrutiny test and the somewhat more relaxed form of judicial review adopted with regard to socio-economic legislation where the courts generally inquire as to whether differentiation is rationally connected to a legitimate state purpose. The justification for the intermediate approach has been set out as follows:

> 'While racial classification should be looked at very carefully, to treat efforts to remedy past injustice with the same disfavour as we treat invidious discrimination itself, would be improper.'[30]

The intermediate level of scrutiny has aimed at protecting those persons subjected to discrimination based upon gender, alienage, or illegitimacy. To the extent that these forms of discrimination are subjected to a lower level of scrutiny they are considered less central to the US experience. In itself this shows the relativity of any such classificatory enterprise. What is important to many is reduced to less of a problem for the judiciary. For example, in *Bowers v Hardwick*[31] homosexuals were not considered to constitute a suspect or quasi-suspect class. Hence proscriptions on sodomy were held not to violate the equal protection clause since they were rationally related to a legitimate state interest.

The three-tier approach to constitutional review of differentiation adopted by the US Supreme Court has influenced other constitutional regimes. The Indian Supreme Court acknowledged the existence of these different standards of review when Matthew J stated:

> 'Laws regulating economic activity could be viewed differently from rules which touch and concern freedom of speech and religion, voting, procreation and rights with respect to criminal procedure.'[32]

However, Sorabjee[33] points out that the Indian Supreme Court has adopted a rational basis of review formulated in these terms: the classification must be grounded in terms of an intelligible differentiation which distinguishes persons that are grouped together from other parties left out of the group. Accordingly differentiation must have a rational basis in terms of the object which the legislation seeks to achieve. This differentiation is justified, if it is not palpably discriminatory, as long as it has a rational basis. In this the burden of so proving is upon the party who so alleges. In seeking to explain the difference between US and Indian jurisprudence, Sarobjee suggests:

> 'The problems of inequality and the perceptions of it are not the same in both countries. In India the source of discrimination does not mean legislation by the states of codified ... or white majority. In India invidious discrimination evolves from religious "personal" customs or practices. In the United States many state laws perpetuate racial discrimination and generally survived a tax based on the equal protection clause for many years.'[34]

---

[29] See in general Greenawallt 'The Unresolved Problems of Reverse Discrimination' (1979) 67 *California LR* 87.
[30] Wright 'Colour Blind Theories and Colour Conscious Remedies' (1980) 47 *U Chicago LR* 213. See also in general Sadurski op cit (n 17) 137–8.
[31] 478 US 186 (1986).
[32] *State of Gujarat v Ambica Mills Limited* AIR 1974 SC 1300 at 1314.
[33] 'Equality in the United States and India' in Henkin & Rosenthal (eds) *Constitutionalism and Rights: The Influence of the United States Constitution Abroad* (1990) 104.
[34] At 103.

Significantly the due process jurisprudence has been employed in anti-discriminatory cases in India. Thus the Supreme Court in the case of *Royappa* found that equality 'and arbitrariness are sworn enemies'. Consequently any arbitrary act, any act which is irrational, capricious, or arbitrary, will be struck down as unconstitutional.[35]

The *Royappa* approach was confirmed by the Supreme Court in *Ajay Hasia v Khalid Mujib*[36] as follows:

'It must therefore now be taken to be well settled that what Article 14 of the Indian Constitution strikes at is arbitrariness because actions that are arbitrary must necessarily involve negation of equality. The doctrine of classification which has evolved by the Court is not a paraphrase of Article 14 nor is it the objective and end of that Article. It is merely a juridical formula for determining whether the legislative or executive action in question is arbitrary and therefore constituting denial of equality. If the classification is not reasonable and does not satisfy the two conditions referred to above the impugned legislative or executive action would plainly be arbitrary and the guarantee under Article 14 would be breached.'

Accordingly the Indian courts have held that art 14 does not forbid a classification between citizens provided that it satisfies two conditions: it must be founded on an intelligible differentiation which distinguishes between persons or things that are grouped together from others left out of the group; and such differentiation must have a rational relation to the object sought to be achieved by the statute in question.[37]

Perhaps the most relevant aspect of the Indian Supreme Court for South Africa's constitutional enterprise has been its willingness to incorporate into fundamental principles of the Constituiton, such as equality, the spirit 'of the Directive Principles of State Policy' contained in the Constitution, which impose obligations on the state to provide a decent standard of living, a minimum wage, just and humane conditions of work, and to raise the level of nutrition and public health.[38] Thus in the case of *Francis Corali Mullin*[39] Bhagwati J declared that the 'right to life includes the right to life with human dignity and all that goes along with it, namely the bare necessities of life such as adequate nutrition, clothing and shelter overhead'. In short, the Indian Supreme Court has exhibited a commitment to an egalitarian society and has sought authority for this approach in the Directives Principles of State Policy. As the court noted in *Pradeep Jain v Union*,[40] 'equality must not remain a mere idle incantation but must become a living reality for the large masses of people'.

An equally important source of comparative jurisprudence for the purposes of interpreting the South African Bill of Rights will probably be that developed in Canada, particularly in the light of the large-scale borrowing from the Canadian Charter of Rights and Freedoms that took place in the formulation of Chapter 3 of the new Constitution.

---

[35] *E P Royappa v State of Tamil Nadu* AIR 1974 SC 555 at 583.
[36] AIR 1981 SC 487 at 499.
[37] See in general Seervai *Constitutional Law of India* (1991) vol I 454–5.
[38] Section 232(4) of the Constitution of the Republic of South Africa provides that in the interpretation of the provisions of the Constitution the provisions of the schedules to the Constitution and the 'afteramble' are to be regarded as of similar weight to the substantive provisions. It is thus open for a South African court to treat these parts of the Constitution in the same way as the Indian court has used the Directive Principles.
[39] AIR 1981 SC 746, particularly at 753.
[40] AIR 1984 SC 1420 at 1432.

Early Canadian law was characterized by a formalistic approach to equality. In *Attorney-General of Canada v Lavell*[41] an Indian married a non-Indian, as a result of which the Registrar deleted her name from the Indian register pursuant to the provisions of the Indian Act of 1970, which provides *inter alia* that a woman who marries a person who is not an Indian is not entitled to be so registered. In dealing with an argument that this provision was in contravention of the equality provision in the Bill of Rights, Richie J noted:

> 'In considering the meaning to be attached to "equality before the law" as those words occur in Section 1(b) of the bill, I think it important to point out that in my opinion this phrase is not effective to invoke the egalitarian concept exemplified by the 14th Amendment of the US Constitution as interpreted by the Courts of that country . . . I think rather that, having regard to the language employed in this second paragraph of the preamble to the Bill of Rights, the phrase "equality before the law" as used in s 1 is to be read in its context as part of the "rule of law" to which overriding authorities are accorded by the terms of that paragraph.'

Accordingly Richie J concluded that the phrase 'equality before the law' as contained in the Bill of Rights is to 'be treated as meaning equality in the administration or application of the law by the law enforcement authorities in the ordinary Courts of the land'.[42]

This approach was followed in *Bliss v A-G, Canada*.[43] In this case the issue before the court related to the entitlement to benefits under the Unemployment Insurance Act of 1971 and in particular the provisions of special conditions for claimants who were pregnant women, conditions that required a period of at least ten weeks of insurable employment before a pregnant woman could take advantage of prescribed benefits. The court rejected the applicant's submissions that she was denied benefits available to all other claimants, both male and female, who had eight weeks of insurable employment and who were capable of and available for work in favour of pregnant women. It concluded that the legislation did not discriminate against pregnant women on the basis of the constitutional right to equality as the law involved a definition of qualifications required for benefits.[44] There existed a major difference between legislation which treated one section of the population more harshly than all other sections by reason of race as compared to legislation which provided additional benefits to one class of women specifying those conditions which entitled the claimant to benefits or which provided a period during which no benefits were available. The court concluded that the first case involved the imposition of a penalty on a racial group to which other persons were not subjected whereas the second case involved the definition of those qualifications required for entitlement benefits. Consequently the limitations imposed upon pregnant women in so far as uninsurance benefits were concerned did not involve the denial of equality of treatment in the administration and enforcement of the law before the ordinary courts.

To an extent these cases prompted a change in the drafting of the equality provision in the Canadian Charter of Rights and Freedoms which was introduced some years later. Section 15(1) of the Charter provides that every individual is equal

---

[41] (1974) 38 DLR (3rd) 481 at 494.
[42] At 494–5.
[43] (1979) 92 DLR (3rd) 417.
[44] At 423.

before the law and under the law and has the right to equal protection and equal benefit of the law without discrimination and, in particular, without differentiation based on race, national or ethnic origin, colour, religion, sex, age, or mental of physical disability. The concept of equal benefit of the law was introduced so as to ensure that the court could examine equality of economic benefits in a manner which had been rejected in the *Lavell* and *Bliss* cases.

Under the Canadian Charter the Canadian Supreme Court has adopted a far less progressive approach to the question of equality and has sought an approach which pays proper attention to 'the content of the law, to its purpose, and its impact upon those to whom it applies, and also to those whom it excludes from its application'.[45]

The *Andrews* case dealt with the question of an admission to the legal profession. Andrews, a British subject permanently resident in Canada, had fulfilled all the requirements for admission to the practice of law in British Colombia except for Canadian citizenship. He commenced proceedings by challenging s 42 of the Barristers' and Solicitors' Act, which required Canadian citizenship for admission, and relied upon s 15 of the Charter which he contended was breached by s 42 of the Barristers' and Solicitors' Act.

The court was required to consider whether a class which is not designated, such as non-citizens, could gain equality benefits in terms of s 15 of the Charter. Wilson J found that a law which barred an entire class of person from certain forms of employment solely on the grounds that they were not Canadian citizens violated the equality provision in that it discriminated against such persons on the grounds of their personal status. She emphasized:

> 'This is a determination which is not to be made only in the context of the law which is subject to challenge but rather in the context of the place of the group in the entire social, political and economic fabric of our society. While Legislatures must inevitably draw distinctions among the governed, such distinctions should not bring about or reinforce a disadvantage of certain groups and individuals by denying them the right freely accorded to others ... In enumerating the specific grounds of s 15 the framers of the Charter embraced those concerns in 1982 but also addressed themselves to the difficulty experienced by disadvantaged on the ground of ethnic origin, colour, sex, age, physical and mental disability. It can be anticipated that discreet and insular minorities of tomorrow will include groups not recognized today. It is consistent with the constitutional status of s 15 that can be interpreted with sufficient flexibility to ensure the "unremitting protection" of equality rights in years to come.'[46]

Of equal significance was the approach of McIntyre J, particularly his statement that

> 'the promotion of equality entails the promotion of a society in which all are secure in the knowledge that they are recognized at law as human beings equally deserving of concern, respect and consideration'.[47]

In the light of this analysis of those aspects of comparative jurisprudence which influenced the drafting of Chapter 3 of the Constitution of the Republic of South Africa it is now possible to examine s 8 of the Constitution, namely the equality provision.

---

[45] *Andrews v Law Society of British Colombia* (1989) 56 DLR (4th) 1 at 13.
[46] At 21. See also *McKinney v University of Guelph* (1991) 76 DLR (4th) 545 at 608–9.
[47] At 16.

## 3 CHAPTER 3 AND THE EQUALITY PROVISION

Section 8 provides as follows:

'(1) Every person shall have the right to equality before the law and to equal protection of the law.

(2) No person shall be unfairly discriminated against, directly or indirectly, and without derogating from the generality of this provision, on one or more of the following grounds in particular: race, gender, sex, ethnic or social origin, colour, sexual orientation, age, disability, religion, conscience or belief, culture or language.

(3)*(a)* This section shall not preclude measures designed to achieve the adequate protection and advancement of the persons or groups or categories of persons disadvantaged by unfair discrimination in order to enable their full and equal enjoyment of all rights and freedoms.

*(b)* Every person or community dispossessed of rights in land before the commencement of this Constitution, under any law which would have been inconsistent with (2) had that subsection been in operation at the time of dispossession shall be entitled to claim restitution of such rights subject to and in accordance with sections 121, 122, 123. *Prima facie* proof of discrimination on any of the grounds specified in subsection (2) shall be presumed to be sufficient proof of unfair discrimination as contemplated in that subsection until the contrary is established.'

The wording of this section differs from a number of the comparative instruments examined above. While it acknowledges the jurisprudence of the US Fourteenth Amendment by providing for equal protection of the law, it separates the fundamental proposition of equality as outlined in s 8(1) from the specific list of prohibited categories as contained in s 8(2). In this s 8 differs from s 15 of the Canadian Charter and art 14 of the European Convention on Human Rights, which integrates the general provisions of equality with an anti-discrimination clause.

Section 8(1) introduces the possibility of a broad judicial examination of questions of equality relating to both formal and substantive issues. While the Canadian cases of *Lavell* and *Bliss* would support an argument that the formulation of equality before the law and equal protection of the law should be construed narrowly, the comparative examination of US and European case law as well as the later case of *Andrews* suggests the possibility of a judicial evaluation of socio-economic legislation and the assessment as to whether such legislation accords with the protection afforded by the phrase 'equal protection of the law'.

The potential for expanding s 8(1) into a fusion of considerations of both procedural and substantive equality is supported by Constitutional Principle V contained in sched 4 to the Constitution. As noted above, s 232(4) of the Constitution provides that in the interpretation of the provisions of the constitution the schedules are to be given the same weight as the substantive provisions. Accordingly the court is enjoined to examine the Constitutional Principles in its interpretation of the substantive provisions of the Act.

This Principle enjoins the legal system to ensure the equality of all before the law and an equitable legal process. Equality before the law includes laws, programmes, or activities that have as their object the amelioration of the conditions of the disadvantaged, including those disadvantaged on the grounds of race, colour, or gender. Principle I commits the Constitution to the achievement of equality between men and women and people of all races. Were these Principles to be used to interpret the provisions of s 8(1) it would appear unnecessary to have included s 8(3) in the Act — namely the provision which ousts affirmative action programmes from constitutional scrutiny under the general equality provision — for an affirmative action programme would fit within the ambit of equality as contained in s 8(1). Accordingly s 8(1) and (3) must be reconciled if the more expansive concept of equality is to be employed in the interpretation of s 8(1). It is submitted that the answer lies in the use of the phrase 'disadvantaged by unfair discrimination' in s 8(3) — i e measures designed to deal with unfair discrimination are placed beyond constitutional scrutiny.

In s 8(2) a series of grounds are outlined including race, gender, sex, ethnic or social origin, colour, sexual orientation, age, disability, religion, conscience or belief, culture, or language. These all point to human characteristics which are either immutable, such as race or age, are difficult to change, such as language or culture, or are so inherently part of the human personality, such as belief, religion, or conscience, that they contribute to the shaping of identity. While this argument might well give a more confined connotation to the listed grounds than is suggested by the phrase 'without derogating from the generality of this provision', the purpose of s 8(2) would appear to ensure that there should be no differentiated treatment on the grounds or elements which are vital to the nature of human identity. The words 'without derogating' from the generality of this provision would thus allow a court to take account of a range of elements of the human personality which have hitherto not been considered in the express words.

Unfair discrimination turns on the application of unjustified criteria for the purposes of classification. Many groups might also be placed in a detrimental position not only as a result of discrimination in the sense of an unfair and unreasonable application of a particular characteristic but rather as a result of the effects of poverty, unemployment, and lack of access to power. The concept of equality which refuses to restrict the concept to purely formal criteria can deal with these considerations notwithstanding that discrimination, whether direct or indirect, is not the primary cause of the social evil.[48]

Amongst the designated criteria are gender and sex. The inclusion of gender implies that the Constitution acknowledges that significant differences between men and women in respect of skills and social roles cannot be explained by biological differences but must be located in social and political origins. As Ann Oakley observes, 'sex is a biological term; gender a psychological and cultural one'.[49] The inclusion of gender as a designated prohibition allows a court to examine those social forces and power relationships which promote discrimination between men and women.

The concept of unfair discrimination doubtless represents an attempt to distinguish between a process of benign and malign distinction. It presupposes that discrimination itself can be freed from a pejorative content. To an extent the policy of affirmative action could be construed to be a form of benign or positive treatment which would therefore fall within the scope of the concept of fair discrimination. However, the question of affirmative action is canvassed in terms of s 8(3). Accordingly it would appear that the distinction between unfair and fair discrimination invites a court to examine the justification for the differentiation in question, its interpretation, and application of the equality provision rather than leaving such

---

[48] See in general Meyerson 'Sexual Equality and the Law' (1993) 9 *SAJHR* 237.
[49] Quoted by Meyerson op cit (n 48).

inquiry to an analysis of the limitation clause, contained in s 33(1). This inquiry is aided by the presumption created in s 8(4) in that *prima facie* proof of discrimination on any of the designated grounds gives rise to a presumption of unfair discrimination until the contrary is established.

It is thus possible that a different justificatory framework can be adopted to ascertain whether discrimination is fair or not, an approach which would be far more difficult were the justificatory grounds restricted to the general limitation clause in terms of s 33(1). Colker[50] argues that different justificatory frameworks can be applied to different forms of discrimination. Thus an approach which is suitable to age discrimination may be inappropriate to sex discrimination. In short Colker argues that:

> 'A more contextual consideration of the substantive right that was being considered would ensure that a court would be "more sensitive" to the importance of the substantive right that was being infringed.'[51]

The concept of discrimination may take one or two forms, direct or indirect, developed largely through US jurisprudence. Thus in *Griggs v Duke Power Company*[52] the US Supreme Court distinguished between direct discrimination, which occurs where a person is disadvantaged simply on the grounds of her race, sex, ethnicity, religion, or whatever the distinguishing feature may be, or on the basis of some characteristics specific to members of that group. Neither motive nor intention are relevant to the determination of whether the detrimental treatment represents discrimination. The court is concerned, however, with the application of either race- or gender-based criteria.[53] Indirect discrimination occurs when policies are applied which appear neutral, but which adversely affect a disproportionate number of a group. Although not always successful, cases of indirect discrimination have been recognized both by municipal and international courts. For example, in *Binder v Canada*[54] there was a complaint by a Sikh employed by the Canadian National Railways that the company's requirement that workers wear hard hats was both a violation of his right to freedom of religion and *de facto* discrimination against persons of the Sikh religion. When the matter reached the Human Rights Committee it was required to interpret the International Covenant of Civil and Political Rights. The Committee held that there was no violation of art 14, but was prepared to entertain an application granted on indirect discrimination. In so far as indirect discriminatory causes are concerned, the inquiry comprises two important stages: the delineation of the groups to be compared, and a decision as to what level of discrepancy between the two groups' ability to satisfy the challenged requirements is necessary to show the disparate impact.[55]

Section 8(3) attempts to immunize affirmative action programmes from constitutional scrutiny. The critical phrase in this section is measures 'designed to achieve the adequate protection and advancement of persons or groups or categories of

---

[50] Colker 'Section 1, Contextuality and the Anti-Disadvantaged Principle' (1992) 42 *U Toronto LJ* 77, particularly at 100–3.
[51] At 103.
[52] Supra.
[53] See also *R v Birmingham City Council: Ex parte Equal Opportunities Commission* [1989] AC 1155 (HL).
[54] (1985) 23 DLR (4th) 481.
[55] See generally Baldus & Kelb *Statistical Proof of Discrimination* (1980).

persons disadvantaged by unfair discrimination, in order to enable their full and equal enjoyment of all rights and freedoms'. The wording in this section invites a court to examine whether there is a rational connection between the means employed in the implementation of the scheme and the object, namely to enable the targeted group to achieve its full and equal enjoyment of all rights and freedoms contained within the Chapter.

So much for the express wording of s 8. Perhaps the most critical issue in the development of equality jurisprudence is not canvassed in the section. Does the section accord constitutional protection to victims of discrimination by private individuals? This question can only be answered by interpreting the provisions of s 7. Section 7(1) provides that the chapter containing fundamental rights shall 'bind all legislative and executive organs of state'. References to both the judiciary and private persons are omitted. The omission of the judiciary from s 7(1), it is argued, means that only legislation, administrative or executive action, and decisions which are contrary to the provisions in the Bill of Rights can be constitutionally evaluated. If this is an accurate reflection of the position, the rules of common and customary law are immune from constitutional attack.

Section 7(2), however, provides that Chapter 3 shall apply to all law in force and all administrative decisions taken and acts performed. This would appear to include any rule, whether of the common law or customary law, as well as legislation. In this the Afrikaans text is helpful. The English text of s 103(2) uses the word 'law'. The Afrikaans text uses the word 'wet'. By contrast the equivalent word 'law' in s 7(2) is translated as 'reg' — i e all law, whether common or statutory law.

Advocates of an exclusively vertical position argue that, notwithstanding the provisions of s 7(2), consideration must be given to s 35(3), which enjoins a court during the process of interpretation of any law and the application and development of the common law or customary law to have due regard to the spirit, purport, and objects of Chapter 3. This would appear to imply that the chapter applies only vertically. Were it to apply horizontally, there would be no need for s 35(3) as all law would fall under the ambit of the Bill of Rights, rendering the provisions of s 35(3) redundant. It would appear, however, that the word 'law' is given a broader context in s 35(3), namely that in interpreting any 'law' account should be taken of the chapter, and then, in so far as the subspecies of law is concerned, namely common law and customary law, in applying and developing such law the court should have due regard to the important objects of the chapter. The courts do not develop statutes; they interpret statutes so that a distinction between the interpretation of statutory law and the application and development of the common law is recognized by the drafters as constituting two different but related tasks. Further, many issues not covered by Chapter 3 are dealt with under the common law. Accordingly it is submitted that s 35(3) is not a fatal flaw to the argument that law as used in s 7(2) applies to all law whether it be legislation, customary law, or common law. In developing the common law to which no provision of Chapter 3 applies, s 35(3) has considerable force.

It is, however, clear that by virtue of the provision of s 7(1), Chapter 3 does not apply to all private relationships. The question arises as to whether private individuals may validly regulate their relationships in such a manner as to violate the substantive provisions contained in Chapter 3. Could two individuals, for example, enter into a restrictive covenant without the agreement being susceptible to constitutional attack?

It is submitted that whenever such relationships come before the courts there is a requirement that the issue be evaluated in terms of the express provisions of the chapter, whether the relationship be created by legislation or common law. Accordingly in such a case the court needs to apply the Bill of Rights in terms of the provisions of s 7(2). For this reason it is submitted that whenever a legal relationship is required to be enforced or confirmed by the courts Chapter 3 will apply, whether that relationship be of a horizontal or vertical character. Accordingly the equality provision contained in s 8 has a reach beyond the restrictive confines of the relationship between the individual and the state. In this, Chapter 3 can contribute significantly to our constitutional enterprise, namely the promotion of an open, democracy based on freedom and equality. By scrutinizing all law which seeks to enforce or consummate a relationship the court can use s 8 to safeguard and promote the spirit, object, and purport of the Constitution, as it is enjoined to do by the express wording of s 35(3).

# PERSONAL RIGHTS: LIFE, FREEDOM AND SECURITY OF THE PERSON, PRIVACY, AND FREEDOM OF MOVEMENT

LOURENS M DU PLESSIS & J R DE VILLE

## 1 GENERAL BACKGROUND

The rights discussed in this chapter are labelled 'personal rights'. All human rights, in so far as they vest in human beings, are of course 'personal'. The rights presently under discussion are, however, 'personal' because essentially they are entitlements or claims of human beings as constitutional subjects in contradistinction to, for instance, juristic persons.[1] The fundamental rights entrenched in Chapter 3 of South Africa's transitional Constitution can vest in juristic persons 'where, and to the extent that, the nature of the rights permit'.[2] The personal rights which will now be looked at are rights to which constitutional subjects which are not human beings are as a general rule not entitled (subject to but a limited number of exceptions). These rights are the right to life;[3] the rights to freedom and security of the person;[4] the right to privacy;[5] and the right to freedom of movement.[6]

The entrenchment of (especially some of) the above rights usually provokes a divergence of opinion on several issues. We shall endeavour not to pre-empt the outcome of the debates on these issues which will inevitably ensue from the adoption of South Africa's transitional Constitution (with its chapter on fundamental rights), but rather to mark out the areas of contention with which these debates will deal.

## 2 THE RIGHT TO LIFE

### 2.1 Nature and scope

The right to life is usually not discussed elaborately in works on domestic constitutional jurisprudence and in some (especially American and Canadian) textbooks no substantive rubric is devoted to it at all.[7] All commentators, however, agree that it

---

[1] Juristic persons can, however, in exceptional circumstances claim some of these rights and, in particular, the right to privacy: see below, 4.4.2.
[2] Section 7(3); see also the German Basic Law art 19.3.
[3] See below, 2.
[4] See below, 3.
[5] See below, 4.
[6] See below, 5.
[7] See e g Gunther *Constitutional Law* 12 ed (1991) 503–53; Stone, Seidman, Sunstein & Tushnet *Constitutional Law* 2 ed (1991) 908–85; Stone, Seidman, Sunstein & Tushnet *1992 Supplement Constitutional Law* 2 ed (1992) 86–146; Tribe *American Constitutional Law* 2 ed (1988) 1337–71; Finkelstein *Laskin's Canadian Constitutional Law II* 5 ed (1986) 1182–220; Hogg *Constitutional Law of Canada* 2 ed (1985) 744; Magnet *Constitutional Law of Canada II* 3 ed (1987) 526–65.

is probably the most basic human right on which all other rights are premised.[8] Its fundamental nature moreover explains its inclusion in some of the earliest formal human rights declarations in the Western hemisphere (notably the Declaration of Virginia of 4 July 1776 and the US Declaration of Independence of 4 July 1776) and its central status in early modern-day human rights theories (notably that of John Locke).

In the second paragraph of the latter declaration it is, for instance, stated 'that all men are created equal; that they are endowed by their Creator with certain inalienable rights; that among these are life, liberty and the pursuit of happiness'. This statement, as well as art 1 of the Virginia Declaration, take their cue from the political philosophy of John Locke (1632–1704), in which the notion of preservation of the self and others is pivotal and which has had a profound influence on human rights thinking in the modern world. In his *Second Treatise of Government*[9] Locke, for example, contends that, in the state of nature, reason prescribes that 'no one ought to harm another in his life, health, liberty, or possessions' and then elaborates as follows:

> 'Everyone, as he is bound to preserve himself, and not to quit his station willfully, so by the like reason, when his own preservation comes not in competition, ought he, as much as he can, to preserve the rest of mankind, and may not, unless it be to do justice on an offender, take away or impair the life, or what tends to the preservation of the life, liberty, health, limb, or goods of another.'[10]

When the human being eventually quits the state of nature ('which, however free, is full of fears and continual dangers') and exchanges it for political society and government, his or her main object remains, according to Locke,[11] the preservation of life, liberty, and estate, which he calls by the general name of property. Similarly the end of political power in the hands of a magistrate is to preserve the members of society in their lives, liberty, and possessions

> 'and so cannot be an absolute, arbitrary power over their lives and fortunes, which are as much as possible to be preserved, but a power to make laws, and annex such penalties to them, as may tend to the preservation of the whole, by cutting off those parts, and those only, which are so corrupt that they threaten the sound and healthy, without which no severity is lawful.'[12]

So paramount is the preservation of human life, however, that society's wrath on the offender can be allayed by the executive exercising its prerogative to 'mitigate the severity of the law, and pardon some offenders . . . where it can prove no prejudice to the innocent'.[13]

It is remarkable how, three centuries after Locke, the right to life is dealt with in very much the same way he did and how certain themes continually recur. Here are four examples:

(a) The paramountcy of the right to life (and life as a human value) is duly acknowledged, but it is dealt with not in the abstract but in its interconnected-

---

[8] Treatises on international law tend to deal with the right to life more extensively.
[9] At 16. See also Wootton (ed) *John Locke Political Writings* (1993) 264.
[10] Loc cit.
[11] *Second Treatise* 9 123; Wootton op cit (n 9) 324–5.
[12] *Second Treatise* 15 171; Wootton op cit (n 9) 350.
[13] *Second Treatise* 14 159; Wootton op cit (n 9) 344.

ness with other rights and values, such as (to refer to one of Locke's own standard expressions) 'liberty' and 'estate'.[14]

(b) The paramountcy of life does not preclude the possibility of 'taking a life' to serve a legitimate end connected with the preservation of the lives of other individuals or the 'life' of society as a whole.[15]

(c) A life must, however, only be taken in compliance with the requirements of non-arbitrariness and/or due process.[16]

(d) Locke hints at the possibility that the right to life includes not only the right to be protected against the deprivation of one's life but also a 'positive' entitlement to that which is necessary for the preservation of life.[17] This theme has recurred in contemporary reflections on the right to life and in recent jurisprudence too.[18]

Contemporary writers continue to proclaim the fundamental nature of the right to life. Katz,[19] for example, describes it (with reference to art 2.2 of the German Basic Law (*Grundgesetz*), in which it is enshrined) as '*eine verfassungsrechtliche Grundentscheidung und gewährleistet oberste Werte und essentielle Grundrechtsgüter*'. Kurt Herndl[20] comments on its significance in modern-day international law as follows:

'Of all the norms of international law, the right to life must surely rank as the most basic and fundamental, a primordial right which inspires and informs all other rights, from which the latter obtain their raison d'être and must take their lead. Protection against arbitrary deprivation of life must be considered as an imperative norm of international law which means not only that it is binding irrespective of whether or not States have subscribed to international conventions containing guarantees of the right, but also that non-derogatability of the right to life has a peremptory character at all times, circumstances and situations.'[21]

The basic nature of the right to life raises methodological perplexities.[22] It cannot be a right to an object or entity of some sort for two reasons:

(a) Life is sometimes associated with human existence as such or with being human in its entirety. This is expressed in colloquial speech as follows: 'Life has meaning'; 'She leads an exemplary life'; 'Never in my life will I do a thing like this'. A human right to the entirety of one's existence can hardly be asserted. Human rights are individualized claims or entitlements to

---

[14] See e g below, 2.2.1 and 2.2.2.
[15] See e g below, 2.3.1, 2.3.3 and 2.3.4.
[16] See e g below, 2.3.1.
[17] See above, nn 9 and 10.
[18] See e g below, 2.2.2.
[19] Katz *Staatsrecht: Grundkurs im öffentlichen Recht* 10 ed (1991) 317. Free translation: 'A fundamental constitutional decision and guaranteed highest value and essential fundamental right.'
[20] In a foreword to Ramcharan (ed) *The Right to Life in International Law* (1985) xi.
[21] See also Dinstein 'The Right to Life, Physical Integrity, and Liberty' in Henkin (ed) *The International Bill of Rights: The Covenant on Civil and Political Rights* (1981):
'The right to life is incontestably the most important of all human rights. Civilised society cannot exist without protection of human life. The inviolability or sanctity of life is, perhaps, the most basic value of modern civilization. In the final analysis, if there were no right to life, there would be no point in the other human rights.'
See further Alen *Treatise on Belgian Constitutional Law* (1992) 192 and Robertson (ed) *Human Rights for South Africans* (1991) 31.
[22] See in general Du Plessis *Vraagstukke Rondom die Lewe Juridies Besien* (1976) 1–3.

demarcated facets of being human from which life, as a characteristically encompassing value, derives its ultimate significance.[23]

(b) Life, cast in a conceptually more manageable mould, is not human existence as such but the nodal point of being human. It is, in other words, the living (human) being's underlying bond with reality. Looked at in this way it is not an identifiable object or entity either. It is, at most, a condition (or 'state of affairs') in which the individual human being has a vital interest.[24] Unlike 'objects', such as freedom or property, life can be taken away from a particular individual but cannot be restored — either in kind or in any other form. The knot with reality, once untied in a particular instance, cannot be redone again.

From both (a) and (b) above it is clear that reality in its diversity is encapsulated in life both as the wholeness and the nodal point of human existence. It has, however, become the rule rather than the exception to narrow the right to life down to the axiomatic imperative 'No one shall be deprived of his or her life'. This is done probably in quest of evading the above methodological perplexities. This has unfortunately resulted in a conceptually inadequate articulation of this pivotal right which, in turn, has inhibited construing it as a right inclusive of the entitlement to what is necessary for the preservation or sustenance of life.

Thus narrowed down, the right to life seems to be of jurisprudentially manageable proportions, and questions raised in relation to it mainly concern the circumscription of normative injunctions in terms of which it is expressed. This explains why issues of social policy, such as capital punishment, abortion, and euthanasia, are associated with the right to life quite readily, while the death of 40 000 children each day as a result of hunger and malnutrition[25] or the numerous deaths caused by armed conflict and crime[26] are not so readily looked upon as right-to-life issues. We contend for the wider meaning of the concept 'right to life' and agree with Ramcharan[27] that all the following issues fall within the scope of the right to life:

- Threats to and loss of life resulting from armed conflict and environmental hazards.

- Failure to meet the survival needs of millions of people, resulting in a phenomenal loss of life. This failure is caused by systemic or structural problems inherent in inequitable international and in national orders.

- Gross and large-scale violations of human rights in situations of armed conflict, during states of emergency, and in the course of refugee outflows or in their aftermath. Arbitrary and summary executions as well as political killings often characterize these situations.

- Disregard for due process of law by law-enforcement, security, and military personnel. Ramcharan[28] points out that the excessive use of force by law-enforcement officials is a particularly acute problem.

---

[23] Robertson op cit (n 21) 29.
[24] See also Van Eikema Hommes *De Elementaire Grondbegrippen der Rechtswetenschap* (1972) 220.
[25] Ramcharan 'The Concept and Dimensions of the Right to Life' in Ramcharan op cit (n 20) 2.
[26] The number for South Africa from January to October 1993 is 3 521, which makes us the second most violent country on earth for 1993.
[27] Op cit (n 25) 8.
[28] Ibid.

- Issues of social policy such as abortion, euthanasia, and capital punishment which do not, however, present difficulties of the same proportions as the first four issues.

It is true that from an international-law perspective such as Ramcharan's the right to life can more readily be understood in terms of its most extensive manifestations. Each of the issues mentioned above, however, to a greater or a lesser extent, has implications in and for domestic constitutional systems and falls within the typical sphere of enforceability of national human rights instruments. The constitutional prevention of violations to the right to life and its corollaries at a national level may moreover obviate an eventual need for international cure. Lastly, as Henkin[29] correctly contends, international human rights law

> 'has destroyed the myth that the manner in which a State treats its own inhabitants is not the concern of anyone else, and the myth that the individual is not a legitimate preoccupation of international law'.

This certainly also holds for the international dimensions of the protection of the right to life, which will next be considered.

## 2.2 International and domestic human rights law

### 2.2.1 *International law*

The right to life (together with the rights to liberty and security of the person[30]) is enshrined in art 3 of the Universal Declaration of Human Rights. However, the more elaborate wording of art 6 of the International Covenant on Civil and Political Rights is usually cited as the international *locus classicus* on the protection of the right to life.[31] Article 6(1) reads as follows:

> 'Every human being has the inherent right to life. This right shall be protected by law. No one shall be arbitrarily deprived of his life.'

Subarticles (2)–(6) circumscribe art 6(1) by providing for the imposition of the death penalty subject to compliance with six requirements.[32]

Noteworthy is the fact that the right to life is described as an inherent right.[33] This is not done in any other international human rights instrument and it is also the only right which the Covenant describes as 'inherent'. It is, however, not quite clear what the implications of this 'inherency' of the right to life are. A first possibility is that the drafters of the Covenant wanted to signal preference for the philosophical position that the existence of rights in a moral or 'natural-law' order precedes their entrenchment in human rights instruments. Secondly, they might have wanted to convey the idea that the right to life is entrenched in customary international law already and that art 6(1) is merely declaratory in nature. And, finally, the use of the adjective 'inherent' may simply be seen as an attestation to the primacy of the right to life, emphasizing 'that it derives from the very fact of a human being's existence'.[34]

---

[29] Henkin 'Human Rights' in *Encyclopedia of Public International Law* VIII (1985) 274.
[30] See below, 3.
[31] See in this regard Dinstein op cit (n 21); Gormley 'The Right to Life and the Rule of Non-derogatability: Peremptory Norms of *Jus Cogens*' in Ramcharan op cit (n 20) 120–59.
[32] See below, 2.3.3.
[33] See in this regard Dinstein op cit (n 21) 114–15.
[34] At 114.

The further requirement laid down by art 6(1) is that the right to life must be protected by law, which probably means that it must be protected by higher forms of legislation, such as the supreme Constitution of a state or statute law enacted by the highest legislature.[35] It is submitted, however, that in legal systems where the common law enjoys an acceptable degree of pre-eminence common-law protection will also meet the requirements of art 6(1). The provision that '[n]o one shall be arbitrarily deprived of his life' will be dealt with later.[36]

Article 2(1) of the European Convention on Human Rights also requires the protection of the right to life by law. It goes on to state that '[n]o one shall be deprived of his life intentionally save in the execution of a sentence of a court following his conviction of a crime for which this penalty is provided by law'. This circumscription must, however, since 1 March 1985, be read in view of the Sixth Protocol to the Convention, which will be looked at later.[37] Article 2(2) also lists circumstances under which intentional deprivation of life is permissible. These will also be discussed later.[38]

The American Convention on Human Rights (art 4(1)) requires the protection of the right to life by law and contains an injunction against any arbitrary deprivation of life. The American Convention, however, goes further and states that this right shall, in general, be protected from the moment of conception.[39]

Article 4 of the African (or Banjul) Charter on Human and Peoples' Rights proclaims the inviolability of the human being and then proceeds to state that every human being shall be entitled to respect for his or her life and that no one may be arbitrarily deprived of this right. No specific reference is, however, made to circumstances under which this right can be circumscribed.

The four regional instruments for the protection of human rights just mentioned are international treaties which, in practice, bind the states which have endorsed them to varying extents. Other international instruments, such as the International Covenant on Civil and Political Rights, also bind states parties to them, but probably also bind states, like South Africa, which have not become parties to them.

The right to life is one of those rights enshrined in the Universal Declaration of Human Rights, which is, as a matter of customary international law, binding on every state irrespective of whether it is a party to any international convention or covenant.[40] It then follows that the more detailed and legally precise restatement of the right to life in the International Covenant on Civil and Political Rights will be binding in a similar way.

Some authors, however, go further, contending that the right to life is '[a]n imperative norm of international law ... generally recognized by the international community as a whole as a norm from which no derogations are permissible'[41] — it is, in other words, *jus cogens*, which is not only binding in the same way as customary international law but also from which no derogations are permissible,

---

[35] At 115.
[36] See below, 2.3.1.
[37] See below, 2.3.3.
[38] See below, 2.3.4.
[39] See also below, 2.3.5.
[40] Henkin op cit (n 29) 271.
[41] Gormley op cit (n 31), especially 121–2; Ramcharan op cit (n 20) 14–17.

even in times of emergency. This does not mean that the right to life is absolutely illimitable,[42] but that it constitutes a norm of *jus cogens* subject to carefully controlled limitations, for instance those in art 6(2)–(5) of the Covenant. The rule of non-derogatibilty also binds states, such as South Africa, which are not parties to international conventions or covenants applicable in this context.

Section 35(1) of South Africa's transitional Constitution requires a court interpreting the chapter on fundamental rights in the Constitution, where applicable, to 'have regard to public international law applicable to the protection of the rights entrenched in this Chapter'. The section uses mandatory language: 'a court shall'. This leaves little doubt that public international law applicable to the protection of life, whether it be regarded as customary international law or *jus cogens*, will have to be taken into account by South African courts in interpreting s 9 of the transitional Constitution, which entrenches the right to life. Should such international law not be *jus cogens* but customary international law, it would still follow that, in terms of the customary international law binding South African courts by virtue of s 35(1), limitations of the right to life will still only be possible in terms of the carefully controlled exceptions permissible under *jus cogens*.

### 2.2.2 *Domestic law (with particular reference to South Africa)*

Hardly any domestic Bill of Rights omits explicit reference to the right to life (usually in conjunction with the rights to freedom and security of the person[43]). There are, however, Bills of Rights, for instance that of Belgium, which do not explicitly refer to the right to life because, as Alen[44] explains, 'this right was so self-evident that it was not deemed necessary to guarantee it explicitly in the text of the Constitution'.

The right to life is mostly mentioned as one of a core of universally accepted fundamental rights without an indication, however, of its philosophical paramountcy. In constitutional jurisprudence it is usually also dealt with in its interconnectedness with other rights and values[45] and is thus, in spite of its universal recognition, rather contextualized in terms of time and place.

In Germany, for instance, the right to life (one of the *Hauptsicherheitsgrundrechte* entrenched in art 2.2. of the Basic Law) enjoys a definite degree of pre-eminence[46] which is reflected in, among other things, the abolition of capital punishment in art 102 of the Basic Law and a generally 'conservative' judicial approach to abortion.[47] This attitude can be attributed to eminently negative experiences dating from the period 1933–45 — for example the large-scale destruction of human life regarded as 'unworthy' (*Vernichtung lebensunwerten Lebens*) or 'liquidation' (*Liquidierung*), all sanctioned by the Nazi regime. Even though, in the scheme of things, the inviolability of human dignity is proclaimed to be the basis for

---

[42] See also below, 2.3.1.
[43] See below, 3.2.
[44] Op cit (n 21) 193.
[45] See above, 213 *(a)*.
[46] Reference was, for instance, made above, n 21 to its description by Katz op cit (n 19) 317 as '*eine verfassungsrechtliche Grundentscheidung und gewährleistet oberste Werte und essentielle Grundrechtsgüter*'.
[47] See also below, 2.3.5 and Kommers *The Constitutional Jurisprudence of The Federal Republic of Germany* (1989) 361.

guaranteeing fundamental rights in the Basic Law,[48] the right to life functions as the *'vitale Basis der Menschenwürde'*.

In the US Bill of Rights, on the other hand, the right to life is not treated as an autonomous entitlement. The Fifth Amendment inter alia states that 'no person shall . . . be deprived of life, liberty, or property, without due process of law'. A similar injunction is contained in the Fourteenth Amendment, which applies to state governments. Issues related to the right to life are in the literature therefore mostly subsumed under the heading 'modern substantive due process'.[49]

Section 9 of South Africa's transitional Constitution simply states that 'every person shall have the right to life'. The reason for the seemingly inadequate reference to this right must be sought in the nature and course of the political process from which the chapter on fundamental rights in the Constitution emerged. A brief explanation is appropriate at this stage.

The Negotiating Council of the Multi-Party Negotiating Process (MPNP) in Kempton Park appointed seven technical committees — of which the Technical Committee on Fundamental Rights during the Transition was one — to assist it in its deliberations in key areas. The Technical Committee on Fundamental Rights was informed that its first task would be to compile a limited list of fundamental rights to be entrenched during the transition. Agreeing to this list in the plenary sessions of the Negotiating Council turned out to be a tug of war between minimalists and optimalists which, in the end, resulted in a compromise.

The minimalists, mainly the African National Congress (ANC) and its allies, argued that the list should include only those rights indispensable to the political process of transition. The optimalists, on the other hand, which were mainly parties who later withdrew from the MPNP to form the Freedom Alliance (FA), contented for the fullest possible list of rights. The South African government/National Party (NP) alliance initially also signalled preference for the optimalist position, but not at all costs.

The minimalist position coincided with the broader political view that the Negotiating Council, as an insufficiently representative — and therefore not really legitimate — political forum, could at most agree to a transitional Constitution. A more representative legislative *cum* constituent assembly, elected in terms of the transitional Constitution, would eventually have to decide on a final Constitution. The minimalists were mainly the parties and alliances believed to enjoy majority popular support. The optimalist position, on the other hand, was underpinned by a strongly held view that the Negotiating Council was the appropriate authority to decide on a final Constitution which should — especially in its chapter on fundamental rights — embody the fullest possible number of absolute guarantees pertaining to a 'final' dispensation. The optimalists were parties and alliances with vested political power interests, but limited popular support, fearing marginalization in a proportionally representative constitution-making process.

The Technical Committee on Fundamental Rights was mandated to identify those rights which would be 'fundamental to the transition', but was not told how long the transition was expected to last and precisely how fundamental the rights

---

[48] See art 1.1 read with art 1.2.
[49] Gunther op cit (n 7) 491–583; Stone et al op cit (n 7) 908–85 and *1992 Supplement* op cit (n 7) 87–146.

identified had to be. The technical committee, in its first progress report, listed the rights which it regarded as basic to the functioning of a democratic system of government. In its second and third progress reports it formulated criteria for the inclusion of rights in the transitional Constitution. The Negotiating Council at no stage really approved of these criteria, but agreed to the inclusion of the list of rights contained in the technical committee's third progress report.

This list of rights is, from a jurisprudential point of view, neither fatally anorectic nor satisfactorily comprehensive. Significant second-generation (socio-economic) and third-generation ('green' and group) rights had, for instance, not been included in the final list. The few rights in these two categories which were indeed included (with the exception of children's rights in s 30) enjoy but restricted protection and the sections entrenching them are also restrictively phrased.

The constitutionalization of the right to life was contentious because of its direct implications for capital punishment and abortion, and hence its inclusion in the chapter on fundamental rights was not certain at all. The technical committee had before it various proposed Bills of Rights. In most of these drafts either capital punishment or abortion or both of them were addressed in one way or another.[50] The minimalist negotiators made it clear from the outset that these two issues were not to be dealt with in any way in Chapter 3 of the transitional Constitution but only in a final Bill of Rights drafted by a truly representative Constituent Assembly. However, in the course of the process they signalled amenability to the notion of entrenching, for the duration of the transition, the moratorium on capital punishment[51] under the heading 'Right to life' in Chapter 3. With this the NP/South African government alliance refused to go along. A *nudum* right to life was consequently entrenched in s 9 of the Constitution and the judiciary (especially the Constitutional Court) will, in due course, have to decide on the constitutionality of both capital punishment and abortion rights. Both the South African Law Commission[52] (in art 4 of its proposed Bill of Rights[53]) and the Democratic Party (DP) (in art 3 of its proposed draft) opt for this 'Solomonic solution'. The Law Commission, however, refers to a right 'to the protection of . . . life', which is more restrictive than the straightforward 'right to life' which was eventually entrenched in the transitional Constitution. It is, for instance, less likely that a right to the protection of life will be construed as inclusive of an entitlement to what is necessary for the preservation or sustenance of life.[54] The DP's proposal, on the other hand, mentions a straightforward right to life, but adds the potentially problematic qualification that 'no person shall be deprived arbitrarily of his or her life'.[55]

Both of the restrictive elements above are present in art 21 of the Constitution of India, which states that '[n]o person shall be deprived of his life or personal liberty except according to the procedure established by law'.[56] This did not, however,

---

[50] The various points of view reflected by (and explained in explanatory notes to) these proposed drafts will be referred to more fully below, 2.3.3 and 2.3.4.

[51] See below, 2.3.3.

[52] See, for an explanation, SA Law Commission *Project 58: Group and Human Rights* Interim Report (1991) 277.

[53] We are referring to the very latest Law Commission draft which was submitted to the Technical Committee on Fundamental Rights at the MPNP as both a discussion document and a draft report, dated May 1993.

[54] See below.

[55] See below, 2.3.1.

[56] The latter part of the provision of course embodies the due process requirement in a better formulation than the DP's. As will be explained below, 2.3.2, this restriction forms an essential part of any formulation of the right to life.

preclude the Indian Supreme Court's finding in *Tellis & others v Bombay Municipal Corporation & others* and *Kuppusami & others v State of Maharashta & others*[57] that the right to life includes the right to livelihood[58] — a conclusion which was to a large extent induced by the Directive Principles of State Policy enunciated in arts 39*(a)* and 41 of the Constitution.[59] The court was called upon to adjudicate the constitutionality of a statute authorizing the demolition of pavement and slum dwellings as well as administrative action under the said legislation. The court held that the demolition of dwellings under conditions of extreme poverty and deprivation in principle amounts to a violation of the right to livelihood and hence the right to life. At the same time, however, it invoked the 'due process' provision in art 21 to justify a strict understanding of the conditions on which an applicant could approach the court to undo administrative action of the sort complained of: it would have to be shown that, in the circumstances of the case, the deprivation of the right to livelihood was not fair, just, and reasonable. This the applicants in the *Tellis* case failed to do and the court concluded that it could therefore not come to their aid.

The narrowing down of the right to livelihood to an entitlement which has effect against the state only if strict requirements of due process have not been met is debatable, and the court's failure to strike down the enabling legislation, which clearly violated this right, is even more questionable. The *Tellis* judgment, however, constitutes a landmark attempt to construe a conceptually comprehensive and realistic right to life which includes the entitlement to what is necessary for the preservation or sustenance of life[60] and which is reflected in the following instructive *dicta*:

> '[T]he question which we have to consider is whether the right to life includes the right to livelihood. We see only one answer to that question, namely, that it does. The sweep of the right to life conferred by Article 21 is wide and far reaching. It does not mean merely that life cannot be extinguished or taken away as, for example, by the imposition and execution of the death sentence, except according to procedure established by law. That is but one aspect of the right to life. An equally important facet of that right is the right to livelihood because no person can live without the means of living, that is, the means of livelihood. If the right to livelihood is not treated as part of the constitutional right to life, the easiest way of depriving a person of his right to life would be to deprive him of his means of livelihood to the point of abrogation. Such deprivation would not only denude the life of its effective content and meaningfulness but it would make life impossible to live. Deprive a person of his right to livelihood and you shall have deprived him of his life.'

The *Tellis* judgment shows overtones of a reluctance to compel organs of the state to 'act positively' in order not only to protect the right to life but also to enhance the conditions for its meaningful enjoyment. In *State of Himachal Pradesh & another v Umed Ram Sharma & others*[61] the Supreme Court, however, dispensed with this reluctance and ordered the completion of a road which would give the impoverished

---

[57] AIR 1987 LRC 351.
[58] See especially at 368 of the judgment.
[59] Ibid.
[60] See the discussion above, and especially the exposition of the scope of the right to life above, 2.1.
[61] AIR 1986 SC 847.

inhabitants of a hilly area comfortable access to the outside world and thus enhance their quality of life. In this case the right to freedom of movement guaranteed in art 19(1)(d) of the Constitution and the state's commitment to the minimalization of various forms of inequality enumerated in art 38(2) permeated the court's understanding of the right to life in art 21 as encompassing not only the right to livelihood as such but also the right to the means of livelihood. The unabated reign of creative judicial activism of this sort can of course obliterate the functional delimitation of executive and judicial powers.[62] The art of constitutional adjudication in this area therefore consists in striking a balance between, on the one hand, creative extensions of the right to life and, on the other, the orderly demarcation of the spheres of state authority according to the tried wisdom of *trias politica*.

The previously mentioned restraints on the human rights debate during the Multi-Party Negotiating Process in South Africa did not only result in unsatisfactorily restricted recognition for second- and third-generation human rights but also precluded meaningful discussion on the vital 'second-generation dimension' of the right to life. One's first impression is that during the transition the enforcement of second- (and third-) generation rights with a life-sustaining dimension, such as the environmental rights entrenched in s 29 or the children's rights entrenched in s 30, will have to cater for the concerns which underpin a comprehensive understanding of the right to life as inclusive of an entitlement to the conditions for staying alive. Nothing, however, precludes the first South African Constitutional Court from demonstrating a boldness similar to that of the Indian Supreme Court in adjudicating issues impacting on the conditions necessary for particularly the poor and the marginalized in society 'to stay alive'. The omission of explicit entitlements to, for instance, the basic necessities of life or health care in the transitional Constitution could in this way be remedied to a limited extent.

## 2.3 The limitability of the right to life

### 2.3.1 *Basic considerations*

C K Boyle[63] comments on the limitability of the right to life and then detects a paradox:

> '[L]ife is not only finite for all, but is not accorded either at the national or international level the status of an absolute right. It is a paradox that torture of a human being which leaves that person alive is never justifiable, whatever the circumstances, while to kill that person in different circumstances may be. Torture is not permissible even to save life, but killing one human being to save another can be.'

The international-law standard that arbitrary deprivation of life is not admissible[64] governs the limitation of or exceptions to the right to life, but is also a guarantee against unjustified killing.[65] The concept of arbitrariness is, however, problematic. It could mean 'action not provided for or in conformity with the law'.

---

[62] See also in this regard Chatrapati Singh 'Right to Life: Legal Activism or Legal Escapism' (1986) 28 *J of the Indian Law Institute* 249.
[63] 'The Concept of Arbitrary Deprivation of Life' in Ramcharan op cit (n 20) 221 at 222–3.
[64] See above, 2.2.1.
[65] Boyle op cit (n 63) 221.

Arbitrariness can then be avoided simply by making a new law or adjusting the existing law.[66]

What is clear, though, is that the notion of non-arbitrariness was introduced in art 6(1) of the International Covenant on Civil and Political Rights 'with the intention of providing the highest possible level of protection of the right to life and to confine permissible deprivations therefrom to the narrowest of limits'.[67] This intention translates into the following international standards for permissible deprivations from the right to life:[68]

- Any deprivation must purport to have a legal basis.
- The deprivation of life must be a proportionate response in the circumstances.
- Determining the justification of any deprivation must be subject to an independent judicial process.
- Deprivation of life may be justified only in defence of life. Accepted practices in many states still fall short of particularly this ideal.

Section 33(1) of South Africa's transitional Constitution is a general circumscription clause providing for the limitation of all the rights entrenched in Chapter 3 and therefore also the right to life. The limitation of any right can be achieved through 'law of general application' (i e legal rules which apply generally and not solely to an individual case) provided that:

(i) the right in question is limited only to the extent that it is reasonable and 'justifiable in an open and democratic society based on freedom and equality',[69] and
(ii) its essential content is not negated.[70]

A list of illimitable rights is included in some Bills of Rights. Illimitability in this particularly technical sense does not, however, mean that the right in question can in actual fact not be limited at all, but merely that it is not limitable by law of general application in the way described above. 'Illimitable' rights can, however, still be limited by other rights entrenched in the Bill of Rights.[71] Since the chapter on fundamental rights in the transitional Constitution is not a full Bill of Rights it was deemed inadvisable to include a list of illimitable rights in s 33(1) because too little room is left for their effectual limitation in terms of the incomplete list of rights included in the chapter itself. The limitation of certain rights is, however, subject to a stricter test than the one which normally applies in that such limitations must, in addition to being reasonable, also be necessary.[72] The right to life as entrenched in s 9 is not among rights in this latter category and its (paradoxical) absence bears

---

[66] In response to the allegation that in offences carrying the death penalty like cases are treated differently, thus indicating a freakish and arbitrary application of capital punishment, some American states, for instance, enacted guided discretion laws fixing lists of mitigating circumstances and thus not requiring juries to consider any and all mitigating circumstances; see Greenberg 'Capital Punishment as a System' (1982) 91 *Yale LJ* 908 at 923.
[67] Ramcharan op cit (n 25) 19.
[68] Boyle op cit (n 63) 239–42.
[69] Section 33(1)(a).
[70] Section 33(1)(b).
[71] Du Plessis & De Ville 'Bill of Rights Interpretation in the South African Context (3): Comparative Perspectives and Future Prospects' (1993) 4 *Stell LR* 356 at 385.
[72] Section 33(1)(aa).

testimony to the controversy surrounding its inclusion in Chapter 3.[73] The conditions for the limitation of the right to life relate directly to the two most contentious issues connected with its constitutional entrenchment: capital punishment, and abortion. Subjecting the limitation of the right to life to a stricter test (which would have been more in conformity with the international standards previously discussed) was therefore, politically speaking, not achievable.

The exclusion of the right to life from the ambit of this stricter limitation test holds the possibility of watering down internationally accepted standards of due process which optimally restrict circumscriptions of the right to life.[74] It can also facilitate a finding of the Constitutional Court that both capital punishment[75] and abortion[76] are permissible limitations of the right to life.

### 2.3.2 Diverse manifestations of 'due process'

Section 34 provides for decidedly strict conditions on which rights can be suspended during a state of emergency, and here the right to life has been listed with those rights which cannot, even under these circumstances and on the said strict conditions, be suspended.[77] The international standard of non-derogatibility, in terms of which no derogations from the right to life are permissible, even in times of emergency,[78] is thus complied with.

It appeared earlier that constitutional statements entrenching the right to life are usually qualified by the due process requirement that any limitation of the right to life must be in accordance with (procedures established by) the law.[79] Section 33(1) of South Africa's transitional Constitution most certainly embodies this qualification since a limitation of the right to life is required to be authorized by law of general application. If the Constitutional Court should opt for a broad understanding of the right to life as inclusive of, for instance, the right to livelihood, this due process requirement will also apply and could then be invoked to harmonize this broader understanding of the right to life with the need to keep *trias politica* intact.[80]

Limitations of the right to life in accordance with the requirements of due process are most often manifest in rights related to criminal law and especially criminal procedure. These rights are discussed more fully elsewhere in this volume.

### 2.3.3 Capital punishment

Article 6(2) of the International Covenant on Civil and Political Rights recognizes capital punishment as a permissible exception to the right to life, but then subject to stringent conditions. It is stated that, in countries which have not abolished the death penalty, a 'sentence of death may be imposed' subject to the following six requirements:

---

[73] See above, 2.2.2.
[74] See below, 2.3.2.
[75] See below, 2.3.3.
[76] See below, 2.3.5.
[77] Section 34(5)(*c*).
[78] See above, 2.2.1.
[79] See e g art 21 of the Constitution of India discussed above, 2.2.2.
[80] See the discussion above, n 62.

- It can only be done for the most serious crimes.[81]
- It must be in accordance with the law in force at the time of the commission of the offence (the principle *nullum crimen sine lege* must, in other words, be observed).[82]
- It must not be contrary to other provisions of the Covenant itself or the Convention on the Prevention and Punishment of the Crime of Genocide.[83] When deprivation of life constitutes the crime of genocide, nothing in art 6 shall authorize any state party to the Covenant to derogate from any of its obligations assumed under the Genocide Convention.[84]
- It can be carried out only pursuant to a final judgment rendered by a competent court.[85]
- Any person sentenced to death shall have the right to seek pardon or commutation of the sentence and may be granted amnesty, pardon, or commutation even without seeking any one of these.[86]
- It shall not be imposed for crimes committed by persons below 18 years of age and shall not be carried out on pregnant women.[87]

Article 6 is concluded with a provision stating that '[n]othing in this article shall be invoked to delay or to prevent the abolition of capital punishment by any State Party to the present Covenant'.[88] The Second Optional Protocol to the Covenant, which was adopted and opened for signature on 15 December 1989 and entered into force on 11 July 1991, is aimed at the abolition of the death penalty.

The American Convention on Human Rights also provides for the imposition of the death penalty in countries which have not abolished it,[89] but then also subject to strict conditions. Among these are prohibitions on the reintroduction of capital punishment in states which have abolished it[90] and on its infliction for political offences 'or related common crimes'.[91] The African Charter on Human and Peoples' Rights, on the other hand, makes no mention of capital punishment and simply states that '[n]o one may be arbitrarily deprived of' the right to life.[92]

It was pointed out earlier[93] that art 2(1) of the European Convention on Human Rights also provides for the intentional deprivation of life in the execution of a sentence of a court following a conviction of a crime for which this penalty is provided by law. However, the Sixth Protocol to the Convention, which entered into force on 1 March 1985 (almost thirty-five years after the Convention itself), deals with the abolition of the death penalty, thereby encapsulating 'the evolution that has

---

[81] Article 6(2).
[82] Ibid.
[83] Ibid.
[84] Article 6(3).
[85] Article 6(2).
[86] Article 6(4).
[87] Article 6(5).
[88] Article 6(6).
[89] Article 4(2).
[90] Article 4(3).
[91] Article 4(4).
[92] Article 4.
[93] See above, 2.2.1.

occurred in several member States of the Council of Europe' which 'expresses a general tendency in favour of abolition of the death penalty'.[94] This Protocol unequivocally requires from states parties to it to abolish the death penalty, not to condemn anyone to such penalty, and not to execute it.[95] An exception in the eventuality of war is allowed.[96]

The death penalty has been a profoundly contentious issue in South Africa not only because it is controversial worldwide but also because it was seen as one of apartheid's instruments of oppression. The constitutionalization of the right to life will most definitely add an unfamiliar dimension to — and raise unexplored themes in — debates on an issue which has been with South Africans for quite some time.

Reform of capital punishment has been part of the process of political reform in South Africa. When, on 2 February 1990, State President F W de Klerk made announcements in his speech at the opening of Parliament which helped set in motion the last phase of political transformation towards full democracy in South Africa, he also announced far-reaching changes in the administration of the death penalty. Because of the momentousness of the other announcements these announcements did not receive the attention they really deserved.[97] The execution of all death sentences was suspended with immediate effect and death sentences not executed were to be reviewed. Other reforms, which later found expression in the Criminal Law Amendment Act,[98] were also announced. These took effect on 27 July 1990 and included the substitution of a discretionary death sentence for the mandatory death sentence and provisions in terms of which persons sentenced to death were granted an automatic right of appeal, the Appellate Division was authorized to substitute its own sentencing discretion for that of the trial court, and a new form of sentencing, real life imprisonment, was introduced. In the wake of these changes the case law regarding the imposition of the death sentence has also undergone significant development which, from an abolitionist point of view, represents progress.[99] At the time of writing this chapter these changes together with the moratorium on the execution of death sentences were still in force.

Various parties and interest groups in South Africa have assumed divergent positions on the death penalty and these are succinctly expressed in their various Bill of Rights proposals. As was previously pointed out, the South African Law Commission and the DP have opted for a 'Solomonic solution' which leaves a final decision on the constitutionality of capital punishment in the hands of the (Constitutional) Court.[100] In the Charter of Fundamental Rights proposed by the previous South African government provision is made, by way of exception to the right to life, for the execution of the death sentence in accordance with art 6 of the International Covenant on Civil and Political Rights.[101]

All the other proposals with regard to capital punishment are overtly abolitionist, taking their cue from art 6 of the Namibian Constitution, which states that:

[94] See the Preamble to the Sixth Protocol.
[95] Article 1.
[96] Article 2.
[97] See also Mureinik 'Editorial Comment: From Moratorium to Reprieve' (1990) 6 *SAJHR* vii–x.
[98] Act 107 of 1990.
[99] See e g Van Rooyen 'South Africa's new Death Sentence: Is the Bell Tolling for the Hangman?' (1991) 4 *SACJ* 79; Bekker 'Die Doodsvonnis: Voor en na 27 Julie 1990' (1993) 6 *SACJ* 57.
[100] See above, 2.2.2.
[101] Article 4(2); see also above for the requirements laid down in art 6 of the Covenant.

'The right to life shall be respected and protected. No law may prescribe death as a competent sentence. No Court or Tribunal shall have the power to impose a sentence of death upon any person. No executions shall take place in Namibia.'

Article 2(3) of the ANC Draft Bill of Rights[102] and art 4(3) of the Charter for Social Justice (a document drafted by a group of Western Cape lawyers)[103] also require the abolition of capital punishment in no uncertain terms, while art 18 of the proposed Constitution of the State of Kwazulu/Natal[104] does so in a slightly more restrained, but nevertheless unequivocal, way.

The general mood in South Africa among political parties and other interest and activist groups (such as Lawyers for Human Rights and the Society for the Abolition of the Death Penalty) seems to be more in line with the abolitionist sentiments reflected in the Sixth Protocol to the European Convention than with the limitedly retentionist position catered for in art 6 of the Covenant. If, during the transition, the Constitutional Court is not going to strike down the provisions of the Criminal Procedure Act[105] providing for the imposition of the death penalty, a future Bill of Rights (by itself or in conjunction with other legislation) will probably provide for its abolition.

The Chief Justice of South Africa, M M Corbett, in a *Memorandum submitted on behalf of the Judiciary of South Africa on the Draft Interim Bill of Rights*, expresses the view (in an 'apolitical' vein, as he is at pains to point out[106]) that s 33(1)(b),[107] in terms of which law of general application can limit a right entrenched in Chapter 3 only if it does not negate its essential content, read with s 9 effectively abolishes the death penalty and outlaws abortion.[108] What the Chief Justice seems to suggest, although he does not say so explicitly, is that taking or ending a life *ipso facto* amounts to a negation of the essential content of the right to life. When the wording of s 33(1)(b) is considered in a literalist way, this indeed seems to be the case. It is, as a matter of fact, hardly conceivable that the right to life can be 'limited' if life is understood as the nodal point of being human or the living (human) being's underlying bond with reality.[109] If, on the other hand, life is understood as human existence as such or being human in its entirety,[110] then the right to life is more readily limitable — either by itself or by limiting other rights pertaining to the quality of life. The same holds if the right to life is understood to include an entitlement to what is necessary for the preservation or sustenance of life.[111] Ending a life, however, raises issues in relation to life as the nodal point of being human and not, in the first place, 'life' in any of its other meanings.

It is not clear from his remarks whether the Chief Justice is familiar with any jurisprudence regarding the interpretation of limitation formulas requiring that the

---

[102] Preliminary Revised Version, February 1993.
[103] Corder, Kahanovitz, Murphy, Murray, O'Regan, Sarkin, Smith & Steytler *A Charter for Social Justice: A Contribution to the South African Bill of Rights Debate* (1992).
[104] This constitution was adopted by the Kwazulu Legislative Assembly on 1 December 1992.
[105] Introduced by the previously referred to Criminal Law Amendment Act 107 of 1990.
[106] See para 1.2 of the Memorandum.
[107] It was clause 28(1)(b) in the draft on which the Chief Justice commented.
[108] Paragraph 13.1.
[109] See above, 215 *(b)*.
[110] See above, 214 *(a)*.
[111] See above, 2.1 and 2.2.2.

essential content of a right shall not be negated or encroached upon. Such formulas can be understood either as embodying the principle of proportionality, in which event the essential content of a right is to be determined from case to case, or as meaning that the essence of every basic right can be understood in the abstract.[112] If the formula in s 33(1)*(b)* is understood as denoting proportionality, then it is still possible to argue that, in certain instances, taking a life is justified on the basis that it is a proportionate response in the circumstances.[113] Such a finding can be facilitated by the fact that the right to life is not subject to the stricter limitation test in s 33(1)*(aa)* of the Constitution.[114] The door nevertheless remains open for an interpretation of s 9 read with s 33(1)*(b)* which will result in the abolition of capital punishment. This will, ironically enough, most probably be the case if s 33(1)*(b)* is construed in a narrow, literalist (and almost 'unconstitutional') way. In the case of abortion the issue is, however, more complicated than this, as will be shown in due course.[115]

Capital punishment as an institution has also come under fire because of the fact that death row can be regarded as cruel, inhuman, or degrading punishment or even torture.[116] Convicted prisoners may, for instance, find themselves on death row for long periods of time precisely because they exercise their right of exhausting all possible review procedures at their disposal.[117]

The question whether a long period on death row can be regarded as torture or cruel, inhuman, or degrading punishment also came up in the southern African context recently. The Zimbabwe Supreme Court in *Catholic Commission for Justice and Peace in Zimbabwe v Attorney-General, Zimbabwe, & others*[118] ordered the permanent stay of the execution of the sentences of four prisoners who were condemned to death for different offences, had been on death row for periods ranging from four years four months and two days to six years and twenty-one days, and were held under harsh and degrading conditions in the condemned section at Harare Central Prison. The court concluded that the incarceration of the condemned convicts under those conditions constituted a violation of s 15(1) of the Zimbabwe Constitution, which contains guarantees against torture or inhuman and degrading punishment. As a result the commutation of their death sentences to life imprisonment was ordered.[119]

### 2.3.4 *Diverse manifestations of 'due process'*

Article 2(2) of the European Convention states that the intentional deprivation of life shall not be regarded as inflicted in contravention of the guarantees provided by art 2 (in respect of the right to life)

---

[112] Du Plessis & De Ville op cit (n 71) 385.
[113] See above, 2.3.1.
[114] See above, 2.3.1.
[115] See below, 2.3.5.
[116] See, for instance, s 11(2) of South Africa's transitional Constitution, which follows the example of numerous international as well as domestic human rights charters in requiring that '[n]o person shall be subject to torture ... [and] inhuman or degrading treatment or punishment'. See also below, 3.7.
[117] See, for instance, Greenberg op cit (n 66).
[118] 1993 (4) SA 239 (ZS).
[119] See, for a discussion of this case, Angus 'Delay before Execution: Is it Inhuman and Degrading Treatment?' (1993) 9 *SAJHR* 432.

'when it results from the use of force which is no more than absolutely necessary:

(a) in defence of any person from unlawful violence;
(b) in order to effect a lawful arrest or to prevent the escape of a person lawfully detained;
(c) in action lawfully taken for the purpose of quelling a riot or insurrection'.

It is submitted that this article sets out standards which are by and large internationally acceptable.[120] The entrenchment of the right to life in s 9 of the 1993 Constitution will subject provisions such as s 49(2) of the Criminal Procedure Act,[121] which 'authorizes would-be arresters and persons who are statutorily empowered to assist with the arrest, to kill a person who resists arrest or takes flight',[122] to hitherto unknown forms of scrutiny which will hopefully not be watered down because limitations of the right to life are not subject to the stricter test in s 33(1)(aa) of the Constitution.[123]

### 2.3.5 Abortion[124]

Reference was previously made to the South African Chief Justice's view that the requirement that law of general application 'shall not negate the essential content' of a right it purports to limit[125] effectively outlaws both capital punishment and abortion. We also indicated that in the case of abortion, matters cannot be all that simple.[126] The Chief Justice's view will hold only if the right to life entrenched in South Africa's transitional (or any other) Bill of Rights is construed as pertaining also to foetal life. The question, in other words, is whether a foetus is a constitutional subject. There are but very few international and domestic human rights charters which explicitly answer this question in the affirmative. Here are examples:

(i) Article 4(1) of the American Convention on Human Rights (to which reference was previously made[127]) requires the protection of the right to life by law and, in general, from the moment of conception. An attempt to introduce a similar provision into art 6 of the International Covenant on Civil and Political Rights failed,[128] though art 6(5) provides limited protection for pre-natal life by requiring that a '[s]entence of death shall not be . . . carried out on pregnant women'.[129]

The United Nations Declaration on the Rights of the Child was adopted on 20 November 1959 as an elaboration of the Universal Declaration. In the third paragraph of its preamble it refers to the special safeguards which children need 'before as well as after birth' while principle 4 requires the provision of special care for the child and his or her mother 'including adequate pre-natal

---

[120] See also Boyle op cit (n 63) 236–9.
[121] Act 51 of 1977.
[122] Du Toit, De Jager, Paizes, Skeen & Van der Merwe *Commentary on the Criminal Procedure Act* (1993) 5-29.
[123] See above, 2.3.1.
[124] Abortion in the context of this chapter refers to the expulsion of a foetus procured through artificial means and does not include natural or spontaneous abortion.
[125] Section 33(1)(b) of the Constitution.
[126] See above, 2.3.3.
[127] See above, 2.2.1.
[128] Dinstein op cit (n 21) 122; for an elaborate exposition of the genesis of both art 3 of the Universal Declaration and art 6 of the Covenant in relation to the issue of protecting pre-natal life, see Smits *The Right to Life of the Unborn Child in International Documents, Decisions and Opinions* (1992) 8–27.
[129] See also above, 2.3.3.

and post-natal care'.[130] On the other hand, the Convention on the Rights of the Child adopted by the General Assembly on 20 November 1989 does not explicitly mention the child's pre-natal condition.[131] In art 1 a child is defined as 'every human being below the age of eighteen years'. Under art 6 states parties to the Convention recognize every child's inherent right to life (art 6(1)) and assume the obligation to 'ensure to the maximum extent possible the survival and development of the child' (art 6(2)).

The American Convention on Human Rights and the Declaration on the Rights of the Child of 1959 are the only international human rights documents which refer specifically to the pre-natal condition of the child. The protection of the right to life from the moment of conception required by the American Convention, however, impedes abortion more directly and significantly than the references to pre-natal safeguards and care in the Declaration, although the latter to at least some degree treats the foetus as a subject of human rights protection.

(ii) In art 40.3.3 of the Irish Constitution 'the State acknowledges the right to life of the unborn child and, with due regard to the equal right to life of the mother, guarantees in its laws to respect, and, as far as practicable, by its laws to defend and vindicate that right'. This provision prompted the High Court in the case of *Attorney General v X*[132] to make an order, at the instance of the Attorney-General, prohibiting a 14-year-old girl (X) to leave Ireland in order to have her pregnancy terminated in England. It was common cause that the pregnancy resulted from X being sexually abused and raped by her friend's father and that there existed a real risk that she might commit suicide if she was compelled to carry the foetus to term. The court *a quo* nevertheless felt itself constrained to make the order sought because failure to do so would inevitably result in terminating the constitutionally protected life of the foetus — an outcome more certain than the likelihood of X committing suicide, since she had 'the benefit of the love and care and support of devoted parents who will help her through the difficult months ahead'. This order was set aside on appeal not on the basis that, in the circumstances, X was entitled to have an abortion but because, on the facts, the Supreme Court concluded that the threat to X's life was more real than the court *a quo* had contemplated. This controversial judgment shows that the constitutionalization of right to life of the foetus is likely to rule out the possibility that women can as of right have an abortion.

In the German Basic Law the right to life of the foetus is not explicitly mentioned but the *Bundesverfassungsgericht* has, since its first jurisprudentially significant ruling on abortion in 1975,[133] consistently held that the protection art 1.3 affords the right to life as such includes pre-natal life from conception. This position was again confirmed in a judgment of 28 May 1993.[134] The state therefore has a duty to

---

[130] For the genesis of this Declaration, see Smits op cit (n 128) 28–39.
[131] At 40–51.
[132] The transcript of the appeal proceedings before the Supreme Court is dated 5 March 1992.
[133] 1 *BVerfGE* 39.
[134] Reported in full as '*Die Entscheidung des Bundesverfassungsgerichts zum Schwangerschaftssabbruch vom 28. Mai 1993*' in a special issue of the *Juristenzeitung* of 7 June 1993.

protect the life of the foetus, also against action by its mother, and a woman has a fundamental legal duty to carry the foetus to term.

In other jurisdictions, notably the US and Canada, constitutional courts, while recognizing the protect-worthiness of foetal life as potential life, have maintained that, especially during the first trimester of pregnancy, the rights of the mother trump those of the unborn child. Accordingly, in *Roe v Wade*[135] the US Supreme Court concluded that the mother's right to privacy entitles her to an abortion, while the Canadian Supreme Court, in *Morgentaler v The Queen*,[136] based the mother's entitlement to abortion on her right to the security of her person. It can also be argued that women's reproductive capacity has been abused to prolong their position of subordination in society and that part of undoing discrimination against women will be to recognize their full and exclusive control over this capacity. Her right to 'equality before the law and to equal protection of the law'[137] will then entitle a woman freely to choose whether she wants to have her pregnancy terminated or not.

What status the South African Constitutional Court will accord pre-natal life is difficult to predict. If it were to take its cue from private law,[138] it will probably not recognize the foetus as a 'subject' bearing the rights which Chapter 3 of the Constitution confers on 'every person'. However, in a recent decision of the Cape Provincial Division there was an *obiter* intimation that legal subjectivity, albeit restricted, could be conferred on the unborn child, especially 'in circumstances where its very existence is threatened'.[139]

It was pointed out previously that (and why) nowhere in South Africa's new Constitution reference is made to pre-natal life or abortion.[140] Views on the abortion issue in the Bill of Rights proposals of various political parties and interest groups in South Africa diverge. The South African Law Commission's and the DP's preference for a 'Solomonic solution' was previously referred to.[141] Both the previous South African government and the ANC have also refrained from mentioning the abortion issue *eo nomine*. The ANC explains the omission in its draft Bill of Rights by saying that the matter should be decided not so much by the (Constitutional) Court but through 'legislative action after democratic discussion in future'. The need for 'informed debate with extensive participation by all interested parties and a respect for differing views' is thereby emphasized. The *Charter for Social Justice*, in its right to life clause (art 4), provides for legislation to permit abortion. Theoretically the right to life of the foetus is thereby not negated, but in practice it is watered down considerably since challenges to legislation violating it are held off. The same idea is expressed more explicitly in a Black Sash National Conference Resolution on Abortion dated 4 April 1993.[142] The proposed

---

[135] 410 US 113, 35 LEd 2d 147, 93 SCt 705.
[136] (1988) 44 DLR (4th) 385 (SCC).
[137] See s 8(1) of the Constitution.
[138] For the South African courts' attitude towards the recognition of the legal subjectivity of the foetus in private law, see in general Du Plessis 'Jurisprudential Reflections on the Status of Unborn Life' 1990 *TSAR* 44 at 49–54 and 'Reflecting on Law, Morality and Communal Mores' (1991) 56 *Koers* 339 at 348–354.
[139] *G v Superintendent, Groote Schuur Hospital, & others* 1993 (2) SA 255 (C) at 259C–G.
[140] See above, 2.2.2.
[141] A clause in the Bill of Rights which states that '[t]he right to life should (*sic*) not derogate from a woman's right to choose an abortion should she wish to do so' is proposed.
[142] *S v De Bellocq* 1975 (3) SA 538 (T); *S v Hartman* 1975 (3) SA 532 (C); see also in general Du Plessis op cit (n 22) 26–32.

Constitution of the State of Kwazulu/Natal, in its art 27 under the heading 'Procreative Freedom', recognizes all people's right to 'terminate unwanted pregnancy when safe'. This provision is not necessarily as far-going as it may at first glance seem. Since the right to life of the foetus is neither ruled out nor circumscribed, it can still be inferred and invoked against the abortion rights provided for in art 27. The reference to 'all people' in art 27 is also problematic. Does it include only 'all mothers' or 'all (natural) fathers' as well? A father could, for instance, argue that his right to prevent an abortion which threatens to destroy his progeny emanates from his procreative freedom and should be weighed against the mother's right to an abortion. The method proposed in the *Charter for Social Justice* therefore makes more effective constitutional provision for allowing women's right to abortion by choice.

### 2.3.6 *Euthanasia (and the right to die)*

The active hastening of the death of a terminally ill patient or a mentally and/or physically seriously handicapped person (euthanasia in the broadest sense, in other words) does not qualify as a justified limitation of the right to life. This has always been the position in South African law though the perpetrators of mercy killing in the narrower sense of the word — in other words, persons who kill terminally ill and intensely suffering patients out of pity — has as a rule been treated with conspicuous leniency.[143] It is unlikely that the constutionalization of the right to life will affect the present position.

A question which will, however, be raised is whether this right has a right to die as its counterpart. Does a person have a constitutional right to decide, in certain circumstances, on his or her own behalf or on behalf of somebody else who cannot decide for him or herself, to have means vital to the sustenance of life withheld and to be allowed to die with dignity? This issue has in modern times been brought to the fore, first, as a result of the ever increasing capability of modern medicine to sustain life artificially and, secondly, by the increasing importance which is attached to patient autonomy reflected in, for instance, the drafting of 'living wills'. Helpful guidelines for dealing with this issue were laid down in a recent decision of the Natal Court in *Clarke v Hurst NO & others*,[144] even though the court did not give the fullest possible recognition to the patient's autonomy to choose. Further developments will most likely take their cue from the *Clarke* decision and the main focus will probably be on the issue of personal autonomy emanating from the right to freedom and security of the person.[145]

### 2.3.7 *Organ transplants*

It is hardly conceivable that the killing of a human being in order to obtain a vital organ for a transplant could ever be permissible under international or domestic law.

---

[143] Strauss 'The "Right to Die" or "Passive Euthanasia": Two Important Decisions, one American and the other South African' (1993) 6 *SACJ* 196.
[144] 1992 (4) SA 630 (D).
[145] See below, 3; see also the US case of *Cruzan v Director, Missouri Department of Health et al* 58 LW 4916 (1990). On the right to die if pregnant, see MacAvoy-Snitzer 'Pregnancy Clauses in Living Will Statutes' (1987) 87 *Columbia LR* 1280.

The practice of transplanting vital organs does, however, raise the issue of formulating a satisfactory legal definition of death — thus far, by and large, an uncatered for concern.

The Human Tissue Act,[146] which presently regulates organ transplants in South Africa, is, however, unlikely to be constitutionally controversial.

## 3 FREEDOM AND SECURITY OF THE PERSON

### 3.1 Introductory remarks

The rights to freedom and security of the person as well as the freedoms from torture and cruel, inhuman, or degrading punishment usually associated with them are most frequently manifested in due process entitlements associated with criminal law and criminal procedure,[147] which are discussed elsewhere. Under the present heading the rights to freedom and security of the person as 'mother rights' (and the 'freedoms from' associated with them) will be considered in outline. Certain issues in relation to these rights and their corollaries are also topical in relation to the right to life — for example, the questions whether a prolonged period on death row constitutes cruel, inhuman, or degrading punishment,[148] whether women have a right to abortion,[149] and whether a terminally ill patient or someone in a vegetative state has 'a right to die'.[150] Though these issues have traditionally also been dealt with mainly in the context of criminal law or criminal procedure, it could be argued that some of them, for instance abortion and the right to die, can to a large extent be decriminalized.

### 3.2 International and domestic human rights instruments

In human rights declarations, charters, or covenants the rights to freedom and security of the person — in certain instances also referred to as the rights to liberty and physical, mental, and moral integrity[151] — are sometimes mentioned as correlates of the right to life and not always interlocked with freedom from torture and cruel, inhuman, or degrading treatment or punishment. Article 3 of the Universal Declaration of Human Rights states that '[e]veryone has the right to life, liberty and security of person'. In art 2.2 of the German Basic Law the right to inviolability of the individual person (*das Recht auf körperliche Unversehrtheit*) is connected with the right to life and entrenched in the same subarticle as freedom of the person (*Freiheit der Person*). Life, liberty, and security of the person are also interconnected in s 7 of the Canadian Charter of Rights and Freedoms, and in the US the right to liberty is subsumed under 'due process' according to the Fifth and Fourteenth Amendments, although, it would seem, not 'modern substantive due process' as is the case with the right to life,[152] but 'procedural due process'.[153]

---

[146] Act 65 of 1983.
[147] See e g Dinstein op cit (n 21) 128–36.
[148] See above, 2.3.3 and nn 116–19.
[149] See above, 2.3.5 and n 136.
[150] See above, 2.3.6 and n 146.
[151] See below, 3.5.
[152] See above, 2.2.2.
[153] Tribe op cit (n 7) 663.

In the African Charter on Human and Peoples' Rights, on the other hand, it is stated in art 4 that 'every human being shall be entitled to respect for his life and integrity of his person', while the rights to liberty and security of the person are enshrined separately in art 6. The International Covenant on Civil and Political rights deals with the rights to life and liberty and security of the person as well as freedom from torture or cruel, inhuman, or degrading treatment or punishment in three separate articles (arts 6, 9, and 7 respectively), while the European Convention on Human Rights follows the same pattern (in arts 2, 5, and 3 respectively). Article 4 of the American Convention on Human Rights deals with the right to life, while the right to physical, mental, and moral integrity as well as freedom from torture or cruel, inhuman, or degrading punishment or treatment are grouped together in art 5 under the heading 'Right to Humane Treatment'. In the Constitution of the Republic of Namibia the right to life and the right to personal liberty are dealt with separately (in arts 6 and 7 respectively) while freedom from torture or cruel, inhuman, or degrading treatment or punishment is dealt with under the heading 'Respect for Human Dignity' (art 8(2)(b)).

All proposed Bills of Rights in the South African context, except the one contained in the proposed Constitution of the State of Kwazulu/Natal,[154] separate the right to life from the rights to freedom and security of the person and mostly (but not in every instance) treat the latter rights in conjunction with freedom from torture or cruel, inhuman, or degrading treatment or punishment.[155] The various proposals, however, treat the rest of the 'package' in widely differing ways.

Section 11 of South Africa's transitional Constitution groups the right to freedom and security of the person as well as freedom from torture, cruel, inhuman, or degrading treatment or punishment together under the heading 'Freedom and security of the person' and does not interlock them with the right to life in s 9. Section 11 reads as follows:

'**11 Freedom and security of the person**
(1) Every person shall have the right to freedom and security of the person, which shall include the right not to be detained without trial.
(2) No person shall be subject to torture of any kind, whether physical, mental or emotional, nor shall any person be subject to cruel, inhuman or degrading treatment or punishment.'

We agree with the drafters of the *Charter for Social Justice* that it is preferable to entrench the right to life and the rights to freedom and security of the person in separate provisions.[156] The question then is whether only one right to freedom and security of the person is entrenched or whether s 11 refers to two rights, namely a right to freedom (of the person[157]) and a right to security of the person. The clear preponderance of authority in both international and domestic human rights law suggests that these are different rights. Difference of opinion is, however, detectable in relation to the scope of the right to freedom.[158]

---

[154] Article 18.
[155] See the ANC Draft Bill of Rights art 2(1), (2), (6) and (7); DP Draft Bill of Rights arts 3 and 5; the NP government's proposals arts 4(1), 5, and 23; *Charter for Social Justice* arts 4 and 6; the SA Law Commission's proposal arts 4, 6, and 7.
[156] Corder et al op cit (n 103) 33.
[157] As to the question whether 'of the person' is implied, see below, 3.4.
[158] Ibid.

The formulation in s 11(1) does not have such a dominant 'due process' ring to it as, for instance, s 7 of the Canadian Charter, which states that deprivation of the right to life, liberty, and security of the person can only be 'in accordance with the principles of fundamental justice'. This latter formulation raises the question whether the right to life, liberty, and security of the person and the right not to be deprived of these are one and the same or two different rights. The view that this is only one right, namely the predominantly due process right not to be deprived of life, liberty, and security of the person, seems to be preferable.[159]

The rights entrenched in s 11(1) are not the rights to personal freedom and security, but freedom and security of the person. This is also clear from the Afrikaans translation: 'vryheid en die sekuriteit van sy of haar persoon'. This freedom and security is therefore primarily 'bodily' or 'somatic' (*körperlich*), but not in an exclusively physical or material sense: it denotes the *de facto* freedom and security of the human being as a psychosomatic unity. The freedom (and in a sense also security) of the human spirit, on the other hand, is guaranteed by safeguarding, for example, freedom of religion, belief, and opinion[160] and freedom of expression.[161] It is of course impossible to determine with mathematical precision where the psychosoma ends and the spirit begins. Perhaps the most adequate way of expressing the scope of s 11 as a whole is to say that it focuses on the human being's somatic existence, which includes the emotional, psychological, and mental attributes most directly related (or incidental) to his or her interaction with a material environment.[162]

### 3.3 Limitation and suspension

Possible limitations (and the suspension) of each and every of the rights entrenched in s 11 of the Constitution will be considered more fully under the headings which follow. All these rights are of course subject to the general limitation clause,[163] which, as previously explained,[164] provides for the limitation of any right entrenched in Chapter 3 by 'law of general application' provided that (i) the right in question is limited only to the extent that it is reasonable and 'justifiable in an open and democratic society based on freedom and equality',[165] and (ii) its essential content is not negated.[166]

All the rights entrenched in s 11 are subject to the stricter limitation test in s 33(1)(*a*). Limitations of these rights must, in other words, in addition to being reasonable, also be necessary. Only the rights (or, actually, the 'freedoms from') mentioned in s 11(2) are non-suspendable under a state of emergency (as envisaged in s 34). This means that the rights to liberty and security of the person (in s 11(1)) can be suspended in consequence of the declaration of a state of emergency, but then only to the extent necessary to restore peace and order.[167] Section 34(6) therefore

---

[159] Hogg op cit (n 7) 743–4.
[160] Section 14(1).
[161] Section 15(1). See also below, 3.4.
[162] See also Katz op cit (n 19) 317–19 and the discussion below, 4.4 and 3.5.
[163] Section 33(1).
[164] See above, 2.3.1.
[165] Section 33(1)(*a*).
[166] Section 33(1)(*b*).
[167] Section 34(4).

stipulates eminently strict conditions under which people can be detained during a state of emergency.

The tendency in international and other domestic human rights instruments has been to list conditions for the limitation of the rights to freedom and security of the person, but not for the 'freedoms from' (for example, torture etc) implied by these rights. The said conditions will be looked at briefly when the specific rights are dealt with.[168] All instances where limitation or suspension is possible are governed, either explicitly or implicitly, by the due process requirement that any limitation or suspension has to be in accordance with the law,[169] which includes original and subordinate legislation as well as common law. The said 'law' must, however, be adequately accessible to all citizens and formulated with sufficient precision to enable the citizen to regulate his or her conduct.[170]

## 3.4 Freedom of the person

The first pivotal question here is how comprehensively 'freedom' (or 'liberty') should be understood. In the US context, where 'liberty of the person' is subsumed under 'due process', the tendency to give the widest possible (and therefore 'most effective') meaning to this concept is understandable. In *Meyer v Nebraska*,[171] for instance, it was said that liberty includes

> 'not merely freedom from bodily restraint but also the right of the individual to contract, to engage in any of the common occupations of life, to acquire useful knowledge, to marry, establish a home and bring up children [and] to worship God according to the dictates of his own conscience and generally to enjoy those privileges long recognized . . . as essential to the orderly pursuit of happiness by free men'.[172]

In German jurisprudence, on the other hand, the concept of freedom of the person is understood relatively narrowly as including '*nur Behinderungen der körperlichen Bewegungsfreiheit, nicht etwa auch die Entfaltungs- und Betätigungsfreiheit*'.[173]

We agree with the drafters of the *Charter for Social Justice* that it is undesirable to give a wide meaning to the concept of 'liberty' when used in conjunction with 'security of the person'. We do not, however, agree that using the word 'liberty' in this context makes an extensive interpretation of 'liberty' inevitable.[174] The German example shows that the narrower meaning is more likely if the right to liberty is couched not in due process language but as a substantive entitlement in its own right. 'Freedom' in s 11(1) can moreover be read as qualified by 'of the person' and in the context of Chapter 3 as a whole this is the preferable reading, since other freedoms have also been entrenched as substantive entitlements, for example freedom of religion, belief, and opinion (which includes academic freedom);[175] freedom of expression (which includes the freedom of artistic creativity and scientific

---

[168] See below, 3.4–3.7.
[169] Or 'the principles of fundamental justice', as s 7 of the Canadian Charter has it — see above, 3.2.
[170] Dinstein op cit (n 21) 129.
[171] 262 US 390, 67 LEd 1042, 43 SCt 625, 29 ALR 1446.
[172] 262 US 390, 399.
[173] Katz op cit (n 19) 319. Free translation: 'merely the impairment of physical freedom of movement, excluding the freedom of personal development and activity.'
[174] Corder et al op cit (n 103) 33.
[175] Section 14(1).

research);[176] freedom of association;[177] freedom of movement;[178] the freedom to choose a place of residence;[179] and the freedom to engage in economic activity.[180] It is of course true that these freedoms to a large extent depend on how free the person (in a psychosomatic sense) is, but this interconnectedness denotes a *de facto* dependence and does not imply that conceptually all the various freedoms entrenched in Chapter 3 derive their meaning from the concept 'freedom of the person' enshrined in s 11(1).[181]

Protection of the freedom of the person is most concretely embodied in safeguards woven into the criminal process. These safeguards are comprehensively embodied in s 25 of the Constitution and are more fully discussed in the chapter on procedural rights. In the event of the suspension of the s 25 safeguards the extraordinary safeguards in especially s 34(6) come into effect.[182]

The fact that art 11 of the International Covenant prohibits the imprisonment of a person merely because he or she is unable to fulfil a contractual obligation, however, shows that infringements of the right to liberty of the person through incarceration does not always fall strictly within the sphere of criminal law and procedure.

In many instances where explicit provision is made for the limitation of the right to freedom of the person, circumstances in and conditions on which a person may be detained are listed.[183] Section 25 does not list any of the circumstances in which detention is justified, but simply states that 'every person who is detained' shall have certain rights and then gives a fairly full list of such rights (which also obtain as conditions on which a person may be detained).[184] A court itself — guided primarily by the limitation and interpretation clauses in Chapter 3[185] and by international and comparative human rights jurisprudence[186] — will have to determine, through its interpretation of s 25, in which circumstances detention does not constitute a violation of the right to freedom of the person.[187] The previous government's proposed Bill of Rights,[188] for example, contains an extensive list of circumstances in which detention is justified.[189] This list is reminiscent of (though even more comprehensive than) the one in art 5(1) of the European Convention.

One of the rights of a detained person is 'to challenge the lawfulness of his or her detention in person before a court of law and to be released if such detention is unlawful'.[190] This, in effect, is an anti-detention without trial measure expressing a

---

[176] Section 15(1).
[177] Section 17.
[178] Section 18.
[179] Section 19.
[180] Section 26(1).
[181] See also Robertson op cit (n 21) 33, where it is pointed out that too broadly understood 'liberty' can become meaningless and that the most common interpretation of the term as used in art 3 of the Universal Declaration therefore probably is 'that of physical freedom, or freedom of the body and movement', i e 'the idea that no one may be held in slavery or otherwise be confined to a place without his or her consent'.
[182] See also above, 3.3.
[183] See e g art 9 of the International Covenant, art 5 of the European Convention, and art 5 of the American Convention.
[184] See s 25(1).
[185] Sections 33 and 35 respectively.
[186] Incorporated into South African law by s 35(1).
[187] And probably also security of the person.
[188] In art 23(2).
[189] It lists fourteen such circumstances.
[190] Section 25(1)(e).

guarantee inherent in the protection of the freedom and security of the person in s 11(1). This does not, however, mean that the reference to detention without trial in s 11(1) has been inserted merely *ex abundati cautela*. It was a political inevitability. Given the history of detention without trial in South Africa, the majority of delegates at the MPNP (many of whom had themselves been incarcerated without trial) insisted that specific reference be made to its exclusion. This provision is a good example of how inevitably a Bill of Rights reflects the peculiarities of the political context from which it evolves. This also explains why, given an unfavourable history of child detention in South Africa, s 30(2) particularly requires that a child who is in detention has 'the right to be detained under conditions and to be treated in a manner that takes account of his or her age'.

### 3.5 Security of the person

At least one South African Bill of Rights proposal, that of the South African Law Commission, leaves the impression that the right to mental and physical integrity is different from the right to security of the person. It deals with the right to the protection of mental and physical integrity and 'personal security' in two different articles.[191] The African Charter does the same with the rights to personal integrity and personal security.[192] The previous government's proposal, on the other hand, mentions only the right to physical and mental integrity[193] and not the right to security of the person.

We submit that 'of the person' denotes the human being's somatic existence as previously defined[194] and that both mental and physical integrity are therefore included in 'security of the person'. This view is supported by the German understanding of *körperliche Unversehrtheit* (inviolability of the body). Katz[195] explains that while the right to life denotes the *körperliche 'Dasein'* (or somatic existence) of the human being, the right to inviolability of the body denotes his or her *körperliche 'Sosein'* (or somatic well-being). It may be that the expression 'inviolability of the body' is somewhat stronger and perhaps more directly to the point than 'security of the person', but then at least the latter includes the former.

Security of the person relates, for instance, to all forms of clinical intervention or all acts which result in physical or mental or psychological injury. The right to security of the person is manifested in the injunctions against torture,[196] cruel, inhuman, or degrading treatment or punishment,[197] and subjecting someone to medical experimentation without his or her free consent.[198] The right to security of the person also raises the questions whether a person has the autonomy to refuse life-prolonging or life-saving medical treatment[199] or whether a woman's autonomous decision to have an abortion (thereby 'doing with her body as she pleases')

---

[191] Articles 6 and 7 respectively.
[192] See above, 3.2.
[193] In art 5.
[194] See above, 3.2.
[195] Op cit (n 19) 318–19.
[196] See below, 3.6.
[197] See below, 3.7.
[198] See art 7 of the International Covenant, which actually brands such experimentation as cruel, inhuman, or degrading treatment.
[199] See above, 2.3.6, 3.1, and n 146.

should be the paramount consideration in procuring an abortion.[200] In Germany the question has also been raised whether environmental rights cannot be said to derive from the right to inviolability of the body. All the above questions have to be answered with due deference to the limits of the right to security of the person. International human rights instruments do not, however, as in the case of the right to freedom of the person, list specific instances or examples of these limits.

## 3.6 Freedom from torture

In Part I art 1(1) of the United Nations Convention against Torture and Cruel, Inhuman or Degrading Treatment or Punishment adopted by the General Assembly on 10 December 1984 'torture' is defined as follows:

> 'For the purposes of this Convention the term "torture" means any act by which severe pain or suffering, whether physical or mental, is intentionally inflicted on a person for such purposes as obtaining from him or a third person information or a confession, punishing him for an act he or a third person has committed or is suspected of having committed, or intimidating or coercing him or a third person, or for any reason based on discrimination of any kind, when such pain or suffering is inflicted by or at the instigation of or with the consent or acquiescence of a public official or other person acting in an official capacity. It does not include pain or suffering arising only from, inherent in or incidental to lawful sanctions.'

Four key elements of this definition are worth noting:[201]

- Torture can have a punitive or any other purpose.
- What induces torture is immaterial. There is, in other words, no 'good reason' for torture.
- Torture (as explicitly stated in s 11(2) of the South African Constitution) can be physical or mental (or emotional). It is, however, not clear to what extent a particular individual's tolerance to pain is a determining factor in establishing whether certain treatment amounts to torture.
- An act of torture is by definition one in which a public official or a person acting in an official capacity participates, to which he or she consents, or in which he or she acquiesces.

A powerful (albeit indirect) mechanism to help restrain public officials (especially policemen) from torturing people (especially suspects in criminal cases) is the exclusionary rule of evidence 'which excludes real, documentary and oral evidence unconstitutionally obtained by those officials who are responsible for the prevention, detection and prosecution of crime'.[202] In the South African law of evidence an inclusionary rule presently prevails.[203] During the MPNP in Kempton Park[204] two of the members of the Technical Committee on Fundamental Rights[205] were decidedly in favour of adding the following paragraph to s 25(3) of the Constitution:

---

[200] See above, 2.3.5, 3.1, and n 136.
[201] Dinstein op cit (n 21) 123.
[202] Van der Merwe 'Unconstitutionally Obtained Evidence: Towards a Compromise between the Common Law and the Exclusionary Rule' (1992) 3 *Stell LR* 173 at 175.
[203] At 178–83.
[204] See above, 2.2.2 for more details of this process.
[205] Professors H M Corder of the University of Cape Town and Lourens M du Plessis.

'Every accused person shall have the right to the exclusion during his or her trial of evidence which was obtained in violation of any right[206] entrenched in this chapter [Chapter 3 of the Constitution]:[207] Provided that the court must be convinced that the admission of such evidence will bring the administration of justice into disrepute.'

Taking its cue from s 24(2) of the Canadian Charter, the proposed provision's aim was to strike a balance between the most extreme effects of the exclusionary rule, on the one hand, and some of the concerns for which the inclusionary rule professedly caters, on the other. Both the South African Law Commission[208] and S E van der Merwe[209] contend for a similar approach.

Other members of the technical committee, however, opposed the inclusion of the said paragraph. It also appeared during bilateral discussions as if there was a difference of opinion among the political parties. The argument against the restricted constitutionalization of the exclusionary rule as proposed was that (even) this will have a detrimental effect on the prevention and combating of crime during what could be an unstable period of political transition. This latter view, which eventually prevailed, was also supported in a submission from an Attorney-General.

In Namibia a restricted exclusionary rule obtains by virtue of art 12(1)(f) of the Constitution, and the Namibia High Court recently confirmed its appositeness in countering torture and cruel, inhuman or, degrading treatment during the interrogation of suspects by police.[210]

In art 2(2) and (3) of the Convention against Torture and Cruel, Inhuman or Degrading Treatment or Punishment it is stated that no exceptional circumstances whatsoever, not even war or a state of emergency[211] or an order from a superior officer or a public authority,[212] can be invoked as justification for torture.[213] These provisions are indicative of the peremptory, nonderogatable nature of injunctions against torture which form part not only of customary international human rights law but has probably also acquired the peremptory character of *jus cogens*.[214] Mention was previously made of the paradoxical element which Boyle[215] detects in the fact that taking a life to save a life or lives, for instance, can be justified under certain circumstances, while torturing a person without killing him or her can never be justified — not even to save a life or lives.[216] Note, however, that there is a limitation to freedom from torture inherent in the definition quoted above: the pain or suffering inherent in or incidental to lawful sanctions does not brand the infliction of the said sanction as torture.

---

[206] Another alternative which was considered was to use the words 'the rights of any person' instead of 'any right'.

[207] The possibility of referring to 'this section' (i e s 25 dealing with criminal due process) only, was also considered.

[208] In art 20(5) of its proposed Bill of Rights.

[209] Op cit (n 202) 195–205.

[210] *S v Minnies & another* 1991 (3) SA 364 (Nm).

[211] Article 2(2).

[212] Article 2(3).

[213] The SA Law Commission has incorporated these provisions in its article on the right to mental and physical integrity (art 6(3)).

[214] Dinstein op cit (n 21) 122; see also above, 2.2.1.

[215] Op cit (n 63) 222–3.

[216] See above, 2.3.1.

## 3.7 Cruel, inhuman or degrading treatment or punishment

The difference between torture and cruel, inhuman, or degrading treatment seems to be a matter of degree determined with reference to the difference in the intensity of the suffering inflicted:

> 'There seems to be, then, a scale of aggravation in suffering which commences with degradation, mounts to inhumanity and ultimately attains the level of torture ..."[C]ruel" ... presumably ... is somewhere between inhuman conduct and torture.'[217]

Degrading treatment must be treatment — resulting from human action — and cannot emerge from, for example, adverse socio-economic conditions by themselves. In certain circumstances such treatment may be an act or acts of unfair discrimination. Examples of conduct which was held to amount to degrading treatment are the following:[218]

(i) committing a person to a mental institution for psychiatric treatment because of his non-conformist political views;
(ii) subjecting immigrants to demeaning procedures such as 'virginity tests';
(iii) admitting a migrant labourer in a country for a long period of time without allowing his family free access to the country;
(iv) medical experimentation without someone's consent, under art 7 of the International Covenant.

By the same token cruel, inhuman, or degrading punishment must be punishment, i e treatment meted out to an offender following his or her conviction and sentencing by a court of law. Punishment of course has an unalterable dimension of humiliation and even degradation. Cruel, inhuman, or degrading punishment must therefore be 'something more severe' than the punishment normally meted out for the offence in question.

The constitutionality of capital punishment is not only a right to life issue.[219] If a prolonged period on death row constitutes cruel, inhuman, or degrading punishment,[220] then certainly the execution of the sentence itself can hardly be said to be something less. Opinions on this matter, however, diverge.

There have over the last few years been a number of significant court decisions with regard to the constitutionality of corporal punishment in the Southern African context. The Zimbabwe Supreme Court has held that sentences of whipping for both adults[221] and juveniles[222] violate the prohibition against inhuman and degrading punishment in s 15(1) of the Constitution of Zimbabwe. The Namibia Supreme Court[223] has come to the conclusion that the imposition of any sentence by any judicial or quasi-judicial authority directing corporal punishment upon any person is in conflict with art 8(2)(b) of the Constitution of the Republic of Namibia.[224]

---

[217] Dinstein op cit (n 21) 123–4.
[218] At 124.
[219] See above, 2.3.3.
[220] See above, 2.3.3, 3.1, and nn 116–19.
[221] *S v Ncube; S v Tshuma; S v Ndhlovu* 1988 (2) SA 702 (ZS).
[222] *S v A Juvenile* 1990 (4) SA 151 (ZS).
[223] In *Ex parte Attorney-general, Namibia: In re Corporal Punishment by Organs of the State* 1991 (3) SA 76 (NmS).
[224] See above, 3.2 for the contents of art 8(2)(b).

Accordingly not only sentences of whipping imposed by a court of law but also allowance for corporal punishment in government schools were held to be unconstitutional.

Finally, there is quite a difference of opinion worldwide as to whether certain judicially imposed punishments, such as solitary confinement or life imprisonment, are cruel, inhuman, or degrading.[225]

## 4 THE RIGHT TO PRIVACY

### 4.1 Introduction

The right to privacy is guaranteed explicitly in the Universal Declaration of Human Rights,[226] the International Covenant on Civil and Political Rights,[227] the European Convention on Human Rights,[228] and the American Convention on Human Rights,[229] but not (explicitly) in the African Charter on Human and Peoples' Rights. This right is also entrenched in most domestic Bills of Rights.

In South Africa this right has, in the absence of a Bill of Rights, often been violated by the legislature and the executive through, for instance, laws conferring wide powers of search and seizure on the police,[230] the prohibition of interracial sexual intercourse and marriage,[231] and interference with correspondence without court authorization.[232] Section 13 is the privacy clause in the South African Constitution and it reads as follows:

> 'Every person shall have the right to his or her personal privacy, which shall include the right not to be subject to searches of his or her person, home or property, the seizure of private possessions or the violation of private communications.'[233]

The right itself can be limited — in terms of the general limitation clause[234] — by law of general application if the limitation (i) is reasonable and justifiable in an open and democratic society based on freedom and equality, and (ii) does negate the essential content of the right. The stricter limitation test in s 33(1)(a) does not apply.

The right to privacy can also be suspended[235] in consequence of the declaration of a state of emergency, but then only to the extent necessary to restore peace and order.[236]

For comparative purposes US and German jurisprudence will next be surveyed in an attempt to identify considerations which could guide South African courts' understanding of s 13 read with s 33(1).

---

[225] Dinstein op cit (n 21) 125.
[226] Article 12.
[227] Article 17.
[228] Article 8.
[229] Article 11.
[230] See e g s 25 of the Criminal Procedure Act 51 of 1977.
[231] Sexual Offences Act 23 of 1957 s 16 (now repealed).
[232] See e g s 71 of the Internal Security Act 74 of 1982 and s 118A of the Post Office Act 44 of 1958.
[233] Section 13.
[234] Section 33(1). See also above, 2.3.1 and 3.3.
[235] In terms of s 34.
[236] Section 34(4).

## 4.2 The United States of America

### 4.2.1 *Privacy defined*

The courts usually quote the following *dictum* of Brandeis J to justify their recognition of a right to privacy:

> 'The makers of our Constitution ... recognized the significance of man's spiritual nature, of his feelings and of his intellect. They knew that only a part of the pain, pleasure and satisfactions of life are to be found in material things. They sought to protect Americans in their beliefs, their thoughts, their emotions and their sensations. They conferred, as against the Government, the right to be let alone — the most comprehensive of rights and the right most valued by civilized men.'[237]

This fundamental right is not mentioned explicitly in the Constitution,[238] but has been held to be guaranteed implicitly in various of its provisions.[239] It has also been held that the general right to privacy includes a number of so-called privacy rights.

In determining whether a particular privacy right ought to be recognized the Supreme Court usually asks itself the question whether such a right is 'implicit in the concept of ordered liberty' in such a way that 'neither liberty nor justice would exist' if it was sacrificed and whether it is 'deeply rooted in this Nation's history and tradition'.[240] This inherent limitation of the scope of the right to privacy has resulted in a narrower understanding of it in the US compared to other jurisdictions.[241]

The right to privacy extends to the home as well as to marriage, procreation, contraception, motherhood, family relationships, child rearing, and education.[242] These rights are said to be substantive privacy rights distinguishable from informational privacy rights (for example, privacy of communication).[243] While the latter rights limit the ability of others to gain, disseminate, or use information about someone, the substantive privacy rights immunize certain conduct of the person holding them.[244] Because of the highly personal, human nature of substantive privacy rights the protection they afford appears to be restricted to natural persons only, whereas juristic persons seem to have a claim to certain informational privacy rights.[245]

Apart from inherent limitations of the scope of protection of the right to privacy,[246] it may also justifiably be infringed if a compelling state interest so requires. An infringing statute must be shown to be necessary and not merely

---

[237] *Olmstead v United States* 277 US 438, 478, 72 LEd 944 956, 48 SCt 564, 66 ALR 376.

[238] The recognition of this right has lead to an interesting debate between those who are of the opinion that the court should keep to the literal text of the Constitution and those who are in favour of a more generous approach in regard to constitutional interpretation. For a discussion, see Stone et al op cit (n 7) 918–20.

[239] Such as the First, Third, Fourth, Fifth, Ninth, and Fourteenth Amendments: *Griswold v Connecticut* 381 US 479, 14 LEd 2d 510, 85 SCt 1678; *Roe v Wade* (supra).

[240] *Bowers v Hardwick* 478 US 186, 92 LEd 2d 140 146, 106 SCt 2481.

[241] Ibid.

[242] See inter alia *Meyer v Nebraska* (supra); *Pierce v Society of Sisters* 268 US 510, 69 LEd 1070, 45 SCt 571, 39 ALR 468; *Griswold v Connecticut* (supra); *Roe v Wade* (supra); *Moore v East Cleveland* 431 US 494, 52 LEd 2d 531, 97 SCt 1932; *Zablocki v Redhail* 434 US 374, 54 LEd 2d 618, 98 SCt 673. According to Rubenfeld 'The Right of Privacy' (1989) 102 *Harvard LR* 737 at 740, the recognition of a right to privacy in these instances hasn't in fact centered on a 'fundamental act' which the law protects (e g abortion, interracial marriage), but the capacity of the impugned statutes 'to direct and to occupy individuals' lives through their affirmative consequences'.

[243] See *Katz v United States* 389 US 347, 19 LEd 2d 576, 88 SCt 507.

[244] Rubenfeld op cit (n 242) 740.

[245] *16A American Jurisprudence 2d Constitutional Law* 606.

[246] See below, 4.2.2.

### 4.2.2 Substantive privacy rights[248]

Various state statutes have been declared invalid because they infringed substantive privacy rights in the absence of a compelling state interest. The following are examples: a Connecticut statute which prohibited any person from using or aiding or abetting the use of contraceptives;[249] a state law which criminalized interracial marriage;[250] a Texas statute which made procuring an abortion a crime except for the purpose of saving the life of the mother;[251] and a city ordinance which narrowly defined 'family' to include only a few categories of related individuals and then limited the occupancy of any dwelling unit to members of the same family.[252] Similarly a conviction for the possession of pornographic films was reversed in *Stanley v Georgia*.[253] It was, however, held recently that the right to read and observe what one chooses in the privacy of the home does not include watching child pornography.[254]

In *Bowers v Hardwick*[255] it was held that the constitutional right to privacy does not include a fundamental right of homosexuals to engage in acts of consensual sodomy. A statute in Georgia which made consensual sodomy a criminal offence even when the acts occurred in the privacy of the home was thus found to be constitutional.

### 4.2.3 Informational privacy rights

Where the courts found that a compelling state interest justifies the infringement of informational privacy rights or where claims to privacy were nebulous or unsubstantiated, statutes complained of were upheld. A statute which required doctors to disclose information to the state about prescriptions for drugs with a high potential for abuse and which also provided for the storage of that information in a central computer file was held not to violate the right to privacy.[256] In *United States v Little*[257] the practice of asking census questions concerning personal and family characteristics and threatening refusal to reply with criminal sanction was upheld since the answers could be used only statistically and would never be disclosed so

---

[247] Per Goldberg J in *Griswold v Connecticut* 14 LEd 2d 510 at 523. In *Planned Parenthood of Southeastern Pennsylvania v Casey* 112 SCt 931, 112 SCt 2791 (1992), the court, however, held (deviating from the decision in *Roe v Wade* (supra)) that the strict scrutiny test does not apply in the case of restrictions on abortion. According to the court, the undue burden standard applies in such cases — a state statute having the effect of placing an undue burden on a woman's decision to procure an abortion would be unconstitutional.

[248] See Maditsi 'The Right of Privacy in America: What Does it Mean?' 1992 *De Rebus* 659.

[249] *Griswold v Connecticut* (supra).

[250] *Loving v Virginia* 388 US 1, 18 LEd 2d 1010, 87 SCt 1817.

[251] *Roe v Wade* (supra).

[252] *Moore v East Cleveland* (supra). Moore, in this case, lived with her son, Dale, and her two grandsons, Dale Jr and John (who were cousins). In terms of the ordinance John could not live in the home because he was not sufficiently related to his uncle, Dale, and his cousin, Dale Jr, to constitute a family within the meaning of the ordinance.

[253] 394 US 557 (1969).

[254] *Osborne v Ohio* 110 SCt 1691 (1990).

[255] Supra. For a critical discussion see Goldstein 'History, Homosexuals, and Political Values: Searching for the Hidden Determinants of *Bowers v Hardwick*' (1988) 97 *Yale LJ* 1073.

[256] *Whalen v Roe* 429 US 589, 51 LEd 2d 64, 97 SCt 869.

[257] 321 F Supp 388 D Del (1971).

as to identify any individual. In *United States v Miller*[258] the court concluded that an individual has no Fourth Amendment[259] expectation of privacy in respect of the information contained in cheques and deposit slips voluntarily entrusted to the bank.[260]

In *Katz v United States*[261] electronic eavesdropping on private conversations was held to constitute a search and seizure impinging on the privacy of communication and therefore subject to Fourth Amendment requirements. The sphere of privacy protected by the Fourth Amendment does not, however, extend very far with respect to the gathering and dissemination of information. In *Smith v Maryland*[262] the court, for example, ruled that no warrant was required before a telephone company, at the behest of law-enforcement officials, could electronically monitor the numbers dialed from a private telephone. The court's reasoning was that as the numbers were transmitted to a third party — the phone company — the dialer could have no 'reasonable expectation of privacy' with regard to the information. The monitoring therefore did not constitute a Fourth Amendment search.

The court's approach in the latter case (as well as in *Miller*) is open to criticism. Tribe[263] argues that it is up to the individual to measure out information about him or herself selectively — to whomsoever he or she chooses. Otherwise, he says,

> 'we would not shield our account balances, income figures, and personal telephone and address books from the public eye, but might instead go about with this information written on our foreheads or our bumperstickers'.

## 4.3 Germany

The most important provisions in the German Basic Law regarding privacy are arts 1.1 (protection of human dignity), 2.1 (right to self-determination), 10 (privacy of posts and telecommunications), and 13 (the inviolability of the home).

### 4.3.1 *The right to self-determination*

In terms of art 2.1 everyone shall have the right to the free development of his/her personality in so far as they do not violate the rights of others or offend against the constitutional order or the moral code. The courts draw a distinction between the right to general freedom of action (*allgemeine Handlungsfreiheit*)[264] and the general personality right (*allgemeine Persönlichkeitsrecht*) protected in this article.[265] The

---

[258] 425 US 435, 48 LEd 2d 71, 96 SCt 1619.

[259] This amendment provides the following: 'The right of the people to be secure in their persons, houses, paper, and effects, against unreasonable searches and seizures, shall not be violated, and no Warrants shall issue, but upon probable cause, supported by oath or affirmation, and particularly describing the place to be searched, and the persons or things to be seized.'

[260] In the words of the court (48 LEd 2d 71 at 79): 'The depositor takes the risk, in revealing his affairs to another, that the information will be conveyed by that person to the Government.'

[261] Supra.

[262] 442 US 735, 61 LEd 2d 220, 99 SCt 2577.

[263] Op cit (n 7) 1391.

[264] This right serves as a safety net for claimants who aver that their fundamental rights have been infringed: '*Geschützt wird jedes menschliche Tun und Unterlassen, sofern es nicht vom Schutzbereich eines anderen Freiheitsrechts erfaßt wird.*' (Free translation: 'Every human act or omission is protected to the extent that it is not affected by the sphere of protection of someone else.') For a discussion, see Jarass & Pieroth *Grundgesetz für die Bundesrepublik Deutschland: Kommentar* (1989) 35–43.

[265] At 34.

personality right must be read with art 1.1 of the Basic Law, which protects human dignity.[266] Together these two articles guarantee for each individual an inviolable sphere of privacy beyond the reach of public authority.[267] Although the general freedom of action is not restricted to natural persons,[268] the sphere of protection of the general personality right makes it clear that only natural persons can lay a claim to this right.

#### 4.3.1.1 Sphere of protection

The personality right includes the right of the individual to decide for him or herself, on the basis of the notion of self-determination, when and within what limits facts about his/her personal life shall be disclosed.[269] The Federal Constitutional Court (FCC) has eloquently verbalized the scope of this right in the following way:

> 'Ein . . . Eindringen in den Persönlichkeitsbereich durch eine umfassende Einsichtnahme in die persönlichen Verhältnisse seiner Bürger ist dem Staat auch deshalb versagt, weil dem einzelnen um der freien und selbstverantwortlichen Entfaltung seiner Persönlichkeit willen ein Innenraum verbleiben muß, in dem er sich selbst besitzt und in dem man in Ruhe gelassen wird und ein Recht auf Einsamkeit genießt.'[270]

The courts have recognized the following aspects of the right to personality:

*(a)* The right to a private, secret, intimate sphere of life. The *Bundesverfassungsgericht* has, for example, held that to require a person to record and register all aspects of his or her personality (even though such an effort is carried out anonymously in the form of a statistical survey) would be a violation of this right.[271] This would also be the case where a doctor's record of a patient who faces a criminal trial is seized without the patient's consent.[272] In a case where the complainant had undergone an operation changing his sex from male to female the court held that human dignity and the right to personality demand that one's civil status be governed by the sex with which one is psychologically and physically identified.[273]

*(b)* The right to determine whether and to what extent others may give a public account of one's life or certain incidents from it. Thus in the *Lebach* case[274] the court held that a German television station would violate the complainant's privacy rights if it broadcast a documentary based on a crime he had committed six years before.

*(c)* The right to one's own image and spoken word. In the *Tape Recording II* case[275] the court held that a private, secret recording, made during a discussion

---

[266] The dignity clause is violated when the state treats persons as mere objects: 1 *BVerfGE* 27; 1969 *NJW* 1707.
[267] 1 *BVerfGE* 27.
[268] Katz op cit (n 19) 314.
[269] 1 *BVerfGE* 65 (41).
[270] 1 *BVerfGE* 27; 1969 *NJW* 1707. (Free translation: 'The state is further not permitted to encroach upon the personal sphere by a comprehensive supervision of the personal relations of the citizens. For the sake of the free development of their personality at their own responsibility, individuals have an intimate sphere where they possess themselves, where they should be left in peace and where they have a right to solitude.')
[271] 27 *BVerfGE* 12 71.
[272] 32 *BVerfGE* 373.
[273] 49 *BVerfGE* 286.
[274] 35 *BVerfGE* 202; 1973 *NJW* 1227.
[275] 34 *BVerfGE* 238.

to conclude a contract, may not be used in criminal proceedings, the applicant being suspected of tax evasion, fraud, and forging documents.[276]

(d) The right not to have statements falsely attributed to oneself.[277] In the *Princess Soraya* case[278] the court held that publication by *Die Welt* of a fictitious interview with the complainant revealing intimate details of her private life invaded her privacy rights.[279]

(e) The right to informational self-determination.[280] This right will be violated if, for instance, automatic data processing and the sharing of statistical data (collected in terms of a census act) with local and regional authorities could result in the reconstruction or release of the personality profiles of particular individuals.

(f) Pregnancy belongs to the intimate sphere of a woman and is constitutionally protected by art 2.1 in conjunction with art 1.1. The right of a woman freely to develop her personality does not, however, confer *a priori* the authority to intrude upon the protected legal sphere of another (*in casu* the unborn child) without a justifiable reason and much less the authority to destroy this sphere as well as the life itself.[281]

### 4.3.1.2 Limitations

The general right to personality may be limited by the public rights (especially fundamental rights) and private rights of others, the notions of decency held by reasonable thinking people, and norms which are formally and materially in accordance with the Constitution, as long as the principles of *Verhältnismäßigkeit* (proportionality) and *Güterabwägung* (balancing) are observed and the *Wesensgehalt* (essence) of the fundamental right respected.[282]

The so-called *Divorce Records* case (*Ehescheidungsakten-Urteil*)[283] illustrates how the court seeks to balance conflicting interests. The complainant, who was a civil servant, challenged the constitutionality of a court turning over his divorce records to the chief examiner in a disciplinary hearing. The divorce court, in the course of divorce proceedings, recorded evidence of the complainant's extramarital affair with his former secretary. A disciplinary hearing was subsequently instituted against the complainant on account of this affair. He was dismissed partly on the basis of the facts divulged by the divorce records. The FCC (*Bundesverfassungsgericht*) held that the applicant's basic rights protected in arts 2.1 and 1.1 of the Basic Law were infringed by the decision of the divorce court to turn over the divorce records. According to the court, such an infringement without the consent of the marriage partners could only be justified if it was found to be in accordance

---

[276] The court held, however, that the public interest may in certain cases outweigh the right to one's own spoken word.
[277] 54 *BVerfGE* 148.
[278] 34 *BVerfGE* 269.
[279] This decision provides an example of how *Drittwirkung* works in practice. The decision of the Federal High Court of Justice (granting monetary relief for non-pecuniary injuries) was held by the FCC not to be in conflict with the Basic Law.
[280] 65 *BVerfGE* 1. For a discussion of this case, see Oliver & Von Borries 'Data Protection and Censuses under the West German Constitution' 1984 *Public L* 199.
[281] 39 *BVerfGE* 1. See also above, 2.3.5.
[282] Article 2.1; Katz op cit (n 19) 315–16.
[283] See Kommers op cit (n 47) 337–40; 1970 *NJW* 555–6.

with the principle of proportionality. This principle requires that an equitable balance be struck between the protection of the private sphere of the individual, on the one hand, and the public interest, on the other. It further requires that the means adopted by the state to infringe a basic right in pursuit of a legitimate purpose must be suitable, necessary, and not out of proportion to that aim. In the light of the fact that there was no determination by the divorce court of the necessity for the disclosure of the entire content of the divorce records in this case, the court concluded that the decision of the divorce court should be set aside.

### 4.3.2 *Privacy of posts and telecommunications*

Article 10 of the Basic Law states that both privacy of correspondence (*Briefgeheimnis*) and privacy of post and telecommunications (*Post- und Fernmeldegeheimnis*) shall be inviolable. This right has been interpreted more generously by the FCC than the similar right recognized by the US Supreme Court in terms of the Bill of Rights.[284]

While some argue that three different rights are protected in this article, most commentators are of the view that art 10 protects one right only:[285] the right to confidentiality of individual communication transmitted in writing or through telecommunication. This right guarantees the free development of the individual personality through the private exchange of information, thoughts, and beliefs.[286]

Any natural person (German or foreigner)[287] or domestic juristic person can claim this right provided that he or she or it acts as the sender of mail or takes part in a telephone conversation.[288]

#### 4.3.2.1 Privacy of posts

This is the most comprehensive of all the spheres of privacy protected in art 10 and the postal administration is under a duty to ensure secrecy in all its spheres of activity.[289] 'Post' does not only include letters but also, for example, packages, parcels, and samples.[290] Not only the content of the mail but also the fact of its transmission, the identity of the sender and receiver, their addresses, and the time and the manner of dispatch are protected.[291] The protection commences the moment the postal article is handed in and it lasts until the time of its delivery at the receiver's address.[292] The postal administration may make no disclosures regarding, for instance, correspondence to either private persons or public bodies except with the permission of the person(s) involved.

#### 4.3.2.2 Privacy of correspondence

Privacy of correspondence protects correspondence against intrusion by public

---

[284] See above, 4.2.3.
[285] Jarass & Pieroth op cit (n 264) 189.
[286] At 188.
[287] See also below, 4.3.3.1.
[288] Jarass & Pieroth op cit (n 264) 191; Von Münch *Grundgesetz-Kommentar* 3 ed (1985) vol 1 480.
[289] Katz op cit (n 19) 358.
[290] Jarass & Pieroth op cit (n 264) 190.
[291] Katz op cit (n 19) 358; Jarass & Pieroth op cit (n 264) 190.
[292] Von Münch op cit (n 288) 484.

bodies or officials in areas and instances where privacy of posts does not afford this protection, for example before the correspondence is handed in at the post office as well as after its delivery. It also protects the flow of correspondence outside the sphere of the postal administration, for example delivery by private persons or the exchange of correspondence inside a big organization. Correspondence includes letters, printed matter, postcards, and telegrams, but not, for instance, newspapers.[293]

### 4.3.2.3 Privacy of telecommunications

Privacy of telecommunications affords privacy protection in the sphere of telecommunication, which includes telegrams, long-distance calls, teleprinters, radio telephones, teletex, and telefax.[294] As in the case of privacy of posts this protection extends to both the content of the communication and information regarding the circumstances in which it took place, for example whether, between whom, and when it took place.[295] Telecommunication which takes place without the assistance of the postal administration (the so-called *außerpostalischer Fernmeldeverkehr*) is also protected.[296]

### 4.3.2.4 Limitations

This right is infringed when a public body reads mail, listens in to or records a conversation of a private person or business, makes an order to do so, or enables a third party to do so.[297] This is also the case when the postal administration or other public body records certain information, such as the time of or the names of participants in a telephone conversation.[298] When one of the participants in a conversation waives his or her right to privacy and a public body listens in, no infringement is at hand, however.[299]

Article 10.2 sets out conditions under which this right may be infringed:

> 'This right may be restricted only pursuant to a law. Such law may lay down that the person affected shall not be informed of any such restriction if it serves to protect the free democratic basic order or the existence or security of the Federation or a *Land*, and that recourse to the courts shall be replaced by a review of the case by bodies and auxiliary bodies appointed by Parliament.'[300]

Parliamentary legislation[301] authorizing infringements upon the right to privacy of posts and telecommunications must mention specifically that this right is to be

---

[293] At 483. He includes the following in his description of correspondence (*Brief*) in this context: '*[J]ede den mündlichen Verkehr ersetzende schriftliche Nachricht von Person zu Person in allen Schrift- und Verfielfältigungsarten, wobei ein konkreter, durch die Sendung individualisierbarer Empfänger oder Empfängerkreis vorhanden sein muß.*' (Free translation: 'Every communication between persons, written instead of oral, in any form of writing and duplication, aimed at a specific receiver or group of receivers, who can be identified from the communication'.)
[294] Katz op cit (n 19) 359.
[295] Ibid.
[296] Von Münch op cit (n 288) 484.
[297] Hesse *Grundzüge des Verfassungsrechts der Bundesrepublik Deutschland* 18 ed (1991) 156; Jarass & Pieroth op cit (n 264) 191.
[298] Jarass & Pieroth op cit (n 264) 191.
[299] Ibid.
[300] Article 10 did not originally include subart 2, which was inserted in 1968. As to the validity of this amendment to the Constitution, see the so-called *Klass* case (30 *BVerfGE* 1). For a discussion, see also Hesse op cit (n 297) 157.
[301] *Formelles Gesetz* (i e legislation by the *Bundestag* or a state legislature) is required: Von Münch op cit (n 288) 489.

infringed,[302] must be sufficiently precise so as not to leave any doubt concerning the subject-matter, purpose, and extent of the possible infringement,[303] and may not encroach on the essence (*Wesensgehalt*) of the right.[304] In addition the measure authorizing the infringement has to be in proportion to the aims of the infringement (*Verhältnismäßigkeitsprinzip*).[305]

The courts interpret the extraordinary clause in the second sentence of art 10.2, in terms of which the power to exclude judicial control is granted, restrictively.[306]

### 4.3.3 *The inviolability of the home*

#### 4.3.3.1 Scope of protection

Article 13.1 of the Basic Law provides that '[t]he home shall be inviolable' and its rationale is the protection of a spatial sphere where an individual can freely do what he or she pleases.[307] In other words, it protects the right of an occupier '*in Ruhe gelassen zu werden*'.[308] Germans, foreigners, domestic juristic persons, and voluntary organizations are all protected under this article.[309] The concept home (*Wohnung*) is interpreted generously and includes guesthouses, hotel rooms, and boats as well as places of business (as long as the relevant area is not freely accessible to the general public).[310]

#### 4.3.3.2 Limitations[311]

Searches (*Durchsuchungen*) may be conducted only in compliance with the requirements of art 13.2. A search in this context is a search by any public body or official (not only by the police) for persons or things or the investigation of facts without the permission of the occupier of a dwelling.[312] Searches carried out on the instruction of authorized bodies other than the judiciary may take place only when the delay in obtaining judicial approval will frustrate the purpose of the search.[313] The requirement of proportionality is applicable especially in the case of searches because they generally involve serious intrusions upon the private sphere. The infringement must therefore be in a proportional (*angemessenen*) relationship with the strength of the suspicion.[314]

---

[302] Article 19.1.
[303] Jarass & Pieroth op cit (n 264) 192, 318.
[304] See art 19.2.
[305] i e requiring the measure to be suitable (*geeignet*), necessary (*erforderlich*), and proportional (in the narrow sense). For an example of a case where the infringement on the right to privacy of posts and telecommunications was held to be justified, see 67 *BVerfGE* 157; 1985 *NJW* 121. In this case the applicant challenged legislation which permitted the control of letters and telephone calls to countries which had signed the Warsaw treaty.
[306] Jarass & Pieroth op cit (n 264) 193.
[307] Katz op cit (n 19) 371.
[308] 75 *BVerfGE* 318 326.
[309] 32 *BVerfGE* 54 72; 42 *BVerfGE* 212 219. All lawful occupiers of *Wohnungen* (therefore also tenants) have a claim to this right. See also Jarass & Pieroth op cit (n 264) 228.
[310] 32 *BVerfGE* 54; Katz op cit (n 19) 371-2; Jarass & Pieroth op cit (n 264) 228. Motor cars and empty-standing houses are, however, excluded.
[311] Apart from the restrictions laid down in art 13.2 and 13.3 the inviolability of the home may, in terms of art 17a.2, also be restricted by laws for defence purposes.
[312] 47 *BVerfGE* 31 36; 51 *BVerfGE* 97 106; 75 *BVerfGE* 318 325.
[313] 51 *BVerfGE* 97 111.
[314] 59 *BVerfGE* 95 97.

In instances other than searches[315] this right may not be encroached upon or restricted except to avert a common danger or a mortal danger to individuals or, pursuant to a law, to prevent imminent danger to public safety and order, especially to alleviate the housing shortage, to combat the danger of epidemics, or to protect endangered juveniles.[316] The FCC has interpreted art 13.3 in such a way that the protection given to different places can differ according to each one's particular need for protection (*Schutzbedürfnis*). The requirements for the limitation of the right to the inviolability of the home are therefore stricter than those which apply when the same right in respect of, for example, business offices is limited.[317]

## 4.4 Conclusions

### 4.4.1 *Sphere of protection*

Section 13 of the South African Constitution, in providing for the right to personal privacy, also gives some indication of its scope by specifying some of the entitlements it entails. The exact scope of this right will, however, still have to be determined in future jurisprudence. Does the right to personal privacy, for instance, include substantive privacy rights (as in the US) or a general personality right (as in Germany)? Does s 13, in other words, entitle an individual to engage in homosexual conduct, to be in possession of pornographic material, or to official recognition of his or her 'new sex' after a sex change operation? Does s 13 give women the right to terminate an unwanted pregnancy (during its early stages at least)? And, finally, does it also guarantee the right to informational self-determination?

'Personal privacy' in s 13 could, for instance, be construed *eiusdem generis*, in which event the right to personal privacy will be restricted to the so-called informational privacy rights explicitly mentioned in the section, and substantive privacy rights (in the American sense) as well as a general right to personality (in the German sense) will be excluded. The words 'which shall include', however, introduces reference to the genus of informational privacy rights and this in itself makes reliance on the *eiusdem generis* rule debatable.

Determination of the exact meaning of s 13 should furthermore be guided by the following considerations:

(a) The constitutional provisions safeguarding human rights and freedoms, contained mainly in Chapter 3 of the Constitution, should be interpreted benevolently (in favour of those protected).[318]

(b) A provision guaranteeing a right or freedom must be read within the context of the other sections in the chapter on fundamental human rights and of the Constitution as a whole.

With these considerations in mind, the application of the *eiusdem generis* rule for the purpose of restricting the scope of guaranteed rights and freedoms becomes

---

[315] e g when a public official listens in on conversations taking place in a room: 65 *BVerfGE* 1 40. On the other hand, no infringement of this right is at hand in the case of the laying down of building requirements: Jarass & Pieroth op cit (n 264) 229.
[316] Article 13.3.
[317] 32 *BVerfGE* 54 75.
[318] *S v Ncube; S v Tshuma; S v Ndhlovu* (supra); *S v A Juvenile* (supra).

wholly inappropriate. This conclusion is furthermore supported by the contention that '[i]f "wide language" is characteristic of the contextual environment in which a provision occurs, it is often assumed that this indicates an exclusion of the *eiusdem generis* rule'.[319]

Apart from giving the right to personal privacy a benevolent interpretation, s 13 must also be read together with similar rights protected in other sections of the chapter, such as the right to human dignity provided for in s 10 as follows: 'Every person shall have the right to respect for and protection of his or her dignity.'

In Germany this right is protected in art 1 of the Basic Law, which is indicative of its paramountcy in the context of the Constitution. The article states that the dignity of man (sic!) is inviolable and must be respected and protected by all state authority. It would, for example, be in conflict with human dignity to treat a person as a mere object. Katz[320] explains the meaning of this right in the following way:

> '*Die unverlierbare Würde des Menschen als Person besteht gerade darin, daß er als selbstverantwortliche Persönlichkeit mit eigenständiger Identität, Wertansprüchen und Leistung, einem menschspezifischen Eigenbereich anerkannt bleibt, Subjekt staatlichen Handelns ist. Der Staat ist primär für den Menschen da und nicht umgekehrt.*'

Human dignity also takes a central place in the new South African Constitution. The right to personal privacy, read with the right to human dignity, should therefore be interpreted as guaranteeing to each citizen an inviolable sphere of privacy beyond the reach of public authority.

### 4.4.2 *Entitlement to the right to personal privacy*

Had a straightforward right to privacy been guaranteed by s 13, it would no doubt have been appropriate for South African courts to rely on German and US case law in order to determine which persons enjoy this protection. Section 7(3) provides that juristic persons shall be entitled to the rights contained in the chapter on fundamental rights where, and to the extent that, the nature of the rights permits. However, by protecting the right to personal privacy, the Negotiating Council of the MPNP apparently intended to depart from the conception of this right in other Bills of Rights. Some parties participating in the process expressed concern at the possibility that, especially during what could be a socially, politically, and economically unstable period of political transition, powerful commercial enterprises may, with examples from other jurisdictions in mind, take undue advantage of the newly introduced protection of fundamental rights in order to try and constitutionalize each and every legal dispute. This in turn could have the effect of undermining the legitimacy of the Bill of Rights at grassroots level. Personal rights — which essentially are entitlements or claims of human beings as constitutional subjects[321] — are particularly prone to such abuse. This concern most clearly shows in the narrowing down in s 13 of 'privacy' to 'personal privacy'.

---

[319] Du Plessis *The Interpretation of Statutes* (1986) 155.

[320] Op cit (n 19) 308. (Free translation: 'Human dignity, which cannot be lost, finds expression in the following: the individual is subject to state action only as a self-responsible personality with an own identity, own values and own achievements, and with a recognized, human focused personal sphere. The state exists primarily for people, not the other way round.')

[321] See above, 1.

The *Concise Oxford Dictionary* defines 'personal' as

'one's own; individual; private . . . done or made in person . . . directed to or concerning an individual . . . existing as a person, not as an abstraction or thing . . .'.

Section 13 in effect thus seems to restrict the protection of the right to privacy to natural persons. This is also implied by phrases such as 'searches of his or her person, home or property', the 'seizure of private possessions', and 'the violation of private communications'. Although the latter wording should not be conclusive, as the question still is whether the nature of the right permits juristic persons to its entitlement, personal privacy clearly suggests the exclusion of legal persons from the operation of this section.

### 4.4.3 *Limitation*

If the effect or purpose of legislation or an executive or administrative act would be to impinge on the sphere of protection guaranteed by the right to personal privacy, it would only be justified (and valid) if the infringement could be brought within the framework of the limitation clause in s 33(1).[322]

Apart from the restriction of the right to privacy to natural persons, it is submitted that the South African courts should not adopt the narrow approach followed in the US with regard to the scope of protection of this right. As was pointed out,[323] the Supreme Court accepts that the Bill of Rights guarantees a general right to privacy. In determining whether specific conduct falls under the protection of this right it is accepted that the scope of the right is subject to certain inherent limitations which, in the absence of a general limitation clause in the Bill of Rights, the courts have had to develop themselves.

A broad and benevolent interpretation, giving full scope to the protection of the right to privacy, should rather be given to s 13. Because s 33(1) as general limitation clause applies to all fundamental rights safeguarded in Chapter 3, this clause should be invoked in order to determine whether a limitation of the right to privacy is justified, and arbitrary limitations not envisaged by the Constitution itself will have to be avoided. The common-law criminalization of sodomy (between consenting male adults) in our view, for example, *prima facie* infringes the right to (personal) privacy (even though conduct of this nature is probably not 'deeply rooted in this Nation's history and tradition')[324] and whether this infringement is a permissible limitation of the said right (in view also of s 8(2), which prohibits discrimination based on sexual orientation) will have to be determined with reference to the general limitation clause. Other contentious issues that the South African courts will have to deal with are abortion,[325] living wills,[326] polygamy, prostitution, same-sex marriages, and (possibly) whether it is within the state's powers to limit the size of families.

It is noticeable that the courts in Germany and the US do not always come up with the same solutions to similar problems because of inter alia the different texts

---

[322] See above, 4.1.
[323] See above, 4.2.1.
[324] See *Bowers v Hardwick* (supra).
[325] See above, 2.3.5.
[326] See above, 2.3.6 and 3.5.

of their Bills of Rights, diverse cultures, and peculiar socio-economic and political circumstances. For the same reasons the South African courts will not necessarily understand the right to privacy and permissible limitations of it in the same way as was done in other jurisdictions. Internationally accepted human rights norms should not, however, be departed from.

## 5 THE RIGHT TO FREEDOM OF MOVEMENT

### 5.1 Introduction

The origins of the fundamental right to freedom of movement can be traced back to the Magna Carta of 1215.[327] Nowadays this right is recognized internationally, as is evident from the Universal Declaration of Human Rights,[328] the International Covenant on Civil and Political Rights,[329] the Fourth Protocol to the European Convention for the Protection of Human Rights and Fundamental Freedoms,[330] the American Convention on Human Rights,[331] and the African Charter on Human and Peoples' Rights.[332]

Once again apartheid South Africa's track-record of respecting the freedom of movement of citizens and residents is eminently unimpressive. This freedom was violated under, for instance, the Black Land Act,[333] the Group Areas Act,[334] the Development Trust and Land Act,[335] and the Black Administration Act.[336] Passports were also refused on numerous occasions[337] under the State President's prerogative powers.[338]

Rights relating to the freedom of movement are guaranteed in three sections of the chapter on fundamental rights. These sections[339] read as follows:

> '**18 Freedom of movement**
>
> Every person shall have the right to freedom of movement anywhere within the national territory.
>
> **19 Residence**
>
> Every person shall have the right freely to choose his or her place of residence anywhere in the national territory.
>
> **20 Citizens' rights**
>
> Every citizen shall have the right to enter, remain in and leave the Republic, and no citizen shall without justification be deprived of his or her citizenship.'

Note that the rights in ss 18 and 19 are guaranteed for every person, while the protection afforded in s 20 is restricted to citizens only. The rights in the three sections are all subject to the general limitation clause (s 33(1)). Section 18, in so

---

[327] See Von Münch op cit (n 288) 503; Carpenter *Introduction to South African Constitutional Law* (1987) 31–2.
[328] Article 13.
[329] Article 12.
[330] Article 2.
[331] Article 22.
[332] Article 12.
[333] Act 27 of 1913 s 1.
[334] Act 36 of 1966.
[335] Act 18 of 1936 ss 25 and 26.
[336] Act 38 of 1927 s 5.
[337] During 1988 210 people were e g refused passports: Robertson op cit (n 21) 96.
[338] See Carpenter 'Passports and the Right to Travel — The South African Perspective' (1990) XXIII *CILSA* 1.
[339] Sections 18, 19, and 20.

far as it relates to free and fair political activity, is furthermore subject to a stricter limitation test.[340] Sections 18–20 are also susceptible to suspension in terms of s 34.

The negotiators at Kempton Park opted for the German rather than the Canadian approach in dealing with the right to freedom of movement and the right of every person freely to engage in economic activity and to pursue a livelihood anywhere in South Africa in different sections and under different headings.[341] The latter right is entrenched in s 26(1). In the Canadian Charter of Human Rights and Freedoms the right to freedom of movement is guaranteed in conjunction with the right to pursue the gaining of a livelihood in any province. This has led to endless difficulties of interpretation.[342]

## 5.2 The United States of America

### 5.2.1 *Interstate travel*

#### 5.2.1.1 Scope of protection

Although the US Constitution does not explicitly guarantee the citizen's right to interstate travel[343] (i e the right to pass into any other state in the country or to reside in it for the purpose of participating in lawful commerce, trade, or business without interference[344]), this right has long been recognized by the Supreme Court as a constitutional right.[345] Its exact source is, however, still in dispute.[346] The reported cases dealing with the right to travel seem to grant protection of this right to natural persons only. Foreigners lawfully within the US have a right to enter and remain in any state with the same rights as citizens.[347]

#### 5.2.1.2 Limitation

The right to interstate travel, like all other constitutional rights, is subject to limitation under certain conditions.[348] Restrictions imposed on the exercise of this right which cannot be shown to be necessary to promote a compelling governmental interest are unconstitutional.[349]

---

[340] Contained in s 33(1)*(bb)* (and not s 33(1)*(aa)*, as is the case with the same test in respect of rights previously discussed — see above, 2.3.1 and 3.3). Section 33(1)*(bb)* lists the rights in respect of which the stricter test applies only in so far as the said rights relate to free and fair political activity.

[341] The SA Law Commission and the previous government submitted in their Bill of Rights proposals that the right to freedom of movement should include the right to engage freely in economic activity and to pursue a livelihood anywhere in South Africa.

[342] See below, 5.4.2. For the position in Germany, see below, 5.3.4.

[343] A citizen's right to travel intrastate is not, however, regarded as a constitutional right. The Supreme Court accordingly refused to declare invalid a city ordinance requiring city employees to be residents of the city: *McCarthy v Philadelphia Civil Service Commission* 424 US 645, 96 SCt 1154, 47 LEd 2d 366.

[344] *16A American Jurisprudence 2d Constitutional Law* 550.

[345] Stone et al op cit (n 7) 875.

[346] The privileges and immunities clauses of art IV s 2 (see e g *Paul v Virginia* 75 US 168, 19 LEd 357) and the Fourteenth Amendment (see e g *Williams v Fears* 179 US 270, 45 LEd 186, 21 SCt 128), the due process clause of the Fifth Amendment (see e g *Jacobson v Massachusetts* 197 US 11, 49 LEd 643, 25 SCt 358), and the nature of the Federal Union (*Shapiro v Thompson* 394 US 618, 22 LEd 2d 600, 89 SCt 1322) have all been suggested as possible sources of this right.

[347] *Graham v Richardson* 403 US 365, 29 LEd 2d 534, 91 SCt 1848.

[348] See e g *Edwards v California* 314 US 160, 86 LEd 119, 62 SCt 164.

[349] *Dunn v Blumstein* 405 US 330, 31 LEd 2d 274, 92 SCt 995; *Shapiro v Thompson* (supra).

### 5.2.1.3 The right to interstate travel as interpreted by the courts

In *Crandall v Nevada*[350] the court, for example, declared unconstitutional a state law which imposed a capitation tax of one dollar on 'every person leaving the State by any [vehicle engaged] in the business of transporting passengers for hire'. The court argued as follows:

'For all the great purposes for which the Federal Government was formed we are one people, with one common country. We are all citizens of the United States, and as members of the same community must have the right to pass and repass through every part of it without interruption, as freely as in our own states.'[351]

State and municipal charges on commercial passengers boarding planes in order to help cover the costs of airport construction and maintenance, however, were found not to violate the right to interstate travel.[352]

In *Edwards v California*[353] a Californian statute prohibiting the transportation of indigent persons into the state was held to be unconstitutional. According to the Supreme Court, a state also violates this right when it tries to prevent residents from travelling to another state to obtain legal abortions or when it prosecutes them for going to another state.[354]

The right of interstate travel also has particular relevance in the context of the equal protection of the laws clause. This right can, according to the Supreme Court, be burdened or 'penalized' by durational residency requirements in state laws.[355] Thus state laws which required one year's residence in a state as a condition to receive welfare benefits[356] and medical care at the state's expense[357] as well as to vote[358] were held to be unconstitutional. Residency requirements as preconditions to instituting an action for divorce against a non-resident,[359] to standing for public office,[360] and to becoming eligible for reduced tuition fees at a state university[361] were, however, not invalidated.

### 5.2.2 International travel

The due process clause of the Fifth Amendment has been held to be the source of the right of Americans to leave the country[362] — a right described by the Supreme

---

[350] 73 US 35, 18 LEd 745.
[351] 18 LEd 745 at 749.
[352] *Evansville-Vanderburgh Airport Authority Dist v Delta Airlines Inc* 405 US 707, 31 LEd 2d 620, 92 SCt 1349.
[353] Supra.
[354] *Bigelow v Virginia* 421 US 809, 44 LEd 2d 600, 95 SCt 2222.
[355] *Shapiro v Thompson* (supra). As the right to interstate travel is a fundamental right, the court tests classifications penalizing this right by means of 'strict' scrutiny as in the case of classifications based on race and other 'suspect' criteria. Compare this with the court's approach to classifications in the economic and social realm which do not involve 'suspect' criteria.
[356] *Shapiro v Thompson* (supra).
[357] *Memorial Hospital v Maricopa County* 415 US 250, 94 SCt 1076, 39 LEd 2d 306 (1974).
[358] *Dunn v Blumstein* (supra).
[359] *Sosna v Iowa* 419 US 393, 95 SCt 553, 42 LEd 2d 532.
[360] *Chimento v Stark* 414 US 802, 94 SCt 125, 38 LEd 2d 39.
[361] *Starns v Malkerson* 401 US 985, 91 SCt 1231, 28 LEd 2d 527.
[362] *Kent v Dulles* 357 US 116, 2 LEd 2d 1204, 78 SCt 1113; *Aptheker v Secretary of State* 378 US 500, 84 SCt 1659, 12 LEd 2d 992; *Zemel v Rusk* 381 US 1, 85 SCt 1271, 14 LEd 2d 179. The general right of locomotion (i e to go where and when one pleases — only restrained in so far as the rights of others may make it necessary for the welfare of all other citizens) has also been held to be a part of the 'liberty' guaranteed by the due process clauses: *United States v Laub* 385 US 475, 17 LEd 2d 526, 87 SCt 574.

Court as 'basic in our scheme of values' and an 'important aspect of the citizen's liberty'.[363] Legislation purportedly infringing it is, however, not judged by the same standards applicable to laws encroaching on the right to interstate travel. Provisions which have an impact on the right to travel abroad thus only have to be rationally based in order to past the constitutionality test.[364] Applying this standard, the Supreme Court in *Califano v Aznavorian*[365] held that a section of the Federal Social Security Act which prohibits supplementary security income payments to needy, aged, blind, and disabled persons for any month spent entirely outside the US was constitutional, even though it affected the right to travel abroad.

## 5.3 Germany

### 5.3.1 *General*

The right to freedom of movement (*Freizügigkeit*) is guaranteed as follows in art 11.1 of the Basic Law: 'All Germans shall enjoy freedom of movement throughout the federal territory.' This right may only be infringed subject to the conditions laid down in subart 2 and art 17a.2.[366]

### 5.3.2 *Meaning of the right to freedom of movement*

The FCC has described freedom of movement as the possibility *'an jedem Ort innerhalb des Bundesgebiets Aufenthalt und Wohnsitz zu nehmen'*.[367] It thus depicts the right of Germans to stay (temporarily) and take up residence (permanently) anywhere within the federal territory. This definition can be broken up in three components, describing (i) the persons who can lay a claim to this right, (ii) the place where this right may be exercised, and (iii) the time period applicable.[368]

#### 5.3.2.1 The personal dimension

This right[369] is guaranteed to all Germans[370] whether they reside within or outside the operational sphere of the Basic Law.[371] To Germans who reside outside the borders of the federal territory art 11 guarantees the right of immigration and entry into the country.[372] Foreigners do not have a claim to this right.[373] Their position is governed by arts 16.2[374] and 2.1.[375]

---

[363] *Kent v Dulles* (supra).
[364] *Califano v Aznavorian* 439 US 170 (1978).
[365] Ibid.
[366] See below, 5.3.6.
[367] 2 *BVerfGE* 266 273; 43 *BVerfGE* 203 211. (Free translation: 'to remain and take up residence at any place in the federal territory'.) This interpretation corresponds with the wording of the *Gesetz betreffende die Grundrechte des deutschen Volks* of 1848, chapter IV art I of the *Paulskirchenverfassung* of 1849, the *Freizügigkeitsgesetz* of 1867, and art 11 of the Weimar Constitution of 1919.
[368] See also Rautenbach *Die Reg op Bewegingsvryheid* (unpublished LLD thesis 1974) 257–8.
[369] The right to freedom of movement is a defensive right (*Abwehrrecht*). It thus does not give a person the right to claim benefits (*Leistungen*) or his removal costs (*Umzugskosten*) from the state to enable a change of residence: Von Münch op cit (n 288) 511.
[370] For a definition of 'Germans' in art 11, see art 116.1 *GG*. It also includes minors.
[371] Katz op cit (n 19) 360.
[372] 2 *BVerfGE* 266 272.
[373] 56 *BVerfGE* 254 258.
[374] The right of asylum.
[375] Rights of liberty.

The personal nature of art 11 as well as the distinction which is drawn between this article and art 12 (which protects the establishment of a business) make it unlikely that domestic juristic persons have a claim to freedom of movement.[376]

### 5.3.2.2 The spatial dimension

The right to freedom of movement includes the right to enter the country with the purpose of staying,[377] to move from state to state (*interterritoriale Freizügigkeit*),[378] from (local) community to (local) community (*interkommunale Freizügigkeit*),[379] and from residence to residence within the same community (*interlokale Freizügigkeit*) as well as for a person to retain the place where he or she is residing.[380] A person taking up a new residence must be treated in the same way as a local resident.[381] This is evident from art 3.1 (guaranteeing equality before the law) and it is further enhanced by art 11.1.

Limitations of the right to freedom of bodily movement (*körperliche Bewegungsfreiheit*) is dealt with in art 104 of the Basic Law. Article 11 therefore does not have as its aim the protection of the individual from arrest and detention. The freedom to leave the country is also not guaranteed in art 11. It has, however, been held that this right is included in the general right of liberty guaranteed in art 2.1.[382] As in the US,[383] the right to international travel is thus distinguished from the right to interstate travel.[384]

### 5.3.2.3 The temporal dimension

While the taking up of permanent residence does not provide much of a problem, it is still in dispute for how long a person has to stay at a specific place before he or she can qualify as 'staying' (*Aufenthalt*). This is important because only if (at least) a person's 'staying' is limited by the state will art 11.2 be applicable. Some are of the opinion that every lingering (*Verweilen*), even for a few minutes, is sufficient to bring a person under the protection of art 11.[385] Jarass & Pieroth,[386] however, support the view that the stay should at least be overnight.

### 5.3.3 *The relationship between art 11 and other fundamental rights*

Since art 12 provides for the right to choose a trade, occupation, or profession, art 11 is not relevant in respect of vocational establishment.[387] Hence a provision

---

[376] Jarass & Pieroth op cit (n 264) 196.
[377] Katz op cit (n 19) 361.
[378] See also art 33.1, which provides that every German shall have the same political rights and duties in every state. A similar article exists in the US Constitution: art 4(2).
[379] Hesse op cit (n 297) 155.
[380] Thus protecting a person against deportation: Jarass & Pieroth op cit (n 264) 195.
[381] Von Münch op cit (n 288) 510.
[382] 2 *BVerfGE* 266 273, 632–4, 895 897; 72 *BVerfGE* 200 245). Hesse op cit (n 297) 155 criticizes this view as being contradictory, seeing that entry into the country is also not explicitly guaranteed in art 11. He is of the opinion that the right to leave the country is — in the light of the history of prohibitions on leaving the DDR — more than mere *allgemeiner Handlungsfreiheit*.
[383] Where the right to international travel is seen to originate from the due process clause of the Fifth Amendment.
[384] See above, 5.2.2.
[385] Von Münch op cit (n 288) 509.
[386] Op cit (n 264) 195.
[387] 12 *BVerfGE* 140 162.

prohibiting prostitutes to operate in a certain area does not infringe on the right guaranteed in art 11.[388] Freedom of movement furthermore exists only within the framework of the law of property. As a result, art 11 does not provide for the right to build a house at a specific place, to lay claim to a specific house, or to pursue a vocation at any place.[389]

### 5.3.4 *Private law*

Article 11 does not impact directly on the private-law relationships of individuals. It can, however, have some importance for the interpretation of private-law norms. The Federal Supreme Court, for example, declared invalid a residence prohibition (obliging someone not to take up residence in a particular city) in an agreement between a divorced couple in view of art 11, read with art 138 of the *Bürgerliches Gesetzbuch*.[390]

### 5.3.5 *Limitations*

Article 11.2 provides the following regarding the limitation of the right to freedom of movement:[391]

> 'This right may be restricted only by or pursuant to a law and only in cases in which an adequate basis of existence is lacking and special burdens would arise to the community as a result thereof,[392] or in which such restriction is necessary to avert imminent danger to the existence or the free democratic basic order of the Federation or a *Land*, to combat the danger of epidemics,[393] to deal with natural disasters[394] or particularly grave accidents,[395] to protect young people from neglect or to prevent crime.'[396]

It is generally accepted that art 11 protects the individual against direct infringements only, for example by making freedom of movement dependent upon conditions, permission, or proof. Indirect interference by the state, in other words, interference which is not aimed at limiting this right, does not infringe the right to freedom of movement. Planning provisions (even those in effect barring certain persons from staying at a particular place) and provisions relating to property tax are therefore excluded from the operation of this article.[397]

Limitations of the right to freedom of movement can in terms of art 11.2 only be effected by (federal or state) legislation or regulations based on legislation.[398]

---

[388] Jarass & Pieroth op cit (n 264) 195.
[389] 2 *BVerfGE* 151.
[390] *BGH* 1972 *NJW* 1414.
[391] Translation as in Karpen (ed) *The Constitution of the Federal Republic of Germany* (1988) 230–1.
[392] This ground — because of the principle of the social state (*Sozialstaatsprinzip*) — will apparently exist only in very special circumstances. It will e g not be applicable in the case of a housing need or where a person is old, sick, or disabled or even because there are no job opportunities for him or her while he or she is willing and able to work (3 *BVerfGE* 135 138–9).
[393] This is every danger for the health or life of people, for property, or for means threatening as a result of the epidemic spreading of infectious diseases in humans, animals, and plants: Von Münch op cit (n 288) 516.
[394] Events caused by elements of nature, e g flooding, earthquakes, volcanic eruptions, droughts, etc.
[395] Catastrophes with a technical cause, e g train, aeroplane, and mine disasters or explosions of weapons arsenals and nuclear reactors.
[396] In terms of this ground it is not necessary or sufficient that a person should already have committed a crime. It is only important whether the commitment of a crime can in all probability be expected and only be averted by placing a restriction on freedom of movement: Von Münch op cit (n 288) 517.
[397] Jarass & Pieroth op cit (n 264) 196.
[398] A further restriction is laid down in art 17a.2.

Such legislation must apply generally and must mention the right to be infringed.[399] The right to freedom of movement may furthermore be infringed only for one of the reasons explicitly laid down in subart 2 and must be in accordance with the principle of proportionality (*Verhältnismäßigkeit*).

## 5.4 Canada

### 5.4.1 *General*

The right to freedom of movement is guaranteed in s 6 of the Canadian Charter of Rights and Freedoms under the heading mobility rights. It has been held that this expression means 'the right of the person to move about, within and outside the national boundaries'.[400]

In this section a distinction is drawn between citizens and permanent residents. Citizens of Canada have the right to enter, remain in, and leave Canada. These rights are not granted to permanent residents. The two substantive rights in s 6(2) are granted to citizens as well as persons who have the status of permanent resident. This is the right (i) to move and to take up residence in any province and (ii) to pursue the gaining of a livelihood in any province. Section 6 does not guarantee a right to freedom of movement to juristic persons.[401]

The rights guaranteed in subsec (2) are subject to limitations laid down in s 6(3) and (4). These limitations may be imposed by any one or more of the following:

*(a)* laws of general application as long as they do not discriminate on the basis of province of residence;
*(b)* laws imposing reasonable residence requirements before entitling someone to publicly funded social services;
*(c)* affirmative action programmes in those provinces where the rate of employment is below the national average.

Section 6 is furthermore made subject to s 1 of the Charter, which provides that the rights set out in the Charter are guaranteed subject 'only to such reasonable limits prescribed by law as can be demonstrably justified in a free and democratic society'.

### 5.4.2 *Problems of interpretation*

In *Law Society of Upper Canada v Skapinker*[402] the Supreme Court had the first opportunity to interpret s 6. In this case the court had to consider the validity of a requirement in s 28*(c)* of the Law Society Act[403] that admission to the Bar of the province of Ontario is restricted to Canadian citizens and other British subjects. Skapinker (replaced in the course of the proceedings by Richardson) was not a citizen but a permanent resident of Ontario who sought admission to the bar.

In regard to s 6(2)*(b)* the court held that it does not establish a separate and distinct (free-standing) right to work divorced from the mobility provisions in which it is

---

[399] Article 19.1.
[400] *Law Society of Upper Canada v Skapinker* (1984) 9 DLR (4th) 161 (SCC).
[401] Hogg op cit (n 7) 14.
[402] Supra.
[403] RSO 1980, c 233.

PERSONAL RIGHTS 261

founded.[404] According to the court, the rights in paras *(a)* and *(b)* both relate to freedom of movement into another province either for the taking up of residence or to work without establishing residence.[405] Since Richardson was not purporting to move to Ontario (he was already resident there) s 6(2)*(b)* afforded him no protection. Section 28*(c)* of the Law Society Act thus did not infringe on Richardson's right to freedom of movement.[406]

This, however, still leaves unanswered a question submitted to the court by the Chief Justice,[407] namely whether s 28*(c)* of the Law Society Act infringes s 6(2)*(b)* of the Charter. With regard to lawyers being permanent residents of Canada and residing in other Canadian provinces there can be little doubt as to the answer.[408]

In *Black v Law Society of Alberta*[409] the validity of two rules of the Alberta Law Society had to be considered by the Supreme Court. The court was in this case squarely confronted with the consequences of its decision in the *Skapinker* case. While the applicants were clearly prejudiced by the provision complained of (limiting their right to pursue a livelihood) they did not intend moving to another province (as required in *Skapinker*) and the Constitution provided them with no other guarantee to pursue a livelihood.

A law firm (Black & Co) was formed in the province of Alberta which was made up exclusively of members of the Law Society of Alberta, some of whom resided in Calgary (Alberta) and some in Toronto (Ontario). All of the partners of Black & Co were also partners of an Ontario Firm (McCarthy & McCarthy). The Law Society of Alberta, however, enacted two rules to try and prevent such interprovincial relationships from continuing. Rule 154 provided the following:

> 'An active member who ordinarily resides in and carries on the practice of law within Alberta shall not enter into or continue in partnership, association or other arrangement for the joint practice of law in Alberta with anyone who is not an active member ordinarily resident in Alberta.'

The second rule, rule 75B, reads as follows: 'No member shall be a partner in or associated with more than one law firm.'

The Supreme Court decided to approach the interpretation of the Charter in the way laid down in *R v Big M Drug Mart Ltd*.[410] There it was said that a generous and purposive interpretation should be adopted. The purpose of the right in question is to be determined with reference to inter alia the character and larger objects of the Charter itself, the language chosen to articulate the specific right, and the historical origins of the concepts enshrined. Following this approach, the court concluded that one of the objects of the drafters of the first Constitution of Canada[411] was the

---

[404] Supra at 181.
[405] Ibid. The mobility element in para *(b)* does not, however, go so far as to require a person to move to another province and become a resident of that province before he or she has a right to gain a livelihood in that province: *Black v Law Society of Alberta* (1989) 58 DLR (4th) 317 (SCC) 338.
[406] Supra at 181.
[407] At 166. The question was framed in the following way: 'Is Section 28*(c)* of the Law Society Act, RSO 1980, Chapter 233, in so far as it excludes from its benefit persons having the status of permanent residents of Canada, inoperative and of no force and effect by reason of Section 6 of The Constitution Act 1982?'
[408] As this was not a direct infringement on the applicant's freedom of movement it might perhaps have availed him rather to have proceeded in terms of s 15 of the Charter (laying down equality rights). This was done with success in *Andrews v Law Society of British Columbia* [1989] 2 WWR 289 (SCC) with regard to a statutory requirement in the province of British Columbia which provided that only Canadian citizens could qualify to practise law in that province. The Supreme Court declared the statutory provision to be of no force and effect.
[409] Supra.
[410] (1985) 18 DLR (4th) 321 (SCC) at 359–60.
[411] The British North America Act, 1867.

creation of a single country with a common market.[412] Inherent in citizenship of a united country is the right to reside wherever one wishes and to pursue the gaining of a livelihood without being restricted by provincial boundaries.[413] Section 6(2) of the Charter was enacted to entrench this right and to make it applicable to citizens and permanent residents alike.[414]

The court, however, tried to avoid the narrow approach followed in the *Skapinker* case by drawing a distinction between working and pursuing a livelihood.[415] While in *Skapinker* much emphasis was placed on the relationship between s 6(2)*(a)* and 6(2)*(b)*, making movement a prerequisite to relying on s 6(2)*(b)*, the court in *Black* held that the words 'to pursue the gaining of a livelihood in any province' in s 6(2)*(b)* 'does not connote the physical movement of the individual to the province'.[416]

According to the court, the expression 'to work in the province' (used in *Skapinker*) might more easily be open to an interpretation requiring physical movement.[417] In order to rely on s 6(2)*(b)* the applicants thus did not have to prove physical movement. As the combined effect of rules 154 and 75B was seriously to impair the ability of the respondents to maintain a viable association for the purpose of pursuing a livelihood and to make such a business arrangement completely unfeasible, the court held that these rules did infringe s 6(2)*(b)* of the Charter.[418]

The question whether the infringement of this right could be justified in terms of s 6(3) or s 1 was answered in the negative. With regard to s 6(3)*(a)* the court held that, contrary to the requirements of this section, both rules discriminate among persons primarily on the basis of their province of present or previous residence.[419] With regard to s 1 it was found that the limitations placed on the applicant's rights were disproportionate to the legislative objectives of the relevant provisions.[420] Rules 154 and 75B were thus held to be in violation of the Charter and of no force and effect.

### 5.4.3 *The right to remain in and leave Canada*

With regard to the right of citizens to remain in Canada[421] it was held by the Ontario Appeal Court in *Re Germany and Rauca*[422] that the Extradition Act (which can have the effect of infringing rights of Canadian citizens to remain in Canada because it creates the possibility of extraditing them to other countries) is a reasonable and justifiable limitation of this right. This view has been approved of by the Supreme Court.[423]

---

[412] *Black v Law Society of Alberta* (supra) at 334.
[413] At 337, 343.
[414] At 337.
[415] At 343.
[416] Ibid, the court holding that 'an interpretation that permits a person to pursue his living throughout Canada does not seem to ... be a meaning that is out of sympathy with mobility'.
[417] At 343.
[418] At 341–2.
[419] At 346.
[420] At 352. See also *R v Oakes* (1986) 26 DLR (4th) 200 at 225–6.
[421] Section 6(1).
[422] (1983) 145 DLR (3rd) 638 (Ont CA).
[423] *Schmidt v The Queen* (1987) 39 DLR (4th) 18 (SCC) 38.

## 5.5 Conclusion

The right to freedom of movement should be distinguished from the rights to freedom and security of the person.[424] It is submitted that a person being detained should not base his or her claim on the infringement of the right to freedom of movement, but should rather rely on ss 11 and 25 protecting and regulating the personal freedom of an individual exhaustively.

Having said this, the exact scope of ss 18, 19, and 20 is still open to interpretation by the courts. Issues that will have to be resolved are inter alia whether the following can be regarded as infringements of the rights entrenched in these sections and whether such infringements (if at hand) can be said to be reasonable (and necessary in the case of s 18 in so far as it relates to free and fair political activity) and justifiable in an open and democratic society based on freedom and equality: residence requirements for admission to a school, university or (provincial) professional association, or for receiving welfare benefits; declaring of a national road a toll road; restrictions upon the types of vehicles being permitted to make use of a national road; permit requirements; building regulations in a residential area; the refusal of passports to citizens and the extradition of citizens.

It is further submitted that only natural persons should have a claim to the protection of the right to freedom of movement as enshrined in ss 18, 19, and 20. Section 26 will then provide sufficient protection for juristic and natural persons to engage in economic activity anywhere within the borders of South Africa.

---

[424] See above, 3.4 and 3.5.

# FREEDOM OF EXPRESSION

## JOHANN VAN DER WESTHUIZEN

## 1 INTRODUCTION

The urge to say something is human. So too, unfortunately, is the reluctance to listen to others. Freedom of expression therefore is essential in any attempt to build a democratic social and political order and a legal system based on constitutionalism and fundamental human rights. Consequently it is a freedom that occupies a prominent place in any catalogue of fundamental rights. Section 15 of Chapter 3 of the Constitution of the Republic of South Africa Act 200 of 1993 recognizes this fundamental right in providing that:

> 'Every person shall have the right to freedom of speech and expression, which shall include freedom of the press and other media, and the freedom of artistic creativity and scientific research.'[1]

It furthermore states that

> '[a]ll media financed by or under the control of the state shall be regulated in a manner which ensures impartiality and the expression of a diversity of opinion'.[2]

Section 15(1) protects speech and expression. The latter includes the former and it is so wide that it could embrace non-verbal or verbal symbolic acts.[3] 'Speech' arguably relates to utterances with some intelligible content intended to inform, ask, or persuade, whereas 'expression' may include appeals to the emotions or the senses, through sound, colour, etc. Section 15 has to be read with several other clauses in the Constitution, dealing with related and potentially complementing and competing rights and freedoms, such as equality, dignity, privacy, religion, belief and opinion, assembly, demonstration and petition, association and access to information, fair trial, and economic activity,[4] as well as with the clauses dealing with the application, limitation, and interpretation of the chapter on fundamental rights.[5]

It is trite that freedom of expression is not absolute. This is the case in all legal systems, although the boundaries of this freedom may vary from one society to another and from one area of expression to another. It is furthermore linked to the history, traditions, culture, and political and social environment of each society, against the backdrop of which it is bound to be interpreted and exercised. The Constitution does not provide a hierarchy of values and such competing values and interests will have to be weighed and balanced by the courts responsible for the development of a new constitutional jurisprudence.[6] This process cannot be a purely

---

[1] Section 15(1).

[2] Section 15(2).

[3] See e g *US v O'Brien* 391 US 367 (1986) (draft card burning); *Tinker v Des Moines School District* 393 US 503 (1969) (the wearing of black armbands to protest against the war); *Clark v Community for Creative Non-Violence* 468 US 288 (1984) (sleeping in public parks). Symbolic expression is also referred to below, 4.1.

[4] Sections 8, 10, 13, 14, 16, 17, 23, 25(3), 26, and 96(3). The concept of human rights revolves around the freedom and equality of human beings, but some tension between these two is present in Chapter 3, also with regard to freedom of expression. The right to information is often viewed as the flipside of the right to free expression. Section 23, protecting access to information, seems to relate more to information held by the state, in so far as such information is required for the exercise or protection of one's rights. Consequently it is not discussed here.

[5] Sections 7, 33, and 35.

[6] See the concise but fine exposition by Marcus 'Freedom of Expression under the Constitution' (1994) 10 *SAJHR* 140. Section 33 requires 'necessity' with regard to the limitation of some rights, though not for others.

legalistic one and is likely to be influenced by an ongoing public debate between different interest groups and by civil society's very exercise of its freedom of speech and expression. Views on the extent and limitation of freedom of expression are also likely to change over time, depending on the development or decay of tolerance and other democratic practices.[7]

In determining whether a particular statutory or other limitation of freedom of expression is constitutional or not the recognition of freedom of expression as a fundamental right in s 15 serves as the starting point. If the limitation seems to infringe this right, it must be measured against s 33, which provides a mechanism for the limitation of fundamental rights and freedoms and which could well be one of the most critical provisions in Chapter 3.[8] This section provides that a fundamental right such as freedom of expression may be limited by law of general application, provided that the limitation shall be permissible only to the extent that it is *reasonable* and *justifiable* in an *open and democratic society based on freedom and equality* and that the limitation shall not negate the *essential content* of the right in question. Such limitation of freedom of expression must furthermore also be *necessary*, but only in so far as the right relates to *free and fair political activity*.[9]

In order to apply the standards contained in s 33 a number of theoretical approaches and comparative sources should be followed or consulted, which are related to the approach followed in constitutional interpretation.[10]

Section 35 provides guidance regarding the interpretation of s 15, as well as of concepts such as 'reasonable', 'justifiable' and 'necessary' in s 33, by stating that a court of law shall promote the values which underlie an open and democratic society based on freedom and equality and shall, where applicable, have regard to public international human rights law, and may have regard to comparable foreign case law.[11] The door for extensive comparative interpretation and creative lawyering is thus fairly wide open. Section 35(3) furthermore states that in the interpretation of any law and the application and development of the common law a court shall have due regard to the spirit, purport, and objects of Chapter 3. A measure of 'horizontal application' to areas of private law thus seems to be possible.

## 2  A BRIEF COMPARATIVE OVERVIEW

### 2.1  International and regional

Freedom of expression is generally recognized as an important fundamental right in international human rights instruments.

---

[7] The assumption that the degree of freedom of expression practised and allowed in a society may depend on its state of democratic development, together with the assumption that freedom of expression is an essential component of democracy, may amount to circular reasoning, of course. The argument will be dealt with under the discussion of hate speech and state security below, 4.1 and 4.2.

[8] See Cachalia, Cheadle, Davis, Haysom, Maduna & Marcus *Fundamental Rights in the New Constitution* (1994) 106–16 as to the different 'stages of enquiry'. Regarding the limits of free expression, see the European *Handyside* judgment, 7/12/1976, Series A vol 24, discussed inter alia by Janis & Kay *European Human Rights Law* (1990) 233.

[9] See s 33(1)(*a*) and (*b*), and in particular s 33(1)(*bb*). This would seem to imply a difference between e g speech and expression with political implications, and speech and expression related to 'non-political' spheres, such as erotica, religion, etc.

[10] The need for a contextual or purposive interpretation is accepted. See e g the chapter by Erasmus in this volume, as well as Cachalia et al op cit (n 8) 109–16, Marcus 'Interpreting the Chapter on Fundamental Rights' (1994) 10 *SAJHR* 92 and, as far as foreign decisions are concerned, the Canadian Supreme Court's decision in *R v Oakes* (1986) 26 DLR (4th) 200.

[11] Section 35(1).

Article 19 of the Universal Declaration of Human Rights[12] proclaims that everyone has the right to freedom of opinion and expression, including freedom to hold opinions without interference, and to seek, receive, and impart information and ideas through any media and regardless of frontiers. So does art 19 of the International Covenant on Civil and Political Rights.[13]

As far as regional protection of the international human rights system is concerned, the African Charter on Human and Peoples' Rights[14] recognizes in art 9 the right of the individual to receive information and to express and disseminate his opinions 'within the law'. The European Convention on Human Rights[15] proclaims freedom of expression, including the freedom to hold opinions and to receive and impart information and ideas in art 10, but provides for the regulation of the media and entertainment and mentions the correspondent duties and responsibilities and limitations to which it may be subjected. Article 4 of the American Declaration of the Rights and Duties of Man[16] protects the right to freedom of investigation, of opinion, and of the expression and dissemination of ideas, by any medium whatsoever. Freedom of thought and expression is also proclaimed in art 13 of the American Convention on Human Rights.

## 2.2 State Constitutions

Freedom of expression seems to be recognized almost universally in Bills of Rights. It is guaranteed in the constitutions of more than 120 states, with Colombia, Gabon, Mali, and Togo among the few exceptions.[17] (The fact that actual freedom of expression does not exist in all the states pretending to protect it in their Bills of Rights clearly illustrates that it is one of those values which is easy to respect in theory, but tempting to violate in practice.)

The First Amendment to the Constitution of the United States of America, stating that 'Congress shall make no law . . . abridging the freedom of speech, or of the press', is probably the world's best-known example of the protection of free expression in a state Constitution and has given rise to a vast body of constitutional jurisprudence.[18]

In Germany art 5 of the Federal Constitution or Basic Law of 1949 protects free expression.[19] Section 2*(b)* of the Canadian Charter of Rights and Freedoms of 1982

---

[12] Adopted and proclaimed by UN General Assembly Resolution 217A (III) of 10 December 1948.

[13] Adopted by UN General Assembly Resolution 2200A (XXI) of 16 December 1966. Article 19(2) recognizes freedom of expression, including freedom to seek, receive, and impart information and ideas of all kinds, regardless of frontiers, either orally, in writing or in print, in the form of art, or through any other media of his choice. Article 19(3) states that the right provided for in para 2 carries with it special duties and responsibilities. It may be subject to certain restrictions, but these shall only be such as are provided for by law and are necessary *(a)* for the respect of the rights or reputations of others and *(b)* for the protection of national security or of public order, or of public health or morals. Article 20 provides for further limitation and restriction by law of war propaganda and 'hate speech'.

[14] Adopted by the OAU Heads of State and Government in Nairobi on 27 June 1981.

[15] Signed in Rome on 4 November 1950.

[16] Proclaimed by the Ninth International Conference of American States on 2 May 1948.

[17] See the SA Law Commission's *Project 58: Group and Human Rights* Working Paper 25 (1989) 112–27.

[18] See in general Tribe *American Constitutional Law* 2 ed (1988) 785 et seq; Emanuel *Constitutional Law* (1991) 412 et seq.

[19] '(1) Everyone shall have the right freely to express and disseminate his opinion by speech, writing, and pictures, and freely to inform himself from generally accessible sources. Freedom of the press and freedom of reporting by means of broadcasts and films are guaranteed. There shall be no censorship. (2) These rights are limited by the provisions of general laws, the provisions of law for the protection of youth, and by the right to inviolability of personal honour. (3) Art and science, research and teaching, shall be free. Freedom of teaching shall not absolve from loyalty to the Constitution.'

recognizes freedom of expression as a fundamental freedom,[20] as does art 19(1)(a) of the Constitution of India.[21] In the Namibian Constitution 'freedom of speech and expression, which shall include freedom of the press and other media' is recognized as one of several fundamental freedoms in art 21.

## 3 SOME PHILOSOPHICAL AND POLICY CONSIDERATIONS REGARDING FREEDOM OF EXPRESSION AND ITS LIMITATION

If the question is asked why freedom of expression is regarded as being of such high importance, one simple answer could be that it is universally recognized as one of the most basic human rights. But why is it so widely recognized as a fundamental human right, at least in theory, even in societies where it hardly exists in practice and by those which are the least tolerant of views that differ from their own?

Numerous philosophers, lawyers, and ideologues have expressed opinions on the philosophical, ethical, and ideological underpinnings of freedom of expression and censorship and an extensive analysis is not possible within the limited scope of this contribution. Only some trends and considerations are pointed out and some guidelines offered.[22]

A number of arguments (some of which have from time to time been rejected as liberal bourgeois obfuscations) has been presented to explain the rationale behind the high ranking afforded to free expression by human rights advocates. One of these is the *quest for the truth* or *market-place of ideas* paradigm. It is argued that the expression of any idea or emotion, whether true, contentious or false, represents a potential contribution to humankind's ongoing search for the truth and its desire to understand the world. Without maximum freedom of expression, science, the arts, political wisdom, and indeed the human spirit cannot develop and progress is not possible. Even blatantly false statements could amount to a step forward in this process, if only in emphasizing what is not true and thus indirectly steering the cause closer to truthful or valuable discoveries. If scientists were prohibited from stating that the earth is round, because the state, the church, and the majority of the population thought it to be flat and therefore regarded their research as witchcraft, we would never have been able to realize that our planet is round. If the likes of Nietzsche could not attack conventional morality by shouting — through his weird and wonderful characters in *Also sprach Zarathustra* — that 'God' is dead and that we killed him because we made him the vehicle of our fears and inhibitions, Western thinking might not have been able to debate morality and to free itself from the Victorian age. If Voltaire and others did not ridicule the monarchy in pre-1789 France, we might not have come to experiment with democracy, and if the genius of Mozart were to be restricted to the mediocre standards of his contemporaries, music might not have developed as it did.

See in general Kommers *Constitutional Jurisprudence of the Federal Republic of Germany* (1989) 366 et seq, 505; Lepa *Der Inhalt der Grundrechte* 6 ed (1991) 111 et seq.

[20] 'Everyone has the following fundamental freedoms: . . . *(b)* freedom of thought, belief, opinion and expression, including freedom of the press and other media of communication.' See Beaudoin & Ratushny *The Canadian Charter of Rights and Freedoms* 2 ed by Carswell (1989) 195 et seq.

[21] 'All citizens shall have the right . . . to freedom of speech and expression.'

[22] As to philosophical and ideological considerations, see e g Meyerson ' "No Platform for Racists": What Should the View of Those on the Left Be?' (1990) 6 *SAJHR* 394; Suttner 'Freedom of Speech' (1990) 6 *SAJHR* 372; Sachs 'Towards a Bill of Rights in a Democratic South Africa' (1990) 6 *SAJHR* 13; Lloyd *The Idea of Law* (1981) 152–8; Tribe op cit (n 18) 785–9; Greenawalt 'Free Speech in the United States and Canada' (1992) 55 *Law and Contemporary Problems* 5; Van Rooyen *Censorship in South Africa* (1987) 1–4; Street *Freedom, the Individual and the Law* 5 ed (1982); Hogg *Constitutional Law of Canada* 3 ed (1992) 961–2.

The assumption that the prime reason for free speech is to ascertain the truth has to a large extent emanated from John Stuart Mill's *On Liberty* and has been carried forward by numerous eminent liberals. To suppress the expression of a view is regarded as harm to the quest for truth, or to claim infallibility, omniscience, or a monopoly on the truth. Different and opposing views must be permitted to compete in the market-place of ideas, from which the most valuable will emerge. In the US Judge Learned Hand stated that the First Amendment 'presupposes that right conclusions are more likely to be gathered out of a multitude of tongues, than through any kind of authoritative selection'.[23]

As a basic starting point the 'quest for the truth' argument is useful. To ignore the fact that where unpopular ideas are suppressed development cannot take place is dangerous. However, attempts to justify all expression on this basis, from serious art and science to racist hate speech and pornography, would appear artificial. Therefore the 'quest for the truth' paradigm has been subjected to serious criticism, also in South Africa. It is argued, for example, that racist views have been proved to have no merit and that there is no possibility that their suppression might be suppression of the truth.[24] The freedom to espouse any view whatsoever may also cater for the egotistic and individualistic interests of those who profit from an unequal and oppressive society.[25] Furthermore, it has been argued that the assumption that truth and progress will arise from competition in the market-place of ideas is closely connected to the capitalist mode of production. Like other commodities, ideas do not always win support in the market because of their intrinsic worth, but because of their appearance and presentation, which may conceal their true character and power. The wealthy also have more access to the most potent media of communication than the poor.[26] False and malicious propaganda could thus be allowed to go very far and to result in much harm before its fallacy is exposed by the mechanisms of a supposedly free market.[27] Free speech should not be viewed in abstract, supra-historical terms and the differing social context of various types of utterance should not be ignored, it is argued.[28] Furthermore, utterances often neither intend nor claim to present some truth or progress towards it, or even to

---

[23] *United States v Associated Press* 52 F Supp 362 at 372, quoted in *New York Times Co v Sullivan* 376 US 254. See in particular the dissenting opinion of Holmes J (joined by Brandeis J) in *Abrams v US* 250 US 616 (1919) within the context of state security. Also see e g Mill *On Liberty*, as well as discussions by Suttner op cit (n 22) 386–90 and Meyerson op cit (n 22) 394. George Bernard Shaw believed that all censorship exists to prevent anyone from challenging current conceptions and existing institutions and that all progress is initiated by challenging current conceptions. Consequently he stated that 'the first condition of progress is the removal of censorship' (in Preface to *Mrs Warren's Profession*, quoted by Stuart *The Newspaperman's Guide to the Law* 5 ed by Bell, Dewar & Hall (1990). See further Tribe op cit (n 18) 785–9.

[24] Meyerson op cit (n 22) 394. See also the Preamble of the International Convention on the Elimination of All Forms of Racial Discrimination, referred to again below, n 55. Because racism has had horrific consequences for humankind and in view of all available evidence, one could only agree. However, there might have been a time when many people firmly believed that claims that people were all equal had no merit at all, or that it had been conclusively proved that the earth was flat. Meyerson later (at 397–8) states that 'conservatives, not progressives, . . . appeal to revealed truth and the infallibility of authority, and . . . want the state to save us from false beliefs'. She wishes to put her faith in the route of 'democracy, debate, reason and autonomy' and believes that progressives 'ask for the truth by demonstration, not revelation, and . . . have always celebrated, not distrusted, thought'.

[25] This argument is discussed by Meyerson op cit (n 22) 394, with reference to Marx and others.

[26] Suttner op cit (n 22) 372; Tribe op cit (n 18) 786 (also referring to other powerful critiques of the market-place model).

[27] Millions of people may have to die in gas chambers or perish at the stake for the world to realize the evils of Nazism or of unfounded beliefs. On the other hand, it could be argued that these practices occurred not because such ideas were not suppressed timeously, but because the expression of opposing ideas and the free dissemination of information were not allowed.

[28] Suttner op cit (n 22) 372.

contain any intelligible thought or idea at all, and amount to the expression of emotions, such as fear, hatred, happiness, or sorrow, or are aimed at stimulating the senses of the party they are addressing, or even to insult or intimidate.

A second reason why freedom of speech and expression is regarded as important is because *speech is an expression of self*. The desire to communicate, to express one's feelings and thoughts, and to contribute to discussion and debate is an essential characteristic of human nature. Therefore freedom of expression is as fundamental a human right as the rights to privacy, religion, belief, and opinion, which are widely recognized in human rights thinking and literature, as well as in the South African Constitution.[29] Solitary confinement and other forms of isolation are well known to have serious psychological and other consequences. Normal human beings want to speak, sing, write, or display colours and insignia and believe that they have something to say in which others should be interested. To prevent a person from expressing a view, belief, or emotion is to deny his or her basic dignity, freedom, and individual autonomy as a human being and thus to violate the most basic human right of all, in Kantian terms.[30] This aspect is linked to the quest for the truth argument. Each individual has the right (and duty) to seek his or her own 'truth', whether it objectively exists or not, in order to develop as a human being. Unjustified restrictions on freedom of expression may thus also infringe other rights, such as freedom of opinion and conscience, as well as privacy. In this context the question whether all expression and utterances could indeed be regarded as *conversation*, or *communication*, or only those intending to convey ideas of some kind (instead of mere insults, threats, or displays aimed at arousing some emotional response) becomes relevant. It is submitted that any expression, verbal or otherwise, which is intended to be observed by one or more other person(s) and to stimulate some intellectual or emotional reaction, is a form of communication, even though it may not be 'speech'.[31]

A third reason for recognizing the importance of free expression, connected to and overlapping the previous two, is that it is *central to the concept and ideal of democracy*.[32] The Canadian Supreme Court pointed out in *Retail, Wholesale and Department Store Union, Local 580 v Dolphin Delivery Ltd* [33] that freedom of expression had not been created by the Charter of Rights and Freedoms, but that it was a fundamental concept which formed the basis of the historical development of the institutions of Western society, and stated:

'Representative democracy, as we know it today, which is in great part the product of free expression and discussion of varying ideas, depends upon its maintenance and protection.'

For a democracy to function, people need access to different viewpoints and policies in order to make choices. Not only political players but anyone who has something to say about socio-political and economic conditions must therefore be free to disclose his or her ideas and to promote perceived solutions. Numerous viewpoints indirectly contribute to the political sophistication of the electorate.

---

[29] Sections 13 and 14.
[30] See e g Kant *Metaphysische Anfangsgründe der Rechtslehre*, also translated as *The Metaphysical Elements of Justice* (by J Ladd) 43–4.
[31] The question also arises within the context of 'hate speech' and pornography, discussed below, 4.1 and 4.4.
[32] Marcus op cit (n 6) 140 mentions mainly this aspect when discussing the 'value of free expression', illustrating his point with references to the Canadian Supreme Court's above-mentioned opinion, as well as the opinion of the US Supreme Court in several cases.
[33] (1986) 33 DLR (4th) 174 (SCC) *per* McIntyre J.

Furthermore, the media must be able to investigate and disclose possible malpractices and abuse of power in an administration and relevant aspects of the professional and private conduct of those putting themselves forward as leaders. The public has a right to information, which is a widely recognized value in free and open societies. Moreover, other important human rights could not be struggled for and realized without the right to free expression, assembly, and association. This is true especially with regard to social and economic rights, which are not always explicitly recognized in Bills of Rights,[34] including the present South African one. These rights — and in particular housing or shelter, education, health care, and employment — are sometimes proclaimed to be more basic than first-generation civil and political rights. Freedom of the press or of the arts means little to the homeless, the illiterate, the starving, and the poor, so it is argued. But freedom of speech, the press, and even the arts is an indispensable tool in pointing out the illnesses and injustices of a society to the world and in campaigning for better education, housing, and health policies.

Freedom of expression thus enables a society to change peacefully. The US Supreme Court has referred to 'unfettered interchange of ideas for the bringing about of political and social changes desired by the people',[35] as well as 'free political discussion to the end that government may be responsive to the will of the people and that changes may be obtained by lawful means, an opportunity essential to the security of the Republic'.[36]

From the perspective of democracy the value of freedom of expression is not only based on the assumption that what people have to say may be true or useful. The constitutional protection of free expression 'does not turn upon "the truth, popularity, or social utility of the ideas and beliefs which are offered" ', the US Supreme Court has stated.[37] When people are free to speak and to campaign they feel that they are playing some role in their society. The perception of participation is created, which serves to legitimize a democratic political dispensation. To be free to express oneself is a recognition of one's dignity and relevance as a human being, even though one may not have much to say — just like the right to vote, even though one single vote is unlikely to influence the outcome of an election. The fact that the denial of free speech and of the right to vote is likely to lead to frustration, anger, and political turmoil — even amongst people who do not seem to care about these rights in a democratic situation — emphasizes this fact.[38]

As with other facets of democracy, the protection of free expression has its prizes and risks. Some degree of abuse is inseparable from the proper use of almost anything and in the case of freedom of expression and of the press this is all too often clear.[39] Furthermore, conceptions of democracy and freedom do of course

---

[34] See e g s 23 of Chapter 3 of the Constitution.

[35] *Roth v United States* 354 US 476, 484 (1957); *New York Times Co v Sullivan* (supra).

[36] *Stromberg v California* 283 US 359, 369; *New York Times Co v Sullivan* (supra). This assumption could involve a theoretical problem, connected to tests such as the 'clear and present danger' standard. See the discussion of hate speech and the advocacy of criminal conduct below, 4.1 and 4.2.

[37] *New York Times Co v Sullivan* (supra) at 270–1, quoting *NAACP v Button* 371 US 415, 445 (1963).

[38] The South African experience bears out this fact. See also the famous statement by Brandeis J in *Whitney v California* 274 US 357, 375–6 (1927):
'Those who won our independence believed . . . that it is hazardous to discourage thought, hope and imagination; that fear breeds repression; that repression breeds hate; that hate menaces stable government; that the path of safety lies in the opportunity to discuss freely supposed grievances and proposed remedies; and that the fitting remedy for evil counsels is good ones.'

[39] This was stated by Madison, quoted in *New York Times Co v Sullivan* (supra). The US Supreme Court also

differ, and some may ask why democracy, self-government, and political participation are to be valued so highly in the first place.[40]

So, it would seem that all of the above three explanations — and several other possible models — look attractive in some ways, but flawed in others. An adequate conception and satisfactory jurisprudence of freedom of expression must draw upon several strands of theory in order to protect a rich variety of modes of expression.[41]

Accepting that freedom of expression as a fundamental right is highly valued from several possible perspectives, but that it is not absolute, the question is when and how it may be limited, as a matter of general policy and also in the context of the spirit of the Constitution. This confronts one with the concept of censorship.[42] Here the issue is not only 'where to draw the line', or what standards or which yardstick to use, but also who is to decide what others are allowed to say, write, sing, hear, see, or read. As far as state control is concerned, two possibilities are normally distinguished: direct control by the criminal law, and administrative control backed up by the criminal law. As a matter of principle the criminal law and the ordinary courts are preferable. The relevant criminal statute normally requires intent on the part of an accused. Furthermore, an administrative board or similar organ is appointed by the executive, often on conditions which hardly encourage independence (such as that members are remunerated per case, and that they have to be re-appointed every few years).[43] On the other hand, it is sometimes argued that censorship frequently involves questions of taste which are not easily dealt with by legal machinery. The English experience, for example, also suggests that the courts are not necessarily more liberal than an administrative organ. An administrative system is aimed at the direct and immediate banning of material or sometimes at the classification of material, whereas the criminal law aims at holding specific perpetrators accountable, thereby deterring others from engaging in the same conduct.[44] Although an administrative system may be desirable in specific areas, the manner in which decisions to prohibit publications or other matter is reached will have to meet the requirements of natural justice contained in s 24 of the Constitution. The cornerstone of administrative censorship in South Africa, the Publications Act 42 of 1974, is likely to fall short of these requirements.[45]

In addition to statutory censorship, self-control by an industry is also possible.[46] Its relation to the Constitution depends inter alia on the so-called horizontal application of the chapter on fundamental rights.

---

stated that 'it is a prized American privilege to speak one's mind, although not always with perfect good taste' (in *Bridges v California* 314 US 252 (1941), referred to in *New York Times Co v Sullivan* (supra)).

[40] See e g Suttner op cit (n 22) 372. See also Tribe op cit (n 18) 787.

[41] Tribe op cit (n 18) 789; Hogg op cit (n 22) 961–2.

[42] In its usual sense the term 'censorship' indicates all legal restrictions proclaimed by state authority. It could also refer to voluntary restrictions, or non-statutory control, by the relevant industry. See Van Rooyen in Joubert (ed) *LAWSA* vol 2 'Censorship' 55.

[43] This has been the case in South Africa with the Directorate of Publications and the Publications Appeal Board, in terms of ss 2, 4, and 35 of the Publications Act 42 of 1974.

[44] Lloyd op cit (n 22) 155. Van Rooyen op cit (n 22) 5, from his perspective as the chairman of the Publications Appeal Board, prefers an administrative process, because it is more effective in banning material and because a process before a criminal court is often too slow. He also regards the administrative process as 'less personal' because the material and not the producer thereof is dealt with.

[45] This submission by Marcus (1990) 10 *SAJHR* 140 at 143 is probably correct. He particularly refers to the decision-making procedure of Publications Committees.

[46] A system of non-statutory control or self-censorship is normally based on an agreement between members of an industry inter alia to accept and act in accordance with a code of conduct. The Press Council and the Broadcasting Complaints Commission of South Africa (BCCSA) of the National Association of Broadcasters (NAB) are

Different areas of speech and expression have widely different connotations and requirements as far as legal limitations are concerned. In view of the considerations discussed above, a few basic and tentative guidelines could be offered:

- The starting point and guiding principle should be that freedom of expression is a fundamental human right, explicitly recognized and guaranteed by the Constitution. Any curtailment thereof has to be clear and precise as to what is expressly forbidden and has to be interpreted narrowly in conformity with the limitation clause.[47] In South Africa's pre-constitutionalism jurisprudence an interesting reference point is to be found in the minority judgment of Rumpff JA in *Publications Control Board v William Heinemann Ltd*[48] (dealing with the banning of Wilbur Smith's book *When the Lion Feeds*): it should be assumed that the legislature in every case where liberty is repressed intends to do so 'only to such extent as it in clear terms declares, and . . . only to such extent as is absolutely necessary'.

- In response to the question whether moral values ought to be enforced by law, it must be accepted that law cannot be separated entirely from morality and from politics. Legal mechanisms are often used to support and strengthen the moral and political values on which a society is believed to be based. It is not undemocratic legally to protect some measure of public morality. However, claims that public morality is indeed at stake have to be treated with circumspection. Furthermore, although a society may have the right to insist on some conformity for the sake of its own existence, it is immoral to force the religious and moral preferences and prejudices of one group upon others. Moreover, intervention by the law must be necessary in the sense that public condemnation is clearly insufficient. It must not be forgotten that — in spite of the earlier-mentioned misgivings about the 'market-place of ideas' model — much could be achieved without the law if individuals and groups in a vibrant civil society actively used their freedom of expression, assembly, and demonstration.[49]

- In the formulation of legal restrictions of free expression, open-ended concepts

examples. As far as the film industry is concerned, the outcome is often a system of classification in order to warn viewers, rather than the banning of films. The Motion Picture Association of America and the British Broadcasting Classification Committee are examples.

[47] The contents and application of s 33 are referred to above, 1. Van Rooyen op cit (n 42) 55 reiterates the statement by Van der Vyver that in South African law a person's rights and competencies extend to all acts and actions not prohibited or restricted by law. Residual freedoms are thus provided for: everything is permitted which is not expressly forbidden. The Constitution now strengthens this approach (as opposed to one where a person is taken to possess only those rights and competencies granted by law). In US law the twin doctrines of *vagueness* and *overbreadth* have in several areas of free speech been used to strike down ordinances. See e g *Hynes v Mayor* 425 US 610 (1976); Emanuel op cit (n 18) 435–42; Tribe op cit (n 18) 1022.

[48] 1965 (4) SA 137 (A) at 160. The full quotation at 160E–G reads as follows:
'The freedom of speech — which includes the freedom to print — is a facet of civilization which always presents two well-known inherent traits. The one consists of the constant desire by some to abuse it. The other is the inclination of those who want to protect it to repress more than is necessary. The latter is also fraught with danger. It is based on intolerance and is a symptom of the primitive urge in mankind to prohibit that with which one does not agree. When a court of law is called upon to decide whether liberty should be repressed — in this case the freedom to publish a story — it should be anxious to steer a course as close to the preservation of liberty as possible. It should do so because freedom of speech is a hard-won and precious asset, yet easily lost. And in its approach to the law, including any statute by which the court may be bound, it should assume that Parliament, itself a product of political liberty, in every case intends liberty to be repressed only to such extent as it in clear terms declares, and, if it gives a discretion to a court of law, only to such extent as is absolutely necessary.'

[49] As to the enforcement of morality by law, the so-called Hart–Devlin debate, with the later contribution by Ronald Dworkin, is well known. See Mill *On Liberty* in general; Lord Devlin *The Enforcement of Morals* (1959); Hart *Law, Liberty and Morality* (1961); Dworkin *Taking Rights Seriously* (1977) 240–65.

such as 'offensiveness' and 'indecency' must be avoided. 'Offensiveness', for example, can easily be used as a vehicle to deal with material which is regarded as unpopular, unpleasant, or disagreeable. Furthermore, political statements in a robust debate or the serious questioning of religious beliefs or practices can offend people and great examples of artistic expression are in fact often intended to do so. As a general rule some demonstration of likely *harm* should be required in order to justify the curtailment of free speech. This does not necessarily have to be concrete harm to particular persons directly affected by the practice in question, or harm which can be proved by evidence acceptable in a court of law. It may consist of some effect on social customs and institutions which seriously influences the social environment in a negative way, and thus affects all or some members of a society indirectly. In determining the significance of such influences the history of a society is a relevant factor, as explained below.

- In considering whether a particular limitation of free expression is reasonable and justifiable in an open and democratic society based on freedom and equality the underlying reasons for the recognition and protection of free speech should be taken note of. As indicated above, many of these relate to the free flow of ideas, which is necessary to enhance democracy, to enable the members of a society to function as dignified and equal human beings, and to strive towards progress. Freedom of expression is not only abused by overstepping the limits of decency or good taste, or by spreading half- or untruths. It is also abused by forces for whom its protection was not intended in the first place, including those who are bent on destroying or undermining democracy instead of enhancing it and on eradicating the equality and liberty of others, rather than on fostering tolerance and discourse. According to German constitutional theory, such forces could forfeit their fundamental rights, according to the principle of 'militant democracy'. History has proved that a democratic system has to defend itself proactively, instead of being destroyed because of its own passive tolerance.[50]

- Finally, the constitutional protection and limitation of freedom of expression has to be interpreted within the context of appreciating where our society comes from and where we want it to go. Today we strive for equality and freedom, openness, reconciliation, and tolerance, and aim to become a truly exemplary democracy in Africa and the world. In doing so we are conscious of a history of denial of these values, of race discrimination, sexism, an obsession with secrecy in the face of perceived onslaughts, and state censorship aimed not only at preserving white minority rule but also at enforcing the morality of a small group by the instrument of the law.[51]

---

[50] Expression may thus have to be limited, in 'self-defence', to protect freedom of expression. See also the discussion of hate speech below, 4.1. As to the concept of 'militant democracy', see Kommers op cit (n 19) 43–4; Hesse *Grundzüge des Verfassungsrechts der Bundesrepublik Deutschland* 17 ed (1990) 694, 714.

[51] On censorship in South Africa, see Van Rooyen op cit (n 22); Van der Westhuizen 'Do We Have to be Calvinist Puritans to Enter the New South Africa?' (1990) 6 *SAJHR* 425; Marcus 'The Wider Reaches of Censorship' (1985) 1 *SAJHR* 69; Haysom & Marcus ' "Undesirability" and Criminal Liability under the Publications Act of 1974' (1985) 1 *SAJHR* 31; Van der Vyver 'Censorship in South Africa by JCW van Rooyen' (1988) 21 *De Jure* 182; Van Rooyen 'Censorship in a Future South Africa: A Legal Perspective' (1993) 26 *De Jure* 283. As far as South Africa's censorship history is concerned, it is also true that the media have enjoyed considerably more freedom than in many other countries and that significant breakthroughs were from time to time achieved in litigation under the Publications Act 42 of 1974.

## 4 SOME SPECIFIC AREAS OF EXPRESSION

### 4.1 Political propaganda and racial hate speech

The considerations underlying the treatment of what is known as 'hate speech' are relevant to several other areas of expression. It is an area where the tension between liberty and equality is particularly relevant. One of South Africa's greatest challenges is to achieve racial harmony and reconciliation after a history of apartheid and struggle. Therefore we hardly need racial bigotry, insults, and threats in our public life. On the other hand, the political debate must be an open and a robust one, which is bound to revolve around race and class differences. People need to be able to vent their frustration, anger, and aspirations in order to achieve a mature democracy. South Africa is likely therefore to have legal restrictions aimed at preventing incitement to racial hatred, as it has had for several decades.[52]

The only law presently on the statute book aimed at restricting racist propaganda or hate speech is s 62 of the Internal Security Act 74 of 1982, stating that any person who utters words or performs any other act with intent to cause, encourage, or foment feelings of hostility between different population groups or parts of population groups of the Republic shall be guilty of an offence and liable on conviction to a fine, imprisonment, or to both such fine and such imprisonment. Other statutory provisions dealing with harm to relations between different sections of the population or bringing a section of the population into ridicule or contempt have recently been abolished.[53]

The need to prevent incitement of racial hatred is recognized in international human rights law as well as in the legal systems of several countries. For example, art 20 of the International Covenant on Civil and Political Rights states:

> '1 Any propaganda for war shall be prohibited by law.
> 2 Any advocacy of national, racial or religious hatred that constitutes incitement to discrimination, hostility or violence shall be prohibited by law.'

Article 4 of the International Convention on the Elimination of All Forms of Racial Discrimination[54] proclaims that state parties shall, amongst other things,

> '[d]eclare an offence punishable by law all dissemination of ideas based on racial superiority or hatred, incitement to racial discrimination, as well as all acts of violence or incitement to such acts against any race group or group of persons of another colour or ethnic origin'.[55]

The US goes further than any other country in affording protection to hate speech.

---

[52] Marcus op cit (n 6) 147 correctly points out that it is ironic that such laws should exist in a country where government policy and practice, more than anything else, has been responsible for inflaming racial passions.

[53] Section 29 of the Black Administration Act 38 of 1927 dealt with the promotion of feelings of hostility between race groups. It provided for the prevention of dissemination of certain doctrines amongst blacks by stating that any person who utters words or does any other act or thing with intent to promote any feeling of hostility between 'Blacks' and 'Europeans' shall be guilty of an offence. Section 47(2) of the Publications Act of 1974 provided for the banning of publications, objects, films, public entertainment, or intended public entertainment if such material was 'undesirable', inter alia if it or any part of it '(c) brings any section of the inhabitants of the Republic into ridicule or contempt; (d) is harmful to the relations between any sections of the inhabitants of the Republic'. Following debates at the Multi-Party Negotiating Process, these provisions were repealed by the Abolition of Restriction on Free Political Activity Act 206 of 1993. With regard to the past application of s 47(2)(c) and (d) of the Publications Act, see e g Van Rooyen op cit (n 42) 69–70 and op cit (n 22) 99–105.

[54] Adopted by General Assembly Resolution 2106A (XX) of 21 December 1965.

[55] It furthermore states that 'States Parties condemn all propaganda and all organizations which are based on ideas or theories of superiority of one race or group of persons of one colour or ethnic origin, or which attempt to justify or promote racial hatred and discrimination in any form and undertake to adopt immediate and positive measures designed to eradicate' such acts and organizations. States parties also agree to declare illegal and to prohibit organizations which promote and incite racial discrimination.

US case law on the issue is well known. One of the most prominent cases is the *Skokie* ruling, which affirmed the right of Nazis to march on a public street in a suburb populated by Jewish concentration camp survivors.[56] In *Brandenburg v Ohio*[57] the right of the Ku Klux Klan publicly to call for the expulsion of blacks and Jews in harsh language[58] was upheld. A state is not permitted to forbid or proscribe advocacy of the use of force or of law violation, except where such advocacy 'is directed to inciting or producing imminent lawless action and is likely to incite or produce such action'.

In other decisions so-called 'fighting words' have emerged as an unprotected category of speech. Fighting words, i e words which are likely to make the person to whom they are addressed commit an act of violence, receive no First Amendment protection because they are not normally part of any 'dialogue' or 'exposition of ideas', although the Supreme Court seems to keep this exclusion within tightly circumscribed bounds.[59] Groups interested in eliminating discrimination against minorities have recently argued that hate speech directed at minorities which have traditionally been disfavoured or discriminated against should be treated exceptionally. This debate has centred on hate speech on campus, a number of universities having enacted codes that inhibit speech expressing hatred or bias towards certain groups. The US Supreme Court found that such a code is not necessarily unconstitutional solely on the ground of its contents, but that it may be overbroad and impermissibly vague under specific circumstances.[60]

Some instances of symbolic expression are particularly relevant within the context of political statements or propaganda. The US Supreme Court has held, for example, that the prohibition of the wearing of black armbands in schools violated the First Amendment rights of students.[61] In view of South African controversies regarding national symbols, the way flag desecration is dealt with is of some relevance. Nearly all states, as well as the federal government, make it a crime to mutilate or otherwise desecrate an US flag. These statutes are aimed at preserving the flag as a symbol of national unity. In *Texas v Johnson*[62] the Supreme Court, by a 5–4 vote in an agonizing opinion, held that a statute to the above-mentioned effect violated the First Amendment, after Johnson had burnt a US flag and chanted (with others who participated in a political demonstration): 'America, the red, white, and blue, we spit on you.' When the US Congress immediately afterwards tried to ban flag-burning the Flag Protection Act of 1989 was also found to be a violation of the First Amendment in a second highly controversial decision.[63]

---

[56] *Smith v Collin* 439 US 916 (1978).
[57] 395 US 444 (1969), especially at 447.
[58] Phrases such as 'there might have to be some revenge taken', Jews should be 'returned to Israel', and a call to '[b]ury the niggers' were used. As another example of rather vile expression of hatred, where white youths burned a cross on the property of a black family, see *RAV v City of St Paul* 112 SCt 2538 (1992).
[59] See *Chaplinsky v New Hampshire* 315 US 568 (1942). In *Cox v Louisiana (Cox I)* 379 US 536 (1965) it was decided that wherever the police have the physical ability to control an angry crowd, as a means of preventing threatened violence, they must do so in preference to arresting the speaker for using 'fighting words'.
[60] *Doe v University of Michigan* 721 F Supp 852 (ED Mich 1989); Emanuel op cit (n 18) 458–60.
[61] *Tinker v Des Moines School District* 393 US 503 (1969). On the other hand, the conviction in terms of a law making it a crime to destroy or mutilate draft cards in public was upheld in *US v O'Brien* (supra). See Emanuel op cit (n 18) 461–7 and, with regard to the 'two-track approach' followed by the courts, Tribe op cit (n 18) 785.
[62] 491 US 397 (1989).
[63] *US v Eichman* 110 SCt 2404 (1990).

Several reasons have been put forward for the uniquely far-reaching protection afforded to hate speech in the US. The principle that limitations on free speech may not be based on disapproval of the content of the speech is at the heart of US constitutional law. A concession on the banning of racist speech may lead to a 'slippery slope' as far as all currently unpopular speech is concerned and further exceptions may be demanded. Another reason is rooted in the exceptional nature of US political culture. Unlike many other nations, the US has been relatively unthreatened by the serious social conflict that has moved several societies to outlaw 'hate speech'. In fact the very freedom to express one's opinion on almost everything and everyone in the strongest terms often seems to play an important role in holding together the many diverse components of US society.[64]

Germany has a different history and German law follows a more restrictive approach. As far as constitutional interpretation is concerned, the 'unity of the Constitution' and its 'hierarchy of values' are guiding principles. Freedom of expression is seen to operate within an interrelated set of other fundamental rights, liberties, rules, and standards and has to be reconciled with the rights and liberties of other persons and groups and social values recognized by the Constitution.[65] The fundamental rights of citizens may be limited or even forfeited in terms of art 18 of the Constitution if used to destroy the democratic constitutional order. Whereas art 21.1 establishes the principle that secures to all political parties the freedom to organize and mobilize the electorate, this freedom is limited by art 21.2. Parties which seek to impair or abolish the free democratic basic order shall be unconstitutional.[66] As far as free speech is concerned, the German Criminal Code prohibits attacks on the human dignity of individuals and groups, as well as incitement of racial hatred.[67]

Unlike the US, the democratic order is perceived to be more endangered by inflammatory racist propaganda in Germany because of its history. A Nazi march through the streets of Skokie may be extremely offensive, but is unlikely to gain many followers or to cause a riot. The situation might have been different in Berlin, especially shortly after World War II or the fall of the Wall. Viewed cynically, an acceptance of this reality could mean that free expression is a fundamental right, but that it can only be allowed in situations where it is unlikely to have any effect, while it has to be banned as soon as it could be taken seriously.[68] And is maximum free expression only affordable in a mature democracy, or does a society become a mature democracy by allowing maximum free expression?

---

[64] As to hate speech in the US in general, see Tribe op cit (n 18) 841–56; Emanuel op cit (n 18) 423–42; Abrams 'Hate Speech: The Present Implications of a Historical Dilemma' (1992) 37 *Villanova LR* 743; Greenawalt op cit (n 22) 5; Cammack & Davies 'Should Hate Speech be Prohibited in Law Schools?' (1991) 20 *Southwestern U LR* 145; Brownstein 'Regulating Hate Speech at Public Universities: Are First Amendment Values Functionally Incompatible with Equal Protection Principles?' (1991) 39 *Buffalo U LR* 1; McGowan & Tangri 'A Libertarian Critique of University Restrictions of Offensive Speech' (1991) 79 *California LR* 825.

[65] See e g Kommers op cit (n 19) 366–8.

[66] See Van der Westhuizen 'The Protection of Human Rights and a Constitutional Court for South Africa: Some Questions and Ideas, with Reference to the German Experience' (1991) 24 *De Jure* 1 and 245 at 251–2. The principle involved is referred to as *'streitbare Demokratie'* or 'militant democracy', which was mentioned above, 3. For a recent opinion of the European Commission of Human Rights regarding dismissal from the civil service of a Communist Party member, see *Dorothea Vogt v Germany*, 30/11/1993, Application No 17851/91.

[67] Articles 130 and 131 of the *Strafgesetzbuch* prohibits *'Volksverhetzung'*, *'Verherrlichung von Gewalt'*, and *'Aufstachelung zum Rassenhass'*.

[68] See below, 4.2, where the 'clear and present danger test' as well as 'ineffective speech' are discussed.

In Canada the most relevant decision is *R v Keegstra*.[69] A high-school teacher communicated anti-semitic teachings to his students in the classroom and was convicted of the public wilful promotion of group hatred in terms of s 319(2) of the Criminal Code. The Alberta Court of Appeal held that although deliberate lies are not protected by s *2(b)* of the Charter of Rights and Freedoms, innocently or negligently made hate speech is. Although s 319(2) had the valid legislative object of preventing harm to the reputation and psychological well-being of target group members, it was unconstitutional because greater harm, such as proof of actual hatred being caused as a result of the impugned expression, was necessary to require the sanction of criminal law.[70] The Supreme Court decided that s *2(b)* permitted context-based restrictions only if the speech is communicated in a physically violent form; that even threats of violence are within the scope of the section's protection; and that legislation prohibiting the public, wilful promotion of group hatred infringed the Charter's guarantee of free speech, because it was an attempt to prohibit communication conveying meaning. However, by a majority of four to three, the court held that under s 1 of the Charter the infringement was a limit demonstrably justifiable in a free and democratic society and that the relevant provision could be upheld.[71]

The arguments and international trends referred to, as well as several voices in the South African debate, seem to indicate that legislation to prevent or limit hate propaganda is called for.[72] To prohibit hate speech or propaganda mainly because it brings a population group 'into ridicule or contempt'[73] or because it is offensive to individuals or groups seems to be unreasonably vague and restrictive. On the other hand, to require the advocacy of racial hatred to be *intended* or *directed* to invite or produce imminent violence, lawless action, or other similar harm *as well as the likelihood of in fact producing such harm*[74] would be ineffective. To prohibit hate speech when it is *intended* to undermine or destroy the underlying values justifying the protection of freedom of expression, namely the *democratic process*, the *free and equal co-existence of human beings* and the *enhancement of knowledge and exchange of ideas* is not unreasonable or unjustifiable in a democratic society based on freedom and equality.[75]

As far as the contents of s 62 of the Internal Security Act (referred to above) are concerned, it has to be noted that a criminal sanction (instead of an administrative banning procedure) is provided for and the intention to bring about hostility between different population groups is required. In principle this provision may not be too far off the mark. Whether the Internal Security Act, which carries with it some

---

[69] (1990) 3 SCR 697. See e g Mahoney 'The Canadian Approach to Freedom of Expression in Hate Propaganda and Pornography' 1992 (55) *Law and Contemporary Problems* 77. See also Beaudoin & Ratushny op cit (n 20) 215–17; Hogg op cit (n 22) 974–5.

[70] *R v Keegstra* (supra).

[71] Section 1 states that the rights and freedoms set out in the Charter are guaranteed 'subject only to such reasonable limits prescribed by law as can be demonstrably justified in a free and democratic society'.

[72] See e g the Constitutional Guidelines of the African National Congress, as well as the organization's draft Bill of Rights published in 1990 and amended in 1993. See also Meyerson, Suttner, and Sachs, all op cit (n 22), as well as the guidelines proposed by these authors. Furthermore, see Van Rooyen op cit (n 51) 291.

[73] Section 47(2)*(c)* of the Publications Act of 1974.

[74] In accordance with *Brandenburg v Ohio* (supra).

[75] Robust arguments and statements, which may even amount to hate speech, may thus qualify for protection if intended e g to contribute to the political debate. In terms of s 33(1)*(b)* the limitation of a right which relates to free political activity must also be *necessary* in addition to being reasonable and justifiable.

historical baggage, is the proper place for such a provision or whether it ought to be accommodated in race-relations, anti-discrimination, or civil rights legislation, is another question.

## 4.2 The advocacy of illegal conduct; state security

Much of what has been said with regard to hate speech also applies to the soliciting of criminal conduct or other crime-related speech, and in particular speech of this nature in the sphere of state security. Historically the massive suppression of freedom of speech, association, and assembly under the banner of state security in South Africa has dwarfed many other concerns. It is common cause that the draconian constellation of 'security legislation' was necessary to sustain the undemocratic and inhuman apartheid system. Therefore it is to be hoped that the situation will be more 'normal' in a democratic situation. However, South Africa's racial and class divisions as well as its political history are not favourable to the immediate blossoming of a conflict-free society. Concerns about national security and crime prevention will have to be addressed within the new constitutional framework.

The Internal Security Act 74 of 1982 has had a profound impact on journalism and free political expression in South Africa.[76] In addition, debate on and the publication of information related to defence, official secrets, and strategic matters have been and are regulated by several statutes.[77] The Correctional Services Act 8 of 1959, the Police Act 7 of 1958, and the Mental Health Act 18 of 1973 furthermore impose restrictions on publications.[78] Many of the restrictions contained in these statutes certainly address legitimate concerns and are not unreasonable or unjustifiable in open and democratic societies. Some are in need of thorough reform, but the detail cannot be addressed in this contribution.

The Publications Act 42 of 1974 still contains a provision related to state security. Section 47(2)(e) provides that matter is deemed to be undesirable if it is prejudicial to the safety of the state, general welfare, or peace and good order. The formulation is vague and open to arbitrariness and it includes conduct which forms part of the democratic process in many societies, thus inhibiting free political activity.

The need for controlled and reasonable security and emergency measures is internationally recognized. Therefore a comparative perspective is useful. The jurisprudence of the US Supreme Court with regard to security and the advocacy of illegal conduct has influenced numerous other legal systems. The first and best known in a long series of decisions was *Schenk v US* [79] in 1919, in which Holmes J advanced both his now famous 'clear and present danger' test and the 'crying "Fire!" in a theatre' example to illustrate that not all speech was constitutionally protected. The defendants were convicted of conspiracy to violate the Espionage Act of 1917 as a result of sending a document advocating peaceful measures to ensure the repeal of the Conscription Act. In the opinion of Holmes J the question

---

[76] See e g Stuart op cit (n 23) 123–42.

[77] e g the Defence Act 44 of 1957, the Post Office Act 44 of 1958, the Armaments Development and Production Act 57 of 1968, the Protection of Information Act 84 of 1982, the National Supplies Procurement Act 89 of 1970, the National Key Points Act 102 of 1980, the Petroleum Products Act 120 of 1977, and the Nuclear Energy Act 92 of 1982. See Stuart op cit (n 23) 144–59.

[78] Stuart op cit (n 23) 161–73.

[79] 249 US 47 (1919).

was 'whether the words used are used in such circumstances and are of such a nature as to create a clear and present danger that they will bring about the substantial evils that Congress have a right to prevent'. Whether the defendants' conduct did in fact pose such a danger was a factual question. Speech could be punished as an attempt to commit an illegal act if it created a clear and present danger that the illegal act would come about, even if the act never in fact occurred. Speech of this nature is not privileged, just as falsely crying 'Fire!' in a crowded theatre is not.[80]

In several cases thereafter the 'clear and present danger' doctrine was further reiterated by Holmes and others until it was generally followed.[81] Modifications and refinements also occurred. In *Abrams v US*,[82] for example, the question was whether the defendants (American socialists of Russian-Jewish birth) had the required intent to interfere with the war effort against Germany when they published Bolshevik leaflets. The majority of the court held that the defendants' primary purpose might have been only to end the Russian revolution, but that one must be held to have intended the effects which one's acts are likely to produce. In his dissent (joined by Brandeis J), Holmes J found that a consequence is not intended unless that consequence is the aim of the deed. In the best-known part of his dissenting judgment, he articulated the (earlier-mentioned) 'market-place of ideas' or 'free trade of ideas' theory and argued that even opinions which one loathes and believes to be fraught with death should not be suppressed. In *Whitney v California*[83] Brandeis J (this time joined by Holmes J) eloquently reiterated the 'clear and present danger' test and found that only the court, not the legislature, could determine whether a particular utterance posed such a danger. During and immediately after World War II the application of the Smith Act of 1940 showed signs of the influence of fears of an international communist threat. In *Dennis v US*,[84] for example, the court theoretically applied the 'clear and present danger' standard, but in a manner affording considerably less protection under the First Amendment, representing a 'temporary eclipse of the Holmes–Brandeis formulation of the . . . test'.[85] After *Dennis* some of the protection was given back in other decisions.[86]

The 'clear and present danger' test has also been criticized. One argument is that it relies upon the factfinder's opinion about the immediacy of the specific threat, which makes political speech vulnerable to mass paranoia in a time of national crisis, which may be stirred up by the government of the day. Another interesting point of criticism, related to the above discussion of democracy and hate speech, is that ineffectiveness is rewarded. Speech is only permissible as long as it is ineffective, it is argued, which seems peculiar in view of the fact that the protection of free speech is regarded as essential in order to bring about political and social change!

---

[80] The example is not entirely appropriate, of course. The false cry of 'Fire!' is understood by its listeners to be a statement of fact, which leaves little time for consideration or rebuttal, whereas the advocacy of measures to resist legislation is an opinion which could be debated and rejected.

[81] See e g the two opinions by Holmes J for a unanimous court in *Frohwerk v US* 249 US 204 (1919) and *Debs v US* 249 US 211 (1919); *Abrams v US* 250 US 616 (1919); *Gitlow v New York* 268 US 652 (1925); and especially *Herndon v Lowry* 301 US 242 (1937). In a pre-*Schenk* decision, *Masses Publishing Co v Patten* 244 F 535 (SDNY 1917), Justice Learned Hand focused solely on the words spoken, and not on the surrounding circumstances and believed that words could be punished if they counsel or advise others to violate the law, making the likely effects of the speech completely irrelevant.

[82] 250 US 616 (1919).

[83] 274 US 357 (1927).

[84] 341 US 494 (1951).

[85] Tribe op cit (n 18) 846.

[86] e g *Yates v US* 354 US 298 (1957).

The courts seem to be most willing to protect free expression at times when it is the least needed. It is easier to allow 'the surreptitious publishing of a silly leaflet by an unknown man' which poses no danger at all and proudly to claim to do so in the name of free speech,[87] than powerful political statements likely to have a real influence on events. It is not an all or nothing situation, however. Speech which falls short of inciting or producing imminent violence or other illegal behaviour or of an onslaught on an existing democratic order may still be highly relevant and influential in a process of social and political change, and it is this category which merits protection. A balance obviously has to be struck and the temptation which has to be resisted is to mistake harsh criticism and robust political attacks for a 'clear and present danger'.

The modern standard applied by the US Supreme Court, which affords greater protection to free speech than ever before, in a situation where the American nation is believed to be relatively free of the dangers of foreign infiltration or the destruction of democracy, is best expressed in *Brandenburg v Ohio*,[88] mentioned earlier in the discussion of 'hate speech'.

The 'clear and present danger' doctrine is not unknown in South Africa. It was often put forward in arguments before the Publications Appeal Board in cases dealing with s 47(2)*(e)* of the Publications Act of 1974, and it has been claimed that the Board held itself guided by this standard, thereby handing down some significant pro-free expression decisions while applying a potentially draconian piece of legislation.[89] US jurisprudence in this regard is likely to have a significant influence on future South African developments.[90]

### 4.3 Religion

Freedom of religion and belief is a very fundamental human right, recognized in the Constitution of South Africa and many other states, as well as under international human rights law.[91] The protection and practice of religion can overlap with and complement freedom of expression. However, it can also provide an excuse for the abuse of free expression or compete with freedom of expression. A speaker who incites racial hatred or advocates criminal conduct in the name of religion will not be able to do so under the protection of free speech, as indicated above.[92] On the other hand, insistence on protecting the religious feelings of citizens may result in the limitation of free expression.

Blasphemy is a common-law criminal offence. It consists of the unlawful and intentional publication of words or conduct whereby God is slandered, or contempt is shown towards God.[93] Even in pre-constitutional legal thinking the trend has been

---

[87] Holmes J described the alleged criminal conduct in *Abrams v US* (supra) with these words.

[88] Supra. See above, 4.1. See also in general Tribe op cit (n 18) ch 12; Emanuel op cit (n 18) 423–42; Leader 'Free Speech and the Advocacy of Illegal Action in Law and Political Theory' 1982 (82) *Columbia LR* 412; Atkey 'Reconciling Freedom of Expression and National Security' (1991) 41 *U Toronto LJ* 38.

[89] From the reasoning of the Board's judgments it is not always clear to what extent the doctrine was followed, but it certainly influenced its thinking. See Van Rooyen op cit (n 42) 70 and Heyns *A Jurisprudential Analysis of Civil Disobedience in South Africa* (unpublished PhD thesis, University of the Witwatersrand 1992) 375.

[90] Marcus op cit (n 6) 145.

[91] See s 14 of the Constitution. See also in general Van der Westhuizen & Heyns 'A Legal Perspective on Religious Freedom' in Kilian *Religious Freedom in South Africa* (1993) 93; Sachs *Protecting Human Rights in a New South Africa* (1990) 43.

[92] See above, 4.1 and 4.2.

[93] *R v Webb* 1934 AD 493 at 496–7.

to interpret this crime restrictively in modern circumstances, as opposed to the position held by common-law writers such as Van der Linden and Van Leeuwen. The mere denial of God's existence or the expression of a *bona fide* opinion about the attributes of God, for example, does not amount to blasphemy.[94] In view of the constitutional protection of free speech, as well as s 35(3), a very restrictive interpretational approach will have to be followed, perhaps to the extent of rendering the crime of blasphemy virtually obsolete.

South Africa is generally regarded as a very religious society and continuing pressure to prohibit free speech which hurts religious feelings by way of administrative censorship can therefore be expected. Section 47(2)*(b)* of the Publications Act of 1974 has thus far provided the mechanism by providing for the banning of material as 'undesirable' when it, or any part of it, is blasphemous or offensive to the religious convictions or feelings of a section of the population. Under this provision films such as *The Last Temptation of Christ* and books such as Rushdie's *The Satanic Verses* and André Brink's *Kennis van die Aand* were banned, and numerous scenes and especially pieces of dialogue (such as exclamations of 'Jesus' and 'Christ') were excised from films and plays by the Publications Appeal Board or Publications Committees, in spite of claims that a restrictive interpretation was given to the concept of 'offensiveness'. The impression was often created that censorship in religious matters was tightened whenever changes on the political front were introduced by the ruling establishment, perhaps in order to pacify conservatives. However, the continuing liberalization in the field of religion, which is obvious when listening to the dialogue in modern films widely available on the cinema circuit, illustrates the unsustainability of religious censorship of this kind.[95]

It is submitted that s 47(2)*(b)* will not survive constitutional scrutiny. First, in providing for the banning of material which is found to be 'blasphemous' (which does not easily happen, in view of the criminal-law position) or 'offensive' it is once again too vague, open-ended, and arbitrary. Secondly, the constitutional protection of freedom of religion and belief in s 14 could hardly be interpreted to include the right of the state to curb the fundamental right to freedom of expression of others in order to protect religious people against being offended. Because of the very nature of religion, discussions thereof and attacks on or the questioning of practices of religious groups are bound to be viewed as offensive by those who disagree. Yet for the very reason that religion is so fundamental to human nature and has such a profound influence on social policy it needs to be debated publicly. Any attempt at limiting freedom of expression in the interests of protecting religion will have to be formulated with great care and caution.

A related and perhaps more complex problem is presented by the phenomenon that the publication of material which is deemed to be blasphemous or offensive can sometimes solicit such a strong and even violent reaction from fundamentalist groups that something akin to a 'clear and present danger' to the peace could in fact be on hand. One possibility is to deal with such material within the context of state security and crime prevention, or even hate speech, but those whose work tends to

---

[94] See e g *Brandwagpers (Edms) Bpk v Raad van Beheer oor Publikasies* 1975 (2) SA 32 (D); *Publications Control Board v Gallo (Africa) Ltd* 1975 (3) SA 665 (A).

[95] Van der Westhuizen op cit (n 51) 427–8, 431–2; Van Rooyen op cit (n 22) 86–98. As to freedom of expression, blasphemy, and the seizure of film, see the opinion of the European Commission of Human Rights in *Otto-Preminger-Institut v Austria* 14/1/1993, Application No 13470/87.

anger fundamentalists often intend to create art or to contribute to a discussion and not to insult or to incite hatred and violence. To prohibit such material because of its likely but unintended and perhaps unforeseen consequences would be to yield to unreasonableness not justifiable in an open democratic society. Other measures are available to deal with public violence and upheaval. The seriousness of some such situations should not be underestimated, though. In practice the powerful lobbying of religious groups may often result in self-censorship on the part of public speakers, publishers, and film distributors who wish to avoid controversy. Classification and warning mechanisms could also be useful to protect sensitive persons, although it is unlikely to satisfy hardliners who do not wish anyone to see, read, or hear material which they regard as objectionable.

### 4.4 Morality, obscenity, pornography

In South Africa the arts, the publishing and film industries, and ordinary people who view themselves as mature, responsible, and often curious members of the human race have been subjected to a system of censorship which was intended to impose the Calvinist morality of a small ruling establishment on the entire population. In its practical application a degree of liberalization certainly took place, but in principle the system was not something conceived in a spirit of liberty and democracy. Because of this systematic suppression of freedom, which was linked to 'state security', attacks on the system have been associated with the cause of liberals and progressives. In this process some legitimate concerns might have been neglected.

In criminal law the Indecent or Obscene Photographic Matter Act 37 of 1967 prohibits the possession of indecent or obscene photographic matter. The definition of such matter is broad and likely to be found unconstitutional.[96]

The common-law criminal offence of public indecency, as well as the Sexual Offences Act 23 of 1957 and the Liquor Act 27 of 1989, prohibits certain kinds of expression in public and has mainly been applied to striptease dancing and sex-related public entertainment. Public indecency consists in unlawfully, intentionally, and publicly performing an act which tends to deprave or corrupt the morals of others or which outrages the public's sense of decency. The common law, as well as the relevant statutory provisions, will have to be interpreted in accordance with the spirit of Chapter 3 of the Constitution in so far as such provisions are not unconstitutional, subject to the discussion of pornography below.[97]

Section 47(2)(a) of the Publications Act of 1974, providing for material to be banned as 'undesirable' if it is deemed to be 'indecent or obscene or harmful or offensive to public morals', has been the main vehicle for the banning of and imposition of restrictions on numerous books, magazines, films, and plays — from serious art to pornographic rubbish — when they contained sex, nudity, or crude language. Although it cannot be argued that law should never be used to enforce or support public morality,[98] there can be little doubt that this section is unconstitutional. The concept of 'offensiveness to public morals' in particular is open-ended and could be used to harbour not only petty prejudices and preferences related to

---

[96] This submission by Marcus op cit (n 6) 144 is probably correct. The definition includes matter depicting lust, homosexuality, lesbianism, intercourse, masochism, sadism, etc, as well as 'anything of a like nature'.

[97] See s 19(6) of Act 23 of 1957; s 160(d)(i) of Act 27 of 1989; *S v W* 1975 (3) SA 841 (T); *S v K* 1983 (1) SA 65 (C).

[98] See above, 3.

morality and taste but also a wide variety of apparently laudable causes which could not be accommodated under more carefully formulated limitations.[99]

This does not mean that all pornographic and similar matter warrants protection as free expression. The question, once again, is to determine where to draw the line in accordance with the principles of reasonableness, democracy, freedom, and equality, and how, coherently and accurately, to define material which is to be restricted, and by whom the restrictions should be enforced.

Against the background of South Africa's history of sexism, discrimination, and violence against women the debate over pornography is particularly relevant. Arguments in recent years over the possible prohibition of pornography, especially in feminist jurisprudence and literature, are mostly founded on a contextualization of its potential harmful effects. A considerable body of material on the issue of some identifiable harm has been produced.[100] Harm may, in the most direct sense, include sexual murder, sexual violence such as assault and rape, sexual abuse of children, and sexual harassment. How to prove a causal link between pornography and sexual harm is a major point of contention. Unconvincing anecdotal evidence aside, it is often argued that there is real evidence of a causal link — or at least a correlation — between pornography and rape, indicating, for example, that pornography is one of several factors which predispose men to rape, inter alia by undermining male inhibitions.[101] Harm also includes the sexual objectification or the subordination of women. Pornography is said to create or perpetuate a stereotypical view of women as not really meaning to say 'no', loving to be used and abused, and even raped. It creates a 'rape culture' and tends to degrade women in their own eyes as well as in the eyes of men.

Furthermore, harm to women may include sex discrimination and the perpetuation of the sexual inequality of women. The fact that pornography — for whatever social or economic reason — often portrays men in a dominant position over women and depicts violence against women constitutes discrimination against women.[102] Even if the the roles are reversed in this portrayal, it still usually happens from the point of view of a male fantasy. In the production of pornography women are also often economically exploited.

Because some forms of pornography are said to create images of hatred or a violent mode of expression, it is equated to 'hate speech' or 'rape speech' by some writers.[103] Pornography and hate speech are similar in their express or implied intent to distort the image of a group or class of people, to deny their humanity, to ridicule or humiliate them to the extent that acts of aggression against them are viewed less seriously. In some pornography there is an inherent threat of violence that takes

---

[99] The Publications Appeal Board consistently proclaimed that a very narrow interpretation was given to this phrase and that it could not be used to ban vulgarity, bad taste, or controversial art, or to force authors and film producers to educate and to moralize. In practice the Board's decisions did not always reflect this approach. See Van Rooyen op cit (n 22) 52–86 and Van der Westhuizen op cit (n 51) 425.

[100] See the contributions of Itzin, MacKinnon, Dworkin, and numerous others in Itzin (ed) *Pornography. Women Violence and Civil Liberties. A Radical New View* (1992). See also Mahoney op cit (n 69) 77; Kutchinsky 'Pornography and Rape: Theory and Practice?' (1991) 14 *Int J of L and Psychiatry* 47; Lahey 'Pornography and Harm — Learning to Listen to Women' (1991) 14 *Int J of L and Psychiatry* 117; Childress 'Reel "Rape Speech": Violent Pornography and the Politics of Harm' (1991) 25 *L and Society Review* 177. See especially Dworkin 'Is there a Right to Pornography?' (1981) *Oxford J of Legal Science* 177.

[101] Itzin 'Pornography and Civil Liberties: Freedom, Harm and Human Rights' in Itzin op cit (n 100) 553.

[102] In the South African context s 8 of the Constitution is thus directly involved. Mahoney op cit (n 69) 94; Dworkin 'Against the Male Flood: Censorship, Pornography and Equality' in Itzin op cit (n 100) at 516.

[103] Mahoney op cit (n 69) 91–103.

away women's choices and undermines their freedom of action. Pornography is 'low-value speech'. If it is produced through the use of violence, force, or coercion, it hardly meets the values underlying the constitutional protection of free expression. It has little to do with truth-seeking or democracy. Feminists are divided, however, on the issue whether pornography should be prohibited by censorship.

Feminist jurisprudence has found its way into Canadian law. In decisions related to the prohibition of 'obscene' material in the Criminal Code and the Charter of Rights and Freedoms it has been held that sexually violent pornography and non-violent dehumanizing pornography are not tolerated by the contemporary community and are therefore obscene, and that the testimony of social scientists shows that social harm does in fact result from certain kinds of pornography.[104]

In the US obscenity was — like defamation and 'fighting words' — categorized as speech unprotected by the First Amendment in *Chaplinsky v New Hampshire*.[105] States are not completely free to define obscenity as they wish and the Supreme Court has attempted to lay down guidelines for what materials may be punished as 'obscene'. It has been stated that all ideas having even the slightest redeeming social importance are to be protected and different standards have been experimented with.[106] None of these attempts to define 'obscenity' has turned out to be particularly successful. It has also been held that the mere private possession of obscene material by an adult may not be made criminal.[107] In order to protect children from pornography, either as an audience or as participants (for example, as photographic subjects), special doctrines have been developed.[108]

In the context of pornography as sex discrimination and the subordination of women, cities such as Minneapolis and Indianapolis have enacted ordinances that distinguish between those sexually explicit materials that subordinate or degrade women and those that do not, banning only the former.[109] Some of these ordinances have been struck down as unconstitutional inter alia because the courts did not regard them as content-neutral, but as amounting to thought control. Speech that subordinates women is forbidden, no matter how great the political or literary merit of the work viewed as a whole may be, whereas speech that portrays women in positions of equality is lawful, no matter how graphic its sexual content.[110]

In several other legal systems matter which is described as pornographic or obscene is to some extent prohibited.[111]

---

[104] See *R v Butler* (1992) 89 DLR (4th) 449 (SCC) in particular, where the owner of a sex shop was found guilty on several charges. The prohibition of obscenity was based on the avoidance of harm to society. Prohibition must not be excessively vague, though, which has been the fatal flaw in attempts to control pornography. See Check 'The Effects of Violent Pornography, Non-Violent Dehumanizing Pornography and Erotica: Some Legal Implications from a Canadian Perspective' in Itzin op cit (n 100) 350; *R v Wagner* (1985) and *R v Ross Wise* (1990), discussed by Check. See Hogg op cit (n 22) 977–9.

[105] 315 US 568 (1942).

[106] e g *Roth v US* (supra); *Jacobellis v Ohio* 378 US 184 (1964); *Miller v California* 413 US 15 (1973). See Tribe op cit (n 18) 904–28.

[107] *Stanley v Georgia* 394 US 557 (1969).

[108] See e g *Ginsberg v New York* 390 US 629 (1968); *New York v Ferber* 458 US 747 (1982).

[109] Some of these ordinances have been drafted by prominent feminists, such as Cathy MacKinnon and Andrea Dworkin. See MacKinnon 'Pornography, Civil Rights and Speech' in Itzin op cit (n 100) 456.

[110] *American Booksellers Assoc Inc v Hudnut* 771 F 2nd 323 (7th Cir 1985), 475 US 1001 (1986).

[111] Article 184 of the German Criminal Code prohibits the distribution of pornography under certain circumstances. As to the Federal Constitutional Court, see Kommers op cit (n 19) 423. In England the Obscene Publications Act of 1959 provides for criminal prosecution as well as civil forfeiture of obscene matter. The Australian censorship system provides for action against films which are 'indecent or obscene' and in New Zealand Act 94 of 1993 regulates the classification of films, videos, and publications and defines 'objectionable' as including sex, cruelty,

There seems to be considerable international consensus that not all forms of pornography and obscene matter qualify for constitutional protection as free expression and that limitations and prohibitions are not necessarily unreasonable. On the other hand, not all erotica or even pornography should be banned. Not only would it violate free expression and perhaps even rights to privacy and freedom of conscience, and even free economic activity (according to some) but it would ignore the possible positive aspects of such matter, such as the elements of creativeness and fantasizing which may sometimes be involved.

That children should be protected, both from being exposed to pornography and from participating in the production thereof, is unquestionable.

As far as the access of adults to sexually explicit material is concerned, the following three categories have been suggested:[112]

(1) sexually violent pornography portraying the overt infliction of pain;
(2) non-violent dehumanizing pornography portraying explicit sex in a degrading way, often involving verbal abuse, and the depiction of human beings as having animal characteristics and women as objects;
(3) sexually explicit erotica portraying nudity and sexual interaction between consenting adults, without aggression, force, violence or abuse.

Based on the considerations discussed above, it is unlikely that the first two categories would be constitutionally protected. The third category, however, should not be prohibited, regardless of the degree of explicitness, in order to avoid censorship which enforces moral prejudices and to allow those who find some value in erotica to exercise a free choice. A classification or warning system could be useful in such cases.

The statutory formulation of a definition of matter which is not protected is bound to be problematic. An attempt could be made accurately to describe certain specific elements expected to be present in harmful pornography. Alternatively, a wider concept, such as 'obscenity' (which has received considerable international recognition), or even just 'pornography', could be used, with the courts having to interpret it narrowly in the light of the constitutional protection of fundamental rights.[113]

Serious concerns about the possible harmful consequences of the portrayal of violence are also relevant in South Africa, as elsewhere, but cannot be discussed in this contribution. Some of the above arguments regarding hate speech and dehumanizing pornography may be applicable.

## 4.5 Arts and science

Section 15(1) of the Constitution specifically mentions the freedoms of artistic creativity and scientific research under the right to freedom of speech and expression. A number of inferences may be drawn from this formulation.

---

and violence being dealt with in a way 'to be injurious to the public good'. See also Lötter *Moraliteitswetgewing en die Suid-Afrikaanse Strafreg* (unpublished LLD thesis, University of Pretoria 1991).

[112] See Check in Itzin op cit (n 100) 350 and *R v Wagner*, discussed by him.

[113] These options are fraught with risk, as the above-mentioned striking down of the city ordinances illustrated. The overall context in which the matter is presented, for example, could not be ignored. The banning of material because of the idea behind it, or on the assumption of harm which is far removed, could well violate the values underlying freedom of expression. South Africa has a history not only of sexism and discrimination but also of censorship and thought control. Finally, the dangers of both censorship and pornography will have to be weighed and taking risks cannot be avoided.

Some modes of expression which cannot readily be described as 'speech' could be specifically protected as artistic creativity. The idea of communication and a free flow of ideas thus assumes a somewhat different perspective. Furthermore, the relevant expression does not have to 'qualify' as a 'work of art'. Artistic creativity, and not art, is protected, which would include experimental and unsuccessful attempts at producing art.

The same applies to 'scientific research'. The process of doing scientific research is protected and encouraged. Statements claiming to present the results of research do not have to be proved to be true or sound. False or unpopular statements are included if they represent *bona fide* scientific activity.

The Publications Act of 1974 makes no special allowance for artistic creativity or scientific research in its determination of what is offensive or harmful to morals or to religious convictions. Not even the taking into account of the nature of the likely readership or viewership of a publication, film, or play was expressly sanctioned. Only after the Publications Appeal Board had been taken on review to the Supreme Court did the Board start to take artistic merit into account, connected to the concept of the likely reader or viewer.[114] Although matter which would otherwise have been banned escaped the censors because it was found to be directed at a small or sophisticated likely readership or viewership, the danger of the censors having to decide whether something is indeed art and what its merits are is a serious one. The inherent freedom of the ordinary reader, viewer, or listener to decide whether something is indeed art, and what its merits are, is taken away by the censors. Thus not only one's right to decide that something has considerable merits is violated but also one's right to decide that it is rubbish. If very risqué material is passed because it has been officially labelled as 'art', the ordinary member of the public finds it hard to decide otherwise and easily comes to the conclusion that he or she is not sufficiently educated or sophisticated to appreciate art. More or less the same considerations apply to the right of the scientific community to evaluate the results of research.

Viewed from a historical perspective, the specific mentioning of artistic creativity and scientific research in s 15(1) may thus be interpreted as a statement against suppressive censorship and a constitutional acknowledgement of the value of science and the arts. Matter which would otherwise not seem to qualify for constitutional protection because of its content may indeed be protected within the context of artistic creativity and scientific research if the nature and manner of presentation thereof merit such a conclusion.[115]

## 4.6 Contempt of court

The criminal offence of contempt of court consists of the unlawful and intentional violation of the dignity, reputation, or authority of a judicial officer in his or her judicial capacity, or of a judicial body, or of the unlawful and intentional interference with the administration of justice in a matter pending before a judicial body.[116] It

---

[114] *Human en Rousseau Uitgewers (Edms) Bpk v Snyman NO* 1978 (3) SA 836 (T); Van Rooyen op cit (n 22) 9, 11, 65–6.

[115] In the pre-constitutional draft *Bill of Rights for A New South Africa* (1990) of the ANC 'freedom of artistic activity and scientific enquiry, without censorship' was recognized in art 5(10). As to freedom of artistic expression, see also the judgment of the European Court of Human Rights in *Müller & others*, 24/5/1988, Series A vol 130.

[116] See Snyman in Joubert (ed) *LAWSA* vol 6 'Criminal Law' 174–91.

manifests itself in a variety of forms, which cannot be discussed here, some of which have their own requirements. Two of the main concerns underlying the existence of the crime are interference with the judicial process, and thus prejudice to the right to a fair trial (manifested mainly in the *sub judice* rule), and the dignity and reputation of the court or of judicial officers (contempt *in facie* or *ex facie curiae*). The present legal position, as articulated in the relevant case law, is bound to be interpreted in view of the constitutional protection of free speech, according to s 35(3) of Chapter 3. The underlying rationale and features of each form of contempt will have to be scrutinized separately.[117]

The US Supreme Court has acknowledged that the state has a strong interest in the fair and efficient administration of justice, but has generally upheld the constitutionality of contempt citations only if a 'clear and present danger' is posed to the administration of justice. Where the case is tried by a judge the court has been reluctant to find a clear and present danger. Where a case is tried before a jury the courts have greater freedom to find such a danger of interference with the just consideration of the case because juries presumably have less resistance to influences than judges. Oral statements or publications attacking a judge's integrity or criticizing the administration of justice will not be punishable by contempt.[118]

## 4.7 The press and other media

### 4.7.1 *General*

The press and the electronic media are subjected to numerous statutory and common-law restrictions, regulating a wide range of aspects, from registration and licensing to content.[119] The right to publish, and to broadcast, is now constitutionally entrenched in s 15(1), which expressly provides that 'freedom of the press and other media' shall be included under the right to freedom of speech and expression.[120]

In view of the history of the South African Broadcasting Corporation and the government's role in setting up the *Citizen* newspaper, s 15(2), which states that all media financed by or under the control of the state shall be regulated in a manner which ensures impartiality and the expression of a diversity of opinion, is to be welcomed.

Only two aspects of freedom of expression of the press and electronic media are briefly discussed here.

### 4.7.2 *Defamation*

Defamation is a private- and a common-law matter. The common law has to be interpreted in the light of the chapter on fundamental rights. The law with regard to defamation, as interpreted by the Appellate Division of the Supreme Court, will thus

---

[117] Section 96(3) of the Constitution prohibits interference with judicial officers in the performance of their functions. See the exposition of Marcus op cit (n 6) 145. See also Cleaver 'Ruling Without Reasons: Contempt of Court and the *Sub Judice* Rule' (1993) 110 *SALJ* 530. See especially the tests laid down in the leading cases of *S v Van Niekerk* 1972 (3) SA 711 (A) and *S v Harber & another* 1988 (3) SA 396 (A), which require reconsideration.

[118] See e g *Craig v Harvey* 331 US 367 (1947); *Bridges v California* (supra); *Wood v Georgia* 370 US 375 (1962); Tribe op cit (n 18) 856–61. See, on the situation in Canada, Beaudoin & Ratushny op cit (n 20) 206 and 211.

[119] See in general Stuart op cit (n 23); Burns *Media Law* (1990).

[120] See above, 4.5 regarding artistic creativity and scientific research, as to the possible significance of this inclusion.

have to be re-interpreted in the light of the Constitution, and is likely to be found wanting.[121]

One of the best-known decisions of the US Supreme Court, *New York Times Co v Sullivan*,[122] which emanated from the civil rights struggle of Martin Luther King and his followers, has become the *locus classicus* on press freedom and defamation for lawyers the world over. The court struck down strict liability as was provided for in the libel law of Alabama. It furthermore articulated a formal rule for future purposes, namely that the First Amendment prohibits a public official from recovering damages for a defamatory falsehood relating to his or her official conduct, unless it is proved that the statement was made with 'actual malice', meaning with knowledge that it was false, or with reckless disregard of whether it was true or false. The court viewed the case as one involving criticism of government policy and stated that debates on public issues had to be uninhibited, robust, and open. *Sullivan* thus established a constitutional privilege for good-faith critics of government officials.[123] Afterwards the 'actual malice' requirement was extended to include public figures, instead of merely public officials.[124]

In South African law defences open to the media have been severely curtailed by the Appellate Division. The media are strictly liable for the publication of defamatory matter,[125] whereas subjective intention is required on the part of the individual. Should *Sullivan* appear to afford too much freedom to the press, the middle option of liability based on negligence, which has been rejected by the Appellate Division, at least deserves consideration. Furthermore, in *Neethling v Du Preez & others; Neethling v The Weekly Mail & others*,[126] which was recently received with great disappointment in press and human rights circles, it was held that a defendant in a defamation action is encumbered with a full *onus* in regard to the defences of truth in the public benefit and of qualified privilege, and that at common law there is no general press privilege.

### 4.7.3  Regulation of the electronic media

Until recently the Radio Act 3 of 1952 and the Broadcasting Act 73 of 1976 have regulated control over broadcasting in South Africa. The Independent Broadcasting Authority (IBA) Act 153 of 1993 is now in operation. This Act provides for an authority, which is independent from political control, to regulate broadcasting activities in South Africa 'in the public interest'. In addition to the issuing of licences and similar matters the regulation of content and a Code of Conduct are provided for. Pre-censorship is not provided for, but monitoring of programme content by a Broadcasting Monitoring Committee is envisaged. Broadcasters who have set up a satisfactory system of content regulation could be exempted from this provision.[127]

---

[121] See Marcus op cit (n 6) 143–4. In view of s 33(2), and especially s 35(3), the chapter on fundamental human rights is probably, it is to be hoped, 'horizontally' applicable to private law as well.
[122] Supra.
[123] Tribe op cit (n 18) 864–5.
[124] *Curtis Pub Co v Butts; Associated Press v Walker* 388 US 130 (1967). As to Germany, see Kommers op cit (n 19) 368–96, and Canada, see Hogg op cit (n 22) 975–6. See also the discussion of the European Court in the *Lingens* case, 8/7/1986, Series A vol 103, and the *Barford* case 22/2/1989, Series A vol 14. With regard to the allegation of racial hate speech and criminal defamation, see *Oberschlick v Austria*, 23/5/1991, Series A vol 20.
[125] *Pakendorf v De Flamingh* 1982 (3) SA 146 (A).
[126] 1991 (1) SA 708 (A).
[127] See e g ss 2, 3–20, 56 and 62 of Act 153 of 1993.

The Broadcasting Complaints Commission of South Africa should be mentioned in this connection. The Commission was established by the National Association of Broadcasters (NAB), an organization of which several broadcasters are members on a voluntary basis, to ensure adherence to certain standards of broadcasting (as embodied in a Code of Conduct), to settle complaints against members of NAB, and to adjudicate upon a complaint where a settlement cannot be attained. This is self-censorship by the industry. The Code deals with news reporting, comment, elections and referenda, privacy, payment for information from a criminal, and general matters related to obscenity, religion, violence, and the interests of children.

The obvious question that arises is whether the kind of control embodied in the IBA Act infringes the constitutional guarantee of freedom of expression. The fact that broadcasting is regulated inter alia by the issuing of licences does not in itself violate free expression. Just as one could not claim freedom of movement as justification for driving on the wrong side of the road, or for piloting an aircraft without a licence and without heeding instructions from airport authorities, so one could not claim freedom of expression to justify pirate broadcasting. In the US, as elsewhere, the courts have accepted that radio and television spectrums are limited and that the airwaves are 'technologically scarce', as a result of which the right of state authorities to regulate and allocate the broadcast spectrum is recognized.[128] Does it follow from the right to technical regulation of frequencies because of scarcities that content can also be controlled? It is one thing to regulate traffic flow in the streets or in the air for considerations of safety, but quite another to prescribe the destination of a motorist or pilot. However, if impartiality and the expression of a diversity of opinion is regarded as important to the concept of free speech in a democratic society based on freedom and equality (as envisaged in s 15(2) with regard to media financed or controlled by the state), a moderate and fair measure of content regulation is not unreasonable. But it is to be noted that the distinction between broadcasting and print-based media on the basis of scarcity of frequencies and channels, which has been accepted over a considerable period of time, is increasingly being subjected to criticism, in view of modern developments in both the print media and broadcasting industries. Cable television, for example, makes access to broadcasting easier than to newspapers, especially where communities no longer have several dailies to choose from.[129]

Whether the independence envisaged for the IBA will in practice materialize, and whether the monitoring of broadcasts can be prevented from steering close to thought control, will depend on the strength of the IBA to resist political pressure. The IBA Act is clearly an improvement on the previous dispensation.

## 5 COMMERCIAL SPEECH

Although the constitutional protection of freedom of speech and expression was not designed for the benefit of advertising or 'commercial speech', this form of speech

---

[128] See e g *Red Lion Broadcasting Co v FCC* 395 US 367 (1969); *CBS v Democratic National Committee* 412 US 94 (1973). Pirate radio stations wishing to broadcast the views of only one political group or subtle and not so subtle racist propaganda could therefore hardly rely on the right to freedom of expression to escape regulation, as some have attempted to do.

[129] Scarcity is thus linked to content regulation — a high degree of scarcity would justify more intensive regulation and even control. If scarcity is not a factor, free expression could only be restricted in terms of the previously discussed norms and not because of technical considerations. See the unanimous decision of the

is becoming increasingly relevant.[130] Advertising companies and other large commercial concerns have — especially over the last twenty years — not hesitated to rely on the constitutional right to free speech to justify controversial advertising campaigns. Many of these concerns are financially in a much better position to litigate to assert their rights than individuals or non-profit-making organizations.

In US constitutional jurisprudence most kinds of commercial speech were traditionally viewed as an 'unprotected category' of speech outside the scope of the First Amendment.[131] In a 1976 decision sometimes referred to as 'the *Virginia Pharmacy* Revolution', the Supreme Court abandoned this rule and held that even 'purely commercial speech' is entitled to constitutional protection.[132] Thereafter a vast body of jurisprudence was built up, fully assimilating commercial speech into the First Amendment. In 1980 a four-part test was laid down to determine whether the regulation of commercial speech violates the First Amendment.[133] The advertising of unlawful products may be prohibited. As far as lawful but harmful products are concerned, a broad ruling was handed down that if the legislature could have outlawed the activity as such, it had the 'lesser power' to ban advertising of the product. It would thus seem that the advertising of liquor or cigarettes could in fact be prohibited.[134] According to Tribe,[135] the Supreme Court's commercial speech doctrine seems poised on a makeshift and unsteady foundation, in the wake of these recent decisions.

Canadian courts have also experienced difficulties in deciding to what extent commercial speech is protected under the Charter. The need for information about available options which could affect people's lifestyles is recognized, but also the need for a balacing of interests.[136]

In South Africa advertising is regulated by several statutes and by the Advertising Standards Authority.[137] To what extent these provisions could be successfully challenged remains to be seen. However, note should be taken of s 7(3) of Chapter 3, which states that juristic persons shall be entitled to the rights contained in the chapter where, and to the extent that, *the nature of the rights permits*. This section corresponds with art 19.3 of the German Constitution. Juristic persons can litigate to enforce their rights when the nature and activities of these entities are such that they relate to the free exercise of the rights of natural persons, or when their activities

---

European Court in *Informationsverein Lentia & others v Austria*, 24/11/1993, that the prohibition to set up and operate a radio or television station constituted a violation of art 10 of the Convention, inter alia because justification for some restrictions could no longer be found in technical considerations because of progress made. See also the European Commission's opinions in *XSA v The Netherlands*, 11/1/1994, Application No 21472/33 and *Nydahl v Sweden*, 11/1/1993, Application No 17505/90.

[130] See Marcus (1994) 10 *SAJHR* 140 at 147–8; Tribe op cit (n 18) 890–904; Emanuel op cit (n 18) 511–23.

[131] *Valentine v Christensen* 316 US 52 (1942).

[132] *Virginia Pharmacy Bd v Virginia Consumer Council* 425 US 748 (1976).

[133] *Central Hudson Gas v Public Service Commission* 447 US 557 (1980). The first question is whether the commercial speech is protected at all under the Constitution. Speech that is misleading and speech which concerns unlawful activity is not protected. Next the court must ask whether the governmental interest asserted in support of the regulation is substantial. The regulation must directly advance this interest and must not be more extensive than is necessary.

[134] *Posadas de Puerto Rico Association v Tourism Company of Puerto Rico* 478 US 328 (1986).

[135] Op cit (n 18) 904.

[136] See the discussion of the *Klein* and *Irwin Toy* cases by Beckton in Beaudoin & Ratushny op cit (n 20) at 204–6. See also Hogg op cit (n 22) 969–72.

[137] See Stuart op cit (n 23) 241–8 and, regarding the ASA, 249–58.

are such that they amount to a meaningful exercise of individual freedom.[138] It may be argued that not all commercial juristic persons can 'speak', within the meaning of Chapter 3, which is intended to protect human liberty and discourse. But advertisers do often have 'something to say' in informing the public about the availability and quality of products and services. It is preferable to recognize commecial speech as speech or expression, subject to the right of the government to impose reasonable and justifiable limitations.

## 6 CONCLUDING REMARKS

It has almost become customary to conclude a contribution on freedom of expression on a sober yet inspiring note, warning against the temptation to ban that with which one disagrees.[139] This is the correct approach. The risks inherent in suppressing speech tend to outweigh the harm sometimes caused by free speech. The harm that may result from speech is almost always overestimated and history is filled with examples of irrational overreaction to the fear of such harm. Men indeed 'feared witches and burnt women'.[140] In case of doubt freedom of speech and expression must get the nod.

But another aspect deserves to be mentioned. The formal legal recognition of freedom of expression does not guarantee substantial liberty and equality. In a society emerging from a historical position where free speech and other aspects of democracy were often denied, the danger exists that the newly guaranteed freedom will not be utilized by those most needing to do so, and at the same time that it will be exploited and perverted by those who have never believed in freedom of speech or granted it to others.

What must be achieved is freedom not only from legal restrictions but from fear, intimidation, and inferior or suppressive education; equality as far as access to media and the confidence to express one's views are concerned; and particularly the willingness to listen to and tolerate the views of others. The legal system can play a role in this process.

---

[138] In 21 *BVerfGE* 362 the German Federal Constitutional Court ruled that the concept of fundamental rights is based on the liberty of the individual as a natural person. Juristic persons could only be assimilated into the sphere of protection of fundamental rights when the activities of such juristic persons embody the freedom of natural persons. Religious organizations and other juristic persons whose aims and activities revolve around the promotion of religious activities or the preaching of a faith have freedom of religion and conscience. See Schlaich *Das Bundesverfassungsgericht* (1985) 103–4; Schwabe *Entscheidungen des Bundesverfassungsgerichts* (1988) 263–6; Hesse op cit (n 50) 115–16; Lepa op cit (n 19) 320–3. As to the opposite regarding freedom of religion in Canada, see *R v Big M Drug Mart Ltd* (1985) 18 DLR (4th) 321 SCC.

[139] See e g Abrams op cit (n 64) 755–6.

[140] *Per* Brandeis J in *Whitney v California* (supra), also referred to by Abrams op cit (n 64) 756. Thomas Aquinas also pointed out — centuries ago — that if a captain's only concern were that his ship should never sink, he would always stay in the harbour.

# FREEDOM OF ASSEMBLY: VOTING WITH YOUR FEET

STUART WOOLMAN & JOHAN DE WAAL

## 1 INTRODUCTION

Protests, assemblies, and mass demonstrations have played a central role in the political struggles of the past forty years. Without the franchise, without representatives in government, without the freedom to engage in open and robust debate with other members of society, and with only limited access to the media, the majority of South Africans had but one mode of political participation available to them: at the right time and place they could 'vote with their feet', they could toyi-toyi, they could *demonstrate*.

Even after the April 1994 election, however, demonstrations and assemblies are likely to continue to be an essential means of political participation. Despite the implementation of a constitutional order which guarantees all South Africans the whole panoply of recognized political rights, the remaining vast disparities in economic and social power mean that many South Africans will continue to have their political experiences primarily mediated by mass gatherings and demonstrations.

Part 2 of this chapter traces the history of assembly in the old order, which made such political experiences difficult, if not impossible, to have. In part 3 we look at some proposals for assembly reform in the new order. We pay particular attention to recent legislation on demonstrations and gatherings, as well as the recommendations of a multinational panel on the subject. In parts 4, 5, and 6 we go on to look at how freedom of assembly jurisprudence has developed in three of the world's major constitutional orders: the US, Canada, and Germany. In each of these three sections we shall examine the extent to which the tests employed by the courts permit clear and unclouded consideration of the competing free speech and public order interests invariably at stake in assembly cases. In part 7 we turn to the interim Constitution and describe the mechanics of a challenge to governmental action restricting the freedom of assembly. In light of the conclusions drawn in parts 3, 4, 5, and 6 we then make substantive recommendations as to how the courts should construe the interim Constitution's provisions on assembly.

## 2 THE OLD ORDER

In South Africa local authorities, national executives, and Parliament have shown little enthusiasm for the practice of assembly.[1] They have demonstrated even less sympathy for assemblers. The following account of South African assembly law

---

[1] Section 15 of the General Law Further Amendment Act 92 of 1970 and s 53 of the Internal Security Act 74 of 1982 require that assemblies receive both the local authority's consent and the approval of a magistrate in the district in which the assembly is to take place. See Dugard *Human Rights and the South African Legal Order* (1978) 187.

specifically concentrates on the ways in which national legislation has suppressed assembly as a form of political participation.

Before 1950 assembly was, to some extent at least, permissively regulated by common law.[2] At common law the crime of public violence serves as the primary limitation on the freedom to assemble. Such a limit seems to secure a relatively wide ambit for public protest and demonstration. However, lest the pre-1950 period start to take on the glow of a golden age, it should be made clear that as South Africa approached the middle of the century increasingly wide powers were granted to the executive to prohibit or control the gatherings of black South Africans.[3]

After 1950 the National Party government accelerated the passage of legislation designed to curtail assembly, especially assembly that took the form of political protest. The National Party began with s 9 of the Suppression of Communism Act.[4] Section 9 allowed the Minister of Justice to prohibit a gathering or an assembly whenever there was in his opinion reason to believe that the objects of communism would be furthered at such a gathering.[5] Sometime thereafter, in response to the ANC's 1952 defiance campaign, the government passed the Criminal Law Amendment Act.[6] The Act increased penalties for crimes committed in the context of political protest.[7] More serious limitations followed when a new Riotous Assemblies Act was passed in 1956.[8]

From this early period of apartheid politics and through the seventies the judiciary showed little awareness of the political context within which they interpreted these

---

[1] Under the Internal Security Acts of 1976 and 1982 the Minister issued a notice annually which declared outdoor gatherings illegal — save for *bona fide* sporting and religious purposes — unless permission was obtained from a magistrate. Demonstrators often ignored the permission requirement, despite the fact that it featured quite prominently — through its selective enforcement — in the state's strategy to suppress political protest. See Haysom 'Licence to Kill — Part 1' (1987) 3 *SAJHR* 3 at 23; Corder & Davis 'A Long March — Administrative Law in the Appellate Division' (1988) 4 *SAJHR* 281 at 289 (the authors of the latter article make clear how difficult it eventually became to obtain permission to assemble.)

[2] At common law the individual is entitled to all rights in so far as they are not expressly prohibited or limited by statute or by the common law itself. Section 52 of the Internal Security Act 74 of 1982 repealed the common law with regard to open-air assemblies. See Ackermann *Die Reg insake Openbare en Staatsveiligheid* (1984) 153.

[3] See ss 25 and 27 of the Black Administration Act 38 of 1927 and the Development Trust and Land Act 18 of 1936. At the time of writing, s 27 of the former Act was still in force. It allows the President to promulgate regulations with reference to 'the prohibition, control or regulation of gatherings or assemblies of Blacks' and 'the observance by Blacks of decency'. Section 38(3)(r) of the Black (Urban Areas) Consolidation Act 25 of 1945 conferred power to the Bantu administration boards, under the supervision of magistrates, to control and restrict the meetings of 'Bantus'. See Mathews *Law, Order and Liberty in South Africa* (1971) 240–2, 249–50; Dugard op cit (n 1) 186–91. Incidentally, the first legislative regulation of assembly after the Union was formed — the provisions of the original Riotous Assemblies Act 27 of 1914 — was adopted to enable the government to deal with white labour unrest. The provisions of this statute infringed the rights to procedural fairness of those involved in protest more than it affected the freedom to assemble.

[4] Act 44 of 1950. The Act was later consolidated into the Internal Security Act of 1982.

[5] The minister could in terms of ss 9 and 5 (which applied to listed persons) give notice to a person prohibiting him from attending any gathering. The provisions gave rise to many court cases involving the definition and meaning of the word 'gathering'. See Forsyth *In Danger for Their Talents* (1985) 148–67; Dugard op cit (n 1) 162–3.

[6] Act 8 of 1953.

[7] Sections 58 and 59 of the Internal Security Act 74 of 1982 were designed to achieve a similar result. See Ackermann op cit (n 2) 164–8. The judiciary also on occasion saw a political motive as an aggravating factor in sentencing. See Cameron 'Civil Disobedience and Passive Resistance' in Corder (ed) *Essays on Law and Social Practice in South Africa* (1988) 219 at 231.

[8] Act 17 of 1956. Initially the Act allowed the Minister of Justice to prohibit any public gathering in order to maintain public peace or to prevent the engendering of racial hostility. However, the 1974 amendments to the Act extended the minister's prohibitory powers to private gatherings. See s 2(1) of Act 30 of 1974. Section 17 of the Riotous Assemblies Act, which deems a person to commit the crime of incitement to public violence if the natural and probable consequences of his act, conduct, speech, or publication would be the commission of public violence by others, was at the time of writing still in force. See Dugard op cit (n 1) 188–90. Demonstrations near Parliament were also outlawed at about this time by the Gatherings and Demonstrations in the Vicinity of Parliament Act 52 of 1973. This Act was not repealed by the Internal Security Act of 1982 and was just recently (in 1992) amended.

statutes. Even when judges intervened to curtail the relatively unfettered discretion of the executive they could state in all seriousness that

> 'freedom of speech and freedom of assembly are part of the democratic right of every citizen of the Republic, and Parliament guards these rights jealously for they are part of the very foundation upon which Parliament rests. Free assembly is a most important right for it is generally only organized public opinion that carries weight and it is extremely difficult to organize it if there is no right of public assembly.'[9]

The Rabie Commission's report — which ultimately culminated in the adoption of the Internal Security Act and the Demonstrations in or near Court Buildings Act[10] — failed to deliver the hoped-for reform of the law.[11] However, at the very least, the hodgepodge of statutory limitations found in various Acts were simplified and consolidated into two statutes.[12]

The mass protests by extra-parliamentary movements in the eighties began soon after these two Acts were promulgated. The government responded by issuing even more restrictive 'emergency' regulations under the Public Safety Act.[13] As these regulations were subordinate legislation, the task of the courts shifted from the interpretation of legislation to judicial review of administrative regulations.[14] As with most of the emergency regulations, a few challenges to the assembly regulations were successful.[15] The majority were not.[16]

February 1990, and the agreement of most parties to the National Peace Accord, ushered in a new era in assembly jurisprudence. For the first time real attempts were made to balance the fundamental rights of protestors, demonstrators, and assemblers against the state's interest in public order, the government's interest in carrying out its tasks, and the general public's liberty interests.

---

[9] *S v Turrel* 1973 (1) SA 248 (C) at 256. (A magistrate's prohibition of a meeting in terms of s 2(1) of the Riotous Assemblies Act was struck down for vagueness on the ground that the order did not specify the meeting in question with sufficient clarity to pass administrative scrutiny.) See also *S v Budlender & another* 1973 (1) SA 264 (C); Kahn 'Freedom of Assembly' (1973) 90 *SALJ* 18. It was not until the late seventies that academic lawyers started to criticize both the assembly legislation and the interpretations rendered by the courts. See e g Van der Vyver *Die Beskerming van Menseregte in Suid-Afrika* (1975) and *Seven Lectures on Human Rights* (1976).

[10] Act 74 of 1982 and Act 71 of 1982 respectively.

[11] Even mainstream legal academics had begun to look at restrictions on fundamental rights with a reasonably critical eye. See Wiechers *Verloren van Themaat Staatsreg* (1981) 142–56; Basson & Viljoen *South African Constitutional Law* (1988) 216–84; Boulle, Harris & Hoexter *Constitutional and Administrative Law* (1989) 20–64; Carpenter *Introduction to South African Constitutional Law* (1987) 83–115.

[12] For a comprehensive analysis of the statutes, see Mathews *Freedom, State Security and the Rule of Law* (1986) 52–6, 139–47; Ackermann op cit (n 2) 149–68. Section 46(1) was employed most frequently. It provided that a magistrate could prohibit — for a maximum of 48 hours — any gathering in his/her district when he/she had reason to apprehend that it would seriously endanger the public peace. Section 46(3) allows the minister to prohibit any gathering in any area for any period of time, if he/she deems it necessary or expedient in the interest of state security or peace or to prevent feelings of hostility between the different population groups.

[13] Act 3 of 1953. For example, reg 7(1) in terms of Proc 109 of 1986 held that '[t]he ... Commissioner may for the purpose of the safety of the public ... issue orders ... (bA) whereby any particular gathering, or any gathering of a particular nature, class or kind, is prohibited at any place or in any area specified in the order.' See Kidd 'Meetings and the Emergency Regulations' (1989) 5 *SAJHR* 471. See also Dugard, Haysom & Marcus *The Last Years of Apartheid: Civil Liberties in South Africa* (1992).

[14] For commentary on these decisions see e g Mureinik 'Pursuing Principle: the Appellate Division and Review under the State of Emergency' (1989) 5 *SAJHR* 60; Basson 'Judicial Activism in a State of Emergency: an Examination of Recent Decisions of the South African Courts' (1987) 3 *SAJHR* 28.

[15] See e g *Natal Newspapers (Pty) Ltd v State President of the Republic of South Africa* 1986 (4) SA 1109 (N): court struck down reg 7(1)(*d*).

[16] See e g *Van der Westhuizen NO v United Democratic Front* 1989 (2) SA 242 (A): court upheld reg 7(1)(*bA*) (quoted above, n 13).

## 3   THE NEW ORDER

The work in the area of demonstrations and gatherings over the past two years signals a hopeful, if not entirely radical, break with past practice. While the National Peace Accord and the interim Constitution's provision protecting freedom of assembly provide the grounds for some of this hope, much of the real thinking and progress on this subject has taken place under the auspices of the Goldstone Commission.

The Commission's first constructive effort at bringing South Africa's law on assembly into line with that of other liberal democracies was to convene a multinational panel of experts to thrash out a new approach to assembly in South Africa.[17] Given the extreme authoritarianism of the National Party regime, it is not surprising that the panel's work on assembly reform in South Africa has as much to do with the transformation of an entire political culture as it does with the transformation of a body of law.

As an initial treatment for the wholesale lack of communication in the past and the deep divides in the present, the panel opens by advising that, where possible, all three concerned parties — local authorities, police, and convenors — should participate in pre-demonstration negotiations.[18] In practice, of course, this means that organizers of a demonstration should be obliged to give notice to the local authorities — as well as the police — of the nature, size, and route of their demonstration.

The panel's next piece of recommended political etiquette consists of a reminder to local authorities and the police that their response to the notice should be predicated on the understanding that their role is to facilitate the demonstration, while minimizing any inconvenience to other citizens.[19] Given this understanding of the local authority's and the police's role and an overall commitment to 'demonstration as of right' for all citizens, in most instances approval for the demonstration should be granted automatically or without much issue. However, should the local authorities object to the time, place, or manner of the demonstrations, negotiations will then ensue between the convenors of the demonstration and the local authorities.

Negotiations, and good political etiquette, do not ensure agreement. Even after negotiations the local authorities may decide for reasons of public convenience and safety that the plans for demonstration should be changed or restricted. As the panel rightly notes, this power to change or restrict a demonstration plan cannot go uncontested.

The only viable check on such local power is to ensure access of demonstrators and protestors to expeditious, vigorous, and independent judicial review. In deciding on the legality or constitutionality of the restrictions the panel urges that judges ought to be guided by the notion that a vibrant democracy requires a relatively permissive approach to demonstrations and gatherings.[20]

---

[17] See Heymann (ed) *Towards Peaceful Protest in South Africa: Testimony of a Multinational Panel Regarding the Lawful Control of Demonstrations in the Republic of South Africa before The Commission of Inquiry Regarding the Prevention of Public Violence and Intimidation* (Pretoria 1992). The panel predicated its approach to and recommendations on the subject on a single primary premise: the right to assemble, demonstrate, protest, and petition is a necessary condition for making good a democratic society's basic commitment to universal political participation.

[18] At 5.

[19] At 9.

[20] At 13. The panel took great pains to make sure that a permissive approach was not understood to mean an absence of limits. The panel argued that legitimate restrictions may be placed on demonstrations so that they do not unnecessarily impede traffic, run into demonstrations by rival groups, bar access to public or private workplaces, or threaten significant property damage. In addition it recommended that legislation on gatherings and

While the remaining bulk of the report is devoted to the sorts of transformations necessary to breed a culture of openness and tolerance — namely changes in the practices of both demonstration organizers[21] and police[22] — it does suggest new legal rules for the use of force. In a dramatic departure from current South African law the panel eschews the use of deadly force in all but the most extreme — and genuinely life-threatening — instances.[23]

The panel's aforementioned suggestions are certainly of the greatest interest. However, what is truly compelling about the report is its fate following publication in 1992. Rather than simply add to the list of position papers on political transformation, the Commission and the panel directly sought to change existing practice by drafting legislation on demonstrations and gatherings that would give effect to the principles enunciated in the panel's testimony. In January 1994, following publication, criticism, and revision of several rough draft bills,[24] the State President signed the Regulation of Gatherings Act.[25]

---

demonstrations ban the carrying of weapons amd the wearing of disguises. More controversially, it advised that speech or expressive conduct likely to incite racial hatred should be proscribed: at 16–19.

[21] At 15. Though a relatively permissive approach to demonstrations is necessary for a liberal democracy to flourish, responsibility for the peaceful execution of a march or protest must be borne by someone. The panel argues that the organizers and convenors of demonstrations are in the best position actually to maintain public order. The panel places this burden on the organizers because it recognizes that the convenors of a demonstration or gathering are more likely to command moral authority with their fellow participants or party members — i e demonstrators are more likely to obey a route change dictated by their organization's leadership and marshals than they are to a similar command by the police or local authorities.

[22] At 23–46. The panel's final set of recommendations is motivated by the understanding that while the demonstrating group's convenors and marshals may be the first, best, and most democratic means of ensuring public order, they are not, and cannot, be the last line of defence. That responsibility falls to the police. The panels also recognizes that because the SAP's role has just as often been that of a disruptor, as opposed to a facilitator, of demonstrations and protests and because the SAP's historical relationship to the majority of South Africans is one of antagonism and distrust, this responsibility will not be easy for the police to discharge. It is perhaps for this reason that the better portion of the panel's report concerns itself with the mechanisms necessary for the wholesale transformation of the SAP into an organization capable of serving the needs of a nascent liberal democracy. With respect to demonstrations the panel had two specific sets of recommendations for changes in SAP operations. The first set of recommendations provided detailed guidelines for facilitating demonstrations. In particular, the panel emphasized the need for the police to act with restraint during spontaneous demonstrations and demonstrations marked by limited and random violations of criminal and civil laws. The panel argues that well-defined and established procedures and sanctions already exist to punish the individual offenders and that the punishment of a few rabble-rousers in no way justifies the curtailment of the peaceful protestors' democratic rights. The second set of recommendations strongly urges that the SAP employ a new methodology for recruiting, training, and equipping police units which deal with demonstrations and riots. To learn these new approaches and methods of policing demonstrations the panel advises the creation of special courses designed to equip officers with the knowledge and skills necessary to mediate the disputes that often arise during protests.

[23] At 23–38. If the police must intervene in the demonstration to prevent serious harm that is absolutely certain to arise or has already arisen, then one must ask what level of force the police should use to contain or, if necessary, disperse a demonstration. To this end the panel advocates adopting the widely accepted principle of 'minimum force'. A commitment to the use of minimum force has two primary repercussions for the policing of demonstrations. First, it limits the use of lethal force to instances of self-defence, protection of the lives of others, and the prevention of other very serious violent crimes. Protection of property, for example, does not justify the use of lethal force. Secondly, minimum force commits the police to using force only where necessary and never more force than necessary. Thus mere disobedience by demonstrators — and even minor property damage — should not be grounds for using even sublethal force. And in those cases where a demonstration begins to spin out of control the police are advised first to use communication, then warnings, and finally as little force as possible to bring the situation under control.

[24] See *Final Report to the Commission of Inquiry Regarding the Prevention of Public Violence and Intimidation by the Committee Established to Inquire into Public Violence at Mass Demonstrations, Marches and Picketing* (Pretoria 1993); *Final Draft of the 'Goldstone' Bill on the Regulation of Gatherings* (Sandton 1993).

[25] Act 205 of 1993. The Act repeals the following statutes and sections of statutes dealing with assembly: Gatherings and Demonstrations in the Vicinity of Parliament Act 52 of 1973 (as amended in 1992); Demonstrations in or near Court Buildings Prohibition Act 71 of 1982; s 46(1) and (2) — but not ss 46(3) — 47, 48, 49, 51, 53, 57, and 62 of the Internal Security Act 74 of 1982; Gatherings and Demonstrations in or near the Union Buildings Act 103 of 1992. The Act states that it should not be understood to repeal any part of the following statutes: Arms and Ammunition Act 75 of 1969 (s 38A sets out the requirements for carrying a gun in public); Dangerous Weapons

To Parliament's credit, the legislation ultimately retains what is one of the most interesting aspects of the panel report, namely the notion of 'demonstration as of right': the notion that the ability to hold a public gathering, assembly, or demonstration is not necessarily contingent upon a local or state authority's approval.[26] Unfortunately the legislation also contains provisions which reflect the difficulty that the political actors and the security establishment have had with making a complete break with the past.

First, the legislation requires that notice for demonstrations or gatherings be provided to local authorities and police seven days in advance.[27] Given that assemblies are often an immediate response to a political action which touches the raw felt need of some segment of the public, it is the rare convenor or 'out-group' that will wait seven days. Furthermore, the primary justification for assembly is the ability of public gathering directly to communicate (some part of) the public will to the state and in so doing perhaps prevent the government from undertaking or continuing a particular act which lacks either public support or some other form of legitimacy. Should a protestor be required to wait the full seven days, the government project could be a *fait accompli* before the public can register its collective ire. This restriction fails to take the new Constitutition's commitment to free expression and broad political participation seriously.

Failing the ability of convenors to give seven days' notice, there are slightly more restrictive provisions for demonstrations carried out on forty-eight hours' notice.[28] These provisions seem to reflect a more realistic assessment of assembly dynamics. However, what is truly worrying about these additional provisions is that failure to meet the forty-eight-hour-in-advance deadline for notice gives the local authorities almost unfettered discretion to issue blanket prohibitions.[29] This extraordinary power to silence opposition is an unnecessarily blunt cudgel to place in the hands of individuals unlikely to place expressive interests on a par with public order

---

Act 71 of 1968 (s 2 permits the minister to prohibit a person or class of persons from bearing arms in public); Control of Access to Public Premises and Vehicles Act 53 of 1985 (allowing the state to control access to public property); Civil Protection Act 67 of 1977; Public Safety Act 3 of 1953; Intimidation Act 72 of 1982; Prevention of Public Violence and Intimidation Act 139 of 1991.

[26] See s 4(3). Consistent with the panel's report, the legislation requires demonstration organizers to give notice to local authorities (but not police) sufficiently far in advance of the gathering to allow for what official response and planning may be deemed necessary. If local authorities see no problem with the demonstration plans as originally conceived, then the demonstration proceeds as scheduled. If, however, the local authorities believe that alternative arrangements may be necessary to safeguard the rights of both demonstrators and non-demonstrators, then provision is made for negotiation.

[27] Section 3(2).

[28] Ibid.

[29] Ibid. Section 4(4)*(b)* holds that if, after a negotiation meeting contemplated in s 4(2)*(b)*, the convenor, authorized member, responsible officer, and other concerned parties do not reach agreement on the gathering's contours, then the responsible officer may restrict the gathering on any of the grounds set out in s 4(4)*(b)*(i)–(iv): to ensure (i) that vehicular or pedestrian traffic, especially during traffic rush hours, is least impeded; or (ii) an appropriate distance between participants in the gathering and rival gatherings; (iii) access to property and workplaces; or (iv) the prevention of injury to persons or damage to property. These restrictions appear at first blush to provide significant limits on the discretion of local authorities to ban gatherings. However, the limitations set out in s 4(4)*(b)* apply only to those instances in which notice has been received, a meeting was convened, and no agreement was reached. It does not speak to limitations on local authorities with respect to spontaneous gatherings and demonstrations, or gatherings where notice was recieved less than forty-eight hours before a gathering and no official response has been made. The police, on the other hand, have almost no power to prohibit a gathering in advance. Under s 9(1)*(c)* their powers are limited to restricting gatherings to a particular place or modifying a demonstration route, and only when a number of different conditions are satisfied. These limits on police power pose their own special problems. What happens when you have illegitimate local authorities in place who are either uninterested in permitting demonstrations or are, perhaps, very interested in seeing a demonstration become a conflict? Without the power to determine a different date or route in advance or to approach a magistrate for a banning order, the police are limited to damage control during a demonstration — hardly the most propitious time to intervene.

concerns. If any legal provision bodes ill for freedom of assembly in South Africa, it is the forty-eight-hour notice deadline.[30] Even expedited judicial review would be no match for local authorities bent on stamping out the spread of dissent through the use of such prohibitions.[31]

Another powerful set of mechanisms for chilling public expression and assembly are the provisions made in Chapter 4 for the imposition of civil liability. If riot damage occurs as a result of a demonstration, each member of the demonstration is jointly and severally liable for the damage caused. Joint and several liability for riot damage creates the potential for huge personal liability. We must ask how many members of the public would be willing to risk personal bankruptcy to challenge some undesirable state of affairs? Only those, we suppose, who have nothing left to lose. However, the freedoms guaranteed in the interim Constitution are intended to protect the expressive interests of all, not just those on the margin. The response to this concern that civil liability requirements will chill speech is that demonstration organizers can always take out demonstration damage insurance prior to a march. That line of argument appears reasonable until you ask whether controversial groups will be able to secure insurance, or whether even a mainstream political group can convince their insurers that they will not attract a violent response for which they may ultimately be held liable. In many instances both controversial and mainstream groups will find insurance either unavailable or far too costly. These groups may decide to take their chances. If they do, however, they run a very real risk that opponents of the group may attempt to hijack the march and cause as much damage as possible, thereby both discrediting and bankrupting the organization and its membership. Civil liability makes assembly a high-stakes game which most assemblers either are bound to lose or are not allowed to play at all.[32]

Finally, on a quick reading of the Act Parliament seems to have taken the security bull by the horns and tackled the problem of the use of deadly force by the police to disperse demonstrations. Section 9(2)(e) provides that the force necessary to prevent the killing or serious injury of persons or the destruction or serious damage

---

[30] The legislation also contains troublesome restrictions on 'hate speech' at assemblies. As these provisions go more to the heart of free expression jurisprudence, we believe that criticism of these provisions should rather occur in the context of an analysis of the legitimate limits on expression. Cf s 8(5) and (6). Another troublesome expression provision in the Act concerns the use of masks during gatherings and marches: s 8(7).

[31] Unfortunately it is not even clear that parties whose rights have been affected by a local authority's decision to ban or impose conditions on a demonstration will receive the expedited judicial review envisioned by the panel. In terms of s 6 the affected party must file an application with either a magistrate or the appropriate Supreme Court within twenty-four hours of the local authority's decision. No provision within the Act guarantees a response within a similarly limited period of time. Even s 6(5), which provides for urgent *ex parte* applications before the Supreme Court, does not assure the allegedly aggrieved party of a full evidentiary hearing. If the applicant can satisfy the Uniform Rules' very stringent criteria of urgency, infringement of a right, and irremediable harm, only then may he/she win a temporary interdict against the local authority's order which allows the demonstration to proceed as originally planned. However, given the *ex parte* nature of the urgent application proceeding, the judge will likely be disposed to hold the decision over until a full hearing set for a later date. Clearly a judgment to postpone the decision to a later date serves the interests of the local authorities and not the interests of the protestors.

[32] One suggested cure for the potential chilling effect of civil liability involves placing the burden on the property owner to show that the organizer did not take 'reasonable steps' to prevent the damage and restricting the ambit of 'reasonable steps'. See Van Zyl 'Marching to a Different Tune: The Regulation of Gatherings Act' (unpublished memorandum on file with authors, 1994). The suggested cure has two problems. First, the reversal of the burden in civil cases is motivated primarily by the belief that the party who bears the burden has some form of privileged access to information which the court requires. The reversal of the burden helps squeeze that information out. The property owner in assembly liability cases cannot be expected to have such information. Secondly, the reversal of the burden is not only unlikely to limit damage claims but it is also unlikely to make the assembly organizer rest easier.

to immovable property or valuable movable property must be 'necessary', 'moderated', and 'proportionate to the circumstances'. It thereby places some 'philosophical' limits on deadly force. However, s 9(2)(d) expressly allows the use of 'firearms and other weapons' for crowd control. Sections 9(3) and 13(1)(b) insulate the common-law defences of self-defence, necessity, and protection of property from the effect of s 9(2)(e). Section 9(2)(d) also permits the use of force where there are apparently 'manifest intentions' to kill or seriously to injure persons or to destroy or seriously damage property. Read together, these provisions create innumerable opportunities for the police to use deadly force to curb 'potentially violent' or 'potentially destructive' demonstrations. While these conditions do not quite swallow the commitment to 'moderated' and 'proportionate' force, they do permit the police to keep their licence to kill.[33]

## 4 FREEDOM OF ASSEMBLY IN THE UNITED STATES

### 4.1 Introduction

In the US freedom of assembly is understood to be foundational for the life of a liberal democracy for two primary reasons. First, it helps create space for collective politics. This space for collective politics is crucial: while a single voice is likely to be drowned out in the political community, a collective voice is far more likely to get its message across. Secondly, assembly is essential for democratic politics because only through meeting and talking with fellow citizens can we critically explore the various beliefs and values which animate our political decisions. It is generally believed that the more we discuss the ideas we seek to put into practice, the better and the more legitimate our political decisions are likely to be.

Given the primacy of place of speech and assembly in a democratic society and the general belief that the more discussion we have the healthier our polity will be, any restrictions on speech and assembly will be carefully scrutinized by US courts. This careful scrutiny does not mean that all forms of speech and all manner of assembly are acceptable. It means that when balancing these rights of speech and assembly against the importance of the state's interest in the laws and regulations restricting these rights the courts will begin their analysis with a general presumption in favour of the expressive activity.

It having been said that there is a presumption in favour of expressive activity over and against the state's interests, it is essential to note that US courts recognize different kinds of expressive activity and accord them different levels of protection. In the pantheon of expressive rights assembly receives perhaps the least amount of judicial solicitude. In short, despite its recognized status as a separate and distinct

---

[33] The conditions for exercise of this licence stand in direct conflict with international instruments on the subject and the accepted practices of most nations. For example, Principle 9 of the Basic Principles on the Use of Force and Firearms by Law Enforcement Officials states that:
  'Law enforcement officials shall not use firearms against persons except in self-defense or defense of others against the imminent threat of death or serious injury or to prevent the perpetration of a particularly serious crime involving grave threat to life ... In any event, intentional lethal use of firearms may only be made when strictly unavoidable in order to protect life.'
Document adopted by the 8th United Nations Congress on the Prevention of Crime and the Treatment of Offenders (1990). Indeed one wonders how the use of lethal force to protect property will square with the interim Constitution's protection of the right to life in s 9.

constitutional right, freedom of assembly has largely been treated as a less important category of free speech[34] — i e for reasons that will shortly become clear, assembly receives the same sort of diminished protection the court accords what it calls expressive *conduct*.

Part of the explanation for this diminished protection is that assembly — like other forms of conduct — is often viewed merely as a condition for freedom of speech, and that it is the nature and *content* of the speech itself which is thought to be of paramount importance. Stated another way, the court has tended to view a political or social gathering as important for what is said at the gathering, rather than for the fact of the gathering itself.[35]

This tendency towards (artificially) separating the speech act from the surrounding conduct reflects the Supreme Court's deeply imbedded bias against extending constitutional protections to groups and its preference for seeing groups merely as a collection of individuals. Thus, because it is the individual and not the group which is important, for the better part of its history the Supreme Court has held that it is the speech or expressive activity of individuals alone which deserves constitutitional protection. As a result, while the court has repeatedly recognized the importance of assembly, it has accorded it a lesser level of protection than 'pure speech'. The distinction between the protection afforded speech and the protection afforded assembly is generally reflected in the court's distinction between the court's protection of the *content* of a belief and the *conduct* employed to express that belief.

Where the government seeks to regulate the *content* of a particular expression it must have a *compelling* interest — not at all an easy test to satisfy.[36] However, where the government simply wishes to regulate the manner in which the expression is made, i e the conduct, the courts grant the government far greater latitude. When the state wishes to restrict expressive conduct in traditionally public forums the courts will uphold those laws which are content-neutral and which are narrowly tailored to effect a significant or important government interest in regulating the time, place, and manner of the expressive activity. Laws regulating non-public forums need only have a reasonable relationship to a legitimate government interest to be upheld. From these brief statements of the tests it should be clear that a regulation seeking to prevent the expression and communication of specific ideas or kinds of ideas is far less likely to be upheld than a regulation of the conduct deemed incidental to the speech.

## 4.2 The public forum doctrine

Assembly is afforded the greatest protection in what are known as public forums. Indeed, some public property is so traditionally identified with the exercise of First

---

[34] Cf *De Jonge v Oregon* 299 US 353 (1937): court recognizes the right of free assembly as separate and distinct from those of free speech and free press, and 'equally fundamental.' See also *Thomas v Collins* 323 US 516 (1945): court not only recognizes the right of free assembly as a separate and distinct right but also extends its protection to any peaceable assembly, be it public, private, political, economic, or social.

[35] Cf Baker 'Unreasonable Reasonableness: Mandatory Parade Permits and Time, Place and Manner Regulations' (1983) 78 *Northwestern U LR* 937: Baker argues that there are strong and independent grounds for protecting assembly and that it should not be treated simply as an adjunct of speech.

[36] Of course a compelling state interest is not necessary if the speech falls into one of several very, very narrow and unprotected categories of speech: obscenity, defamation, 'fighting words', words creating a clear and present danger to public order, and misleading or false advertising.

Amendment rights of speech and assembly that a blanket denial of public access to this property for the purpose of exercising these rights is forbidden. The Supreme Court has held that streets, parks, and sidewalks all fall into this category of public property. In declaring that citizens effectively have a 'guaranteed access' to streets, parks, and other public forums the court in *Hague v CIO* wrote as follows:

> 'Wherever the title of streets and parks may rest they have immemorially been held in trust for the use of the public and, time out of mind, have been used for purposes of assembly, communicating thoughts between citizens, and discussing public questions. Such a use of the streets and public places has, from ancient times, been a part of the privileges, immunities, rights and liberties of citizens. The privilege to use the streets and parks for communication on national questions may be regulated in the interest of all: it must not, in the guise of regulation, be abridged or denied.'[37]

Again, the fact that the public has guaranteed access to streets, parks, and sidewalks for their expressive activities does not mean that such access cannot be restricted.[38] It does mean that the restriction must pass a fairly demanding test.[39] This test for restricting assembly in public forums has three parts. First, the restriction must be content-neutral — i e the restriction cannot be based on the content or subject-matter of the communication being controlled.[40] Secondly, the restriction must be 'narrowly tailored' to serve a 'significant government interest'. To be 'narrowly tailored' a regulation must not substantially burden the expressive conduct more than necessary to further the significant government interest.[41] Thirdly, the restriction must 'leave open alternative channels for communication of the information' or allow the assembly to take place elsewhere or at another time.[42] This test may seem a bit abstract. A few case examples may help to see what is at stake for assembly and expressive conduct and what a court does when it applies this test.[43]

Perhaps the most famous series of legal battles to deal with free assembly and expressive conduct in the US occurred in the late seventies and revolved around plans by the Nationalist Socialist Party — an American neo-Nazi group — to stage a march and rally in Skokie, Illinois — the home of some 5 000 holocaust survivors. To prevent the march and rally the city of Skokie enacted several ordinances designed to neutralize, if not absolutely bar, the demonstration. These ordinances

---

[37] 307 US 496, 515–16 (1939).

[38] See Kalven 'The Concept of the Public Forum: Cox v Louisiana, 1965' *Sup Ct Rev* (1965) 1. Kalven argues for a broad, guaranteed — and therefore largely unrestricted — access to public forums.

[39] See *United States v Grace* 461 US 171, 177 (1983): with respect to a recognized public forum, 'the government may enforce reasonable time, place and manner restrictions as long as the restrictions are content neutral, are narrowly tailored to serve a significant government interest, and leave open ample alternative channels of communication'.

[40] See e g *Chicago Police Department v Mosely* 408 US 92 (1972): ordinance allowing labour picketing near schools, but barring other grounds for picketing, is declared invalid as a content-based restriction; *Boos v Barry* 485 US 312 (1988): law forbidding display of banners or signs critical of a foreign government within 500 feet of said government's embassy is constitutionally invalid as a content-based restriction.

[41] See *Ward v Rock Against Racism* 491 US 781 (1989): ordinance requiring performers appearing at city theatre to use city-owned sound equipment is a regulation *narrowly tailored* to effect the city's significant interest in preventing excessive noise. See also *Clark v Community for Creative Non-Violence* 468 US 288 (1984): significant government interests that warrant protection and may justify infringement of expressive conduct include traffic safety, sanitation, public peace and order, noise control, and personal privacy.

[42] See *Metromedia, Inc v San Diego* 453 US 490 (1981): ban on all billboards eliminated a 'well-established means of communication used to convey a broad range of different kinds of messages,' and a means of communication for which there is no meaningful surrogate.

[43] For an excellent discussion of the various interests at stake when public spaces are used for expressive conduct, see *Niemotko v Maryland* 340 US 268, 273 (1951).

included one preventing the dissemination of literature promoting racial hatred and another preventing the wearing of uniforms or clothing which possessed offensive symbolic significance. In *Collin v Smith* the Seventh Circuit found these ordinances unconstitutional and rejected the town's claim that it had the right to prevent such an offensive display.[44] Despite the potential 'infliction of psychic trauma on the resident Holocaust survivors', the court wrote that the First Amendment demands that 'public expression of ideas may not be prohibited merely because the ideas are themselves offensive to some of their hearers'.[45] In short, the restrictions of expressive conduct must remain content-neutral.[46]

Though the most notorious of legal battles over assembly and expressive conduct, the Skokie litigation was not really ground-breaking with respect to the public forum doctrine. The ambit of the right to free assembly and the public forum time, place, and manner test were first greatly expanded during the freedom marches of the Civil Rights movement.

In 1961 187 black college and high-school students assembled on the sidewalk and street in front of the state house in Columbia, South Carolina to protest racially discriminatory laws still on the state's books. They listened to speeches, sang hymns, and talked amongst themselves. They never threatened violence nor did they become unruly. Despite the quiet and peaceful nature of their protest, they were arrested for and convicted of breaching the peace. When the Supreme Court finally received their appeal in 1963 it struck down the convictions. The court noted that the protest took place in an historically recognized public forum and that there had been no threat of violence by the demonstrators nor evidence of the use of 'fighting words'. In addition, the court wrote:

> 'The circumstances of this case reflect an exercise of these basic constitutional rights [of freedom of speech and free assembly] in their most pristine and classic form ... The Fourteenth Amendment [which incorporates the First Amendment] ... does not permit a State to make criminal the peaceful expression of unpopular views.'[47]

Similarly in 1965 2 000 students gathered in front of a Louisiana courthouse to stage a peaceful protest of the trial of twenty-three of their fellows arrested for picketing stores with segregated lunch counters. The demonstrators initially had police permission to assemble in the street before the courthouse. However, when they began milling about on the sidewalk the police arrested them. In reversing the

---

[44] 578 F 2d 1197 (7th Cir 1978).

[45] At 1206, quoting *Street v New York* 394 US 576, 592 (1969).

[46] See *Collin v Smith* 447 F Supp 676, 702 (ND Ill 1978): articulating the basic underlying conviction animating the near-absolutist position on free speech, the District Court wrote that 'it is better to allow those who preach racial hate to expend their venom in rhetoric, rather than to be panicked into embarking on the dangerous course of permitting government to decide what its citizens may say and hear'. See also *Terminiello v Chicago* 337 US 1 (1949): words that simply make the listeners angry is not sufficient to bar speech; incitement to violence is necessary. As noted earlier, freedom of assembly applies as much to social as to political gatherings:
> 'Where freedom of assembly ... [is] involved, "mere public intolerance or animosity cannot be the basis for abridgement". Thus, the right to "gather in public places" for "social" as well as political purposes "cannot be subject to suspension" even "through the good-faith enforcement of a prohibition against annoying conduct". In this context, government cannot limit the freedom of those whose "ideas ... lifestyle or physical appearance is resented by the majority of their fellow citizens".'

Tribe *American Constitutional Law* 2 ed (1988) 1409–10, quoting *Coates v Cincinnati* 402 US 611, 612, 615 (1971).

[47] *Edwards v South Carolina* 372 US 229 (1963). See also *Brown v Louisiana* 383 US 131 (1966): court struck down breach of peace convictions of African-American students who had peaceably assembled in a public library to protest silently against whites-only policy.

demonstrator's convictions the Supreme Court relied on precedents permitting peaceful labour picketing and its recent decision in *Edwards* and held that such a peaceful non-disruptive assembly on public land could not be criminalized under the Constitution.[48] It wrote:

> 'The rights of free speech and assembly, while fundamental in our democratic society, still do not mean that everyone with opinions or beliefs may address a group at any public place and at any time. The constitutional guarantee of liberty implies the existence of an organized society maintaining public order, without which liberty itself would be lost in the excesses of anarchy ... [However,] it is clearly unconstitutional to enable a public official to determine which expressions of view will be permitted and which will not or to engage in invidious discrimination among persons or groups either by the use of a statute providing a system of broad discretionary licensing power or, as in this case, the equivalent of such a system by selective enforcement of an extremely broad prohibitory statute.'[49]

That last statement by the *Cox* court reveals two other important characteristics of time, place, and manner restrictions: (1) they must provide clear guidelines for the specific conduct being regulated and restricted; (2) they cannot give a public official the relatively unfettered discretion to decide what kind of expressive conduct is permissable.[50]

Indeed, in *Shuttlesworth v Birmingham* the Supreme Court struck down an ordinance which failed both for lack of specificity and for the unbridled power it gave to Birmingham's city commission.[51] The court found that Birmingham's parade-permitting procedures gave the city commission the power to refuse permits on the basis of such vague criteria as 'public welfare, safety, health, decency and public morals'.[52] This vague criterion allowed the commission to wield arbitrary power and refuse permits on the slightest whim. In this case the city commission's whim was to prevent a civil rights protest. The court held that such a permitting scheme violated both free assembly and free speech rights, and struck down the Birmingham ordinance.[53]

## 4.3 Non-public forums

In the aforementioned cases the space in which the assembly or expressive conduct took place was deemed a public forum. As a result the petitioners were entitled to the rather strong protections of the time, place, and manner test. However, what constitutes a public forum has itself been the focus of a significant amount of assembly and expressive conduct litigation, and such litigation has been one of the preferred occasions for curbing the right to free assembly.

For example, in *Adderly v Florida* the court held that the students protesting the

---

[48] *Cox v Louisiana* 379 US 536 (1965).

[49] At 554, 557.

[50] See *Gregory v Chicago* 394 US 111 (1969): convictions for disorderly conduct of a group of peaceful demonstrators pressing for school desegregation were struck down because the statute was vague and gave the police almost unlimited discretion to decide what constituted a 'diversion tending to a breach of the peace'.

[51] 394 US 147 (1969).

[52] At 149.

[53] See Blasi 'Prior Restraints on Demonstrations' (1970) 68 *Mich LR* 1481: Blasi discusses municipalities' use of large fees for policing and sanitation as prior restraints on public assemblies, as well as permit denials on grounds of anticipated fears of public violence and hostile audience responses. See e g *Lovell v Griffin* 303 US 444 (1938): since city manager's power to reject a permit application was unlimited, and not limited by concerns for public cleanliness or orderly conduct, court deemed the ordinance to be void on its face; *Lakewood v Plain Dealer Publishing Co* 468 US 750 (1989): municipal ordinance granting mayor unfettered discretion to issue permits allowing newspaper-vending machines on public property unconstitutional.

arrest of fellow students who had attempted to enter a whites-only theatre did not have the right to gather on jail grounds.[54] The court found that the state normally is given the widest latitude to control activity in prisons and on prison grounds, and the state was within its rights to order dispersal of the crowd and arrest those protestors who refused to leave. It reasoned that '[t]raditionally, state capitol grounds are open to the public. Jails, built for security purposes, are not.'[55] The court noted, however, that had the sheriff ordered the crowd's dispersal based upon the content of the speech, the order would not have been content-neutral and would have been a violation of the right to free speech.

Similarly in *Greer v Spock* the court upheld two regulations barring political activities on a military base.[56] In justifying its conclusion the court wrote that the purpose of a military base is

> 'to train soldiers, not to provide a public forum ... The notion that federal military reservations, like municipal streets and parks, have traditionally served as a place for free public assembly and communication of thoughts by private citizens is historically and constitutionally false.'[57]

As non-public forums, venues such as jails, military bases, and sometimes schools will generally be subject to greater regulation by the state.[58] Indeed, a government regulation on the time, place, and manner of assembly and expressive conduct in a non-public forum will be upheld if it satisfies the following two-part test. First, it must be viewpoint-neutral, i e the regulation need not be content-neutral, but may in fact allow speech on some subjects and not others. However, as viewpoint-neutral, when the government does permit speech on a subject it must permit differing views on the subject.[59] Secondly, it must be reasonably related to a legitimate government interest.[60]

## 4.4 The problem with the public forum and non-public forum doctrines

The problem with both the public forum and non-public forum doctrines is that they tend to focus too much attention on the physical location of the government-owned property on which the expressive conduct is to take place and thereby divert attention away from the real interests at stake.[61] In other words, the 'geographical' analysis

---

[54] 385 US 39 (1966).

[55] At 41.

[56] 424 US 828 (1976).

[57] At 838.

[58] But see *United States v Grace* 461 US 171 (1983). The petitioners challenged a statutory provision which barred display of organizational banners on Supreme Court grounds and sidewalks. The court did not address the constitutionality of the actual statutory provision, but only its effect on the right of the petitioners and public to use the surrounding sidewalk to carry out their expressive activities. The court held that the 'public forum' doctrine could not be understood to mean that public property that abuts government property dedicated to some use other than as a forum for public assembly and expression somehow loses its character as 'public forum property.'

[59] See *Widmar v Vincent* 454 US 263 (1981): if a state college allows various student groups to use classrooms for meetings, it cannot restrict use based on the content of a group's speech and therefore cannot prohibit religious groups from using the classroom.

[60] Reasonably related really only means rationally related. See *Bethel School District v Fraser* 478 US 675 (1986): since public-school activities such as school newspapers or assemblies are *not* public forums, schools can control their content for legitimate pedagogical reasons.

[61] See e g Dienes 'The Trashing of the Public Forum: Problems in First Amendment Analysis' (1986) 55 *Geo Wash LR* 109; Farber & Nowak 'The Misleading Nature of Public Forum Analysis: Content and Context in First Amendment Adjudication' (1984) 70 *Va LR* 1219; Note 'A Unitary Approach to Claims of First Amendment Access to Publicly Owned Property' (1982) 35 *Stan LR* 121; Lee 'Lonely Pamphleteers, Little People, and the Supreme Court: The Doctrine of Time, Place and Manner Regulations of Expression' (1986) 54 *Geo Wash LR* 757; Tribe op cit (n 46) 992–3.

employed fails to get down to the real crux of the matter: a comparison of the various governmental ends at stake in the use of public property for its intended purposes with the competing First Amendment values served by the expressive activity in question. The result is that expressive conduct (and assembly) cases are often heavily influenced, if not entirely determined, by whether or not the particular location is first categorized as a public forum or a non-public forum.

Two of the cases referred to above, *Brown v Louisiana* and *Adderly v Florida*, reflect this subordination of substance to form. In *Brown* the court employed the public forum analysis in finding unconstitutional the breach of peace convictions of African-American students who had engaged in peaceful silent protest within a public (whites-only) library. In *Adderly*, on the other hand, the court employed the non-public forum doctrine and held that the students — protesting the arrest of fellow students who had attempted to enter a whites-only theatre — did not have the right to gather on a jail driveway. It is hard to understand why the inside of a library — a place for quiet contemplation — is declared a public forum and thus a potentially appropriate venue for public protest and the government driveway fronting a jail is a non-public forum and a far more easily restricted venue for public protest. Given the nature of the two locations, one might have thought a reversal of the assignations was appropriate.

But even this reversal of assignations would not have helped to reveal the real interests at stake and the underlying rationales of the judgment. The *Brown* court's decision to strike down the convictions ultimately has to be understood as a reflection of the court's belief that the prosecutions were motivated by the expressive content of the protest — the opposition to Jim Crow laws — and were thus unconstitutional as an infringement of free speech. The *Adderly* court, on the other hand, held the arrests of the protesting students constitutional because it did not view the arrests as content-based and found the restrictions on the space fronting a jail to be legitimate time, place, and manner restrictions. Unfortunately, by focusing on the labels 'public forum' and 'non-public forum' the decisions 'divert attention away from the real first amendment issues'.[62]

To be fair and accurate, the characterization of a place as a public forum or a non-public forum does not completely determine a judicial decision nor do public forum and non-public forum analyses entirely eschew balancing of interests.[63] However, the assignation does determine the test used. And as Farber & Nowak note, and the aforementioned cases suggest, '[c]lassifying a medium of communication as a public forum' will weight the analysis heavily in favour of the speaker and 'may cause legitimate governmental interests to be thoughtlessly brushed aside'.[64] On the other hand, classifying it as a non-public forum will weight the

---

[62] See Farber & Nowak op cit (n 61) 1234.

[63] See Dienes op cit (n 61) 114–15. Dienes cites both *United States v Grace* 461 US 171 (1983) and *Heffron v International Society for Krishna Consciousness* 452 US 640 (1981) as evidence that at least within the limited parameters of the public forum test the courts make 'a real effort to articulate the competing interests involved'. The *Grace* court employs the public forum test and finds that the government's interest in controlling the sidewalks abutting the Supreme Court too weak to justify a ban on expressive conduct in the form of handbilling, picketing, and protests. The *Heffron* court also employed the public forum test, but found that the government's limitation on the distribution of goods or materials at a state fair to certain set locations was justified by its interest in traffic and crowd control and further supported by the ready availability of other channels for communication.

[64] Farber & Nowak op cit (n 61) 1224.

analysis heavily in favour of the government and 'may lead courts to ignore the incompatibility of challenged regulations with first amendment values'.[65]

This critique of public forum and non-public forum analysis also reveals a fairly obvious solution: do away with the jurisprudence of labels. Employ instead a balancing test which gives adequate effect to the free speech interests and public order interests at stake and which permits 'a more candid, open delineation of [these] competing considerations'.[66]

### 4.5 Assembly on private property

Of all the types of venue used for assembly and expressive conduct, private forums are the easiest for the government to regulate. Because individual privacy interests compete on a rather equal constitutional footing with free expression concerns the government regulation need only be reasonable. That is, the issue the court grapples with in these private forum cases concerns not the time, place, and manner of the assembly, but the extent to which the privacy and property interests of the owner are disturbed. For example, a municipal ordinance may require a private homeowner's consent before commercial solicitation is valid.[67] In addition in most instances the court has let stand ordinances which bar picketing or demonstration in front of private residences.

The more difficult question for the court has been what to do with private commercial property such as shopping centres. In *Amalgamated Food Employers v Logan Valley* the court held that, given the 'public' nature and function of shopping centres, they were subject to the same First Amendment standards as any downtown business block.[68] As a result the court found that the picketing of a store in the mall charged with unfair labour practices fell within the protection of the First Amendment.

However, four years later the court severely curbed the application of the 'public function' doctrine to commercial property. In *Lloyd v Tanner* it found that the handing out of anti-war leaflets in a shopping mall did not warrant constitutional protection.[69] Unlike the *Logan Valley* labour protest targeting a particular store, the court felt that this general protest could be just as easily accomplished in an alternative public location such as the street in front of the mall.[70] However, to the

---

[65] Ibid.
[66] Dienes op cit (n 61) 111. See also Tribe op cit (n 46) 992–3: '[Thus], it might be considerably more helpful if the court were to focus more directly and explicitly on the degree to which the regulation at issue impinges on the first amendment interest in the free flow of information'; Note op cit (n 61) 121: Note favours elimination of the conceptual distinction between public and non-public forums and argues that the courts should simply examine the competing interests and uphold the restrictions on expressive conduct and assembly 'only when the restrictions are the least restrictive means of serving a compelling state interest'.
[67] See *Breard v City of Alexandria* 341 US 622 (1951).
[68] 391 US 308 (1968). The court was effectively applying and extending the 'public function' doctrine developed in *Marsh v Alabama* 326 US 501 (1946). The *Marsh* court, however, was concerned with the state action doctrine and not freedom of assembly.
[69] 407 US 551 (1972).
[70] See also *Hudgens v NLRB* 424 US 507 (1976): striking labourers do not have First Amendment right to picket in front of store in mall. Cf *Pruneyard Shopping Center v Robins* 447 US 74 (1979): state constitutions may grant more expansive protections to speech and assembly than Federal Constitution, and thus permit and protect political solicitation in a private shopping centre, as long as the restrictions on the use of the private property do not amount to a taking without compensation or contravene some other federal constitutional provision. See Harrington 'Free Speech, Press and Assembly Liberties under the Texas Bill of Rights' (1990) 68 *Texas LR* 1435.

extent that the assembly and protest have a particular target within the mall, and cannot otherwise effectively communicate their position, *Logan Valley* may still be good law and permit access to private mall property.

Even if the spirit of *Logan Valley* can somehow be salvaged from the restrictions on the use of private property for expressive conduct set out in *Lloyd* and later cases, the cases when read together underscore the extent to which assembly is truly the poor person's media. In a modern society, where most communication, political and otherwise, is electronically disseminated, public assembly has a greatly diminished role. What 'out-groups' in contemporary society really require is access to the 'now' traditional public forums — radio, television, and cinema. Unfortunately the line of cases just discussed provides almost no support for the proposition that because the airwaves serve an important 'public function' there should be some provision made for broader public access to the media. Where the Supreme Court has taken up this issue it is the First Amendment interests — as well as the property interests — of the private broadcasters to say what they please without substantial government intervention that are of primary concern.[71]

## 5  FREEDOM OF ASSEMBLY IN CANADA

### 5.1  Introduction

Of all the areas of constitutional law which may be litigated under the Canadian Charter of Rights and Freedoms, the law on the right of peaceful assembly is perhaps the most underdeveloped.[72] Indeed, at this writing, but a handful of reported cases involve claimants seeking what protection that Charter right affords.[73]

Several possible explanations exist for this phenomenon. First, the Charter has been around for only ten years and one would not expect every right granted in it to have been contested in that brief period of time. Secondly, most sectors of Canadian society — from the police to the protestors — agree on the appropriate parameters for assemblies and demonstrations. Thus there has been no fertile breeding ground for the kinds of conflict which would lead to constitutional litigation on the issue. These two explanations have much to recommend them.

---

[71] Despite early approval — in *Red Lion Broadcasting Co v FCC* 395 US 367 (1969) — of the Federal Communications Commission's 'fairness doctrine', which requires television and radio stations to provide fair coverage of political campaigns and other public issues, later decisions severely curtailed public access to the media. See e g *CBS v Democratic National Committee* 412 US 94 (1973): as part of their 'journalistic discretion' television stations have right to refuse request by individual or political party or commerical organization to purchase broadcast time; *Miami Herald Pub Co v Tornillo* 418 US 241 (1974): striking down law entitling political candidate right to editorial space to respond to political attacks. But see *CBS, Inc v FCC* 453 US 367 (1981): court approves statutory enlargement of a right of access to broadcast media for candidates for federal elective office.

[72] The Charter's text for right of peaceful assembly reads as follows: '2. Everyone has the the following fundamental freedoms: . . . *(c)* freedom of peaceful assembly.' Constitution Act 1982, RSC 1985, Appendix II, No 44, Schedule B, Part I, s 2*(c)*.

[73] See *Canadian Civil Liberties Association* (1992) 91 DLR (4th) 38 (see text below); *Butler v R* (1983) 5 CCC 356 (FCTD): transfer of prisoner from a prison in which he was member of a group practising aboriginal rights to another prison in which no such group existed did not violate his right of assembly; *Re United Assn of Journeymen & Apprentices of Plumbing Industry of US and Canada, Local 740 and Pitts Atlantic Construction Ltd* (1984) 7 DLR (4th) 609 (Nfld CA): statute prohibiting secondary picketing did not violate freedom of assembly; *BCGEU v AG British Columbia* (1985) 20 DLR (4th) 339 (BCCA): statute barring picketing in front of courthouse infringed freedom of assembly, but upheld on s 1 grounds; *Fraser v AG Nova Scotia* (1986) 24 CRR 78, 193 (NSSC): provisions of Act which prevented civil servants from attending partisan political rallies violated freedom of assembly; *R v Skead* (1984) 4 CNLR 108 (Alta Prov Ct): refusal of permit for peaceful march and later charge of obstruction declared unconstitutional infringement of freedom of assembly.

However, even if a number of assembly cases were to be litigated in the not too distant future, it is highly probable that assembly jurisprudence itself would remain underdeveloped. The reason for this is that in Canada, as in the US, the law on freedom of assembly has quickly come to be understood as a part of or an adjunct to freedom of expression jurisprudence.[74] As we have already seen in the US case law, freedom of speech jurisprudence exerts a strong gravitational pull on what may otherwise be matters adjudicated under a freedom of assembly clause because it possesses a conceptual category which subsumes the subject-matter found in freedom of assembly jurisprudence: expressive conduct.

Expressive conduct draws attention not so much to the meaning or content of expression, but to the manner or mode in which the expression is communicated. Thus expressive conduct cases will involve governmental restrictions ranging from the use of loudspeakers, to the wearing of tee-shirts, to the burning of flags, to the public display of political posters and banners, to the distribution of handbills, to the picketing of businesses, to marching on city hall, to protests which occupy a government office. As the last few examples suggest, cases which may otherwise solely implicate assembly concerns — the picketing of businesses, the marching on city hall, the protests which occupy a government office — are treated as expressive conduct cases.

## 5.2 Expressive conduct and the Supreme Court

The Supreme Court of Canada has addressed the doctrine of expressive conduct just once: in *Committee for the Commonwealth of Canada v Canada* ('*CCC*').[75] At issue in *CCC* was the plaintiffs' freedom to distribute handbills and carry placards promoting their political positions in a public airport terminal concourse. The airport prohibited all expressive activity and made no distinction between commercial solicitation and political advocacy. The plaintiffs sought a declaration that the government officials in charge of the airport had infringed upon their right to freedom of expression under s 2*(b)* and that a public airport terminal concourse constituted a public forum in which expressive activities protected by the fundamental freedoms and rights of the Charter could take place. Unfortunately the court's decision to uphold the lower court's grant of the declarations provided no clear guidance on the subject. Instead, the decision generated six different opinions and three very different tests. The Supreme Court's decision is interesting not only because it generated these three different tests regarding the restriction of expressive conduct on public property but also because the three tests, each in its own separate way, illustrate some of the pitfalls associated with freedom of assembly jurisprudence. Because South Africa's constitutional analysis of both assembly and expression is likely to follow the form of Canada's decisions, if not the exact substance, we set out and discuss these three tests in detail.

---

[74] Viewing assembly as a subcategory of expression was not always the norm in Canada. In the pre-Charter case of *AG of Canada v Dupont* (1978) 2 SCR 770 at 797 the Supreme Court held that

'Demonstrations are not a form of speech but of collective action. They are of the nature of a display of force rather than that of an appeal to reason, their inarticulateness prevents them from becoming part of language and reaching the level of discourse.'

Yet such a distinction between assembly and expression can hardly be said to safeguard assembly — for the content of the distinction made in *Dupond* suggests that there is nothing really worth protecting. Force alone does nothing to advance the democratic or pluralistic ends which normally justify freedom of assembly.

[75] (1991) 77 DLR (4th) 385.

Chief Justice Lamer begins his treatment of expressive conduct on public property by rejecting the public forum/non-public forum distinctions made in US expressive conduct and assembly jurisprudence. Lamer CJ can hardly be faulted for wanting to avoid sterile categories which, as we have already noted, seem to deflect attention away from the real values and interests at stake.

Lamer CJ instead decides to craft a simple test in which the interest of the individual in expressing herself in a public forum so as to reach a large number of her fellow citizens is balanced against the government's interest in ensuring that 'the services or undertaking offered by government are operated effectively and in accordance with their intended purpose'.[76] In so doing he rejects the argument that s 2(b) considers only the interests of the person wishing to express an idea. He asserts, instead, that the individual's interest in expression is legitimately circumscribed by the interests of both the government and the rest of the citizenry.

The first problem with this test is that it dramatically expands the categories of expression and expressive conduct which do not enjoy constitutional protection under s 2(b). Lamer CJ insists that his general limitation on expression is in accord with the previous limitations on expression set out by the Supreme Court in *Irwin Toy*.[77] However, in *Irwin Toy* only violent expressive conduct was deemed to fall outside the protection of s 2(b). Here Lamer CJ quite clearly holds that expression which interferes with the effective operation of a government-owned space also falls outside the protection of s 2(b). This new unprotected category of expression would represent a deep incursion into an expansively understood and relatively unfettered sphere of activity.

The second problem with this test is that it does the balancing of individual interests and governmental interests within the freedom of expression clause. While that may be appropriate and necessary under the US Constitution — which has only the bald text of the First Amendment to guide expressive conduct adjudication[78] — it is quite unusual and unnecessary in Canadian Charter adjudication. After all, the Charter has the all-important limitation clause, s 1. The limitation clause permits governmental restrictions on fundamental freedoms and rights provided that the state can show that the restrictions are reasonable and justifiable in a free and open democratic society.[79] Thus the balancing of individual interests against governmental interests usually occurs in the context of s 1 review.

---

[76] The Chief Justice also states the test this way at 395:
'[T]he individual will only be free to communicate in a place owned by the state if the form of expression he uses is compatible with the principal function or intended purpose of that place . . . The interest which any person may have in communicating in a place suited for the purpose cannot have the effect of depriving the citizens as a whole of the effective operation of government services and undertakings.'

[77] *Irwin Toy Ltd v Quebec* (1989) 58 DLR (4th) 577.

[78] Under the US Constitution the balancing of competing governmental and individual interests occurs within the fundamental right provision itself.

[79] See *R v Chaulk* (1990) 62 CCC (3d) 193 at 216–17: setting out the test for s 1 of the Charter developed in *R v Oakes* (1986) 26 DLR (4th) 200. The *Oakes* test has the following two prongs: first, the objective of the impugned provision must be of sufficient importance to warrant overriding a constitutionally protected right or freedom — it must relate to concerns which are pressing and substantial in a free and democratic society before it can be characterized as sufficiently important; secondly, assuming that a sufficiently important objective has been established, the means chosen to achieve the objective must pass a proportionality test. This test has three parts. The first part requires that the government restriction of the right be 'rationally connected' to its objective and not be arbitrary, unfair, or based upon irrational considerations. The second part requires that the government restriction impair the right or freedom as 'little as possible'. The third part requires that the restriction's effects on the limitation of rights and freedoms are proportional to the objective. For more on the balancing of expressive interests and governmental interests within s 1 and the *Oakes* test, see MacKay 'Freedom of Expression: Is It All Just Talk?' (1989) 68 *Can Bar Rev* 713.

Part of the reason, if not the entire reason, that Lamer CJ locates the test for expressive conduct in public spaces within s 2(b) is that he decides that the regulation in question is not a 'law' within the meaning of s 1. Thus he is unable to do the necessary balancing in the context of s 1.

However, Lamer CJ's cramped reading of the word 'law' has severe repercussions. First, it means that the significant body of balancing analysis law that had developed under s 1 must necessarily be ignored. Secondly, and more importantly, it creates the potential for two separate bodies of case law to develop on expressive conduct in public spaces. The first body of case law will flow from impugnable regulations and discretionary acts reviewed under s 2(b)'s balancing test. The second body of case law will flow from impugnable laws reviewed under the s 1 balancing test. This bifurcation of the test for expressive conduct into a s 2(b) test for regulations and a s 1 test for laws not only creates the undesirable potential for confusion but will also likely result in the establishment of different tests for the very same sort of problem.

The final reason for rejecting Lamer CJ's approach to the problem of expressive conduct on public property is that while the Lamer test may have the virtue of candor regarding the balancing of interests, the balancing test itself provides very little specific guidance as to which individual interests and governmental interests warrant protection. Save for his specific factual finding that the distribution of handbills and the carrying of placards in a public airport concourse are protected activities, Lamer CJ tells us neither what kinds of expression are and are not compatible with government operations nor what counts as the 'effective' operation of government.

Like Lamer CJ, L'Heureux-Dube J also attempts to distance herself from the public/non-public forum distinctions made in US jurisprudence. Her opinion, however, engenders few of the same basic problems raised by the Chief Justice's opinion. Unlike Lamer CJ, she recognizes that the different structures of the US Constitution and the Canadian Charter of Rights and Freedoms dictate that the 'balancing tests be undertaken at different stages of the analysis'.[80] As a result, while the guarantee of freedom of expression under s 2(b) may not be absolute, 'it should be given a large and liberal application'. This interpretation of s 2(b) seems consistent with previous construals of s 2(b)'s ambit.[81]

Adoption of a 'large and liberal' interpretation of s 2(b) means that any government law with the purpose or effect of restricting expressive activity — save for violent expressive activities — is going to be deemed an infringement of the right to freedom of expression under s 2(b) of the Charter.[82] This understanding of the

---

[80] *CCC* (supra) at 411.

[81] See *Irwin Toy Ltd v Quebec* (supra) at 606: 'We cannot . . . exclude human activity from the scope of the guaranteed free expression on the basis of the content or the meaning being conveyed. Indeed, if the activity conveys or attempts to convey meaning, it has expressive content and *prima facie* falls within the scope of the guarantee'; *R v Keegstra* (1990) 61 CCC (3rd) 1 at 24: the content or meaning of an expression or expressive conduct is not relevant to a determination as to whether s 2(b) has been infringed.

[82] Under *Irwin Toy*, to determine whether there has been an infringement of s 2(b), one first asks: Is the activity 'expressive activity?' If so, one then asks: Is the expressive activity 'unprotected?' That is, is the expressive activity violent or does it threaten violence? If the expressive activity is found to be protected, one then asks whether the purpose of the government expression is to restrict the protected expression. If so, then the analysis moves to s 1 to see whether the restriction is reasonable and justifiable. If the purpose of the law is not to restrict expression, then one asks whether the actual effect of the law is to restrict expression. If the plaintiff claims that the law in question has the effect of restricting her protected expressive activity, she must first show her expressive activity

s 2(b) test means that if the expression is protected, then the question of whether restrictions of expression on government property are justifiable is going to be determined under s 1, and not under s 2(b).

Before setting out her balancing test under s 1 L'Heureux-Dube J observes that two considerations provide the outer boundaries for discussion of expressive activity on public property. On the one hand, she notes that if the public did not have the right to free expression on public property, there would be little meaningful opportunity for most citizens to express their beliefs. Only those few individuals or groups who possessed access to mass media or control over sufficiently large locations for group gatherings would be able to express fully and effectively their beliefs. Limitation of the right to expression to those few wealthy or powerful individuals able to control the means of communication would thereby undermine the basic purposes of the Charter's guarantee of free expression: to provide the grounds for 'the free exchange of ideas, open debate on public affairs, the effective working of democratic institutions and the pursuit of knowledge and truth'.[83] On the other hand, it seems equally clear that not all government property was intended for or is necessary for making good the promise of open and robust public debate. Access to 'internal government offices, air traffic control towers, prison cells or judges' chambers' does not promote democratic values to any greater degree than access to more readily accessible public spaces within government buildings, concourses in airports, the sidewalk outside a courtroom, or open areas fronting prisons.[84]

In determining what sorts of public areas are appropriate for expressive activities, L'Heureux-Dube J rejects the use of rigid American forum categories.[85] L'Heureux-Dube J offers a more flexible approach to expression in what she calls 'public arenas'. She identifies a number of criteria designed to guide a court attempting to determine whether a government-owned property is open to expressive activity.[86]

If, after a consideration of these criteria, a place is deemed to qualify as a public arena fit for expressive activity, the court then asks whether the government's restrictions on expressive activity are reasonable and justifiable in a free and open democratic society. The court, however, is not obliged to adhere rigidly or mechanistically to the *Oakes* test. It is instead the spirit of the *Oakes* test that should be followed.[87] According to L'Heureux-Dube J, the spirit of the *Oakes* test dictates that

---

serves one of the following three ends: (1) the seeking after truth and knowledge; (2) participation in the political and social affairs of the community; (3) diversity in individual self-fulfilment and human flourishing. Having made that showing, she must then show that the law, regulation, or action in question had the effect of restricting her protected activity.

[83] *CCC* (supra) at 426.

[84] Ibid.

[85] For a Canadian critique of the US public forum doctrine, see Moon 'Access to Public and Private Property under Freedom of Expression' (1988) 20 *Ottawa LR* 339.

[86] The six criteria are: (1) the traditional openness of such property for expressive activity; (2) whether the public is ordinarily admitted as a matter of right; (3) the compatibility of the property's purpose with such expressive activity; (4) the impact of the availability of such property for expressive activity on the achievement of s 2(b)'s purposes; (5) the symbolic significance of the property for the message being conveyed; (6) the availability of other public arenas in the vicinity for expressive activities.

[87] The Attorney-General of Ontario argued that it would be difficult if not impossible for the state to show that a measure restricting expressive activity impaired the speaker's expressive rights as little as possible. Thus no legislation could be saved by s 1. Both L'Heureux-Dube J and McLachlin J agreed that neither the *Oakes* test nor s 1 could be read so restrictively. See *USA v Controni* (1989) 48 CCC (3d) 193 at 218–19: 'In the performance of the balancing task under s 1 . . . a mechanistic aproach must be avoided'; *Keegstra* (supra) at 28: it is 'dangerously misleading to conceive of s 1 as a rigid and technical provision, offering nothing more than a last chance for the state to justify incursions into the realm of fundamental rights'; *Edward Books & Art Ltd v R* (1986) 35 DLR (4th) 1

a second set of criteria be used in determining the reasonableness of the government's content-neutral time, place, and manner restrictions.[88]

There are two primary problems with L'Heureux-Dube J's test. First, despite her stated belief that not all public property is appropriate for expressive activity, she holds that every restriction of expressive activity on public property is an infringement of freedom of expression. It is hard to understand how, if you have no right to engage in expressive activity on certain public properties, your right to freedom of expression can possibly be infringed. Thus the simplicity and desirability of holding all restrictions of expressive activity to be infringements of s *2(b)* is undermined by the well-justified belief that not all expression on public property deserves constitutional protection.

Secondly, holding that all restrictions of expressive activity on public property are infringements of s *2(b)* takes all of the balancing out of s *2(b)* and places it in s 1, where balancing usually occurs. For L'Heureux-Dube J, this choice has the following unfortunate result. A court employing the L'Heureux-Dube approach to assembly could wind up doing two different balancing tests within s 1. The first test requires the court to determine whether a particular piece of public property counts as a public arena given the kind of expressive activity being engaged in. If the property is found to be a public arena, the court must undertake a second balancing test and decide whether the value behind the government's restriction of the expressive activity outweighs the value behind the expressive value taking place in that particular public arena. The problem here is not so much incoherence, but a lack of elegance: both balancing tests effectively ask whether the expressive activity is compatible with the property's purpose and whether other public arenas in the vicinity are available and appropriate for the expressive activities. If, as L'Heureux-Dube J says, one wants to get away from the rigid categories of public forum analysis, it is not at all clear why one has first to establish the existence of a 'public arena' before deciding on the justifiability of the government's restrictions. It seems just as easy to do the balancing of the interests in favour of the expressive activity on the public property and the interests in favor of the government restriction in one fell swoop by simply aggregating the criteria.

Between Lamer CJ's balancing all the interests within s *2(b)* and L'Heureux-Dube J's balancing all the interests within s 1, there exists a middle ground. It is this middle ground that McLachlin J's opinion attempts to occupy. Contrary to L'Heureux-Dube J, McLachlin believes that only some expression on public property is protected by s *2(b)*. There must therefore be a threshhold test within s *2(b)* to determine what kinds of public property permit expressive activity. However, McLachlin J rejects Lamer CJ's position that s *2(b)*'s guarantee only

---

at 41, arguing that while there are two prongs to the s 1 test as set out in *Oakes*, 'the nature of the proportionality test [the second prong] would vary depending on the circumstances. Both in articulating the standard of proof and in describing the proportionality requirement, the court has been careful to avoid rigid and inflexible standards.'

[88] This second set of criteria reads as follows: (1) the more significant the purpose of the measure, the greater the latitude for regulating time, place, and manner of expression; (2) the extent to which the restriction is tailored to its objectives, such that it does not overreach its purpose; (3) whether the restrictions are designed in a manner free from excessive official discretion or undue arbitrariness; (4) whether adequate alternative avenues of expression are left open; (5) the extent to which the restriction ensures that the property at issue can be effectively used by the government and the public for the governmental function or activity for which it was intended, apart from its use as a public arena for expression.

protects expression on public property if it does not unduly impair the function of the particular piece of public property and that all the balancing of interests occurs under s 2(b). Instead, she argues that if the threshhold for s 2(b)'s protection is met, the analysis moves on to s 1 for the more delicate balancing of interests.

While McLachlin J's opinion has the virtue of splitting the baby between L'Heureux-Dube J and Lamer CJ, it is, among other things, a bit short on substance. For example, McLachlin J tells us that the protection afforded by s 2(b) lies somewhere between absolute government control of expression on public property and *prima facie* protection for all expression on public property. As for the actual mechanism for determining a s 2(b) infringement, McLachlin J says only that the test for public expression on government property must be 'based upon the values and interests at stake and not [on] . . . the particular types of government property'.[89] Unfortunately she does not specify what the competing interests are or how they are to be weighted. The only direction she gives is that 'the task at this stage should be primarily definitional rather than one of balancing, and that the test should be sufficiently generous to ensure that valid claims are not excluded for want of proof'.[90] Given the imprecision of this language, it is not at all clear whether this stipulative exercise effectively provides the grounds for a Canadian version of the public forum doctrine — despite McLachlin J's stated wish to distance herself from this doctrine — or whether it comports with the kind of categorical analysis we suggest below.

If, after this initial test, the expressive activity on public property is deemed to be protected by s 2(b), then one asks whether the government's restriction is justified under s 1. Here McLachlin J provides a far more robust and useful test. According to this s 1 balancing test, the state's interest in regulating expression on public property is determined by two primary criteria: (1) the extent to which it legitimately seeks to 'control the content of the expression', for example, hate speech; (2) the extent to which it legitimately seeks to control the consequences of expressive activity on public property: i e the extent to which the expressive activity is compatible with the property's purpose or function. The competing individual or group interest in the expressive activity is determined by asking the following questions: (1) 'How suitable is the location for the effective communication of the message to the public?'; (2) 'Does the property in question have symbolic significance for the message being communicated?'; (3) 'Are there other public arenas in the vicinity in which the expression can be disseminated?'; (4) 'What does the claimant lose by being denied the opportunity to spread his or her message in the form and in the time and place asserted?' Of course, McLachlin J's s 1 test suffers from a similar problem as L'Heureux-Dube J's second s 1 test — it repeats much of the analysis which occurred within s 2(b). The vague values and interests McLachlin J asks us to consider in s 2(b) must in large part be the same as those values and interests which she explicitly identifies in her s 1 test.

However, the major problem with McLachlin's approach to expressive conduct is not with this second half of the test, but with the first. As we have already noted, it is highly unusual, if not entirely contrary to practice, to undertake balancing tests

---

[89] *CCC* (supra) at 454.
[90] Ibid.

within a s 2 fundamental freedom. The simple reason for this is that s 1 provides the proper context for such balancing. Furthermore, with respect to freedom of expression, no balancing has ever been done within the right itself. At most a category of expression has been found to fall outside the provision's protection.

This last point suggests a possible solution to the problems which seem to plague both L'Heureux-Dube J's s 1 and McLachlin J's s 2*(b)* tests for expressive activity. Rather than engage in a balancing test within s 2*(b)*, it seems more appropriate to craft categories of expressive conduct on public property which do not deserve s 2*(b)*'s protection; i e categories of expressive conduct which are deemed not to serve the values which animate the freedom may be legitimately excluded from the freedom's protective ambit. This tact would have the virtue of remaining consistent with both *Irwin Toy*'s excising the category of violent expressive activity and the Charter's structural commitment to doing balancing within the limitation clause and not the s 2 freedoms. In addition one would at the same time eliminate much of the redundancy which exists in either L'Heureux-Dube J's s 1 double-balancing test or in McLachlin J's dual s 2*(b)* and s 1 balancing tests. According to this value-based categorical approach, certain kinds of places could be deemed off-limits to public demonstration because they do not serve the values which animate the freedom or because they can *never* safely suffer protest. For example, top-security military bases or places which may involve dangers to the greater public, such as control rooms for nuclear reactors, may all fall within a category of places which can never safely suffer protest.[91] If a demonstration or expressive activity did not take place in one of those few specified places, then it would be deemed protected by s 2*(b)*. The analysis would then move to s 1 to see whether, when the interests of the state and the individual are balanced, the restriction is justified.

### 5.3 Learning from other expressive conduct and assembly cases

Because of the limited guidance which the decision in *CCC* offers, it is useful to look at what lower Canadian courts have done in other expressive conduct and assembly cases. For example, we have thus far pressed the thesis that assembly follows expression. This thesis finds support in the recent case of *Canadian Civil Liberties Association v Canada* (*'CCLA'*).[92] Although the court in *CCLA* does not expressly recognize the connection between expression and assembly jurisprudence, it is worth noting that the ease with which the court dispenses with the freedom of expression claim makes it especially easy for the court then to dismiss the freedom of assembly claim. In *CCLA* the issue was whether certain sections of the Canadian Security Intelligence Service Act which authorized the Canadian Security Intelligence Service (CSIS) to use highly intrusive surveillance techniques to determine whether members of the Canadian public are involved in activities designed either to overthrow the Canadian government or to foment violence abroad were violative of the Charter.[93] The Canadian Civil Liberties Association (CCLA) sought a declaration that the impugned sections of the CSIS Act were unconstitu-

---

[91] Admittedly, a potential danger exists that we shall revisit the very same problems of a public forum doctrine on s 2*(b)*. However, if one gives s 2*(b)* a very large and liberal interpretation, and proscribes expressive activity in only those few public spaces which can safely suffer *no* protest, assembly, or demonstration, one avoids the rigidity problems of the US doctrine and permits flexible analysis of expressive conduct in the context of s 1.
[92] (1992) 91 DLR (4th) 38.
[93] Sections 12, 21–26.

tional on the grounds that these sections did not so much seek to regulate unlawful activity as they sought to restrict potentially lawful activity protected by the rights to expression, assembly, association, life, liberty, and security.

The court spent the better part of its decision rejecting the argument that the vagueness and breadth of the term 'activity' in the CSIS Act could lead to the 'chilling' and effective suppression of expressive activity protected under s 2*(b)* of the Charter. Thus, when the court finally arrived at the question of whether the CSIS Act infringed upon the right of peaceable assembly, it was able to dispense with the issue in a highly abbreviated manner. The court held that while it appeared that the surveillance of some marches and organizations had apparently deterred some individuals from participating in some assemblies, it did not necessarily follow that the surveillance contemplated and authorized in the CSIS Act had either the purpose or the effect of restricting the freedom of peaceable assembly. Consistent with its view that the 'chilling effect' doctrine had as yet no place in Canadian free expression jurisprudence, it likewise held that the 'chilling effect' doctrine had no place in the review of peaceful assembly claims.

In addition to our thesis that assembly generally follows expression it may be possible, based upon some lower-court decisions, to put forward one more general thesis about Canadian expressive conduct and assembly cases. The thesis has two parts or sides. First, to the extent that an expressive activity serves democratic ends and only incidentally impairs the use of public property, the courts will find the activity *prima facie* protected and only subject to those regulations which minimally impair the expressive activity and are proportionate to the state's desired end. However, where the expressive activity is primarily commercial in nature and requires the relatively permanent use of public property the courts have generally held that the activity is not protected by s 2*(b)*, and that even if it is, it may be justifiably restricted by the state.

The case of *City of Edmonton v Orchard ('Forget (Re)')*[94] illustrates the first half of the thesis. In *Forget* an Alberta appeals court had to grapple with an Edmonton municipal by-law which prohibited the affixing of posters to utility poles, traffic lights, and other city-owned structures. The defendants had affixed posters to utility poles to announce a public meeting and were charged with a violation of the city by-law. The defendants challenged the by-law as an infringement of their freedom of expression guaranteed under s 2*(b)* of the Charter. The Alberta Court of Queen's Bench held that generally a person is entitled to use public property in her exercise of a fundamental freedom unless the person's use of the public property seriously interferes with the use of the public property by other persons or the city.[95] In this case the placing of posters which announced a public meeting on utility poles was clearly a use of public property protected by s 2*(b)*. The court held that while preventing the visual blight of public postering on lampposts may be a pressing and substantial concern, the absolute ban on postering was neither essential nor proportionate to the desired end of preserving the city's aesthetic appearance, and thus could not be justified under s 1. The court suggested, however, that less restrictive

---

[94] (1990) 74 DLR (4th) 547.
[95] At 557.

measures regulating the use of posters on public property could have been employed and would have passed constitutional muster.

The flip-side of our thesis is reflected in *Canadian Newspapers Co v Victoria*[96] and *Canadian Newspapers Co v Montreal*.[97] In *Canadian Newspapers Co v Montreal* the court held that freedom of expression does not require that a private party be permitted permanently to use public property to run their newspaper business — even though the business involves an expressive activity. Otherwise, the court argued, any person or group engaged in expressive activity could legitimately lay claim on an ongoing basis to a particular piece of public property needed to carry out their expressive activity. Similarly in *Canadian Newspapers Co v Victoria* the British Columbia Court of Appeal held that a Victoria municipal by-law barring placement of paper-vending machines on public property did not infringe the company's freedom of expression. First, the court held that the city was entitled to protect its own commercial interests — the aesthetic appeal of the city necessary for the tourist trade — at the expense of the commerical interests of the newspapers. Secondly, given that the newspapers have many others means of distribution, the court held that the newspapers' freedom of expression was minimally impaired.[98]

## 6 FREEDOM OF ASSEMBLY IN GERMANY

### 6.1 Introduction

In Germany assemblies have not only been used by demonstrators to articulate complaints against and demands of the state. In the past assemblies have also been instrumental in the state's repression of dissent. Thus, while protest by popular civic action groups may have been directly responsible for the fall of the DDR (East Germany), and have strongly influenced the environmental and defence policies of the BRD (West Germany), state-ordered propaganda marches and demonstrations in Nazi Germany and the DDR have had a terrifying effect on dissidents and will not be easily forgotten.[99]

---

[96] (1990) 63 DLR (4th) 1.

[97] [1988] RJQ 482.

[98] See also *New Brunswick Broadcasting Co v Radio, Television & Telecommunications Commission* (1984) 13 DLR (4th) 77. The Federal Court of Appeal held that licence renewal requirements for television stations were justifiable limitations on the plaintiff's right to expression. More generally, the court opined that freedom of expression did not entitle one to the use of someone else's property to engage in the expressive activity, even if the property in question was public property. Cf *Re Canadian Newspapers Co and Director of Public Road and Traffic Services of City of Quebec* (1986) 36 DLR (4th) 641. The Quebec Superior Court held that an absolute ban on newspaper-vending machines was not a justifiable infringement of the right to freedom of the press. The right to freedom of the press was deemed to include a right to publish and distribute. The court's holding suggests that some more limited and narrowly tailored restrictions on vending machines would be justifiable.

[99] The Assembly Act of 1934 assigned wide powers of control over assemblies to the executive. Permission was required for all assemblies except those of the NSDAP and its branches. Practically no rules existed to guide the executive in their decisions and the permission to assemble could be recalled or be subjected to conditions at any time. See *Das Gesetz zur Regelung der öffentliche Sammlungen und sammlungsähnlichen Veranstaltungen* — 5.11.1934. In 20 *BVerfGE* 150 157–8 the court declared this pre-constitutional statute to be unconstitutional and void. The court reasoned that the statute was a disproportionate infringement of art 2.1 *GG* (general freedom to develop the personality) and the *Rechtsstaat* and separation of powers principles. See Scholler & Birk *Verfassungsrecht und Verfassungsgerichtsbarkeit* (1988) 47; Von Münch & Kunig *Grundgesetzkommentar* (1992) 534. For the history of freedom of assembly in Germany, see Schwäble *Das Grundrecht der Versammlungsfreiheit (art 8 GG)* (1975) 17–45; Müller *Wirkungsbereich und Schranken der Versammlungsfreiheit, in besondere im Verhältnis zur Meinungsfreiheit* (1974) 15–40.

This history explains the elaborate regulation of the freedom to assemble under current German law. The Basic Law *(GG)*,[100] a substantial amount of ordinary legislation,[101] and an array of judicial decisions[102] together form an intricate web of protection for the freedom of assembly. Yet despite these protections the practice of the freedom remains extremely controversial. Mass protests and demonstrations have become increasingly difficult to regulate. Very often agitators present at the demonstrations exploit volatile group dynamics for destructive ends. Because of the mass of people present at any given assembly, however, it is difficult, if not impossible, for the police to identify and act against the individual offenders. As a result, the costs involved in policing demonstrations have increased dramatically over the past several years, as have calls for tougher controls.[103]

## 6.2 The extension of the term 'assembly'

The term 'assembly' in art 8.1 of the Basic Law covers public and private assemblies, protest marches, and demonstrations.[104] Although opinion differs as to the exact number, it is clear that more than one person will be necessary to form an assembly.[105] In addition, to constitute an assembly those present must further aim to form or express an opinion and this common goal must unite them.[106] An assembly

---

[100] Article 8 *GG* reads: '(1) All Germans have, without notification or permission, the right to assemble peacefully and unarmed. (2) The right to assemble in the open-air may be restricted by or pursuant to a statute of parliament.' The formulation has changed little from art 7.29 of the Paulskirche Constitution of 1848 and art 123 of the Weimar Constitution of 1919.

[101] The most important piece of legislation is the Assembly Act of 1953 (*VersammlG*). For the full text and interpretation see Dietel & Gintzel *Demonstrations- und Versammlungsfreiheit Kommentar zum Gesetz über Versammlungen und Aufzüge vom 24 Juli 1953* 9 ed (1989).

[102] The most important judicial decision is the *Brokdorf* decision of the Federal Constitutional Court (FCC), 69 *BVerfGE* 315.

[103] Costs of policing a single assembly have run up to DM30 million (more than R60 million). See Zitzmann *Öffentliche Versammlungen unter freiem Himmel und Aufzüge* (1984).

[104] A public assembly concerns public affairs, is open to all, and requires no invitation. The difference between a public assembly and a private assembly will not be discussed here. The distinction is only really relevant for the limitations placed on the right to assemble. See Dietel & Gintzel op cit (n 101) 24, 69.

[105] Opinion on the number of people needed to constitute an assembly differs from two persons (Herzog *Maunz-Dürig-Herzog Grundgesetz Kommentar* (1991) 8-20) to three (Hoffmann-Riem *Reihe Alternativkommentare Kommentar zum Grundgesetz für die Bundesrepublik Deutschland* (1984) 751) to a greater number of participants (Frowein 'Versammlungsfreiheit und Versammlungsrecht' 1969 *NJW* 1081n10).

[106] See 56 *BVerwGE* 63 69 (information stand of political party does not constitute an assembly); *BVerwG* 1989 *NJW* 2411 at 2412; 69 *BVerfGE* 315 343. See Von Münch & Kunig op cit (n 99) 541, 97–103; Frowein '*Die Versammlungsfreiheit vor dem Bundesverfassungsgericht*' 1985 *NJW* 2376. Hoffmann-Riem op cit (n 105) 752 argues that the communication of ideas in conjunction with others makes assembly special and worthy of protection. The court seems to have aligned itself with this view in the *Brokdorf* decision. See 69 *BVerfGE* 315 343–5. Thus, for the court, assembly and freedom of opinion are inextricably linked. Herzog op cit (n 105) 8-21-2 takes isssue with the dominant opinion. He argues that there must be an internal connection between participants in the sense that they must consciously want to be together. However, as Herzog believes that assembly is not only functional to democracy but also to the free development of the individual's personality in the context of a group, he does not require that assemblers must have the common objective of communicating their beliefs. The implication is that assemblies which merely seek to satisfy the individual's need to be with others will be covered by art 8 *GG* and not merely by the less protective art 2.1 *GG*. Thus it appears that Herzog sees freedom of assembly as a concretization of, or as instrumental for, the freedom of development of the personality (art 2.1 *GG*). Unfortunately Herzog's definition, while generous, leaves assembly without sufficient contours to justify the higher level of protection afforded to it by art 8 *GG*. Another dissenting view is held by Mangoldt & Klein *Das Bonner Grundgesetz* (1966) 304–5. They insist that the assemblers should not merely aim to communicate a common belief, but that belief should also concern 'public affairs' to qualify for art 8 *GG* protection. This argument may have a foundation in the history of the freedom — see Schilder *Het recht tot vergadering en betoging* (1989) 137 — but not in the decisions of the courts. Mangoldt & Klein's viewpoint should also be understood in the context of their propagation of the democratic-functional theory of interpreting rights (see above, 98). This theory of interpreting rights has been criticized for giving higher levels of protection to the 'political' use of rights. See Schwäble op cit (n 99) 74–84.

therefore differs from a crowd merely desiring to be together or from an audience listening to a rock concert or from spectators looking at an accident or a soccer match or a showroom window.

## 6.3 The meaning of 'freedom of assembly' as an objective principle

Freedom of assembly is not simply a subjective right of the individual to be used against the state. It is also an objective principle which expresses part of the nature of the German democratic order. Given the foundational nature of freedom of assembly for the German polity, all subordinate legal rules are required to respect this 'objective meaning'. The objective component of the freedom to assemble serves as a corrective to the representative democratic process in Germany. On this account, assembly represents a direct form of popular sovereignty. This direct form of sovereignty functions as a counterweight to the massive power and influence granted political parties by the Basic Law.[107] Such a view of assembly also seems to be historically accurate. For example, in the sixties frustrations with official channels for communicating demands to the government — especially during the time of the Great Coalition between the SPD (Social Democrats) and the CDU (Christian-Democrats) — led to a resurgence of interest in extra-parliamentary opposition and, particularly, a resurgence in public protests and demonstrations.

Today freedom of assembly still remains an important political tool for those who feel that their demands are not being given serious attention by the state. In large part assembly is used by discrete minorities, or so-called 'out-groups', as well as by groups concerned about a single issue, such as consumer protection or environmental protection. All these groups find it difficult to organize and present their concerns within the confines of representative politics.[108] For them the freedom to assemble makes democracy visible and legitimate in addition to countering feelings of helplessness and isolation.[109] In this way majority rule is stabilized by allowing minorities to influence decisions of the majority.[110] The extent to which citizens make use of assembly therefore not only reflects on the political consciousness of citizens in a political system but may also be said to be a yardstick of the ability of the exisiting political leadership to integrate divergent views in society.[111]

---

[107] See 69 *BVerfGE* 315 345.

[108] See Hoffmann-Riem op cit (n 105) 749.

[109] See 69 *BVerfGE* 315 346; Dietel & Gintzel op cit (n 101) 1. Freedom of assembly and association are especially important for groups in society, such as minors and foreigners, who are denied the franchise. Unfortunately the protection of neither freedom is extended to foreigners in the Basic Law and they are therefore dependent on — the less protective — art 2.1 *GG*. Alternatively, foreigners may rely on art 11 of the European Convention on Human Rights (status of a statute), art 1.1 of the Assembly Act, and art 1.2 of the Association Act. See Herzog op cit (n 105) 14; Scholz *Maunz-Dürig-Herzog Grundgesetz Kommentar* (1991) 9-64. Minors become subjects of the basic rights when they reach the necessary maturity to exercise the right in question. What is particularly unsatisfactory about this situation is that groups who are denied access to the formal political process are also denied the full protection of the Basic Law to express their opinions in other ways. In the past such restrictions were of course quite common. After the Paulskirche Constitution was suspended in 1851 one of the characteristics which the regulation of assembly by the different German states had in common was that women and the youth, who were denied the vote, were also not allowed to participate in public meetings. Article 12 of the *Reichsvereinsgesetz* of 1908 contained an equally bizarre provision: the use of languages other than German at meetings was criminalized. See Schilder op cit (n 106) 125–6.

[110] 69 *BVerfGE* 315 347.

[111] See Von Münch & Kunig op cit (n 99) 536.

In addition to providing an alternative mode of communication for the politically marginal groups in society[112] freedom of assembly also ensures the continuation of communication between voters and representatives. Thus not only may assembly serve as a warning to the government of the unpopularity of its policies but it may also help to identify pressing problems which arise in the time between elections.[113]

Not everyone agrees with the Federal Constitutional Court (FCC or *Bundesverfassungsgericht*) that the objective meaning of freedom of assembly is exhausted by its functionality to democracy. Some authors have argued that because the individual often needs to develop his/her personality in the context of a group, assemblies which serve this end also deserve constitutional protection. Put in other terms, the formation of opinions through group participation is but one end of assembly. Relaxation and companionship are also ends of free assembly that may be deemed worthy of protection.[114]

## 6.4 The content of 'assembly' as a right

As a right, freedom of assembly provides the individual with a number of defences against state power.[115] First, as is made clear from the text of art 8.1 *GG*, permission or absolutely mandatory registration or notice requirements are unconstitutional. Secondly, freedom of assembly is understood not only to include the act of assembling but also to encompass the collective activities resulting from the assembly:[116] the courts see various forms of communal conduct, including non-verbal forms of expression, as protected.[117] Thirdly, the preparations and the organization (advertisement, invitations, finding the venue and speakers, transport to the assembly), the administration of the assembly under own leadership (determination of intermissions, closure), and participation (to be present, talk, interrupt) are also included.[118] Fourthly, under most circumstances assemblers have the right to disperse in an appropriate time after the assembly has ended.[119] Finally, freedom of assembly also protects the individual from state coercion to join an assembly.[120]

---

[112] See 69 *BverfGE* 315 347. New dangers seem inherent in this alternative form of communication. People resort to assembly because their demands are not given any media coverage; but often demonstrators do not believe that the problem can be overcome by sticking to legitimate means of protest. It therefore becomes necessary to break the law. The media, by giving disproportionate attention to illegal forms of protest, reinforce this belief. Another danger is that radical groups may, by making use of well-orchestrated mass meetings, skew public opinion about their real support and importance. See Von Münch & Kunig op cit (n 99) 536; Hoffmann-Riem op cit (n 105) 750.

[113] 69 *BVerfGE* 315 347.

[114] Schilder op cit (n 106) 120; Herzog op cit (n 105) 88. The goal of the assembly has, to the extent mentioned above, been incorporated in its definition and the individual's need, simply to be together with others, is given the lesser protection of art 2.1 *GG*.

[115] The effect of art 19.3 *GG* is that the protection offered by freedom of assembly is extended to juristic persons to organize assemblies and participate therein through their organs or delegates. Article 19.3 *GG* states that the basic rights shall apply to domestic juristic persons to the extent that the nature of such rights permits. Freedom of assembly differs from freedom of association in that the assembly itself does not have the right to assemble or any other rights. In other words, no collective right of the assembly to exist is recognized since the assembly is not a juristic person. The existence of the assembly is protected indirectly through the rights of participants and the organizer. See Herzog op cit (n 105) 15–16.

[116] See Dietel & Gintzel op cit (n 101) 22.

[117] 69 *BVerfGE* 315 343.

[118] Ibid.

[119] See Dietel & Gintzel op cit (n 101) 37. Article 13.2 *VersammlG* places a duty on participants to disperse immediately when the police intervene to terminate an assembly.

[120] 69 *BVerfGE* 315 343. According to Herzog op cit (n 105) 13, the individual is only protected from being compelled by the state to join a private assembly. Article 8 *GG* will therefore not apply to assemblies, such as civic meetings, which are organized by the state itself in terms of art 28.1.3 *GG*. Herzog's view derives from decisions

This fear of state pressure to participate in assemblies probably plays a role in the almost unequivocal refusal to place the state under a duty to encourage assembly by making the means for its exercise available.[121] On the other hand, this policy also means that no permission from the state is necessary for using public streets.[122] As in the US and Cananda, the state may refuse to make other types of public forums available as long as it does not discriminate improperly.

In addition to providing access to the streets and equal access to other public forums the FCC has held that the administrative procedures surrounding the right to assemble must be assembly-friendly.[123] Duties to co-operate for both assembly leadership and the police have been derived from the statutory requirement to notify.[124] In short, the duty to co-operate clearly obliges both sides to abstain from provocation and is designed to isolate and remove violent elements in mass demonstrations.[125]

Despite this duty of co-operation the court has yet to decide whether there is a duty on the state to protect assemblers from interference by third parties.[126] The assemblers may of course rely on ordinary police laws for their protection. In addition the Assembly Act further prohibits interference with the orderly completion of public assemblies.[127]

The court has also accorded assemblers few rights against other parties within the assembly itself. In principle the assemblers have, on the basis of art 8.1 *GG*, no right to meaningful participation vis-à-vis the organizers and the leadership. Participants who feel that they cannot make themselves heard have to resort to an alternative assembly.[128] The Assembly Act, however, distinguishes between the right to organize, lead, and participate in an assembly. As these rights may clash, it

---

of the FCC to the effect that the individual may not rely on freedom of association, but has to resort to the lesser protection of art 2.1 *GG*, to abstain from public association. This interpretation of freedom of association by the court is highly controversial and has been heavily criticized. It would therefore be unwise to extend its operation to assembly.

[121] In *BVerwG* 1986 *NJW* 738 the court refused to grant a mother the costs of transport to enable her to protest against a reduction of the state child allowance. See Schilder op cit (n 106) 152; Herzog op cit (n 105) 5. However, the state may be compelled, on the basis of the equality clause, to make means available to the extent that similarly situated assemblers were assisted in the past. See Schilder op cit (n 106) 154.

[122] Feldmeier *Politische Meinungsäusserung auf öffentlichen Strassen* (1982) 164.

[123] 69 *BVerfGE* 315 355.

[124] Ibid.

[125] At 356–7. The duty to co-operate also entails that the police refrain from prohibitory measures even when such measures can pass administrative and constitutional scrutiny. The duty to co-operate is justiciable to the extent that the willingness of the police or the assemblers to co-operate and negotiate may play a role in the outcome of an administrative court's decision: it may reflect on the tenability of the police's prognosis of the likelihood of violence resulting from an assembly. See Herzog op cit (n 105) 41. If the police are willing to talk, but the demonstrators not, then it will be much more difficult to argue that the police prognosis was wrong and that the decision to ban lacked proportionality. The opposite will be true when the police showed themselves unwilling to negotiate. Von Münch & Kunig op cit (n 99) 547–8 criticize the constitutionalization of duties to co-operate for resulting in the re-interpretation of a freedom into a duty of co-operation. They also warn against the derivation of 'a handbook of assembly' from art 8.1 *GG*.

[126] See 69 *BVerfGE* 315 355. The FCC has made it clear that the police's first responsibility is to act against the anti-assemblers. However, no duty to protect was found. See the decision reported in 1970 *Juristenzeitung* 283, 285. See also Herzog op cit (n 105) 17; Dietel & Gintzel op cit (n 101) 45; Hoffmann-Riem op cit (n 105) 761. The latter authors affirm the existence of such a duty as part of the freedom to assemble. The derivation of the duty, it is argued, not only follows from the importance attached to the freedom of assembly by the court but also flows from police practice. The conclusion is further supported by the authors' presupposition that assembly, as an avenue for the resolution of disputes in open society based on the rule of law, must be encouraged and made possible by the state and police.

[127] Article 2.2 *VersammlG*.

[128] Von Münch & Kunig op cit (n 99) 545.

contains regulations to deal with conflicts between the leaders, organizers, and participants.[129] Under the Act the leader may determine the course of the assembly and exclude people who disrupt or disturb the meeting. However, as long as participants keep to the schedule as determined by the leader they may not be excluded from participating.[130]

## 6.5 Conditions placed on assembly: 'peaceful' and 'without arms'

Assembly in Germany is protected so long as it is peaceful and without arms. The effect of these conditions is different from that of limitations. If the conditions of 'peacefulness' and 'without arms' are not met, then the protection of art 8 *GG* falls away. No question of the proportionality of state action need arise. The effect is therefore akin to a determination that a meeting is not covered by the definition of assembly. There is, however, an important addendum. Since violent and armed assemblies are expressly prohibited in the Basic Law they may also not be protected by any other freedom, including the freedom to develop the personality (art 2.1 *GG*).[131]

The content given to the terms 'peaceful' and 'without arms' is crucial to understanding the extent of the prohibition. According to the dominant opinion, 'peaceful' is to be understood with reference to arts 5.3 and 13.1.2 *VersammlG*. They provide that assemblies may be prohibited when facts exist which show that the organizer or his/her supporters intend to cause violence or unrest. The term 'violence' as it is used in the criminal law has too wide an ambit.[132] In German assembly jurisprudence not every unlawful disturbance of law and order or infringement of the rights of others is understood to be 'violent'. An assembly, or assembly members, are deemed violent only if act(s) of physical violence against person or property (but not merely clothes) are committed or threatened.[133] For example, the use of sit-ins to blockade entrances, roads, and railway lines was not initially accepted as peaceful by the ordinary courts. In time, however, the FCC made it clear

---

[129] Articles 6–12 *VersammlG*. See also Dietel & Gintzel op cit (n 101) 74–8. The assumption of the Assembly Act that 'a leader' exists creates a problem. See 69 *BVerfGE* 315 359. In modern massive demonstrations several organizations often demonstrate together so that several leaders exist, none of whom may be able to negotiate on behalf of more than his or her followers. It may even be artificial to speak about a common goal or an internal connection between the assemblers in these demonstrations. Assemblies without leaders are also protected. See Hoffmann-Riem op cit (n 105) 749, 772. But presumably the absence of leadership may be taken into account by the police when they determine whether violence is likely to erupt and when they consider the proportionality of action against the assembly. See 69 *BVerfGE* 315 359.

[130] See Zitzmann op cit (n 103) 48–53. These provisions apply to both indoor and outdoor public assemblies.

[131] See Dietel & Gintzel op cit (n 101) 53; Herzog op cit (n 105) 8–11.

[132] 73 *BVerfGE* 206 248.

[133] 69 *BVerfGE* 315 360; 73 *BVerfGE* 206 248. Hoffmann-Riem op cit (n 105) 753 argues that it should be kept in mind that assembly is primarily used by those who are unsatisfied with the status quo. A wide interpretation of the term 'peaceful' is therefore necessary to prevent the state from exploiting the conditions in order to censor unpopular ideas.

that these forms of protest are constitutionally protected, though they may be limited in terms of art 8.2 *GG*.[134]

Disguised participation and the use of defensive weapons were prohibited in a 1985 amendment to the Assembly Act and may now be punished with a monetary fine.[135] The court has yet to pronounce on the constitutionality of these amendments, but it seems clear that the whole assembly may not be prohibited when some participants wear masks since no inference of violence may be drawn from disguises alone. Whether disguised participants themselves are protected by art 8 *GG* remains unclear.[136]

What is true for disguises is also true for random acts of violence. When some members of an assembly resort to violence (by throwing stones at the police, for example), while the majority of the participants remain peaceful, the assembly remains protected. This result is necessary to prevent a peaceful assembly from being hijacked by violent supporters or opponents.[137] In these cases the police are obliged to act solely against the violent minority. What is not clear is whether the peaceful participants must actively distance themselves from the violence or whether it suffices that they do not encourage or sympathize with the troublemakers.[138] However, creating such distance appears desirable. For if the police

---

[134] The *BGH* argued (see *BGH* 1969 *NJW* 1770 at 1773), as some commentators still do, that pressure to listen becomes coercion to listen — and therefore violent — in the cases of blockades and sit-ins. In *BGH* 1982 *NJW* 189 the court confirmed the convictions of students who disrupted lectures. The students' demonstration was not considered peaceful and was therefore not protected by the Constitution. See further Schilder op cit (n 106) 144–6. In 73 *BVerfGE* 206 248 the FCC ruled that blockades and sit-ins are peaceful, but that the state may put limitations on and even criminalize such actions in appropriate situations. The consequence of the court's acceptance of blockades and sit-ins as peaceful is most important: the state will have to pass proportionality scrutiny every time it takes actions against these forms of protest. More specifically, the prohibition or breaking-up of outdoor blockades and sit-ins will be possible only if the requirements of art 15 *VersammlG* are met. This means that in most cases the state will be permitted to break up the blockade only if it presents 'an immediate threat to the public security and order'. In cases where alternatives routes for traffic are available and the blockade is a relatively short one prohibition may not be a proportional remedy. See Ott '*Rechtsprobleme bei der Auflösung einer Versammlung in Form eines Sitzstreiks*' 1985 *NJW* 2384 at 2385–6. Presumably the scope for breaking up indoor blockades will be even more limited. A caveat needs to be added to the above. It seems clear that when obstruction becomes the objective of the assemblers in order to force compliance with their demands the protection of the freedom of assembly will fall away. See 73 *BVerfGE* 206 250. The communication of beliefs is then clearly the incidental effect of the obstruction. Hoffmann-Riem op cit (n 105) 755 offers the example of a blockade which intentionally prevents the completion of a nuclear power station. It will not be 'peaceful' since the demonstrators are trying to coerce others and are not interested in allowing others to form an opinion. Their action is simply geared towards ensuring that their opinion — that the construction of the nuclear power station should be prevented — is complied with. See also Dietel & Gintzel op cit (n 101) 30. Herzog op cit (n 105) 24–5 states that intentional blockading is protected by art 2.1 *GG*. It is not clear why this should be the case. Assemblies which are not peaceful are not given any constitutional protection. If the obstruction or disruption is intentional, then the assembly will not be protected. When the obstruction is the incidental effect of the assembly the personal freedom of others (art 2.2.2 *GG*) may provide grounds for limiting the duration of such assemblies and for their eventual dissolution. See 73 *BVerfGE* 206 247; Herzog op cit (n 105) 48. Sit-ins should be treated in similar fashion. The fact that the Assembly Act does not apply to non-public, indoor sit-ins should not make any difference.

[135] *Gesetz zur Änderung des Strafgesetzbuches und des Versammlungsgesetzes* of 18.7.1985

[136] Frowein op cit (n 106) 2378 argues that there is no room for disguised participation in an assembly because, as the court has stated, demonstrators propagate their opinions through their physical presence in public: 69 *BVerfGE* 315 345. Disguised individuals are not publicly present. Kühl '*Demonstrationsfreiheit und Demonstrationsstrafrecht*' 1985 *NJW* 2379 at 2380 is not prepared to go as far as Frowein. Kühl argues that disguised participation must be protected as long as good ground exists for disguise. As long as the police regularly videotape assemblies and as long as the police may confiscate film recordings made by the media, disguise may be necessary to avoid personal or occupational problems resulting from participation. The Assembly Act recognizes that there may be a legitimate ground for wearing a disguise: art 17a.3.2 confers a discretion to police to allow disguised participation in cases of foreigners who fear persecution from the governments of their countries of origin. Dietel & Gintzel op cit (n 101) 43 state that the individual may in principle decide whether she wants to participate anonymously or openly.

[137] 69 *BVerfGE* 315 361.

[138] Schilder op cit (n 106) 142.

cannot distinguish between the perpetrators of violence and the rest of the assembly, then the assembly may be terminated.[139]

The prohibition against the carrying of arms closely corresponds to the condition that assemblies must be peaceful.[140] If armed individuals participate, the police should first try to prevent their further armed participation before the assembly as a whole may be prohibited.[141] The use of protective devices (such as shields and helmets) has been prohibited by the Assembly Act on the basis that they stimulate aggression among participants and onlookers by showing a readiness to engage in violence.[142] The carrying of defensive weapons may, however, be grounds for police action against the whole assembly — as opposed to the individuals carrying the defences — only when it is shown that demonstrators intend to provoke a response and are gearing themselves for the reaction from counter-demonstrators or from the police. In these cases the carrying of defensive weapons is an indication that the assemblers do not intend to be peaceful.[143]

## 6.5 Limitations on assembly

Article 8.2 *GG* provides for legislative limitations on outdoor assemblies. The Assembly Act gave effect to this provision in 1953.[144] The statute does not contain an exhaustive list of limitations and additional limitations of freedom of assembly may have to be tolerated when its exercise conflicts with other constitutionally protected goods, especially the fundamental rights of others.[145] Conflicts of this nature will, of necessity, be resolved on a case-by-case basis. However, *ad hoc* adjudication does not mean that no principles exist for their resolution. Indeed, the unity of the constitution demands that these conflicts are to be resolved by proportionally limiting the right(s) which carries less weight in the concrete case.[146] The prohibition of an assembly can therefore only be considered when more elementary constitutional-legal goods are endangered. Thus infringements of the less

---

[139] In instances where police control measures seem unlikely to be effective a preventative prohibition may also be justified. See 69 *BVerfGE* 315 362; Herzog op cit (n 105) 44.

[140] Article 2.3 *VersammlG* further prohibits the transportation, provision, or distribution of weapons to assemblies. The definition of 'arms' obviously includes shooting and cutting weapons, but other objects such as bottles and sticks may also, depending on the intention of the carrier, qualify as arms. It is debatable whether rotten eggs, tomatoes, or paint, when used to embarrass opponents, are to be included in the definition. See Schilder op cit (n 106) 150.

[141] See Dietel & Gintzel op cit (n 101) 59.

[142] Article 17a *VersammlG*. A further objection is that the shields hinder the police in enforcing the law.

[143] See Herzog op cit (n 105) 26.

[144] The limitations enumerated in the Assembly Act are the product of the legislature's effort to give effect to art 8.2 *GG* by balancing the freedom to assemble with other constitutionally protected goods. The Assembly Act may, of course, be subjected to constitutional scrutiny. To pass constitutional muster the limitations must be proportional and may not encroach on the essence of the freedom of assembly. According to art 19.1 *GG* and art 8.2 *GG*, legislation which seeks to limit assembly must also be general, i e it may not be directed at a specific assembly. In addition the legislation must deal exclusively with the freedom to assemble in order to qualify as an exploitation of art 8.2 *GG*. Other statutes which are not promulgated in terms of art 8.2 *GG* and which do not specifically direct themselves at freedom of assembly — Sunday laws, traffic regulations, and the regulation of the use of loud speakers — further limit the right. See Schilder op cit (n 106) 178–83; Herzog op cit (n 105) 43. Demonstrations in the vicinity of the Federal and *Länder* Parliaments and the FCC are prohibited in terms of the *Bannmeilengesetze* (protecting certain areas around the various Parliaments).

[145] According to the court, freedom of assembly, like all other fundamental rights protected in the Basic Law, has 'immanent' limitations. The high value placed on the freedom of assembly in the value system of the Basic Law means that the legislature and the executive should be particularly alert to the operation of the principle of proportionality when limiting the right to assemble. For examples of the court's approach to 'immanent' limitations in general, see e g 28 *BVerfGE* 243 261; 30 *BVerfGE* 173 193; 32 *BVerfGE* 98 108; 47 *BVerfGE* 327 369.

[146] 69 *BVerfGE* 315 349.

elementary rights of third parties, which necessarily results when a number of people assemble, will have to be tolerated.[147]

Public outdoor assemblies are affected by the following provisions of the Act.[148] First, the organizer has a duty to notify (not necessarily in writing) the responsible government official of a public assembly forty-eight hours before it is to take place.[149] According to the Act, assemblies may be banned if there was no notification or if the assembly differs considerably from the information given in the notification.[150] The FCC has, however, ruled that the duty to notify does not apply to spontaneous demonstrations.[151] In cases where the assembly is organized within a very short period of time a derogation of the time-limit has been held to be the appropriate solution.[152] The court also ruled that even where the duty applies a failure to comply with notification does not automatically justify a banning order. The principle of proportionality has to be observed by the executive.[153]

Secondly, public outdoor assemblies may be banned if public security and public order is directly threatened.[154] While the term 'public security' has well-defined parameters,[155] the use of 'public order' has been criticized on the grounds that it is so 'vague' a term that it can be exploited to censor unpopular or unconventional views.[156] The FCC has nevertheless found it to be constitutional on the condition that it is interpreted restrictively and in accordance with the principle of proportionality. Banning is allowed only in circumstances where important goods of the community are directly and clearly threatened.[157]

---

[147] See Frowein op cit (n 106) 2377. The application of the principle of proportionality does not, however, mean that individuals may, in assembly form, engage in conduct which would be illegal in normal circumstances.

[148] Almost all the provisions of the Assembly Act apply solely to 'public' assemblies. The effect of the limited application of the Assembly Act is that private outdoor assemblies, which are not open to the public or do not concern themselves with public affairs, are not subject to the provisions of the Act. It is only the prohibition against the wearing of uniforms to express a common political conviction that applies to all forms of assembly: art 3 *VersammlG*. Uniforms are prohibited on the grounds that the aggressive military connotations associated with uniforms could inhibit onlookers. Schwäble op cit (n 99) 194 criticizes the prohibition on the ground that it is overbroad. It permits the proscription of all uniforms, including, for example, a white cloth with a peace sign. While the wearing of uniforms to display an aggressive militant attitude might have been banned on good grounds, it is difficult to justify the banning of uniforms which possess no such meaning, but simply reflect solidarity. Article 3.2 *VersammlG* contains an exception for youth organizations.

[149] Article 14 *VersammlG*.

[150] Article 15.2 *VersammlG*.

[151] 69 *BVerfGE* 315 350.

[152] *BVerfG* 1992 *DVBl* 149 at 150; Schilder op cit (n 106) 193. If organization starts less than forty-eight hours before the assembly is to take place (*Eilversammlungen*), then the time limit can obviously not be observed.

[153] 69 *BVerfGE* 315 351. The court held that the executive must take into consideration that a single group or person may not be able to accept responsibility for the notification of the entire demonstration. The absence of the notification may, however, result in the police having no alternative other than issuing a banning order since there may not be enough time left for the police to prepare for the assembly.

[154] Article 15.1 *VersammlG*.

[155] The term 'public security' includes protection of individual interests and 'subjective rights' (life, health, property) and community interests (the institutions of the state and the legal order).

[156] The term 'public order' includes those prevailing societal and moral norms which are considered to be vital for an ordered civil society. See Schilder op cit (n 106) 196–7.

[157] See 69 *BVerfGE* 315 352–4. The court applied the principle of reciprocal interaction: the objective working of the fundamental right is used to limit the effect of the limiting legislation. The operation of the principle of proportionality would further entail that government action in terms of art 15 *VersammlG* must be clear, suitable, possible to adhere to, necessary, and proportional in the narrow sense. In a decision of the Federal Administrative Court (*BVerw* 1982 *NJW* 1008 at 1009) it was made clear that banning may not be resorted to if less infringing measures will suffice to avert the danger. *In casu* participants carried banners with inscriptions which insulted the Chilean Head of State and the Chilean Ambassador. In so doing they committed a criminal offence in Germany. The court held that the confiscation of banners was a proportional response by the police. In general the police are required to balance the conflicting expressive and public order interests. Thus where a demonstration impedes traffic the police must balance the public's interest in the free flow of traffic against the interest of the demonstrators in the particular venue (maybe another street could be used with less consequences for the flow of traffic, but with

Thirdly, the police may exclude participants who overtly disturb the public order in open-air meetings. Indeed, they must do so, rather than break up the assembly.[158]

The founders of the Basic Law and the legislature assumed that public indoor assemblies are far less likely to lead to disturbances than public outdoor assemblies. The Assembly Act provides for their limitation in only a few specified instances.[159]

No limitations — other than the wearing of uniforms — are enumerated for non-public indoor or outdoor assemblies in the Basic Law or in the Assembly Act. The freedom of assembly, nevertheless, has immanent limits. For example, in 1969 the NPD (a far-rightwing political party) planned a meeting in Saarbrücken. Leftist groups made clear that they intended to prevent the meeting from happening. In its opinion the court makes it quite clear that the police's first responsibility is to act against anti-assemblers. However, by upholding the constitutionality of the banning order the primary thrust of the court's opinion is ultimately that the police may justifiably prevent a non-public indoor assembly when,

> 'despite all conceivable preparation, including stringent police action, the public order will not only be burdened seriously, but the lives and health of third parties (not merely snooping bystanders) who are not participating and therefore worthy of protection, will be seriously and inevitably endangered.'[160]

Thus, while it is quite apparent that the police have some obligation to protect the assemblers, it is not clear what efforts they are obliged to make or what financial costs the public is expected to bear so that they can make those efforts.[161]

Finally, the freedom of assembly for persons in 'special status relationships' (soldiers, students, and prisoners) may be subjected to further limitations. These limitations vary and are contingent upon the nature of the relationship.[162]

## 6.6 State infringements of assembly

Police observation, escorting, or recording of the people present (or their car registration numbers) may be deemed an infringement of the freedom to assemble or the right to informational self-determination.[163] However, general observation (by helicopter, for example) may be necessary for a proper assessment of the

---

the same effect for the demonstrators) and the police must also consider factors such as the time and duration of the assembly, the seriousness of the disruption of traffic (number of motorists affected), and the number of assemblers. It should be remembered that where the objective of the assemblers is to barricade and obstruct the flow of traffic the assembly is not protected. According to the court, the hindrance of traffic is only to be tolerated when it is the unavoidable and incidental effect of the exercise of the freedom to assemble.

[158] Articles 18.3 and 19.4 *VersammlG*. For a detailed discussion, see Zitzmann op cit (n 103) 107–74. As long as the leader is capable and willing to act against the troublemakers the police may not act. Trouble caused by persons who are clearly not part of the assembly must be controlled by the police in accordance with the general police laws, and not the Assembly Act (at 182).

[159] An indoor public assembly may be prevented from taking place if the organizer's right to assemble has been withdrawn in terms of art 9.2 *GG* (associations), art 18 *GG* (individuals), or art 21.2 *GG* (political parties), if there are to be armed participants, if a violent activity is intended, or if opinions and expressions which have been criminalized are to be communicated. Under art 5 *VersammlG* the dissolution — as opposed to prevention — of a public indoor assembly is justified in similar circumstances.

[160] 1970 *Juristenzeitung* 283 at 285. The lives and health of the peaceful assemblers are surely also worthy of protection. See Herzog op cit (n 105) 29.

[161] See Schilder op cit (n 106) 224.

[162] 39 *BVerfGE* 334 367 (government bureaucrats' freedom of assembly inherently limited by the '*Treuepflicht*' of art 33.5 *GG*); *BVerwG* 1987 *NJW* 82 at 84 (free speech in the military; officers of higher rank in the military may be required to refrain from active political involvement); 57 *BVerfGE* 29 (soldiers may be prohibited from wearing their uniforms at political meetings).

[163] As derived from art 2.1 *GG* in 65 *BVerfGE* 1.

situation, and even more direct recording of events and persons (by video-camera and other recording devices) may be legitimate when the purpose is to secure evidence for criminal prosecution.[164]

While some forms of police observation may therefore be constitutional, it is clear that burdening peaceful participants with civil liability for damages caused by others or the cost of policing the assembly is unconstitutional. The potential for chilling speech and assembly is just too great for such remedies to be allowed.[165]

### 6.7 Relationship of assembly with other rights

In German jurisprudence it is said that rights concur when a person may rely on more than one right in a particular situation. Conversely, rights are said to collide when reliance on a right by one person conflicts with the reliance by another person on the same right or on another right. When rights collide they limit each other, but what happens when rights concur?

Freedom of assembly concurs in some situations with the freedom of movement (art 2.2.2 *GG*). An assembly may also find itself protected by both the freedom of assembly and artistic freedom (art 5.3 *GG*).[166] Freedom of association and assembly often concur where an association embarks on assemblies and utilizes them for the organized formation of its will.[167] Assemblies used by political parties to propagate their political programme are privileged and may only be restricted once the political party has been declared unconstitutional by the FCC in terms of art 21.2 *GG*. The right to picket, which forms part of the freedom to assemble, is also protected as part of the trade union freedoms (art 9.3 *GG*).

In many ways the differentiated and special order of limitations in the Basic Law have strengthened the protection offered by the fundamental rights. However, in cases where more than one right is implicated a weakness in the system becomes apparent. Since the ambit of legitimate limitations differs from one right to the next, different rights will be protected with varying intensity and the same action will likely receive different levels of protection, depending upon the right under which it is analysed. To the extent that one wishes to see one's constitutional challenge upheld, it is important to determine which right is apt to elicit the greatest judicial solicitude.[168]

For example, freedom of assembly complements free speech in that it makes collective communication possible. The freedoms therefore concur to this extent. But the different nature and levels of protection offered by the two should not be lost sight of.[169] For while open-air assemblies may be limited by (special) legislation, freedom of speech may be limited only by general legislation, with the result

---

[164] See Hoffmann-Riem op cit (n 105) 764.
[165] See Dietel & Gintzel op cit (n 101) 51. Schwäble op cit (n 99 158–61 makes it clear, however, that when a causal connection exists between the damage and the conduct of the organizers or participants then liability may be attached to such conduct. The same would be true if a violent outcome was desired by the organizer.
[166] Watney *Die Reg op Vrye Vergadering* (LLM thesis, 1988) 42. See also Rautenbach *Die Reg op Bewegingsvryheid* (LLD thesis, 1974).
[167] The most common example of which is the meetings of association members. See Dietel & Gintzel op cit (n 101) 56.
[168] Some rights stand in special relationships to one another. Article 8 *GG* is *lex specialis* vis-à-vis art 2.1 *GG* (general freedom to develop the personality) and displaces art 2.1 *GG* in its area of operation. Thus the limitations of art 2.1 *GG* (rights of others, constitutional order, and the *boni mores* of the community) may not be transplanted onto the freedom to assemble.
[169] See Dietel & Gintzel op cit (n 101) 28.

that there is far less room for limiting free speech than for limiting open-air meetings.[170] It is therefore of the utmost importance to decide which right — and which set of limitations — applies.[171]

## 7 RECOMMENDATIONS

### 7.1 Introduction

In this final section we begin by taking a brief look at the actual mechanics of a freedom of assembly challenge under the interim Constitution. We then suggest a relatively skeletal test for the Constitutional Court to apply when faced with such a challenge. To round out the discussion we take this skeletal test through its paces with a few hypotheticals.

### 7.2 The mechanics of a constitutional challenge to a governmental restriction on freedom of assembly

The interim Constitution protects freedom of assembly under s 16:

> 'Every person shall have the right to assemble and demonstrate with others peacefully and unarmed, and to present petitions.'

Though the clause itself does not say what the exact parameters of this freedom are, we do know that in determining whether some particular governmental action unjustifiably infringes some particular person's freedom of assembly the court's analysis will have to take the following basic form. First, the court will have to ask whether or not the petitioner's conduct falls within the sphere of activity protected by the freedom of assembly. Secondly, if the court decides that the petitioner's conduct is protected, it must then decide whether the governmental action actually infringes the freedom. Thirdly, if the governmental action infringes the freedom, the court must then ask if the infringement is justifiable. Under the interim Constitution this last determination is made not within the context of the freedom of assembly clause, but within s 33 — the limitation clause.[172]

---

[170] For examples of the court's jurisprudence on the limitations to free speech: 7 *BVerfGE* 198; 12 *BVerfGE* 124; 20 *BVerfGE* 162 176; 42 *BVerfGE* 143 150; 60 *BVerfGE* 234 240; 62 *BVerfGE* 230 243–4.

[171] Herzog op cit (n 105) 12 proposes that the limitations to free speech should apply to the content of the speech generated by participants and that the limitations to assembly should apply to the collectivity, the organizing and the participation in the assembly. Similarly, he argues, where the content of the belief at religious assemblies or the programmes of political parties or associations present problems the constitutionality of limitations has to be determined with reference to the special rights, i e arts 4, 21, and 9 *GG* respectively. But where the problem results from the coming together of people the limitations to freedom of assembly govern the situation. The solution proposed by Müller op cit (n 99) 73–4 is quite similar: art 8 *GG* (freedom of assembly) applies when the assembly is the means for expressing an opinion, but art 5 *GG* (freedom of speech) applies to the content of the opinion expressed. It is, however, doubtful whether the problem of concurring rights is avoided by such artificial distinctions which deny that both rights apply to the situation. See Schilder op cit (n 106) 168.

[172] The text of the limitation clause reads, in relevant part, as follows:
'(1) The rights of this chapter may be limited by law of general application provided that such limitation —
  (a) shall be permissible only to the extent that it is —
    (i) reasonable; and
    (ii) justifiable in an open and democratic society based upon freedom and equality; and
  (b) shall not negate the essential content of the right in question,
and provided further that any limitation to
(aa) a right entrenched in s 10, 11, 12, 14 (1), 21, 25 or 30(1)(d) or (e) or (2); or
(bb) a right entrenched in s 15, 16, 17, 18, 23, or 24, in so far as such rights relate to free and fair political activity,
  shall, in addition to being reasonable as required in paragraph (a)(i), also be necessary.'

To determine whether the government's restriction on assembly passes constitutional muster subsec (1) of the limitation clause requires that the court begin by asking the following three questions:

(i) Is the restriction on the right of assembly 'reasonable'?
(ii) Is the restriction on the right of assembly 'justifiable in an open and democratic society based upon freedom and equality'?
(iii) Does the restriction on the right of assembly negate the 'essential content of the right'?

To pass constitutional muster all governmental limitations or infringements on assembly must answer (i) and (ii) affirmatively, and (iii) negatively. In addition, however, those governmental actions which restrict *political* assemblies must answer a fourth question affirmatively: (iv) Is the restriction on the right of assembly 'necessary'?

## 7.3 The substance of a constitutional test for governmental restrictions on freedom of assembly

The above section sets out the basic prongs of a constitutional test for a governmental restriction on assembly. Here we shall look a bit more closely at each of the prongs and suggest slightly more detailed contours. To a significant extent we shall track our discussion of Canadian jurisprudence on the subject. This choice is natural. Though the Canadian law may be underdeveloped, the constitutional structure of assembly analysis is virtually identical.

### 7.3.1 *Does the petitioner's conduct fall within the sphere of activity protected by the freedom of assembly?*

Section 16 is not without some readily identifiable limits. Like the German Basic Law, s 16 leaves unprotected assemblies or demonstrations which are not peaceful or involve armed participants. Additional conditions and limitations on assembly may, however, be effected by the Constitutional Court. In deciding on additional limitations when interpreting s 16 we suggest that the court be extremely circumspect and that it give the clause a 'large and liberal' effect.

The justification for this liberal interpretation has been detailed above in the discussion of the Canadian jurisprudence. In short, it is both unnecessary and undesirable for the majority of limitations and conditions to be placed upon assembly to be dealt with in the context of s 16. It is unnecessary because most government restrictions on assembly can be handled within a balancing test set out within the limitation clause. It is undesirable because many of the same sorts of considerations that would go into a balancing test for assembly interests within s 16 would appear in a balancing test for assembly concerns within the limitation clause. To have both the s 16 test and the limitation clause test weighing largely identical competing interests is clearly redundant and more than likely to lead to analytical confusion.

The solution of course is to undertake very different sorts of analyses within s 16, on the one hand, and within the limitation clause, on the other. It seems appropriate, given s 16's language and the Constitution's structure, to take a rather categorical approach to the recognition of restrictions on assembly within s 16: s 16 already prohibits armed assemblies or unpeaceful assemblies. It should be left to the court to work out additional categories of conduct which also fail to serve the values underlying the freedom and which therefore should not receive constitutional protection. That having been said, it is important to note that we are not advocating the creation of a number of new categories of unprotected assembly under s 16. The US experience with the public forum doctrine reflects the problems with assembly tests that tend to emphasize names at the expense of the real governmental and expressive interests at stake. What we are advocating is the careful creation of a few categories which reflect the belief that the expressive interests in play either do not serve the values underlying the freedom or can *never* outweigh competing governmental interests, public order interests, or private interests. Under such an approach certain kinds of places would likely be deemed strictly off-limits to public demonstration: for example, top-security military bases, the control rooms for nuclear reactors, the President's residence, or the inside of a private person's home.[173] Such a categorical approach avoids the rigidity and sterility of the US doctrine: few public places would be left unprotected by s 16 and most of the careful analysis and balancing of state interests and expressive interests would take place within the limitation clause. At the same time the categorical exclusion approach recognizes that the freedom was not enshrined in the Constitution to protect all activity that could nominally be housed under the term 'assembly,' but was intended to protect an identifiable set of values. Thus assembly acitivies which fail to serve the values which animate the freedom may be legitimately excluded from the freedom's protective ambit.

### 7.3.2 *Does the governmental action infringe the freedom of assembly?*

If the express purpose of the governmental action in question is to restrict the right of assembly, then the analysis proceeds to the balancing test under the limitation clause. The more difficult question to answer is what to do with a governmental restriction that does not have the express purpose of restricting assembly, but allegedly has the effect of restricting assembly.

There are at least two ways to go with this question. Following the Canadian model, we could require that the assembly activity for which protection is sought serve at least one of a specified set of desirable social ends: (1) the pursuit of knowledge or truth; (2) political participation, broadly construed; (3) self-realization; (4) cultural diversity. If the assembly can be shown to serve one of these ends, the petitioner would then be obliged to show that the governmental restriction has the effect of restricting her activity. If she can prove effect, then the analysis proceeds to the balancing test under the limitation clause.

A potentially more generous approach to the question of a restrictive effect on assembly is the US 'chilling effect' doctrine. According to this doctrine, expression of any form, including assembly, is chilled when people whose speech is not constitutionally proscribable are intimidated into not exercising their right to speak by a law punishing some form of expression.

---

[173] As we have already noted, access to internal government offices, presidential suites, air traffic control towers, prison cells, or judges' chambers does not promote democratic values to any greater degree than access to more readily accessible public spaces within government buildings, concourses in airports, the sidewalk outside a courtroom, or open areas fronting prisons.

A restriction on assembly may chill expressive conduct and assembly in two ways. First, it may be overbroad, i e the code may sweep into its proscriptive coverage not only expression which may be constitutionally forbidden but also speech which is protected by free speech guarantees.[174] The danger of an overbroad statute is that it 'hangs over people's heads like a Sword of Damocles . . . That [a] Court will ultimately vindicate a person if his speech is constitutionally protected is of little consequence — for the value of the Sword of Damocles is that it hangs — not that it drops.'[175] To prevent such an effect US courts will find overbroad statutes unconstitutional. In determining whether a statute is overbroad the court will look beyond the litigant before the court to a putative class of future speakers or assemblers who would forego protected expression rather than chance running foul of the law.[176]

A restriction on assembly may also have a chilling effect if it is vague. Given that a person faced with a vague statute will not know whether her expression will be constitutionally protected, she will likely refrain from speaking or assembling.[177] A statutory provision will be held void for vagueness if the expression forbidden by it is so unclearly defined that people 'of common intelligence must necessarily guess at its meaning and differ in its application'.[178]

The US 'chilling effect' doctrine is more generous than the Canadian approach in two obvious ways. First, it does not require a showing that the assembly or expression is socially desirable. Secondly, where a statute is overbroad it allows the court to go beyond the litigant before it to strike down constitutionally offensive legislation.[179] Given our relatively maximalist approach to freedom of assembly, we believe that the 'chilling effect' doctrine provides the basis for a more suitable test for restrictive effect.

### 7.3.3 Is the government's infringement of the freedom of assembly justifiable?

A complete test for assembly under the limitation clause is clearly beyond the scope of this chapter. A discussion of such a test would be primarily focused on the special, and as yet radically indeterminate, jurisprudence of the limitation clause.[180] However, there are two important aspects of a test for assembly under the limitation clause that we can, and indeed must, address. The first involves the balancing of competing governmental and expressive interests to be undertaken under the limitation clause. The second concerns the differential treatment which the limitation

---

[174] See *Thornhill v Alabama* 310 US 88 (1940).

[175] *Arnett v Kennedy* 416 US 134, 231 (1974) (Marshall J dissenting).

[176] See *Maryland v Joseph Munson* 467 US 947 (1984): overbreadth found where there is no sharp line between protected and proscribed speech.

[177] While vagueness and overbreadth seem similar, and often overlap, they are distinct concepts. For example, if a statute says that 'No person may expressly advocate criminal conduct', it will be deemed overbroad. We know what is proscribed — thus it is not vague — but it certainly will sweep constitutionally protected expression into its ambit. Conversely, if a statute reads, 'No person may engage in speech that the state may constitutionally restrict', it will be deemed vague. While there is no danger of sweeping constitutionally protected speech into the coverage of the statute, it is impossible to tell what kind of expression is covered. The citizen is left to guess.

[178] See *Connally v General Construction* 269 US 385 (1926).

[179] According to the current US jurisprudence, a litigant cannot claim a statute was vague if the litigant's action was clearly and unequivocally proscribed by the statute. See *RAV v St Paul* 112 SCt 2538 (1992).

[180] For such a discussion, see Woolman 'Riding the Push-Me Pull-You: Constructing a Test that Reconciles the Conflicting Interests which Animate the Limitation Clause' (1994) 10 *SAJHR* 60.

clause gives to assembly which is 'related to free and fair political activity' and assembly which is apolitical.

### 7.3.3.1 The balancing test

Having reached this stage of the overall test for freedom of assembly, we can assume that the assembly or demonstration in question is protected and has been infringed by some form of governmental action. What is left for us to decide is whether or not the restriction is justifiable.

As we have already noted, the general manner in which this question is decided will be a function of the test for limitations set out by the court. However, whatever the general nature of the limitations test, there are still quite a few questions a court needs to ask if it is to give an assembly case a thorough hearing. These questions must reflect the wide range of competing governmental interests, public order interests, private interests, and expressive interests that may be at stake in any given assembly case.[181]

The court may begin by asking whether the public is ordinarily admitted to the property as a matter of right. Should the answer to that question be negative, it would clearly weigh in favor of the governmental or private interest. If the answer is in the affirmative, the court may want to ask what could otherwise be described as a public forum question: is the property in question traditionally open to expressive activity?[182] If this question is answered in the affirmative, then the expressive activity could be said to have a leg up.

It may be, however, that the place in question is open to the public, but is not normally associated with expressive activity. Since not all publicly accessible places are easily transformed into assembly or demonstration grounds the next sort of question would inquire into the compatibility of the property's purpose with such expressive activity. If the property is government-owned, the court may ask to what extent the restriction simply ensures that the property at issue can be effectively used by the government and the public for the governmental function for which it was intended, or the extent to which it is designed to suppress expression. If the property is privately owned, the court may ask to what extent the property serves a public function and to what extent the expressive activity infringes on the property and privacy rights of the owner.

Another standard question in deciding whether or not a restriction on assembly is legitimate is the relative ease with which a demonstration can be relocated to another 'more suitable' venue — i e one which gives rise to fewer conflicts of interest. One could first ask whether other forums in the vicinity are available for expressive activities. If such alternative forums are not available, then one may ask more generally whether adequate alternative avenues of expression are left open.

Of course, sites for demonstrations are often selected because of their close

---

[181] A prefatory note: if the following questions seem to reflect a preoccupation with governmental or public order interests, it is important for the reader to remember that a significant portion of the expressive interests have been recognized by according the expressive conduct the protection of s 16.

[182] We use the term 'tradition' here quite loosely. Tradition should be understood in the context of the general practice of liberal democracies and not simply the practices of the 'old' South Africa. To import the distortions of the old order into the practice of the new order would undermine the entire project of constitutionalizing the foundations of a liberal democratic order.

relationship to the issue being contested. Alternative sites or avenues of expression may well diminish the impact of the demonstration or protest. Thus the court should inquire into the symbolic significance of the property for the message being conveyed. The more closely related the property is to the message, the greater the weight to be given to the expressive interests.

Finally, there are what may be known as proportionality questions or criteria. In one sense proportionality requires that the more important the state interest — the government interest, the public order interest, the private interest — the greater the latitude for restriction of the assembly. In another sense proportionality requires that the government restriction be closely tailored to meet its objectives. Thus the court must ask whether or not the restriction overreaches its purpose. This last proportionality question should resonate with our previous discussion of the 'restrictive effect' or 'chilling effect' of a government action. These questions, however, have less to do with a government infringement of the right, and more to do with the reasonableness of the restriction.[183]

A test which includes this list of questions may legitimately be said to lack precision. However, we believe that both its flexibility and its close attention to the wide range of interests at stake more than make up for the rejection of Ockham's razor.

### 7.3.3.2 The different levels of scrutiny for political and apolitical assemblies

We noted above that governmental actions which restrict *political* assemblies must be 'necessary' in addition to being 'reasonable'. Government actions which restrict other sorts of assembly must simply be reasonable. For example, assemblies which serve largely commercial purposes — such as a business convention — or purely recreational purposes — such as a sporting event — or entirely aesthetic purposes — for example, a rock concert — would be subject to reasonable government restrictions. Rallies for political parties or particular social causes, on the other hand, could only be restricted if the government action were deemed both reasonable and necessary.

The distinction seems simple enough. It does, however, raise two questions. First, how does one differentiate political assemblies from non-political assemblies? Secondly, what does it mean for a restriction on assembly to be 'reasonable' or 'reasonable and necessary'?

❐ Oranges, naartjies, and mineolas

The aforementioned examples appear to suggest a neat dividing line between political and non-political assemblies. But how is one to classify a concert put together to raise money for AIDS research, a play about corruption in the present government, or even a business convention where the primary focus is on changing the copyright laws for computer software and other intellectual property? All three

---

[183] One question that goes to both the 'chilling effect' and the reasonableness of a restriction is whether the restriction is designed in a manner free from excessive official discretion or undue arbitrariness. To the extent that excessive official discretion to cancel demonstrations or throw people in jail keeps people with legitimate expressive interests off the streets, it chills expression. To the extent that open-ended official discretion to cancel demonstrations is used for the more specific task of keeping people off the Parliament grounds, it lacks proportionality and the quality of reasonableness.

assemblies possess characteristics associated with political assemblies. At the same time it is unlikely that all the attendees are politically motivated.

One answer to this question is that the answer doesn't matter all that much. First, most of the these borderline assemblies are apt to take place on private property. As such, they both receive the protections afforded private property owners from government interference and do not implicate the governmental property and public order concerns that are subject to restrictions. Secondly, to the extent that there are restrictions on what goes on at these private assemblies, they are likely to target the content of the assembly and not the assembly itself. Content restrictions must be said to implicate freedom of expression — or freedom of thought, opinion, and belief — and not freedom of assembly, if there is to be any meaningful distinction between the coverage of the two clauses.[184]

Let us assume, however, that assembly concerns are implicated in restrictions on these private assemblies. Our maximalist approach to assembly suggests that if the petitioners are able to make the showing that the primary purpose of the assembly is political, then they are entitled to the benefits of the protection afforded political assemblies.[185]

☐ 'Reasonable' and 'reasonable and necessary'

As we noted above, if an assembly is categorized as political, the restriction on it must be both reasonable and necessary. If it is non-political, the restriction must only be reasonable. Without going into the details of the limitation test itself it is possible to note briefly the difference in effect of these two levels of scrutiny of assembly.[186]

If a governmental restriction on assembly must be both reasonable and necessary, it means that expressive and assembly interests are going to be far more privileged than the governmental interests. Thus when we do our balancing test it is clear that the assembly will receive a thumb on the scale and that the government restriction is far less likely to survive judicial scrutiny. On the other hand, if the government need only show that the restriction on assembly is reasonable, the converse will be the case and the restriction is far more apt to survive judicial scrutiny.

---

[184] Furthermore, even if a freedom of assembly challenge is brought with respect to content-based restrictions, the constitutional protections afforded by the freedom of expression or freedom of thought, belief, and opinion clauses are likely to be much stronger.

[185] For a relevant and excellent discussion of the distinction between, as well as the difficulties of distinguishing between, political and non-political expression, see Spitz 'Eschewing Silence Coerced by Law: The Political Core and Protected Periphery of Freedom of Expression' (1994) 10 *SAJHR* 301.

[186] The notion of levels of scrutiny reflected in the limitation clause is borrowed from US constitutional jurisprudence. Earlier drafts of the limitation clause and interpretation clause made the debt explicit by stating that the clauses which now receive 'reasonable and necessary' review would receive 'strict scrutiny'. However, it would be dangerous to import the US version of levels of scrutiny into South African limitations jurisprudence. These levels of scrunity developed primarily within equal protection litigation under the Fourteenth Amendment — though they function within fundamental rights jurisprudence as well — and serve very particular purposes in US constitutional law. Those purposes differ quite profoundly from those ends which motivated the creation of the limitation clause and its varying levels of review. In short, strict scrutiny in US equal protection jurisprudence is designed to provide constitutional protection against laws which discriminate on the basis of race or nationality. On the other hand, the limitation clause's 'reasonable and necessary' review is designed to ensure greater judicial solicitude for those rights and freedoms which are deemed absolutely foundational for a liberal democratic order.

## 7.4 Testing the test: easy, hard, and real cases

### 7.4.1 *An easy case*

Several hundred students from the University of the North gather on the street outside the Yale Road gates of Wits West Campus to protest the inequitable funding of historically black and historically white universities. Speeches are made, petitions are passed around, and the crowd engages in responsive cheering. There is no violence nor threat of violence. Police arrive on the scene. After spending several minutes cordoning off the Wits campus the police ask the demonstrators to stop milling about on the sidewalk of Yale Road. The demonstrators refuse. Without warning, the police fire tear gas into the crowd. Those demonstrators who are unlucky enough to be stunned by the gas are arrested by the police on charges of disorderly conduct. The Witwatersrand Local Division then convicts all the accused demonstrators of these charges.

The first two prongs of our test are rather easily satisfied by this scenario. This assembly is intended to further the sorts of interests protected by s 16 and does not appear to fall into one of the categories expressly or implicitly left unprotected by the section. The police response and the unfettered grant of power to use such unjustifiable force constitutes governmental action which infringes the right of assembly.

Moving on to our third prong, we find that a quick review of the balancing test questions suggests that the expressive interests far outweigh the governmental interests at stake. First, the protesting students — and the public generally — do have access to the streets and sidewalks as a matter of right. Secondly, such locations are traditionally open to public protest. Thirdly, no mention is made in the account of governmental services or private activity being unduly disrupted. Nor is mention made of a blockade which impedes movement. Fourthly, as Wits is an historically white university, the demonstration at the Wits campus is obviously symbolically linked to the underlying purpose of the protest. Fifthly, the unfettered discretion given to the police to disperse the protest and the overly broad ambit of the disorderly conduct laws — especially as applied in this case — appear to constitute restrictions on assembly which are not proportionate to the ends of crowd control and public order. Finally, given that this is a political assembly, the government's action must be both reasonable and necessary. Such a requirement makes it even more difficult to sustain the government's actions in this case. The reviewing court would, in all likelihood, find for the petitioners and strike down the convictions.

### 7.4.2 *A hard case*

Members of the PAC gather at a police station in Cape Town to protest the previous day's arrest of several PAC executives on charges of disrupting the Constituent Assembly. After handing their petition to the police demanding the immediate release of the PAC executives, they sit down on the floor of the front foyer office of the police station and lock arms. When the police ask them to disperse the protestors refuse. The protestors are arrested and convicted on charges of criminal trespass and breaching the peace.

The first prong of our test is not so easily satisfied by this scenario. Although peaceful and unarmed, it is not clear whether the protest takes place in a venue which can ever, or rather *never*, tolerate expressive conduct. Police stations understandably have security concerns that require a significant amount of control over the station building. One can understand that protests within the charge office or near the jail cells would be intolerable. On the other hand, because police enforcement of the law gives almost as much meaning to the law as the words of the laws themselves and because citizens must have the capacity to bring unjust enforcement of the law directly to the attention of the police, we would certainly permit demonstration outside a police station. The foyer appears to occupy a middle ground. Given the closeness of the question, we may wish to leave a decision as to whether demonstration in a police station foyer compromises security to the more flexible and detailed analysis undertaken under the limitation clause.

The second prong gives us fewer problems if we find that the demonstration in the foyer is protected. The legal grant of power to arrest and the exercise of that power under these circumstances clearly constitute governmental action which infringes of the right of assembly.

If we find that the protest is protected and the right of assembly infringed, we move on to the third prong. Unlike our first case, we find that the governmental interests and the expressive interests are closely balanced.

First, the PAC — and the public generally — probably do not have access to a police station foyer as a matter of right. Secondly, police foyers are not traditionally open to public protest. Thirdly, while it is not clear to what extent governmental services are being disrupted by a protest in a foyer, it must impede movement. Much of the way this last consideration cuts will depend upon the nature of the protest — how calm or raucus it is. A raucus protest would pretty clearly not be compatible with the purposes of a police station. Fourthly, an alternative venue, such as the street or sidewalk fronting the police station, is probably available and just as appropriate for the protest. Fifthly, criminal trespass laws for the inside of a police station may well be a proportionate means for effecting public order ends.

On the expressive interests side is the fact that the demonstration at the police station is clearly linked to the underlying purpose of protesting unfair law enforcement and an effective way of getting the attention of those in charge. In addition, because this protest is political in nature, the government's action must be both reasonable and necessary.

Given the careful scrutiny which must be given to these criminal trespass laws, the reviewing court will not find it easy to reach a conclusion. However, the security interests, the non-traditionality of the forum, and the ready availability of close and appropriate venues would provide grounds for sustaining the convictions.

### 7.4.3 A 'real' case

The government announces that it will raise the petrol price by 18c to R2,00 per litre. Several taxi unions, other affected industries, and numerous private individuals call for a massive protest on the streets near Parliament the next day. Under s 3(2) of the Regulation of Gatherings Act, and on the grounds that twenty hours is insufficient time for municipal officials and police to ensure the general public's safety, the local authority issues a banning order prohibiting the protest.

As with the easy case, the first two prongs of our test are rather easily satisfied by this scenario. A street demonstration over a political decision is protected by s 16.

The local authority's banning order constitutes governmental action which infringes the right of assembly.

However, when we move to the limitation clause analysis, the public order interests and the expressive interests appear to be relatively closely balanced. The local authority has a responsibility to provide for traffic control and freedom of movement for the non-protesting public. The local authority will argue that the forty-eight-hour rule is proportionate to this end. The local authority may also argue that an extra twenty-four hours for the demonstration will not change the nature of the debate: the petrol price increase will not have taken effect and will remain a contestable issue.

On the other hand, the protesting taxi drivers and their fellow citizens do have access to the streets and sidewalks as a matter of right. And as we have noted before, these locales are traditionally open to public protest. The streets near Parliament, while not especially symbolically linked to the object of the protest, are being used to catch the attention of a concerned body. To that extent they serve an important expressive function. A protest of a petrol price hike effected by the government is a political assembly, which receives the highest level of constitutional protection.

The most important feature of this scenario weighing in favour of the expressive interests is the ability of the government to use the forty-eight-hour rule in a relatively unfettered manner to suppress political positions with which it disagrees. The ability to use public order concerns as a cloak for the government's political agenda directly undermines the protections which a liberal and democratic constitutional order is supposed to provide. For this reason alone the court of first impression would find itself well advised to lift the banning order and declare the forty-eight-hour notice rule unconstitutional.

### 7.4.4 *Another 'real' but easy case*

The Afrikaner Volksfront (AVF) calls for a public meeting of its membership to protest the national legislature's decision to desegregate South African public schools through a forced busing programme in which some white students are to be sent to historically black schools and some black students are to be sent to historically white schools. The demonstration organizers also announce plans to march through a predominantly black neighbourhood. AVF supporters turn out in numbers. The vast majority make a point of publicly brandishing their arms. Police officials and local authorities deny permission for the march and cordon off the route area on the grounds that the armed procession is intentionally intimidatory and more than likely to lead to violence. The AVF files suit against the local authority's decision, claiming that the Arms and Ammunitions Act permits the public display of weapons and that the prevention of the march violates their right to assemble and demonstrate.

The AVF claim doesn't make it beyond the first prong. Only peaceful and unarmed gatherings, demonstrations, and assemblies are constitutionally protected. Thus the armed AVF march is unprotected activity. Since the Regulation of Gatherings Act — which must be construed so as not to detract from the Arms and Ammunition Act — permits police and local authorities to disperse gatherings and marches where life and property are threatened the local authorities were apparently acting lawfully. Any questions about their actions are strictly matters of statutory interpretation and do not implicate the constitutional protection of assembly.

## 8 CONCLUSION

Despite the compelling narrative which accompanies each of the previous four examples, the test adumbrated above does not purport to generate uniquely specifiable results for individual assembly cases. However, what it should do is help to produce an acceptable range of decisions. It serves this more limited goal in three ways. First, it raises the questions which any court should ask in almost every assembly inquiry. Secondly, it raises these questions in a manner which ensures that the various interests at play are apparent to the court. Thirdly, it is designed to ensure that the expressive interests at stake are not routinely subordinated to the public order interests of the government.

It is perhaps trite to observe that legal academics have the tendency to take a political, economic, or cultural problem and disguise it as a legal problem open to a technical solution. However, this caveat still retains real force with respect to our conclusions about freedom of assembly. Whatever the test set out by the Constitutional Court, whatever the restrictions passed by Parliament, the real parameters of assembly will be determined by the willingness of those who demonstrate and those who police demonstrations to abide by the 'new' norms of a liberal democratic society.

# FREEDOM OF ASSOCIATION: THE RIGHT TO BE WE

STUART WOOLMAN & JOHAN DE WAAL

> The most natural privilege of man, next to the right of acting for himself, is that of combining his exertions with those of his fellow-creatures, and of acting in common with them. I am therefore led to conclude that the right of association is almost as inalienable as the right of personal liberty. No legislator can attack it without impairing the very foundations of society.
>
> Alexis de Toqueville *Democracy in America*

> An active civil society which is represented by legitimate political and social [associations] at the local level is as essential to the attainment of democracy as an agreement at the national level. It is only through a vibrant . . . civil society [that] . . . the process of democratisation might well be pushed through to the ultimate stage of economic socialisation.
>
> Dennis Davis *South Africa and Transition*

## 1 INTRODUCTION

### 1.1 The multiple grounds for freedom of association

Whether a person is a classical liberal, like de Toqueville, or a social democrat, like Davis, chances are she'll identify freedom of association as one of the essential ingredients for a flourishing liberal democracy. However, why she identifies association as foundational may well depend upon whether it is her politics, her culture, her religion, her family life, her class, or her race that she wishes to see served. As we shall see, associational freedom serves many masters.

For the politically minded, associational freedom is foundational because it makes participatory politics meaningful and genuinely representative politics possible. Political associations enable individuals collectively to channel their otherwise divergent energies towards the realization of shared ends. That is, unless he's Ross Perot, Silvio Berlusconi, or Harry Oppenheimer, an individual is unlikely to have either the ability or the resources necessary to mount an effective campaign to convince large numbers of his peers that his position on a particular subject is correct. However, a group of like-minded individuals — with their collective insight, effort, and resources — is far more likely to make itself heard. Once heard, the members of such a group have the opportunity to influence fellow members of society. If they are able to influence a sufficiently large number of their fellow citizens, they can perhaps translate their influence into the election of representatives. These representatives, who wield the real power, may then effect the desired political change. Associations thereby provide the bridge from individual efforts to collective political action.[1]

---

[1] The argument for constitutionally protecting political association can also be stated in the negative. One oft articulated justification for associational freedom is that associations act as a brake on majoritarian tyranny. De Toqueville argues — in line with what we have already suggested above — that associations make it possible

Freedom of association need not only be a vehicle for political participation. Whom we love, how we love them, whom we live with, how we live together, whom we like, how we engage them — these decisions about our most intimate, most meaningful relationships may also be protected by the freedom of association. The justification for this protection is that such relationships form an absolutely integral part of our self-understanding and that we, as individuals, must have relatively unfettered control over such decisions. If we are to be truly free to make these self-defining choices, then we need the protection provided by the freedom of association in order to prevent the state from exercising too substantial an influence over our decisions about whom to love and how to love them.

This justification for protecting intimate associations under the freedom of association — that the state should not be able to determine the most significant aspects of our self-definition — could also provide the grounds for extending that same protection to cultural associations. Cultural practices and affiliations — like intimate relationships — often form an integral part of our self-understanding. Cultural associations sustain these practices and affiliations. If, therefore, we wish to safeguard these basic or primordial attachments from undue state interference, then we must be willing to place cultural associations securely within the freedom's protective sphere.

Individual or collective control over self-definition does not exhaust the grounds for protecting cultural associations. Others may wish to protect cultural associations for more instrumental reasons. They may argue that cultural associations act as effective buffers between the individual and state power or suggest that the more and varied our cultural associations, the more enriched our national culture and our individual lives.

Instrumental goals also support the extension of the freedom's protection to associations which have been created to advance the social and economic interests of various groups and, perhaps, society as a whole. Business associations, for example, may realize certain efficiencies or advances through the sharing of price, product, and technical information. Optimally, and ultimately, the benefits of such shared knowledge should flow to the consumer in the form of lower prices and better products. Associations made up of individuals from historically disadvantaged groups, communities, or classes may also realize certain efficiencies and advances: for those particular individuals and communities. If we believe that the social or

---

for individuals and minorities to challenge existing political majorities. The first challenge consists simply of a demonstration of numerical strength. The second challenge consists of developing arguments designed to persuade members of the existing majority to switch their allegiance and ultimately turn the present minority into the majority. Associations on this account make majorities fluid. And the more fluid the majority, so the argument goes, the less likely it will be to squash a minority: members of a fluid majority may well recognize that they could be on the receiving end should allegiances shift once again. See de Toqueville *Democracy in America* (1835) 223.

Davis offers a more contemporary, sophisticated, and relevant variant of de Toqueville's thesis when he argues that only the continued success of grassroots and intermediate associations can ensure that the benefits of political liberation result in economic and social liberation. At present the large political parties — the ANC and the NP — have reached an agreement which secures the interests of big political parties in the new dispensation. From eliminating constituencies to preventing MPs from crossing the aisle, the major parties have increased simultaneously their security of tenure and diminished their direct accountability to the electorate. While the 1994 election will give us an unprecedented multiracial democracy, a government of pacted elites unresponsive to the needs and demands of the electorate threatens to give us a democracy of a very impoverished sort. Davis persuasively argues that only local and intermediate political associations can apply the sort of pressure necessary to spur the party elites into action. See Davis *South Africa and Transition: From Autocracy to What?* (1992) 18 Centre for Applied Legal Studies Working Papers 23–29.

economic uplift of subordinated groups is a sufficiently pressing goal, then we may want to insulate such associations from significant state interference. Freedom of association could then be understood to support a labour union's right to bargain collectively, a university's right to admit only women, or a law society's right to admit only black South Africans.

The foregoing analysis suggests that the sphere of liberty secured by the freedom of association is important for two very basic reasons. First, the sphere of liberty secured by the freedom enables individuals (and groups) to pursue or maintain those attachments which they believe are constitutive of their being. Such attachments might be intimate, cultural, religious, or social. Secondly, the sphere of liberty secured by the freedom enables individuals (and groups) to realize a most important instrumental goal: a rich and varied civil society. This rich and varied civil society in turn serves many ends: facilitating social debate and participatory politics, providing a buffer between the individual and the state, sustaining a vibrant culture, and ensuring economic progress and advancement.

If one looks hard enough, the foregoing analysis also implies that if we withdraw constitutional protection from these associations, our ability to protect individuals from the abuses of state power will be significantly diminished. Given that behind every occasionally abusive state lies a totalitarian monster, it should now be clear why de Toqueville claims that one cannot attack associational freedom without impairing the very foundations of an open and democratic society.

## 1.2 The conflict between association and equality

In each of the aforementioned justifications for freedom of association we have rather cryptically alluded to undue state interference in the affairs of political, intimate, cultural, social, or economic associations. We did not say why the government would interfere or what form that interference would be likely to take. At this stage of South African history we believe that the most likely grounds for government interference with an association's affairs would be the government's desire to promote equality. Government interference intended to promote equality will probably take one of three forms: (1) an outright banning of the association on the grounds that its professed aims or beliefs are inconsistent with the requirements of an open and democratic society based upon freedom and equality, or (2) a requirement that the association open up its membership to include all interested members of society on the grounds that membership exclusivity is inconsistent with the overridingly important goal of equality, or (3) a requirement that the internal organization of a political association must conform to basic democratic principles.

The outright banning of an association is at once the most extreme form of government interference and the form least likely to be employed. Certain democratic states — 'fighting democracies' — believe that banning is a legitimate response to associations which aim to undermine or destroy the state's free and democratic constitutional order. As we shall see, even these fighting democracies are highly circumspect in employing such a drastic measure. They generally require clear evidence of a concerted effort to destroy the constitutional order before they will impose a ban. The more difficult question for associational theory is whether banning an association is justified when it is simply the association's 'beliefs' which offend the state's commitment to an open and democratic society based upon freedom and *equality*. Such a banning is at bottom a question of what one may and may not say. It is therefore a freedom of expression issue. It is only derivatively a question about freedom of association and what beliefs an association may articulate. Given that banning an association for its expressive activities is primarily a freedom of expression issue, we have decided to leave most questions about content-based bans on speech and association to those who would write on the legitimate bounds of freedom of expression.

The second and third forms of government interference — legislation making illegal certain kinds of restrictive membership policies and legislation requiring that political parties structure their internal affairs in a more egalitarian way — are relatively pure association issues. They will engage us throughout the chapter.

Control over membership policies goes directly to the heart of associational freedom. Membership policies are after all about how the association chooses to constitute itself. Because the selection of members for an association is such a critical choice one must be aware that laws which force a change in the membership policies of an association *may* alter the essential character of that association. If one believes political pluralism, cultural diversity, individual autonomy, and social uplift — the very bases of a liberal democratic society — may be threatened by forced changes in associations' membership criteria, then some associations should perhaps be given the power to police their boundaries and thereby prevent the capture of the association by individuals or groups who wish to change the association's aims — i e individuals and groups who invest significant resources and effort in the creation of a particular kind of enterprise should have the power to police the membership of the organization in order to ensure that it remains true to its founding tenets. The question then is when, or under what conditions, is an association entitled to exercise its right to determine its membership criteria free from external intervention? Or conversely, when can society's commitment to equality trump an association's control over its membership criteria? For each type of association we look at, it will be asked when that kind of association should have its selection criteria protected, and when that same kind of association should have those criteria 'expanded' in the service of society's commitment to equality.

With respect to the third form of government interference — legislation requiring that political parties structure their internal affairs in a more egalitarian way — the basic question is: to what extent does the state's interest in the integrity of a democratic electoral process justify the infringement of the party's associational right to order its affairs as it wishes? If you begin from the premise that political parties are largely 'private orderings' created to pursue private ends, then the state will have to go some distance to demonstrate its need to meddle. If, on the other hand, your departure point is that political parties are essential for a functioning representative democracy, then you would argue that party structures must be democratic in order to serve democracy and that any deviation from democratic principles in the party's internal affairs must be justified. When we look at the case law and legislation regarding political parties we shall see how different nations mediate this tension between the party members' interest in ordering their own affairs and the state's interest in making sure that all members actually have the equal right and power to participate in their party's decision-making processes.

## 1.3 The structure of the discussion

The bulk of this chapter looks at the association jurisprudence of three of the world's major constitutional orders. In part 2 we examine the development of association jurisprudence in the US. We pay particular attention to the existing justifications for expressive associational freedom and intimate associational freedom. We then examine the extent to which US freedom of association jurisprudence supports constitutional protection for cultural, social, and economic associations. In part 3 we look at Canadian freedom of association jurisprudence. The Charter's relative youth means that Canada's association case law is somewhat underdeveloped. However, because the structure of South African constitutional analysis is likely to be similar to Canadian constitutional analysis in important respects, it is still worth making a quick survey. In part 4 we turn to Germany and the vast body of association legislation and case law which has been built up over the past forty years. The better part of this section is devoted to the independent and special protections afforded political parties under the Basic Law. In part 5 we return to South Africa and look briefly at its rather ignominious tradition of associational freedom. Finally, in part 6 we make several recommendations as to how those provisions in the interim Constitution which affect association should be construed. These recommendations are driven largely by the belief that the other rights enshrined in the Constitution provide relatively clear direction as to the kinds of associations which merit constitutional protection.

Our treatment of association contains one notable lacuna. Labour associations receive scant independent attention. They are discussed solely in terms of the development of case law in each of the three major constitutional orders we survey. We decided to pay diminished attention to labour associations for two simple reasons: first, labour associations have an entire chapter devoted to them elsewhere in the book; secondly, we believe that since the labour unions' associational interests operate at a sufficient distance from other sorts of associational interests, they are best handled by labour-law specialists.

## 2 FREEDOM OF ASSOCIATION IN THE UNITED STATES

### 2.1 Introduction

No express mention is made of the freedom of association in the text of the US Constitution. However, despite the lack of textual support, the Supreme Court has recognized a constitutional right to associate.

The court first identified a constitutional right to associate in *NAACP v Alabama*.[2] In *NAACP v Alabama* the state of Alabama had attempted to stop the NAACP — a civil rights organization — from operating within the state on the grounds that it had failed to comply with all the public disclosure and registration requirements of 'foreign corporations' 'doing business' in the state. The NAACP believed itself exempt from these requirements. While expulsion proceedings were pending, the state moved for production of the NAACP's membership lists. The NAACP refused.

---

[2] 357 US 449 (1958).

It argued that the state could not compel disclosure without violating the organization's associational rights.

In considering the NAACP's appeal the Supreme Court advanced several of its own arguments in favour of the recognition of this ostensibly new right to associate. First, the court argued that a right to association is justified on the instrumental grounds that public and private debate on issues of political and social importance are 'undeniably enhanced by group association'.[3] Secondly, the court asserted that the right to associate must be seen as an essential aspect of the 'liberty' guaranteed by the Fourteenth Amendment. Without such a liberty people would have their ability to express their beliefs on political, cultural, religious, and economic matters significantly impeded, if not entirely denied.[4]

In applying the new right to the case before it the court found that the trial court's production and disclosure order would work a 'substantial restraint upon the exercise by [the NAACP's] members of their right of freedom of association'.[5] In particular the court found that revelation of the NAACP's membership would inevitably result in its members being subjected to 'economic reprisal, loss of employment, threat of physical coercion and other manifestations of public hostility'.[6] Since the state's action would have the effect of severely undermining the NAACP members' constitutional right to associate, and could not be justified by reference to some compelling state interest, the court held that the state's action was unconstitutional and that the disclosure order would have to be quashed.[7]

In *NAACP v Button* the court extended the right to associate to include the right of groups to engage in litigation designed to further the group's political aims.[8] The court found that the state of Virginia's interest in regulating the legal profession did not provide a sufficiently compelling justification for proscribing the political advocacy being engaged in by the NAACP.

However, *Button* is interesting not so much for the case holding itself, but for the manner in which that holding was expanded in several cases which followed. In *Brotherhood of Railroad Trainmen v Virginia*,[9] *United Mine Workers v Illinois Bar Ass'n*,[10] and *United Transportation Union v State Bar of Michigan*[11] the court found that unions had a right to associate which included a right to litigate cases in the interests of the organization and their individual members. While the *Brotherhood of Railroad Trainmen* court found that 'the Constitution protects the associational rights of the members of the union precisely as it does those of the NAACP' and the *United Transportation Union* court held 'collective activity undertaken to obtain meaningful access to the courts is a fundamental right within the protection of the First Amendment', these cases do not actually involve litigation designed to express

---

[3] At 460.
[4] Ibid.
[5] At 462.
[6] Ibid.
[7] See also *Bates v Little Rock* 361 US 516 (1960): court reversed conviction of NAACP official for failing to turn over records on grounds that it interfered with NAACP's freedom of association and that the state had no compelling interest in the documents sought.
[8] 371 US 415 (1963).
[9] 377 US 1 (1964).
[10] 389 US 217 (1967).
[11] 401 US 576 (1971).

the political beliefs or to realize the political agenda of the association. Thus, despite the court's attempt to tie these cases closely to the NAACP cases which preceded them, these cases do not simply promise protection to engage in other First Amendment activities such as speech, assembly, or petition. Rather, the cases appear to protect a somewhat more general right to engage in associational activities.[12]

Whatever the parameters of this more general right, it was inevitable that once the court recognized the right to associate it would then have to address two closely related questions. First, is there, implicit in the right to associate, a right not to associate? Secondly, is there, implicit in this right to not associate, or dissociate, a right to discriminate in the selection of the association's membership?

The court addressed the first question in *Abood v Detroit Board of Education*.[13] The court recognized that the freedom of association — and the correlative freedom not to associate — could not permit dissenting employees to object to the collection of union dues for collective bargaining purposes. Such a holding would make collective bargaining almost impossible. However, the court did hold that dissenting employees did possess a right to 'refuse to associate' with respect to 'ideological union expenditures not directly related to collective bargaining'. The court held that the dissenting union members could not be forced, under the First Amendment, to support particular political parties or organizations which expressed positions to which they did not adhere.

As for the right to discriminate in membership selection, the court, in *Norwood v Harrison*, found that while 'invidious private discrimination may be characterized as a form of exercising freedom of association protected by the First Amendment, . . . it has never been accorded affirmative constitutional protection'.[14] Thus, although the court withheld support for a constitutionally protected right to discriminate in one's associations, the court did say that it could be characterized as a necessary part of the exercise of other First Amendment rights such as speech, petition, assembly, and religion.

The tougher question of when discriminatory membership practices would lack the penumbral protection of these other First Amendment rights and could fall before some compelling or legitimate state interest was not addressed until the mid-1980s. In three gender equality cases, *Roberts v United States Jaycees*,[15] *Board of Directors of Rotary International v Rotary Club of Duarte*,[16] and *New York State Club Association v City of New York*,[17] the Supreme Court revealed that the traditional US solicitude for private voluntary associations which discriminate is fast disappearing. Antidiscrimination legislation passed in the 1960s and 1970s had already barred discrimination in the formerly 'private' areas of housing, education, public accommodation, and employment. In *Roberts*, *Rotary Club*, and *New York State*

---

[12] But see Tribe *American Constitutional Law* 2 ed (1988) 1011–12, citing *Garcia v Texas State Board of Medical Examiners* 421 US 995 (1975). Tribe argues that *Garcia's* rejection of a health maintenance organization's claim that it had a constitutional right to associate for medical ends supports the proposition that associational rights are recognized by the court only when they serve some other important First Amendment interest such as speech, assembly, or petition.
[13] 431 US 209 (1977).
[14] 413 US 455 (1973).
[15] 468 US 609 (1984).
[16] 481 US 537 (1987).
[17] 487 US 1 (1988).

*Club Ass'n* the court, in concert with the human rights codes of various states, severely curtailed the wide latitude which private clubs and associations had previously had to constitute themselves. These human rights codes made it clear that it was no longer enough for clubs to say that the boys just want to be with the boys because boys will be boys. According to this trio of decisions, an association's right to differentiate in its membership policies must have one or two more sophisticated and acceptable justifications. Either the freedom of association claim must involve the right to engage in expressive activities protected by the First Amendment or it must be designed to protect the associational right to 'enter into and maintain certain intimate relationships'. Since the associations could not be said to serve either purpose their associational claims were rejected.

What these cases did not determine, however, was the specific nature of these more sophisticated justifications for discriminatory membership policies. To the extent that membership policies are designed to ensure the expression of views propounded by the original membership, they are protected by both the freedom to associate and the freedom of expression. However, the freedom of association for expressive purposes is not absolute. States may pass laws restricting freedom of expression and association in order to promote a compelling state interest. What remains unclear is just what sorts of infringement on expressive association are justified by what kinds of compelling state interest. Similarly it seems clear that, at a very general level, 'the Bill of Rights . . . must afford the formation and preservation of certain kinds of highly personal relationships a substantial measure of sanctuary from unjustified interference by the State'.[18] The difficulty, as Laurence Tribe notes, lies 'in deciding what constitutes unjustified interference by the State and what types of relationships deserve constitutional protection'.[19] As yet the cases have provided neither precise nor coherent guidelines for determining the kinds of intimate associations immune from state intervention.

In the following sections we shall look more closely at the existing justifications for and limitations on political and intimate associations. We shall also suggest additional types of associations which deserve constitutional protection. Finally, for each type of association we shall ask when they should have their discriminatory practices protected and when they should have them enjoined and eliminated in the service of a society's commitment to equality.[20]

## 2.2 Expressive and political association

The US Supreme Court has recognized expressive association as an instrumental safeguard of the right to free speech. Protection of expressive association recognizes that the ability to associate with others is indispensable to effective advocacy in a mass society. Through a collective effort organized individuals can make themselves

---

[18] *Roberts* (supra) at 615.
[19] Tribe op cit (n 12) 1401–2.
[20] For an excellent treatment of the conflict between the freedom to dissociate and equality concerns, to which this analysis is particularly indebted, see Marshall 'Discrimination and the Right of Association' (1986) 81 *Northwestern U LR* 68. Few authors argue that the right to association includes an absolute right to dissociate. But see McGee 'The Right to Not Associate: The Case for an Absolute Freedom of Negative Association' (1992) 23 *UWLA LR* 123.

heard and understood, whereas alone, 'their voices would be faint or lost'.[21] In short, groups designed and created to promote a particular political or social viewpoint are clearly covered by the protections of the First Amendment.

Free speech, assembly, and petition jurisprudence further supports the proposition that since advocating discrimination is constitutionally protected the formation of organizations to advance such advocacy should also be protected.[22] However, the value considerations supporting these rights also support the notion that the fit between the expressive association's political and social viewpoints and its discriminatory membership policies ought to be rather tight, i e an expressive association's discriminatory policies ought to be part of or closely linked to its advocacy for a certain way of life, if the discrimination is to be deemed justified. Where the discriminatory membership policies do not serve the expressive ends of the organization the state should be deemed to have a legitimate interest in stepping in — on equality grounds — to end the discriminatory practice. For example, an environmental advocacy organization such as Greenpeace would not be entitled to exclude Muslim men of Pakistani descent from the organization because such discrimination would have nothing to do with the positions that the organization maintains. On the other hand, a neo-Nazi organization may discriminate in its membership policies against Jews. This discrimination would be consistent with its belief that Jews should be deported or returned to Israel.[23]

The legitimacy of the state's intrusion into the affairs and discriminatory membership policies of the major political parties has been more easily recognized and effected because state action, and consequently constitutional condemnation, has been so much easier to find. For example, in *Smith v Allwright* the court held that a Democratic Party rule barring blacks from participating in the party's primaries elections contravened the Fifteenth Amendment's right to vote. The court justified its decision on the grounds that through the presence of the Democrat primary winner of the general ballot the state would be deemed to have endorsed the racially discriminatory practices of the party.[24] Similarly in *Terry v Adams* the court found that the Jaybird Democratic Association invariably determined the Democratic Party nominee in pre-primary elections in a particular part of Texas. State action could be found both in the state's legitimation of the process through its placing of the candidate on the official ballot and the fact that this Democrat candidate was

---

[21] *Citizens Against Rent Control v Berkeley* 454 US 290, 294 (1981). The court has also recognized that freedom of expressive association protects groups that publicly pursue common 'social, legal and economic' ends or ideals in addition to those groups which pursue expressly political ends: *City of Dallas v Stanglein* 490 US 19, 25 (1989).

[22] See *Brandenburg v Ohio* 395 US 444 (1969): in allowing the Ku Klux Klan publicly to articulate virulently racist and anti-semitic beliefs the court held that free speech, free press, and free assembly protections do not permit state to proscribe the advocacy of force to effect political, social, or economic change or forbid assemblies designed to promote such beliefs, save where the advocacy or assembly will produce imminent lawless action; *Collin v Smith* 578 F 2d 1197 (7th Cir 1978): in permitting a neo-Nazi group to march through a Jewish suburb the court wrote that 'public expression of ideas may not be prohibited merely because the ideas are themselves offensive to some of their hearers'.

[23] By contrast, the petitioners in *Roberts*, *Rotary Club*, and *New York State Club Association* would still not benefit from this test because they would be unable to establish that they have expression as their primary purpose. In *Roberts* the court established what would be an even more stringent requirement for this test. It held that even if the Jaycees were understood to have made political expression a primary goal of the organization, they had not shown that the inclusion of women in the organization would alter the character of the organization or the positions it espoused. We reject this burdensome qualification of the test on the grounds that such an empirical showing would be difficult, if not impossible, to make. The qualification would likely swallow the test.

[24] 321 US 649 (1944).

almost assured of winning the particular seat in question. Having found state action, the court could hold that the barring of black Democratic Party members from the Jaybird's proceedings violated the Fifteenth Amendment.[25]

However, where there is no state action, and the political party affairs being interfered with are deemed private, the state must show that a compelling state interest justifies interference with the associational rights of the party. Thus, for example, in *Cousins v Wigoda* the Supreme Court found an Illinois law on the election of convention delegates to be an unconstitutional infringement of the Democratic Party's associational right to choose its delegates according to its own rules. The state of Illinois' interest in preserving the fairness of a national convention was held to be insufficiently compelling to warrant the state's interference.[26] Likewise, in *Tashjian v Republican Party of Connecticut* the court held that a statute barring independent voters from participating in Republican Party primaries violated the party's 'First Amendment right to enter into political associations with individuals of its own choosing'.[27] Despite this natural predisposition to favour the right of association, the court has on occasion held that the state has a sufficiently compelling interest in maintaining the integrity of the electoral process to warrant interference in the internal workings and membership policies of the political parties.[28] What the court has yet clearly to decide is when the state's interest in the integrity of the electoral process is of sufficient importance to infringe upon the party's associational rights.[29]

## 2.3 Intimate association and cultural association

### 2.3.1 *Intimate association*

As we noted above, the Bill of Rights affords a 'certain kind of highly personal relationships a substantial measure of sanctuary from unjustified interference by the State'.[30] Unfortunately the court has refused to identify exactly which kinds of personal relationships merit constitutional protection. Even more unfortunate is that where the court has chosen to identify those relationships which receive judicial solicitude and those which do not the results are often incoherent, if not logically

---

[25] 345 US 461 (1953). See Tribe op cit (n 12) 1119. Tribe argues that the aforementioned cases and others, known collectively as the White Primary Cases, stand for the 'proposition that all activities of political parties that are closely related to the nomination of a candidate who will receive some preferential state treatment' implicate the state and are therefore potentially subject to constitutional proscriptions.

[26] 419 US 477 (1975). See also *Democratic Party of the United States v Wisconsin* 450 US 107 (1981): court struck down Wisconsin law requiring delegates to vote in compliance with results of the state's open primary as an unconstitutional interference with the party's associational right to choose its delegates as it sees fit.

[27] 479 US 208 (1986). See also *March Fong Eu v San Francisco County Democratic Central Committee* 489 US 214 (1989): court declares unconstitutional, as violation of First Amendment, California election law prohibition on candidate endorsements by party central committees during primary elections.

[28] See e g *Marchioro v Chaney* 442 US 191, 196 (1979): upholding a Washington law requiring that the major parties have a State Committee with two representatives from each county on grounds that a state's interests in conducting elections in a 'fair and orderly fashion is unquestionably legitimate'. See also Easterbrook 'Implicit and Explicit Rights of Association' (1987) 10 *Harvard J of L & Pub Pol* 91 at 97, arguing that the court's decisions which interfere with associational freedom in this area simply reflect the court's belief that the association under scrutiny has an immoral or objectionable agenda.

[29] For an extended commentary on this conflict between the state's interest in the integrity of the election process and a political party's associational rights, see March 'Fong Eu v San Francisco County Democratic Central Committee: Tension between Associational Rights of Political Parties and Fair Elections' (1990) 16 *J Contemp L* 381.

[30] *Roberts* (supra) at 615.

contradictory. To return to the *Roberts* decision for a moment: Brennan J notes there that the reason shelter is afforded intimate associations 'reflects the realization that individuals draw much of their emotional enrichment from close ties with others'.[31] Unlike the freedom of political or expressive association, this right to intimate association is not instrumental. Rather it seeks to protect certain kinds of relationships from intrusion by the state simply because it is widely felt that these relationships are so central to our lives, so inextricably linked to our self-understanding, so 'intimate to the degree of being sacred', that the state should play little or no role in their construction and operation.[32]

Although the US Supreme Court has protected intimate associations for some time, it has not until recently expressly identified itself as protecting associations. Intimate associations have usually been protected by the right to privacy. The result of this conceptual dependence is that because the body of law developed under privacy lacks coherence the constitutional protection offered to intimate associations also lacks coherence.[33] The incoherence of the court's decisions in the area of privacy and intimate associations is rather readily revealed through a comparison of two cases, *Griswold v Connecticut*,[34] and *Bowers v Hardwick*.[35]

In *Griswold v Connecticut* the Supreme Court struck down a Connecticut statute which forbade the use of contraceptives and the counselling of people in their use. At least one justice found that the state's interest in preventing the use of contraception was not so sufficiently compelling as to warrant the impairment of a right 'implicit in the concept of ordered liberty', as well as a right that formed an integral part of the 'basic values which underlie our society': the right to marital privacy. However, *Griswold* is not just about the right to marital privacy. With the statute struck down and contraception widely available, *Griswold* is ultimately about the freedom to have private intimate recreational sexual relations free from the fear of unwanted pregnancy or venereal disease.

In *Bowers v Hardwick* an adult male was charged with violating the Georgia sodomy statute by engaging in a sexual act with another man in his own bedroom. The statute defined sodomy as committing or submitting to 'any sexual act involving the sex organs of one person and the mouth or anus of another'. The court rejected Hardwick's challenge to the constitutionality of the statute on the grounds that neither the text of the Constitution, nor court precedents, nor the traditions of the country supported the claim that intimate homosexual contact falls within a

---

[31] Ibid. Elsewhere in the opinion (at 620), Brennan J notes that this freedom of intimate association also protects 'deep attachments and commitments to the necessarily few other individuals with whom one shares . . . distinctly personal aspects of one's life'.

[32] *Griswold v Connecticut* 381 US 479, 486 (1965): court recognizes constitutional right to privacy. See also Karst 'The Freedom of Intimate Association' (1980) 89 *Yale LJ* 624.

[33] Thus far privacy rights — and therefore intimate associational rights — have generally been limited to traditional familial relationships, contraception, procreation, and heterosexual sex. See e g *Skinner v Oklahoma* 316 US 535 (1942): court recognizes limited right to reproductive autonomy and strikes down law permitting state to sterilize repeat felons; *Griswold v Connecticut* 381 US 479 (1965): striking down law making use of contraceptives by married couples a crime; *Eisenstadt v Baird* 405 US 438 (1972): holding that the right of privacy means that individuals, whether married or single, are free from government interference into their decisions as to whether or not to bear a child; *Roe v Wade* 410 US 113, 153 (1973): holding that the right of privacy encompasses a 'woman's decision whether or not to terminate her pregnancy'; *Carey v Population Services International* 431 US 678 (1977): striking down law proscribing commercial distribution of contraceptives.

[34] 381 US 479 (1965).

[35] 478 US 186 (1986).

protected sphere of liberty.[36] Furthermore, the court was unwilling to create a new fundamental right in order to override clear legislative choices.

If, as we have suggested, *Griswold* is ultimately about the freedom to have private intimate recreational sexual relationships free from the fear of unwanted pregnancy or venereal disease, and free from state intrusion, then it is difficult to understand the decision in *Bowers* — which also concerns private intimate sexual relations. For if a hypothetical heterosexual couple is permitted to engage in safe-sex sexual relations because we regard such intimate acts as essential to their self-definition, then it remains impossible to understand why a homosexual couple cannot engage in intimate acts which they likewise regard as fundamental to their particular self-definition. This inconsistency undercuts the legitimacy of *Griswold* and makes the privacy or intimate association right articulated there seem less an essential ingredient of a scheme of ordered liberty and more a reflection of the raw prejudices of the bare majority in *Bowers*.[37]

A similar inconsistency in the treatment of intimate associations can be detected in *Moore v City of Cleveland*[38] and *Village of Belle Terre v Boraas*.[39] In *Moore* an East Cleveland zoning ordinance limited occupancy of particular dwellings to 'single families'. However, 'single families' was so strictly construed by the ordinance that it effectively prevented a grandmother from living with her son, a grandson by this son, and a grandson by another child. Citing close to half a century's worth of privacy cases, the Supreme Court struck down the ordinance on the grounds that the ordinance struck too deeply into the well-protected sphere of family or domestic autonomy.

In *Belle Terre*, however, the court sustained a very similar ordinance which restricted land use in the town to single-family dwellings occupied by individuals related either by blood, marriage, or adoption. The ordinance was challenged by several unrelated college students living together in what would otherwise be a 'single-family' dwelling. The court dismissed the challenge on the grounds that such zoning requirements fall squarely within the town's police powers and were rationally related to the legitimate ends the town sought to effect.

What is difficult to understand about the latter case is why the associational rights or privacy rights of these students were accorded such little weight. Given the town's significant interference with the constitution of its inhabitant's domestic associations, one would have thought that the court would have demanded the production of compelling reasons or interests to justify the interference and exclusion. What it

---

[36] The court in *Bowers* rejected Mr Hardwick's claim in large part because it purportedly failed to satisfy the two-prong test set out in *Palko v Connecticut* 302 US 319 (1937). This test determines whether the due process clause of the Fourteenth Amendment incorporates certain fundamental rights. The judges held that a right to homosexual intimacy was neither (1) part of 'the very essence of a scheme of ordered liberty' nor (2) 'a principle of justice so rooted in the traditions and consciences of our people as to be ranked as fundamental'. On reasonably close inspection, however, it becomes clear that the *Palko* test is not much of a test at all. First, the notion of ordered liberty is sufficiently elastic to include just about any right that a justice feels deserves protection. Secondly, the requirement that the 'proposed' right be 'rooted in tradition' functions largely as a conservative break on the recognition of rights to engage in activities which offend conventional morals. The result of such a highly subjective test is that justifications for the recognition of a right to intimate association for some relationships are almost wholly inconsistent with the justifications for the denial of a right to intimate association for other kinds of relationships.

[37] For an interesting analysis of the totalitarian implications of *Bowers* and a more compelling justification for freedom of intimate association, see Rubenfeld 'The Right of Privacy' (1989) 102 *Harvard LR* 737.

[38] 431 US 494 (1976).

[39] 416 US 1 (1973).

received was a laundry list of small-town concerns almost wholly unrelated to the legal relationship of the occupants in a single-family dwelling — population growth, traffic levels, rental costs, and the community aesthetic. One would think that a family of ten would be far more likely to have an untoward effect on these ends than would an unrelated gang of four.

The only plausible explanation of the court's decision is that because it did not see any semblance of a family in the Boraas et al household the court refused to extend the protections for intimate association to it. But as we have already seen, the privacy rights which tend to support this right to intimate association are not limited to families. Decisions recognizing the right to read pornography in the privacy of one's home[40] or to purchase non-medical contraception[41] can hardly be recognized as supporting the traditional picture of the family. Thus the rejection of Boraas's claim cannot rest on the court's previous privacy decisions.

A more plausible rationale for the court's decision not to recognize the household's associational rights does not appear in the case law until some thirteen years later in *Roberts*. In *Roberts* the court suggested several criteria for recognition of a right of intimate association: the size and purpose of the association, the selectivity of membership, and the insularity of the group. The Boraas household was comprised of students from a local college who had no binding purpose for living together other than convenience and could not be described as especially insular or selective. It is possible therefore that under the *Roberts* test the court would have found that the household was not an intimate association entitled to constitutional protection.[42]

### 2.3.2 Cultural association

Brennan J's four aforementioned *Roberts* criteria appear to set relatively clear limits on the kinds of intimate association entitled to constitutional protection. Under this test the Jaycees, the Rotary Club, or your average eating club do not qualify as intimate associations: members have only a passing familiarity with one another, the membership is neither small nor insular, and expression is incidental to the purpose of the organization. While it may be true that some members of these organization do form the kind of deep, abiding, and highly personal relationships protected by *Roberts*, these relationships do not require constitutional protection of the association. A deep friendship should, one would imagine, survive inside or outside these rather amorphous associations.

It would seem, following *Roberts*, *Rotary Club*, and *New York State Club Ass'n*, that expressive associations and intimate associations are the only kinds which merit constitutional protection. However, as Brennan J himself casually suggests in *Roberts*, there may be other associations which deserve judicial solicitude:

> 'Without precisely identifying every consideration that may underlie this type of constitutional protection, we have noted that certain kinds of personal bonds have played a critical role in the

---

[40] *Stanley v Illinois* 405 US 645 (1972).
[41] *Carey v Population Services International* (supra).
[42] Of course this new test would not save the *Belle Terre* result. The ordinance would still not be rationally related to the laundry list of reasons given for it.

culture and traditions of the Nation by cultivating and transmitting shared ideals and beliefs; they thereby foster diversity and act as buffers between the individual and the power of the State.'[43]

Brennan J's language seems to point to an additional right of freedom of cultural association. Extension of the freedom of association to include the freedom of cultural association could be justified on two primary grounds.

First, the freedom would help to preserve national, ethnic, or religious communities and identities. This aim already has significant support in the court's existing body of jurisprudence. In tacit recognition of this right the court has on various occasions permitted Amish parents to educate their children at home,[44] allowed Catholics to educate their children in private school,[45] struck down legislation barring the teaching of foreign languages,[46] and prohibited undue interference with Native American tribal autonomy.[47]

The preservation of these communities is important because our cultural groups do not simply provide us with poker partners or excuses for having a picnic. They often provide us with our most basic constitutive attachments. In other words, our identity as individuals may often be determined in large part by our membership in a particular cultural group.[48]

By identifying cultural attachments with our constitutive attachments or sources of self-definition we come much closer to the kind of values which support constitutional protection for familial relationships. Both familial relationships and cultural attachments are important because they provide us with our primary bonds and with what we recognize as the most essential elements of our selves.

Secondly, the preservation of cultural communities serves a liberal-democratic system's overarching aim of pluralism. Pluralism sees the value of preserving cultural entities as an end in itself. Cultural pluralism is understood to enrich the entire national culture, not solely through the development of individuality but through the interaction of diverse traditions, communities, and practices which help to make up and forge a national identity.[49]

Of course cultural associations have their dark side. The insularity associated with cultural associations often results in lack of understanding of and care for other communities in the polity. Instead of lessening prejudice, reinforcing the insularity of cultural associations may actually heighten it.

Given their very real potential for increasing prejudice and social strife, we do

---

[43] *Roberts* (supra) at 615.
[44] *Wisconsin v Yoder* 406 US 205 (1972).
[45] *Pierce v Society of Sisters* 268 US 510 (1925).
[46] *Meyer v Nebraska* 262 US 390 (1923).
[47] *Santa Clara Pueblo v Martinez* 436 US 49 (1978).
[48] As Kenneth Karst has noted, cultural groups establish many of our 'primordial affinities'. These affinities 'not only provide a tie to other people, but also offer us our very selves': 'Paths to Belonging: The Constitution and Cultural Identity' (1986) 56 *NC LR* 303. See also Karst *Paths to Belonging: Equal Citizenship and the Constitution* (1989).
[49] Cultural pluralism supports three more strong constitutional values. First, a commitment to cultural pluralism ensures the presence of diverse perspectives. These diverse perspectives in turn foster and enhance public debate. Under the market theory of truth this debate results in better decision-making because important public issues are more fully ventilated. Secondly, the promotion of cultural pluralism is also understood to result in greater mutual tolerance — the more you see, so the argument goes, the more you respect the traditions of others. Finally, and perhaps most importantly, cultural associations often serve as a buffer between the state and the individual. Cultural associations serve as a buffer in two ways: first, they often provide support for individuals in their legal battles with the state; secondly, when operating as expressive associations they ensure that an individual's interests are not simply articulated in a weak singular voice, but have the effective force of numbers.

not believe that a cultural association may discriminate as it pleases. As with the protection afforded expressive associations, we would want to require a showing that a cultural organization's discriminatory practices affirmatively promote the identity and community which the cultural association serves.[50] Thus a professional association that admits only Zulus and teaches leadership skills and provides other professional training would not satisfy this test: its ultimate purpose is economic and not cultural. On the other hand, the restrictive membership practices of an association dedicated to maintaining Zulu traditions and celebrating Zulu heritage would be justifiable: the association is designed to promote and protect Zulu culture.

Against this last justification for permitting discriminatory membership policies by cultural associations it might be argued that anyone interested in a particular culture should be able to join the appropriate cultural organization. Unlike political groups or households, which must be relatively 'closed' in order to achieve their ends, one might argue that cultural organizations need not be exclusive in order to sustain a heritage. In addition one might press the argument that cultures are the sorts of things which evolve over time and which actually benefit from contact with non-members.

While superficially appealing, this argument for cultural openness suffers from an important defect: it underestimates the possibility of 'capture' — by sufficiently large numbers of individuals from outside the original group joining the group and changing its driving purpose or direction. Where a cultural organization has built up a valuable infrastructure — buildings, equipment, books, etc — it becomes especially attractive for those who wish to employ those tools for other ends. If we are to take cultural associations seriously, then individuals and groups who invest significant resources and effort in the creation of a particular cultural organization must have the right to police the membership of the organization in order to ensure that it remains true to its founding tenets.

## 2.4 Two additional grounds for protecting freedom of association: anti-orthodoxy and the empowerment of historically disadvantaged groups

### 2.4.1 *Anti-orthodoxy*

> 'If there is any fixed star in our constitutional constellation, it is that no official, high or petty, can prescribe what shall be orthodox in politics, nationalism, religion or other matters of opinion or force citizens to confess by word or act their faith therein.'[51]

Opposition to state-enforced orthodoxy is a cornerstone of US constitutional politics. In short, this US brand of liberalism holds that individuals should be free to 'create, articulate and explore different visions of society' without having to conform their behaviour to a state-enforced morality.

However, in applying antidiscrimination legislation to at least some private clubs the state will be asking them to conform to such a state-enforced morality. For those clubs not engaged in commercial or quasi-public undertakings the state's sole interest in eliminating the discriminatory membership practice is ideological —

---

[50] See Marshall op cit (n 20) 90–1.
[51] *West Virginia State Bd of Educ v Barnette* 319 US 624, 642 (1943).

i e the state wishes to send a message to the club members, and the society as a whole, that it is committed to equality.

This ideological commitment to equality threatens the commitment to pluralism. While we have suggested that this commitment to pluralism is protected by the freedom of expressive association, it is most vigorously defended through the rights of free speech and assembly.

For example, in *Coates v City of Cincinnati* the petitioners took issue with a city ordinance that proscribed any 'annoying' congregation of three or more people on a public sidewalk.[52] The court struck down the ordinance because it served to bar assembly in its purest form and was animated by nothing more than the town's moral biases. Similarly in *Shelton v Tucker* the court struck down a law forcing public-school teachers to file annual affidavits declaring the organizations or associations to which they had either belonged or contributed in the previous five years.[53] The court wrote that the Constitution not only protects expressive associations against the compelled disclosure of membership lists but also protects an individual's affiliation with an 'unpopular minority organization', including 'social' or 'avocational' groups. What truly offended the court in both these cases was the state's methods. The court rejected the use of private individuals to teach others a state-endorsed lesson in what constitutes a just society.

This approach to associational concerns is wholly in keeping with the court's free speech jurisprudence. In *Wooley v Manard* the state of New Hampshire was prevented from making individuals the vehicle for disseminating a piece of ideology — the motto 'Live Free or Die' on licence plates — no matter how acceptable it was to most New Hampshireans.[54] The court held that the state's interest in disseminating this message could not outweigh the individual's First Amendment right not to be the courier for such a message.

Just as the state is not permitted to make individuals the couriers for particular ideological messages, it is also not permitted to prevent individuals from making what may be ideologically offensive statements. Thus when individuals, groups, and the state itself are confronted with dignitary harms the right of free speech does not permit the government to suppress such speech. Rather it holds that the proper response of both political and civil society to repugnant speech is additional speech, education, political mobilization, and pressure.

If, however, we allow the state to use its remedial powers to override the membership policies of private associations for the symbolic purpose of eliminating dignitary harms, then we go quite a way towards allowing the state to run rampant in the sphere of individual conscience. We thereby permit the state to make individuals, and the groups of which they are a part, the couriers for its ideological aims. As one commentator has argued, this very significant grant of power to the state is 'potentially' totalitarian in its dimensions.[55] From this anti-totalitarian perspective the right to discriminate in one's associations can profitably be seen as a prophylactic measure designed to provide a brake on government power.

We should not be understood as suggesting that the state does not have an abiding

---

[52] 402 US 611 (1971).
[53] 364 US 479 (1960).
[54] 430 US 705, 717 (1977).
[55] See Rubenfeld op cit (n 37) 737.

and legitimate interest in ending discrimination. We want to argue only that the state should concentrate its energies on ending discrimination in some circumstances, and not in others. Where the associations are clearly public, quasi-public, or commercial enterprises — such as businesses or universities — the state has a clear interest in ensuring that all individuals have equal access to these institutions. However, where the institutions provide largely psychic benefits the elimination of discrimination is primarily symbolic and designed to enforce a particular social vision. In a situation where the state's interest is almost purely ideological the private association, along with its discriminatory policies, ought to be constitutionally protected.[56]

### 2.4.2 *Empowerment of historically disadvantaged groups*

Even if we reject out of hand the proposition that white male associations may discriminate against females and blacks as they wish, we may not immediately want to say that organizations which are all-female or all-black may not, likewise, discriminate in their membership policies. We would like to argue, at least initially, that separatism imposed by historically disadvantaged communities has a very different practical value and symbolic cast than separatism imposed by the historically dominant groups in a community.

Given the historical and existing relationships between communities in South Africa, no one could legitimately assert that exclusion of men from a women's legal defence organization or whites from a black political action group connotes the inferiority of males and whites or somehow perpetuates the vast inequalities in power between men and women, whites and blacks. On the other hand, it seems clear that institutional separatism enforced by white groups or males groups does actually reinforce both their privileged positions and the stereotypes associated with the differences in status between men and women, whites and blacks.

Naturally the objection to permitting membership discrimination by women's or black associations, but precluding such discrimination in historically male or white associations, is that this asymmetrical treatment is unprincipled. However, while the treatment of these groups is asymmetrical with respect to sex in one instance and race in the other, this differential treatment is not asymmetrical and unprincipled with respect to power. From the perspective of our commitment to equality and eradicating historical disadvantage it is the elimination of the significant differences in power between the sexes and races which matters. This purpose might well justify the 'asymmetrical' treatment.

Let us suppress, for the moment, the criticism that such asymmetrical treatment violates the interim Constitution's commitment to equal protection of the law. Let us assume that everyone is in favour of the constitutionally recognized commitment to affirmative action to redress grievous historical wrongs and everyone believes that asymmetrical treatment of sex- and race-based associations is justified on the grounds that we want to eliminate historically determined inequalities. Even so we would want to qualify the conditions under which associations representing disadvantaged groups may discriminate in their membership policies. We would want

---

[56] See Note 'State Power and Discrimination by Private Clubs: First Amendment Protection for Nonexpressive Associations' (1991) 104 *Harvard LR* 1835.

to hold that these associations may discriminate in their membership policies only when the association and the membership policy is designed to help remedy the presence of inequality in the society.[57]

If we accept this test, we still have two empirical questions left to answer. First, how do we identify which groups have been historically disadvantaged? What sort of statistics do we use to measure continued disadvantage? This last question about continued disadvantage is important. One assumes that when the disadvantage disappears so does the basis for the discriminatory membership practices.

Secondly, we have to ask what separatist institutions, if any, promote the equality which we seek? If in fact coeducational institutions were found to result in less stereotypical attitudes towards the opposite sex, better education for all concerned, and greater professional success for the women alumni than that achieved by their single-sex college counterparts, then the empirical basis for maintaining single-sex schools so as to eliminate inequality would not exist.

Even if we are empirically satisfied with the answers to those two questions, endorsing asymmetry of treatment for advantaged and disadvantaged groups is hardly unproblematic. Deborah Rhodes suggests that:

> 'Separatist education, like other forms of separatist affiliation, offers the vices and virtues of a ghetto: it provides support, affiliation and self-esteem for subordinate groups, but often at the price of perpetuating attitudes that perpetuate subordination.'[58]

In short, single-sex or race institutions are at best a palliative. What is of foremost importance is that mainstream institutions be challenged and changed to eliminate the attitudes and practices which perpetuate subordination.

## 3  FREEDOM OF ASSOCIATION IN CANADA

### 3.1  Introduction: freedom of association[59] and labour relations

Freedom of association litigation in Canada has almost entirely concerned labour relations. Unfortunately for the unions, the court's preoccupation with labour relations has not redounded to their benefit.

In a series of 1987 cases known as the 'labour trilogy,' the Supreme Court held that the Charter's guarantee of freedom of association does not include a right to bargain collectively or a right to strike. The rationale for this holding was set out in a fragmented opinion in *Reference re: Public Service Employee Relations Act*.[60] In upholding legislation which contained prohibitions and restrictions on strikes and collective bargaining by certain classes of public employees three justices held that the right to bargain collectively or the right to strike were simply creatures of statute and not part of the sphere of activity protected by the Charter's right to freedom of

---

[57] This justification parallels our previous requirements that expressive associations which discriminate may do so only where the discrimination is actually a part of their expressive activities and that cultural associations may discriminate only where it serves to preserve the cultural identity and community.

[58] 'Association and Assimilation' (1986) 81 *Northwestern U LR* 106 at 143.

[59] The Charter's text for freedom of association reads as follows: '2. Everyone has the following fundamental freedoms: . . . (d) freedom of association' (Constitution Act 1982, RSC 1985, Appendix II, No 44, Schedule B, Part I, s 2(d)).

[60] 1987 (38) DLR (4th) 161.

association. Another justice held that the freedom of association belongs solely to the individual, not to the group formed through the exercise of that individual right. As a result, because an individual can neither bargain collectively nor strike, the right to bargain collectively or strike could not be part of the fundamental right to associate.[61] The reasoning set out in *Reference re: Public Service Employee Relations Act* was then closely tracked in *PSAC v Canada*.[62] In *PSAC* the Supreme Court held that legislation which extended several federal civil servant collective bargaining agreements and removed their right to strike for two years did not violate the freedom of association. Rounding out the trilogy is the court's decision in *Saskatchewan v RWDSU*.[63] In *RWDSU* Saskatchewan legislation temporarily prohibiting a strike by dairy workers and compelling arbitration was held not to violate the freedom of association.

Despite the court's resistance to finding that a right to strike and a right to bargain collectively falls within s 2(d)'s ambit, its freedom of association decisions have not been entirely inimical to labour's interests. Indeed, a recent decision by the court frees unions to use union funds to engage in a wide range of political and social activities unrelated to collective bargaining. In *Lavigne v OPSEU*[64] a union member argued that the mandatory check-offs for dues collected by his appointed collective bargaining unit forcibly compelled him to associate with the political causes financially supported by the unit and thereby unjustifiably infringed his right to freedom of association. A unanimous court rejected the applicant's claim on several different grounds.

La Forest, Sopinka, and Gonthier JJ found that the union's expenditures in support of nuclear disarmament or in opposition to the Sky Dome were not closely related to the union's function as an effective collective bargaining agent and thereby effectively compelled the union member to associate with 'political' beliefs to which he did not adhere. Thus s 2(d) of the Charter was in fact infringed. However, the three justices held that this restriction on freedom of association was justified and saved under the Charter's limitation clause. First, the court found the state had two pressing and substantial objectives in permitting unions to compel dues for political and non-collective bargaining ends: promoting union democracy, and enabling unions to participate fully in public debates on a range of political, social, cultural, and economic issues. Secondly, it found that the mandatory check-off was rationally related to these ends, proportional to the goal of broader union participation, and a minimal impairment of the right to associate.

Wilson, L'Heureux-Dube, and Cory JJ read s 2(d) far more restrictively — or affirmatively. They held that while s 2(d) secures the freedom to associate with others for a common purpose, it does not include a right *not* to associate. As the

---

[61] Dickson CJ and Wilson J held, in dissent, that freedom of association should be understood as the freedom to combine together in the pursuit of common purposes and the advancement of common causes. This broader reading of association, unlike the politically evasive reading of the plurality or the reductive reading of McIntyre J, means that this collective bargaining association ought to include the right to withdraw services collectively under s 2(d). On this account the legislation prohibiting collectively bargaining and strikes by certain classes of government employee was an infringement of s 2(d). In addition, because the legislation provided no other effective or fair means of bargaining in place of the right to strike or bargain collectively the legislation's prohibitions constituted unjustifiable limitations on the right to associate and could not be saved under s 1.

[62] 1987 (38) DLR (4th) 249.

[63] 1987 (38) DLR (4th) 277.

[64] 1986 (33) DLR (4th) 174.

applicant had not been prevented from joining or forming an association, his right to associate had not been infringed.

McLachlin J took a more Solomonic approach. She held, as did La Forest, Sopinka, and Gonthier JJ, that implicit within s 2(d)'s freedom of association is the right not to be compelled to associate. However, McLachlin J reasoned that mandatory check-offs do not implicate this right not to be compelled to associate because there is too attenuated a relationship between the union dues paid by the member and the political positions ultimately adopted by the union. Unlike a person being coerced into saluting a flag or being forced to display a car licence plate with a particular motto, a person who merely pays dues to an organization cannot be understood as the unwilling bearer or supporter of that organization's political agenda.[65]

## 3.2 Other problems in association litigation under the Charter

Despite the fact that freedom of association claims have arisen in but a few instances outside the labour context,[66] it is highly likely that the Supreme Court will soon be obliged to decide whether a private association has a right to engage in discriminatory membership practices under s 2(d).

It is unlikely that such private associations are going to be attacked with the direct aid of the Charter. Following the Supreme Court's decision in *Retail, Wholesale and Department Store Union Local 580 v Dolphin Delivery Ltd*,[67] it is relatively clear that the Charter's rights and freedoms apply to and serve as restrictions only on

---

[65] As Thornicroft notes in 'Compulsory Payment of Union Dues — Use for Collective Bargaining and Non-Bargaining Purposes: Lavigne v The Ontario Public Service Employees Union' (1992) 71 *Can Bar R* 153, the Canadian Supreme Court's opinion, however fragmented, represents a wholesale rejection of the 'fair share' doctrine worked out by the US Supreme Court in a long line of cases starting with *International Associational Machinists v Street* 367 US 740 (1961). See also *Abood v Detroit Board of Education* 431 US 209 (1977); *Ellis v Brotherhood of Railway, Airline and Steamship Clerks* 466 US 435 (1984); *Chicago Teachers Union v Hudson* 475 US 292 (1986); *Communications Workers of America v Beck* 487 US 735 (1988); *Lehnert v Ferris Faculty Association* 111 SCt 1950 (1991). The fair share doctrine as originally conceived permitted union members ideologically opposed to causes supported by union funds to recoup that percentage of their union dues used for those causes. Under the present incarnation of the fair share doctrine union members may challenge the union executive to demonstrate that union expenditures serve the ends of collective bargaining. If, after the union supplies the requested accounts, the member is still not satisfied, an arbitrator is asked to assess the propriety of the expenditures.
Lower-court rulings reinforce this reading of *Lavigne*. In *Assn of Professional Engineers of Saskatchewan v SGEU* (1992) 91 DLR (4th) 694 the Saskatchewan Court of Queen's Bench held that the plaintiff's rights of association were not violated by a provision of the Institute Act certifying an academic bargaining unit or by provisions of the Trade Union Act requiring mandatory union dues check-off and making union membership a condition of employment for new employees. Following *Lavigne*, the court held that certification of bargaining units, mandatory dues check-offs, and requirement of union membership are necessary for maintaining well-recognized balance of power in labour relations. In addition new employees are not forced to join or associate with the union, except as a condition of employment — and no one is forcing them to accept this employment.

[66] See e g *Osborne v Canada* (1991) 82 DLR (4th) 321: Supreme Court holds that Act prohibiting public employers from engaging in work for a candidate or political party violates freedom of expression under s 2(b) of the Charter and can be tacitly understood as finding a violation of freedom of association, though it expressly chose not to address that claim in this context; *Jones v Ontario, Rheaume v Ontario* (1992) DLR (4th) 11: Ontario Court of Appeal rejects claim that legislation requiring public official to take leave of absence in order to run for office constitutes an infringement of the freedom of association; *Alex Couture v Canada* (1991) 83 DLR (4th) 577: Quebec Court of Appeal holds that federal competition legislation does not infringe the freedom of association with respect to mergers; *Cheema v Ross* (1991) 82 DLR (4th) 213: British Columbia Court of Appeal holds that municipal ordinance prohibiting sound amplification on public property that can be heard on private property for over fifteen minutes does not deny freedom of association because demonstration was permitted to continue after the sound equipment was removed; *Canadian Civil Liberties Assn v Canada* (1992) 91 DLR (4th) 39: legislation permitting security service to collect information through intrusive surveillance techniques held not to deny freedom of association.

[67] (1986) 33 DLR (4th) 174.

legislative and executive action. Common-law and judicial decisions unrelated to legislative and executive action are not subject to the Charter. Under this fairly restrictive version of the state action doctrine private associations — even if they serve a 'public function' — are unlikely to be reached by an equality clause action.[68]

However, this restrictive state action doctrine does not immunize private associations from attack by ordinary legislation. A human rights code, for example, could state that private clubs which serve food and offer accommodation to the public may not discriminate on the basis of race or gender. Private associations which discriminate would then find it difficult to attack the legislation in the same way as such legislation has been attacked in the US. The reason for this is that while *Lavigne* appears to stand for the proposition that freedom of association includes a right not to be compelled to associate, it does not hold that the Charter also protects the right of associations to engage in discriminatory membership policies. An all-men's club faced with a human rights code barring discriminatory membership policies would not therefore have recourse to a freedom of association defence.[69] Thus, while the public/private distinction of the state action doctrine immunizes the private discriminatory club from direct attack under the equality clause, the freedom of association clause does not insulate the private club from attack by ordinary legislation.

## 4 FREEDOM OF ASSOCIATION IN GERMANY

### 4.1 A brief history of association in Germany

Only towards the middle of the nineteenth century did freedom of association find expression as a right in a German law.[70] Earlier political arrangements prevented the development of associational freedom in a number of different ways. The feudal orders of the Middle Ages were dominated by 'corporations'. These corporations determined the better part, if not the entirety, of an individual's social, political, and economic relationships. Such socially determined caste-like structures stand in sharp contrast to the rather open, fluid, and choice-sensitive free associations we know today. The absolutist states which followed the feudal systems were hostile to both free associations and the corporative structures. Both corporations and associations were viewed as undesirable competition for scarce social goods and fragile political structures.[71] The French Revolution, though often understood as a progressive moment, actually placed further brakes on the development of freedom of association. The commitment to radical individualism and in particular the notion of the *volonté générale* made it conceptually impossible for the drafters of the Declaration of Peoples and Civil Rights of 1789 to recognize a right to freedom of

---

[68] See Freeman 'Justifying Exclusion: A Feminist Analysis of the Conflict between Equality and Associational Rights' (1989) 47 *U Toronto LJ* 269.

[69] Following the Supreme Court's ruling upholding hate speech codes in *R v Keegstra* (1990) 61 CCC (3rd) 1, it is reasonable to conclude that legislation prohibiting discrimination in private clubs or associations which have a 'public function' would also be deemed constitutional — i e even if the anti-discrimination legislation were found to violate the freedom of association under s 2(d), it would very likely be saved as a justifiable limitation under s 1.

[70] For a really exceptional philosophical-historical analysis of the development of the right to freedom of association in Germany, see Müller *Korporation and Assoziation* (1965).

[71] Rinken *Kommentar zum Grundgesetz für die Bundesrepublik Deutschland* (1989) vol 1 780–1.

association. Indeed, the virulent opposition to associations resulted, for example, in the *Loi le Chapelier* of 1791. The *Loi* declared every form of trade union unlawful and criminal.

Despite these previous attempts to suppress freedom of association, the rise of industrialism and the nation state, as well the influence of liberal thinkers, made free associations the dominant form of organization in nineteenth-century German civil society. The freedom found expression as a constitutional right for the first time in the Paulskirche Constitution towards the end of the German *Vormärz* (1789–1849). That recognition, however, was short-lived. Shortly thereafter the liberal movement and its 1849 Constitution collapsed. In its place arose a positivist legal order which insisted on a strict separation of state and society. As a result, legal theorists dismissed associations as vehicles for vital public functions.[72] Thus, whilst the influence of socially powerful associations was increasing, they were accorded little official recognition and afforded almost no protection by the law.

Associations enjoyed a moment's protection under the Weimar Constitution. However, in Nazi Germany the Weimar constitution was suspended and free associations were replaced by corporative organizations closely aligned with the fascist regime.[73] Indeed, the distinctions between the organs of the state, the Nazi party, and all other associations in civil society — whether political, cultural, social, or economic — withered under Hitler's policy of *Gleichschaltung*.[74] Only after World War II and the promulgation of the Basic Law did German society finally enjoy the full panoply of protections offered by the freedom of association.

### 4.2 Article 9.1 *GG*: the general freedom of association

Article 9 of the Basic Law (*Grundgesetz* (*GG*)) protects both the general freedom to associate (*Vereinigungsfreiheit*) and the specific freedoms to form trade unions and employer associations (*Koalitionsfreiheit*).[75] Although these freedoms are related in a legal-technical sense, they are sociologically and structurally different human rights and are consequently treated in different chapters of this publication.[76] Freedom to associate for religious purposes is protected primarily by the freedom of religion clause. It is therefore dealt with elsewhere.[77] Associational freedom for

---

[72] At 782–3.
[73] At 784.
[74] *Gleichschaltung* literally means 'to bring into line'.
[75] Article 9 *GG* reads:
   '(1) All Germans shall have the right to form associations and societies.
   (2) Associations, the purposes or activities of which conflict with criminal laws or which are directed against the constitutional order or the concept of international understanding, are prohibited.
   (3) The right to form associations to safeguard and improve working and economic conditions is guaranteed to everyone and to all trades, occupations and professions. Agreements which restrict or seek to impair this right shall be null and void; measures directed to this end shall be illegal. Measures taken pursuant to Article 12a, to paragraphs (2) and (3) of Article 35, to paragraph (4) of Article 87a, or to article 91, may not be directed against any industrial conflicts engaged in by associations within the meaning of the first sentence of this paragraph in order to safeguard and improve working conditions.'
[76] For an analysis of the freedom to form trade unions and employer associations in Germany, see Scholz in Maunz-Dürig-Herzog *Grundgesetz Kommentar* (1991) 9-37.
[77] Article 140 *GG* incorporates the Weimar Constitution's arts 136–139 and art 141. In other words, the same provisions which never served freedom of religion in Weimar Germany now do so effectively in contemporary Germany.

political parties, though protected by a separate article — art 21 — is included in our discussion. It is, however, treated separately. The reason for this separate treatment is that art 21 *GG* is *lex specialis* vis-à-vis art 9 *GG*, i e while political parties are associations which qualify for art 9 *GG* protection, in so far as art 21 *GG* differs, art 9 *GG* becomes inapplicable.[78]

### 4.2.1 *The term 'association'*

The meaning of the term 'association' in art 9.1 *GG* is of central importance for determining the scope of protection offered by the freedom of association. The Associations Act provides some insight. It defines association to include

'every association in which, irrespective of its legal form, more than one natural or juristic persons freely unite to pursue a common objective for a longer period of time and subject themselves to an organized structure of decision-making for this purpose'.[79]

In order to qualify for constitutional protection an association must establish itself through a constitutive act which creates a legal bond between members. The mere collaboration between individuals will therefore not suffice for protection under art 9.1 *GG*. However, in certain circumstances such collaboration will be protected by the freedom to assemble.[80] The Act's time requirement will be broadly construed. An association brought into existence for a fixed period of time or a particular goal will qualify for protection.[81]

The protection of art 9.1 *GG* does not depend on the goal of the association.[82] In principle therefore the free association of partners, shareholders, or members in business enterprises should enjoy constitutional protection.[83] The exact position of big public companies is, however, far from clear. The Federal Constitutional Court (FCC) has stated that the interests of shareholders in such companies should be

---

[78] Schnorr *Öffentliches Vereinsrecht* (1965) 83–4.
[79] Article 2.1 of the Associations Act of 1964 (hereafter also referred to as the *Vereinsgesetz* or simply '*VereinsG*'). See Rinken op cit (n 71) 800; Reichert, Dannecker & Kühr *Handbuch des Vereins- und Verbandsrecht* (1987) 769.
[80] Scholz in Maunz-Dürig-Herzog *Grundgesetz Kommentar* (1991) 9–69.
[81] Von Mutius '*Die Vereinigungsfreiheit gem. Art. 9.1GG*' 1984 *Jura* 193 at 194. See also Reichert, Dannecker & Kühr op cit (n 79) 770; Merten '*Vereinsfreiheit*' in Kirchhof & Isensee (eds) *Handbuch des Staatsrechts der Bundesrepublik Deutschland* (1989) 789.
[82] 50 *BVerfGE* 290 354. This is not to say that the association's goals will not receive constitutional protection. On the contrary, it is difficult to imagine an associational objective which will not be protected by one of the following freedoms: the general freedom to act (art 2.1 *GG*), freedom of speech (art 5.1 *GG*), freedom of religion (art 140 *GG*), freedom to do art and scientific research (art 5.3 *GG*), freedom to assemble (art 8 *GG*), or the freedom to practise a profession and hold property (arts 12, 14 *GG*). Moreover, constitutional protection for the goals of associations such as the family, churches, trade unions, or political parties have led to greater protection for these associations themselves. The important consequence of art 9.1 *GG* lies, however, in the protection it offers to associations independent of the goals they pursue. No *association* will therefore receive less protection than the minimum offered by art 9.1 *GG*. See Merten op cit (n 81) 776. The US Supreme Court, on the other hand, seems to derive all the protection for the association from existing constitutional protections for the association's goals. The danger of such an approach is that it may drain the separate protection of the freedom of its content. Moreover, an inappropriate level of protection may result from this inextricable link between protection of the goal and protection of the association. For example, a court may not necessarily want to subject state regulation of an expressive association to the same high level of scrutiny as state regulation of the association's exercise of its right to freedom of speech.
[83] The sole proprietorship will of course not receive art 9.1 *GG* protection. It is, however, protected indirectly by art 19.3 *GG*, which confers the protection of the fundamental rights to juristic persons in so far as the nature of the rights permits. The 'juristic person' concept includes the sole proprietorship. Thus, in so far as the sole proprietorship can be instrumental in the enjoyment of human rights, it is protected.

qualified as property interests rather than associational interests.[84] Such a denial of protection could have consequences for the legislature's ability to control cartels through anti-trust legislation. In so far as they have subjected themselves to a common organizational structure, business cartels constitute protected associations. At the moment their regulation by the state therefore needs to be justified as a proportional limitation of the right of association.[85]

Public associations are not protected by the freedom of association. Because of the state's involvement in public associations such associations are not 'freely' constituted.[86] Private associations with compulsory membership also fall outside the freedom's protection.[87]

### 4.2.2 Meaning of 'association' as an objective principle

The principle of 'free social association' has been described by Konrad Hesse as follows:

> 'The social system found by the Basic Law may neither take the form of status-based corporatism, as characteristic of older social orders, nor that of planned formation and organization by the state in accordance with the values of a ruling group, as occurred in the totalitarian state more recently.'[88]

---

[84] 50 *BVerfGE* 290 355. See also 4 *BVerfGE* 7 26; 14 *BVerfGE* 263 273 (take-over not considered an infringement of art 9.1 *GG*). In 50 *BVerfGE* 290 the 1976 Co-determination Act was attacked on the ground that it infringed shareholders' freedom to associate. It was argued that the presence of workers on the supervisory board of the company had resulted in foreign control of the company. The court rejected this argument on the basis that the act did not achieve parity of representation of workers and shareholders on the supervisory board and that the issue of foreign control therefore did not arise. The remark of the court to the effect that shareholders' interests in the company were not associational was merely *obiter dictum*. The court nevertheless made it clear that the 'big public companies are hardly the type of association envisioned by art 9.1 *GG*' (50 *BVerfGE* 290 358) and that the 'existence and the operation of such companies requires extensive legal regulation in order to protect their members, creditors, workers and the public interest' (at 359). Merten op cit (n 81) 791 criticizes the court's characterization of shares in public companies as merely property interests of a multitude of shareholders. He argues that shareholding includes rights to participate in shareholders' meetings and in the administration of company affairs, the right to information, and the right to dispute decisions of the board. The court's position is, however, supported by the majority of commentators. Rinken op cit (n 71) 800 argues that the personal influence of shareholders disappear in big public companies with a wide distribution of small shareholders. See also 50 *BVerfGE* 290 355. In such companies it is the monetary contribution — and not the personal influence of the shareholder — that matters. A conglomeration of monetary contributions in public companies is not worthy of art 9.1 *GG* protection. This is after all the reason why a foundation does not qualify for art 9.1 *GG* protection. In small private companies, on the other hand, the company is often little more than an extension of the personality of its majority shareholder. The influence of the other shareholders is often so negligible that it seems artificial to refer to these companies as associations. Wollburg *Die Anwendbarkeit des Artikels 9 abs.1 Grundgesetz auf Kapitalgesellschaften* (1984) and Kunze *Unternehmensrechtreform und Artikel 9 Absatz 1 GG* (1976) 19 make a similar argument. They point to the high percentage of companies with only other juristic persons as members. In such cases, they argue, there is almost no human association to speak of. Schnorr op cit (n 78) 70 doubts whether it is possible to determine who the members in public companies are at a specific moment in time. It is therefore quite artificial to speak of an association where it is impossible to determine who its members are. It is even more difficult to make the case that companies are associations when one takes into account the fact that members may not always be in the position to dissolve the company. Another argument against the inclusion of companies under art 9.1 *GG* protection is that the companies do not need the protection offered by the freedom of association. Companies of the size envisaged by most co-determination schemes are capable of looking after their interests with or without constitutional protection.

[85] Scholz op cit (n 80) 9–71.

[86] 10 *BVerfGE* 89 102; 10 *BVerfGE* 354 361–2 (medical doctors' association); 12 *BVerfGE* 319 323; 15 *BVerfGE* 235 239; 38 *BVerfGE* 281 297; 27 *BVerwGE* 228 230; 32 *BVerwGE* 308 310 (student medical aid scheme); *BVerwG* 1962 *NJW* 1311 at 1312. The court's approach makes little sense unless it is understood to reflect the view that an association opens itself to more penetrating regulation if it fulfils public — as opposed to private — functions.

[87] Some private associations, such as legal and medical professional associations, are constituted to fulfil a watchdog function. In order to do so effectively these associations may on occasion have to compel all members of a particular profession to join the association. In Germany the legal and medical professional associations are statutory bodies with compulsory membership. They are therefore excluded from protection on two grounds.

[88] Hesse *Grundzüge des Verfassungsrechts der Bundesrepublik Deutschland* 18 ed (1991) 168. Hesse's formulation was employed by the court in 50 *BVerfGE* 290 353, *BVerfG* 1979 *NJW* 699 at 705.

This description points to the value of freedom of association in preventing a totalitarian or repressive social order. However, it fails to identify the positive functions of the freedom which make it so important for the shaping of the constitutional order envisaged by the Basic Law.

In modern societies, where no strict separation exists between state and society, associations often fulfil vital public functions. As representative of their members' interests, they constitute institutional channels of communication between the organs of the state and society. Within the association demands are aggregated, articulated, and, by excluding unpopular alternatives, selected for presentation to the state.[89] Moreover, by informing their members of government decisions the associations play a role in advancing state policy.[90] Indeed, associations have become so important for the furtherance of state policy that the administration and implementation of policy have increasingly been left to private associations. Their independence, and in particular the fact that they are not bound to the constraints of public-law norms, render associations more effective executors of the law.[91]

Naturally there are inherent dangers in having too close a relationship between state and free associations. If too close a relationship forms, associations are no longer able to fulfil their 'checking' function on state power. Another danger lies in the fact that the significance of private associations exercising public functions has never been recognized in public law. On the contrary, the associations remain regulated solely by private-law norms. As a result, *Rechtsstaat* concerns exist about private assocations exercising public functions. The primary concern, however, lies in the disjunction between the public function of the association and the lack of public control over the association's internal decision-making processes.[92] Normally associations exercise relatively unfettered control over their decision-making processes. This high degree of autonomy, many believe, is not justified where the association exercises public functions which affect third parties, the state, and even its own members.[93]

A proper analysis of the meaning of any freedom requires some discussion of the place occupied by the freedom in the total scheme of protection offered by the Constitution. That is not to say that the meaning of one freedom is to be derived

---

[89] See Rinken op cit (n 71) 788.

[90] See Rinken op cit (n 71) 789; Brangsch '*Rechtsberatung und Rechtshilfe durch Verbände*' 1953 *NJW* 732 (legal advice to members); Benda '*Rechts- und staatspolitische Vereinigungen —Entwicklung, Wesen und Wirksamkeitsvoraussetzungen*' in *Ein Jahrzehnt Gesellschaft für Rechtspolitik (1974–1984)* (1984) 55 at 63. Benda argues that the Constitution itself needs a sufficient degree of support in the community in order to operate effectively. Ultimately such support must be demonstrated through personal engagement because the real threat to the Constitution lies in the belief of large parts of the population that they are excluded from important decision-making processes. Political associations ameliorate this threat by enabling the citizen to participate in public affairs. In so doing they strengthen the normativity of the Constitution and contribute to the building of consensus in society.

[91] The autonomy of unions and employers to determine the compensation for employment constitutes the most important example of associations regulating an entire social area. See Rinken op cit (n 71) 789 for other examples.

[92] Rinken op cit (n 71) 806 raises another concern: the increasing acceptance of and reliance on associational fulfilment of public functions must lead to the institutionalization of the associations' 'public functions'. This institutionalization in turn may lead to the re-interpretation of the freedom into a duty to share responsibility for the welfare of others. Moreover, such institutional protection may lead to the emergence of group of 'socially relevant associations'. Presumably these associations should then receive more constitutional protection and may even be able to claim financial support from the state.

[93] The debates surrounding associational autonomy raise most profound questions about the nature of the democratic *Rechtsstaat* and indeed the whole enterprise of constitutionalism. See generally Teubner *Organisationsdemokratie und Verbandsverfassung: Rechtsmodelle für politisch relevante Verbände* (1978). See also Rinken op cit (n 71) 791–7, 811; Krüger '*Die Stellung der Interessenverbände in der Verfassungswirklichkeit*' 1956 *NJW* 1217.

simply from another freedom. Nor is it meant to suggest that the spheres of protection offered by the different freedoms cannot overlap. It just reflects the belief that the Constitution should be interpreted as a whole. In following this holistic approach some commentators have argued that the freedom to associate supplements the protection for free development of the personality offered by art 2.1 *GG*. The freedom to associate, it is said, fulfils the same function for the group as free development fulfils for the individual.[94] Since the Basic Law's conception of human self-worth is community-bound the roots of freedom of association may also be found in art 1.1 *GG* protection of human dignity.[95] However, we believe that freedom of association is most closely aligned with and is designed primarily to reinforce the other expressive or political freedoms, e g assembly, speech, petition, and the protection for political parties.

### 4.2.3 Content of 'association' as a right

Article 9.1 *GG* contains a double right of association: that which belongs to the individual and that which belongs to the association. The individual's rights protect his/her freedom to establish an association and, subject to the control of the association, to join and to take part in an association's activities.[96] The freedom to establish an association includes the freedom to determine whether to form an association as well as the freedom to decide the objectives and the legal form of the association. In principle state controls which prevent the formation of associations — such as a system of concessions — are unconstitutional.[97] A duty of registration is, however, an acceptable limitation of the freedom as long as the limits of the doctrine of proportionality are observed.[98]

In so far as the association obtains protection through the operation of art 19.3 *GG*[99] the associational activities are obviously subject to the same legal regulations and limitations as those of the individual.[100] However, as was stated above, the court regards the activities which are central to the existence of the

---

[94] See Rinken op cit (n 71) 799. According to an extreme version of this view, all the specific fundamental rights are concretizations of art 2.1 *GG*.
[95] 4 *BVerfGE* 7 15; 20 *BVerfGE* 290.
[96] 10 *BVerfGE* 89 102; 10 *BVerfGE* 354 361; 27 *BVerwGE* 228 230. Since the individual's rights to join and resign from the association most often raises questions relating to the *Drittwirkung* of the freedom of association these specific rights will be discussed in that context.
[97] See Scholz op cit (n 80) 9–78; Von Mutius op cit (n 81) 195.
[98] 7 *BVerwGE* 125 135; 25 *BVerwGE* 272 276. In these two cases the Federal Administrative Court made clear that student organizations do not have the right to be recognized — and registered — by the university administration. Also the administration does not necessarily infringe on a student organization's freedom of association when it scraps the organization from the registration roll and thereby withdraws all the privileges associated with registration from the organization.
[99] Article 19.3 *GG* extends the protection offered by the fundamental rights to both juristic persons with legal personality and others, but public juristic persons — in so far as they exercise public functions — may not receive the protection of any of the fundamental rights. See 3 *BVerfGE* 383 391; 21 *BVerfGE* 362 369; 23 *BVerfGE* 353 372; 25 *BVerfGE* 198 205; 26 *BVerfGE* 228 244; 35 *BVerfGE* 263 271; 39 *BVerfGE* 302 312; 45 *BVerfGE* 63 78; Merten op cit (n 81) 787. The inquiry in terms of art 19.3 *GG* turns on the nature of the right in question. In order to make this determination the court has attached importance to the following considerations: can the association exercise the right in question? does the association find itself facing a similar threat as natural persons (45 *BVerfGE* 63 79; 61 *BVerfGE* 82 105)? are the formation and the activities of the association the expression of the free development of a natural person (21 *BVerfGE* 362 369; 61 *BVerfGE* 82 101; 68 *BVerfGE* 193 205)?
[100] 30 *BVerfGE* 227 243; 50 *BVerfGE* 290 353.

association as protected directly by art 9.1 *GG*.[101] At the most general level the collective rights of the association include the right to exist and the right to engage in activities.[102] More particularly, these activities include the right to keep and solicit new membership and to determine the name and *domicilium* of the association and its legal form.[103] More controversial, however, is the court's recognition of a freedom to form a will without outside interference.[104] The FCC regards this autonomy to make and to amend internal rules as of crucial importance for the association. In the *Co-determination* case the court stated that

> '[f]reedom of association guarantees for both members and the association self-determination over their own organization, its process of decision making and the management of its affairs. Without such self-determination there can be no talk of a free association; foreign control will undermine the aim of the art 9.1 *GG* protection.'[105]

---

[101] In other words, the association itself is also protected by art 9.1 *GG*. See 13 *BVerfGE* 174 175; 30 *BVerfGE* 227 241; 50 *BVerfGE* 290 354. Scholz op cit (n 80) 9–50 disagrees: he derives all protection for associational activities and all protection for the existence of the association from art 19.3 *GG*. Scholz, in other words, denies the existence of any collective rights of the association. Von Feldman *Vereinigungsfreiheit und Vereinigungsverbod Eine kritische Darstellung des Umfangs und der Schranken der Vereinigungsfreiheit nach dem Grundgesetz und dem Vereinsgesetz* (1972) 22, on the other hand, argues that all protection for the association, including all the protection for associational activities, follows from art 9.1 *GG*. This interpretation makes art 19.3 *GG* unnecessary. Kunze op cit (n 84) 16, 23 and Ballerstedt '*Von den Grenzen der Vereinigungsfreiheit*' 1952 *Der Öffentliche Dienst* 161 suggest application of art 2.1 *GG* and its limitations to the activities of the association. This approach, which sees the limitations to art 2.1 *GG* as applicable to all fundamental rights, is, however, rejected by the court and most other commentators. Schwerdtfeger *Zur Verfassungsmässigkeit der paritätischen Mitbestimmung* (1978) and *Mitbestimmung und Grundgesetz* (1972) argues that, in so far as the association seeks to realize its goals, other fundamental rights — but not art 9.1 *GG* — are applicable. Article 9.1 *GG* is affected only when state action is directed at the collectivity itself. Schwerdtfeger's approach merely reformulates the notion that the association's activities receive no greater protection than that of the individual. Merten op cit (n 81) 795 distinguishes between external and internal activities. The latter, such as the right to solicit membership, hold meetings, elect office bearers, and formulate decisions, are protected by art 9.1 *GG* itself. In addition Merten sees the association's privacy, especially control over its data, as protected by art 9.1 *GG*. See also Reichert, Dannecker & Kühr op cit (n 79) 773. The debate is important since the freedom of association offers much stronger protection than several other rights. It will consequently be much more difficult for the state to control the activities of the association if they are protected by the freedom of association rather than those other (weaker) rights.

[102] 13 *BVerfGE* 174 175; 30 *BVerfGE* 227 241; *BVerfG* 1979 *NJW* 706; 54 *BVerwGE* 211 219. Unless one protects an association's ability to undertake collective activities in one way or another, the freedom to associate will be meaningless. Why? Members may not transfer their human rights or use thereof to the association. See 16 *BVerfGE* 147 158; Ramm *Die Freiheit der Willensbildung zur Lehre von der Drittwirkung der Grundrechte und der Rechtsstruktur der Vereinigung* (1960) 30–1.

[103] In 30 *BVerfGE* 227 241 the court invalidated legislation which, in order to avoid confusion, prevented an association from disputing different types of elections under the same name. The court found the legislation to be a disproportionate infringement of the freedom of association. The infringement of the association's choice of name meant that the association couldn't engage in its activities freely. See Von Mutius op cit (n 81) 195; Merten op cit (n 81) 793.

[104] The seventies and early eighties witnessed a heated debate in Germany over 'the internal freedom of association'. See Schmitz *Innere Vereinsfreiheit* (1976); Schmidt '*Die "innere Vereinsfreiheit" als Bedingung der Verwirklichung von Grundrechten durch Organisation*' 1977 *Zeitschrift für Rechtspolitik* 255. Schmitz neatly sets out the problems which need to be confronted. First, how can individuals be protected against a state which is controlled by massive associations? In other words, how can individuals be protected from the indirect influence of associations? Secondly, how can individuals be protected from the power which massive associations wield directly over their lives? Thirdly, how can the individual who belongs to an association be protected against abuse of power by those in control of the association? These problems have already been raised in the context of the objective meaning of the freedom of association. Proponents of the 'internal freedom of association' argue that in so far as the external functions of the association become public the exercise of power needs some sort of democratic legitimacy. This legitimacy can be provided, it is then argued, by democratizing the internal decision-making structures of the association. Constitutional support for this argument is usually found in the democratic, *Rechtsstaat*, and social state principles. Article 21.1 *GG* is further relied on. It is argued that, since politically, socially, and economically powerful associations enjoyed a public status comparable with political parties these associations should also be required to exhibit democratic internal structures. The 'internal freedom to associate' thus encompasses the demand for management to be elected by an equal vote of all members, rights to internal dissent, and rights to form an internal opposition and to a transparent mode of decision-making. Smitz's concerns cannot be addressed by democratization of the internal structures of asociational decision-making alone. More penetrating forms of interference are therefore discussed below.

[105] 50 *BVerfGE* 290 354.

The court's position is controversial, if not incoherent. Claims of workers to co-determination,[106] proposals to standardize and limit the forms of acquiring juristic personality,[107] the public's demand for more information about the company's affairs,[108] and the demand for fair internal disciplinary procedures,[109] all stand in direct conflict with the association's right to 'internal autonomy'.

As these conflicting interests suggest, the court's very generous interpretation of internal autonomy does not preclude all state regulation of the association's decision-making processes. Regulations of an 'integrating' (*Ausgestaltung*) nature are permissible and indeed required by the Constitution. The Constitution requires the legislature to make a multitude of legal forms available to accommodate the different types of association and their needs.[110] In the words of the court:

'Freedom of association is to a greater or lesser degree dependent on regulation which integrates the free associations and their lives into the general legal order and guarantees legal certainty, the rights of members, third parties and the public interest. The constitutional guarantee of freedom of association therefore necessarily presupposes legislative regulation in order to attain practical significance. This necessity has always belonged to the content of art 9.1 *GG* . . . .'[111]

---

[106] As was pointed out above, the constitutionality of 'foreign' control of the company did not arise in the *Co-determination* case since the workers had no parity of representation on the supervisory boards established in terms of the Co-determination Act. The court did, however, state that the interests of the shareholders may not be of an associational nature. Badura *Paritätische Mitbestimmung und Verfassung* (1985) sees this particular Act as affecting the periphery of the freedom of association, but not its essence. In other words, he considers the Act a proportional limitation of the shareholders' freedom to associate. There is little doubt that the Act is constitutional. Still, the question remains: when exactly will co-determination become unconstitutional? Various propositions are put forward in the vast literature on the relationship between co-determination, freedom of association, and other fundamental rights. Naendrup *Mitbestimmung und Verfassung* (1972) 24 sees implications for the shareholders' freedom of association only when the use of membership rights becomes meaningless for shareholders. Naendrup warns against affording more constitutional protection to the already powerful associations than to individuals. He also argues that the existing commercial-law system may not be 'frozen' by protecting it from legislative reform. Support for his last argument can be found in 50 *BVerfGE* 290 355. Nagel *Paritätische Mitbestimmung und Grundgesetz* (1988) 35 sees shareholding, at least in the kind of companies normally affected by co-determination legislation, as the combination of monetary contributions and not the association of people. He relies on decisions of the court — 4 *BVerfGE* 7 26; 14 *BVerfGE* 263 273 — which do not consider forced restructuring, mergers, or take-overs as implicating art 9.1 *GG*. Pernthaler *Qualifizierte Mitbestimmung und Verfassungsrecht* (1972) 22–6 and *Ist Mitbestimmung verfassungsrechtlich messbar? Eine Analyse der Entscheidung des BVerfG über das Mitbestimmungsgesetz* (1980) 87–92, on the other hand, argues for institutional protection of the ability to form a will autonomously as long as the association seeks to realize a legitimate goal. In the case of companies the linkage between membership, ownership, and management guarantees that the companies' will is formed autonomously. The forced participation by third parties, according to Pernthaler, violates the institutional protection offered by the freedom of association to shareholders. Schwerdtfeger *Mitbestimmung und Grundgesetz* (1972) 203 suggests that art 9.1 *GG* is affected only if the co-determination legislation discloses a belligerence towards associations as a form of business enterprise. In other words, the legislation may not single out the association, as a form of business enterprise, for special treatment. Simitis, Kübler & Schmidt *Mitbestimmung als Gesetzgebungsaufgabe zur Verfassungsmässigkeit des Mitbestimmungsgesetzes* (1978) 71–76 argue that the autonomy of the association is in itself not worthy of protection. The degree to which associational autonomy deserves constitutional protection depends instead on the objectives of the association. The constitutionality of co-determination in the case of most companies must therefore be determined with reference to art 14 *GG* (right to property). See Kunze op cit (n 84) 1–27; Bleckmann *Allgemeine Grundrechtslehren* (1989) 804–7; Rinken op cit (n 71) 802.

[107] Kunze op cit (n 84) 34–72 mentions the proposal that companies with more than, say, 20 000 workers should not have a choice as to their legal form or articles of association. One problem with this proposal is that art 9.1 *GG* may be interpreted as guaranteeing protection for existing legal forms as institutes of private law. But even if such an interpretation is not accepted, it would still seem difficult to deny that the implication of 50 *BVerfGE* 290 355 is that the legislature must make the essential prerequisites for the exercise of the freedom available. Some variety of legal form will have to be part of those essential prerequisites.

[108] See Kunze op cit (n 84) 28–33.

[109] At the moment the exclusion of members raises a constitutional issue only in so far as the principles of ordinary law, which governs disciplinary procedures, are to be interpreted with reference to the *Rechtsstaat* principle. See *BGH* 1958 *NJW* 1867; *BGH* 1954 *NJW* 834; *OLG Stuttgart* 1955 *NJW* 833.

[110] See Rinken op cit (n 71) 809; Merten op cit (n 81) 782. In other words, the objective component of the right places a duty on the state to make that minimum of legal forms available which enable individuals to realize their objectives collectively. According to Scholz op cit (n 80) 9–74, this does not mean that existing 'integrating' regulations, which confer recognition upon the association, obtain constitutional protection.

[111] 50 *BVerfGE* 290 354–5.

Such legislative intervention must, however, honour the objective meaning of the freedom. In other words, the principles of free association and collective self-determination and the organization's capacity to function through its organs may not be impaired.[112]

The freedom not to associate is also protected by art 9.1 *GG*.[113] The dominant opinion regards this freedom not to associate as the logical and necessary correlative of the freedom to associate — i e if the individual is denied the freedom to dissociate, his or her positive freedom to join or establish an association is also infringed.[114] The freedom not to associate includes the right not to establish the association, to stay out of existing associations, to dissolve an association, and to resign from an association.[115]

The court has, however, restricted the scope of protection offered by the freedom not to associate to state compulsion to join a private association. The constitutionality of public bodies with compulsory membership has been tested against the general freedom of self-realization (art 2.1 *GG*). Within the limited protection offered by this provision the court has confirmed state compulsion to join where the public association seeks to fulfil a legitimate public function.[116] Legitimate public

---

[112] See Scholz op cit (n 80) 9–74.

[113] See 4 *BVerfGE* 7 26; 10 *BVerfGE* 89 102; 38 *BVerfGE* 281 297; 50 *BVerfGE* 290 354. The recognition of the right not to associate is of course extremely controversial in the labour context. A discussion of art 9.3 *GG* (freedom to form unions and employer associations) falls outside the scope of this chapter. It should be mentioned that the court has confirmed that a worker does have a right not to associate with the union, but has ruled that this right not to associate is not implicated when the organized workforce receives different treatment than other workers: 31 *BVerfGE* 297 302. It is only when direct pressure is applied to join the union that the right not to associate is affected. The court explicitly left open the question whether the right not to associate is to be derived from art 9.3 *GG*. See Von Prondzynski *Freedom of Association and Industrial Relations: A Comparative Study* (1987).

[114] Merten op cit (n 81) 796 argues that since the decision on 'how' to exercise the freedom is protected by the freedom the decision not to exercise the freedom at all must also necessarily form part of the scope of the freedom's protection.

[115] See Scholz op cit (n 80) 9–80.

[116] 4 *BVerfGE* 7 26; 10 *BVerfGE* 89 102; 10 *BVerfGE* 354 361; 11 *BVerfGE* 105 126; 12 *BVerfGE* 319 323; 38 *BVerfGE* 281 297; 27 *BVerwGE* 228 230; 32 *BVerwGE* 308 312; 39 *BVerwG* 100 102; *BVerwG* 1962 *NJW* 1311 at 1312. The basis of the court's jurisprudence seems to be that, because the individual may only rely on art 9.1 *GG* for establishing private associations, he/she may also only rely on art 9.1 *GG* for staying out of private associations. See Rode '*Negative Vereinigungsfreiheit und Zwangmidgliedschaft in öffentlichen Körperschaften*' 1976 *Die Öffentliche Verwaltung* 841 at 842. Friauf '*Die negative Vereinigungsfreiheit als Grundrecht*' in *Festschrift für Rudolf Reinhart* (1972) 395 points to one problem with the court's reasoning: the individual who desires to stay out of a public association does not want to usurp public power in any way. Moreover, as Rode argues, many public corporations with compulsory membership were established by private individuals or groups. After these individuals or groups proved that the corporation satisfied certain conditions the state had a mere ministerial discretion to confer public status upon them. The main problem with the court's approach, however, lies in the derivation of the scope of protection offered by the freedom not to associate from the positive freedom to associate. The protection offered by the former might indeed be very different (wider, for example) to that of the latter freedom. The court has in similar fashion deduced the content of the freedom not to act from the freedom to act (art 2.1 *GG*). The court's jurisprudence in the area of the freedom not to associate may indeed be the result of seeing the freedom of association as a concretization of the freedom to act. According to Etzrodt *Der Grundrechtshutz der negativen Vereinigungsfreiheit* (1980) 47–71, the principle of free formation of social groupings, which represents the objective meaning of the freedom of association, militates against restricting the negative freedom of association to state compulsion to join private associations. According to Etzrodt, the intensity with which a fundamental right protects cannot depend on legal form. The court's approach found more favourable comment in the work of Starck *Verfassungsrecht in Fällen. Entscheidungen des Bundesverfassungsgerichtes. Vereinigungsfreiheit* (1975) 43. Starck reminds critics of the courts that the state may choose to fulfil its tasks without making use of associations and in doing so it avoids being bound by art 9.1 *GG* completely. The result, according to Starck, would be a net loss of individual freedom. Merten op cit (n 81) 799 argues that the opinion of the court is clearly supported by the intent of the framers. Moreover, state compulsion to join a public association differs from state compulsion to join a private association in at least two ways: first, the state is not as free as individuals to form associations; secondly, the effect of compulsion differs since compulsion to join a public association does not necessarily result in identification with that (public) association. See also Hamacher *Die Bedeutung der Vereinigungsfreiheit für Zwangzusammenschlüsse unter der Herrschaft des Grundgesetzes* (1972) 39–76. Hamacher describes the nature of compulsion in associations such as the Chambers of Commerce, professional societies, and social security associations.

functions are described as functions which — by their nature — cannot be fulfilled by private initiative. While these public functions do not belong to the category of state functions which are normally fulfilled by the executive itself, the community has a heightened interest in their fulfilment.[117]

Freedom of association does not direct or require the state to subsidize associations. Indeed, the 'freedom' to associate can only in exceptional instances be interpreted to require state support.[118] Consequently, the freedom of association does not afford individuals or the association the right to demand state conferral of juristic personality.[119]

Freedom of association does not operate directly against third parties (*Drittwirkung*). The objective meaning of the right does of course influence the interpretation of all private law.[120] According to private law, an association may be forced to accept an applicant as a member when its refusal intentionally causes the applicant harm in a *contra bonos mores* manner. Given the Basic Law's influence on private law, a court's interpretation of the *contra bonos mores* requirement must reflect the objective meaning of the freedom of association. For example, when the association has monopolistic control over a particular benefit and the applicant meets all the requirements for entry a refusal to grant the applicant membership will be *contra bonos mores*.[121]

---

[117] 38 *BVerfGE* 281 299; *OLG Hamburg Beschl* 1952 *NJW* 943: forced membership of law society not unconstitutional. Mronz *Körperschaften und Zwangmitgliedschaft. Die staatsorganisations- und grundrechtliche Problematik der Zwangsverbände aufgezeigt am Beispiel von Arbeitsnehmerkammern* (1973) 119–42 criticizes the 'sociological nature' of the term 'public function'. Mronz suggests that it be replaced with the term 'tasks of the state'. The latter term has a legal-constitutional origin and allegedly lends itself to more precise definition. Mronz's proposals are aimed at giving the test of the court some 'bite'.

[118] See Merten op cit (n 81) 780.

[119] A connection between the limitation of the freedom of association and the granting of juristic personality does exist: the state authority responsible for the prohibition of associations may object to the granting of juristic personality to a particular association. The association will then have to be banned within a month, otherwise the objection will lapse. See art 63 *BGB* (*Bürgerliches Gesetzbuch*); Schnorr op cit (n 78) 54. The withdrawal of an association's legal personality by a public authority must, however, be distinguished from the banning of an association. The former may already be effectuated when the association's activities threaten the general welfare or when the association pursues other objects than the ones mentioned in its memorandum. An association may only be banned in terms of art 9.2 *GG*. Loss of legal capacity does not of course result in loss of art 9.1 *GG* protection. See 58 *BVerwGE* 26 33–5; Reichert, Dannecker & Kühr op cit (n 79) 773; Schnorr op cit (n 78) 57; Von Feldman op cit (n 101) 34.

[120] In principle the individual may therefore contractually bind herself to establish, belong to, or not to belong to a particular association for a period of time. The courts will, however, refuse to give effect to the contract when it ties the individual to a particular association in a *contra bonos mores* way. Article 39 *BGB* lays down the criteria relating to maximum periods of notice. The effect of the provision is that notice requirements will be enforced as long as they are not unreasonably long. See Reichert, Dannecker & Kühr op cit (n 79) 774. The limited and indirect nature of the *Drittwirkung* of the freedom of association stands in stark contrast to the increasing influence of associations over the lives of their members, their employees, third parties, and in society generally. See Lengsfeld *Das Recht zum Verbot verfassungswidriger Vereinigungen und der Ausgleich zwischen Interessen des Staates und Rechten der Individualsphäre* (1965) 38–9; Von Mutius op cit (n 81) 198–9; Merten op cit (n 81) 782.

[121] This right to demand admittance to an association is based upon a private-law code provision (art 826 *BGB*). Different provisions apply to political parties (art 10 *PartG* (Political Parties Act of 1967)), business cartels (art 27 *GWB*), and trade unions. When the state orders the association to accept a member the association's freedom of association is *prima facie* infringed. The state action will therefore have to pass proportionality scrutiny in every case. The state will have to consider the alternatives to forcing the association to accept a person. In some instances another form of relief may exist which will satisfy the applicant's demands. In other circumstances an amendment to the association's articles of association may even be ordered to accommodate the applicant. Usually such an order is reserved for situations where an amendment poses no serious threat to the association and the applicant cannot be accommodated in any other way. By making race a criterion for membership the association violates art 1.3 *GG* (human dignity). This provision operates directly against third parties. Alternatively, such associations may be prohibited in terms of art 9.2 *GG* from directing themselves against the elementary principles of international law. See Lengsfeld op cit (n 119) 49; Birk '*Der Aufnahmezwang bei Vereinen und Verbänden*' (1972) *Juristenzeitung* 343; Scholz op cit (n 80) 9–84. Existing members are protected against unreasonable exclusion in a similar way.

## 4.3 Article 9.2 *GG* — limiting the freedom of association

The principle of proportionality remains the crucial device for determining the constitutionality of the limitations of fundamental rights. This principle has three requirements. First, it implies that the means of limiting the right in question must be suitable to achieve the state's objective. Secondly, the limitation must be necessary — in the sense of the least restrictive means available — to achieve the state objective. Thirdly, the deleterious effects of the infringement must be proportional to the benefits realized by achievement of the state objective.

Limitations of the freedom of association may be generally divided into three groups: preventive measures, repressive measures, and measures aimed at the activities of the association. Courts normally consider the prevention of the association's establishment to be a greater infringement than the association's repression. Repression is in turn considered to be a greater infringement than state control of the association's activities.[122] These three types of limitation are considered separately below.

### 4.3.1 *Preventive controls*

Preventive controls are precluded in instances where the association may be repressed in terms of art 9.2 *GG*. Repression is in such cases the appropriate measure of state control prescribed by the Basic Law.[123] Since the control of business cartels has an economic aim repression is not possible in terms of art 9.2 *GG*. Oddly enough, because the repressive measures are not available, prevention of the cartel's formation now becomes a potential method of control.

### 4.3.2 *Supression or banning*

The association may be suppressed or banned if the state can meet the requirements of art 9.2 *GG*. Article 9.2 *GG* is concretized in two ways: the Associations Act, and the principle of proportionality.[124] Thus the executive not only needs to abide by the — largely procedural — requirements of the Act but must also be able to justify every banning order under the principle of proportionality.[125]

One should also remember that art 9.2 *GG* does not contain an exhaustive list of all possible limitations of the freedom of association. It merely provides that the association may be suppressed if it violates general criminal laws or if it directs itself against the constitutional order or the general principles of international law.[126]

---

[122] 55 *BVerwGE* 175 181; 37 *BVerwGE* 344 361–2; 61 *BVerwGE* 218 220; Demme '*Die Grenzen der Vereinigungsfreiheit besonders in Hinblick auf den Gesetzesvorbehalt des Art.12.1.2GG*' 1967 *Gewerbearchiv Zeitschrift für Verwaltungs-, Gewerbe- und Handwerkersrecht* 199.

[123] A requirement of mere registration is, however, constitutionally permissible. See Scholz op cit (n 80) 9-93; Rinken op cit (n 71) 808.

[124] The Associations Act of 1964 replaced the *Reichsvereinsgesetz* of 1908. The provisions of the Act may of course also be subject to constitutional scrutiny.

[125] The vague grounds for banning are not concretized in the Associations Act. The question whether the state may ban depends largely on whether banning is a proportional means to achieve one of the ends mentioned in art 9.2 *GG*. The courts have developed some guidelines in this area, but the executive has to consider each banning carefully since the application of the principle of proportionality depends on the facts of the particular case. See Bleckmann op cit (n 106) 810.

[126] In addition to these enumerated limitations, and like all fundamental rights entrenched in the Basic Law, the freedom of association has 'immanent' limitations which flow from its relationships with other constitutionally protected goods. Banning, however, may only be effectuated in terms of the grounds mentioned in art 9.2 *GG*.

An association may be banned if its aims or activities violate criminal laws. An unlawful aim may be attributed to the association when it forms part of its statutes or when the aim is pursued by the organ(s) or the people who form the will of the association. The members do not have to agree or even be aware of the pursuance of the unlawful aim of the conducting of illegal activities. On the other hand, the illegal activities of some of the members may not be attributed to the association — i e unless those activities determine the character of the organization. This determination is contingent upon the nature of the unlawful aims and activities and the relationship between the lawful and the unlawful aims and activites. If the aims and activities involve merely negligent acts or offences of a not especially serious nature (*Ordnungswidrigkeiten*), the banning of the association will not be jusitifiable. Similarly, if the unlawful aim or activity is less central for the association compared to other legitimate aims or activities, the banning of the association will not be justifiable.[127]

The second ground for banning mentioned in the Basic Law requires proof that the association directs itself against the 'constitutional order'.[128] For an association to direct itself against the constitutional order it must aim to undermine, destroy, or impair the constitutional order in a material way.[129]

A reviewing court will not look only at the grounds for the banning. It will also pay especially careful attention to the procedures employed. These procedures are laid down in the Associations Act.[130] Under this Act the Federal Minister of Interior and the *Länder* Ministers of Interior are respectively responsible for the investigation and banning of national and regional associations.[131] The banning order issued by the aforementioned ministers must be in writing, reasons must be furnished, a member of the association's executive must be informed, and the order must be published in the official government publication.[132] The banning order automatically includes all divisions, branches, or subsidiaries of the association. However, service and replacement associations are not affected.[133]

---

[127] Scholz op cit (n 80) 9-97–8; Reichert, Dannecker & Kühr op cit (n 79) 777–8; Von Mutius op cit (n 81) 199.

[128] The term 'constitititutional order' has the same meaning as the term 'free and democratic order' used in art 18 *GG* and art 21.2 *GG*. Article 21.2 *GG* concerns the possibility of a forfeiture of the individual's fundamental rights. Article 21.2 *GG* deals with the banning of political parties. The meaning of the term will be analysed in the latter context. The other term used in art 9.2 *GG*, 'the principles of international understanding', has a wider application than a breach of the peace as defined by art 26 *GG*. All the elementary principles of international law are included.

[129] See *BVerwG* 1954 *NJW* 1947: the prohibition of the FDJ, the communist youth movement, was declared to be constitutional.

[130] Article 2.2 *VereinsG* makes clear that the provisions of the Act do not apply to political parties and religious associations.

[131] Article 3.2 *VereinsG*; Reichert, Dannecker & Kühr op cit (n 79) 781. In keeping with German 'co-operative federalism' the *Länder* governments, and therefore the local police, may be relied on for help in the investigation process and the eventual execution of the banning order. See arts 4–5 *VereinsG*. Special provisions relating to searches and seizures apply. See art 4 *VereinsG*; Von Feldman op cit (n 101) at 62–71; Schnorr op cit (n 78) 129–48.

[132] Article 3.2.4 *VereinsG*; Schnorr op cit (n 78) 125; Von Feldman op cit (n 101) 71. Despite the wording of art 9.2 *GG*, which seems to suggest that an association which falls within its scope is prohibited, a constitutive and formal act — the banning order — is necessary before an association can be considered prohibited. See 55 *BVerwGE* 175 177; art 3.1 *VereinsG*; Bleckmann op cit (n 106) 812; Reichert, Dannecker & Kühr op cit (n 79) 776.

[133] In determining whether a related association is affected by the banning order the court regards political affiliations as less important than organizational structure. A further factor to be considered is whether the associations have the same or different membership. See Schnorr op cit (n 78) 120. Article 8 *VereinsG* prohibits the formation of replacement associations of a banned association. The banning authority is also responsible for determining whether an association replaces a banned association. This determination may of course be taken on review. But the decision to ban the original association may not be disputed in such proceedings.

The banning order usually has three parts: the prohibition, the order of dissolution, and the confiscation of the assets of the association.[134] All three parts may be attacked in the administrative courts. The association may object to the banning order within a month after the publication of the order. This objection suspends the execution of the banning order unless the banning authority deems the banning order, in the public interest, to be immediately executable.[135] The banning order becomes unimpeachable (*unanfechtbar*) either when the one-month objection period lapses or when all legal remedies against it have been exhausted.[136] After this point criminal-law remedies may be used to enforce the banning order.[137]

Objections may also be raised against any order intended to execute the banning order. Objections to such orders must be raised in the normal administrative courts. However, if the validity of the banning order is also attacked in the Highest Federal or *Land* court, the administrative courts will have to suspend their proceedings until the constitutionality of the banning order is settled.[138] This suspension of execution proceedings is crucial. It bars the state from confiscating the assets of the association and effectively destroying the association before a court can determine the validity of the banning order.[139] However, the association must also be prevented from squandering its assets. The banning order therefore has the effect of freezing the association's assets.[140] Once all legal remedies against the banning order and its execution have been exhausted — and the order is upheld — the association may be liquidated.[141]

A final caveat needs to be added concerning the state's powers to suppress associations. The principle of opportunity confers upon the administration the power to use means other than banning to fulfil the objectives of art 9.2 *GG*. For example, the administration may choose to issue a warning, place a ban on certain activities of the association, or do nothing at all, even though the banning of the association may be constitutionally justifiable.[142]

---

[134] Article 3.1 *VereinsG*. See Schnorr op cit (n 78) 103–4.

[135] Article 74.1 *VwGO* (*Verwaltungsgerichtsordnung* — Rules of the Administrative Courts). The validity of an objection against the banning order is decided, depending on the banning authority, by the Highest Federal or *Land* Administrative Court. The association may of course also object to an order of immediate execution. The court will then have to determine whether immediate execution is legitimate in the light of public interest concerns. See Von Feldman op cit (n 101) 71–4; Schnorr op cit (n 78) 155.

[136] Article 7 *VereinsG*.

[137] Individuals who try to keep the organizational structure of the banned association intact are guilty of a criminal offence. See art 20 *VereinsG*; arts 85–86 *StGB* (*Strafgesetzbuch*).

[138] Article 6 *VereinsG*.

[139] The process of review might even end up before the FCC and can therefore take several years. In the mean time the legal status of the association hangs in the air. The provisions in the Associations Act dealing with suspension of execution, immediate execution, and the unimpeachability of the banning order, discussed above, try to address this problem. Trade unions and employers' associations may also be prohibited on art 9.2 *GG* grounds, but according to art 16.1 *VereinsG*, such prohibitions come into effect only upon confirmation by a court. Religious associations may not be subjected to the provisions of the Act. See Spiller *Das Vereinsverbot nach Geltendem Verfassungsrecht* (1967) 55; Von Feldman op cit (n 101) 15.

[140] Article 10 *VereinsG*.

[141] Members' rights and duties and the relationship between the association and its workers remain unchanged until all legal remedies against the validity of the banning order have been exhausted. See Von Feldman op cit (n 101) 76–83; Schnorr op cit (n 78) 175–219. Liquidation takes place in terms of arts 10–13 *VereinsG*. Claims of third parties against the association which arose out of a relationship of collaboration with the association or claims which are attempts to circumvent effective confiscation will not be recognized by the liquidator. The assets of third parties which were placed under the control of the association to further its unconstitutional aims may also be confiscated. See art 12 *VereinsG*; Schnorr op cit (n 78) 122–3.

[142] See Scholz op cit (n 80) 9–102; Schmidt *Die Freiheit verfassungswidriger Parteien und Vereinigungen. Zur Schrankenlehre in Rahmen von Art. 21.2GG und Art. 9.2GG* (1983) argues that, since the constitution prohibits certain associations, the recognition of the principle of opportunity undermines the normativity of the constitution. Spiller op cit (n 139) 88–95 disagrees. He argues that the purpose of art 9.2 *GG* is to protect the constitutional order:

### 4.3.3 *Limitations on the activities of the association*

The last kind of government restriction places limitations on the association's activities.[143] Some limitations on activities result from the concurrence of human rights. The protection offered by the freedom of association concurs with the protection offered by other rights when the freedom of association is the means for exercising other human rights. In such cases the special enumerated limitations of both rights are applicable.[144] Other limitations flow from the collision of human rights. The most important example of collision is the clash between the freedom of members of cartels to associate with the constitutionally protected right to property and free economic activity.[145]

## 4.4 Article 21 *GG*: political parties

The Basic Law, through the incorporation of art 21 *GG*, is the first German Constitution to afford independent and special protection to political parties.[146]

### 4.4.1 *The term 'political party'*

The term 'political party' is defined in the Political Parties Act.[147] In order to comply with the definition a party must aim to participate in the formation of the political will of the people in the ways foreseen by the Basic Law. The party must therefore participate in elections and must be serious about obtaining representation in the Federal or *Länder* Parliaments.[148] The party must have a programme and

---

the propaganda value generated for the association by a prohibition may indeed result in a bigger threat to the constitutional order than toleration of the association. In any event this determination should be made by the minister and not by the courts.

[143] Etzrodt op cit (n 116) 39, 72–89 points to the confusion concerning the limitations of the right not to associate. Etzrodt at 128–49 agrees with the majority of commentators that art 9.2 *GG* is not applicable and that no specific limitations are therefore enumerated in the Basic Law for the right not to associate. 'Immanent' limitations may, however, be developed for this right.

[144] Most activities of the association are therefore protected subject to the limitations of the art 2.1 *GG* general freedom of action. In other words, these activities of the association may be limited by laws protecting morality, the constitutional order, and the rights of others. The protection offered by the freedom of assembly further often concurs with that of the freedom to associate. The limitations of the former may in some cases impair the association's freedom to from its will without state interference. See Ramm op cit (n 102) 33–4.

[145] Strickrodt '*Das Kartellverbot in verfassungsrechtlicher Betrachtung*' 1955 *NJW* 1697. Dürig '*Art.9 Grundgesetz in der Kartellproblematik*' 1955 *NJW* 729 argues that the legislature may justify its regulation of cartels with reference to public order concerns. Most other commentators, however, suggest that proportional limitation of cartels' freedom of association has to further other constitutional concerns. This debate has become mute after the court rejected the basis of Dürig's reasoning, which was that the limitation triads of art 2.1 *GG* may also be applied to art 9.1 *GG*.

[146] Article 21 states:
'(1) The political parties shall participate in the forming of the will of the people. They may be freely established. Their internal organization must conform to democratic principles. They must publicly account for the sources of their funds.
(2) Parties which, by reason of their aims or the behaviour of their adherents, seek to impair or abolish the free democratic basic order or to endanger the existence of the Federal Republic of Germany, shall be unconstitutional. The Federal Constitutional Court shall decide the question of their constitutionality.
(3) Details shall be regulated by federal laws.'
The incorporation of art 21 *GG* should be seen against the historical background of the small, and often fragmented, political parties which existed in Weimar Germany. It is often argued that these parties gave rise to the weak coalition governments which lacked the political will to act against anti-democratic movements.

[147] Article 2 of the Political Parties Act of 1967 (*PartG*). See also 3 *BVerfGE* 383 403; 24 *BVerfGE* 260 264; 47 *BVerfGE* 198 222.

[148] 24 *BVerfGE* 260 264. Initially it seemed as if the court required that the party must be represented in Parliament before it could qualify as a political party for the purposes of art 21 *GG*. See 4 *BVerfGE* 375 383; Piepenstock *Politische Vereinigungen unter dem Grundgesetz* (1971) 16. Today a political party's status is not dependent on its success at the ballot box.

demonstrate a certain degree of stability and permanence in its pursuit of parliamentary representation.[149]

### 4.4.2 Objective meaning of the protection for political parties

Public opinion and the political will of the people are not formed by political parties alone. The government, the press, the unions, and normal associations all play a role in this process. The difference is that political parties are indispensable institutions of mediation between people and the state.[150] In order to enable parties to fulfil this mediating role between people and state principles of multi-party democracy and public opposition,[151] equal opportunities for parties,[152] the freedom to promote the political programme of the party and to compete in elections,[153] as well as the independence of the parties from outside interference have been derived from art 21 *GG*.

### 4.4.3 Content of 'political party' as a right

Since political parties are also associations art 21 *GG* provides political parties with the same protections afforded individuals and other associations under the freedom of association. Still, a few differences between the subjective content of the two freedoms warrant mention. Generally speaking, there is greater scope for the direct operation of fundamental rights in the relationship between the political party and its members than between the association and its members. Party members may rely on their freedom of opinion within the party and can be expected to be treated equally by the party.[154] The freedom of political parties to decide on their membership is

---

[149] 5 *BVerfGE* 77 84. Piepenstock op cit (n 148) 17–18 argues that there is often very little difference between the programmes of political parties and those of political associations. Like a political association, a party's programme may focus on a single regional issue. Despite such similarities, the party, unlike the association, will still qualify for art 21 *GG* protection. This argument leads Piepenstock to conclude that the differentiation between the level of protection afforded to political parties and political associations is unwarranted. See also Maunz-Dürig-Herzog *Grundgesetz Kommentar* (1991) 21-10.

[150] In the German Constitution the institutional role which political parties play in the representation of the will of the people is acknowledged by their protection in a distinct provision of the Constitution. Most commentators deny such institutional protection to general associations. They argue that art 9 *GG* makes the formation of associations possible, but not necessary. Moreover, legal concepts, such as 'the company', do not enjoy protection and the legislature is free to amend and even abolish these established legal institutions. The discretion of the legislature is much more limited with regard to political parties.

[151] The freedom to establish political parties guarantees a multi-party system. Further to ensure such a system, no permission or licence may be required to form a political party.

[152] This principle guarantees all parties an equal opportunity to become the majority party. It is derived from art 21 *GG*. However, art 3.1 *GG* (the general equality clause) is also sometimes considered in this context. See 4 *BVerfGE* 31 40 (requirement to show support does not discriminate against parties representing national minorities); 4 *BVerfGE* 273 280; 12 *BVerfGE* 10 28; 52 *BVerfGE* 63 88 (tax deductions for financial contributions to parties may infringe on equality of opportunity); 7 *BVerfGE* 99 107. The length and quality of time allotted to a party on television depends on the significance of the party. The degree of success in the last election may not, however, be the sole consideration when determining the party's significance. In addition factors such as the length of time in existence, the party's continuity and membership, the extent of the party's organization, its representation in Parliament, and participation in the government must also be considered. See 7 *BVerfGE* 99 107; 14 *BVerfGE* 121 132, 137; 20 *BVerfGE* 56 116; 47 *BVerfGE* 198 225; 48 *BVerfGE* 271 277. Individuals also have equal opportunity to be elected to government in terms of art 38.1 *GG*. The court (41 *BVerfGE* 399) therefore declared unconstitutional legislation which excluded independent candidates from state funding.

[153] 3 *BVerfGE* 19 26; 20 *BVerfGE* 56 116.

[154] See Reichert, Dannecker & Kühr op cit (n 79) 753–4.

also limited by the prohibition of discrimination.[155] Finally, party members may not be subjected to notice requirements and are free to resign at any time.[156]

Parties also stand in a different relationship to the state than normal associations. For example, political parties may not be refused access to public property for the holding of their meetings.[157] More importantly, political parties are for some purposes considered to be constitutional organs. Thus, in so far as the parties' right to participate in the formation of the will of the state is allegly infringed, the party may gain direct access to the FCC in order to press its claim.[158]

### 4.4.4 *The internal order and the publicity of a party's financial affairs*

The Basic Law interferes with the freedom of political parties to regulate their internal affairs in two ways: the parties' internal organization must conform to democratic principles, and the parties must publicly account for their funding sources.

The internal order of the party encompasses the drafting and formulation of the articles of association, the procedures at membership meetings, the election of the various committees, the nomination of candidates, and the determination of the rights and duties of the members.[159] The rules which govern the internal order must meet the democracy requirement in the following ways. First, the rules must specify that party issues are reserved for resolution at membership meetings. Secondly, members must be able to participate actively and on an equal basis in the decision-making process.[160] Thirdly, free expression of opinion must be possible at membership meetings. Fourthly, the will of the majority must prevail.[161] Therefore the determination of party policy by the bureaucracy or leader — according to the so-called *Führer* principle, for example — or by foreign governments fails to satisfy the democracy requirement.[162] Fifthly, the party rules must provide for the formation of the party structures from the bottom up, i e all members must have an equal chance of being elected to the party executive. Sixthly, the executive must answer to the membership at general meetings. Finally, exclusions from the party may not be arbitrary. Thus, while total fidelity to the party programme may never be required, the party may have a disciplinary organ which may exclude those who do not subscribe to the party's ideals.[163]

---

[155] Article 3.1 *GG* therefore limits art 21.1 *GG*. A political party may not discriminate on the basis of race or gender. The only permissible ground for refusing an applicant, it seems, is that the applicant does not subscribe to the party programme. See Reichert, Dannecker & Kühr op cit (n 79) 753.

[156] The internal rules of the party may require written notice of resignation, but nothing more. See Reichert, Dannecker & Kühr op cit (n 79) 753.

[157] 31 *BVerwGE* 368 369; *BVerwG* 1990 *NJW* 135.

[158] 4 *BVerfGE* 27 30; 4 *BVerfGE* 375 378; 6 *BVerfGE* 84 102; 7 *BVerfGE* 99 103; Maunz-Dürig-Herzog op cit (n 149) 21-33-4. In other circumstances the party, like all other associations, will have to rely on the constitutional complaint procedure. See *BVerfG* 1990 *NJW* 3002.

[159] The Political Parties Act and the European, Federal, and *Länder* Election Laws contain detailed regulations in this regard. For example, art 21 of the Federal Electoral Act determines that candidates for federal elections must be elected by a meeting of the members, or a representative group of such a meeting, or the permanent representation of such meeting. See Reichert, Dannecker & Kühr op cit (n 79) 750–68.

[160] 2 *BVerfGE* 1 40.

[161] See Maunz-Dürig-Herzog op cit (n 149) 21-24.

[162] This, despite the fact that the content of the party programme does not belong to the internal order, but rather to the external activities of the party. See Maunz-Dürig-Herzog op cit (n 149) 21-23.

[163] Article 10.4 *PartG* determines that a member may be excluded only if he/she intentionally contravenes the internal rules, requirements of loyalty, or solidarity, or if he/she rejects the fundamental beliefs of the party. The contraventions or rejections must be significant and serious damage must result to the party. See Maunz-Dürig-Herzog op cit (n 149) 21-25.

All internal party decisions taken in contravention of the democracy requirement are void. While no explicit provision for punishment is made, the undemocratic internal order may be of such a nature that it renders the party unconstitutional in terms of art 21.2 *GG*.[164]

According to the Basic Law, parties must make public information relating to their funding sources and the respective amounts of their contributions. The parties are therefore not constitutionally protected from revelations regarding their financial dependence on particular funders.[165] Today the requirement of publicity has largely become a mute topic: the state is the major contributor to party coffers.

The constitutionality of state financial support to political parties has been the subject of many complicated court decisions. The court has made clear that the legislature is under no constitutional duty to provide the political parties with the financial support necessary for them to fulfil their functions. However, the legislature may support political parties as long as the latter do not limit themselves to financial support from the state and as long as the transparency and fairness of the political process is not impaired.[166]

In 1966 the FCC declared unconstitutional Parliament's practice of funding out of the annual budget all those party activities which relate to the formation of public opinion.[167] The court held that the formation of the will of the people is a complex process and that the role played by the political parties, though important, is but one element of that process. This process may be influenced by many forms of relationships of dependence. But the court argued that ultimately the people must drive the state and not the other way around. Thus the formation of the will of the people must in principle be a 'state-free process'.[168] Under this interpretation the Basic Law relies on the citizen's eagerness and competence to organize and support political parties. Political parties may, however, be compensated for the direct costs they incur in contesting a particular election since in this capacity the parties fulfil an indispensable public function.[169] This compensation is, however, given subject to the condition that the party obtain at least 0,5 % of the vote in the election.[170]

---

[164] See 2 *BVerfGE* 1. See also Maunz-Dürig-Herzog op cit (n 149) 21-28.

[165] In practice the political parties do not always discharge this obligation satisfactorily. One excuse for non-compliance may lie in the conflict between the duty to publicize and the contributor's art 38 *GG* right to secrecy of his or her political beliefs. See Maunz-Dürig-Herzog op cit (n 149) 28-9.

[166] See 20 *BVerfGE* 56 99, 102; 73 *BVerfGE* 1 86.

[167] See 20 *BVerfGE* 56. State funding of the political-educational activities of the political parties was also invalidated. The court said that a proper distinction cannot be drawn between promotion of the party's programme and the education of the public.

[168] This explains why political parties remain, despite the public functions they often fulfil, bodies regulated by private law. Indeed, the court's conception of democracy as a 'state-free' process has resulted in all associations retaining their private-law status. Even trade unions and employer associations are considered to be bodies of private law. See Scholz op cit (n 80) 9–53; Maunz-Dürig-Herzog op cit (n 149) 9-46.

[169] Leibholz et al *Kommentar an der Hand Rechtsprechung des Bundesverfassungsgericht* (1989) arts 21–3 argue that the court's decision rests on an archaic view of a state–society dichotomy. They reject this view inter alia on the ground that the independence of the political parties is nowadays threatened not by the state, but by the rich and powerful in society. Piepenstock op cit (n 148) 35–8, on the other hand, agrees with the court, arguing that it is a characteristic of undemocratic regimes to integrate all political association into the state. Piepenstock also regrets state support for political associations which support the government's policy. Piepenstock's work, written in the early seventies, fails to take into account more recent developments in the court's jurisprudence. The court has subsequently interpreted the term 'election campaign' so expansively that the impact of its original decision has been relativized. The parties may, for example, be compensated by a lump sum calculated on an amount (currently put at DM2,50 (just more than R5,00)) for every potential voter. See 24 *BVerfGE* 299 335; 73 *BVerfGE* 1 96. Costs incurred are further calculated on what can be considered necessary, under the prevaling political, economic, and social conditions, for conducting a political campaign. See 20 *BVerfGE* 56 115; 73 *BVerfGE* 1 95.

[170] See art 18 *PartG*. See also 24 *BVerfGE* 300 339; 41 *BVerfGE* 399 421.

The FCC has also declared unconstitutional legislation which permitted tax deductions for political donations. Such deductions were deemed an infringement of the equality clause because richer individuals will inevitably have more to gain from such donations than poor citizens.[171]

### 4.4.5 Article 21.2 GG: the prohibition of political parties

According to the Basic Law, the FCC is the only body which may restrict the political activities of or ban a political party.[172] The court may only make such a determination when it is petitioned to do so by the Federal government, the Federal Senate (*Bundesrat*), or the Lower House of the Federal Parliament (*Bundestag*). As a result, the FCC has a monopoly over decisions which affect the continued existence of political parties.

Before the court has made such a decision the party — along with its members and supporters — may not be threatened by any legal sanctions. Political parties are thereby 'privileged' associations.[173] However, the privilege applies only when the state takes legal action against the political activities of the political party.[174]

Article 21.2 *GG* establishes the basis for a 'fighting' or 'militant' democracy. The court's power to prohibit parties enables the 'fighting democracy' to defend itself against the enemies of the free and democratic order.[175] The court declared the

---

[171] 8 *BVerfGE* 51 68; 24 *BVerfGE* 300 360; 52 *BVerfGE* 63 88; 69 *BVerfGE* 92 107; 73 *BVerfGE* 40 71.

[172] 5 *BVerfGE* 85 140; 40 *BVerfGE* 287 291; 47 *BVerfGE* 130 139. Articles 43–47 of the FCC Act (*BVerfGG*) set out the procedures to be observed.

[173] The conflict between the party privilege and civil servants' duty to loyalty (art 33 *GG* — *Treuepflicht*) confronted the court in 39 *BVerfGE* 334. The court had to decide whether an applicant may be refused employment in the civil service on the basis of his/her affiliations with an anti-constitutional — but not banned — political party. The court stated that the duty to loyalty is necessary because the executive can only be expected to realize its constitutional goals if it may appoint civil servants who positively support the basic order established by the Basic Law. *In casu* the court found no conflict between the duty to loyalty and the party privilege. The party privilege does not protect members or supporters of political parties in their capacity as members of or applicants to the civil service. The anti-constitutional activities of the applicant may therefore form the basis for a refusal to employ. An opposite result, the court held, would make the duty to loyalty unenforceable. For the opposite view, see Rudolph 'Die Mitgliedschaft von Beamten und Angestellten des öffentlichen Dienstes in nicht verboten verfassungsfeindlichen Parteien und Vereinigungen' 1967 *Deutsches Verwaltungsblatt* 647.

[174] 12 *BVerfGE* 296 305; 13 *BVerfGE* 123 126; 13 *BVerfGE* 155 166; 47 *BVerfGE* 130 140; 47 *BVerfGE* 198 230. The 'privilege' is interpreted restrictively. See e g 40 *BVerfGE* 287. This case — the *National Democratic Party* case — raised the question of how far the government may go in gathering and publishing information about the activities of anti-constitutional parties and groups. The decision concerned a government report which described the National Democratic Party (NPD — an extreme rightwing party often accused of displaying neo-Nazi tendencies) as a 'party engaged in anti-constitutional goals and activities', as a 'radical rightwing party and an enemy of freedom', and as 'a danger to the free and democratic basic order'. Despite its report, the government never petitioned the FCC for a declaration of unconstitutionality. The NPD therefore challenged the report as an infringement of the party's privilege accorded by art 21.1 *GG*. First, the court held that all organs of the state have the duty to protect the free and democratic basic order. The government has a choice of means, however. It may petition for a declaration of unconstitutionality or it may decide to wage the battle against unconstitutional political parties in the political arena. There is, in other words, no duty on the government or any other organ of the state to petition the court for a declaration of unconstitutionality. Secondly, the court held that the party privilege of the NPD was not infringed. The Minister of Interior made clear that the government intended to fight the NPD at the ballot box. The publication was held to be part of this strategy. The court described the report as an 'information bulletin' and said that it did not even amount to administrative action against the NPD. In fact it was not found to constitute legal action against the NPD at all and could therefore not infringe the party privilege. See Schmidt op cit (n 142) 195.

[175] The provision was included as a response to the Nazis' use of the freedom guaranteed by the Weimar Constitution. In the present Italian Constitution the risk of a political party with such a belligerent attitude towards the existing constitutional order is acknowledged, but, according to the Constitution, this risk is inherent to a democratic order. The Fascist Party is, however, forbidden by name in the Constitution. In the *Communist Party* case (5 *BVerfGE* 85) the court commented on the problematical relationship between art 21.2 *GG* and art 5 *GG* (freedom of speech). The court said that the art 5 *GG* neutrality towards the content of speech is qualified by those

following principles to be essential components of the free and democratic basic order: a legal system which excludes violent or arbitrary use of state power; the rule of law based on sovereignty and self-determination of the people; democratic majority rule; equal chances for all political parties; the right to form and practise opposition; the protection of the fundamental rights enumerated in the Basic Law; separation of powers and the independence of the courts; and the responsibility of government to Parliament.[176] In the *Communist Party* case the court held that the mere rejection of the free and democratic order by a political party does not suffice to justify a banning if that rejection is not accompanied with an active, fighting, and aggressive attitude towards this order. The party must actually aim to destroy or undermine the free and democratic order in a concerted manner.[177] The isolated acts of a few members will not suffice.

The court will make the prohibition determination without considering the following factors: the chances of the party realizing its untoward objective; postponement of the programme's implementation due to unfavourable conditions. The unconstitutional objective must, however, exist at the time when the constitutionality of banning the party is considered.[178]

The FCC also determines the consequences of a declaration of unconstitutionality. The court may order that the party's property be confiscated and/or that no replacement organizations be allowed and/or that the representatives of the party lose their mandates in the Federal or *Länder* Parliaments.[179]

## 5  FREEDOM OF ASSOCIATION IN SOUTH AFRICA

If, as Nietzsche said, the truth is a useful lie, the following falsification of the historical record should prove to be even more useful. For purposes of space and analytical simplicity this section operates *as if* the bulk of the apartheid government's restrictions on 'purely' associational freedoms were designed primarily to undermine political opposition to the apartheid government. Or, more accurately, we write as if the apartheid government's laws restricting associational freedom were not intended to realize racial separatism as well as suppress political association. We treat laws designed to effect racial separation as though they constituted a distinct regime of laws.[180]

---

provisions which protect the essence of the Basic Law's value system. These values, which were entrenched by a super majority, must be defended even if it results in a limitation of the freedom of speech.

[176] See Doehring 'The Special Character of the Constitution of the Federal Republic of Germany as a Free and Democratic Basic Order' in Karpen (ed) *The Constitution of the Federal Republic of Germany* (1988) 26.

[177] See 5 *BVerfGE* 85 (*Communist Party* case). The political philosophy to which the party subscribes is relevant to the extent that the theory underlies the party's actions.

[178] Von Feldman op cit (n 101) 31 makes clear that the act of banning the political party is not a retributive one, but rather a preventative action.

[179] In the *Socialist Reich Party* case, 2 *BVerfGE* 1, the court suggested that it might be possible for a banned political party to continue to exist in the form of a political movement in the community.

[180] Apartheid legislation clearly infringed everyone's freedom to associate: it compelled black, white, Indian, and coloured South Africans to live separately (Group Areas Act 41 of 1950); it required these groups to use separate public facilities (Separate Amenities Act 49 of 1953); it denied individuals the freedom to choose a sexual partner or spouse (Prohibition of Mixed Marriages Act 55 of 1949 and the Immorality Act 23 of 1957). The Status Acts of the TBVC states denationalized many black South Africans and forced them to accept the citizenship of the Bantustans. The 1983 Constitution of South Africa divided Parliament into three separate Houses for coloured, Indian, and white South Africans. Ultimately, however, these particular laws were not about the freedom to associate. These statutes were about white domination.

We shall not defend this conceptual distinction with any real conviction. Obviously, the Group Areas Act, the Separate Amenities Act, and the Mixed Marriages Act all impinged directly upon our ability to associate. Their aim was to keep people apart and to ensure white domination. The question motivating the distinction is whether we are likely to see similar anti-social measures adopted under a new government operating within a new constitutional dispensation. We think not. The new Constitution unequivocally rejects the radical forms of inequality and discrimination represented by the aforementioned racist laws.

There are, however, forms of apartheid-era association legislation that may have constitutional-era equivalents. As we noted in the introduction, these constitutional-era Acts will likely declare certain forms of political association illegal because they pose some kind of threat to an open and democratic South African society based upon freedom and equality. However, unless we wish to revisit the sins of the past on the present we believe great care should be taken before we resort to banning. Our trip through South Africa's house of past banning horrors is therefore largely designed to serve a cautionary function. We stop at each important banning Act just long enough to identify it.

In 1950 the National Party Parliament passed its first major piece of anti-political association legislation — the Suppression of Communism Act.[181] Despite the apparently narrow target suggested by its name, the Act was successfully employed for more than twenty-five years to suppress all 'radical' opponents of apartheid. The Act not only outlawed the Communist Party of South Africa expressly but also empowered the State President to ban any association which he believed to support any of the objects of the communist movement. What's more, the State President could ban the association without giving it notice or the opportunity to be heard.[182] Not content to employ a legal variant of the 'rooi gevaar,' the 1960 Parliament added the Unlawful Organizations Act to its quiver of banning arrows.[183] Under this Act and its 1963 amendments the ANC and the PAC were banned on the grounds that 'they seriously endangered the safety of the public [and] the maintenance of the public order'.[184] In addition to its public order proscriptions the Act created a host of lesser offences which enabled the executive and the security apparatus to punish individuals suspected of furthering the aims of opposition associations.[185]

By the mid-70s Parliament had introduced two new banning Acts. The first, the Prohibition of Political Interference Act, banned all forms of multiracial political

---

[181] Act 44 of 1950.

[182] Section 2(2). See *South African Defence and Aid Fund v Minister of Justice* 1967 (1) SA 31 (C) and *South African Defence and Aid Fund v Minister of Justice* 1967 (1) SA 263 (A): upheld ban of the South African Defence and Aid Fund, an organization which sought to provide legal defence for those opponents of apartheid who were persecuted by the state. In *R v Sisulu* 1953 (3) SA 276 (A) it was acknowledged by the Appellate Division that the provisions of the Act were so broad that women protesting against existing matrimonial property arrangements could e g be prosecuted under the Act if they were to contravene a municipal by-law. For more on the incredible breadth of proscriptive powers under the Act, see Mathews *Law, Order and Liberty in South Africa* (1971) 54–72, 76–96; Dugard *Human Rights and the South African Legal Order* (1978) 155–63; Forsyth *In Danger for their Talents* (1985) 147–67.

[183] Act 34 of 1960.

[184] Section 1(1) of the Unlawful Organizations Act. See Mathews op cit (n 182) 69–72, 240–1; Dugard op cit (n 182) 163–7. Before the passage of this Act the ANC and the PAC were already effectively banned in many rural areas under the Black Administration Act 38 of 1927.

[185] See Mathews op cit (n 182) 96–108.

association.[186] The intent, naturally, was to fracture existing coalitions and to prevent new ones from forming. The second, the Affected Organizations Act, was also designed to prevent new opposition from forming — this time by cutting off foreign funding for their activities.[187]

The Suppression of Communism Act was replaced by the Internal Security Act in 1976. The latter Act was in turn transformed into the Internal Security Act of 1982.[188] Neither of these two statutes will be remembered as major advances in the fight for freedom of association.[189] Yet when compared to the emergency regulations that followed they appear rather tame. In terms of the emergency regulations the minister could, without giving notice or hearing to anyone, prohibit all the activities of an association.[190]

The last four years of National Party rule witnessed a pretty dramatic reversal in that party's treatment of political opposition. While dirty-tricks campaigns and paramilitary responses have not entirely disappeared, opposition parties such as the ANC and the PAC have been able to operate publicly and participate in official political structures. Law followed political change in the form of two Acts: the Internal Security and Intimidation Amendment Act and the Abolition of Restrictions on Free Political Activity Act.[191] In tandem these Acts repealed much of the anti-political association legislation on the books.

The final nail in the coffin of this anti-political association legislation is s 17 of the 1993 Constitution. It is to the task of generating an appropriately pro-political association interpretation of the freedom of association clause that we now turn.

## 6 THE 1993 CONSTITUTION'S PROTECTION OF FREEDOM OF ASSOCIATION

In this final section we attempt to delineate the 'appropriate' parameters of freedom of association under the Constitution. Our analysis is divided into two general

---

[186] Act 51 of 1968; Mathews op cit (n 182) 206–8; Dugard op cit (n 182) 167–8; Ackermann *Die Reg insake Openbare Orde en Staatsveiligheid* (1984) 172–4. The Act was repealed by the Abolition of Restrictions on Free Political Activity Act 206 of 1993.

[187] Act 31 of 1974. See Dugard op cit (n 182) 168–73; Mathews *Freedom, State Security and the Rule of Law* (1986) 115–17. Parliament later passed another Act with a very similar, if not identical, aim: the Disclosure of Foreign Funding Act 26 of 1989.

[188] Act 74 of 1982.

[189] Section 4(1) of the Act conferred extraordinary powers on the minister to declare an organization unlawful when the minister was satisfied that the organization endangers the security of the state or the maintenance of law and order, promotes communism, or carries on the activities of an unlawful organization. In making these decisions the minister was subject to the most nominal of restraints. See, concerning the banning of organizations in terms of the Act: Mathews op cit (n 187) 101–17; Ackermann op cit (n 186) 77–82; concerning restrictions of the individual's freedom to associate in terms of the Act: Mathews op cit (n 187) 124–39; Ackermann op cit (n 186) 85–99; concerning the Act's provisions with regard to the furthering of the aims of an unlawful organization: Mathews op cit (n 187) 50–1; Ackermann op cit (n 186) 44–8.

[190] Regulation 23 of 24 February 1988 amended reg 96 of 11 June 1987 by the insertion of s 6A. The UDF and many other dissident organizations were frequent targets of this provision. The legislation's objective was quite obviously to provide a mechanism for silencing political opposition without having to deal with the consequences of a banning. See generally on the state of emergency Mathews op cit (n 187) 192–215.

[191] Acts 138 of 1991 and 206 of 1993 respectively. In the 1991 Act the subjective discretion requirement for ministerial action was replaced by an objective requirement: if the minister has reason to believe that an organization seeks to achieve its aims by violence, threats of violence, or the propagation of violence, he/she could ban the organization by notice in the *Government Gazette*. In the 1993 Act all references to 'disturbance' and 'disorder' as legitimate grounds for banning the association have been deleted. In addition the minister had to act on the advice of the Transitional Executive Council before he/she could exercise any banning powers.

parts.[192] First, we identify the kinds of association protected by s 17 and the kinds of association which do not deserve constitutional protection. Secondly, having identified which kinds of association merit constitutional protection, we then suggest when these various freedoms of association may be justifiably limited in the service of some important government objective.

## 6.1 Associations protected and associations left unprotected under s 17

We have, it is hoped, effectively developed at least one theme throughout this chapter: though there exist independent justifications for freedom of association, associational freedom is often most powerfully justified by reference to other constitutional imperatives. These imperatives are readily apparent in the Constitution.

The Constitution's guarantees of freedom of expression, political rights, and freedom of assembly bolster political associational freedom. Privacy, dignity, and equality rights support intimate associational freedom. Language, cultural, educational, and religious rights, as well as the principle of self-determination, all buttress cultural associational freedom. Economic activity and property rights provide additional protection for the freedom to form economic associations. Social associational freedom appears well served by the Constitution's general commitment to freedom and openness as well as the penumbral protections of various liberties, including expression, religion, privacy, culture, and dignity. Finally, the Constitution's affirmative commitment to redressing past inequalities, as well as equality and economic activity rights, reinforces disadvantaged-group associational freedom.

The last paragraph's list of kinds of associational freedom, along with their supporting constitutional rights, should suggest that there are few kinds of association which fail to serve the values which undergird the freedom and which therefore enjoy no constitutional protection. Given the freedom's wide protective ambit, it is perhaps more appropriate to ask what kinds of association do not serve the values underlying the freedom and definitely should not enjoy any constitutional protection. We offer two candidates: criminal associations, and associations which directly threaten the constitutional order.

### 6.1.1 *Criminal associations*

Our approach to constitutional analysis requires that we be circumspect about finding that an association lacks all constitutional protection. Why? Remember that under the limitation clause the court will ask the state (or the party seeking to uphold the limitation) to demonstrate that the interests that motivated the restriction on the associational activity outweigh the interests in the associational activity. The

---

[192] The division of our analysis into two sections reflects the bifurcated analysis required by Chapter 3. The first stage of analysis involves a simple threshold test, in this case: is the petitioner's associational activity protected by s 17? At this stage one's determination is a function of whether the associational activity serves the values which animate the freedom. If it is protected — and the government is found to have restricted the activity in question — then the analysis moves to the second stage. The second stage of analysis involves the far more complicated limitation clause test. Under the limitation clause the court will ask the state to demonstrate that its interests in the restriction are sufficiently reasonable and/or necessary to justify the restrictions on the individual's or group's ability to exercise the affected right.

limitation clause creates a framework for unclouded consideration of the competing interests at stake. We see no reason to substitute clumsy definitional exclusions crafted under a particular freedom for the careful balancing of governmental interests and associational interests which takes place under the limitation clause. This insight into the structure of constitutional analysis under the Constitution supports articulating as narrow a prophylactic rule under s 17 as possible.

Even with a highly circumspect approach and a narrow prophylactic rule some associations clearly fall outside the clause's protective ambit. Associations designed to achieve criminal ends are one such kind of association.

Criminal associations fall outside the clause's protective ambit because they fail to serve any of the ends which we have identified as supporting a freedom of association guarantee in the first place. Criminal associations do not help to realize a rich and varied civil society or any of the macrosocial ends which flow from such a society. While we do not wish to underestimate the positive contributions of some subversion for social growth, we would be on safer ground arguing that criminal associations actively undermine the open and democratic society based upon freedom and equality to which the Constitution says we aspire. Similarly, while criminal associations may aid certain subversive forms of self-realization, these forms of self-realization cannot be safeguarded without threatening the free democratic constitutional order itself. Thus the failure to realize either positive social ends or acceptable forms of self-realization justify the categorical exclusion of criminal associations from the freedom's protective ambit.

Of course this approach is open to the criticism that by excluding criminal associations from the protection of the freedom we suppress artificially the very sort of question the Constitution says the court should be asking, i e is the criminal statute in question unconstitutional on the grounds that it violates the freedom to associate? While the criminal association exclusion does have the potential to cover associations which, although presently criminalized, should be entitled to constitutional protection, there are possible ways around the problem. First, the threshold test for criminal associations need not simply entail a mechanistic application of the existing criminal law to the association in question. What counts as a criminal association excluded from the protection of the freedom could itself be the subject of a more subtle discrimination by the court as to which criminal associations definitely do not and cannot serve the values underlying the freedom and which criminal associations may just serve those values. Secondly, even if the criminal association which we wish to see protected did not survive under the more subtle threshold test, it is more than likely that the association in question could find constitutional solace elsewhere. As we have repeatedly noted, the associations which warrant constitutional protection are almost invariably protected by some other constitutional right. Thus, while it is conceivably possible that the 'criminal' association in question may fail to secure protection under our more subtle test, if it warrants constitutional protection, it will likely find it elsewhere.

### 6.1.2 *Associations which directly threaten the constitutional order*

Failure to effect acceptable forms of self-realization or macrosocial ends also justifies the categorical exclusion of associations which directly threaten the constitutional order from the freedom's protective ambit. As with criminal associations, the difficulty with this exclusion is in determining the extension of the phrase 'directly threaten the constitutional order'.

Our judicious approach to exclusions suggests that only those organizations which possess the military capacity to subvert that order and have demonstrated clearly their intent to use that capacity should fail to secure constitutional protection. This rule draws a distinction between associations which merely advocate the government's overthrow — which deserve at least *prima facie* protection — and associations which demonstrate through military preparation and action that they are bent on non-peaceable governmental change. The former deserve at least *prima facie* protection under both freedom of expression and freedom of association. If they are going to be restricted, then the government must be able to justify the restriction under the limitation clause.

Two examples may help make clear the distinction between the two kinds of association. Imagine that the Fourth International Association (FIA) produces literature which advocates a worker revolt against their capitalist exploiters and the state aparatus which supports them. FIA has no military capacity, let alone an intent to use it. FIA would therefore remain protected by s 17. The Federation of Optomologists and Urologists (FOU) has acquired tanks, helicopter gunships, surface-to-air missiles, and enough artillery for years of intensive warfare. They have employed 10 000 mercenaries to do their bidding and fighting. They have demanded immediate state recognition of the independence and importance of their professions, as well as a large chunk of the PWV. FOU troop movements on several farms in the Eastern Transvaal suggest that they are ready to go. Unlike FIA, FOU directly threatens the free and democratic constitutional order of South Africa. Under our proposed prophylactic rule, s 17 would not offer FOU any succour. FOU is, to our minds, the paradigmatic example of an association which fails to receive the protections afforded most associations by s 17.

## 6.2 Justifiable limitations on protected associations

Unless you are FOU or Mafia s 17 is likely to afford your association some protection. However, the court's inquiry does not end with the determination that the association and its activities are *prima facie* protected. The court now employs the limitation clause test to determine whether the limitation on the petitioner's associational freedom is justifiable and therefore constitutional.

### 6.2.1 *Different levels of scrutiny under the limitation clause*

On its face the limitation clause bifurcates the test for associational freedom. Political associations — or more accurately associations related to free and fair political activity — are given the highest level of protection under the reasonable and necessary restriction test. Restrictions on other forms of association have their fidelity to the Constitution measured by the weaker reasonable restriction test.[193]

We believe, however, that the associational hierarchy is far more complex than the limitation clause's bifurcated system of review suggests. If most associational rights are buttressed by other constitutional rights, then the nature of the review they

---

[193] For a detailed discussion of this bifurcated system of limitation clause tests, see Woolman 'Riding the Push-Me Pull-You: Constructing a Test that Reconciles the Conflicting Interests Which Animate the Limitation Clause' (1994) 10 *SAJHR* 60.

receive will in substantial part be contingent upon the level of review accorded the buttressing right. Thus varying degrees of scrutiny will exist for associational rights. Political associations might still receive the highest level of judicial solicitude. But intimate associations, if buttressed by dignity, or cultural associations, if buttressed by religion, might also receive 'reasonable and necessary' protection. Economic associations will not receive the highest level of protection, buttressed as they are by property rights or economic activity rights. However, the mere fact that other constitutional imperatives support economic associations suggests that they will receive greater judicial solicitude than associations which lack such support.

Even this rendering of the scrutiny afforded associational rights does not capture the truly complex character of the analysis. As we shall see, the justifications for banning or interference in membership policies or regulating internal affairs will vary substantially from associational context to associational context. Most importantly, however, the success of the state in providing justifications for its interference may not necessarily correlate with the level of protection offered the association — i e some highly protected associations may be very susceptible to state intervention, while some associations which receive little express judicial solicitude under the limitation clause are less likely to be interfered with justifiably. In general the more public the functions of the association, the more likely it is to be subject to legitimate state intervention.

### 6.2.2 Banning, opening up membership policies, and meddling in internal affairs

#### 6.2.2.1 Political associations and political parties

In most jurisdictions state action which aims to limit political association is usually subjected to higher levels of judicial scrutiny than state action which aims to limit other forms of association The explanation for the increased protection is that political associations and parties fulfil indispensable functions in liberal democracies. The Constitution has recognized the special position occupied by political associations and parties by requiring that, in so far as the right of association relates to free and fair political activity, limitations must not only be reasonable but also necessary in an open and democratic society based upon freedom and equality.

And yet, despite this rather stringent test, it may often be easier for the state to justify its limitations on political associations and parties than for the state to justify its limitations on other less well-protected forms of association. At first blush this result seems counter-intuitive, if not contradictory. However, the result begins to make sense when one recalls that the proportionality of a limitation does not depend solely upon the value of the associational interest asserted but also depends upon the importance, intensity, or weight of the state interest offered as justification for the limitation. Thus the public nature of the functions fulfilled by political associations not only legitimizes the higher level of protection offered to them but also serves as the justification for significant state interference with such associations. On the other hand, while associations which serve few if any public or quasi-public functions may not be deserving of any special degree of constitutional protection, they are less apt to be the object of state interference because the state possesses fewer compelling reasons to interfere in their affairs.

◻ Membership policies

We have suggested earlier in this chapter that the membership policies of political associations and political parties may only legitimately discriminate against applicants either in the service of the expressive ends of the association or when the applicants do not subscribe to the association or party programme.[194] Otherwise the state may step in to eliminate the discrimination in the furtherance of an important state objective, such as equality. For example, the state may require that a 'Save the White Rhino' campaign not discriminate against black applicants. The limitation's objective will be the overridingly important goal of equality. The campaign, in response, will not be able to offer a legitimate reason for its discrimination. It cannot tie the discrimination either to its expressive ends or to the applicant's 'incorrect' beliefs. The state's limitation on the campaign's membership policy will in all likelihood be viewed as justifiable.

Political parties, as the US and German case law suggests, may be subject to even stricter state controls than political associations because they play an even more public role. Thus let us assume that a Green (Environmental) Party excludes white applicants. Assume also that the state attacks the discriminatory membership policy in pursuit of its equality objectives. The attack will be found justifiable on two grounds. As above, the Green Party cannot tie its discriminatory membership policies either to its expressive ends or to the applicant's 'incorrect' beliefs. In addition the state may argue that democracy requires that political demands are made by representative groups of interested individuals.[195] A representative group of interested individuals means black and white alike.

◻ Internal affairs

State interference with the internal rules of political associations may require balancing of a slightly more complex nature. This complex balancing of interests is especially evident with respect to state interference in the affairs of political parties. There exists quite obviously a close relationship between political parties and the state. The state may feel that this close relationship requires intervention in the party's internal affairs to ensure that the party serves its representative function in a representative democracy. Indeed, the courts generally accept the state's contention that representative democratic politics demands that the members of political parties elect the candidates of their political party to represent them in elections. The courts, however, are less apt to require that all political party decisions are made democratically. Such broad interference strikes too deep into the heart of the parties' associational freedom. This interference is even less likely to be tolerated in the absence of substantial state funding of political parties. The greater the divorce between the state and the parties — the less the parties operate as state organs — the less justification there will be for the regulation of parties' internal rules.[196]

---

[194] The programmes of political parties normally contain such vague principles that it will be very difficult for the parties to discriminate against any applicant.

[195] Individuals must be allowed to join those political parties which espouse their beliefs. Otherwise a small clique is allowed to dominate the articulation of a political demand.

[196] Furthermore, the costs of observing an all-encompassing democracy requirement may make it nearly impossible for the political party to operate at all.

❐ Banning

We can think of few acceptable grounds for the banning of *prima facie* protected political parties, at least not on associational grounds. In the absence of a showing that a political association is not constitutionally protected under the freedom of association the banning will probably have to be justified as a legitimate limitation of the freedom of expression. As we stated in our introduction, the grounds for banning expression are treated elsewhere in this book and will not be rehearsed here.

6.2.2.2  Intimate and cultural associations

With associations that are supported by some other constitutional right or imperative, distinctions are rarely made between state regulation of the goal and state regulation of the association as the means to achieving that goal. Consequently the degree of protection afforded the association is often derived from the constitutional protection for the association's objective. This conflation of goal and means is hardly problematic with respect to intimate associations. The intimate associational goal and its means are inextricably linked. As a result, intimate associations normally receive the strong constitutional protection which flow from privacy rights or human dignity rights.

At the same time there exist few reasons for the state to regulate these forms of association. Few public goods are at issue in intimate associations. Furthermore, where equality is an issue it usually cuts against, and not in favour of, traditional forms of state intervention. For example, the Constitution is committed to sexual orientation equality. That commitment directly undermines state attempts to restrict intimate sexual relationships. Indeed, the commitment might well require the state to recognize homosexual marriages.[197]

Cultural (and religious) associations will generally find themselves in a similarly advantageous position. To the extent that these associations stick to *bona fide* religious and cultural activities they will be relatively immune to state intervention. If cultural or religious associations can demonstrate that their discriminatory membership policies legitimately help to preserve their communities' religious or cultural life, then the associational right to determine membership should trump the state's interest in equality. And for good reason: the state's interest in equality here is rather weak. The goods provided by such associations are less public than those provided by other types of association — political and economic — which are legitimately subject to far greater state control.[198]

While there may be the odd good reason to open up the membership policies of cultural and religious associations, there are no good reasons for state interference

---

[197] State control of intimate association could be distinguished from state recognition of such associations. Still, it will be difficult to justify state recognition of a heterosexual marriage and the refusal of the state to confer a similar status on gay or lesbian unions. The refusal to acknowledge polygamous marriages is different. The polygamous marriage scenario finds the equality argument on the other side. It is supported instead by cultural rights. It seems perfectly reasonable for the equality argument in this case to trump the state's interest in maintaining cultural traditions. However, even if the state refused to confer legal status on the relationship between three women and a man, it would be on far less secure ground in preventing the three women and a man from living together and from concluding their own agreement to support such an arrangement.

[198] State interference with the membership policies of such associations will only pass constitutional muster when that policy does not support the exercise of the cultural or religious rights of the members, but has some ulterior political or economic purpose.

in the internal affairs of such associations. The internal affairs of such associations are generally linked to some concrete vision of religious or community life. In a liberal society the state should have no role to play in the construction of these particular visions of the good life.

### 6.2.2.3 Economic associations

Quite a different set of considerations apply to business associations. In all the jurisdictions described in this study the state is entitled to place substantial limitations upon economic associations. While the specific reasons for the low level of protection afforded these associations may differ from jurisdiction to jurisdiction, and context to context, the general reason remains the same: business associations control the distribution of important social (or public) goods and must be subject to rules of fair play. In addition, where economic regulations are deemed to strike too far into the heart of the association's membership policies or internal affairs the constitutional attack on the regulations is more likely to rely on a taking of property rights argument than it is on an infringement of associational rights argument. For example, in some jurisdictions shareholders in juristic persons often enjoy little freedom of association protection. In such jurisdictions the shareholders' meeting is seen as the means for exercising shareholders' property rights. The protection for the shareholder's association, if recognized, is then derived almost entirely from the right to property.

### 6.2.2.4 Empowering associations

Associations which aim to empower historically disadvantaged groups support the Constitution's commitment to affirmative action and real equality. These associations may need to have discriminatory policies if they are to be able to police their resources and be in a position to achieve their constitutionally protected objective. When faced with such an association the state may be hard pressed to show that it has an interest in regulating the membership policies of such an association on racial or gender equality grounds. After all, it is the constitutionally protected goal of realizing real racial and gender equality through affirmative action which justifies the exclusion in the first place.

However, to pass constitutional muster the association should at least have to demonstrate two things. First, it should have to show that its membership is historically disadvantaged and continues to be disadvantaged. Secondly, it should have to show that the exclusive membership policy promotes the goal of substantive equality. A black lawyers association will have little trouble making the first showing. If not legally barred from the rolls, black lawyers have been prejudiced at every step of the way and presently constitute but a minority in the legal profession. The second showing may be more difficult. The association will have to demonstrate that a separate association will serve black lawyers better than the larger and more general law association.

### 6.2.2.5 Small social associations

This last general type of association does not really receive support from other constitutional rights. Still, small social associations do provide the opportunity for some self-realization.

Despite the absence of additional constitutional support, small social associations are unlikely targets for state interference. First, the state is unlikely to bother with small associations because it will generally have much larger fish to fry. Secondly, even if the state did wish to bother, there are few good reasons for interference. For example, it is hard to imagine why the state would have a real interest in regulating either the membership policies or the internal order of a nine-boy neighbourhood chess club that discriminated against girls. Given that the club does not fulfil any public function — such as selecting players for a South African National Team — and does not exercise a monopoly over this particular social good, the state cannot argue that it has some substantive vision of equality which it is trying to realize in this case by opening up the membership. If perhaps the club could award grandmaster points, then the state may have a compelling motivation. However, where, as here, the club serves the 'purely' local and social ends of its members the state's interest in opening up the membership is 'purely' ideological. Unless we wish to grant the state the power to enforce its ideology at every turn — which carries the threat of totalitarianism — such purely ideological grounds for interfering in an association's affairs should be rejected.

# ADMINISTRATIVE JUSTICE

### HUGH CORDER

## 1  PHILOSOPHICAL BACKGROUND

This chapter is concerned with control over executive power through the Constitution. Few lawyers or political commentators in the late twentieth century would deny that the growth of executive power ranks with the development of the constitutionalisation of human rights as one of the two most important features of government during the last fifty years. The origins of and reasons for this expansion of the power of one branch of government, chiefly at the expense of the legislature, are many and varied[1] and need not detain us here. We need only recognize *the fact* that most modern governments rely to a great degree for the effective execution of their policies on a large and powerful public administration, acting often in a discretionary manner.

The main challenge which faces all constitutional systems which aspire to democracy is to devise and implement structures and measures whereby the bureaucracy, having been appropriately *empowered*, can necessarily be held *accountable* for its actions. Thus the administrative law of most legal systems has developed markedly during this century, both in 'common-law' and 'civil-law' jurisdictions.[2] Equally, there remains much to be done by way of reform in this area of the law,[3] although some countries, such as Australia,[4] have taken highly innovative steps to heighten accountability.

One of the areas in which relatively little change has occurred, however, forms the subject of this chapter and straddles the growth of executive power and the constitutional protection of human rights. In other words, should the statutory or common-law right to review administrative action be elevated to constitutional status? If so, exactly how should this 'right' be formulated, and to and against whom should it be available? Should the grounds for review be spelt out, should the review function be confined to the courts, and what types of administrative action should be subject to review?

These are some of the questions which arise for discussion in this context, and which will be considered below. It is clear that the answers given to these questions will be system-specific and that there is no 'one right answer' to such questions. Much will depend on the political context and the philosophical foundations of the legal system concerned, for there are good reasons in certain circumstances for regarding the 'constitutionalization' of administrative justice as a retrograde step.

---

[1] For a review of this process, see e g Craig *Administrative Law* 2 ed (1989), particularly chs 1 and 2.

[2] For an overview of the legal systems typical of the British Commonwealth, see Corder *Empowerment and Accountability* (1991). For a masterly summary treatment of civil law systems, see Schwarze *European Administrative Law* (1992), especially at 97–206.

[3] See Justice All Souls *Administrative Justice: Some Necessary Reforms* (1988).

[4] See Allars *An Introduction to Australian Administrative Law* (1990).

The essential issue which underlies the discussion which follows is the attempt to strike a constructive balance through the law between executive empowerment and accountability within a democratic environment. Whether a provision of the Constitution has a part to play in this legal relationship is the particular focus. In addition attention will be paid to two crucial concomitants of any such review procedure: the role of an 'ombudsman' and freedom of information provisions.

## 2   COMPARATIVE AND INTERNATIONAL BACKGROUND

In the vast majority of the legal systems of the world the source of the accountability to law of the executive is to be found in legislation and the common law (including of course judge-made law, through the doctrine of precedent).

Accountability takes many forms and is sought through a range of structures. Thus the commonest grounds on which review of administrative action is based are expressed in the 'principle of legality',[5] which includes requirements of lawfulness (*intra vires* action) and fairness (including procedural and substantive reasonableness). While the ordinary courts of almost every legal system participate in this process of review, many countries (and particularly those in the civil-law tradition) have developed a complete set of specialist courts to undertake such review functions[6] or have set up independent tribunals parallel to the ordinary courts.[7] It is particularly (although not exclusively) in this latter type of system that the scope of review is widened from procedural regularity to embrace appeals on the merits of administrative decisions.

Very few countries therefore provide for a constitutional right to administrative justice in their bills or charters of fundamental rights and freedoms. Many would view such a specific 'right' as being unnecessary as they would argue that the ability to challenge unlawful administrative action at law could be sustained generally by the application of, for example, the right to equality (including non-discrimination) to any act or omission of the executive branch of government.[8]

The Constitution of Namibia, however, which has special relevance for South Africans, does provide for a right to administrative justice.[9] The provision reads as follows:

'Administrative bodies and administrative officials shall act fairly and reasonably and comply with the requirements imposed upon such bodies and officials by common law and any relevant legislation, and persons aggrieved by the exercise of such acts and decisions shall have the right to seek redress before a competent Court or Tribunal.'

It will be noticed that this article imposes a positive duty on the public administration to meet the requirements of legality, fairness, and reasonableness in all their actions and grants persons 'aggrieved' by administrative action the right to seek redress before a court or tribunal.

---

[5] See e g Schwarze op cit (n 2) 212–60.
[6] As e g in Western Europe.
[7] As e g in Australia, the UK, and the US.
[8] For a clear view of the way in which this has worked in Canada, see Evans 'Administrative Appeal or Judicial Review: A Canadian Perspective' 1993 *Acta Juridica* 47 at 68–70.
[9] Constitution of the Republic of Namibia 1990 art 18.

This signifies a change from the former position in Namibian (and South African) administrative law in the following respects:

- Fairness and reasonableness now become requirements for *valid* administrative action (and thus, in the reverse, recognized grounds for challenging administrative action).

- The group of persons who will have legal standing to question the validity of administrative action is widened to include all those 'aggrieved' by such action (as opposed to those who have a 'direct, personal interest' in the matter).

- Those aggrieved now have a constitutional right — which can only be ousted by legislative action under strict conditions — to question the validity of administrative action and seek an appropriate remedy.

- The way is opened for the creation of tribunals other than the ordinary courts to be the appropriate forum for review (including the probability that appellate jurisdiction could be conferred on such bodies).

These changes represent important advances in administrative justice, but have yet to be tested in the superior courts of Namibia.

A different approach, which endeavours to avoid some of the difficulties adverted to above,[10] can be found in the proposals for a Constitution of the UK,[11] which provides for administrative justice by casting the onus on Parliament to legislate for judicial review of administrative acts and omissions, a general duty on public authorities to give reasons for their decisions, and for effective remedies.[12] Legal standing is accorded to all who have a 'significant interest' in the matter.[13] In addition provision is made[14] for a Commission for Public Administration with wide-ranging investigative, review, research, remedial, and reporting powers, and a duty to establish a complaints procedure is imposed on every public authority.[15] Thus the Constitution creates the framework for legislative action and failure by Parliament to fulfil its constitutional duties would presumably be actionable in court.

Other than these two examples, there is little evidence of *direct* provision for a constitutional right of review of administrative action internationally. On the other hand, such a right is *indirectly* achieved through causing all executive action to be subject to the rights and freedoms duly constitutionalized and further providing for a citizen's right to enforce such rights through a competent court of law. Furthermore, some modern Constitutions provide for access to at least that information held by the state, as well as the establishment, powers, and functions of the office of 'ombudsman'. In this regard we can refer once more to the constitution of Namibia,[16] and to the proposed Constitution of the UK.[17] It seems, on the other hand, that the relative modernity of the concern about administrative accountability has produced a situation in which most legal systems are content to provide for

---

[10] In the text preceding n 8.
[11] Institute for Public Policy Research *The Constitution of the United Kingdom* (1991).
[12] Article 118.1.
[13] Article 118.2.
[14] In art 119.
[15] By art 120.
[16] Chapter 10, referring to the Ombudsman.
[17] Op cit (n 11) arts 28 and 29.

freedom of information[18] and ombudsman surveillance[19] in ordinary legislation rather than elevating such matters to the constitutional plane. In this respect therefore the 'lateness' with which South Africa has reached the stage of having to draft a written Constitution, including a statement of protected rights, is in fact an advantage which most of the participants in the constitutional debate have grasped readily, as will be seen in the next section.

## 3 STATE OF THE DEBATE IN SOUTH AFRICA

The significant aspect of the South African constitutional 'debate', such as it is, is that almost every serious participant accepts without question that administrative justice is a goal worth constitutionalizing, both in the form of a right to some degree of judicial review, as well as in providing for freedom of information and the office of ombudsman (or public protector, as it is called in the 1993 Constitution). It is instructive to review the various proposals in this regard, in the chronological order in which they have been published.

### 3.1 The South African Law Commission

The South African Law Commission[20] proposes the following:

'Article 12: Freedom of Speech
Everyone has the right to freedom of speech and other forms of expression and to obtain and disseminate information.'

'Article 31: Review of administrative acts and subordinate legislation
Everyone has the right to have civil disputes settled by a court of law and to have recourse to the Supreme Court to review, by virtue of its inherent jurisdiction, any subordinate legislation and any executive act and any administrative act.'

'Article 32: Rules of natural justice
Everyone has the right to have the rules of natural justice applied in administrative proceedings and actions in which, on the grounds of findings of fact and of law, the rights or legitimate expectations of an individual or a group are infringed or likely to be infringed, and in such cases every person having an interest in the matter has the right to be furnished on demand with the reasons for a decision.'

'Article 37: Ombudsman
(a) There shall be a permanent full-time Ombudsman who shall on his or her own initiative or in response to representations made —
    (i) investigate complaints of maladministration by executive or administrative bodies or persons, including the violation of human rights as contained in this Bill;
    (ii) investigate complaints against state institutions or administrative bodies or officers or employees thereof regarding unfair, unjust and discourteous conduct which.infringes or has infringed human rights as contained in this Bill;
    (iii) act on behalf of groups or individuals, including patients in hospitals, taxpayers, pensioners, prisoners, children and other groups, whose individual rights have been

---

[18] See Bayne *Freedom of Information* (1984) and Mathews *The Darker Reaches of Government* (1978).
[19] See the British Parliamentary Commissioner Act of 1967 and the Australian Ombudsman Act of 1976.
[20] *Project 58: Group and Human Rights* Interim Report (1991) (released in November of that year), published on 1 February 1993.

prejudiced or are likely to be prejudiced by a specific act or acts by the executive authority or the administration;
(iv) generally watch over the upholding and respecting of human rights by the executive and administrative bodies and officers, and himself or herself take the initiative in protecting the human rights set forth in this Bill;
(v) institute enquiry as to whether or not acts done by the executive or administrative authorities under powers conferred by subordinate or delegated legislation and which appear to infringe the human rights set forth in this Bill are unconstitutional;
(vi) through investigation, mediation, conciliation and negotiation endeavour to reach a settlement between the complainant and the body or person complained of, which may include obtaining an apology, revoking a decision or ruling, reconsidering the complainant's application or request, or effecting a change in policy or practice;
(vii) co-operate with the Human Rights Commission with a view to attaining the aims and objects of the Commission;
(viii) in respect of every investigation carried out by him or her report in writing, at least once each year, to the highest legislative body concerning his or her findings relating to the infringement of human rights and the steps and actions taken or recommended by him or her, such report to be published for general information simultaneously with submission thereof to that legislative body.
(b) Further provision shall be made in the Constitution for the functions of the Ombudsman.'

It seems that these provisions are unlikely to change in any significant respect in the Commission's final report. These clauses must be seen against the background of the Commission's valuable work on the reform of judicial review and its proposal to Parliament that a Judicial Review Act, spelling out the grounds for review and related matters, should be adopted.[21] This strategy — of enshrining the principle of the matter in the Constitution, while leaving the detail to statute — is a sound one, which underlies most of the suggested formulations which follow and which is likely to be chosen by a future government.

## 3.2 Constitution of the State of KwaZulu/Natal

While it provides expressly for freedom of information and the office of ombudsman, the Constitution of the State of KwaZulu/Natal[22] appears not to do so in respect of the right to review administrative action. The following articles do, however, relate to the issue.

'Article 16: Justiciability of rights
All rights and freedoms recognized and guaranteed under this Constitution shall be justiciable to the fullest practical and reasonable extent. In case of a violation of the rights and freedoms recognized and guaranteed under this Constitution any aggrieved party shall be entitled to be heard by a court of record on the basis of urgency and, upon showing a *prima face* [sic] violation of rights, shall be granted preliminary relief pending the final disposition of the case.'

'Article 29: Human rights in the Constitution
All fundamental human rights and all those other rights which are inherent to fundamental human needs and aspirations as they evolve with the changes and growth of society, and as they will be recognizable on the basis of the principles underlying the provisions of this Constitution,

---

[21] SA Law Commission *Project 24: Report on the Investigation into the Courts' Powers of Review of Administrative Acts* (November 1992).
[22] Adopted by Resolution of the KwaZulu Legislative Assembly on 1 December 1992.

are hereby entrenched in this Constitution and in their essential content shall not be modified by virtue of constitutional amendments.'

'Article 57: Freedom of Information

Any citizen has the right to access and receive any information or document which is in the possession of the State or Regional governments or of any of the commissions or agencies established in this Constitution, provided that such document or information is not privileged as established by law to protect privacy, commercial secrets or national and State security. During the process of judicial review of the government's decision to withhold information, the court shall have the power to examine *in camera* the information withheld.'

'Article 103: The Ombudsman

a. The Ombudsman shall be independent and subject only to this Constitution and to the law. No public official shall interfere with the exercise of the Ombudsman's functions or shall refuse full assistance as it may be needed. The Ombudsman's salary are [sic] set forth by the law and shall not be inferior to the salary of a Minister. The office of the Ombudsman drafts and proposes to the General Assembly its own budget.

b. The Ombudsman shall either be a judge, a lawyer or an advocate. The Ombudsman shall be appointed by General Assembly on the recommendation of the Judicial Service Commission. The Ombudsman shall hold office for a non-renewable six year term. The functions of the Ombudsman include the investigation of the complaints concerning violations of rights and freedoms, abuse or use for political purposes of power, corruption and misappropriation of public monies, unfair, harsh, insensitive or discourteous treatment of anyone in the State by a public official, including police, defence forces and prison personnel, manifest injustice, or conduct of a public official which would properly be regarded as unlawful, oppressive or unfair.

c. The Ombudsman shall have the power to take appropriate action to call for the remedying, correction and reversal of injustices and violations of laws and regulations through the most fair, proper and effective means, including:
   — negotiation and compromise between the parties concerned,
   — causing the complaint along with the Ombudsman's findings to be reported to the superior of the offending party,
   — referring the matter to the Director of Public Prosecution, with a recommendation,
   — bringing proceedings in a competent Court for suitable remedies to secure the termination of the offending action or conduct, the compensation of the victims and/or the modification of the offending procedures,
   — bringing proceedings before the Constitutional Court to challenge the constitutionality of legislation, or before a court to challenge the validity of regulations,
   — reviewing laws in force before the enactment of this Constitution to ascertain their consistency with the principles and provisions of this Constitution so as to make recommendations to the Governor and the General Assembly.

d. The Ombudsman shall have the power to compel the appearance of witnesses and the production of documents and records relevant to his or her investigation. The Ombudsman shall also have the power to cause anyone contemptuous of his or her subpoenas to be prosecuted before a competent Court.

e. The Ombudsman shall submit an annual report to the General Assembly on the exercise of his or her powers and functions.

f. The Ombudsman may be removed from office before the end of his or her term by the Governor acting on the recommendation of the Judicial Service Commission. The Ombudsman may only be removed from office on the grounds of mental incapacity or for gross misconduct. The Judicial Service Commission shall conduct the investigation and report to the Governor and the General Assembly.

g. The Ombudsman shall empower assistant district Ombudsmen who shall serve in decentralized offices on the basis of districts designated by the Ombudsman with the aim of maximizing the accessibility of the Ombudsman's services and protection.

### 3.3 *The Charter for Social Justice*

The *Charter for Social Justice*, a suggestion for a Bill of Rights for South Africa drafted by a group of lawyers from Cape Town,[23] assumes that the office of ombud will be provided for outside the chapter of the Constitution dealing with the protection of rights, but does propose the following in regard to administrative review and freedom of information:

> 'Article 23
> 
> Anyone adversely affected by an improper or unreasonable administrative act shall have the right to seek redress from an independent court and any other body or tribunal established for such purpose.'
> 
> 'Article 24
> 
> (1) Everyone has the right of access to information held by any authority performing governmental functions.
> 
> (2) Everyone has the right of access to that information which is necessary for the implementation of his or her rights.'

### 3.4 South African government proposals

The South African government proposals for a Charter of Rights[24] fail to provide in specific terms for a right to review administrative action, being satisfied with a general jurisdictional provision and the entrenchment of the rules of natural justice, as follows:

> 'Article 28
> 
> (1) Every person shall have the right to have any dispute settled by a court of law.
> 
> Article 29
> 
> Every person shall have the right —
> 
> *(a)* to have the rules of natural justice applied in administrative proceedings where, on the ground of findings of fact or of fact and law, his or her rights or reasonable expectations are or may be infringed;
> 
> *(b)* that in such a case the reasons for any decision be furnished on demand to him or her.

The government does provide for a right to obtain and disseminate information,[25] but shares the view of the compilers of the *Charter for Social Justice* that the office of ombudsman belongs elsewhere in the Constitution.

### 3.5 The African National Congress (ANC)

The ANC deals fully with each of these matters,[26] as follows:

> 'Article 2: Personal Rights
> 
> (26): The Right to Judicial Review
> 
> Any person adversely affected in his or her rights, entitlements or legitimate expectations by an

---

[23] Hugh Corder, Steve Kahanovitz, John Murphy, Christina Murray, Kate O'Regan, Jeremy Sarkin, Henk Smith & Nico Steytler *A Charter for Social Justice* published on 10 December 1992.

[24] Published on 1 February 1993.

[25] In art 9(1).

[26] In *ANC Draft Bill of Rights* (Preliminary Revised Version) of February 1993.

administrative or executive act shall be entitled to have the matter reviewed by an independent court or tribunal on the grounds of irregularity, including abuse of authority, going beyond the powers granted by law, bad faith, or such (gross) unreasonableness in relation to the procedure or the decision as to amount to manifest injustice.

NOTE: This clause will in all likelihood have to be revised in the light of recommendations of the workshop, held in Cape Town early in 1993, on the future of Administrative Law and also after further discussions.'

'Article 4: Freedom of Speech, Assembly and Information

(3) All men and women shall be entitled to all the information necessary to enable them to make effective use of their rights as citizens, workers or consumers.

'Article 17: Enforcement

Ombud

(13) With a view to ensuring that all functions and duties under the Constitution are carried out in a fair way with due respect for the rights and sentiments of those affected, the office of Ombudsman [sic] shall be created.

(14) The Ombud shall be appointed by the State President subject to confirmation by the Senate.

(15) The Ombud shall be appointed for a term to be determined by Act of Parliament, and may only be removed by the President, acting on the advice of the Senate, on grounds of gross misconduct or mental incapacity.

(16) The Ombud shall be independent in the carrying out of his or her functions and shall serve in a full-time capacity and may open offices in different parts of the country.

(17) The Ombud shall receive and investigate complaints from members of the public concerning abuse of power or unfair, insensitive, capricious, harsh, discourteous or unduly delayed or discriminatory treatment of any person by any official of government at national, regional or local level, or any attempt by such official to extort benefits or corruptly to receive favours.

(18) In accordance with his or her findings, the Ombud may initiate legal proceedings, refer the matter for prosecution, negotiate a compromise, issue a public communication, or make a report to the department or organ concerned containing recommendations with a view to remedying the improper conduct, preventing repetition, and, where appropriate, making amends, including compensation.

## 3.6 The Democratic Party

The Democratic Party also resists a provision relating to the Ombudsman, but provides for the other issues as follows:[27]

'Article 14: Right to Administrative Justice

14.1 No person shall be affected adversely by a decision made in the exercise of public power which is unlawful, unreasonable or procedurally unfair;

14.2 every person adversely affected by a decision made in the exercise of public power shall be entitled to be given reasons, in writing, for the decision.

'Article 15: Right to information

Every citizen shall have the right to obtain from the State, and from any organ of State or Government, with due expedition, all information:

15.1 concerning the organization of such organ, its decisions and decision-making procedures, its rules and policies;

15.2 held by the State concerning such citizen.

---

[27] See *Freedom under the Rule of Law: Advancing Liberty in the New South Africa* of May 1993.

N.B. This article must be specifically read together with the derogation clause contained in article 18.'

## 3.7 Elements of Chapters 3 and 8 of the transitional Constitution

Finally, in this review of proposals made for entrenching rights related to administrative justice in the 'final' South African constitution, we must take note of elements of Chapters 3 and 8 of the transitional Constitution[28] drawn up by the Multi-Party Negotiating Process (MPNP) at the World Trade Centre, Kempton Park. The following clauses are particularly relevant:

'Section 23: Access to Information

Every person shall have the right of access to all information held by the State or any of its organs at any level of government in so far as such information is required for the exercise or protection of any of his or her rights.

'Section 24: Administrative Justice

Every person shall have the right to —
(a) lawful administrative action where any of his or her rights or interests is affected or threatened;
(b) procedurally fair administrative action where any of his or her rights or legitimate expectations is affected or threatened;
(c) be furnished with reasons in writing for administrative action which affects any of his or her rights or interests unless the reasons for such action have been made public; and
(d) administrative action which is justifiable in relation to the reasons given for it where any of his or her rights is affected or threatened.

'CHAPTER 8: The Public Protector

110 Establishment and appointment

(1) There shall be a Public Protector for the Republic.

(2) The President shall, whenever it becomes necessary, appoint as the Public Protector a person —
(a) nominated by a joint committee of the Houses of Parliament composed of one member of each party represented in Parliament and willing to serve on the committee; and
(b) approved by the National Assembly and the Senate by a resolution adopted by a majority of at least 75 per cent of the members present and voting at a joint meeting:

Provided that if any nomination is not approved as required in paragraph (b), the joint committee shall nominate another person.

(3) The first appointment of a person as the Public Protector after the commencement of this Constitution shall be made within 60 days of the first sitting of the Senate under this Constitution.

(4) The Public Protector shall be a South African citizen who is a fit and proper person to hold such office and who —
(a) is a Judge of the Supreme Court of South Africa; or
(b) is qualified to be admitted as an advocate and has, for a cumulative period of at least 10 years after having so qualified:
   (i) practised as an advocate or an attorney, or
   (ii) lectured in law at a university; or
(c) has specialized knowledge of or experience for a period of at least 10 years in the administration of justice, public administration or public finance.

(5) Unless the new constitutional text provides otherwise, the Public Protector shall hold office for a period of 7 years.

---

[28] See the Constitution of the Republic of South Africa Act 200 of 1993.

(6) The remuneration and other terms and conditions of employment of the Public Protector shall be as prescribed by or under an Act of Parliament, and such remuneration shall not be reduced, nor shall such terms and conditions be adversely altered, during his or her term of office.

(7) The Public Protector shall not perform remunerative work outside his or her official duties.

(8) The Public Protector may be removed from office by the President, but only on the grounds of misbehaviour, incapacity or incompetence, determined by a joint committee of the Houses of Parliament, composed as provided in subsection (2)*(a)*, and upon receipt of an address from both the National Assembly and the Senate requesting such removal.

(9) A Public Protector who is the subject of an investigation by the joint standing committee of Parliament in terms of subsection (8), may be suspended by the President pending a decision in such investigation.

111 Independence and Impartiality

(1) The Public Protector shall be independent and impartial and shall exercise and perform his or her powers and functions subject only to this Constitution and the law.

(2) The Public Protector and the persons appointed in terms of section 113(1) shall have such immunities and privileges as may be assigned to them by or under Act of Parliament for the purpose of ensuring the independent and impartial exercise and performance of their powers and functions.

(3) No organ of state and no member or employee of an organ of state nor any other person shall interfere with the Public Protector or a person appointed under section 113 in the exercise and performance of his or her powers and functions.

(4) All organs of the state shall accord such assistance as may be reasonably required for the protection of the independence, impartiality, dignity and effectiveness of the Public Protector in the exercise and performance of his or her powers and functions.

112 Powers, Functions and Duties

(1) The Public Protector shall, in addition to any powers and functions assigned to him or her by any law, be competent —

*(a)* to investigate, on his or her own initiative or on receipt of a complaint, any alleged —
  (i) maladministration in connection with the affairs of government at any level;
  (ii) abuse or unjustifiable exercise of power or unfair, capricious, discourteous or other improper conduct or undue delay by a person performing a public function;
  (iii) improper or dishonest act, or omission or corruption, with respect to public money;
  (iv) improper or unlawful enrichment, or the receipt of any improper advantage, or promise of such enrichment or advantage, by a person as a result of an act or omission in the public administration or in connection with the affairs of government at any level or of a person performing a public function; or
  (v) act or omission by a person in the employ of government at any level, or a person performing a public function, which result in unlawful or improper prejudice to any other person;

*(b)* to endeavour, in his or her sole discretion, to resolve any dispute or rectify any act or omission by —
  (i) mediation, conciliation or negotiation;
  (ii) advising, where necessary, any complainant regarding appropriate remedies; or
  (iii) any other means that may be expedient in the circumstances; or

*(c)* at any time prior to, during or after an investigation —
  (i) if he or she is of the opinion that the facts disclose the commission of an offence by any person, to bring the matter to the notice of the relevant authority charged with prosecutions; or
  (ii) if he or she deems it advisable, to refer any matter which has a bearing on an investigation, to the appropriate public body or authority affected by it or to make an appropriate recommendation regarding the redress of the prejudice resulting therefrom or make any

other appropriate recommendation he or she deems expedient to the affected public body or authority.

(2) Nothing in subsection (1) shall be construed as empowering the Public Protector to investigate the performance of judicial functions by any court of law.

(3) The Public Protector shall conduct an investigation under subsection (1) with due regard to the circumstances of each case, and shall for the purposes of such investigation, in addition to such powers as may be prescribed by law, but subject to the provisions of this Constitution and the law of privilege, be competent to —
 (a) direct any person to appear before him or her to give evidence or to produce any document in his or her possession or under his or her control which in the opinion of the Public Protector, has a bearing on the matter being inquired into, and may examine such person for that purpose; and
 (b) enter, or authorize another person to enter, any building or premises and there to make such investigation or inquiry as he or she may deem necessary, and seize anything on those premises which in his or her opinion has a bearing on the purpose of the investigation.

(4) The Public Protector or any member of his or her staff shall be competent, but not compellable, to answer questions in any proceedings in or before a court of law or any body or institution established by or under any law, in connection with any information which in the course of his or her investigation has come to his or her knowledge.

(5) Recourse to, or the exercise and performance of any powers and functions of, the Public Protector shall not oust the jurisdiction of a court of law to hear any matter or cause whatsoever.

(6) The Public Protector shall report in writing on his or her activities to Parliament at least once every year.

113 Staff and expenditure
(1) The Public Protector may appoint, on such terms and conditions of service as may be determined by or under a law, such persons as may be necessary for the discharge of the work of the office of the Public Protector.

(2) The Public Protector may delegate any of his or her powers or functions to persons referred to in subsection (1) subject to such conditions as shall be determined by or under a law.

(3) Expenditure incidental to the exercise and performance of the powers and functions of the Public Protector in terms of this Constitution or under any other law shall be defrayed from money appropriated by Parliament.

114 Provincial public protectors
(1) A provincial legislature may, subject to subsections (2) and (3), by law provide for the establishment, appointment, powers and functions of a provincial public protector and for matters in connection therewith.

(2) A provincial law referred to in subsection (1) shall not in any way derogate from the powers and functions of the Public Protector.

(3) A provincial public protector shall be appointed by the Premier of a province in consultation with the Public Protector, provided that the appointment shall be confirmed by resolution of a majority of at least two-thirds of all the members of the provincial legislature.

(4) A provincial public protector shall exercise and perform his or her powers and functions in consultation with the Public Protector, who shall have concurrent jurisdiction in the provinces.

These proposals reveal the emphasis which the main political parties and the negotiating structures have placed on the constitutional protection of administrative justice, but they also reveal inevitable differences of opinion.[29] That these differ-

---

[29] Some of which had become clear in 1991 in a published exchange of views on the meaning of the ANC proposals between Marcus & Davis 'Judicial Review under an ANC Government' (1991) 7 *SAJHR* 93 and Sachs 'From the Violable to the Inviolable' (1991) 7 *SAJHR* 98.

ences are strongly felt became clear during the discussions leading up to the compromise formulation of ss 23 and 24 at the MPNP, which occupied a considerable amount of time of the technical and *ad hoc* committees concerned with the protection of fundamental rights.[30] That they are also of considerable professional interest had been evident earlier in the year, when a gathering[31] of many of South Africa's leading academic and practising administrative lawyers, with the assistance of some foreign experts in the field, debated the desirability and formulation of a right to administrative justice. The outcome of the latter event has been reported as follows:[32]

'IV Constitutional entrenchment of a right to administrative justice

The workshop did not have sufficient time to debate a proposal to incorporate a clause in the Constitution to entrench the right to administrative justice, although the leading political parties and the South African Law Commission have included such clauses in their draft bills of rights, and several submissions on the desirability of constitutional entrenchment and on the terms of any such entrenchment were made during the process leading to the publication of this Declaration. In the light of these comments, the proposal rendered below was circulated among the participants by the workshop convenor. It met with wide-ranging fundamental criticisms. As a result, [it was] decided [that] the circulated clause, together with a synopsis of the principal objections, [should be published] as a touchstone for further debate and consideration.

(i) Draft judicial review clause:

*(a)* Anyone adversely affected by a decision made in the exercise of public power shall have the right to a decision which is lawful, procedurally fair and in accordance with the principles of equality and rationality, and shall have the right to seek redress from an independent court and any other body or tribunal established for that purpose.

*(b)* Subclause *(a)* shall not be construed as an exhaustive statement of the grounds upon which decisions made in the exercise of public power may be reviewed.

*(c)* In the exercise of the power of review, due weight shall also be given to the principles of good governance and the need to empower all public authorities to undertake programmes to remedy social, political and economic disadvantages.

(ii) Comments received:

*(a)* Some respondents felt strongly that judicial review of administrative acts or abstentions should derive from the terms of the Bill of Rights in general and needed no specific entrenchment.

*(b)* Others felt that the entrenchment of requirements for validity, such as those embodied in subclause *(a)*, would engender expansive judicial review at the expense of programmes for socio-economic reconstruction.

*(c)* Yet others felt that such an extension of the judicial power to review administrative acts or abstentions is indispensable for securing administrative justice. In particular, this last group felt that the effect of subclause *(b)* would be to render those requirements for validity not mentioned in subclause *(a)* susceptible to legislative ouster clauses, and that subclause *(c)* would destroy the entire basis of entrenchment by too easily granting immunity from review to officials ostensibly pursuing socio-economic reform programmes. One suggestion to resolve this last problem was the inclusion of the words 'legally prescribed' after 'to undertake' in subclause *(c)*.'

---

[30] A fact in the personal experience of the writer.
[31] A workshop on the theme 'Administrative Law for a Future South Africa', held from 10–13 February in Cape Town, a summary report of which is contained in *The Breakwater Declaration* 1993 (also published in (1993) 8 *SAPR/PL* 152–6). Many of the papers delivered on that occasion are published in Bennett et al (eds) *Administrative Law Reform* (1993).
[32] See *The Breakwater Declaration* part IV.

There can be little doubt that the enforcement of such rights to administrative justice will be much contested in the courts and is likely to be much used. It is precisely the fear that such rights could be misused to hold up vitally necessary social reform measures that has persuaded many lawyers to resist the constitutionalization of the standard of 'reasonableness' as a ground of review of administrative action, and has led to the formulation which introduces the notion of 'justifiability' in relation to the reasons given for an administrative act.[33] While only litigation will produce some guidelines as to how the courts are likely to interpret such rights, there is no doubt that even the compromise proposals adopted by the MPNP considerably strengthen the potential for achieving administrative accountability in the future.

The following aspects constitute particular progress: the constitutionalization of (i) procedural fairness, including the rules of natural justice in a wide range of circumstances; (ii) the giving of reasons for administrative action; and (iii) the virtual elimination of 'ouster clauses', which in the past served to limit the review jurisdiction of South African courts to some degree. These rights are naturally subject to possible legislative curtailment, in terms of the general limitations clause,[34] but it is unlikely that substantial undermining of these rights will satisfy the relatively strict requirements of that clause. This is particularly the case in the light of the guarantee of the right of access to court which is contained in Chapter 3.[35]

There are naturally several aspects of the formulations adopted in the interim Constitution which are capable of at least more than one interpretation and which may cause the courts some difficulties. Among these are the following:

(i) The various thresholds or gateways to review, with 'rights', 'legitimate expectations', and 'interests' being referred to, which may be 'affected' or 'threatened'. While such standards differ for each form of relief, such complexity should not be insurmountable.
(ii) The concept of lawfulness in s 24*(a)* is particularly susceptible of a wide or narrow interpretation, co-terminous with the notions of wide and narrow '*ultra vires*' — already familiar ideas in our courts;
(iii) The flexible meaning given to the content of procedural fairness, which will depend to a great degree on the circumstances of each case.
(iv) What will constitute the publicizing of reasons for administrative action, such as to deny the right to obtain such reasons independently under s 24*(c)*.
(v) Whether the justifiability of administrative action (which will inevitably lead the reviewing body to consider the *merits* of such action, thus breaching the theoretical barrier between appeal and review) under s 24*(d)* should be confined to those reasons already obtained pursuant to s 24*(c)*, an approach which would not only be unlikely but also wrong.[36]
(vi) The inter-relationship between the standing provisions of Chapter 3[37] and the various thresholds contained in s 24.[38]

---

[33] See s 24*(d)* of the Constitution.
[34] Section 33 of the Constitution.
[35] Section 22. This section, by its reference to 'another independent and impartial forum', admits of the possibility that administrative tribunals could be established on a wider basis.
[36] Especially as the right to justifiability is available once a right is threatened, a circumstance which does not entitle the aggrieved party to a right to reasons under s 24*(c)*.
[37] Contained in s 7(4).
[38] Many of these concerns are raised and discussed by Mureinik 'A Bridge to Where? Introducing the Interim Bill of Rights' (1994) 10 *SAJHR* 31 at 38–44 in his typically perceptive and incisive style.

As to the efficacy of the constitutional provisions relating to access to information and the Public Protector, there can be little doubt that much will depend upon the speedy enactment of detailed legislation in order to provide structures and substance to realize these formal grants of remedies. Indeed, a Parliamentary Act to give greater clarity to many of the questions just raised can also be expected in the sphere of administrative justice.

In sum therefore it can be stated safely that, despite the uncertainties and problems inherent in the constitutional provisions described, they mark a real measure of formal progress in comparison with the current state of judicial review of administrative action. More than this, it is submitted that they contain the seeds of a greater degree of administrative justice than exists in many a legal system, if sensitively and constructively nurtured. Ultimately of course judicial and legislative commitment will be the crucial determinants of success.

# PROCEDURAL RIGHTS

JOHN MILTON, MICHAEL COWLING, GRAHAM VAN DER LEEUW, MATHEW FRANCIS, PJ SCHWIKKARD & JAMES LUND

## 1 INTRODUCTION

The rights discussed in this chapter relate to that branch of national law which is termed 'procedural' law. Procedural law is distinguished from 'substantive' law, which is that part of the legal system concerned with the rights attributed to and legal duties imposed upon particular persons in particular circumstances. Procedural law sets out the legal machinery whereby rights and duties are declared or enforced; it is thus 'the machinery as distinguished from the product'.[1]

To illustrate: substantive law prohibits driving at a speed greater than the specified limit; procedural law determines how the traffic police are to set up speed traps and prove in court that a driver has exceeded the speed limit.

Procedure, in legal terms, thus denotes a process or series of actions which must be performed or followed in order to give effect to principles of the substantive law.

The characterization of legal procedure as essentially a mechanical process may seem to imply that procedure is not something concerned with substantive human and civil rights and therefore a subject for consideration in a Bill of Rights.

In fact the contrary is true. The course of a procedure may well have a decisive effect on the exercise or enjoyment of a human or civil right. Procedural rules, for instance, will prescribe how a trial is to be conducted. If those rules are not shaped by principles of fairness, the trial will not be a fair trial. In the result the systems of procedure of most civilized countries are constructed not only to be efficient and expeditious but according to standards of fairness and justice.

The proper observance of established and agreed procedures constitutes what is termed 'due process of law'. In most legal systems there is a constitutional right to due process of law. In other words, it is a basic civil right of the citizen that in judicial matters the authorities meticulously observe the due process of established legal procedure.

## 2 PROCEDURE IN CRIMINAL PROCEEDINGS

### 2.1 Philosophical background

Typically, criminal procedure comprises three more or less distinct stages:

- Investigation (wherein is involved: detention of persons for purposes of interrogation or examination; searching of person or property; seizure of property for evidential purposes; arrest of suspected offenders).
- Prosecution (wherein is involved the decision to prosecute the accused person and the formulation of the charges to be brought).

---

[1] *Poyser v Minors* (1881) 7 QBD 329 at 333.

- Adjudication (wherein is involved the trial of the charges against the accused; the receiving of evidence; and the imposition of punishment).

In some systems, notably that of the United States of America, the right to due process of law is seen as involving not only the observance of prescribed procedure but also the observance of these according to the sense of justice. Too great an emphasis on individual rights could compromise the ability of the state adequately to regulate its citizens in order to attain the minimum standards of protection and order necessary for peaceful co-existence.[2] On the other hand, placing undue emphasis on law and order at the expense of the protection of the fundamental human rights and freedoms of the individual will result in the system becoming oppressive.[3]

## 2.2 Comparative review

### 2.2.1 *Adversarial vs inquisitorial systems*

All modern systems of criminal procedure can be categorized as being either adversarial or inquisitorial. The adversarial model is typical of the Anglo-American jurisdictions, the inquisitorial model of the Continental systems.

In the inquisitorial model pre-trial investigations are conducted by a state-appointed judicial officer; the process of adjudication is conducted by a presiding judge, whose task it is to examine the evidence and interrogate the witnesses. The attorneys for the defence and the state play only a supplementary role.

In the adversarial model, by contrast, the evidence is gathered by non-judicial personnel and presented at a trial in which the prosecution and defence appear in a combatative confrontation, the judge playing a passive role in the nature of a neutral umpire ensuring that the parties observe the rules of evidence and procedure.[4]

There is a dispute as to which of these systems is more just and equitable.[5] However, as Dugard states, it is generally recognized today 'that an equitable system of criminal justice may be achieved under either system, provided that adequate procedural safeguards are afforded to the individual'.[6]

### 2.2.2 *Pre-trial procedures*

The investigation of crime is, in all legal systems, a function of the police. In Continental systems the magistracy, however, enjoys investigatory powers and has the power to instruct the police as regards investigation. In the adversarial system, by contrast, the judiciary has no investigatory role, this being left to the police, sometimes in consultation with the independent public prosecutor.

---

[2] Cf Paciocco 'The Development of Miranda-like Doctrines under the Charter' (1987) 19 *Ottawa LR* 49, who refers to 'the line between laudable protections for the rights of accused persons and self-destructive zealotry which causes criminals to run free, regardless of what they did, because of what may or may not have been done to them'.
[3] Burchell & Milton *Principles of Criminal Law* (1991) 66–7.
[4] Dugard *Introduction to Criminal Procedure* (1977) 1.
[5] For useful discussions of the issues in this debate, see Damaska 'Evidentiary Barriers to Conviction and Two Models of Criminal Procedure: A Comparative Study' (1972) 121 *U Pennsylvania LR* 506, especially at 583ff.
[6] Op cit (n 4) 117.

### 2.2.2.1 Search and seizure

In all systems it is recognized that the police exercise the powers of search of person or premises, the power to seize property uncovered in such searches, and the power to arrest persons whose possible guilt is indicated by the evidence discovered during the investigation.

The right to search, seize, and arrest is, however, not left entirely in the discretion of the police. In both inquisitorial and adversarial systems these powers may be exercised only with the authorization of a magistrate. It is, however, universally recognized that there may be circumstances in which the police may act without prior magisterial authorization. In inquisitorial systems, where the magistracy has greater authority over the police investigation, the control of the police discretion is less stringent. In adversarial systems the determination of when police may exercise discretionary powers of search, seizure, and arrest are more closely scrutinized by the judiciary. In these systems arrests effected in excess of the powers allowed give rise to civil liability, while evidence obtained by impermissible searches and seizures may[7] be held to be inadmissable.

Pre-trial procedures constitute an important consideration in the formulation of a Bill of Rights for two main reasons: in the first place, whereas it is conceded that law enforcement officials may require special powers in order to conduct criminal investigations, such powers will inevitably constitute a violation of the ordinary fundamental rights and freedoms of the individual.[8] Secondly, there exists the risk that abuses at the pre-trial stage could well taint the fairness of the subsequent criminal trial.

Thus many Bills of Rights provide protection against the improper exercise of pre-trial investigative powers. The US Constitution, by the Fourth Amendment, confers on individuals the right 'to be secure in their persons, houses, papers, and effects, against unreasonable searches and seizures'. Section 8 of the Canadian Charter of Fundamental Rights and Freedoms guarantees the 'right to be secure against unreasonable search and seizure'. The courts of both these countries have interpreted the search and seizure provisions as protecting not merely rights to private property but also the citizen's right to privacy.[9] Thus search and seizure in public places can also be unlawful and hence both the Canadian Charter and the US Fourth Amendment guarantee a broad and general right to be secure from unreasonable search and seizure. In similar vein art 13 of the Constitution of the Republic of Namibia recognizes the right to privacy[10] and expressly provides[11] that all searches must be judicially authorized unless delay in obtaining such authorization will prejudice the objects of the search.[12]

---

[7] But not necessarily. See below, 4.2.

[8] The powers of search and arrest constitute also 'the first and most effective weapons in the arsenal of every arbitrary government. Human personality deteriorates and self-reliance disappears where homes, persons and possessions are subject at any hour to unheralded search and seizure by the police': *Brinegar v US* 338 US 160 (1949).

[9] This was first enunciated in the US in *Kurz v US* 88 SCt 507 (1967) and followed by the Canadian Supreme Court in *Southam Inc v Hunter* (1984) 2 SCR 145.

[10] Article 13(1).

[11] Article 13(2).

[12] On the matter of reliance upon evidence obtained through an illegal search or seizure, see below, 4.2.

## 2.2.2.2 Arrest

Arrest and detention of persons suspected of having committed a crime clearly constitute a drastic inroad into the fundamental right of freedom of the person. The power of arrest is vested in the police as a necessary adjunct of their role of maintaining law and order and investigating suspected criminal offences. Lest this power be abused at the expense of the citizen's right to personal freedom, most systems restrict the police power of arrest by requiring that, as a general rule, police may not arrest without the warrant of a judicial officer, which shall not be granted without there being sufficient cause shown to justify the infringement of the liberty of the subject.

The Fourth Amendment of the US Constitution provides that 'no warrants shall issue, but upon probable cause, supported by oath or affirmation', and 'particularly describing ... the persons ... to be seized'. The Namibian Constitution states that no person shall be subject to 'arbitrary arrest or detention'.[13] It does not elaborate on what is meant by 'arbitrary', but it should be presumed that this should not only apply to arrests that are not authorized but should also cover cases that may be legally authorized but fail to comply with basic due process standards.

## 2.2.2.3 Interrogation

A fundamental civil right, particularly under adversarial systems, is the privilege against self-incrimination or, as it is also known, the right to silence. However, such right would be rendered meaningless if a suspect were to incriminate himself prior to the trial as a result of extensive interrogation at the hands of law enforcement officials, resulting in statements made by him during such interrogation being used at the subsequent trial. The US Supreme Court, in the landmark case of *Miranda v Arizona*,[14] held that a suspect must be informed of his right to silence as well as the concomitant right to be advised by legal counsel. Failure to so would render any admission or confession obtained during the interrogation inadmissible.

The Canadian Charter, however, does not contain any express right to silence.[15] But s 10*(b)* recognizes the right to be informed of the right to counsel and it has been held that failure to warn a suspect of such right could result in the exclusion of any statement made by the suspect.[16] The Namibian Constitution protects suspects against self-incrimination at the trial stage only,[17] although any evidence obtained contrary to art 8(2)*(b)* (which prohibits torture and cruel, inhuman, and degrading treatment) is inadmissible.[18]

### 2.2.3 *The prosecution*

In every legal system the power to prosecute offenders is vested in the state. From a constitutional point of view the important question that arises is whether the

---

[13] Article 11(1).
[14] 384 US 436 (1966).
[15] Sections 11*(c)* and 13 prevent self-incrimination, but only during formal proceedings, and hence not at the pre-trial stage.
[16] *R v Collins* (1937) 1 SCR 265.
[17] In terms of art 12(1)*(f)*.
[18] See below, 4.2.

discretion to prosecute should be vested in the prosecutor alone. In the US, for instance, there exists an almost absolute discretion in the public prosecutor whether or not to pursue a charge. This absolute power has been criticized on the ground that it results in arbitrary and unequal treatment of offenders.

In other systems the discretion to prosecute is confined, either by statutory obligations to do so (as under art 152 of the German *Strafprozessordnung*) or by review of the prosecutor's decision not to prosecute (as provided for by arts 171–175 of the German *Strafprozessordnung*) or, as in the English law, by recognizing a right in private citizens to institute a 'private' prosecution.

### 2.2.4 *Adjudication*

In principle every legal system seeks to provide the accused with a fair trial. What constitutes the elements of a fair trial is the subject of the debate regarding the merits of the adversarial and inquisitorial systems.

In the US the Fifth Amendment establishes the adversarial nature of the criminal process by preserving and enforcing the right to silence throughout the entire trial. This also applies at the pre-trial stage.[19] It even extends to the court being prevented from drawing an adverse inference from an accused's failure to testify when there is a strong case against him.[20] But the basic provision concerning the right to a fair trial is contained in the Fourteenth Amendment, which guarantees that no person shall be deprived of life, liberty, or property without 'due process of law' within the context of 'equal protection of the laws'. These provisions have provided the springboard for the development of fair procedures which, to take but a single example, have extended to the right of an indigent accused to be provided with a legal representative in serious cases.[21]

In terms of the Canadian Charter the general due process provision is contained in s 7, which holds that everyone has the 'right to life, liberty and security of the person and the right not to be deprived thereof except in accordance with the principles of fundamental justice'. As is the case with the Fifth and Fourteenth Amendment of the US Constitution this section provides the broad base from which fair trial procedures have been developed.[22]

In contrast, the Namibian Constitution does not contain an all-embracing provision regarding fair trial procedures. Article 7 merely confirms the rule of law by requiring that no one shall be deprived of personal liberty except according to procedures established by law. Thus it is necessary to have to resort to specific provisions contained in art 12 in order to ascertain fair trial procedures guaranteed in the Constitution. Thus art 12(1)(*a*) provides for a fair and public hearing by an independent, impartial, and competent court. In addition other tenets of fair trial procedures are set out in this article,[23] including the right not to testify.[24] At this stage it is not possible to determine whether the courts will develop the concept of a 'fair and public hearing' to cover other aspects of a fair trial not specified in art 12.

---

[19] See above, 2.2.2.3.
[20] *Griffin v California* 380 US 609 (1965).
[21] *Gideon v Wainwright* 372 US 335 (1963).
[22] Friedland 'Criminal Justice and the Charter' (1983) 13 *Manitoba LJ* 549 at 555.
[23] For example, the presumption of innocence (art 12(1)(*d*)) and *audi alteram partem* (art 12(1)(*e*)).
[24] Article 13(1)(*f*).

## 2.3 South Africa

### 2.3.1 *Introduction*

The South African criminal procedure system is derived from the common law, as amplified, modified, and supplemented by extensive statutory enactment, presently contained in the Criminal Procedure Act 51 of 1977. The basic system is derived from English law and thus is adversarial in nature and character. However, over the years the South African system of criminal procedure, particularly as regards pre-trial procedures, has acquired certain distinctive features of inquisitorial systems.[25] In addition the Constitution of the Republic of South Africa[26] contains a chapter that sets out certain fundamental rights guaranteed by the Constitution, for example the rights to life, liberty, equality, privacy, etc. Many of these rights will impact upon the existing rules of criminal procedure and hence will be dealt with below.

### 2.3.2 *Pre-trial procedures*

#### 2.3.2.1 Search and seizure

Search and seizure is currently regulated by chapter 2 of the Criminal Procedure Act, which employs the standard of reasonable belief that a particular article located on certain premises is connected with the commission of an offence. The test is therefore objective and thus the courts have been empowered to set the standard. The general requirement is that information justifying the suspicion should be placed before a justice of the peace, justifying the latter to issue a search warrant authorizing a particular search and seizure operation.[27] However, provision is also made[28] for the conducting of search and seizure operations without a warrant in circumstances where a warrant would have been granted, but the delay in obtaining one would have defeated the objects of the search.[29]

Section 10 of the Constitution preserves the right to dignity, whereas s 13 prescribes that everyone is entitled to 'the right to his or her personal privacy, which shall include the right not to be subject to searches of his or her person, home or property, the seizure of private possessions or the violation of private communications'. On the face of it this appears to be an absolute prohibition, which would mean that it would have the effect of overriding the provisions contained in chapter 2 of the Criminal Procedure Act providing for search and seizure operations in certain defined circumstances. This in turn would deprive the police of an essential tool and technique of the criminal investigative process, viz the power to search persons and premises and to seize suspect articles.

However, the right to privacy as enunciated in s 13 must be read in conjunction with any permissible limitations on this right in terms of s 33(1) of the Constitution. The latter provides that rights entrenched in the Constitution may be limited by law of general application, provided that such limitation is reasonable, justifiable in an

---

[25] Identified and discussed below, 2.3.4.3.
[26] Act 200 of 1993.
[27] In terms of s 21 of the Act.
[28] Ibid.
[29] *LSD Ltd v Vachell* 1918 WLD 127.

open and democratic society based on freedom and equality, and does not negate the essential content of the basic right to privacy. This limitation recognizes the basic right of search and seizure, but it will have to be carefully weighed against the entrenched right to privacy.

Therefore the courts will closely have to scrutinize any search and seizure action in order to ensure that it complies with the above standard. This applies particularly in the case of searches without a warrant, but will also entail courts having to assess the decision to issue a search warrant in the first place. The courts will also have to ensure that authorized searches are conducted in a decent and orderly manner, although it is doubtful that the Bill of Rights takes the matter any further than the standards set out in s 29 of the Criminal Procedure Act, which stipulates that searches shall be conducted with strict regard to decency and order.

An example of a legislative provision that is unlikely to comply with the standards contained in the Bill of Rights is s 25 of the Criminal Procedure Act. The section empowers a police official to enter any premises where he/she suspects on any grounds that any offence has been committed or is being planned at a particular place. Dugard has referred to this section as forming part of the drastic process[30] and it is submitted that the courts are likely to strike down a provision of this nature on the basis that it inherently violates the standard of privacy contained in the Bill of Rights.

It is submitted that these provisions confer upon the courts sufficient flexibility to devise a standard that is capable of striking a balance between the protection of the rights of individual privacy, on the one hand, without undermining the forces of law and order, on the other. The fact that the Bill of Rights requires that all invasions of privacy can only be limited by law of general application prevents law enforcement authorities from embarking on unauthorized operations even where other conditions (such as reasonable cause, justifiability in an open and democratic society, and necessity)[31] exist. This is important because there must be legislation regulating such issues as the procedure for the issuing and execution of search warrants and the circumstances under which searches without a warrant may take place. Section 35(2) prescribes that any existing law which *prima facie* exceeds the limits of s 13 shall only be invalid to the extent that it is not capable of a more restricted interpretation that preserves the essence of the said right.

### 2.3.2.2 Arrest and detention

The Criminal Procedure Act makes provision for the arrest of suspects with or without a warrant.[32] Detention following arrest is regulated by s 50 of the Act, which stipulates that any arrested person should be charged and brought to court within forty-eight hours. The detention without trial provisions that once were a feature of South African procedure[33] have been repealed, with the exception of s 29 of the Internal Security Act, which makes provision for detention without trial for a period of ten days. In addition the Criminal Law Second Amendment Act of 1992[34] and

---

[30] Op cit (n 4) 65.
[31] As prescribed by s 33(1).
[32] See ss 43 and 40 respectively.
[33] For example, ss 28 and 29 of the Internal Security Act 74 of 1982.
[34] Act 126 of 1992. See s 23.

the Drugs and Drug Trafficking Act 1992[35] allow the detention of persons believed to be withholding information concerning offences relating, respectively, to certain weaponry or drugs.

At the outset the Bill of Rights sets broad parameters in the form of recognition of the right to respect for and protection of individual dignity.[36] In more specific terms provision is made for every person to enjoy the 'right to freedom and security of the person which shall include the right not to be detained without trial'.[37]

As in the case of search and seizure the above provisions must be interpreted in the light of the limitations permitted in terms of s 33. This means that the right to freedom and security of person in terms of s 11(1) may be limited provided such limitation is reasonable,[38] justifiable in an open and democratic society based on freedom and equality,[39] and does not negate the essential content of the right.[40] In addition s 33(1)*(bb)* expressly stipulates that any limitation to this right must be necessary.

It is submitted that ss 10 and 11 do not preclude the basic right to arrest persons, provided such arrest complies with the requirements of reasonableness and necessity contained in s 33(1). Both the ANC and the previous government drafts contained detailed lists of exceptions to the right to freedom and security of the persons, e g detention of recalcitrant witnesses for the prevention of the spreading of infectious diseases and the detention of mentally disabled people, alcoholics and drug addicts, and illegal immigrants. The current Bill of Rights has not adopted this approach. This means that the courts are empowered in general terms to scrutinize any decisions to arrest in order to ensure compliance with those standards of due process.

As far as the justification of arrest is concerned the previous government's draft Bill of Rights provided for arrest and detention on the basis of a reasonable suspicion that the detainee has committed an offence.[41] The ANC draft goes further in this respect by stipulating that no persons shall be arrested or detained for any purpose other than that of bring them to trial on a criminal charge.[42] Although the current Bill of Rights is silent on this issue, it is submitted that reasonable suspicion of the commission of an alleged offence should provide the basis for arrest in terms of the bill. This is supported by s 25(2), which sets out certain rights for any person arrested 'for the alleged commission of an offence'.

Any person who has been arrested is entitled to be promptly informed in a language which he or she understands of the reason for the arrest and detention[43] as well as of the right to remain silent.[44] Section 25(2)*(b)* confirms the forty-eight-hour rule in terms of which an accused must be charged before a court before the expiry of forty-eight hours.[45] An arrested person is also entitled to be informed of the reason

---

[35] Act 140 of 1992. See s 12.
[36] Section 10.
[37] Section 11(1).
[38] Section 33(1)*(a)*(i).
[39] Section 33(1)*(a)*(ii).
[40] Section 33(1)*(b)*.
[41] Section 23(2)*(a)*.
[42] Article 2(10).
[43] Section 25(1)*(a)*.
[44] Section 25(2)*(a)*.
[45] This accords with s 50 of the Criminal Procedure Act 51 of 1977.

for any further detention. It is submitted that the entrenchment of the basic right of freedom and security of the person,[46] read in conjunction with the further rights of an arrestee[47] and the limitations prescribed in s 33, set out basic standards of due process that prohibit arbitrary arrest and instead confine arrest and detention within the parameters of acceptable standards of individual liberty, while at the same time creating a balance with the necessary requirements of proper law enforcement. To this end it would appear that these provisions will override the decision in *Duncan v Minister of Law and Order*,[48] where the court expanded the purpose of arrest to include mere investigation in order to confirm a suspicion that did not exist at the time.

### 2.3.2.3 Detention without trial

Although the Bill of Rights guarantees freedom and security of the person, it is silent on the question of detention without trial under normal circumstances of the operation of law. As pointed out above, present legislation makes provision for two types of detention without trial: for purposes of interrogation concerning acts of terrorism and related offences,[49] and unlawful possession of certain weaponry.[50]

Both these provisions contain certain safeguards:[51] the decision to detain is objectively justicable (i e the commissioned police officer must have reason to believe); the initial detention period is ten days and can only be extended for further ten-day periods at the instance of a Supreme Court judge where the detainee (or his or her legal representative) will be given an opportunity to submit reasons in writing as to why the detention should not be extended.[52] In the event of detention being extended by a judge the detainee is entitled to be furnished with the grounds of arrest[53] as well as the reason why further detention is considered necessary.[54] Access to and visits by district surgeons and magistrates are also required.[55] As far as the Criminal Law Second Amendment Act is concerned, a person can only be detained once a magistrate has agreed to issue a warrant for the arrest and detention of the detainee on the request of the prosecutor on grounds of information upon oath.[56] Thereafter the detention must be confirmed by a magistrate within forty-eight hours and thereafter every ten days;[57] a detainee may make representation in writing to a magistrate[58] and the maximum period of detention shall not exceed thirty days,[59] but the courts will have to determine whether these sufficiently ameliorate the

---

[46] In terms of s 11(1) of the Constitution.
[47] In terms of s 25.
[48] 1984 (3) SA 460 (T) at 466.
[49] In terms of s 29 of the Internal Security Act 74 of 1982.
[50] In terms of s 23 of the Criminal Law Second Amendment Act 126 of 1992.
[51] For example, under the Internal Security Act.
[52] In terms of s 29(3)*(d)*(ii).
[53] Section 29(3)*(a)*(i).
[54] Section 29(3)*(a)*(ii).
[55] Section 29(9).
[56] Section 23(1) of the Criminal Law Second Amendment Act 126 of 1992.
[57] Section 23(3)*(a)*.
[58] Section 23(3)*(c)*.
[59] Section 23(4).

harshness of detention without trial in order to satisfy the basic standards of due process inherent in the Bill of Rights.

On the other hand, the Bill of Rights does make provision for the declaration of a state of emergency, which in turn allows for the suspension of the right to freedom and security of the person to the extent necessary to restore peace and order.[60] Express provision is made for detention without trial[61] subject to certain conditions such as judicial review of the decision to detain within ten days after detention,[62] as well as a right to further review on application after the expiry of the ten-day period.[63] In addition a detainee is granted access to court[64] as well as a legal representative[65] and a medical practitioner.[66] Finally, the state is obliged to furnish written reasons justifying the detention at least two days before any review hearing.[67] It is submitted that these safeguards must set the basic minimum standards for all legislation that provides for detention without trial and hence the Internal Security and Criminal Law Second Amendment Acts should be tested against it.

To this end there are certain basic safeguards set out in s 25(1) of the Constitution that guarantee a basic standard of treatment in respect of all detainees.[68] In this respect the following rights are applicable: to be informed of the reason for the detention;[69] to be detained under conditions consonant with human dignity, which includes adequate nutrition, reading material, and medical treatment;[70] to legal representation which will be funded by the state where substantial injustice would otherwise result;[71] access to family members, religious counsellors, and medical practitioners of choice;[72] and the right of access to the courts for purposes of challenging the detention.[73]

### 2.3.2.4 Bail

Bail is a mechanism for restoring the liberty of a detained person, while meeting the interests of the administration of justice by ensuring that the accused should stand trial.[74]

The South African courts have adopted the approach that they do not enjoy any inherent jurisdiction to grant bail[75] and hence any power to allow bail must be derived from the statutory authority conferred by the Criminal Procedure Act 1977.[76] Although s 60(1) of the Act confers upon an accused the right to apply for

---

[60] Section 34(4) of the Constitution.
[61] In terms of s 34(6).
[62] Section 34(6)(c)(i).
[63] Section 34(6)(c)(ii).
[64] Section 34(6)(d).
[65] Section 34(6)(e).
[66] Section 34(6)(f).
[67] Section 34(6)(g).
[68] This includes arrestees who are detained pending trial, detainees who are detained for other purposes, and sentenced prisoners.
[69] Section 25(1)(a).
[70] Section 25(1)(b).
[71] Section 25(1)(c).
[72] Section 25(1)(d).
[73] Section 25(1)(e).
[74] Du Toit et al *Commentary on the Criminal Procedure Act* 9-1.
[75] See *Beehari v Attorney-General, Natal* 1956 (2) SA 59 (N); *S v Kaplan* 1967 (1) SA 634 (T) at 636A–B.
[76] *Chunilall v Attorney-General, Natal* 1979 (1) SA 236 (D).

bail, it is left to him/her to initiate the application. The onus is on the applicant to show cause on a balance of probabilities,[77] a rule which can work considerable hardships on accused persons.[78] The Bill of Rights guarantees the right of every arrested person 'to be released from detention with or without bail, unless the interests of justice otherwise require'.[79] This appears to infer that the onus rests on the state to justify denial of bail. This is an important improvement on the Criminal Procedure Act because it is no longer incumbent upon the accused to bring an application. In terms of the Criminal Procedure Act the presiding officer does not bear any responsibility to initiate a bail application and should an accused fail to do, so that is the end of the matter.[80]

It is submitted that s 25(2)(d) places a duty on judicial officers to inquire into the question of the accused's release and the onus will rest on prosecutors to establish grounds whereby the interests of justice require that an accused should not be released. It is further submitted that the test as to whether the interests of justice require that an accused should not be released embraces the existing recognized principles governing the decision to grant or refuse bail, viz the risk concerning whether the accused will stand trial; interference with state witnesses or the police investigation; the commission of further offences by the accused; and whether or not the accused's release will endanger the maintenance of law and order, public safety, or national security.[81]

Finally, there are several other aspects concerning bail that will be strengthened by the entrenchment of a right to bail in a Bill of Rights. Thus courts must ensure that proper bail inquiries are held and that presiding officers do not simply accept the recommendations of public prosecutors or investigating officers. Courts must also ensure that the amount of bail set is not excessive.[82] A final consideration is that a Bill of Rights underscores the fact that the granting of bail is essentially a judicial function and hence statutory provisions which empower the executive to usurp this function[83] will be struck down by the courts.[84]

### 2.3.3 *Prosecution*

The principle of compulsory prosecution does not apply in the South African criminal justice system. Attorneys-General and the public prosecutors who are controlled by them have a discretion whether or not to prosecute.[85] Neither the executive nor the judiciary can interfere in the exercise of this discretion. Courts have refused to order an Attorney-General to prosecute[86] or to interdict an Attorney-General from prosecuting where he has decided to do so.[87]

---

[77] Van der Berg *Bail —A Practioner's Guide* 11.
[78] See Cowling 'Bail and the Search for a New Theoretical Approach' (1991) 4 *SACJ* 65.
[79] Section 25(2)(d).
[80] Cowling op cit (n 78) 66.
[81] Du Toit et al op cit (n 74) 9-8Bff.
[82] This was considered in *S v Mohamed* 1977 (2) SA 531 (A).
[83] For example, s 61 of the Criminal Procedure Act empowers the Attorney-General to prevent the granting of bail in certain circumstances. In addition s 21 of the Criminal Law Second Amendment Act provides that no one charged with a special offence shall be released on bail unless authorized in writing by the Attorney-General.
[84] See *Smith v Attorney-General, Bophuthatswana* 1984 (1) SA 196 (B) for an example of the relationship between a Bill of Rights and this provision.
[85] Attorney-General Act 92 of 1992.
[86] *Gillingham v Attorney-General* 1909 TS 572.
[87] *Allen v Attorney-General* 1936 CPD 302.

Private prosecutions are permitted in certain limited circumstances.[88] It is permitted in order to avoid illegal retaliation by an individual who feels aggrieved by an Attorney-General's decision not to prosecute. A private prosecutor must show a peculiar and substantial interest in the issue of the trial.[89]

### 2.3.4 Adjudication

#### 2.3.4.1 Fair trial

The extent to which the procedure of criminal trials in South Africa can be described as fair is difficult to gauge. The courts have tended to scrutinize criminal trials in order to ensure that there has not been a departure from those formalities, rules, and principles of procedure required by law.[90] However, not every irregularity is fatal and proceedings will be set aside only where there has been a failure of justice which in turn results in the accused suffering prejudice in the sense that he would not have been convicted in the absence of the irregularity.[91] However, if the irregularity impairs an aspect of the procedures which is fundamental to a proper administration of justice, the proceedings as a whole are tainted and hence will be set aside irrespective of the likelihood of subsequent conviction.[92] Examples of this type of failure of justice have occurred where the impartiality of the presiding officer is questioned;[93] the ability of the accused to follow the proceedings is in doubt;[94] and where the accused's right to arrange legal representation is compromised.[95] This must all be viewed in the context of the broad principles of due process that confer upon an accused the right to be fully informed of the charge against him as well as the right to present his case subject to the privilege against self-incrimination.

Section 25(3) of the Bill of Rights entrenches the right to a fair trial. This is followed by a number of specific rules which provide such basic guarantees as the right to a public trial within a reasonable time[96] and to be informed with sufficient particularity of the charge.[97] The bill also entrenches the fundamental essentials of the adversarial system, such as the presumption of innocence and the right to silence.[98] What is of interest in this respect is the express reference of the right to remain silent during plea proceedings. It is submitted that the courts will have to scrutinize judicial interrogation in terms of s 115 of the Criminal Procedure Act in order to ensure that this right is properly protected. This is especially in view of the fact that the right to silence embraces the right not to be involuntarily questioned.[99] On this basis it can be argued that this provision will override s 20(4)*(b)*(i) of the Criminal Law Second Amendment Act,[100] which allows a judicial officer to draw

---

[88] Criminal Procedure Act 51 of 1977 s 7.
[89] Section 7(1)*(a)*.
[90] *S v Xaba* 1983 (3) SA 717 (A) at 728D.
[91] *S v Davids; S v Dladla* 1989 (4) SA 172 (N) at 193.
[92] Ibid.
[93] *S v Sallem* 1987 (4) SA 772 (A).
[94] *Pachourie v Additional Magistrate, Ladysmith, & another* 1978 (3) SA 986 (N).
[95] *S v Mkhize* 1978 (3) SA 1067 (T).
[96] Section 25(3)*(a)*.
[97] Section 25(3)*(b)*.
[98] In terms of s 25(3)*(c)*.
[99] See *R v Camane* 1925 AD 570.
[100] Act 126 of 1992.

an adverse inference from an accused's failure to indicate the basis of his/her defence on pleading not guilty. In keeping with the basic characteristics of the adversarial model an accused cannot be compelled to testify against himself or herself[101] and is also guaranteed the basic right to adduce and challenge evidence.

Otherwise certain rights — such as the right to legal representation;[102] non-retroactivity;[103] *autrefois acquit* and *convict*;[104] and appeal and review[105] — are also guaranteed. Finally, an accused is also entitled to be tried in a language which he or she understands[106] and to be sentenced within a reasonable time after conviction.[107]

It is submitted that entrenching the right to a fair trial in a Bill of Rights will have the effect of strengthening the hand of the courts in enforcing standards of due process and fairness. Although the latter have not been expressly conferred with powers of setting aside proceedings on the basis of failure to comply with the said basic due process standards, a strong case can be made in favour of courts impliedly enjoying such powers. This means that it would not be necessary for the courts to concern themselves with the issue of whether an accused has been prejudiced in the sense that he would probably not have been convicted but for the irregularity. This is especially so in light of the fact that the Bill of Rights expressly enables individuals to apply to the courts for appropriate relief in the case of any infringement of any of the entrenched rights contained in the bill.

Therefore the fact that the Bill of Rights expressly lists certain fundamental rights serves to indicate that the courts are empowered to intervene and to set aside legal proceedings that do not conform to the standard set by the rules. It must also be borne in mind that the list is not exhaustive. Section 25(3) refers to the general right to a fair trial, and the rights thereafter listed[108] are included. This does not exclude any other rights that are inherent in the concept of a fair trial and therefore the above list must be regarded as merely providing examples by way of illustration.

It is submitted that in general terms the provisions contained in the Bill of Rights concerning the actual conduct of the trial do not take the matter much further than the existing position. However, the guaranteeing of such rights as the right to silence, the presumption of innocence, non-compellability as a witness in order to prevent involuntary self-incrimination, and the right to adduce and challenge evidence bring about constitutional confirmation of the adversarial nature of the South African criminal procedure system. On the other hand, the entrenchment of all of the rights contained in s 25(3) will enable the courts to overcome a major weakness in the South African criminal procedure system: the fact that 'drastic' provisions undermining various aspects of the right to a fair trial are enacted in other legislation.[109] These provisions would be struck down by the courts to the extent that they conflict with a Bill of Rights.

---

[101] In terms of s 25(3)(*d*) of the Constitution.
[102] In terms of s 25(3)(*e*). This is dealt with more fully below, 2.3.4.2.
[103] Section 25(3)(*f*).
[104] Section 25(3)(*g*).
[105] Section 25(3)(*h*).
[106] Section 25(3)(*i*).
[107] Section 25(3)(*j*).
[108] i e, s 25(3)(*a*)–(*j*).
[109] The Internal Security Act 74 of 1982, the Abuse of Dependence-producing Substances and Rehabilitation Centres Act 41 of 1971, and the Criminal Law Second Amendment Act 126 of 1992 serve as examples in this regard.

## 2.3.4.2 The right to legal representation

It cannot be denied that in many situations the absence of legal representation in a criminal trial can cast serious doubt as to whether such trial was fair and in accordance with due process.[110]

In South African law s 73 of the Criminal Procedure Act provides for an 'entitlement' — rather than a right — to legal representation after arrest[111] and during criminal proceedings,[112] which imposes upon a presiding judicial officer the obligation to inform an accused of such 'right'[113] and of the various institutions (such as the Legal Aid Board) that may be approached for legal assistance.[114] In addition the presiding officer is also obliged to give an accused a reasonable opportunity to obtain legal assistance.[115] The above provisions are obviously necessary to give real effect to the entitlement and have already been recognized by the courts when interpreting s 73 of the Criminal Procedure Act. It has been held that it was desirable for presiding judicial officers to inquire whether accused persons wished to engage a legal representative,[116] while in *S v Radebe; S v Mbonani*[117] it was held that in certain circumstances (i e complexity of charge, seriousness of the case, etc) a failure to inform an accused of his right to legal representation could be construed as a failure of justice. This could also apply in appropriate circumstances to advising the accused that he is entitled to apply to the Legal Aid Board for assistance. In addition it was held in *S v Davids; S v Dladla*[118] that once the question of legal representation had been canvassed by the presiding judicial officer the accused should be 'afforded every reasonable opportunity to arrange for his representation'.

The debate on the question of whether an accused who is not represented at his/her trial has been given a fair trial was initiated by the courts when the Natal Provincial Division held in *S v Khanyile*[119] that in certain serious cases of a complex nature where it appears that, taking account of the accused's intellectual capacity and educational level, he is not able to properly defend himself, such trial will miscarry on the basis that it is 'intolerably unfair'.[120] *Khanyile* was overruled by the Appellate Division in *S v Rudman & another; S v Mthwana*,[121] but for reasons which were pragmatic rather than principled.[122]

The right to a legal representative is recognized in the following situations:

---

[110] This issue has been discussed above, 2.2.2.3 in an international and comparative context.
[111] Section 73(1).
[112] Section 73(2).
[113] *S v Radebe; S v Mbonani* 1988 (1) SA 191 (T).
[114] In terms of s 26(1)(g)(ii).
[115] In terms of s 26(1)(g)(iii).
[116] See e g *S v Mthethwa; S v Khanyile* 1978 (2) SA 773 (N).
[117] Supra at 196F–I.
[118] Supra at 194I.
[119] 1988 (3) SA 795 (N) *per* Didcott J.
[120] The actual provisions of this test were formulated by Didcott J in the subsequent case of *S v Davids; S v Dladla* (supra) at 185B–C.
[121] 1992 (1) SA 343 (A).
[122] At present it is generally recognized that leaving unskilled and incompetent persons to defend themselves in criminal trials is manifestly unfair. But the Appellate Division is not prepared to hold that such unfairness is so fundamental as to result in a failure of justice. The reasoning in the *Rudman* case indicates that the courts are not averse to the concept of a broad right to legal representation (cf at 392G), but rather that the conferral of such a right is, in the present constitutional set-up, something that cannot be properly undertaken by the courts.

1.  Persons who have been detained.[123] This includes sentenced prisoners, but, from the perspective of the criminal process, it should apply immediately upon arrest. Although s 25(2), which expressly confers certain specific rights on an accused upon arrest, does not list the right to legal representation, these latter rights are in addition to those set out in s 25(1) that are applicable to detainees.
2.  Accused persons during the course of a criminal trial.[124]
3.  Persons detained under a state of emergency.[125]

As far as situations 1 and 2 above are concerned, such persons are entitled to the practitioner of their choice. In addition this right is more than a mere entitlement (as was the case in s 73 of the Criminal Procedure Act) because the Bill of Rights further stipulates that where substantial injustice would otherwise result such persons would be provided with legal representation at state expense.

It is submitted that the test for determining whether or not substantial injustices would result could well be modelled along the lines of that formulated by Didcott J in *S v Davids; S v Dladla*.[126] Thus, if it were to be shown that an indigent accused was confronted with a serious case that was complex in nature while at the same time lacking the intellectual capacity or educational level to properly defend him- or herself, this would amount to a substantial injustice if such person were not provided with a legal practitioner at state expense.

Section 25(1)*(c)* and (3)*(e)* also provides for a detained, arrested, or accused person to be promptly informed of such right. This entrenches the principle established in *S v Radebe; S v Mbonani*,[127] where it was held the failure to inform an accused of this right could result in a failure of justice. What is of importance in this respect is that s 25(1)*(c)* expressly refers to detainees (which, it is submitted, includes persons who have been arrested for the alleged commission of an offence[128]). This means that all arrestees must be informed of this right to legal representation as soon as is reasonably possible after arrest.

Until now this issue has only been considered once the accused has been brought before the court. It is submitted that entrenching the right to be informed of the right to legal representation immediately upon arrest is to be welcomed because many irregularities can occur at this stage prior to the accused being brought before the court for trial. This is especially in view of the fact that the South African criminal procedure system has certain inquisitorial elements (such as the fact that pre-trial confessions, admissions, and pointings-out are admissible at a subsequent trial and that an accused may be subjected to inquisitorial-style interrogation on a plea of not guilty in order to indicate the basis of his defence). Therefore it can safely be said that the right to legal representation should operate immediately upon arrest, and this is what s 25(1)*(c)* purports to do. This includes the provision of such a representative at state expense should substantial injustice otherwise result.

---

[123] Section 25(1)*(c)* of the Constitution.
[124] Section 25(3)*(e)*.
[125] Section 34(6)*(d)*.
[126] Supra.
[127] Supra.
[128] This is based on the fact that s 25(2) confers rights on arrested persons that are additional to those contained in s 25(1) and that apply in respect of detained persons.

### 2.3.4.3 Inquisitorial features

Although the form of trial provided for by the South African criminal procedure is based on the adversarial model, there has been a significant assimilation of inquisitorial-type procedures into the trial process. These include judicial interrogation of the accused at the plea stage (whereby a presiding judicial officer is authorized to question an accused at the outset of a trial in order to induce him to indicate the basis of his defence).[129] A further instance of this tendency is provided by the Criminal Law Second Amendment Act of 1992. This Act, in s 18, enables the Attorney-General to issue a certificate designating certain offences to be 'special offences'. Such offences must entail murder, robbery with aggravating circumstances, violence, or intimidation. The presiding officer in any trial concerning a 'special offence' is empowered to enter into the inquisitorial mode of questioning the accused who pleads not guilty as to the basis of his/her defence and to draw an unfavourable inference from any failure to give an explanation. So too the fact that confessions,[130] admissions,[131] and pointing-out[132] are admissible against an accused in a subsequent trial undermines drastically the accused's right to silence and so diminishes the adversarial nature of this stage of the process.

While it is clear that the prosecution may benefit from these inquisitorial elements in the process, the accused could well be doubly disadvantaged by being subjected to the worst of both worlds. This is because, although the inquisitorial system generally allows for some form of judicial interrogation during the pre-trial stage of the investigation, it is undertaken at the instance of a legally trained magistrate. Thereafter all relevant information (including exculpatory evidence) is compiled in a dossier and placed before the presiding judge. The fact that the latter is empowered to play an active role in the proceedings and generally conducts all the questioning of witnesses means that he can come to the assistance of the unskilled accused. By contrast, in South Africa an accused (particularly if he/she is unrepresented and unskilled) is not so protected and is left at the mercy of police interrogators who, during the pretrial stage, are empowered to undermine his/her right to silence by obtaining confessions, admissions, and pointing-out from him/her. Thus the safeguards present in the procedure of judicial interrogation in the inquisitorial system do not exist.

This inquisitorial process continues right up to the plea stage of the trial where the accused is subjected to further questioning — this time by the presiding judicial officer at the trial — and can be induced to make all kinds of damaging admissions. Thereafter the accused is further disadvantaged as a result of the fact that the trial is now converted into an adversarial process whereby the presiding officer suddenly becomes a passive umpire who is not empowered to come to the assistance of the accused. This is especially important with the cross-examination of state witnesses.

In this regard s 25(2)(a) of the Constitution expressly refers to the right of an arrested person not only to remain silent but also to be informed of the consequences of making any statement. In addition s 25(3) confers upon every accused person the

---

[129] In terms of s 115(2) of the Criminal Procedure Act.
[130] In terms of s 217 of the Criminal Procedure Act.
[131] In terms of s 219A of the Act.
[132] In terms of s 218 of the Act.

# PROCEDURAL RIGHTS

right to a fair trial, while s 25(3)(c) entrenches the right to be presumed innocent and to remain silent during plea proceedings and trial and not to testify during trial. This is reinforced by a provision to the effect that an accused is not a compellable witness against him- or herself.[133]

These provisions clearly reinforce the adversarial system and would presumably result in the striking down of s 115(2) of the Criminal Procedure Act as well as s 20 of the Criminal Law Second Amendment Act. In the case of the former persistent silence in the face of interrogation by the presiding judicial officer could well result in an adverse inference being drawn. In the latter Act the court is required to draw an adverse inference in the case of persistent silence, which, it is submitted, is in direct conflict with the entrenched right to silence contained in the Bill of Rights.

## 3 PROCEDURE IN CIVIL PROCEEDINGS

### 3.1 Philosophical background

In some areas of the law the need to constitutionalize important rules and principles is immediately apparent and long-recognized: for example, civil liberties, criminal procedure, and evidence. Civil procedure issues, by contrast, while they have been constitutionalized to some extent in some jurisdictions,[134] have typically not been seen as constitutionally central. This may be because there is less scope for state coercion of the individual in this realm, with the traditional Bill of Rights being directed primarily at protecting individuals against the might of the state.

In the adversarial model of civil procedure the legal process was seen as being in the hands of the litigants, who controlled the proceedings. The role of the state was that of adjudicator and, if necessary, enforcer (state force being available to vindicate the interests of the successful litigant rather than the state itself). The prevailing liberal notion of a Bill of Rights as a shield against the might of the state therefore had little obvious application to civil procedure. This model of a Bill of Rights meant that the economically advantaged had access to the courts, whilst the indigent were often effectively denied justice. However, even on this narrow view of a Bill of Rights as a shield there is a strong case for constitutionalizing the right to basic fairness in civil matters.

Increasingly, however, it is apparent that a Bill of Rights that operates only as a shield, and not also as a sword, may perpetuate social inequality and injustice. It is in this context that the access to justice movement, which has been gaining momentum over time, is critically important to the practical implementation of the South African Bill of Rights.[135]

The idea of access to justice holds that it is not enough to provide formal access to the courts in the way that the traditional liberal notion of a Bill of Rights would, at best, seek to do; unless the economic, organizational, and educational barriers to access to the courts are also addressed formal access to justice is a hollow, if not cynical, gesture. The theory of a Bill of Rights as a sword gives rise to a strong claim

---

[133] In terms of s 25(3)(d).
[134] See below, 3.2.
[135] See e g Cappelletti (ed) *Access to Justice* (a series published under the auspices of the Florence Access-To-Justice Project). A succinct overview is provided by Cappelletti 'Access to Justice as a Theoretical Approach to Law and a Practical Programme for Reform' (1992) 109 *SALJ* 22.

for the constitutionalization of rights that will ensure substantive, and not merely formal, access to justice. This will in some areas mean dealing with second- and third-generation rights, although not all proposed mechanisms for ensuring substantive access to justice involve such rights.

## 3.2 Comparative international situation

The Bill of Rights in the US Constitution and subsequent Amendments (Amendments I–X) have a significant impact on the law of civil procedure. The most important provisions are the due process clauses in the Fifth and Fourteenth Amendments, which are applicable to the federal government and the several states, respectively. The Fifth Amendment provides that no person shall 'be deprived of life, liberty, or property, without due process of law'; the Fourteenth Amendment is to similar effect. In the civil procedure context the due process clauses require that legal proceedings be conducted in accordance with a minimum standard of procedural fairness or justice.[136] A judgment obtained against a person without compliance with due process is unconstitutional and liable to be set aside. Thus, for example, a judgment will not be binding against a party to whom adequate notice was not given. The underlying due process values of fairness and justice are well illustrated by the rules relating to the exercise of jurisdiction by courts over non-residents, i e the circumstances in which a person may be forced to defend legal proceedings in a court situated somewhere other than where he or she resides. The US Supreme Court has held that a court may exercise jurisdiction over a non-resident only if doing so satisfies 'traditional notions of fair play and substantial justice'.[137] In the Bill of Rights itself only the Seventh Amendment exclusively addresses a civil procedure issue; it preserves the right to a jury trial in suits at common law (as opposed to those in equity).

The Namibian Constitution expressly guarantees the right to a fair trial by stating that '[i]n the determination of their civil rights and obligations . . . all persons shall be entitled to a fair and public hearing by an independent, impartial and competent Court or Tribunal established by law . . '.[138] The German Basic Law, by contrast, does not make any provision for a fair trial; it simply states that in the courts everyone shall be entitled to a hearing in accordance with the law.[139]

The idea of substantive access to justice is a relatively recent one and finds no expression, in the civil context at least, in the US Constitution. The Sixth Amendment confers on an indigent accused the right to state-funded counsel in certain cases,[140] but there is no such general right in civil matters. However, the Namibian Constitution, being a more recent document, does constitutionalize an important aspect of substantive access to justice. It requires the state actively to promote and maintain the welfare of the people by adopting policies aimed at achieving stated objectives. One of these policy objectives is 'a legal system . . . [that seeks] to

---

[136] The due process clauses have an impact that reaches far wider than the realm of civil procedure. See e g Tribe *American Constitutional Law* 2 ed (1988) 629–32 and 663–768 (procedural due process), 1673–87 (structural due process), and 553–86 and 1302–1435 (substantive due process).

[137] *International Shoe Co v State of Washington, Office of Unemployment Compensation and Placement* 326 US 310, 316 (1945).

[138] Article 12(1)(*a*).

[139] See Hirte 'Access to the Courts for Indigent Persons: A Comparative Analysis of the Legal Framework in the United Kingdom, United States and Germany' in (1991) 40 *ICLQ* 91 at 110–20.

[140] See e g *Gideon v Wainwright* (supra).

promote justice on the basis of equal opportunity by providing free legal aid in defined cases with due regard to the resources of the State ...'.[141] The German Basic Law does not provide for substantive access to justice, but significant extra-constitutional provision has been made in this regard. Indigent persons have access to legal aid in civil cases.[142] In addition state-funded projects, such as the City of Hamburg's Public Legal Advice and Mediation Centre, seek to make justice accessible to all.[143] Similarly the simplified Stuttgart Model of civil procedure, used in some types of cases, facilitates access to justice.[144] Thus, while substantive access to justice is not constitutionalized in Germany, substantial extra-constitutional provision exists.

## 3.3 South Africa

The Constitution confers on every South African citizen a wide range of rights hitherto not enjoyed by him or her. However, these rights will be no more than illusory if the rank and file have no means of approaching courts to enforce their rights. Within the context of civil litigation the Constitution has considerably widened the access to formal justice for potential litigants. These measures include (1) extra-judicial avenues for the protection of fundamental rights; (2) procedural fairness in trials; and (3) a liberalization of the rules relating to *locus standi* (legal standing). Each measure is discussed in turn.

### 3.3.1 *Extra-judicial protection*

The Constitution introduces mechanisms which of their own accord are designed to protect and enforce rights guaranteed under the Constitution. These mechanisms are the office of the Public Protector and the establishment of a Human Rights Commission.

#### 3.3.1.1 The Public Protector

Section 110 makes provision for the establishment of the office of Public Protector at a national level, whilst s 114 empowers the Premier of a province to appoint a provincial public protector. The Public Protector will essentially perform the role of an ombudsman,[145] an office which has long been recognized as a popular extra-judicial antidote to administrative excesses.[146] High status is accorded to the office of Public Protector and the Constitution contains provisions regarding the

---

[141] See art 95*(h)*.
[142] See Kaplan, Von Mehren & Schaefer 'Phases of German Civil Procedure' (1958) 71 *Harvard LR* 1193 (Part I) and 1443 (Part II) for a somewhat dated, but otherwise useful, account of civil procedure in the Federal Republic of Germany. State legal aid is discussed at 1467–70. A more recent discussion may be found in Baumgartel 'Germany' in Zemans (ed) *Perspectives on Legal Aid* (1979) 150.
[143] See Falke, Bierbrauer & Koch 'Legal Advice and the Non-Judicial Settlement of Disputes: A Case Study of the Public Legal Advice and Mediation Centre in the City of Hamburg' in Cappelletti *Access to Justice* vol II 103. Similar centres exist in Lübeck, Berlin, and Bremen. See Baumgartel op cit (n 142) 154–6.
[144] See Bender 'The Stuttgart Model' in Cappelletti *Access to Justice* vol II 431.
[145] The term 'public protector' is certainly more user-friendly than that of 'ombudsman'.
[146] See e g Boulle, Harris & Hoexter *Constitutional and Administrative Law* (1989) 209 and Baxter *Administrative Law* (1984) 287–92.

independence of this office and the prohibition on interference with the Public Protector's duties which are similar to those regarding the judiciary.[147]

The Public Protector may either on his or her own initiative, or upon receipt of a complaint, investigate any allegation of maladministration against any government agency. It has been granted wide powers to fulfil its functions and one cannot gainsay the fact that this office could well provide citizens with a relatively accessible and cheap means of securing redress against the executive.

### 3.3.1.2   The Human Rights Commission

Section 115 makes provision for the establishment of a Human Rights Commission which is entrusted with the task of promoting and protecting fundamental rights. The Commission may on its own initiative, or on receipt of a complaint, investigate any alleged violation of fundamental rights. Apart from its watchdog role, the Commission has one obvious benefit to litigants: it is empowered to provide financial assistance to the complainant and any other affected person to enable them to seek redress in an appropriate adjudicatory forum.[148]

### 3.3.2   *Procedural fairness in civil trials*

The Constitution provides expressly, and in some detail, for a fair trial in respect of criminal matters.[149] The rights of civil litigants, on the other hand, are limited to a guarantee of minimum standards of procedural fairness. In terms of s 8, read with s 22, every person is not only entitled to have justiciable disputes settled by an independent and impartial court of law (or similar forum) but is guaranteed the right to equal treatment by, and protection of, the courts.

Independence and impartiality are fundamental to the judicial process. This aspect of a fair hearing is underwritten by the fact that the judiciary is institutionally independent from the other branches of government.

The equality aspect of a fair hearing should ideally ensure that a litigant's right and capacity to participate fully in the trial is not dependent on irrelevant criteria such as race, gender, language, or social and economic status.[150] This entails inter alia that a litigant will have an equal opportunity to put his or her case to the court. A litigant is to some extent assisted by s 107, which provides that a party to litigation is entitled to use the language of his or her choice and to insist that proceedings be interpreted in a language understood by the litigant. Traditionally the practice has been for civil litigants to provide an interpreter at their own expense.

It is arguable, however, that the guarantee of equality in judicial proceedings is seriously compromised by the fact that indigent persons are not guaranteed the services of a legal representative. Given the adversarial nature of civil proceedings in South Africa, an indigent representing him- or herself can hardly be said to be on an equal footing in the court room with an opponent who has the financial resources to engage the services of a legal representative. Ironically those litigants who are detained pursuant to civil causes may have a far stronger constitutional right to being

---

[147] Cf s 111(1), (2) and (3) with s 96(2) and (3).
[148] Section 116(3) of the Constitution.
[149] Section 25.
[150] See 'The Right to a Fair Hearing' in Robertson (ed) *Human Rights for South Africans* (1990) 75.

granted state assistance for obtaining the services of a legal representative. Section 25(1) provides that every person, including a sentenced prisoner, shall have the right to consult with a legal practitioner and to be provided with the services of a legal practitioner by the state 'where substantial injustice would otherwise result'. This provision is typically directed in the first instance at the detention of criminals, suspected criminal offenders, and preventative or interrogative detention. However, the language used would permit its application to those detained pursuant to civil proceedings such as arrests to found jurisdiction and arrests *tanquam suspectus de fuga*. There is, moreover, no reason in principle why all detainees should not enjoy the protection of the law.

### 3.3.3 *Locus standi and substantive justice*

Traditionally the South African law of *locus standi* has been relatively restrictive in that the courts have required a personal, sufficient, and direct interest before a litigant is given standing in court. This has posed fewer problems in matters of an essentially private-law nature than in the realm of public law. In public law, e g administrative law, the interest of a litigant may well be shared with the public at large; the litigant may therefore be unable to meet the personal interest requirement.[151] Similarly, representative organizations have on occasion been denied standing on the basis that their interest, as opposed to that of their members, is insufficiently direct.[152] There are of course cases that have taken a contrary view,[153] but the issue has remained a potentially troublesome one.

These particular standing problems raise acute concern in the context of enforcing some types of social rights which have been included in the Constitution. The enforcement of, for example, those rights relating to the environment[154] will typically involve issues affecting the public at large, making it potentially difficult for a litigant to establish a personal interest. These issues are also such that in many cases they will be the concern of public interest organizations rather than individuals. This will raise the question of whether the interest of the organization is sufficiently direct to meet the standing requirement.[155]

The Constitution has anticipated these potential problems by adopting and entrenching a very liberalized notion of legal standing: in the process the *actio popularis* has been resuscitated and class actions introduced into South African law. Section 7 provides that the following persons may also bring an action for the protection and enforcement of any fundamental rights recognized by the Constitution:

(a) an association acting in the interests of its members;
(b) an individual acting on behalf of someone who is not in a position to seek such relief in his or her own name;

---

[151] The decisions in *Bamford v Minister of Community Development and State Auxiliary Services* 1981 (3) SA 1054 (C) and, more recently, in *Jacobs en 'n ander v Waks en andere* 1992 (1) SA 521 (A) go some way to meeting this concern.

[152] *South African Optometric Association v Frames Distributors (Pty) Ltd t/a Frames Unlimited* 1985 (3) SA 100 (O); *Noll v Alberton Frames (Pty) Ltd* 1989 (1) SA 730 (T).

[153] *Transvaal Indian Congress v Land Tenure Advisory Board* 1954 (2) SA 506 (T); *Ex parte Natal Bottle Store-Keeping and Off-Sales Licensees' Association* 1962 (4) SA 273 (D).

[154] Section 29 provides: 'Every person shall have the right to an environment which is not detrimental to his or her health or well-being'.

[155] This problem has arisen in the US in *Sierra Club v Morton* 405 US 727 (1972).

*(c)* a person acting as a member or in the interest of a group or class of persons; and
*(d)* a person acting in the public interest.

This more generous approach to legal standing will greatly facilitate the enforcement of rights on behalf of those persons who are perhaps ignorant of their rights or do not have the capacity, financial or otherwise, to bring an action on their own.

### 3.3.3.1 Class actions

It is of course not only legal access to the courts that is in issue here. In most cases the barrier to access will be financial rather than legal. South Africa's legal aid budget is notoriously small and is unable adequately to meet the present demands made upon it, much less those that may arise out of a Bill of Rights.[156] The financial restrictions on a future South African state are likely to be very real and it is naïve to expect that the state will be able to provide comprehensive legal aid. The practice of charitable representation by legal practitioners is important, but also of inherently limited impact.[157]

A more feasible way of facilitating financial access to the courts could be by way of class actions which, as noted above, have now been constitutionalized. A class action, in which a named plaintiff brings legal proceedings on behalf of a wide class of persons, may spread the costs of the action throughout the class. However, if class actions are to enhance financial access to the South African courts on constitutional matters, the courts must be empowered to award damages for breach of constitutional rights. The financial impetus to pursue class actions lies ultimately in the damages awarded to a successful class; without damages the financial obstacles, while diminished, remain and are compounded by logistical problems concerning payment of fees. Moreover, if one is to look to the damages ultimately paid to the class to meet the costs of the action, then logically no fee should be payable if the action fails, i e a contingency fee. In South Africa lawyers may not as a general rule charge contingency fees; however, if the class action is to facilitate access to the courts, this will need to change.

### 3.3.3.2 *Amicus curiae* briefs

A policy, rule, or law allowing interested individuals and organizations to present legal arguments in cases to which they are not parties would further promote substantive access to justice. This practice is widespread in the US; the written arguments submitted by such parties are known as *amicus curiae* briefs.[158] Access

---

[156] See generally McQuoid-Mason *An Outline of Legal Aid in South Africa* (1982).

[157] Chapter V.

[158] The term '*amicus curiae*' literally means 'friend of the court'. In South Africa the term is frequently used to refer to an advocate who represents a party to an action at the request of the court. See e g *S v Ward* 1992 (1) SA 271 (B) (Attorney-General appointed as an *amicus curiae* to an indigent mother in a maintenance action) and *S v Koopman* 1991 (1) SA 474 (NC) (counsel appointed as an *amicus curiae* to an indigent accused in a criminal trial). In the sense in which the term is used in the text, *amicus curiae* bears the meaning ascribed to it in *Black's Law Dictionary* 5 ed (1979) 75: 'A person with strong interest in or views on the subject matter of an action [who] may petition the court for permission to file a brief, ostensibly on behalf of a party but actually to suggest a rationale consistent with its own views. Such *amicus curiae* briefs are commonly filed in appeals concerning matters of broad public interest; for example civil rights cases.' *Amici curiae* in this meaning of the term are also known in South African law. See e g *In re Rome* 1991 (3) SA 291 (A) (Pretoria Bar Council represented by an *amicus curiae* in an

to the courts is enhanced when representative organizations, while not parties to an action, are permitted to place their arguments before the court on matters of constitutional importance. In this way no individual is saddled with the prohibitive costs of an action and even the representative organization does not have to meet the costs of a full-blown legal proceeding. Moreover, it is a well-established rule of South African law that costs may not be awarded against an *amicus curiae*.[159] A practice whereby the courts allow the widespread use of *amicus curiae* briefs in South Africa in matters of constitutional importance would therefore greatly enhance access to the courts.

## 3.4 Conclusion

It is submitted, in conclusion, that the Constitution in South Africa has entrenched certain key rights relating to civil procedure. The right of formal access to the courts and the right to a fair trial, *albeit* limited to procedural fairness, in civil matters have been included in express terms in the Constitution. The issue of substantive access to justice will, however, have to be dealt with in a different way. The right to legal aid in civil matters, for example, raises difficult questions concerning the allocation of scarce resources and it is probable that measures such as class actions and *amicus curiae* briefs will have to be used in the interim. Nevertheless one should not lose sight of the fact that legislative reform guaranteeing the right of all indigent persons to legal representation is necessary if the capacity of such persons to enforce their rights is not to be dependent on what they earn.

## 4 EVIDENCE IN JUDICIAL PROCEEDINGS

### 4.1 Philosophical background

The adjectival nature of the law of evidence has been identified in the following way: '[S]ubstantive law lays down what has to be proved in any given issue and by whom, the rules of evidence relate to the manner of its proof.'[160]

The basic function of the rules of evidence is to assist a court in reaching the most 'correct' decision based on relevant and reliable evidence. The law of evidence, however, pertains to both civil and criminal matters. In its criminal relation the law of evidence has acquired another function: that of ensuring procedural fairness and justice are complied with.

In this regard, as in other facets of procedural law relating to the criminal justice process, it is necessary to balance the 'interests of society at large in knowing that those persons who have committed crimes will be convicted on the presentation of all relevant evidence, and on the other hand the need to protect individuals against the improper gathering of evidence'.[161]

---

application by a person for admission as an advocate) and *Hurter v Hough* 1989 (3) SA 545 (C) (Law Society of the Cape represented by an *amicus curiae* in an application, brought by a private party, for the removal of an attorney from the roll).

[159] See *Ex parte De Vos* 1953 (2) SA 642 (SR).

[160] In *Tregea v Godart* 1939 AD 16.

[161] Skeen 'The Admissibility of Improperly Obtained Evidence in Criminal Trials' (1988) 3 *SACJ* 389. Skeen uses the term 'improperly obtained evidence' interchangeably with 'illegally obtained evidenced'. However, he notes the following distinctions between the terms: 'Technically illegally obtained evidence is evidence gathered

It is not only the 'due process' provisions in a Bill of Rights that influence the application of the rules of evidence. An 'equality clause' may require the amendment of existing evidentiary rules to ensure that they are not in effect discriminatory.

## 4.2 Comparative international situation

Almost every legal system has had to confront the problem whether evidence that has been obtained in ways that violate the civil or human rights of the subject may nevertheless be admitted at the trial.

Traditionally English courts have applied the 'reliability' principle in determining admissibility in this context. If the illegally obtained evidence is considered to be reliable, it will be admitted. Thus involuntary confessions are excluded because they are regarded as unreliable. However, if the police obtain physical evidence as a consequence of information contained in the involuntary confession, that evidence will be admissible on the basis of its reliability.[162] The harshness of this crime-control-orientated approach has been ameliorated by the existence of a judicial discretion to exclude evidence where the Judges Rules[163] have been breached or where it would be unfair to the accused.[164] Recent cases would appear to indicate that prevailing judicial attitudes increasingly regard the discretion as an instrument to deter improper police behaviour.[165]

The courts in the US have provided one response to the problem by stringently excluding illegally or improperly obtained evidence. In both the federal[166] and state[167] courts evidence discovered as a result of a violation of the constitutional rights of an accused may not be admitted into evidence.

However, the rigid exclusionary approach of US courts has been the subject of much internal debate.[168] This approach has not found a following in other jurisdictions, where a more flexible discretionary approach is preferred.[169]

Although constitutional entrenchment has gone a long way in upholding the ideal

---

as a result of a gross violation of a suspect's rights which may lay the perpetrator of the State open to liability, whereas improperly obtained evidence may result from some deceit which may be unfair or improper without bearing the additional taint of being illegal.' When the term 'improperly obtained' evidence is used in the following pages, it is intended to include 'illegally obtained' evidence.

[162] In the US such evidence would be inadmissible 'as fruit of the poisonous tree'.

[163] Administrative directions formulated by the judges upholding some of the rudimentary notions of due process. The original Judges Rules have been replaced by a statutory and much more detailed Code of Practice relating to the detention, treatment, and questioning of persons by police officers.

[164] This discretion was initially developed through the case law (see *Kuruma, Son of Kainu v R* [1955] AC 197, [1955] 1 All ER 236; *R v Sang* [1980] AC 402 (HL), [1979] 2 All ER 1222). Later it was given statutory effect by s 78 of the Police and Criminal Evidence Act 1984.

[165] Dennis 'Confessions: Evidentiary Issues and their Solutions' (Unpublished paper delivered at a conference of the Society for the Reform of Criminal Law *Reform of Evidence*, Canada 1992).

[166] *Weeks v US* 232 US 383 (1914).

[167] *Mapp v Ohio* 367 US 643 (1961). The holding in *Weeks* was extended to the states on the basis that the Fourteenth Amendment prohibits the states from abridging 'the privileges or immunities of citizens of the United States', from depriving any person of life, liberty, or property without due process and from denying any person the equal protection of the laws. These provisions can receive content from the Bill of Rights and this 'mechanism' has been used to apply the Fourth and Fifth Amendments to the states effectively.

[168] The following questions are central to the debate: 'Is the rule constitutionally required or a creature of judicial creation? Is the primary purpose of the rule deterrence or police misconduct or the maintenance of judicial integrity?' See Kaczynski 'Admissibility of Illegally Obtained Evidence: A Comparative Study' in Redden (ed) *Modern Legal Systems Cyclopedia* vol 1A at 1A.80.18.

[169] For example, in Scotland, Ireland, and Australia improperly obtained evidence is excluded in the absence of an excuse or condonation. See Skeen op cit (n 161).

of due process in the US, the effectiveness of the constitutional provisions have depended to a large part on judicial interpretation.

In contrast, the Namibian Constitution of 1990 does not rely on judicial interpretation for the implementation of the exclusionary rule. Article 12*(f)* provides:

> 'No persons shall be compelled to give testimony against themselves or their spouses . . . and no Court shall admit in evidence against such persons testimony which has been obtained from such persons in violation of Article 8(2)*(b)*[170] hereof.'

The Namibian exclusionary rule applies only to evidence obtained in violation of art 8(2)*(b)*.[171] It would therefore appear that other improperly obtained evidence (e g evidence obtained as a consequence of an unauthorized search in breach of art 13) would be admissible.[172]

In many respects the Namibian provisions are very similar to art 136a of the German Code of Criminal Procedure,[173] which contains the following provision:

> '(i) The freedom of determination and manifestation of the defendant's will shall not be impaired through ill-treatment, fatigue, subjugating to bodily trespass, application of drugs, through torturing, deceiving or hypnosis . . . Threats with any measure outlawed . . . and the promise of any advantage not provided for by the law is prohibited.
> (ii) . . . Statements obtained in violation of this prohibition must not be used in evidence, not even with the consent of the accused.'

The German Code highlights the dangers of specificity in drafting. The detailed nature of art 136a.i has enabled the courts to hold that a statement made by an accused while illegally detained need not necessarily be excluded.[174]

It is submitted that the Namibian courts would be free to take a broader approach than the German courts because of the generality of the words 'cruel, inhuman or degrading treatment or punishment'.

The Namibian High Court has also suggested that the rules of evidence may be found wanting when tested against the equality clause in the Constitution. The case in point is *S v D*,[175] in which Frank J held that the cautionary rule applicable to sexual offences could well be in violation of the equality clause. The efficacy of this argument will depend on the court's approach in interpreting the equality clause. To date there are no reported cases dealing directly with the Namibian 'equality' clause.[176]

## 4.3 South Africa

### 4.3.1 *The exclusionary rule*

A general principle of excluding improperly obtained evidence is not recognized in

---

[170] The allusion is to evidence obtained by torture or other 'cruel, inhuman or degrading treatment'. See art 8(2)*(b)*.
[171] Article 8(2)*(b)* provides: 'No person shall be subject to torture or to cruel, inhuman or degrading treatment or punishment.'
[172] See *S v Minnies* 1991 (3) SA 364 (Nm), the only reported case to date dealing with these provisions.
[173] Germany, being a civil-law system, is inquisitorial in nature. The traditional approach of civil-law systems was that prosecutorial and judicial control over the police was an effective deterrent to improper policing, and that consequently a general exclusionary rule was not necessary.
[174] See Redden op cit (n 168) at 1A.80.60.
[175] 1992 (1) SACR (Nm).
[176] Article 10.

South African law, the traditional approach of the courts being that all evidence that is relevant is admissible, no matter how it was obtained.

This position is somewhat ameliorated by a discretion to exclude evidence which would operate unfairly against the accused.[177] However, this discretion has tended to be interpreted restrictively so as to apply only where its prejudicial effect outweighs its probative value.[178]

On the other hand, there are several *dicta* that reflect the view that to condone improper police conduct is not in the interests of the proper administration of justice. These cases go no further than to uphold the privilege against self-incrimination.[179] Despite these developments it is doubtful whether at common law our courts have a discretion to exclude evidence on the basis of fairness.[180]

Unfortunately, although the new Constitution upholds many of the ideals of due process, there is no specific provision for the exclusion of evidence obtained in breach of the Constitution.[181] This is a surprising omission since the majority of draft Bills of Rights[182] presented during the negotiation period included such exclusionary clauses. The previous government and KwaZulu Bills were silent on this issue. However, the draft Bills of the African National Congress, the South African Law Commission, and the *Charter for Social Justice* all contained prohibitions on the admission of improperly obtained evidence.

These Bills reflected three different approaches: an absolute exclusion, a discretionary exclusion, and no exclusionary rule at all. The divergent approaches illustrate the tension between the ideals of the crime control model and due process. Those in favour of the exclusionary rule argue that 'the primary function or goal of a criminal justice system is not merely to secure the conviction of an accused, but to ensure that a conviction takes place in terms of a procedure which duly and properly acknowledges the rights of an accused at every critical moment during the pre-trial, trial and post-trial stages'.[183] If it is accepted that there must be certain checks and balances to ensure that the standards for the fair administration of justice are upheld, the question that follows is whether there should be a strict exclusionary rule.

In the US serious doubts have been cast on the efficacy of the strict exclusionary rule. Its critics argue that its deterrent value is limited in that it will not prevent

---

[177] *Kuruma, Son of Kainu v R* (supra); *S v Mushimba* 1977 (2) SA 829 (A).

[178] See *R v Sang* (supra); *S v Maphalele* 1982 (4) SA 505 (A); *S v Mushimba* (supra); *S v Mbatha* 1985 (2) SA 26 (D); *S v Ramgobin* 1986 (4) SA 117 (N); *S v Holshausen* 1983 (2) SA 699 (D). Note that prejudice in this context usually refers to 'procedural prejudice' such as delay, expense, confusion of issues, the trying of collateral matters, etc. However, in *Shell SA (Edms) Bpk v Voorsitter Dorperaad van die Oranje Vrystaat* 1992 (1) SA 906 (O) the court held that it has a discretion to exclude evidence obtained by improper means and that this discretion applied in both civil and criminal matters.

[179] See e g *R v Maleleke* 1925 TPD 491; *S v Nel* 1987 (4) SA 950 (W); *S v Sheehama* 1991 (2) SA 860 (A); *S v Khumalo* 1992 (2) SACR 411 (N).

[180] See Hoffmann & Zeffertt *The South African Law of Evidence* 4 ed 513 for general discussion.

[181] The only specified mechanism for relief is to be found in s 7(4)(*a*), which provides that '[w]hen an infringement of or threat to any right entrenched in this Chapter is alleged, any person referred to in paragraph (*b*) shall be entitled to apply to a competent court of law for appropriate relief, which may include a declaration of rights'.

[182] The following proposed Bills of Rights have been considered: *ANC Draft Bill of Rights* (preliminary revised version February 1993); the *South African Government Proposals on a Charter of Fundamental Rights* 2 February 1993; SA Law Commission *Project 58: Group and Human Rights* Interim Report (1991); *The Constitution of the State of KwaZulu/Natal* December 1992; Corder et al *A Charter for Social Justice* December 1992: hereinafter referred to as 'the Bills'.

[183] SA Law Commission op cit (n 182) 7.324 at 392.

'improper' police behaviour carried out in good faith. Furthermore, its application frequently frustrates an accurate determination of the facts by courts of law. Consequently perpetrators of serious crimes are acquitted in circumstances which appear senseless to the public. These considerations have led a number of jurisdictions to adopt a policy of discretionary exclusion.[184]

Another question that arises is whether the exclusion of such evidence should be presumed and then included as an exception. Conversely, should the evidence be included and then exceptionally excluded? It is submitted that if the integrity of the Constitution is to be preserved, any evidence obtained in violation of rights guaranteed in Chapter 3 must be excluded subject to a discretion to admit it according to the dictates of public policy. The approach of the courts to improperly obtained evidence will be determined by a process of judicial interpretation. Section 35 sets guidelines for the interpretation of its provisions and requires the promotion of 'the values which underlie an open and democratic society based on freedom and equality'. The exclusion of evidence obtained in breach of the Constitution would accord with the broad purpose of these principles. In the absence of a discretion to exclude improperly obtained evidence the accused has no effective remedy availabe to him/her. Civil actions are inappropriate in the absence of quantifiable damages and the high financial costs involved mean that in most instances they remain a theoretical remedy. Reliance on internal police disciplinary measures has an extremely poor history, few policeman being prepared to approach the prosecution of their fellow colleagues with any rigour.

### 4.3.2 The presumption of innocence[185]

The adversary system is traditionally seen as an essential component of the due process ideal.[186] Deeply embedded in this concept is the presumption of innocence. This presumption is not a prediction of outcome, but a directive to law enforcement officers as to the way in which they are to treat accused persons.

The presumption of innocence in the South African common law has been interpreted as a general rule of policy in terms of which the prosecution is required to bear the onus of proof on all issues.[187] An exception to the rule can be found in the requirement that an accused bears the onus when a defence of insanity is raised. There are also numerous statutory exceptions to the rule.

Section 25 of the Constitution entrenches the right to remain silent. However, the courts will have to determine the extent to which this right prohibits the use of presumptions to assist the prosecution. The standpoint of the South African Law Commission[188] is that statutory presumptions 'which place an onus of proof on an accused person are without foundation and should be done away with'. The Commission said nothing about the only common-law exception to the presumption of innocence, that the accused bears the onus with regard to the defence of insanity.

---

[184] For example, Scotland, Ireland, and Australia.
[185] Purists may define rules such as those pertaining to the presumption of innocence and the onus of proof as being rules of procedure or substantive law and not evidence. They are included in the present discussion simply because of the fact that they are traditionally dealt with in evidence texts.
[186] Packer *The Limits of the Criminal Sanction* 157.
[187] Hoffmann & Zeffertt op cit (n 180) 284ff; *R v Britz* 1949 (3) SA 292 (A).
[188] *Project 58: Group and Human Rights* Interim Report (1991) 390.

On the other hand, the authors of *A Charter for Social Justice*[189] state that the prohibition is not absolute and 'that certain presumptions may well be regarded as constitutional (when successful prosecutions would be impossible without their use) in terms of a general circumscription clause'.

Section 35(2) of the Constitution provides:

'No law which limits any of the rights entrenched in this Chapter, shall be constitutionally invalid solely by reason of the fact that the wording used *prima facie* exceeds the limits imposed in this Chapter, provided such a law is reasonably capable of a more restricted interpretation which does not exceed such limits, in which event such law shall be construed as having a meaning in accordance with the said more restricted interpretation.'

It would thus appear possible that the courts may in the future take the approach that where a presumption affects only a evidentiary burden and not the overall burden of proof it will not be viewed as falling foul of the Constitution.

### 4.3.3 Privilege

#### 4.3.3.1 The privilege against self-incrimination

Provisions upholding the privilege against self-incrimination[190] (or the right to remain silent) are to be found in both the Criminal Procedure Act[191] and the Civil Proceedings Evidence Act.[192]

The statutory provisions regulating the admissibility of confessions and admissions are a further reflection of this privilege. Section 219A of the Criminal Procedure Act requires that before an informal[193] admission is admitted it must be proved to have been made voluntarily. However, this protection against self-incrimination is limited in that the courts have continued to apply the common-law interpretation of the 'voluntary' requirement.[194] In terms of this, voluntariness is compromised only if the admission is 'induced by any promise or threat proceeding from a person in authority'.[195] Section 25(2)(c) of the Constitution directs that an arrested person has a right 'not to be compelled to make a confession or admission which could be used in evidence against him or her'. This may well have the effect of nullifying the requirement that the duress must flow from a person in authority.

The Criminal Procedure Act provides broader protection in the case of confessions.[196] Not only must the confession be made voluntarily before it can be admitted but it must also be made in sound and sober senses without undue influence. If it is made to a peace officer other than a magistrate or justice of the peace, it must be written down and confirmed in the presence of a magistrate or a justice of the peace. Once such a confession is reduced to writing the onus rests on the accused to prove that the requirements of admissibility have not been met. This often has the effect

---

[189] Corder et al op cit (n 182) 44 — hereinafter referred to as 'the *Charter*'.

[190] In terms of this privilege a person may refuse to answer a question that may expose him/her to a criminal charge.

[191] Sections 203, 217, and 219A of Act 51 of 1977.

[192] Sections 14 and 42 of Act 25 of 1965. The right to remain silent is also well established in the common law.

[193] The word 'informal' is used to distinguish an extra-judicial admission from formal admissions made in the pleadings or in court.

[194] *S v Yolelo* 1981 (3) SA 1002 (A).

[195] *R v Barlin* 1926 AD 459 at 462. See also *S v Peters* 1992 (1) SACR 292 (E).

[196] Section 217.

of obscuring the reality of the situation. A frightened accused who remains in the custody of those who might have persuaded him/her to confess may well be too scared to appraise a magistrate of the true conditions in which s/he came to make the confession. There are thus good policy reasons for holding that this presumption does not accord with the constitutional presumption of innocence.

The Judges Rules[197] have the potential to alleviate the position of the accused who is brought to a confessing state of mind. Unfortunately the tendency of the courts has been to view them as merely administrative directions and they have been accorded little weight.[198] Certain provisions found in the Judges Rules have at last been given the status of law by s 25(2)(a), which requires every arrested person to be 'promptly informed, in language which he or she understands, that he or she has the right to remain silent and to be warned of the consequences of making any statement'. Unfortunately there is no specification that statements made by such persons must be taken down in the language which it was made.[199] Consequently there remains a risk of inaccuracy in the recording of statements. This is not the only provision in the Judges Rules not reflected in the Constitution. However, there is no reason why these rules should not be used by the courts to assist in determining whether or not an accused was compelled to make a confession or admission.

Probably the most significant departure from the privilege against self-incrimination is to be found in s 218(2) of the Criminal Procedure Act. In terms of this section,

> 'evidence may be admitted at criminal proceedings that anything was pointed out by an accused appearing at such proceedings or that any fact or thing was discovered in consequence of information given by such accused, notwithstanding that such pointing-out or information forms part of a confession or statement which by law is not admissible in evidence against such accused at such proceedings'.

Until recently evidence obtained as a consequence of an 'involuntary' pointing-out was held to be admissible even if induced by violence.[200] This exception to the privilege against self-incrimination was severely curtailed in *S v Sheehama*.[201] The court held that a pointing-out had to be made freely and voluntarily before evidence obtained as a consequence thereof was admitted. However, the court left open the question whether the common-law privilege against self-incrimination is superseded when the pointing-out contains the requisite element of discovery.[202] Levinsohn J in *S v Khumalo*[203] held that the reliability principle has been disapproved of in our law; consequently 'the theory of confirmation by subsequently discovered facts' must by implication be rejected.[204] The status of the *Khumalo*

---

[197] The Judges Rules were formulated at the South African Judges Conference in Cape Town in 1931, their purpose being to protect an accused from unfair practices by the police.
[198] Hiemstra (1963) 80 *SALJ* 187 at 206; Hoffmann & Zeffertt op cit (n 180) 222; cf *S v Colt* 1992 (2) SACR 120 (E).
[199] See rule 9 of the Judges Rules.
[200] Since *R v Samhando* 1943 AD 608 this approach was consistently applied by the courts until 1985, when the *dictum* of Hoexter JA in *S v Magwaza* 1985 (3) SA 29 (A) initiated a debate that culminated in an implied rejection of *Samhando* in *S v Sheehama* (supra).
[201] Supra.
[202] As was held in *R v Samhando* (supra).
[203] Supra.
[204] In terms of the reliability principle all reliable evidence must be admitted. Consequently, if the unreliability of evidence is cured by the subsequent discovery of a fact, that evidence should then be admitted.

decision is dubious in the light of a recent *obiter dictum* in *S v Jordaan*[205] which upheld the exception to the privilege against self-incrimination.

Fortunately s 25 of the Constitution, which clearly protects the right to remain silent, will strengthen the arguments of those who reject the reliability principle.

### 4.3.3.2 'Family' privilege

Although distinct from the privilege against self-incrimination, the law of evidence recognizes a marital privilege in terms of which spouses have the right to refuse to disclose communications made between themselves during the course of their marriage.[206] The spouses may elect to waive the privilege. The rationale for the privilege is founded on an age-old recognition of a family's right to privacy.[207] Article 2.22 of the ANC draft Bill of Rights extended the existing marital privilege to communications made between parent and child. Although this right is not specified in the Constitution, it is submitted that the right to privacy should be interpreted so as to bestow an equivalent privilege on communications made between parent (or other caretaker) and child. Recognition of this right would also eradicate the existing anomaly in the Criminal Procedure Act. This Act compels parents to be present at the trial of a juvenile,[208] permits them to assist their child,[209] and makes them compellable witnesses for the prosecution.[210]

### 4.3.3.3 State privilege

The doctrine of state privilege enables the executive branch of government to refuse to disclose information in its possession on the ground that public interest would be jeopardized by its production.[211] Section 66 of the Internal Security Act[212] empowers the responsible minister or the administrator of a province to refuse to disclose information on the basis that to do so would prejudicially effect state security. If this claim of privilege is made in its proper form (no reasons need be given), the courts are ousted and they may not order disclosure of the information. Where this privilege is claimed on grounds of public policy that do not effect the security of the state the court may overrule the minister where it is satisfied that the minister's objection to disclosure is unjustifiable or unreasonable.[213]

The ambit of state privilege will obviously be curtailed by s 23 of the Constitution, which provides:

'Every person shall have the right of access to all information held by the state or any of its organs

---

[205] 1992 (2) SACR 498 (A).

[206] Section 198 of Act 51 of 1977; s 10 of Act 25 of 1965.

[207] See Hoffmann & Zeffertt op cit (n 180) 244, where they express the underlying rationale as follows: '[P]ublic opinion would find it unacceptable if spouses were forced to disclose communications from each other.'

[208] Section 73 of Act 51 of 1977.

[209] Ibid.

[210] Section 192. The US courts have held that the right to privacy enables parent/guardian to claim privilege from disclosure with regard to confidential communications from a child/ward. See *In re A & M* 61 AD 2d 426, 403 NYS 2d 375 (1978); *People v Fitzgerald* 101 Misc 2d 712, 422 NYS 2d 309; *In re Michelet P v Gold* 10 AD 2d 68, 419 NYS 2d 704 (1979); *In re Ryan* 123 Misc 2d 854, 474 NYS 2d 931.

[211] For a general discussion on the negative implications of state privilege, see Mathews *Freedom, State Security and the Rule of Law* (1986) 174ff.

[212] Act 74 of 1982.

[213] See Hoffmann & Zeffertt op cit (n 180) 269 for general discussion.

at any level of government in so far as such information is required for the exercise or protection of his or her rights.'

There can be no doubt that the effective ousting of the court's jurisdiction contained in s 66 of the Internal Security Act will cease to be effective, and once it is established that the information is necessary to enable a person to exercise or protect her rights the minister will have a very onerous task establishing that the privilege claimed is reasonable and necessary.

### 4.3.4 *Hearsay*

The right to cross-examine is protected in s 25(3)*(d)* of the Constitution. This could possibly impact on the admission of hearsay evidence.[214] At present the law of evidence provides that hearsay evidence is generally inadmissible subject to certain exceptions. In terms of the Law of Evidence Amendment Act[215] hearsay will be admitted where: the party against whom the evidence is to be adduced agrees to its admission; the person upon whose credibility the probative value of such evidence depends himself testifies at such proceedings; and where the court taking into account a broad variety of factors is of the opinion that it would be in the interests of justice to admit such evidence.

Although the admission of hearsay obviously makes severe inroads into the right of cross-examination, it is permitted in many jurisdictions where it is sufficiently reliable and does not prejudice the accused.[216] It is submitted that the present formulation of the exceptions to the hearsay rule accords with these principles and its application is likely to remain unchanged.[217] However, the right of cross-examination will have to be borne in mind should reforms such as the admission of videotape evidence in child sexual abuse cases be introduced.

### 4.3.5 *Equality*

In terms of s 8(1) of the Constitution every person has a right 'to equality before the law and to equal protection of the law'. Subsection (2) prohibits both direct or indirect discrimination on the basis of 'race, gender, sex, ethnic or social origin, colour, sexual orientation, age, disability, religion, conscience, belief, culture or language'.

International comparisons have shown that the precise wording of the equality clause together with the interpretative approach of the courts will determine whether or not a provision is discriminatory.

The interpretive guidelines found in s 35 require the court to take a purposive approach in interpretation. If this approach is taken, many evidentiary provisions that appear to be neutral may yet be found to be discriminatory in that they have 'a

---

[214] Hearsay evidence is defined in s 3(4) of the Law of Evidence Amendment Act 45 of 1988 as evidence, whether oral or in writing, the probative value of which depends upon the credibility of any person other than the person giving such evidence.
[215] Section 3 of Act 45 of 1988.
[216] Even the US permits hearsay evidence to be admitted in exceptional circumstances despite the provisions of the Sixth Amendment guaranteeing the right to confront witnesses.
[217] It is submitted that the statutory provisions applying to documentary and computer evidence will also not be seriously challenged by a Bill of Rights.

disparate disadvantaging impact on certain individuals and groups'.[218] For example, the cautionary rule applicable to women in sexual offence cases, although applying to both men and women, is rather lopsided in its impact. The cases clearly reveal that it is based on a discriminatory and discredited view of women.[219] Furthermore, the vast majority of complainants are women; therefore men as a group tend to escape its disadvantaging effects.

Similarly, if effective equality is sought, a court may well be entitled to take into account disadvantages suffered by witnesses and complainants in order to ensure that they have equal access to justice. This could be a basis for introducing law reform programmes to enable children and other vulnerable witnesses to testify 'in more conducive' environments.

Ultimately it will be the interpretive approach taken by the courts that will determine the extent of the constitutional impact on the law of evidence.

## 5  PUNISHMENT

### 5.1  Philosophical background

Judicial punishment will inevitably involve an interference with or loss of one or more constitutionally guaranteed rights.[220] The Constitution recognizes this as legitimate.[221] However, whilst those who have committed a crime (as proved by their conviction) cannot complain of the infringement of their rights by legitimate punishment, this does not mean that they are deprived of all or even most constitutional rights on conviction: in principle they retain all rights except those that are necessarily lost or restricted as a result of the conviction or punishment.[222] Convicted persons are entitled to constitutional protection in relation to the process, the rules, and the principles by which the sentence is determined in relation to the type of punishment that is imposed and in relation to the way in which that punishment is executed.

### 5.2  Comparative review

Provisions for a fair trial obviously apply equally after conviction to the sentencing stage, as is already established under our common law.[223] Although discretion is not incompatible with the provisions usually contained in Bills of Rights, it must be exercised in a rational and consistent manner if it is not to offend provisions relating to a fair trial and equality.[224] But this does not mean that the constitutional

---

[218] Sheppard 'Recognition of the Disadvantaging of Women: The Promise of *Andrews v Law Society of British Columbia*' (1989) 35 *McGill LJ* 207 at 213.

[219] See e g *S v Balhuber* 1987 (1) PH H22 (A) at 40; *S v F* 1989 (3) SA 847 (A) at 854; *R v Rautenbach* 1949 (1) SA 135 (A) at 143; *R v W* 1949 (3) SA 772 (A) at 780; *S v M* 1992 (2) SACR 188 (W).

[220] Richardson 'Time to Take Prisoners' Rights Seriously' (1984) 11 *J of L and Society* 1 at 6.

[221] It clearly falls within the general provision for limitations contained in s 33(1). But it is also recognized, for instance, in prohibition of cruel, inhuman, or degrading punishment and in the reference to detention of prisoners in s 25(1).

[222] Cf Diemont J in *Hassim v Officer Commanding, Prison Command, Robben Island* 1973 (3) SA 462 (C) at 472H–473A. See also the discussion of s 33(1) below.

[223] e g *S v Jabavu* 1969 (2) SA 466 (A) at 472E.

[224] Cf *Furman v Georgia* 408 US 233, 33 LEd 2d 346 (1972). See also Polyviou *The Equal Protection of the Laws* (1980) 523; Kress *Prescription for Justice* (1980) 59ff. In the US the reasoning has been partly based on the prohibition of cruel and unusual punishment, but it is suggested that the absence of reference in the South African Constitution to unusual punishment does not alter the position.

requirement of equality requires the imposition of equal sentences for apparently equal crimes: no US court has adopted that view,[225] and it is unlikely that a South African court would do so.[226] Indeed equality requires courts to take account of the differences in each case, and it is therefore arguable that mandatory sentences would be contrary to an equal protection clause.[227]

In relation to the severity of punishment, the US Supreme Court has accepted the view that the ban on cruel and unusual punishment in the Eighth Amendment is based on 'nothing less than the dignity of man' and 'must draw its meaning from the evolving standards of decency that mark the progress of a maturing society'.[228] This supports a principle that the punishment must, in the light of evolving standards, be proportionate to the nature and seriousness of the crime.[229]

A similar interpretation has been given to the prohibition of 'inhuman or degrading punishment or treatment' appearing in many modern Constitutions.[230] This phrase is construed disjunctively so as to prohibit (i) inhuman punishment, (ii) degrading punishment, (iii) inhuman treatment, and (iv) degrading treatment,[231] and it applies at three different levels. First, it prohibits punishment or treatment that is 'acknowledged to be inherently inhuman or degrading'.[232] In such a case no moderation or control will justify the punishment or treatment.[233] Secondly, it extends to punishments that are disproportionate to the nature or seriousness of the offence, 'the punishment being so excessive as to shock or outrage contemporary standards of decency'.[234] Thirdly, it may apply to the way in which punishment or treatment is imposed or executed, in which case provisions relating to a fair trial or equal treatment may also be in issue.[235] Whilst courts have been willing to accept, as a starting point, the dictionary definitions of the words 'inhuman' and 'degrading', they have emphasized that the decision ultimately depends on an evolving value judgment reflecting the norms, aspirations, and experiences of the particular society moderated by the values accepted by the international community.[236]

---

[225] See *Furman v Georgia* (supra).
[226] Cf *S v Giannoulis* 1975 (4) SA 867 (A); *S v Marx* 1989 (1) SA 222 (A).
[227] Cf *Woodson v North Carolina* 428 US 280, 49 LEd 2d 944 (1976) (mandatory death sentence struck down because it involved the imposition of a penalty without regard to the particular circumstances of the crime or the offender).
[228] *Trop v Dulles* 356 US 86, 100–1, 2 LEd 2d 630, 642 (1958). This approach has been followed in numerous subsequent decisions.
[229] See e g *Weems v United States* 217 US 349, 54 LEd 793 (1910); *Coker v Georgia* 433 US 584, 53 LEd 2d 982 (1977); *Solem v Helm* 463 US 277, 284, 77 LEd 2d 637, 645 (1983); Kress op cit (n 224) 69.
[230] In *S v Ncube; S v Tshuma; S v Ndhlovu* 1988 (2) SA 702 (ZS) at 716H–J Gubbay JA held that the US Supreme Court decisions were 'at the very least, helpful in establishing the basic concept against which [such protection] should be construed', despite the differences in the US provisions.
[231] *Tyrer v United Kingdom* (1978) 2 EHRR 1 at 9; *S v Ncube; S v Tshuma; S v Ndhlovu* (supra) at 714–15; *Ex parte Attorney-General, Namibia: In re Corporal Punishment by Organs of State* 1991 (3) SA 76 (NmS) at 86.
[232] Gubbay JA in *S v Ncube; S v Tshuma; S v Ndhlovu* (supra) at 715G.
[233] *Ex parte Attorney-General, Namibia: In re Corporal Punishment by Organs of State* (supra) at 86.
[234] Gubbay JA in *S v Ncube; S v Tshuma; S v Ndhlovu* (supra) at 715H–I. Contrast *R v Runyowa* 1966 (2) SA 495 (PC), criticized in *Ncube's* case at 716.
[235] See e g the discussion of the death sentence and imprisonment below, 5.2.1 and 5.2.3.
[236] *S v Ncube; S v Tshuma; S v Ndhlovu* (supra) at 717; *Ex parte Attorney-General, Namibia: In re Corporal Punishment by Organs of State* (supra) at 86–7, 95–6; *S v Tcoeib* 1993 (1) SACR 274 (Nm). See also *Tyrer v United Kingdom* (supra) para 30; *S v Chabalala* 1986 (3) SA 623 (BA) at 626–7, 628D–E; *S v Petrus* (1985) LRC (Const) 699 (Botswana CA) 714g; Sieghart *The International Law of Human Rights* (1983) 162–72.

## 5.2.1 Death sentence

Courts have been reluctant to hold that the death penalty is per se inhuman, cruel, or degrading. In the well-known case of *Furman v Georgia*[237] the US Supreme Court held the death sentence to be unconstitutional in that (as at 1972) it was imposed and carried out in an arbitrary, capricious, and discriminatory manner in violation of the cruel and unusual clause and, according to some opinions, also the equal protection and due process clauses. But, following changes in state legislation to provide for guided discretion in the imposition of the death sentence, the Supreme Court has since 1976 frequently upheld the constitutionality of the death penalty for murder.[238] On the other hand, the death penalty for crimes other than murder may be unconstitutional on the ground that it is disproportionate and excessive.[239]

In some jurisdictions the wording of the Constitution has been decisive. For instance, in Bophuthatswana the Appellate Division has held that the prohibition of 'inhuman and degrading treatment or punishment' could not override the express acceptance of the death penalty in a clause that made the right to life subject to 'the execution of a sentence of a court following ... conviction of a crime for which this penalty is provided by law'.[240] But it is debatable whether the court was correct in also holding that the way in which the death sentence was applied was constitutional, particularly in view of its mandatory imposition for murder in the absence of extenuating circumstances.[241]

Article 6(2) of the International Covenant on Civil and Political Rights requires that the death penalty be imposed only for the most serious crimes in accordance with the law in force at the time of the commission of the crime. It can also only be carried out pursuant to a final judgment rendered by a competent court. The Covenant further stipulates that anyone sentenced to death shall have the right to seek pardon or commutation of the death sentence, and that such sentence shall not be imposed for crimes committed by persons below 18 years of age and shall not be carried out on pregnant women.[242]

## 5.2.2 Whipping

It is widely accepted that the whipping of an adult offender is both inhuman and degrading[243] — a view that is also reflected in a number of South African court judgments.[244] Greater reluctance may be shown in declaring the whipping of

---

[237] Supra.
[238] Starting with *Greg v Georgia* 428 US 153, 49 LEd 2d 859 (1976). The literature on the subject is vast. For a useful review of the Supreme Court cases, see John E Theuman's Annotation in 90 LEd 2d 1001.
[239] Cf *Coker v Georgia* (supra) (rape of an adult woman with no particularly aggravating circumstances); *Enmund v Florida* 458 US 782, 73 LEd 2d 1140 (1982) (robbery).
[240] *S v Chabalala* (supra). See also the Malaysian cases cited at 629 and Lord Morris (*obiter*) in *R v Runyowa* (supra) at 498F.
[241] *Woodson v North Carolina* (supra).
[242] Article 6(4) and (5).
[243] *S v Ncube; S v Tshuma; S v Ndhlovu* (supra); *S v Petrus* (supra); *Ex parte Attorney-General, Namibia: In re Corporal Punishment by Organs of State* (supra). See also the authorities cited in these cases.
[244] e g *S v Kumalo* 1965 (4) SA 565 (N) at 574; *S v Masondo* 1969 (1) PH H58 (N); *S v Masia* 1968 (1) SA 271 (T); *S v Kantor* 1972 (4) SA 683 (O) at 684B; *S v Ruiters* 1975 (3) SA 526 (C) at 530; *S v Nkoana* 1985 (2) SA 395 (T) at 401; *S v Machwili* 1986 (1) SA 156 (N) at 157H–I; *S v Motsoesoana* 1986 (3) SA 350 (N) at 357I; *S v Ndaba* 1987 (1) SA 237 (T) at 241–2, 245A–B; *S v V* 1989 (1) SA 532 (A) at 543D–E. It is also significant that a recent White Paper proposes the abolition of whipping as a punishment for prison disciplinary offences.

juveniles to be unconstitutional,[245] though this has been done by the European Court of Human Rights[246] and by the courts in Zimbabwe[247] and Namibia,[248] in the latter case extending the prohibition also to corporal punishment inflicted in government schools.[249]

### 5.2.3 *Imprisonment*

Although imprisonment is undoubtedly 'degrading' and probably also 'inhuman' or 'cruel' in the ordinary meaning of those terms,[250] no court is likely to declare imprisonment, even for life, unconstitutional for it is a form of punishment that is universally accepted and often expressly or impliedly recognized by the Constitution.[251] Rather, the debate revolves around the extent to which prisoners' rights are curtailed and the way in which imprisonment is carried out.[252]

Until the 1960s and 1970s courts in both the US and Europe tended to adopt a 'hands-off' approach. The prevailing view was that prisoners had a status[253] that involved inherent limitations on their rights so that it was unnecessary to justify wide-ranging limitations regarded as a natural and normal consequence of imprisonment.[254] That view has now been rejected and it has been recognized that, like other citizens, prisoners have rights that can be limited only if the state justifies the particular restriction.[255] But the requirement of state justification may be more apparent than real because the courts often appear uncritically to accept the assertions of prison authorities.

The US Supreme Court has held that while 'convicted prisoners do not forfeit all constitutional protections by reason of their conviction and confinement',[256] their constitutional rights are subject to restrictions and limitations which 'arise from both the fact of incarceration and from valid penological objectives — including deterrence of crime, rehabilitation of prisoners, and institutional security'.[257] However, the appropriate test to be applied in balancing these considerations has, until *Turner v Safley*,[258] been a matter of uncertainty. In *Turner's* case the court rejected the strict

---

[245] The South African judges have generally been less critical of its application to juveniles, regarding it as a desirable alternative to imprisonment.
[246] *Tyrer v United Kingdom* (supra).
[247] *S v A Juvenile* 1990 (4) SA 151 (ZS).
[248] *Ex parte Attorney-General, Namibia: In re Corporal Punishment by Organs of State* (supra).
[249] A view shared by Dumbutshena CJ (*obiter*) in *S v A Juvenile* (supra). Contrast *Campbell and Cosans v United Kingdom* (1982) 4 EHRR 293.
[250] *S v Tcoeib* (supra) at 285h–i. See also *S v Chabalala* (supra) at 628E–F and the remarks of Thirion J, dissenting, in *S v Motsoesoana* (supra) at 372E–G.
[251] *S v Tcoeib* (supra).
[252] See generally Van Zyl Smit *South African Prison Law and Practice* (1992) 59ff; Krantz *The Law of Corrections and Prisoners' Rights* 3 ed (1986); Van Zyl Smit & Dunkel (eds) *Imprisonment Today and Tomorrow — International Perspectives on Prisoners' Rights and Prison Conditions* (1991); Fowles *Prisoners' Rights in England and the United States* (1989).
[253] 'Slaves of the State', according to *Ruffin v Commonwealth* 62 Va 790 (1871), and in an 'extraordinary authority relationship', according to German law: see Van Zyl Smit op cit (n 252) 59–60. Several American states provided for 'civil death', entailing a loss of civil rights: Rubin *Law of Criminal Correction* 2 ed (1973) 704.
[254] Van Zyl Smit op cit (n 252) 59ff; Beaven 'Prisoner's Access' (1979) 95 *LQR* 393.
[255] Beaven op cit (n 254); Richardson op cit (n 220) 8–10; Fowles op cit (n 252) 98–9. South African courts have adopted a similar view: *Hassim v Officer Commanding, Prison Command, Robben Island* (supra) at 472H–473A; *Mandela v Minister of Prisons* 1983 (1) SA 938 (A) at 957E.
[256] *Bell v Wolfish* 441 US 520, 545, 60 LEd 2d 447, 472 (1979) (a case that in fact involved awaiting-trial prisoners).
[257] *O'Lone v Estate of Shabazz* 482 US 342, 348, 96 LEd 2d 282, 290 (1987). See also *Bell v Wolfish* (supra).
[258] 482 US 78, 96 LEd 2d 64 (1987). For discussion of *Turner's* case, see e g Norris (1991) 64 *Temple LR* 1109; Roberts (1990) 27 *Am Crim LR* 545.

scrutiny test that requires a compelling state interest to justify the infringement of fundamental rights. Instead it adopted a less demanding 'reasonableness' test: 'when a prison regulation impinges on inmates' constitutional rights, the regulation is valid if it is reasonably related to legitimate penological interests'.[259] The court adopted this test to 'ensure that courts afford appropriate deference to prison officials' charged with and trained in running institutions, and to avoid 'unnecessary intrusion of the judiciary into problems particularly ill-suited to "resolution by decree" '.[260] As a result of this (now well-established) deference to the judgment of prison authorities, the US courts have shown increasing reluctance to uphold prisoners' rights when those rights are alleged to impinge on the daily administration of prisons, especially if they are alleged to affect internal order or security.[261]

The approach has been similar in other jurisdictions, such as Zimbabwe.[262] And the European Court of Human Rights, while appearing to require state justification, has been generous in accepting that a restriction on a prisoner's rights falls within one of the recognized exceptions; for instance, that a prohibition on correspondence is 'in accordance with the law and is necessary in a democratic society' for public safety or the prevention of disorder.[263]

Space does not permit a detailed consideration of the many different types of rights that may be affected by imprisonment.[264] Suffice it to say that the courts have been fairly willing to grant procedural rights to prisoners, presumably because that is an area in which they do not feel any obligation to defer to the experience of prison authorities. This has been especially true of access to the courts and to legal advice, which are of course fundamental to the exercise of all other rights. Courts have been equally willing to intervene where there has been a denial of basic rights such as provision of food, clothing, and medical care.

It has been argued that prisoners should be accorded 'positive rights' in the sense of rights that impose on the prison authorities a duty to act for the benefit of the prisoner.[265] Prisoners are placed in a situation in which most of their rights can be exercised only with the active assistance of the prison authorities, and whilst the usual 'negative rights' (involving a duty not to interfere) are often translated into 'positive rights', this, it is argued, has proved unsatisfactory.

---

[259] At 89. The court went on (at 89–90) to set out four factors relevant to the application of the test. Briefly, these were (i) a requirement of a valid, rational, and direct connection between the regulation and the alleged state objective which must be legitimate; (ii) whether alternative means of exercising the right remain open to the prisoner; (iii) the impact that acceptance of the prisoner's alleged right will have on guards, other prisoners, and the allocation of prison resources; (iv) the presence or absence of ready alternative solutions as evidence of the reasonableness of the prison regulation.

[260] *O'Lone v Estate of Shabazz* (supra) at 290.

[261] See e g *Bell v Wolfish* (supra) (various practices, including body-cavity searches, relating to awaiting-trial prisoners); *Jones v North Carolina Prisoners' Union* 433 US 119, 53 LEd 2d 629 (1977) (prohibition on meetings and soliciting for union membership); *Rhodes v Chapman* 452 US 337, 69 LEd 2d 59 (1981) (double-bunking alleged to involve overcrowding); *O'Lone v Estate Shabazz* (supra) (Muslims prevented from attending weekly *Jumu'ah* religious service).

[262] *Conjwayo v Minister of Justice, Legal and Parliamentary Affairs* 1992 (2) SA 56 (ZS). See also the Indian cases cited at 61 of the report.

[263] Richardson op cit (n 220) 9–10. See also the discussion in Fowles op cit (n 252) 63ff.

[264] Reference may be made to Fowles op cit (n 252); Krantz op cit (n 252); Palmer *Constitutional Rights of Prisoners* (1991). A useful brief account of some aspects with particular reference to South African law is Labuschagne 'Deliktuele Beskerming van die Bewegingsvryheid van die Gevangene' (1993) 4 *Stell LR* 130.

[265] Richardson op cit (n 220) 23; Van Zyl Smit op cit (n 242) 65–6.

## 5.2.4 Fines

Fines are unlikely to attract constitutional challenges in the normal course of events, but it is highly arguable that imprisonment of indigent offenders for failure to pay fines that are beyond their means is discriminatory and contrary to the requirement of equal protection since it amounts to imprisonment for being poor.[266]

## 5.3 South Africa

Issues relating to the sentencing process and the general severity of the punishment, touched on in the comparative review, need not be repeated here. The interpretation of the prohibition of 'cruel, inhuman or degrading treatment or punishment' contained in s 11(2) of the Constitution is likely[267] to follow the well-established model of foreign jurisdictions discussed above.

However, the constitutional protection of convicted persons' rights in relation to the imposition and execution of particular types of punishment will to a large extent depend on how the courts interpret and apply the provisions of s 33(1) of the Constitution. That section permits limitations that are reasonable and 'justifiable in an open and democratic society based on freedom and equality', provided that the limitation does 'not negate the essential content of the right'. The first part of this provision accords with the widely accepted view that convicted persons retain all rights subject only to such restrictions that the state can justify. The requirement that the essential content of the right must not be negated appears to mean that a right can be limited, but not entirely lost, as a result of the punishment. This could be problematic, for instance, where imprisonment affects rights such as freedom of the person, of association, or of movement. Presumably it could be argued that some residual aspect of those rights remain, though it is questionable whether the remainder could be described as the 'essential content'. Be that as it may, the preservation of the essential content of the right would have most impact in relation to the death sentence, as discussed below.

In the case of some rights s 33(1) has an additional requirement that the limitation must also be necessary. The section therefore seems to adopt something like the approach of the US courts in distinguishing two classes of constitutional rights: (i) fundamental rights where the limitation must be both reasonable and necessary, requiring compelling state interest; (ii) other rights which require only that the limitation be reasonably related to a legitimate penological objective.

### 5.3.1 Death penalty

Unlike the various draft proposals, which expressly allowed or abolished the death penalty, the Constitution is silent on this controversial issue. As already indicated above, courts elsewhere have been reluctant to hold that the death penalty is per se cruel, inhuman, or degrading. Nevertheless it is suggested that the death penalty would be unconstitutional in that it would 'negate the essential content' of the right

---

[266] Westen (1969) 57 *California LR* 778; Polyviou op cit (n 224) 522ff and the authorities there cited; *Tate v Short* 401 US 395, 28 LEd 2d 130 (1971).
[267] Cf s 35(1).

to life provided for by s 9 and therefore fall outside the limitations permitted by s 33(1).

### 5.3.2 Imprisonment

Section 25 grants prisoners (and other detained persons) certain positive rights which impose duties on the state to provide 'conditions consonant with human dignity', nutrition, reading material, and medical treatment. Also included are the right to legal assistance and opportunities to communicate with relatives, religious counsellors, and medical practitioners. These rights can be limited only if it is both reasonable and necessary to do so. The express provisions of s 25 do not, it is submitted, exclude the application to prisoners of the general rights available to all citizens, even though the usable content of some of those rights may be very limited by reason of the imprisonment. In each case the intrusion into the right must be justified, the test for that justification depending on whether the right in question is (as a result of s 33(1)) classified as fundamental or not.[268]

South African law distinguishes prisoners' rights from prisoners' privileges.[269] The latter are accorded or withdrawn in the discretion of the prison authorities and are unenforceable. It is submitted that this distinction cannot survive since most of the so-called privileges fall within the entrenched constitutional rights that can be limited only on the appropriate level of state justification being shown.[270]

### 5.3.3 Whipping

Whilst the Constitution is silent on the validity of this punishment, it is likely that the courts will follow other jurisdictions in holding whipping — at least of adults — to be inhuman and degrading in contravention of either s 10 or s 11(2) or both. Not only have the South African courts previously described whipping in those terms but it would have to be shown that the retention or imposition of whipping was necessary in addition to being reasonable and justifiable.[271] It is suggested that this latter consideration and the international trends could lead to the same conclusion in relation to the whipping of juveniles.

---

[268] See the discussion of s 33 at various places in this work.
[269] *Hassim v Officer Commanding, Prison Command, Robben Island* (supra); *Goldberg v Minister of Prisons* 1979 (1) SA 14 (A). For a detailed and critical discussion of prisoners' 'privileges', see Van Zyl Smit op cit (n 252) 97–9, 192ff.
[270] Section 33(1). Cf Van Zyl Smit op cit (n 252) 59ff; Labuschagne op cit (n 264) 132.
[271] Section 33(1)*(aa)* places s 10 and s 11 in this category.

# CONSTITUTIONALIZATION OF LABOUR RIGHTS

## DENNIS DAVIS

More than half a century ago Benjamin Cardozo said: 'The chief law makers may be, and often are, the judges because they are the final seat of authority. Every time they interpret contract, property, vested rights, due process of law, liberty, they necessarily enact into law parts of the system of social philosophy.'[1] As most Bills of Rights are premised on the protection of the individual from the power of the state, a philosophy which distinguishes between the public and private spheres has dominated constitutional jurisprudence particularly in North America. The tension between the individual and the collectivity is particularly evident in the constitutional adjudication of workers' rights.

Not all constitutions safeguard workers' rights. The omission of express provisions dealing with collectivities has profoundly affected US constitutional jurisprudence. Whereas legislative protection of workers began to develop in the late nineteenth century in Europe, US courts began to use the Constitution to strike down as unconstitutional reforms such as minimum wage and maximum hour limitations for factory workers. Initially the US Supreme Court adopted a somewhat more enlightened approach. In *Holden v Hardy*[2] the court held that the federal Constitution is not violated when a state limits the maximum number of hours of work per day that can be worked in underground mines. This decision was, however, given a restrictive interpretation in that it was found to have emphasized the state's official concern in protecting the workers against health and safety hazards involved in mining operations which were more extraordinary than experienced in other enterprises. In *Muller v Oregon*[3] state law limiting the hours of employment for women was upheld on the grounds that it directly served to protect the health of women and thus the public welfare in protecting the health of child-bearers.

This period of enlightened jurisprudence did not last for long. In *Lochner v New York*[4] the Supreme Court declared void state law limiting the number of hours per day that a person could be employed as a baker on the grounds that it interfered with the liberty of selling one's labour and was subjecting that liberty to unreasonable restraints. The decision in *Lochner* was followed in other cases, the Supreme Court declaring void a federal law designed to regulate the employment of children and prohibiting interstate commerce and goods produced in plants which employed children below the age of 14 or which employed children between the ages of 14 and 16 but beyond specific hours. The court found such regulations a matter of local

---

[1] Cardozo *The Nature of Judicial Process* (1949) 171.
[2] 169 US 366 (1898).
[3] 208 US 412 (1908).
[4] 198 US 45 (1905).

concern and thus beyond the scope of federal power.[5] In *Adkins v Children'Hospital*[6] the court held that statutory minimum wages for women were constitutionally barred on the grounds of the price paid for labour when set by broadly applied standards had no direct relationship to preserving health or the public welfare and thus unduly restricted the freedom to contract.

The court went further than the simple curtailment of health, safety, and minimum wage legislation. In *Adair v United States*[7] the court held that Congress could not prohibit anti-union discrimination by the railroads on the grounds that the common good was not adequately served by this law. Therefore legislation could not be justified which interfered with the individual's freedom to choose the terms and conditions under which contracts were entered into. Shortly thereafter, in the *Danbury Hatters* case,[8] the court affirmed the civil suit for treble damages against the union on the basis that the union had violated the Sherman Anti-Trust Act by promoting a boycott against a hat manufacturer who refused to recognize the union as its employees' collective bargaining representative.

It was only during the era of Roosevelt's New Deal that the Supreme Court began to view labour legislation more sympathetically. In *West Coast Hotel Company v Parrish*[9] the court overruled the *Adkins* case and found that the legislature was constitutionally entitled to introduce greater equity in the market place by establishing minimum wages designed to counteract the unequal bargaining position of workers. In *NLRB v Jones & Laughlin Steel Corporation*[10] the court upheld the legality of the National Labour Relations Act as well as the authority of Congress to enact laws which created a national retirement insurance system which induced the states to adopt unemployment programmes and which established minimum wages and overtime payment requirements for employment directly and indirectly effecting interstate commerce.

From the inception of the New Deal era interventionist legislation rather than the Constitution became the major source of worker protection. Apart from the NLRB and associated legislation, Title VII of the Civil Rights Act of 1964 has had a significant impact upon employment practices. It prohibits employment discrimination by employers and employment agencies and membership discrimination by labour unions on the base of race, colour, religion, sex, or natural origin. It established the Equal Employment Opportunity Commission as a federal agency which, although not having enforcement powers, was supplemented in the Act by powers given to the US Department of Justice, which is empowered to attack practices of discrimination, particularly large-scale discriminatory practices. In 1972 the Equal Employment Opportunity Act amended Title VII to broaden the power of the EEOC so as to seek enforcement of the law in the courts. Amendments covered state and local governments as well as the executive branch of the federal government, excluding the courts and the legislative bodies, and empowered the US Attorney-General to pursue suits against states and local governments. Individual

---

[5] *Hammer v Dagenhart* 247 US 251 (1918).
[6] 261 US 525 (1923).
[7] 208 US 161 (1908).
[8] 208 US 274 (1908).
[9] 300 US 379 (1937).
[10] 301 US 1 (1937).

complaints, the right to sue, and private actions were retained and extended to actions against federal, state, and local government. Initially the Act excluded from its coverage small employers and organizations with a decreasing number from a hundred to twenty-five employees after its first five years of existence. This was later reduced to fifteen.

Notwithstanding this legislation, the Constitution has continued to have an important impact upon labour relations. In particular the courts' interpretation of the First Amendment provision relating to freedom of association is of considerable significance to labour law. Indeed, not until *Citizens against Rent Control v Berkley*[11] did the Supreme Court find that individuals acting together have a right of association to be as free to pursue lawful aims as they would if the same individuals pursue their aims acting separately. As a result of a series of cases the courts have interpreted the right of association to include disassociation, which had the result of weakening majoritarian bargaining, closed-shop agreements, and the organizational cohesion of unions in general.[12]

The individualistic approach to interpretation regarding freedom of association has not only been confined to America. Its impact upon labour law has been considerable in Canadian jurisprudence. Like the US Bill of Rights, the Canadian Charter of Rights and Freedoms, introduced in 1982, did not include an express provision on workers' rights, but did include a provision protecting freedom of association. This clause has had a significant impact on labour law.

The first reported Canadian decision on freedom of association and collective bargaining was the *Broadway Manor Nursing Home* case[13] in which the Ontario High Court was required to consider the Inflation Restraint Act of 1982, which extended the life of the terms and conditions of collective agreements covering public-sector employees for up to two years, suspended the right of some of the affected public servants to strike down that period of time, and removed the right which other public servants had to refer compensation issues to arbitration. Two of the applications turned on whether the consequences of the statute was to extend collective agreements or simply to extend their terms and conditions. The court adopted a liberal reading to the provision of freedom of association and ruled that

---

[11] 454 US 290 (1981).

[12] See the approach of the court in the judgments in *NAACP v Alabama ex R E L Patterson* 357 US 449 (1958); *Shelton v Tucker* 364 US 479 (1960); and in the area of labour law *Abood v Detroit Board of Education* 431 US 209 (1977). *Abood* involved employees in the public rather than private sector and an agency shop rather than a union shop agreement. Under an agreement adopted by a school board and a union pursuant to state law, every non-union employee was required to pay to the union 'a service fee equal in amount to union dues' as a condition of employment. That scheme was challenged by dissenting employees who objected to (1) fees for 'collective bargaining in the public sector' and (2) 'ideological union expenditures not directly related to collective bargaining'. Steward J's majority opinion, while recognizing a right to 'refus[e] to associate', rejected the first challenge and sustained only the second objection. A separate opinion by Powell J, joined by Burger CJ and Blackmun J, as well as another separate opinion by Rehnquist J, argued that the first challenge should also be sustained.

Steward J relied in part on earlier cases that had sustained, largely on statutory grounds, compulsory dues in the private sector. He insisted that in the public sector, as in the private sector, the interests in the operation of a collective bargaining system in assuring labour peace and in avoiding the risk of 'free riders' overcame the objectors' First Amendment interests 'in not being compelled to contribute to the costs of exclusive union representation'. Powell J's opinion countered that the earlier cases had not explored the constitutional issues and that the majority here had adopted an unnecessary 'sweeping limitation of First Amendment rights' by failing to apply 'strict scrutiny'. He concluded: 'I would [require] the State to come forward and demonstrate, as to each union expenditure for which it would exact support from minority employees, that the compelled contribution is necessary to serve overriding governmental objectives.'

[13] (1984) 4 DLR (4th) 231.

freedom of association included freedom to engage in conduct reasonably constant with the lawful objects of association. What this meant for trade unions was the freedom to form joint trade unions to bargain and strike. Indeed O'Leary J held that the right to organize and to bargain collectively would be made virtually meaningless if the right to strike was not recognized. Consequently the Inflation Restraint Act was found to be offensive to the Charter to the extent that it stopped workers from opting for a new union and bargaining on non-monetary issues during the period in terms of which the Act froze such negotiations.

This approach was not followed in subsequent decisions. In *Reference re Public Service Employer Relations Act*[14] the court was required to decide whether the imposition of compulsory arbitration in place of the right to strike and lock out offended the provisions of the Charter. The court rejected the submission that freedom of association protected disassociational rights subject to the limitations inherent in s 1 of the Charter. In the absence of evidence that the substitution of compulsory arbitration for the right to strike undermined the ability of the trade union movement the court was not prepared to find that there was a group right for union members to strike in terms of the express provision of freedom of association. In *Retail, Wholesale and Department Store Union v Saskatchewan*[15] the Chief Justice concluded, 'where an act is capable of being performed by a person alone or in association, then only if the person acting alone is forbidden to perform the act, is the person acting in association forbidden'.[16] Where an action, however, can only be taken in association the freedom of associ-ation clause protects such act only where there is no intention to cause harm to some or others.

In a number of cases the Canadian courts have confirmed that freedom of association means choice and thus freedom of disassociation. In *Re Lavigne & OPSEU*[17] the court held that the compulsory union dues check-off clause between a government agency and a union was constitutionally impermissible as being a breach of the freedom of association clause to the extent that such dues were applied by the union to social rather than bilateral collective bargaining issues. In this the Canadian court followed the US Supreme Court decision in *Abood v Detroit Board of Education*.[18]

The individualistic approach of the Canadian Supreme Court to workers' rights was, however, best illustrated in *Retail, Wholesale and Department Store Union v Dolphin Delivery Limited*.[19] The case concerned an industrial dispute between the Retail, Wholesale and Department Store Union and Purolator Courier Inc. The union, which represented locked-out employees of the company, believed that Dolphin Delivery Ltd, another courier, was acting in collaboration with Purolator. The union was intent on picketing Dolphin's premises, but before it could do so the company sought and obtained from the British Columbia Supreme Court and injunction preventing picketing. The injunction was granted on the basis that the alleged relationship between Dolphin and Purolator was unproved and that the

[14] (1985) 16 DLR (4th) 359.
[15] (1985) 19 DLR (4th) 609.
[16] At 619.
[17] (1985) 29 DLR (4th) 321.
[18] Supra.
[19] (1986) 33 DLR (4th) 174.

union's proposal of secondary picketing amounted to the common-law tort of inducing breach of contract between Dolphin and its employees. The matter had to be resolved under common law because Purolator, an interprovincial undertaking, was subject to federal labour law and there was no provision in federal legislation regarding the legal status of secondary picketing. The question was whether secondary picketing was a protected activity under the express provision of the Charter regarding freedom of expression.

In delivering the majority judgment of the Supreme Court McIntyre J found that the Charter did not apply to 'private litigation, divorced completely from any connection with government'.[20] He also held that the Charter applies to the common law 'only insofar as the common law is the basis of some governmental action but not insofar as the regulation of relations amongst private actors is concerned'.[21] Thus where the Charter did not apply to the common law 'the judiciary ought to apply and develop the principles of the common law in a manner consistent with fundamental values enshrined in the constitution'.[22]

A number of commentators have pointed to the individualistic approach inherent in the *Dolphin* case in which the Charter was interpreted as limiting state action and arming individuals with a negative set of formal rights to repel attempts at governmental interference.[23] As Dixon CJ stated in *Hunter v Southam Inc*, the purpose of the Charter 'is to constrain governmental action inconsistent with rights and freedoms . . . [I]t is not in itself an authorization for government action.'[24] By emphasizing the individualism inherent in the Charter, common-law protection of private property and freedom of contract remains immune from constitutional attack and a whole sphere of private relations is immunized from the law. Within the context of worker rights this form of *laissez faire* individualism is utterly incompatible with an interventionist statute which seeks to redress the imbalance of social forces so as to achieve an equilibrium in industrial relations.

This approach to labour law has not been confined to North America.[25] In *Young, James and Webster v UK* [26] the European Court of Human Rights was required to interpret British legislation of 1974–1976 which allowed British Rail to dismiss three existing employees who refused to join any of the three rail unions when a closed-shop agreement came into effect. The majority of the court held this to be an infringement of the employees' rights to freedom of association. Six of the judges found that art 11(1) of the European Convention of Human Rights (the freedom of association clause) implied a negative right to dissociate. The three dissenting judges (from Denmark, Sweden, and Iceland) held that there was no logical link between the rights to associate and dissociate.

Common-law judges have followed a similar approach. In *Learie Collymore v AG*[27] the Privy Council interpreted a certain Trinidad legislation which prohibited

---

[20] At 191.
[21] At 195.
[22] At 198.
[23] See in general Hutchinson & Petter 'Private Rights — Public Wrongs: the Liberal Lie of the Charter' (1988) 38 *U Toronto LJ* 278.
[24] (1985) 11 DLR (4th) 641 at 650.
[25] In general see Lord Wedderburn *Employment Rights in Britain and Europe, Selected Papers in Labour Law* (1991) ch 5.
[26] (1982) 4 EHRR 38.
[27] [1970] AC 538 (PC) at 548.

strikes and lock-outs and imposed compulsory arbitration before an industrial court. The Trinidad Constitution declared that freedom of association and assembly were protected. Lord Donovan denied that abridgement of the rights of free collective bargaining and of the freedom to strike are abridgements of the right of freedom of association. The jurisprudential sleight of hand accomplished in protesting union freedoms and simultaneously denying its cause of action is well illustrated in the following passage of the judgment.

> 'Moreover, trade unions need more than "freedom of association". They need to establish an organization. This involves setting up some kind of headquarters, and appointing officers to man it. Branches may also have to be set up either in districts where the union has sufficient members or in particular plants or offices. Arrangements must be made for the due collection, usually weekly, of subscriptions. Recognition by the employer must be obtained as a prelude to collective bargaining. Arrangements have to be made for industrial action in the event of collective bargaining failing either wholly or partly. All this is something over and above freedom of association. It involves a union having freedom also to organize and to bargain collectively: and it is not surprising, therefore, to find this right the subject of a separate Convention (No 98) of the International Labour Organization.'[28]

Similarly the Supreme Court of India interpreted the constitutional right to form associations or unions as not incorporating any right to engage in collective bargaining or strike action.[29]

By contrast, Continental systems of labour law have experienced a different judicial performance particularly as a result of the constitutional entrenchment of workers' rights. In West Germany the Constitutional Court has interpreted the right to form associations for the safeguarding of improvements of working and economic conditions[30] as empowering associations to be given the opportunity to engage in activities typically undertaken by such enterprises, such as collective bargaining. This constitutional provision has been interpreted to contain a number of additional safeguards for collective action. Associations may take steps to protect and increase their membership. Furthermore, the article has been interpreted to include the protection of the freedom pertaining to association as to exercise the activity specified in the Constitution such as the safeguarding and improving of working and economic conditions. Article 9.3 has been interpreted to guarantee with the freedom of association the freedom of collective bargaining and the foundation of a system of collective agreements. The court has held that were it not for these provisions, associations would not be able to fulfil their functions, i e to arrange working life in detail by collective agreements in a sphere left open by state regulation.[31] The functional link between industrial action and collective bargaining means that the former can only be taken by a union with the objective of influencing the subject-matter of collective agreements. This implies the curtailment of official and political strikes. Furthermore, industrial action is subject to an *ultima ratio* principle, i e that industrial action can only be used as a last means once all alternative measures of negotiation have been exhausted.[32]

---

[28] Ibid.
[29] *All India Bank Employees' Association v National Industrial Tribunal* AIR 1962 SC 171.
[30] Article 9.3 of the Basic Law.
[31] See in general Mischke (1992) 13 *ILJ* 1 at 3.
[32] See Mischke op cit (n 31) 4.

In France the constitutional right to join a union of one's choice in the context of other union rights and the overall *liberte syndicale* 'implies a right to take normal union activity for the member or the activist'.[33] Similarly in Sweden the right of association, which is entrenched in the Constitution, read together with s 7 of the Joint Regulation of Working Rights Act of 1976, has been interpreted to include the right to make use of membership of an organization and further that the right of association is inextricably linked to the right to bargain collectively.

A number of provisions in the German Basic Law have had a less progressive impact on labour relations. Article 6 of the Basic Law provides special protection to marriage and family and grants mothers protection and care of the community. Article 6.1 requires the legislature to take the needs of both the woman and the family into account when the woman's needs conflict with the needs of her family. Article 12a.i provides that only men may be drafted. Article 20, which contains the *Sozialstaatsprinzip*, restricts the interpretation of the equal rights protection, calling upon the legislature to play an active role in shaping society. It requires the legislature to determine who is disadvantaged and to enact legislation to equalize social differences.

These particular provisions are of considerable significance when read together with art 3 of the Basic Law, which sets out the principle of equality in three separate provisions. First, it provides that every person is equal before the law. The second clause specifically addresses the relationship between men and women as being important in decisions concerning equal treatment by providing that men and women have equal rights. The third clause prohibits individuals from being disadvantaged or privileged because of certain specified attributes, one of which is gender. The equality provision has proved somewhat problematic with regard to the German court's approach to the implementation of standards of equal treatment between men and women in the workplace. Apart from the area of equal pay, the equal rights provisions have had a limited effect on the relationship of employers to their employees. The provision has not been seen as an obstacle to preferential treatment of men and women by private employers. Biological differences justify differential treatment, provided that the biological difference makes differential treatment necessary or even desirable in so far as the individual is concerned. Only in a few cases have the courts held that legislative provisions requiring differential treatment in the workplace have violated the Basic Law. In short, constitutional principles had a limited impact upon promoting substantive equality in the German workplace.[34]

Arguably the most extensive constitutional entrenchment of workers' rights is to be found in the Italian Constitution. Adopted in 1948 after World War II, the Constitution includes a range of workers' rights, including the right to form associations without authorization (art 18), organization in trade unions (art 39), and the right to strike (art 40). Following the Constitution, the Workers' Statute of 1970 was passed and includes rights to carry on union activities, not to be penalized for joining or not joining a union, and for participating in a strike. Within the structure of the

---

[33] Wedderburn op cit (n 25) 149.
[34] See in general Harvey 'Equal Treatment of Men and Women in the Workplace: Implementation of the European Community's Equal Treatment Legislation in the Federal Republic of Germany' (1990) 38 *Am J Comp L* 31.

Constitution and the Workers' Statute the freedom of association clause has been interpreted to have both an individual and collective freedom, albeit that it is the individual who generally exercises such freedoms. Trade union activity which is guaranteed includes recruitment in organizations, self-protection, and bargaining.

Article 40 has placed major limitations on the managerial prerogative. The court has declared unconstitutional an employer's right to substitute other workers recruited from outside in the place of strikers.[35] The recognition of the right to strike in Italy implies that the considered abstention from work does not constitute a breach of contract, but rather a cause of legitimate suspension of the individual employment relationship, and thus the employer cannot dismiss the strikers during a strike period. However, an individual employee participating in a unlawful strike violates his obligations in terms of the contract and is liable to disciplinary action by the employer, including dismissal. The Italian courts have limited the right to strike on the basis that the notion of the strike itself contains limitations and by the reconciliation of other constitutionally recognized rights.

In some countries the lock-out has also been recognized constitutionally. In France, Italy, and Portugal there is a refusal to recognize the lock-out. These countries recognize the lock-out as a freedom but not as a right. Portugal categorically rejects the lock-out in art 60 of its Constitution and France and Italy reject that parity can be drawn between strike and lock-out with particular reference to the exclusive constitutional guarantees of strikes. In short the lock-out is characterized as a breach of the employment contract. In these jurisdictions the lock-out is allowed as a defence against unlawful attacks, i e as a form of self-help.

## INTERNATIONAL PROTECTION OF LABOUR LAW

A series of international standards have been adopted by the International Labour Organization (ILO). In particular there are important ILO instruments and freedoms of association, including Convention 87, concerning the freedom of association and protection of the right to organize, and Convention 98, concerning the application of the principle of the right to organize and bargain collectively. Convention 87 contains four main provisions. First, it provides that workers and employers without distinction shall have the right to establish and join organizations or their own choosing without previous authorization. Secondly, workers' and employers' organizations shall have the right to draw up their constitutions and rules, to elect their representatives, to organize the administration and activities, and to formulate their programme. Thirdly, there is a prohibition against the suspension and dissolution of workers' and employers' organizations by administrative authority; and, fourthly, workers' and employers' organizations shall have the right to establish and join federations and confederations, which will have the same rights as their constituent organizations, and to affiliate with international organizations of workers and employers.

Convention 98, which does not apply to the armed forces, police, and public servants engaged in the administration of justice, has as its objective the protection

---

[35] Treu *International Encyclopedia for Labour Law and Industrial Relations* (R Blanpain (ed)) vol 5 at para 472. See also Treu 'State Regulation and Job Security' (1992) 13 *ILJ* 1053.

of workers against anti-union discrimination in respect of their employment and of workers' and employers' organizations against interference by each other. It also calls for measures appropriate at national conventions to encourage and promote the full development of collective bargaining.

Other important ILO documents have been published. Convention 135 concerns the protection and facilities to be afforded workers' representatives in the undertaking, Convention 141 concerns the organization of the rural workers and their role in economic and social development, Convention 151 concerns protection of the right to organize and procedures for determining conditions of employment in the public service, and Convention 153 concerns the promotion of collective bargaining. Convention 141, which takes into account the difficulties encountered with regard to the organization of rural workers, confirms the principles of Conventions 87 and 98 and suggests the adoption of measures designed to promote the effective development of rural workers' organizations. Convention 151, which applies to public employees who are not covered by Convention 98, includes protective measures against anti-union discrimination and negates interference by public authorities in the affairs of public employees' organizations. It also contains provisions on various other issues such as the facilities to be afforded to the representatives of public employees' organizations and the procedure to determine the terms and conditions of employment of public employees whether through collective bargaining or otherwise.

A number of other international organizations have adopted standards of protecting freedom of association. Important safeguards are included in the United Nations instruments such as the Universal Declaration of Human Rights (arts 20 and 23), the International Covenant on Economic and Social and Cultural Rights of 1966, and the 1966 International Covenant on Civil and Political Rights (art 22). Amongst regional instruments containing provisions for freedom of association are the American Declaration of the Rights and Duties of Men of 1948 (art 22), the European Convention for the Protection of Human Rights and Fundamental Freedoms of 1950 (art 11), and the European Social Charter of 1961 (Part II arts 5 and 6).

The Social Charter has a number of important provisions, including art 5, which commits the state to ensuring freedom for workers and employers to form and join organizations for the protection of their economic and social interests. Article 6 obliges the state to ensure effective collective bargaining, promotion of joint consultation and voluntary negotiations for collective agreements, as well as the right to strike, although only in regard to conflicts of interest and not in breach of obligations in collective agreements, as well as subject to any restrictions imposed by the state that, prescribed by law, are necessary in a democratic society for protection of the rights and freedoms of others and for the protection of international public security, health, or morals. However, the European Convention on Human Rights has been the more important document in shaping national labour law in Europe. Whereas the Charter allows for complaints only to the committee of experts (independent nominees' reports are sent to the Committee of Ministers with recommendations for the attention of the states and parties concerned), the European Convention on Human Rights allows parties to complain to the European Commission and to the Court of Human Rights, which can (and does) award damages to individuals. Unfortunately, deprived of the collective standards expressed in the

Charter, the European Court of Human Rights has been unable to develop its jurisprudence and it reflects the needs of workers collectively organized. Thus in the *Belgium Police Union*[36] and *Swedish Engine Drivers Union*[37] cases the court concluded that states must recognize that union members are protected by trade unions, but it did not accept the Commission's view that collective bargaining could be an essential part of the recognized rights. The court held that a public-sector union had no right to make collective agreements with or be consulted by the state where it was the employer, for 'not only is this latter right not mentioned in art 11(1) but neither can it be said that all Contracting States incorporated it in their national law practice, or that it is indispensable for the effective enjoyment of trade union freedom'.[38]

Furthermore, in *X v Germany*[39] the court did not recognize that a teacher as a public servant had a right to strike and that there was no contravention of art 11(1) by virtue of such prohibition. Reference has already been made to the case of *Young, James and Webster v UK*[40] with regard to the European Court of Human Rights' approach to art 11. This approach was extended in *Cheall v UK*.[41] In this case the applicant preferred to belong to one union rather than another since he felt that the former would represent his interests rather more effectively than the latter had previously done. He was initially admitted to the union, which then expelled him in order to comply with their obligations not to admit a former member of an affiliated union without enquiring whether there was any objection from that quarter. The applicant complained that the UK, in affording him no protection with respect to his expulsion, had violated his right to freedom of association in terms of the Convention. The right was not simply that of joining the union but also the right to remain a member of a union of his choice. The Commission rejected the claim, saying that in an exercise of rights under art 11(1) the unions must remain free to decide questions concerning admission to and expulsion from the union in accordance with union rules.[42]

It is interesting to note that the Commission's approach is similar to that of the House of Lords, which had said of Mr Cheall's litigation,[43] 'freedom of association can only be mutual; there can be no right of an individual to associate with others who are not willing to associate with him'. In this case the Commission seemed to take the approach that freedom of association gives to trade unions a measure of autonomy in regulating their affairs, including the right to refuse to associate with those whom they consider to be prejudicial to their interests. Unlike the earlier *Young* case, there appears to be some recognition by the Commission as opposed to the court of the collectivity of union interests.

The EEC Treaty also has implications for workers. In terms of art 119 members are obliged to establish and retain the principle of equal pay for men and women for

---

[36] *National Union of Belgium Police v Belgium* (1975) 1 EHRR 578.
[37] *Svenska Lokmannaforbunder v Sweden* (1976) 1 EHRR 617.
[38] Wedderburn op cit (n 25) 143.
[39] (1985) 7 EHRR 461.
[40] Supra.
[41] [1983] 1 All ER 1130, (1986) 8 EHRR 74.
[42] At 75.
[43] [1983] 1 All ER 1130 at 1136. See in general Leader 'The European Convention on Human Rights, The Employment Act of 1988 and the Right to Refuse to Strike' (1991) 12 *ILJ* 39.

equal work. This article has been held to create a binding right on the member states that a litigant could appeal on the basis of the article to domestic courts and that the latter should apply the principles of the article.

Directive 75/117 provides that the principle of equal pay prohibits discrimination on the grounds of sex for elements of remuneration and conditions of remuneration. The internal legal system must provide that all provisions and tariff agreements, wage or salary agreements, and factory agreements, as well as individual employment contracts, must be compatible with this principle and, if not, are void and are to be declared void. Furthermore, notices or dismissals solely on the grounds that the worker raises his or her claim to equal pay out of court or in court are to be declared inadmissible with the national legal system. With regard to the workers and obligations the obligation to publish the applicable provisions of equal pay must be established. The European Court of Justice has dealt with the scope of these provisions. In one case a stockroom manageress was paid less than the man who had for some months previously held the same position. She sought to establish a right to equal pay by means of a comparison with the former male employee. The European Court ruled that the principle of equal pay for equal work is not confined to situations in which man and woman are contemporaneously doing equal work for the same employer.[44]

## CONCLUSION

In *Law, Legislation and Liberty* Hayek has written: '[T]he term "freedom of organization" — a hallowed battle cry of labour and political organizations — carries overtones ... in conflict with the reign of law on which a free society rests.' The organizational powers of unions 'will probably require limitations by general rules of law far more narrow than those it has found necessary to impose by law in the actions of private individuals'.[45] As Wedderburn has noted, this form of individualism 'recoils from freedom of association the more it incorporates an effective right to organize'.[46]

The case of *Lochner* is perhaps the quintessential example of the Supreme Court relying on an image of the neutrality of the common law and thereby curtailing the impact of interventionist labour legislation. More than seventy-five years later Laurence Tribe can state in his leading work on US constitutional law that

> 'the basic justification for judicial intervention under *Lochner* — that the courts were restoring the natural order which had been upset by the legislature — is increasingly perceived as fundamentally flawed. There was no "natural" economic order to upset or restore, legislative or judicial decision in any direction could neither be restrained nor justified on any such basis ... [T]he belief that there just was no transcendent body of binding general common law ... ultimately devastated *Lochner's* due process doctrine that legislatures may not upset the "natural" conditions of contract and property enshrined in common law categories and their logical entailments.'[47]

The fact that *Lochner* has been overturned should logically have resulted in the

---

[44] See Crisham 'The Equal Pay Principle, Some Recent Decisions in the European Court of Justice' 1981 *Common Market LR* 601.
[45] *Law, Legislation and Liberty* (1979) vol 3 89.
[46] Op cit (n 25) 151.
[47] Tribe *American Constitutional Law* (1988) 447.

demise of the common-law vision as neutral and fair. Yet, as other US commentators have noticed, the premises of *Lochner* continue to exert a considerable influence within US jurisprudence. As Sunstein notes:

> '[T]he provision of welfare is treated differently because it is in some respects new and in any event hedged with limitations and reservations. Here *Lochner's* premises, having to do with neutrality and inaction, account critically for current constitutional doctrine with respect to 'affirmative' rights.'[48]

As other decisions, such as the *Dolphin* case of the Canadian Supreme Court, have shown, the individualism of the market plays a considerable influence in the interpretation of the Constitution in general and the application of workers' rights in particular. Given a Labour Relations Act which attempts to promote industrial democracy by means of the dilution of importance of the concept of freedom of contract, it will be important for South African constitutional jurisprudence to circumvent the *Lochner* route in order to give effect to such a collective enterprise.

Comparative jurisprudence indicates that unless the collective rights of workers are entrenched in a code in such a manner so as to be interpreted so as to promote collectivity the more individualistic principles of the Bill of Rights tend to trump collective interests, thereby counterpoising the freedom of the individual to that of the collectivity. The blending of collective and individual rights is well summarized by Kahn Freund in the following passage:

> 'Freedom of organization has two social and therefore two legal functions. It is a civil liberty, a human right, an aspect of freedom of association . . . [I]ts existence and adequate guarantees for its exercise are, however, also indispensable to conditions for the operation of collective labour relations.'[49]

An interesting example of where a constitutional provision has had a significant influence on labour jurisprudence is in the Indian case of *National Textile Workers' Union v Ramakrishnan*.[50] In this case the company employed approximately 1 000 workers and the thirteen shareholders were all from the same family. A petition for the winding-up of the company was initiated as a result of a deadlock between the shareholders. One group of shareholders petitioned as both contributories and creditors on the grounds of inability of the company to pay its debts and on grounds of justice and equity. An interim injunction issued in the proceedings prevented the workers at one plant from claiming under the Employees' State Insurance Scheme. This led to an apprehension that the employees might not have received wages. The court *a quo* took the view that, although all parties had an interest in winding up, including employees, this was not sufficient to give such employees the right of a hearing. The Supreme Court set aside the order and instructed that the unions should be heard. The majority of the court found that

> 'the concept of a company has undergone radical transformation in the last few decades. The traditional view of a company was that it was a convenient mechanical device carrying on trade and industry, a mere legal framework providing a convenient institution or container for holding and using the powers of company management . . . Today social scientists and thinkers regard the company as a living, vital and dynamic social organism with firm and deep-rooted affiliations with

---

[48] Sunstein 'Lochner's Legacy' (1987) 87 *Columbia LR* 873 at 882.
[49] As quoted by Wedderburn op cit (n 25) 142.
[50] AIR 1983 SC 75. See in general Cottrel (1990) 39 *ICLQ* 434.

the rest of the community in which it functions. It would be wrong to look upon it as something belonging to the shareholders.'[51]

In arriving at this conclusion the court was influenced by art 43A of the Indian Constitution, i e the Directive Principle which provides that in interpreting the Constitution the court shall take account that the state shall take steps, by suitable legislation or in any other way, to secure the participation of workers and the management of undertakings, establishments, or other organizations engaged in any industry. Of this Directive Principle Bhagwati J said: '[I]t is therefore idle to contend . . . that the workers should have no voice in the determination of the question of whether the enterprise should continue to run or be shut down under an order of Court.'[52] In short, the existence of the Directive Principles such as art 43A allowed the court to introduce a collective notion into its interpretation of company law, thereby safeguarding worker interests. *Ramakrishnan* is thus a good example of interpretive principles of a Constitution influencing the manner in which courts develop their substantive and procedural areas of law.

It is also clear from this overview that a number of rights in a Bill of Rights impact upon the rights of workers other than an express section dealing with workers' rights. In particular freedom of association, which is generally recognized as a fundamental right, impacts significantly on the interpretation of workers' rights. Provisions such as freedom of assembly and freedom of expression affect picketing and other forms of union organization. Depending upon the exact wording of a Charter, the obligation of the court is to harmonize individual and collective interests so as to recognize the rights of workers rather than to undermine them.

## CHAPTER 3 OF THE NEW CONSTITUTION

Section 27 of the new Constitution guarantees a series of fundamental rights for both workers and employers. The section provides as follows:

**'Labour relations**

(1) Every person shall have the right to fair labour practices.

(2) Workers shall have the right to form and join trade unions, and employers shall have the right to form and join employers' organizations.

(3) Workers and employers shall have the right to organize and bargain collectively.

(4) Workers shall have the right to strike for purposes of collective bargaining.

(5) Employers' recourse to the lock-out for the purpose of collective bargaining shall not be impaired, subject to s 33(1).'

The initial impact of this section may well be limited as a result of the insulation of labour legislation that promotes fair employment practices, orderly and equitable collective bargaining, and the regulation of industrial action. In terms of s 33(5)*(a)* such legislation shall remain of full force and effect until repealed or amended by the legislature. Section 33(5)*(b)* provides that if a proposed enactment amending or repealing a law referred to in para *(a)* deals with a matter in respect of which the National Manpower Commission or any other similar body which may replace such Commission as competent in terms of the law then in force to consider and make

---

[51] *National Textile Workers' Union v Ramakrishnan* (supra) at 81 (*per* Bhagwati J).
[52] At 83–4.

recommendations, such proposed enactment shall not be introduced in Parliament unless the commission or any similar body has been given an opportunity to consider the proposed enactment and to make recommendations with regard thereto.

Section 33(5) is designed to insulate existing labour legislation from inquiry under Chapter 3. It is significant that the phrase 'notwithstanding the provisions of this chapter', which would have given the exemption under s 33(5) primacy over the rights guaranteed in Chapter 3, was excluded.[53] Consequently it is possible that an argument based on the theory which attaches importance to drafting history with the intention of insulation of existing legislation could be weakened.[54]

The express wording of s 33(5)*(a)*, which provides that existing law must promote fair employment practice, orderly and equitable collective bargaining, and the regulation of industrial action for it to remain in force, arguably invites a court to test existing legislation against these criteria before finding that such legislation shall remain in force. The laws which s 33(5)*(a)* is intended to insulate from constitutional scrutiny are the Labour Relations Act 28 of 1956, the Public Service Labour Relations Act 102 of 1993, the Education Labour Relations Act 146 of 1993, and the Agricultural Labour Act 147 of 1993.

Given the provisions of s 33(5)*(a)*, s 27 is only applicable to those categories of employee and employer who are not covered by the four statutes. At present this would include domestic workers, teachers at private schools, academics at universities and technikons, and certain limited categories of public servants such as town clerks, directors-general, and those persons employed in terms of the common law of employment. Clearly the requirement that every person has the right to fair labour practices will have a substantial effect on the common law of employment. Thus the common-law rule that an employer may not terminate on notice without reason will be unconstitutional, for it clearly violates the principle of fair labour practices. In short, the ordinary courts will now have an unfair labour practice jurisdiction.[55]

The controversy relating to the application of Chapter 3 began during the deliberations at the Technical Committee on Fundamental Rights. One of the earlier reports openly supported the horizontal application of fundamental rights and sought to give legal effect by making the chapter binding on not just the legislative and executive organs of state but the judicial organs as well. The intention behind this recommendation was that if the courts were so bound, they would have to apply Chapter 3 in every case that came before them, including cases where an individual asserted a right against another private individual body or institution. Reference to judicial organs was deleted from s 7(1) so that it was made binding only on the legislative and executive organs of the state. However, in terms of s 7(2) Chapter 3 shall apply to all law in force. Furthermore, s 33(2) subjects the common and customary laws to the rights contained in Chapter 3 by rendering any common-law limitation of such rights unconstitutional unless its limitation conforms with the requirements of s 33(1).

Furthermore, s 35(3) enjoins a court to have due regard to the spirit of the

---

[53] Technical Committee on Fundamental Rights during the Transition, 10th Progress Report (5 October 1993).
[54] Mureinik 'Bridge to Where? An Introduction to the Interim Bill of Rights' (1994) 10 *SAJHR* 31 at 44.
[55] See Cachalia et al *Fundamental Rights in the New Constitution* (1994) 91.

important objects of the chapter when interpreting, applying, or developing common law or customary law. It has thus been suggested that while applying to the common law, Chapter 3 does not apply to all transactions either because the common law does not govern the transactions or because the rights do not have any bearing on the arrangement.[56]

This proposition highlights the important point that a Bill of Rights is a shield and not a sword. In other words, the Bill will not provide positive rights to an applicant against another individual or private institution. However, once the latter attempts to enforce a relationship against the former in terms of the law the Bill of Rights can well apply as a shield, notwithstanding its horizontal application. For this reason s 27 will have longer-term implications for the development of labour law irrespective of whether the employee is employed by the public or private sector. Consequently an employer may in certain cases seek relief in either the industrial court under the unfair labour practice jurisdiction provided by the Labour Relations Act or in the Supreme Court in terms of the common law.

Section 27 will also put an end to the possibility of an argument that s 17, the right to freedom of association, undermines those principles of collective bargaining and the right to strike which have been developed in terms of the unfair labour practice jurisdiction contained in the Labour Relations Act. The specific inclusion of the right to bargain collectively and the right to strike invites a court to reconcile the jurisprudence relating to freedom of association with the provisions of s 27. Accordingly many of the difficulties encountered by comparative law will not be applicable within the South African context.

Although the provisions of s 27 constitute minimum rights, the open-textured nature of the section will allow both the ordinary courts and the Constitutional Court to develop a parallel labour jurisprudence.

Of particular interest is s 27(5), which provides that employers' recourse to the lock-out for the purpose of collective bargaining shall not be impaired, subject to s 33(1). Unlike the other subsections of s 27, employers do not have a right to lock out workers. In terms of the Labour Relations Act there is a statutory recognition of a lock-out in the event that certain procedures are followed.

Compliance with the procedures laid down in s 65 affords an employer immunity from prosecution and in terms of s 79(1) of the Labour Relations Act an employer will then be protected against a claim for wages by affected employees.[57]

On this basis it would appear that there is already a right to a lock out in our law. Consequently the word 'recourse' as opposed to a right could mean that such a 'right' has no constitutional status and can be restricted on the basis of the general limitation clause contained in s 33(1).

This argument is fortified by the fact that the limitation clause is expressly included in s 27(5). It is thus submitted that the word 'recourse to lock out' has been employed to confirm that there is no general right to lock out in present South African law and that the existing immunity from prosecution, were a lock-out to

---

[56] See Cheadle *Current Labour Law* (1994) 98.
[57] See Wallis *Labour and Employment Law* (1993) para 56. However, see Rycroft & Jordaan *South African Labour Law* 2 ed (1992) 292, where s 65 is interpreted restrictively to exclude protection against an action for breach of contract. The use of the word 'recourse' would then afford even weaker protection.

take place, can itself be amended if the state is able to prove the justification grounds contained in s 33(1).

The apparent reason as to why none of the other provisions of s 27 are expressly made subject to s 33(1) is because all labour legislation has been subjected to its own express provision, s 33(5). However, while under existing legislation it could be argued that rights to fair labour practices, to form and join trade unions, and to organize and bargain collectively exist under present law, strike and lock-out action are limited to an immunity from criminal proceedings in the event that there is compliance with the provisions of s 65 of the Labour Relations Act. In other words, there is no general right to strike in terms of present South African law. Accordingly none of the labour legislation purportedly immunized from constitutional attack in terms of s 33(5)*(a)* accords a right to strike for the purpose of collective bargaining. Hence, were such a right to be granted in terms of an amendment to the Labour Relations Act, another Parliament could curtail this right, but only within the terms of the justification grounds provided for in s 33(1), the general limitation clause.

# PROPERTY RIGHTS, LAND RIGHTS, AND ENVIRONMENTAL RIGHTS*

A J VAN DER WALT

## 1 PHILOSOPHICAL BACKGROUND

### 1.1 Theories of property

#### 1.1.1 *Introduction*

Philosophers, lawyers, and politicians have justified the existence and protection of private individual property almost as often and as vehemently as they have criticized it. The justification of private property was discussed by the Greek philosophers and the classical Roman lawyers, but in a fundamental sense this debate is a typically modern one, especially regarding the inherent tension between the public sphere and the private sphere which underlies it. In this context the problem of property has been described as a clash between two sets of values — the value of liberty and the value of justice.[1] According to this view, justice demands equality, whereas liberty requires room for individuality, thereby precipitating a classic confrontation between claims for the equal distribution of property or the promotion of social interests, on the one hand, and for the protection of individual property, on the other.

This tension strikes at the heart of all property theories. In order to avoid a fatal schism between justice and liberty a theory of property must justify the existence of private property without denying the promotion of equality. In fact, however, most theories of property justify either the existence and protection of private property or the existence of more or less fundamental state powers to interfere with private property in order to promote social justice and equality.

#### 1.1.2 *Moral property theories*

Moral arguments in favour of property seek to justify the privatization of property — the removal of objects from the public or common sphere and reserving them for

---

\* The author gratefully acknowledges the financial support of the Alexander von Humboldt Foundation (Bonn) and the Institute for Research Development at the Human Sciences Research Council (Pretoria), without which the research for this project would not have been possible. Views and opinions expressed here are those of the author, and should not be attributed to either institution.

[1] Minogue 'The Concept of Property and its Contemporary Significance' in Pennock & Chapman (eds) *NOMOS XXII: Property* (1980) 3 at 3, 24. See further Honoré 'Ownership' in Guest (ed) *Oxford Essays in Jurisprudence* (1961) 107; Exshaw 'The Right of Private Property' in Bridge et al (eds) *Fundamental Rights* (1973) 73; Becker *Property Rights: Philosophic Foundations* (1977); Macpherson (ed) *Property: Mainstream and Critical Positions* (1978); Van den Bergh *Eigendom: Grepen uit de Geschiedenis van een Omstreden Begrip* (1988); Schwartländer & Willoweit (eds) *Das Recht des Menschen auf Eigentum* (1983); Waldron (ed) *Theories of Rights* (1984); Munzer *A Theory of Property* (1990).

the exclusive benefit of a specific individual. As a rule these theories justify not only the acquisition and protection of private property in general but also its exclusivity, autonomy, and absoluteness, which means that interferences with private property should be limited to the minimum. These theories are usually based upon either first occupation or labour.

First-occupation theories justify private property with reference to the actual occupation of a previously unoccupied object. These theories reflect the requirements for the original acquisition of ownership by occupation in Roman law: an actual act of occupation, exercised with the will to acquire ownership of a previously unoccupied object. Famous proponents of this theory such as Grotius, Kant, and Hegel stress the fact that the occupation of a previously unoccupied object involves an act of will by the occupier, and justify the acquisition of the right on the basis of the exercise of will and the temporal precedence of the occupation.[2]

Modern manifestations of this theory tend to concentrate less upon the actual first occupation of property since unoccupied property has become uncommon in the contemporary world. However, these theories still find moral justification for property in the fact that it embodies the will and provides room for the development of the personality of the occupier. According to these theories, property is the external sphere within which an individual exercises and enjoys his/her freedom, and usually their justifications of private property argue from the existence of body rights and personal rights to property rights with regard to the outside world.[3] In this context it is characteristic of these theories that they emphasize the individual's right to exclude others from his/her private property, whereas many contemporary property theories tend to focus on the right not to be excluded from social and public property.

Labour theories justify the acquisition of private property from a slightly different perspective. Locke, who is considered the most important advocate of this theory, argues that everyone has property rights with regard to his/her own person so that everyone has property in his/her own labour and, by extension, in everything upon which labour has been spent.[4] In a slightly different version of the theory Locke emphasizes the fact that labour adds value to an object and that a person is entitled to an object if its value has been enhanced as a result of that person's labour.[5] These theories resemble the requirements for the original acquisition of ownership through manufacture in Roman law: the creation of a new object through the labour and effort of one subject who uses the property or material of another without permission. This applies equally to previously unoccupied and previously owned objects. It is important to note that Locke, whose aim was to describe the limits of sovereign monarchical power, justifies private property in this theory on the basis of natural and not human law.

---

[2] See Grotius *De Jure Praedae* (1604–1605) ed by Hamaker (1868) *Hagae Comitum* 214–16; *De Jure Belli ac Pacis* (1625) ed by Kanter van Hettinga-Tromp (1939) *Lugdunum Batavorum* II.2; *Inleidinge tot de Hollandsche Rechtsgeleerdheid* (1619–1621) ed by Dovring, Fischer & Meijers (Leyden 1952) II.I.16; Kant *Metaphysik der Sitten* part I para 14 in *Sämmtliche Werke* ed by Hartenstein (Leipzig 1868) vol 7 62; Hegel *Grundlinien der Philosophie des Rechts* part I para 44 in *Sämmtliche Werke* ed by Glockner (Stuttgart 1952) vol 7 97.

[3] See in this regard Cohen 'Self-ownership, World-ownership, and Equality' in Lucash (ed) *Justice and Equality Here and Now* (1986) 108; 'Self-ownership, World-ownership, and Equality: Part II' (1986) 3/2 *Social Philosophy & Policy* 77.

[4] See Locke *Two Treatises of Government* (1698) ed by Laslett (1960) Second Treatise para 27 328–9.

[5] See Locke op cit (n 4) para 28 329–30.

Moral arguments in favour of property rely upon a strong relationship between property and the person. In the first-occupation theories this relationship exists in the fact that the act of occupation embodies the will of the occupier in the property. According to Kant, the acquisition of property is justified if the act of occupation is in accordance with the moral law and if anybody else's subsequent use or occupation of the property would constitute an injury to the occupier.[6] According to Hegel, the acquisition of property amounts to the establishment of personal freedom in the external sphere of objects by imbuing the property with the will of the person.[7] Through this externalization of personal freedom a person not only acquires property but also realizes his/her own reason, will, and personality.[8] In fact, in Hegel's case property rights are regarded as the basis of the right to life and liberty.[9] This relationship between person and property implies that if anybody else commits acts of use or occupation with regard to the property, he/she causes injury to the occupier. The influence of this argument is demonstrated by the fact that nineteenth-century German legal theory treats possessory infringements as delicts against the person of the possessor rather than mere infringements of property rights.[10]

In the labour theories the relationship between the person and his/her property is constituted by the personal effort or value which is added to the property through the person's labour. Locke does not distinguish between personal property and productive property and his theory can at most justify the acquisition of the former, resulting in a paradox: the labourer who actually does the work collects a salary, while the entrepreneur for whom value accumulates does not need to do actual physical work in the production process at all.[11] In this sense the labour theories illustrate the limitations of the person–property relationship, thereby necessitating a distinction between personal and productive property.

In the relatively recent 'new property' theories it is argued that the nature of property (and therefore of property rights) is changing and that the classic perception of property as 'thing'-ownership is being replaced by a new perception of property as the right to participate in (or not to be excluded from) socio-economic and political benefits. According to these theories, the new property consists of a variety of benefits or 'handouts' granted by the welfare state in the process of the just distribution of wealth, based upon increased taxation.[12] In the process property as 'thing-ownership' is increasingly replaced by rights to participate in social benefits such as social security, pensions, medical security, workers' rights, state contracts, state benefits (such as housing), and so on. In one sense this new property is still

---

[6] See Kant op cit (n 2) 27.

[7] See Hegel op cit (n 2) part 1 paras 41–71 88–129.

[8] See Stillman 'Property, Freedom and Individuality in Hegel's and Marx's Political Thought' in *NOMOS XXII: Property* op cit (n 1) 130 at 131–2.

[9] See Stillman op cit (n 8) 131–2. Olivecrona '*Die zwei Schichten im naturrechtlichen Denken*' (1977) 63 *ARSP* 79 at 81ff argues that Grotius' theory follows a similar pattern, in which the owner's person or *suum* forms the centre from which rights to the outside world emanate.

[10] See Von Savigny *Das Recht des Besitzes: eine civilistische Abhandlung* (1803) 7 ed by Rudorff (1864, reprinted 1967) 48–50.

[11] See Minogue op cit (n 1) 9–10.

[12] See Reich 'The New Property' (1964) 73 *Yale LJ* 733; Anderson 'Takings and Expectations: Toward a "Broader Vision" of Property Rights' (1989) 37 *U Kansas LR* 529; Large 'This Land is Whose Land? Changing Concepts of Land as Property' 1973 *Wisconsin LR* 1039; Van Alstyne 'Cracks in "the New Property": Adjudicative Due Process in the Administrative State' (1977) 62 *Cornell LR* 445.

person-related, but it also represents a fundamental shift away from classic moral arguments in favour of property since it does not allow justifications based upon the will or individuality of the property holder.[13] In fact this view of the 'new property' displays a shift away from the individual and towards the public sphere, as is demonstrated by the fact that the 'new property' is not so much the right exclusively to hold (private) property as the right not to be excluded from (public) property. In the process the focus of property theories is shifting towards participatory rights with regard to common property and away from exclusive rights to individual property. Obviously this development is of the utmost importance for constitutional and human rights theory since it implies a shift away from defensive and performance rights towards participatory rights. Macpherson[14] has argued that a similar change in the traditional perception of property was necessitated by the obsessive individualism of liberal theory and that a broadened perception of property which includes both the right to exclusive use of personal property and the right not to be excluded from the benefit of social assets would be better suited to a modern liberal democracy than the narrow traditional concept of exclusive 'thing'-ownership. In fact arguments in favour of the 'new property', especially when they are inspired by utility rather than moral considerations, are often difficult to distinguish from instrumental theories aimed at a socially responsible perception of ownership.

Closely related to the theories of the 'new property' is another recent perception in terms of which the traditional concept of property is in a process of disintegration or fragmentation. Theories of property in this category focus on the traditional perception of property as 'thing'-ownership and the ways in which it is changing, and they variously describe the process of change as the 'erosion',[15] 'fragmentation',[16] 'disintegration',[17] or 'dephysicalization'[18] of property. Two aspects of the development described by this perception demonstrate the fact that perceptions of property rights are moving away from the private individual towards the public or social sphere: property rights increasingly relate to incorporeal social benefits rather than to corporeal things and property rights that still relate to things are increasingly being limited and restricted by legislation protecting social interests.

---

[13] The moral justification of property rights based upon the investment of a person's will or labour in a corporeal thing physically occupied or produced does not apply in the case of property in the form of shares in a company or an interest in a state pension fund. It is one thing to argue that property rights with regard to a piece of land personally cultivated or with regard to tools of one's trade are necessary for the development of personality or individuality, but it is much harder to make the same argument stick with regard to shares or a state pension. Obviously Reich op cit (n 12) is forced to defend exactly this argument, but it is less convincing than in the classic moral arguments regarding corporeal property.

[14] Macpherson 'Liberal-Democracy and Property' in Macpherson op cit (n 1) 199.

[15] This term is used to describe what is perceived as a diminution of property rights through the increasing imposition of legislative restrictions and limitations. See Van der Walt 'Introduction' in Van der Walt (ed) *Land Reform and the Future of Landownership in South Africa* (1991) 1–7.

[16] This term is used to indicate that a more or less unitary right or group of rights is being fragmented into a larger number of rights that are not necessarily unified conceptually or systematically. See Van der Walt 'The Fragmentation of Land Rights' (1992) 8 *SAJHR* 431. In some cases the same concept is used interchangeably with 'disintegration'.

[17] This term is used to indicate that the right of property is undergoing an inescapable transformation which brings about the dissapearance of its original private individual character. See Grey 'The Disintegration of Property' in *NOMOS XXII: Property* op cit (n 1) 69–85; Underkuffler 'On Property: an Essay' (1990) 100 *Yale LJ* 127; Gray 'Property in Thin Air' (1991) 50 *Cambridge LJ* 252.

[18] This term is used to indicate that property rights increasingly relate to incorporeals rather than to things. See Vandevelde 'The New Property of the Nineteenth Century: the Development of the Modern Concept of Property' (1980) 29 *Buffalo U LR* 325; Horwitz 'The Transformation in the Conception of Property in American Law, 1780–1860' (1973) 40 *U Chicago LR* 248; Horwitz *The Transformation of American Law, 1780–1860* (1977) ch II.

An important aspect of 'fragmentation' theories of property is that property rights are not regarded as a unitary class. Instead, the nature and content of property rights are determined with due regard for the nature of the object, the identity of the subject, and the possible social implications of the use and exploitation of the object.[19] The most obvious and influential examples of such a differentiated treatment of objects of property rights are the distinctions between personal and productive property, on the one hand, and between land and movable property, on the other. Both distinctions play a major role in the debate concerning the limits and social implications of property exploitation. Property theories concerned with the diversification or fragmentation of property rights often stress the importance of the nature, context, and social function of specific property objects since these factors can and should determine the content and nature of specific property rights — the definition, content, and limits of the right to a pencil must obviously be different from the right to nuclear material. In this context the unique position and function of land is often pointed out and many theories argue or assume that all rights to land should be defined and treated with due regard to its unique character as a vital but finite resource.

### 1.1.3 *Instrumental property theories*

Instrumental property theories, in contrast to the moral theories, are characterized by the fact that they all treat property as a means to an end and not as an end in itself. These theories are consequently not focused on the moral justification of private individual property, but rather on the function of a system of protected property rights in society. In this category theories based on utility, anti-property theories, and restrictive theories can be distinguished.

Utility theories resemble the moral theories in that they also seek to justify the existence of private property based on the premise that all humans need securely protected property rights in order to attain a reasonable standard of happiness, which is the ultimate goal. The protection of property is therefore not seen as an end in itself, but as a means to an end. These theories as propounded by the likes of Hume and Hobbes are not really interested in the inherent qualities or characteristics of property as such, but rather in its function in providing a requirement of human and social life.[20] The same theme is taken up in similar theories which also treat property as a means to a social end and which consequently tend to judge the importance of individual property rights with due regard for the rights of others and the interests of society. Rawls, for instance, justifies both the current distribution and the possible redistribution of property on the basis of distributive justice, arguing that inequality can be allowed to the extent that it can justifiably be said to improve the position of the worst off in society.[21] This means that both the protection and the justifiable

---

[19] In Dutch theory this is known as the 'pluriformity' of property; see Slagter 'Eigendom en Privaatrecht' 1976 *Rechtsgeleerd Magazijn Themis* 276; Van Neste 'Eigendom Morgen' 1983 *Tijdschrift voor Privaatrecht* 479; Van Goch 'Naar een Gedifferentieerd Eigendomsbegrip' (1982) 8 *Recht en Kritiek* 82; Schut 'Naar een meer Pluriforme Regeling van het Eigendomsrecht?' 1981 *Rechtsgeleerd Magazijn Themis* 329; Slagter 'Eigendom en Pseudo-eigendom' in *Quod Licet: Kleijn-bundel* (1992) 357–74.

[20] See Hume *Treatise of Human Nature* ed by Selby-Bigge (1960) book III part II para II 484–8. It is important to note that some authors employ both moral and instrumental theories or a combination of both; see Locke op cit (n 4) Second Treatise paras 36–7 334–7; Pennock 'Thoughts on the Right to Private property' in *NOMOS XXII: Property* op cit (n 1) 171–86.

[21] See Rawls *A Theory of Justice* (1971) 75.

infringement of privileged property positions are judged not with regard to the rights or claims of the rich, but with regard to its effects for the poor. In this context some of the instrumental theories closely resemble theories concerned with the fragmentation or dephysicalization of property in the sense that they perceive property not as individual 'thing-ownership', but as a productive asset which may be manipulated for social purposes, so that rights to property are both defined and restricted by an overriding social goal such as economic development or the promotion of greater social equality and justice.[22]

Instrumental property theories based upon the social utility of property differ from the classic moral theories in that they acknowledge that the protection of individual interests does not provide an automatic guarantee for social justice and equality and therefore they mostly insist that the perception and institution of ownership must leave room for the protection of others and the overriding interests of society. Usually theories in this category state that the interests of others and of society establish limits and responsibilities that are inherently part of individual property rights, which must be subject to some state interference. In terms of this approach the limits of private property rights are defined by statutory provisions outlining the right and/or duty of state organs to promulgate legislation which restricts private property and which provides for expropriation, together with provisions stating the social purposes for which state interference or expropriation are justified and the principles regarding compensation for such interference or expropriation.[23]

Contemporary property theories striving towards social justice and equality do not necessarily reject the idea that an individual person needs a sphere of individual freedom which should be inviolate both with regard to others and to the state, but they no longer accept the idea that such a sphere of individual freedom requires a guaranteed right to dispose freely and autonomously of private property. Therefore these theories limit either the kind or the amount of property that is protected. According to some theories, only personal property, which is destined directly to serve the immediate needs of the individual, requires state protection. Some theories protect a wider range of property interests, but only up to a certain amount, while others protect all property, but only to a certain extent.[24] Perhaps the best recent example of this approach is the work of Underkuffler,[25] who argues that the inclusion of a public or social element in the perception of property rights can eliminate the tension between private and public which characterizes this concept. This approach resembles the German *Immanenztheorie*, which implies that the public element of limitations and restrictions imposed upon private property is inherently part of property as such and not an exceptional and temporary addition to a fundamentally private and autonomous right.[26]

---

[22] See Horwitz (1973) op cit (n 18) 248–90.

[23] See in this regard generally Caldwell 'Rights of Ownership or Rights of Use? The Need for a New Conceptual Basis for Land Use Policy' 1975 *Environment LR* 409; Wadley 'The Emerging "Social Function" Context for Land Use Planning in the United States: a Comparative Introduction to Recurring Issues' (1988) 28 *Washburn LJ* 22.

[24] See generally Van der Walt 'The Future of Common Law Landownership' in Van der Walt op cit (n 15) 30–4; Van der Walt '*De Onrechtmatige Bezetting van Leegstaande Woningen en het Eigendomsbegrip: een Vergelijkende Analyse van het Conflict tussen de Privaat Eigendom van Onroerend Goed en Dakloosheid*' (1991) 17 *Recht en Kritiek* 329.

[25] Underkuffler op cit (n 17) 127–48; as well as Underkuffler 'The Perfidy of Property: Review of Nedelsky's *Private Property and the Limits of American Constitutionalism*' (1991) 70 *Texas LR* 293.

[26] See in general Van der Walt op cit (n 15) 442n57. Cf below, 2.2.2 for a discussion of German law.

Anti-property theories also stress the interests of the group and of others and the ways in which those interests suffer injury or prejudice if the protection of individual property is exaggerated. Most of the anti-property theories focus on negative social results of a strictly protected individual right to private property, such as the creation and continuation of social and economic inequality, but not all of them are actually in favour of the wholesale abolition of property. In fact, just like the moral arguments, most anti-property arguments are also concerned with the relationship between property and the person and on the effect property relationships have on the freedom of the individual. According to Marx, for instance, self-earned private property such as that of an artisan can contribute to the individuality of the owner, even though the effects of this kind of property are limited since they lack the diversity which is typical of developed social relationships.[27] Capitalist private property, which is the result of salaried labour, is regarded as destructive of individuality and personal freedom.[28] Socialized property, on the other hand, forms a sound basis for individuality and freedom because of its context in a developed society.[29] This theory does not deny the importance of property for the development of personal freedom, but rather argues that the structure and function of property rights must be of a socialized rather than an individual nature in order to promote such personal freedom in the proper social context.[30] In terms of this approach a distinction between personal and other forms of property is vital.

A different kind of anti-property argument is proposed by Caldwell,[31] who argues that rational and responsible land-use planning requires a whole new conceptual framework which is not dominated and frustrated by the traditional perception of property as an autonomous right of disposal. According to Caldwell, property rights, and especially property ownership, should be abolished and replaced by use rights, which can be defined and controlled more effectively.

## 1.2 The constitutional guarantee of property

It is a moot point whether the private right to individual property requires (and deserves) constitutional protection above and beyond the normal remedies offered by private law. It is significant that the idea of constitutional protection of property emerged as part of Locke's labour theory in an effort to define the limits of sovereign power. In terms of Locke's theory the existence of individual property rights are justified on the basis of the labour argument specifically in order to protect those rights against interference by the sovereign. The US Constitution is a classic example of a property clause cast in this mould, providing constitutional protection for life, liberty, and property as the parameters of personal freedom and individuality. In this form the property clause is part of a specific perception of the social function of property relationships, namely that private property forms a guaranteed enclave

---

[27] Marx *Das Kapital* ed by Dietz (1966) (based on Engels 4 ed (1890)) vol I 789–91.
[28] Marx op cit (n 27) 789–91. According to Stillman op cit (n 8) 153, this criticism lies at the root of Marx's criticism of capitalism.
[29] Marx op cit (n 27) 618, 791.
[30] Grey op cit (n 17) 76, 79 points out that the relationship between capitalist and socialist views of property is more complex than it seems since the dissolution or integration of the capitalist concept of property is inherent to the process of capitalism as such.
[31] Caldwell op cit (n 23) 409–25.

of individual freedom within which the individual is shielded from the threats posed by society. Nedelsky[32] argues that this preoccupation with property and its constitutional protection has shaped and distorted basic notions about the nature of individual rights and the structure of democracy by depicting the individual as an autonomous but isolated and threatened entity that needs to be protected from the threats posed by his/her fellow citizens and society by a wall of rights.

This view of the relationship between individuals and society and the implications it holds for the constitutional protection of property are not accepted universally. Concern about the possible creation of an imbalance as a result of strong constitutional protection of private property is common to most contemporary theories of property aimed at the realization of social justice and equality. As a rule the tension between constitutionalism and democracy or between the constitutional guarantee of private property and the need for social restructuring and affirmative action towards greater social equality becomes the central point for discussions about the need and the justification of a constitutionally guaranteed right to private property.[33] The question is whether it is possible to justify the constitutional protection of property rights without thereby implicitly granting the individual a superior position against other individuals and society. In South Africa, however, the inclusion of a property clause was never seriously debated and the current debate is focused on the formulation and interpretation of a property clause and on the inclusion and effects of surrounding clauses and other legislation concerned with expropriation, compensation, and affirmative action.

Traditionally property clauses contain certain standardized elements which may be refered to as the guarantee clause, expropriation clause, and restriction clause respectively. The guarantee clause states that property or some right with regard to property is guaranteed, while the expropriation clause provides that property may be expropriated and sets out the purposes for and conditions under which expropriation may take place. The restrictions clause stipulates that property rights may be restricted or curtailed for certain stated purposes without such restriction amounting to an expropriation or requiring compensation. In many cases the property clause does not include a restriction clause and it is merely assumed that restrictions and limitations of private property which do not amount to expropriations are permissible. The distinction between expropriation and non-expropriatory restrictions is usually one of the most difficult issues regarding a constitutional property clause. Either the guarantee clause or the expropriation clause (or the whole property clause) may be subjected to a due process clause, which means that takings and/or restrictions of entrenched property rights must conform to the due process of law in order to be valid.

In terms of constitutional theory both the guarantee clause and the expropriation clause (containing due process and compensation requirements) can usually be described as defensive guarantees, whereas the restrictions clause can have both defensive (in the form of due process requirements) and participatory (in the sense

---

[32] Nedelsky *Private Property and the Limits of American Constitutionalism* (1990). See the review by Underkuffler op cit (n 25) 293–316. See on the comparative overview of constitutional protection of property in general Van der Walt 'Comparative Notes on the Constitutional Protection of Property Rights' (1993) 19 *Recht en Kritiek* 263.

[33] See, in the South African context, Van der Walt 'Towards the Development of Post-apartheid Land Law: an Exploratory Survey' 1990 *De Jure* 1; Van der Merwe 'Land Tenure in South Africa: Changing the Face of Property Law' (1990) 1 *Stell LR* 321.

of its social programmatic content) characteristics. As a rule none of these clauses creates performance rights in the sense that they provide citizens with rights to demand positive actions or services from the state, although some guarantee clauses in the 'new property' context may be interpreted as guarantees of existing property rights to certain state services and actions. It is also possible to interpret certain restrictions clauses (especially with regard to environmental conservation) and other clauses dealing with affirmative action or socio-economic rights in such a manner that they provide performance rights. In this regard it is interesting to note that more recent property theories, especially those in the 'new property' tradition, tend to treat constitutional property rights as participatory (defensive or performance) rights with regard to common or public property or resources rather than as exclusive defensive rights with regard to individual property. This represents a fundamental shift in constitutional thinking about the protection of property.

## 2  COMPARATIVE OVERVIEW

### 2.1  International human rights instruments

#### 2.1.1  *The Universal Declaration of Human Rights (1948)*

The Universal Declaration of Human Rights adopted by the General Assembly of the United Nations in 1948 provides in art 17 that everyone has the right to own property alone as well as in association with others and that no one shall be arbitrarily deprived of property. Article 29 states that everyone has duties to the community and that the exercise of rights and freedoms is subject to limitations as determined by law for the purpose of securing due recognition and respect for the rights of others and of meeting the just requirements of morality, public order, and the general welfare in a democratic society.

#### 2.1.2  *The International Convention on the Elimination of all Forms of Racial Discrimination (1965)*

This convention adopted by the General Assembly of the United Nations in 1965 determines in art 5*(d)*v that state parties undertake to eliminate racial discrimination in all forms and to guarantee the right of everyone to own property alone as well as in association with others.

#### 2.1.3  *The European Convention on Human Rights (1950)*

Article 1 of the First Protocol to the European Convention for the Protection of Human Rights and Fundamental Freedoms (1950) provides that every natural or legal person is entitled to the peaceful enjoyment of their possessions and that no one shall be deprived of their possessions except in the public interest and subject to the conditions provided for by law and by the general principles of international law. These provisions shall not, however, impair the right of a state to enforce such laws as it may deem necessary to control the use of property in accordance with the general interest or to secure the payment of taxes or other contributions or penalties.

### 2.1.4 *The American Declaration of the Rights and Duties of Man (1948)*

Article 23 of the Declaration states that every person has the right to own such private property as meets the essential needs of decent living and helps to maintain the dignity of the individual and of the home.

### 2.1.5 *The American Convention on Human Rights (1969)*

Article 21 of the Convention provides that everyone has the right to the use and enjoyment of their property and that the law may subordinate such use and enjoyment to the interest of society. No one shall be deprived of her/his property except, upon payment of just compensation, for reasons of public utility or social interest and in the cases and according to the forms established by law. The article states explicitly that usury and the exploitation of man by man shall be prohibited by law. Article 27 also provides for the suspension of guarantees in times of war, public danger, or other emergencies.

### 2.1.6 *The African Charter on Human and Peoples' Rights (1981)*

The African (or Banjul) Charter adopted by the Organization of African Unity in 1981 provides in art 14 that the right to property shall be guaranteed. This right may only be encroached upon in the interest of public need or in the general interest of the community and in accordance with the provisions of appropriate laws. Article 21 provides further that all peoples shall freely dispose of their wealth and natural resources and that this right shall be exercised in the exclusive interest of the people. Articles 27–29 determine that every individual has duties towards his family, society, and the state; that all rights and freedoms shall be exercised with due regard for the rights of others, collective security, morality, and common interest; and that every individual shall have the duty to respect and consider fellow beings without discrimination.

## 2.2 National Constitutions

### 2.2.1 *Classic property clause: United States of America*

#### 2.2.1.1 Content and structure

What is usually referred to as the US Bill of Rights is contained in the amendments to the Constitution of the United States of America. The property clause is contained in the Fifth and Fourteenth Amendments. According to the Fifth Amendment, no person shall 'be deprived of life, liberty, or property, without due process of law; nor shall private property be taken for public use without just compensation'. The Fourteenth Amendment extends this guarantee to state legislation by providing that no state shall 'deprive any person of life, liberty, or property, without due process of law'. This may be regarded as a classic property clause in that it protects the individual's right to property together with the right to life and liberty against undue state interference. In the sense referred to above[34] this property clause consists entirely of an expropriation clause coupled with a due process clause, which is aimed

---

[34] See above, 1.2.

primarily at ensuring the enforcement of due process of law in the event of takings of individual rights. The context and formulation makes it clear that the idea is to ensure constitutional protection for an inviolate enclave of private freedom against state interference.

In terms of this provision the US courts and authors distinguish between the powers of eminent domain and police power.[35] Eminent domain is the state's right to expropriate private property for public purposes or for the public good, and the property clause ensures that this power is exercised according to due process of law and against just compensation. The state's police power, on the other hand, is the state's right to control the use of property and to take steps to ensure the proper functioning of normal state duties with regard to public safety, health, and well-being. The steps normally taken in the process of fulfilling these duties almost always encroach upon private property rights in one way or another, but they do not amount to a taking of property and they do not justify compensation. Jurisprudence on the US property clause deals either with the question whether a certain state interference amounts to a taking or an exercise of the police power or with the question whether a taking was effected according to due process requirements.

### 2.2.1.2 Scope of protection

The interpretation of the property clause in the US Constitution demonstrates a trend to include a growing number of rights, interests, and entitlements under the protection of the Fifth and Fourteenth amendments. This trend, which has been described as the 'dephysicalization' of property,[36] was the origin of the theory of 'new property'.[37] According to this theory, the property clause originally guaranteed rights with regard to corporeal things, but this kind of 'thing'-ownership has been replaced in modern society by a variety of social and economic interests and benefits so that it became necessary to attach an increasingly wider interpretation to the property clause in order to secure constitutional protection for the new forms of property. The original focus of this theory of 'new property' was on economic and social benefits such as state contracts, pension and medical benefits, employment rights, and so on, but it can also be applied to social rights such as workers' rights, political rights such as the right to vote, and others.

However, there are indications that this theory is now regarded with less enthusiasm than used to be the case.[38] One of the criticisms levelled against the theory is that the increasing extension of the concept of property and the concomitant dephysicalization of property tends to blur the distinction between expropriation and the exercise of police power, so that it becomes extremely difficult to classify the revocation of a state licence as either a taking or a legitimate exercise of control

---

[35] See Badenhorst 'Transfer Developments Rights in America: Just Compensation, Fair Compensation or No Compensation?' 1987 *TSAR* 214–22, 352–61; Murphy 'Insulating Land Reform from Constitutional Impugnment: an Indian Case Study' (1992) XXV *CILSA* 129 ((1992) 8 *SAJHR* 362); Murphy 'Property Rights in the New Constitution: An Analytic Framework for Constitutional Review' (1993) XXVI *CILSA* 211 ((1993) 56 *THRHR* 623); Chaskalson 'The Problem with Property: Thoughts on the Constitutional Protection of Property in the United States and the Commonwealth' (1993) 9 *SAJHR* 388; Van der Walt op cit (n 32) 267–70.

[36] See Horwitz op cit (n 18); Vandevelde op cit (n 18) 333.

[37] See Reich op cit (n 12); and cf above, 1.1.2.

[38] See Van Alstyne op cit (n 12); Epstein 'No New Property' (1990) 56 *Brooklyn LR* 747.

over property.[39] Another criticism is that this trend tends to redefine the whole of private law by sucking more and more of it into the sphere of property.[40] This resulted, on the one hand, in the concept of property being expanded so as to include almost anything with value, which extends the protection of the property clause in the Bill of Rights. On the other hand, it makes the concept of property less determinate, thereby making it possible for authors such as Anderson and Underkuffler to devise new interpretations of property which leave room for a reconciliation between the individual and public spheres. The main problem with the 'new property' theory is that it falls between two theoretical chairs. On the one hand, it is based firmly on and attempts to extend the limits of the traditional exclusivist perception of individual property rights, viewed as part of the person-related trio of 'life, liberty, and property'; but, on the other hand, it tends in the direction of other contemporary theories, which place their emphasis on the right of individuals to participate in (or not to be excluded from) social and public wealth and resources rather than on the exclusivity of individual property.

The scope of the protection provided by this property clause must be judged from two different but related perspectives. The first perspective is concerned with the distinction between takings and exercises of the police power, and then the question usually is whether a specific state interference with property amounts to a taking, for which compensation must be paid, or whether it is an exercise of the state's regulatory police power, for which no compensation is paid. Decisions which tend to extend the scope of the property clause by characterizing a wider group of state actions as takings are usually of a more reactionary nature, as was characterized by the development of the concept of 'inverse condemnation' or constructive takings. The second perspective is concerned with the due process requirement, and then the question was usually whether or not the aim of a certain law which intereferes with private property was reasonable. Conservative or reactionary decisions in this regard tended to declare a wide range of industrial and social welfare legislation unconstitutional, as demonstrated by the *Lochner* era. In the final analysis both aspects relate to the conflict between individual and social interests and the approach of the courts was instrumental in developing theories for the solution of this conflict.

### 2.2.1.3 Individual rights and social interests

The tension between the protection of individual rights and the promotion of social interests becomes apparent in the US context in the distinction between expropriations[41] and the exercise of police power. Obviously there is a grey area between expropriation and the exercise of police power and a large part of jurisprudence on the property clause is concerned with this distinction. The problem may be described as an effort to find a suitable rule of interpretation which makes it possible to explain why some encroachments upon private property must be suffered without compen-

---

[39] See Anderson op cit (n 12) 529–62; Peterson 'The Takings Clause: In Search of Underlying Principles: Part I' (1989) 77 *California LR* 1301; Peterson 'The Takings Clause: In Search of Underlying Principles: Part II' (1990) 78 *California LR* 55; Rose 'Property Rights, Regulatory Regimes and the New Takings Jurisprudence — An Evolutionary Approach' (1990) 57 *Tennessee LR* 577.

[40] See Vandevelde op cit (n 18), especially 362–7. Chaskalson op cit (n 35) 406 has shown that by the early 1980s the full range of 'new property' rights have been accorded constitutional protection by the US Supreme Court. At 406–8 he indicates that similar extensions have taken place in Commonwealth countries.

[41] Or 'takings' as they are known in terms of the Fifth Amendment.

sation, while others justify the payment of compensation.[42] Several theories have been developed in this regard in order to find a suitable theoretical explanation of the relationship between private individual property rights, on the one hand, and the interests of society and the powers of the state, on the other.

Anderson[43] argues, on the basis of the theory of 'new property', that property rights must be defined with regard for the owner's legitimate expectations about the interests that will be protected by law, although these expectations have to be 'tempered by a public interest condition', which entails that expectations can only be reasonable and legitimate if they are tempered by the realization that restrictions of property rights in the public interest must be expected. Underkuffler[44] devises a similar attempt to solve the conflict between the protection of private individual property and the public interest by defining property not as a private sphere of individual liberty which is protected from state interference, but rather as a mediating force between the individual and the state. This is done by pointing out that the state context, which involves all kinds of limitations and restrictions imposed for the public benefit, is a necessary prerequisite for the definition and exercise of individual rights. These theories offer justification for state encroachments upon private property rights as well as explanations of the distinction between eminent domain and police power. The important point of these theories is that they represent state encroachments upon private property not as temporary or unnatural and exceptional restrictions of a fundamentally unlimited right, but as inherent and unavoidable public aspects of a private right — the private right itself cannot exist without this public or social element, which provides the basic philosophical or theoretical justification for both expropriations and the exercise of police power.

A second aspect of takings jurisprudence which highlights the tension between individual rights and social interests is concerned with reactionary or conservative interpretations of the property clause, resulting in a situation where almost any encroachment upon private property amounts to a taking, with the result that all state efforts at the limitation of or control over the use and exploitation of property is frustrated. It is often said that the US takings jurisprudence indicates a tendency, which varies from time to time,[45] to use property rights as 'an instrument to roll back entitlements under social welfare programmes or other legal changes that have been made to foster equality'.[46] This conservative tendency is the cause of fears that a property clause, especially in this classic form, might be used to block or delay

---

[42] There are more refined aspects of the conflict which are left untouched by this discussion, such as the 'unconstitutional conditions doctrine'; see Been ' "Exit" as a Constraint on Land Use Exactions: Rethinking the Unconstitutional Conditions Doctrine' (1991) 91 *Columbia LR* 473; Radin 'Evaluating Government Reasons for Changing Property Regimes' (1992) 55 *Albany LR* 597; Sullivan 'Governmental Interests and Unconstitutional Conditions Law: A Case Study in Categorization and Balancing' (1992) 55 *Albany LR* 605; Michelman 'Discretionary Interests — Takings, Motives, and Unconstitutional Conditions: Commentary on Radin and Sullivan' (1992) 55 *Albany LR* 619.

[43] Op cit (n 12) 529–62.

[44] Op cit (n 17).

[45] See in general literature mentioned above, nn 43 and 44, as well as Tribe *American Constitutional Law* (1988) 568ff; Nedelsky op cit (n 32) 203–76; Epstein *Takings: Private Power and the Power of Eminent Domain* (1985) 161ff. Chaskalson op cit (n 35) 403 argues that this tendency highlights the essential arbitrariness of the US case law.

[46] The classic US cases usually referred to in this context are *Lochner v New York* 198 US 45 (1905); *Coppage v Kansas* 236 US 1 (1914); *Pennsylvania Coal Co v Mahon* 260 US 393 (1922). A more recent example of a possible return to this extreme position is the minority judgment in *Keystone Bituminous Coal Association v De Benedictus* 107 SCt 1232 (1987). See Michelman 'Takings, 1987' (1988) 88 *Columbia LR* 1600; Bauman 'Property Rights in the Canadian Constitutional Context' (1992) 8 *SAJHR* 344 at 359; Anon 'The Supreme Court — Leading Cases 1992' (1992) 106 *Harvard LR* 269.

efforts to promote social welfare and justice in the form of restructuring and affirmative action programmes. In the final analysis the actual interpretation of a property clause will probably be determined largely by the socio-political and economic approach followed by the courts and the question is whether socio-economic programmes of this nature should be at the mercy of an appointed judiciary.

The distinction between expropriation and police powers was complicated in the US by the concept of 'inverse condemnation', which refers to cases where an ostensible exercise of the state's regulatory police powers resulted in an effective taking or expropriation. This tendency must be characterized as reactionary as it tends to extend the range of compensatable takings and restrict the range of non-compensatable exercises of the police power.[47] This concept embodies an effort to increase the sphere of individual sovereignty that is insulated from state interference by the Constitution.

### 2.2.2 Social property clause: Federal Republic of Germany

#### 2.2.2.1 Content and structure

Article 14.1 of the German Basic Law (1949)[48] states that ownership and the law of succession are guaranteed and that its content and limits are determined by statute.[49] Article 14.2 provides that ownership entails duties for the owner and that its exercise should serve the public interest.[50] Ever since the promulgation of these provisions they have caused a debate concerning the correct interpretation of the balance between protected individual ownership and the interests of the community. This may be regarded as an example of a social property clause in that it is supposed to embody the constitutional guarantee of individual property within the context of social equality and justice. This is the result of a compromise between a traditional capitalist guarantee of private individual ownership and a socialist guarantee of social equality, and the Federal Constitutional Court (FCC) seems to have adopted the idea that it must be interpreted as such.[51]

#### 2.2.2.2 Scope of protection

The first part of art 14.1 is a guarantee clause and it actually contains two guarantees: a guarantee of ownership as institution,[52] and a guarantee of private ownership

---

[47] See in this regard Chaskalson op cit (n 35) 395–401. See further Michelman 'Property as a Constitutional Right' (1981) XXXVIII *Washington and Lee LR* 1097; Sax 'The Constitution, Property Rights and the Future of Water Law' (1991) 28 *Public Land and Resources Law Digest* 53; Ely *The Guardian of Every Other Right: A Constitutional History of Property Rights* (1992).

[48] *Grundgesetz für die Bundesrepublik Deutschland* (1949). See for commentary in general Rittstieg *Eigentum als Verfassungsproblem: zu Geschichte und Gegenwart des Bürgerlichen Verfassungsstaates* (1976); Badura *Staatsrecht: Systematische Erläuterung des Grundgesetzes für die Bundesrepublik Deutschland* (1986) 138–43; Stein *Staatsrecht* 11 ed (1988) 250–65; Maunz et al (eds) *Grundgesetz Kommentar* (1990) vol II 14.1–14.284. See further Ockermann *Die soziale Bindung des Eigentums in der Bundesrepublik Deutschland, ihren Nachbarlanden und den Vereinigten Staaten von Amerika* (1974); Ramsauer *Die faktischen Beeinträchtigungen des Eigentums* (1980); Wendt *Eigentum und Gesetzgebung* (1985); Van der Walt op cit (n 32) 270–5.

[49] '*Das Eigentum und das Erbrecht werden gewährleistet. Inhalt und Schranken werden durch die Gesetze bestimmt.*'

[50] '*Eigentum verpflichtet. Sein Gebrauch soll zugleich die Allgemeinheit dienen.*'

[51] See in this regard Stein op cit (n 48) 250–1.

[52] *Wesensgehaltgarantie, Institutsgarantie,* or *Einrichtungsgarantie*; which must be read with art 19.2 of the Basic Law, which provides that no fundamental right may be encroached upon in its essential aspects: '*in keinem Fall darf ein Grundrecht in seinem Wesensgehalt angetastet werden.*'

against state interference.[53] It is important to note that this article provides a guarantee of ownership,[54] although the theory of property rights is known to German legal theory via US law.[55] Ownership as defined and protected by the German civil code pertains to 'thing'-ownership only,[56] but in line with general constitutional theory the ownership which is protected by art 14 is interpreted widely by the FCC so as to include not only 'thing'-ownership but all patrimonial rights and claims with regard to public wealth which were acquired through the owner's own work or effort. Mere interests and future possibilities are not included.[57] Originally the FCC followed the interpretation of the civil courts with regard to ownership as guaranteed in art 14,[58] but subsequently the FCC decided that the content of ownership in art 14 had to be determined from the Constitution itself.[59]

Consequently a dual concept of ownership is recognized in German law.[60] On the one hand, the content and limits of ownership as a civil-law institution are contained in civil law. For this purpose ownership is interpreted narrowly as 'thing'-ownership, and the extensions known as 'new property' in US law are not recognized. In this context ownership is regarded as an unlimited right — art 14 does not set limits to this right, but merely declares statutory restrictions valid.[61] For purposes of interpretation of the Basic Law, on the other hand, ownership is interpreted as ownership of all patrimonial rights and claims acquired through the owner's own work or effort, which is narrower than the US concept of 'new property' in that it excludes interests or claims not acquired through personal endeavour.[62] In this public-law context ownership is regarded as a relationship between the individual and the state so that the content and limits of ownership for this purpose must be determined with regard to the Basic Law and not from civil law. According to the second part of art 14.1, the content and limits of ownership for this purpose are defined by the totality of statutes which at a specific time influence the position of an owner.[63] If that indicates that an owner does not have a specific entitlement at

---

[53] *Rechtstellungsgarantie* or *Bestandsgarantie*. See Baur *Lehrbuch des Sachenrechts* 15 ed (1989) 213; Badura op cit (n 48) 138–9; Stein op cit (n 48) 251, 254; *Grundgesetz Kommentar* op cit (n 48) 14.22–14.25, 14.128–14.130.

[54] '*Das Eigentum*', as opposed to '*Sachenrechte*' or 'property rights'.

[55] See Dubischer et al (eds) *Kommentar zum Bürgerlichen Gesetzbuch* (1983) vol 4 *Sachenrecht* 24–5. See further Häberle '*Vielfalt der Property Rights und der verfassungsrechtliche Eigentumsbegriff* 1984 *Archiv des öffentlichen Rechts* 36.

[56] *BGB* art 903 determines that the owner of a thing can dispose of property at will and exclude everybody else from it, in so far as this is not in conflict with laws or the rights of others: '*Der Eigentümer einer Sache kann, soweit nicht das Gesetz oder Rechte Dritter entgegenstehen, mit der Sache nach Belieben verfahren und andere von jeder Einwirkung ausschliessen.*'

[57] 14 *BVerfGE* 288 293; 30 *BVerfGE* 292 334; 53 *BVerfGE* 257 291. See Baur op cit (n 53) 213; Badura op cit (n 48) 139; Stein op cit (n 48) 251–2; Wendt op cit (n 48) 31; *Grundgesetz Kommentar* op cit (n 48) 14.44–14.45, 14.71, 14.73–14.84.

[58] 50 *BVerfGE* 290 339.

[59] 52 *BVerfGE* 1 29; 58 *BVerfGE* 300 311.

[60] See Baur '*Möglichkeit und Grenzen des Zivilrechts bei der Gewährleistung öffentlicher und sozialer Erfordernisse im Bodenrecht*' (1976) 176 *Archiv für die civilistische Praxis* 97; Badura '*Möglichkeit und Grenzen des Zivilrechts bei der Gewährleistung öffentlicher und sozialer Erfordernisse im Bodenrecht*' (1976) 176 *Archiv für die civilistische Praxis* 119; *Grundgesetz Kommentar* op cit (n 48) 14.28–14.29.

[61] Baur op cit (n 53) 213.

[62] See above, n 57.

[63] See Kübler ' "*Eigentum verpflichtet*" *—eine zivilrechtliche Generalklausel?*' (1960) 159 *Archiv für die civilistische Praxis* 236; Kimminich '*Grenzen der Sozialbindung des Eigentums*' (1980) 10 *Agrarrecht* 177; Stein op cit (n 48) 252.

that stage, it does not form part of ownership. The totality of statutes which determine the content and limits of ownership in terms of the Basic Law at a specific stage defines the object and scope of the right guaranteed by art 14 and indicates when compensation for encroachments upon that right is required.

### 2.2.2.3 Individual rights and social interests

The second part of art 14.1 provides that the government must give substance to the concept of ownership by defining its content and limits through legislation. This provision is interpreted in conjunction with art 14.2 to create a responsibility resting upon the government to determine, through the promulgation of suitable legislation, the content and limits of ownership within the context of social and public interests.[64] In this way the social contextuality or bounds of property is established.[65] After World War II the idea was that this kind of legislation should be aimed at the promotion of social interests and consequently examples of this process can be found in statutes dealing with housing law and the law of landlord and tenant,[66] land-use planning and control,[67] and environmental conservation.[68]

The theory concerning the true relationship between individual ownership and public interests that was originally accepted most widely is that proposed by Martin Wolff,[69] who argues that ownership is the unlimited right to use property as one sees fit and that limitations and restrictions of this basically unlimited right must be seen as exceptions laid down by the state in the interests of weaker citizens and for the promotion of civil social order.[70] This pandectist perception is inspired by the view that ownership is part of the natural freedom of all humans, which means that it cannot be affected fundamentally by temporary exceptions and limitations required by the specific needs of time and place.[71] This argument resulted in a fundamental

---

[64] The theoretical explanation of this tension between the protection of private ownership and public interests has given rise to a huge literature; see e g Ekey *Die Verminderung von Eigentümerrechten im Spannungsfeld zwischen Art. 14 I S. I GG und Art. 14 I S. 2 GG* (1988); Schmitt-Kammler 'Ungelöste Probleme der verfassungsrechtlichen Eigentumsdogmatik' in *Festschrift der rechtswissenschaftlichen Fakultät zur 600-Jahr-Feier der Universität zu Köln* (1988) 821ff; Schoch '*Die Eigentumsgarantie des Art. 14 GG*' 1988 *Jura* 113ff.

[65] See Badura op cit (n 48) 140; Stein op cit (n 48) 253; Wendt op cit (n 48) 176–83; *Grundgesetz Kommentar* op cit (n 48) 14.119–14.121. See further Kübler op cit (n 53) 236–93; Badura '*Die soziale Schlüsselstellung des Eigentums*' (1973) 1 *Bayerische Verwaltungsblätter* 1.

[66] See in this regard Pergande '*Die Kündigung von Wohnraum und die Sozialklausel im neuen Mietrecht*' (1964) 17 *NJW* 1925; Müller-Gatermann '*Soziales Mietrecht und Eigentumsgarantie*' (1985) 38 *NJW* 2628; Sonneschein '*Die Entwicklung des privaten Wohnraummietrechts 1986 bis 1988*' (1990) 43 *NJW* 17. Developments in this field are concerned with providing housing for certain economic and social groups, improvement of the social and legal position of tenants, and promoting effective and beneficial use of residential and office premises through the regulation of changes in the use of premises or non-use of premises.

[67] See Jürgens *Die Beschränkungen des Grundeigentums im Rahmen der Städteplanung auf Grund der neuesten Gesetzgebung* (1965); Nawroth '*Das Bodeneigentum in einer sozialen Wirtschafts- und Gesellschaftsordnung*' in *Die Funktion des Grundeigentums in der Sozialordnung der 70er Jahre: Referate des 9. Deutschen Volksheimstättentages* (1970) 31–9; Sendler '*Zum Funktionswandel des Eigentums in der planenden Gesellschaft*' 1975 *Gewerbe-Archiv* 353; Nawroth '*Privateigentum als Problem der Raumordnungspolitik*' 1982 *Die neue Ordnung* 252. In this case the legislation in question is concerned with control over the use, development, and exploitation of land.

[68] See Weyreuther '*Zum Grundrechtsschutz des Waldeigentums*' (1980) 2 *Natur und Recht* 137; Pestalozza '*Eigentum verpflichtet*' (1982) 35 *NJW* 2169; Soell '*Die Bedeutung der Sozialpflichtigkeit des Grundeigentums bei der Landschaftspflege und dem Naturschutz*' (1983) 98 *Deutsche Verwaltungsblätter* 241.

[69] Wolff '*Reichsverfassung und Eigentum*' in *Festschrift für Wilhelm Kahl* (1923) 3ff.

[70] See in this regard also Weber '*Eigentum als Rechtsinstitut: Beurteilungsstand und Entwicklungstendenzen*' 1978 *Zeitschrift für Schweizerisches Recht* 161 at 170–1.

[71] See Sontis '*Strukturelle Betrachtungen zum Eigentumsbegriff*' in Paulus, Diederichsen & Canaris (eds) *Festschrift für Karl Larenz zum 70. Geburtstag* (1973) 981 at 984.

distinction between the essence of ownership, on the one hand, and the practical substance or content of ownership as determined by legislation at a specific time, on the other.[72] With regard to its essence ownership is regarded as static, formal, and abstract, while changes, restrictions, limitations, and diversities which characterize the specific content of ownership in any given context are seen as unessential, temporary, and exceptional. In terms of this theory art 14 preserves the essence of ownership, while providing for temporary, exceptional, and unessential limitations and restrictions as demanded by the requirements of a specific social context.

Some authors[73] have promoted the alternative theory that limitations and restrictions are inherent to ownership,[74] and that ownership is restricted by the social function of every specific object.[75] These theories are mostly inspired by the perception that it is factually false and morally misleading to regard all restrictions and limitations upon ownership as exceptions, especially in contemporary society. Similar convictions inspire the so-called theory of 'smaller ownership', which entails that the correct balance between the protection of individual ownership and social interests should be found by cutting private ownership back to size.[76] According to this theory, private ownership is supposed to create a private enclave of individual freedom and while that enclave should be protected vigorously under the Constitution, it should be done within the limits of its original scope, which is defined by the meaning of ownership for the development of the individual personality. Outside that enclave individual rights must make room for social or public interests. In effect this would mean that different spheres of ownership must be distinguished according to the nature of each object and its proximity to the individual personality so that the state's power to encroach upon property rights would vary according to the sphere in which it is exercised. This theory has in turn been criticized on the basis that it amounts to the abolition of private ownership as an institution, contrary to the guarantee provided by art 14.1.[77]

According to the theory followed by the FCC, its task in terms of art 14 is to give effect to both the fundamental guarantee of private ownership and the duty to serve the social interest and to bring about a just balance between the interests of those involved.[78] The idea is to constitute a just balance between the interests of the individual and the interests of society, with the common good serving as point of orientation and as limit for the restriction of ownership.[79] It is the duty of the legislature to define the content and limits of ownership through legislation[80] and

---

[72] The former is usually referred to as '*der Eigentumsbegriff*' and the latter as '*der Eigentumsinhalt*'.

[73] See Meier-Hayoz '*Vom Wesen des Eigentums*' in *Revolution des Technik — Evolutionen des Rechts: Festgabe für Karl Oftinger* (1969) 171–86.

[74] The so-called *Immanenztheorie*.

[75] The so-called *Funktionseigentum*; see Pawlowski '*Substanz- oder Funktionseigentum? Zum Eigentumsbegriff des geltenden Rechts*' 1965 *Archiv für die civilistische Praxis* 395. See further Liver '*Eigentumsbegriff und Eigentumsordnung*' in Faistenberger & Mayrhofer (eds) *Privatrechtliche Beiträge: Gedenkschrift Franz Gschnitzer* (1969) 247–65; Riegel '*Verfügungs- oder Nutzungseigentum? Einige Ueberlegungen zum Eigentumsbegriff*' 1975 *Bayerische Verwaltungsblätter* 412 at 413; Georgiades '*Eigentumsbegriff und Eigentumsverhältnis*' in Baur, Larenz & Wieacker (eds) *Beiträge zur europäischen Rechtsgeschichte und zum geltenden Zivilrecht: Festgabe für Johannes Sontis* (1977) 149 at 150.

[76] See especially Pawlowski op cit (n 75); Rey '*Dynamisiertes Eigentum*' 1977 *Zeitschrift für Schweizerisches Recht* 65 at 65–7; Weber op cit (n 70) 170–1.

[77] See Weber op cit (n 70) 174; Baur op cit (n 60) 97–118; Badura op cit (n 60) 119–44.

[78] *BVerfG* 1981 *JZ* 828; 52 *BVerfGE* 1 29.

[79] 25 *BVerfGE* 112 118. See further *Grundgesetz Kommentar* op cit (n 48) 14.121–14.122.

[80] 25 *BVerfGE* 112 117.

it is accepted that such legislation can limit the exercise of private ownership, but it may not disregard or terminate the institution of private ownership completely[81] since ownership has an important function in the provision of personal freedom of the individual.[82] Since the nature and function of the object has a bearing on the scope of the legislature's duty to determine the scope of ownership the impact of restrictions will increase in so far as the object has a smaller personal or individual and a larger social function.[83]

This approach is supposed to embody the correct balance between individual and social interests and provide justification for constitutional encroachments upon individual ownership, but it does not provide an infallible distinction between expropriations and the exercise of police power. The expropriation clause is contained in art 14.3, which provides that expropriation is permissible only for purposes of public benefit and that it must take place in terms of a law which prescribes the manner and measure of compensation. Just compensation must be determined with reference to a fair balance between the interests of those affected and the public interest. In cases of conflict about the measure of compensation recourse may be had to the normal courts.[84] Originally the civil courts approached this question on the basis of equality by reasoning that any encroachment which affected only one individual was an expropriation,[85] but lately encroachments with regard to land-ownership are judged with due regard for the situation and context of property.[86] In terms of this approach the character of every piece of land is determined by its situation in a specific area, including the state of nature and of the land around it, and by its general use and situation and accordingly the owner must accept that the scope of his/her right is affected by this character of the property so that certain limitations and restrictions may apply to it and affect the owner's entitlements to use and enjoy it without compensation.[87] The test is whether a reasonable owner who does not lose sight of public interests would forgo certain uses of the land considering its position and environmental situation.[88]

### 2.2.3 No property clause: Canada

Originally the Canadian Constitution of 1960 contained an unentrenched non-justiciable Bill of Rights which could be revoked by Parliament and which did not provide the courts with the power to review statutes. This Bill of Rights, which is

---

[81] 24 *BVerfGE* 367 389.
[82] 14 *BVerfGE* 288 293; 24 *BVerfGE* 367 389; 42 *BVerfGE* 64 77; 42 *BVerfGE* 263 293.
[83] 21 *BVerfGE* 73 83; 31 *BVerfGE* 229 242; 36 *BVerfGE* 281 292; 37 *BVerfGE* 132 140; 42 *BVerfGE* 263 294. See *Grundgesetz Kommentar* op cit (n 48) 14.147–14.198.
[84] 'Eine Enteignung ist nur zum Wohle der Allgemeinheit zulässig. Sie darf nur durch Gesetz oder auf Grund eines Gesetzes erfolgen, das Art und Ausmass der Entschädigung regelt. Die Entschädigung ist unter gerechter Abwägung der Interessen der Allgemeinheit und der Beteiligten zu bestimmen. Wegen der Höhe der Entschädigung steht im Streitfalle der Rechtsweg vor dem ordentlichen Gerichten offen.' See generally Badura op cit (n 48) 141–2; Stein op cit (n 48) 257–60; *Grundgesetz Kommentar* op cit (n 48) 14.132–14.147.
[85] *BGHZ* 6, 270 277, 278: the so-called *Sonderopfertheorie*. See *Grundgesetz Kommentar* op cit (n 48) 14.140.
[86] *BGH* 1988 *NJW* 3201 (*BGHZ* 105, 15): the so-called *Situationsgebundenheitstheorie*. See Böhmer 'Die Rechtsgeschichtlichen Grundlagen der Abgrenzungsproblematik von Sozialbindung und Enteignung' 1985 *Der Staat* 157; Stein op cit (n 48) 260–2; *Grundgesetz Kommentar* op cit (n 48) 14.144.
[87] See Baur op cit (n 61) 216.
[88] See also 7 *BVerwGE* 297 299; 15 *BVerwGE* 3 335; *BVerwG* 1977 *NJW* 945; *BVerwG* 1981 *NJW* 2137.

contained in an ordinary statute, remains in force and contains specific protection for property rights by providing the right to the enjoyment of property and not to be deprived of property except by due process of law.[89] The property right so provided is, according to Bauman,[90] 'a relatively feeble and underemployed right,' because the Bill of Rights is not entrenched. Furthermore, it applies to the federal Parliament and it seems to be restricted to the property of individual persons. Several provincial Bills of Rights also provide explicit protection of property rights.[91]

However, in 1982 the new enforceable Canadian Charter of Rights and Freedoms was accepted as part of the Constitution.[92] One of the remarkable features of the Charter is that it does not contain an explicit guarantee of property rights.[93] Originally it was argued by some that the protection of life, liberty, and security of the person in s 7 of the Charter included at least some of the economic rights often associated with property, but this contention was dismissed by the courts.[94] Reasons put forward for the omission include uncertainty about the range of rights that would be included in the category of property protected by a constitutional property clause,[95] previous experience with the earlier unentrenched constitutional provision regarding property,[96] the conviction that vital aspects of life, liberty, and personal security that are often associated with and protected by the property clause are sufficiently covered by the sections dealing with personal rights,[97] opposition from provincial governments fearing that the inclusion of a property clause might hamper the solution of specific provincial problems,[98] and, finally, the fact that it is a highly controversial question whether property is in fact such a fundamental right that it should rank with other rights that are guaranteed in the Charter.[99]

The exclusion of property rights from the Charter of Rights and Freedoms does not mean that property owners enjoy no protection. Provinces and the federal government acquire the right to expropriate property from the Constitution,[100] but in each case there are explicit procedural provisions which guarantee due process of law. There is, however, no explicit provision which guarantees the payment of compensation, although it is usual for the relevant statutes to provide for payment of adequate compensation.[101] Bauman[102] argues that property owners are also protected by a number of common-law rules. In the same context it is worth mentioning that several other Constitutions, although they do not contain a Bill of Rights, provide some sort of protection of property rights in the form of an expropriation clause which requires due process of law.[103]

[89] Section 1(a). See Bauman op cit (n 46) 349. See further Van der Walt op cit (n 32) 275–7.
[90] Op cit (n 46) 250.
[91] See Bauman op cit (n 46) for examples.
[92] Part I of the Constitution Act 1982, being Schedule B of the Canada Act 1982 (UK), s 11. See De Villiers, Van Vuuren & Wiechers *Human Rights: Documents that Paved the Way* (1992) 247. See further McCullough 'Parliamentary Supremacy and a Constitutional Grid: the Canadian Charter of Rights' (1992) 41 *ICLQ* 751; Bauman op cit (n 46) 344–61.
[93] This omission is not generally welcomed; see Bauman op cit (n 46) 344–5.
[94] See Bauman op cit (n 46) 353.
[95] See Bauman op cit (n 46) 345, 346–7.
[96] See Bauman op cit (n 46) 345, 348–52.
[97] See Bauman op cit (n 46) 345, 352–4.
[98] See Bauman op cit (n 46) 345, 350.
[99] See Bauman op cit (n 46) 345, 352–5.
[100] Sections 92(13) and 91 of the Constitution Act 1982 respectively; see Bauman op cit (n 46) 351.
[101] See Bauman op cit (n 46) 351.
[102] Op cit (n 46) 352.
[103] For instance, the Dutch constitution — see below, 2.2.6.

## 2.2.4 Directive Principles of State Policy: India

Originally the Indian Constitution of 1950 contained a property clause. Article 19(1) provided that all citizens shall have the right to acquire, hold, and dispose of property and art 19(5) authorized certain restrictions of that right in the interests of the general public. Article 31 contained an expropriation clause which required expropriations to take place by authority of a law which provides for compensation. Compensation either had to be determined in the law, or the method of its calculation had to be laid down.[104] Both the expropriation clause and the restrictions clause drew upon the US example,[105] and it is therefore not surprising that the distinction between expropriation and police powers came to the attention of the Indian courts.[106] With regard to compensation for expropriations the courts decided that the amount or the method of calculation specified by each statute enabling expropriation had to conform to the equal value of the property taken,[107] which resulted in an amendment which ousted the courts' jurisdiction concerning the validity of expropriation laws on the basis that the compensation provided for was inadequate.[108] A further controversy was followed by an amendment which replaced the word 'compensation' in art 31 with 'an amount'.[109] After thirty years of controversy about land tenure reform and agricultural reform the 44th Amendment was adopted, which deleted arts 19(1)(f) and 31 from the list of fundamental rights in the Constitution and subsequently property rights were removed from the Constitution altogether.

Apart from the fundamental rights in the Indian Constitution, the Directive Principles of State Policy[110] have also played a role in influencing and shaping state policy.[111] One of these principles requires the state to direct its policy towards assuring 'that the ownership and control of material resources of the community are so distributed as best to subserve the common goal'.[112] A wrangle between the courts and the legislature concerning the relative force of fundamental rights and Directive Principles[113] was resolved by the *State of Tamil Nadu* decision,[114] in which it was stated that the Directive Principles were not legally enforceable, but they nevertheless had to be harmonized with the fundamental rights. This struggle between fundamental rights and the Directive Principles embodies the Indian effort to reconcile the protection of individual rights with the promotion of socio-economic reform and restructuring. In this case the eventual decision was to avoid litigation concerning the constitutional protection of property by removing property from the list of fundamental rights and to promote social restructuring by way of the Directive Principles.

---

[104] See in general Murphy (1992) op cit (n 35) 129–55; Van der Walt op cit (n 32) 277–8.
[105] Murphy (1992) op cit (n 35) 132–4.
[106] See Murphy (1992) op cit (n 35) 134–40 for a discussion of Indian case law.
[107] See Murphy (1992) op cit (n 35) 140–3 for a discussion of case law.
[108] See Murphy (1992) op cit (n 35) 133n7 for the revised text of art 31.
[109] See Murphy (1992) op cit (n 35) 143n47 for the full revised text of art 31.
[110] Contained in art 39 of the Constitution.
[111] See in general De Villiers 'The Socio-economic Consequences of Directive Principles of State Policy: Limitations on Fundamental Rights' (1992) 8 *SAJHR* 188. See further the example concerning housing policy discussed by Budlender 'Towards a Right to Housing' in Van der Walt (ed) *Land Reform and the Future of Landownership in South Africa* (1991) 45–52.
[112] Article 39(b); see De Villiers op cit (n 111) 193–5.
[113] See in general De Villiers op cit (n 111) 193–5 for a discussion of case law.
[114] AIR 1984 SC 725.

## 2.2.5 African Constitutions

### 2.2.5.1 Namibia

Article 16 of the Namibian Constitution provides that all persons shall have the right in any part of the country to acquire, own, and dispose of all forms of immovable and movable property individually or in association with others and to bequeath their property to their heirs or legatees. Parliament may by legislation prohibit or regulate as it deems expedient the right to acquire property by non-citizens.[115] The state or a competent body or organ authorized by law may expropriate property in the public interest subject to the payment of just compensation in accordance with requirements and procedures to be determined by statute.[116] Provision for the exercise of police power and affirmative action is made in art 23, in terms of which legislation for the advancement of those who have been socially, educationally, and economically disadvantaged by discriminatory laws and practices of the past is excluded from the equality clause in art 10.

The National Conference on Land Reform and the Land Question held in Namibia in 1991[117] submitted a number of proposals regarding land reform that affect the application of the property clause. Relevant submissions include the following: that foreigners should not be allowed to own farmland, although they should be allowed to develop it on a leasehold basis; that land owned by absentee landlords should be expropriated; that land held by persons who own very large tracts of land or more than one farm should be expropriated; that underutilized and abandoned land should be reallocated and made productive; that some sort of restitution with regard to injustices of the past regarding landholding should be devised; that a charter of rights for farmworkers should be drawn up; and that state assistance to farmers be revised in favour of beginner farmers. It was also advised that communal areas be retained for the time being; that land boards be introduced to administer the allocation of communal land; and that steps be taken to alleviate the plight of disadvantaged communal landholders and farmers.

The Namibian property clause is an example of an attempt to approach social restructuring and land reform within the context of constitutionally protected property rights, although it is not yet quite clear what form the land reforms are going to take or how they are going to be reconciled with the Bill of Rights.

### 2.2.5.2 Other African states

Several different approaches are followed in other African countries. Certain Constitutions contain expropriation and restriction clauses, while others also contain a guarantee clause. Some Constitutions are geared towards socialism and provide guarantees of personal property only.

The Bill of Fundamental Rights contained in the Nigerian Independence Constitution of 1960 contains no guarantee clause, but only a relatively detailed

---

[115] Article 16(1). See further in this regard Bhalla & Ojwang 'Property Rights and the Constitution: The Position of Aliens in Kenya' (1990) 6 *Lesotho LJ* 127; Van der Walt op cit (n 32) 278.

[116] Article 16(2).

[117] See in general Van Wyk 'The Namibian Land Conference — A First Step Towards Addressing a Burning Problem' (1992) 7 *SAPR/PL* 30.

expropriation clause[118] and restriction clause.[119] Section 16 of the Constitution of Zimbabwe (1979) as amended in 1990, art 8 of the Botswana Constitution, art 18 of the schedule to the Constitution of Zambia, art 13 of the Constitution of the Republic of Uganda, art 11 of the Constitution of Sierra Leone, art 40 of the Constitution of the Federal Republic of Nigeria, and art 8 of the Constitution of Mauritius contain similar broadly formulated expropriation clauses which provide for expropriation for public purposes and against compensation as well as restriction clauses. Section 2(1)(iv) of the Republic of Malawi Constitution Act 23 of 1966 contains only an expropriation clause. The Constitutions of the Republic of Senegal,[120] the Somalia Democratic Republic,[121] and the United Republic of Tanzania[122] all provide a guarantee of private property together with a right of expropriation and a restriction clause.

Article 12 of the Constitution of the Peoples' Republic of Mozambique recognizes and guarantees personal property, while art 13 stipulates that obligations are attached to private property and that its use should not be to the detriment of the interests defined in the Constitution. Article 30 of the Constitution of the Peoples' Republic of the Congo (Brazzaville) stipulates that the state regulates the collective and individual enjoyment of the means of production and art 31 provides that the land is the property of the people. All land titles and customary rights are abolished. However, any person may dispose freely of the produce of the land, the fruit of his own labour. Article 33 guarantees the private ownership and right of inheritance with regard to all property other than land, but no one may use property to the detriment of the community. Limitations of ownership may be imposed in the general interest and expropriation can occur according to law. Article 34 guarantees individual ownership of citizens. Individual ownership is based on revenues from work and concerns all property other than land, consisting mainly of items of ordinary use, convenience, and personal consumption. Article 21 of the Zaïrean Constitution provides a guarantee of individual and collective property which may not be jeopardized except by law and for reasons of public interest and against prior fair indemnity.

### 2.2.6 *Other examples*

#### 2.2.6.1 Irish Free State

Article 43 of the Irish Free State Constitution (1922) provides for private property rights. Interestingly enough this property clause explains its theoretical or philosophical foundations explicitly, stating that the state acknowledges that man, as a rational being, has the natural right, antecedent to positive law, to the private ownership of external goods.[123] The state accordingly guarantees to pass no laws attempting to abolish the right of private ownership or the general right to transfer, bequeath, and inherit property.[124] On the other hand, it is also acknowledged that

---

[118] Article 42(1).
[119] Article 42(2).
[120] Article 12.
[121] Article 28.
[122] Article 24.
[123] Article 43.1.1.
[124] Article 43.1.2.

the exercise of private property rights ought in civil society to be regulated by the principles of social justice,[125] and accordingly the state is allowed to delimit by law the exercise of these rights with a view to reconciling their exercise with the exigencies of the common good.[126]

#### 2.2.6.2 Malaysia and the Netherlands

The Malaysian Constitution of 1957 contains a very simple property clause in art 13, which states that no person shall be deprived of property save in accordance with law[127] and against adequate compensation.[128] The Dutch Constitution, which enjoys the status of a normal statute and is not entrenched, safeguards fundamental rights in Chapter 1 and, although it does not include a direct guarantee clause, art 14 provides an expropriation clause. The Constitution also provides that it will be the concern of the government to secure the means of subsistence of the population and to achieve the distribution of wealth,[129] to provide social security,[130] and to keep the country habitable and to protect and improve the environment.[131]

#### 2.2.6.3 Brazil

Article 5 of the Constitution of Brazil guarantees for every resident of the country the right to equality, life, liberty, security, and property. In art 5.XXII–5.XXVI this general guarantee is set out in more detail, stating that the right to own property is guaranteed, that ownership of property shall attend to its social function, that the law shall establish the procedure for expropriation for public use or need or for social interest, against just and prior compensation in money, and that in the event of imminent public danger the proper authority may use private property against compensation for damage. Small rural properties used by families are guaranteed against attachment for debts incurred in the process of production. The right to inheritance is guaranteed in art 5.XXX.

### 2.3 Environmental rights

The Stockholm Declaration[132] declares that man has the fundamental right to freedom, equality, and adequate conditions of life in an environment of a quality that permits a life of dignity and well-being, and adds that man bears the solemn responsibility to protect and improve the environment for present and future generations. A number of Constitutions contain environmental clauses in this spirit that amount to state policy guidelines:[133] the Dutch Constitution provides that the authorities must keep the country habitable and must protect and improve the

---

[125] Article 43.2.1.
[126] Article 43.2.2.
[127] Article 13(1).
[128] Article 13(2).
[129] Article 20.1.
[130] Article 20.2–20.3.
[131] Article 21.
[132] Adopted by the first United Nations Conference on the Human Environment in 1972; see principle I.
[133] See in general Witzsch 'The Right to a Healthy and Decent Environment in a New Lesotho Constitution?' (1990) 6 *Lesotho LJ* 167 at 172.

environment;[134] the Greek Constitution obliges the state to protect both the natural and the cultural environment;[135] the Constitution of Sri Lanka requires the state to protect and improve the environment for the benefit of the community;[136] the Swiss Constitution empowers the federal authorities to protect the environment and to take steps against pollution and noise;[137] the Austrian Federal Constitutional Law of 1984 obliges federal, state, and municipal authorities to protect the environment;[138] and the Indian Constitution includes the protection of the environment under the policy objectives to be strived for by the state.[139]

Witzsch[140] distinguishes these Constitutions from others which contain environmental rights, meaning that they do not simply lay down policy directives, but actually supply citizens with an enforceable right against the government. Examples of these are the Constitutions of Turkey[141] and Hungary.[142] The environmental clauses in the Constitutions of Portugal[143] and Spain[144] are formulated as rights but interpreted as policy guidelines.[145] A similar constitutional right to a safe and clean environment has been proposed for Lesotho[146] and the United States of America.[147]

## 3 THE SOUTH AFRICAN PROPERTY CLAUSE I: PROPOSALS AND VIEWPOINTS

### 3.1 Introduction

Prior to and during the Multi-Party Negotiating Process (MPNP) at Kempton Park, which lead to the acceptance of the 1993 Constitution, various parties and groups had published their proposals for a new Constitution and Bill of Rights and most of these proposals included a property clause. The property clause in the Constitution was such an important and controversial issue that it seems necessary to discuss it against the background of its development. This section is focused on the various proposals and viewpoints regarding a property clause that were published during the negotiations, while the transitional property clause is discussed in the next section. The property clause in the transitional Constitution is finally evaluated against the background of the proposals.

---

[134] Article 21. Like all the fundamental rights mentioned in the Constitution this article is not judicially enforceable, since the Constitution is an ordinary Act and not a *Grundnorm*-type constitution. See Algra *Positief Recht Volgens het NBW* (1984) 47.
[135] Article 24.
[136] Article 27(14).
[137] Article 24*sept*.
[138] See Witzsch op cit (n 133) 172.
[139] Article 48A. See further Pathak 'Human Rights and the Development of the Environmental Law in India' (1988) 14 *Commonwealth Law Bulletin* 1171; Glazewski 'The Environment, Human Rights and a New South African Constitution' (1991) 7 *SAJHR* 167 at 176–80.
[140] Op cit (n 133) 173.
[141] Article 56.
[142] Witzsch op cit (n 133) 173.
[143] Article 10.
[144] Article 45(1).
[145] Witzsch op cit (n 133) 173.
[146] Ibid.
[147] Chiappinelli 'The Right to a Clean and Safe Environment: A Case for a Constitutional Amendment Recognizing Public Rights in Common Resources' (1992) 40 *Buffalo U LR* 567 at 604–11.

The South African debate on the Bill of Rights was hardly ever primarily concerned with the question whether a Bill of Rights should in principle include a property clause. The inclusion of such a clause was generally accepted as a political reality,[148] and the main point of debate even amongst those who are opposed to the inclusion of a property clause is how it should be formulated. This is demonstrated by the proposals and comments of a group of Western Cape lawyers[149] who thought that there should be no property clause, but nevertheless accepted that the eventual Bill of Rights would contain one and therefore dedicated most of their discussion to the formulation and discussion of a property clause which leaves room for the promotion of social justice and affirmative action. In effect therefore the parties to the South African debate usually either propagated the inclusion of a fairly traditional property clause or they were in principle opposed to the inclusion of a property clause, but nevertheless argued in favour of a restrictive and socially responsible formulation. The transitional Constitution includes a property clause as was predicted all along, but it is still worth while paying attention to some of the arguments against a property clause.

## 3.2 Arguments against a property clause

The main argument against a property clause is that property is a controversial and ambiguous concept. Judging from the history of constitutionally protected property rights, it is difficult to predict which rights will actually be protected by the courts, which makes it difficult for a government to embark on a programme of social or economic restructuring. In the second place it is often feared that the inclusion of a property clause in a Bill of Rights might sanctify and institutionalize imbalances in the current distribution of wealth, and more particularly of land and other productive property. Traditionally a property clause tends to have a more or less reactionary effect by protecting and institutionalizing the status quo and therefore its constitutional entrenchment is controversial at a time of socio-political change and restructuring.

For that reason most of the arguments against a property clause originate from concern about the effect of a property clause on the social and economic restructuring of the South African community. It is feared that the property clause may frustrate future attempts at land reform or land tenure reform, agricultural reform, housing reform, affirmative action with regard to land rights, and so on.[150] The reactionary effect of a traditional property clause may be enhanced by the fact that such a property clause tends to be interpreted widely, with the result that a large number of commercial and social rights are protected as property, thereby extending the reach of a conservative property clause. It has also been argued in the same context that an extensive interpretation of a fairly traditional property clause will

---

[148] See Murphy (1993) XXVI *CILSA* 211 at 214; Chaskalson op cit (n 35) 408–11; Van der Walt op cit (n 32) 263.
[149] Consisting of Hugh Corder, Steve Kahanovitz, John Murphy, Christina Murray, Kate O'Regan, Jeremy Sarkin, Henk Smith, and Nico Steytler. See Corder et al *A Charter for Social Justice: A Contribution to the South African Bill of Rights Debate* (1992) 60–5.
[150] See Hund 'A Bill of Rights for South Africa' (1989) 34 *Am J Jurisprudence* 23 at 31; Sachs 'Towards a Bill of Rights in a Democratic South Africa' (1990) 6 *SAJHR* 1 at 4, 6–8; Van der Walt op cit (n 33) 43; Dugard 'A Bill of Rights for South Africa?' (1990) 23 *Cornell Int LJ* 441 at 459–60.

formalize and perpetuate the systematic dominance of ownership in South African property law with negative results for much needed development and reinforcement of other land rights.[151] However, John Murphy[152] has argued that such an extensive interpretation of a property clause in the 'new property' tradition is not necessarily to be avoided since it can serve a mediating function between individual interests and government power, provided the interpretation of the property clause is accompanied by explicit recognition of this mediating function of property. That would mean that property is not regarded as 'a factually and interpretively discoverable truth' and that the interpretation of the property clause is aimed at 'finding the socially desirable limits of collective interference with individual economic activities'.[153] This possibility is explored further in the discussion of the property formulations below.[154]

The South African Law Commission's Working Paper 25 and Interim Report on group and human rights[155] noted the warnings that a property clause which protects private property too zealously might obstruct future governments' efforts to promote equality and justice, but the draft Bill of Rights proposed by the Law Commission nevertheless includes a property clause.[156] In view of the fact that the African National Congress (ANC)[157] and the National Party government both favoured a Bill of Rights with a property clause hardly anybody argued against the inclusion of a property clause very strenuously, although a number of authors have maintained that a property clause should not be included in the Bill of Rights at all[158] or that it should at least be subject to exceptions or limitations in order to permit the government to address existing inequalities and injustices.[159] In fact, however, the whole debate was focused on the formulation of the property clause in an attempt to find a formulation which provides a guarantee of property rights in the traditional sense while still leaving scope for social and economic restructuring and affirmative action.

In what follows below, the main proposals for a property clause are discussed, up to and including the formulations that were proposed in the seventh and tenth progress reports of the Technical Committee on Fundamental Rights during the Transition. This analysis is followed by a discussion of the property clause that was eventually accepted by the Negotiating Council as part of the Constitution.

---

[151] See Van der Walt op cit (n 33) 431–50. In this context Chaskalson op cit (n 35) 403 has drawn attention to the essentially arbitrary nature of US court decisions on the constitutional property clause.

[152] (1993) XXVI *CILSA* 211 at 217, with reference to Underkuffler op cit (n 17) 141. Also in favour of such an interpretation are Lewis 'The Right to Private Property in a New Political Dispensation in South Africa' (1992) 8 *SAJHR* 305 and the group of Western Cape lawyers (see Corder et al op cit (n 149) 61–2).

[153] Murphy (1993) XXVI *CILSA* 211 at 217.

[154] See below, 3.4.1.

[155] SA Law Commission *Project 58: Group and Human Rights* Working Paper 25 (1989) 462–3, 464–6, 468–9; Interim Report (1991) 358–9.

[156] See below, 3.3.2 for a full discussion of the Law Commission's proposals.

[157] See below, 3.3.1 for a full discussion of the proposals put forward by the African National Congress.

[158] See Van der Merwe 'Land Tenure in South Africa: A Brief History and some Reform Proposals' 1989 *TSAR* 663 at 692; Van der Walt 'Developments that may Change the Institution of Private Ownership so as to meet the Needs of a Non-racial Society in South Africa' (1990) 1 *Stell LR* 26 at 46–47; Van der Walt op cit (n 33) 42–3; Van der Walt 'The Fragmentation of Land Rights' (1992) 8 *SAJHR* 431 at 446–50.

[159] See Robertson 'Land and Human Rights in South Africa: A Reply to Marcus and Skweyiya' (1990) 6 *SAJHR* 215 at 219–22; Corder et al op cit (n 149) 60–5.

## 3.3 Proposals for a property clause

### 3.3.1 *African National Congress*

The Bill of Rights proposed by the ANC is based largely upon the Freedom Charter,[160] although many of the points raised in the Freedom Charter have since been amended. The Freedom Charter does not mention the right to private property and in fact seems to be aimed at nationalization of certain resources[161] rather than the protection of individual property, as can be seen from the principles that the national wealth of the country shall be restored to and shared by the people and that all land shall be redivided amongst those who work it.

The constitutional guidelines published by the ANC in 1988 to stimulate debate on the constitutional future[162] make more specific recommendations regarding private property. In the section on the economy it is stated that property for personal use and consumption will be constitutionally guaranteed, but from the sections on affirmative action, the economy, and land it becomes clear that land is not regarded as personal property for that purpose and that the state shall determine and limit the rights and obligations attaching to ownership. In a working document on the Bill of Rights published by the ANC in 1990[163] this approach is worked out in more detail in art 11, which deals with the economy, land, and property.

Article 11.2 states that every person and lawfully constituted body is entitled to the peaceful enjoyment of their possessions, including the right to acquire, own, and dispose of property. However, natural resources and minerals not belonging to anyone when the Constitution comes into operation shall belong to the state.[164] According to art 11.7 and 11.8 nobody shall be deprived of their possessions except on grounds of public interest or utility, and then only pursuant to a law and subject to just compensation which takes into account the need to establish an equitable balance between the public interest and the interest of those affected.[165] In case of a dispute over the amount or method of payment of compensation recourse is to be had to a special tribunal, with an appeal to the courts.[166] The state shall also have the right to regulate the economy[167] and to take steps to overcome the effects of past statutory discrimination and to implement the required measures to control the use and exploitation of property.[168]

The ANC published a revised Bill of Rights in 1993.[169] This document contains two separate clauses concerned with property. Article 13 is a revised version of the

---

[160] As adopted at the Congress of the People, Kliptown, 26 June 1955.

[161] The statement in the preamble that 'South Africa belongs to all who live in it' is probably not meant to refer to land rights, but rather to political sovereignty. However, the aim of nationalization is clear enough from other principles stated in the Charter.

[162] African National Congress 'Constitutional Guidelines for a Democratic South Africa' (1989) 5 *SAJHR* 129. In the introduction it is stated that the time has come 'where the Freedom Charter must be converted from a vision for the future into a constitutional reality'.

[163] African National Congress *A Bill of Rights for a New South Africa* (1990).

[164] Article 11.3.

[165] Article 11.9.

[166] Article 11.10.

[167] Article 11.1.

[168] Article 11.11.

[169] African National Congress *ANC Draft Bill of Rights: Preliminary Revised Version* February 1993 (1993) Centre for Development Studies, University of the Western Cape. See further Murphy (1993) XXVI *CILSA* 211 at 212–13; Van der Walt op cit (n 32) 282–7.

earlier art 11. The guarantee clause in art 13(1) states that all South Africans shall, without discrimination, have the right to undisturbed (instead of peaceful) enjoyment of their personal (a new qualification) possessions, and individually, in association, or through lawfully constituted bodies be entitled to acquire, hold, or dispose of property. A new subart (2) states that the content and limits of these rights and the rights to inheritance shall be determined by law. Subarticle (3), which is also new, provides that property rights impose obligations and that their exercise should not be in conflict with the public interest. Both subarticles (2) and (3) are evidently inspired by the second part of art 14.1 and by art 14.2 of the German Basic Law. The new expropriation clause in art 13(4)[170] states that the taking of property shall only be permissible according to law and in the public interest, which shall include the achievement of the objectives of the Constitution. In terms of art 13(5) any such taking shall be subject to just compensation, which shall be determined by establishing an equitable balance between the public interest and the interest of those affected. Disputes regarding compensation are to be resolved by a special independent tribunal, with an appeal to the courts, as was the case with the earlier art 11.[171] Article 13(7), which is identical to the earlier art 11(1), still prescribes the guiding principle of economic legislation in terms of the establishment of collaboration between the public, private, co-operative, communal, and small-scale family sectors with a view to reducing inequality, promoting growth, and providing goods and services for the whole population.[172] Article 13(8) contains the restriction clause, which once again refers to economic principles by stating that the clause shall not be interpreted as impeding legislation such as might be deemed necessary in a democratic society with a mixed economy which may be adopted with a view to providing for the regulation or control of property or for its use or acquisition by public or parastatal authorities in accordance with the general interest, or which is aimed at preserving the environment, regulating or curtailing cartels or monopolies, or securing the payment of taxes or other contributions or penalties.[173] Article 13(9) states that this property clause shall be read subject to and in harmony with art 12, which deals with land and the environment.

The restriction clause is in a sense extended by art 14, which deals with affirmative action. Article 14(1) provides that nothing in the Constitution shall prevent the enactment of legislation or the adoption by a public or private body of

---

[170] Article 23 also contains a new additional expropriation clause dealing with the expropriation and commandeering of property in times of national defence or emergency. In essence the article allows for temporary or final expropriation, commandeering, and use and consumption of property for purposes of national defence or emergency; that once it is no longer required it should be returned to its owner unless it was consumed for the purpose for which it was commandeered; that compensation shall be payable with due regard for the needs and interests of the state in the particular situation and the needs of the person affected; and that the measures in question may provide that compensation shall not be paid for temporary loss of the property unless it was used by the person affected for income. Since this is an exceptional exclusion provision with regard to national emergencies it does not really affect the principles contained in the property clause.

[171] Now art 13(6).

[172] In a note it is mentioned that this kind of clause could perhaps rather be included in a section called Directives of State Policy and that there is much argument about the question whether principles governing economic life should be included in the Constitution at all. In this regard it is interesting to note that the German Basic Law, upon which much of this clause was modelled, was drafted in an explicit attempt to avoid prescribing a specific economic regime; see above, 2.3.2.

[173] Once again a note mentions the fact that the reference to a mixed economy may be unnecessarily provocative to those who favour either an extensive free market or considerable state intervention and that it is not normal to prescribe either of these in the Constitution.

special measures of a positive kind designed to procure the advancement and opening up of opportunities, including access to land, and the general advancement of social, economic, and cultural spheres, of people who in the past have been disadvantaged by discrimination.[174] Article 15 deals with positive measures that have to be taken to remove inequality.

The detailed new art 12 dealing with land and the environment must be read together and in harmony with art 13.[175] Article 12(1) and (2) repeats the principles stated in the Freedom Charter, namely that the land, the waters, and the sky and all the natural assets which they contain are the common heritage of the people of South Africa, who are equally entitled to their enjoyment and responsible for their conservation; and that the system of property rights in relation to land shall take into account that it is the country's primary asset, the basis of life's necessities, and a finite resource. These provisions are probably meant to have a programmatic and interpretive effect. Article 12(3)–(13) deals with rights to the land.

Article 12 states that South Africa belongs to all who live in it[176] and that access to land and other living space is the birthright of all South Africans.[177] No one shall be removed from their homes except by an order of court, which shall take into account the existence of reasonable alternative accommodation.[178] Legislation shall provide that the system of administration, ownership, occupation, use, and transfer of land is equitable, directed at the provision of adequate housing for the whole population, promotes productive use of land, and provides for stable and secure tenure.[179] Furthermore, legislation shall provide for the establishment of a tribunal for land claims which shall have the power to adjudicate upon land claims made on legal or equitable grounds, specifically with regard to the return of land to or compensation of people dispossessed by forced removals or the award of land or rights to land to claimants on the basis of use or occupation.[180] Legislation shall also provide access to affordable land to be given as far as possible within the limits of available resources to those who were historically deprived of land and land rights.[181] All such legislation shall guarantee fair procedures and be based on the principle of achieving an equitable balance between the public interest and the interests of those affected,[182] and any redistribution of land or interests in land required to achieve these objectives shall be subject to just compensation according to the same equitable balance.[183] Disputes regarding compensation shall be heard by an independent tribunal with an appeal to the courts.[184] Article 12(12) and (13) provide that all natural resources below and above the surface area of the land, including the air, and all forms of potential energy or minerals which are not

---

[174] In a note it is specified that this article is not supposed to override other provisions in the Bill of Rights, and specifically not the property clause, which contains its own special provisions with regard to affirmative action dealing with land. Perhaps this interpretive principle should be made explicit in the text.
[175] See art 13(9).
[176] Article 12(3).
[177] Article 12(4).
[178] Article 12(5).
[179] Article 12(6).
[180] Article 12(7).
[181] Article 12(8).
[182] Article 12(9).
[183] Article 12(10).
[184] Article 12(11).

otherwise owned at the commencement of the Constitution shall vest in the state acting as trustee for the whole nation and that the state shall have the right to regulate the exploitation of all natural resources, grant franchises, and determine royalties subject to payment of just compensation in the event of interference with any existing title, mining right, or concession. Article 12(14)–(17) deals with environmental rights.[185]

### 3.3.2 South African Law Commission

The working paper of the South African Law Commission[186] states that the right to private property is guaranteed, with the proviso that expropriation can be provided for by legislation when it is in the public interest to do so against fair compensation. The new art 22 of the Interim Report[187] states that everyone has the right individually or jointly with others to be or to become the owner of private property or to acquire or have a real right in private property or to become entitled to any other right.[188] Legislation may authorize the expropriation of any property or right in the public interest against payment of just compensation, which in the case of a dispute shall be determined by a court of law.[189]

### 3.3.3 KwaZulu/Natal Indaba

The Bill of Rights proposed by the KwaZulu/Natal Indaba in 1986[190] provides that everyone has the right lawfully to own and occupy property anywhere in the province[191] and that no one may be deprived of property without due process of law in terms of a law which authorizes expropriation for the public benefit and which provides that equitable and fair compensation be promptly paid.[192] Article 7(3) provides, somewhat redundantly, that land and natural resources shall not be expropriated except for the common good and in accordance with laws providing for equitable compensation.

### 3.3.4 The previous South African government

The former South African government's proposals for a Bill of Rights were published early in 1993.[193] The property clause is obviously based on the Law Commission's proposals, although it provides much stronger protection for individual property rights. Article 18(1) provides that everyone shall have the right individually or with others to acquire, possess, use, and dispose of any form of movable and immovable property, including disposal by way of testamentary disposition or intestate succession. Article 18(2) provides that, subject to the

---

[185] See in this regard below, 3.5.
[186] Article 15; see the Working Paper op cit (n 155) 478. See in general Murphy (1993) XXVI *CILSA* 211 at 212; Van der Walt op cit (n 32) 285–6.
[187] Article 22; see the Interim Report op cit (n 155) 693–4.
[188] Article 22*(a)*.
[189] Article 22*(b)*.
[190] See 1986 *Natal U L and Society R* 175. See in general Van der Walt op cit (n 32) 286.
[191] Or region KwaZulu/Natal. See art 7(1).
[192] Article 7(2).
[193] Republic of South Africa *Government's Proposals on a Charter of Fundamental Rights* (1993) Government Printer. See in general Van der Walt op cit (n 32) 286.

expropriation clause, no one shall be deprived of property without a judgment or order of court. Property may be expropriated for public purposes subject to the payment within a reasonable period of compensation as agreed to. In the absence of such an agreement compensation must be paid in cash as determined by a court of law according to the market value of the property.[194] Everyone shall have the right not to be subjected to taxes which have a confiscatory effect or which make unreasonable inroads upon the enjoyment, use, or value of property.[195]

### 3.3.5 *Other proposals*

The group of Western Cape lawyers[196] propose a property clause which is aimed at establishing an equitable balance between individual and social interests. Article (1)[197] states that everyone has the right to the enjoyment of his/her property. Article (2) establishes that no one shall be deprived of his/her rights and interests in property unless such action is taken in the public interest, in accordance with due process of law, and subject to the payment of appropriate compensation. Appropriate compensation shall be determined by establishing an equitable balance between the public interest and the interest of those affected. Article (3), which is unique to this group's proposals, states that no law enacted within seven years of the commencement of the Constitution with the purpose of affirmatively reforming land tenure and access to land shall be declared invalid for a period of ten years after its enactment on the grounds that it is inconsistent with or takes away or abridges any rights conferred by the Bill of Rights, nor shall it be declared invalid retroactively. Articles (4) and (5) determine that no one shall be removed from their homes except in terms of a court order, such court order not being granted unless the existence of appropriate alternative accommodation is taken into account.

Article 9 of the draft Bill of Rights published by the Democratic Party[198] states that every person shall have the right, in any part of South Africa, to acquire, own, or dispose of any form of movable or immovable property, individually or in association with others. It is stated that legislation may authorize the expropriation of property in the public interest subject to the proper payment of equitable compensation which, in the event of a dispute, shall be determined by an ordinary court of law.

The South African Chamber of Business proposes a Charter of Economic, Social and Political Rights which is based on basic adherence to a market economy. Part I contains economic rights and principles, and art 1.1 grants everyone the right to own property, alone as well as in association with others, including communal ownership as found in traditional communities. Article 1.2 provides that no one shall be deprived of property without due process of law and compensation. Article 2 guarantees the right to the rewards of one's own endeavours, and states that this right shall be subject only to such limitations as are prescribed by law and are

---

[194] Article 18(3).
[195] Article 18(4).
[196] Corder et al op cit (n 149) 60.
[197] There are only subarticles and no main article numbers since the group believes in principle that its proposed Bill of Rights should contain no property clause at all.
[198] *Freedom Under the Rule of Law: Advancing Liberty in the New South Africa: Draft Bill of Rights* May 1993.

necessary in a democratic society in the public interest and the promotion of the public health and well-being. Article 25 also determines that everyone's exercise of rights and freedoms shall be subject to such limitations as are determined by law solely for the purpose of securing due recognition and respect for the rights and freedoms of others and for meeting the just demands of morality, public order, and the general welfare in a democratic society.

### 3.3.6 *Technical Committee on Fundamental Rights during the Transition*

The Technical Committee on Fundamental Rights during the Transition, which advised the Negotiating Council and parties at Kempton Park, produced several progress reports, the seventh and tenth of which are of interest for the property clause.

In clause 23(1) of its seventh progress report[199] the Technical Committee proposed a property clause that guarantees the right of every person to acquire, hold, and dispose of rights in property. Clause 23(2) states that expropriation of property[200] by the state shall be permissible in the public interest and subject to agreed compensation or, failing agreement, to just and equitable compensation as determined by a court of law, taking into account all relevant factors, including the use to which the property is being put, the history of its acquisition, its market value, the value of the owner's interest in it, and the interests of those affected. Clause 23(3) states that nothing in clause 23 shall preclude measures aimed at restoring rights in land to or compensating persons who have been dispossessed of rights in land as a consequence of any racially discriminatory policy, where such restoration or compensation is feasible. The interesting aspects of this clause are the formulation '*rights in property*' instead of 'ownership' or just 'property'; the fact that judicial calculation of compensation is subjected to a number of explicitly enumerated factors; and the fact that affirmative land action is explicitly justified as being possible and lawful in terms of the Constitution.

The property clause proposed in clause 28 of the Technical Committee's tenth progress report[201] is substantially different from and better than the earlier version. Clause 28(1) states that every person shall have the right to acquire and hold rights in property and, to the extent that the nature of the right permits, to dispose of such rights. In a note the change is explained as an effort to cater for communal as well as individual rights. Clause 28(2) provides for expropriation of rights in property by the state and in the public interest subject to the expeditious payment of either agreed compensation or, failing agreement, of compensation to be determined by a court of law as just and equitable, taking into account all relevant factors. This time the factors that were specified in the earlier version are left out. A new subclause (3) states that expropriation of rights in property for the purpose of restoring rights in land to persons who have been dispossessed of these rights as a consequence of any racially discriminatory policy shall for the purposes of subclause (2) be deemed to be expropriation in the public interest. This is complemented by a new subclause (4),

---

[199] Dated 29 July 1993. See in general Van der Walt 'The Impact of a Bill of Rights on Property Law' (1993) 8 *SAPR/PL* 296, where this proposal is analysed.

[200] This formulation was improved in the tenth report by inserting 'rights in' before 'property' to bring it in line with clause 23(1). See in this regard Van der Walt op cit (n 199) 304–6.

[201] Dated 5 October 1993.

which states that every person who was dispossessed of rights in land in terms of any racially discriminatory policy has a right to restitution or, where such restitution is not feasible, to compensation or any other suitable remedy. Parliament must enact a law setting out the conditions, procedures, and mechanisms by which this right can be enforced and for the calculation of compensation, and to determine a date as the cut-off point for historical land claims.

## 4  THE SOUTH AFRICAN PROPERTY CLAUSE II: THE 1993 CONSTITUTION

The property clause is contained in s 28 of the Constitution.[202] Section 28(1) remains exactly as it was in the tenth progress report of the Technical Committee, but it is followed by a new s 28(2), which states that no deprivation of any rights in property shall be permitted otherwise than in accordance with a law. This section was probably supposed to act as a 'due process clause' similar to the US one, but the term 'deprivation' was an unhappy choice, as is pointed out later. Subsection (3) of s 28 was amended to read that where any rights in property are expropriated pursuant to a law referred to in subsec (2) such expropriation shall be subject to the payment of agreed compensation or, failing agreement, the payment of such compensation and within the period determined by a court of law as just and equitable, taking into account all relevant factors. In the case of the determination of compensation the factors that were mentioned in the seventh progress report and omitted in the tenth progress report are once again to be taken into account.

The property clause in s 28 is complemented by a special (and extensive) section on the restitution of land rights which appears in ss 121–123. Section 121(1)–(3) more or less repeats clause 28(4) of the tenth progress report in providing a claim to restitution of dispossessed land rights except that it is determined explicitly that the cut-off date for historical land claims shall not be earlier than 19 June 1913, while racially discriminatory policies causing land dispossession are defined more accurately with reference to laws which would have been been invalid had s 8(2) been in operation at the time of the dispossession. Provision is further made that these claims for restitution shall be subject to the conditions, limitations, and exclusions that may be prescribed by the proposed Act of Parliament and that these claims shall not be justiciable by a court of law unless they have been processed in accordance with the Act by a commission established for that purpose by the Act.[203] Section 121(5) makes it clear that no such claim shall be instituted before the Act is promulgated.

Claims fall into various categories. A number of claims for restitution can be investigated, mediated, and settled by the commission that is envisaged.[204] Other claims that remain unsettled are lodged with the courts and in this case the commission can draw up reports and other evidence to be presented to the court at the hearing.[205] The court can settle these claims by way of restitution of the

---

[202] See in general Van der Walt 'Notes on the Interpretation of the Property Clause in the New Constitution' (1994) 57 *THRHR* 181.
[203] Section 121(6).
[204] See in general s 122(1).
[205] Section 122(1)*(c)*.

dispossessed rights, granting of an appropriate alternative right with regard to alternative land, payment of compensation, or any alternative relief, depending on the circumstances.[206] Restoration can take place if the state certifies that restoration is feasible and if the relevant land is 'in the possession of the state', or if the state certifies that, although the land is 'in the possession of a private owner',[207] restoration is feasible by way of purchase or expropriation of the land. Section 123(2) specifies that this last procedure will be followed only if it is just and equitable, taking into account all relevant factors, including the history of the dispossession, the hardship caused, the use to which the property is being put, the history of the acquisition of the land by the owner, the interests of the owner and others affected by the expropriation, and the interests of the dispossessed. Expropriation in terms of this subsection shall be subject to payment of compensation calculated in the manner set out in s 28(3).

If the state certifies that a restoration is not feasible or if the claimant wants alternative relief, the court may order granting of an appropriate alternative right to available alternative state land or payment of compensation or any other relief.[208] Compensation shall be determined by the court as just and equitable taking into account all factors, including the circumstances that prevailed at the time of the dispossession, any compensation paid upon the dispossession, and other factors prescribed by the Act. If the court grants alternative relief, it shall take into account and make an appropriate order with regard to compensation that was paid to the claimant upon dispossession.[209]

In terms of s 121(4) the procedure described here does not apply to rights in land that were expropriated in terms of the Expropriation Act 63 of 1975 or any other law incorporating that Act or its provisions regarding payment of compensation if just and equitable compensation as contemplated in s 123(4) was paid in respect of such expropriation.

## 5  THE SOUTH AFRICAN PROPERTY CLAUSE III: COMPARISON AND EVALUATION

*General*
The proposals of the main political parties leave the impression that the proposed property clauses have been drafted for the benefit of political negotiators in order to supply them with concession and compromise materials. It is therefore difficult to assess which parts of the proposals are really to be taken seriously. However, it would appear that all parties approached the property clause with a view to hedging their proposals against opposition from all sides and consequently many of the proposals bristled with all kinds of qualifications, exceptions, and exemptions. It is very much a question of whether it is salutory to formulate a Bill of Rights and a property clause on the basis of political give and take and whether any Bill of Rights and property clause surrounded by so many qualifications can serve their purpose.

---

[206] Section 123.
[207] Section 121(1)*(a)* and *(b)*.
[208] Section 121(3).
[209] Section 121(4)*(a)* and *(b)*.

If there is so much doubt and uncertainty about the function and effects of a property clause, it may be better to reconsider its inclusion.

The point of departure must be that the property clause should provide basic protection for private property rights within a theoretical and constitutional framework which incorporates both individual and social interests, neither of which should be perceived and treated as exceptions. The outdated perception of property as an exclusive and unlimited private right which should not be interfered with is unsuitable and it is better to base the property clause on the modern perception of property rights, which leaves room for a wide range of different and contextualized property rights that derive their very nature and content from their actual context, including the social and public aspects of that context. This means that the social, environmental, physical, and other characteristics of property determine the nature, scope, limits, and protection of each right so that both the scope of the property holder's entitlements towards the property and the scope of state powers to interfere with it are inherently determined by the context.

One of the important results of this approach is that land deserves special treatment because it is a special, vital, and limited resource, the use and exploitation of which have serious social implications for all. Therefore the scope of land users' rights to use and exploit land and the scope of the state's power to interfere with and control land use can never be determined abstractly — the special nature of land and the circumstances of each case have to be considered. This also means that the adherence to ownership as the fundamental and most important land rights should be abandoned so that the development of a wide range of divergent land rights for different kinds of land and for different uses of land can be promoted.

## 5.1 Guarantee clause

### 5.1.1 *Proposals*

Most of the proposals include a property clause in the traditional framework of a guarantee clause plus an expropriation clause, although they approach the formulation of these clauses differently.

One group formulates the guarantee clause by simply stating that everyone shall have the right to acquire, possess, enjoy, use, and dispose of property.[210] Some of them prefer to be more specific by stating that these rights may be acquired, held, and exercised individually or jointly with others,[211] or that these rights include ownership and other real rights,[212] or that they apply to both movable and immovable property,[213] or that the right of disposal includes the right to dispose by way of testamentary disposition or intestate succession.[214] The other group prefers to guarantee not private property as such, but the peaceful enjoyment of one's possessions[215] or the enjoyment of one's property.[216] The second approach, which is

---

[210] Proposals of the Law Commission, the KwaZulu/Natal Indaba, and the South African government.
[211] Proposals of the Law Commission and the South African government.
[212] Proposals of the Law Commission and the South African government.
[213] Proposals of the South African government.
[214] Proposals of the South African government.
[215] Proposals of the African National Congress.
[216] Proposals of the group of Western Cape lawyers.

focused on the actual enjoyment of property rights, derives from an attempt to escape the liberalist and individualist overtones of the ownership-dominated traditional property clause, which provides a much more abstract blanket protection of property rights as such, regardless of their use and enjoyment. The differences between the two formulations should not be exaggerated since some formulations of the second group also state that the peaceful enjoyment of one's possessions includes the right to acquire, own, and dispose of property,[217] which means that in the end the two formulations could well be interpreted similarly.

The enumeration of entitlements associated with property[218] in some proposals is a redundancy unless certain entitlements are left out on purpose. For the same reason the specific mention of testamentary and intestate disposition in the previous government's proposals is superfluous, as is the statement that the clause applies to both movable and immovable property. Far from clarifying the property clause, these provisions seem to have a merely political function to ensure that certain specific entitlements enjoy constitutional protection or to prevent the promulgation of restrictions on certain entitlements or pertaining to land only. Such a cynical attitude towards the formulation of a Bill of Rights can only cause confusion and uncertainty.

Several authors[219] have pleaded for a wide and flexible rather than a precise and specific formulation of the property clause, albeit for different reasons. A wide and unqualified guarantee clause has important consequences. In constitutional theory the guarantee of property is usually interpreted widely to include, in addition to ownership and other real rights to movable and immovable things, at least some of the rights constituting the so-called 'new property',[220] namely rights to incorporeal property such as intellectual property, commercial interests such as goodwill, and certain social rights and economic benefits such as labour rights, rights of action, participation in social insurance schemes, and other welfare entitlements. The Western Cape group of lawyers prefer such a wide interpretation of their guarantee clause[221] and several authors agree with them that such an interpretation of the property clause will be beneficial. In this respect it is worth noting how the German courts have restricted such a wide interpretation to the products of personal endeavour, while excluding mere interests and future possibilities not yet realized.

Carole Lewis[222] argues that the test of 'excludability',[223] which is described as the physical, legal, and moral ability to keep an object or a right for oneself to the exclusion of others, should be used to determine whether a right qualifies as a property right or not. The benefits of this approach are that the concept of property

---

[217] This is not so clear in the case of the proposals of the group of Western Cape lawyers, but the same conclusion can be reached from the implications of the expropriation clause.

[218] Especially in the proposals of the South African government, but also in the proposals of the Law Commission and the African National Congress.

[219] See Lewis op cit (n 152) 389–430; Van der Walt (1992) 8 *SAJHR*) 431; Murphy (1993) XXVI *CILSA* 211 at 216–17.

[220] See the discussion of the theory of 'new property' above, 1.1.2.

[221] See Corder et al op cit (n 149) 61; Murphy (1993) XXVI *CILSA* 211 at 217. Compare also Verloren van Themaat 'Property Rights, Workers' Rights and Economic Regulation — Constitutional Protection for Property Rights in the United States of America and the Federal Republic of Germany: Possible Lessons for South Africa' (1990) XXIII *CILSA* 53.

[222] Op cit (n 152) 392–408.

[223] Borrowed from Gray op cit (n 17) 268.

is flexible and adaptable, that property rights are regarded as relative and restricted rights from the outset, and that it allows for moral considerations to prevail when determining whether or not to grant constitutional protection to a property right. John Murphy[224] supports this approach for its flexibility and the fact that it allows for moral considerations to influence the protection of property. Murphy is in favour of a combination of this approach and that of Laura Underkuffler, who defines property in such a way that it loses its individualist connotations and acquires a more complex nature, according to which individual liberties are 'understood and interpreted within a collective context of both support and constraint'.[225]

However, despite the attractions of the interpretive approaches of Lewis and Murphy, the theory of 'new property' is no longer universally followed or admired.[226] Van der Walt[227] has argued that the 'new property' theory does not really succeed in escaping from the traditional liberalist paradigm because it relies too heavily on simple conceptual expansion without attempting actually to abandon the traditional framework. Others have argued, with reference to US[228] and German[229] law, that the theory of 'new property' does not provide a satisfactory framework for the theoretical explanation of socially responsible property theories and perceptions. It is noticeable that the idea of 'propertization' on the basis of excludability still remains firmly within the framework of the traditional perception of ownership as an exclusive and individual right, whereas many contemporary theories (including the original 'new property' theory) aimed at solving the tension between the private and the public spheres now tend to develop a new perception of property as the right not to be excluded from (or to participate in) public or social wealth, property, or resources. These new theories can be and often are assimilated within the theory of 'new property', but their point of departure is different from the old-fashioned liberalist idea of exclusivity.

It is interesting to note that some of the guarantee clauses proposed for South Africa do not allow interpretation based upon the theory of 'new property' because they are framed on the basis of the 'peaceful enjoyment of possessions' or the 'enjoyment of property'. This formulation of the guarantee clause was perhaps meant to avoid traditional individualist interpretations of an abstract property right, but the result is that they restrict the guarantee clause to one aspect of property — its enjoyment — which does not really fit in with the theory of 'new property'. It is possible to interpret a traditional property clause, which guarantees the right to property, in such a manner that it includes the right to work and the right to social pension and medical benefits, but it is not so easy to see how the Constitution can protect the peaceful possession or the enjoyment of these rights. In short, the theory of 'new property' is a typical product of the traditional abstract perception of property and aimed at extending the benefits of that perception of property, and it does not seem logical to argue in favour of such an extension of traditional property

---

[224] (1993) XXVI *CILSA* 211 at 217.
[225] Op cit (n 17) 141.
[226] See above, 2.3.1 and 2.3.2 for a discussion of the US and German situations.
[227] Op cit (n 158) at 439–40.
[228] See particularly Van Alstyne op cit (n 12) 457–70; Epstein op cit (n 43) 747–75; Chaskalson op cit (n 35) 407–8.
[229] See above, n 57.

rights within the framework of a new guarantee clause aimed at restricting traditional property rights.

Besides the 'new property' debate a second implication of the guarantee clause has to be considered. In a sense the protection of private property is already guaranteed in the expropriation clause,[230] as demonstrated by the classic US example, which raises the question of what the function of the positive guarantee clause[231] is. In German constitutional theory[232] the guarantee clause is interpreted as creating a constitutional guarantee of the institution of private property as such, meaning that the state cannot make laws which amount to the abolition of this institution through nationalization or disproportionate taxation. Obviously such a general institutional guarantee of private property[233] implies a constitutional guarantee of a certain economic and social programme which allows for the implementation of social democratic principles, but only in so far as they are compatible with the continued protection of the institution of private property. Once again it seems unlikely that the same interpretation can be followed with regard to the guarantee clauses proposed for South Africa. The fairly traditional proposals for the guarantee clause, such as those of the Law Commission and the South African government, might allow such an interpretation, except for the fact that the specific mention of certain entitlements in these proposals tends to obstruct an interpretation in favour of a general institutional guarantee. At the very least the mention of these entitlements makes the guarantee clause so specific that its programmatic effects may become unacceptable. On the other hand, the 'peaceful possession' or 'enjoyment' guarantee clauses do not seem to allow for this kind of interpretation at all. In fact it seems likely that the bodies who promote these proposals have never contemplated the possibility that the property clause can guarantee not only individual property rights but also the institution of private property as such.

In view of these considerations the question is whether this part of the property clause should not have been left aside entirely to avoid the impression of duplication or redundancy, which can only create confusion and uncertainty.[234] If the guarantee clause were left out of the property clause entirely, the same protection of private property rights could still have been attained by way of the expropriation clause, which provides for due process and compensation, and the restriction clause, which requires due process and equality. It is probable, however, that the positive guarantee

---

[230] As contained in art 13.4 of the African National Congress proposals, art 22*(b)* of the Law Commission proposals, art 7(2) of the KwaZulu/Natal Indaba proposals, art 18(3) of the South African government proposals, and art (2) of the Western Cape lawyers' proposals.

[231] As contained in art 13.1 of the African National Congress proposals, art 22*(a)* of the Law Commission proposals, art 7(1) of the KwaZulu/Natal Indaba proposals, art 18(1) of the South African government proposals, and art (1) of the Western Cape lawyers' proposals.

[232] See above, 2.2.2 for a full discussion of the German property clause.

[233] It is important to note that the German guarantee clause in question protects ownership, which is of course not such a wide concept as property.

[234] If it is assumed that this part of the clause does not provide an extra (redundant) guarantee of private property or an anti-discrimination provision, it may be argued that the words 'entitled to the peaceful possession of their property' are aimed at something similar to the Dutch and German criminal provisions regarding the guarantee of the 'home peace'. ('*Huisvredebreuk*' in art 138 of the Dutch Criminal Code and '*Hausfriedensbruch*' in art 123 of the German Criminal Code; see Van der Walt op cit (n 24) 334–6, 339–40.) Such an interpretation would tie in well with art 12.5 and art 2.25–2.26 of the African National Congress proposals and arts (4)–(5) of the Western Cape lawyers' proposals op cit (n 149). However, it is very much a question of whether this was the intention of the drafters of these articles, and it is more probable that they are simply repetitive or redundant formulations resulting from an effort to couch the clause in a more or less traditional form.

of property rights will be used for its psychological value in allaying fears of large-scale nationalization.

### 5.1.2 *The 1993 Constitution*

As was indicated, the new Constitution provides a guarantee of 'rights in property' in s 28(1). This formulation was not promoted in any of the original proposals and is unique in many respects.

This guarantee clause virtually ensures a very wide interpretation of the property clause because of the term 'rights in property'.[235] Its formulation is unique in the sense that it has not been used in any of the better known property clauses and it actually came as a surprise that such a formulation was opted for. In a sense this formulation avoids the US and German 'new property' debate about the inclusion or exclusion of non-corporeal rights because the formulation itself more or less explicitly opts for a wider rather than a narrow interpretation of the rights in property that are to be included in the constitutional guarantee. In fact this formulation seems to envisage an even wider protection of property rights than was achieved in the US by way of the 'new property' theory.

It is logical that such a wide formulation will lead to a wide interpretation which includes both real and personal rights in material property as well as other patrimonial rights with regard to incorporeals such as shares, state contracts, jobs, and so on. Such a wide interpretation of the property clause will very probably extend the constitutional guarantee of existing property rights further than was intended. Even though the final wording of the clause makes the 'new property' debate unnecessary, it seems certain that the US extensive approach will ensure that a wide range of (inevitably existing) 'new property' rights will enjoy the constitutional guarantee provided by s 28(1).

An interesting aspect of the guarantee clause is the differentiation between the right to acquire, hold, and dispose of rights in property in terms of s 28(1). The rights to acquire and hold property are protected without qualification, whereas the right to dispose of it is protected only 'to the extent that the nature of the right permits'. According to a note in the tenth progress report of the Technical Committee, this formulation was meant to accommodate communally held property rights, but as it stands it may be applied to all situations where the right of disposal is limited for some reason. In a sense it represents some awareness of the diversity of property rights, but it does not really go far enough actually to realize a diversified right to property.

The guarantee clause in s 28(1) can be seen as a positive guarantee of rights in property in the sense mentioned above and therefore it might seem to lend itself to an interpretation similar to the German approach, in terms of which the positive guarantee clause provides a guarantee of the institution (of ownership) rather than individual rights, whereas individual rights are protected by the negative expropriation clause. To a certain extent the idea of a construction in favour of a guarantee of the institution is reinforced by s 33(1), which provides for statutory limitations of the entrenched rights. In terms of this section one of the provisos for such a

---

[235] See in this regard Van der Walt op cit (n 202) 191.

limitation to be valid is that it should not 'negate the essential content' of the right in question. However, this German approach is typical for the German property clause, which provides a guarantee of ownership, whereas the South African 'rights in property' formulation does not fit into this theoretical distinction. Ownership is a well-established and fundamental institution of private law, but 'rights in property' is such a wide and general term that it is hard to see how it can be equated with or regarded as a legal institution. The difference in formulation and practical considerations[236] make it unlikely that such an interpretation will be followed in South African law.[237] It would nevertheless be interesting if legislation (aimed at some form of nationalization) were to be challenged on the basis of this theoretical construction, arguing that such legislation undermines the continued existence of a socio-economic system which makes it possible for everybody to acquire, hold, and dispose of rights in property.

An interesting and no doubt controversial aspect of the property clause in the Constitution is its vertical and horizontal enforcement. In terms of s 7(1) the Constitution and the rights entrenched in it are meant to be enforced against state organs — in other words, vertically. However, the tenth progress report of the Technical Committee has already mentioned the possibility of allowing some 'horizontal seepage' of these rights and s 35(3) of the Constitution seems to make such seepage possible. This subsection stipulates that a court 'shall have due regard for the spirit, purport and objects' (sic)[238] of Chapter 3 of the Constitution '[i]n the interpretation of any law and the application and development of the common law and customary law'. An example illustrates the possible effect of this provision.

In terms of the common law it is possible for a landowner to select prospective lessees of his/her property on the basis of race, gender, or religious belief. Section 28(1) of the Constitution guarantees the landowner's rights in property and s 33(3) provides that the entrenchment of rights in the Constitution shall not be construed as depriving anyone of common-law or customary-law rights that are not inconsistent with Chapter 3 of the Constitution. In view of these considerations the landowner may be justified in arguing that his/her right of disposal, including the 'right' to rely on factors relating to race, gender, or religious beliefs in selecting prospective lessees, is upheld and guaranteed by the Constitution. Moreover, this argument seems to be strengthened by the fact that the entrenched rights can only be enforced against the state and not against other citizens. On the other hand, a prospective lessee might argue that s 8(2) of the Constitution guarantees his/her right not to be discriminated against on the basis of race, gender, or religious beliefs and that common-law property rights, including the right of disposal, are upheld by s 33(3) and guaranteed by s 28(1) only in so far as they are not inconsistent with the Constitution itself. The questionable common-law 'right' to rely upon discriminatory factors when selecting prospective lessees must therefore be interpreted and applied by a court of law with due regard for the spirit, purport, and objectives of Chapter 3, which means that a court of law must heed the constitutional anti-discrimination provision when applying common-law principles on the horizontal

---

[236] Such as the accessibility of sources.
[237] See Van der Walt op cit (n 202) 194.
[238] What was meant was probably 'objectives'.

level. In this manner the entrenched rights in Chapter 3 may, and possibly should, gain horizontal effect through a process of interpretive 'seepage', thereby extending the scope of s 28(1) quite drastically.

## 5.2 Expropriation clause

### 5.2.1 *Proposals*

Despite the fact that most of the proposals discussed above provide for the possibility of expropriation against compensation, they display different approaches to the formulation of the expropriation clause.

The 1990 ANC proposals have been criticized severely by the Law Commission in its Interim Report,[239] especially for the provisions regarding compensation in art 11.8–11.10 and 11.11. According to the Law Commission, art 11 provides the state with the necessary powers 'to introduce naked nationalization without compensation, without any testing right for the courts, without protection for those prejudiced'.[240] In its turn this criticism has been subjected to critical analysis by Murphy[241] and others.[242] Murphy in particular took the Law Commission to task for having 'fallen victim to the anti-nationalization hysteria gripping the white community in South Africa'.[243] In his view[244] the Law Commission's criticism is largely the result of a misunderstanding of art 11.8, which was supposed to restrict the state's right of eminent domain and not to elevate it above judicial intervention, as it is understood by the Law Commission.[245] Moreover, the absence of compensation for interferences with private property in art 11.11 should not be regarded as underhanded nationalization because that article deals with the state's police power, which is usually not subject to compensation. Murphy argues that the Law Commission's criticism of the ANC proposals is unjustified and that these proposals do not differ much from the Law Commission's own proposals in the same context.[246] In broad outline this is true since all the proposals allow for expropriation in the public interest and against just compensation and all of them make provision for some sort of adjudication of disputes concerning compensation. More or less the same applies with regard to the 1993 proposals of the ANC.

The one obvious difference, however, is the fact that just compensation in terms of the ANC proposals should be calculated with due regard for the creation of an equitable balance between the interests of the community and of the person affected, whereas the National Party government proposals state specifically that just compensation in case of a dispute should be determined according to the market value of the property. The ANC approach was probably borrowed from the German Basic Law[247] in an effort to establish a more balanced view of the relationship between

---

[239] SA Law Commission op cit (n 155) 359–65.
[240] At 364.
[241] Murphy 'A Note on the SA Law Commission's Interpretation of the Property Rights in Article 11 of the ANC Bill of Rights' (1992) 7 *SAPR/PL* 12.
[242] See Corder et al op cit (n 149) 63.
[243] Murphy op cit (n 244) 27.
[244] Murphy op cit (n 244) 16–18.
[245] Murphy op cit (n 244) 19, 21.
[246] See above, 3.3.2 for a discussion of the Law Commission's proposals.
[247] See above, 2.2.2 for a complete discussion of the German Basic Law. See further Corder et al op cit (n 149) 63; and cf Nicholas Haysom 'Democracy, Constitutionalism and the ANC's Bill of Rights for a New South Africa' (1991) 7 *SAJHR* 102 at 106. The ANC proposals are discussed in full by Murphy op cit (n 244) 18–27.

private property and social justice and equality. This difference is the result of diverging approaches, the previous government being interested mainly in compensation for the affected individual, while the ANC strives to establish a balance between individual and social interests.[248] Of course one may argue that compensation should always strive for an equitable balance between individual and social interests.[249] Compared with the ANC the proposal of the Western Cape lawyers, which refers to 'appropriate compensation', which shall also be determined by establishing an equitable balance between the public interest and the interest of those affected, may be too vague because of its use of the untechnical and vague term 'appropriate'. The ANC proposal that expropriation be allowed not only in the public interest but also for public utility, including the achievement of the objectives of the Constitution, is unnecessary since the achievement of the objectives of the Constitution should be in the public interest in any case.

The expropriation clause should be brief and simple and should leave detailed provisions to an expropriation Act. The expropriation clause should merely state the principle that private property can be expropriated for public purposes, that compensation should be paid, and that due process should be adhered to.

### 5.2.2 *The 1993 Constitution*

The property clause in the new Constitution follows traditional formulations of the expropriations clause, although certain aspects of it are not quite clear.[250]

Section 28(2) was obviously included to provide a 'due process' clause according to the US model, but it creates unnecessary confusion because of the use of the term 'deprivation'. This term suggests that something is taken away, which may seem to make it applicable to expropriations only, thereby leaving the courts to find their own way in searching for a solution to the very difficult question of distinguishing between expropriations and exercises of the police power. It seems unlikely that exercises of the police power (such as planning, health, and conservation laws) were not meant to be subject to the due process clause as well and they have to be distinguished from expropriations in order to avoid the conclusion that planning, health, and conservation laws should make provision for compensation. Instead of facilitating the distinction between expropriation and exercises of the police power this provision will probably confuse the issue more than is necessary.

The expropriation clause in s 28(3) reverts to the formula of the Technical Committee's seventh progress report by including a number of factors that have to be taken into account when a court has to decide upon the amount of compensation that is just and equitable. The factors enumerated are clearly meant to force the court to accept a certain approach when taking this decision, namely an approach in terms of which not only the narrow market-oriented factors related to the owner's financial interests are considered but also a wider range of socially relevant factors concerned with the circumstances under which the owner acquired and uses the land and the interests of others who are affected by it. It is noticeable that this provision applies

---

[248] Murphy (1993) XXVI *CILSA* 211 at 228–30 discusses the implications for a standard of compensation of his proposals concerning constitutional review.

[249] And, similarly, that compensation which is not promptly paid is not equitable. In this regard the proposal of the KwaZulu/Natal Indaba is perhaps unnecessary.

[250] See Van der Walt op cit (n 202) 195–9.

only to the one case and not to decisions regarding the question whether the expropriation itself is just and equitable. The same factors are also brought into play when a court has to decide whether a law which restricts the entrenched rights in property is reasonable and justifiable in an open and democratic society based on freedom and equality[251] and when a court has to decide whether it is just and equitable to expropriate land for restitution to someone who was previously dispossessed of it.[252]

One of the most obvious problem areas regarding the exercise of the state's expropriation powers is expropriation for the purpose of affirmative action with regard to access to land and land rights[253] and for the purpose of land restitution. Once the principle of affirmative action aimed at redressing the imbalances with regard to access to land is accepted as one of the aims of the Constitution the expropriation clause permits the expropriation of private property rights towards that purpose, against just compensation as determined by the expropriation clause. The special sections of the Constitution that deal with restitution of land rights make it clear that expropriations for this purpose qualify as expropriations 'for public purposes' in terms of s 28(3) of the Constitution.

## 5.3 Restriction clause

### 5.3.1 *Proposals*

Once private property rights and the right of expropriation are explicitly provided for in a Bill of Rights it is advisable to include a reference to police power to preclude the possibility of confusion and uncertainty. Police power involves the exercise of state powers in the course of the administration and control of state functions whereby private interests are defined, curtailed, or otherwise affected without amounting to expropriation, and consequently compensation is normally not paid for the effects of these powers on private rights and interests. All land-use planning and control and environmental measures taken by the state fall into this category since they necessarily affect private property rights. One of the most important aspects of interpretation of a property clause will be concerned with the distinction between the expropriation clause and the police power referred to in the restriction clause since the courts will have to distinguish between the two in individual cases in order to decide whether a specific limitation or taxation constitutes expropriation and whether compensation is payable or not.[254]

The majority of proposals make provision for the exercise of the state's police power in the form of limitations of the fundamental rights guaranteed in the Bill of

---

[251] Section 33(1).
[252] Subsection (5) of the special section on restitution of land rights.
[253] See in this regard Sachs 'Rights to the Land' in *Protecting Human Rights in a New South Africa* (1990) 104 at 116–18; 'Towards a Bill of Rights in a Democratic South Africa' (1990) 6 *SAJHR* 1 at 8–9; Budlender op cit (n 111) 45–52; Budlender 'The Right to Equitable Access to Land' (1992) 8 *SAJHR* 295 at 299, 302–3; Du Plessis 'Regstellende Aksie met Betrekking tot Grond' 1991 *Tydskrif vir Regswetenskap* 140; Omar *The Role of the Bill of Rights for a Democratic South Africa: Key Issues* (1992) 12. The question of affirmative action and the exercise of police powers also concerns the inclusion of socio-economic rights in the Bill of Rights and the co-ordination of property rights and socio-economic rights such as housing rights. See in this regard the chapter on socio-economic rights by Bertus de Villiers below, 599.
[254] See the discussion by Murphy op cit (n 244) 18–27, where the distinction is applied to the ANC proposals; and especially Murphy (1993) XXVI *CILSA* 211 at 223–8, where the distinction between the expropriation power, police power, and taxation is discussed at length.

Rights. The ANC proposals do so directly in the property clause itself, which contains a provision[255] to the effect that the guarantee clause and expropriation clause shall not be interpreted in any way impeding the right of the state to adopt measures deemed necessary in any democratic society for the control, use, or acquisition of property in accordance with the general interest, or to preserve the environment or to regulate or curtail monopolies or to ensure the payment of taxes or other contributions or penalties. This provision should be read together with the new art 13.3, which states that property rights impose obligations and that their exercise should not be in conflict with the public interest, and art 13.2, in terms of which the content and limits of property rights shall be determined by law. The Law Commission[256] and the previous government[257] proposals provide, in a general clause, for the 'circumscription'[258] or the limitation of all fundamental rights protected by the Bill of Rights. The KwaZulu/Natal Indaba proposals contain a similar clause[259] dealing with the restriction of rights and freedoms.

All these proposals determine that the fundamental rights, including property rights, may be limited or restricted by way of legislation for the sake of public interests or safety, provided that the right in question is not in effect abolished or in its essence encroached upon. In fact this provision should be interpreted in such a manner that the exercise of police powers may be excessive in that they actually amount to an expropriation (in which case the expropriation clause will apply) or in that they actually affect the very essence of the right as such, in which case they should be unconstitutional. In the second case this kind of provision with regard to the state's police powers contains the institutional guarantee which was read into the guarantee clause of the German Basic Law, so that once again the necessity of a guarantee clause for a South African Bill of Rights may be questioned. Article 18(4) of the erstwhile government's proposals is concerned with such a fundamental encroachment through excessive taxation.

The restriction clause should lay down the principle that the state can and should control the use and exploitation of private property, that such control need not amount to expropriation, and that they do not require compensation as long as they satisfy the equality principle.

### 5.3.2 *The 1993 Constitution*

As indicated above, the property clause in the new Constitution does not contain a clear provision with regard to exercises of the state's police powers and furthermore the development of a distinction between expropriation and the police power is hampered by the use of the term 'deprivation' in s 28(2), which acts as a due process clause.

The only clause that can be utilized in construing a sensible provision for police powers is s 33, which deals with limitations of the entrenched rights. Section 33(1) provides that the rights entrenched in Chapter 3 of the Constitution may be limited

---

[255] Article 13.8.
[256] Article 34(1).
[257] Article 35(1).
[258] A term probably borrowed from the German Basic Law, which provides that the contents and limits of the guaranteed right of ownership shall be described by way of legislation; see in general above, 2.3.3.
[259] Article 14(1)–(3).

by a law of general application provided that such limitation shall be permissible only to the extent that it is reasonable and justified in an open and democratic society based on freedom and equality, and provided that the limitation shall not negate the essential content of the right in question. Section 33(2) provides that limitations of certain entrenched rights may also be necessary, but the rights in property protected in s 28(1) are not included in this group.

On the basis of this provision it is possible to argue that laws concerned with matters such as land-use planning and control, conservation, health, and so on can place limitations upon private rights in property, provided that the law applies generally and not to an individual, the limitation does not negate the essential content of property rights, and that the limitation is reasonable and justifiable. One may assume that limitations of this nature are not meant to require compensation as long as they conform to these provisions. The question is, however, where to draw the line between limitations of this nature and expropriations. It seems possible that a construction similar to the US 'inverse condemnation' or constructive expropriation can be fitted into this framework in order to push the borderline between the two situations towards the expropriations side, thereby extending the area in which encroachments by state action require compensation.

Obviously borderline cases will occur[260] in which the courts will have to determine whether a particular encroachment upon private property rights amounts to an expropriation or to a restriction. Murphy[261] has proposed a model of review in terms of which the presence and effects of an encroachment upon constitutional rights may be established and dealt with. Matthew Chaskalson[262] has concluded from his analysis of US jurisprudence on takings that US case law in this regard is essentially arbitrary, and that the *ad hoc* way in which the courts approach this matter makes it very difficult to develop clear and consistent principles, especially if the outcome of the conflict between social and individual interests is influenced by political motives. Van der Walt[263] argues that this kind of arbitrary result is almost inevitable in a situation where the courts are expected to fulfil everybody's expectations and allay everbody's fears with regard to property rights. To a very substantial degree the outcome of this debate about the distinction between expropriations and regulatory powers will be an indication of the success or failure of the Constitution in providing a solution for the fundamental conflict between individual and social interests.

## 5.4 Rights in land

### 5.4.1 *Proposals*

Of all the proposals only the ANC deemed it necessary to treat land differently from other property rights. In terms of the modern fragmentation theories discussed above it is necessary to treat land differently because it is such a unique, vital, and limited resource. In practical terms this approach means that rights in land and the state's

---

[260] As they do in most other jurisdictions with even vaguely similar constitutional provisions; see above, 2.3.1, 2.3.2. See further the discussion by Murphy op cit (n 244) 18–27.
[261] (1993) XXVI *CILSA* 211 at 228–33.
[262] (1993) XXVI *CILSA* 211 at 395–401. See also Chaskalson 'The Property Clause: Section 28 of the Constitution' (1994) 10 *SAJHR* 131 at 134–9.
[263] Op cit (n 32) 295.

power to limit and restrict those rights should be treated in a way that suits the unique character of the object as well as the essential interests of all people in the sensible use and exploitation of this resource. This thought was expressed in the Freedom Charter and in art 12 of the ANC proposals, which stated that the land, the waters, and the sky and all the natural assets which they contain are the common heritage of the people of South Africa, who are equally entitled to their enjoyment and responsible for their protection, and that the system of property rights should take into account that it is the country's primary asset, the basis of life's necessities, and a finite resources. A constitutional property clause including and based upon this idea would reflect modern views about property rights very well and would indeed be a unique and progressive provision.

### 5.4.2 *The 1993 Constitution*

The Constitution does not treat land as a unique object of rights in property except for the fact that the special sections on restitution of land rights are focused on land rights only and not on all objects of dispossessed rights. In a sense these sections do signify that land is regarded as a unique and important object, but unfortunately this idea is not taken into account in the property clause itself at all.

The only indication of a diversified view of rights in property is the fact that s 28(1) does not treat the acquisition, holding, and disposal of rights in property the same. The right to acquire and hold property is guaranteed without any qualifications, but the right to dispose of it is protected only 'to the extent that the nature of the right permits'. This qualification does indicate a measure of awareness of the diversity of rights in property, but it does not necessarily affect land rights in particular. A note in the tenth progress report of the Technical Committee indicated that this formulation was used in order to accommodate communal land holdings as opposed to individually held rights, but of course the same argument applies to land or any other property that is co-owned in the form of so-called bound co-ownership, or any other situation where the rights of disposal are restricted for some reason. Apart from this provision rights in property are presented and entrenched as a homogenous body of rights and no provision is made for differences brought about by the differences in the objects or the subjects concerned nor for the effect of the exercise of these rights upon society at large.

## 5.5 Environmental rights

### 5.5.1 *Proposals*

The ANC proposals provide explicitly for the protection of environmental rights. Article 12 provides that the environment[264] is the common heritage of the people of South Africa and of all humanity, that everyone shall have the right to a healthy and ecologically balanced environment and the duty to defend it,[265] and that the state shall take the necessary steps to conserve, protect, and improve the environment.[266] In the 1993 revised proposals the old art 12.1 is moved over to the introductory part

---

[264] Including the land, the waters, and the sky: art 12.1.
[265] Article 12.2.
[266] Article 12.3–12.5.

of the article on land and the environment,[267] but for the rest the proposals regarding environmental rights remain the same.[268]

The Law Commission proposals state simply that everyone has the right not to be exposed to an environment which is dangerous or seriously detrimental to human health and well-being and the right to the protection and conservation of that environment.[269] The erstwhile government's proposals contain a similar provision.[270]

Glazewski[271] welcomes the environmental clause proposed by the ANC in 1990 and points out that it contains three vital elements: an individual environmental human right, an obligation on the state to undertake positive environmental action, and a citizen's duty to defend (which should actually include a duty to protect and conserve) the environment.[272]

### 5.5.2 *The 1993 Constitution*

The Constitution provides in s 29 that every person shall have the right to an environment which is not detrimental to his or her health and well-being. Compared with the remarks of Glazewski referred to above it is clear that this provision is rather bloodless, especially as it takes away the explicit duty upon the state to take steps to enforce this right. In the process the right that is created becomes a typical third-generation right with all the uncertainties concerning enforcement that usually accompanies such a right.

---

[267] Article 12.1.
[268] Article 12.14–12.17.
[269] Article 30.
[270] Article 32.
[271] Op cit (n 139) 167–84.
[272] Glazewski op cit (n 139) at 183.

# FAMILY RIGHTS

JUNE SINCLAIR

## 1 INTRODUCTION

Until recently the inclusion of a chapter on family law in a book dealing with constitutional law and a new Bill of Rights would have seemed odd, even inappropriate. The conventional division between public and private law has produced in South Africa a family-law jurisprudence almost devoid of reference to the fundamental human rights of persons *qua* family members. And it has produced family-law syllabuses and a body of academic writing largely confined to the explication of the black-letter rules that govern the relationship of family members *inter se*. The role of the state in according or denying fundamental rights to those members through its statutory regulation of the family has not been challenged. The result has been an overall impoverishment in this field of endeavour.

The constraints of the past are being shed. South Africa is entering a new constitutional era, anxious to provide guarantees of basic human rights and freedoms. These rights and freedoms extend beyond the public domain of interaction between the state and its citizens. They assume major importance within the so-called private context of the family so that state and private regulation of the rights of family members *inter se* is seen as a matter of concern from a human rights perspective. Within the public domain a multitude of laws and policies governing taxation, pensions, and rights to housing and health care affect power relations between family members. The entrenched societal expectation that women are inexorably and exclusively responsible for rearing children, coupled with the structure of paid labour and its assumption that the ideal worker is a man with no child-care responsibilities, play a fundamental role in determining which of two partners in an intimate relationship becomes financially dependent on the other. The human capital depreciation that flows from the subordination of career advancement to familial responsibility frequently also entails financial dependence on the state for women when the relationship ends.

A rich comparative literature demonstrates that within the family unit women (and children) occupy positions that leave them deeply at risk, and men occupy dominant positions that facilitate economic independence. This statement about the private sphere is not startling. It mirrors the position of women within the public sphere of employment.

In this chapter considerable attention is given to the position of women within society and the family. It cannot be justifiable to describe the legal rules governing families without drawing sharp attention to the inferior position to which society and the law have relegated women. And the enterprise of connecting family law to the debates about equality is now enriched and made more challenging by the inclusion in the Bill of Rights of clauses guaranteeing sex equality, dignity, security of the person, privacy, and special protection for children. How clauses of these kinds will impact upon the existing rules governing families and how private discrimination, especially within the public world of work, affect family relationships and may be eradicated will remain vexed questions. Some insights into the context and nature of the difficulties may provide a basis for the future development of this area of the law. That development will undoubtedly be infused with new vitality as the issues of public and private discrimination are confronted and equality between men and women assumes the importance it deserves. Until recently the major challenges lay in the drafting of an instrument of fundamental rights; now they lie in interpreting it.[1]

## 2 THE RADICAL NATURE OF THE TRANSFORMATION OF FAMILY LAW

Profound transformation of the legal relationship between family members *inter se* and between the family and the state has taken place in Western industrialized societies during this century.[2] Similar transformations have occurred in the past, such as the transition from ecclesiastical to secular administration of family law.

---

[1] It is Chapter 3 of the (interim) Constitution of the Republic of South Africa Act 200 of 1993 that contains what is being termed the Bill of Rights. Recent legislation that has altered the law of the family is dealt with in the relevant places. A complicating feature of the preparation of this chapter has been that other chapters cover equality, personal rights, and labour law. All of these topics affect families and individual members of families. A certain overlap is therefore unavoidable. Also, the chapter on family law should arguably cover every aspect of this branch of the private law upon which the Bill of Rights will have an impact and it clearly encompasses a detailed discussion of children's rights. This piece does not attempt full coverage and, in particular, covers children's rights only in passing. It does not deal at all with fiscal legislation that discriminates against women and married women in various ways. (Although separate taxation of husbands and wives has been achieved over the past few years, there are still differences in, for example, tax rates, rebates, and allowances.) Its aim rather is to open the debate among family lawyers and public lawyers about equality in intimate relationships and some of the connections between seemingly discrete branches of law. It attempts to stress that the boundaries we create between these branches serve to do no more than facilitate the assimilation of the content of a mass of legal rules. They should not blind us to the fact that developments in many areas of the law affect families and are thus not only legitimately the concern of family lawyers but unjustifiably ignored by them.

[2] See Glendon *State, Law, and Family: Family Law in Transition in the United States and Western Europe* (1977) and the sequel to this work, *The Transformation of Family Law: State, Law, and Family in the United States and Western Europe* (1989) ch 1. One crucial example of dramatic change in the family and in the workplace is the number of women working outside the home. Jacobson 'Pregnancy and Employment: Three Approaches to Equal Opportunity' (1988) 68 *Boston U LR* 1019 offers figures for the US: 44 per cent of the labour force is female (over fifty million women). The two-parent household with the husband the sole breadwinner constitutes less than 10 per cent of American families, while single-parent families account for 16 per cent of all families. Jacob 'The Changing Landscape of Family Policy and Law' (1988) 21 *L and Society R* 743 points out that nearly half of all American marriages end in divorce, cohabitation has 'increased markedly . . . the birth rate is well below the replacement level . . . [T]he proportion of illegitimate births has almost quintupled from 37,9 per 1 000 live births in 1940 to 184,3 per 1 000 in 1980' (ibid). '[P]reschool child care has shifted from the mother in the home to someone else . . . outside the home' (at 744). A Central Statistical Services news release (PO302 of 29 November 1990) reveals, as mid-year estimates for South Africa for 1990, that out of an economically active population of 11 073 000, 33,3 per cent (3 687 000) are women; 65,4 per cent (2 411 000) of those women are African (and they represent 21,7 per cent of all economically active persons); 17,9 per cent (660 000) of those women are white. See further Le Roux 'The Economically Active Married Woman and Dual Income Couples' in Steyn, Strydom, Viljoen & Bosman (eds) *Marriage and Family Life in South Africa: Research Priorities* (1987) 317; Church 'Legal Aspects Relating to the Greater Participation of Women in the South African Economy and Concomitant Decrease in Population Growth' (1990) 31 *Codicillus* 26; Van Zyl 'What do Women Want from the Law?' (1992) 109 *SALJ* 509 at 512–13. Ginwala, Mackintosh & Massey *Gender and Economic Policy in a Democratic South Africa* (UK: Open University Development Policy and Practice Working Paper No 21, April 1991) contest statistics that reflect large numbers of women as being not economically active. The authors contend that statistics commonly reflect only registered workers who may be unemployed and those in full-time employment. They point out that in 1988 a UNESCO study gave 800 000 as the number of registered domestic workers and 2 000 000 as the number unregistered. Official statistics therefore distort, by underestimating, the extent to which women are working outside their homes (at 11).

But the current period of rapid change seems to 'strike at the most basic assumptions' underlying marriage and the family.[3]

> 'While the family has remained fundamental to social organisation, the present generation has witnessed considerable relaxation in the grip which the marriage institution has held over family life ... This has been the result of changes in public opinion which has come to place a high value on respect for individual fulfilment and free choice, on tolerance of diversity of styles in personal relationships and on concern for the well-being of all persons in society.'[4]

Itself a country where considerable political and socio-economic movement is taking place, South Africa occupies a distinctive position in the context of developments in the legal relationship between family members and between the state and the family. Its heterogeneous society is 'fissured by differences of language, religion, race, cultural habit, historical experience and self-definition'[5] and consequently reflects widely varying expectations about marriage, family life, and the position of women in society. Its geographical isolation from and protracted political ostracism by countries with which there were once strong ties stifled here the impetus that precipitated major reforms in other places. These factors weighed heavily in inhibiting the evolution of our law of marriage and of our conception of sex equality. The current transition from racial domination to a constitutional dispensation that guarantees fundamental rights is making the experiences of our African neighbours and also of Europe, the Commonwealth, and North and South America more accessible to us. From them we could learn to fashion a better legal dispensation for South African families, and particularly for women. The resolution of our political problems will in turn enhance the possibility of economic recovery to enable an improved theory of family law to be put into practice.

The make-up of South African society is not unique. Responses to the pluralism and diversity of US society provide instructive comparisons in this context. They gave birth to the idea that democracy in family law demands neutrality rather than the imposition of ideologies or behavioural patterns of any one dominant group upon others. In practical terms this neutrality is seen to have provoked a decrease in the legal regulation of marriage.[6] Nevertheless, despite the apparent policy of withdrawal that has emerged in the US, far-reaching reforms in the economic and child-related fields of marriage (encompassing divorce) have occurred there. Changes of an equally fundamental nature, representing a move away from Christian tradition and towards the modern ideal of individual freedom, coupled with a growing concern for the welfare of children, are discernible also in Europe,

---

[3] Eekelaar 'The Place of Divorce in Family Law's New Role' (1975) 38 *Modern LR* 241. Brinig & Carbone 'The Reliance Interest in Marriage and Divorce' (1988) 62 *Tulane LR* 855 at 865 say that if the 'nineteenth century produced major changes in marriage and divorce, the twentieth century witnessed a wholesale revolution'.

[4] Zuckerman 'Formality and the Family — Reform and Status Quo (1980) 96 *LQR* 248. Rutherford 'Beyond Individual Privacy: A New Theory of Family Rights' (1987) 39 *U Florida LR* 627 at 652 says '[t]he pendulum of family rights has swung from absolute preference for the family unit to absolute preference for individuals', creating conflict requiring a new approach to create a balance between individualism and familialism.

[5] The quotation is from a leader-page article in *Business Day* 26 June 1990 by Ken Owen.

[6] Rheinstein & König *International Encyclopedia of Comparative Law* vol IV *Persons and Family* (1974) ch 1 'Introduction' 9 para 10 remark that the dominant ideology in a pluralistic society must be one of tolerance. Glendon *Transformation of Family Law* 14 observes that secular family law in some countries which follow the occidental pattern of regulation of family matters refrains from articulating a common morality. 'It confines itself merely to defining the current outer limits of permissible diversity ... while leaving maximum room for choice and ... individual liberty.'

where there is a larger measure of uniformity in societal expectations about marriage.

It is not clear that the failure of the South African legislature until 1979[7] and 1984[8] to take the first meaningful steps to bring our law of marriage into line with that in societies with some comparable characteristics was attributable either to our geographical isolation or to a commitment to neutrality.[9] It was the political impasse brought on by the pernicious policy of apartheid that inhibited international exchange of ideas. And it was our status as political pariahs that prevented the free flow of information about the development of family law and the position of women in Western societies and constrained research here. The policy of apartheid, moreover, demanded the enactment and enforcement of barbarous laws that deformed the legal system as a whole and family law and family life with it.

The failure for a considerable time to modernize our law left the legal system based on rules which formed the basis of Western systems of family law prior to the dramatic reforms effected virtually everywhere during the last thirty years. And even our important matrimonial property reform of 1984 waited four further years to be extended to Africans. The persistence for so long of legal rules shaped by religious tenets, and which ignored both equality between men and women and the cultural heritage of the majority of South Africans, resulted in serious discrepancies between laws and mores and brought the legal system into disrepute. But in a pluralistic society such as ours a very difficult question is always 'whose mores?'

> 'Even if one were to believe that a unitary system of [family] law could be developed and applied to clearly identified problems, which law should be selected? Which problems should it address? Which values should be given prominence? Whose image of the world ... should prevail?'[10]

Are the policies expressed in our current attitudes to the recognition of African

---

[7] When the Divorce Act 70 of 1979 was enacted, to substitute marriage breakdown for fault as the main ground for divorce.

[8] When the Matrimonial Property Act 88 of 1984 revolutionized the proprietary consequences of marriage. Most of these changes were not extended to the civil marriages of Africans until the commencement of the Marriage and Matrimonial Property Law Amendment Act 3 of 1988, on 2 December 1988. The categorization in this chapter of our population into whites, coloureds, Asians, and Africans (blacks) for the purpose of describing family-law legislation is one used not out of preference, but because without it a clear exposition is not possible.

[9] Concerning geographical isolation, it must be noted that from African countries immediately to the north there has been none. And, as to developments abroad, South African academics and members of the Law Commission have had access to the comparative literature. The inhumanity of the apartheid apparatus reveals an ideology far removed from neutrality. What has been done to families in the name of preserving white supremacy has been done deliberately and with scant regard for the suffering and deprivation that has ensued. Sachs *Protecting Human Rights in a New South Africa* (1990) 64, in the essay 'The Constitutional Position of the Family in a Democratic South Africa', describes the laws that deliberately split up families. He refers to the migrant labour system, the establishment of single-sex hostels in which no family life was permitted, and the hated s 10 of the Native Urban Areas Act, which was specifically designed to prevent African women and children from living with their husbands and fathers in the towns. He stresses that the damage done to the family in South Africa must not be seen simply to be a consequence of industrialization or urbanization. (See also Mndaweni 'Limping Marriages in the New South Africa?' (1991) XXIV *CILSA* 215.) These incontrovertible observations notwithstanding, it cannot be denied that the diversity among the various groups comprising South African society does present a problem to the lawyer investigating the fairness of existing laws and their operation, intent on promoting coherence between the law and social practices, and eager to cultivate public acceptance and effective application of enacted reforms. This problem is exacerbated when change is contemplated in areas likely to generate emotive responses. Thus the legal regulation of intimate relationships in South Africa has its own special difficulties, not unlikely to produce an attitude of withdrawal on the part of legislators and, ultimately, judges. Inaction nevertheless cannot be passed off as neutrality. And particular vigilance is called for now because the operative system has been inherently evil and immanently inimical to family stability.

[10] Fineman 'Societal Factors Affecting the Creation of Legal Rules For Distribution of Property at Divorce' (1989) 23 *Family LQ* 279 at 282. For discussion of a unitary system of marriage law which tolerates cultural and religious diversity in South Africa, see Sachs op cit (n 9) 70–6.

and Muslim marriages, in the rules of divorce, matrimonial property, and parental power, for example, enacted by the (minority) group sufficiently powerful to make them law, ahead of or behind patterns of behaviour held desirable by other groups? Is the law defining marriage and family and regulating family relations, both directly and indirectly, being used to retard social change or beneficially to restructure societal attitudes along new lines? Or is it, in this context, neutral?[11]

To offer unequivocal responses to these kinds of questions would be dogmatic and rash. But posing them is important, especially now that the era of reconstruction of our society and our legal system is upon us. Laws enacted to prop up the apartheid system, such as the Population Registration Act, the Group Areas Act, and the Land Acts that denied black people fair access to immovable property, and policies designed to deter urbanization, such as those that have retarded the provision of urban housing for black people, are now relics of our unfortunate past. But their disappearance from the statute book is insufficient. Measures (requiring considerable financial resources) to redress the harm that has been done can only be seen as legitimate demands by individuals and communities against whom these laws and policies were directed. Without appropriate remedial development programmes to provide the basic necessities of health care, education, and housing the restoration of stable family life will not be achieved.

Some insight into the direction that reform in the law affecting intimate relationships may take may be gained from a brief reference to selected aspects of the transformation of marriage and family law that has been occurring in other places. At the beginning of this century many underlying assumptions about marriage were common to most Western legal systems. In South Africa, too, little flexibility existed in formulating suggestions for reform. But the major upheaval in Western nations has eroded the traditional concept of Western marriage as a lifelong commitment terminable only for just cause; as a community of life, the sanctity and importance of which outweighs the pursuit of individual success and happiness;[12] and as a support institution that guarantees the housewife-mother permanent maintenance from her breadwinner-husband.[13] Even the importance of the status that formal marriage offers is seen to be withering away.[14] The English Law Commission, in

---

[11] Rheinstein & Glendon *International Encyclopedia of Comparative Law* vol IV *Persons and Family* (1980) ch 4 'Interspousal Relations' 4 para 1 assert that the law does not always aim only at conformity with mores, but can be used as an instrument of retardation by conservative regimes and of restructuring by avant garde regimes. Freeman & Lyon *Cohabitation Without Marriage* (1983) 25 consider that the law serves not only to reproduce social order — it actually constitutes and defines that order. 'Law defines the character and creates the institutions and social relationships within which the family operates' (ibid).

[12] The introduction of marriage breakdown as the main or sole basis for divorce in Western jurisdictions is the obvious manifestation of the ideal of individualism, in terms of which marriage is believed to be concerned primarily with personal happiness and fulfilment.

[13] Two bases were traditionally advanced to justify a woman's right to lifelong maintenance. One was the 'contract theory', whereby the husband undertook to provide financial support in exchange for the services of his wife. Laws reflecting this attitude are now considered to be unjust to husbands and inimical to the attainment of economic independence and equality by wives. Blackstone *The Commentaries on the Laws of England* 4 ed (1876) by R M Kerr vol I at 418 predicated the husband's obligation to maintain his wife upon the unipersonality of husband and wife. This justification has been adequately negated. Ellman 'The Theory of Alimony' (1989) 77 *California LR* 1 at 5 reflects the modern view that the financial need of one spouse at the termination of a marriage does not lead inevitably to the conclusion that the other spouse is the one who must meet that need. The movement is away from stereotyped role-allocations towards a new ideal of equality and financial independence.

[14] Glendon *Transformation of Family Law* 16. This is borne out by the enormous increase worldwide in the number of people who now choose to live together without marriage.

its Report of 1988 entitled 'Facing the Future: A Discussion Paper on the Ground for Divorce', describes the changes thus:

> 'Socio-economic developments seem to have led to a change in the nature of marriage in Western society. What has been called "institutional" marriage, which largely entails economic functions and the provision of domestic services, has been replaced by what may be called "companionate" marriage, which requires a continuing successful emotional relationship... A number of factors... may have contributed to this changed view of marriage. First, the values of society generally have changed, with greater emphasis on pursuit of individual success and happiness and less on religious and ethical doctrines. Secondly, income and wealth today depend upon trade and employment rather than inherited property. This has emancipated more young people from their parents' control... [I]t has enabled couples to marry, or set up home together, as soon as they please, and even... to apply consumer society's "throwaway attitude" to marriage. Thirdly, the "emancipation" of women has changed women's expectations of what marriage should provide for them... The other side of the coin may be that the "emancipation" of women has also emancipated men from the traditional responsibility generated by the dependence and vulnerability of their wives.'[15]

These changes have not been completed,[16] nor are they occurring at the same rate in different countries. Recent reforms, considered to have been implemented to reflect new and sound policies, are in several places already being criticized. Rejection of the premises upon which these reforms were predicated and dissatisfaction with their effects are being manifested.[17] The content and significance of

---

[15] Report No 170 of May 1988 para 2.19.

[16] Katz, in a review of the excellent book by Fox & Quitt *Loving, Parenting and Dying: The Family Cycle in England and America, Past and Present* (1980), published in (1983) 17 *Family LQ* 96, points out that the history of the family is the 'hot' field in Anglo-American history. Historians are asking how the changing character of the family relates to social change generally (at 97). Some appreciation of these changes and their relationship to the law governing families is indispensable for family lawyers. In South Africa racial segregation has produced and entrenched differences between communities, making analysis of emerging trends and the identification of appropriate policies exceedingly difficult — Burman 'Capitalizing on African strengths: Women, Welfare, and the Law' (1991) 7 *SAJHR* 215.

[17] Sweden is an example of a country that embarked upon enormous social experiments in the late sixties and seventies. Professor Jacob F Sundberg, in a monograph entitled *Family Law in Turmoil — The Norsemen on the Move* (1979), eruditely traces the experimental journey in family law undertaken by the highly literate, remarkably homogeneous Swedes. Extensive reforms to entrench the principle of neutrality between different lifestyles generated changes that emptied marriage of most of its consequences. The reforms concentrated on the contractual nature of living in the same household regardless of formal marriage, the status of children whether born in or out of wedlock, the integration of maintenance and social welfare to ensure that dependants received their entitlement from the state, which then recovered a contribution from the provider, and the improvement of the rights of unmarried fathers in relation to custody and adoption of their children. The author concludes, acerbically, that the experiments were a trip to nowhere. The ticket for the voyage was bought by mistake; the journey turned out to be enormously expensive; and it was discovered that no return coupon was included in the price (at 35).

The English Law Commission, in its Report on the Financial Consequences of Divorce No 103 of October 1980 para 1, alluded to the serious and sustained criticism of the judicial discretion to divide property on divorce only ten years after radical reform introduced it. The criticism culminated in a reformulation of the guidelines and objectives that govern the exercise by English courts of their adjustive discretion — see the Matrimonial and Family Proceedings Act 1984, succinctly analysed by Cretney & Masson *Principles of Family Law* 5 ed (1990) 384ff. The original aim, to place the parties in the financial position in which they would have been had the marriage not broken down, often entailing lifelong maintenance for former wives, has been abandoned. The new goal is a clean break between the spouses, primary consideration being given to the interests of children. Dewar *Law and the Family* 2 ed (1992) 297 reports that the 1984 Act is widely criticized as being contradictory in its objectives and falsely premised on the myth that ex-wives are parasites living on the earnings of their former husbands. He considers the need for further reform in the light of criticisms about the uncertainty of the operation of the judicial discretion and the restrictive category of assets capable of division on divorce. The sharing of pension benefits is strongly advocated by Dewar (see 298). Reconsiderations of matrimonial property rules in Sweden and West Germany reveal a belief that systems based on a partnership involving the sharing of *all* assets are extreme, and that only a sharing of the matrimonial home and its contents should be implicit in modern relationships — see Glendon *State, Law and Family* 161–2; Eekelaar (1982) 45 *Modern LR* 420 at 421; Saldeen's discussion of the 1986 Swedish bill proposing a new Marriage Code (1987–8) 26 *J Family L* 197 at 200. And on the question of sharing career assets (e g enhanced earning capacity derived from a professional education, or goodwill in a business), Eekelaar 'Equality and the Purpose of Maintenance' (1988) 15 *J of L and Society* 188 considers that the ideology of equality is pressed too far. It demands 'equality of result stretching into the long-term future', which may be incoherent and objectionable because it assumes that if the spouse who is the claimant had not married, she

these events, amply documented in a rich comparative literature, must be adverted to in analyses of the 'black-letter' law of marriage in South Africa. So too, within the context of formulating policy, must the implication be highlighted that family law is everywhere in a state of flux and in conceptual disarray. We are passing through a period of unsettled assumptions.[18] Legal rules acceptable to us today may soon be considered unsuitable; ideas and ideals, such as real rather than mere formal equality of the sexes, previously impossible to incorporate into the legal system or inculcate in society, may achieve the acceptance they require to become law and to become inherent in social mores. This ambivalence that exists in society and in individuals and the lack of fixed ideas about what marriage is and should be have been described as 'but an aspect of the alienation of modern [wo]man'.[19]

## 3   STATE AND FAMILY: FAMILY AUTONOMY AND THE PUBLIC/PRIVATE DICHOTOMY

In addition to the changing social ideas about marriage and the decline in most legal systems of canon-law precepts a markedly different posture adopted by the state towards the family requires scrutiny. A diminution in the regulation of the formation

would have pursued an economically independent and fruitful career and the marriage prevented her from doing so. In fact, he asserts, she most probably would have married someone else and chosen the same lifestyle (at 192–3). The widespread move in the US towards equitable distribution on divorce in the common-law separate-property states provokes Oldham 'Is the Concept of Marital Property Outdated?' (1983–4) 22 *J Family L* 263 at 266 to challenge the partnership ideal, advanced as the justification for this development, on a different more fundamental ground. It is ironic, he says, that this form of judicially imposed sharing has finally been widely accepted during an era when fewer and fewer marriages can be characterized as long-term partnerships. He advocates the limitation of equitable distribution to cases of long marriages or marriages involving children. Reservations such as this one, about the extent to which the much cherished partnership ideal should be implemented, contrast sharply with the sharing cult that precipitated the frenetic search in the US in particular for more and more property susceptible of division on divorce. And it is still said there that it was the divorce revolution that, at a minimum, sought to achieve recognition of marriage as a financial partnership (Levy 'An Introduction to Divorce-Property Issues' (1989) 23 *Family LQ* 147 at 159). Weitzman 'Marital Property: Its Transformation and Division in the United States' in Weitzman & Maclean (eds) *Economic Consequences of Divorce* (1992) 85 argues that whatever the complaints against equitable distribution may be, there can be no question of a return to strict title untempered by discretion. She points to the blurring of the distinction between community-property and common-law (separate property) states (at 89), and questions the fairness of equitable versus equal division of property. She alerts us to the fact that equal division often compels the sale of the family home, which prejudices the woman and children (at 101). Reconciling tensions between division based on entitlement and division based on need is possible, she believes, but only through the recognition of more new property susceptible of division — especially career assets, i e earning capacity (at 88, 138). In England, too, there is a stark contrast between the recommendations of co-ownership of the matrimonial home made by the English Law Commission in 1973 (see Law Com No 52), in 1978 (see Law Com No 86), and in 1982 (see Law Com No 115), and the rejection of its proposals in 1982 by the government. Hoggett 'Recent Reforms in Family Law: Progress or Backlash?' (1987) 11 *Dalhousie LJ* 5 documents the rise and fall of the marital partnership principle in English law. She concludes that the removal in 1984 of the objective of placing the parties in the position in which they would have been had the marriage not broken down and the failure to replace this unworkable objective with some other principle to encourage a fair sharing of property on divorce, coupled with the government's rejection of co-ownership of the matrimonial home, signals the abandonment of the concept of marital partnership (at 19). Yet more recent developments suggest contrarily that the partnership ideal still thrives in England. It finds renewed expression in the Report of the Law Commission on Family Law: Matrimonial Property No 175 of December 1988, which proposes joint ownership of all movable property used by both spouses. The omission of the matrimonial home from the proposal is explained as a desire to avoid controversy and not as a rejection of the principle of sharing immovable property. One might therefore conclude that the objections to devices for sharing frequently go either to the extent or to the time of the application of this ideal rather than to the ideal itself. What seems to be emerging is a need to give expression to the notion of partnership of certain assets *during* the marriage and not only on its dissolution. Whatever the future brings, this adumbrated survey serves to show how rapidly policies thought to be equitable gain and lose credibility as we stumble on in the search for fairness for husbands and wives.

[18] Glendon 'Modern Marriage Law and its Underlying Assumptions: The New Marriage and the New Property' (1980) 13 *Family LQ* 441 at 442.

[19] By Rheinstein & Glendon op cit (n 11) 191 para 244.

and dissolution of marriage[20] and a concomitant preoccupation with the regulation of economic and child-related features of marriage, divorce, and non-marital cohabitation has occurred.[21] The introduction of judicial power to vary ownership of property to give effect to the notion that marriage is an economic partnership; judicial power to issue garnishment orders directing employers to deduct money from a person's income before it reaches his pocket; the assimilation effected by the courts and by legislatures of the consequences of cohabitation to the consequences of marriage; and the development of elaborate systems of juvenile justice and child-welfare — these are examples of state intervention which some see as the erosion of individual and family autonomy.[22] Yet not everyone agrees with this evaluation of the recent legislation. Katherine O'Donovan observes that

> '[c]onventional academic discussion of state intervention in family and personal life is based on the premise that legislation which directs the management of these areas is not only a problem, but the only problem. Critics of . . . state [intervention] hold the family up as a universal good. What they overlook is that the nuclear family which they so admire reflects a particular culture within a particular set of social relations: it is the family form of the nineteenth-century bourgeoisie.'[23]

---

[20] Referred to above as a move away from Christian tradition and towards greater individual freedom. Smart 'Regulating Families or Legitimating Patriarchy? Family Law in Britain' (1982) 10 *Int J of the Sociology of L* 129 at 131 describes this withdrawal by saying that 'matrimonial law has begun to abandon its punitive treatment of those who fail to marry . . . and those whose marriages fail'. At the federal level in the US there has been a 'notable reduction in . . . legislative and judicial activism pertaining to domestic relations laws', reports Wardle 'United States of America: All Quiet on the Federal Front' (1986–7) 25 *J Family L* 269.

[21] Some examples from the comparative literature give a sense of the kind of intervention that has occurred, and the reaction to it. Davis 'Introduction: "Rethinking" American Family Law' (1985) 61 *North Dakota LR* 185–6 identifies the two issues of importance in family law there to be economic, encompassing alimony, child support, and division of property, and 'people' issues, encompassing custody, child abuse, abortion, and adoption. Fineman op cit (n 10) 281 asserts that the 'state has abandoned . . . its concern with the formalities attending entry into marriage and the designation of acceptable reasons for divorce. Instead, there is increasing focus on the internal aspects of family life with need for protection of individuals within the family structure, and the desirability of the imposition of egalitarian standards as the contemporary justification for state regulation . . . This shift of state regulatory focus is consistent with the view that marriage is a voluntary . . . union of equals which either may terminate "at will" if it does not satisfy their desires and needs.' Freeman 'Introduction: Rethinking Family Law' in Freeman (ed) *The State, the Law, and the Family* (1984) 1 itemizes domestic violence, cohabitation, autonomy in child-rearing practices, divorce, post-divorce maintenance, and the extent to which the welfare state is replacing the conventional state as the issues upon which the debate about state intervention focuses in England.

[22] Smart op cit (n 20) 142–3 criticizes the assaults on the traditional principle of non-intervention in family life. She refers to the mounting concern over the welfare of children, which has 'led to a steady increase in the demand for welfare reports . . . to assist the judiciary . . . to make decisions about the future of children which are based on welfare, rather than legal, criteria' (at 142). Freeman 'Questioning the Delegalization Movement in Family Law: Do We Really Want a Family Court?' in Eekelaar & Katz *The Resolution of Family Conflict* (1984) 7 at 13 expressed agreement with others that 'an unjustified professionalization [has occurred] of issues that are "in fact beyond the present reach of expert understanding" '. He reiterated his concern and disquiet about the wide powers assumed by the local state in relation to children and the inadequate surveillance of the ways in which these powers have been exercised in the piece 'England: New Responses to Old Problems' (1987–8) 26 *J Family L* 69 at 73. Since his comments the Children Act of 1989 has reversed this trend. It adopts a policy discouraging judicial intervention and replacing parental rights with parental responsibility; it acknowledges parental autonomy and curtails the use of wardship. But already doubts are being expressed about whether this Act provides sufficient protection for children (Freeman (1992) 6 *Int J of L and the Family* 52).

[23] O'Donovan *Sexual Divisions in Law* (1985) 14–15. Barton 'Children: The International Perspective' (1989) 19 *J Family L* 369 at 371 observes that child-care professionals walk a tightrope of disapproval in their work — 'damned if they do intervene and damned if they do not'. Dingwall & Eekelaar 'Rethinking Child Protection' in Freeman (ed) *The State, the Law, and the Family* (1984) 93 at 104 and 110 challenge assertions that state intervention did grow. The assertions are, they contend, without empirical foundation and ideologically misconceived. It seems that, despite conflicting views on this subject, disquiet about the incidence of state intervention contributed to the policy underlying the Children Act of 1989, which is now one of non-intervention. Shifts like this one in policy and in the laws that give effect to it demonstrate how uncertain the reform of family law can be. And yet it is that very uncertainty that can be seen as a strength of the legal system in which it is found, for it permits the refinement of policies not serving the interests of society. Non-intervention can be a rigid unarticulated policy the effects of which frequently escape scrutiny. Tension and ongoing interplay between the need for a certain defined policy and the quest for flexibility of approach are more likely to produce satisfactory responses than dogmatic adherence to rigid principles or abandonment of the search for a clear programme. The right balance is the (elusive) goal.

O'Donovan cogently points out that not legislating entails a value judgment that can entrench oppression inherent in traditional conceptions of marriage just as legislating can. Thus the absence of state intervention does not mean that the state has no position. Nor can it be inferred that, if left to their own devices, individuals would regulate their lives free from prejudices imposed by the legislature or society and in a way that would conduce to justice and equality. The state's unarticulated position permeates the unregulated fields through its regulation of what it regards as 'public'. 'Both private and public law are suffused with the ideology of the family, which operates on gendered subjects.'[24]

The apparent penetration of intimate personal relationships by bureaucratic regulation and administration has provoked controversial writings on the distinction between issues that are properly seen as 'public', i e suitable for regulation by the law, and those deemed 'private', i e falling within a zone that has in traditional liberal thought been considered sacred and to require protection from intrusion by the state. This public/private dichotomy has assumed a special significance in family law and especially in feminist legal scholarship, where it has been used to explain the subordination of women and, inter alia, their persistent economic dependence on men and the state. Feminist writings frequently attack not so much the intrusion of the state into the family, but rather state protection and approbation of the privatized nuclear family which is traditionally based on a sexual division of labour. The criticism is that the state classifies the family as a private arena in order to justify its failure to intervene in matters such as marital rape and domestic violence, where women are the victims of the patriarchal domination deriving from the power delegated by the state to men.[25]

---

[24] O'Donovan op cit (n 23) 203. Hutchinson & Petter 'Private Rights/Public Wrongs: The Liberal Lie of the Charter' (1988) 38 *U Toronto LJ* 278 at 285 make the same point in relation to Canada. They observe that the claim of the state to sovereignty 'implies that a decision not to intervene and regulate, or mere inaction, is as much a governmental responsibility as a decision to do so'. The state 'is equally implicated in the retention of the status quo. Acquiescence and action are merely opposite sides of the same governmental coin.'

[25] O'Donovan op cit (n 23) 181; Rose 'Beyond the Public/Private Division: Law, Power and the Family' (1987) 14 *J of L and Society* 61; Thornton 'The Public/Private Dichotomy: Gendered and Discriminatory' (1991) 18 *J of L and Society* 448 at 459. As Hutchinson & Petter op cit (n 24) 286 point out, leaving power in the hands of an individual within the so-called private sphere amounts in effect to a delegation by the state to the individuals it chooses of power that can be wielded in a largely unchecked and democratically unaccountable way. In the South African context there is strong evidence of the suspect nature of the non-interventionist approach. One of the reasons for the rejection by the Joint Committee of Parliament (see its report on the Criminal Law and Criminal Procedure Act Amendment Bill, No 6 of 10 Feb 1989) and by Parliament itself of the Law Commission's recommendation (contained in the report *Project 45: Women and Sexual Offences in South Africa* (1985)) that the marital rape exemption be abolished was that it was not proper for the state to intrude in the marital relationship. Since then the (previous) government has done so (to attract votes in the April 1994 election?) by enacting the Prevention of Family Violence Act 133 of 1993, which came into operation on 1 December 1993 (Proc R124 *Reg Gaz* 5211 of 1 December 1993). Section 5 abolishes the exemption entirely, with none of the strings attached that were trenchantly criticized in respect of previous legislation and draft bills dealing with marital rape. The paucity of attention that has been given to the problem of domestic violence in South Africa and the reports of women that police are reluctant to come to their aid in cases of domestic violence are further examples. The 1993 Prevention of Family Violence Act is a belated but welcome attempt to rectify the situation. Delegation by the state to the husband of authority over the family was also exemplified by the archaic common-law notion that the husband is its 'head'. A choice was made by the government not only not to interfere with that notion but expressly to retain it by the enactment of s 13 of the Matrimonial Property Act 88 of 1984. That Act abolished the marital power (prospectively) and s 13 clearly put beyond any doubt that the abolition was intended to confer adult status upon married women without detracting from the common-law position of pre-eminence of husbands in the family. The Act was none the less publicly portrayed as seeking to create out of marriage a partnership of equals. Now husbands have lost the marital power and possibly their headship of the family (s 29 and s 30 (the latter amending s 13 of the Matrimonial Property Act by deleting the reference to the husband as head of the family) of the General Law Fourth Amendment Act 132 of 1993, which came into operation on 1 December 1993 (Proc R123 *Reg Gaz* 5211 of 1 December 1993)). (See below, n 61 for the argument that the abolition of the reference in s 13 to the husband's position as head of the

Professor Michael Freeman writes, for example, that the powerful ideology of liberal theorists that the state should refrain from intervention in the 'private' lives of individuals has served to deny protection to women and children, the elderly, the mentally ill, the handicapped, and others traditionally cared for in the home, by women. The state defines particular areas as private to mystify us and to control its own ideologies relating to the family. Far from being a liberal stance protecting areas of freedom, this insistence on the privacy of the family is designed to perpetuate male domination and female subordination, which are seen by the state as crucial to the 'assumed stability of the family unit'.[26]

The insistence also entails an argument that the protection of individual rights of members of the family will threaten the family's existence. Such an argument is tenable only if one accepts that justice is somehow incompatible with the intimacy, harmony, altruism, generosity, and loyalty that we seek in our private lives. The argument is surely spurious. Families are essential to society and the makers of laws and policies should be profoundly concerned to ensure that the place within which we raise children and seek love and comapanionship to mitigate the harshness of (public) life is a place where the justice that governs other institutions prevails.[27]

Recent writings challenge assertions that the state has pervasive control over relationships between men and women and that state activity represents the unfolding of a plan dictated by the inexorable logic of capitalism and/or patriarchy. They seek to explicate the complex conglomeration of institutions and agencies that make up the modern state. They reveal that some state action serves the interests of women, some the interests of men, and some the interests of both or neither.[28]

Nikolas Rose,[29] among others, considers the public/private debate limiting and productive of overly simple criticisms of family law. He is sceptical about feminist

---

family, without express legislative abrogation of the common-law rule, leaves the common law intact.) The common law of guardianship and the refusal of the state until late in 1993 to interfere in this 'private' sphere to create parental equality was for long another area of concern and a further legitimate criticism of the 1984 Act. The very recent 1993 amendment to s 13 of the Matrimonial Property Act (referred to above) did not encompass the law relating to guardianship, although previous drafts of the legislation that became the General Law Fourth Amendment Act 132 of 1993 did create equal guardianship of parents during marriage. At the 'last minute', one might say, the government rushed through the Guardianship Act 192 of 1993. This Act was assented to on 22 December 1993, but was not in force as at 28 February 1994. The major change effected by it confers upon mothers of legitimate children rights of guardianship equal to those exercised by the father of such children. It repeals s 13 of the Matrimonial Property Act. Other aspects of the law regulating the parental power still require scrutiny — see below, 5.1.2 and 5.1.3.

[26] See his inaugural lecture as Professor of English Law at University College London, entitled 'Towards a Critical Theory of Family Law' (1985) 38 *Current Legal Problems* 153 at 168 and 174. See also Zimring 'Legal Perspectives on Family Violence' (1987) 75 *California LR* 521, who points out that life's 'greatest moments occur behind closed doors. So too do some of modern life's most outrageous exploitations.' For O'Donovan op cit (n 23), the collapse of the distinction between public and private is essential to the attainment of fairness and equality (at 206). The private 'is a sphere of battery, marital rape, and women's exploited labour' (at 181). Rhode *Justice and Gender: Sex Discrimination and the Law* (1989) 133 tells us that '[m]ale physical violence and female economic dependence reinforce patriarchical patterns. Over time, the asymmetrical allocation of domestic roles perpetuates the gender stereotypes that perpetuate subordination.' She advocates preservation of the valuable aspects of traditional roles and protection of the functions performed by the family, rather than the 'family' as traditionally defined. To achieve this will require the abandonment of public/private distinctions and concentration on the disadvantages that flow from gender (at 133–4). See further Olsen 'The Family and the Market: A Study of Ideology and Legal Reform' (1983) 96 *Harvard LR* 1497 at 1510; Naffine *Law and the Sexes: Explorations in Feminist Jurisprudence* (1990) 69–71; Hutchinson & Petter op cit (n 24).

[27] Larson 'The Sexual Injustice of the Traditional Family' (1992) 77 *Cornell LR* 997 at 999.

[28] One may add of course, in the South African context, that a great deal of state action in the past has served the interests only of those wishing by coercion to maintain the supremacy of whites, or white men. Black men and women alike were the victims, although it cannot be contested that black (African) women have endured a disproportionate share of suffering.

[29] 'Beyond the Public/Private Division: Law, Power and the Family' (1987) 14 *J of L and Society* 61.

attempts to explain the position of women which attribute all manifestations of disadvantage and lack of empowerment to a conspiracy between husbands and the state to keep the family 'private' and which see the state as the embodiment of exclusively male interests. Rose rejects the view that women have been passive victims or duped collaborators in family reforms over the last century. And he rejects the view that women are inexorably forced into the private domain of family by the inequitable structures of the labour market and educational institutions and the lack of child-care facilities. He concludes that family law is but one component of a complex network of powers which link domestic, sexual, and parental relations with social, economic, and political objectives. Essentially his point is that women have become subjected to the power of men not simply through coercion and domination but also through their own commitment to a project of subjective fulfilment, a project in which familialism has a central role. They have internalized the norms of motherhood in a way that has contributed to their subordination.

Rose's arguments, it is clear, do not challenge the fact that women's interests have been and frequently are subordinated to other interests. They suggest rather that 'the state is a battleground and that state policy is a reflection of feminist as well as of patriarchal, of working-class as well as of capitalist interests, ideologies, and power'.[30] More effective than attempts to find one coherent explanation of all aspects of gender inequality would be efforts to identify specific problems and to uncover the conditions and assumptions that have produced them and the relations of advantage and disadvantage that they entail.[31]

The male sphere is commonly described as the 'public world of work, of politics and of culture'. The separate female sphere is 'the private world of family, home, and nurturing support for the separate public activities of men'.[32] This notion that the world of remunerative work and the world of the family are separate spheres is considered to be what has fostered the economic and social subordination of women. It has done so by deeming the qualities necessary for success in the home unnecessary, even unsuitable, for the workplace and by entrenching the idea that the consignment of women to the home is inevitable because of their different reproductive capacity. Lucinda Finley calls for a legal framework based on the 'premise that [since] work and family are the two most important defining aspects of the lives of men and women, the idea that these two aspects of human existence occupy separate spheres must be replaced with legal policies . . . that appreciate that public and private are a continuum, with each defining and affecting the other'.[33] We must move towards 'workplace policies that make it possible for both women and men to combine their work lives with involvement in the family'.[34]

Insistence on the assumptions underlying laws and policies that conventionally categorize husbands as breadwinners and wives as homemakers brings oppression

---

[30] See Elliot 'The Family: Private Arena or Adjunct of the State' (1989) 16 *J of L and Society* 443 at 453. Goodall ' "Public and Private" in Legal Debate' (1990) 18 *Int J of the Sociology of L* 445 at 451 postulates that although important to the structure of law, the public/private dichotomy is not central to it. She reminds us that there are forms of oppression in society other than the subordination of women.

[31] Rose op cit (n 29) 74–5.

[32] Finley 'Transcending Equality Theory: A Way out of the Maternity and the Workplace Debate' (1986) 86 *Colorado LR* 1118–19.

[33] Op cit (n 32) 1182.

[34] Ibid. See also Teitelbaum 'Family History and Family Law' (1985) 5 *Wisconsin LR* 1135; Bennett 'The Economics of Wifing Services: Law and Economics on the Family' (1991) 18 *J of L and Society* 206.

to women who wish to escape from these roles. It also denies to men the enriching aspects of parenting. Research suggests that the oppression for women takes on this form: the greater the disparity between husband and wife in economic resources, the greater the husband's dominance in decision-making is likely to be. Disadvantage is then compounded by the fact that the inferior vocational advancement, and hence financial status, and hence decision-making power experienced by a woman, fosters further unfair distribution between her and her husband of domestic burdens such as child care and care of the aged — which in turn further limits her occupational advancement.

This circle of disempowerment must be seen in the context of the alarming incidence of breakdown of intimate relationships which create and foster dependence for women while they last and leave behind persistent dependence when they fail. The post-breakdown dependence is then exacerbated by ineffective mechanisms for the enforcement of support obligations of fathers towards the children of their failed marriages. These phenomena have led to what is termed 'the feminization of poverty'.[35]

---

[35] See Graycar & Morgan *The Hidden Gender of Law* (1990) 69. The authors point out that this phrase, used in many parts of the world, is believed to have been coined by Pearce 'The Feminization of Poverty: Women, Work and Welfare' (1978) 11 *Urban and Social Change Review* 28. They say that in Australia in 1985, 89 per cent of female sole parents were receiving social-security payments, yet only 40 per cent were participating in the workforce. This comparatively low figure is accounted for by the conditioning of Australian women to be dependent on men. The conditioning occurs mainly through education (at 70–1). Parker 'Rights and Utility in Anglo-Australian Family Law' (1992) 55 *Modern LR* 311 at 314 points to research which provoked the emergence of the Child Support Scheme in Australia because it revealed the drastic drop in the standard of living of women who became sole parents on divorce. The research showed that men improved their pre-divorce standard of living. Parker refers to research identifying similar patterns in England and in the US. For the position in England see Eekelaar & Maclean *Maintenance after Divorce* (1986). See also Neave 'Living Together — The Legal Effects of the Sexual Division of Labour in Four Common Law Countries' (1992) 17 *Monash U LR* 14 at 15. On the plight of single-parent families headed by women in the US, see Bruch 'One-Parent Families in the United States: Changing Law and Economics' in Meulders-Klein & Eekelaar (eds) *Family, State and Individual Economic Security* vol I (1988) 265. Rhode op cit (n 26) 126 cites data for the US revealing that women are twice as likely as men to be poor; that female single parents are five times more likely than men to be poor; that two-thirds of all indigent adults are women. Given that 90 per cent of single-parent families in the US are headed by women, it is not surprising that half of these families are below the poverty line. In addition, race exacerbates the position — three-quarters of poor black and half of poor Hispanic families are headed by women. See also the report that 84,7 per cent of married white women and 75,6 per cent of married non-white women in the US in 1980 were financially dependent on their husbands, in Esseks 'Redefining the Family' (1990) 25 *Harvard Civil Rights–Civil Liberties LR* 183n3. Rhode 'The "No-Problem" Problem: Feminist Challenges and Cultural Change' (1991) 100 *Yale LJ* 1731 notes further that the 'workforce remains highly gender segregated and gender stratified, with women of color at the bottom of the occupational hierarchy. Full-time female employees earn less than two-thirds of the annual wages of male workers, and a Black female college graduate on the average earns no more than a white male high school dropout' (at 1733). She points out that the increasing feminization of poverty has sharpened class divisions and left intact racial subordination (at 1734). Gimenez 'The Feminization of Poverty: Myth or Reality?' (1990) 17 *Social Justice* 43 eruditely exposes the causes of the phenomenon to which the title of her article refers. She cites, in particular, unpaid labour in the home and underpaid labour in the workforce and documents her assertions with copious data. While unemployment is a cause of poverty among men, it is usually remedied when a job is found. For women, poverty endures despite full-time employment (at 45). Sachs 'The Constitutional Position of the Family in a Democratic South Africa' in op cit (n 9) 67 points out that African people have been denied their traditional family-based support systems and at the same time excluded from the mainstream of state-based social benefits (such as they are). He asserts that 'social security law leans heavily towards benefiting most those who already have the most'. Thus pensions for whites have been considerably higher than those for blacks; whites receive more protection from unemployment insurance and workers' compensation law than do blacks. The study of Burman & Berger 'When Family Support Fails: The Problems of Maintenance Payments in Apartheid South Africa' (1988) 4 *SAJHR* 194 and 334 is a stark account of the plight of black women and their children. Burman 'Capitalizing on African Strengths: Women, Welfare, and the Law' (1991) 7 *SAJHR* 215 (also published in Bazilli (ed) *Putting Women on the Agenda* (1991) 103) cites figures supplied by the Medical Officer of Health for Cape Town for 1988/9, which reveal that 68,2 per cent of all African children born in 1988/9 were born outside of any form of marriage. She suggests that, although it is not possible to quantify the number of children being brought up in female-headed households in Cape Town, it seems likely that the vast majority of children will spend part of their growing years in one. This is so mainly because of the high rate of marriage breakdown (over 50 per cent of African marriages in

Child care is a particular and prominent context within which the public/private dichotomy has yielded gender disadvantage. There appears to be widespread feeling that it is inappropriate for the state to initiate comprehensive child-minding facilities; that it is up to the mother, or the parents, to make alternative arrangements for the care of children if their mother is not going to fulfil her role as nurturer. This reticence and implicit disapproval of a mother's decision to work outside the home manifests itself not only in the paucity of facilities subsidized by the state — it is apparent also in the lack of adequate regulation of the private facilities that are available. Tax laws, too, allow no deduction of the child-care costs inevitable for the working mother. A carefully planned system of child care subsidized by the state, but provided ideally by employers, is required. It must replace the *ad hoc* unsatisfactory arrangements that too many women, by reason of their financial predicaments, have no choice but to accept.[36] Not only would some of the implications of gender discrimination be diminished by such a development; the country, critically short of qualified personnel, would derive fuller advantage from the considerable resources it has invested in training women by enabling more of them to pursue their talents while continuing to discharge their procreative and nurturing desires and responsibilities.

Calls for improved facilities, however, must not be seen as acceptance that these specific ameliorations would suffice to eradicate disadvantage and disempowerment flowing from gender and create equality within families. The problem is much more complex than that. It derives largely from the inexorable delegation to women of the primary responsibility for rearing children and the assumption that the unremunerated work of the homemaker is not work. Power relations within the family need to be scrutinized and the burdens of its members more equitably defined. There will have to be a change in the structure of the workplace and a change in the attitude of employers to women who work outside their homes. There will have to be a constitutional commitment to equality for women which is enforced to ensure that constraints which the public/private dichotomy imposes are thrown off. Wherever the inequality resides and whatever its source, it needs to be eradicated.

Mary Ann Glendon, analysing the transformation of family law in the US, England, West Germany, and France, concludes that the principal unresolved problems for family law and policy in the jurisdictions she lists remain those relating

---

Cape Town end in *de facto* divorce) and because women with illegitimate children who subsequently marry often leave their children in the care of their single or divorced mothers. The failure of the fathers of these children to pay maintenance makes the burden of their mothers an intolerable one, not mitigated much by the inadequate state maintenance grants, which are available, inter alia, only if the man is dead, disabled, a pensioner, in prison for more than a year, or has vanished (at 216). See further Burman 'First-World Solutions for Third-World Problems' in Weitzman & Maclean (eds) *Economic Consequences of Divorce* (1992) 367 at 375–7 and, more generally, Sinclair *An Introduction to the Matrimonial Property Act 1984* (1984) 4–13.

[36] Until recently local authorities regulated only child-care facilities catering for more than six children, but during 1992 Provincial Administrations gave the go-ahead for municipalities to pass by-laws regulating all child-minders. Television programmes and newspapers have highlighted the unsatisfactory position in South Africa, but the commentaries are confined largely to child care for whites. The plight of black mothers who have to seek employment to shelter and feed their children and who are far too often the sole providers of sustenance to their offspring is largely ignored. See further Burman 'Marriage Break-up in South Africa: Holding Want at Bay?' (1987) 1 *Int J of L and the Family* 206; 'Maintaining the One-Parent Support in South Africa: Law and Reality' in Meulders-Klein & Eekelaar op cit (n 35) 507; 'Capitalizing on African Strengths: Women, Welfare, and the Law' (1991) 7 *SAJHR* 215 at 219 (for suggestions for the involvement of the state and the community in the development of child-care facilities for African children); Caine 'Maternity Rights of Black Working Mothers' (1989) 5 *Responsa Meridiana* 444.

to the situation of women who are raising children, fulfilling the role of caretaker and homemaker, and working outside the home. Their remuneration, status, and job security are ubiquitously inferior to those of their male counterparts.[37] These problems, inextricably bound up with the constitutional question of equality, will demand close scrutiny in South Africa for a long time.

## 4  FORMAL EQUALITY VERSUS REAL EQUALITY

Feminist writings in the comparative legal literature have devoted much attention to the subordination of women, occasioned in the main by their child-care responsibilities, and to the inability of women to achieve economic equality with men in employment despite formal equality in the law. The formal equality to which the research refers is that achieved by the eradication of express discrimination based on sex or gender and by the inclusion in Constitutions, charters of rights, and ordinary legislation of provisions demanding such things as the equal protection of the law for all and outlawing sex and gender discrimination.

These writings have perceived and powerfully portrayed how women for long believed that the achievement of formal equality in the law would guarantee actual equality in society and in their homes. They demonstrate that the achievement of formal equality in the law, important though that clearly is, should be regarded as no more than a first stage in the quest for real equality. They demonstrate more specifically that the poverty being experienced by divorced and single mothers heading one-parent families will not be overcome as long as current assumptions about the family and the responsibility for parenting persist and the present male-oriented structure of paid employment remains unchallenged. And they demonstrate that within marriage real meaning for the notion that marriage is a partnership of equals will require much more than bland laws and commendable accompanying platitudes. Feminism has directly challenged the perpetuation of the traditional family by asking why, with its sex-specific division of labour and the consequential economic disempowerment and vulnerability of mothers, the family should be immune from the demands for justice that are so prevalent in other institutions in society.

### 4.1  Equal treatment, special treatment, dominance, and disadvantage

Another fundamental aspect of the debate about sexual equality, particularly in relation to economic disadvantage endured by divorced or single mothers, has been the case for special treatment rather than equal treatment. The issue is often termed 'equality analysis'. A full discussion of it here would inappropriately repeat subject-matter more properly located in the chapter on equality, but certain observations are indispensable.

Inherent in the notion of equal treatment or formal equality, based on the Aristotelian theory that like persons must be treated alike, is the proposition that persons in different situations must be treated differently. Feminist writers

---

[37] *Transformation of Family Law* 307. Chapman 'Violation Against Women as a Violation of Human Rights' (1991) 17 *Social Justice* 54 at 57 states that '[w]omen make up over half the world's population and perform two-thirds of its work, but receive one-tenth of its income and own less than one hundredth of its property'.

criticizing formal equality point out that men and women are not the same, that women should not be made to strive to be like men in order to enjoy fair treatment, and that the quest for equal treatment has obscured the fact that the legal system is based on a male model.[38] Its male bias is revealed by the way laws are constructed — the adult male being the norm, women, children, and the feeble-minded being the exceptions.

The bias is acutely felt in the labour market, where the premise is that the ideal worker is a man with no child-care responsibilities. While men are raised to believe that they have the right and the responsibility to perform as ideal workers, women are raised to believe that their commitment to work must be defined to accommodate their child-care responsibilities. They therefore have a tendency to select jobs that will allow them to fulfil their responsibilities, even if such jobs pay less and offer fewer opportunities for advancement. This 'choice' is a major factor contributing to their impoverishment and inability to attain a degree of economic independence that would free them from reliance on men and the state for maintenance.

Catharine MacKinnon points out that under the standard of sameness, i e formal equality, women are measured according to their correspondence with men so that equality for women is judged by their proximity to man's measure. Under the difference standard women are measured according to their lack of correspondence with men so that their womanhood is judged by their distance from man's measure. In both instances, note, the law holds women to a male standard and calls that sex equality.[39] The male-biased conception of gender neutrality has allowed some women to enter male preserves, but only those who have been able to construct for themselves 'a biography that somewhat approximates the male norm'.[40] It abandons women who most need the protection of real equivalence, for they are the ones least similar to the men whose situation sets the standard against which entitlement to 'equal treatment' is measured. For this reason the Aristotelian model of equality is doomed by its own conception to prevent the sex equality that it is designed to achieve.[41] 'Equality analysis is of little use to women who would like to question the male-oriented values and norms upon which the workplace is built.'[42]

It was recognition of the fact that problems such as rape, sexual harassment, discrimination based on pregnancy, abortion, family violence, and pornography do not lend themselves to resolution via rules demanding equal treatment for men and women that led to the 'differences approach'. This approach sought to remove from the legal system and from society the use of differences between men and women to justify essentially unfair treatment of women. The problem with it was how to

---

[38] MacKinnon *Feminism Unmodified: Discourses on Life and Law* (1987) 33 describes the sameness branch of the doctrine of formal equality as 'granting women access to what men have access to: to the extent that women are no different from men, we deserve what they have'.

[39] MacKinnon op cit (n 38) 34.

[40] MacKinnon op cit (n 38) 37, and 'Reflections on Sex Equality under Law' (1991) 100 *Yale LJ* 1281 at 1289, where she criticizes the courts for their assimilationist approach, by which men say to women, 'be like us and we will treat you like we treat each other'. Rhode op cit (n 26) 304 warns that women's gradual absorption into prevailing social networks as they strive to achieve the male standard will result in assimilation but not alteration of the closed networks of privilege. The danger is that influential women who achieve membership of the male club lose interest in challenging existing structures. Rhode sees the need to avoid this kind of acculturation as one of the most critical issues confronting feminism. She stresses the danger of acculturation again in her article 'The "No-Problem" Problem: Feminist Challenges and Cultural Change' (1991) 100 *Yale LJ* 1731 at 1761.

[41] MacKinnon op cit (n 38) 44.

[42] Finley op cit (n 32) 1182.

identify those differences between the sexes that are relevant for legal purposes. Should such differences be inherent, i e biological, such as the capacity unique to women to become pregnant, or could they arise also from a particular upbringing and the stereotyped role allocations that place women in a disadvantaged position in the market?[43]

The response to this question was to try to evolve a theory of 'special rights' for women which would accord with the so-called 'real' differences between the sexes. It focused primarily on obtaining pregnancy and maternity leave from paid employment. The effort expended on the exercise was enormous, the results considered disappointing. The exercise was criticized as narrowing the feminist debate by accepting as correct the existing criteria used to define the differences between men and women.[44] It encourages the law's tendency to act upon a frozen slice of reality.[45] It overlooks that gender differences, being based on social conditioning, are mutable. It ignores, moreover, that there are fundamental differences between different groups of women. The white middle-class well-educated woman who claims to know 'what women want' is not 'universal woman', if there is such a being.[46] Subordination for millions of women is not merely a question of gender, but also of race, class, and religion.[47] Angela Harris is an example of a feminist trenchantly critical of those whose 'gender essentialism' overlooks race as a critical factor in the subordination of women. To black women the story feminists tell is about women who are 'white, straight, and socio-economically privileged'.[48] Harris attacks the 'installation of white women on the throne of essential womanhood'[49] and denies that there is a monolithic 'women's experience'.[50]

---

[43] Scales 'The Emergence of Feminist Jurisprudence: An Essay' (1986) 95 *Yale LJ* 1373 at 1375. The models of 'identical treatment with biological exceptions' and of 'treatment according to all differences' (i e including those socially constructed) are succinctly explained in an extract from the work of Elizabeth Sheehy, which appears in Graycar & Morgan op cit (n 35) 41–2. Of the first model, Sheehy notes the disadvantages of stereotyping women according to biological difference and of failure to alter women's subordinated position; of the second, Sheehy warns again of the danger of entrenchment of differences between men and women that disempower women and of the potential use of the model to oppress women further by keeping them out of certain jobs. 'Differences', she points out, is a legal construct; it does not directly focus on subordination.

[44] Scales op cit (n 43) 1376; Rhode op cit (n 26) 82; Daly 'Reflections on Feminist Legal Thought' (1990) 17 *Social Justice* 7 at 17. See also MacKinnon op cit (n 40) 1296–7; Daly op cit 11–13.

[45] Scales op cit (n 43) 1376.

[46] Petersen 'Perspectives of Women on Work and Law' (1989) 17 *Int J of the Sociology of L* 327 at 333, enquiring whether there are anything like a woman's standpoint or perspective, refers to the 'fractured identities' of black women, Asian women, native American women, working-class women, lesbian women. These differences among women may force the abandonment of the idea of 'universal' woman. Rhode op cit (n 35) 1790 says: 'There is no "generic woman", nor any monolithic "woman's point of view".'

[47] Minow 'Introduction: Finding our Paradoxes, Affirming Our Beyond' (1989) 24 *Harvard Civil Rights–Civil Liberties LR* 1 at 4; Dowd 'Work and Family: The Gender Paradox and the Limitations of Discrimination Analysis in Restructiring the Workplace' (1989) *Harvard Civil Rights–Civil Liberties LR* 79 at 80.

[48] Harris 'Race and Essentialism in Feminist Legal Theory' (1990) 42 *Stanford LR* 581 at 588. See also Clark 'Race, Class, Gender, and Sexuality: On Angela Y Davis "Women, Culture, and Politics" ' (1990) 17 *Social Justice* 195 at 197. For a perspective from England, see Smart 'Law's Power, the Sexed Body, and the Feminist Discourse' (1990) 17 *J of L and Society* 194 at 200.

[49] Op cit (n 48) 603.

[50] Op cit (n 48) 588. She illuminates, by way of example, the different experiences of black and white American women in relation to rape. As slaves, and even after emancipation, the majority of black American women were domestic servants in white households where they were uniquely vulnerable to sexual harassment and rape by their masters or employers. But, as slaves, no crime of rape existed in respect of them and, as employees, rape laws were ineffective against black and white men because black women were regarded as 'promiscuous by nature' (at 599). In contrast, white women have enjoyed partial formal protection against sexual brutalization. ' "Rape" . . . was something that only happened to white women; what happened to Black women was simply life' (ibid).

For women to continue to affirm difference in order to justify special benefits, MacKinnon asserts, is to affirm the characteristics of powerlessness.[51] For her, questions of equality are questions of the distribution of power and of hierarchy rather than biological or gender difference. The issue to confront is domination and disadvantage, not equality analysis. She therefore proposes that the question in any challenge of a policy or a rule should be whether it integrally contributes to the maintenance of an underclass or a deprived position because of gender.[52]

The attraction of MacKinnon's approach is that it permits the inclusion of issues into the equality debate that are kept outside of it by the conventional sameness/ difference approach to sex equality. Rape, battery, sexual harassment, prostitution, and pornograghy are drawn in, whereas they are not confronted by 'sex equality law in its difference garb' because they happen predominantly, if not exclusively, to women.[53] The issues of disproportionate poverty among women and their concentration in low-paying jobs are other critical areas that can be brought into high relief by this formulation of inequality, but which usually remain unperceived by those preoccupied with equality analysis and the identification of sameness and difference.

## 5 THE CONSTITUTIONAL PROTECTION OF SEX AND GENDER EQUALITY IN SOUTH AFRICA

The contextual background sketched above of women in families and in society sets the scene for the constitutional framework proscribing laws, practices, and structures which exploit sex and gender.[54]

It might be asked again here why an exposition of aspects of South African family law should be so concerned with women's rights. First, the position of women within the private sphere of marriage and the effect of marriage and family commitments on their position in public life are inextricably linked. These issues, it might also be

---

[51] MacKinnon op cit (n 38) 38–9, commenting on the work of Gilligan *In A Different Voice* (1982), stresses that the special treatment approach provides a double standard that does not give to women the dignity of the single standard. Gilligan considers that women reason differently, that they are compassionate and nurturing, and think in terms of relationships, while men are competitive, aggressive, and assume hierarchical relationships. MacKinnon confesses an 'affection' for this approach, but ultimately rejects it as failing to see that these special qualities are not really 'ours'; they are qualities that male supremacy has attributed to women for its own use. Accepting these so-called differences merely means accepting subjection. Feminists are deeply divided on the 'Different Voice' issue. Gilligan's assumption that women freely choose to be how she describes them is open to attack. Society and its expectations exert insurmountable pressures on most women to demonstrate their goodness, their femininity, by displaying the characteristics that Gilligan attributes to their inherent nature. Subordinating career aspirations in favour of child-nurturing is frequently a manifestation of such pressure rather than one of truly free choice.

[52] MacKinnon *Sexual Harassment of Working Women* (1979) 117. Meyerson 'Sexual Equality and the Law' (1993) 9 *SAJHR* 237 makes a similar case for the abandonment of the preoccupation with sexual difference, which she describes as a sterile debate and the product of an obsession with the concept of discrimination (at 254). She calls for attention to be paid to decreasing 'the extent to which sexual differences translate into unfair disparities of power, income and status between the sexes' (at 253). Her coined expression for disadvantage is 'unfair group inequality' (at 254).

[53] MacKinnon op cit (n 38) 40.

[54] The terms 'sex' and 'gender', although clearly and necessarily distinguishable, are often used interchangeably in the literature. The use of either here is intended to cover both biological differences and those flowing from socialization unless the context demands the distinction between the terms to be expressed. On the failure of draft proposals for a Bill of Rights for South Africa to appreciate the distinction, see Meyerson (1993) 9 *SAJHR* 291. Section 8 of the 1993 Constitution cites sex and gender as separate grounds upon which unfair discrimination is outlawed.

noted, have a profound effect on men who marry,[55] and most men marry. Secondly, the common corollary of marriage is divorce, the consequences of which make an examination of the relative social and economic positions of men and women important. Finally, the era of constitutional reform has dawned in South Africa. The impact on the substantive rules of private law of guarantees of equality and equal protection and the prohibition of unfair discrimination on the grounds of sex and gender demands attention.

The answer to the question posed about the significance of women's rights in a study of family law will also depend on one's broader conception of the boundaries of the subject. A traditional approach would accept unquestioningly the status of women within the family and society and proceed to expound the current rules regulating formal marriage. A more adventurous approach would raise some difficult issues. How can a discussion of family law ignore the fundamental rights of individual members of the family? Why do so many intimate relationships not culminate in formal marriage, and how should the law respond to this phenomenon? If the one-parent family (headed so often by women), the extended family, the family comprising one man and several wives, and homosexual or lesbian couples are encountered sufficiently frequently within a particular society, one may query whether laws regulating and protecting families and their members should not recognize these relationships. Why should women be assumed to be financially dependent on their husbands during marriage, but expected by divorce courts spontaneously to be able to cultivate financial independence when their marriages are terminated?[56] Why can women not fulfil this expectation? Does the division of labour within the home, creating a 'double shift' for women who work outside the home, contribute to their disadvantage and could it be modified? Why do women continue to experience violence and battery within marriage and in intimate relationships outside of marriage, despite formal protection provided to them by the law? What should be done about the plight of women and children whose poverty has been exacerbated by apartheid and the migrant labour system in particular and also by the high rate of default by men in making maintenance payments after divorce?[57]

---

[55] Especially when the marriage breaks down and the post-divorce financial security of the wife and children competes with the ability of the man to support a second family. Nhlapo 'International Protection of Human Rights and the Family: African Variations on a Common Theme' (1989) 3 *Int J of L and the Family* 1 at 10 makes the important point that in the African context family matters cannot be dissociated from issues of women's rights: 'Most of the sex inequalities in traditional society stemmed from the African conception to marriage.'

[56] In South Africa the questionable view that a divorced woman should be expected to be independent finds expression in *Claassens v Claassens* 1981 (1) SA 360 (N) at 369E–F, where Didcott J said that '[t]hose anxious about poverty here are unlikely . . . to find divorce a major cause of it nowadays. The independence and self-sufficiency of women is argued so persuasively and, by the growing number who support themselves through their own efforts, demonstrated so frequently that, as a general thesis, it can hardly be doubted any longer.' Cf *Grasso v Grasso* 1987 (1) SA 48 (C); *Pommerel v Pommerel* 1990 (1) SA 998 (E).

[57] Cf Sachs op cit (n 9) 64 in the essay 'The Constitutional Position of the Family in a Democratic South Africa' where he describes how under apartheid the 'splitting of families became deliberate policy enforced by law'. Legislation 'was specifically designed to prevent African women and children from living with their husbands and fathers in the towns' (at 66). Further on the migrant labour system and the plight of rural African women under apartheid, see 'The Nature of Women's Oppression', a paper presented by the Natal Organization of Women at the Malibongwe Conference in Amsterdam in January 1990. Burman & Berger 'When Family Support Fails: The Problems of Maintenance Payments in Apartheid South Africa' (1988) 4 *SAJHR* 194 and 334 starkly reveal the plight of single-parent families headed by African women. The authors found that awards of maintenance are too low and that the incidence of default by men is very high. The extent and administration of state grants is also hopelessly inadequate.

The premise of this excursus is that South Africa stands ready to question the assumptions that have formed the basis of its laws regulating and affecting intimate human relationships. Unless attention is given to the issues cited below only as examples the new mould will reproduce the inequities of the old; the society may achieve non-racialism, but it will not achieve sexual equality.[58] And 'a programme for the liberation of South Africa which does not take the issue of gender discrimination seriously is incomplete',[59] even for traditional family lawyers.

In which broad areas is discrimination felt? Within what is known as 'the public sphere' women universally suffer disadvantage in employment. Preferences for hiring males, the concentration of women in lower-paid jobs and in part-time work, the wage differential between men and women, the higher risk of dismissal and lower chance of promotion, the intractable question of maternity leave: these are some of the crucial issues to be faced. Thus the workplace must be one focus. Because labour law will be examined in another chapter this focus will not be explored here. But the omission should not be taken to imply that the structure of the paid labour system should be of no concern to the family lawyer. The oppression of women in the workplace cannot be resolved without confronting the role of women in the home. Their lone domestic responsibility and the characterization of (unpaid) domestic work as women's work are features of the patriarchal structure of our society and of the system of paid labour that inhibit the achievement by women of their full potential.[60]

Within the 'private sphere', i e marriage and the family, the unambiguous premise of the South African common law was that the husband is pre-eminent. Take for example these rules: in the absence of an antenuptial contract excluding it, the marital power placed the husband in a position of guardianship over his wife; the husband is the head of the family; a husband could not be guilty of raping his wife; a married woman followed the domicile of her husband; and a father was the natural guardian of his legitimate children. After years of government obduracy and unsuccessful campaigning by champions of women's rights (and in a frenetic attempt by the National Party to capture the votes of women in the April 1994 election) changes to these discriminatory rules were effected suddenly and recently to produce conformity between the content of this branch of private law and the growing public demand for constitutional guarantees of equality between the sexes.[61] Within the customary law of Africans the premise of patriarchy is even more

---

[58] Sachs op cit (n 9) 57 comments that if sexism is not abolished, the transition from apartheid to post-apartheid will be little more than 'the handing over of power from one gang of men to another'.

[59] Murray & O'Regan 'Putting Women into the Constitution' in Bazilli (ed) *Putting Women on the Agenda* (1991) 33 at 45.

[60] Murray & O'Regan op cit (n 59) 43.

[61] The marital power was abolished, but only prospectively, by s 11 of the Matrimonial Property Act 88 of 1984. The abolition applied only to marriages celebrated after the coming into operation of the 1984 Act (on 1 November 1984). Further, this amelioration of the position of white, coloured, and Asian women did not apply to marriages governed by the Black Administration Act 38 of 1927 (essentially civil marriages between Africans). It was not until the coming into operation of the Marriage and Matrimonial Property Laws Amendment Act 3 of 1988 (on 2 December 1988) that the marital power was abolished for such marriages, and only provided they were celebrated after its commencement. These two statutes therefore left intact the marital power operating in marriages celebrated prior to their commencement. On 1 December 1993 the General Law Fourth Amendment Act 132 of 1993 came into operation. It abolishes the marital power from all existing marriages in which it was operating, thus finally cleansing our system of an anachronism (s 29). The same Act amends s 13 of Act 88 of 1984 to delete the reference to the husband's position as head of the family (s 30). The difficulty here is that the husband's position is a rule of the common law that was given renewed expression when it was included in s 13 of the Matrimonial Property Act

fundamental and has not received the same attention of the legislature. For example, the Black Administration Act places African women (except those residing permanently in Natal) married at customary law under the guardianship of their husbands, thus leaving them with limited capacity to contract and to own property.[62] On the death of the husband the wife falls under the guardianship of his male heir, who may even be the woman's son. Thus a system of perpetual tutelage denies African women full status.[63] Family law, encompassing but not limited to the civil law of marriage, must therefore be another focus.

Three common kinds of clause impinge on these matters in international covenants and conventions and in Constitutions. One is the common guarantee of equality and equal protection before or under the law, which dovetails with the prohibition of discrimination on the grounds, inter alia, of sex and gender; the second seeks to preserve the institution of marriage; and the third gives recognition to the anxiety of the state to protect 'the family'. Only the first of these survived the negotiation process and finds expression in the new South African Constitution.[64]

Whether such clauses prohibit both public (state) and private violations (between citizens) depends on the drafting, and the question whether they should do so is a highly controversial one.[65] Section 7(1) of the Constitution specifies that Chapter 3

---

in 1984. It is arguable now that the deletion of the statutory reference to it, without an express abrogation of the rule, leaves the common law intact. Lending force to this argument is the fact that the other common-law rules enacted into s 13 — pertaining to domicile and guardianship — have been removed from s 13 and expressly modified by statute (see below, 545). The companion to the General Law Fourth Amendment Act, the Prevention of Family Violence Act 133 of 1993, which also came into operation on 1 December 1993, abolished the marital rape exemption. Until its enactment a husband who had forced his wife to have intercourse against her will could be charged only with assault and the court was required in sentencing to regard as an aggravating circumstance the fact that he could have been convicted of rape but for the marriage (s 1 of the Criminal Law and Criminal Procedure Act Amendment Act 39 of 1989). The Domicile Act 3 of 1992 made provision for all persons over the age of 18 years to acquire a domicile of choice. It came into operation on 1 August 1992 (Proc R76 of 1992 *GG* 14166 of 20 July 1992). Section 1 of the Guardianship Act 192 of 1993 creates for parents of legitimate children equal powers of guardianship and repeals s 13 of the Matrimonial Property Act 88 of 1984. The Act was asssented to on 22 December 1993, but was not in operation as at 28 February 1994.

[62] Section 11(3)*(b)* of Act 38 of 1927.

[63] See 'Cultural and Traditional Practices and how they Retard or Enhance Women's Emancipation and Participation in the Development of South Africa' (paper presented by the Border Region of the Organization of Women at the 1990 Malibongwe Conference in Amsterdam). See further on the legal position of African women under customary law *The Legal Situation of Women in Southern Africa* (1990), a publication of the Women and Law in Southern Africa Research Project, which contains comprehensive surveys of the legal status of women in Botswana, Lesotho, Mozambique, Swaziland, Zambia, and Zimbabwe.

[64] Marriage and family (which might be protected in one clause) do not feature in the Bill of Rights in Chapter 3 of the Constitution. Article 6.1 of the West German Basic Law of 1949, by contrast, provides that marriage and the family qualify for the special protection of the state. And the African Charter on Human and Peoples' Rights, in art 18, declares the family to be 'the natural unit and basis of society', 'the custodian of morals and traditional values', which shall be protected by the state. See also Van Wyk 'Safeguards for the Family: A South African Perspective' (1990) 1 *Stell LR* 186. Various draft Bills of Rights debated in South Africa over the last few years did include protection for marriage and the family. In the Bill of Rights proposed by the SA Law Commission in its *Project 58: Group and Human Rights* Interim Report (1991), family rights included the protection of the integrity of the family and freedom to marry a person of one's choice, although monogamy featured prominently as the marriage in contemplation (art 19). The previous government's draft Charter of Fundamental Rights, published in February 1993, protected the integrity of the family (art 12). The ANC's revised Draft Bill of Rights, also published in February 1993, contained the rights to establish a family, to marry, and of marriage based on free consent (art 2(29)). The Democratic Party's draft Bill of Rights protected the right to marry and establish a family (art 10). Whether the disappearance of these rights from Chapter 3 of the interim Constitution was altogether regrettable is far from clear. The interpretation of the word 'family', for example, would undoubtedly not have produced a harmonious chorus. Moreover, preserving the 'family' may to some mean preserving the national interest, while to others it will signify the preservation of patriarchy — see Murray 'Democracy, the Family and the African Charter on Human Rights' (paper published in the proceedings of the Fourth Annual Conference of the African Society of International and Comparative Law, Dakar, April 1992) 187.

[65] I have spoken of the family as the private sphere and the workplace as the public sphere. This dichotomy should not be confused with the term 'private discrimination' and the controversial question whether the reach of the Bill of Rights should extend to outlaw discrimination perpetrated by individuals. Thus discrimination by a private

shall bind 'all legislative and executive organs of state'. The judiciary and private persons are omitted — a formulation that invites comment.

The omission of the judiciary suggests that only legislation and administrative action that violate the Bill of Rights may be attacked, while the rules of the common law and of customary law that have not been enacted into a statute remain immune. But s 7(2) goes on to say that Chapter 3 shall apply 'to *all law* in force and all administrative decisions taken and acts performed' (my emphasis) during the operation of the Constitution. 'All law in force' is an expression wide enough to cover any rule, whether residing in the common law, in written or unwritten customary law, or in legislation. On the other hand, the correspondence between s 7(1) and s 7(2) would appear at first glance and logically to require that the words 'all law in force' in s 7(2) be taken to apply to the legislative organ referred to in s 7(1), and that the words 'all administrative decisions taken and acts preformed' in s 7(2) be taken to apply to the executive organs of state referred to in s 7(1). Attributing this meaning to the two subsections would achieve a narrow congruence between the two subsections, but would compel an emasculated application of the Bill of Rights. Rules of the common law and of unwritten customary law that violate the principles enshrined in the Constitution would be beyond the scrutiny of the courts and could be applied by the courts with immunity. Such a result would be a shame. But, further, the law would be so complicated as to be incomprehensible.

There are rules of the common law and of customary law that have been partly or wholly enacted into legislation. One example from the common law is the rule in s 5 of the Matrimonial Affairs Act,[66] which provides that the father of a legitimate child may appoint a testamentary guardian to the child, but not to the exclusion of the mother. In doing this it imported into legislation, by necessary implication, the discriminatory rule of the common law that the father is the natural guardian of the legitimate child and thus the only one of the parents entitled to make a testamentary appointment of a guardian. Section 5 circumscribed the father's common-law power to appoint a testamentary guardian to the exclusion of the mother, but did not extend any right of appointment to the mother.[67] Would the rule of pre-eminence of the father, described above, be classified as one of the common law, or was it fully translated into legislation by s 5, or would it be classified as a mixture of the two? The question does not admit of an easy answer and is one that happily will not have to be asked if the Guardianship Act of 1993 is put into operation. Another example of the undesirability of distinguishing between common-law and statutory violations of the Bill of Rights is the rule of the common law that makes the mother of an illegitimate child its natural guardian to the exclusion of the father of the child. It is one that fathers may wish to attack. It finds oblique expression in s 72 of the Administration of Estates Act,[68] which makes provision for the granting of letters of tutorship by the Master to a person appointed (only) by the mother of an

---

employer against female employees, say, is private discrimination occurring within what I have termed the public sphere of work.

[66] Act 37 of 1953.

[67] These rules have now been superseded by equal powers of guardianship of parents of legitimate children and the denial to both parents of the right to appoint a testamentary guardian while the other parent is alive, unless sole guardianship has been awarded to one of them, by the enactment in December 1993 of the Guardianship Act 192 of 1993. This Act was not in force as at 28 February 1994.

[68] Act 66 of 1965.

illegitimate child to be its testamentary guardian. Although the rule that selects the mother as the sole guardian has its roots in the common law, its application is dealt with in the statute. Does this fact render it vulnerable to attack for discriminating against fathers of illegitimate children?

The enterprise of deciding which rules of the customary law of Africans reside in legislation and which remain partly or wholly unwritten would be an enormous and difficult one. Unwritten African customary law permits, for example, a husband to have more than one wife (polygyny). The Marriage and Matrimonial Property Law Amendment Act[69] amends the Black Administration Act 38 of 1927[70] to permit a civil marriage between persons married to each other according to African customary law, provided that the man is not also a partner in a subsisting customary marriage with another woman. It prohibits both partners in the subsisting customary marriage from marrying another person at civil law. The customary marriage is raised by this legislation to the status of an impediment to a civil marriage other than a civil marriage between the parties to the customary marriage. Yet customary marriage is not fully recognized in our law. The provision also clearly acknowledges the polygynous nature of African customary marriages. If polygyny, as opposed to polygamy, which encompasses polyandry, is discriminatory against women, the question arises whether this discrimination resides in legislation, or in the unwritten customary law, or in both? Why should we have to answer such a question?

To achieve a broader congruence between s 7(1) and (2) of the Constitution, therefore, and one which would obviate an analysis of whether or not a rule being questioned resides sufficiently in legislation to be vulnerable to attack, the words 'all law' should be given their literal meaning. The result would clearly be more in keeping with the spirit of guaranteeing fundamental rights and would avoid the gymnastics of interpretation that a narrow interpretation would compel. Against this interpretation, however, is the fact that s 4(2), a general clause outside the chapter on fundamental rights, declares that the Constitution shall bind all legislative, executive, and judicial organs of the state. The difference in wording between it and s 7(1) would be without significance if the judiciary were held to be covered by s 7. Also, s 35(3) suggests that 'law' means only legislation, for it speaks separately of 'the interpretation of any law' and 'the application . . . of the common law and customary law', as if the word 'law' did not encompass common and customary law.

The omission of private persons from s 7(1) appears to imply no horizontality so that private individuals may validly regulate their rights *inter se* in violation of the Bill of Rights, unless to do so is proscribed by ordinary legislation. Thus sexually and racially discriminatory employment practices in the private sector, outlawed in labour legislation, would be unlawful despite the fact that the Bill of Rights does not reach them. But private discrimination based on race, deriving, say, from a pact between owners of immovable property to dispose of their houses only to persons who are white, since there is no ordinary legislation preventing such a contract would be immune and hence enforceable. A contract between a man and a woman discriminating against the woman, and agreed to by her (perhaps because of an

---

[69] Act 3 of 1988 s 1.
[70] Section 22(1) and (2) are the relevant provisions.

unequal balance of power between the parties, but not entailing duress), such as an undertaking by a wife, but not by her husband, not to enforce the common-law (reciprocal) duty of spousal support, would pose questions about whether the wife could resist a claim for support by her destitute husband and whether he could rely on the contract to resist a claim by his destitute wife. Could one argue that, because such contracts entail reliance on the 'law' of contract and because the Bill of Rights applies to all law in force and outlaws race and sex discrimination, deals like these would not stand? If one could, the effect would be to import into our law a doctrine of unconscionability that would substantially broaden the reach of the Bill of Rights.

It is regrettable that vital issues like these will have to await elucidation by the courts. There was much debate about the reach of the Bill of Rights during the long period preceding its enactment.[71] One would have hoped that the outcome of that debate would have yielded a clearer result.

## 5.1 The prohibition of discrimination based on sex or gender

Section 8 of the Constitution guarantees to every person equality before the law and the equal protection of the law. It expressly outlaws unfair discrimination, direct or indirect, on one or more of a number of listed grounds, including sex and gender, but without limiting the grounds to those listed.

The implications of this clause are manifold and are dealt with in the chapter on equality. Only some that may be of special interest to family lawyers follow. Several raise the question of inequality experienced by women and require an examination of other constitutional guarantees, but the discussion ranges beyond the confines of the feminine. The first question, abortion, is dealt with also in the chapter on personal rights. Reproductive autonomy is vital to the domain of family law, wherever else it may be covered.

### 5.1.1 *Abortion*

Abortion is not commonly regarded as a question of sex equality. The law regulating it is often uncritically taught in family-law courses and mentioned in passing or studied technically in courses on criminal law. Since men do not become pregnant, the argument runs, unfair treatment of women who do is not an instance of sex discrimination.[72] The debate about abortion and about the legal basis upon which it should be permitted is endless and positions are influenced by a range of factors

---

[71] The Bill of Rights proposed by the SA Law Commission op cit (n 64) proscribed only certain legislative, executive, and administrative acts (arts 1 and 40). The previous government's proposals, contained in the Charter of Fundamental Rights published in February 1993, conferred rights upon the individual against the state (arts 1 and 2). The ANC proposals, contained in its preliminary revised version of February 1993, were not clear as to the operation of the Bill of Rights. While art 2.26 spoke of interference by administrative or executive act and art 15.8 advised that special legislation could be passed to require private bodies to provide for affirmative action, art 17.1 declared that the Bill of Rights would bind the state and, *where appropriate*, social institutions and persons. The Democratic Party's draft Bill of Rights of May 1993 bound not only the state but also private persons (art 1, read with art 2(3)).

[72] MacKinnon op cit (n 38) 251 and op cit (n 40) 1318–24 describes this argument, and rejects it, proclaiming with a cogency that bears reading to be appreciated that 'forced motherhood is sex inequality' (at 1319). Clauses in a Bill of Rights outlawing sex discrimination risk being interpreted not to cover legislative restriction on abortion also because the discrimination is regarded as being against pregnant women, not all women, and thus is not discrimination based on sex. But since the discrimination in both cases is against a class of women it seems unduly restrictive an interpretation to deny relief sought under the sex discrimination clause. The combination of discriminatory factors should not prevent relief sought on one even where the particular clause does not deal with

such as culture and religion.[73] Within marriage, and in legal systems where abortion is permitted, the question whether a wife should have the final and only say about abortion is also controversial.

In the US the Supreme Court in *Roe v Wade*[74] held that a woman's constitutional right to privacy prevented a state from forbidding abortion. This recognition of women's autonomy in the 'private' sphere of reproduction, however, is what has been used to justify failures on the part of the federal government to provide funding necessary to make the abortion choice meaningful to those women who cannot afford medically acceptable procedures. The duty of the state not to prohibit abortion in this sphere of privacy has come to mean also that it has no duty to intervene to protect the choice that its non-intervention guarantees. The negative right does not translate into a positive claim to safe subsidized abortion facilities.

Catharine MacKinnon's analysis of the 'privacy' basis of US abortion law is a complaint about the failure of the law to locate women within a context of coercion, of male domination. Her views have important implications for other issues also not seen as questions of sex discrimination. She asserts that the legal concept of privacy has

> 'shielded the place of battery, marital rape, and women's exploited labor; has preserved the central institutions whereby women are deprived of identity, autonomy, control and self-definition; and has protected the primary activity through which male supremacy is expressed and enforced. Just as pornography is legally protected as individual freedom of expression — without questioning whose freedom and whose expression and at whose expense — abstract privacy protects abstract autonomy, without inquiring into whose freedom of action is being sanctioned at whose expense.'[75]

For MacKinnon abortion is not a privilege for which women should have to supplicate to men, but a right based on sex equality, one to which women must have access through proper state funding. The procreation of a child, she argues, makes demands upon a woman's time. Time is what makes up a life. To interfere with the right of any woman to decide whether or not to carry a child to term and to fail to take steps to provide access to acceptable medical procedures deprives her of the right to control her life. It is an instance of inequality. It is discrimination against women.[76]

Adducing equality to ground the right to abortion (which would include sterilization) is compelling in the employment context: the demands of motherhood inhibit a woman's ability to fulfil her potential, to be financially independent, and to compete on an equal basis with men so that she can avoid dependence on an erstwhile

---

discrimination deriving from such a combination (but see Meyerson 'Sexual Equality and the Law' (1993) 9 *SAJHR* 237). Fortunately s 8 of our Bill of Rights expressly avoids the problem by outlawing discrimination on one or more of a number of grounds and by specifying that the list is not exhaustive.

[73] Ashe 'Conversation and Abortion' (1988) 82 *Northwestern U LR* 387 at 388 refers to the 'truly discordant' and 'deeply divided' voices of women on the abortion issue.

[74] 410 US 113 (1973). See also *Webster, Attorney General of Missouri & others v Reproductive Health Services & others* 106 LEd 410 (1989), considered as signalling a move on the part of the US Supreme Court to retreat from, if not overrule, *Roe* (Campbell 'The Constitution and Abortion' (1990) 53 *Modern LR* 238 at 243–5). The case of *Planned Parenthood Federation v Casey* 947 F 2d 682 (1991) is seen in a similar way.

[75] Op cit (n 38) 101 and see also op cit (n 40) 1311–12.

[76] 'Unthinking ERA Thinking' (1987) 54 *U Chicago LR* 759 at 767. 'Because forced maternity is a sex equality deprivation, legal abortion is a sex equality right. "Women's access to legal abortion is an attempt to ensure that women and men have more equal control over their reproductive capacities, more equal opportunity to plan their lives and more equal ability to participate fully in society than if legal abortion did not exist" ' (Mackinnon op cit (n 40) 1323, quoting from the LEAF factum in *Borowski v Attorney General for Canada* (1989) 1 SCR 342).

male partner or the state when the intimate relationship breaks down. The argument does, however, underplay the fact that, if parenting responsibilities were shared in the way that feminists argue they ought to be and if employers were compelled to structure their requirements for a workforce in a way that took account of the human life cycle, including the need for fathers to participate in nurturing their children, the demands of child-rearing, albeit not child-bearing, would not entail the same disadvantage to women that they entail now. The argument from time would be diminished. It rests moreover upon the premise that although a child is the product of man and woman, woman, because the experience of procreation is more prejudicial to the fulfilment of her potential than it is for that of man, should have the right to override the wishes of the child's father and the community. The equality argument asserts *a fortiori* that a man who wants his child aborted in the face of a woman's wish to carry it to term must fail. What is not clear is that the right to reproductive autonomy will be won more easily by women through an argument, albeit a cogent one, for sex equality than by the asssertion of constitutional rights to privacy, dignity, and security of the person.

The context of these arguments assumes considerable importance for South Africa. The Bill of Rights contains an equality clause that is coupled with equal protection of the law, a right-to life clause, a clause guaranteeing human dignity, one guaranteeing security of the person, and a privacy clause.[77] It is silent on the question of abortion. The Constitutional Court will be faced with the conventional conflict between protagonists of free choice and those of protection of the foetus as a person. It will have to grapple with the division of opinion about the true source of reproductive rights and the proper interpretation of clauses that appear to conflict with the right to life. In the many drafts preceding the final version of the Bill of Rights the matter of abortion was located, either expressly or in the commentaries, solely within the context of the right to life. It is on this clause that the public debate about abortion focuses.

The annexation of commentary about abortion to the clause on the right to life deserves attention, given that in our legal system no one would argue that a foetus is a bearer of constitutional rights. The Roman-Dutch law incorporates a special fiction of the Roman law, the *nasciturus* rule, to overcome the absence of legal personality of the foetus in order to permit it, for example, to inherit from a person who dies prior to its birth. This fiction protects specific interests. It would not be required, nor would the crime of abortion exist, if the foetus were ordinarily a bearer of rights in our law. Abortion would simply be murder.[78] The new Constitution does

---

[77] Sections 8, 9, 10, 11, and 13, respectively, of Chapter 3 of the Constitution.
[78] The question whether a foetus has a right to life that can be protected from abortion by the common-law *nasciturus* rule (explained by Boberg *The Law of Persons and the Family* (1977) 9–18) was addressed in *Christian League of Southern Africa v Rall* 1981 (2) SA 821 (O). The applicant approached the court for the appointment of a *curator ad litem* to represent the foetus against its mother, the respondent, who sought to have it lawfully aborted in terms of the Abortion and Sterlization Act 2 of 1975. It was held that the applicant had no *locus standi in judicio*. Apart from this impediment, the court found that the *nasciturus* rule could not be invoked to prevent an abortion. The rule protects benefits that may accrue to a foetus (such as an inheritance or a claim for damages for prenatal injuries) provided that the child is subsequently born alive. It holds in suspense those rights, but does not clothe the unborn child with legal personality. The court endorsed the view that a foetus has no right to life which can be enforced by its father or a third party and held that there was no legal basis for the appointment of a *curator* to protect the foetus from an abortion sanctioned by the law. (See further *G v Superintendent, Groote Schuur Hospital* 1993 (2) SA 255 (C).) The *Rall* judgment excited conflicting responses from academics — see Bedil (1981) 98 *SALJ* 462; Van der Vyver (1981) 44 *THRHR* 305; Davel (1981) 14 *De Jure* 361; Verster (1981) *Obiter* 153; and Du Plessis 'Jurisprudential Reflections on the Status of Unborn Life' (1990) *TSAR* 44 at 52. Du Plessis is critical of the decision for adopting too narrow a view of the interests of the applicant and for failing adequately to protect

nothing to enlarge the category of bearers of constitutional rights to include the unborn. Thus it is surely in the interpretation of other clauses, such as equality and equal protection, dignity, security of the person, and privacy that the abortion debate should occur. And the debate, on this analysis, does not entail a competition between the constitutional rights of the pregnant woman and those of the foetus. There can be no such competition until the fundamental proposition of our law that rights and obligations accrue only from birth is altered expressly to accommodate the foetus.

Take *Roe v Wade*[79] on this point. The duty of states not to deprive a person of life without due process of law[80] was not regarded by the US Supreme Court as depriving a woman of the right to privacy in choosing abortion because the court was in no doubt that a foetus was not considered to be a person with constitutional rights.[81] And the 1988 Canadian Supreme Court's decision in *R v Morgentaler*,[82] striking down Canada's abortion law on the ground that it violated the Charter's right to security of the person, was unaffected by a Charter right protecting life.[83]

Ronald Dworkin[84] argues that the real question in the abortion debate is obscured by the language. The real question is not whether the foetus is a form of life or whether it is a person, but whether it is the bearer of constitutional rights. And he points out that no judge or politician has advanced the claim that a foetus is a constitutional person. If it were, all states would be obliged to forbid abortion in the way they forbid murder. Any unilateral addition by a state to the category of bearers

---

the interests of one of its wards (ibid). Leaving aside the controversy surrounding the precise import of the *nasciturus* rule, one can discern without difficulty that the views of the various authors are coloured by their moral stance on the question of abortion. Those who subscribe to the 'right to life' of the foetus, entailing the assumption that the foetus is a person with legal rights, will support the view that preventive protection should have been accorded in this case.

[79] Supra.

[80] In terms of the Fourteenth Amendment.

[81] Glendon makes this point about *Roe v Wade* in her appraisal of the Canadian position — (1989) 83 *Northwestern U LR* 569 at 580. See also her book *Abortion and Divorce in Western Law* (1987) 34–5.

[82] (1988) 1 SCR 30.

[83] Glendon (1989) 83 *Northwestern U LR* at 580 makes this point in discussing the fact that only one of the majority judges in the *Morgentaler* case, Wilson J, was eager to instruct the legislature on the limits of its authority to regulate abortion. Despite her exposition of the import of 'liberty' in s 7 of the Canadian Charter of Rights and Freedoms, Wilson J did not consider it necessary to explore the implications of the right to 'life', also contained in s 7. Glendon regards the basis of the Canadian court's decision to be narrow and confined to a ruling that it was certain procedural requirements in the Canadian legislation of 1969 that violated a pregnant woman's right to security of the person under s 7 of the Charter. Weinrib, on the other hand, does not. For her the *Morgentaler* decision signifies that a pregnant women's liberty includes the substantive right to access to abortion. It gives shape to the idea that women are 'Charter rights-holders first, breeders second' ('The *Morgentaler* Judgment: Constitutional Rights, Legislative Intention, and Institutional Design' (1992) 42 *U Toronto LJ* 22 at 68 and 76). Whether procedural or substantive or a combination of these, at the end of the day the finding rendered Canadian abortion regulation invalid and the decision was hailed as one showing that the judiciary was becoming attuned to the interests of women. This landmark decision was followed by *Tremblay v Daigle* (1989) 2 SCR 530. Here the Supreme Court declined to rule on the question whether 'everyone' in s 7 of the Canadian Charter included a foetus because the Charter applies only if state action or a law infringes the rights contained in the Charter, whereas the case concerned an attempt by a man to prevent a woman carrying his child from aborting it. No claim was made by him that state action or a law was infringing his rights. But the Supreme Court did hold that a foetus was not a person within the meaning of the Quebec Charter of Human Rights and Freedoms, which accords every human being a right to life. Greschner 'Abortion and Democracy for Women: A Critique of *Tremblay v Daigle*' (1990) 35 *McGill LJ* 633 notes three important aspects of the judgment which advance the rights of women: First, the attitude of the court revealed empathy with pregnant women seeking abortion; secondly, the court recognized that for constitutional adjudication the question whether a foetus is a person is a normative not a genetic or biological one; thirdly, the court accepted that women and men are not in identical positions regarding reproduction (at 657). Greschner regrets the omission of a ruling by the court on the interpetation of the right to life contained in s 7 of the Canadian Charter. Uncertainty about the constitutional rights of a foetus leaves the right of a woman to have an abortion unclear, she says. She also points out that a decision to afford to a foetus a constitutional right to life would profoundly affect the lives of Canadian women (at 667).

[84] 'The Concept of Unenumerated Rights' (1992) 59 *U Chicago LR* 381 at 398–405.

of constitutional rights abridges the rights of the known national constitutional population and is therefore not permissible. The question whether a foetus is a person does not therefore resolve the conflict about the right of a pregnant woman to an abortion. She is not only a person but a bearer of constitutional rights. The foetus may be termed a person, as it is in the legislation of certain states, as long as by that rubric it is not intended to declare that the foetus is also the bearer of constitutional rights.

Dworkin terms the responsibility of the state to protect individual citizens from harm a derivative responsibility; he terms the responsibility to protect common values and the public moral space in which all must live a detached responsibility.[85] The debate about abortion is not about a derivative responsibility to the foetus since the foetus is not a citizen; it is about the detached responsibility of the state to protect the intrinsic value of human life and how this responsibility can be balanced against the pregnant woman's constitutional right to procreative autonomy. Dworkin accepts therefore that states do have a right to protect the interests of the foetus, just as they can protect the interests of animals, who are also not the bearers of constitutional rights. This yields a legitimate interest to regulate abortion, but not the right to legislate in ways that abrogate the fundamental rights of women who are members of the national constitutional population.

*Roe*, explains Dworkin, upholds the woman's constitutional right to procreative autonomy, but it does not entail that states should not display the collective view about the appropriateness of abortion and the intrinsic value of human life. Equality, equal protection, basic liberty, and privacy, in his analysis, do not prevent governments from pursuing a goal of responsible decision-making on the part of citizens.[86] But these fundamental rights constrain the right of government to compel conformity about the intrinsic value of human life by forbidding abortion. Further, the woman's rights to both personal and religious freedom, for Dworkin, guarantee her prerogative to decide whether or not to bear a child. To fail to respect a woman's reproductive autonomy, he says, is to take over her body for purposes she does not share, which is partial enslavement, a serious deprivation of her liberty. The sanctity of human life is a foundational but contestable value, served best by a state which permits people to attach their own meaning to it. A woman forced to bear a deformed child or a child doomed to impoverishment and inadequate education, or a child whose existence will cripple the woman's own life 'is forced to act . . . in defiance of her own beliefs about what respect for human life means . . .'.[87] Convictions about how and why human life has intrinsic importance are so fundamental to overall moral personality, Dworkin says, that they take on a religious character. Constitutional freedoms of conscience and religious belief thus additionally entail the freedom to decide whether to bear a child.[88]

What Dworkin shows us is that there is more than one constitutional basis for preventing the state from forbidding abortion on request. And he points out that this overlap between different provisions in a Bill of Rights reinforces the culture of

---

[85] Op cit (n 84) 396.
[86] Op cit (n 84) 410 and 411–15.
[87] Op cit (n 84) 412.
[88] Op cit (n 84) 412–15 and 424–5. Freedom of conscience and of religion are protected in s 14 of the South African Constitution.

commitment to just government that the US Constitution enshrines.[89] The same commitment is evident in the comparable provisions of the new South African Constitution.

The difficult question that remains to be answered for South Africans then is not whether a pregnant woman has a constitutional right to abortion, but whether a decision like the one in *Roe* is an appropriate balance between the woman's right to procreative autonomy and the state's interest in protecting the sanctity of human life. *Roe* acknowledged the right of the state to regulate abortion in the second trimester and to outlaw abortion (subject to certain exceptions) in the third. Dworkin accepts this balance on the basis that from approximately the beginning of the third trimester the foetus is viable, i e it is capable of independent existence. At that moment, he argues, the constitutional right of the pregnant woman becomes less powerful and the state's interest more powerful. The state's position is transformed from a detached responsibilty to protect the sanctity of life into a derivative responsibility to protect the viable foetus. This cut-off of the woman's prerogative still affords her ample time to reflect about the continuation of the pregnancy. What the state is in effect doing is compelling her to exercise her right during the first six months of the pregnancy. It is doing so on the ground that during the last three months 'the difference between pregnancy and infancy becomes more a matter of location than development'.[90]

The danger in this line of argument is that it in effect contradicts the firm view that the foetus is not a citizen whose rights the state has a responsibility to protect. It confers legal personality on the foetus before birth, on the ground that the foetus is so much like a person after the point of viability. Is this likeness enough to make the foetus to all intents and purposes a bearer of constitutional rights, a competitor with a member of the known constitutional population? A preferable approach may be to claim simply that the state's compelling interest to protect the sanctity of human life overrides the pregnant woman's constitutional rights during the last trimester.

Similar points about the competing interests of the woman and the foetus are made, less rigorously than by Dworkin, by Mary Ann Glendon, in the course of her comparison between the decisions of the US Supreme Court and the 1975 decision of the West German Federal Constitutional Court (FCC).[91] Glendon remarks that Americans think of abortion issues as involving individual rights — either the right to life of the foetus or the right of a woman to privacy. For her this approach locks two seemingly irrevocably opposed positions into a framework that she sees as rigid and impoverished when compared with the German court's evaluation of the character of the right to life. The FCC sees this right as a value of the community rather than as something attaching to the foetus. The court is more concerned with the obligation of the state to promote the public value than it is with any rights the value might give to individuals.[92]

Glendon attempts to show, in her approbation of the German law, that in a society

---

[89] Op cit (n 84) 425, countering a criticism that to Dworkin *Roe* is the 'Wandering Jew of constitutional law'.
[90] Op cit (n 84) 429.
[91] The development of the West German law is described by Glendon *Abortion and Divorce* 25–33. The celebrated decision of the FCC is its judgment of 25 Feb 1975, 39 *BVerfGE* 1. References to two English translations of the judgment are offered by Glendon op cit at 167n75.
[92] Op cit (n 91) 38.

deeply divided on the question of abortion an accommodation can be achieved if legislation permitting abortion in the early months of pregnancy, and outlawing it except in extreme cases and with strict procedures in the later months, communicates the state's message that women should be encouraged and assisted to choose maternity over non-maternity.[93] She asserts in addition that the law itself can assist in the formation of a consensus 'by influencing the way people interpret the world around them as well as by communicating that certain values have a privileged place in society'.[94]

The South African Abortion and Sterilization Act 2 of 1975 permits abortion only in the narrowest of circumstances. The preliminary procedures that must be complied with are so cumbersome that they effectively deny access to abortion even when it is countenanced by the law.[95] Grounds for a legal abortion at any stage of pregnancy are: the continued pregnancy must endanger the life of the woman or constitute a serious threat to her physical or mental health; or there must exist a serious risk that the child will suffer a physical or mental defect that will render it irreparably seriously handicapped; or the foetus must have been conceived as a result of unlawful intercourse, defined as rape or incest, or as a result of illegitimate intercourse, entailing that the woman was, due to a mental handicap, unable to comprehend the implications of coitus.[96]

On the spectrum of Western laws South Africa would be grouped with countries that permit abortion only on 'hard' grounds and in terms of highly restrictive procedures.[97] The social problem of illegal abortions remains utterly unaddressed by our legislation,[98] not only because of the restrictive grounds but also because of

---

[93] Op cit (n 81) 18, 40, 59. Put another way, the legislation permitting abortion communicates the state's disapproval of abortion.

[94] Op cit (n 81) 59.

[95] The procedure to be followed for a legal abortion requires that two independent medical practitioners must certify the existence of the ground relied upon; neither may participate in the abortion; and they may not be in partnership with one another or employed by the same person. Other provisions further define the necessary qualifications of the medical practitioners, require that the abortion must take place in a state-controlled hospital, and demand that the superintendent of the hospital give consent for the operation and reports it to the Department of Health and Welfare. See ss 3, 5, 6, and 7 of the Act. For a trenchant criticism of the procedures see Hansson & Russell 'Made to Fail: The Mythical Option of Legal Abortion for Survivors of Rape and Incest' (1993) 9 *SAJHR* 500 at 506–11.

[96] Section 3 of the Act. A serious threat to mental health cannot be established on the mere assertion of the woman that she is upset at the prospect of having a child. Hansson & Russell op cit (n 95) 521, however, cite the statistic that of 1 027 legal abortions performed in 1992 77 per cent were on psychiatric grounds. For an account of the history of the legislation and some of the parliamentary discussions, see Sinclair 'Women's Rights and Family Law' in Lee (ed) *Values Alive: A Tribute to Helen Suzman* (1990) 135 at 143. See further Boberg op cit (n 78) 18–21; Van der Vyver & Joubert *Persone- en Familiereg* 2 ed (1985) 70–2; Hansson & Russell op cit (n 95) 500–6.

[97] Glendon *Abortion and Divorce* 15. But once the abortion falls within the terms of the Act and the procedures have been complied with the court has no discretion to grant an interdict prohibiting the operation: *G v Superintendent, Groote Schuur Hospital* (supra).

[98] Official statistics show that there were 541 legal abortions in 1978; 347 in 1980; 712 in 1985; 963 between 1 July 1988 and 31 June 1989 and 868 from July 1989 to June 1990 (Annual Reports of the Department of National Health and Population Development). In the *Debates of Parliament* 10 February 1993 col 14 it is stated that 1 027 legal abortions occurred in 1992 (cited by Hansson & Russell op cit (n 95) 521). See further Sarkin-Hughes 'A Perspective on Abortion Legislation in South Africa's Bill of Rights Era' (1993) 56 *THRHR* 83 at 84. The Reports reveal that during the twelve-month period from 1989 to 90 there were officially 38 020 cases of removal of the residue of pregnancy (excluding natural miscarriages). Only a small percentage of legal abortions are performed on women who are not white. For the period 1 July 1988–30 June 1989, for example, of the 963 legal abortions only 228 (23,7 per cent) were performed on black, coloured, and Asian women, while 735 (76,3 per cent) were performed on white women. In the *Daily Mail* newspaper of 9 July 1990 a report estimated that 300 000 backstreet abortions are performed annually. This is also the figure given by the Abortion Reform Action Group (ARAG) *The Star* 30 November 1988. The incidence is said to be particularly high among poor women in rural areas where medical facilities are minimal.

the inhibiting and intrusive bureaucratic procedures that must be followed before a legal abortion can be performed. African custom regards abortion as taboo,[99] yet the incidence of illegal abortion among African women is alarmingly high.[100] Marriage in customary law is an alliance between two kinship groups. Its purpose is to realize 'goals beyond the immediate interests of the particular husband and wife'.[101] This important feature of African culture highlights the danger of believing that the position of the African woman and that of the typical Anglo-American feminist can simply be equated.[102] It demonstrates the possibility that there could be strong anti-abortion sentiment among African people more committed to the principles of indigenous custom than to the eradication of sexual oppression or to guarantees of equality and privacy. There is, however, a feeling among those who have been grappling with the conflict between rules of customary law and the fundamental rights contained in the Constitution that those aspects of customary law which

---

[99] Children are regarded as a form of wealth and security for old age in African culture. Barrenness of a wife entitles her husband to marry a seedraiser or to claim back from his sterile wife's family the *lobolo* he has paid for her. An ANC paper entitled 'Sexual Abuse and Aggression Against Women' (Lusaka 1989) 2, describing family tradition and social practice among Africans in South Africa, contains the following statement: 'The determination of the family size is generally an exclusive prerogative of men, irrespective of wives' feeling or state of health. Failure to reproduce "male progeny", considered guarantors to the continuity of the family lineage, is blamed on women . . . The man and/or his family turn to ostracize her or encourage the husband to find an alternative. The trauma for the female is beyond description in such cases.'

[100] At Baragwanath Hospital in Johannesburg it has been reported that twenty-five women are admitted each day with incomplete illegal abortions; three of them die; a significant number are under the age of 20 years (see *The Star* 21 November 1990). Education is regarded as a crucial factor in population control. Since 60 per cent of South Africa's black population resides in rural areas where there is a tendency among the poor to educate boys before girls women are dragged into the vicious circle of poverty, illiteracy, poor health, and multiple pregnancies (see *The Star* 10 May 1993). There is a powerful argument to be made for population development that includes abortion. The results of studies cited by Sarkin-Hughes op cit (n 98) 85 show that 'no family planning programme has succeeded anywhere in the world without it'.

[101] Nhlapo 'Customary Law and the Family' (draft paper, August 1990) 5.

[102] Nhlapo 'International Protection of Human Rights and the Family: African Variations on a Common Theme' (1989) 3 *Int J of L and the Family* 1 at 10. It is, however, also true that several issues central to the abortion debate in Western jurisdictions remain controversial in African countries. This fact is born out by the analysis of Cook & Dickens 'Abortion Laws in African Commonwealth Countries' (1981) 25 *J of African L* 60. Countries such as Botswana, the Gambia, Malawi, Mauritius, Nigeria (Northern States), and the Seychelles have what the authors call a 'basic' law, which simply prohibits abortion and makes it a crime. Following English judicial pronouncements on what constitutes the essential element of unlawfulness for the purpose of this crime, these jurisdictions, by interpretation, exempt from criminal sanction abortion to preserve a woman's life or health, including her mental health. Countries that have what the authors call a 'developed' law have given expression to the exceptions mentioned above in their legislation. These include Ghana, Kenya, Nigeria (Southern States), Sierra Leone, and Uganda. Only Zambia and Zimbabwe are said to have 'advanced' laws because their legislation positively lists grounds permitting abortion. While Zimbabwe's law permits abortion on the ground of risk to life or grave risk to permanent health of the woman and serious physical or mental handicap to the child, Zambia's laws recognize, in addition, serious danger to physical or mental health and the socio-medical ground of general health and welfare of the pregnant woman and/or of her existing children. It can be seen that apart from Zambia all of these juridictions have, at least in theory, strict abortion laws. But the interpretation of 'health' justifying abortion varies from one to another and converts strict grounds into relatively easy abortion regulation in some if the woman has the resources to obtain the necessary medical certification. Abortion law on the books does not resemble abortion practice in any of the juridictions, where illegal abortion and its tragic consequences are widespread. Cook & Dickens stress that a serious deficiency in the laws of these juridictions is that they discriminate against the poor woman. 'Mature women and their daughters with financial means can often obtain safe, lawful termination of pregnancy. They can acquire medical evidence to bring themselves within the physical and mental health-preserving licence of . . . developed law. The poor and especially their young tend to depend for health care upon local public services, and perhaps upon traditional healers.' Medical facilities are scarce, in some areas non-existent, making it unavoidable for a woman without resources who feels unable to continue with a pregnancy to resort to self-induced abortion or abortion carried out by an unskilled person in unhygienic circumstances. The danger to life and health and the risk of infertility for young women are some of the serious consequences in these places.

entrench the inferior position of women are properly to be subordinated in favour of the fundamental rights referred to above.[103]

It is not surprising that our new Constitution is silent on the question of abortion, leaving the matter to be decided by the Constitutional Court, at the instance of an individual or a group of individuals. South Africans brought up according to Western norms and those who adhere to African custom were not able to produce a sufficiently powerful lobby to provoke explicit resolution of the problem in the new Bill of Rights or via an amendment to the ordinary legislation.[104]

The question for the Constitutional Court will be whether the rights contained in the Constitution render invalid our restrictive Abortion and Sterilization Act and, if so, what amendments would be required to rectify the Act's violation of fundamental rights. Whatever the answer, it is unlikely entirely to satisfy either the pro-life or the pro-choice protagonists.[105]

Acknowledgement of the pregnant woman's right to reproductive autonomy, coupled with a message that the state disapproves of abortion, that abortion is a matter of great import not to be regarded as a method of birth control and not permitted after a certain stage in the gestation period, would go a long way to accommodate the pro-choice lobby, although many feminists would be left

---

[103] Nhlapo op cit (n 102) 18 suggested that such rules of customary law be de-emphasized. The status of customary law in the new Constitution was a controversial issue during the negotiation process. The outcome and the future of customary law is discussed below, 5.1.5. The African Charter on Human and Peoples' Rights, while expressing a strong concern for the preservation of African values, contains a clause which ensures tha elimination of every discrimination against women and also ensures the protection of the rights of women, as stipulated in international declarations and conventions (Nhlapo op cit (n 102) 14 and Murray op cit (n 64) 194–7). See also Sachs's general remark in 'Towards a Bill of Rights in a Democratic South Africa' (1990) 6 *SAJHR* 1 at 19.

[104] The important reality, however, is that whether or not the right to an abortion is officially sanctioned, women will continue to exercise it regardless of the state of the law. The reality of their suffering and endangered health under the present restrictive dispensation and the suffering of children for whom they cannot provide the necessities of life simply cannot be brushed aside. The views of pro-lifers, simply put, place the interests of the foetus before those of the mother without taking account of the awful reality that each year 25 million pregnancies are terminated illegally throughout the world, and about 300 000 of these occur in South Africa (Hansson & Russell op cit (n 95) 522). And the moral conflict between the interests of the mother and those of the foetus is not susceptible of dogmatic resolution. This is borne out in the literature. Take, for example, the review article of Tribe *Abortion: the Clash of Absolutes* (1990) by pro-lifers Calhoun & Sexton 'Is It Possible to Take Both Fetal Life and Women Seriously? Professor Lawrence Tribe and his Reviewers' (1992) 49 *Washington and Lee LR* 437. South African views on the competing interests of the foetus and the pregnant woman range over the full spectrum. See, for example, the statement of Du Plessis op cit (n 78) 56, that '[a] state involving itself in the protection of unborn life is not meddling in the private affairs of its citizens. Nor is it making moral choices which can best be made at a personal level. It is simply protecting life — which is its duty.' And again at 59: 'A true liberalization of abortion legislation will be directed at the increased protection of the foetus' basic right to live — not at its increased subversion.' This author suggests that the Act be amended so as to provide for judicial proceedings in each case where a legal abortion is sought and that a *curator ad litem* be appointed to represent the unborn child. He calls for the proceedings to be 'adversary in nature leaving the curator the right to cross-examine witnesses' (ibid). (If this is a significant reflection of public opinion on how to balance the interests of the foetus and the pregnant woman, the case for an abortion law that recognizes the reality of the situation in this country will be a difficult one to win.) See further Van Oosten 'Inadequacies in the Promotion of Life Before Birth in South Africa' (1990) 9 *Medicine and Law* 769 and the essays in Van Niekerk (ed) *The Status of Pre-Natal Life* (1991). For an opposing view, see Sarkin-Hughes op cit (n 98) 87, who asserts that society's interest in protecting life is laudable, but its role in preventing abortion should be no more than an advisory one. Compulsion which infringes the civil rights of pregnant women is for him unacceptable. See also Leyshon 'Abortion: In Search of a Constitutional Doctrine' (1991) 10 *Medicine and Law* 155 and 219 for the view that a constitutional right to abortion will probably be conceded in South Africa, but that the uncertainty surrounding the acceptance by a court of the complex and highly controversial arguments of pro-life and pro-choice protaganists demands an explicit clause in the Bill of Rights dealing with the right to abortion. Hansson & Russell op cit (n 95) 503–4 seem persuaded that there is a definite likelihood that a new government in South Africa will reform our legislation governing abortion, although they warn against underestimating the power and militancy of the anti-abortion lobby. For these authors abortion is a question of equality (at 505).

[105] Glendon *Abortion and Divorce* 41 says of the US that public opinion will not support the positions of activists in the pro-life or the pro-choice movements. If this is true also of South Africans, and it may well be, it suggests that the court will feel constrained to opt for a compromise of some kind.

dissatisfied. The right to choose abortion in the earlier months of pregnancy would undoubtedly assist the vast majority of women seeking to terminate an unwanted pregnancy. Under the present dispensation they are deprived of any meaningful choice and perceive themselves to be discriminated against by the men who make them pregnant and by the men who have made and acquiesced in the laws that they consider to be discriminatory. A compromise of this kind would not satisfy feminists favouring untrammelled freedom of choice and demanding judicial assertion that their various constitutional rights prohibit not only the outlawing of but also procedural restrictions on abortion. They would resent any judgmental stance of legislation formulated, somewhat grudgingly, and with a clear message of disapproval, as a concession against penal consequence. Pro-lifers would have to concede that the state's message accords with their beliefs, but would reject the rights conferred by the Constitution.

The compromise leaves both sides unsatisfied. Yet on the whole it can produce a climate of tolerance not achieved by total victory for one side and total defeat for the other, a climate conducive to further debate and evaluation of the law without the extremes of the profit-making abortion mills encountered in the US or the tragic deaths from illegal abortion occurring here now. We could do worse for our fissured society than a solution that does give women control over their reproductive functions,[106] but which permits the legal system to arrogate to itself the power to urge widely shared moral values about the sanctity of life upon the society it governs.[107]

### 5.1.2 *The parental power*

In many jurisdictions this label would be regarded as unsatisfactory. The emphasis has changed from the power of the parents to the reponsibilities of the parents and the rights of the child.

In our law the parental power is made up of two quite distinct elements: guardianship and custody. The common law provides that the natural guardian of a child born in wedlock (a marital child, a legitimate child) is its father, while that of a child born out of wedlock (an extra-marital child,[108] an illegitimate child) is its mother.[109] A guardian is empowered to take decisions regarding both the child's property and its person. A custodian has control over the day-to-day life of the child. On divorce the major issues are custody and access, for they determine with whom the child will live and hence which of the parents will be confined to a right of access (visitation). Orders pertaining to guardianship are rare. Custody of young children is nearly always granted to mothers, leaving fathers as guardians — a split that is impractical and conducive to discord.

---

[106] Glendon *Abortion and Divorce* 18 says: 'Let us remember that France, like the United States, was deeply and bitterly divided on the abortion question. The legislation that was adopted there may be a mélange of elements pleasing to few and offensive to many, yet, since its passage, France has had no continuing high-level turmoil on the issue of abortion.'

[107] State funding of abortion is crucial to the success of any liberalization of the law. It would not in any event be acceptable to acknowledge the right of the state to counsel women against abortion without insisting also that the state respect the right to choose abortion by making available safe medical facilities to all women.

[108] The label for the illegitimate child created by the Children's Status Act 82 of 1987.

[109] This proposition is not controversial; it is amply supported by authority. See, for example, the authorities cited by Boberg op cit (n 78) 315n1, 458, 333n37.

It is necessary to set out the common law of guardianship of legitimate children, despite the fact that it has been changed by the Guardianship Act of 1993[110] because, as at 28 February 1994, this Act was not yet in force.

At common law a mother of a legitimate child is said to share the parental power with the child's father, 'although the rights of the father are superior to those of the mother'.[111] For the mother, sharing is confined to custody and the need for her consent to be obtained for the adoption of her child [112] or its marriage while it is a minor. In other spheres she is excluded from the role of guardian. The father, in his capacity as the natural guardian of the child, administers its property, gives consent to legal transactions, and makes up for the child's deficient *locus standi in judicio*. The Matrimonial Affairs Act 37 of 1953 remedied the unfairness of the common law which provided that, in the event of a disagreement between the parents about consent to the marriage of the minor, the father's wishes would prevail. The 1953 Act demanded the consent of both parents for the marriage and laid down that consent withheld by either parent had to be replaced by a judge of the Supreme Court.[113] The 1953 Act also changed the common-law rule that a father could appoint a testamentary guardian to succeed him, to the exclusion of the mother of the child. It permitted him to appoint such a guardian, but only to act jointly with the mother.[114] Since the mother had no right at common law to appoint any testamentary guardian to succeed her, and none was conferred upon her by the 1953 Act, she could not appoint a guardian to act jointly with the father after her death.[115]

These inequalities have been removed by the Guardianship Act 192 of 1993, not in operation as at 28 February 1994. Husbands and wives are to share equally the right to make decisions affecting their children and will have the same rights to appoint testamentary guardians to succeed them.[116] Each is to be entitled independently to exercise any right or power and to carry out any duty arising from guardianship except in matters pertaining to consent to the marriage of the minor, adoption, removal of the child from the Republic, the application for a passport, or the alienation or encumbrance of immovable property belonging to the minor.[117] In

---

[110] Act 192 of 1993.

[111] Boberg op cit (n 78) 458.

[112] Section 18(4)(*d*) of the Child Care Act 74 of 1983.

[113] Section 5(4) of the Matrimonial Affairs Act 37 of 1953 and s 25(4) of the Marriage Act 25 of 1961.

[114] Section 5(3)(*b*) of Act 37 of 1953.

[115] The rules described here assume that no court order interfering with the parental power has been made.

[116] Section 1(1) and (2) of the 1993 Act. In fact the right of a father to appoint a testamentary guardian to act jointly with the mother is removed by s 2 of the 1993 Act. It effects amendments to s 5 of the Matrimonial Affairs Act 37 of 1953 to provide that only where a court has awarded sole guardianship to a parent or where that parent is the surviving natural guardian of a child is he or she entitled to appoint a testamentary guardian.

[117] Section 1(2) of the 1993 Act. The history of the Guardianship Act is worth recording. After decades of unsuccessful lobbying by champions of parental equality the National Party government, in clause 51 of the draft bill entitled The Abolition of Discrimination Against Women GN 158 *GG* 14591 of 19 February 1993, created equal rights of guardianship during marriage and equal rights to 'dispose' of guardianship and custody during marriage. The wording was unhappy. It is clear that the legislation was drafted hurriedly and as a political ploy to secure votes in a forthcoming election. By the end of June 1993 another bill, The Promotion of Equality between Men and Women Bill, superseded the first and did not contain such a clause. Moreover, the reference to s 13 of the Matrimonial Property Act (in clause 31) differed from the repeal of s 13 that was contemplated in the Abolition of Discrimination Bill — the later bill retained that part of s 13 of the Matrimonial Property Act which stated that nothing in the 1984 Act would affect the husband's position relating to guardianship. First the flurry, then a strange retreat, followed by a somewhat unexpected Christmas present in the form of the Guardianship Act, assented to on 22 December 1993, creating equal guardianship and repealing s 13 of the Matrimonial Property Act.

these cases the consent of both parents is required unless a competent court orders otherwise.

The common law regulating the parental power in respect of illegitimate children remains unaffected by the recent Guardianship Act. It too is discriminatory, against fathers, in providing that the mother of the illegitimate child alone has the parental power. She is its guardian and its custodian. She may consent to its adoption without the concurrence of the child's father.[118] The father has no inherent right to guardianship of the child, even on the death of the mother, or to custody, although he has the same duty to maintain it as he has in respect of his legitimate children.[119]

Although there is considerable dissension about a father's entitlement to access to his illegitimate child, the recent spate of cases overwhelmingly declares that he has no 'inherent right' to access. None denies that he may approach the court to be granted access.[120] The Full Bench of the Transvaal Provincial Division in *B v P* held that all he need show is that, on a balance of probabilities, the child's best interests would be served by granting him access and that such relief will not unduly interfere with the mother's right of custody.[121] Only the case of *Van Erk v Holmer*[122] contests the inferior position of the father of an illegitimate child. Van Zyl J found that the old authorities do not provide a clear answer to the question whether the father has an inherent right of access. They simply do not deal with the situation. The reason is probably that few fathers of illegitimate children were in those times anxious to publish their extramarital procreative achievements for reasons of severe social constraint. The learned judge was acutely alive to changed mores and the growing number of illegitimate children born to women having no stable relationship with the father, but to an ever greater extent to women who live or have lived in stable marriage-like relationships with the fathers of their children. He surveyed the academic writing on the subject, the Law Commission report of 1985 on illegitimate children,[123] the comparative law, and current social mores. He concluded that, in the absence of clear authority on the point, and given the worldwide trend towards treating legitimate and illegitimate children equally, he was free to confer upon the father of an illegitimate child an automatic right of access with which the court would interfere, in the interests of the child, at the instance of the mother, if necessary. His decision, he asserted, was born of reasonableness, justice, equity, and public policy.[124] It was clearly intended to reflect the best interests of the child.

---

[118] Section 18(4)(*d*) of the Child Care Act 74 of 1983.
[119] The duty of support is based on the blood relationship, not on the status of the child.
[120] See *F v L* 1987 (4) SA 525 (W); *F v B* 1988 (3) SA 948 (D); *W v S* 1988 (1) SA 475 (N); *D v L* 1990 (1) SA 894 (W); *B v P* 1991 (4) SA 113 (T); *Van Erk v Holmer* 1992 (2) SA 636 (W); *S v S* 1993 (2) SA 200 (W); *B v S* 1993 (2) SA 211 (W) and the unreported decisions referred to in *S v S*: *J v O* case 1407/90; *T v V* case 2840/91; *K v G* case 10433/92; and *B v V* case 35144/91.
[121] Supra at 117. Some previous decisions had required exceptional or compelling reasons to be proved — see *Douglas v Mayers* 1987 (1) SA 910 (Z); *F v L* and *F v B* (supra).
[122] Supra.
[123] Investigation into the Legal Position of Illegitimate Children, Project 38 of 1985.
[124] Supra at 648 and 649.

The judgment has provoked a mini-storm, ranging from commendation, through concern, to condemnation.[125] In the short period since its delivery it has been departed from several times by judges in the same division.[126] The multifarious arguments advanced in favour and against the finding are disturbingly cogent. Some

---

[125] The judgment accords with earlier views expressed about previous decisions, inter alia, by Boberg 'The Sins of the Fathers and the Law's Retribution' (1988) 18 *Businessman's Law* 35; Van Onselen 'TUFF — The Unmarried Fathers' Fight' 1991 *De Rebus* 499; Ohannessian & Steyn 'To See or not to See? — That is the Question' (1991) 54 *THRHR* 254; and Eckhard 'Toegangsregte tot Buite-egtelike Kinders — Behoort die Wetgewer in te Gryp?' 1992 *TSAR* 122. Church '*Secundum Ius et Aequitatem Naturalem*: A Note on the Recent Decision in *Van Erk v Holmer*' (1992) 33 *Codicillus* 32 welcomes the commendable recognition of the Roman-Dutch heritage of equity and compliments the court for its judicial activism. She does, however, caution us that attention needs to be paid to the position in African customary law, where the concept of illegitimacy is unknown and where children born out of wedlock would remain members of their mother's group. (Further on the position in customary law see Burman 'The Category of Illegitimate Children in South Africa' and Clark & Van Heerden 'The Legal Position of Children Born Out of Wedlock: A Comparative and Predictive Analysis', both in Burman & Preston-Whyte (eds) *Questionable Issue? Illegitimacy in South Africa* (1992) 21, and 36 at 43–6, respectively.) Clark 'Should the Unmarried Father have an Inherent Right of Access to his Illegitimate Child?' (1992) 8 *SAJHR* 565 is cautious and prefers the view that the father has no inherent right and bears the onus of proving the best interests of the child. Goldberg 'The Right of Access of a Father of an Extramarital Child: Visited Again' (1993) 110 *SALJ* 261 acknowledges the need for change in the law, but suggests that *Van Erk* goes too far. She proposes the *via media* — that once the father proves paternity and an existing commitment to the child a presumption should arise that it would be in the child's interest for the father to have access. This presumption could be rebutted by the mother. (One obvious difficulty with this formulation is that the father's commitment to the child is not always potestative to him — the mother may deliberately thwart his efforts and even refuse maintenance offered by him, knowing that to accept it would assist in creating the presumption that she would have to rebut. But the criticism does not yield an ideal alternative. There is no ideal since the competing interests of the parents are very difficult to reconcile with the interests of the child.) Kruger, Blackbeard & De Jong 'Die Vader van die Buite-Egtelike Kind se Toegangsreg' (1993) 56 *THRHR* 696 consider *Van Erk* to have been wrongly decided. While they support the rejection of the decision by Flemming J in *S v S* (supra), they call for legislation recognizing an automatic right for the father (at 703). Hutchings 'Reg van Toegang vir die Vader van die Buite-egtelike Kind — Outomatiese Toegangsregte — Sal die Beste Belang van die Kind Altyd Seevier?' (1993) 56 *THRHR* 310 feels that the judgment in *Van Erk* subordinates the interests of the child to those of the father. In aligning herself with the views of Sonnekus & Van Westing 'Faktore vir die Erkenning van 'n Sogenaamde Reg van Toegang vir die Vader van 'n Buite-egtelike Kind' 1992 *TSAR* 232 she calls for legislative intervention. The latter authors (at 241) consider that family law cannot be uncoupled from moral standards. They say that 'indien morele en godsdiensstandaarde nie met betrekking tot die gesin, as die kern van die gemeenskap, gehandhaaf word nie, die gemeenskap as geheel op 'n hellende vlak kom.' For Sonnekus & Van Westing the *Van Erk* judgment is unsatisfactory. It affords to men who beget illegitimate children the same rights as those who procreate within marriage. And the assimilation of cohabitation with marriage, for them, is undesirable and poses a threat to society. (See also at 235–6.) Assertions about unacceptable ('ongewens') behaviour are backed by citations of Roman and German authority! Their *ex cathedra* assumption is that those who treat marriage and cohabitation alike have the intention to degrade marriage.) The authors propose that a father of an illegitimate child would at least have to show voluntary acceptance of parental responsibility and the existence of a parent–child relationship involving commitment to the child and its mother to perusade a court to grant access (at 241, and see also 253, where they consider that proving these elements will not be difficult. Where one parent is antipathetic to the other, however, there will surely be difficulties.) The pontificating and aspersive tone of these authors is unacceptable. Diversity of thought and lifestyle is a fact of our society. Those with deep convictions of the kind expressed by the authors must be free to practise what they believe. But it is a different thing to adopt a punitive stance towards some members of society because they do not share those convictions. The choice not to marry or to marry according to religious or cultural custom that produces consequences different from our civil marriage must be respected. Factors not punitive in nature may indeed yield a result that differentiates between those who marry according to the civil law and those who do not. (Those who deliberately choose not to marry may object to having all the consequences of marriage foisted upon them.) It is the arrogation of power to impose a particular lifestyle on a community and to punish those who do not comply that is objectionable. What is nevertheless clear is that the authors' primary purpose is to elevate the interests of the child to the pre-eminent position. With this no one would quarrel, although it should be recognized that in a contest between the parents over the child someone has to bear the onus of proof. There has to be some starting premise. This compels a choice between litigating parents prior to the investigation of the child's interests. See further below, n 128 for ways of reducing the starkness of the choice. A strong claim for tolerance, an acceptance of diversity of modern lifestyles, and the abolition of differentiation between marital and extramarital children, entailing, in the context of access, an inherent right for the father who accepts responsibilities towards his illegitimate children, is made by Labuschagne 'Persoonlikheidsgoedere van 'n Ander as Regsobjek: Opmerkinge oor die Ongehude Vader se Persoonlikheid- en Waardevormende Reg ten aansien van sy Buite-egtelike Kind' (1993) 56 *THRHR* 414.

[126] See *S v S* (supra); *B v S* (supra). See also the following unreported decisions, referred to by Flemming J in *S v S* (at 203) as instances of judges, after the *Van Erk* decision, regarding themselves bound by the Full Bench decision in *B v P* (supra): Streicher J in *T v V* case 2840/91; Roux J in *K v G* case 10433/92; and Daniels J in *B v V* case 35144/91.

authors concentrate, for instance, on the potential plight of mothers confronted with irresponsible men intent on disrupting the lives of their newly reconstructed families; others focus on the plight of men denied the opportunity to bond with their offspring by women motivated by spite after the breakdown of an intimate relationship. None of the widely varying circumstances alluded to occurs ubiquitously in our society. Nor does the enigmatic expression 'the best interests of the child', to which so many resort as *the* criterion, yield an obvious answer to the problem.

This discussion does not have as its aim a reconciliation of the disparate views on both extremes of the spectrum or even the formulation of the typical panacea, the *via media*. The issue as postulated in the writings and in the most recent Law Commission paper[127] requires one to select the status quo, perhaps with some modification, but essentially requiring the father to approach the court for relief and to discharge an onus of proving that the interests of the child demand access, or to select the opposite position, conferring rights upon the father, perhaps with some modifications to appease the mother. Such a position would require the mother to approach the court and to discharge the onus of proving that it is not in the best interests of the child that the father should have access.[128]

There is another dimension to the problem, adverted to in some of the commentaries on our recent cases, but not central to any.[129] It is one that deserves special

---

[127] *Project 79: A Father's Rights in Respect of his Illegitimate Child* Working Paper 44. The closing date for comments on this paper was 30 April 1993.

[128] A number of the authors who have commented on the cases offer variants of these solutions. The Law Commission's paper op cit (n 127) ends with two draft bills. The first leaves the father with no automatic right of access, but the right to approach the court for an order that must be in the best interests of the child. The factors that the court must take into account in considering whether to make an order are enumerated — the relationship between the parents, between the child and the parents, the effect on the child of separation from a parent, the attitude of the child, any other fact. The draft also provides that the father of a child born as a result of rape (or *in vitro* fertilization) may not approach the court for an access order. The second draft bill confers an automatic right of access upon the father (but not a gamete donor), provided that the child is not the product of his having raped the mother. The court can interfere with his right in the best interests of the child. It is the mother here who would have to show that access is not in the best interests of the child. The United Nations Convention on the Rights of the Child, adopted by the General Assembly in 1989, demands respect for the right of the child to maintain personal relations and direct contact with both parents on a regular basis unless to do so would be contrary to the child's best interest (art 9). Where the child is capable of having a view on this matter it has a right to express its view, which must be given due weight, according to the age and maturity of the child (art 12).

[129] Sonnekus & Van Westing op cit (n 125) 234 refer to the US approach of protecting the father's constitutional right to maintain a role in his child's upbringing, and they dismiss it; Goldberg op cit (n 125) 271–3 refers to the developing concept of children's rights in international conventions and moves on to discuss the position in the US. Her concern, however, is to identify qualifying factors that will reinforce the claim of a father of an illegitimate child to a right of access or to veto a proposed adoption. She then deals with visitation rights for grandparents. There is no discussion of constitutionally guaranteed equality as between the parents or of equal protection of the law or of protection of the family. Robinson 'Die Ouer–Kind Verhouding in die Lig van 'n Menseregteakte — 'n Beknopte Oorsig oor die Posisie in Duitsland' 1992 *SAPR/PL* 228 is not concerned, as the writers mentioned above are, only with the position of the illegitimate child and its father's plea for access. He commences his article with reference to the impending enactment of a Bill of Rights in South Africa and warns that aspects of our law of parent and child that violate the Bill of Rights will be struck down (at 228–9). He ends with the suggestion that the parent–child position might usefully be regulated constitutionally and that parental responsibility should replace the concept of parental rights/power. The article is a detailed exposition of the German law, but it contains no analysis of which aspects of our private law might fall foul of constitutionally protected rights such as equality, equal protection, and the protection of children. Clark & Van Heerden op cit (n 125) 52–3 give useful insights into the position in the US. Their contribution, however, deals with a wide range of issues, so that the constitutional protection of the rights under discussion and the potential violation of those rights by our current law do not feature prominently. Labuschagne op cit (n 125) also deals with a wide range of social and legal issues pertaining to the parental power. He does include a discussion of the protection of the father's right as a fundamental right, particularly equal protection of the law, in the context of a discussion of the position in the US, of which he approves. This author's contribution comes closest to tackling the problem from a perspective wider than the competition between the parents *inter se*. He adverts also to the child's own right to a relationship with its father (at 418–21).

attention here. We have a new Constitution which includes a Bill of Rights that outlaws unfair discrimination, entrenches equality between men and women, equal protection of the law, privacy, and the protection of children.[130] The question is whether either of the options postulated above would satisfy a Constitutional Court that the rights so entrenched are not being infringed by the laws that currently regulate parental responsibility to the child born outside of formal marriage.

The question, moreover, runs deeper than access by a father to his illegitimate child. It encompasses guardianship, custody, and adoption. And it will also include the position of legitimate children until the Guardianship Act of 1993 is brought into operation. At the time of writing the law currently in force and regulating the parental power provokes a number of questions: can it be said that laws which differentiate between mothers and fathers regarding their rights to make decisions affecting their children are not discriminatory on the grounds of sex? What of a law that differentiates between married and unmarried men regarding the same kinds of rights? Why (as will be the case until the commencement of the Guardianship Act) should a woman who marries the father of her child have fewer rights in respect of the child not only than her husband but also than a woman who elects not so to marry? Why (as will be the case until the commencement of the Guardianship Act) should a man who marries the mother of his child enjoy pre-eminence over its mother? Why should he be denied any automatic parental privileges if the mother of his child refuses to marry him? Why is it assumed that mothers make better custodians when marriages are dissolved? How will the Constitutional Court deal with legal rules that have evolved within a system that discriminates against women, against illegitimate children, and against the fathers of those children?

The answer depends on the reach of the Bill of Rights. And this is a controversial matter, which was discussed earlier in this chapter.[131] On the basis of the content of the rules described above, however, the court will be hard pressed not to strike them down. It must surely have been partly in appreciation of this fact, although mainly, one suspects, to gain votes, that the National Party government by-passed its Law Commission and produced a flurry of legislation in 1992 and 1993 to improve the position of women.[132] It did nothing for the fathers of children born out of wedlock.

The fact that the underlying premise of our current law on the parental power is contended to be in the best interests of the child will not obviate the need to test the rules against the Bill of Rights. And many years will pass before all the issues have been canvassed via litigation. A sounder approach would be to recognize that our law governing parental responsibility is still in urgent need of reform. It requires more than the piecemeal improvement effected by the Guardianship Act in relation

---

[130] See ss 8, 13, and 30. Section 30(1)(b) guarantees to every child 'parental care', suggesting that unwarranted denial of a parental right such as access to a father may also be a denial of fundamental rights to the child.

[131] In the introductory remarks to section 5 'The constitutional protection of sex and gender equality in South Africa'. It was pointed out there that the better interpretation of s 7 of the Constitution would be that rules of the common law which violate the rights enshrined in the constitution ought not to be immune from attack. The exercise of deciding whether a particular rule, such as that conferring exclusive parental rights on the mother of an illegitimate child (used in that discussion as an illustration), is entirely a rule of the common law or one that has also found express or implied expression in legislation would be difficult and not worth while. The spirit in which South Africans have accepted a new constitutional dispensation to eradicate discrimination demands an appropriate and early resolution of this problem of interpretation.

[132] The Domicile Act 3 of 1992, the General Law Fourth Amendment Act 132 of 1993, the Prevention of Family Violence Act 133 of 1993, and the Guardianship Act 192 of 1993 are all examples of the National Party government's sudden change of heart about the need for equality between men and women.

to legitimate children and the tinkering evident in the recent report of the Law Commission, which offers compromise solutions to the problem of access for fathers of illegitimate children. These compromises are not without merit; they simply fail to locate the issue within the broader context of a constitutional framework that makes a clear coherent commitment to equality and equal protection, while enshrining children's rights, including the right to parental care.

What we require is a comprehensive recrafting of the rights and responsibilities of parents and their children, taking into account the justification for state intervention to protect widely shared societal values, and also the diversity of cultural and religious convictions within our country.[133] Thus, it may be concluded, for example, in accordance with similar rulings in the US, that the state may legitimately permit adoption of a child, dispensing with the normal requirement of both parents' consent[134] in certain circumstances. It may be that a man who begets a child by rape has no inherent rights at all as a parent.[135] But at the end of the day, we are left with the task of formulating general principles comprehensively to govern the issue of parental responsibility which cater for the large majority of cases without the need for judicial intervention and which conform with the principles set forth in the new Constitution. In the light of a Bill of Rights that commits itself to equality and equal protection, and in the light of the insistence in international conventions such as the United Nations Convention on the Rights of the Child and the European Convention on Human Rights that illegitimate children be not discriminated against,[136] we should reform our law of parent and child to incorporate full sharing of all parental rights and responsibilities, regardless of whether the child is born in or out of wedlock. This would mean joint guardianship, joint custody, and automatic rights of access in cases where joint custody is departed from by a court or by agreement. No adoption could take place without the consent of both parents. The court must clearly retain wide powers to intervene to alter all of these automatic incidents of parental responsibility whenever the interests of the child require that it should do so.[137]

---

[133] Attention is given by Clark & Van Heerden op cit (n 125) 59–60 to the difficult issue of pluralism. They deal with the position of children born of customary, Hindu, and Muslim marriages. At civil law these children are illegitimate, while within those systems they are not. 'The problem is whether there should be a single legal regime of marriage . . . irrespective of background or culture; or whether preference should be given to a legally recognized plurality of marriage systems.' This is indeed a grave problem, raised here, but left unanswered, save for one comment. To the extent that such systems contain rules that deny equality (to women, mostly) they may well have to give way, for the right to equality should prevail (see further below, especially 558–72).

[134] As to which, cf *Caban v Mohammed* 441 US 380 (1979) and *Lehr v Robertson* 463 US 248 (1983), discussed by Wintjen 'Make Room for Daddy: A Putative Father's Rights to his Children' (1990) 24 *New England LR* 1059 at 1074–7. See also Goldberg op cit (n 125) 271; Heaton 'Should the Consent of the Father of an Illegitimate Child be Required for the Child's Adoption?' (1989) XX *CILSA* 346; Labuschagne op cit (n 125).

[135] See the draft bills proposed by the Law Commission op cit (n 127). Strange situations can be envisaged where this rule might be harsh. Take a man who lives with a woman and who desperately wants a child with her. She is less committed to the relationship, does not want children, and refuses intercourse on a particular occasion, fearing pregnancy. He insists, without physical violence, on intercourse without contraception. He is guilty of rape. If a child were born of that intercourse, which the mother did not want and thus abandoned, but which the father adored, it may well be in the interests of the child to give parental responsibility to the father. Legislation that disqualifies him should make provision for exceptional cases.

[136] As to which see Clark & Van Heerden op cit (n 125) 51; Forder 'Constitutional Principle and the Establishment of the Legal Relationship between the Child and the Non-Marital Father: A Study of Germany, the Netherlands and England' (1993) 7 *Int J of L and the Family* 40 at 73–92; Clive 'Reform of the Law on the Child in the Family' 1992 *Juridical Rev* 109; Kodilinye 'Is Access the Right of the Parent or the Right of the Child? A Commonwealth View' (1992) 41 *ICLQ* 190 at 192–4.

[137] At the instance of either parent or the child itself and even other persons with a clearly defined interest. Where the parents are not living together, who should have custody of the child, whether the parents should retain joint custody despite the separation, the matter of access, including access for grandparents, and whether guardianship

A fundamental premise of equality between parents[138] would give real meaning to attempts to remove the stigma attaching to children whose parents for whatever reason do not marry.[139] It would accord with the reality that most family situations are not pathological. Being illegitimate is not pathological. Where the interests of the child demand judicial intervention to vary the law's preference for shared parental responsibility the court would make whatever arrangement it believes would best protect the child. Stereotyped assumptions that child care is woman's work and that fathers do not want to or cannot take care of their children would be diminished. The law would be sending the signals that conform to the letter and spirit of the Bill of Rights.

Competition and conflict between warring parents would doubtless continue. But where there is no war, and in most cases there is none, individual men and women would be treated alike. Respect would be shown for their choice whether or not to marry or to marry according to religious or cultural customs that produce consequences different from those inherent in the civil law of marriage. And their children would be legally unaffected by that choice.

### 5.1.3 *Inequality within marriage*

Several glaring inequalities ensuing from the law of marriage were removed by the previous government in legislation passed at a late stage of negotiations for a new constitutional dispensation. A large measure of formal equality has been achieved, and will be documented here. What will not be traversed again in this section are the more subtle forms of inequality within marriage and within other intimate relationships deriving from stereotyped role allocations for women and their lone domestic responsibility. These points were made in earlier parts of this chapter and must feature in the section on divorce. It is at the time of the breakdown of intimate relationships that the human capital depreciation entailed in them for women becomes a crucial issue for family lawyers. Financial security for women heading one-parent families, which is a matter of equality for women, is an elusive goal.

The most notable example of a glaring inequality in our law was the marital power. Our common law provided that on marriage, unless the marital power was

---

can continue to be shared, are questions that will require determination. Only where the best interests of the child require it should a parent be deprived of the opportunity of preserving a meaningful relationship with his or her child. No presumption that a mother makes a better parent should operate to favour her claim for custody.

[138] Can women fairly make constitutional claims for equality and still insist that it would be unfair for them if fathers were to be given equal rights in respect of their illegitimate children? It seems that the answer must be no.

[139] Note the recommendations of the Scottish Law Commission in its Report on Family Law No 135 of 1992, commented upon by Clive op cit (n 136), that illegitimacy should be abolished and that both parents should have full rights and responsibilities in respect of their children, whether born in or outside of marriage. The Scottish Commission's draft bill would remove what is regarded as an anomaly, namely that the father of an illegitimate child has no rights until these are conferred by a court. Clive (at 114) cites the following examples to demonstrate the incoherence of the current law in Scotland. They serve admirably to demonstrate the deficiencies of our own: 'Two families live next door to each other. Both consist of father, mother and two children . . . Both are happy, well-adjusted families in which the children are loved and well cared for. In one the father and mother are married to each other. In the other they are not, because the mother disapproves of marriage on principle. In the first family the father has full parental responsibilities and rights. In the second he does not.' And Clive's second example: 'Mr X abandoned his wife when she was pregnant with his child. He has never seen his child or shown any interest in her. Legally he has full parental responsibilities and rights. Mr Y lives in a stable relationship with the mother of his child, but is not married to her. He plays a full parental role in relation to the child. Legally he does not have full parental responsibilities and rights.' Can it seriously be argued that the law is serving the best interests of the children in question?

excluded by antenuptial contract, a wife was relegated to a status similar to, but in many respects worse than, that of a minor. Under the perpetual tutelage of her husband, who administered her and his property, the married woman had limited contractual capacity and limited *locus standi in judicio*.

The abolition of the marital power by the Matrimonial Property Act 88 of 1984 was billed by the then government as creating out of marriage a partnership of equals. But despite strong calls for this reform to apply across the board, to African marriages and to all existing marriages in which the marital power was operating, the Act affected only marriages celebrated after its coming into operation (1 November 1984) and those not governed by the Black Administration Act of 1927.[140] It took until 1988, when the Marriage and Matrimonial Law Amendment Act[141] repealed the legislative provision rendering the consequences of the civil marriages of Africans different from those ensuing from the marriages of persons of other races, to extend the abolition of the marital power to the marriages of Africans. And then the 1988 Act was made to apply only to such marriages celebrated after its commencement (2 December 1988).

Thus the civil marriages of South Africans of all races celebrated after 2 December 1988 produce the same consequences[142] — in the absence of an antenuptial

---

[140] See s 11 of the Act, which was made subject to s 25, which expressly excluded marriages governed by the Black Administration Act 38 of 1927 — the civil marriages of Africans. (Section 25 was amended in 1988.)

[141] Act 3 of 1988. It contained no specific section abolishing the marital power from the civil marriages of Africans. But the legislative provision which rendered the consequences of a marriage between two black persons (and, it is submitted, between a black man and a woman of another race) different from those of the marriages of persons of other races — s 22(6) of the Black Administration Act 38 of 1927 — ceased to exist from the date of commencement of the Marriage and Matrimonial Property Law Amendment Act 3 of 1988. Further, s 25(1) of the Matrimonial Property Act 88 of 1984, which rendered the provisions of Ch II of the 1984 Act (i e the abolition of the marital power) inapplicable to marriages governed by the Black Administration Act, was deleted from the 1984 Act by the 1988 Act. A marriage between two blacks (or between a black man and a woman of another race) celebrated after 2 December 1988 therefore produces the same consequences as those that flow from the marriages of persons of other races. It should be noted that the consequences of s 22(6) were inter alia that the marriage was automatically out of community unless, by way of a declaration, community was introduced. Unless an antenuptial contract was entered into the marital power applied regardless of the matrimonial property system. Those whom this dispensation affected very rarely entered into antenuptial contracts. The result was that virtually every woman who married a black man became subject to the marital power. Very few would have resorted to the mechanisms provided to eradicate it (a court application or a notarial contract).

[142] This is not to say, however, that the civil marriages of all South Africans produce the same consequences. Differentiation based on race in the national law has been removed, but a problem is that the laws of the self-governing territories and the erstwhile 'independent' (TBVC) states do not always coincide with the laws operating in the rest of South Africa. The reasons are that in some instances legislation has been enacted in those places which differs from the national law and in other cases those places took over much of our national law when they acquired the capacity to legislate, made some or no amendments, but have not incorporated all of the changes that have been occurring here. So, for example, the Marriage and Matrimonial Property Act 3 of 1988 would not apply in those territories or states unless expressly imported. KwaZulu and Transkei are used here to provide examples of the kinds of problems that could occur. The KwaZulu Act on the Code of Zulu Law 16 of 1985, passed by the Legislative Assembly of KwaZulu, repeals s 22(6) of the Black Administration Act in its schedule, but it re-enacts the content of s 22(6) in s 35(1) of the Code. The civil marriages of persons subject to the KwaZulu Code therefore are governed by the position as it was prior to the 1988 reform of the South African Parliament. In particular the KwaZulu Code also stipulates that a married woman is under the marital power of her husband (s 27(3)). The differences between the marriage laws of South Africa and those of Transkei are even more substantial: the Marriage Act 21 of 1978 repeals, inter alia, s 22(6) of the Black Administration Act (schedule), creates for civil and customary marriages an automatic system of separation of property without the need for an antenuptial contract (s 39), recognizes customary marriages as equal in status to civil marriages and capable of subsisting simultaneously with them (s 3), provides that in both civil and customary marriages the wife shall be under the guardianship of her husband (s 37), and, finally, that although it is possible by antenuptial contract or declaration to create community of property, the marital power of the husband can in no way be affected (s 39). These differences, which represent examples from only one self-governing territory and one 'independent' state — there are other differences — must be seen against the fact that, as from the commencement of the 1993 Constitution on 27 April 1994, the founding statutes that gave effect to the policy of separate development disappear. (These are repealed in Schedule 7 of the Constitution.) The 'national territory' of South Africa (s 1) includes all of the self-governing territories and the

contract, the marriage is in community of property. Women enjoy full legal status and, if the marriage is in community of property, they have the same right to administer jointly owned property that their husbands have.[143] However, but for the enactment of the General Law Fourth Amendment Act in 1993,[144] which came into operation on 1 December 1993,[145] the marital power would have persisted in hundreds of thousands of marriages celebrated either before the commencement of the 1984 Act or before the commencement of the 1988 Act. This anachronism would have remained part of our law until all the marriages in which the marital power applied had been dissolved. And it was the date of the marriage and the race of the parties that would have determined whether the marital power applied — criteria hardly likely to have passed judicial scrutiny for compliance with the Bill of Rights.

The General Law Fourth Amendment Act of 1993 'repeals' the common-law rule that gave the husband marital power 'over the person and property of his wife' and abolishes any marital power that any husband might have been exercising immediately prior to the coming into operation of the Act.[146] It finally cleansed our legal system of this inequality for wives and avoided an inevitable striking down by the Constitutional Court. There will, however, be major conflicts between the laws of self-governing territories and the TBVC states, on one hand, and the national law of South Africa, on the other.[147] The KwaZulu Code of Zulu Law,[148] for example, stipulates that a married woman shall be subject to the marital power of her husband.[149] Neither the Marriage and Matrimonial Property Law Amendment Act 3 of 1988 nor the General Law Fourth Amendment Act 132 of 1993 was made to apply in KwaZulu. The marital power also operates in Transkei, for example, and cannot be excluded by antenuptial contract.[150] The South African statutes of 1988 and 1993 referred to here were not imported by Transkei. The repeal by the Constitution[151] of the founding statutes that gave effect to the policy of separate development creates one 'national territory'[152] within which the national laws, such

---

TBVC states. The Constitution (s 229) preserves all laws in force in the area where they applied at the time of the commencement of the Constitution until they are repealed or amended by a competent authority. The civil marriages of all South Africans therefore do not and will not produce the same consequences until the matter is regulated further. See also below on the irreconcilability of the laws of these territories and states and the national law.

[143] Chapter III of the Matrimonial Property Act sets out a system of equal concurrent administration of the joint estate. The basic premise is that either spouse may perform any juristic act in connection with the joint estate, but there follows a long list of transactions that cannot be entered into without the concurrence of the non-contracting spouse. The provisions are complex, have not been the subject of clarifying judicial decisions, and are in certain respects deficient in creating a proper balance between the interests of a spouse whose consent was not obtained and the third party with whom the offending spouse has contracted in violation of the consent provisions. A detailed analysis of this issue is beyond the scope of this chapter. See further Sinclair op cit (n 35) 15–24.

[144] Act 132 of 1993.

[145] GN R123 *GG* 15308 of 1 December 1993 (*Reg Gaz* 5211).

[146] Section 11(1) and (2). Section 11(3) automatically replaces the marital power with the concurrent administration provisions of the Matrimonial Property Act in all marriages affected by the reform and s 11(4) provides that no transaction effected prior to the abolition of the marital power shall be affected by the change. Thus it is still possible that a contract entered into by a wife without her husband's consent or a transaction by a husband in fraud of his wife's rights, for example, may become the subject of litigation. For this reason it remains necessary to include in expositions of the law of marriage an explanation of the implications of the marital power. But that level of detail is beyond the scope of this chapter.

[147] In several respects. Only the differences relating to the matrimonial property systems and the marital power are alluded to here as examples.

[148] Act 16 of 1985 of the KwaZulu Legislative Assembly. See above, n 142.

[149] Section 27(3). The section permits the exclusion of the marital power by antenuptial contract, but only where the civil marriage is out of community.

[150] Section 39 of the Transkei Marriage Act 21 of 1978.

[151] In schedule 7 of the Constitution.

[152] Section 1 of the Constitution.

as the two Acts of 1988 and 1993, apparently apply. There is no provision in the Constitution to the effect that the national laws of South Africa will not apply in any territory or area in which they did not apply at the time of the commencement of the Constitution. By contrast, there is a special constitutional provision preserving the laws of self-governing territories and the TBVC states in the area of those territories and states until such laws are repealed or amended.[153] When the content of these preserved laws is irreconcilable with national law, as it is in relation to the example of the marital power used here, which will take precedence?

What seems clear is that the Constitutional Court could order that, to the extent that the preserved law offends against the Bill of Rights or any part of the Constitution, it is invalid (and the national law applies if it is consistent with the Constitution) or must be corrected within a specified period.[154] The insistence on an inferior legal status for women by way of the marital power certainly offends against the guarantee of equality. But if the preserved law does not violate the Bill of Rights and is not inconsistent with the Constitution, yet is irreconcilable with national law, the question 'which law prevails?' persists.[155] The answer may very well be that by necessary implication the preservation of the laws of the self-governing territories and the 'independent' states entails the non-application of the national law (common and statutory) in those areas to the extent that there is a conflict. (Whether there is indeed a conflict, and its extent, may not always be obvious and may itself have to be resolved via litigation.)

What emerges from all of this is that for the ordinary citizen, and even the experts, the law is inordinately complex. To make the fundamental right of equality for women a reality may require protracted litigation followed by a period of waiting for appropriate legislation. To discover what matrimonial property system applies to a particular marriage will be a question not easy to answer. The sooner conflicts between national law and the law of the various territories and states are resolved, the better for all South Africans. A code of family law drawing together the disparate common-law and statutory rules and making uniform their application is overdue.

Aside from the problems attendant upon civil marriage, there is the customary marriage of Africans and the religious marriage of Muslims. Both systems, which

---

[153] Section 229 provides that all laws that were in force in any area prior to the commencement of the Constitution will remain in force in such area until repealed or amended.

[154] Section 229 is expressly made subject to the Constitution. Section 4(1) renders of no force or effect any law that is inconsistent with the Constitution. Section 98(5) requires the Constitutional Court to declare invalid laws inconsistent with the Constitution, but permits the court to specify a period within which the defect must be corrected. The marital power or any form of guardianship of a husband over his wife cannot survive these provisions. Whether in a marriage in community concurrent administration would automatically replace the marital power/guardianship or whether the court will use its power to direct that remedial legislation be passed is a matter of conjecture.

[155] The re-enactment of the content of s 22(6) of the Black Administration Act 38 of 1927 into s 35(1) of the KwaZulu Code, creating an automatic system of separation of property without an antenuptial contract and permitting community of property only if this is introduced by declaration, is a fine example of the problem. There are others, from KwaZulu and from the other self-governing territories. The same is true of the provision in the Transkei Marriage Act 21 of 1978, which creates an automatic system of separation of property and provides for the introduction of community by way of antenuptial contract or declaration (s 39). And here too there are other examples from Transkei and from other 'independent' states. (See also above, n 142.) This matrimonial property dispensation is irreconcilable with South African common law and with s 2 of the Matrimonial Property Act 88 of 1984, but is not in itself inconsistent with the Constitution. The common law provides for automatic community in the absence of an antenuptial contract, and s 2 of the Matrimonial Property Act provides for the accrual system to operate in marriages out of community unless this system is excluded in the antenuptial contract. Since the repeal of s 22(6) of the Black Administration Act 38 of 1927 automatic community has applied nationally to South Africans of all races. See further below, n 224.

permit polygyny, subject women to a status inferior to that of their husbands. Aspects of African customary and Muslim law and the impact on them of the 1993 Constitution will be discussed below, but it should be mentioned here that African women married at customary law (except those living in Natal) are deemed by statute[156] to be minors subject to the guardianship of their husbands. The abolition of the marital power from the civil law of marriage therefore has not freed them from inequality.

Another anachronism from our common law, and one that was expressly imported into the Matrimonial Property Act in 1984, is the rule that the husband is the head of the family.[157] By virtue of this special status the husband is accorded the decisive say in all matters concerning the common life of the spouses; he may choose where and how the spouses should live. Until the substitution of breakdown for fault as the main ground of divorce[158] this rule carried the sanction that a disobedient wife could be sued, for example, for malicious desertion if she failed to follow her husband when he elected to change the couple's place of residence. Now her recalcitrance can be relied on by her, or by her husband, to prove irretrievable breakdown of the marriage. Her behaviour would, however, still entail the loss of her right to be supported while the marriage subsists, although on dissolution of the marriage she could qualify for post-divorce maintenance despite it.[159] In other words, the content of the rule is largely hortatory. But it is also unacceptable. It should not have been included in the 1984 legislation and it clearly violates the right, entrenched in s 8 of the Constitution, not to be unfairly discriminated against on the ground of sex. The question to be asked now is whether it has been destroyed by the General Law Fourth Amendment Act of 1993.[160]

Certainly an attempt was made in the latter Act to deprive the husband of his pre-eminent status via the removal of the reference in s 13 of the Matrimonial Property Act to the headship of the family.[161] But the problem is that the source of the rule is the common law. The enactment of the rule into s 13 of the Matrimonial Property Act was unnecessary to preserve it and therefore merely declaratory of what the position would have been had there been no statutory reference to it. On

---

[156] Section 11(3)(b) of the Black Administration Act 38 of 1927. The exemption from this Act of women in Natal was brought about by s 1 of the Laws on Co-operation and Development Amendment Act 91 of 1985; that for women in KwaZulu by the KwaZulu Legislative Assembly's KwaZulu Act on the Code of Zulu Law 6 of 1981, superseded by the KwaZulu Act on the Code of Zulu Law 16 of 1985. But *both* codes dictate that women are subject to the guardianship of their husbands (s 27(3) in both cases). The schedule to the Transkei Marriage Act 21 of 1978 also repeals s 11(3), but re-enacts its content into s 37. KwaZulu and Transkei are used as examples here. There are others.

[157] Section 13 of Act 88 of 1984. In its widest sense the marital power includes three elements: the husband's power over his wife's person, his power over her property, and his power as head of the family. The Matrimonial Property Act recognized these elements explicitly. Section 11 abolished the power that the husband has 'over the person and property of his wife'; s 12 went on to explain that the effect of the abolition was to remove restrictions on the capacity of a wife to contract and to litigate; s 13, *ex abundanti cautela*, expressly stipulated that the abolition of the marital power would not affect the law relating to the position of the husband as head of the family. (It also preserved the status quo for domicile and guardianship, but these issues have been the subject of separate legislative amelioration — see below, 545).

[158] By the Divorce Act 70 of 1979.

[159] Section 7(2) of the Divorce Act 70 of 1979 permits a court to award maintenance even to a spouse who has caused the breakdown of the marriage.

[160] Act 132 of 1993, which came into operation on 1 December 1993.

[161] Section 30 of the General Law Fourth Amendment Act amends s 13 of the Matrimonial Property Act by removing from it the reference to the headship of the family and the law of domicile, leaving intact only the reference to guardianship. The last vestige of the section is repealed by the Guardianship Act 192 of 1993, which, however, had not come into operation by 28 February 1994.

this argument, its removal from s 13 on its own does nothing to the common law. And one should not overlook that in respect of the other two aspects of the common law specifically, but equally unnecessarily, mentioned in s 13 of the 1984 Act[162] there has been express legislative alteration of the common law in addition to the removal of the references in s 13. The one aspect is the common law of domicile, which dictated that a married woman follows the domicile of her husband — altered by the Domicile Act 3 of 1992, to allow all persons over the age of 18 years to acquire a domicile of choice regardless of marital status. The other is the law of guardianship, which dictated that the guardian of a legitimate child is its father — altered by the Guardianship Act 192 of 1993, not yet in force, but giving parents of legitimate children equal rights of guardianship. It seems then that the husband is still the head of the family. Wives who flout the authority of their spouses to choose where and how to live may lose their right to be maintained unless they proceed to have the marriage dissolved on the ground of irretrievable breakdown. The prospect is dim of litigation in the Constitutional Court to remedy this lingering instance of spousal inequality. In its hurry to garner the votes of women in the forthcoming election the National Party government by-passed the Law Commission and passed a flurry of legislation, not all of it effectual.

Marital rape and marital violence are topical issues in several jurisdictions. An exemption from prosecution for rape enjoyed by a husband in respect of his wife is widely seen as discriminatory against (married) women. In 1985 the South African Law Commission recommended the abolition of the marital rape exemption from the South African law,[163] but its views were rejected by a Joint Committee of Parliament.[164] In 1989 the Criminal Law and Criminal Procedure Act Amendment Act laid down that whenever a man is convicted of an assault on his wife and, but for the marriage, he could have been convicted of rape the court shall regard the latter fact as an aggravating circumstance in determining sentence.[165] This provision attracted the criticism that, while it is undoubtedly true that a sensitive enlightened judge might impose a sentence no lighter than the one he would have imposed had the conviction been one for rape, the champions of the abolition of the exemption could not be expected to content themselves with the hope that all judicial officers would respond appropriately. There is, it was also pointed out, no justification for charging a man with a different offence when he rapes his wife. Women are entitled to expect the law to regard sexual abuse by husbands of their wives just as seriously as sexual abuse of a stranger, a mistress, or a cohabitant.

The Prevention of Family Violence Act of 1993, which came into operation on 1 December 1993, abolishes the marital rape exemption, providing that a husband

---

[162] Because the abolition of the marital power which the husband has over the person and the property of his wife (by s 11 of the 1984 Act) could not have altered the law relating to domicile or to guardianship. The husband had these powers by virtue of discrete rules of the common law. His wife followed his domicile even where the marital power was excluded by antenuptial contract. Similarly his guardianship of the children of the marriage did not depend in any way on his having the marital power.

[163] Women and Sexual Offences, Project 45 of 1985.

[164] See Announcements, Tablings and Committee Reports No 6 of 10 February 1989, Report of the Joint Committee on the Criminal Law and the Criminal Procedure Act Amendment Bill. The arguments of the Joint Committee were utterly spurious. One worth repeating here was that the state should not interfere in the private realm of marital relationships (to make the rape of a wife rape, when it already regarded such behaviour as assault)!

[165] Section 1 of Act 39 of 1989.

may be convicted of the rape of his wife.[166] But it goes further than that. It attempts also to address the criticism that violence against women has not been given the attention or visited with the opprobrium it deserves. Although the law formally outlaws it, women remain in the main its victims. Police are said to be notoriously reluctant to become involved in a 'domestic dispute', despite the fact that the law is being broken. Until men are appropriately punished and appropriately educated against using their superior physical strength on women, and until women who are the victims of this abuse see it as an instance of inequality that must be stopped rather than endured, our society will remain one in which countless women are forced to live out their lives in fear of what men will do to them.[167]

The Family Violence Act sets out new simplified procedures for obtaining restraining orders against 'a party to a marriage', defined broadly, and commendably, to include partners of customary unions and persons who live together as if they were married — cohabitants. The judge or magistrate granting the interdict is required also to issue a warrant of arrest. The procedure for and consequences of arrest are then set out in the Act.[168] An important but controversial provision is that which requires, on pain of criminal liability, a range of persons who ordinarily come into contact with children to report circumstances which give rise to the suspicion that the child has been deliberately ill-treated.[169] All in all, the Act represents an attempt to deal with an aspect of the inequality of women that is rarely seen as such and to protect children at risk of abuse.

Equality of the spouses within marriage raises vexed questions about reproduction. It was advocated above that abortion must be the decision of the pregnant woman. A conflict between that proposition and the right of each spouse to decide on 'the number and spacing of the children', a right contained in art 16*(e)* of the

---

[166] Act 133 of 1993 s 5. See GN R124 *GG* 15308 of 1 December 1993 (*Reg Gaz* 5211). See also Campanella 'The Marital Rape Exemption Resurrected' (1994) 111 *SALJ* 31, where the cases dealing with the exemption prior to the legislative abolition are analysed. There is a substantial body of South African writing on the exemption, not referred to here because the statutory abolition renders it largely academic. The sentencing of husbands for rape and the definition of the crime itself, however, are issues that will require ongoing attention.

[167] Judges too need to become more discerning about coercion and the abuse of women. The judgment of Van den Heever J in *Coetzee v Coetzee* 1991 (4) SA 702 (C) amply demonstrates a cause for grave concern. A woman sought a divorce on the ground that her marriage had broken down. Evidence revealed that she was the sole supporter of her four children; that she had not left the matrimonial home or the matrimonial bed because her husband had threatened to kill her if she did; and that she had nowhere else to go. The husband was unemployed and drank excessively. Intercourse occurred at times, under threat of assault. The woman was deeply afraid of this man. According to the court, she deserved no sympathy and no relief. It denied her a divorce, expressing no wonder that her husband had not taken the summons seriously, seeing that his life at the table and in bed continued as usual. When intimacy continues in circumstances that fall short of rape, it held, a divorce cannot be granted. How stark must the difference be between coercion and free choice for the court to see marriage breakdown, let alone oppression?

[168] Dicker 'The Prevention of Family Violence Act: Innovation or Violation' 1994 *De Rebus* 212 is critical of the Act's 'apparent disregard of the *audi alteram partem* principle' in that it provides for the granting of an interdict without the respondent's being heard. Only after service of the interdict does it appear that the respondent is afforded the opportunity to apply for amendment or setting aside. For Dicker the protection of the victim of violence comes at an 'unacceptably high price' (at 215) and the legislation violates the due process requirement of the Constitution. He does not say where he finds the due process clause in the Constitution. Indeed there is none that is obvious. Yet it does not seem unrealistic to read due process into the clause protecting freedom (liberty) and security of the person (s 11(1)). It may even be possible to argue that due process may be read into the clause demanding equal protection of the law (s 8(1)). Also, Dicker cites the distinction between a judge or magistrate sitting in chambers and the court over which he or she presides (at 214). The functions performed in chambers are said to be quasi-administrative. If this be so, the administrative justice provision of the Constitution (s 24) may be invoked.

[169] Section 4. The provision ties in well with s 30(1)*(d)* of the Constitution, which entrenches the right of children not to be neglected or abused. The effectiveness of the Prevention of Family Violence Act and the content of the fundamental right remain to be evaluated.

United Nations Convention on the Elimination of All Forms of Discrimination Against Women, is obvious. It is ironic that the implication of this right in this particular Convention is that women should not have sole say over the procreation of children; that a husband should have an equal right to decide such things as whether pregnancy should ensue from intercourse, whether a foetus should or should not be carried to term, and how soon after the birth of one child another should be conceived. In cases of disagreement between the spouses the wish of one must prevail over the other. Unless the Convention is intended to take away from a woman the right to control her bodily functions and to produce precisely the kinds of inequalities that it is intended to eliminate, which is inconceivable (the *mot juste* in these circumstances), it is surely her will that must prevail. This interpretation would accord with the decision of the European Commission in *Paton v UK*, which rejected the contention that a father has any right to interfere with a decision of the pregnant woman to have an abortion.[170] A second problem is sterilization.[171] Since one of the fundamental objects of marriage is said to be the procreation of children it must be asked whether each spouse should have the right to be sterilized without the concurrence of the other. The answer, it is suggested, should be positive. An aggrieved spouse who believes that a marriage without any or more children no longer has any purpose has the remedy of divorce on the ground of irretrievable breakdown. That is cold comfort to him or her, but for the law to demand concurrence would in any event entail the creation of a sanction for non-compliance, which could only realistically be divorce. And the demand would detract from what it is suggested is the overriding principle of individual autonomy in the matter of reproduction.

### 5.1.4 *Inequality on divorce*

Stereotyped role allocation for women has been a major source of their impoverishment. In addition great changes have occurred in the transmission of family wealth.

> 'Whereas of old, wealth transmission from parents to children tended to center upon major items of patrimony such as the family farm or the family firm, today for the broad middle classes, wealth

---

[170] (1980) 3 EHRR 408, discussed by Douglas 'The Family and the State Under the European Convention on Human Rights' (1988) 2 *Int J of L and the Family* 76 at 85, in the context of art 25 of the European Convention on Human Rights. The husband in this case had already been refused an injunction in the English High Court (in *Paton v British Pregnancy Advisory Service Trustees* [1979] 1 QB 276) to prevent his wife from proceeding with the abortion, which was lawful in terms of the English Abortion Act of 1967. The question whether a (former) cohabitant has the right to interdict his partner from having an abortion which would amount to an offence under the English legislation was left open in *C v S* [1987] 1 All ER 1230. The most recent South African case on abortion held that the court has no discretion to prevent the operation if the abortion is legal and the procedures of the Abortion and Sterilization Act 2 of 1975 have been complied with — *G v Superintendent, Groote Schuur Hospital* (supra). In this case the mother of a girl aged 14 years sought unsuccessfully to restrain her from aborting a child conceived as a result of rape.

[171] Sterilization of a healthy person for contraceptive reasons is not covered by our Abortion and Sterilization Act (which deals only with the sterilization of a person incapable of consenting thereto) and was considered unlawful in the Roman-Dutch law. But see *Edouard v Administrator, Natal* 1989 (2) SA 368 (D), where the court held (inter alia) that sterilization has become an accepted form of contraception in our society (at 376). (An appeal against the decision was unsuccessful — 1990 (3) SA 581 (A).) The case does not answer the question whether a medical practitioner who successfully sterilizes a married woman without the consent of her husband would be liable in delict for an intentional interference with *consortium*. If reproductive rights are a matter of equality, privacy, dignity, and other individual rights enshrined in the Constitution, as has been argued here, both men and women should have control over their reproductive capacity regardless of marital status. Their decisions as individuals alone should govern the consequences of sterilization. An aggrieved spouse's remedy is divorce on the ground of irretrievable breakdown, but not an interference with reproductive autonomy. Non-liability of the practitioner follows.

transmission centers on a radically different kind of asset: *the investment in skills*. In consequence, intergenerational wealth transmission no longer occurs primarily upon the death of the parents, but rather, when the children are growing up, hence, during the parents' lifetime.'[172]

Despite this preoccupation with what is known as 'human capital', which might compensate for the decline in the transmission of traditional property, the socialization and education of girls do not equip them, in the same way as boys are equipped, to pursue successful financial careers as adults.[173] Young women still rely heavily on the dangerous notion that they will marry, have children, and be supported throughout their lives by their husbands.

Within marriage the unequal distribution of the domestic burden, which has its own further effect of channelling married women into lower-paid part-time jobs,[174] inhibits the development of a stable career and diminishes the chances that a married woman has of securing 'a good job with good fringe benefits' — Professor Charles Reich's definition of 'new property'.[175] After divorce, the incidence of which is ever increasing, it is not surprising that women are unable suddenly to compete for scarce jobs and to become financially independent. Deborah Rhode lists inequalities like these as major causes of what is termed 'the feminization of poverty'.[176] In the US 90 per cent of single-parent families are headed by women and half of these families remain below the poverty line. In addition race exacerbates the position — three-quarters of poor black and half of poor Hispanic families in the US are headed by women.[177] There is no doubt that these trends are manifest in South Africa and that African women in particular suffer more acutely, and from similar causes. But the apartheid apparatus, especially the migrant labour system, occasioned special additional hardship for them. And that hardship is not alleviated by social security that serves to cushion the effect of poverty in some jurisdictions.[178]

Three major strands in other legal systems have been developed in recognition of the inability of women, especially those with child-care responsibilities, to

---

[172] Langbein 'The Twentieth-Century Revolution in Family Wealth Transmission' (1988) 86 *Michigan LR* 722 at 723.

[173] It is trite that the choice of subjects for girls at school and even at university is frequently influenced by this notion. In families that can afford tertiary education for some, but not all, of their children it is not uncommon to find that boys are preferred, not on merit.

[174] Many women who take up employment during marriage do so out of economic necessity, not with a view to establishing careers. And many men consider economic necessity to be the only justification for a wife's going out to work.

[175] Reich, in a seminal article entitled 'The New Property' (1964) 73 *Yale LJ* 733 elucidated the changes in the nature of wealth and property that have occurred during this century. The two world wars impoverished the propertied classes. Employment and employment-related benefits have become the assets which determine both economic and social status. This theme is taken up and developed by Langbein op cit (n 172). The changes, and they describe what has happened to a sector of South African society also, have had a profound effect on the family (see Glendon *The New Family and the New Property* (1981) 3, 91).

[176] Op cit (n 26) 126. She cites data for the US revealing that women are twice as likely as men to be poor; that female single parents are five times as likely as men to be poor; that two-thirds of all indigent adults are women. For fuller documentation of this issue see above, n 35 and the works cited.

[177] Ibid.

[178] Sachs op cit (n 9) 67, in the essay 'The Constitutional Position of the Family in a Democratic South Africa', points out that African people have been denied their traditional family-based support systems and at the same time excluded from the mainstream of state-based social benefits (such as they are). Despite efforts by the government to narrow the gap, pensions for whites are still higher than those for blacks; whites receive more protection from unemployment insurance than blacks. See also Burman & Berger 'When Family Support Fails: The Problems of Maintenance Payments in Apartheid South Africa' (1988) 4 *SAJHR* 194 and 394, which starkly reveals the plight of single-parent families headed by African women; and Burman 'Maintaining the One-Parent Support in South Africa: Law and Reality' in Meulders-Klein & Eekelaar op cit (n 35) 507.

achieve some degree of financial security. One is the modification of the law of matrimonial property to ensure that on divorce women share assets built up during marriage. Another is the refinement of the law compelling private maintenance. And the third is the development of sophisticated social security systems to alleviate the poverty and hardship occasioned by the breakdown of intimate relationships.

Of the first strand reform saw the development in some jurisdictions of highly structured matrimonial property systems, such as the deferred sharing of acquests (*Zugewinngemeinschaft*) and equalization of pension benefits (*Versorgungsausgleich*) of the German law;[179] in others it resulted in a judicial discretion to redistribute property on divorce, of which the English law is a prime example.[180]

South Africa, a country whose common law was based on universal community of property and of profit and loss, has incorporated both of these features into its matrimonial property law.[181] There can be no doubt that the introduction of the accrual system (which amounts to a deferred sharing of profits of spouses married out of community) and the provision for judicial interference with the consequences of complete separation of goods via the transfer of property from one spouse to the other on divorce, have mitigated the harsh consequences that ensue from a system that excludes all sharing. Such a system conatradicts the widely accepted view that marriage produces a form of partnership.

Not to be overlooked, however, is that the accrual system is frequently excluded in the antenuptial contract in situations which reflect the choice of the party whose estate is most likely to increase (the husband), rather than the informed choice of both parties.[182] In such marriages the judicial discretion cannot remedy any injustice

---

[179] See the Equality Act of 1957 and arts 1363ff and 1587ff of the *BGB*.

[180] The enactment of the Matrimonial Proceedings and Property Act of 1970 (the provisions of which were consolidated in 1973 in the Matrimonial Causes Act) was considered to be a major advance for women on divorce. Mitigating the consequences of a matrimonial property regime that dictated strict separation of property, the Act made possible, by way of a judicial discretion on divorce, the sharing of assets such as the matrimonial home and even business assets of the husband, on the basis that the parties should as far as possible be placed in a position as if the marriage had not broken down (the minimal loss principle). The Act was amended after much controversy by the Matrimonial and Family Proceedings Act of 1984. This legislation inter alia abandoned the minimal loss principle, introduced the 'clean break' principle, and attenuated maintenance obligations of ex-husbands to their former wives. Divorced women immediately became more dependent on the state in order to support the one-parent families headed by them. See further below, nn 198, 199. For a complete account of the power of the English courts to make financial orders on divorce, see Cretney *Principles of Family Law* 5 ed (1990) ch 19; Dewar *Law and the Family* 2 ed (1992) ch 8.

[181] Marriages with the standard-form antenuptial contract always excluded sharing. Since the enactment of the Matrimonial Property Act 88 of 1984 marriage by such an antenuptial contract carries with it the accrual system, based on the German *Zugewinngemeinschaft*, unless this consequence is expressly excluded (s 2 of the Act). These consequences were made to ensue in the same way from the civil marriages of Africans by virtue of the Marriage and Matrimonial Property Law Amendment Act 3 of 1988, which made it necessary for Africans to enter into an antenuptial contract to avoid community of property and of profit and loss. (Until the 1988 legislation was enacted s 22(6) of the Black Administration Act, as interpreted by the Appellate Division in *Ex parte Minister of Native Affairs: In re Molefe v Molefe* 1946 AD 315, rendered the civil marriages of blacks automatically out of community, but the husband had the marital power. Community could be introduced in certain circumstances by way of a declaration.) The judicial discretion to divide property on divorce was also a creation of the 1984 Matrimonial Property Act. It was designed to mitigate the harshness of complete separation of goods in marriages celebrated before the introduction of the accrual system. The wording of s 36 (which amended s 7 of the Divorce Act 70 of 1979) suggested that it did not apply to a civil marriage governed by the Black Administration Act (i e a marriage between two Africans and a marriage between an African man and a woman of another race), although in one case it was held to apply to a marriage between Africans — *Mathabathe v Mathabathe* 1987 (3) SA 45 (W); cf *Milbourn v Milbourn* 1987 (3) SA 62 (W). Since the enactment of the 1988 Act it is clear that the discretion applies to these marriages, but only if they are out of community and were celebrated prior to the coming into operation of the 1988 legislation.

[182] A surprising degree of ignorance about the proprietary consequences of marriage persists among women. It is often the attorney of the husband or of the husband's father, if the parties are young, who drafts the antenuptial contract. And if the prospects of increased wealth for the husband are good, the likelihood increases that the accrual system will be excluded.

that may flow from the chosen system. The reason is that the judicial discretion is formulated in a highly restrictive way.[183] The provision permits a redistribution of property by the court on divorce only (inter alia) if the marriage was celebrated with an antenuptial contract excluding all forms of sharing prior to the commencement of the Matrimonial Property Act of 1984.[184] The equivalent provision for the civil marriages of Africans requires that the marriage was celebrated out of community prior to the commencement of the Marriage and Matrimonial Property Law Amendment Act of 1988.[185] The inevitable demise of the judicial discretion will occur when all such marriages celebrated prior to the commencement of the two Acts have been dissolved.

It must be questioned whether this differentiation based on the date of marriage will withstand the scrutiny of the Constitutional Court. As has been said above, many couples are marrying after the two commencement dates with antenuptial contracts which, by excluding the accrual system, are creating marriages in which no sharing of family assets takes place. Such a system was regarded by the legislature as unsatisfactory and sufficiently dangerous for and unfair to women that its harshness had to be mitigated via the introduction of the discretion.[186] Now there is developing another group of people, more often than not women, equally at risk, but who are denied the relief granted to their counterparts who married, fortuitously, before the cut-off dates. What argument can be advanced to justify the different treatment of people in identical circumstances? What can be adduced to palliate the sense of unfairness that women feel who are now emerging impecunious from broken marriages from which the accrual system was excluded?

It is important to try to answer these questions. The Law Commission did so in 1990.[187] It rejected a proposed extension of the judicial discretion to marriages

---

[183] The judicial discretion was created by s 36 of the Matrimonial Property Act 88 of 1984, which amended s 7 of the Divorce Act 70 of 1979. For comment on the unduly restrictive formulation see Sinclair op cit (n 35) 47–52.

[184] Act 88 of 1984, which commenced on 1 November 1984.

[185] Act 3 of 1988, which commenced on 2 December 1988.

[186] It must be stressed that the discretion can be invoked by husbands and wives, and has been. But there is little doubt that its fundamental purpose was to protect women who were emerging from failed marriages with no assets, no job, no employment benefits, little or no chance of successfully entering the labour market in middle age, and the responsibility in many cases of caring for the children of the marriage on parsimonious maintenance, which inevitably declined with inflation, if it was paid at all. After years of campaigning by persons who encountered and appreciated the plight of these women and their children Parliament came to the rescue with the introduction of the judicial discretion. The remedy has saved a sizeable number of divorced women from financial disaster and society from some of its many penurious one-parent families. Lest it be claimed that this assertion is an exaggeration, given the small number of judicial decisions reflecting the implementation of the discretion, a counter-argument must be offered in anticipation. Nearly all divorces are undefended and the financial matters are regulated by a settlement incorporated into the court's order. This fact does not support a claim that the judicial discretion plays no part in such divorce settlements. Parties bargain in the shadow of the law. Private ordering of the consequences of divorce depends upon the bargaining chips that the law provides to the parties. The very fact that the court has the power to intervene to do justice between the parties by way of its discretion compels fairer settlements. It compels settlements that do not produce for women the financial risk that complete separation of property without the possibility of redistribution produces.

[187] It undertook an investigation into the extension of the judicial discretion inter alia to marriages celebrated after the commencement of the 1984 Act, from which the accrual system had been excluded — see its report, *Project 12: Review of the Law of Divorce* (1990). In the draft bill appended to its working paper for comment the Commission proposed the extension where the court could be satisfied that exceptional circumstances justified equitable distribution of assets between the spouses. This proposal elicited favourable comment from judges, practising lawyers, and academics. My view that the discretion should apply more broadly (see Sinclair op cit (n 35) 48–50) features prominently in the report and attracted a lot of support (although the wording proposed to effect the extension was, I thought, inauspicious). But there was also strong opposition, notably from two prominent academics who could not condone the interference with contractual choice that the discretion entails and who consider that the entire notion of a judicial discretion does not sit happily in our law of matrimonial property, largely

celebrated after the cut-off dates mainly on the grounds that extension would introduce legal uncertainty about the outcome of divorce and would interfere with the contractual preference for total separation of property expressed by the parties at the time of the marriage.[188] As to uncertainty, it is preferable to the rigid irremediable harshness acknowledged to derive from complete separation of property. Indeed it is preferable to irremediable harshness caused by any highly structured matrimonial property system.[189] The so-called uncertainty introduced in 1984 for some marriages has not produced the flood of litigation that the critics predicted. But it has made much fairer the basis for the settlement of proprietary issues on divorce. It has mitigated the harshness of choices made inopportunely at the time of marriage.[190]

This fact leads to the question of interference with the contractual choice of the parties. First, let it be stressed that the principle of non-interference did not deter

because it produces uncertainty. The General Council of the Bar contended that there was no justification for the extension because parties about to marry are fully apprised of the consequences of excluding the accrual system in the antenuptial contract by way of the expert financial advice they receive from attorneys. Yet the Association of Law Societies, representing attorneys, favoured the amendment. The Bar Council also felt that the law has never had as its object to protect the foolish (who, it is worth remembering, are also the weak and the vulnerable). The Commission acknowledged that there was a difference of opinion on the matter. It made much of the issue of vested rights flowing from contractual choice, and of the issue of uncertainty, and rejected the idea of the extension. Its main contention was that a more broadly applicable discretion would amount to an alternative matrimonial property system that would render superfluous the accrual system because sharing would take place *ad hoc* by court order. The last argument is flawed because it assumes that the existence of a discretion demands that the courts should ordinarily intervene to alter the proprietary consequences of marriage chosen by the parties. This is not the way proponents of the broader discretion see it operating. The judicial power should be, and is (see the negative formulation in s 7(4) of the Divorce Act 70 of 1979), a residual one, employed only to avoid injustice — see Sinclair 'Divorce and the Judicial Discretion — In Search of the Middle Ground' (1989) 106 *SALJ* 249. The arguments about contractual choice and uncertainty are dealt with below, 551f.

[188] See ch 3 para 1.3.10 of its report.

[189] My view has for long been that the discretion should apply to all marriages, regardless of the proprietary system. Undue harshness can flow from unalterable equal sharing in a marriage in community of property, just as it can flow from complete separation of property. Take a marriage of very short duration in which one spouse suddenly amasses a fortune in virtue of work done (like the writing of a novel) over ten years prior to the marriage. Is inexorable equal sharing not unjust? Undue harshness can also arise where the accrual system has not been excluded. One example is where the statutory accrual system has been modified (as it seems it can be — s 2 speaks of its application 'except in so far as that system is expressly excluded') to exclude the major profit-bearing asset(s) of one spouse (s 4(1)(*b*)(ii)). Another is where it has not been modified to reflect the change in the value of money, required by the Act (s 4(1)(*b*)(iii)), and inflation has reduced the profit to zero, leaving a wealthy spouse with no obligation to share accumulated or any other assets and the impecunious spouse with no right to anything. Here the accrual system is no better than complete separation of property would have been. In none of these cases can the judicial discretion rectify a poor choice by a spouse which has produced grossly inequitable discrepancies in wealth. The need is for broad residual judicial power to intervene to prevent injustice wherever it is found. (For a trenchant criticism of what equal division has and has not done for women in California, see Weitzman *The Divorce Revolution* (1985) 104–9. And for an analysis of the uncertainty deriving from the judicial discretion see Discussion Paper 54 of 1993 of the Australian Law Commission, entitled *Equality before the Law*. At paras 8.7–10 this important paper laments the fact that there is no starting point of equality in the division of property, which renders too uncertain the outcome of divorce litigation. It pleads for equal sharing to be the basic assumption informing the allocation of property and for the retention of the discretion of the court to vary equal sharing. South African law already has the advantage of structured matrimonial property systems to create the necessary starting point. What is being pleaded for is a broader discretion to mitigate harshness that flows from the rigid application of the systems. Such a solution would achieve for us what the Australian Law Commission is recommending for Australia.)

[190] See above, n 182. The words of Glendon op cit (n 175) 66 are instructive here. Discussing the reliance on antenuptial contracts to regulate the proprietary interests of the parties at the time of divorce, she says: 'There is no reason to think that increased use of marriage contracts would enable the economically weaker spouse to bargain for property division and future economic security in case the marriage terminates by divorce. On the contrary, European and US experience, and common sense, indicate that such contracts . . . would probably more often be used by the stronger party to contract out of or to restrict property division . . .'. Even if we assume that the parties bargain on an equal footing at the time of marriage, the simple truth is that it is not possible to predict what injustice may flow from the strictures of a rigid unalterable matrimonial property system. This is the crux of the argument for adjustive judicial power regardless of the governing matrimonial property system.

the legislature from introducing the discretion for marriages celebrated before the cut-off dates. The sacrosanctity subsequently flaunted to justify non-interference had been sacrificed in 1984 and again in 1988.[191] What changed was that the contractual choices open to women became nicer after the introduction of the accrual system in 1984. Whereas previously the effective choice[192] was between full legal status plus no sharing and subjection to marital guardianship plus community, the choice became one between full legal status plus deferred profit sharing or full legal status plus community. But the change in choices does not support the claim that people are now more able to predict their fortunes when they express a contractual preference at the time of marriage. And further, the parties are often unequally situated at that time; the choice of the economically stronger often prevails. There is absolutely no evidence to suggest that choices made now by intending spouses are informed choices, whereas those made prior to the cut-off dates were ill-informed and therefore legitimately subjected to judicial interference.

If the purpose of the adjustive discretion is to avoid injustice, and that was the justification adduced for its introduction into our legal system, then the date of one's marriage and the range of the available choices should not constrain the power of the court. It has to be recognized that the premise of adjustive judicial power is to avoid grossly inequitable discrepancies in the financial positions of the parties on divorce. Such discrepancies do not depend solely or even fundamentally on the nature of the matrimonial property system. All that can be said is that some systems, notably complete separation of property, are more likely than others to produce injustice. If this is so, then at the very least, whenever complete separation of property applies, the court should be able to intervene. And this is what the argument being advanced here is about. Although it advocates as a matter of justice the application of the judicial discretion across the spectrum of matrimonial property systems, its more limited purpose is the constitutional argument that the current criterion is unsound: the date of the marriage cannot serve to differentiate between people in identical circumstances. The Constitutional Court should strike down this criterion because it is arbitrary; it unfairly discriminates against people married according to the system of complete separation of property on the ground of the date of their marriage. The discrimination takes the form of denying to those people a remedy to relieve injustice that is granted to persons married with an identical system, but earlier. That the differentiation has a disparate unfair impact on women is a further possible ground for attack, but a harder one to substantiate.[193]

What is the significance to South Africans of the constitutional challenge to the formulation of the judicial discretion? For couples who live on their salaries and do

---

[191] It will undoubtedly be argued that this sacrifice was made on a temporary basis until all the marriages to which the discretion applies have been dissolved and on the understanding that this ugly excrescence would ultimately disappear from our legal system. But it is unlikely that this view of the discretion will save the law from its present unconstitutionality. The argument about the appropriateness of adjustive judicial power is one between those who favour the granting of typically Anglo-American discretionary powers to the judiciary and those who prefer the certainty more prevalent (but not uncompromisingly insisted upon) in the Continental systems. That is a different argument, not pursued here.

[192] Since anything that is not illegal, immoral, or impossible may be included in an antenuptial contract parties have always been able to create their own matrimonial property systems. In fact few depart from the standard-form contracts that develop in relation to a particular system. But one notable exception was the creation by parties of versions of an accrual system in their antenuptial contracts prior to the enactment of the Matrimonial Property Act. The contracts were often based on the evolving proposals of the Law Commission.

[193] The same may be true of the exercise by the court of its power, as evidenced by the cases.

not have the opportunity to amass property the matrimonial property system that governs their marriage does not turn out to be the panacea for the poverty that will be experienced most acutely by the divorced woman. For the poor, matrimonial property law is as important as an elaborate estate planning exercise. But for many thousands of people the matrimonial home[194] and a share in pension and other retirement benefits accumulated during marriage make the difference between forced reliance on exiguous welfare and some form of financial security. To these people the sharing of property acquired by joint effort is crucial. To be denied an equitable remedy on the ground of the date of one's marriage is unacceptable.

The second major strand of development in this field has been in the law regulating the private maintenance obligation. At common law the duty of support between husband and wife terminated when the rationale for its existence ceased to exist. It was by statute, in many jurisdictions, that the continuation of the husband's duty to maintain his wife was extended beyond the date of divorce. Post-divorce maintenance is still relied on by countless divorced women, not only for their own support but also for the support of the children in their custody. But this mechanism too has proved inadequate.[195] A major problem encountered universally is the high rate of default by men liable to support families with which they do not live.[196] Elaborate statutory devices to locate defaulters and to compel them to pay or face imprisonment have been introduced to ensure compliance, but on the whole these have proved to be inadequate. The point is that default is not always a reflection of the morality of the debtor; it is increasingly a reflection of the fact that one pay packet is not sufficient to sustain more than one family. And since a large proportion of divorced men remarry they use that pay packet to support the family with which they are currently living. A consequence of this fact has been the propagation of the view that it is fair to expect the victims of marriage breakdown to be cared for by the state.[197]

Both the introduction of principles of partnership to ensure the sharing of matrimonial property and the acknowledgement that a lifelong duty of support enduring beyond divorce is harsh and ineffective have been used as justifications for the curtailment of the duty of support between divorced persons in countries

---

[194] Even if it is not owned. The right to council housing is important. It arose in the context of forfeiture of benefits in a marriage in community of property in *Persad v Persad* 1989 (4) SA 685 (D). Didcott J held a lease entitling a husband by virtue of marriage to occupy a council house to be a patrimonial benefit and ordered forfeiture of it in favour of the wife. Since it qualified as property for forfeiture it would in an appropriate case qualify for redistribution in terms of the discretion.

[195] For the position in England, as an example, see Eekelaar & Maclean op cit (n 35). The 1984 Matrimonial and Family Proceedings Act was premised on the belief that divorced women were living (parasitically) off their former husbands. In fact there is little if any evidence that they were doing so. Its aim was to abolish the mythical 'meal-ticket for life'; it separated child support from support of a divorced spouse, emphasized the clean-break principle, and resurrected matrimonial misconduct as a factor affecting awards of maintenance. After 1984 divorced women continued to become more and more dependent on the state in order to support the one-parent families headed by them. But the failure of the private maintenance obligation was not compensated for by increased benefits from the state.

[196] Copious reference to the comparative literature documenting this problem cannot be undertaken here, but a useful survey of the approaches in a number of foreign jurisdictions can be obtained from Van Zyl 'Post-Divorce Support — Theory and Practice' (1989) 22 *De Jure* 71. Burman & Berger op cit (n 57) 194 and 334 starkly reveals the plight of single-parent families headed by African women. The authors found that awards of maintenance are too low and that the incidence of default by men is very high. The extent and administration of state grants is also hopelessly inadequate.

[197] This is the thesis of Gray *The Reallocation of Property on Divorce* (1977) 327.

such as the US, England, and West Germany.¹⁹⁸ In those jurisdictions and others, for they are no more than examples, the compensatory measure has been welfare payments to women caring alone for minor children. This is the third major strand of development referred to above.

Sophisticated social security systems developed in many places to cater inter alia for one-parent families with dependent children testify to the transfer of the duty to support the victims of marriage breakdown from husbands to the state. The evidence from most places, however, is that the cost is too high to be sustained. The erosion of welfare benefits by inflation and actual cuts in welfare budgets are amply documented in the literature of the jurisdictions referred to.¹⁹⁹ Largely for this reason the private maintenance obligation, although it is deficient, persists and ways to improve compliance with it continue to be sought.

The South African law of marriage has tended to follow, albeit belatedly, Western trends. It has certainly done so in the reform of matrimonial property law and it continues to impose post-divorce obligations on husbands in favour of their wives.²⁰⁰ (The parental duty of support rests upon the blood relationship and remains unaffected by the dissolution of the parents' marriage.) But the inability of fathers to support two families is as much of a reality here as it is elsewhere. There has also been an infiltration of the widely held sentiment that women can be expected to achieve financial independence after divorce, although our courts have expressed different views on the extent to which this expectation should affect orders for maintenance.²⁰¹ The incidence of default by maintenance debtors is alarmingly

---

¹⁹⁸ What was overlooked in England when the Matrimonial Causes Act of 1973 was enacted to provide for the sharing of property on divorce and the continuation of the duty of support even in favour of a woman who had been responsible for the breakdown of her marriage was that divorced women would remarry far less frequently than divorced men. The latter soon found themselves in the position of having to support two families on one income — something most of them simply could not do. In 1984 the law had to be changed again to reduce the liability for maintenance of ex-husbands to their former wives. The meal-ticket for life fell away. In Germany, too, entitlement to maintenance after divorce was restricted to exceptional cases by the Marriage Law Reform Act of 1977. The legislation provides for maintenance only in cases where one spouse cannot find adequate employment because of career prejudice occasioned by the marriage or cannot be expected to work after the divorce. There is no doubt that the sting of this curtailment is felt by women.

¹⁹⁹ In England, for example, the curtailment of the private maintenance obligation was not compensated for by increased benefits from the state; Indeed, precisely at the time that women became entitled to the same National Insurance Benefits as men, the value of these benefits declined for everyone and became less significant as a source of income maintenance. Divorced women, especially those caring for children, have therefore experienced formal equality, but coupled with increasing poverty. See Smart 'Feminism and Law: Some Problems of Analysis and Strategy' (1986) 14 *Int J of the Sociology of L* 109 at 115–16. See also Eekelaar & Maclean op cit (n 35). Douglas 'Individual Economic Security for the Elderly and the Divorced: A Consideration of the Position of England and Wales' in Meulders-Klein & Eekelaar op cit (n 35) 491 at 505–6 emphasizes the expectation in English law that divorced and elderly people should be independent. She points out that there are more women in each of these groups than there are men. Their inferior capacity to earn has resulted in increased poverty for them, which neither the private maintenance obligation after divorce nor state support has been able to redress. For a description of the decline of aid for women heading one-parent families in the US, see Law 'Women, Work, Welfare, and the Preservation of Patriarchy' (1983) 131 *U Pennsylvania LR* 1249 at 1274–5, 1320.

²⁰⁰ Observation of divorce proceedings and perusal of court files reveal that awards of post-divorce maintenance for black women are more rare than they are for white women. This impression is confirmed by Burman 'Maintaining the One-Parent Support in South Africa: Law and Reality' in Meulders-Klein & Eekelaar op cit (n 35) 507 at 511.

²⁰¹ Much of course depends on the circumstances of the particular case. Nevertheless a sense of the predilection of the judge can sometimes be obtained from the way the judgment reads. It has been accepted by the Appellate Division that an order for financial provision which achieves a 'clean break' between the parties (implying no ongoing duty of support) is desirable in the right circumstances (see *Beaumont v Beaumont* 1987 (1) SA 967 (A) at 992–3; *Katz v Katz* 1989 (3) SA 1 (A) at 11; *Archer v Archer* 1989 (2) SA 885 (E) at 894–5). Didcott J, in *Claassens v Claassens* (supra) at 369E–F, said that '[t]hose anxious about poverty here are unlikely . . . to find divorce a major cause of it nowadays. The independence and self-sufficiency of women is argued so persuasively and, by the growing number who support themselves through their own efforts, demonstrated so frequently that, as a general

high.[202] It has provoked amendments to the Maintenance Act to improve compliance.[203] But South Africa is not a welfare state. It has no social security system comparable to those in Europe, the US, and the Commonwealth countries, the laws and policies of which have influenced the development of our law.

It is unlikely that the incidence of divorce and family breakdown is going to be reversed. The search for individual happiness, regardless of the cost, is likely to continue to encourage people whose personal relationships become unfulfilling to change their partners. While this phenomenon persists and while women continue to suffer the consequences of the kinds of inequalities alluded to above, post-divorce poverty among them and their children will remain a fact of our lives. What is to be done about it?[204]

Within the context of sex equality it has already been said that laws and policies which inhibit the attainment by women of their true potential in employment must be extirpated. A restructuring of the system of paid employment, to assist mothers to discharge their child-care responsibilities and to inculcate in fathers acceptance that they too are parents with those responsibilities, must be undertaken. The complexity and restrictions within our law of husband and wife which, because of infelicitous formulation, prevent a redistribution of property between spouses on divorce to ensure financial security for dependent women and children must be attended to. Better enforcement of the duty of support between spouses and of parents to their children must, despite the hardship it occasions, be pursued. It may even be that a system should be developed to provide for payment of maintenance by the state to the creditor, leaving the state to pursue the debtor for its own account. The expectation that divorced women can achieve financial independence and the imposition of a 'clean break' on divorce are issues that must be approached by judges with due circumspection. Women, on the other hand, must come to realize that housewife-marriage has become a luxury which few can afford and which the law cannot encourage. The ethos that all individuals must pursue their talents and work to fulfil their potential must be extended to women — from the time they are girls. Women must strive for the equality that has become part of their rhetoric, for equality is not a gift; it is something that will have to be worked for.

The area of fundamental innovation, however, is the development of a social

---

thesis, it can hardly be doubted any longer.' Cf *Kroon v Kroon* 1986 (4) SA 616 (E); *Grasso v Grasso* (supra); *Pommerel v Pommerel* (supra) at 1001–4, all containing negative responses to the idea that a divorced woman should be expected to enter the labour market. The issue is a difficult one and generalizations that do not take into account the special circumstances of the case can be misleading. A balance has to be sought between competing propositions. On the one hand, children generally benefit from having their mothers at home during their early years. A choice by parents able to do so to extend this benefit to them should not be overturned simply on the ground that the spouses become divorced. On the other hand, women who remain out of the labour market for too long lose marketable skills and find it very difficult to make up the lost time in later years. They place themselves at risk. Post-divorce poverty becomes a real danger unless their husbands are and remain wealthy and generous. It is submitted that in South Africa today women should be expected and assisted to develop careers for themselves and their child-care responsibilities should be shared more equitably with their partners. Housewife marriage entrenches the dependence of one adult on another, often in circumstances where the dependence is unwarranted, and even in childless marriages. It militates against the achievement of equality for women.

[202] Burman & Berger op cit (n 196) 339–44.

[203] The Maintenance Amendment Act 2 of 1991, which came into force on 1 March 1992 (Proc 15 *GG* 13802 of 28 Feb 1992). For a summary of the main provisions see Sinclair (1992–3) 31 *J of Family L* 461 at 464–5; Keyser 1991 *Annual Survey of South African Law* 7–11.

[204] For discussion of the options open to us and some suggestions from the comparative literature, see Sinclair op cit (n 35) 1–13. See also Burman op cit (n 200) 528–32.

security system to cushion the effect of divorce and of the breakdown of intimate relationships which do not culminate in marriage (or, *ex hypothesi*, divorce), but which produce the same dependencies. The provision of welfare is a controversial issue, largely beyond the scope of this discussion. That notwithstanding, it is contended that an intensive study must be commissioned to investigate the foundations for a social security system here. The extent of poverty and deprivation in this land far exceeds that experienced in jurisdictions from which we have gleaned so much. Reform of the private law has been demonstrated there to be insufficient to counter the effects of serial marriage.[205] Social security has proved insufficient too. But together, private maintenance and state assistance are better than either on its own. South Africa cannot ignore the need to nurture the next generation by providing it, and those it has chosen to be its caretakers, with the basic necessities of life.

One final question to be raised in connection with inequality on divorce is the question of who should be the caretaker of the children of divorced parents.[206] The issue of parental responsibility in general was canvassed above and equality between parents was urged as the appropriate starting point for the law. Unlike the matter of guardianship, no formal legal rule dictates which parent is entitled to custody. The court is required to make its order to serve 'the best interests of the child'. But this is a notoriously elusive concept.[207] There is no doubt that our courts favour women over men to be custodians of minor children after divorce.[208] The assumption that mothers will make better caretakers in a milieu of increasing participation by them in the labour market requires re-examination.

The constitutional question that arises here is whether fathers are entitled to an equal chance to obtain custody of their children after divorce. Countless court orders granting custody to women without a serious consideration of the possibilities for an award of joint custody have been made. Indeed our courts are not enthusiastic about joint custody, although it has on occasion been ordered.[209] Equality between the spouses appears to entail a reversal of this position. The questions are how the change could, and whether it should, be brought about. Although there is no formal

---

[205] The English Law Commission Report on the Financial Consequences of Divorce No 112 of 14 December 1981 para 4 considered as a basic issue the limits of what the private law can achieve.

[206] It is a question not entirely dependent on marriage and its corollary, divorce. Who should care for the children of former cohabitants is also at issue.

[207] See Heaton 'Some General Remarks on the Concept "Best Interests of the Child" ' (1990) 53 *THRHR* 95; Schafer 'Joint Custody' (1987) 104 *SALJ* 149 at 153, who points out in his extremely useful article that 'our courts are all too frequently cast in the Solomonic role of having to choose between competing parents, each of whom would be a fit custodial parent, and where in addition there is evidence of a strong bond between the child and both of them'. The enormous body of comparative literature on the application of this principle testifies to its indeterminacy.

[208] The maternal-preference rule, also known as the tender-years doctrine, is well known in our law — see Schafer op cit (n 207) 154–5. The author asserts that it can no longer go unchallenged (at 155).

[209] The reluctance of the courts even to give effect to joint custody agreements is apparent from cases such as *Heimann v Heimann* 1948 (4) SA 926 (W) and *Edwards v Edwards* 1960 (2) SA 523 (D). A notable departure from this view came after the widening of the court's discretion by the Divorce Act 70 of 1979 (see s 6(3)) in *Kastan v Kastan* 1985 (3) SA 235 (C). Here the court incorporated the terms of an agreement providing for joint custody into its order. By contrast, the court refused to do so in *Schlebusch v Schlebusch* 1988 (4) SA 548 (E), disagreeing with the views of Schafer op cit (n 207). The court was at pains to stress that *Kastan* did not represent 'a departure from existing principles . . . or a stepping stone to the granting in future of joint custody at the mere request of the parties' (at 551). One wonders how joint custody could be awarded in circumstances where one parent wants nothing to do with the children. It seems appropriate to grant the request of the parents for joint custody in all cases unless the court is convinced that to do so would be inimical to the interests of the children. The judge in *Schlebusch* viewed with concern 'any trend towards the granting of joint custody orders' (at 551). (See the criticism of this case by Schoeman 'Gesamentlike Bewaring van Kinders' (1989) 52 *THRHR* 462 at 465–6.)

legal rule favouring mothers, a statement by a judge that custody of minor children ought to be given to their mother may, depending on the reach of the Bill of Rights,[210] be open to attack under the equality clause. But the difficulty with most judicial pronouncements is that they will be specific to the facts of the case and will assert that the finding accords with the best-interest principle. Formal equality could more effectively be achieved by giving expression to the right of fathers to be custodians in legislation requiring an award of joint custody[211] unless the interests of the child demand a different order.

A dispensation like this would impose upon a parent seeking variation of the normal joint custody rule the onus of proving that it is inappropriate in the circumstances. Some may consider this solution to be unduly harsh on women, who are most often primary caretakers[212] of minor children and who would most often be seeking variation. It may well be argued that the court deciding custody should first ascertain which of the two parents is the primary caretaker and apply a presumption that that parent deserves custody unless the other can prove that a different order would better serve the interests of the children. The argument would be that the formal equality inherent in a joint custody dispensation entails actual inequality for women.[213] It is not without force. But by implication it sanctions the inequality now experienced by fathers because our society and the labour market are structured in such a way as almost inevitably to make mothers primary caretakers. Further, the inexorable delegation by society to women of parenting responsibilities is not a good thing for mothers, or fathers, or children.[214]

Not without diffidence it is suggested that equality of parental responsibility in the law is the correct message. It assumes that children have a fundamental right to preserve the strongest possible bond with both of their parents despite the breakdown of the parental relationship.[215] It would encourage equitable sharing of parental responsiblity, which would in turn conduce to the broader achievement of real equality for women. While the law continues to regard housework and childcare as women's work, men will remain free from these obligations and women will be denied equal opportunities to fulfil their potential to become financially independent

---

[210] Dealt with above in the introductory part of section 5 'The constitutional protection of sex and gender equality in South Africa'.

[211] The expresssion is not uniformly interpreted by judges or academics nor is there a definition that transcends national boundaries. Schafer op cit (n 207) 155–8 discusses the two components of joint custody — physical custody and legal custody. Joint custody need not entail the child's moving on a weekly or monthly basis from the one parent's home to the other's, as is often thought. In England, for example, joint custody implies shared legal custody, permitting both parents to participate in decisions about the child's future, while its permanent home is with one parent, the other having access. See also Schoeman op cit (n 209) 464.

[212] Discussed as an alternative criterion to the best-interests principle by Clark 'Custody: The Best Interests of the Child' (1992) 109 *SALJ* 391 at 395–6.

[213] I am indebted to Felicity Kaganas, of Brunel University, for sharing her views with me on this matter.

[214] The roles society allocates to women and to men need to be challenged, as was asserted in the first part of this chapter. To insist on preferential treatment in the law for mothers in this context could be a contributory factor in undermining efforts to change the way we are socialized. Men are impoverished by society's implicit demand that they not share the homemaking and parenting function. Children in turn are deprived by it of the opportunity to develop the bond with their fathers that they have more chance of developing with their mothers.

[215] In accordance with the fundamental right entrenched in s 30(1)(b) of the Constitution to parental care, not — it should be stressed — maternal care. Schafer's words are instructive, albeit that they may overstate the incidence of the sentiments they express: 'It has been amply demonstrated that children always maintain an intense desire to have contact with both their parents, and that a divorce does little to diminish this desire . . . Joint custody ensures a continuing relationship between the child and both its parents so that it need not feel . . . rejected by the absent parent. The result is that loyalty conflicts are largely eliminated' (op cit (n 207) 158). See also Schoeman op cit (n 209) 464.

of men and the state for their maintenance. Joint custody as the starting point would, moreover, be problematic only in pathological post-divorce situations. In the vast majority of cases the parents work out their own preferred solutions.[216] Doing so within the parameters of a rule granting them equal rights would be in keeping with the spirit of the Constitution and in line with developments in other countries. In the difficult matters it does not seem unfair, nor is there any obvious contradiction of the best-interest principle, to endow both parents with the same opportunity to be granted custody of their children and both with the same opportunity to contest the application of the rule.[217]

### 5.1.5 *African customary marriages and Muslim marriages*

Nearly all of what has been said above assumes a fully recognized civil marriage that complies with the formalities of the Marriage Act 25 of 1961 and is afforded the protective, adjustive, and supportive measures of the law. Two kinds of intimate relationships to which the full range of family laws has not been extended, but which are ubiquitous in South Africa, will be given brief attention here. They are African customary marriages and religious Muslim (and Hindu) marriages.

Both African customary marriages and those of Muslims (and Hindus) are potentially polygynous and for this reason are not regarded as valid by our law.[218] But there has been statutory recognition of customary marriages for limited purposes. For example, s 31 of the Black Laws Amendment Act 76 of 1963 entitles a widow of an African customary marriage to recover damages arising from the death of her breadwinner husband. Also the customary marriage was raised by the Marriage and Matrimonial Property Law Amendment Act 3 of 1988 to the status of an impediment to a civil marriage except between the partners to the customary marriage.[219]

These relationships, whether polygynous or not, create family units and questions arise about their recognition as valid marriages and the rights of the parties within them. The chapter on fundamental rights in the interim Constitution states, in the clause on religion, belief, and opinion,[220] that nothing in the chapter shall preclude *(a)* legislation recognizing a system of personal and family law adhered to by

---

[216] See Schafer op cit (n 207) 150.

[217] On the ground, for example, that one is manifestly the primary caretaker and that the other has no real interest in the child's welfare. The equal treatment in the law would conduce to the preservation of the child's bond with both parents. But there is of course the counter-argument that women are often in a weaker position than men, financially and because they are more risk-averse, to litigate to enforce their rights. As primary caretakers they would be the likely applicants for judicial interference with the norm. And this could prove harsh. There is no perfect choice. Patronizing women with special treatment as opposed to empowering them via increased access to the courts and sensitive judicial responses in appropriate cases may be the less harmful one for all concerned.

[218] Section 3 of the Marriage Act 25 of 1961 does make special provision for the appointment of priests of any Indian religion to be marriage officers. Provided that the marriage is solemnized in accordance with the Act by such a marriage officer it is recognized as a legal monogamous marriage. It is those marriages not solemnized in accordance with this dispensation that are in issue in this discussion.

[219] Section 1*(a)* and *(b)* of the Marriage and Matrimonial Property Law Amendment Act amends s 22(1) and (2) of the Black Administration Act 38 of 1927. The changes render a person who is a partner in a customary marriage incompetent to contract a civil marriage with any person other than the partner in the customary marriage. The definitions of 'marriage' and 'customary union' in s 35 of the Black Administration Act, however, reveal that the customary marriage is left in a twilight zone. While it is an impediment to a civil marriage, it is not fully recognized. Other examples of limited statutory recognition are to be found in s 27 of the Child Care Act 74 of 1983, in relation to adoption; s 4(3) of the Workmen's Compensation Act 30 of 1941; and s 21(13) of the Insolvency Act 24 of 1936.

[220] Section 14(3).

persons professing a particular religion, and *(b)* legislation recognizing the validity of marriages concluded under a system of religious law subject to specified procedures.

Precisely what this means is not clear, but undoubtedly the provision relates only to legislation, which at this stage does not exist. It seems that if legislation is passed recognizing, for example, the system of Muslim family law, it will be immune from attack under the Constitution even if aspects of the protected system violate fundamental rights by being unfairly discriminatory on the grounds of sex. African customary family law, on the other hand, is not a system adhered to by persons professing a *particular* religion. It may be argued that African custom is so deeply entrenched in the culture of Africans as to be for them 'religious' in character, but it surely cannot be said that African customary family law is connected to persons professing a particular religion. Some ardent adherents to it are Christians, others are not. The system of African customary family law therefore, even if it is expressly recognized in legislation, would not, it seems, be immune from attack. The inferior position of women within it is a major point at issue. Should Muslim women be denied the right of constitutional challenge that African women would retain in these circumstances?

The separate constitutional treatment of the narrower issue, the validity of marriages, may produce a different result. The provision lays down that legislation recognizing the validity of marriages concluded 'under a system of religious law', subject to specified procedures, is not precluded by anything in the chapter on fundamental rights. Potentially polygynous Muslim marriages would again clearly be covered. African customary law, although not adhered to by persons professing a particular religion, could nevertheless be argued to be a system of religious law on the basis alluded to above, namely that it is so fundamental to African culture as to take on a religious character. This interpretation would render legislation recognizing the validity of both Muslim and African customary marriages immune from attack, even were the Constitutional Court to pronounce, for example, that polygyny, fundamental to both kinds of marriages, is discriminatory against women. The equality clause is trumped by legislation under s 14.

The future of customary law is uncertain. By virtue of the amendment to s 126 and to Schedule Six of the Constitution, effected by s 2 of the Constitution of the Republic of South Africa Amendment Act 2 of 1994, matters of indigenous and customary law are placed within the special competence of provincial legislatures. Parliament retains its competence to make laws on these matters, but a law passed by a provincial legislature shall, subject to certain (very widely couched) exceptions, prevail over an Act of Parliament dealing with the same matter.[221] There is also evident in the Constitution an intention to preserve the institution of traditional leaders. Chapter 11 provides for a Council of Traditional Leaders to advise the national government on matters pertaining to traditional authorities, indigenous law and custom, or any matter of national interest. It also provides for a House of Traditional Leaders in each province to advise provincial legislatures on matters of

---

[221] Section 126(3) as amended. Section 126(4) provides further that an Act of Parliament shall prevail over provincial legislation, as provided for in the exceptional cases in s 126(3), only if it applies uniformly in all parts of South Africa. Section 184(5) clearly envisages that Parliament will legislate on matters pertaining to indigenous law and custom, but it must be read subject to the provisions of s 126(3).

indigenous law and custom, and for the recognition of existing traditional authorities exercising powers and functions in accordance with existing laws and customs. On the other hand, it is clear that neither the provincial legislatures nor Parliament will be bound by the views of the traditional leaders.[222]

Whereas the traditional leaders may be concerned to preserve aspects of indigenous law and custom even when they are not consistent with the fundamental rights enshrined in Chapter 3 of the Constitution, Parliament would probably not. The inclinations of different provincial legislatures will surely vary.[223] An area of great difficulty is that of equality for women. But among women themselves there is a high degree of dissension about the value of traditional custom that relegates them to a status of subordination to men.[224]

The interpretation of s 7 of the Constitution raises the additional difficulty that written customary law may be subject to the constraints of the Constitution, whereas unwritten customary law (applied by the courts) may not because it does not reside in legislation. This issue was dealt with in the introductory part of this section and will not be traversed again here.[225] But it is of great importance in determining the future of customary law.[226]

In what follows, some of the rules of African customary marriage and marriage by Muslim rites are adverted to to focus attention upon the options for pluralism or unification and to draw attention to conflicts with the constitutional right to equality.

---

[222] Sections 183(2) and 184(5) of the Constitution provide delaying mechanisms where there are objections from traditional leaders to proposed legislation.

[223] Customary law is not rendered immune from constitutional attack. In relation to previous drafts of the Constitution there were attempts by the traditional leaders inter alia to exempt customary law from the equality provision of the Constitution, which provoked considerable public debate (see Davis 'Two Clauses that Mar the Bill of Rights' *Weekly Mail & Guardian* 15–21 October 1993; Mureinik 'Customary Law is Faring Well' *The Star* 15 October 1993; Rantao 'The Forgotten Women' *Sunday Star* 5 December 1993; Nhlapo 'Throwing the Baby out with the Bathwater' Supplement to the *Weekly Mail & Guardian* December 1993). The complexity of the constitutional situation is enormous. The collapse of the boundaries of the 'independent' national states and the self-governing territories on 27 April and the coming into being of the new provinces produce a multiplicity of conflicting laws applying simultaneously in some of the provinces. Take, for example, the new province of Eastern Cape. Laws passed by the former Ciskei and Transkei Parliaments governing marriage, for example, which differ from each other and from national law, will remain in force in the areas formerly covered by those legislatures (s 229 of the Constitution). National law will apply in areas that were part of the old South Africa, but presumably not in the areas incorporated by the Constitution (that is, where s 229 applies — see above, 541ff, and below, n 271). There will therefore be three different sets of rules governing marriage in this one province. The internal conflict of laws problems do not bear thinking about. A solution to this problem must be found as soon as possible, and the problem is not confined to customary law. The interface between civil and customary marriages will be one of the most difficult issues to reslove.

[224] It was reported by Collinge 'Women Come out Fighting' *The Star* 23 February 1994 that the 700 delegates to the Community Land Conference in Bloemfontein were happy to support women's rights to own land and not to be discriminated against in the laws of inheritance, but were sharply divided on the question of polygyny and the rejection of the widow's obligation to marry her husband's brother (a reference to the levirate).

[225] It was urged that a broad interpretation of s 7 was the one to be preferred. A narrow coherence between s 7(1) and (2) would emasculate the Bill of Rights and compel the nearly impossible enterprise of determining which rules of customary law have been sufficiently imported into legislation to make them subject to judicial scrutiny by the Constitutional Court. (See also Rantao above, n 223.) To compound the difficulty there is also a difference between 'official customary law', i e customary law applied by the courts, and 'living' or 'non-official' customary law practised but not applied by the courts — see Bekker & Maithufi 'The Dichotomy between "Official Customary Law" and "Non-official Customary Law" ' (1992) 17 *TRW* 47.

[226] The term is not precise because customary law differs from one tribal group to another. However, there are elements common to most systems (see *Seymour's Customary Law in Southern Africa* 5 ed by J C Bekker (1989) xxxv). Codification of certain systems of customary law, moreover, has stultified its development. And there is an acknowledged wide gap between customary law crafted by professional lawyers and expressed in the textbooks, the case law, and the legislation, on one hand, and current African social practice, on the other. Customary law is seen by many to have been deeply alienated from its community origins (see Bennett 'The Compatibility of African Customary Law and Human Rights' in Bennett et al (eds) *African Customary Law* (1991) 18 at 18–19, 20 and 25 (also published as 1991 *Acta Juridica*); and Chanock 'Law, State and Culture: Thinking about "Customary Law" after Apartheid' in the same volume, 52 at 55–7).

### 5.1.5.1 Patriarchy

The extent to which African customary law is compatible with the notion of the fundamental right of equality that resides in the Constitution received considerable attention in a volume of essays entitled *African Customary Law*.[227] Several of the authors point to the patriarchal nature of customary law. It is stressed that 'human rights emphasize the individual while customary law emphasizes the group or community'.[228] And 'in patriarchal societies group interests are framed in favour of men'.[229] Although it is true that our civil law is also based on patriarchy, women have made substantial gains in achieving formal equality within that system. This is not true of African customary law, which remains more fundamentally premised on patriarchal notions that are largely unchallenged and highly controversial. T R Nhlapo's observation is that a marriage 'where men acquire rights over women and children but not vice versa, and where these rights are secured by the movement of cattle, has a direct bearing on the perpetual minority of women'.[230] He asks what it is about custom that is inimical to women's rights, and responds that it is 'everything that emanates from an attitude to women in marriage and in the family which sees them solely as adjuncts to the group . . . rather than as valuable in themselves and deserving of recognition for their human worth on the same terms as men'.[231]

The needs of the larger group, however, have changed. Procreation to ensure the survival of the group, for example, epitomized in the institution of the sororate and the levirate,[232] is seen nowadays in terms of population growth to inhibit economic progress. Other values too, which made sense in pre-colonial times, are 'dysfunctional in today's formal society'[233] and international system of capital. But with a deeper understanding of the nature, origin, and function of these customs it ought to be possible to salvage 'a usable residue' of 'Africanness' which will enhance the human rights ideal in family law.[234]

In relation to Muslim family law, also based on patriarchy and entailing deep inequalities for women, it is accepted that formal recognition of personal systems of law based on religious or cultural beliefs could create inconsistencies with guarantees of equality in the Constitution.[235]

### 5.1.5.2 Polygyny

African customary marriages and Muslim marriages have been refused recognition as valid marriages in our legal system on the argument that polygyny is 'reprobated

---

[227] Op cit (n 226).

[228] Bennett op cit (n 226) 18 at 23.

[229] Nhlapo 'The African Family and Women's Rights: Friends or Foes?' in Bennett et al op cit (n 226) 135 at 137, 144. Bennett *A Sourcebook of African Customary Law for Southern Africa* (1991) 301–11 explains that in sub-Saharan Africa male dominance is still the norm.

[230] Nhlapo op cit (n 229) at 138.

[231] Nhlapo op cit (n 229) 138–9.

[232] The former requiring a younger sister to take the place of a wife unable to produce children, the latter entitling the relative of a deceased to exploit the procreative capacities of the widow.

[233] Nhlapo op cit (n 229) 145.

[234] Nhlapo op cit (n 229) 141.

[235] See Cachalia 'Citizenship, Muslim Family Law and a Future South African Constitution' (1993) 56 *THRHR* 392 at 395; Moosa & Bosch 'Muslim Family Law Must meet the Changes' Supplement to the *Weekly Mail & Guardian* December 1993.

by the majority of civilized peoples, on the ground of morality and religion'.[236] In the case of *Ismail v Ismail*,[237] declaring invalid a religious Muslim marriage not celebrated in terms of the Marriage Act, the Appellate Division added that 'in view of the growing trend in favour of the recognition of complete equality between marriage partners, the recognition of polygamous unions . . . may even be regarded as a retrograde step'.[238]

The constitutional question now is whether polygyny is discriminatory against women and, if so, what to do about it. Albie Sachs,[239] discussing the recognition of Hindu and Muslim marriages and African customary marriages, considers a unitary system recognizing only one form of marriage rite and denouncing all others to be intolerant. He offers a softer solution — a single South African marriage law enabling various rites (in a church, a village, a homestead, the court, in whatever language) to constitute due solemnization of a fully recognized marriage that would enjoy all the supportive, adjustive, and protective measures of the law. But, interestingly, he requires that within such a dispensation the marriage officers of the various communities would have to satisfy themselves that the 'pre-requisites of a proper marriage were present', including monogamy.[240] The difficulty with the approach is that it would appear to leave outside the protection of family law persons who participate in the practice of polygyny. And even though the practice may be declining, to the extent that it remains part of the family system of some communities the formal legal rules make for 'paper law'.[241] The exclusivity of the legal system would ignore the victims inter alia of family breakdown.

The basis of Sachs' proposal is commendable — that polygyny is not compatible with the notion of sex equality in a democratic South Africa.[242] He appears to be correct. But his view is not undisputed and not without consequential problems.

Felicity Kaganas and Christina Murray[243] remark that within African customary law it is difficult to envisage a polygynous household in which the husband does not dominate. They consider it arguable that polygyny facilitates stereotyping and the objectification of women to a greater degree than monogamy does. Links are forged between groups through the exchange of women and cattle. Polygyny serves the purpose of increasing a man's labour force for the expansion of his agricultural

---

[236] *Seedat's Executors v The Master (Natal)* 1917 AD 302 at 307. The Appellate Division in *Ismail v Ismail* 1983 (1) SA 1006 (A) at 1026 added that it is 'contrary to the accepted customs and usages which are regarded as morally binding upon all members of our society'. The implicit exclusion of Africans and Muslims from 'society' invites criticism (see also Kerr (1984) 101 *SALJ* 445).

[237] Supra.

[238] At 1024. As Kaganas & Murray 'Law, Women and Family: The Question of Polygyny in a New South Africa' in Bennett et al op cit (n 226) 116 at 125 point out, the court appeared to be oblivious of the effect of its concern for the equality of women. The case arose out of a claim for maintenance by a woman married according to Muslim rites. The result of the court's finding that the marriage was invalid was to deprive her of a right to be supported by her husband.

[239] 'The Constitutional Position of the Family in a Democratic South Africa' in op cit (n 9) 64 at 72.

[240] Ibid. Sachs at 76 points to the 'universalization of certain family-law concepts, permitting a broad degree of freedom to pursue religious and cultural practices, but laying down certain common norms'. One of these is monogamy. See also Cachalia op cit (n 235) 396.

[241] See Bennett's statement that there is telling evidence suggesting that reforms affecting delicate matters like patriarchy 'are either ignored or actively combated' (op cit (n 226) 32). See the same author to the same effect at 34.

[242] See his statement op cit (n 240) in the piece 'Judges and Gender' 53 at 55 that 'in areas where polygamy [sic] still exists, monogamy enters the list of women's claims'.

[243] Op cit (n 238) 128.

holding and maximizes the possibility of numerous offspring, another important source of labour. The authors speculate that 'symbolically polygyny may have become so closely associated with the oppression of women that it could be seen as incompatible with a social order in which the liberation of women is a recognized goal'.[244] Yet they are concerned to identify the benefits to women of the system of multiple wives. It enables the sharing of domestic and farm work, provides companionship, reduces sexual demands made on each wife, facilitates the spacing of children, and may even promote independence through freeing wives to engage in economic activites and to join self-help groups.[245]

C R M Dlamini[246] defends polygyny much more strongly and explains the security it afforded to women in traditional rural societies. He considers polygyny in modern times as a possible compromise between a happy marriage and divorce (the high rate and ease of which in Western societies amounts to serial polygamy). He rejects the idea that polygyny is discriminatory against women and states that it is 'calculated to protect the woman who cannot find a single man to marry and is prepared to settle for a married man. The first wife, who may be aggrieved, is lucky still to have a husband, and may even be given the status of the great wife.'[247] Some of his arguments are unlikely to impress women wanting equality between the sexes.

These diverse views reveal that moral condemnation of one form of marriage in favour of another is unhelpful.[248] It becomes even more problematic when a party to a potentially polygynous marriage that has in fact been monogamous is denied the protection of the law. The circumstances of *Ismail's* case are in point here. Within the social and historical context, decisions about how the law should respond to polygyny need to be taken with great care. One obviously to be rejected would be allowing women to have more than one husband — in other words, permitting polygamy. Another might well be the outlawing of polygyny, for this would oust polygynous relationships from the protection of the law that they enjoy now. Customary wives in polygynous relationships are at present, for example, entitled to enforce a duty of support against their husbands during the subsistence of the marriage. And they can claim damages from a third party who deprives them of this source of support.[249] Severe prejudice would be occasioned to them if outright rejection of the system entailed that these remedies were removed.

Kaganas & Murray conclude that patriarchy rather than polygyny is the problem and that women need to challenge patriarchy to achieve equality. They caution against assuming that polygyny is the cause of oppression to women in customary marriages, although they recognize that within many polygynous marriages women do suffer oppression.[250] The question one wants to ask is whether a polygynous relationship could realistically be freed from its patriarchal bonds. While it is obvious that patriarchy can and does exist without polygyny, must not polygyny disappear for patriarchy to begin to be destroyed?

---

[244] Op cit (n 238) 129.
[245] Op cit (n 238) 130.
[246] 'The Role of Customary Law in Meeting Social Needs' in Bennett et al op cit (n 226) 71.
[247] Op cit (n 246) 77–8.
[248] See also Kaganas & Murray op cit (n 238) 132.
[249] The limited recognition of customary marriages is discussed below, 564, especially n 252.
[250] Op cit (n 238) 134.

In the event that the Constitutional Court is seized of a claim that polygyny discriminates against women the source of the offending notion might require identification.[251] Polygyny, as has been said above, is a fundamental unwritten notion underlying both African customary and Muslim marriages. But it finds legislative expression also in the Black Administration Act 38 of 1927. Section 22(1) of that Act, for example, lays down that a couple between whom a customary 'union' subsists may marry each other at civil law, provided that the man is not also a partner in a subsisting customary union with another woman.[252] Here is implicit recognition of the polygynous nature of the African customary marriage. No parallel legislative provision for Muslim marriages could be found.

On the assumption that polygyny does fall within the ambit of the Constitution and that it is found to be discriminatory, what should the Court do? Simply to declare that polygyny is inconsistent with the Constitution and therefore outlawed[253] would create undue confusion. It is submitted that the only feasible option in these circumstances would be to invoke the proviso in s 98(5) of the Constitution to order that legislation be passed within a specified period prohibiting polygyny prospectively; preserving the existing rights of women and children involved in polygynous unions; and fully recognizing customary marriages and Muslim (or Hindu) marriages celebrated in specified circumstances after the reforming legislation.

This 'solution' will not be without its problems. First, attention is drawn again to the fact that in those communities in which polygyny remains fundamental and is still practised it would probably continue whatever the law may dictate. The effect of the court's intervention may simply be to remove from the law's consciousness (and limited protection) those who participate (some more truly out of free choice than others) in polygyny. The law's message to women would be that they indulge in this prejudicial practice at their peril. That message may or may not serve in the future to deter them.

Another point that may be raised in objection is that the current refusal of the legal system fully to recognize African customary and Muslim (and Hindu) marriages because of their polygynous nature amounts to unfair discrimination based on culture in the first instance and religion in the second.[254] Section 8(2) of the Constitution expressly prohibits both. The fact that the civil law of marriage is available to Africans and Muslims, as it is not, by contrast, to gay or lesbian

---

[251] The difficulty of interpreting s 7 of the Constitution was raised at the beginning of this section. It is not entirely clear that the Bill of Rights applies to unwritten customary law.

[252] This raises the customary marriage to the status of an impediment to a civil marriage except between the partners to the customary marriage. Section 22 of the Act regulates the civil marriages of Africans and the interface between civil marriage and customary marriage. To avoid competing interests of a customary wife and the wife of a civil marriage the provision goes on to prohibit a marriage officer from solemnizing the marriage of an African man until he has taken from him a declaration that he is not a partner in a customary union with any woman other than the one he intends marrying (s 22(3)). Prior to the amendment of s 22 by the Marriage and Matrimonial Property Law Amendment Act 3 of 1988 it was possible for a man married at customary law to take a different civil-law wife. The customary marriage was automatically dissolved by the civil marriage, but the material rights of the customary wife and her chidren were protected by s 22(7), which stipulates that these rights shall in no way be affected by the civil marriage and that the widow and children of the civil marriage shall have no greater rights in respect of the estate of the husband than they would have had had the civil marriage been a customary 'union'. Since there are still many situations of this kind, caused by civil marriages celebrated prior to the elevation of customary marriages to the status of an impediment, s 22(7) remains on the statute book.

[253] See s 4(1) of the Constitution.

[254] The refusal of our legal system to reecognize Muslim marriages has long since been a cause of grievance in the Muslim community — see Cachalia op cit (n 235) 398.

couples,[255] may not be a sufficient answer to such objection. Insistence on the monogamy that forms part of our common-law definition of marriage as 'the legally recognized union for life of one man and one woman, to the exclusion of all others while it lasts'[256] may infringe the culture and religion grounds in s 8. In this situation the court would be faced with a conflict between protecting equality on the ground of sex, which, on the assumption outlined above, would require it to strike down polygyny, and preventing discrimination based on culture and religion. It is submitted that here the court should choose to protect sex equality at the expense of culture and religion. The reason is that s 14(3) expressly provides the legislature with the opportunity to insulate from attack under the equality clause family law systems adhered to by persons professing a particular religion and the validity of marriages concluded under a system of religious law.[257] Until it exercises that legislative prerogative to trump sex equality, sex equality should prevail. Indeed if the opposite answer, namely one protecting culture and religion over sex equality under s 8, were the correct one to resolve the conflict, there would have been no need for s 14(3).

### 5.1.5.3 *Lobolo*

The institution of bridewealth (known variously as *lobolo, lobola, bohadi*) is a contract between the groom and the bride's father in terms of which, traditionally, cattle was delivered to the bride's father in consideration of the transfer of the woman and her reproductive capacity from the father's family to that of the husband. One of the major purposes of *lobolo* was to provide security for the woman if the marriage ended through no fault of hers. It remains an essential element of a valid customary marriage in many uncodified systems of African customary law[258] and is not an uncommon accompaniment to the civil marriages of Africans. Section 11(1) of the Black Administration Act 38 of 1927 lays down that it shall not be lawful for any court to declare that the custom of *lobolo* is repugnant to public policy. Bridewealth is thus a protected institution. But it has not been subjected to constitutional scrutiny against a Bill of Rights demanding equality before the law and outlawing unfair discrimination.

Objections to the payment of bridewealth are frequently heard by feminists.[259] They take the form that the payment of *lobolo* treats women as property,[260] objectifies them, commercializes marriage,[261] and has been corrupted.[262]

---

[255] Gay and lesbian marriages are entirely prohibited. It seems that our common-law definition of marriage, insisting as it does on heterosexuality, unfairly discriminates against persons on the ground of their sexual orientation — also expressly prohibited by s 8. To say to homosexuals that their incapacity is relative — they can marry, but they must marry a person of the opposite sex — is unlikely in my view to be a good enough answer.

[256] 'Marriage' is statutorily defined in s 35 of the Black Administration Act as 'the union of one man with one woman in accordance with any law for the time being in force in any Province governing marriages, but does not include any union contracted under Black law and custom . . .'.

[257] It was said earlier in this section in relation to this clause that customary law may be so fundamental to Africans that it takes on a religious character and may be regarded as a system of religious law.

[258] Cf s 38 of the KwaZulu Act on the Code of Zulu Law 16 of 1985 and s 38 of the Natal Code of Zulu Law (Proc R151 *GG* 10966 of 9 October 1987).

[259] A muted objection to the fact that men have to pay *lobolo* while women get their husbands for nothing comes from Dlamini op cit (n 246) 71 at 79.

[260] Place 'Women and Children in Southern Africa: An Introduction' in *Women and Children at Risk in Southern Africa* (Conference Proceedings Boston (1990)) 9.

[261] Sachs op cit (n 239) 71.

[262] Stella Sigcau, as reported by Graham 'Women's Struggle Still Far From Over' *The Star* 7 December 1993.

J M T Labuschagne[263] traces the history and functions of *lobolo* and points out that many of them are still of importance. *Lobolo* serves to validate the marriage, to join the two families, to stabilize the marriage, to protect the wife against maltreatment by her husband. But this author, outside the context of the constitutional debate, concludes that the societal expectation of autonomy for women will be the one factor most likely to lead to the disappearance of *lobolo*.[264] T W Bennett, discussing the historical significance of *lobolo*, states that 'even a superficial knowledge of customary marriage would show that the wife is neither a slave nor a chattel'.[265] He traces the various anthropological theories explaining *lobolo* and finds it surprising that the institution has survived the onslaught of missionaries, colonial governments, and courts.[266] But he concludes that customary marriage has become commericalized and that there is justification for the claim that bridewealth contributes to the subordination of women.[267] He goes on to say that the institution is now dysfunctional, having none of the benefits previously claimed for it.

> 'Because it is now paid in cash, bridewealth is dissipated to defray day-to-day expenses instead of being kept as financial security for the divorced or widowed wife. The entire institution of marriage is said to be undermined: men cannot afford to pay the sums asked of them, so they enter into informal unions, which condemns their offspring to a status of illegitimacy. In a community which is already desperately poor, the continued practice of bridewealth seems irrational and self-destructive.'[268]

Sandra Burman,[269] on the other hand, sees possibilities for the updating of the institution so that it might serve its original purpose of providing a safety net for the woman and her children. She advocates the investigation of the acceptability to the community of a 'Bridewealth Fund', something akin to a Retirement Annuity Fund.[270]

### 5.1.5.4 Legal capacity

Of all the features of customary law that subordinate women, this one appears to be the most objectionable. Section 11(3) of the Black Administration Act 38 of 1927 provides that African customary wives, except those living in Natal, are deemed to be minors and are subject to the guardianship of their husbands.[271] Section 11A,

---

[263] 'Regsakkulturasie, *Lobolo*-funksies en die Oorsprong van die Huwelik' (1991) 54 *THRHR* 541.
[264] At 553.
[265] Bennett op cit (n 229) 196.
[266] At 201.
[267] Ibid.
[268] At 202. Cf Dlamini op cit (n 246) 79, who argues that to abolish *lobolo* would be dysfunctional; that the insitutiton serves to express the views and convictions of black society on what characterizes a valid marriage; and that black women do not regard it as an affront to their dignity.
[269] 'Capitalizing on African Strengths: Women, Welfare and the Law' (1991) 7 *SAJHR* 215.
[270] At 220–1.
[271] The exclusion from this disability of women in Natal was brought about by s 1 of the Laws on Co-operation and Development Amendment Act 91 of 1985. Section 11(3) of the Black Administration Act was made inapplicable in KwaZulu as from the enactment of the KwaZulu Act on the Code of Zulu Law 6 of 1981 (now superseded by Act 16 of 1985). The KwaZulu and Natal codes (see above, n 258) state that every black person 'shall be either a family head or an inmate subject to the family head in all family matters' (s 12); and that 'a Black shall become a major in law on marriage or on attaining the age of twenty-one years' (s 14). Yet s 27(3) of both codes states that a married woman shall be under the marital power of her husband, provided that the marital power can be excluded by antenuptial contract in a marriage out of community. Section 27 deals with other rules of the civil law pertaining to guardianship of legitimate and illegitimate children, and the impression is thus created that subsec (3) deals only with African marriages celebrated in terms of the civil law. The question is whether women in Natal and KwaZulu

however, exempts women from customary law for certain purposes related to leasehold, sectional title, and ownership of immovable property.[272] An African wife has only limited capacity to own property and limited *locus standi in judicio*.[273] What she earns becomes the property of her house and thus subject to the control of her husband. The marital power of the husband in customary law is described as 'vast' by Nhlapo.[274] The author explains that the husband has the final say in matters concerning both the person and property of his wife. He can dictate what she should wear, with whom she may associate, and whether she may seek employment or consult a doctor. In some systems the marital power even includes the right to administer corporal punishment.

This constellation of rules governing status and capacity, some written into legislation and some not,[275] clearly conflict with the right to sex equality contained in the Bill of Rights. Certain African leaders point out that the notion of equality for women is 'foreign to African culture'.[276] But Nhlapo concludes that, although it may take time, it should be possible to de-emphasize aspects of African tradition that are incompatible with the attainment of human rights and yet to retain those aspects that genuinely conduce to the welfare of all.[277]

---

married at customary law have been freed from s 11(3)(b) and the guardianship of their husbands only to become subject to their marital power. If s 27(3) applies only to civil marriages and has no bearing on customary marriages (and this is possible in KwaZulu because that self-governing state was given power to regulate civil and customary marriages), the odd result is that in KwaZulu African women who marry at civil law and whose antenuptial contracts do not exclude the marital power are in a worse position than women married at customary law. They have only limited capacity to contract and no *locus standi in judicio*, whereas the customary wife is treated as a major in law. The position in Natal is that s 27 of the Natal Code states the civil law of South Africa as it was in 1987, when the code was promulgated. The difficulty is that it has not apparently been updated to incorporate the changes introduced by the Marriage and Matrimonial Property Law Amendment Act 3 of 1988, which abolished the marital power prospectively from African civil marriages. Nor does it reflect the eradication of the marital power from the South African civil law of marriage by the General Law Fourth Amendment Act 132 of 1993. Its only application, as it stands, could be to customary marriages, for the Natal Code cannot compete with the civil law. (The fact that there is no comparable section in the Natal Code to s 35 of the KwaZulu Code lends credence to the fact that the Natal Code intended only to regulate customary law. Section 35 of the KwaZulu Code regulates the consequences of a civil marrige in KwaZulu. Section 22(6) of the Black Administration Act 38 of 1927, prior to its repeal in 1988, regulated the consequences of the civil marriages of Africans in the old South Africa.) No such uncertainties arise in relation to the Marriage Act of Transkei (Act 21 of 1978). That Act makes it clear that in both civil and customary marriages a woman is subject to the guardianship of her husband (s 37) and that no antenuptial contract can affect the marital power of the male party to a marriage (s 39). These provisions cannot be reconciled with the South African civil law or the right of women to full legal status and equality enshrined in the Bill of Rights. The position is inordinately complex because the collapse of the boundaries of the 'independent' states and the self-governing territories on 27 April produces a national territory and provinces with legislative power to regulate customary and indigenous law. The province of Eastern Cape, as described in Schedule 1 of the Constitution, consists of Transkei, Ciskei, and parts of the old South Africa. In each of these areas different laws govern the status of African women, married at civil and at customary law. Such laws will remain in force in those areas until they are altered (s 229 of the Constitution). Imagine the internal conflict of laws problems within this province (used merely to illustrate a ubiquitous problem), to say nothing of those that will arise between the provinces. Unifying legislation to enable people to know what rules govern their marriages is urgently required — see above, n 223.

[272] The provision was first inserted in 1985 to enable financial institutions to provide finance to African women to acquire homes. It is couched in wide terms and, in respect of the acquisition of ownership, there is no express limitation to immovable property. But the intention of the legislature was clearly to provide for the circumstances referred to here.

[273] The position is different in KwaZulu. In terms of s 13 of the Natal and KwaZulu Codes of Zulu Law, any black person may acquire movable or immovable property. The Law Commission, in its *Project 51: Marriages and Customary Unions of Black Persons* (1986), recommended that black women be given full capacity to own property in their own names; that their husbands be prevented from dealing with the property without their consent; and that they have full *locus standi in judicio* (para 11.2.5.4 and clause 5 of the draft Customary Law Amendment Bill, contained in the report). But its recommendations have not been implemented.

[274] 'International Protection of Human Rights and the Family: African Variations on a Common Theme' (1989) 3 *Int J of L and the Family* 1 at 16.

[275] And thus the subject of the controversy about the reach of the Bill of Rights.

[276] See Nhlapo op cit (n 274) at 5.

[277] Op cit (n 274) at 18; and see the same author op cit (n 229) 146, where he calls for the discovery of ways to ensure that cherished African values are not expressed in a form that 'depersonalizes' women.

Muslim family law knows no concept that deprives a married woman of capacity to own property, to conclude contracts, or to litigate without her husband's consent. 'The Roman Dutch concept of the marital power is completely alien to Islamic law.'[278]

### 5.1.5.5 Dissolution of marriage

Unilateral repudiation by a husband of his wife is a feature of African customary and Muslim marriage. In the latter it is known as *talaq*.[279] In the former the issue of the return of bridewealth is fundamental to the dissolution of marriage and, unless the husband acts with good cause, he is required to forfeit what he has paid.[280] The wife has no power to end her marriage. She is dependent on the guardian who received the *lobolo* to negotiate the divorce on her behalf.[281] In both systems a husband is obliged to support his wife during the marriage. Section 5(6) of the Maintenance Act 23 of 1963 deems a black male to be the husband of a woman associated with him in a customary union and thus legally liable to maintain that woman. On dissolution of a civil marriage by divorce the spousal duty of support ends unless the court orders in terms of s 7 of the Divorce Act 70 of 1979 that it should continue. A Muslim husband is required to render support to his wife for three months after divorce. The issue of post-dissolution maintenance in African customary law does not arise, for it is assumed that the woman will return to her guardian's home.[282]

There is no provision in either system for the division of property on divorce, as there is in terms of the civil law. Section 7 of the Divorce Act provides for a judicial discretion to divide property on divorce in certain types of civil marriages,[283] and in terms of the matrimonial property systems of community and the accrual system sharing of property between spouses occurs. Muslim religious marriages are automatically out of community of property and no obligation to share arises.[284] An African woman married at customary law has limited capacity to own property and no right to any part of the matrimonial estate on dissolution by divorce.[285]

The different treatment of these women gives rise to concern. And it should not be overlooked that even those to whom the Divorce Act and the law of matrimonial property apply frequently experience grave financial hardship after the termination of their marriages. It is not clear that the solution lies in applying to them the rules of the civil law. One problem would be compliance, which the woman in need is in no position to compel; another would be the futility of maintenance orders and division of property for people whose poverty cannot be solved within the private

---

[278] Cachalia op cit (n 235) 401.

[279] Cachalia op cit (n 235) at 401–2; *Ismail v Ismail* (supra) at 1024.

[280] In terms of the KwaZulu and Natal Codes (see above, n 258) a customary marriage can be dissolved only by order of a competent court (s 36(1)) on grounds based squarely on the fault principle (s 48), but acknowledging also irretrievable breakdown of the marriage.

[281] Bennett op cit (n 229) 255; Kaganas & Murray op cit (n 238) 130.

[282] See, for example, Bennett op cit (n 226) 26n66; Bennett op cit (n 229) 275, 277; Kaganas & Murray op cit (n 238) 123.

[283] Discussed above, n 181.

[284] Cachalia op cit (n 235) 401.

[285] Bennett op cit (n 226) 26 and n 66.

law of the family. Without the intervention of the state to cushion the effect of failed marriages of whatever kind, divorced women and their children will remain at risk.

Dissolution of African customary and Muslim marriages by death raises a number of issues, including the dependant's action in cases where the husband's death is caused by a third party and the vexed question of succession.

While the death of an African wife dissolves her marriage, the death of the husband does not; his wife falls under the guardianship and protection of her husband's heir.[286] That person may be the woman's son or some other male relative of the husband. Prior to legislative intervention a widow had no action against a third party responsible for the death of her husband because her right to be supported was not lost and because the customary marriage, potentially polygynous, is not recognized as a marriage.[287] Section 31 of the Black Laws Amendment Act 76 of 1963 created a cause of action for widows in this situation, thereby recognizing for this limited purpose the African customary marriage.[288] There is no comparable right for widows of Muslim (or Hindu) marriages and no rationale for excluding them from this protection.

Testamentary succession is unknown in African customary law, while the law of Islam dictates that a testator can bequeath no more than one-third of the estate to persons other than the heirs prescribed by the *Quran*.[289]

The customary law of succession is governed by the principle of primogeniture in the male line. Regulation 2 of the Regulations for the Administration and Distribution of the Estates of Deceased Blacks[290] provides that the estate of a deceased black on intestacy devolves according to black law and custom. Ordinarily this would result in the estate's devolving upon the eldest son of the first or great customary wife (which leaves the customary wives themselves at risk[291] and has often created a disastrous situation for the civil-law wife). The competing interests of customary wives and their children, and a civil-law wife and hers, will become a relic of the past as a result of the prohibition on civil marriage during the subsistence of a customary marriage, except between the partners to the customary marriage, introduced by s 1 of the Marriage and Matrimonial Property Law Amendment Act 3 of 1988.[292]

A Muslim wife has an entrenched right to inherit from her husband. If there are

---

[286] In certain systems, where the death of the wife deprives the husband of her full reproductive potential, the institution of sororate requires a younger sister to take her place. The levirate, on the other hand, entitles a relative of a deceased husband to exploit the procreative capacity of the widow. The survival of these institutions under the Constitution is clearly doubtful. In KwaZulu and Natal the respective Codes provide that a marriage is dissolved by the death of either party (s 36(1)). In the uncodified systems the marriage between the widow and her husband's heir may be dissolved in much the same way as the marriage between the original parties.

[287] *SANTAM Bpk v Fondo* 1960 (2) SA 467 (A).

[288] *Pasela v Rondalia Versekeringskorporasie van Suid-Afrika Bpk* 1967 (1) SA 339 (W). There are serious difficulties of compliance with the technical aspects of s 31, especially the requirement of the certificate confirming the marriage (s 31(2)) — see for example Paterson 'Is there still a Difference Between a Common-law Marriage and a Customary Union?' (1992) 109 *SALJ* 18).

[289] Cachalia op cit (n 235) 402n76. In *Davids v The Master* 1983 (1) SA 458 (C) it was held that 'spouse' in s 49(1) of the Administration of Estates Act 66 of 1965 did not include a woman married according to Muslim rites.

[290] R200 *GG* 10601 of 6 February 1987.

[291] See Bennett 'The Conflict of Personal Laws: Wills and Intestate Succession' (1993) 56 *THRHR* 50 at 53.

[292] Which amended s 22 of the Black Administration Act 38 of 1927. But it should not be forgotten that this legislation was enacted for the old South Africa and was not made to apply in all the 'independent' states and self-governing territories. On the protection of the material rights of the widow and children of a customary marriage against the claims of the civil-law wife and her children, by s 22(7), see above, n 252.

no children of the marriage, she is entitled to one-quarter of the estate; if there are children, she receives one-eighth.[293]

A question that requires attention is whether the provisions of the Maintenance of Suriviving Spouses Act 27 of 1990 apply to the customary marriages of Africans and Muslim (and Hindu) marriages. After a long struggle by academics this legislation afforded to a surviving spouse the right to claim maintenance out of the estate of the deceased spouse.[294] The Act stipulates that where a 'marriage' is dissolved by death after the commencement of the Act the surviving spouse has a claim for maintenance in so far as he or she cannot provide for himself or herself.[295] On the basis of the meaning of 'marriage' in the civil law it seems that only civil-law marriages are covered by the Act. But s 5(6) of the Maintenance Act 23 of 1963 deems a black male to be the husband of a woman associated with him in a customary union for the purposes of determining whether he is a person legally liable to maintain. On the basis of this provision it has been asserted that the widow of a customary marriage may invoke the provisions of the 1990 Act.[296] The connection seems tenuous,[297] but the question of the applicability of this legislation to surviving spouses in African and Muslim (and Hindu) marriages is an important one. It would be desirable for the Act to apply in all cases.

### 5.1.5.6 The law of evidence

In this field the non-recognition of potentially polygynous marriages produces unfortunate results for both spouses. Since the passing of the Law of Evidence Amendment Act 45 of 1988 a spouse in a civil marriage is a competent, but not a compellable, witness in a criminal prosecution against the other.[298] It seems odd that, in the face of several instances of legislative recognition of the African customary marriage for specified purposes,[299] the non-compellability rule does not extend to these spouses. Indeed, avoiding any uncertainty, the Criminal Procedure Act deems spouses in these marriages to be unmarried.[300] In *S v Vengetsamy*[301] non-compellability was extended to a Hindu marriage not legally recognized, but the correctness of this decision is doubted.[302]

---

[293] Cachalia op cit (n 235) 403.

[294] The celebrated case which denied a widow the right to support out of her deceased husband's estate is *Glazer v Glazer NO* 1963 (4) SA 694 (A).

[295] Section 2(1).

[296] By Van Heerden 'Onderhoudsverpligtinge Voortspruitend uit 'n Gebruiklike Huwelik' (1993) 56 *THRHR* 670 at 673.

[297] The obstacle is the meaning of 'marriage', which the author does not address. But for an argument that s 5(6) imports the customary-law duty of support into the civil law and thus grounds a dependant's action at the instance of an African customary widow, without the need to resort to s 31 of the Black Laws Amendment Act 76 of 1963, see Paterson op cit (n 288) 20–1. On this kind of reasoning it may be arguable that an African widow of a customary marriage is also a surviving spouse entitled to claim maintenance. (Section 2(1) of the 1990 Act speaks of a 'survivor', defined in s 1 as 'the surviving spouse in a marriage'.) Clearly the widows of Muslim (and Hindu) marriages are not covered. Bennett's view (op cit (n 291) 63) is that the Maintenance of Surviving Spouses Act does not apply to African customary marriages.

[298] Section 6 of the Law of Evidence Amendment Act 45 of 1988 amended s 195 of the Criminal Procedure Act 51 of 1977. Prior to 1988 the spouse was neither competent nor compellable. There are exceptional cases where the spouse of an accused is both competent and compellable to give evidence for the prosecution (s 195(1)).

[299] See above, n 219.

[300] Section 195(2).

[301] 1972 (4) SA 351 (D).

[302] By Hoffmann & Zeffertt *The South African Law of Evidence* 4 ed (1988) 386; Van Niekerk, Van der Merwe, Van Wyk & Barton *Privilegies in die Bewysreg* (1984) 190; Isaacs 1972 *Annual Survey of South African Law* 389. See also *S v Johardien* 1990 (1) SA 1026 (C), in which *Vengetsamy* was not approved and not followed.

In civil as well as in criminal proceedings one spouse cannot be compelled to disclose communications made to him or her by the other spouse during the marriage.[303] Although this privilege applies also to marital communications made during the subsistence of a putative marriage,[304] it does not apply to spouses in a customary marriage. And it was held in *S v Johardien*[305] that the privilege does not apply to a marriage by Muslim rites.

The constitutional challenge looming here is that the refusal to extend to African customary and Muslim (and Hindu) spouses the same protection of their relationship that is extended to persons married at civil law amounts to unfair discrimination on the ground of culture and religion, respectively.

## 6 MONITORING EQUALITY THROUGH THE GENDER COMMISSION

Having decided expressly to recognize the difference between sex and gender in the equality clause[306] by enumerating both as grounds upon which it is impermissible to discriminate unfairly against any person, the drafters of the Constitution abandoned the distinction in ss 119 and 120, which are the provisions creating the 'Commission on Gender Equality'. Curiously this omission creates another distinction, and one that we should hope is without a difference. It is the distinction between human rights and gender equality. We must surely assume that sex equality is too closely linked to gender equality not to be covered by the aims of the Commission on Gender Equality. It would be absurd if the matter of sex equality had to be the prerogative of the Human Rights Commission, also to be set up in terms of the Constitution,[307] and that of gender equality confined to its own special Commission. But it may be worse if both sex and gender equality are to be excluded from the ambit of the Human Rights Commission.

The Commission on Gender Equality is to be created by Act of Parliament in order to promote gender equality and to advise and make recommendations to Parliament or any other legislature on laws affecting gender equality and the status of women. In what way is this Commission's purpose supposed to differ from that of the Human Rights Commission?[308] Will women, undeniably human, be able to resort to the commission of their choice to raise their complaints about violations of fundamental rights? Was it wise to provide specially and separately for issues of gender (and sex), or are we falling into the trap of marginalizing discrimination against women so that men, concerned with human rights, can safely ignore more than half of the population, immune from criticism? Feminists need to think long and hard about their long-term goals.

---

[303] Sections 10(1) and 12 of the Civil Proceedings Evidence Act 25 of 1965; ss 198 and 199 of the Criminal Procedure Act 51 of 1977.
[304] Section 10(2) of the Civil Proceedings Evidence Act 25 of 1965; s 198(2) of the Criminal Procedure Act 51 of 1977.
[305] Supra.
[306] Section 8.
[307] See ss 115–118.
[308] The sections providing for the Human Rights Commission are much more detailed and elaborate than the provisions for the Gender Commission. The Human Rights Commission will be obliged to report at least annually to the President. Does one detect an air of greater seriousness about human rights than about gender (read women's) rights?

This chapter attempts to demonstrate that the work of any Commission concerned with fundamental rights will entail, inter alia, a thorough investigation of many of the rules that govern intimate relationships. Equality between men and women in their public lives is inextricably linked to the power relations that the law creates for them in their homes and within their families. And the complex combination of sex and race defies separation. The diversity of South Africa's peoples presents unique challenges in this regard and the emotive nature of the enterprise of regulating intimate relationships will test the metal of the men and women who are to be charged with this important responsibility. For the liberation of our country from oppression to be the victory we all seek, sex and gender will have to receive the same attention that race must receive. Racial equality without equality for women will render that victory incomplete and the slogan 'human rights for all' a hollow call.

# CULTURE, EDUCATION, AND RELIGION

### CHARLES DLAMINI

## 1 INTRODUCTION

South Africa is a country characterized by cultural and religious diversity. For this reason it has been described as a 'multi-lingual, multi-faith, multi-cultural, and multi-political' country.[1] The kaleidoscopic panorama of cultures, religions, and languages is both a strength and a weakness. While this cultural and religious pluralism adds to the colourfulness of the country, to enable these cultures, religions, and languages to coexist harmoniously in one geographical territory is not an easy task. The reason for this is that these cultures and religions often clash. Although the differences may not be too great, people tend to exaggerate and accentuate the differences in order to justify preferential treatment for their own particular group. There is a streak in human nature which makes people feel better than others upon whom they look down. Differences in culture may provide such a pretext. Because culture and religion are closely connected with emotions people are extremely sensitive to the way these are treated by outsiders. This brings about an element of rivalry and tension.

With the history of racism and discrimination in this country it is obvious that the cultures and religions of those who have suffered past discrimination are often vulnerable largely because one of the perennial problems is that one group will often regard itself and its culture and religion as superior to those of the other groups. This provides a source of endless conflict.

Culture, education, and religion are interwoven. Religion is part of the culture of a people. Education is the instrument through which both culture and religion are transmitted from one generation to another and that is why these should be dealt with together. Culture is often difficult to define. It may be defined in a narrow or a broad sense. In the narrow sense it refers to a situation where a person has attained a high degree of intellectual, moral, and artistic development so as to be regarded as a 'cultured' person.[2] In a broader sense culture denotes all those practices, institutions, and beliefs of a group of people which uniquely identify the group. These are adopted as a means of survival or for purposes of enriching life. Malinowski defines culture as that complex whole, which includes knowledge, belief, art, law, morals, customs, and all other capabilities and habits, acquired by man as a member of society.[3] Religion entails the norms that regulate the relationship

---

[1] Sachs 'A Bill of Rights for South Africa: Areas of Agreement and Disagreement' (1989) 21 *Columbia Human Rights LR* 13; Sachs *Protecting Human Rights in a New South Africa* (1990) 23.
[2] Robertson *Human Rights for South Africans* (1991) 197.
[3] Malinowski *The Dynamics of Culture Change* 5 imp (1958) 1.

between human beings and their creator or deity and between members of the community.

From this it is clear that culture, religion, and education are regarded as fundamental to human existence. One of the reasons for the idea of human rights is to protect those values which are fundamental to human existence from interference by the state. It is to ensure that the law keeps in touch with those values and interests and protects them instead of violating them. In this regard the law is not an end in itself, but a means to an end. Its end is human welfare and development.[4] If culture and religion are fundamental to human existence, it means that there can be no human welfare and development if culture and religion are adversely affected by legal norms. Legal positivism, which separates law and morality, has on occasion been responsible for the denial of this truth — with disastrous consequences.[5] This has led to the realization that there are certain values which should be protected from easy violation or change.

Culture and education belong to the category of economic, social, and cultural rights, or second-generation rights. Second-generation rights are somewhat problematic because, unlike first-generation rights, which are largely negative in nature, they are positive and impose obligations on the government to use resources to provide for the basic needs of the people. This distinction between these two categories of rights has come under heavy criticism as being inaccurate. The argument is that the distinction is not that first-generation rights are costless and second-generation rights are costly because the realization of first-generation rights does involve cost. A better approach is not to emphasize this distinction. For this reason both first- and second-generation rights need to be respected and to be protected in the Constitution. Although second-generation rights are more difficult to realize and may not be easily justiciable, they are not impossible to realize.[6] Their realization is more a question of political will than of law.[7] Notwithstanding these arguments, certain second-generation rights involve more costs in their realization and may therefore be more difficult to realize than first-generation rights.[8]

## 2 CULTURE

### 2.1 Introduction

If culture is essential to human existence, then individuals have a right to culture. The right to culture is aimed at preventing people from being treated unequally on account of their culture. It is possible to pay lip-service to non-discrimination and yet to discriminate against certain groups by treating their culture unfavourably.

---

[4] Hahlo & Kahn *The South African Legal System and Its Background* (1968) 26; Cardozo *The Nature of the Judicial Process* (1921) 66.

[5] For a discussion of this aspect, see Hart *The Concept of Law* (1961) 151ff; Hart 'Positivism and the Separation of Law and Morals' (1958) 71 *Harvard LR* 593; cf Forsyth & Schiller 'The Judicial Process, Positivism and Civil Liberty' (1981) 98 *SALJ* 218ff.

[6] For a discussion of this subject, see Haysom 'Constitutionalism, Majoritarian Democracy and Socio-economic Rights' (1992) 8 *SAJHR* 451ff; Mureinik 'Beyond a Charter of Luxuries: Economic Rights in the Constitution' (1992) 8 *SAJHR* 464ff; see also Beddard & Hill (eds) *Economic, Social and Cultural Rights: Progress and Achievement* (1992).

[7] Hill 'Rights and their Realisation' in Beddard & Hill op cit (n 6) 10.

[8] Davis 'The Case Against the Inclusion of Socio-economic Demands in a Bill of Rights Except as Directive Principles' (1992) 8 *SAJHR* 475ff.

Culture is, however, not static but variable. It changes as a result of a number of factors. Cultures also influence each other, especially if they coexist in one geographical unit. This influence may not be easily perceptible, but it is none the less there. Although it has been said that culture is indispensable to human existence, this is not always so. Some cultural practices may be objectionable to outsiders for a variety of reasons. They may be harmful to health and hygiene or may be discriminatory.[9] Whether or not a cultural practice is objectionable on the ground that it is injurious should not be determined arbitrarily or subjectively, but in accordance with universal human rights norms in order to avoid bias or unfairness in judging it. Invidious discriminatory cultural practices should not be condoned and should not override human rights norms on the basis of cultural relativism. Apparently discriminatory practices may, however, be justified on the grounds of consent.[10]

In the past there was a belief that there was one predetermined direction for cultural development. This facilitated cultural assimilation or integration. Today, however, this is perceived as cultural imperialism. In general no culture is superior to another. This realization has allowed greater cultural diversity. Implicit in this is that all cultures must be respected. This further prevents one culture from dominating others. The right to culture entails the right to be different.

Cultural diversity requires cultural tolerance if there is to be mutual and peaceful coexistence. Cultural tolerance depends on the understanding of the cultures of others. Such understanding may be slow in forthcoming and may be realized only after much harm has been done. Conflict often emanates from cultural intolerance, which often stems from lack of understanding of the cultures of others. History has amply demonstrated this. In order to circumvent this cultural intolerance and consequent conflict various international and regional instruments have provided for the protection of the right to culture. A brief discussion of these is apposite. These instruments are no doubt based on the experiences of various countries and peoples.

## 2.2 Comparative international situation

One of the earliest instruments for regulating the interaction between cultures is art 27 of the Universal Declaration of Human Rights of 1948. This article stipulates that everyone has the right freely to participate in the cultural life of the community, to enjoy the arts, and to share in scientific advancement and its benefits.[11] The purpose of this provision is to protect cultural diversity while at the same time supporting the evolution of a common culture. A similar provision appears in a number of conventions and political manifestos. These conventions provide ample evidence of the universal recognition of cultural rights.

Article 15 of the International Covenant on Economic, Social and Cultural Rights of 1966 provides that states recognize the right of everyone 'to take part in cultural life'. The International Labour Organization Convention on Indigenous and Tribal

---

[9] Robertson op cit (n 2) 198.
[10] For a discussion of this aspect, see Teson 'International Human Rights and Cultural Relativism' (1985) 25 *Virginia J of Int L* 869ff.
[11] Article 27(1) of the Universal Declaration of Human Rights of 1948.

Populations of 1957[12] seeks to protect the cultural values of indigenous and tribal populations. This shows an awareness of the need to protect the cultural practices of all peoples and not only those of the West. The International Convention on the Elimination of All Forms of Racial Discrimination[13] enjoins states which are parties to the Convention to recognize the right of every person — irrespective of race, colour, or national or ethnic origin — to equality before the law as regards cultural rights. Moreover, the International Covenant on Civil and Political Rights makes provision for persons who belong to ethnic, religious, or linguistic minorities not to be denied the right, in community with other members of their group, to enjoy their own culture.[14] The purpose of these conventions is to protect minorities against discrimination on the ground of their culture. While these instruments provide for cultural diversity, they do not forestall the development of a common culture. The development of a common culture is often necessitated by considerations of nation-building and the desire to remove conflicts in the culture of a people who find themselves in one geographical area. A common culture may also evolve from constant contact between members of different cultures. This evolution of a common culture should, however, be based on the free volition of the groups concerned and not on coercion or forced assimilation.

As pointed out above, the protection of a right to culture is a product of hindsight. In the past people from Western countries tended to look down upon and consequently to treat shabbily the cultural practices of non-Westerners. This was part of the philosophy of imperialism which gave rise to feelings of cultural superiority on the part of European people. This view, which regarded pre-colonial Africa as an unorganized and undeveloped part of the world, was a parochial European notion which reached the peak of its development during the latter part of the nineteenth and the beginning of the twentieth centuries.[15] This view was eminently ethnocentric and was not conducive to the development of peace and mutual understanding. It suited the early colonists to bolster the virtues of European culture, which was supposed to replace primitive backwardness in the process of 'civilizing' the 'native' peoples, who were characterized as childlike or mentally retarded and therefore unable to take care of themselves.[16] Obviously this paternalistic view is no longer acceptable.

Besides these international instruments, various countries recognize a constitutional right to culture or provide for the protection of the culture of minorities. The right to culture is often closely connected to education because education is the means through which culture is transmitted from one generation to another. Moreover, the issue of language is relevant to education. Language is part of the culture of a people.

Article 29(1) of the Constitution of India provides that any section of the citizens residing in the territory of India or any part thereof having a distinct language, script, or culture of its own has the right to conserve the same. Clause (2) stipulates that

---

[12] 107 of 1957.

[13] Article 5 of the International Convention on the Elimination of All Forms of Racial Discrimination of 1965.

[14] Article 27 of the International Convenant on Civil and Political Rights of 1966.

[15] Sanders *International Jurisprudence in African Context* (1979) 49; Shapera *Government and Politics in Tribal Societies* (1956) 1ff.

[16] Santa Cruz *Racial Discrimination* (1971) 8; see also Fredrickson *White Supremacy* (1981) 7n2.

no citizen should be denied admission to any educational institution maintained by the state or receiving aid out of the state funds on the grounds only of religion, race, caste, or language.[17] This article protects two different but related rights. It protects the distinct language, script, or culture of a section of the citizenry and it also guarantees the right to an individual citizen not to be discriminated against only on the grounds of religion, race, caste, or language in the matter of admission to educational institutions.

Article 30 of the Indian Constitution guarantees religions and linguistic minorities the right to establish and administer educational institutions of their choice. The state is precluded, in granting aid to educational institutions, from discriminating against any educational institution on the grounds that it is under the management of a minority, whether based on religion or language.

In order to claim the protection of art 29(1) of the Indian Constitution the claimants must prove that they are a section of the citizens of India, residing in the territory of India or any part thereof, having a distinct language, script, or culture and that the distinct language, script, or culture is their own. These requisites must be proved simultaneously in order successfully to rely on art 29(1).[18]

In a number of cases where minorities have challenged attempts to violate minority rights guaranteed in arts 29 and 30 of the Indian Constitution the judiciary has consistently upheld the rights of the minorities embodied in those articles. It has ensured that the ambit of the minority rights is not narrowed. The general approach has been to see to it that nothing is done to impair the rights of minorities in the matter of their education and that the scope of the provisions of the Constitution dealing with those rights should not be unnecessarily limited. A general principle which runs through the various decisions of the courts is that the provisions relating to minority rights should not be rendered nugatory by narrow judicial interpretation. On the contrary, minorities should be made to feel that they are as much part of the country as the majority; they should have a sense of belonging and an awareness that they are treated equally. They should also be conscious of the fact that their religion, culture, language, and script are being conserved and that their educational institutions are being protected. The same generous, liberal, and sympathetic approach should be adopted by the courts in interpreting arts 29 and 30 of the Constitution as the one that was adopted by the constitution-makers in drafting those fundamental rights.[19]

Although the Canadian Charter of Rights and Freedoms[20] makes provision for equality under the law in s 15(1), which seeks to ensure that ethnic minorities in Canada do not suffer discriminatory treatment, ss 16–20 of the Charter provide for the protection of the cultural identity of linguistic and ethnic minorities by guaranteeing the equality of the French and English languages. The rationale for such protection is that the general equality provision provides for formal equality, which is attained when linguistic and cultural minorities are placed on an equal footing

---

[17] Article 29 of the Indian Constitution of 1949.
[18] Kumar *Cultural and Educational Rights of the Minorities under Indian Constitution* (1985) 98.
[19] *DAV College Bhatinda v State of Punjab* AIR 1971 SC 1731; *Ahmedabad St Xavier College Society & others v State of Gujarat* AIR 1974 SC 1389; *State of Bombay v Bombay Education Society & others* AIR 1954 SC 561; *Rev Father W Proost v State of Bihar* AIR 1969 SC 465; see also Kumar op cit (n 18) 97ff.
[20] Part I of the Canadian Constitution Act 1982.

with the majority. Material or substantial equality, however, can result from a recognition that a minority and a majority are not in comparable situations and that the same treatment applied to different situations inevitably produces inequality. Formal equality entails that a minority is served by the cultural, religious, and educational institutions of the majority. This integration into the cultural mainstream results in a rapid disintegration of all the distinctive features which make up a minority people and consequently leads to assimilation.[21]

In 1976 Canada ratified the International Covenant on Civil and Political Rights, which provides for equality and non-discrimination in arts 2(1) and 26, and for the right of ethnic, religious, and linguistic minorities 'to enjoy their own culture, to profess and practice their own religion, or use their own language' in art 27. As a consequence of ratifying the Covenant Canada was obliged to bring its domestic law into line with the provisions of the Covenant. Section 15(1) of the Charter is the domestic equivalent of arts 2(1) and 26 of the Covenant. The rights protected in ss 16–20 of the Charter are equivalent to the rights protected in art 27 of the Covenant. However, although the Charter makes adequate provision for the protection of the official language rights, i e English and French, it falls short of the standard required by art 27 of the Covenant regarding other minority languages.[22]

Education is the chief instrument for preserving and protecting a minority language or culture. Yet even art 27 of the Covenant does not address this adequately. It is generally accepted that the Covenant requires only that the state parties should allow minorities to set up private schools at their own expense and to provide for instruction in their own language. The state is not obliged to assist minorities, either financially or materially, to establish minority public schools. Similarly, while the Charter guarantees members of the francophone and anglophone minorities the right to have their children educated out of public funds in their respective languages at elementary and secondary levels where there are enough children to justify this, no similar provision is made for other minorities.[23]

Section 27 of the Charter provides that the Charter should be interpreted in a manner consistent with the preservation and enhancement of the multicultural heritage of Canadians. It is only through the application of this interpretative provision that the courts can give meaningful effect to the protection of cultural rights. This can be done if s 27 serves to limit the scope of the other provisions of the Charter and thereby ensuring the protection or enhancement of cultural diversity. It could also be used to interpret the Charter as implicitly containing linguistic and cultural rights other than those expressly mentioned.[24]

While provisions relating to the protection of minorities largely complement the right to equality, they may also be regarded as divergent. The courts should be able to interpret these provisions in such a way that the fundamental assumptions on which the Constitution is based are not violated. The principle of multiculturalism recognizes that all cultural collectivities which make up society are of equal

---

[21] Woehrling 'Minority Cultural and Linguistic Rights and Equality Rights in the Canadian Charter of Rights and Freedoms' (1985) 31 *McGill LJ* 52.
[22] Woehrling op cit (n 21) 57.
[23] Woehrling op cit (n 21) 58–9.
[24] Woehrling op cit (n 21) 60ff.

importance and dignity.[25] Cultural identity is a necessary component of human dignity.[26]

From the aforegoing discussion it is clear that in countries with cultural diversity the right to culture is particularly important. While discrimination based on ethnic features is generally proscribed, cultural pluralism is provided for in many Constitutions. South Africa has a lot to learn from this because it is a country that is characterized by cultural pluralism.

## 2.3 State of the debate in South Africa

Now that a Bill of Rights forms part of the South African interim Constitution,[27] international jurisprudence is of more than passing interest. Section 31 of the interim Constitution provides that every person has a right to use the language and to participate in the cultural life of his or her choice. In interpreting and applying this provision the court will have recourse to international jurisprudence on the issue.

Although a distinction is often drawn between first-generation and second-generation rights, this distinction is sometimes not helpful. Besides the fact that these rights are often interdependent and mutually reinforcing, there are second-generation rights which do not impose positive obligations on the government, but which are negative, e g the right to culture. The right to culture does not require the government of the country to employ resources to develop a particular culture, but obliges the government to allow people to practise their own culture. As has been shown above, this view may be criticized on the ground that those who have the means will be able to develop their own culture, while those who do not will be unable to do so. This may not result in equality but in inequality. The South African Law Commission, in considering the inclusion of second-generation rights in a Bill of Rights, found that in dealing with this issue we should not be dogmatic but flexible. Consequently those second-generation rights which could be couched in negative terms like the first-generation rights should be protected in a Bill of Rights and those which could not may be accommodated in directive principles.[28] When it comes to the right to culture, however, this view may not be adequate, given the decades of discrimination in this country.

Although the right to culture was accepted by most of the draft proposals for a Bill of Rights[29] and it is provided for in the interim Constitution, its interpretation will raise interesting questions which the courts will have to answer in a judicious manner in order to realize substantial equality in the area of culture.

---

[25] Woehrling op cit (n 21) 67ff.
[26] Clements 'Misconceptions of Culture: Native Peoples and Cultural Property under Canadian Law' (1991) 48 *U Toronto LJ* 4.
[27] Chapter 3 of the Constitution of the Republic of South Africa Act 200 of 1993.
[28] SA Law Commission *Group and Human Rights* Interim Report (1991) 536–7; cf Didcott 'Practical Workings of a Bill of Rights' in Van der Westhuizen & Viljoen (eds) *A Bill of Rights for South Africa* (1988) 58ff.
[29] Sachs *Protecting Human Rights* 24ff; clause 5(11) of the ANC's draft Bill of rights; clause 13 of the Democratic Party's draft Bill of Rights; clause 26 of the Multi-Party Negotiating Council's draft Bill of Rights; clause 18 of the SA Law Commission's draft Bill of Rights.

Culture is often viewed as a group right[30] or collective right.[31] Although a culture is practised by a certain group, it does not necessarily mean that the group itself has a right to culture. To regard the group as the bearer of the right may lead to a number of problems. It is better to regard the individual as the bearer of this right. It is ultimately the individual that must practise the culture, although cultural practices have generally to be observed in a group context.

Cultural rights are sometimes perceived as being in conflict with the right to equality. This is because some cultural practices may allow or promote inequality or discrimination and because allowing different cultural practices may amount to differential treatment. There is general consensus that the protection of a right to culture should not be an excuse for invidious discrimination on the basis of race, ethnicity, language, or gender. There should be general protection of cultural diversity without derogating from the principle of non-discrimination or equality. This allows for groups to protect what they regard as their own way of life while doing away with objectionable features which are universally or widely disapproved of. The right to non-discrimination or equality or dignity does not mean cultural sameness or similarity. It simply means that as citizens South Africans are equal and have the same right to dignity, to be treated as human beings, and not to be discriminated against on racial or ethnic grounds. But as people they have the right to distinguish themselves culturally. This brings about a distinction between invidious discrimination and benign differentiation.

From the above discussion it is clear that education is important for the protection and transmission of culture. For this reason the right to education is next to be considered.

## 3 EDUCATION

### 3.1 Introduction

Education is particularly important for purposes of teaching people about themselves and their environment so that in understanding themselves and their environment they may be able not only to survive but also to live life to its full. So important is education that in many (but not all) societies there is a constitutional right to education. The right to education is included in the Constitutions and Bills of Rights of at least fifty-nine countries, while in the Constitutions of seventy countries no mention is made of this right. This does not imply that the latter group does not treat education seriously. On the contrary, it does. In this group one finds countries such as the Federal Republic of Germany, Norway, the Netherlands, Sweden, and the United States of America, all of which recognize that right.[32] This shows that practice may be stronger and more effective than written declarations.

While the US Constitution provides for equal protection of the law, it does not guarantee equal access to education. As a result, there is no provision which requires that each and every American be afforded the opportunity to receive an education.[33]

---

[30] On the issue of group rights, see Venter 'Menseregte, Groepsregte en 'n Proses na Groter Geregtigheid' 1986 *SAPR/PL* 202ff; Erasmus ' 'n Akte van Menseregte vir Suid-Afrika' 1987 *SAPR/PL* 100–3.

[31] Woehrling op cit (n 21) 55.

[32] SA Law Commission op cit (n 28) 326.

[33] Rhodes 'We the People and the Struggle for a New World: The Constitution of the United States of America and International Human Rights' 1987 *Howard LJ* 997ff.

Despite this, the importance of education was underscored in the case of *Brown v Board of Education of Topeka*[34] by Warren CJ:

> 'Today, education is perhaps the most important function of state and local governments. Compulsory school attendance laws and the great expenditures for education both demonstrate our recognition of the importance of education to our democratic society. It is required in the performance of our most basic public responsibilities, even service in the armed forces. It is the very foundation of good citizenship. Today it is a principal instrument in awakening the child to cultural values, in preparing him for later professional training, and in helping him to adjust normally to his environment. In these days, it is doubtful that any child may reasonably be expected to succeed in life if he is denied the opportunity of an education. Such an opportunity, where the state has undertaken to provide it, is a right which must be made available to all on equal terms.'

The idea of a right to education can be traced back to the traditional concept of the natural duty of parents to take care of and bring up their children. This parental responsibility gradually and increasingly became associated with furthering the development and needs of children instead of conforming to the wishes of the parents. Emphasis has shifted towards formal education as an indispensable part of upbringing. Today this right is considered as primarily the right of all children to be educated. The duty to provide education has shifted from parents to society. Owing to the possibility of parents failing to exercise this power because of ignorance or selfishness, compulsory education, funded by the state up to a minimum age, has become the norm.[35]

Education is closely related to culture because it is the medium through which culture is transmitted from one generation to another. This is why education in one's mother tongue is one of the primary means by which culture is acquired. The right to choose the type of education which a person is to receive is important 'for the exercise of the right to develop freely one's culture'.[36]

The importance of education is underlined by the fact that governments regard it as a powerful instrument. It can be used to control the minds of young people, although this has not always completely succeeded. The importance of education lies in the fact that it develops the human mind to think critically about issues. Even a mind that has been indoctrinated with a particular ideology is capable of eventually discovering the falsity of that ideology and rejecting it. It also equips people with the knowledge that enables them to acquire certain skills and expertise. Education is a good example of how various categories of right are interdependent. As democracy requires informed participation in the political process, education is indispensable for such informed participation. Illiteracy therefore undermines democracy.[37]

Education is therefore fundamental to human existence. It is the process through which human beings develop to full humanity or maturity. This development is acquired through the acquisition of knowledge which makes a difference in the human condition.

---

[34] 347 US 483 (1954).
[35] Van der Westhuizen 'A Post-Apartheid Educational System: Constitutional Provisions' (1989) 21 *Columbia Human Rights LR* 113; cf MacFarlane *The Theory and Practice of Human Rights* (1985) 125–9.
[36] Robertson op cit (n 2) 199–200.
[37] Amankwa 'Constitutions and Bills of Rights in Third World Nations: Issues of Form and Content' (1981) XIV *CILSA* 185ff.

Notwithstanding what has been said above, the right to education imposes a duty on the state to provide education for children. The fundamental question is: what is the content of this right as regards quality, duration, and cost? This raises the further question of whether the right to education requires the provision of equal, identical, or similar education. Should the emphasis be placed on equality or on fairness and legitimacy? The questions are not new. America, for instance, has had to grapple with the very same problem. The answers to these questions have given rise to three approaches: the conservative position, the modern liberal position, and the social democratic school.

The conservative position is mainly concerned with the protection of basic rights and is non-distributive. It does not impose an obligation on the government to distribute funds equally. Moreover, it is non-interventionist in that it does not vest the state with powers to compel citizens to make use of the benefits of education. It ensures legal or formal equality.[38] This approach merely guarantees equal opportunities in education.

According to the liberal position, there is a need for the protection of basic rights and equal opportunities or admission. In addition it grants the citizen certain minimum benefits as regards basic education. What distinguishes this school from the conservative one is the scope of the opportunities offered. Both of them proceed from the premise that the state is expected to provide equal opportunities.[39]

These approaches have been severely criticized. In the words of Salomone:

'This formula can be radically misleading. It is more accurately articulated as equality of opportunity to develop with talents that are highly regarded in a given group. Only those who are superior in the desired qualities have the opportunity to develop them and the gap between the highest and the lowest inevitably widens. While equality of opportunity has been defined as equal access to social goods, it can translate into constructive exclusion for those individuals who fail to possess certain qualities. An opportunity is an opportunity only for those who may or may not make use of it.

Modern-day liberal proponents of equality of opportunity consider this conception as narrow, coldly artificial, and fundamentally unfair. They condemn it for taking people simply as they are and for judging them without asking why one performs better than the other. True equality of opportunity requires, so they argue, that we modify those aspects of people's circumstances that prevent them from performing up to their natural abilities.'[40]

As a result of criticism of this kind, a third school of thought, the social democratic school, came into being. This school places emphasis not only on equal opportunities but also on the equal apportionment of all the benefits. This school is distributionist and obliges the government to provide the pupil with benefits for enabling him or her to use the available opportunities. It also imposes an obligation on the pupil to use the benefits.[41]

Whereas the liberal school looks at the individual and the personal benefits to be derived from economic and social advantages, including education, the social democratic school focuses on the general welfare of society by teaching that society as a whole benefits if an improvement of the individual's achievement takes place

---

[38] Salomone *Equal Education Under Law* (1986) 23.
[39] SA Law Commission op cit (n 28) 321.
[40] Salomone op cit (n 38) 24–5.
[41] SA Law Commission op cit (n 28) 329.

as a result of a redistribution in favour of the disadvantaged. For the social democratic school the ultimate goal of justice in education is the attainment of equal status and conditions. As Salomone puts it:

> 'Equality is here viewed as an end in itself. Adherents to this position would sacrifice the total general welfare to produce greater equality for those at the bottom of the distributive ladder.'[42]

As these different schools of thought demonstrate, there is no one approach which can be regarded as perfect. Moreover, the needs of education are not static, but change according to the exigencies of the situation. More on this will be said below.

## 3.2 Comparative international situation

Perhaps the oldest provision on the right to education is that found in art 26 of the Universal Declaration of Human Rights. It stipulates that everyone has a right to education, which should at least be free in the elementary and fundamental stages. It also provides that elementary education should be compulsory. Technical and professional education should be made generally available and higher education should be equally accessible to all on the basis of merit.[43] The Declaration further provides that education should be directed to the full development of the human personality and to the strengthening of human rights and fundamental freedoms. Moreover, it should promote understanding, tolerance, and friendship among all nations and racial or religious groups, and should further the activities of the United Nations for the maintenance of peace.[44] Parents are vested with a prior right to choose the kind of education to be given to their children.[45]

A similar provision is contained in the International Covenant on Economic, Social and Cultural Rights. This Covenant recognizes the right to education and stipulates that education should be purposive and 'directed to the full development of the human personality and the sense of its dignity'. It should also strengthen respect for human rights and fundamental freedoms as well as facilitate effective participation in a free society, promote understanding, tolerance, and friendship among all nations and all racial, ethnic, or religious groups, and further the activities of the United Nations for the maintenance of peace.[46] In order to realize this right primary education should be free and compulsory; secondary education in its various forms should be made generally available and accessible to all by every appropriate means and by the progressive introduction of free education. Similarly, higher education should be made accessible to all on the basis of ability and by the progressive introduction of free education. 'Fundamental education shall be encouraged or intensified as far as possible for those persons who have not received or completed the whole period of their primary education'; and 'the development of a system of schools at all levels shall be actively pursued, an adequate fellowship system shall be established, and the material conditions of teaching staff shall be continuously improved'.[47]

---

[42] Salomone op cit (n 38) 26.
[43] Article 26(1).
[44] Article 26(2).
[45] Article 26(3).
[46] Article 13(1).
[47] Article 13(2).

There are two ways of interpreting these provisions: the weak, and the strong. According to the strong interpretation, there should be maximum state control of education. The weak interpretation, on the other hand, entails minimum state control over education. While the state is supposed to provide the resources and facilities to enable education to take place, parents and communities are expected to make significant contributions. The parents and communities at local level have the responsibility of determining what is taught and by whom it is taught. Personal needs are regarded as a priority and education is regarded as a private matter where freedom is emphasized over equality. The strong interpretation, on the other hand, emphasizes that people should have the same opportunities to receive the same quality of education. The state not only has to provide the finances for the provision of education but it also has to control issues such as what is taught, how it is taught, and by whom. The state has even to decide on the kind of education to be pursued, whether it is to be academic, technical, or commercial, according to social need. Social needs enjoy priority over personal needs. Education seen as a public matter implies that equality is regarded as being more important than freedom.[48]

The weak interpretation coincides with the conservative school and the strong interpretation coincides with the liberal and social democratic schools referred to above.

Article 26 of the Declaration emphasizes the purposive role of education in the development of the personality and social attributes such as tolerance. This confirms the view that education is instrumental to the understanding of the various cultures and hence of developing a tolerant attitude towards them. Article 26, however, does not mention the economic functions of education. This omission is further evidenced by the fact that it does not refer to schooling as the major source of education in modern societies. For a considerable period of time education has been closely linked to schooling. This arose from the process of industrialization which 'requires a mass schooling system to provide a labour force with appropriate skills and attitudes, and a child-minding service to enable parents to work.'[49]

Whereas art 17 of the African Charter on Human and Peoples' Rights of 1981 stipulates that '[e]very individual shall have the right to education', art 2 of the First Protocol to the European Convention on Human Rights[50] is couched in negative terms and provides that '[n]o person shall be denied the right to education'. This is because at the time of the signing of this Protocol in 1952 the member states could not assume the burden of an unlimited guarantee to provide education.[51]

In the *Belgian Linguistic Case*[52] the European Court of Human Rights decided that the scope of the right to education means that persons within the territory of member states can make use of the existing educational system. In this case six

---

[48] Robertson op cit (n 2) 187–8.

[49] Robertson op cit (n 2) 188.

[50] The European Convention on Human Rights was signed in Rome on 4 November 1950. For a discussion of the First Protocol to the Convention, see Clarke 'Freedom of Thought and Educational Rights in the European Convention' 1987 *The Irish Jurist* 28ff.

[51] When the draft text of the European Convention was signed it did not include an article on education. On 20 March 1952 the First Protocol to the Convention was approved and included, as art 2, an amended version of the text on education which was originally intended to be included in the Convention. The Convention came into force on 3 September 1953, and the First Protocol on 18 May 1954. See Clarke op cit (n 50) 28.

[52] Series A, vol 6, Judgment of 23 July 1968.

groups of French-speaking applicants who resided in Brussels and in the Flemish part of Belgium claimed that the linguistic system of education in Belgium violated the European Convention and its First Protocol. Belgium had refused to establish, subsidize, or maintain primary schools in the Dutch-speaking regions, where French was the medium of instruction. The Belgian government contended that the right to education did not entail any positive obligation on the part of the government.

The majority of the Commission decided that the right to education placed no positive obligation on the state and did not bind the state to provide education or to subsidize private education. The Commission none the less concluded that art 2 gave everyone the right to education. In the case of Belgium, a modern highly industrialized state, the right to education included nursery, primary, secondary, and higher education.

The European Court of Human Rights decided that Belgium's refusal to establish, subsidize, or maintain primary school education in the Dutch-speaking region was not a violation of art 2 of the First Protocol. On the other hand, the court noted that the right to education would be meaningless unless there was a recognition of the right to be educated in the official language or in one of the official languages. The right to education was held to entail some form of regulation and uniformity by the state. This could vary in time and place according to the particular needs of the community.

The shift from one school of thought to another in the provision of education is amply demonstrated by the US experience, where various approaches to education have been formulated. This provides evidence of the fact that no one approach can provide answers to all situations.

Until 1954 America allowed racially segregated schools as a result of the approval of the 'separate but equal' doctrine by the US Supreme Court in *Plessy v Ferguson*.[53] This doctrine often meant that there was no equality in segregated schools owing to the fact that a larger amount of state funds was spent on white children than on black pupils in many of the southern states.[54] Consequently the National Association for the Advancement of Colored People (NAACP) challenged the 'separate but equal' doctrine before the courts, arguing that it violated the Fourteenth Amendment's guarantee of 'equal protection of the laws'.

In 1954, in *Brown v Board of Education of Topeka*[55] the US Supreme Court decided that in the field of public education the doctrine of 'separate but equal' has no place on the ground that separate educational facilities are inherently unequal. Warren CJ declared:

> 'Segregation of white and colored children in public schools has a detrimental effect upon the colored children. The impact is greater when it has the sanction of law, for the policy of separating the races is usually interpreted as denoting the inferiority of the Negro group. A sense of inferiority affects the motivation of a child to learn. Segregation with the sanction of law, therefore, has a tendency to retard the educational and mental development of Negro children and to deprive them of some of the benefits they would receive in a racial[ly] integrated school system.'

In order to implement the mandate of the *Brown* decision and to desegregate schools, school boards concentrated on 'busing' and the rezoning of school districts.

---

[53] 163 US 537 (1896).
[54] Salomone op cit (n 38) 41.
[55] Supra at 494.

'Busing' simply meant that black children were fetched by bus from near and far to attend 'white' schools and that white children were conveyed to 'black' schools in order to ensure a balance in the ratio of black and white children and to ensure that this ratio in the schools corresponded with the population in the whole area.[56] In *Davis v Board of School Commissioners of Mobile County*[57] the US Supreme Court held that a school board and district court were required to do all they could to achieve the greatest possible degree of desegregation, taking into account the practicalities of the situation, and that they should consider the use of all available techniques for that purpose, including the restructuring of attendance zones.

This marked the beginning of a 'compensatory' education approach, which dominated federal policy for the next two decades and led to the major redistribution of the society's educational resources.[58] As time went by, however, emphasis shifted away from the individual pupil and individual interests and group interests became more important. In the words of Salomone:

'What had started out in *Brown* as equality premised on respect for the individual began to evolve as a manifestation of group consciousness and group rights. During that decade, the conflict between individual autonomy and social justice, between diversity and equality, came to the fore of the policy debate. By mid-decade, a Republican executive had locked horns with a Democratic legislature on such issues as busing to achieve racial balance, the education rights of the handicapped, and the preferred approach to federal financing of educational services. And by the end of the decade, demands for parental choice and federal aid to non-public education became louder and more organized than ever.'[59]

It soon became clear that not only was the ideal of equality expensive to attain but also that it clashed with individual freedom and autonomy. When resources diminished and costs escalated in the 1970s equality began to yield to diversity. Mandatory busing aimed at achieving a racial balance was superseded by freedom of association. 'And so public sentiment turned against the concept of group rights in favour of individual liberty.'[60]

Salomone sums up the current position as follows:

'Where does this all leave the equality mandate of *Brown* three decades down the road? Obviously, not to the racial hostility and blatant segregative policies of the 1950's. Nevertheless, with federal commitment on the downside, equality of educational opportunity has assumed a different contour for different groups. For racial minorities, there are indicators of a return to pre-*Brown* separate but equal programmes and facilities. For linguistic minorities, equal means *effective* as measured against a *whatever works* standard. More than a decade of controversy surrounding proper goals and methodology has brought us full circle back to assimilation as the end, English language instruction as the means, and achievement test scores as the measure of success for children whose dominant language is not English. Cultural pluralism, maintenance programmes and effective development are now vague memories of a not so distant past. As for handicapped students, equal education translates merely into the provision of *some* benefit — a sharp departure from the *maximization of potential* goals of the 1970's. For all these groups, recent federal policies define equality of educational opportunity not as *equal* nor necessarily *more is equal*, but *different*

---

[56] Van der Vyver '*Brown v Board of Education*: A Survey of the American Desegregation Programme' (1974) 91 *SALJ* 510.
[57] 402 US 33, 37 (1970).
[58] Salomone op cit (n 38) 30.
[59] Salomone op cit (n 38) 194–5.
[60] Salomone op cit (n 38) 194.

treatment that is circumscribed by considerations of financial cost and administrative burden. As for women, equality had never gone beyond equal treatment *per se* — there has been no affirmative action for female students. However, weakened enforcement, narrow court rulings, and limited financial resources pose the threat of regression to *less than equal* services and a perpetuation of gender-defined roles.'[61]

The conclusion to be drawn from the aforegoing is that the right to education is not an absolute one. Salomone redefines the right underlying equal educational opportunity as 'an amalgam of the 1960's concept of a "minimum floor" of basic services, combined with the process-oriented reforms of the early 1970's tempered by the economic realities and political concerns of more recent years'.[62] She further points out that what is important is to recognize that each child 'has a right to a minimally adequate education that is appropriate to its needs'. Instead of asking 'how much education?' we should ask what type of education is necessary to permit the individual to participate effectively in the democratic process and to enjoy the personal benefits that learning brings, within limits set by individual potential.[63] This is more appropriate because it shifts the emphasis from the group to the specific needs of individual students. On the issue of the struggle to implement the equality mandate of *Brown* Salomone states that *Brown* has taught the lesson that

'the road between moral precept and public policy is rough and winding. It has also taught us that political consensus eventually evaporates in the air of rhetorical excess to the right or the left. Nevertheless, we must not be immobilized by equality's limitations but rather energized by its substantive force. We now know that equality as a policy goal in itself is unrealistic. Equality of results is limited by economic conditions and by differences in individual potential. But we also know that equal treatment alone often does not suffice. In fact, justice demands a pluralistic perspective on equality whereby *equality for all* means different or more is equal for some. We may never achieve the equality ideal, but it must continue to serve as a guiding principle and legal norm that we use to define educational rights. This conception of equality as a direction for educational policy making is moral and economic necessity.'[64]

There is a variety of issues which impact on the right to education. Article 2 of the First Protocol to the European Convention on Human Rights also protects the religious and philosophical convictions of parents in relation to the education of their children. In the *Belgian Linguistic Case* the European Court of Human Rights intimated that while art 2 does not imply that in the area of education states should respect the linguistic preferences of the parents, they should take note of their religious and moral values. But the interests of the child will prevail if they are met in a positive way and if they clash with the views of the parent.

*Kjeldsen & others v Denmark*[65] raised the acceptability of a Danish law which made sex education compulsory in all state schools. This law, which was enacted after a long process of inquiry, required sex education to be spread over different subjects and to be adapted to the age of the pupil. Before this, sex education in the schools was offered in an optional class from which parents could remove their children if they wished. In this case the applicants contended that by making sex

---

[61] Salomone op cit (n 38) 195.
[62] Salomone op cit (n 38) 201.
[63] Salomone op cit (n 38) 202.
[64] Salomone op cit (n 38) 203.
[65] Series A, vol 23, Judgment of 7 December 1976.

education compulsory in all state schools the government had violated the applicants' right to ensure that the education of their children conformed with their religious and philosophical convictions. The government responded by saying that the parents were free to send their children to private schools if they so wished. The Commission rejected this contention.

The European Court held that the system did not necessarily violate the European Convention on Human Rights or the First Protocol and that integrated and compulsory sex education in schools did not militate against the applicants' religious and philosophical convictions. For this reason art 2 had not been infringed. This was based on the fact that art 2 requires the state to respect the rights of parents while at the same time exercising its functions in education. These functions included the planning of curricula. In fulfilling its functions the state was required to ensure that the information was disseminated in an objective manner that did not attempt to indoctrinate. According to the court, the Danish sex education programme was aimed at educating children early in matters such as illegitimacy, abortions, and sexually transmitted diseases, which it viewed as seriously threatening the social norms of the country. There had been no attempt to indoctrinate.

The conflict between the right of the parent to have his child educated according to his religious views and philosophical convictions and the right to education of a child and the government's obligation to offer such education was also raised in the Canadian case of *R v Jones*.[66] In this case a parent whose children were considered truants, but who contended that he had educated them at home, and had the constitutional right to do so, was prosecuted under the Schools Act of Alberta. In terms of this law all Canadian parents are responsible for the education of their children who are within the compulsory school-going age. The parent is required either to ensure that a child within the prescribed ages attends public school or to prove to the satisfaction of the appropriate authorities that the child is under efficient instruction at home or is being educated at a recognized or approved private school. Children who are receiving efficient instruction at home as certified by an official with the public school authorities are exempted from the requirement of attendance.

The accused, who was a pastor of a fundamentalist church, had refused to apply for certification. He argued that he had the right to bring up his children as he saw fit and to refuse to send his children to a public school or apply for any exemption or approval. His lawyers attempted to produce evidence that the child was receiving efficient instruction outside school. This evidence was disallowed because the statutory scheme dealing with certification had not been complied with. It was then contended that the legislation in question violated s 7 of the Charter in that the legislation contained a provision which prevented the accused from tendering evidence to rebut the charge against him and that the threatened penal provisions, which included imprisonment, deprived the accused of his liberty to bring up his children as he deemed appropriate according to his conscience. The trial judge accepted this.

On appeal, the Alberta Court of Appeal reversed the trial judge's decision and held that the father of the truant child could have applied for a certificate as required by legislation. If he had received the certificate, his freedom to educate his children

---

[66] (1984) 10 DLR (4th) 765.

would have been protected. When the father appealed to the Supreme Court of Canada,[67] the court dismissed the appeal and held that there had been no violation of the liberty provision of the Charter, even assuming that that liberty includes the right of parents to educate their children as they see fit. In this case the accused had not been deprived of that liberty in a manner that conflicted with s 7 of the Charter. If, however, the school authorities exercised their power in an unfair or arbitrary manner, the Charter's reference to liberty could be invoked. A balance must be struck between the statutory requirement of compulsory schooling and the liberty of the individual parent to educate his or her children as he or she sees fit. Balancing this issue involves balancing fairness and efficiency, which should be done with a certain amount of pragmatism.[68]

### 3.3 State of the debate in South Africa

Education in South Africa has always been open to serious criticism. This has largely been due to the policy of apartheid, which legalized inequality in education based on racial separation. The government supported not simply the policy of 'separate but equal' but the more obnoxious policy of 'separate and unequal.' The education system in the country has been characterized by central state control, the purpose of which has been to entrench inequality.[69]

The most notorious education law was the Bantu Education Act of 1953,[70] which laid the foundation of apartheid education for Africans. Before 1953 the control of African education had been in the hands of the provinces and most schools were run by the churches. The purpose of centralizing the control of African schooling in the hands of the government was ideological and, in the words of H F Verwoerd, it was to ensure that race relations were improved. As he put it:

> 'Racial relations cannot improve if the wrong type of education is given to Natives. They cannot improve if the result of Native Education is the creation of frustrated people who, as a result of the education they received, have expectations in life which circumstances in South Africa do not allow to be fulfilled immediately, when it creates people who are trained for professions not open to them, when there are people who have received a form of cultural training which strengthens their desire for the white-collar occupations to such an extent that there are more such people than openings available. Therefore, good racial relations are spoilt when the correct education is not given. Above all, good racial relations cannot exist when the education is given under the control of people who create wrong expectations on the part of the Native himself.'[71]

When the Bantu Education Act was passed the majority of church schools were closed in order to ensure strict control of what was taught in the schools. The considerable increase in the numbers of children attending school, especially primary schools, led to the deterioration of the quality of education owing to inadequate financing. What characterized apartheid education was the gross inequality in the financing of education, with the African population being the worst

---

[67] (1986) 2 SCR 284.
[68] For a discussion of this subject, see Khan 'Canadian Constitutional Guarantee of "Liberty" as it Affects Education and Children' 1993 *J of L and Education* 335ff. On the issue of funding separate schools, see *Reference re an Act to Amend the Education Act* (1986) 25 DLR (4th) 1; see also Stainsby '*Plus ça change* . . .: Education and Equality Rights in the Supreme Court' (1988) 46 *U Toronto LJ* 259ff.
[69] Robertson op cit (n 2) 189.
[70] Act 47 of 1953.
[71] *House of Assembly Debates* col 3576 17 September 1953.

funded. The decentralization of education as a result of the creation of the homelands did not change the picture because control remained in the hands of the central government. Gross inequalities prevailed in the African schools. These included high teacher–pupil ratios, unqualified or underqualified teachers, lack of books, libraries, and laboratories, and a high drop-out rate. 'This is accompanied by rigid ideological control over what is taught and how it is taught with a strong racist bias that asserts the superiority of European culture and people and the inferiority of African culture and people.'[72]

The creation of the tricameral parliamentary system in 1983 did not alter the situation, but entrenched the racial division in education by the establishment of 'own affairs' and 'general affairs' regimes. Although schools fell under 'own affairs', the control of financing and the standardization of syllabi and examinations remained a 'general' affair under the control of the central government. This situation led to the proliferation of education departments. The gross inequalities of apartheid education and the poor conditions in African schools led to resistance on the part of African pupils, especially from 1976 onwards.[73] This has led to the crisis in black education.

As a response to this the De Lange Commission was established in 1980 to attempt a reform of African education. The De Lange Commission considered the fundamental principles for the provision of education in South Africa and was of the opinion that the right to education should be guaranteed.[74] As the Commission pointed out:

'Equal education opportunity can only be developed within a political system where all people participate in a just sharing of power. Therefore, the process of redistributing educational resources and creating equal educational opportunity must take place concurrently in the major changes in the South African political structure.

To ensure equitable educational opportunity for all children and young people, resources for education should be allocated in such a way that per capita expenditure on schooling should be the same for all races. This implies that one race group should not enjoy a more favourable teacher–pupil ratio than another, but well qualified teachers should be distributed among the schools without regard to the race of the pupils, that uniform standards could be applied in the provision and equipping of schools and that beyond the school system equal opportunities for employment and further study should be available to all on the basis of ability. This further implies that a process of integration should be set in motion, so that race ceases to be a factor in determining which school is attended by any particular child, and that Black and White people should share equally in the control and development of education for children of all races. Thus, any decentralization in the organization and control of education should be on a regional basis and not according to racial criteria.'[75]

The guidelines for the reform process provided by the De Lange Commission did not produce many positive results. Boycotts and stayaways by students and teachers have been the order of the day since the mid-1980s.[76] This, however, does not mean

---

[72] Robertson op cit (n 2) 190.
[73] Robertson op cit (n 2) 191; see also Kane-Berman *Soweto: Black Revolt White Reaction* (1978).
[74] *Principles for the Provision of Education in the RSA* (1981). The De Lange Report, as it came to be known, is summarized in 1981 *Survey of Race Relations in South Africa* 338.
[75] De Lange Report op cit (n 74) 203.
[76] Robertson op cit (n 2) 191.

that the De Lange Report has been of no significance. It has exercised considerable influence on the thinking about the provision of education in South Africa.

Dissatisfaction with black education led to the emergence of the idea of 'people's education'. The concept is highly contentious and lacks precise definition.[77] The term originated from a meeting between a delegation of the Soweto Parents Crisis Committee (SPCC) and the African National Congress (ANC) in Harare in 1985 to discuss the crisis in black education. The ANC advised students to return to school and not to boycott education in accordance with the policy of 'liberation first, education later', but to clamour for 'people's education for people's power'. Schools were regarded as ideal places where students could be organized and students were persuaded to try to change schools from within.[78]

In subsequent years attempts have been made to give clarity and meaning to the concept 'people's education'. Although no agreement has been reached, consensus has been achieved on a few features of 'people's education'. The idea is based on principles of non-racialism, democracy, and the participation of students, parents, and teachers in educational structures. Educational aims are to be shaped according to these principles. These aims are to develop critical and creative abilities in students and to teach them to work collectively and non-competitively.[79]

If the idea of people's education is controversial and ambiguous, the definition of 'people' is even less clear. 'People' has been said to refer to an alliance of social forces against apartheid which is informed by the ideals of non-racialism and democracy. Within this group the working class must play a leading role.[80]

Although the right to education is a second-generation right which imposes an obligation on the state to provide education, it is regarded as so important that it should be entrenched in the Constitution. Proposals for a Bill of Rights which preceded Act 200 of 1993 recognized the right to education and to free and compulsory education up to a certain level.[81] Section 32 of the interim Constitution provides that everyone has a right 'to basic education and to equal access to educational institutions'. It also entitles a person 'to instruction in the language of his or her choice where this is reasonably practicable'. It further entitles an individual 'to establish, where practicable, educational institutions based on a common culture, language or religion, provided that there shall be no discrimination on the ground of race.'

The right to education recognized in the Constitution is blended with the rights to culture and to religion. People are free to establish schools based on language or culture without being entitled to discriminate against those who have a different culture or religion. The interpretation of this section will inevitably raise a number of problems relating to the meaning and content of this right.

---

[77] Christie *The Right to Learn* 2 ed (1991) 268; Levin 'People's Education and the Struggle for Democracy in South Africa' in Unterhalter et al (eds) *Apartheid Education and Popular Struggles* (1991) 117ff; Sebidi 'Towards the En-fleshment of a Dynamic Idea: The People's Education' in Mphahlele (ed) *Education for Affirmation* (1987) 49ff.

[78] Christie op cit (n 77) 268ff; Levin op cit (n 77) 118.

[79] Christie op cit (n 77) 270–1; Levin op cit (n 77) 124–5; Sebidi op cit (n 77) 54ff.

[80] Christie op cit (n 77) 283–4; Levin op cit (n 77) 120–2.

[81] Robertson op cit (n 2) 124; see also Sachs *Protecting Human Rights* 43; see clause 11(6) and (7) of the ANC's draft Bill of Rights; clause 12 of the Democratic Party's draft Bill of Rights; clause 27 of the Multi-Party Negotiating Council's draft Bill of Rights; clause 21 of the SA Law Commission's draft Bill of Rights.

Academic freedom is an important component of education. The interim Constitution contains two clauses that deal with this freedom. First, s 14, which recognizes the right to 'freedom of conscience, religion, thought, belief and opinion', provides that this freedom 'shall include academic freedom in institutions of higher learning'. Secondly, s 247 prohibits the national government and provincial governments from unilaterally altering the rights and powers of the governing bodies of existing educational institutions. This goes some way towards recognizing the autonomy of educational institutions.

## 4  RELIGION

### 4.1  Introduction

Religion forms an essential part of human life. Consequently the right to religious freedom, which includes freedom of conscience and freedom of thought, is regarded as the most sacred of all freedoms. It is 'the basic condition and foundation for all other human rights and the fundamental test for the authentic progress of any society'. Respect for religious freedom is an 'acknowledgement that human beings are more than individuals in a market, cogs in a social wheel, or products of various social forces. Their dignity commands respect because it comes from a deeper than human source.'[82]

The movement to achieve religious freedom is one of the oldest, dating back to the sixteenth century, if not to the Roman Empire.[83] Although this right was one of the first to gain international recognition, it remains one of the weakest as regards general recognition and enforcement. Throughout history people have been persecuted for their faith. The reason for this is that people are generally not content with trying to persuade others to their way of thinking 'by reason, preaching, dialogue, exhortation, or example; but frequently make use of force, and sometimes even torture, murder, or massacre in an attempt to achieve this purpose'.[84]

In spite of this, religion continues to play an important part in the spiritual life of people and in the culture of nations.[85] The right to religion is a negative right. It requires the state to tolerate different religions and not to impose any religious belief on its people. Religion is another area where the right to be the same and the right to be different coexist. While all people should be treated on the basis of equality and non-discrimination when it comes to other civil and political rights, in matters of belief people should be allowed to differ. This entails the right to believe and the right not to believe at all. It further entails 'the right to worship in our own ways, to organize our own religious communities, to consecrate our own holy places, and acknowledge our own holy texts, to appoint our own religious leaders, and follow our own rituals and dietary practices. At the constitutional level, this raises questions of the right to religious expression, freedom of association, and the rights of privacy or personal conscience in an affirmative sense.'[86]

Religious freedom may encompass more than 'religion' in the conventional

---

[82] Robertson op cit (n 2) 124; see also Little, Kelsay & Sachedina *Human Rights and the Conflicts of Culture: Western and Islamic Perspectives on Religious Liberty* (1988) 26.
[83] Little et al op cit (n 82) 13ff.
[84] Robertson op cit (n 2) 124.
[85] Sachs *Protecting Human Rights* 43.
[86] Sachs *Protecting Human Rights* 44.

sense. Religious organizations and followers of certain religions often do not confine themselves to matters of worship. They question injustice or oppression in the pursuit of their religious beliefs and this inevitably brings about a clash between religion and politics. While tyrannical regimes may profess to guarantee freedom of religion in terms of worship, they may be reluctant to extend this to the expression of political or social consequences of religious belief or to allow action to put these consequences into practice.[87]

The reason for this dichotomy is that religion and politics 'embrace in differing ways the whole of human life'. Both religious movements and political movements (or governments) hold their own views of what human beings, individually and collectively, should be. They may differ on their point of departure. 'While religions stem from and work in areas of inspiration and conviction, political movements are concerned with maintaining the social and legal framework for the human community.'[88]

It is essential that the separation of church and state should be respected, although not in an absolute way. The state and the church have to co-operate and collaborate with each other in certain matters, without the state legislating on matters of religion.[89]

## 4.2 Comparative international situation

Article 18 of the Universal Declaration of Human Rights provides that everyone has the right to freedom of thought, conscience, and religion. This right is regarded as including the freedom to change one's religion or belief and the freedom, either publicly or privately, individually or in community with others, to manifest one's religion or belief in teaching, practice, worship, and observance.[90] (A similar provision is made in the International Covenant on Civil and Political Rights.[91])

Teaching entails the right to give religious instruction, especially to the young, and the right to run educational institutions, including schools, colleges, and universities. Practice relates to the freedom to express the beliefs and instructions of a particular religion. Worship involves the right to assemble, pray, and hold religious services in public and in private. Observance entails the right to fulfil the requirements of one's religion on special days or during special seasons.[92]

The First Amendment of the US Constitution provides that 'Congress shall make no law respecting an establishment of religion or prohibiting the free exercise thereof'.[93] This article guarantees freedom of religion. Although freedom of religion is guaranteed in the US Constitution, it does not imply that the freedom to express one's religious belief is unlimited. A typical example is that of the practice of polygamy. In the case of *Reynolds v United States*[94] it was held that although polygamy was permitted in the Mormon Church as part of its religious belief, it

---

[87] Sachs *Protecting Human Rights* 44.
[88] Robertson op cit (n 2) 124.
[89] Robertson op cit (n 2) 125.
[90] Article 18 of the Universal Declaration of Human Rights.
[91] Article 18 of the International Covenant on Civil and Political Rights of 1966.
[92] Robertson op cit (n 2) 123.
[93] Article 1 of the US Bill of Rights of 1791.
[94] 98 US 145 (1878).

none the less remained prohibited under the criminal law. Delivering the judgment of the court, Waite CJ posed the question whether those who recognize polygamy as part of their religion are exempted from the operation of the law in terms of the First Amendment. He concluded that if 'those who did not make polygamy a part of their religious belief would be found guilty and punished, while those who did must be acquitted and go free', this would introduce a new element into criminal law. He stressed that laws are made to regulate actions and while they could not interfere with mere religious belief and opinions, they could do so with religious practices. This narrow interpretation of freedom of religion obviously undermines such a freedom. It surely cannot be argued that the framers of the Constitution intended that the 'free exercise' clause would be subject to the existing criminal law.

In the case of *Everson v Board of Education of Township of Ewing*[95] it was said that the First Amendment created a wall of separation between church and state. In this case the court decided that the wall of separation had not been breached when tax money was used to reimburse parents for the transportation by bus of their children to and from Catholic parochial schools. The minority, however, held such use of public money to be a violation by the state of the provision of the First Amendment that no law should be made 'respecting an establishment of religion'.

Another case where freedom of religion was limited to an unwarranted degree is that of *Employment Division, Department of Human Resources v Smith*.[96] In this case the claimants were private drug counsellors who were dismissed from their jobs for using peyote, a drug with a narcotic effect. The claimants argued that the drug was used in conjunction with sacramental rites of the Native American Church. In terms of an Oregon statute and administrative regulation this is an offence and there is no exception for religious use. Because the dismissals were for misconduct, based on the applicants' illegal possession of a drug, they were disqualified from unemployment benefits. The state court twice held that the claimants' 'free exercise of religion' rights had been violated. The US Supreme Court disagreed. According to Scalia J, the 'free exercise' clause 'does not relieve an individual of the obligation to comply with a valid and neutral law of general applicability on the ground that the law prescribes (or proscribes) conduct that the religion prescribes (or proscribes)'.[97] The court rejected the claimants' reliance on *Sherbert v Verner*[98] and similar cases[99] by limiting those cases to the factual context of unemployment compensation. Although the *Smith* case also involved such a claim, the denial of benefits was based on a generally applicable criminal statute which proscribed the use of drugs. According to the court, the 'free exercise' clause does not automatically allow an exemption from a neutral generally applicable statute.

In referring to precedent the court invoked the prohibition of polygamy[100] and the rejection of draft exemption claims of religious objectors to particular wars.

---

[95] 330 US 1 (1947); see also Mousin 'Confronting the Wall of Separation: A New Dialogue Between Law and Religion on the Meaning of the First Amendment' 1992 *Depaul LR* 1ff.
[96] 110 SCt 1595 (1990).
[97] At 1600; cf *United States v Lee* 455 US 252 (1982).
[98] 374 US 398 (1963).
[99] *Thomas v Review Board, Employment Division* 450 US 707 (1981); *Hobbie v Unemployment Appeals Commission* 480 US 136 (1987).
[100] Citing *Reynolds v United States* (supra).

Religious practice had prevailed in the past, the court reasoned, because of the presence of some other constitutional protection, usually free speech, in addition to the 'free exercise' interest. In prior 'free exercise' cases the court had relied on the balancing test, which required governmental actions that substantially burdened the free exercise of religion to be justified by a compelling governmental interest.[101] In the *Smith* case the court held that the test did not apply to general criminal prohibitions. The court held the balancing test to be inapplicable to 'free exercise' claims because in using the balancing test the court must either evaluate the centrality of the religious practice involved or give all religious conduct, whether trivial or crucial, the same protection.

The decision in the *Smith* case has been severely criticized because it seriously undermines the free exercise of religion.[102] It shows that although the Constitution protects the free exercise of religion, the courts are not prepared to countenance a practice simply because it is practised in the context of the free exercise of religion. Although the framers guaranteed freedom of religion, it is obvious that they had Christianity in mind and not other religions.[103]

In *Abington School District v Schempp*[104] the US Supreme Court declared a statute requiring the reading of verses from the bible and the reciting of the Lord's prayer in public schools to be a violation of the First Amendment. The court ruled that religious exercises of this kind infringed the rights of the plaintiffs in this case and as a result public school officials were prohibited from authorizing religious exercises on school premises. Although the daily devotions were not compulsory and the plaintiffs had the option to leave the classroom during the exercise, the Supreme Court none the less decided that the option to abstain did not provide due process of law.[105]

The European Convention on Human Rights provides in art 9 that 'everyone has the right to freedom of thought, conscience and religion'. It has been decided that art 9 does not place an obligation on a state to distribute books to prisoners which they consider essential for their religious and philosophical beliefs.[106] In *X v United Kingdom*[107] the Commission held that the refusal by prison authorities to distribute to a prisoner a book which, although it basically dealt with a religious theme, also discussed the martial arts, was a violation of the prisoner's right to freedom of religion, but was necessary for the 'protection of the rights and freedoms of others'.

The issue of the religious freedom of Jehovah's Witnesses has always been a prickly one. In *Grandrath v Federal Republic of Germany*[108] a member of the Jehovah's Witness sect refused to undergo compulsory military service on the

---

[101] Citing *Gillette v United States* 401 US 437 (1971).
[102] Kmiec 'The Original Understanding of the Free Exercise Clause and Religious Diversity' 1991 *U Missouri LR* 591ff; Rains 'Can Religious Practice be Given Meaningful Protection After *Employment Division v Smith*?' 1991 *U Colorado LR* 687ff.
[103] Rains op cit (n 102) 690ff.
[104] 374 US 203 (1960).
[105] Cf *West Virginia Board of Education v Barnette* 319 US 624 (1943); *Illinois ex rel McCollum v Board of Education* 333 US 203 (1948).
[106] *X v Austria* Application 1753/63; Yearbook of the European Convention on Human Rights VIII (1965) 174.
[107] Application 6886/75; Decisions and Reports of the European Commission of Human Rights No 5 (1976) 100.
[108] Report of 29 June 1967, Yearbook of the European Convention on Human Rights X (1967) 626.

grounds of conscience and, in addition, refused to undergo civilian service in lieu of military service, in terms of art 4(3)(b) of the European Convention, on the basis that it interfered with his duties as a minister. The question that arose was whether the substituted civilian service constituted an interference with the applicant's right to manifest his religious beliefs in terms of art 9. Under West German law full-time ministers of religion were exempted from all service. However, Jehovah's Witnesses do not have full-time ministers — all members are ministers. The Commission found that the situation would be untenable where numbers of people could evade substituted service on the grounds that they were ministers. As a result the Commission held that this was a case for the application of art 9(2), which limits freedom to manifest one's religion in the interests of public safety and for the protection of public order. For this reason it held that substituted service was not a violation of the applicant's freedom to manifest his religious belief.

Jehovah's Witnesses throughout the world have caused controversy in the manifestation of their religious beliefs. They have challenged governments and other churches on the basis of their belief. They have refused to participate in wars, to do compulsory military service, and to salute a flag. Their children have suffered in some schools because of their belief. In the process they have succeeded in asserting their rights and forced governments to recognize them.[109]

The conflict between manifestation of religious belief and some other public interest is exemplified by the case of *X v United Kingdom*,[110] which related to a UK law which made it compulsory for motor-cyclists to wear helmets. The applicant, a Sikh, contended that the act of removing his turban in order to don the helmet was a violation of his right to religious freedom. Although the Commission agreed with this contention, it pointed out that it was necessary and justified for the protection and safety of the public.

The religious beliefs of employees may conflict with their working conditions. The conflict between religious holidays and work programmes poses particular problems. This usually arises with communities such as Orthodox Jews, the Worldwide Church of God, and the Seventh Day Adventists, all of whom observe the Sabbath from sunset on Friday to sunset on Saturday. If an employer allows Christians to observe their 'Sabbath' (which is Sunday as the Lord's Day), but does not allow members of other religions the same right, the practice could be construed as a violation of the right to manifest one's religious belief. Moreover, if an employer recognizes Christian holidays (such as Christmas or Easter), members of other religions can claim the same as far as their religious festivals are concerned. To deny these could similarly be challenged as an infringement of the right to manifest one's religion.[111]

### 4.3 State of the debate in South Africa

South Africa is a religious country. Sometimes it is referred to as a Christian country. On closer inspection, however, it appears that merely lip-service is paid to

---

[109] For a discussion of Jehova's Witnesses in Canada, see Kaplan 'The Supreme Court of Canada and the Protection of Minority Dissent: The Case of the Jehovah's Witnesses' 1990 *U New Brunswick LJ* 65ff.

[110] Application 7992/77; Decisions and Reports of the European Commission of Human Rights No 14 234.

[111] *R v Ontario Labour Relations Board ex parte Trenton Construction Workers Association* 1963 DCR 593; see also Naidu *Fundamental Rights: A Bill of Rights for South Africa* (1988) 169–70.

Christianity. Although the preamble to the 1983 Constitution professed humble submission to Almighty God, and although s 2 stated that 'the people of the Republic of South Africa acknowledge the sovereignty and guidance of Almighty God', there is no evidence that the laws of the country have been tested against the will of God.[112] On the contrary, many laws that were passed by Parliament in the past were a violation of God's law as revealed in scripture.

Although there has been no religious intolerance of Christianity in South Africa, the same cannot be said of other religions. Moreover, even when it comes to Christianity, the government in the past did not allow the free expression of Christian convictions. Through its policy of apartheid and the laws enacted thereunder it violated the fundamental principles of Christianity — love for one's neighbour and treating others as one would like to be treated. People of colour were singled out for legally sanctioned discriminatory treatment. Those who opposed these policies and practices in the name of Christianity were ruthlessly suppressed. This discredited the government's claim to be a Christian government.[113]

Despite this abuse of Christianity on the part of the National Party government, there is no doubt that religion will always form a fundamental part of South African society. The question of how religion should be treated can be approached from various starting points. The most appropriate one is that of having a secular state where there is free interaction between the state and religious organizations. These organizations would be autonomous, although they could collaborate with the state on matters of mutual interest. There is no question of the suppression of religion nor is there a possibility of the creation of one state religion. This is to be accompanied by the constitutional protection of religion, enabling religious organizations and communities to operate freely and without interference from the government of the day.[114]

Proposals for a Bill of Rights before the adoption of the interim Constitution supported the protection of religious freedom.[115] Section 14 of the new Constitution guarantees 'freedom of conscience, religion, thought, belief and opinion'. It further provides that 'religious observances may be conducted at state or state-aided institutions under rules established by the appropriate authority for that purpose, provided that such religious observances are conducted on an equitable basis and attendance at them is free and voluntary'. This provision will ensure that prayer and bible reading are not prohibited in public schools and that South Africa will not follow the example of the US.

## 5 CONCLUSION

The Bill of Rights is a prominent feature of our interim Constitution. The rights to culture, education, and religion are among the most important entrenched in the Bill of Rights. From the above examination of these rights it is clear that the exercise of

---

[112] Robertson op cit (n 2) 126.
[113] Robertson op cit (n 2) 126–8.
[114] Sachs *Protecting Human Rights* 46–7.
[115] Clauses 2(34) and 5 of the ANC's draft Bill of Rights; clause 6.1 of the Democratic Party's draft Bill of Rights, stipulating that everyone shall have freedom of conscience and religion and consequently the state shall not favour one religion over another; clause 8 of the Negotiating Council's draft Bill of Fundamental Rights; clause 19 of the SA Law Commission's draft Bill of Rights.

these rights gives rise to problems which were not envisaged at the time of the framing of the Constitution. The courts will therefore be required to give substance to these rights in the process of interpretation. The rights to culture and religion are particularly sensitive because cultural and religious practices are closely connected with the emotions of the people. In interpreting and applying the provisions of the Bill of Rights in relation to these rights the courts in this country will be guided by a rich international and comparative jurisprudence.

# SOCIAL AND ECONOMIC RIGHTS*

### BERTUS DE VILLIERS

## 1 INTRODUCTION

The inclusion and protection of social and economic rights in a Bill of Rights is one of the main issues in dispute not only in South Africa but also in a range of other countries. In the South African debate there has been growing consensus since the early 1990s that a justiciable Bill of Rights should be included in a new Constitution. It has, however, not been that easy to reach agreement on the contents of such a Bill of Rights. It is especially with regard to social and economic rights that major differences have arisen between the various parties. The contents of the Bill of Rights with regard to social and economic rights as put forward by these parties depended on their respective philosophical approaches to the role of the state in a future dispensation. Those parties that advocated limited state powers were largely opposed to the inclusion of wide-ranging social and economic rights, while those in favour of extensive state powers supported the inclusion of such rights in the Constitution.

The opening bids of the political parties made it clear from the outset that the issue of social and economic rights was at the heart of a new political, social and economic dispensation. The African National Congress (ANC) advocated a Bill of Rights that included far-reaching social and economic rights, such as the freedom from hunger and the right to shelter, good health and employment. According to the ANC proposals, these freedoms should constitute justiciable rights which place a legal obligation upon the state to address the social and economic disparities in society. The National Party (NP), on the basis of the approach adopted by the South African Law Commission in its recommendations on a Bill of Rights, favoured the protection of traditional civil and political rights and freedoms and argued against the inclusion of social and economic rights on the basis that such rights would require an activist and interventionist state and that would be contrary to the principle of the separation of powers.

The protection of social and economic rights is not only a major topic in the South African constitutional and economic debate but is gaining momentum in other parts of the world as well. Where previously the debate on social and economic rights had been limited to mainly developing countries, it is now being conducted in developed countries and international organizations which in the past have almost exclusively been involved in the furtherance of the traditional civil and political rights and freedoms.

---

\* The much appreciated support rendered to me by the *Alexander von Humboldt Stiftung* is hereby acknowledged. The views expressed in this chapter do not necessarily reflect their views or opinion.

The shift in the human rights debate on the protection of social and economic rights towards a more balanced approach has been necessitated by, among other things, the changing environment in which people and governments find themselves. The role of the state is being defined differently today than at the turn of the century, with new problems and expectations in the social and economic spheres requiring a more active state that can address — alone or in partnership with other organizations — the social and economic ills and disparities of society.

In essence the difference between the proponents and opponents of the protection of social and economic rights centres on the question whether the state should have a passive and non-interventionist role in the protection of fundamental rights or whether the state should be under a justiciable legal obligation to adopt an active and interventionist role in order to address socio-economic inequalities and disparities. This difference does not so much concern the question whether the state should have an obligation towards the poor, but whether the state should be placed under a legal and justiciable obligation, or rather a political and moral obligation, to attend to these matters.

The intensity of the international debate on social and economic rights increased after World War II when the welfare state came to the fore and increasing attention was given to the plight of people in developing countries.[1] Up to that stage conventional wisdom had been that only the traditional civil and political rights, such as the right to equality before the law, freedom of movement, expression, and association, the right to life and property, and procedural matters, ought to be protected in a Constitution. The post-war period witnessed greater awareness of the position of the poor, which in turn gave impetus to the debate on social and economic rights. Berenstein summarizes the new debate as follows:

> 'Where the state was previously expected to adopt a *laissez-faire* approach, new calls are made for state interventionism. Individuals argue that in addition to their freedom rights, the state must initiate programs to ensure that equality between individuals is also attained.'[2]

The traditional approach, according to which it is argued that only 'passive' and 'negative' duties can be placed on the state (preventing the state from interference in the activities of the individual) and not 'active' and 'positive' duties (requiring state interference in the furtherance of the individual's interests), has come under fire because of the unscientific and impractical nature of the distinction. As Müller argues:

> '[I]t is difficult to divide the protection of rights in negative and positive duties . . . Thus the protection of the right to life, recognized as a civil and political right, requires not merely forbearance on the part of the state, but also positive action.'[3]

The aims of this chapter are threefold: to examine the background to socio-economic rights, referring to developments in international law; to investigate the

---

[1] The difficulties faced by developing countries in particular in protecting the traditional civil and political rights and freedoms in the absence of the economic prosperity enjoyed by some developed countries are illustrated in the following quotation from the Teheran Proclamation (13 May 1968, endorsed by the UN General Assembly): 'The widening gap between the economically developed countries and developing countries impedes the realization of human rights in the international community.'

[2] Berenstein 'Reflections of Human Rights' 1988 *Human Rights LJ* 165.

[3] Müller 'Fundamental Rights in Democracy' 1983 *Human Rights LJ* 131.

provision of directive principles for state policy; and to reflect on the most recent developments in the South African debate.

## 2  FUNDAMENTAL RIGHTS: THE LOCKEAN APPROACH

The foundation of the modern concept of the human rights theory can be traced back to the writings of the philosopher John Locke (1632–1704) in his monumental work *Two Treatises of Civil Government* (1690), in which he argues that all individuals have the right to be protected against arbitrary government actions. According to him, all individuals find themselves party to two social pacts: *pactum unionis* and *pactum subjectionis*. The first is aimed at the establishment of a civil society, while the latter constitutes a framework in terms of which individuals agree that a government is instituted with the duty to protect the natural rights of everyone.[4] This means that the execution of the powers and functions of government are limited by the supreme will of the people and the provisions of natural law.[5] The government therefore may not, in terms of the social contract that exists between it and the population, (mis)use its powers to encroach upon the fundamental rights and freedoms of individuals. The binding nature of natural law is defined as follows: 'Thus the law of nature stands as an eternal rule to all men, legislators as well as others.'[6]

This approach was later echoed in the American and French Revolutions, where the supremacy of the popular will over that of the state was given concrete form. The first constitutional document that included this notion was the Constitution of the State of Virginia (1776):

> 'All men are by nature equally free and independent and have certain rights, of which, when they enter into a state of society, they cannot by any compact deprive or divest their posterity: namely the enjoyment of life and liberty, with the means of acquiring and possessing property and pursuing and obtaining happiness and safety.'[7]

The theory of social contact thus regarded as self-evident the unalienable right of people to govern themselves by means of elected representatives whose authority is limited by the ultimate will of the people. The Universal Declaration of Human Rights, adopted in 1948, formulates this principle as follows:

> 'The will of the people shall be the basis of authority of government; this will shall be expressed in periodic and genuine elections which shall be by universal and equal franchise and shall be held by secret vote or by equivalent free voting procedures.'[8]

The protection of fundamental rights cannot be viewed in isolation from the political system prevailing in a country. Representative and responsible government, separation of powers, and democratic checks and balances are some of the factors that contribute to a culture conducive to the successful protection of human rights. Dahl describes the relationship between democracy and human rights as follows:

---

[4] *Two Treatises of Civil Government* (1967) para 2 11 135.

[5] 'Locke conceived all natural rights in the same line as property, that is to say, as attributes of the individual person born with him, and hence as indefeasible claims upon society and government. Such claims can never justly be set aside, since society itself exists to protect them; they can be regulated only to the extent that is necessary to give them effective protection': Sabine *A History of Political Theory* (1964) 528.

[6] Quoted in Lloyd *Introduction to Jurisprudence* (1979) 117.

[7] Article 1.

[8] Article 21(3) Universal Declaration of Human Rights (1948) GA Res 217A (III), 3(1) UN GAOR Res 71.

'It seems to me beyond question that the most comprehensive systems of political rights and liberties exist in democratic countries. That this is so is scarcely surprising. For one thing, extensive political rights and liberties are *integral* to democracy.'[9]

The Lockean approach, which in later years was reflected in numerous Constitutions and other human rights documents, in essence provides for the state to adopt a *laissez-faire* approach regarding its role, responsibilities, and duties towards its citizens. The state has the duty to refrain from interfering in the sphere of individual rights and freedoms and consequently it is obliged to provide a framework within which the individual can enjoy maximum freedom from state action.[10]

The core of the Lockean philosophy regarding the protection of fundamental rights can be summarized as follows:

- The individual is legally entitled to an environment that is free of undue state interference. Any unlawful acts committed by the state that encroach on the rights of individuals can be nullified by a competent court of law.[11]

- The rights of individuals are defined in 'negative' terms, in that they can prevent state interference in the lives of individuals, while individuals cannot legally require the state to assist them in the realization of their rights or the improvement of their social and economic welfare.

- The state has the duty towards individuals to withhold itself from any unlawful action that may encroach upon the rights of individuals. The state is under no legal obligation (in contrast to the moral and political obligations that it may have) to take positive action in support of individuals regarding their social and economic situation.

The rights of individuals in terms of the Lockean approach are generally referred to as 'first-generation' rights in that they define the area of individual exclusivity where state action is prohibited.[12] The state has no legal duty to improve the economic, social, and welfare[13] position of individuals.[14]

## 3 THE RISE OF SOCIAL AND ECONOMIC RIGHTS

The emphasis placed on the protection of fundamental rights in accordance with Lockean philosophy has come under wide-ranging criticism since the turn of this century, and especially since World War II. The rise of the welfare state, new approaches to the role of the state, and the socio-economic plight of individuals not only in developing countries but also in poverty-stricken urban and rural areas in

---

[9] Dahl 'Democracy and Human Rights under Different Conditions of Development' in Eide & Hagtvet (eds) *Human Rights in Perspective* (1992) 235.

[10] De Villiers 'Socio-economic Rights in a New Constitution: Critical Evaluation of the Recommendations of the South African Law Commission' (1992) 3 *TSAR* 422.

[11] Beinart 'The Liberty of the Subject' 1953 *THRHR* 30.

[12] 'Traditional human rights, sometimes called first-generation rights to indicate their historical primacy in bills of rights and other human rights instruments, create the ground rules for democratic government. The right of equality before the law, freedom of expression, movement, association, rights of life, liberty and property are all designed to create a zone beyond which the state will not encroach, thereby leaving a space of uncoerced political activity': Davis 'The Case Against the Inclusion of Socio-economic Rights in a Bill of Rights Except as Directive Principles' (1992) 8 *SAJHR* 475.

[13] Epstein 'The Uncertain Quest for Welfare Rights' 1985 *Brigham Young U LR* 201–29.

[14] Pollack *Human Rights* (1971) 231.

developed countries have raised questions as to the theoretical and practical validity of the approach that only first-generation rights ought to be included in a Bill of Rights.

The twentieth century has witnessed various efforts to extend the categories of justiciable rights for inclusion in human right documents.[15] In addition to the first-generation civil and political rights proposals have also been made for the protection of second- and third-generation rights. The following content is given to the respective categories of rights:[16]

- First-generation rights refer to the traditional liberal civil and political rights, which in turn are divided into procedural and substantive rights. The following are examples of procedural rights: protection against arbitrary arrest; protection against detention without trial; the right to a public trial, to information regarding the charges, to legal assistance and to be tried in a language you understand. The substantive rights include the right to be treated equally and the freedom of religion, expression, assembly, association, and movement.

- Second-generation rights refer especially to various aspects of social, cultural, and economic rights, such as the rights to employment, social security, shelter, family assistance, education, mother-tongue education, and state support of cultural activities.[17]

- Third-generation rights refer especially to the right to self-determination,[18] peace, development,[19] and a protected environment.[20]

The protection of second- and third-generation 'rights' has been one of the most intensely debated topics in constitutional and international human rights law. It is increasingly being realized that the political, social, and economic circumstances in which the Lockean approach was formulated differ in crucial respects from those of the twentieth century. The protection of only civil and political rights is, given the demands of modern society, unrealistic and does not address the realities which confront governments and populations.[21]

---

[15] 'We could say that the full historical appearance of the economic, social and cultural rights beginning in the 19th century has been growing since that time and has produced a modified and complex concept of fundamental rights by integrating and completing the classical liberal conception': Peces-Barba 'Reflections on Economic, Social and Cultural Rights' 1981 *Human Rights LJ* 285.

[16] Claude & Weston (eds) *Human Rights in the World Community* (1989) 17–18.

[17] Ganji *The Realization of Economic, Social and Cultural Rights: Problems, Policies, Progress* United Nations (1975) E/CN 4/1108 Rev 1.

[18] Dinstein 'Collective Human Rights of Peoples and Minorities' 1976 *ICLQ* 102; Kiss 'The Peoples' Right to Self-Determination' 1986 *Human Rights LJ* 165–75; Partsch 'Recent Developments in the Field of Peoples' Rights' *Human Rights LJ* 177–82.

[19] 'Moreover, as for the right of development, those who oppose it, overlook the development dimension of individual human rights, as it comes to the fore in the right to self-determination of peoples and in everyone's entitlement to a social and international order, in which all universally recognized human rights can be fully recognized': Chowdhury & De Waart 'Significance of the Right to Development: An Introductory View' in Chowdhury, Denters & De Waart *The Rights to Development in International Law* (1992) 7.

[20] 'Man has the fundamental right to freedom, equality and adequate conditions of life, in an environment where equality permits a life of dignity and well-being . . . Man bears a solemn responsibility to protect and improve the environment for future generations': Principle 1, *Stockholm Declaration on the Human Environment* (1972).

[21] 'A crucial dimension of human nature is its dependence on social, historical and behavioral contexts. Negative rights theory adheres to a further assumption about human nature as axiomatic, when it is merely optional. It presents individuals as self-determining, as best capable of preserving their own interests, as indeed self-developing. This evokes a theory of human nature as self-sufficient, independent, and capable of rational pursuit of enlightened self-interest. It encourages an overly formal and abstract discussion of human rights': Freeden 'Human Rights and Welfare: A Communitarian View' 1990 *Ethics* 490.

Maclachlan summarizes the change that has taken place in socio-economic circumstances as follows:

> 'Locke's democratic society found its final condemnation in the slums and squalor of Western cities and in the exploitation of human and physical resources purely in the interest of individual wealth and property.'[22]

The Lockean approach to the protection of fundamental rights has from a contemporary perspective been criticized for the following reasons as being incomplete:

- The human rights debates of the eighteenth century were dominated not only by the surrounding circumstances but especially by the philosophers of the day — who all had a Western orientation. Since then new arguments regarding the role of the state in the protection of fundamental rights have come to the fore, not only in the West but especially in developing countries as well as in international law.[23] 'From the practical experience in many developing states, it is evident that in most states of the world, human rights as defined by the West are rejected, or, more accurately, are meaningless.'[24]

- The type of socio-economic problems that are being faced today by populations in developing and developed countries are of such a nature that extensive state involvement is required to address them.[25] The traditional *laissez-faire* approach cannot solve the critical problems of illiteracy, education, unemployment, housing shortages, and starvation. The state consequently has a moral, political, and legal obligation to take steps, whether alone or in partnership with others, to improve the quality of life of all individuals. Contemporary experience makes it clear that 'without at least some modicum of such basic necessities as food, shelter and clothing, the enjoyment of other rights appears highly theoretical'.[26]

- It is theoretically unsound to distinguish between civil and political rights, on the one hand (first-generation rights), and social and economic rights (second-generation rights), on the other, on the basis that the former constitute only negative (passive) rights, while the latter are positive rights requiring an active state. There are numerous rights in the category of civil and political rights that also require positive state action, such as the right to a fair trial, the right to vote, the right to legal representation,[27] and so on. It is therefore not accurate to

---

[22] Maclachlan *Human Rights in Retrospect and Reality* (1986) 13.

[23] Khushalani 'Human Rights Issues in Asia and Africa' 1983 *Human Rights LJ* 430. He argues that human rights theory in the West should be interpreted against the background of the historical circumstances in which it was born. 'It is important to note that the seventeenth and eighteenth centuries were times of dramatic changes in the economic and social fabric of western Europe. The communal bonds of feudalism had collapsed and extended family ties were disrupted by the Industrial Revolution. A capitalist system came into existence and a new industrial class rebelled against the constrainst of government, demanding political participation and political freedoms and arguing the ethics of the social contract' (at 413–14).

[24] Ibid.

[25] 'The colonial experience left new, "liberated" states with such a legacy of economic underdevelopment that the regaining of human dignity in these states have come to be viewed primarily in economic terms... Accordingly economic, social and cultural rights are regarded as core human rights': Beukes & Fourie 'Economic and Social Human Rights: An Exploratory Survey' 1988 *TRW* 18.

[26] Ginsburg & Lesser 'Current Developments in Economic and Social Rights: A United States Perspective' 1981 *Human Rights LJ* 241.

[27] The fundamental importance of the right to legal representation was formulated in *Gideon v Wainwright* 372 US 343, 344 (1963) as follows: '[A]ny person haled into court, who is too poor to hire a lawyer, cannot be assured a fair trial unless councel is provided.'

distinguish between the two categories of rights on the basis of 'positive' and 'negative' state action.[28]

- The law is a living organism and should therefore reflect the needs, requirements, and values of the society in which it functions. The protection of human rights cannot occur in the abstract or in a vacuum which is isolated from the community and bearers of the rights. In a similar way that the historical and social forces of the seventeenth and eighteenth centuries influenced the development of civil and political rights the circumstances and requirements of the twentieth century should mould a framework for the protection of social and economic rights.[29]

The right to life should be interpreted not only as a protection against being arbitrarily deprived of life but should for instance also include the right to medical assistance, hospitalization, and nutrition.[30]

The proponents of social and economic rights raise various arguments in support of their position, of which the following are examples:

- The inclusion of these rights in the category of justiciable human rights is justified by the requirements, needs, and circumstances of modern society.[31] The law as a living organism must reflect those requirements rather than entangle itself in a philosophical framework based on the requirements of eighteenth-century society. This does not mean that all socio-economic 'ideals' and 'objectives' can be translated into justiciable 'rights'. Hauserman summarizes the argument as follows:

  'Insisting that economic, social and cultural rights are of equal importance to the other branches of human rights is not intended to paper over the cracks by ignoring the difficulties which inevitably arise in their full realization . . . But what can be stated is that in deciding these (spending) priorities, international human rights laws require states, both rich and poor, to allocate sufficient funds to ensure that all members of their population live in conditions appropriate to guarantee their health and dignity, before allocating funds to those programmes and projects less immediately concerned with human welfare.'[32]

- Social and economic rights may increase the obligation of the state to act positively, but that does not justify the exclusion of the category of rights from a Bill of Rights. A number of first-generation rights also require positive state

---

[28] 'We cannot, however, make a neat distinction around the axis "negative/positive" between civil and political rights on the one hand and economic, social and cultural rights on the other': Eide 'Realization of Social and Economic Rights and the Minimum Threshold Approach' (1989) 10 *Human Rights LJ* 36.

[29] The fact that social and economic rights may require a different role of the state does not mean that the social and economic rights are of lesser value. 'There are certain rights which require positive action by the state and which can be guaranteed only so far as such action is predicable, while others merely require that the state shall refrain from prejudicial action': Sharma *Directive Principles and Fundamental Rights* (1990) 103.

[30] 'The fact that many jurists have interpreted the right to life in a restrictive and narrow-minded way by limiting it to the sole right of not being arbitrarily deprived of life in no way alters the scandalous nature of this contradiction . . . Admittedly, this dimension of the right to life is one of capital importance. But there is another equally important "positive" aspect: not only the right not to die (and this includes dying of hunger), but also the right to life (and not merely to vegetate, subsist or survive), to live in dignity': Leuprecht 'Reflections on Human Rights' 1988 *Human Rights LJ* 165.

[31] Kooijmans argues that the protection of social and economic rights is as important for the full development of human capacities as is the protection of civil and political rights. 'The realization of these rights (social and economic) is as necessary for human development as freedom of speech and respect for private life. Only if one continues to look at human rights as pre-State rights, will economic, social and cultural rights never fit into the category of human rights': Kooijmans 'Human Rights — Universal Panacea?' 1990 *Netherlands Int LR* 320.

[32] Hauserman 'Myth and Realities' in Davies (ed) *Human Rights* (1988) 152.

action, which means that the distinction between first and second-generation rights, in so far as it is based on a 'passive' versus an 'active' state, is invalid.

- Social and economic rights have become well developed in international law and in various formal international documents that bear the signatures of a wide variety of countries. These countries are politically, morally, and even legally obliged to include the provisions of the international law to which they are party in their constitutional law.

- The implementation of social and economic rights may, because of limited resources, be done in a gradual manner without ignoring their fundamental nature. The International Covenant on Economic, Social and Cultural Rights provides a case in point:

    'Each State party to the present Covenant undertakes to take steps, individually and through international assistance and co-operation, especially economic and technical, to the maximum of its available resources, with the view to achieving progressively the full realization of the rights recognized in the present Covenant by all appropriate means, including particularly the adoption of legislative measures.'[33]

- A number of the social and economic rights have become refined to the extent that they have either been included in some Constitutions or they can be included — e g the right to protection of the family;[34] mother-tongue education;[35] a minimum wage;[36] equality of employment opportunities;[37] and collective bargaining.[38]

The opponents of the inclusion of social and economic rights in a Bill of Rights have a number of arguments to substantiate their position. The following are examples of some of these arguments:

- The ideals reflected by social and economic 'rights' are laudable, but they do not constitute justiciable rights. Politically and morally they ought to play an important role in the formulation of government policies, but they do not constitute rights in the same way as the civil and political rights do.[39]

- Social and economic 'rights' are programmatic in nature, which would require the judicial branch to become involved in policy matters which normally belong on the agenda of the legislature.[40] This would constitute a breach of the

---

[33] International Covenant on Economic, Social and Cultural Rights (1966) GA Res 2200 (XXI), 21 UN GAOR, Supp (No 16) 49.

[34] Article 14(3) of the Constitution of Namibia reads as follows: 'The family is the natural and fundamental group unit of society and is entitled to protection by society and the State.'

[35] Section 23 of the Constitution of Canada.

[36] Article 7 of the Constitution of Brazil determines that 'the following are rights of city and rural workers . . . a minimum wage nationwide, established by law, capable of satisfying their basic living needs and those of their families', as quoted in De Villiers, Van Vuuren & Wiechers *Human Rights: Documents that Paved the Way* (1992) 279.

[37] Article 16 of the Constitution of India provides that 'there shall be equality of opportunity for all citizens in matters relating to employment or appointment to any office under the State.'

[38] Article 37 of the Constitution of Spain determines that '[t]he law shall guarantee the right to collective labour bargaining between workers' and employers' representatives, as well as the binding force of the agreements'.

[39] 'The implementation of these *claims* is a political matter, not a matter of law, and hence not a matter of rights' (my emphasis): Vierdag 'The Legal Nature of the Rights granted by the International Covenant on Economic, Social and Political Rights' 1978 *NYIL* 103. Van Niekerk also argues that socio-economic rights 'will definitely not constitute principles of administrative law or civil private law': Van Niekerk 'Categories of Fundamental Rights and Constitutional Reform in South Africa' 1990 *SAPR/PL* 87.

[40] 'This [recognition of social and economic rights] results not only in giving the courts an influence on the state budget by granting claims to social and cultural rights, but also entails leaving it up to the courts to provide a closer

principles of the separation of powers.⁴¹ The first-generation rights are regarded as 'self-executing', while social and economic rights require legislative and other state actions.⁴²

- Social and economic rights do not comply with the necessary requirements of 'practicability', 'paramount importancy', and 'universality' and could therefore only constitute claims and not justiciable rights.⁴³

- The definition of social and economic rights is vague, ambiguous, and could differ not only between countries but also within a country.⁴⁴ This problem could be exacerbated by the various welfare, social, and economic programmes in place in a country.

## 4 SOCIAL AND ECONOMIC RIGHTS: A PERSPECTIVE FROM INTERNATIONAL LAW

The recognition and protection of social and economic rights have gained more ground in international law than in the various state constitutional and legal frameworks. Four international documents that can be referred to in order to illustrate this are the Universal Declaration of Human Rights; the Covenant on Social, Economic and Cultural Rights; the European Social Charter; the African (or Banjul) Charter on Human and Peoples' Rights.

The United Nations has since its establishment endeavoured to improve the position of social, economic, and cultural rights vis-à-vis civil and political rights. The Universal Declaration of Human Rights⁴⁵ contains various provisions related to social and economic rights, such as the right to social security;⁴⁶ the right to work, favourable conditions of work, equal pay for equal work, and a just and favourable remuneration;⁴⁷ and the right to a standard of living adequate for the health and well-being of the person and his family, including food, clothing, housing, and medical care.⁴⁸

The United Nations, however, soon experienced difficulties regarding the first-versus second-generation debate with the adoption of two separate covenants dealing with human rights. The Covenant on Civil and Political Rights⁴⁹ deals only with the traditional civil and political rights, while the Covenant on Economic,

---

definition of the actual object of these rights. And this again may have a decisive influence on the separation of state powers': Starck 'Europe's Fundamental Rights in the Newest Garb' 1982 *Human Rights LJ* 116.

[41] Starck op cit (n 40).

[42] Vierdag op cit (n 39) 83 states that 'social rights are often said to be not "real" not "legal" rights, but "programmatic" rights, or "promotional" rights'.

[43] Cranston as quoted in Basson *Die Ontwikkeling van Ekonomiese Regte met 'n Arbeidsregtelike Perspektief* (Unpublished LLD thesis, Unisa 1990) 117.

[44] 'This typical social right which requires affirmative action on the part of the State is, of necessity, so ill-defined that it would be extremely difficult to identify what, for example, are "just and favourable conditions of work", and even if it were possible to reach agreement on the precise details of the goal in view, its implementation would require such constant supervision as to necessitate an unprecedented change in the nature of the judicial function': Jaconelli *Enacting a Bill of Rights* (1986) 101.

[45] Universal Declaration of Human Rights (1948).

[46] Article 22.

[47] Article 23.

[48] Article 25.

[49] International Covenant on Civil and Political Rights (1966) GA Res 2200 (XXI), 21 UN GAOR, Supp (No 16) 52.

Social and Cultural Rights[50] makes provision for social, economic, and cultural rights. One of the reasons for the separate covenants was the influential role of the developed countries in comparison to that of the developing countries at the time of the drafting of the conventions.[51] A similar exercise today could lead to a different outcome.

The signatories to the two covenants decided to distinguish between the two documents on the basis that the civil and political rights could be implemented immediately, while the social, economic, and cultural rights could not take immediate effect because of their programmatic nature. The civil and political rights were also regarded as 'real' rights, meaning that they were justiciable, while the social and economic rights were regarded only as 'ideals' or 'objectives'.[52] The problem of placing social and economic rights on the same footing as civil and political rights was described as follows:

> 'Civil law distinguished between obligations leading to formal results and obligations to take action. In the present case civil and political rights, and some economic rights, might connote obligations that would produce actual results; most economic and social rights however, could only give rise to obligations to take action.'[53]

The Covenant on Economic, Social and Cultural Rights recognizes, among others, the following social and economic rights of individuals: the right to work;[54] just and favourable conditions of employment;[55] equal pay for equal work, safe working conditions;[56] social security;[57] and the 'widest possible' protection to the family.[58] The states that are party to the Covenant undertake to initiate steps 'to the maximum of its available resources'[59] with the view to realizing the rights.[60] This formulation prevents a state from being forced to provide services beyond its capabilities and although the formulation may have certain weaknesses, it allows for 'flexibility, making it possible for states to comply with their obligations in ways which correspond to their particular situation'.[61]

A difficulty with the operationalization of some of the above and other social and economic rights and the setting of universally acceptable benchmarks for the realization of such rights is that capacities, standards, priorities, and resources in countries differ substantially. This raises the question of whether one could not develop a 'minimum threshold for human rights realization'.[62] This would mean

---

[50] International Covenant on Economic, Social and Cultural Rights (1966) GA Res 2200 (XXI), 21 UN GAOR, Supp (No 16) 49.

[51] Lippman 'Human Rights Revisited: The Protection of Human Rights under the International Covenant on Civil and Political Rights' 1978 *Netherlands Int LR* 272.

[52] Simsarian 'Progress in Drafting Two Covenants on Human Rights in the United Nations' (1952) 46 *Am J Int L* 711.

[53] Ramcharan 'Human Rights and the Law' in Davies op cit (n 32) 121.

[54] Article 6.

[55] Article 7.

[56] Article 7*(a)*.

[57] Article 9.

[58] Article 10.

[59] Article 2.

[60] A Committee on Economic, Social and Cultural Rights was established in 1987 to encourage and monitor the implementation of these provisions. Their task, however, is complicated by the vagueness of the obligations flowing from the social and economic rights, the unsatisfactory guidance given to state parties on how to report on their compliance with the provisions, and the non-involvement of NGOs in monitoring social and economic rights. Eide op cit (n 28) 49.

[61] Eide op cit (n 28) 37.

[62] Eide op cit (n 28) 45.

that thresholds would be used to measure indicators such as nutrition, infant mortality, unemployment, income, and life expectancy. A national standard could be developed in such a way, which would enable the identification of problem areas and communities, the setting of priorities, and the launching of programmes. A 'core list of rights' accompanied by minimum thresholds could for instance include rights to food, health, and employment.[63]

The European Social Charter[64] was signed in 1961 after the Committee of Members of the Council of Europe had announced in 1954 that the purpose of such a social charter would be to determine the social objectives that the member states would seek to achieve.[65] The Social Charter should be seen as complementary to the European Convention on Human Rights, although the former focuses on rights that require certain state intervention, while the latter provides for the protection of the traditional civil and political rights. The rights acknowledged in the Social Charter are not binding and can at best be described as social objectives. The 'rights' contained in the Social Charter are of lesser value that the 'rights' provided for in the European Convention on Human Rights. Berenstein argues for instance that the inclusion of some of the social and economic rights in the European Convention would confer upon them 'a higher value because they would be raised to the rank of fundamental rights'.[66]

The introduction to the Social Charter consequently states that the contracting parties 'accept as the aim of their policy, to be pursued by all appropriate means, the attainment of conditions in which the following rights and principles may be effectively realized'.

The following are examples of some of the aims that are recognized in the Social Charter:

- In order to exercise the right to work the parties undertake as a primary aim to achieve the highest possible level of employment, to grant free employment services to all workers, and to offer training and vocational guidance to all workers.[67]
- To ensure the right to just conditions of work the parties undertake to provide reasonable working hours, public holidays with pay, and resting periods with pay.[68]
- The right to protection of health will be promoted by means of measures such as the provision of educational facilities regarding the promotion of health and the prevention of possible epidemic and other diseases.[69]
- The right to social security will be realized by the establishment of a system of social security and compliance with standards as laid down by the International Labour Convention.[70]

---

[63] Andreassen, Smith & Stokke 'Compliance with Economic and Social Human Rights: Realistic Evaluations and Monitoring in the Light of Immediate Obligations' in Eide & Hagtvet op cit (n 9) 260.
[64] Signed in 1961. European Treaty Series No 48; 12 *European Yearbook* 397.
[65] De Villiers et al op cit (n 36) 83.
[66] Berenstein 'Economic and Social Rights: Their Inclusion in the European Convention on Human Rights' 1981 *Human Rights LJ* 266.
[67] Article 1.
[68] Article 2.
[69] Article 11.
[70] Article 12.

The Council of Europe Parliamentary Assembly attempted in 1978 to develop criteria for the inclusion of the rights provided for in the Social Charter in the Convention on Human Rights.[71] They identified the following criteria:

- the right must be fundamental;
- it must enjoy general recognition;
- it must be defined precisely;
- it must be enforceable.

The Organization of African Unity (OAU) adopted the African Charter on Human and Peoples' Rights in 1981,[72] which came into force in 1986 after being ratified by a majority of members of the OAU.[73] The Charter contains various provisions relating to social and economic rights such as:

- the right to work under equitable and satisfactory conditions as well as to receive equal pay for equal work;[74]
- the right to enjoy the 'best attainable' state of health;[75]
- the right to education, participation in cultural life, and the 'promotion and protection of morals and traditional values' by the state;[76]
- the protection of the family as the 'natural unit and basis of society' by the state, as well as the assistance afforded by the state to the family as the custodian of morals and traditional values.[77]

The African Charter could be interpreted as non-binding in the sense that there are insufficient guarantees to the effect that states are legally obliged to uphold the rights and there is no express guarantee that the rights have to be protected by the states. The social and economic rights provided for in the African Charter are all, individually and collectively, 'geared towards development'.[78] The African Charter has many weaknesses, but it represents an important attempt to develop an African framework for the protection of rights and freedoms against the background of international experience.

Experience of the protection of social and economic rights in international law is varied. The arguments that have been raised against the inclusion of social and economic rights in state Constitutions have, albeit to a lesser degree, also been experienced on the international level. The developments in international law have, however, been of such a nature that Peces-Barba concludes as follows:

---

[71] Recommendation 838 (1978), para 12, stated that 'in order to be incorporated in the Convention, any right must be fundamental and enjoy general recognition, and be capable of suffiently precise definition to lay legal obligations on a State,rather than simply constitute a general rule'.

[72] 27 June 1981 at Nairobi, Kenya.

[73] M'Baye & Ndiaye 'The Organization of African Unity (OAU)' in Vasak *The International Dimensions of Human Rights* (1982); Motshekga 'The African Charter on Human and Peoples' Rights — Its Importance to Human Rights Thinking in South Africa' 1989 *Codicillus* 31–50.

[74] Article 15.
[75] Article 16.
[76] Article 17.
[77] Article 18.

[78] Dlamini 'Towards a Regional Protection of Human Rights in Africa: The African Charter on Human and Peoples' Rights' (1991) XXIV *CILSA* 199.

'It is true that one can no longer speak, even from the most classic positions of juridical science, of an en bloc rejection of economic, social and cultural rights which, at least in part, adopt techniques of organization similar to those of the rights of liberal origin.'[79]

The position of social and economic rights in international law can be summarized as follows:

- There is a realization that the classic distinctions that have been drawn between civil and political rights (first generation), on the one hand, and social, cultural, and economic rights (second generation), on the other, are not based on sound theory or praxis. Various social, economic, and cultural rights have been refined to the extent that they have been included in justiciable and enforceable Bills of Rights, such as the right to education, protection of the family, and equal pay for equal work.

- States have been more generous in their support of social and economic rights on the international level by means of treaties and other agreements than in their support for the inclusion of similar provisions in their respective state Constitutions and human rights documents.

- International law has not been able to develop sufficient remedies and enforcing mechanisms to ensure that the social and economic rights agreed upon are enforced. It would seem as if the major mechanisms remain political rather than judicial in nature.

- There is a realization that the definition and application of social and economic rights may differ between countries on the basis of subjective factors such as resources, state of the economy, and national and regional average standards. It is difficult, if not impossible, to provide a universally acceptable definition of the practical content of some of the social and economic rights. Even if a 'minimum threshold' is determined, it would 'vary with the nature of the national situation and societies, depending whether they are in the Third World, in developing economies, whether it be an industrial society, a subsistence culture in a rural setting, and varying from country to country and region to region'.[80]

- The debates on and relevance of social and economic rights are not limited to Third World developing countries. Various highly developed countries are faced with social and economic problems that require state intervention and assistance to individuals and communities. It can therefore be expected that the process of refining social and economic claims in order to include them in human rights documents as justiciable rights will continue.

- The role and value of a non-justiciable social charter (in addition to the Bill of Rights) in which certain social and economic aims and ideals are contained should not be underestimated as a means of focusing political and moral attention on the plight of people as well as providing a framework within which a Bill of Rights should be interpreted. Although governments cannot judicially be forced to comply with certain of these aims, that does not void them of relevance in the influencing and formulation of government policies.

---

[79] Op cit (n 15) 289.
[80] Lack 'Human Rights and the Disadvantaged' 1989 *Human Rights LJ* 54.

## 5 SOCIAL AND ECONOMIC RIGHTS IN STATE CONSTITUTIONS

The Constitutions of various countries have either been amended through the years or were originally formulated in a manner that provided for the protection of some social and economic rights. In most cases the rights are formulated in a way which respects the separation of powers and which does not allow the judiciary to become involved in the discretion of the legislature to set priorities and determine budgets for social and economic reforms.

The US Constitution is regarded as a prime example of a Constitution where the traditional civil and political rights of individuals are protected and no reference is made to modern-day social and economic rights. Despite this, the US has played a leading role in the drafting of international documents such as the Universal Declaration of Human Rights, in which provision is made for social and economic rights. It is therefore argued that 'to understand the issues in economic and social rights in the US, it is essential to recognize that there are rights not defined or even mentioned in our Constitution'.[81] The basis of this argument is that the rights provided for in the US Bill of Rights are not a complete list and that other sources, such as international law, must be employed to determine the full range of rights that individuals have. A similar argument was raised by the Irish courts when the directive principles of state policy in that country were seen as a possible 'source' of new rights.[82] Black even argues that certain clauses of the US Bill of Rights could and indeed should be interpreted as a 'source' of new rights.[83] He believes that the Preamble could (as in the case of the directive principles in Ireland and India) also serve as a source of new rights as well as give additional content to rights already recognized.

Although the federal Constitution of the US does not contain social and economic rights, some state Constitutions (New York's, for example) provide for rights such as the commitment to a minimally adequate level of subsistence. The courts have upheld these rights, but have rejected them as federal rights.[84] The Supreme Court, for example, has referred to welfare benefits as 'more like property than gratuity'.[85] The economic and social rights that individuals have in the US find their origin in ordinary statutory rather than constitutional provisions.[86] This means that whatever services the state offers must comply with the provisions of the Bill of Rights, but the nature of the programmes and the priorities remains a legislative function and discretion. The state can therefore not constitutionally be obliged to develop certain social and economic programmes.[87]

---

[81] Ginsburg & Lesser op cit (n 26) 236.

[82] *Murtagh Properties v Cleary* IR (1972) 330.

[83] 'I see the Ninth Amendment not as in itself "referring" to any particular right or rights, but rather as commanding us to use the methods available in our legal system in an ongoing search for "unenumerated" rights': Black 'Further Reflections on the Constitutional Justice of Livelihood' (Rubin Lecture, Columbia Law School, 20 March 1986) 5.

[84] Ginsberg & Lesser op cit (n 26) 239.

[85] *Goldberg v Kelly* 397 US 254 (1970).

[86] 'In constitutional principle the United States is a welfare State not by constitutional mandate but by grace of Congress and the legislatures': Henkin 'Economic-Social Rights as "Rights": A United States Perspective' 1981 *Human Rights LJ* 229.

[87] States could consequently provide for inadequate welfare payments to families (*Dandrige v Williams* 397 US 471 (1970)); subsidies for education within states may differ because they are determined on a local level (*San Antonio Independent School District v Rodriguez* 411 US 1 (1973)); and provision could be made for mandatory retirement (*Massachusetts Board of Retirement v Murgia* 427 US 307 (1976)).

A number of Constitutions in Western Europe contain provisions that can be termed social and economic rights and objectives. Most of these Constitutions 'describe accepted welfare-state and cultural-state objectives, which are for the greater part the real prerequisites for the enjoyment of rights of liberty'.[88] In most cases the 'rights' are formulated in a manner that either makes them non-justiciable or they are included in a chapter on directive principles and state duties. The arguments that have been raised above against the protection of social and economic rights have also been raised against the inclusion of such rights in justiciable Bills of Rights in various European countries.[89]

Some of the social and economic rights, duties, and obligations that are contained in the Constitutions of Western Europe are assistance to married couples and families,[90] the right to free primary education,[91] the right to work and protection of workers,[92] health support,[93] and protection of the environment.[94]

On the African Continent the recent Constitution of Nigeria contains a chapter on fundamental rights and one on directive principles. The same applies to the Constitution of Namibia. The Namibian Bill of Rights provides for the 'normal' range of civil and political as well as some social and economic rights that have become associated with human rights documents internationally. Most of the rights require limited state action for the realization of the right. Even in the case of affirmative action the state may undertake such programmes, but cannot legally be obliged to do so.[95] In the case of education the state is under a legal duty to provide primary education.[96]

A whole chapter in the Namibian Constitution is devoted to Principles of State Policy,[97] in which, according to international use, provision is made for certain social and economic goals and objectives without justiciable rights being created. Some of the principles of state policy include the active encouragement of trade unions,[98] fair employment practices, access to public services, an acceptable standard of living and nutrition, and the protection of the environment.

Fourie provides the following reasons why, against expectations, not more provision has been made in the Namibian Bill of Rights for justiciable social and economic rights:

- The independence process and drafting of the Constitution was 'circumscribed' by liberal Western opinion and pressure.

- The 'perception' that it is difficult to define and give legal effect to social and economic rights.

---

[88] Starck op cit (n 40) 114.

[89] Stark op cit (n 40) 116 summarizes the arguments as follows: the inclusion of social and economic rights in state Bills of Rights 'results not only in giving the courts an influence on the State budget by granting claims to social rights, but also entails leaving it up to the courts to provide a closer definition of the actual object of these rights. And this again may have a decisive influence on the separation of State powers.'

[90] Greece art 16; Portugal art 67; Switzerland art 26.

[91] Ireland art 42.

[92] Netherlands art 1.18; Greece art 22.

[93] Greece art 21; Portugal art 65.

[94] Netherlands art 1.20; Greece art 24.

[95] Article 23.

[96] Article 20.

[97] Chapter 11.

[98] Article 95.

- The spirit of compromise between opposing parties. However, he doubts whether all the parties were fully aware of the extent of the compromise and the implications thereof.[99]

Only time will tell what role the principles will fulfil in the developing of a just social and economic dispensation in Namibia. It can be expected that the legislature and judiciary will follow the active Indian rather than the conservative Irish approach to the implementation of the directive principles. Should this happen, the principles may become a source of 'new' rights and may also provide the basis for extensive state programmes aimed at social and economic development, even if it means placing limits on the fundamental rights of individuals.

## 6 DIRECTIVE PRINCIPLES: CLAIMS RATHER THAN RIGHTS

A phenomenon that has been evident in international and constitutional law since World War II is the provision for certain social, economic, cultural, and other directive principles or aims in constitutional and other documents. It was shown in the previous section how such aims have been included in international agreements such as the Covenant on Economic, Social and Cultural Rights and the European Social Charter. A number of states have also included in their Constitutions what can be termed directive principles of state policy. Examples are Ireland,[100] India,[101] Nigeria,[102] Spain,[103] Portugal,[104] and Namibia.[105] A number of the German *Länder* (federal states) have similar provisions in their Constitutions and consideration is being given to the inclusion of directive principles as *Staatsziele* (aims of the state) in the Basic Law (federal Constitution).[106]

The inclusion of the directive principles of state policy in the respective state Constitutions was preceded by the typical debates on the protection and enforcement of social and economic 'rights'. The use of directive principles to complement and support human rights documents has been influenced by various circumstantial developments, such as the moral and political importance of recognizing certain of the social and economic claims of individuals and communities in the Constitution, the difficulty of defining all these claims in a manner that would allow them to be regarded as legally enforceable rights, and developments in international law where the rigid distinction between civil and political rights (on the one hand) and social, economic, and cultural rights (on the other) has been replaced by a more balanced approach.

It is not uncommon for modern-day Constitutions to contain a chapter dealing with fundamental rights (providing for civil and political rights and for some social

---

[99] Fourie 'The Namibian Constitution and Economic Rights' (1992) 8 *SAJHR* 367–8.
[100] Article 45 Directive Principles of Social Policy.
[101] Articles 36–51 Directive Principles of State Policy.
[102] Articles 14–22 Fundamental Objectives and Directive Principles of State Policy.
[103] Articles 39–52 Governing Principles of Economic and Social Policy.
[104] Article 9 Basic Tasks of the State.
[105] Articles 95–101 Principles of State Policy.
[106] *Abstimmungsergebnisse zu den Themenkomplexen 'Staatsziele und Grundrechte' (ausser Art. 3 und 6 GG) Gemeinsame Verfassungskommission Sekretariat, 24 Februar 1993*; Löcke '*Soziale Grundrechte als Staatszielbestimmungen und Gesetzgebungsaufträge*' 1982 *Archiv des öffentlichen Rechts* 15; Merten '*Über Staatsziele*' 1993 *Die öffentliche Verwaltung* 386.

and economic rights) as well as a chapter dealing with directive principles of state policy in which the social and economic ideals of the nation are formulated.

The inclusion of a chapter on directive principles in state Constitutions has been underpinned by a number of considerations, including the following:

- Certain social, economic, and cultural claims have not been refined sufficiently to be regarded as justiciable rights, but this does not mean that such claims are of lesser importance. States should therefore be placed under a political and moral obligation, as defined by the Constitution, to develop their policies in accordance with certain national priorities and needs.

- The directive principles do not allow the courts to become involved in the legislative process where social and economic policy is determined, but at the same time the courts can use the directives to interpret the Bill of Rights, legislation, and other government actions.

- The directive principles allow states to develop policies that are feasible in terms of their abilities rather than setting standards that may be applicable to some states but not to others. The allocation of resources and the determination of priorities are consequently a political and not a judicial matter.

- The inclusion of directive principles in state Constitutions is in line with developments in international law, where recognition is given to justiciable rights and to other social and economic claims. The nature of the relationship between the rights and claims is in a constant state of flux.

Two countries that have had practical experience in the application of directive principles are Ireland and India. Their experiences have differed, with the directives becoming much more central to the legal and legislative process in India that in Ireland.

## 6.1 Ireland: the failure of directive principles

Ireland was in the vanguard when it included directive principles in its Constitution in the late 1930s. The drafters of the Constitution regarded the document as more than a technical legal framework and felt that it should also reflect the aspirations, hopes, and ideals of the nation in general.[107] The purpose of the inclusion of the directive principles was that they should serve as a guideline for social justice according to which future governments would have to respond, develop policies, and set priorities.[108] Owing to their non-justiciability, the value of the directive principles is that they place moral and political, rather than legal, obligations on the state.[109]

The purpose and potential value of the directive principles were set out as follows during the debates in the constituent assembly in 1937:

> 'They will be there as a constant headline, something by which the people as a whole can judge their progress in a certain direction; something by which the representatives of the people can be judged as well as the people judge themselves as a whole. We will judge our progress in a certain

---

[107] Morgan *Constitutional Law in Ireland* (1985) 12.
[108] Bartholomeu *The Irish Judiciary* (1971) 12.
[109] 'The principles of social policy . . . shall not be cognisable by any court under any provision of the constitution': art 45.

direction by asking how far we have advanced in that direction. They are intended to be directive to the legislature.'[110]

The main purpose of the directive principles is clear from these and other debates: to serve as a 'socio-economic charter' for generations to follow.[111] The following three arguments provided the basis for the inclusion of the directives in the Irish Constitution:

- First, the Constitution was regarded as more than a technical legal document. It should reflect the aspirations of the people and the directive principles provide a basis for this. While the rest of the Constitution provides the legal framework for governance, the directive principles are the 'soul' of the Constitution.

- Secondly, the Constitution must recognize the duty of the state towards the poor, illiterate, and impoverished sections of the population.[112] As a result, generations to come will be under a constitutional obligation to devise policies that address the urgent social and economic needs of the general population.

- Thirdly, the directive principles will serve as a checklist and benchmark for all political parties and interest groups to evaluate their social and economic policies.[113]

The directive principles are described by the Constitution as not justiciable,[114] although they do place a constitutional duty on the state to 'promote the welfare of the whole people by securing and protecting as effectively as it may a social order in which justice and charity shall inform all the institutions of the national life'.[115]

The approach to the directive principles has gone through various phases, although at no stage has the legislature or the courts used the directives as actively as had been intended by some of the founding fathers of the Constitution.

The first phase was characterized by a conservative and rigid interpretation of the directive principles. This resulted in the principles being regarded as of relevance only to the legislature and not of any use to the courts in the settling of disputes.[116] Limited reference was made in legislation to the aims of the directive principles in order to justify the particular legislation.[117] The basic approach of the courts to the directive principles can be summarized as follows:

'It puts the State under certain duties, but they are duties of imperfect obligation since they cannot be enforced or regarded by any court of law, and are only directions for the guidance of Parliament.'[118]

The second phase of the application of the directive principles witnessed a gradual

---

[110] *Constituent Assembly Debates* 11 May 1937 (69).

[111] De Villiers op cit (n 10) 429.

[112] 'Our social system is not anything like what it ought to be . . . [I]t ought to be our constant endeavour to try to remedy it. One of the best ways of remedying it is to set out definitely objectives which you should try to reach': *Constituent Assembly Debates* 11 May 1937 (71).

[113] Chubb *The Constitution and Constitutional Change in Ireland* (1978) 49.

[114] 'The Court has no jurisdiction to substitute the impugned enactment with a form of enactment which it considers desirable or to indicate to Parliament the appropriate form of enactment which should be substituted for the impugned enactment': *Somjee v Minister of Justice* IR (1982) 142.

[115] Article 45.1.

[116] *Buckley v Attorney General* IR (1950) 57.

[117] Article 6.1 of the Central Bank Act, 1942 contained a quotation from the Directive Principles stating that in the control of credit 'the constant and predominant aim shall be the welfare of the people as a whole'.

[118] *Comyn v Attorney General* IR (1950) 142.

increase in the use of the principles as the issue of social and economic rights became more relevant.[119] In the *Ryan* case the court argued for the first time that certain rights that were not explicitly mentioned in the Constitution could be derived from the directive principles.[120] The new approach of the courts was that the Bill of Rights might not be exhaustive and that the directive principles could at least serve as a guiding document for interpreting the Bill of Rights in a modern manner.

The third phase regarding the interpretation of the directive principles was entered when a court argued in 1972 that individuals could have certain natural rights that were not necessarily provided for explicitly in the Bill of Rights. The directive principles could therefore be used to extend the 'personal' rights as provided for by the Constitution. Such 'implied' rights could be derived from the Christian religion, the nature of the Constitution, or the provisions of the directive principles. The court concluded as follows:

> 'The opening passage [providing for the non-justiciable nature of directive principles] does not mean that the courts may not have regard to the limits of the Article, but that they have no jurisdiction to consider the application of these principles in it in the making of laws. This does not involve the conclusion that the courts may not take it into consideration when deciding whether a claimed constitutional rights exists.'[121]

The current approach of the courts is therefore that although the directive principles do not constitute justiciable rights, they could be used to interpret the Constitution or even serve as a source of 'new' rights. In this way the directive principles could be used to determine the intention of the legislature more effectively.[122] The courts have been reluctant to use the directive principles in a manner that would affect the separation of powers between legislature and judiciary.[123] The Bill of Rights may also be interpreted more creatively, which would allow some clauses such as those on personal rights to be given new content, covering fields such as education and quality of life in general.[124]

This new approach is reflected in *Landers v Attorney General*,[125] where the question was raised whether the legislature could limit the right of a child to sing in a nightclub or whether such limitation would be in conflict with the right to freedom of contract. The court found that the chapter on directive principles[126] imposes on the state the obligation of endeavouring to ensure that the strength and health of workers, men and women, and the tender age of children shall not be abused for the purpose of reaching a general conclusion as to what may fairly be embraced by the expression 'the exigencies of the common good'. The court concluded therefore that

---

[119] Burne & McCutcheon *The Irish Legal System* (1989) 280.

[120] *Ryan v Attorney General* IR (1965) 294.

[121] *Murtagh Properties v Cleary* (supra) at 330.

[122] Grimes & Horgan *Introduction to the Law in the Republic of Ireland* (1981) 73; *Byrne v Ireland* IR (1972) 241; Casey 'Changing the Constitution' in McConnell *The Irish Constitution* (1989) 152.

[123] The court has declared explicitly that it cannot 'enquire as to whether the Parliament has implemented what are described as the "principles of social policy" ': *O'Brien v Manufacturing Engineering Co Ltd* IR (1973) 334.

[124] Walsh 'Existence and Meaning of Fundamental Rights in the Field of Education in Ireland' 1981 *Human Rights LJ* 323.

[125] IR (1982) 109.

[126] Article 45.4.2: 'The State shall endeavour to ensure that the strength and health of workers, men and women, and the tender age of children shall not be abused and the citizens shall not be forced by economic necessity to enter vocations unsuited for their sex, age or strength.'

the legislature could in the common interest place limits on the child's freedom of contract.

The directive principles in Ireland have, notwithstanding the above developments, not been exploited to their full potential by either the legislature, political parties, or the judiciary. Although it has been generally accepted that the directive principles are non-justiciable, the moral and political role they might have fulfilled has not materialized. In few cases have the principles been used as an instrument of interpretation by the courts and, to a very limited extent, as a possible source of new rights.

## 6.2 India: the success of Directive Principles

India followed the example set by Ireland by also including in its Constitution a chapter on Directive Principles of State Policy.[127] The Indian Directive Principles are far more extensive and cover a larger field that those in the Constitution of Ireland. The Indian Directive Principles originated in the constitutional and political experience and history of India. The modern-day concept of directive principles is basically a continuation of the ancient *Raja Dharma*, which placed the king under an obligation to tend to the poor and infirm.[128]

The drafters of the Indian Constitution attempted to find a balance between the seemingly conflicting claims of individual liberties and social justice.[129] The importance of socio-economic renewal as a prerequisite for the effective protection of fundamental human rights was realized.[130] The Directive Principles had to pave the way for the establishment of what was called an 'economic democracy'.[131] It was feared that if the desperate social and economic position of the population was not in some way addressed, the fundamental rights and freedoms provided for in the Bill of Rights could be reduced to mere 'paper rights'.[132]

The debate that led to the distinction between fundamental rights and directive principles is only partially reflected in the first- versus second-generation rights differences. The chapter on fundamental rights, after all, contains various rights that fall outside the category of civil and political rights. The chapter on fundamental rights is characterized by its individual nature as well as the limits that are placed upon unlawful state action. The Directive Principles, on the other hand, do not contain justiciable rights, but they do place the state under a moral and political obligation to devise policies that will realize certain social and economic goals.[133]

---

[127] Articles 36–51.

[128] Reddy 'Fundamentalness of Fundamental Rights and Directive Principles in the Indian Constitution' 1980 *J of the Indian Law Institute* 403.

[129] Sharma *Justice and the Social Order in India* (1984) 176.

[130] De Villiers 'Directive Principles of State Policy and Fundamental Rights: The Indian Experience' (1992) 8 *SAJHR* 30.

[131] Jain *Indian Constitutional Law* (1978) 549. Nehru formulated the aim of an economic democracy as follows: 'India's immediate goal can only be considered in terms of the exploitation of her people. Politically, it must mean independence and cession of British connection, economically and socially, it must mean the ending of all special class privileges and vested interests.' Quoted by Bhagwati J in *Minerva Mills Ltd v Union of India* AIR 1980 SC 1843.

[132] Sharma op cit (n 129) 179.

[133] The intention of the drafters was that the Directive Principles should have a 'peculiar binding character' and that any party that ignored the principles would in fact be ignoring the constitution: Kagzi *The Constitution of India* (1989) 933.

The fundamental rights are therefore basically the 'mark of a world in which the government has no jurisdiction', while the Directive Principles require positive state action to address social and economic problems.[134]

The Constitution expressly declares the Directive Principles non-justiciable.[135] They constitute the moral and political soul of the Constitution and are in essence 'letters of instruction' to all future governments. The principles cannot, however, be regarded as having no practical significance by the state. They place a constitutional, albeit not a justiciable, duty upon all levels of government to undertake social and economic reform by determining that the principles 'shall be fundamental in the governance of the country and it shall be the duty of the State to apply these principles in making laws'.[136]

The application and interpretation of the Directive Principles have gone through various phases since their inception. The following are the main elements of the phases:

During the first phase the fundamental rights were regarded as 'sacrosanct' and supreme over the Directive Principles.[137] This meant that any legislation that was in conflict with the Bill of Rights, even if such legislation endeavoured to further the aims of the Directive Principles, would be null and void. The approach of the courts was expressed as follows:

> 'The Directive Principles of State Policy, which by art 37 are expressly made unenforceable by a court, cannot override the provisions found in part 3 [Bill of Rights] which, despite other provisions, are expressly made enforceable. The chapter on fundamental rights is sacrosanct and not liable to be abridged by any Legislative or Executive act or order . . . .'[138]

During this phase the courts regarded the Directive Principles as being of relevance only to the legislature, with all laws that were in conflict with the Bill of Rights being void.[139] The legislature consequently was in a position where, even if it wanted to develop programmes aimed at fulfilling the Directive Principles, the courts, because of their restrictive approach to the Directive Principles, nullified social and economic reconstruction programmes.

The second phase of the application of the Directive Principles witnessed more intense efforts to harmonize the Bill of Rights with legislation aimed at providing for social and economic restructuring. The courts were forced by political and other pressures to pay greater attention to the directives and to treat them as complementary to the Bill of Rights.[140] The courts were often criticized for their unwillingness 'to appreciate the insights of the Constitution and needs of society' in respect of social change, and for not having 'shown the evidence of foresight of the inevitable, futuristic projections'.[141]

---

[134] *State of Kerala v Thomas* AIR 1976 SC 516.

[135] Article 37: 'The provisions contained in this Part (Directive Principles) shall not be enforceable by any court, *but the principles therein laid down are nevertheless fundamental in the governance of the country and it shall be the duty of the State to apply these principles in the making of laws*' (emphasis supplied).

[136] Article 37.

[137] De Villiers op cit (n 130) 41.

[138] *Madras v Champakam Dorairajan* AIR 1951 SC 226.

[139] Refer for instance to *M H Quareshi v State of Bihar* AIR 1958 SC 731; *State of Bihar v Kameshwar Singh* AIR 1952 SC 252; *In re Kerala Education Bill* AIR 1959 SC 995.

[140] De Villiers op cit (n 130) 43.

[141] Sharma op cit (n 129) 26.

The state argued in various cases before the courts that it (the state) was under a constitutional obligation to fulfil the duties placed on it by the Directive Principles and that in order to do so certain limitations had to be placed on human rights.[142] In a watershed case the court was faced with the question whether the Minimum Wage Act 1948, which was promulgated in the furtherance of the Directive Principles, infringed the right of freedom of contract. The court argued that the Directive Principles and fundamental rights had to be interpreted in a 'complementary and supplementary' fashion to each other, and with reference to the dispute in question it concluded:

> 'Freedom of contract does not mean freedom to exploit. The provisions of the Constitution are not erected as barriers of progress. They provide a plan for orderly progress towards the social order contemplated by the preamble of the Constitution ... While rights conferred under Part 3 [Bill of Rights] are fundamental, the directives given under Part 4 [Directive Principles of State Policy] are fundamental in the governance of the country. We see no conflict on the whole between them. They are complementary and supplementary to each other.'[143]

The third phase in the application of the Directive Principles has thus far been characterized by an even greater awareness by the judiciary of the need for social and economic restructuring and of the obligations placed upon the state by the Directive Principles of State Policy.[144] The new approach of the courts is based primarily on two arguments: the founding fathers expressly included the Directive Principles in the Constitution in order to place the state under a constitutional obligation and not under a mere moral and/or political obligation to undertake social and economic reforms; secondly, a concerted effort is required by the legislature, executive, and judiciary to find solutions to the desperate problems facing millions of people. The 'conservative' approach taken by the courts during the first three decades limited the ability of the state as whole to fulfil its constitutional obligations.[145]

The new approach recognized the role of the judiciary as crucial in 'trying to force the government to create favourable conditions for effective realization of the new individual, collective, diffuse rights'.[146] The 1970s witnessed various efforts by Parliament to amend the Constitution in an endeavour to give the Directive Principles primacy over certain individual rights.[147] The courts initially in the *Minerva Mills* case rejected such endeavours as unconstitutional because they were aimed at 'destroying' the guarantees set out in the Bill of Rights.[148] Later the *Minerva Mills* case was set aside when the courts found that certain legislation which was aimed at nationalizing mines in the furtherance of the Directive Principles was valid, notwithstanding the fact that it placed limits on fundamental rights.[149]

In the landmark ruling of *State of Tamil Nadu v Abu Kavier Bai*[150] the court ruled

---

[142] *Sajjan Singh v State of Rajasthan* AIR 1965 SC 845.
[143] *Chandra Bhawan Boarding and Lodging Bangalore v The State of Mysore* AIR 1970 SC 2042.
[144] De Villiers op cit (n 130) 45.
[145] Refer e g to *Maneka Gandhi v Union of India* (1978) 1 SCC 248.
[146] Singh 'Judicial Socialism and Promises of Liberation: Myth and Truth' 1986 *J of the Indian Law Institute* 338.
[147] Twenty-fifth Amendment (1971) and Forty-second Amendment (1976).
[148] *Minerva Mills Ltd v Union of India* (supra).
[149] *Sanjiev Coke Mfg Co v M/S Bharat Coking Coal Ltd* AIR 1983 SC 239.
[150] AIR 1984 SC 725.

that the court had the duty to harmonize the Directive Principles with the Bill of Rights even if the Directive Principles were not justiciable. The court laid down new guidelines for evaluating a statute when it was in conflict with the Bill of Rights. Such a statute could be upheld if, first, there was a direct nexus between a Directive Principle and the state, secondly if the link was reasonable, and, thirdly, if the limitation was in the public interest.

The courts therefore no longer view the Directive Principles as of lesser importance that the Bill of Rights and are willing to 'restrict the scope of fundamental rights in order to accommodate the Directive Principles'[151] and to use the principles to give new content to human rights.[152]

It took years for the Directive Principles to develop to their originally intended status. Their impact on Indian society has been extensive and could have been even greater had the courts opted for a different approach in their interpretation of the Directive Principles and fundamental rights.[153] A few of the areas where the principles have been implemented are provisions regarding minimum wages;[154] the participation of workers in the management of companies;[155] equal pay for equal work;[156] and the fixing of prices.[157]

## 7  SOCIAL AND ECONOMIC RIGHTS IN SOUTH AFRICA

The social and economic restructuring of South Africa lies at the heart of the transformation process. The extension of the political rights to participate in the democratic process may come to nothing if people do not experience an improvement in their welfare, education, employment, housing, and other areas where huge gaps have developed as a result of discriminatory policies and practices. South Africa, as a developing country, may find it difficult to convince its millions of squatters and poverty-stricken people that the protection of civil and political rights is of value to them if they do not have the material, intellectual, and social ability and circumstances to make use of such rights.

There is general agreement in South Africa that the state, acting on its own and in partnership with the private sector, has a responsibility in fields such as housing, welfare, education, and employment. The disputed question is whether the state could and should be placed under a legal obligation in terms of a Bill of Rights to undertake certain actions and develop assistance programmes or if it is purely a matter for legislative and political discretion to develop such programmes.

Three basic arguments have been put forward regarding the possible protection

---

[151] Sathe 'Constitutional Law' 1983 *Annual Survey of Indian Law* 219; Narain 'Judicial Law Making and the Place of Directive Principles in the Indian Constitution' 1985 *J of the Indian Law Institute* 222.

[152] Refer e g to *Tellis v Bombay Municipal Corporation* 1987 Commonwealth Law Reports 351 in which the Directive Principles were used to give a wide meaning to the 'right to life' in order to protect slum dwellers from eviction.

[153] De Villiers op cit (n 130) 188–99.

[154] *UPSE Board v Hari Shankar* (1979) ASC 69. The definition of what is meant by 'minimum wage' is clouded in vagueness and uncertainty and depends on numerous surrounding circumstances. In *Reserve Bank Employers Association v Reserve Bank* (1966) 1 SCR 25 at 48 the court concluded that 'our political aim is "living wage" though in actual practice, living wage has been an ideal which has eluded our efforts like an ever-reaching horizon and will remain so for time to come'.

[155] *National Textile Workers' Union v P R Ramakrishan* AIR 1983 SC 75.

[156] *Federation of AIC and CE Stenographers v Union of India* AIR 1988 SC 1291.

[157] *Sonia Bhalai v State of Andra Pradesh* AIR 1981 SC 1274.

of social and economic rights in South Africa: (i) those supporting their inclusion in a Bill of Rights; (ii) those that hold that social and economic rights may be included, but only in so far as they place 'negative' duties upon the state; and (iii) those that are also in favour of the inclusion of some social and economic rights in a Bill of Rights and in addition the inclusion of directive principles of state policy to set out certain aims of the state.

## 7.1 Inclusion of social and economic rights

The Freedom Charter,[158] which was adopted by the ANC in 1956, contains various provisions relating to the social and economic rights of individuals and the role of the state in addressing certain basic human needs. The Charter emphasizes the role of the state as a primary agent in the redistribution of wealth and the restructuring of the economy. The following are some of the provisions contained in the Charter:

- 'the state shall help the peasants with implements, seeds, tractors and dams to save the soil and assist the tillers';
- 'men and women of all races shall receive equal pay for equal work';
- 'there shall be a national minimum wage';
- 'the government shall discover, develop and encourage national talent for the enhancement of our cultural life';
- 'adult illiteracy shall be ended by a mass state education plan';
- 'slums shall be demolished and new suburbs built where all shall have transport, roads, lighting, playing fields, crèches and social centres'.

The rights and ideals contained in the Freedom Charter are in a certain sense a combination of the contents expected in a Bill of Rights and directive principles or aims of state policy. Some of the provisions were formulated as 'rights', such as the right to equal language treatment, the forming of trade unions, and freedom of movement, while other provisions were formulated in a more general and vague manner — resembling aims and objectives of the state rather that justiciable rights.

The late 1980s and early 1990s witnessed two important developments in the human rights field, with the ANC publishing its proposed Bill of Rights and the government appointing the South African Law Commission to investigate the protection of individual and minority rights. The proposals put forward by the ANC and the Law Commission respectively correlated to some extent in respect of the protection of civil and political rights, but differed quite fundamentally in the approach to the protection of social and economic rights.

The ANC in its 1988 constitutional guidelines[159] provided for a Bill of Rights containing civil and political, social and economic, and cultural and environmental rights. Various social and economic rights which have been refined sufficiently for inclusion in the Bills of Rights of other countries were acknowledged by the ANC, for instance the right of workers to form trade unions; equal pay for equal work; safe, clean, and dignified working conditions;[160] and the rights of children.[161]

---

[158] Adopted at the Congress of the People on 26 June 1955. De Villiers et al op cit (n 36) 379.
[159] *Discussion Document: Constitutional Proposals and Structures for a Democratic South Africa* (1988).
[160] Article 6.
[161] Article 9.

Various other social and economic rights that require extensive state involvement in their realization were also included as justiciable rights, such as the right to freedom from hunger, the right to shelter, the right to protection of health, the right to work,[162] and environmental rights.[163] These rights were qualified to the extent that the state should, in accordance with its 'available resources', undertake to achieve 'basic social, educational, economic and welfare rights for the whole population'.[164]

The ANC-proposed Bill of Rights has come under fire for its programmatic nature and the danger that the separation of powers may be encroached upon.[165] The response to this argument has been that the distinction between first- and second-generation rights has become blurred and that many Constitutions, such as those of Ireland, India, and Namibia, provide for similar rights in their directive principles of state policy.[166] Murphy has argued that the social and economic rights are indeed 'self-executing', and that the mere fact that they require the mobilization of resources does not justify an 'undermining' of social rights as rights.[167]

While the distinction between first- and second-generation rights has become blurred, the ANC argument fails when it compares the directive principles in the said countries with the justiciable rights proposed by the ANC. In all of those countries the directive principles are, because of their programmatic nature, explicitly made non-justiciable. The same can be said of the reference by Sachs to the European Social Charter as a rationale for the inclusion of a 'floor of minimum standards' in the Bill of Rights, the Social Charter after all being non-justiciable itself.[168] The reference to these cases (where social and economic rights are formulated as directives rather than rights) actually weakens rather than strengthens the ANC's arguments in favour of extensive social and economic rights.

The difficulties faced in the application of some of the social and economic rights proposed by the ANC have been recognized. Sachs, however, argues that such difficulties should not lead to such rights being 'abandoned', but that 'appropriate methods' should be found to make them 'realizable'.[169] He suggests therefore that what is required for the realization of social and economic rights is a formula that takes account of 'affordability and the issue of appropriate forms of enforcement'.[170] Affordability, according to this argument, would be based on a balance between the 'duty to spend' and the 'obligation to fulfil'. The implication of the inclusion of social and economic rights in a Bill of Rights would be that 'judicial decision-making' would be extended beyond 'judicial review'.

---

[162] Article 10.
[163] Article 12.
[164] Article 10.
[165] Mr Justice Didcott has proposed three basic arguments against the inclusion of certain social and economic rights: the Bill of Rights is a protective device, or shield, rather than a sword; secondly, the financial costs that would be incurred in realizing social and economic rights may be beyond the means of the country; thirdly, it would require the judiciary to involve itself in a matter that was primarily a legislative issue: SA Law Commission *Project 58: Group and Human Rights* Interim Report (1991) 533.
[166] Haysom 'Democracy, Constitutionalism and the ANC's Bill of Rights for a New South Africa' 1991 *Social Justice* 45.
[167] Murphy 'Second Generation Rights and the Bill of Rights in South Africa' 1992 *SA Sociological Review* 31.
[168] Sachs 'Watch Out — There's a Constitution About' 1992 *South Africa International* 188.
[169] Sachs *Advancing Human Rights in South Africa* (1992) 111.
[170] Op cit (n 169) 112.

## 7.2 Excluding social and economic rights

The South Africa Law Commission (whose findings and recommendations were accepted by the previous government) concluded in its investigation on the distinction between first- and second-generation rights that 'it is important not to lose sight of the fact that there is no clear dividing line between the first- and second-generation rights and there are some rights that do not obviously belong to one category or the other'.[171] The Law Commission argued that before claims could be regarded as justiciable rights and consequently included in a Bill of Rights, they must be defined in a manner that would prevent the state from interfering with them.[172] Social and economic rights do not, according to the Law Commission, qualify for inclusion in a Bill of Rights because of their programmatic nature and the positive action that is required of the state in respect of them.

The Law Commission argued that some of the social and economic 'rights' may be laudable from a moral and political point of view, but that they do not comply with the prerequisites for inclusion in a justiciable Bill of Rights.[173] According to the Law Commission, the emphasis in capitalist countries falls on the passive duties of the state towards the individual, whereas in socialist countries the active duties of the state are emphasized. It concludes that 'it is clear that in international law and in the Constitutions of a number of states in which the said rights have been enshrined there are not really any practical enforcement mechanisms to speak of.'[174]

The Law Commission consequently identified the following options for addressing the protection of social and economic rights. First, they could be ignored, with only civil and political rights being protected.[175] Secondly, all social and economic 'claims' could be included as justiciable rights.[176] Thirdly, provision could be made for directive principles of state policy in which some of the social and economic ideals are contained.[177] Fourthly, provision could be made for those social and economic rights that do not require positive state action to be included in a Bill of Rights alongside civil and political rights.[178]

The approach of the Law Commission can be criticized for various reasons, including the following:[179]

- Its distinction between rights and aims on the basis that such rights require only negative state action, while social and economic rights are essentially claims for positive action, is outdated. As has been indicated, various civil and political rights also require positive state action in order to realize a particular right.[180]

---

[171] *Project 58: Group and Human Rights* Interim Report (1991) 126.
[172] At 495.
[173] At 500.
[174] At 514.
[175] This would, according to the Law Commission, ignore the needs of millions of people and is therefore not acceptable (at 532).
[176] Such an approach may leave the state in the position where it has not the means to fulfil the obligations placed on it by the judiciary (at 535).
[177] The Law Commission is critical of this option because the directives would be of 'little legal significance' (at 536).
[178] At 537.
[179] De Villiers op cit (n 10) 426–7.
[180] Haysom for instance argues that 'once the basis of the distinctions between political/civil and socio-economic rights are shown to be, at best, one of degree — then both the legal and political arguments on which it rests fall away to the extent that they rely on an absolute correlation between enforceability and first-generation rights': 'Constitutionalism, Majoritarian Democracy and Socio-Economic Rights' (1992) 8 *SAJHR* 457.

- If limited resources are the main reason for the exclusion of certain rights, then the enforceability of the rights should rather be made dependent on certain limitations. It is for instance not uncommon for the right of state-supplied mother-tongue education to be dependent on the availability of resources, the concentration of students, and other limitations. It is also not correct to presume that there are no costs involved in the protection of civil and political rights. As Mureinik has pointed out, 'judges often make decrees which entail massive expenditure without any regard to the budgetary consequences, particularly by way of enforcing first-generation rights'.[181]

- The distinction between rights protected in 'capitalist' and 'socialist' countries is only of limited value. Various 'capitalist' countries have included some social and economic rights in their Constitutions, such as Japan,[182] Spain,[183] Portugal,[184] and some state Constitutions in the US, as well as numerous international treaties, to which 'capitalist' and 'socialist' are parties, which recognize social and economic rights.

- It is not clear what led the Law Commission to conclude that the inclusion of a chapter on directive principles with certain socio-economic ideals 'would wreck the whole process of negotiations and plunge the country into chaos'.[185] Directive principles have become one of the most widely used methods in international and constitutional law not only to recognize certain social and economic ideals and claims but also to serve as a source of new rights as time passes. These dimensions have unfortunately not been investigated by the Law Commission.

- The neglect or even ignoring of social and economic rights in the South African circumstances is a denial of reality, the turning of a blind eye to the needs of people, an undermining of the legitimacy of a Bill of Rights.[186]

## 7.3 Protecting social and economic rights and directive principles

The possibility of providing for the protection of social and economic rights in a Bill of Rights and simultaneously of providing for certain social, economic, and other aims in a chapter on directive principles of state policy has been suggested. Glazewski argues that the Indian experience with human rights and directive principles has shown that 'some of the obstacles' faced in the human rights debate can be 'diffused'.[187] He suggests that the provisions of a Bill of Rights and directive principles could be used in support of each other, whereby new content could be given to justiciable rights. The directive principles could be used to 'elaborate' on

---

[181] Mureinik 'Beyond a Charter of Luxuries: Economic Rights in the Constitution' (1992) 8 *SAJHR* 466.
[182] The state shall endeavour to promote and extend social welfare: art 25.
[183] The right to health care: art 43.
[184] The right to a healthy and ecologically balanced human environment: art 66.
[185] SA Law Commission op cit (n 171) 536.
[186] 'To deny the existence of any rights except the ones associated with political freedoms, to marginalise rights which some lawyers may consider as non-justiciable, is to accept the bias in favour of the powerful; it is to accept a truncated view of humanity; it is like throwing a rope of sand to the poor and the dispossessed': Asmal 'Victims, Survivors and Citizens — Human Rights, Reparations and Reconciliation' (1992) 8 *SAJHR* 509. See also Basson op cit (n 43) 154.
[187] Glazewski 'The Environment, Human Rights and a New South African Constitution' (1991) 7 *SAJHR* 182.

particular human rights and therefore by incorporating directive principles 'a court is assisted in its task to determine the point of balance between individual and collective rights'.[188]

The inclusion of directive principles alongside a Bill of Rights does not mean that the recognition of social and economic rights is neglected or by-passed. The directive principles should not be seen as replacing social and economic rights, but rather as supporting them by placing the state under a constitutional obligation to further certain aims. The directive principles would therefore supplement the social and economic rights and increase their importance.[189] Provision for directive principles need not, as Mureinik suggests, be motivated by an effort to recognize social and economic rights without making them 'constitutional rights'.[190] The recognition of social and economic fundamental rights as well as directive principles on national aims could be considered.

Murphy is also of the opinion that directive principles could 'enhance second-generation rights as moral values'.[191] Such directive principles could, according to him, 'act as organizational norms directing the public power to the creation of public services for the promotion of an egalitarian society'. The inclusion in the Constitution of directive principles in addition to a Bill of Rights could have the following benefits:[192]

- Provision could be made in certain circumstances for directive principles, owing to the obligations placed upon the state, to have more authority than fundamental rights.

- The directive principles could serve as a basis for interpreting the Constitution and for giving guidance and direction to all tiers of government.

- The directive principles could provide 'judicial standards for structuring the exercise of administrative discretion'.

Davis makes a case against the inclusion of social and economic rights in the Constitution, except as directive principles of state policy.[193] His support for a chapter on directive principles is based on the following arguments: First, that although directives cannot be used to compel a government to implement directives, they could, as in the Indian case, have a marked effect on constitutional jurisprudence.[194] Secondly, directive principles fulfil more than a pragmatic purpose because they provide a framework and commitment for social and economic reconstruction. Thirdly, the inclusion of directives 'is an exercise in constitutional integrity for it announces clearly and unequivocally that second- and third-generation rights can only be protected by way of negative constitutional review'.[195]

---

[188] At 183.
[189] De Villiers op cit (n 10) 435.
[190] Mureinik op cit (n 181) 468. See also Haysom op cit (n 180) 462, who views the inclusion of directive principles as an indication of 'relegating' social and economic rights.
[191] Murphy op cit (n 167) 39.
[192] Murphy op cit (n 167) 41.
[193] Davis 'The Case Against the Inclusion of Socio-Economic Demands in a Bill of Rights Except as Directive Principles' (1992) 8 *SAJHR* 475.
[194] At 468.
[195] At 487. 'Whether the detailed inclusion of second- or third generation rights should be included in a Bill of Rights is a moot point given the difficulty of judicial enforceability': Davis 'Remaking the South African Legal Order' 1991 *Social Justice* 78.

## 7.4 Social and economic rights in the 1993 Constitution

Observers of the political and negotiating processes in South Africa may find surprisingly few the provisions regarding social and economic rights or directive principles of state policy in the transitional Constitution. This surprise is justified if one takes into account international developments concerning social and economic rights, the practical circumstances of poverty, unemployment, and illiteracy in which millions of South Africans find themselves, the development of the theoretical debate on these matters in South Africa, and the historical support that organizations such as the ANC and PAC have given to the recognition of social and economic rights.

The Bill of Rights in the transitional Constitution contains more than the traditional civil and political rights, with provision for educational,[196] workers',[197] and environmental[198] rights. The drafters have clearly attempted to go about their task in a manner that emphasizes the mainly passive role of the state in the protection of rights, limiting the ability of the courts to question policy decisions on the basis of their compliance with the realization of social and economic rights and ideals.

## 8 CONCLUDING REMARKS

The debate on the protection of social and economic rights in South Africa, and in other parts of the world, has not been completed. South Africa cannot in its search for a stable and just democratic dispensation afford to elevate certain rights above the level of others. Rights and their content cannot be divorced from reality and society. The world constantly experiences the development of 'new' rights and the dynamic interpretation of 'old' rights. The role of the state is also not cast in stone, but can be modified as circumstances change. The South African Constitution with its Bill of Rights and, perhaps after time, directive principles of state policy, must in order to be legitimate, realistic, and practical contain all the rights and fundamental principles upon which the governance of the country is to be built. The exclusion of individual rights of whatever generation or ignorance of fundamental principles regarding the governance of the country must be avoided.

The following concluding comments can be made regarding the protection of social and economic rights in South Africa:

- South Africa will shortly find itself party to various international treaties and agreements in which recognition is given to the importance of social and economic rights. The country will be morally, politically, and even legally obliged not only to act in terms of international law but also to integrate such provisions into its own municipal law.

- The rigid distinction between categories of rights on the basis that some require only 'negative' state action while others require 'positive' action, with the former being recognized and the latter not, is theoretically and practically unsound. The difference between some rights in the respective categories of

---

[196] Section 33.
[197] Section 28
[198] Section 30.

rights has become blurred to the extent of disappearing totally. More flexibility is required in the definition of rights and remedies in order to develop a Bill of Rights in which rights of all 'generations' will be well defined and justiciable.

- The Bill of Rights ought to be more than a reflection of historical forces and should contain more than just the rights that had been identified two centuries ago in totally different circumstances. Social and economic rights, as with civil and political rights, have to be moulded and sculptured by societal forces. In this way the Bill of Rights will be a reflection of the inner soul of the population, rather than a historical document with little, if any, emotional and legitimate public base. In such a way all fundamental rights of individuals can be protected and not only those belonging to a particular class, category or generation.

- Various social and economic aims and ideals have in the past few decades been sufficiently refined to be included in the Bills of Rights of other countries. It goes without saying that the Bill of Rights will be seriously undermined if all the social and economic dreams and ideals of the population are elevated to justiciable rights. The rights included in the Bill of Rights must be clearly defined in terms of their subject, object, remedy, and limitations in order to be legitimate and effective.

- The inclusion of social and economic rights in the Bill of Rights need not prejudice the separation of powers between the judiciary and legislature. The duty of the courts would not be to rule on political questions that fall within the sphere of Parliament. The courts would, however, be entitled to use the Bill of Rights as a benchmark once political decisions have been taken, in order to review statutes, programmes, and budgets and to judge their compliance with all the rights set out in the Bill of Rights.

- Consideration could be given to the inclusion of directive principles of state policy in the Constitution. Such inclusion should not be viewed as replacing the inclusion of social and economic rights in the Constitution. Quite the contrary. Directive principles could place a constitutional duty upon all tiers of government to work towards certain aims and goals in addition to the protection of social and economic rights. The directive principles could become the soul of the Constitution, serving as a guiding beam for all governments. The inclusion of directive principles could have the following benefits: first, such principles would place all government agencies under a constitutional duty to direct their programmes in a particular direction; secondly, they could serve as an instrument for interpretation by the courts; thirdly, provision could be made for fundamental rights in certain circumstances and under defined conditions to be limited by laws promulgated in the furtherance of the directive principles; and, fourthly, the directive principles could in time to come serve as a source of new rights.

# LIMITATION AND SUSPENSION*

### GERHARD ERASMUS

## 1 INTRODUCTION

Fundamental or human rights[1] are exercised within the context of a specific society. They are as a rule not absolute and are limited by the rights of others and by the legitimate needs of society. Public order, safety, health, morals, and democratic values are generally recognized as justifying the imposition of limitations on the exercise of various fundamental rights.[2] The enforcement of human rights is to be matched by 'accommodations in favour of the reasonable needs of the State to perform its public duties for the common good'.[3] The organs of state have to balance conflicting demands and rights. Such limitations are as a rule of a permanent nature and are normally contained in a special 'limitation clause' in a constitution or international human rights instrument.

A different type of 'limitation' applies in times of public emergency threatening the 'life of the nation'. Special measures may be required to protect the state and society during such periods. It may then be necessary for the state to suspend temporarily its obligation to protect fundamental rights. The conditions under which this may happen are usually found in a special 'suspension' or 'derogation clause'.[4]

Limitation and suspension differ in character and scope and in the circumstances in which they may be imposed. Their lawful application also depends on different conditions and requirements. Certain fundamental rights may not be subject to suspension, yet may be limited.[5] Both limitation and suspension are exceptional and should be construed and applied strictly.[6] Suspensions are intended to have a temporary character, being permissible for the duration of the emergency only. Limitations, on the other hand, are as a rule of a permanent nature.

The inclusion of limitation and suspension clauses in the 1993 Constitution will have far-reaching consequences. The extent of the changes can be better understood if the Constitution is seen in its historical, 'technical', and value contexts. This Constitution represents a breach with the past. It heralds a new chapter in the legal and political life of South Africa. It must be applied and interpreted in these terms.

This 'newness' will have theoretical and practical consequences. When the Preamble speaks of a 'new order' it refers to a new political reality for all South Africans founded on a new legal construct which, of necessity, will have to be

---

* The author acknowledges John Dugard's valuable editing and comments.
[1] In Chapter 3 of the Constitution the term 'fundamental rights' is used.
[2] Kiss 'Permissible Limitations on Rights' in L Henkin (ed) *The International Bill of Rights* (1981) 290 at 295.
[3] Higgins 'Derogations under Human Rights Treaties' 1976/77 XLVIII *BYIL* 281 at 283.
[4] International human rights documents and literature usually employ the term 'derogation'. The Constitution of 1993 speaks of 'suspension'. A 'derogation clause' is therefore similar to a 'suspension clause'. The South African terminology will be used here.
[5] Freedom of thought, conscience, and religion are often cited as examples of non-derogable ('non-suspendable') rights that are, however, subject to limitation. See e g Kiss op cit (n 2) 290. See further below, 3.5
[6] See below, 2.4.

applied and interpreted in an original fashion. This new order is *sui generis*. Its future meaning will come to depend on the application (and discovery) of the values immanent in the Constitution, the founding contract of a new society. However, the Constitution is at the same time also a very 'modern' instrument which can benefit from the development of an international human rights jurisprudence since World War II.

## 1.1 Historical background

None of the pre-1993 South African Constitutions contained Bills of Rights or their concomitant limitation clauses. Fundamental rights had first to be recognized and secured before it became feasible to consider limiting and balancing their exercise. Yet no constitutional protection of fundamental rights existed. Admittedly at common law the courts could protect certain 'fundamental rights',[7] but these protections could be overruled by the Acts of a sovereign Parliament. Sovereignty of Parliament was the *Grundnorm*[8] of the South African constitutional and legal order.

In such a system there could be no room for a supreme Constitution. Even the jurisdiction of the courts could be, and often was, excluded through Acts of Parliament. Judicial review of Acts of Parliament was impossible and no constitutional yardstick for doing so existed.

This deficient system applied with respect to all South Africans. Its most offensive characteristics, however, found application under apartheid. Apartheid rule was premised on racial classification and discrimination. The very system was anathema to the idea of fundamental rights and their protection. By denying black South Africans many fundamental rights, by excluding them from participation in government, and by removing the basis for legal redress for these wrongs, not only fundamental rights but the very constitutional basis for their recognition were denied.

The magnitude of the changes brought about by the Constitution of 1993 should be viewed against this background. This is a supreme Constitution containing a comprehensive Bill of Rights, including a proper limitation clause in s 33. Such a clause forms part and parcel of the day-to-day implementation of fundamental rights.

The powers of the state in times of public emergency is another area of South African public law most fundamentally altered by the new Constitution. The idea that the state is entitled to protect the public order and to curtail the rights of the individual in times of war or internal rebellion is generally accepted. It is also found in South African common law. The Roman law basis for this is contained in the principle *salus rei publicae suprema lex*. It is said to be founded on notions of self-defence and necessity.[9] From English law we have inherited the concept of martial law as part of the prerogative powers.[10]

---

[7] Carpenter *Introduction to South African Constitutional Law* (1987) 100, 104. She singles out *habeas corpus* and the *interdictum de homine libero exhibendo* as examples.

[8] For a discussion of this term in constitutional law, see Carpenter op cit (n 7) 142.

[9] Carpenter op cit (n 7) 105.

[10] At 106.

For the enforcement of apartheid rule common law did not suffice. In the past many glaring infringements of human rights occurred under 'states of emergency', which were declared in terms of legislation such as the Public Safety Act 3 of 1953. Together with other 'security legislation',[11] this Act authorized detention without trial as well as infringements of other basic human rights and freedoms such as freedom of association, free speech, freedom of movement, and rights relating to a fair trial.

These wide executive 'emergency' powers coexisted with other apartheid measures which denied political and civil rights and freedoms to the majority of South Africans. Together they maintained and enforced that illegitimate order.

An essential characteristic of these 'emergency powers' was that their exercise was largely beyond judicial control.[12] The judicial protection of the individual was for all practical purposes non-existent.[13]

The proposal to include a suspension clause in the new Constitution was a controversial one. The abuses of the recent past have engendered a profound suspicion of states of emergency. Eventually the concept of emergency powers for the state was accepted. However, the issue is now regulated by s 34, under the heading 'State of Emergency and Suspension'. This is the constitutional provision which now allows suspension of the obligation to respect and enforce fundamental rights. Such a suspension will be permissible only under strictly circumscribed conditions which are regulated by the Constitution.

This particular clause and the powers contained therein cannot be interpreted as if they are continuations of the pre-1993 dispensation. They are based on a completely new legal footing and are to be construed as forming part of a new and original legal and constitutional order. Emergency powers are now to be exercised in terms of a system which aims at the *protection* of fundamental rights.

## 1.2 The new constitutional framework

A proper understanding of limitation and suspension under the 1993 Constitution requires a brief discussion of some of the features of the new constitutional framework. The Constitution of 1993 creates for the first time a *supreme* and *justiciable* Constitution. It contains in Chapter 3 a Bill of Rights consisting of a set of fundamental rights and freedoms. Sections 33 and 34 (the limitation and suspension clauses) form an integral part of this Chapter.

All organs of state are now under a constitutional obligation to respect these fundamental rights. Indeed the whole of the Constitution has in fact to be viewed in this way: 'This Constitution shall bind all legislative, executive and judicial organs of state at all levels of government.'[14] The omission of any reference to the judiciary in s 7(1) is unfortunate. Section 4(2) expressly states that the courts are bound by the Constitution. This flows logically from the very nature and scheme of things.

---

[11] See Dugard *Human Rights and the South African Legal Order* (1978); Mathews *Freedom, State Security and the Rule of Law* (1986); Carpenter op cit (n 7) 112.

[12] For a discussion, see Haysom 'States of Emergency in a Post-Apartheid South Africa' (1989) 21 *Columbia Human Rights LR* 139 at 146 et seq.

[13] The 'ouster' clause in s 5*(b)* of the Public Safety Act 3 of 1953 e g prohibits judicial pronouncement on the validity of emergency regulations.

[14] Section 4(2).

Under Chapter 3 the judiciary has to provide 'appropriate relief' when breaches of constitutional obligations occur. The same duty exists with respect to the remainder of the Constitution in terms of ss 98 and 101. This is possible only if the judiciary is bound by the Constitution. No democratic rule-of-law state based on the ideas of constitutionalism and separation of powers would otherwise be possible.

The Constitution shall also be the 'supreme law of the Republic'.[15] All laws (including the common law[16]) and executive actions will have to conform to the Constitution in order to be valid. Acts of Parliament, 'irrespective of whether such law was passed or made before or after the commencement of this Constitution,'[17] are now subject to judicial inquiry into their constitutionality. In cases of infringement the courts, and the new Constitutional Court in particular, will provide the necessary judicial remedies.[18] The judiciary will henceforth protect the individual when breaches of fundamental rights occur and will also rule on all other constitutional issues.[19]

Thus a completely new legal order has been established; one which does away with the sovereignty of Parliament. The Constitution itself is now 'sovereign'.

The fact that the Constitution is supreme will also have a direct impact on executive acts. The Constitution will be the ultimate source of authority for all valid executive action. Legislation enabling executive action will have to comply with the Constitution. Executive action not permitted by the Constitution or in conflict with its provisions will be unconstitutional and invalid.[20] Infringements of basic rights and freedoms, often resulting from wide discretionary powers, will not be beyond the reach of the courts anymore.[21] The Constitution will provide a yardstick for determining their validity.

Prerogative powers deriving from common law will as a rule also cease to exist. The executive branch cannot retain 'inherent' or common-law powers going beyond the ambit of the supreme Constitution.[22] All executive powers will have to be

---

[15] Section 4(1).

[16] A distinction has to be drawn between common law of a public-law nature (e g the prerogatives, which are to be superseded by the Constitution) and common law as a source of private law. Chapter 3 of the Constitution does not deal with private-law relationships directly. Private-law areas may indirectly be influenced in future through the values contained in the Constitution, as indicated in s 35(3). See also below, 1.3 'Basic constitutional values'. Note that s 229 on the continuation of existing laws contains no reference to common law. That the common law must continue to apply, at least in areas of private law, is obvious. Transactions concluded before this Constitution will remain valid and binding.

[17] Section 98(2)(c). This section deals with the jurisdiction of the new Constitutional Court. The Supreme Court will enjoy the same power in terms of s 101(3)(c). For the effect of amendments, see s 232(2)(b).

[18] Sections 7(4), 98(4).

[19] Disputes between national and provincial governments (federal issues) will be constitutional issues. The Constitutional Court has jurisdiction (under s 98(2)(e)) over 'any dispute of a constitutional nature between organs of state at any level of government'. See also ss 98(2)(b) and 101(3)(d).

[20] This flows from the supremacy clause in s 4. See also ss 75 and 81(1).

[21] The extent to which this happened in the case of emergency regulations is well documented. For one such analysis, see Rabie 'Failure of the Brakes of Justice: *Omar v Minister of Law and Order*' (1987) 3 *SAJHR* 300–11; Haysom op cit (n 12).

[22] The existence and scope of a prerogative have traditionally been determined by common law. To that extent the courts might have reviewed a prerogative. The manner in which it is exercised may not: *Sachs v Dönges NO* 1950 (2) SA 265 (A). This rule has been altered in *Boesak v Minister of Home Affairs* 1987 (3) SA 665 (C), where 'illegality, irrationality and procedural impropriety' have been recognized as grounds for judicial review, relying on the judgment of Lord Diplock in *Council of Civil Service Unions v Minister for the Civil Service* [1984] 3 All ER 935 (HL). See in this regard Boulle, Harris & Hoexter *Constitutional and Administrative Law* (1989) 178 et seq and 248 et seq. Note that s 229 on the continuation of existing laws contains no reference to common law. That the common law must continue to apply, at least in areas of private law, is obvious. (See s 35(3).) Private-law relationships, however, fall beyond the primary focus of Chapter 3, which addresses the vertical state–individual relationship, as confirmed in s 7(1).

provided for expressly or by necessary implication in the Constitution itself. When exercising such powers the Constitution and particularly the provisions on fundamental rights will have to be complied with.

## 1.3 Basic constitutional values

Section 35 contains guidelines on how this Constitution, and specifically Chapter 3, should be interpreted and applied.[23] It refers to certain 'values' which underlie the new legal order and which the courts are obliged to promote. Even in the interpretation of ordinary laws, including the common law and customary law, the courts 'shall have due regard to the spirit, purport and objects' of Chapter 3.[24] These values will therefore also apply to rulings with respect to limitation and suspension.

This is a basic-values-oriented Constitution. Constitutional jurisprudence will predominantly be concerned with substance, not merely process. Some of the implications of this orientation can be demonstrated by reference to the US system, where constitutional law is often depicted as a matter of process only.[25] Yet even in the USA

> 'the Constitution's most procedural prescriptions cannot be adequately understood, much less applied, in the absence of a developed theory of fundamental rights that are secured to persons against the state — a theory where derivation demands precisely the kinds of controversial substantive choices that the process proponents are so anxious to leave to the electorate and its representatives.'[26]

Traditional notions about statutory interpretation will not be sufficient in developing a theory of constitutional interpretation. As one commentator on the Canadian Charter of Rights and Freedoms has pointed out:

> '[I]t is necessary to ascertain the values which that provision was designed to protect . . . The purposive approach best achieves this end . . . Charter methodology should not be circumvented by the mechanical application of one of the traditional rules of statutory interpretation.'[27]

A *purposive* approach is possible only if the values contained in the Constitution are first determined. In the words of a well-known Canadian judgment: 'To identify the underlying purpose of the Charter right in question . . . it is important to begin by understanding the cardinal values it embodies.'[28]

---

[23] For a more comprehensive treatment of this particular aspect, see Davis, Chaskalson & De Waal above, 1.
[24] Section 35(3).
[25] Values, according to that view, are selected by the political process. The US Constitution, it is argued, is only concerned with procedural fairness in individual disputes and with ensuring participation in government. See the discussion by Tribe *Constitutional Choices* (1985) 9 et seq. Tribe criticizes this approach.
[26] Tribe op cit (n 25) 11. The German Basic Law (*Grundgesetz*) of 1949 is manifestly value-oriented. 'The substantive values represented by these traditions [liberalism, social welfare, Christianity] are enormously important in the interpretation of the Basic Law': Kommers *The Constitutional Jurisprudence of the Federal Republic of Germany* (1989) 37.
[27] *Per* L'Heureux-Dube J of the Supreme Court of Canada, in *Thomson Newspapers v Canada (Director of Investigation and Research, Restrictive Practices Commission)* (1990) 1 SCR 425. Quoted by Schabas *International Human Rights Law and the Canadian Charter — A Manual for the Practitioner* (1991) 25. (Section 7 of the Canadian Charter deals with 'Life, liberty and security of person.') The 'purposive' approach has found earlier expression in *Hunter v Southam Inc* (1984) 2 SCR 145 at 155.
That a new approach will have to be developed has also been recognized by local decisions. See *Smith v Attorney-General, Bophuthatswana* 1984 (1) SA 196 (B) at 199: 'This Court and its Appellate Division have been schooled in the positivist tradition which applies statutes according to their strict meaning as construed from the words used. Although the "intention of the Legislature" plays a robust part in interpretation, it does so only where the words allow of more than one reasonable construction. The approach to a Bill of Rights is entirely different and it is totally opposed to positivism.'
[28] *R v Oakes* (1986) 1 SCR 103, (1986) 26 DLR (4th) 200.

What are the substantive values of the Constitution of 1993? From what philosophical traditions do they originate? Who will 'discover' and apply these values? How will our 'theory of fundamental rights' be developed and interpretive difficulties resolved?

The answers to these questions will be supplied by the courts (especially the new Constitutional Court) and by constitutional commentators and writers. The text of the Constitution will be the primary focus of analysis. Section 35(1) contains an important guideline in this regard:

'In interpreting the provisions of this Chapter a court of law shall promote the values which underlie an *open* and *democratic society* based on *freedom* and *equality* and shall, where applicable, have regard to public international law applicable to the protection of the rights entrenched in this Chapter, and may have regard to comparable foreign case law.'[29]

Further guidance is provided by the Preamble, which recognizes the need 'to create a new order in which all South Africans will be entitled to a common South African citizenship in a sovereign and democratic constitutional state in which there is equality between men and women and people of all races so that all citizens shall be able to enjoy and exercise their fundamental rights and freedoms'. There is also an epilogue on 'National Unity and Reconciliation'. It proclaims that South Africa's future is to be 'founded on the recognition of human rights, democracy and peaceful co-existence and development opportunities for all South Africans'.[30]

During the drafting of the Constitution of 1993 a 'solemn pact' was concluded which is recorded in a Schedule to the Constitution under the rubric 'Constitutional Principles'.[31] These principles reflect the values which governed the constitutional negotiations. They also constitute an immutable framework for the final Constitution to be adopted by the Constitutional Assembly elected in April 1994.

It seems reasonable to expect that the final Constitution will not deviate radically from the document of 1993. Rather, it will be the final seal on the negotiated transition which started after the abolition of apartheid. It will come into operation after April 1999.[32] The first 'constitutional principles' were adopted before formal negotiations started.[33] The fundamental rights embodied in the final Constitution will be modelled on Chapter 3 of the 1993 Constitution, confirming the basic idea of constitutional continuity.[34]

The basic values underpinning the Constitution derive from the various provisions of Chapter 3, the Preamble, the epilogue, and the Constitutional Principles. These values include inter alia democracy, constitutionalism, the rule of law, freedom, and equality. These are broad concepts. They include further dimensions such as an open society, control over the exercise of power, the effective protection

---

[29] Emphasis added.

[30] The interpretation of the epilogue and the Schedules to the Constitution is dealt with in s 232(4). They 'shall not have a lesser status than any other provision of this Constitution'.

[31] Listed in sched 4. For their legal status, see s 232(4).

[32] Constitutional Principle XXXIII provides: 'The Constitution shall provide that, unless Parliament is dissolved on account of its passing a vote of no-confidence in the Cabinet, no national election shall be held before 30 April 1999.'

[33] The idea of prior constitutional principles being adopted before negotiations for a new constitution start, and determining the nature of the final product, is not new or unique. The same approach was e g followed in Namibia. See Wiechers 'Namibia: The 1982 Constitutional Principles and their Legal Significance' 1989/90 *SAYIL* 1 et seq.

[34] See Constitutional Principle II, sched 4.

of fundamental rights, separation of powers, the independence of the judiciary, and freedom of information.

These values find their embodiment in an important new constitutional concept, the *Rechtsstaat* or 'constitutional State' referred to in the Preamble. A 'constitutional State' provides a framework of rules and institutions which determines how state power has to be exercised. It also contains legal values which direct state action. The application and interpretation of the Constitution should therefore recognize and give effect to both the formal and material (substantive) qualities and the objectives embodied in this concept. It constitutes a basic constitutional norm which serves as the final criterion when state action is measured against the Constitution. In this sense it is of particular importance for the judiciary. The 'values' discussed here are really constitutional and legal values which are 'real' and applicable. They are contained in a supreme Constitution and are therefore binding.

What are the formal and material characteristics of the constitutional state? In a *formal* sense the constitutional state will be based on separation of powers; individual human rights (with particular emphasis on equality); protection of the individual through an independent judiciary; the maxim *nulla poena sine lege*; the idea that all state action must originate in a formal legal source; legal certainty and 'predictability' (through inter alia requiring proportionality for state behaviour and prohibiting retroactive legislation), and the existence of formal legal rules. This last requirement involves the participation of a popularly elected legislature in the enactment of legal rules; it lays down that the law should be of general application; and that the legislature too is bound by the law.[35]

In a *material* sense the constitutional state means that state power is inherently subject to certain higher constitutional values and should be exercised in a manner that will further these values (such as human dignity, freedom, and equality). In this way the constitutional state will be realized. This Constitution and these values are preconditions for the exercise of power. The government of the day exercises power on the basis of and through the Constitution and the law — not because it is 'in power'.

These values will become operational through legislation and adjudication. Choices of substance (including choices about their hierarchical order[36]) will have to be made.

The extent to which these values are universal and their application in South Africa will have to be assessed. An 'open and democratic society' must display universally acknowledged minima, while accommodating local conditions. The courts must find the right balance through the guidance of the Constitution.

Ours is a highly divided society with marked socio-economic and cultural disparities and differences.[37] Although the Constitution contains very little in terms

---

[35] Kriele *Einführung in die Staatslehre — Die geschichtlichen Legitimitätsgrundlagen des demokratischen Verfassungsstaates* (1975) 14; Van Wyk *Persoonlike Status in die Suid-Afrikaanse Publiekreg* (Unpublished LLD dissertation, Unisa 1979) 72–76; Basson & Viljoen *Suid-Afrikaanse Staatsreg* 2 ed (1988) 229–31.

[36] The framers of the German Basic Law are said to 'have arranged these values in a hierarchical order, the most important of which is a "free democratic basic order" crowned by the principle of "human dignity".' Kommers op cit (n 26) 54.

[37] Constitutional Principle XI states: 'The diversity of language and culture shall be acknowledged and protected, and conditions for their promotion shall be encouraged.'

of socio-economic rights and embodies no 'directive principles',[38] references to the 'promotion of national unity', 'restructuring' of the country,[39] the special needs of women,[40] the restitution of land,[41] the development of customary law,[42] as well as some specific socio-economic matters[43] are found. The attainment of legitimacy, justice, and stability will require that these concerns remain on the agenda. They will no doubt also influence judicial choice.

The constitutional values of the new South African order must always be viewed against the background of a history of racial discrimination, exclusion, and domination. The 'new order' to which the Preamble refers will largely depend on achieving equality. The right to 'human dignity' embodied in s 10 will become an important measure and criterion in this regard.

The Constitution of 1993 is also the embodiment of a *negotiated* agreement. It contains many compromises. This resulted from the nature of the transition and the nature of the society for which a new dispensation had to be worked out. South Africa did not undergo 'decolonization' leading to the final departure of a former regime and its complete replacement by a new government. This Constitution has to guide a divided South African society into a new dispensation. It constitutes the contract under which the various parties and groups enter that process. Future peace and stability will also depend on whether the agreement is honoured. These considerations will have to be kept in mind when the Constitution is applied and interpreted.

Another historical pointer is to be found in the international order. The efforts to abolish apartheid found considerable support in public international law and in the resolutions and programmes of action of various international organizations.[44] The Constitution was written after the demise of totalitarian communism in Eastern Europe. It coincides with a new international emphasis on individual freedom, freedom of economic activity, and the effective protection of fundamental rights. The reference in s 35 to 'public international law applicable to the rights entrenched in this Chapter' is concomitant to South Africa rejoining the international community. That community itself is endeavouring to formulate a 'new international order', the successor to the era of the Cold War.[45]

The courts will be required to give concrete meaning to constitutional values in the context of specific disputes. The rights referred to in Chapter 3 are not goals; rather they are *enforceable law*. Public international law and the use of comparable foreign decisions (where appropriate) will be indispensable. In many countries, as well as in public international law, the implications of many of the classic freedoms

---

[38] For the meaning and constitutional impact of directive principles, or 'principles of State policy' as they are called in Namibia, see Erasmus 'Die Grondwet van Namibië' (1990) 3 *Stell LR* 277 at 309. The Constitutional Principles in sched 4 of the 1993 Constitution often display the same promotional character as is commonly found in directive principles.

[39] In the Preamble. The epilogue expressly recognizes the need for reconciliation and reconstruction.

[40] Chapter 8.

[41] Ibid.

[42] Section 35(3); Constitutional Principle XIII.

[43] Education, the rights of children, and labour relations are dealt with in Chapter 3.

[44] For a discussion, see Erasmus 'The International Relations Context of the Freedom Charter' in Steytler (ed) *The Freedom Charter and Beyond — Founding Principles of a Democratic South African Legal Order* (1991) 233.

[45] See in this regard Henkin 'International Law after the Cold War' *American Society of International Law Newsletter* Nov–Dec 1993 1. He foresees that the removal of the ideological influence of the Cold War period will result in changes in the protection of human rights, collective security, nationality, and the subjects of international law.

(e g expression, assembly, privacy, religious exercise, equal protection, and property rights) have become established, as have concepts such as 'public order' and 'an open and democratic society'.

The Constitution also recognizes the *pre-constitutional* nature of fundamental rights. According to the Preamble, 'all citizens shall be able to enjoy and exercise their fundamental rights and freedoms'. These are rights which already exist; they are not created through legislation or even the Constitution. Therefore they cannot be withdrawn by legislative action. They vest in people by nature of their common humanity. The Constitution 'acknowledges' these rights and affords them specific protection.[46] This is achieved through the device of constitutional supremacy; the Constitution binds all the organs of the state.

The pre-constitutional nature of fundamental rights requires that legislative limitations on their exercise will have to be such as to leave the 'essential content' untouched. As s 33(1)*(b)* makes clear, limitations 'shall not negate the essential content of the right in question'. All laws will be measured against the higher values of the Constitution. The onus of proof will be on the state to justify each and every limitation, in particular to show its constitutional validity. The person(s) affected will not have to prove the existence of the fundamental right claimed.

## 1.4 The relevance of public international law

The Constitution is international-law-friendly. It incorporates public international law and provides for the application of international human rights law when the fundamental rights of Chapter 3 are to be interpreted. This pro-international-law orientation seems to be a deliberate choice and another of the constitutional 'values'.

The theoretical basis for invoking public international law when *interpreting* the fundamental rights of Chapter 3 is provided in s 35(1).

In interpreting the provisions of this Chapter a court of law shall promote the values which underlie an open and democratic society based on freedom and equality and *shall*, where applicable, have regard to public international law applicable to the protection of the rights entrenched in this Chapter, and *may* have regard to comparable foreign case law.[47]

Another provision of the Constitution, s 231, incorporates public international law as part of the law of the land.[48] It refers to both international agreements and customary international law. (This section covers several aspects: it confirms that public international law binds South Africa vis-à-vis other states; it provides for the continuation of existing international agreements; it regulates the procedure for the ratification of international agreements; and it lays down principles for the direct domestic application of public international law as part of municipal law.)

International human rights law now becomes applicable through two constitutional devices — as an instrument of *interpretation* and by virtue of the incorporation of the *substance* of public international law into municipal law. Much of the latter will include international human rights law.[49]

---

[46] This is the position generally adopted in Constitutions providing for fundamental rights. See e g Kommers op cit (n 26) 38.

[47] Emphasis added.

[48] See the chapter on international human rights by John Dugard elsewhere in this volume.

[49] For a list of most of the treaties and customary law on human rights, see Henkin 'Human Rights' in Bernhardt (ed) *Encyclopedia of Public International Law* vol 8 268. He writes at 270: 'The Universal Declaration of Human

How will public international law be proved and utilized? South African lawyers will have to become familiar with the discipline in order to be able to argue its content and application. In short, public international law will have to be treated in the same way as other areas of municipal law. Its original sources such as treaties, custom, and general principles will have to be available and known, together with academic commentaries, textbooks, and case law. In addition, the work and publications of certain international organizations will have to be made accessible.

The second source of reference mentioned in s 35(1), comparable foreign case law, will frequently also contain, in addition to the application of local municipal law, analyses of public international-law material and of the judgments of other tribunals applying international human rights law.[50] Even the judgments of the European Court of Human Rights will become relevant.

The fact that South Africa is at present party to very few international agreements on human rights is no obstacle to invoking international human rights law for the purposes of s 35(1). Human rights protection in South Africa does not depend on this country being party to international human rights conventions. These rights are claimed in terms of Chapter 3 of the Constitution. Section 35(1) invokes public international law primarily for the purpose of interpretation and determining their scope, not for proving the existence of the fundamental right at issue.

A considerable part of international human rights law will in any event also apply locally in terms of s 231(4) by virtue of being customary international law. Unlike international agreements, customary international law needs no express parliamentary 'approval' in order to become part of the law of the land. It should be stressed that customary international law creates obligations also for states not party to specific conventions.[51] This may include international humanitarian law (*jus in bello*), which is recognized in s 227(2) of the Constitution. This area of public international law may apply to domestic conflicts and public emergencies.[52]

International human rights law will be applicable whenever a fundamental right contained in Chapter 3 is interpreted. For example, if freedom of expression under s 15 is invoked, the meaning and application ascribed to this concept elsewhere or under international law becomes relevant. All South African courts will be able to consult and use public international law when ruling on matters under Chapter 3. It will not be the exclusive domain of the Constitutional Court.

International human rights law and foreign case law will be of particular importance when the limitation and suspension of rights are assessed. Issues such as the onus of proof, extent of protection, nature and scope of countervailing considera-

---

Rights is the accepted general articulation of recognized human rights. With some variations, the same rights are recognized by the Covenant on Civil and Political Rights and the Covenant on Economic, Social and Cultural Rights.' These universal instruments are often collectively called the International Bill of Rights. See also Kirby 'Human Rights — Emerging International Minimum Standards' (1993) 19 *Commonwealth Law Bulletin* 1252. See further Dugard op cit (n 48).

[50] See Schabas op cit (n 27) for the Canadian position.

[51] Henkin op cit (n 49) 271 writes: 'It is plausible to conclude that as of the early 1980's a State, though not party to any covenant or convention, is guilty of a violation of customary international law, if as State policy, it practices, encourages or condones genocide, slavery or slave trade, the killing or causing the disappearance of individuals, torture or other cruel, inhuman or degrading treatment or punishment, systematic racial discrimination, or consistent patterns of gross violations of internationally recognized human rights.' Some rights may even be *jus cogens*.

[52] See Burgos 'The Application of International Humanitarian Law as Compared to Human Rights Law in Situations Qualified as Internal Armed Conflict, Internal Disturbances and Tensions, or Public Emergency, With Special Reference to War Crimes and Political Crimes' in Kalshoven & Sandoz (eds) *Implementation of International Humanitarian Law* (1989) 1 et seq. See also Sieghart *The International Law of Human Rights* (1983) 117.

tions, the meaning and ambit of grounds for limitation, and techniques of balancing will often be clarified by comparative and international inquiry.

What happens if the public international law binding upon South Africa protects a particular fundamental right more comprehensively than Chapter 3? The various provisions of the Constitution are interrelated. Section 231 provides a constitutional basis for invoking international-law principles in the domestic courts. International law complying with the requirements of s 231 forms part of the law of the land. More comprehensive international human rights may therefore find domestic application, if necessary through a purposive interpretation of the Constitution. The courts should adopt the interpretation most consonant with the state's international obligations. This is in line with the existing presumption in favour of international law.[53]

Every time a fundamental right is to be interpreted the courts are under a constitutional duty to promote the values inherent in a system favouring democracy and fundamental rights as required by s 35(1). This provides a basis for flexibility and a pro-fundamental rights orientation. International human rights law can and must be used to indicate the direction and choice which will satisfy the obligation to promote the values inherent in the Constitution.

Should South Africa become party to a universal or regional human rights convention equipped with adjudicating bodies, a new need will arise. Domestic and international judgments and rulings will have to be synchronized. An element of supra-nationalism may develop in terms of which the state will be bound to honour its international legal obligations. If a right of individual petition to such supra-national bodies is adopted, domestic judgments may be 'appealed' against.[54]

## 2 LIMITATION

### 2.1 Why a limitation clause?

The introduction to this chapter explained that fundamental rights or freedoms are in general not absolute. Their boundaries are set by the rights of others and by the legitimate needs of society. The state is involved in balancing these rights and needs. This task as a rule is pursued through legislation. Overall constitutional control is achieved by providing for a general limitation clause, as in the case of s 33, or through specific limitations to particular rights.[55]

If, for example, it is argued in a given case that action taken in terms of a specific statute infringes a right entrenched in one of the earlier provisions of Chapter 3, it will first have to be determined whether that right has in fact been infringed. This will require an investigation into the nature and scope of the particular right. (When doing so a court will have to keep s 35(1) in mind and will have to 'promote the values which underlie an open and democratic society based on freedom and

---

[53] Dugard *International Law —A South African Perspective* (1994) 46; Schabas op cit (n 27) 26.

[54] For an example of how these issues are dealt with in other systems, see e g Riedel 'Assertion and Protection of Human Rights in International Treaties and their Impact in the Basic Law' in Starck (ed) *Rights, Institutions and Impact of International Law According to the German Basic Law* (1987) 197 et seq; Wilson 'The Domestic Impact of International Human Rights Law' (1993) 19 *Commonwealth Law Bulletin* 1246 for the Australian position. See further Dugard op cit (n 48).

[55] This is the approach adopted in international instruments such as the European Convention and the International Covenant on Civil and Political Rights (ICCPR).

equality'.) If the first question is answered in the affirmative, the state may then argue that the contested action is nevertheless acceptable because it can be justified as a permissible limitation under s 33. This final determination will then be made under the limitation clause, not the earlier provision providing for the right under discussion. Section 33 provides the guidelines for the courts to use when deciding on the constitutionality of limitations. It has to be applied in all instances concerning the infringement of a fundamental right.

A limitation clause is to be distinguished from a derogation or suspension clause as contained in s 34. The latter applies in times of public emergency. A limitation clause, on the other hand, is of a permanent nature. Its application forms part of the normal enforcement of fundamental rights and freedoms.

## 2.2 The constitutional context of section 33

By making limitations an inherent part of a Bill of Rights, as is the case in the Constitution of 1993, an important indication is given as to the nature of such a clause. It forms part of the normal protection and enforcement of the rights contained in Chapter 3. It permits limitations on certain constitutionally recognized grounds and on those grounds only. In this manner it also limits the limiting power of the state. Section 33 thus also protects the rights entrenched in Chapter 3.

The power to limit and balance rights does not give an unfettered discretion. It has to result in a finely balanced exercise that permits the unfolding of these rights in a manner that will result in their optimal application in society. A limitation clause is necessary in order to ensure the meaningful enjoyment of fundamental rights and freedoms, not to create a new source of power for the state to be used for curtailing them.

When seen in this light it becomes logical to interpret limitations restrictively. The application of s 33 should fit into the original value system underpinning the Constitution.[56] Fundamental rights constitute an important facet of these values. They are recognized and protected by the state, not granted; thus these rights cannot be withdrawn at whim. When interpreting s 33 the general obligation contained in s 35(1) should again be borne in mind.

The role of the state with respect to fundamental rights contains several dimensions. It is under constitutional obligation to respect, protect, and promote these rights. The state is required to create conditions and space for their enjoyment and to provide for appropriate relief and remedies when they are threatened or infringed.[57] It is obliged to restrain itself when regulating their exercise. In certain instances it will also be obliged to restrain third parties from infringing the rights of others. This may entail the use of criminal sanctions, provided it meets the requirements of the Constitution. One such area is expressly recognized in s 33(4), which provides for 'measures designed to prohibit unfair discrimination' by private persons contained in 'law of general application'. It may also be necessary for the state to regulate commercial and other private spheres. Finally, it is required to take the legitimate needs of society into account.

In performing these functions the legislation providing for the regulation of

---

[56] See above, 1.3.
[57] Section 7(4).

fundamental rights will have to conform with the parameters set by s 33. This is why human rights litigation practically always involves the interpretation of a limitation clause. Even Constitutions that do not include an express limitation clause have to develop limitation grounds in order to ensure the proper protection of fundamental rights. This usually happens through the judgments of the courts or through constitutional amendments. The new South African Constitution is a 'modern' document which contains an express limitation clause which should facilitate the application of Chapter 3. Comparative foreign case law will be more suitable if selected from similar national and international approaches.[58]

Section 33 forms part of a *supreme* Constitution. Legislation and the law in general, as well as executive action, must be in conformity with the Constitution, including s 33. The fundamental rights entrenched in Chapter 3 do not deny the existence of other rights or freedoms as conferred by common law, customary law, or legislation. However, these rights must be consistent with the fundamental rights of Chapter 3.[59] All forms of limitation of fundamental rights will have to meet the requirements of s 33. There is no other source permitting another set of criteria for the limitation of the rights entrenched by Chapter 3. Even when a state of emergency is declared s 33 will continue to apply.[60] The rights not temporarily suspended will for the duration of the public emergency continue to be regulated and protected under s 33.

## 2.3 The structure of section 33

Although the Constitution contains a single limitation clause, it should be pointed out that several other provisions in Chapter 3 contain qualifications. Section 14, for example, permits legislation recognizing certain religious practices and institutions. Media financed by the state or under its control shall be regulated in a manner which will ensure impartiality and diversity of opinion.[61] Access to information held by the state will be possible in so far as such information is required for the exercise or protection of a person's rights.[62]

Important additional limitation grounds are contained in s 25(1)*(c)* and (2)*(b)* and *(d)* and deal with the administration of criminal justice. Limitations in the interest of the administration of justice are generally recognized and are also inherent in the idea of an open and democratic society. These are only some of the examples[63] of qualifications which will have to be taken into account when these rights are affected. The following discussion will focus on s 33 only.

Section 33 is of general application and in principle applies to all the rights entrenched in Chapter 3.[64] This does not mean that all the various rights may be

---

[58] The US Constitution does not contain a limitation clause. This fact has to be taken into account when selecting comparative case law. See in this regard Woolman 'Riding the Push-Me Pull-You: Constructing a Test that Reconciles the Conflicting Interests which Animate the Limitation Clause' (1994) 10 *SAJHR* 60 at 68. The Canadian courts too have not imported 'the entire US framework for resolving constitutional questions involving individual rights and freedoms into Canada'. Colker 'Section 1, Contextuality, and The Anti-Disadvantage Principle' (1993) 42 *U Toronto LJ* 77 at 110.
[59] Section 33(3). This may provide a ground for the horizontal application of certain fundamental rights.
[60] Section 34(5)*(c)*.
[61] Section 15(2).
[62] Section 23.
[63] Others are to be found in ss 8(2), 26(2), 28(3), and 32*(c)*.
[64] Section 33(1).

limited in an identical manner. Human dignity, for example, will have to be treated differently from freedom of movement. Permissible restrictions on human dignity are far more difficult to foresee. Each case and each right will also have to be dealt with on its own merits. Although the same limitation grounds apply, their impact on the various rights, the nature of the essence of a right, and the thresholds involved will differ. In a Canadian judgment this point was explained along the following lines:

> 'A wide range of rights and freedoms are guaranteed by the Charter, and an almost infinite number of factual situations may arise in respect of these. Some limits on rights and freedoms protected by the Charter will be more serious than others in terms of the nature of the right or freedom violated, the extent of the violation, and the degree to which the measures which impose the limit trench upon the integral principles of a free and democratic society.'[65]

Section 33 contains two different tests or thresholds for valid limitation. As a result the rights entrenched in Chapter 3 are grouped into two different categories for the purpose of applying s 33. The rights entrenched in ss 10, 11, 12, 14(1), 21, 25 and 30(1)*(d)*, *(e)*, and (2), as well as the rights entrenched in ss 15, 16, 17, 18, 23, and 24, inasmuch as they relate to free and fair political activity, may only be limited by: (i) law of general application, (ii) which is reasonable and *necessary*, (iii) which is justifiable in an open and democratic society based on freedom and equality, (iv) and which does not negate the essential content of the right in question.

The remaining rights may only be limited by: (i) law of general application, (ii) which is reasonable, (iii) which is justifiable in an open and democratic society based on freedom and equality, (iv) and which does not negate the essential content of the right in question.

The requirements of s 33 are interrelated and cumulative and should all be met.

The final part of s 33 contains provisions on labour rights created under legislation pre-dating the Constitution. Such provisions apparently are to be insulated and 'shall remain of full force and effect until repealed or amended by the legislature'. They do not relate to the principles typically involved in a limitation clause and will not be discussed.

## 2.4 Application and interpretation of a limitation clause

Limitations should be interpreted strictly.[66] The general rule is the protection of the right or freedom; the limitation is the exception. A limitation may only be applied in so far as is necessary for preserving the values enumerated in the limitation clause. It may not be applied in a manner resulting in the complete suppression of the right or freedom.

It must first be considered whether or not there has been an interference with the protected right and, if so, whether or not this interference was justified in the light of the limitation provisions. The operation of a limitation clause does not involve a

---

[65] *R v Oakes* (supra) at 228 (DLR).
[66] Sieghart op cit (n 52) 91; Kiss op cit (n 2) 290; *Handyside v United Kingdom* European Commission of Human Rights (EUCM) 5493/72, 30 Sept 1975. In *R v Oakes* (supra) at 225 it is called a 'stringent standard of justification.' See also below, n 69.

choice between two conflicting principles; it concerns a single principle which is subject to certain limitations.[67]

In applying s 33 a court will first inquire whether the petitioner's conduct falls within the ambit of the right or freedom on which he or she relies. If a political meeting has, for example, been banned, it must first be shown that holding such a political meeting is protected under Chapter 3. In other words, the scope of the right relied upon will be analysed. It must then be shown that the official banning of that meeting amounts to an infringement of the right to assemble. The facts supporting these arguments will have to be adduced by the petitioner. It must also be recalled that in terms of s 7(4) not only an infringement but also a 'threat to any right' entitles a person to appropriate relief.

If these first requirements have been met, the state will then have to demonstrate that the banning (limitation) is justifiable and therefore constitutional because it meets the requirements of s 33(1). In other words, the state will have to show that the limitation is reasonable, justifiable in an open and democratic society based on freedom and equality, and does not negate the essential content of the right. (In those categories where required necessity will also have to be demonstrated.) This latter part of the court's function will require that it evaluate the arguments and evidence produced by the state and determine the importance of the interest invoked as justification for limiting the enjoyment of the right under discussion. This involves the balancing of the enjoyment of a fundamental right against the interests of the state on which it relies for justifying the limitation. This last function goes to the heart of constitutional review. It requires that the values and purpose of the Constitution should be given full recognition and application.

It has been held in respect of the criteria which must be addressed by the proponent of a limitation on a right or freedom that 'the onus of proof is on the party seeking the limitation, and the standard of proof is the civil standard, proof by a preponderance of probabilities'.[68] Where evidence is required to satisfy the requirements of a limitation clause, which will generally be the case, 'it should be cogent and persuasive and make clear to the court the consequences of imposing or not imposing the limit . . . A court will also need to know what alternative measures . . . were available.'[69] It is fair that the state will have to put before the court the facts on which it relies; they are as a rule not available to the petitioner.

Those who wish to oppose restrictions on rights should also be free to produce relevant evidence in order to rebut the state's claims. This may often include evidence on the impact of restrictions on society, such as sociological data. (Concepts such as the US Brandeis brief may become useful devices.)

---

[67] This is demonstrated in the *Sunday Times v United Kingdom* decision of the European Court of Human Rights, 6538/74, 2 EHRR 245.
[68] *Edwards Books and Art Ltd v R* (1986) 2 SCR 713, (1987) 35 DLR (4th) 1 at 41.
[69] *R v Oakes* (supra) at 225–6 (DLR). The court further ruled: 'The onus of proving that a limit on a right or freedom guaranteed by the Charter is reasonable and demonstrably justified in a free and democratic society rests upon the party seeking to uphold the limitation. It is clear from the text of s 1 that limits on the rights and freedoms enumerated in the Charter are exceptions to their general guarantee. The presumption is that the rights and freedoms are guaranteed unless the party invoking s 1 can bring itself within the exceptional criteria which justify their being limited. This is further substantiated by the use of the word "demonstrably" which clearly indicates that the onus of justification is on the party seeking to limit' (at 227).

In 1984 a set of principles, known as the 'Siracusa Principles',[70] were drawn up by a group of international-law experts to guide the interpretation of the limitation clauses in the International Covenant on Civil and Political Rights. These principles were summarized as follows:

'1. No limitations or grounds for applying them to rights guaranteed by the Covenant are permitted other than those contained in the terms of the Covenant itself.
2. The scope of a limitation referred to in the Covenant shall not be interpreted so as to jeopardize the essence of the right concerned.
3. All limitation clauses shall be interpreted strictly and in favor of the rights at issue.
4. All limitations shall be interpreted in the light and context of the particular right concerned.
5. All limitations on a right recognized by the Covenant shall be provided for by law and be compatible with the objects and purposes of the Covenant.
6. No limitation referred to in the Covenant shall be applied for any purpose other than that for which it has been prescribed.
7. No limitation shall be applied in an arbitrary manner.
8. Every limitation imposed shall be subject to the possibility of challenge to and remedy against its abusive application.
9. No limitation on a right recognized by the Covenant shall discriminate contrary to Article 2, paragraph 1.
10. Whenever a limitation is required in the terms of the Covenant to be "necessary," this term implies that the limitation:
    (a) is based on one of the grounds justifying limitations recognized by the relevant article of the Covenant,
    (b) responds to a pressing public or social need,
    (c) pursues a legitimate aim, and
    (d) is proportionate to that aim.
    Any assessment as to the necessity of a limitation shall be made on objective considerations.
11. In applying a limitation, a state shall use no more restrictive means than are required for the achievement of the purpose of the limitation.
12. The burden of justifying a limitation upon a right guaranteed under the Covenant lies with the state.
13. The requirement expressed in Article 12 of the Covenant, that any restrictions be consistent with other rights recognized in the Covenant, is implicit in limitations to the other rights recognized in the Covenant.
14. The limitation clauses of the Covenant shall not be interpreted to restrict the exercise of any human rights protected to a greater extent by other international obligations binding upon the state.'

This extensive list goes beyond approaches to interpretation *stricto sensu*. It is in essence a complete 'checklist' of all the principles applicable to limitations. It is nevertheless a useful list in the light of s 35(1), which requires regard for international human rights law.

The remainder of the discussion will endeavour to identify and discuss the 'elements' involved in the application of this limitation clause. The approach adopted is as suggested by the formulation of s 33(1).

---

[70] These principles contain a full explanation of the limitation and derogation provisions in the International Covenant on Civil and Political Rights. The full text of their report appears in the (1985) 7 *Human Rights Quarterly* 1–88. See further below, 3.2.

## 2.5 Law of general application

Limitations have to be contained in 'law of general application'. This formulation seems broad enough to include parliamentary legislation, the laws of the new provincial legislatures, and the rules of common law.[71] Acts of Parliament enacted before 27 April 1994 will also be included, as will provincial ordinances and perhaps municipal by-laws. Those laws were adopted during a period when no Bill of Rights or a supreme Constitution existed. They should be construed in that light. Regulations are as a rule of a delegated nature and should be based on empowering statutes. Measures taken by the executive should be excluded unless clearly authorized by general legislation.

New legislation will have to be drafted in a manner which will take the requirements of s 33 into account. Reasonableness, clarity, and respect for the 'essential content' of all fundamental rights will now constitute new requirements for drafters. It should be remembered that bills before Parliament may also be challenged before the Constitutional Court for unconstitutionality.

All 'forms of law' will have to be general and must be adequately accessible. The ordinary person should be able to form a clear picture of the legal rules involved. Rules should also be clear and be formulated with sufficient precision.

Limitations must be established by general rules. Arbitrary restrictions on rights will be inconsistent with s 33, as will all discriminatory measures.

## 2.6 Determining the scope of right

The first part of the application of a limitation clause involves the question whether certain conduct is protected by a right or freedom guaranteed by Chapter 3. It often happens that an application for judicial protection fails in this early stage already.

Other chapters in this book deal with the various individual rights and freedoms. A ruling on the content of a right, however, forms part of the application of a limitation clause as well. What forms of conduct are for example protected by 'freedom of expression'? Does it include racist speech? Does it include conduct?

This part of the judicial investigation should be conducted within the context of a comprehensive approach to the Constitution. What is the *purpose* of a right and what are the *values* contained in the Constitution? The language used for formulating a particular right should be interpreted within this context.

The balancing between the rights of an individual and the interests of society should not be invoked too early. It does not belong to this part of the investigation. Balancing only occurs once the state has demonstrated and identified those interests which will trigger the application of the limitation grounds provided for in s 33. Recognizing certain conduct to fall within the scope of a particular right does not terminate the investigation. It also does not mean that such a right may not be limited.

## 2.7 When is a limitation justifiable in an open and democratic society?

Although sometimes discussed as part of the reasonableness requirement, this

---

[71] The term 'law' in the European Convention on Human Rights has been held to include statute law, unwritten law, subordinate legislation, and royal decrees. See Sieghart op cit (n 52) 92; *Klass v Federal Republic of Germany* (5029/71) 2 EHRR 214.

element (the justification permitted by an open and democratic society) seems to be an independent one. This is the manner in which s 33(1)(a)(ii) treats it. In the Canadian case of *R v Oakes*[72] reasonableness was discussed in a way that linked it to the identification of those limitations which are justifiable in a free and democratic society:

> 'To establish that a limit is reasonable and demonstrably justified in a free and democratic society, two central criteria must be satisfied. First, the objective, which the measures responsible for a limit on a Charter right or freedom are designed to serve, must be "of sufficient importance to warrant overriding a constitutionally protected right or freedom": *R v Big M Drug Mart Ltd*. The standard must be high in order to ensure that objectives which are trivial or discordant with the principles integral to a free and democratic society do not gain s 1 protection. It is necessary, at a minimum that an objective relate to concerns which are pressing and substantial in a free and democratic society before it can be characterized as sufficiently important.'

What is introduced here is the first phase of the balancing of, on the one hand, the rights and interests of an individual and, on the other hand, the interests of a democratic society as represented by the state. The state may limit the exercise of Chapter 3 rights only in so far as permitted by s 33. It is for the Constitutional Court ultimately to weigh the two sets of interests in the light of all the factors provided for by s 33.

The official ground or consideration invoked by the state must be compatible with democratic rule. This is the ultimate standard against which limitations must be measured. In the words of *Oakes*:

> 'Inclusion of these words [free and democratic society] as the final standard of justification for limits on rights and freedoms refers the Court to the very purpose for which the Charter was originally entrenched in the Constitution: Canadian society is to be free and democratic. The Court must be guided by the values and principles essential to a free and democratic society which I believe embody, to name but a few, respect for the inherent dignity of the human person, commitment to social justice and equality, accommodation of a wide variety of beliefs, respect for cultural and group identity, and faith in social and political institutions which enhance the participation of individuals and groups in society. The underlying values and principles of a free and democratic society are the genesis for the rights and freedoms guaranteed by the Charter and the ultimate standard against which a limit on a right or freedom must be shown, despite its effect, to be reasonable and demonstrably justified.'[73]

What this quotation makes quite clear is that the purpose of a limitation in this context is to further the basic objectives of democratic rule.

Democracy is in certain circumstances compatible with restrictions on political freedoms and freedom of expression. European societies (more than in the US) have at times invoked such restrictions in order to protect community interests and to prevent sedition, libel, blasphemy, or obscenity. In Germany the doctrine of a capable or defensible democracy (*streitbare Demokratie*) has been developed inter alia in response to terrorism. In terms hereof democracy has to prevent the exploitation of democratic freedoms for the purpose of destroying democracy. This extraordinary measure will presumably be taken only when there is a threat to the life of the (democratic) nation and should therefore be dealt with in terms of a suspension (derogation) clause.

---

[72] Supra at 227 (DLR).
[73] At 225 (DLR).

Under the European Convention democracy has been explained with respect to liberal objectives such as individual self-fulfilment, the attainment of truth, participation in decision-making, pluralism, openness, tolerance, and a balance between stability and change and between the individual's liberty and the utilitarian 'greater good of the majority'.[74] Democratic rule, constitutionalism and the constitutional state are concepts which, in addition, stress the importance of control over the exercise of state power.

In the case of South Africa the complete criterion is one which requires justifiability in 'an open and democratic society based on freedom and equality'. What this entails in addition or as qualifications and what impact South African conditions will have, will have to be determined when specific measures are balanced against the values of the Constitution. There is the danger that 'democracy' and 'equality' are potentially in tension with each other. It may, as a result, be difficult to make a final choice. It could then be tempting to read into the South African Constitution and society an element of uniqueness, as has been done in other dispensations.[75]

There may be grounds for supporting such an argument. This is a Constitution for South African society. This society displays certain characteristics. The Constitution of 1993 is the product of a process which recognizes all these characteristics, including its diversity. Unique institutions have been created for the purpose of governing and transforming it. The government of national unity, for example, is rather *sui generis*. It is not a typical coalition government because a single party has won a clear and absolute majority. However, majority government was not formed; all parties that have gained more than 5 per cent support in the election for the national legislature are also represented in the Cabinet.

Judicial scrutiny of the legislature's policies cannot be 'undemocratic'. The Constitution is supreme and binds all organs of the state. Section 7, in addition, provides that Chapter 3 'shall bind all legislative and executive organs of state at all levels of government'. Judicial scrutiny is indeed a constitutional obligation.

Not just any officially invoked objective will be acceptable. A limitation must be shown to give effect to another constitutional guarantee. Trivial objectives will be rejected. An acceptable one will have to relate to concerns which are 'pressing and substantial in a free and democratic society'. It has been suggested that

> 'administrative convenience and the saving of costs should not justify the overriding of constitutional guarantees. After all, if you are going to allow rights to be trumped by efficiency concerns, you might as well have left their protection to the hurly-burly of the legislative process. On the other hand, if the government restriction is motivated by the desire to give substantive effect to another constitutional guarantee, the restriction is clearly of a substantial and pressing nature: its presence in the Constitution testifies to its importance.'[76]

There is the danger that the determination of what is acceptable in an open and democratic society takes place at too great a level of generality or too abstractly. In order to avoid such dangers some modifications, such as the 'contextual approach,' have been proposed:

---

[74] Sieghart op cit (n 52) 93.
[75] See in this regard Colker op cit (n 58) 83 for a discussion of the 'anti-disadvantage principle' and how it should be applied in Canada, which is said to display liberal traditions as well as traditions of 'multiculturalism'.
[76] Woolman op cit (n 58) 86.

'First, rather than ask what governmental interests are sufficiently *important* to the government in order to justify an infringement of a substantive right, a contextual approach would try to understand what kinds of justifications are legitimate in the light of the distinctive nature of the right being infringed; and, second, it would assess the legitimacy of the justification for the infringement from the perspective of the plaintiff, the group purported to be protected by the legislature, society at large and the government.'[77]

'Contextualization' as used here is not unknown to South African law. In the law of delict, for example, the balancing of interests is a well-developed (and essential) concept. It is accepted that many factors will influence the balancing process.

> '*Factors influencing the balancing process* Various factors may play a role in the process of determining the reasonableness of the defendant's conduct: these include the nature and extent of the harm and of the foreseeable or foreseen loss; the possible value to the defendant or to society of the harmful conduct; the costs and effort of steps which could have been taken to prevent the loss; the degree of probability of the success of preventive measures; the nature of the relationship between the parties; the motive of the defendant; economic considerations; the legal position in other countries; ethical and moral issues; the values underlying a bill of human rights; as well as other considerations of public interest or public policy.'[78]

This may be a useful modification in those instances where it will focus more directly on the impact of an infringement in a particular case. Limitations formulated in broad statutory terms may then be used in a more subtle manner if measured against the particularities of a specific case. The impact on different rights may also differ. This may lead to more subtle balancing; it will not do away with balancing.

## 2.8 Reasonableness, necessity, and proportionality

Section 33 creates two categories of test. Limitations to certain rights must be both reasonable and necessary. Others must be only reasonable. The effect of this is that a stricter test will be required with respect to certain rights. Limitations on such more 'important' rights will meet with stricter judicial scrutiny. These rights, and they are identified, will enjoy extra protection from the judiciary. This will have the further effect that the problem of 'levels of scrutiny', as developed in US jurisprudence,[79] is to some degree already addressed in the Constitution. Future South African judgments may therefore experience less need for consulting US decisions; the South African Constitution entails an express limitation clause (which is absent from the US Constitution) and levels of scrutiny are provided. The substantive content of the two tests can now be determined with more clarity and certainty.

In devising a suitable test for reasonableness some general considerations should be kept in mind. The test to be developed is to serve the implementation of the new Constitution, which introduces a completely new dimension to South African law. The application of reasonableness in other areas of South African law (such as delict and criminal law) is well developed and may be helpful. It should, however, be remembered that the relationship between the state and an individual protected by an enforceable Bill of Rights is a very specific one. Reasonableness for the purpose of s 33 should be developed in order to give effect to the objectives of Chapter 3

---

[77] Colker op cit (n 58) 81.
[78] Neethling, Potgieter & Visser *Law of Delict* (1993) 34.
[79] Woolman op cit (n 58) 67–71.

and the Constitution in general. In public law the individual needs specific protection against the more powerful state.

Proportionality is inherent in the requirement of reasonableness. The *Oakes* judgment is often cited as a useful authority on reasonableness and proportionality, although the relevant provision of the Canadian Charter of Rights and Freedoms refers only to 'such reasonable limits prescribed by law as can be demonstrably justified in a free and democratic society'. Section 33 of the South African Constitution also does not refer expressly to proportionality. The German approach is also to require proportionality. Proportionality is inherent in the idea of the 'constitutional state'.[80]

The relevant *Oakes dictum* reads as follows:

> '[O]nce a sufficiently significant objective is recognized, then the party invoking s 1 must show that the means chosen are reasonable and demonstrably justified. This involves "a form of proportionality test": *R v Big M Drug Mart Ltd* ... Although the nature of the proportionality test will vary depending on the circumstances, in each case courts will be required to balance the interests of society with those of individuals and groups. There are, in my view, three important components of a proportionality test. First, the measures adopted must be carefully designed to achieve the objective in question. They must not be arbitrary, unfair or based on irrational considerations. In short, they must be rationally connected to the objective. Second, the means, even if rationally connected to the objective in this first sense, should impair "as little as possible" the right or freedom in question: *R v Big M Drug Mart Ltd*. Third, there must be a proportionality between the *effects* of the measures which are responsible for limiting the Charter right or freedom and the objective which has been identified as of "sufficient importance".'[81]

At this stage of the investigation into the constitutionality of an infringement the state will have to satisfy three requirements. The first is that the limitation must be rationally connected to its objective, which is to be identified. This means that it must be carefully designed. Limitation measures should not be arbitrary or unfair.

The second element holds that even if a rational connection exists, the means should do as little 'damage' as possible. In terms of the third requirement the limitation should be proportional to the objective and should only result in attaining that particular effect as justified by a 'sufficiently important' objective. It goes almost without saying that the aim pursued must be legitimate.

The enquiry into effects should go further and take into account the nature of a specific right. Restrictions may have different effects, depending on the nature of the right. The impact of limitations on the ultimate criterion — the proper functioning of an open and democratic society based on freedom and equality — should always be borne in mind. In the words of the *Oakes* judgment:

> Even if an objective is of sufficient importance, and the first two elements of the proportionality test are satisfied, it is still possible that, because of the severity of the deleterious effects of a measure on individuals or groups, the measure will not be justified by the purposes it is intended to serve. The more severe the deleterious effects of a measure, the more important the objective must be if the measure is to be reasonable and demonstrably justified in a free and democratic society.[82]

This may result in a requirement that alternatives be considered.

In order to perform this function the judiciary will have to do the necessary

---

[80] Kommers op cit (n 26) 59 and 425; Van Wyk op cit (n 35) 74.
[81] At 228 (DLR).
[82] At 227 (DLR). The German cases also stress the need for necessity, suitability, and the prohibition of excess in the measures taken: Badura *Staatsrecht* (1986) 84.

balancing throughout. The further salutary consequence will be that reasons for official acts and policies will have to be given, thus benefiting the ideal of more open government.

## 2.9 Respect for the essential content of a right

The nature of fundamental rights was explained in the introduction. The legislature does not grant these rights as a matter of choice; they flow from the Constitution. Therefore the legislature may also not take them away through limitations. The purpose should be to enhance fundamental rights through a sympathetic regulation. Over-broad executive discretions should be viewed critically. Limitations must meet the objective to regulate the exercise of rights in a democratic manner.

What constitutes the essential content of a fundamental right? The basic core of a right must always remain. Respect for the essential content of a right provides a final boundary for limitations. Beyond that it will result in denial of a right.

The German Basic Law and the Namibian Constitution recognize the need to protect the essential content of rights. Both these Constitutions also prohibit discrimination. The Namibian Constitution requires that legislation providing for limitations 'shall not be aimed at a particular individual'. It is also required that such laws shall be 'specific and identify the Article or Articles on which authority to enact such limitation is claimed to rest'.[83]

In the German system a distinction is drawn between the objective and subjective contents of a right.[84] The objective content refers to the values and practices which are typical of a free, democratic, and constitutional state. A democratic society exists only when certain rights and freedoms are guaranteed and only if it is possible for them to be implemented and enjoyed. Once a limitation prevents this the essence of the objective content of a right is negated.

The subjective content of a right refers to those values and practices that particular individuals and groups enjoy. Once such individuals or groups are prevented from exercising such rights as a result of a limitation the essence of the subjective content of the right is negated.

This methodology seems to be devised as a further tool for the proper identification and protection of the basic values inherent in a supreme Constitution based on democratic rule and the ideals of the constitutional state.

## 3 STATE OF EMERGENCY AND SUSPENSION

### 3.1 The justification for section 34

The decision to include a provision on states of emergency and the suspension of fundamental rights in the 1993 Constitution was controversial. Many opposed its inclusion because of serious human rights abuses in the past. Some argued that a Bill of Rights should not allow for the suspension of the very rights it has to protect.

---

[83] Article 22 of the Namibian Constitution.
[84] For a discussion see Woolman op cit (n 58) 72. See also Von Münch *Grundgesetz Kommentar* (1985) vol 1 777. Woolman considers this typology as being the result of a civil-law system without the benefit of precedent. The fact is that South Africa has no precedents on enforceable human rights to rely on. Greater awareness of refinements developed elsewhere will always be useful.

There is also the disturbing tendency for states of emergency often to become 'perpetual'.[85]

Not all 'emergencies' justify an official state of emergency and the suspension of fundamental rights. Only those which threaten the life of a nation require exceptional measures. The best way to prevent abuse of this power and unlawful infringement of fundamental rights is to provide for comprehensive constitutional checks in such situations. In times of emergency the protection of fundamental rights becomes all the more important. Section 34 is such an emergency clause which may only be implemented under the control of a supreme Constitution which provides for extensive judicial and legislative controls.

The absence of such a provision in a Constitution is no guarantee that exceptional powers will not be invoked. Even countries without explicit derogation clauses in their Constitutions sometimes find it necessary to invoke emergency powers.[86] Such measures are then justified by invoking 'implied provisions', common-law grounds, prerogative powers, martial law, the principle of *salus reipublicae suprema lex*, or the right of the state to self-defence, or necessity. The danger is that these grounds may suggest some 'extra-constitutional' source of executive power which is beyond normal constitutional and judicial control.

A clear and adequate provision in a justiciable Constitution provides for a more satisfactory and transparent treatment of this subject-matter. It is also the best way to restrict emergency powers to the truly exceptional instances when ordinary measures have become inadequate to protect the life of the nation. The 1993 Constitution now governs this whole area. Concepts such as prerogative powers, martial law, and other common-law provisions which in the past excluded effective judicial control can no longer apply.

## 3.2 The relation to other fundamental rights

Section 34 forms part of the Bill of Rights of the Constitution. This provides an important guideline with respect to its interpretation. Suspension of rights should be interpreted strictly and the formalities and requirements should always be adhered to. The ultimate aim remains the protection of society by safeguarding fundamental rights, constitutionalism, and democratic government. The purpose is never to protect the government of the day.

The interpretation of s 34 should be based on the new and original basis provided for by the Constitution of 1993. Previous judgments have become largely irrelevant. New guidelines, in addition to the text of s 34, are in terms of s 35(1) to be gleaned from public international law and foreign case law. Most international human rights conventions contain derogation clauses.[87] Their implementation reveals useful guidelines and case law. The international-law requirements with respect to public emergencies do not flow from international agreements only. They are provided for in customary international law as well.[88]

---

[85] Ellmann 'A Constitution for all Seasons: Providing Against Emergencies in a Post-Apartheid Constitution' 1989 *Columbia Human Rights LR* 163 at 167.

[86] See the US case of *Korematsu v United States* 323 US 214 (1945), where it was stated, *per* Frankfurther J: 'Therefore the validity of action under the war power must be judged wholly in the context of war. That action is not to be stigmatized as lawless because like action in times of peace would be lawless.'

[87] See Oraá *Human Rights in States of Emergency in International Law* (1992) 7–10. The African Charter is one of the exceptions.

[88] Oraá op cit (n 87) 209 et seq.

The International Law Association has approved a set of minimum standards, referred to as the 'Paris Minimum Standards of Human Rights Norms in a State of Emergency'.[89] These standards govern all aspects related to the declaration and administration of states of emergency. The 'Siracusa Principles' were drawn up by experts in public international law in 1984. They deal with limitation and derogation as developed under the International Covenant on Civil and Political Rights.[90]

The South African courts have already indicated their preparedness to adhere to other international standards, such as the 'Standard Minimum Rules' on the treatment of prisoners. In *S v Daniels*[91] this was done without any detailed analysis of their legal status. The Supreme Court simply accepted them as 'riglyne vir die behandeling van gevangenes wat deur talle lande as 'n bloudruk vir hulle gevangenisstelsels beskou word'. It also took judicial notice of the fact that prison authorities in South Africa already follow a policy of adhering to these guidelines. This seems to suggest that international state practice and standards are acceptable as a yardstick for executive action. After the coming into effect of the 1993 Constitution they may serve the additional purpose of elaborating and explaining certain provisions of Chapter 3.

A suspension clause should be distinguished from a limitation clause. The latter will not provide adequate legal guidance in times of a public emergency.[92] A limitation clause authorizes restrictions on fundamental rights under 'normal' conditions. A suspension clause, on the other hand, provides for temporary suspension of rights and operates only in exceptional situations when a public emergency threatens the life of the nation.

The following discussion will deal with the formal and substantive requirements applicable to a state of emergency and the suspension of fundamental rights.

### 3.3 The existence of an exceptional threat

What is the precise definition of the kind of emergency which justifies the suspension of fundamental rights? Section 34(1) requires that such an emergency shall be declared only 'where the security of the Republic is threatened by war, invasion, general insurrection or disorder or at a time of national disaster, and if the declaration is necessary to restore peace and order'.

The use of the word 'where' (in Afrikaans 'waar') is unfortunate. At first glance it suggests location, instead of the more logical requirement that *when* certain conditions prevail, *then* an emergency may be declared. (This is the type of formulation adopted with respect to a 'national disaster'.)

Certain exceptional conditions must exist before an emergency may be declared. This is also the internationally accepted approach. Both the European Convention and the International Covenant on Civil and Political Rights (ICCPR) indicate *when* an emergency may be declared.[93]

---

[89] Comprehensively discussed in Chowdhury *Rule of Law in a State of Emergency: The Paris Minimum Standards of Human Rights Norms in a State of Emergency* (1989).
[90] For a discussion see Ghandi 'The Human Rights Committee and Derogation in Public Emergencies' 1989 *GYIL* 323 at 350 et seq.
[91] 1991 (2) SACR 403 (C). See also *S v Staggie* 1990 (1) SACR 669 (C).
[92] Higgins 'Derogation under Human Rights Treaties' (1976–7) XLVIII *BYIL* 281 at 286.
[93] Article 15, European Convention: 'In time of war or other public emergency . . .'; art 4 ICCPR: 'In time of public emergency . . .'.

The following requirements with respect to the nature of the threat must be met:

(a) The emergency must be actual or imminent. There must be a real threat of war, invasion, general insurrection or disorder, or a national disaster must already exist. A 'preventive emergency' will be unlawful.[94] Convincing proof of the existence of an imminent threat will be required. This requires a factual judgment of the evidence available.[95]

(b) The emergency must be of exceptional magnitude. This usually requires a threat to the whole of the population.[96] An emergency experienced in one part of the country only but affecting the whole nation will satisfy this requirement. A localized emergency affecting only the local population may be problematic, although some commentators find it acceptable.[97] Chowdhury[98] provides the following useful discussion:

> 'Relying upon the decision of the European Court in *Ireland v UK*, Buergenthal points out that a public emergency need not engulf or threaten to engulf the entire nation before it can be said to "threaten the life of the nation". One must distinguish between the seriousness of a threat and the geographical boundaries in which the threat appears or from which it emanates. A public emergency which threatens the life of a nation "could presumably exist even if the emergency appeared to be confined to one part of the country — for example, one of its provinces, states or cantons — and did not threaten to spill over to other parts of the country". A contrary interpretation, argues Buergenthal, would be unreasonable "since it would prevent a state party from declaring a public emergency in one of its remote provinces where a large-scale armed insurrection was in progress merely because it appeared that the conflict would not spread to other provinces".'

(c) The life of the nation must be threatened. This requirement is found in both the European Convention and the ICCPR. This has been interpreted by the European Court in the *Lawless Case* to 'refer to an exceptional situation of crisis or emergency which affects the whole population and constitutes a threat to the organized life of the community of which the state is composed . . .'.[99] Another commentator interprets this requirement to mean 'a crisis situation affecting the population as a whole and constituting a threat to the organized existence of the community which forms the basis of the State'.[100]

Section 34 unfortunately deviates from this requirement and employs a formulation of uncertain content: 'the security of the Republic'. The concept of 'state security' formed the basis for previous states of emergency, which were widely condemned because of wide executive discretion, human rights abuses, and lack of judicial protection.

'Security' is qualified in s 34(1) by linking it to war, invasion, general insurrection or disorder, or national disaster. This creates another problem. Lists are incomplete (as this one is[101]) and cannot anticipate all possible

---

[94] Ghandi op cit (n 90) 352.

[95] In the *Lawless Case* (ECHR, Series A Vol 3 1961) an Irish declaration of emergency was accepted as lawful in the light of the 'imminent danger to the nation' caused by the IRA in Northern Ireland. In the *Greek Case* (Commission, 1969) it was rejected.

[96] *Lawless Case* (supra) para 29.

[97] Oraá op cit (n 87) 28–9.

[98] Op cit (n 89) 25.

[99] *Lawless Case* (supra) para 28.

[100] Questiaux, quoted by Chowdhury op cit (n 89) 14. See also Ghandi op cit (n 90) 351.

[101] Civil wars and internal unrest, generally viewed as states of emergency when justified by the exigencies of the situation, are omitted. See Oraá op cit (n 87) 33.

manifestations. Each case has be to judged on its own merits, taking into account the overriding concern for the continuance of a democratic society.

The list provided in s 34(1) creates an additional and serious problem. A 'state of war' is the first of the conditions listed as justifying a public emergency. Section 82(4) empowers the President to declare a 'state of national defence'. Nowhere is any official empowered to declare war, apparently with the objective in mind of bringing the South African position in line with the United Nations Charter. Article 2(4) of the UN Charter states that all members 'shall refrain in their international relations from the threat or use of force against the territorial integrity or political independence of any State, or in any other manner inconsistent with the Purposes of the United Nations'. Article 51 permits only individual or collective self-defence.

Section 34(1) should clearly have referred to a 'state of national defence' and not 'war'. As it now stands a state of war is possible because s 34 foresees it. However, nothing in the Constitution regulates its declaration. (It seems that the technical committee drafting s 82 of the Constitution forgot to inform the drafters of Chapter 3.) This introduces the danger of unwritten or prerogative powers being retained, which will undermine the supreme character of the Constitution and its comprehensive control of executive powers. There are no powers beyond those provided for in this Constitution.

The international standard used is one which puts the emphasis on the gravity of the circumstances.[102] That facilitates subsequent judicial scrutiny.

As a result of the unfortunate formulation found in s 34(1) another international standard ('to the extent strictly required by the exigencies of the situation') has been lost. The Siracusa Principles deal with this standard in considerable detail and list severity, duration, and geographic scope as requirements.[103] A more satisfactory application of the proportionality test would then also have been possible. Proportionality is inherent in the words 'strictly required'.

It should be possible to deal with certain events such as strikes, less severe natural disasters, or even internal strife by imposing 'normal' restrictions on freedom of movement or assembly as provided for in a typical limitation clause. Such events do not as a rule constitute a threat to the life of the nation. The real test is the gravity of the situation and whether the measures taken are necessary 'to the extent strictly required by the exigencies of the situation'.

---

[102] The international standard referred to here includes arts 15 and 4 of the European Convention and ICCPR respectively and subsequent judicial practice and academic commentaries. The European Convention, art 15(1), reads:
  '(1) In time of war or other public emergency threatening the life of the nation any High Contracting Party may take measures derogating from its obligations under this Convention to the extent strictly required by the exigencies of the situation, provided that such measures are not inconsistent with its other obligations under international law.'
The ICCPR, art 4(1), reads:
  '1. In time of public emergency which threatens the life of the nation and the existence of which is officially proclaimed, the States Parties to the present Covenant may take measures derogating from their obligations under the present Covenant to the extent strictly required by the exigencies of the situation, provided that such measures are not inconsistent with their other obligations under international law and do not involve discrimination solely on the ground of race, colour, sex, language, religion or social origin.'
[103] Ghandi op cit (n 90) 355.

Economic difficulties per se, unaccompanied by an additional crisis, should not constitute a threat to the life of the nation. The opinion has also been expressed that 'prolonged economic problems of underdevelopment are not inherently temporary phenomena and are thus incompatible with the requirement that the threat to the life of the nation be exceptional'.[104] It may conceivably be necessary to resort to emergency measures in order to secure the supply of essential goods and services under exceptional circumstances.[105] The lawfulness of such measures will depend on the gravity of the situation, whether the measures are proportionate to the need, and whether the limitation powers are insufficient.

(d) A state of emergency must be a measure of last resort. If the ordinary law of the land can deal with the needs of a situation, a state of emergency is not permissible. The normal provisions of the law should first be exhausted.[106] They include the limitation clause providing for everyday constitutionally acceptable limits to the exercise of human rights.[107] Section 34(1) seems to recognize this principle by requiring that a state of emergency will be declared only if 'necessary to restore peace and order'.

(e) A state of emergency must be a temporary measure. This flows from its very nature. Suspension of rights must therefore end when the threat has disappeared. 'Permanent states of emergency' are unlawful.[108]

Section 34 is basically in conformity with this requirement. Once peace and order is restored an emergency should end.[109] It shall be of force for not longer than twenty-one days 'unless it is extended for a period of not longer than three months or consecutive periods of not longer than three months at a time by resolution of the National Assembly'.[110] Each such extension will have to be justified in terms of the requirements for lawful emergencies and any superior court shall be competent to examine each extension in terms of all the substantive and procedural requirements provided for.

### 3.4 Official proclamation and judicial control

A state of emergency cannot exist unless officially declared. Its proclamation must be by an authority competent and legally empowered to do so. The reason for such a proclamation is to announce publicly the existence of an exceptional situation and to inform the public about the special conditions, powers, suspension of rights, controls, and remedies which will apply. Such a declaration and all subsequent regulations should contain sufficient information to explain the reasons for the emergency, when it will come into effect, and the scope and effect of any suspension of rights. A *de facto* state of emergency is not permitted.

These requirements are to ensure respect for the rule of law, constitutionalism,

---

[104] From the discussion on the adoption of the Siracuse Principles, quoted by Ghandi op cit (n 90) 352. See also the next requirement under *(e)*.
[105] Oraá op cit (n 87) 31 and the sources mentioned there.
[106] Oraá op cit (n 87) 29–30.
[107] Ghandi op cit (n 90) 355.
[108] Oraá op cit (n 87) 30.
[109] Section 34(1).
[110] Section 34(2).

and a Bill of Rights. They also find support in public international law.[111] Under international human rights agreements states are in addition required to inform other state parties and supervisory bodies in international organizations.

Public announcement and justification will help to prevent arbitrariness, lead to a greater appreciation of the seriousness of such an exceptional state of affairs, and secure greater transparency. Judicial and political control with respect to both announcement and implementation are necessary to ensure the achievement of these goals.

Section 34 provides for practically all these requirements. The following may be pointed out:

*(a)* All powers with respect to the proclamation of emergencies flow from the Constitution and laws passed in terms thereof. Prerogatives and wide discretionary powers no longer exist.

*(b)* A state of emergency is to be declared with future effect ('A state of emergency shall be proclaimed prospectively . . .'[112]).

*(c)* No rights may be suspended unless a state of emergency is first proclaimed.

*(d)* An Act of the new Parliament will have to be adopted to provide for the power to declare an emergency. The fact that emergencies are foreseen to be proclaimed 'under' an Act of Parliament suggests the passing of a general empowering Act which provides for subsequent executive action.

*(e)* Such an Act will have to comply with all the requirements of s 34 and the Constitution in general in order to be valid. The Constitutional Court may decide its constitutionality, as it may do with respect to all bills and Acts of Parliament.[113]

Section 34(3) provides for a critical role for the judiciary. 'Any superior court shall be competent to enquire into the validity of a declaration of a state of emergency, any extension thereof, and any action taken, including any regulation enacted, under such declaration.'

May judgment be passed on the substance of the proclamation (the need for it, its justification) or only on procedural matters? Does the 'political' nature of the decision to proclaim an emergency exclude judicial control?

The 'validity' of a state of emergency must inevitably include those substantive grounds justifying its proclamation. Sufficient factual proof of the existence of the threat of war, invasion, insurrection, etc should be supplied in order to justify the extraordinary device which a state of emergency is. In addition it will also have to be shown that 'a state of emergency is necessary to restore peace and order' and why less severe measures will not suffice. Such facts are constitutional preconditions for declaring an emergency.

Care should be taken not to continue with former practices and approaches inhibiting judicial control or to introduce new doctrines which compromise the Constitution. It is a supreme Constitution which has to give effect to the objectives of the constitutional state and an enforceable Bill of Rights. The judiciary has a constitutional obligation to protect and enforce this Constitution. This inevitably entails effective control over all exercise of power which may violate the Constitution.

---

[111] Oraá op cit (n 857 34 et seq; Ghandi op cit (n 90) 352–3; ICCPR art 4(1).
[112] Section 34(1).
[113] Under s 98(2)*(c)*.

Section 34 forms part of a Bill of Rights, the ultimate purpose of which is to protect fundamental rights. Suspension is an extraordinary power and decisions to proclaim emergencies should be subjected to strict judicial scrutiny. All organs of the state now have to respect and promote the new constitutional order, which is based on the 'sovereignty' of the Constitution. The sovereignty of Parliament is over.

*(f)* The executive branch will be responsible for the actual proclamation of an emergency and for specific regulations in order to give effect to it. This is a decision to be taken by the President[114] in consultation with the Cabinet.[115]

*(g)* A state of emergency shall last for not more than twenty-one days. Extension for periods not exceeding three months or consecutive periods of three months is possible. Such an extension requires a resolution by a two-thirds majority of all the members of the National Assembly. This provides for control by the legislature and is an important example of checks and balances. An elected legislature is to demand convincing proof before extension will be granted.

*(h)* Certain substantive constitutional limits are set for a law, regulations, or executive action dealing with public emergencies. No retrospective crimes may be created, state responsibility cannot be avoided, and certain fundamental rights are considered non-derogable and may therefore not be suspended during an emergency.[116]

*(i)* Judicial remedies and relief are provided for, covering all aspects of an emergency, its declaration, and all steps taken thereunder. This inter alia includes issues such as the constitutionality of the Act proclaiming an emergency referred to in s 34(1), the declaration of an emergency, control over subsequent action (including the *ultra vires* principle), and relief for individuals acting under s 7.

Section 34(4) provides an important yardstick for judicial review. Rights may be suspended only 'to the extent necessary to restore peace and order'. This is a clear proportionality test[117] and permits judicial investigation into the object and effect of suspension and of the cause of the emergency. The state will, by necessity, have to provide proof justifying its measures.

An even more effective and better known yardstick would have been the one generally found in international agreements. Derogation from obligations under such agreements is permitted only 'to the extent strictly required by the exigencies of the situation'.[118]

*(j)* The Constitution's jurisdictional provisions must be taken into account. Only a 'superior court' may enquire into the validity of a declaration of a state of emergency, its extension, and 'any action taken, including any regulation enacted, under such declaration'. This latter formulation is unfortunate. It apparently excludes the jurisdiction of lower courts with respect to executive acts and human rights protection otherwise enjoyed. The lower courts do,

---

[114] Section 82.
[115] Section 82(3). Until 1999 the Cabinet will be consistuted according to the principles of 'government of national unity'.
[116] Section 34(5). The non-suspendable rights are discussed below, 3.5.
[117] On proportionality, see further below, 3.6.
[118] ICCPR art 4(1); European Convention art 15(1).

however, have jurisdiction with respect to at least those aspects of an emergency dealing with detained people.[119]

(k) The position of persons detained during an emergency (the term 'detention without trial' is avoided) is dealt with extensively. Provision is made for notification of relatives, publication of the names of detainees, judicial review of the duration of detention, access to legal representatives, and medical services. The state 'shall . . . submit written reasons' justifying detention or extension thereof.[120] This suggests that the executive branch is required to provide reasons and to provide substantive grounds for the further detention of a detainee.

### 3.5 Non-derogability of certain fundamental rights

#### 3.5.1 *Non-derogable rights*

Even in times of emergency there are certain rights that may not be suspended. The state has to refrain from suspending certain non-derogable rights. Extra care should be taken during a public emergency to ensure strict respect for the law. The Constitution and the law in general do not cease to apply during an emergency. It is a legal condition governed by those provisions in the Constitution provided for by s 34. The courts and other organs of the state will continue to function and responsibility for unlawful behaviour will still ensue.

Apart from the obligation not to suspend certain fundamental rights a state must also

> 'take special precautions in time of public emergency to ensure that neither official nor semi-official groups engage in a practice of arbitrary and extrajudicial killings or involuntary disappearances, that persons in detention are protected against torture and other forms of cruel inhuman or degrading treatment or punishment, and that no persons are convicted or punished under laws or decrees with retroactive effect'.[121]

Public international law is of considerable importance in this regard. Under customary international law no state may suspend or violate the right to life; freedom from torture or cruel, inhuman, or degrading treatment or punishment, and from medical or scientific experimentation; the right not to be held in slavery or involuntary servitude; and the right not to be subjected to retroactive criminal penalties.[122]

Section 34(5)(c) lists the following non-derogable rights: non-discrimination;[123] life;[124] human dignity;[125] freedom from torture;[126] freedom from servitude and forced labour;[127] religion, belief and opinion;[128] fair labour practices;[129] the forming of trade unions and employers' organizations;[130] the right of children not to be

---

[119] Section 34(6) and (7). See further below, 3.5.2.
[120] Section 34(6)(g).
[121] Siracusa Principle 59.
[122] Siracusa Principle 69.
[123] Section 8(2).
[124] Section 9.
[125] Section 10.
[126] Section 11(2).
[127] Section 12.
[128] Section 14.
[129] Section 27(1).
[130] Section 27(2).

subject to neglect or abuse or exploitative or hazardous labour practices;[131] the right of detained children to be treated in a manner that takes account of their age;[132] and the protection provided for by the limitation clause.[133] The entrenching section too may not be suspended.

The right to be free from a retroactive application of criminal law is also protected, although it appears elsewhere.[134] It should have been included in the list of non-derogable rights. It is generally recognized as one of the most fundamental human rights, never to be suspended.[135]

This is an extensive list and requires some clarification. A suspension clause is based on a principle which limits the right of the state to take measures suspending certain human rights standards when it faces an emergency. Why should certain fundamental rights be non-derogable? In terms of what criteria should they be selected? It is difficult to detect any single set of criteria from the wide list provided in s 34.

The first important consideration is that s 34 provides for all emergencies — from a localized natural disaster to a full-scale war.[136] There remain no extra-constitutional powers such as martial law which will allow stricter emergency measures. If, for example, the rights of workers to join and form trade unions and of employers to form their own organizations are non-derogable, as they are under s 34(5)(c), then such rights are protected and may be fully exercised even during a drawn-out and full-scale war.

To argue that such rights may be limited under s 33 is to miss the important difference between a limitation and a derogation (suspension) clause. The former is of permanent application — in normal and 'peaceful' times. It provides for the regulation by the state of the exercise of fundamental rights, never for their suspension.[137] Suspension is only possible under s 34. If the latter singles out certain rights and puts them beyond the reach of suspension, then they are permanently non-derogable.

To make the list of non-derogable rights as wide as possible in the belief that a pro-rights approach is thereby displayed is mistaken. The exact opposite may be achieved. To include rights which are not particularly at risk in emergencies could have an adverse psychological effect.[138] In the case of war, which is the gravest emergency, more extreme needs are experienced than in situations of less gravity. The temptation may then arise to resort to 'implied' powers going beyond s 34 in order to suspend certain rights because of extreme need despite the fact that they are listed in s 34 as non-derogable. Justifications may be 'discovered' elsewhere in the Constitution.[139] That will undermine the effect and finality of s 34 as well as the supreme nature of the Constitution as a whole. It should be accepted, as is clearly shown by the practice under international human rights treaties, that not all rights

---

[131] Section 30(1)(d) and (e).
[132] Section 30(2).
[133] Section 33(1) and (2).
[134] Section 34(5)(a).
[135] Oraá op cit (n 87) 125. It appears in international human rights instruments with derogation clauses.
[136] Section 34(1).
[137] Section 33(1)(b). The 'essential content' of a right may never be negated under the limitation clause.
[138] Oraá op cit (n 87) 125.
[139] One such category may be a state of 'national defence', which is not mentioned in s 34, but which s 82(4)(b)(i) allows for.

have the same relevance with regard to suspension and public emergencies. Those rights which are more important also need closer and stricter scrutiny when the necessity for suspension (and proportionality) is determined.[140]

The approach should rather be to identify a criterion in terms of which to determine non-derogability. That is why a 'threat to the life of the nation', which is found in most international instruments,[141] is such a central concept. If some examples are still to be included, a shorter list is to be preferred. It will give strength to the category of such rights. Only those rights which are absolutely fundamental and permanently indispensable for the protection of human beings should be included. They are the rights whose suspension can never be justified because their exercise will not hamper the protection of the life of the nation.

International instruments contain four common non-derogable rights: the right to life; the right to be free of torture or inhuman or degrading treatment; 'freedom from slavery or servitude'; and the right to be free from a retroactive application of penal laws. These rights are generally accepted to be not only norms of customary international law but also norms of *jus cogens*.[142]

Certain international agreements, such as the 1949 Geneva Conventions on the Laws of War for the protection of war victims (to which South Africa is a party) and its 1977 Protocols (to which South Africa is not a party), contain important principles and indications of non-derogable rights. Under the 1977 Additional Protocol II the following rights with respect to penal prosecution shall be respected under all circumstances by state parties to the Protocol:

*(a)* the duty to give notice of charges without delay and to grant the necessary rights and means of defence;
*(b)* conviction only on the basis of individual penal responsibility;
*(c)* the right not to be convicted, or sentenced to a heavier penalty, by virtue of retroactive criminal legislation;
*(d)* the presumption of innocence;
*(e)* trial in the presence of the accused;
*(f)* no obligation on the accused to testify against himself or to confess guilt; and
*(g)* the duty to advise the convicted person on judicial and other remedies.[143]

Some ILO conventions contain a number of rights dealing with such matters as forced labour, freedom of association, equality in employment, and trade union and workers' rights which are not subject to derogation during an emergency; others permit derogation, but only to the extent strictly necessary to meet the exigencies of the situation.[144]

3.5.2 *Detainees*

Chapter 3 of the Constitution provides for two categories of detainees. Section 25 deals with 'detained, arrested and accused persons' under the fair trial provisions.

---

[140] Oraá op cit (n 87) 169.
[141] The ICCPR (art 4(1)), the European Convention on Human Rights (art 15(1)), and the European Social Charter (art 30(1)).
[142] Oraá op cit (n 87) 125.
[143] Siracuse Principle 67.
[144] Siracusa Principle 68.

Section 34(6) deals with detainees held under emergency powers. Only this latter category of detainees is considered in this Chapter.

Persons detained under a state of emergency should be protected against arbitrary detention and the right to due process of law should be provided for. Section 34(6) provides for most of what is required in this regard. Although the protection is listed as 'conditions' of detention, it amounts to rights which 'shall' be protected. The broad provisions of s 7(4) will allow for the necessary *locus standi* to ensure compliance. That is why 'an adult family member or friend of the detainee shall be notified of the detention as soon as is reasonably possible'. The other conditions relate to the official publication of the names of detainees, access to courts, legal representation and access thereto, and access to a medical practitioner of the detainee's choice.

Further protection should include safeguards against incommunicado detention and to ensure humane treatment, judicial review of the period of detention and of its lawfulness, notification, general due process standards, and protection against interrogation abuses and against changes in the application of the law of evidence. Not all of these safeguards appear in s 34.

When the due process provisions of s 25 or those recognizing the freedom and security of the person under s 11 are suspended the detention has to be reviewed by a court of law within ten days. The court 'shall order the release of the detainee if it is satisfied that the detention is not necessary to restore peace or order'.[145] This amounts to full substantive judicial control. 'If a court of law, having found the grounds for a detainee's detention unjustified, orders his or her release, such a person shall not be detained again on the same grounds unless the state shows good cause to a court of law prior to such re-detention'.[146]

These are minimum guarantees which have to ensure the correct application of a suspension clause with respect to detainees as required by the principle of proportionality.[147] The right of the state to take measures in times of an emergency is always conditioned by the principle of proportionality, which holds that measures must be strictly required by the exigencies of the situation.

It is important to emphasize the non-derogable character of these remedies. Many of them are based on the minimum guarantees contained in the four 1949 Geneva Conventions on the Laws of War and its subsequent Protocols. South Africa is party to the 1949 Conventions. The principles of public international law contained in the conventions may become domestically applicable, especially through customary international law, in terms of ss 227(2)*(e)* and 231(4) of the Constitution. International humanitarian law increasingly includes human rights standards applicable to internal strife and uprisings.[148]

## 3.6 Proportionality

Proportionality has already been discussed under the limitation clause. It is a general principle of law that finds application in several areas, especially in human rights.

---

[145] Section 34(6)*(c)*.
[146] Section 34(7).
[147] See further below, 3.6.
[148] See e g Meron *Human Rights in Internal Strife: Their International Protection* (1987).

It is of particular importance in the context of the suspension (derogation) of rights. Here it is the main substantive criterion to assess the legality of the suspension measures taken by the state in situations of emergency. Suspension measures must be proportionate to the threat. That is why a central criterion such as 'a public emergency threatening the life of the nation' is so important. Its absence from s 34 is detrimental to the meaningful operation of the requirement of proportionality and the use of comparative case law. Practically all international human rights instruments employ this concept.

Proportionality applies after the first suspension measures have been taken. Circumstances change during the existence of an emergency and the gravity of the situation can vary. Measures dealing with the emergency must also vary accordingly. Proportionality must exist in each of the phases. Once the emergency has ended or its gravity diminishes the suspension measures no longer have any justification.

International practice has generated the following principles with respect to the proportionality of suspension measures:

'1 Measures derogating from human rights standards can be taken only when the ordinary provisions of the law and the limitations foreseen for peacetime are not enough to deal with the emergency.
2 The mere existence of a public emergency threatening the life of the nation, within the meaning of the derogation clause, does not justify *ipso facto* every derogation from human rights standards. Each measure of derogation taken in a lawfully declared emergency should be necessary and proportionate to the threat.
3 Each measure of derogation has to bear a relation to the threat; in other words, there must be a link between the facts of the emergency and the measures taken.
4 The measures of derogation taken by the government should potentially be able to overcome the emergency. This, however, does not mean that the judgment on the strict necessity of the measures will depend on the fact that the measures actually overcome the emergency.
5 At the same time, the fact that a government did not take preventive measures before the emergency arose or at an earlier stage does not affect its right to take derogating measures once the emergency has arisen. The necessity and the proportionality of the measures should be judged in the light of the current state of emergency.
6 As far as the rights recognized in the human rights treaties are concerned, not all rights have the same relevance. Therefore those rights which are more important need closer and stricter scrutiny when the necessity for derogation and the proportionality to the threat are judged.
7 In assessing whether a derogating state has complied with the principle of proportionality the monitoring organs have to take into account not only the need for bringing the derogating measures into operation but also the manner in which the derogating measures have been applied in practice.
8 In analysing the principle of proportionality, the monitoring bodies should take into account not only the necessity and proportionality of a given measure, e g administrative detention, but also the necessity and proportionality of the suspension of some of the guarantees linked with the derogated right, e g the writ of *habeas corpus*.
9 In order to assess the proportionality of the derogating measures the monitoring bodies should analyse the other less grave alternatives open to the government in dealing with the emergency.
10 In assessing the compliance with the principle of proportionality special importance should be attached to the necessary safeguards taken by governments in order to avoid abuses.
11 In order to analyse the proportionality of the measures and the sufficiency of the safeguards against abuses attention should be paid to every different phase of the emergency.
12 . . . [s]tates of emergency are essentially temporary; in other words, they are only justified as

long as the emergency lasts. Consequently all measures of derogation are justified only as long as the emergency lasts. Therefore a derogating measure is not strictly required by the situation if it continues to be in force once the emergency has ended.'[149]

## 3.7 Non-discrimination

The principle of non-discrimination finds application in the context of suspension clauses too. Some international instruments prohibit discrimination on grounds of race, colour, sex, language, religion, or social origin. It is also a requirement of customary international law. A general non-discrimination clause elsewhere in a Bill of Rights should be adequate to ensure respect for equality also when public emergencies are declared and suspension measures are taken.

## 3.8 Consistency with other international legal obligations

International instruments often determine that the right of a state to take suspension measures in times of emergencies is limited by the condition that such measures must not be inconsistent with the state's other obligation under international law.[150] This will have the effect of raising requirements to the most optimal standards contained in other such instruments or in customary international law.

---

[149] Oraá op cit (n 87) 169–70.
[150] See ICCPR art 4(1); European Convention on Human Rights art 15(1).

# SELECTED BIBLIOGRAPHY

## ACCORDING TO CHAPTERS

### DEMOCRACY AND CONSTITUTIONALISM: THE ROLE OF CONSTITUTIONAL INTERPRETATION

Ackerman B *We the People* (Belknap Press 1991)
Alexy R *Theorie der Grundrechte* (Nomos 1985)
Alexy R *A Theory of Legal Argumentation* (Clarendon Press 1989)
Alexy R 'Grundrechte als subjektive Rechte und als objektive Normen' (1990) 29 *Der Staat* 49
Aristotle *The Politics of Aristotle* (trans E Barker) (1966) Book III, XII
Asmal K 'Constitutional Courts — A Comparative Survey' (1991) XXIV *CILSA* 315
Austin G *The Indian Constitution: Cornerstone of a Nation* (Oxford UP 1974)
Badura P 'Der Sozialstaat' (1989) 42 *Die öffentliche Verwaltung* 482
Bakshi PM (ed) *The Constitution of India: Comments and Subject Index* (New Delhi 1990)
Barendt E 'The Influence of the German and Italian Constitutional Courts on their National Broadcasting Systems' 1991 *Public Law* 93
Baxi U *Courage, Craft and Contention: The Indian Supreme Court in the Eighties* (Eastern 1985)
Baxi U *The Indian Supreme Court and Politics: Mehr Chand Memorial Law Lectures* (Eastern 1980)
Baxi U 'The Post-Emergency Supreme Court: A Populist Quest for Legitimation' in Baxi U *The Indian Supreme Court and Politics: Mehr Chand Memorial Law Lectures* (Eastern 1980)
Baxi U 'Taking Suffering Seriously: Social Action Litigation in the Supreme Court of India' *The Review* no 29 (December 1982) 37
Beatty DM 'The Rule (and Role) of Law in a New South Africa: Some Lessons from Abroad' (1992) 109 *SALJ* 408
Beatty DM *Talking Heads and the Supremes: The Canadian Production of Constitutional Review* (Carswell 1990)
Bekker JC 'Interaction between Constitutional Reform and Family Law' 1991 *Acta Juridica* 1
Benda E 'The Constitutional and Legal Situation of German Industrial Society and the Historical Development of Social Change' in Wellenreuther H (ed) *German and American Constitutional Thought: Contexts, Interaction and Historical Realities* (Berg 1990) 478
Berger R *Government by Judiciary* (Harvard UP 1977)
Berger R 'Constitutional Interpretation and Activist Fantasies' 1993 *Kentucky LJ* 1
Bethge H *Zur Problematik von Grundrechtskollisionen* (Vahlen 1986)
Betterman KA *Die verfassungskonforme Auslegung: Grenzen und Gefahren* (Müller 1986)
Bhagwati PN 'Human Rights as Evolved by the Jurisprudence of the Supreme Court of India' 1987 *Commonwealth Law Bulletin* 236
Bhagwati PN 'Judicial Activism and Public Interest Litigation' (1985) 23 *Columbia J of Transnational Law* 561
Bhagwati PN 'Public Interest Litigation' (1986) 2 *The Commonwealth Lawyer* 61
Bickel AM *The Least Dangerous Branch* (Bobbs-Merrill 1962)
Bila JJ et al 'A Rare Example of Sociological Jurisprudence and Judicial Realism in South Africa' (1989) 106 *SALJ* 595
Bjornlund EC 'The Devil's Work? Judicial Review under a Bill of Rights in South Africa and Namibia' (1990) 26 *Stan J Int L* 391
Blaauw LC 'The *Rechtsstaat* Idea Compared with the Rule of Law as a Paradigm for Protecting Rights' (1990) 107 *SALJ* 80
Blaauw LC 'Alternatives to Military Service' (1989) 5 *SAJHR* 240
Blair PM *Federalism and Judicial Review in West Germany* (Clarendon Press 1981)
Boldt H 'Federalism as an Issue in the German Constitutions of 1849 and 1871' in Wellenreuther H (ed) *German and American Constitutional Thought: Contexts, Interaction and Historical Realities* (Berg 1990) 259
Bork RH 'Neutral Principles and Some First Amendment Problems' (1971) 47 *Ind LJ* 1
Bork RH *The Tempting of America: The Political Seduction of the Law* (Free Press 1990)
Böckenförde EW 'Grundrechte als Grundsatznormen. Zur gegenwärtigen Lage der Grundrechtsdogmatik' (1990) 29 *Der Staat* 1
Böckenförde EW 'Grundrechtstheorie und Grundrechtsinterpretation' (1974) 27 *NJW* 1529
Böckenförde EW 'Die Methoden der Verfassungsinterpretation —Bestandaufnahme und Kritik' (1976) 29 *NJW* 2089

Brest P 'The Fundamental Rights Controversy: The Essential Contradictions of Normative Constitutional Scholarship' (1981) 90 *Yale LJ* 1063
Brest P 'The Misconceived Quest for the Original Understanding' (1980) *Buffalo U LR* 204
Brewer-Carias AR *Judicial Review in Comparative Law* (Cambridge UP 1989)
Bungert H '*Zeitgenössische Strömungen in der amerikanischen Verfassungsinterpretation*' (1992) 117 *Archiv des öffentliches Rechts* 71
Calebresi G 'The Supreme Court — Forward' (1991) 105 *Harvard LR* 80
Calliess R-P '*Strafzwecke und Strafrecht*' (1989) 42 *NJW* 1338
Cameron E 'Judicial Accountability in South Africa' (1990) 6 *SAJHR* 251
Cappelletti M 'Judicial Review of the Constitutionality of State Action: Its Expansion and legitimacy' 1992 *TSAR* 256
Carter SL 'Constitutional Adjudication and the Indeterminate Text: A Preliminary Defense of an Imperfect Muddle' (1985) 94 *Yale LJ* 821
Cassels J 'Judicial Activism and Public Interest Litigation in India: Attempting the Impossible' (1989) 37 *Am J Comp L* 495
Chinnapa Reddy 'Socialism, Constitution and the Country Today' 1983 *AIR Journal* 33
Choper JH *Judicial Review and the National Political Process* (U Chicago Press 1980)
Clark DS 'The Selection and Accountability of Judges in West Germany: Implementation of a *Rechtsstaat*' (1988) 61 *Southern California LR* 1795
Corder H & Davis D 'The Constitutional Guidelines of the African National Congress: A Preliminary Assessment' (1989) 106 *SALJ* 633
Cottrell J 'Indian Judicial Activism, the Company and the Worker: A Note on *National Textile Workers' Union v Ramakrishnan*' (1990) 39 *ICLQ* 433
Craig P 'Public Interest Litigation' (1987) 29 *J Indian Law Institute* 502
Cunningham 'Public Interest Litigation in the Indian Supreme Court: A Study in the Light of American Experiencxe' (1987) 29 *J Indian Law Institute* 504
Currie DP 'Positive and Negative Rights' (1986) 53 *U Chicago LR* 864
Currie PN '*Positive und Negative Grundrechte*' (1986) 111 *Archiv des öffentliches Rechts* 230
Dahl RA 'Decision-making in a Democracy: The Supreme Court as a National Policy-maker' (1957) 6 *J Pub L* 279
De Jager FJ 'Dubbele Blootstelling in die Duitse Reg' 1985 *TSAR* 161
De Jager FJ 'Geweld by Inhegtenisneming in die Duitse Reg' 1989 *TSAR* 24
Denninger E 'Judicial Review Revisited: The German Experience' (1984–5) 59 *Tulane LR* 1013
Diestelkamp B '*Die Verfassungsentwicklung in den Westzonen bis zum Zusammentreten des parlamentarischen Rates* (1945–1948)' (1989) 42 *NJW* 1312
Dorf MC *On Reading the Constitution* (Harvard UP 1991)
Du Plessis LM & De Ville JR 'The Bill of Rights: Interpretation in the South African Context: Diagnostic Observations' (1993) 4 *Stell LR* 59
Dugard J 'A Bill of Rights for South Africa' (1990) 23 *Cornell Int LJ* 441
Dugard J *Human Rights and the South African Legal Order* (Princeton UP 1978)
Dworkin R *Life's Dominion* (Knopf 1993)
Dworkin R 'Unenumerated Rights: Whether and How *Roe* should be Overruled' (1992) 54 *U Chicago LR* 381
Dürig G 'An Introduction to the Basic Law of the Federal Republic of Germany' in Karpen U (ed) *The Constitution of the Federal Republic of Germany* (Nomos 1988) 11
Ebsen I *Das Bundesverfassungsgericht als Element gesellschaftlicher Selbstregulierung: eine pluralistische Theorie der Verfassungsgerichtsbarkeit im demokratischen Verfassungsstaat* (Duncker & Humblot 1985)
Ebsen I 'The *Bundesverfassungsgericht* and Industrial Democracy after the Second World War' in Wellenreuther H (ed) *German and American Constitutional Thought: Contexts, Interaction and Historical Realities* (Berg 1990) 444
Ely JH 'Another Such Victory: Constitutional Theory and Practice in a World Where Courts are No Different from Legislatures' (1991) 77 *Va LR* 833
Ely JH *Democracy and Distrust: A Theory of Judicial Review* (Harvard UP 1980)
Fabricius HJ 'Aspects of Abortion Reform in West Germany' (1976) 39 *THRHR* 72
Fernandez L 'The Law, Lawyers and the Courts in Nazi Germany' (1985) 1 *SAJHR* 124
Forsyth CF 'Interpreting a Bill of Rights: The Future Task of a Reformed Judiciary?' (1991) 7 *SAJHR* 1
Frankel FR *India's Political Economy, 1947–1977: The Gradual Revolution* (Princeton UP 1978)
Frowein JA 'Administrative Structures for the Protection of Human Rights' (1990) 53 *THRHR* 250
Gamillscheg F '*Die Verwirklichung der Grundrechte durch die Gerichte in Arbeits- und Sozialrecht*' in Heyde W & Starck C (eds) *Vierzig Jahre Grundrechte in ihrer Verwirklichung durch die Gerichte* (Beck 1990)
Geiger W '*Das Bundesverfassungsgericht im Spannungsfeld zwischen Recht und Politik*' (1985) *EuGRZ* 401

Gerber P *'Die Rechtssetzungsdirektiven des Bundesverfassungsgerichts'* (1989) 16 *Die öffentliche Verwaltung* 698
Ghouse M & Dhavan R *The Supreme Court: A Socio-legal Critique of its Juristic Techniques* (Tripathi 1977)
Ghouse M 'The Right to Property and Planned Development in India' in Dhavan R & Jacob A (eds) *Indian Constitution: Trends and Issues* (Tripathi 1978) 80
Giesen D 'From Paternalism to Self-determination to Shared Decision-making' (1988) *Acta Juridica* 107
Goerlich H 'Fundamental Constitutional Rights: Content, Meaning and General Doctrines' in Karpen U (ed) *The Constitution of the Federal Republic of Germany* (Nomos 1988)
Gold MPA 'Comment: *Andrews v Law Society of BC*' (1989) 34 *McGill LJ* 1063
Götz V *'Die Verwirklichung der Grundrechte durch die Gerichte im Zivilrecht'* in Heyde W & Starck C (eds) *Vierzig Jahre Grundrechte in ihrer Verwirklichung durch die Gerichte* (Beck 1990) 39
Grimm D *'Vierzig Jahre Grundgesetz'* (1989) 42 *NJW* 1305
Gusy C *Parliamentarischer Gesetzgeber und Bundesverfassungsgericht* (Duncker & Humblot 1985)
Gusy C *Richterliches Prüfungsrecht* (Duncker & Humblot 1985)
Häberle P *Verfassung als öffentlicher Prozess. Materialien zu einer Verfassungstheorie der offenen Gesellschaft* (Duncker & Humblot 1978)
Häberle P 'Menseregte as Tema van 'n Demokratiese Staatsregteorie' (1982) 7 *TRW* 5
Habermas J *Strukturwandel der Öffentlichkeit* 2 ed (Luchterhand 1990)
Hazard N 'Commentary on the "Fundamental Values" Controversy' (1981) 90 *Yale LJ* 1110
Herrmann J 'Development and Reform of Criminal Procedure in the Federal Republic of Germany' (1978) XI *CILSA* 183
Hesse K *Grundzüge des Verfassungsrechts der Bundesrepublik Deutschland* 18 ed (Müller 1991)
Hesse K *Verfassungsrecht und Privatrecht* (Müller 1988)
Heun W *Funktionell-rechtliche Schranken der Verfassungsgerichtsbarkeit: Reichweite und Grenzen einer dogmatischen Argumentationsfigur* (Nomos 1992)
Heyns CH ' "Reasonableness" in a Divided Society' (1990) 107 *SALJ* 279
Hiemstra VG 'Constitutions of Liberty' (1971) 88 *SALJ* 45
Hiemstra VG 'Suid-Afrika Terug in die Wêreld langs die Weg van die Regsstaatbeginsel' 1985 *TSAR* 3
Hogg P 'Interpreting the Charter of Rights' (1990) 28 *Osgoode Hall LJ* 817
Huber B 'The Protection of the Environment in German Criminal Law' (1990) XXIII *CILSA* 84
Huber B 'Safeguarding of Prisoners' Rights under the New West German Prison Act' (1978) 2 *SACC* 229
Hucko E *Von der Paulskirche zum Museum Koenig Vier deutsche Verfassungen* (Bundesanzeiger 1984)
Hutchinson AC 'Waiting for Coraf' (1991) 41 *U Toronto LJ* 350
Hübner H 'Basic Problems of Codification and Modern Tendencies in the German Civil Law' 1977 *TSAR* 22
Ipsen HP 'Constitutional Review' in Starck C (ed) *Main Principles of the German Basic Law* (Nomos 1983) 108
Ipsen HP *'Über das Grundgesetz — nach 25 Jahren'* (1974) 27 *Die öffentliche Verwaltung* 289
Jarass HD 'Grundrechte als Wertentscheidungen bzw objektivrechtliche Prinzipien in der Rechtsprechung des Bundesverfassungsgericht' (1985) 110 *Archiv des öffentlichen Rechts* 363
Karpen U 'Freedom of Expression' in Karpen U (ed) *The Constitution of the Federal Republic of Germany* (Nomos 1988) 102
Karpen U *'Grundgesetz, Konsens und Wertewandel'* (1987) 8 *Juristische Schulung* 593
Karpen U 'The Rule of Law' in Karpen U (ed) *The Constitution of the Federal Republic of Germany* (Nomos 1988) 169
Kirchhof P *'Gegenwartsfragen an das Grundgesetz'* (1989) 10 *Juristenzeitung* 453
Klarman MJ 'The Puzzling Resistance to Political Process Theory' (1991) 77 *Va LR* 747
Klein HH *Die Grundrechte im demokratischen Staat* (Kohlhammer 1972)
Kohli (ed) *India's Democracy* (Eastern 1988)
Kommers DP 'Abortion and the Constitution: The United States and West Germany' (1977) 25 *Am J Comp L* 255
Kommers DP *The Constitutional Jurisprudence of the Federal Republic of Germany* (Duke UP 1989)
Kommers DP 'German Constitutionalism: A Prolegomenon' (1991) 40 *Emory LJ* 837
Kommers DP *Judicial Politics in Western Germany: A Study of the Federal Constitutional Court* (Sage 1976)
Korinek K *'Verfassungsgerichtsbarkeit im Gefüge der Staatsfunktion'* (1981) *VVDStRl* 34
Koriоth S *'Die Bindungswirkung normverwerfender Entscheidungen des Bundesverfassungsgerichts für den Gesetzgeber'* (1991) 30 *Der Staat* 549
Kötz H 'The Role of the Judge in the Court-room: The Common Law and Civil Law compared' 1987 *TSAR* 41
Kröger K *'Die Entstehung des Grundgesetzes'* (1989) 42 *NJW* 1318

Kunig P 'German Constitutional Law and the Environment' (1982–3) *Adelaide LR* 318
Kunig P 'The Principle of Social Justice' in Karpen U (ed) *The Constitution of the Federal Republic of Germany* (Nomos 1988) 189
Kühne J-D 'Civil Rights and German Constitutional Thought 1848–1871' in Wellenreuther H (ed) *German and American Constitutional Thought: Contexts, Interaction and Historical Realities* (Berg 1990) 199
Landfried C 'Introduction' in Landfried C (ed) *Constitutional Review and Legislation* (Nomos 1988) 12
Levinson S 'Law as Literature' (1982) 60 *Texas LR* 373
Luhmann N *Grundrechte als Institution: ein Beitrag zur politischen Soziologie* (Duncker & Humblot 1965)
Luhmann N *Legitimation durch Verfahren* (Luchterhand 1969)
Lübbe-Wolff G 'Safeguards of Civil and Constitutional Rights — The Debate on the Role of the Reichsgericht' in Wellenreuther H (ed) *German and American Constitutional Thought: Contexts, Interaction and Historical Realities* (Berg 1990) 353
Macedo S 'Originalism and the Inescapability of Politics' (1990) *North Western U LR* 1203
Mahrenholz EG '*Verfassungsinterpretation aus praktischer Sicht*' in Schneider HP (ed) *Verfassungsrecht zwischen Wissenschaft und Richterkunst* (Müller 1990) 53
Maltz EM 'The Prospects for a Revival of Conservative Activism in Constitutional Jurisprudence' (1990) 24 *Ga LR* 629
Michaelman FI 'Constitutional Method' (1992) 59 *U Chicago LR* 91
Mischke E 'The Inseperability of Powers: Judge-made Law in the German Legal System' (1992) 7 *SAPR/PL* 253
Morton, Russell & Withey 'The Supreme Court's First Hundred Charter of Rights Decisions: Statistical Analysis' (1992) 30 *Osgoode Hall LJ* 1
Motala Z 'Independence of the Judiciary, Prospects and Limitations of Judicial Review in terms of the United States Model in a New South African Order: Towards an Alternative Judicial Structure' (1991) XXIV *CILSA* 285
Müller F *Die Positivität der Grundrechte: Fragen einer praktischen Grundrechtsdogmatik* (Duncker & Humblot 1990)
Müller F 'The Judge and Unjust Law: A German Perspective' (1985) 10 *TRW* 152
Müller F '*Zur sogennanten subjektiv- und objektivrechtlichen Bedeutung der Grundrechte. Rechtsvergleichende Bemerkungen aus Schweizer Sicht*' (1990) 29 *Der Staat* 33
Müller N *Die Rechtsprechung des Bundesgerichts zum Grundsatz der verfassungskonformen Auslegung* (Stämpfli 1980)
Murphy J 'Insulating Land Reform from Constitutional Impugnment: An Indian Case Study' (1992) 8 *SAJHR* 362
Murphy WF & Tanenhaus J *Comparative Constitutional Law: Cases and Comments* (St Martins Press 1977)
Nedelsky J *Private Property and the Limits of American Constitutionalism: The Madisonian Framework and its Legacy* (U Chicago Press 1990)
Nedelsky J 'Reconceiving Rights as Relationship' (Paper delivered at the Gender and Law Conference, Centre for Applied Legal Studies, University of the Witwatersrand, Johannesburg, 20 March 1993)
Nehm '*Die Verwirklichung der Grundrechte im Prozessrecht und Strafrecht*' in Heyde W & Starck C (eds) *Vierzig Jahre Grundrechte in ihrer Verwirklichung durch die Gerichte* (Beck 1990) 173
Nichol GR 'Bork's Dilemma' (1990) 76 *Va LR* 337
Nierhaus M '*Grundrechte aus der Hand des Gesetzgebers? —Ein Beitrag zur Dogmatik des Art 1 Abs 3 GG*' (1991) 116 *Archiv des öffentlichen Rechts* 72
O'Regan C 'Possibilities for Worker Participation in Corporate Decision-making' 1990 *Acta Juridica* 113
Olivier PJJ 'Die Duitse Konstitusionele Hof: 'n Riglyn vir 'n Nuwe Suid-Afrikaanse Bestel?' 1992 *TSAR* 667
Ortiz DR 'Pursuing a Perfect Politics: The Allure and Failure of Process Theory' (1991) 77 *Va LR* 721
Ossenbühl F '*Die Interpretation der Grundrechte in der Rechtsprechung des Bundesverfassungsgericht*' (1976) 29 *NJW* 2100
Peiris GL 'Public Interest Litigation in the Indian Subcontinent: Current Dimensions' (1991) 40 *ICLQ* 65
Perry MJ 'The Legitimacy of Particular Conceptions of Constitutional Interpretation' (1991) 77 *Va LR* 669
Philippi KJ *Tatsaschenfeststellung des Bundesverfassungsgerichts* (Heymann 1971)
Pieters D 'Social Fundamental Rights in National Constitutions' (1987) 2 *SAPL/PR* 68
Posner RA 'Democracy and Distrust Revisited' (1991) 77 *Va LR* 641

Post RC 'Jurisdictional Unity, Cultural Hegemony and the Impetus for Human Rights' in Wellenreuther H (ed) *German and American Constitutional Thought* (Berg 1990) 242
Rabie A 'A Constitutional Right to Environmental Integrity: A German Perspective' (1991) 7 *SAJHR* 208
Rautenbach IM & Watney MM 'Oorsig van die Reg op Vrye Vergadering in die Federale Republiek van Duitsland' 1990 *TSAR* 641
Reese K 'The Need for Democratic Consent for Private Property' (1976) IX *CILSA* 81
Rehnquist WH 'The Notion of a Living Constitution' (1976) 54 *Texas LR* 693
Reifner U 'The Bar in the Third Reich: Anti-Semitism and the Decline of Liberal Advocacy' (1986) 32 *McGill LJ* 97
Richter I & Schuppert GF *Casebook Verfassungsrecht* 2 ed (Beck 1991)
Robinson JA 'Die Ouer–Kind Verhouding in die Lig van 'n Menseregteakte — 'n Beknopte Oorsig oor die Posisie in Duitsland' (1992) 7 *SAPR/PL* 228
Rostow EV 'The Supreme Court and the People's Will' (1958) 33 *Notre Dame LR* 573
Rudolph LI & Rudolph SH *In Pursuit of Lakshmi: The Political Economy of the Indian State* (U Chicago Press 1987)
Säcker H *Das Bundesverfassungsgericht* 4 ed (Bonn Bundeszentrale für Politische Bildung 1989)
Sattler '*Die Verwirklichung der Grundrechte durch die Gerichte im Verwaltungsrecht*' in Heyde W & Starck C (eds)*Vierzig Jahre Grundrechte in ihrer Verwirklichung durch die Gerichte* (Beck 1990) 127
Schauer F 'The Calculus of Distrust'(1991) 77 *Va LR* 653
Schenke WR '*Der Umfang der bundesverfassungsgerichtlichen Überprufung*' (1979) 27 *NJW* 1321
Schenke WR *Verfassungsgerichtsbarkeit und Fachgerichtsbarkeit* (Müller 1987)
Schenke WR *Die Verfassungsorgantreue* (Duncker & Humblot 1977)
Schenke WR '*Vierzig Jahre Grundgesetz*' (1989) 14 *Juristenzeitung* 653
Schlaich K '*Die Verfassungsgerichtsbarkeit im Gefüge der Staatsfunktion*' (1981) *VVDStRl* 98
Schlaich K *Das Bundesverfassungsgericht: Stellung, Verfahren und Entscheidungen* 2 ed (Beck 1991)
Schmitt C *Verfassungslehre* (Duncker & Humblot 1928)
Schmitt C *Der Hüter der Verfassung* (Möhr 1931)
Schneider HP '*Verfassungsgerichtsbarkeit und Gewaltenteilung*' (1980) 33 *NJW* 2103
Schneider HP '*Verfassungsinterpretation aus theoretischer Sicht*' in Schneider HP & Steinberg R (eds) *Verfassungsrecht zwischen Wissenschaft und Richterkunst* (Müller 1990) 52
Schulze C 'Notes on Judicial Review of Administrative Action in the Federal Republic of Germany' (1992) 7 *SAPR/PL* 290
Schumann E *Bundesverfassungsgericht, Grundgesetz und Ziuvilprozess* (Heymann 1983)
Schuppert GF *Funktionell-rechtliche Grenzen der Verfassungsinterpretation* (Athenäum 1980)
Schuppert GF '*Self-restraint der Rechtsprechung. Überlegungen zur Kontrlldichte in der Verfassungs- und Verwaltungsgerichtsbarkeit*' (1988) 24 *DVBl* 1191
Schwartz P 'The Computer in German and American Constitutional Law: Towards an American Right of Informational Self-determination' (1989) 37 *Am J Comp L* 675
Seervai HM *Constitutional Law of India* (Tripathi 1984)
Sendler H '*Vierzig Jahre Rechtsstaat des Grungesetzes: Mehr Schatten als Licht?*' (1989) 42 *Die öffentliche Verwaltung* 482
Starck C '*Über Auslegung und Wirkungen der Grundrechte*' in Heyde W & Starck C (eds) *Vierzig Jahre Grundrechte in ihrer Verwirklichung durch die Gerichte* (Beck 1990) 10
Stern K 'The Genesis and the Evolution of European-American Constitutionalism: Some Comments on the Fundamental Aspects' (1985) XVII *CILSA* 187
Stern K 'A Society Based on the Rule of Law and Social Justice' 1981 *TSAR* 241
Stern K *Das Staatsrecht der Bundesrepublik Deutschland* (Beck 1988)
Sunstein C 'Free Speech Now' (1992) 59 *U Chicago LR* 255
Thomashausen A 'Local and Regional Autonomy: The Comparative Law Approach to Residential and Spatial Conflicts' (1985) XVIII *CILSA* 297
Thomashausen A 'Savings Clauses and the Meaning of the Phrase "Acceptable in a Democratic Society" — A Comparative Study' (1989) XXX *Codicillus* 56
Trengove SM 'Judicial Ideologies in the Interpretation of a Bill of Rights in South Africa' (1992) 6 *Responsa Meridiana* 118
Tribe LH *Abortion: The Clash of Absolutes* (Norton 1992)
Tribe LH 'The Puzzling Persistence of Process-Based Constitutional Theories' (1980) 89 *Yale LJ* 1063
Tribe LH & Dorf MC *On Reading the Constitution* (Harvard UP 1992)
Tushnet M 'Darkness on the Edge of Town: The Contribution of John Hart Ely to Constitutional Theory' (1980) 89 *Yale LJ* 1037
Van der Merwe D 'A Moral Case for Lawyer's Law' (1992) 109 *SALJ* 619
Van Doren J 'Critical Legal Studies and South Africa' (1989) 106 *SALJ* 648
Van Eikema Hommes HJ '*De materiële Rechtsstaatidee*' 1978 *TSAR* 42

Van Wyk AH 'Matrimonial Property Systems in Comparative Perspective' 1983 *Acta Juridica* 53
Van Wyk DH 'Suid-Afrika en die Regstaatsidee' 1980 *TSAR* 152
Van Zyl Smit D 'Is Life Imprisonment Constitutional? The German Experience' 1992 *Public Law* 263
Venter F 'Die Publieke Subjektiewe Reg — 'n Voorraadopname' (1991) 54 *THRHR* 349
Venter F 'The Western Concept of Rights and Liberties in the South African Constitution' (1986) XIX *CILSA* 99
Verloren van Themaat A 'Property Rights, Workers' Rights and Economic Regulation — Constitutional Protection for Property Rights in the United States of America and the Federal Republic of Germany: Possible Lessons for South Africa' (1990) XXIII *CILSA* 53
Vogel K *Das Bundesverfassungsgericht und die übrigen Verfassungsorgane* (Lang 1988)
Von Arnim HH *Staatslehre der Bundesrepublik Deutschland* (Vahlen 1984)
Von Beyme K 'The Genesis of Constitutional Review in Parliamentary Systems' in Landfried C (ed) *Constitutional Review and Legislation* (Nomos 1988) 27
Von Bismarck SL & Partsch CJ 'Revolution and Continuity: Constitutional Developments in the Five New States of the Federal Republic of Germany and their Influence on the Amendment of the Constitution of the Federal Republic, the Basic Law' (1992) XXV *CILSA* 156
Von Brünneck A 'Constitutional review and Legislation in Western Democracies' in Landfried C (ed) *Constitutional Review and Legislation* (Nomos 1988) 225
Wechsler H 'Towards Neutral Principles of Constitutional Law' (1959) 73 *Harvard LR* 1
Wellington HH 'Common Law Rules and Constitutional Double Standards: Some Notes on Adjudication' (1973) 83 *Yale LJ* 221
West R 'Progressive and Conservative Constitutionalism' (1990) 88 *Mich LR* 641
Wieland J '*Der Zugang des Bürgers zum Bundesverfassungsgericht und zum US Supreme Court*' (1990) *Der Staat* 351
Wischermann N *Rechtskraft und Bindungswirkung verfassungsgerichtlicher Entscheidungen* (Duncker & Humblot 1979)
Wolfe C 'The Result-Orientated Adjudicator's Guide to Constitutional Law' (1992) 70 *Texas LR* 1325
Zajadlo J '*Überwindung des Rechtspositivismus als Grundwert des Grundgesetzes. Die verfassungsrechtliche Aktualität des Naturrechtsproblems*' (1987) 26 *Der Staat* 207
Zeidler W 'The Federal Constitutional Court of the Federal Republic of Germany: Decisions on the Constitutionality of Legal Norms' (1987) *Notre Dame LR* 504
Zimmerman R 'Judges shall be Independent and Subject only to the Law' (1985) 48 *THRHR* 291
Zimmermann R 'Self-determination, Paternalism or Human Care? Suicide and Criminal Responsibility in South African and German Law' 1979 *TSAR* 183
Zimmerman R & Du Plessis J 'Grondtrekke en Kernprobleme van die Duitse Verrykingsreg' 1992 *Acta Juridica* 57

## INTRODUCTION TO THE SOUTH AFRICAN CONSTITUTION

African National Congress *ANC Draft Bill of Rights. Preliminary Revised Version February 1993* (1993)
African National Congress *ANC Regional Policy* (1992)
African National Congress 'Constitutional Guidelines for a Democratic South Africa' (1989) 5 *SAJHR* 129
African National Congress *Ready to Govern* (1993)
African National Congress *What is a Constitution?* (1990)
Asmal K 'Victims, Survivors and Citizens — Human Rights, Reparations and Reconciliation' (1992) 8 *SAJHR* 509
Ballinger M *From Union to Apartheid. A Trek to Isolation* (Juta 1969)
Barrie G & Carpenter G 'Ethics and Insider Trading in Local Government: Or a Case of the Law and the Profits' (1994) 9 *SAPR/PL* 74
Barrie G & Carpenter G 'The Legal Framework within which Local Government Functions' (1993) 8 *SAPR/PL* 269
Basson D & Viljoen HP *Suid-Afrikaanse Staatsreg* 2 ed (Juta 1988)
Berger PL & Godsell B *A Future South Africa. Visions, Strategies and Realities* (Human & Rousseau 1988)
Booysen H & Van Wyk DH *Die '83-Grondwet* (Juta 1984)
Boulle LJ 'The Likely Direction of Constitutional Change in South Africa over the Next Five Years' in Dean WHB and van Zyl Smit D *Constitutional Change in South Africa* (Juta 1983) 70.
Boulle LJ *South Africa and the Consociational Option* (Juta 1984)
Boulle LJ, Harris B & Hoexter C *Constitutional and Administrative Law* (Juta 1989)
Brand RH *The Union of South Africa* (Clarendon Press 1909)
Cameron E 'Legal Chauvinism, Executive-mindedness and Justice — L C Steyn's impact upon South African Law' (1982) 99 *SALJ* 38

Cameron E 'Nude Monarchy: The Case of the South African Judges' (1987) 3 *SAJHR* 338
Carpenter G 'The Changing Face of South African Public Law' 1993 *SAPR/PL* 1
Carpenter G *Introduction to South African Constitutional Law* (Butterworths 1987)
Coetsee HJ 'Hoekom nie 'n Verklaring van Menseregte nie?' 1984 *TRW* 5
Corder H & Davis D 'The Constitutional Guidelines of the African National Congress: A Preliminary Assessment' (1989) 106 *SALJ* 633
Corder H et al *A Charter for Social Justice. A Contribution to the South African Bill of Rights Debate* (Dept of Public Law, University of Cape Town 1992)
Davenport TRH *South Africa: A Modern History* 4 ed (Southern 1991)
Davis D *South Africa and Transition: From Autocracy to What? A Preliminary Analysis about a Tentative Process* Centre for Applied Legal Studies Working Paper 18 (1992)
Dlamini CRM 'The Influence of Race on the Administration of Justice in South Africa' (1988) 4 *SAJHR* 37
Dugard J *Human Rights and the South African Legal Order* (Princeton UP 1978)
Dugard J 'The Quest for Liberal Democracy in South Africa' 1987 *Acta Juridica* 237
Dugard J 'The South African Constitution 1910–1980' in Mellett H et al (eds) *Our Legal Heritage* (Butterworths 1982)
Dugard J 'Towards a Liberal Democratic Order for South Africa' (1990) 2 *Revue Africain de Droit International et Comparé* 361
Du Plessis LM 'The Genesis of the Chapter on Fundamental Rights in South Africa's Transitional Constitution' (1994) 9 *SAPR/PL* 1
Du Plessis LM 'Glosses to the Working Paper of the South African Law Commission on Group and Human Rights (with Particular Reference to the Issue of Group Rights)' (1989) 52 *THRHR* 421
Du Plessis W 'Korrupsie en Meeluistering: Magsbeperking of Magsbehoud' 1992 *SAPR/PL* 238
Erasmus MG 'Towards a New Constitution: What are the Issues?' 1991 *De Rebus* 665
Forsyth CF *In Danger for their Talents* (Juta 1985)
Forsyth CF & Schiller JE *Human Rights: The Cape Town Conference* (Juta 1979)
Frederickse J *The Unbreakable Thread. Non-racialism in South Africa* (Ravan Press 1990)
Friedman S (ed) *The Long Journey. South Africa's Quest for a Negotiated Settlement* (Johannesburg Centre for Policy Studies 1993)
Haysom N 'Negotiating a Political Settlement in South Africa' in Moss G & Obery I (eds) *South African Review 6. From 'Red Friday' to Codesa* (Ravan Press 1992) 26
Heunis J 'Transitional Executive Council' in de Villiers B (ed) *The Birth of a Constitution* (Juta 1994) 20
Kennedy HJ & Schlossberg AM *The Law and Custom of the South African Constitution* (Juta 1935)
Lodge T *All Here and Now: Black South African Politics in the 1980s* (Ford Foundation 1992)
Lodge T *Black Politics in South Africa since 1945* (Ravan Press 1983)
Mathews AS *The Darker Reaches of Government* (Juta 1978)
Mathews AS *Freedom, State Security and the Rule of Law* (Juta 1986)
May HJ *The South African Constitution* 2 ed (1949); 3 ed (Juta 1955)
Maylam P *A History of the African People of South Africa: From the Early Iron Age to the 1970s* (David Philip 1986)
Moss G & Obery I (eds) *South African Review 6. From 'Red Friday' to Codesa* (Ravan Press 1992)
Motimele MM & Semenya IM *Constitution for a Democratic South Africa* (Skotaville 1993)
Motlhabi M *Black Resistance to Apartheid* (Skotaville 1984)
Murphy J 'The Independent Electoral Commission Act 1993' (1993) 8 *SAPR/PL* 283
National Party *Constitutional Rule in a Participatory Democracy* (1991)
Nicolson D 'Ideology and the South African Judicial Process — Lessons from the Past' (1992) 8 *SAJHR* 50
Nürnberger K et al (eds) *A Democratic Vision for South Africa* (Africa Enterprise 1991)
Odendaal A *Vukani Bantu! The Beginnings of Black Protest Politics in South Africa to 1912* (David Philip 1984)
Polley JA (ed) *The Freedom Charter and the Future* (Idasa 1988)
Rautenbach IM & E F J Malherbe *Staatsreg* (1993)
Rycroft AJ et al (eds) *Race and the Law* (Juta 1987)
Sachs A *Protecting Human Rights in a New South Africa* (Oxford UP 1990)
Schrire R (ed) *Critical Choices for South Africa. An Agenda for the 1990s* (Oxford UP 1990)
South Africa Government *A Bill of Rights for South Africa* (1993)
South African Law Commission *Project 58: Group and Human Rights* Working Paper 25 (1989)
South African Law Commission *Project 58: Group and Human Rights* Interim Report (1991)
South African Law Commission *Report on Constitutional Models* (1991)
Steytler N (ed) *The Freedom Charter and Beyond. Founding Principles for a Democratic South African Legal Order* (Wyvern Publications 1992)
Suttner R & Cronin J *The Freedom Charter in the Eighties* (Ravan Press 1986)

Thompson LM *The Unification of South Africa 1902-1910* (1969)
Van der Vyver JD 'Comments on the Constitutional Guidelines of the African National Congress' (1989) 5 *SAJHR* 13
Van der Vyver JD *Die Grondwet van die Republiek van Suid-Afrika: Wet 110 van 1983* (Lex Patria 1984)
Van der Westhuizen J & Viljoen HP *A Bill of Rights for South Africa. 'n Menseregtehandves vir Suid-Afrika* (Butterworths 1988)
Van Vuuren DJ & Kriek DJ *Political Alternatives for South Africa. Principles and Perspectives* (MacMillan 1983)
Van Wyk D 'The Making of the Namibian Constitution: Lessons for Africa' (1991) XXIV *CILSA* 341
Van Wyk DH, Wiechers M and Hill R (eds) *Namibia Constitutional and International Law Issues* (Verloren van Themaat Centre, Unisa 1991)
Van Zyl Slabbert F *The Quest for Democracy. South Africa in Transition* (Penguin 1992)
Vorster MP & Viljoen HP 'Die Nuwe Grondwetlike Bedeling' 1979 *TSAR* 201
Wacks R 'Judges and Injustice' (1984) 101 *SALJ* 266
Wiechers M 'The Fundamental Laws Behind our Constitution' in Kahn E (ed) *Fiat Iustitia: Essays in Memory of Oliver Deneys Schreiner* (Juta 1983) 383
Wiechers M ' 'n Monument in die Suid-Afrikaanse Regsontwikkeling: Die Werkstuk van die Suid-Afrikaanse Regskommissie oor Groeps- en Minderheidsregte' (1989) 52 *THRHR* 311
Wiechers M *VerLoren van Themaat Staatsreg* 3 ed (Butterworths 1981)
*Working Documents for CODESA 2. 15 & 16 May 1992* vol 1 & 2.

## INTERNATIONAL HUMAN RIGHTS

Alston P 'Making Space for New Human Rights: The Case of the Right to Development' (1988) 1 *Harvard Human Rights Yearbook* 3
Alston P 'Out of the Abyss: The Challenges of Confronting the New UN Committee on Economic, Social and Cultural Rights' (1987) 9 *Human Rights Quarterly* 332
Alston P & Simma B 'First Session of the UN Committee on Economic, Social and Cultural Rights' (1987) 81 *Am J Int L* 747
Alston P & Simma B 'Second Session of the UN Committee on Economic, Social and Cultural Rights' (1988) 82 *Am J Int L* 603
Barrie GN 'The Apartheid Convention after Five Years' 1981 *TSAR* 280
Booysen H 'Convention on the Crime of Apartheid' (1976) 2 *SAYIL* 56
Booysen H *Volkereg* 2 ed (Juta 1989)
Bossuyt MJ 'The Development of Special Procedures of the United Nations Commission on Human Rights' (1985) 6 *Human Rights Law Journal* 179
Bossuyt MJ *Guide to the 'Travaux Préparatoires' of the International Covenant on Civil and Political Rights* (Nijhoff 1987)
Brassey M et al *The New Labour Law* (Juta 1987)
Brierly JL *The Law of Nations* 6 ed (Clarendon Press 1963)
Brownlie I *Basic Documents on Human Rights* 3 ed (Clarendon Press 1991)
Buergenthal T 'The Inter-American System for the Protection of Human Rights' in Meron T (ed) *Human Rights in International Law. Legal and Policy Issues* (Clarendon Press 1984) 439
Buergenthal T 'Proceedings against Greece under the European Convention on Human Rights' (1968) 62 *Am J Int L* 441
Buergenthal T, Norris R & Shelton D *Protecting Human Rights in the Americas* 2 ed (Engel 1986)
Burgers H & Danelius H *The United Nations Convention against Torture* (Kluwer 1988)
Burke K et al 'Application of International Human Rights Law in State and Federal Courts' (1953) 18 *Texas J Int L* 291
Cassese A (ed) *The International Fight against Torture* (Nomos 1991)
Cassese A 'A New Approach to Human Rights: The European Convention for the Prevention of Torture' (1989) 83 *Am J Int L* 128
Castberg F *The European Convention on Human Rights* (Sijthoff 1987)
Charlesworth H, Chinkin CM & Wright S 'Feminist Approaches to International Law' (1991) 85 *Am J Int L* 613
Clark B 'The Vienna Convention Reservations Regime and the Convention on Discrimination against Women' (1991) 85 *Am J Int L* 281
Cockram G-M *Interpretation of Statutes* 3 ed (Juta 1987)
Cook RJ 'Bibliography: The International Right to Non-discrimination on the Basis of Sex' (1989) 14 *Yale J Int L* 161
Crawford J (ed) *The Rights of Peoples* (Clarendon Press 1988)
De Zayas A, Moller JT & Opsahl T 'Application of the International Covenant on Civil and Political Rights under the Optional Protocol by the Human Rights Committee' (1985) 28 *GYIL* 9

Delmas-Marty M *The European Convention for the Protection of Human Rights* (Nijhoff 1991)
Devenish GE *The Interprewtation of Statutes* (Juta 1992)
Dlamini CRM 'Towards a Regional Protection of Human Rights in Africa: THe African Charter on Human and Peoples' Rights' (1991) XXIV *CILSA* 189
Drzemczewski AZ *European Human Rights Convention in Domestic Law: A Comparative Study* (Clarendon Press 1983)
Duffy PJ 'English Law and the European Convention on Human Rights' (1980) 29 *ICLQ* 585
Dugard J 'Apartheid: A Case Study in the Response of the International Community to Gross Violations of Human Rights' in Cotler I & Eliadis FP (eds) *International Human Rights Law Theory and Practice* (1992) 301
Dugard J 'International Human Rights Norm in Domestic Courts: Can South Africa Learn from Britain and the United States?' in Kahn E (ed) *Fiat Justitia. Essays in Memory of Oliver Deneys Schreiner* (Juta 1983) 220
Dugard J *International Law: A South African Perspective* (Juta 1994)
Dugard J 'The Legal Effect of United Nations Resolutions on Apartheid' (1966) 83 *SALJ* 44
Dugard J *The South West Africa/Namibia Dispute* (U California Press 1973)
Evans M & Morgan R 'The European Convention for the Prevention of Torture: Operational Practice' (1992) 41 *ICLQ* 590
Evatt E 'Eliminating Discrimination Against Women' (1991) 18 *Melbourne U LR* 435
Fawcett JES *The Application of the European Convention on Human Rights* 2 ed (Clarendon Press 1987)
Fincham CBH *Domestic Jurisdiction* (Sijthoff 1948)
Fischer DD 'Reporting under the Covenant on Civil and Political Rights: The First Five Years of the Human Rights Committee' (1982) 76 *Am J Int L* 142
Forsythe DP (ed) *Human Rights and Development. International Views* (MacMillan 1989)
Fox DT 'Inter-American Commission on Human Rights Finds United States in Violation' (1988) 82 *Am J Int L* 601
Frost LE 'The Evolution of the Inter-American Court of Human Rights: Reflections of Present and Former Judges' (1992) 14 *Human Rights Quarterly* 171
Garber L & O'Connor CM 'The UN Sub-Commission on the Prevention of Discrimination and Protection of Minorities' (1985) 79 *Am J Int L* 168
Greenberg J 'Race, Sex and Religious Discrimination in International Law' in Meron T (ed) *Human Rights in International Law. Legal and Policy Issues* (Clarendon Press 1984) 307
Guest I *Behind the Disappearances: Argentina's Dirty War Against Human Rights and the United Nations* (U Pennsylvania Press 1990)
Hahlo HR & Kahn E *The South African Legal System and its Background* (Juta 1968)
Harris DJ *The European Social Charter* (U Press of Virginia 1984)
Henkin L (ed) *The International Bill of Rights* (Colorado UP 1981)
Heunis JC *United Nations versus South Africa* (Lex Patria 1986)
Higgins R 'The European Convention on Human Rights' in Meron T (ed) *Human Rights in International Law. Legal and Policy Issues* (Clarendon Press 1984) 495
Humphrey 'The Universal Declaration of Human Rights: Its History, Impact and Judicial Character' in Ramcharan BG (ed) *Human Rights: Thirty Years After the Universal Declaration* (Nijhoff 1984)
Jennings R & Watts A (eds) *Oppenheim's International Law* 9 ed (Longman 1992)
Keightley R 'International Human Rights Norms in a New South Africa' (1992) 8 *SAJHR* 171
Kiwanuka RN 'The Meaning of "People" in the African Charter on Human and Peoples' Rights' (1988) 82 *Am J Int L* 80
Kuper L *Genocide* (Yale UP 1982)
Lauterpacht H 'The Universal Declaration of Human Rights' (1948) 25 *BYIL* 354
Lerner N *The UN Convention on the Elimination of All Forms of Racial Discrimination* 2 ed (Sijthoff 1980)
Macdonald R St J, Matscher F & Petzold H *The European System for the Protection of Human Rights* (Nijhoff 1993)
Mann FA *Studies in International Law* (Clarendon Press 1973)
McGoldrick D *The Human Rights Committee. Its Role in the Development of the International Covenant on Civil and Political Rights* (Clarendon Press 1991)
McKean WA *Equality and Discrimination under International Law* (Clarendon Press 1983)
Meron T 'Enhancing the Effectiveness of the Prohibition on Discrimination against Women' (1990) 84 *Am J Int L* 213
Meron T 'The Meaning and Reach of the International Convention on the Elimination of All Forms of Racial Discrimination' (1985) 79 *Am J Int L* 283
Motshekga MS 'The African Charter on Human Rights and Peoples' Rights — Its Importance to Human Rights Thinking in South Africa' (1987) 30 *Codicillus* 31

Özgur OA *Apartheid, the United Nations and Peaceful Change in South Africa* (Transnational Publishers 1982)
Reierson K & Weissbrodt D 'The Forty-Third Session of the UN Sub-Commission on the Prevention of Discrimination and Protection of Minorities: The Sub-Commission under Scrutiny' (1992) 14 *Human Rights Quarterly* 232
Rich R 'The Right to Development: A Right of Peoples' in Crawford J (ed) *The Rights of Peoples* (Clarendon Press 1988) 39
Robertson AH & Merrills JG *Human Rights in Europe* 3 ed (Manchester UP 1993)
Robertson M (ed) *Human Rights for South Africans* (Oxford UP 1991)
Robinson N *The Genocide Convention* (Institute of Jewish Affairs New York 1960)
Rodley NS *The Treatment of Prisoners under International Law* (Unesco 1987)
Schabas WA *International Human Rights Law and the Canadian Charter* (Carswell 1991)
Schwelb E 'The International Convention on the Elimination of All Forms of Racial Discrimination' (1966) 15 *ICLQ* 996
Sieghart P *The International Law of Human Rights* (Clarendon Press 1983)
Stavros S *The Guarantees for Accused Persons under Article 6 of the European Convention on Human Rights* (Nijhoff 1993)
Strydom HA 'View on International Measures for the Protection of Minorities' (1992–3) 18 *SAYIL* 134
Titus Z *The Applicability of the International Human Rights Norms to the South African Legal System — with Specific Reference to the Role of the Judiciary* (1993 LLD Leiden)
Tolley H *The UN Commission on Human Rights* (Westview Press 1987)
Umozurike UO 'The African Charter on Human and Peoples' Rights' (1983) 77 *Am J Int L* 902
UN publication *Human Rights: A Compilation of International Instruments* (1988)
Van Dijk P & Van Hoof GJH *Theory and Practice of the European Convention on Human Rights* 2 ed (Kluwer 1990)
Van Zyl Smit D *South African Prison Law and Practice* (Butterworths 1992)
Welch CE 'The African Commission on Human and Peoples' Rights: A Five Year Report and Assessment' (1992) 14 *Human Rights Quarterly* 43
Weston BH, Lukes RA & Hnatt KM 'Regional Human Rights Regimes: A Comparisdon & Appraisal' (1987) 20 *Vanderbilt J Transnational Law* 585
Woolfrey DJG 'The Application of International Labour Norms to South African Law' (1986–7) 12 *SAYIL* 1356
Zuijdwijk TJ *Petitioning the United Nations* (St Martin's Press 1982)

## EQUALITY AND EQUAL PROTECTION

Aristotle *Nichomachean Ethics* (Ross ed 1925) vol III
Colker R 'Section 1, Contextuality and the Anti-Disadvantaged Principle' (1992) 42 *U Toronto LJ* 77
Freeman AD 'Legitimizing Racial Discrimination through Anti-Discrimination Law: A Critical Review of the Supreme Court Doctrine' (1978) 62 *Minnesota LR* 1049
Greenawalt K 'The Unresolved Problems of Reverse Discrimination' (1979) 67 *California LR* 87
Kelsen H *What is Justice?* (U California Press 1971)
Meyerson D 'Sexual Equality and the Law' (1993) 9 *SAJHR* 237
Minow M 'Justice Endangered' (1987) 101 *Harvard LR* 10
Sadurski W 'Equality Before the Law: A Conceptual Analysis' (1986) 60 *Australian LJ* 131
Seervai HM *Constitutional Law of India* (Tripathi 1991)
Sorabjee SJ 'Equality in the United States and India' in Henkin L (ed) *Constitutionalism and Rights: The Influence of the United States Constitution Abroad* (Columbia UP 1990) 104
Westen P 'The Empty Idea of Equality' (1982) 95 *Harvard LR* 537
Wright JS 'Colour Blind Theories and Colour Conscious Remedies' (1980) 47 *U Chicago LR* 213

## PERSONAL RIGHTS: LIFE, FREEDOM AND SECURITY OF THE PERSON, PRIVACY, AND FREEDOM OF MOVEMENT

Alen A *Treatise on Belgian Constitutional Law* (Kluwer 1992)
Angus L 'Delay before Execution: Is it Inhuman and Degrading Treatment?' (1993) 9 *SAJHR* 432
Bekker PM 'Die Doodsvonnis: Voor en na 27 Julie 1990' (1993) 6 *SACJ* 57
Boyle CK 'The Concept of Arbitrary Deprivation of Life' in Ramcharan BG (ed) *The Right to Life in International Law* (Nijhoff 1985) 221
Carpenter G 'Passports and the Right to Travel: The South African Perspective' (1990) XXIII *CILSA* 1
Carpenter G *Introduction to South African Constitutional Law* (Butterworths 1987)
Corder H et al *A Charter for Social Justice: A Contribution to the South African Bill of Rights Debate* (Department of Public Law, University of Cape Town 1992)

Dinstein Y 'The Right to Life, Physical Integrity, and Liberty' in Henkin L (ed) *The International Bill of Rights: The Covenant on Civil and Political Rights* (Columbia UP 1981) 114
Du Plessis LM *The Interpretation of Statutes* (Butterworths 1986)
Du Plessis LM 'Jurisprudential Reflections on the Status of Unborn Life' 1990 *TSAR* 44
Du Plessis LM 'Reflecting on Law, Morality and Communal Mores' (1991) 56 *Koers* 339
Du Plessis LM *Vraagstukke rondom die Lewe Juridies Besin* (PU vir CHO, Potchefstroom 1976)
Du Plessis LM & de Ville JR 'Bill of Rights Interpretation in the South African Context (3): Comparative Perspectives and Future Prospects' (1993) 4 *Stell LR* 356
Du Toit E et al *Commentary on the Criminal Procedure Act* (Juta 1993)
Finkelstein N *Laskin's Canadian Constitutional Law II* 5 ed (Carswell 1986)
Goldstein AB 'History, Homosexuals, and Political Values: Searching for the hidden Determinants of Bowers v Hardwick' (1988) 97 *Yale LJ* 1073
Gormley WP 'The Right to Life and the Rule of Non-derogatability: Peremptory Norms of Jus Cogens' in Ramcharan BG (ed) *The Right to Life in International Law* (Nijhoff 1985) 120
Greenberg J 'Capital Punishment as a System' (1982) 91 *Yale LJ* 908
Gunther G *Constitutional Law* 12 ed (Foundation Press 1991)
Henkin L 'Human Rights' in *Encyclopedia of Public International Law* VIII (North-Holland 1985) 268
Hesse K *Grundzüge des Verfassungsrechts der Bundesrepublik Deutschland* 18 ed (Müller 1991)
Hogg PW *Constitutional Law of Canada* 2 ed (Carswell 1985)
Jarass HD & Pieroth B *Grundgesetz für die Bundesrepublik Deutschland: Kommentar* (Beck 1989)
Karpen U (ed) *The Constitution of the Federal Republic of Germany* (Nomos 1988)
Katz A *Staatsrecht: Grundkurs im öffentlichen Recht* 10 ed (Müller 1991)
Kommers DP *The Constitutional Jurisprudence of The Federal Republic of Germany* (Duke UP 1989)
Locke J *Second Treatise of Government* (Liberal Arts Press 1952)
MacAvoy-Snitzer J 'Pregnancy Clauses in Living Will Statutes' (1987) 87 *Columbia LR* 1280
Maditsi A 'The Right of Privacy in America: What Does it Mean?' 1992 *De Rebus* 659
Magnet JE *Constitutional Law of Canada II* 3 ed (Carswell 1987)
Mureinik E 'Editorial Comment: From Moratorium to Reprieve' (1990) 6 *SAJHR* vii
Oliver P & von Borries R 'Data Protection and Censuses under the West German Constitution' 1984 *Public Law* 199
Ramcharan BG 'The Concept and Dimensions of the Right to Life' in Ramcharan BG (ed) *The Right to Life in International Law* (Nijhoff 1985) 1
Rautenbach IM *Die Reg op Bewegingsvryheid* (1974 LLD thesis Unisa)
Robertson M (ed) *Human Rights for South Africans* (Oxford UP 1991)
Rubenfeld J 'The Right of Privacy' (1989) 102 *Harvard LR* 737
Singh C 'Right to Life: Legal Activism or Legal Escapism' (1986) 28 *Journal of the Indian Law Institute* 249
Smits PW *The Right to Life of the Unborn Child in International Documents, Decisions and Opinions* (1992 dissertation Leiden)
South African Law Commission *Project 58: Group and Human Rights* Interim Report (1991)
Stone GR et al *Constitutional Law* 2 ed (Little, Brown & Co 1991)
Strauss SA 'The "Right to Die" or "Passive Euthanasia": Two Important Decisions, One American and the Other South African' (1993) 6 *SACJ* 196
Tribe LH *American Constitutional Law* 2 ed (Foundation Press 1988)
Van Eikema Hommes HJ *De Elementaire Grondbegrippen der Rechtwetenschap* (Kluwer 1972)
Van der Merwe SE 'Unconstitutionally obtained Evidence: Towards a Compromise between the Common Law and the Exclusionary Rule' (1992) 3 *Stell LR* 173
Van Rooyen JH 'South Africa's New Death Sentence: Is the Bell tolling for the Hangman?' (1991) 4 *SACJ* 79
Von Münch I *Grundgesetz-Kommentar* 3 ed (Beck 1985)
Wootton D (ed) *John Locke Political Writings* (Penguin Books 1993)

## FREEDOM OF EXPRESSION

Abrams F 'Hate Speech: The Present Implications of a Historical Dilemma' (1992) 37 *Villanova LR* 743
African National Congress *A Bill of Rights for a New South Africa* (Centre for Development Studies, University of the Western Cape 1990)
Atkey RG 'Reconciling Freedom of Expression and National Security' (1991) 41 *U Toronto LJ* 38
Beaudoin GA *The Canadian Charter of Rights and Freedoms* 2 ed (Carswell 1989)
Brownstein AE 'Regulating Hate Speech at Public Universities: Are First Amendment Values Functionally Incompatible with Equal Protection Principles?' (1991) 39 *Buffalo LR* 1
Burns Y *Media Law* (Butterworths 1990)

Cachalia F et al *Fundamental Rights in the New Constitution* (Juta 1994)
Cammack M & Davies S 'Should Hate Speech be Prohibited in Law Schools?' (1991) 20 *Southwestern U LR* 145
Check, JVP 'The Effects of Violent Pornography, Non-Violent Dehumanizing Pornography and Erotica: Some Legal Implications from a Canadian Perspective' in Itzin C (ed) *Pornography. Women Violence and Civil Liberties. A Radical New View* (Oxford UP 1992) 350
Childress SA 'Reel "Rape Speech": Violent Pornography and the Politics of Harm' (1991) 25 *Law and Society Review* 177
Cleaver C 'Ruling Without Reasons: Contempt of Court and the *Sub Judice* Rule' (1993) 110 *SALJ* 530
Devlin, Lord *The Enforcement of Morals* (Oxford UP 1965)
Dworkin R 'Against the Male Flood: Censorship, Pornography and Equality' in Itzin C (ed) *Pornography. Women Violence and Civil Liberties. A Radical New View* (Oxford UP 1992) 516
Dworkin R 'Is There a Right to Pornography?' 1981 *Oxford Journal of Legal Science* 177
Dworkin R *Taking Rights Seriously* (Duckworth 1977)
Greenawalt K 'Free Speech in The United States and Canada' (1992) 55 *Law and Contemporary Problems* 5
Hart HLA *Law, Liberty and Morality* (1961)
Haysom N & Marcus G ' "Undesirability" and Criminal Liability under the Publications Act of 1974' (1985) 1 *SAJHR* 31
Hesse K *Grundzüge des Verfassungsrechts der Bundesrepublik Deutschland* 17 ed (Müller 1990)
Heyns CH *A Jurisprudential Analysis of Civil Disobedience in South Africa* (unpublished PhD thesis, University of the Witwatersrand 1992)
Itzin C 'Pornography and Civil Liberties: Freedom, Harm and Human Rights' in Itzin C (ed) *Pornography. Women Violence and Civil Liberties. A Radical New View* (Oxford UP 1992) 553
Itzin C (ed) *Pornography. Women Violence and Civil Liberties. A Radical New View* (Oxford UP 1992)
Kommers DP *Constitutional Jurisprudence of the Federal Republic of Germany* (Duke UP 1989)
Kutchinsky B 'Pornography and Rape: Theory and Practice?' (1991) 14 *Int J Law and Psychiatry* 47
Lahey KA 'Pornography and Harm — Learning to Listen to Women' (1991) 14 *Int J Law and Psychiatry* 117
Leader SL 'Free Speech and the Advocacy of Illegal Action in Law and Political Theory' (1982) 82 *Columbia LR* 412
Lepa M *Der Inhalt der Grundrechte* 6 ed (Bundesanzeiger 1991)
Lloyd D *The Idea of Law* (Penguin 1981)
Lötter S *Moraliteitswetgewing en die Suid-Afrikaanse Strafreg* (1991 LLD thesis, University of Pretoria)
MacKinnon C 'Pornography, Civil Rights and Speech' in Itzin C (ed) *Pornography. Women and Civil Liberties. A Radical New View* (Oxford UP 1992) 456
Mahoney K 'The Canadian Approach to Freedom of Expression in Hate Propaganda and Pornography' (1992) 55 *Law and Contemporary Problems* 77
Marcus G 'Interpreting the Chapter on Fundamental Rights' (1994) 10 *SAJHR* 92
Marcus G 'The Wider Reaches of Censorship' (1985) 1 *SAJHR* 69
McGowan DF & Tangri RK 'A Libertarian Critique of University Restrictions of Offensive Speech' (1991) 79 *California LR* 825
Meyerson D ' "No platform for Racists": What Should the View of Those on the Left Be?' (1990) 6 *SAJHR* 394
Mill JS *On Liberty* (Blackwell 1948)
Sachs A *Protecting Human Rights in a New South Africa* (MacMillan 1990)
Sachs A 'Towards a Bill of Rights in a Democratic South Africa' (1990) 6 *SAJHR* 13
Schlaich K *Das Bundesverfassungsgericht* (Beck 1985)
Schwabe J (ed) *Entscheidungen des Bundesverfassungsgerichts* 5 ed (1991)
Snyman CR 'Criminal Law' in Joubert (ed) *LAWSA* vol 6 (1981)
South African Law Commission *Project 58: Group and Human Rights* Working Paper 25 (1989)
Street H *Freedom, the Individual and the Law* 5 ed (Penguin 1982)
Stuart KW *The Newspaperman's Guide to the Law* 5 ed (Butterworths 1990)
Suttner R 'Freedom of Speech' (1990) 6 *SAJHR* 372
Tribe LH *American Constitutional Law* 2 ed (Foundation Press 1988)
Van der Vyver JD 'Censorship in South Africa by JCW van Rooyen' (1988) 2 *De Jure* 182
Van der Westhuizen JV 'Do We Have to be Calvinist Puritans to Enter the New South Africa' (1990) 6 *SAJHR* 425
Van der Westhuizen JV 'The Protection of Human Rights and a Constitutional Court for South Africa: Some Questions and Ideas, with Reference to the German Experience' (1991) 24 *De Jure* 1
Van Rooyen JCW 'Censorship' in Joubert WA (ed) *LAWSA* vol 29 (1994)
Van Rooyen JCW 'Censorship in a Future South Africa: A Legal Perspective' (1993) 26 *De Jure* 283

## FREEDOM OF ASSEMBLY: VOTING WITH YOUR FEET

Ackermann M *Die Reg insake Openbare en Staatsveiligheid* (Butterworths 1984)
Anon 'A Unitary Approach to Claims of First Amendment Access to Publicly Owned Property' 35 (1982) *Stan LR* 121
Baker CE 'Unreasonable Reasonableness: Mandatory Parade Permits and Time, Place and Manner Regulations' (1983) 78 *North Western U LR* 937
Basson DA 'Judicial Activism in a State of Emergency: An Examination of Recent Decisions of the South African Courts' (1987) 3 *SAJHR* 28
Basson DA & Viljoen HP *South African Constitutional Law* 2 ed (Juta 1988)
Blasi V 'Prior Restraints on Demonstrations' (1970) 68 *Mich LR* 1481
Boulle L, Harris B & Hoexter C *Constitutional and Administrative Law* (Juta 1989)
Cameron E 'Civil Disobedience and Passive Resistance' in Corder H (ed) *Essays on Law and Social Practice in South Africa* (Juta 1988) 219
Carpenter G *Introduction to South African Constitutional Law* (Butterworths 1987)
Corder H & Davis D 'A Long March — Administrative Law in the Appellate Division' (1988) 4 *SAJHR* 281
Denninger E et al *Reihe Alternativkommentare Kommentar zum Grundgesetz für die Bundesrepublik Deutschland* (Luchterhand 1984)
Dienes CT 'The Trashing of the Public Forum: Problems in First Amendment Analysis' (1986) 55 *Geo Wash LR* 109
Dietel A, Gintzel K & Kniesel M *Demonstrations- und Versammlungsfreiheit Kommentar zum Gesetz über Versammlungen und Aufzüge vom 24 Juli 1953* 9 ed (Heymann 1989)
Dugard J *Human Rights and the South African Legal Order* (Princeton UP 1978)
Dugard J, Haysom N & Marcus G *The Last Years of Apartheid: Civil Liberties in South Africa* (Ford Foundation 1992)
Farber DA & Nowak JE 'The Misleading Nature of Public Forum Analysis: Content and Context in First Amendment Adjudication' (1984) 70 *Va LR* 1219
Feldmeier T *Politische Meinungsäusserung auf öffentlichen Strassen* (1982 dissertation Münster)
Forsyth C *In Danger for Their Talents* (Juta 1985)
Frowein JA *'Versammlungsfreiheit und Versammlungsrecht'* 1969 *NJW* 1081
Haysom N 'Licence to Kill — Part 1' (1987) 3 *SAJHR* 3
Heymann PB (ed) *Towards Peaceful Protest in South Africa: Testimony of a Multinational Panel Regarding the Lawful Control of Demonstrations in the Republic of South Africa before The Commission of Inquiry Regarding the Prevention of Public Violence and Intimidation* (HSRC, Pretoria 1992)
Kalven H 'The Concept of the Public Forum: Cox v. Louisiana, 1965' *Sup Ct Rev* (1965) 1
Kidd M 'Meetings and the Emergency Regulations' (1989) 5 *SAJHR* 471
Kühl K *'Demonstrationsfreiheit und Demonstrationsstrafrecht'* 1985 *NJW* 2379
Lee WE 'Lonely Pamphleteers, Little People, and the Supreme Court: The Doctrine of Time, Place and Manner Regulations of Expression' (1986) 54 *Geo Wash LR* 757
MacKay AW 'Freedom of Expression: Is It All Just Talk?' (1989) 68 *Canadian Bar R* 713
Mathews AS *Freedom, State Security and the Rule of Law* (Juta 1986)
Mathews AS *Law, Order and Liberty in South Africa* (Juta 1971)
Maunz-Dürig-Herzog *Grundgesetz Kommentar* (Beck 1991)
Moon R 'Access to Public and Private Property under Freedom of Expression' (1988) 20 *Ottawa LR* 339
Mureinik E 'Pursuing Principle: The Appellate Division and Review under the State of Emergency' (1989) 5 *SAJHR* 60
Müller W *Wirkungsbereich und Schranken der Versammlungsfreiheit, in besondere im Verhältnis zur Meinungsfreiheit* (Duncker & Humblot 1974)
Ott S *'Rechtsprobleme bei der Auflösung einer Versammlung in Form eines Sitzstreiks'* (1985) 38 *NJW* 2384
Rautenbach I *Die Reg op Bewegingsvryheid* (1974 LLD thesis Unisa)
Schilder AE *Het Recht tot Vergadering en Betoging* (Gouda Quint 1989)
Scholler H & Birk D *Verfassungsrecht und Verfassungsgerichtsbarkeit* (Müller 1988)
Schwäble U *Das Grundrecht der Versammlungsfreiheit (Art 8 GG)* (Duncker & Humblot 1988)
South Africa *Commission of Inquiry Regarding the Prevention of Public Violence and Intimidation by the Committee Established to Inquire into Public Violence at Mass Demonstrations, Marches and Picketing Report* (Government Printer 1993)
Spitz D 'Eschewing Silence Coerced by Law: The Political Core and Protected Periphery of Freedom of Expression' (1994) 10 *SAJHR* 301
Tribe LH *American Constitutional Law* 2 ed (Foundation Press 1988)
Van der Vyver JD *Die Beskerming van Menseregte in Suid-Afrika* (Juta 1975)

Van der Vyver JD *Seven Lectures on Human Rights* (Juta 1976)
Von Mangoldt H & Klein F *Das Bonner Grundgesetz* (Vahlen 1966)
Von Münch I *Grundgesetz Kommentar* (Beck 1992)
Watney MM *Die Reg op Vrye Vergadering* (1988 LLM dissertation RAU)
Wiechers M *Verloren van Themaat Staatsreg* (Butterworths 1981)
Woolman S 'Riding The Push-Me Pull-You: Constructing a Test that Reconciles the Conflicting Interests which Animate the Limitation Clause' (1994) 10 *SAJHR* 60
Zitzmann J *Öffentliche Versammlungen unter freiem Himmel und Aufzüge* (1984 dissertation München)

## FREEDOM OF ASSOCIATION: THE RIGHT TO BE WE

Ackermann M *Die Reg insake Openbare Orde en Staatsveiligheid* (Butterworths 1984)
Anderson JL 'March Fong Eu v San Francisco County Democratic Central Committee: Tension between Associational Rights of Political Parties and Fair Elections' (1990) 16 *J Contemp L* 381
Anon 'State Power and Discrimination by Private Clubs: First Amendment Protection for Non-expressive Associations' (1991) 104 *Harvard LR* 1835.
Badura P *Paritätische Mitbestimmung und Verfassung* (Beck 1985)
Ballerstedt F *'Von den Grenzen der Vereinigungsfreiheit'* 1952 *Der Öffentliche Dienst* 161
Birk R *'Der Aufnahmezwang bei Vereinen und Verbänden'* 1972 *Juristenzeitung* 343
Bleckmann A *Allgemeine Grundrechtslehren* (Heymann 1989)
Brangsch H *'Rechtsberatung und Rechtshilfe durch Verbände'* 1953 *NJW* 732
Davis D *South Africa and Transition: From Autocracy to What?* Centre for Applied Legal Studies Working Papers 23 (1992)
De Tocqueville A *Democracy in America* (Colonial Press 1900)
Demme H *'Die Grenzen der Vereinigungsfreiheit besonders in Hinblick auf den Gesetzesvorbehalt des Art 12.1.2GG'* (1967) 13 *Gewerbearchiv Zeitschrift für Verwaltungs-, Gewerbe- und Handwerkersrecht* 199
Doehring K 'The Special Character of the Constitution of the Federal Republic of Germany as a Free and Democratic Basic Order' in Karpen U (ed) *The Constitution of the Federal Republic of Germany* (Nomos 1988) 26
Dugard J *Human Rights and the South African Legal Order* (Princeton UP 1978)
Dürig G *'Art. 9 Grundgesetz in der Kartellproblematik'* 1955 *NJW* 729
Easterbrook FH 'Implicit and Explicit Rights of Association' (1987) 10 *Harvard J L & Pub Pol* 91
Etzrodt W *Der Grundrechtshutz der negativen ereinigungsfreiheit* (Lang 1980)
Forsyth C *In Danger for their Talents* (Juta 1985)
Freeman J 'Justifying Exclusion: A Feminist Analysis of the Conflict between Equality and Associational Rights' (1989) 47 *U Toronto LR* 269
Friauf KH *'Die Negative Vereinigungsfreiheit als Grundrecht'* in Pleyer K et al (eds) *Festschrift für Rudolf Reinhart* (Schmidt 1972) 389
Hamacher E *Die Bedeutung der Vereinigungsfreiheit für Zwangzusammenschlüsse unter der Herrschaft des Grundgesetzes* (1972 Rheinisches Friedrich-Wilhelms Universität dissertation)
Hesse K *Grundzüge des Verfassungsrecht der Bundesrepublik Deutschland* 18 ed (Müller 1991)
Karst K 'The Freedom of Intimate Association'(1980) 89 *Yale LJ* 624
Karst K 'Paths to Belonging: The Constitution and Cultural Identity' (1986) 56 *North Carolina LR* 303
Karst K *Paths to Belonging: Equal Citizenship and the Constitution* (Leibholz 1989)
Krüger H *'Die Stellung der Interessenverbände in der Verfassungswirklichkeit'* 1956 *NJW* 1217
Kunze T *Unternehmensrechtreform und Artikel 9 Absatz 1 GG* (Heitmann 1976)
Leibholz G, Rinck H-J & Hesselberger D *Grundgesetz für die Bundesrepublik Deutschland* 7 ed (Schmidt)
Lengsfeld M *Das Recht zum Verbot verfassungswidriger Vereinigungen und der Ausgleich zwischen Interessen des Staates und Rechten der Individualsphäre* (1965 dissertation Münster)
Marshall WP 'Discrimination and the Right of Association'(1986) 81 *North Western U LR* 68
Mathews AS *Freedom, State Security and the Rule of Law* (Juta 1986)
Mathews AS *Law, Order and Liberty in South Africa* (Juta 1971)
Maunz-Dürig-Herzog *Grundgesetz Kommentar* (Beck 1991)
Merten D 'Vereinsfreiheit' in Kirchhof P & Isensee J (eds) *Handbuch des Staatsrechts der Bundesrepublik Deutschland* (Müller 1989)
Mronz D *Körperschaften und Zwangmitgliedschaft die staatsorganisations- und grundrechtliche Problematik. Der Zwangsverband aufgezeigt am Beispiel von Arbeitsnehmerkammern* (Duncker & Humblot 1973)
Müller F *Korporation and Assoziation* (Duncker & Humblot 1965)
Nagel B *Paritätische Mitbestimmung und Grundgesetz* (Nomos 1988)

Pernthaler P *Ist Mitbestimmung Verfassungsrechtlich messbar. Eine Analyse der Entscheidung des BVerfG über das Mitbestimmungsgesetz* (Duncker & Humblot 1980)
Pernthaler P *Qualifizierte Mitbestimmung und Verfassungsrecht* (Duncker & Humblot 1972)
Piepenstock W *Politische Vereinigungen unter dem Grundgesetz* (Duncker & Humblot 1971)
Ramm T *Die Freiheit der Willensbildung zur Lehre von der Drittwirkung der Grundrechte und der Rechtsstruktur der Vereinigung* (Fischer 1960)
Reichert B, Dannecker F-J & Kühr C *Handbuch des Vereins- und Verbandsrecht* 4 ed (Luchterhand 1987)
Rhodes DL 'Association and Assimilation' (1986) 81 *North Western U LR* 106
Rinck H-J *Kommentar zum Grundgesetz für die Bundesrepublik Deutschland* (Luchterhand 1989)
Rode K *'Negative Vereinigungsfreiheit und Zwangmidgliedschaft in öffentlichen Körperschaften'* (1976) 29 *Die öffentliche Verwaltung* 841
Rubenfeld J 'The Right of Privacy' (1989) 102 *Harvard LR* 737
Rudolph W *'Die Mitgliedschaft von Beamten und Angestellten des Öffentlichen Dienstes in nicht verboten Verfassungsfeindlichen Parteien und Vereinigungen'* 1967 *Deutsches Verwaltungsblatt* 647
Schmidt T *Die Freiheit Verfassungswidriger Parteien und Vereinigungen. Zur Schrankenlehre in Rahmen von art. 21.2GG und art. 9.2GG* (Duncker & Humblot 1983)
Schmidt W *'Die "innere Vereinsfreiheit" als Bedingung der Verwirklichung von Grundrechten durch Organisation'* (1977) 10 *Zeitschrift für Rechtspolitik* 255
Schnörr G *Öffentliches Vereinsrecht* (Heymann 1965)
Schwerdtfeger G *Unternehmerische Mitbestimmung der Arbeitnehmer und Grundgesetz* (Athenäum 1972)
Schwerdtfeger G *Zur Verfassungsmässigkeit der paritätischen Mitbestimmung* (Decker 1978)
Simitis S, Kübler F & Schmidt W *Mitbestimmung als Gesetzgebungsaufgabe zur Verfassungsmässigkeit des Mitbestimmungsgesetzes* (Nomos 1976)
Spiller W *Das Vereinsverbod nach geltendem Verfassungsrecht* (Schmitt & Meyer 1967)
Starck C *Verfassungsrecht in Fällen. Entscheidungen des Bundesverfassungsgerichtes: Vereinigungsfreiheit* (Nomos 1975)
Strickrodt G *'Das Kartellverbot in verfassungsrechtlicher Betrachtung'* 1955 *NJW* 1697
Teubner R *Organisationsdemokratie und Verbandsverfassung: Rechtsmodelle für politisch relevante Verbände* (Mohr 1978)
Thornicroft K 'Compulsory Payment of Union Dues — Use for Collective Bargaining and Non-Bargaining Purposes: Lavigne v. The Ontario Public Service Employees Union' (1992) 71 *Canadian Bar R* 153
Tribe LH *American Constitutional Law* 2 ed (Foundation Press 1988)
Von Prondzynski F *Freedom of Association and Industrial Relations: A Comparative Study* (Mansell 1987)
Von Feldman P *Vereinigungsfreiheit und Vereinigungsverbod. Eine kritische Darstellung des Umfangs und der Schranken der Vereinigungsfreiheit nach dem Grundgesetz und dem Vereinsgesetz* (Goldmann 1972)
Von Mutius A 'Die Vereinigungsfreiheit gem. Art. 9.1GG' 1984 *Jura* 193
Wollburg R *Die Anwendbarkeit des Artikels 9 abs.1 Grundgesetz auf Kapitalgesellschaften* (1984 dissertation München)
Woolman S 'Riding the Push-Me Pull-You: Constructing a Test that Reconciles the Conflicting Interests Which Animate the Limitation Clause' (1994) 10 *SAJHR* 60

## ADMINISTRATIVE JUSTICE

'Administrative Law for a Future South Africa', workshop held from 10–13 February in Cape Town, a summary report of which is contained in *The Breakwater Declaration* 1993 (also published in (1993) 8 *SAPR/PL* 152).
Allars M *An Introduction to Australian Administrative Law* (Butterworths 1990)
African National Congress *ANC Draft Bill of Rights: Preliminary Revised Version* (Centre for Development Studies, University of the Western Cape 1993)
Aronson M & Franklin N *Review of Administrative Action* (Law Book Co 1987)
Baxter L *Administrative Law* (Juta 1984)
Bayne P *Freedom of Information* (Law Book Co 1984)
Bennett TW et al (eds) *Administrative Law Reform* (Juta 1993)
Boulle L, Harris B & Hoexter C *Constitutional and Administrative Law* (Juta 1989)
Canada Law Reform Commission *Towards a Modern Federal Administrative Law* (1987)
Corder H et al *A Charter for Social Justice: A Contribution to the SA Bill of Rights Debate* (Department of Public Law, University of Cape Town 1992)
Corder H *Empowerment and Accountability* (SA Constitution Studies Centre 1991)
Craig PP *Administrative Law* 2 ed (Sweet & Maxwell 1989)

De Villiers B, van Vuuren DJ & Wiechers M (eds) *Human Rights Documents that Paved the Way* (Human Sciences Research Council 1992)
Evans JH et al *Administrative Law: Cases, Text and Materials* (Montgomery 1989)
Evans JM 'Administrative Appeal or Judicial Review: A Canadian Perspective' 1993 *Acta Juridica* 47
Harlow C & Rawlings R *Law and Administration* (Weidenfeld 1984)
Institute for Public Policy Research *A British Bill of Rights* (1990)
Institute for Public Policy Research *The Constitution of the United Kingdom* (1991)
Jowell J & Oliver D (eds) *New Directions in Judicial Review* (Stevens 1988)
Justice-All Souls Committee *Administrative Justice: Some Necessary Reforms* (Clarendon Press 1988)
Kirby M 'Effective Review of Administrative Acts: The Hallmark of a Free and Fair Society' (1989) 5 *SAJHR* 321
Mahomed I 'Disciplining Administrative Power — Some South African Prospects, Impediments and Needs' (1989) 5 *SAJHR* 345
Marcus G & Davis D 'Judicial Review under an ANC Government' (1991) 7 *SAJHR* 93
Mathews AS *The Darker Reaches of Government* (Juta 1978)
Parker C 'The "Administrative Justice" Provision of the Constitution of the Republic of Namibia: A Constitutional Protection of Judicial Review and Tribunal Adjudication under Administrative Law' (1991) XXXIV *CILSA* 88
Sachs A 'From the Violable to the Inviolable: A Soft-nosed Reply to Hard-nosed Criticism' (1991) 7 *SAJHR* 98
Schwarze J *European Administrative Law* (Sweet & Maxwell 1992)
South African Law Commission *Project 58: Group and Human Rights* Interim Report (1991)
South African Law Commission *Project 24: Report on the Investigation into the Courts' Powers of Review of Administrative Acts* (1992).
Wesley-Smith P *Constitutional and Administrative Law in Hong Kong* (China and Hong Kong Law Studies Ltd 1988)
Wiechers M *Administrative Law* (Butterworths 1985)

## PROCEDURAL RIGHTS

African National Congress *ANC Draft Bill of Rights: Preliminary Revised Version* (Centre for Development Studies, University of the Western Cape 1993)
Baxter L *Administrative Law* (Juta 1984)
Beaven A 'Prisoner's Access' (1979) 95 *LQR* 393
Bender R 'The Stuttgart Model' in Cappelletti M (ed) *Access to Justice* (Sijthoff 1978) vol II 431
Boulle LJ, Harris B & Hoexter C *Constitutional and Administrative Law* (Juta 1989)
Burchell JM & Milton J *Principles of Criminal Law* (Juta 1991)
Cappelletti M 'Access to Justice as a Theoretical Approach to Law and a Practical Programme for Reform' (1992) 109 *SALJ* 22
Cappelletti M (ed) *Access to Justice* (Sijthoff 1978)
Corder H et al *A Charter for Social Justice: A Contribution to the SA Bill of Rights Debate* (Department of Public Law, University of Cape Town 1992)
Cowling MG 'Bail and the Search for a New Theoretical Approach' (1991) 4 *SACJ* 65
Damaska M 'Evidentiary Barriers to Conviction and Two Models of Crimiinal Procedure: A Comparative Study' (1972) 121 *U Pensylvania LR* 506
Dennis I 'Confessions: Evidentiary Issues and their Solutions' unpublished paper delivered at a *Conference of the Society for the Reform of Criminal Law Canada* (1992)
Du Toit E et al *Commentary on the Criminal Procedure Act* (Juta 1987)
Dugard J *Introduction to Criminal Procedure* (Juta 1977)
Falke J, Bierbrauer G & Koch K-F 'Legal Advice and the Non-Judicial Settlement of Disputes: A Case Study of the Public Legal Advice and Mediation Centre in the City of Hamburg' in Cappelletti M (ed) *Access to Justice* (Sijthoff 1978) vol II 103
Fowles AJ *Prisoners' Rights in England and the United States* (Avebury 1989)
Friedland ML 'Criminal Justice and the Charter' (1983) 13 *Manitoba LJ* 549
Hiemstra VG 'Abolition of the Right not to be Questioned' (1963) 80 *SALJ* 187
Hirte HA 'Access to the Courts for Indigent Persons: A Comparative Analysis of the Legal Framework in the United Kingdom, United States and Germany' (1991) 40 *ICLQ* 110
Hoffmann HL & Zeffertt DT *The South African Law of Evidence* 4 ed (Juta 1988)
Kaczynski SJ 'Admissibility of Illegally Obtained Evidence: A Comparative Study' in Redden KR (ed) *Modern Legal Systems Cyclopedia* Hein vol 1A at 1A.80.18.
Kaplan B, von Mehren AT & Schaefer R 'Phases of German Civil Procedure' (1958) 71 *Harvard LR* 1193; 1443
Krantz S *The Law of Corrections and Prisoners' Rights* 3 ed (West 1986)
Kress JM *Prescription for Justice* (Ballinger Publishing Co 1980)

Labuschagne JMT 'Deliktuele Beskerming van die Bewegingsvryheid van die Gevangene' (1993) 4 *Stell LR* 130
Mathews AS *Freedom, State Security and the Rule of Law* (Juta 1986)
McQuoid-Mason DJ *An Outline of Legal Aid in South Africa* (Juta 1982)
Norris JW *'Turner v Safley* 482 US 78' (1991) 64 *Temple LR* 1109
Paciocco DM 'The Development of Miranda-like Doctrines under the Charter' (1987) 19 *Ottawa LR* 49
Palmer JW *Constitutional Rights of Prisoners* 4 ed (Anderson 1991)
Polyviou PG *The Equal Protection of the Laws* (Duckworth 1980)
Richardson G 'Time to Take Prisoners' Rights Seriously' (1984) 11 *J Law and Society* 1
Roberts LG *'Turner v Safley* 482 US 78' (1990) 27 *American Crim LR* 545
Sheppard NC 'Recognition of the Disadvantaging of Women: The Promise of *Andrews v Law Society of British Columbia*' (1989) 35 *McGill LJ* 207
Sieghart P *The International Law of Human Rights* (Clarendon Press 1983)
Skeen A 'The Admissibility of Improperly Obtained Evidence in Criminal Trials' (1988) 3 *SACJ* 389
South African Law Commission *Project 58: Group and Human Rights* Interim Report (1991)
South Africa *Government Proposals on a Charter of Fundamental Rights* (1993)
Steytler, N 'The Right to a Fair Trial' in Robertson M (ed) *Human Rights for South Africans* (Oxford UP 1990) 75
Tribe LH *American Constitutional Law* 2 ed (Foundation Press 1988)
Van der Berg J *Bail — A Practioner's Guide* (Juta 1986)
Van Zyl Smit D & Dunkel F (eds) *Imprisonment Today and Tomorrow — International Perspectives on Prisoners' Rights and Prison Conditions* (Kluwer 1991)
Van Zyl Smit D *South African Prison Law and Practice* (Butterworths 1992)
Westen DA 'Fines, Imprisonment and the Poor: "Thirty Dollars or Thirty Days" ' (1969) 57 *California LR* 778

## CONSTITUTIONALIZATION OF LABOUR RIGHTS

Cachalia F et al *Fundamental Rights in the New Constitution* (Juta 1994)
Cheadle H *Current Labour Law* (Juta 1994)
Cottrell J 'Indian Judicial Activism, the Company and the Worker: A Note on National Textile Workers' Union v Ramakrishnan' (1990) 39 *ICLQ* 433
Crisham CA 'The Equal Pay Principle, Some Recent Decisions in the European Court of Justice' 1981 *Common Market LR* 601
Harvey RA 'Equal Treatment of Men and Women in the Workplace: Implementation of the European Community's Equal Treatment Legislation in the Federal Republic of Germany' (1990) 38 *Am J Comp L* 31
Hutchinson AC & Petter A 'Private Rights — Public Wrongs: The Liberal Lie of the Charter' (1988) 38 *U Toronto LJ* 278
Leader S 'The European Convention on Human Rights, The Employment Act of 1988 and the Right to Refuse to Strike' (1991) 12 *ILJ* 39
Mureinik E 'Bridge to Where? An Introduction to the Interim Bill of Rights' (1994) *SAJHR* 31
Rycroft A & Jordaan B *A Guide to South African Labour Law* 2 ed (Juta 1993)
Sunstein C 'Lochner's Legacy' (1987) 87 *Columbia LR* 873
Technical Committee on Fundamental Rights during the Transition, 10th Progress Report (5 October 1993)
Treu T 'Italy' in *International Encyclopedia for Labour Law and Industrial Relations* vol 5 (Kluwer)
Treu T 'State Regulation and Job Security' (1992) 13 *ILJ* 1053
Tribe LH *American Constitutional Law* 2 ed (Foundation Press 1988)
Von Hayek FA *Law, Legislation and Liberty* (Routledge & Kegan 1979)
Wallis MJD *Labour and Employment Law* (Butterworths 1993)
Wedderburn KW *Employment Rights in Britain and Europe. Selected Papers in Labour Law* (Lawrence and Wishart 1991)

## PROPERTY RIGHTS, LAND RIGHTS, AND ENVIRONMENTAL RIGHTS

African National Congress *ANC Draft Bill of Rights: Preliminary Revised Version* (Centre for Development Studies, University of the Western Cape 1993)
African National Congress *A Bill of Rights for a New South Africa* (Centre for Development Studies, University of the Western Cape 1990)
African National Congress 'Constitutional Guidelines for a Democratic South Africa' (1989) 5 *SAJHR* 129

African National Congress 'The Structure of a Constitution for a Democratic South Africa' (1991) 7 *SAJHR* 233
Anderson JL 'Takings and Expectations: Toward a "Broader Vision" of Property Rights' (1989) 37 *U Kansas LR* 529
Anon 'The Supreme Court — Leading Cases 1992: Property' (1992) 106 *Harvard LR* 269
Asmal K 'Victims, Survivors and Citizens — Human Rights, Reparations and Reconciliation' (1992) 8 *SAJHR* 491
Badenhorst PJ 'Transfer Development Rights in America: Just Compensation, Fair Compensation or No Compensation?' 1987 *TSAR* 214; 352
Badura P *Staatsrecht: Systematische Erläuterung des Grundgesetzes für die Bundesrepublik Deutschland* (Beck 1986)
Badura P '*Möglichkeit und Grenzen des Zivilrechts bei der Gewährleistung öffentlicher und sozialer Erfordernisse im Bodenrecht*' (1976) 176 *Archiv für die civilistische Praxis* 119
Badura P '*Die soziale Schlüsselstellung des Eigentums*' (1973) 1 *Bayerische Verwaltungsblätter* 1
Bauman RW 'Property Rights in the Canadian Constitutional Context' (1992) 8 *SAJHR* 344
Baur F '*Möglichkeit und Grenzen des Zivilrechts bei der Gewährleistung öffentlicher und sozialer Erfordernisse im Bodenrecht*' (1976) 176 *Archiv für die civilistische Praxis* 97
Baur F *Lehrbuch des Sachenrechts* 15 ed (Beck 1989)
Becker LC *Property Rights — Philosophic Foundations* (Routledge & Kegan Paul 1977)
Been V ' "Exit" as a Constraint on Land Use Exactions: Rethinking the Unconstitutional Conditions Doctrine' (1991) 91 *Columbia LR* 473
Bhalla RS & Ojwang JB 'Property Rights and the Constitution: The Position of Aliens in Kenia' (1990) 6 *Lesotho LJ* 127
Blaustein AP & Flantz GH (eds) *Constitutions of the World* (Oceana)
Böhmer W '*Die Rechtsgeschichtlichen Grundlagen der Abgrenzungsproblematik von Sozialbindung und Enteignung*' 1985 *Der Staat* 157
Brooks DHM 'Albie Sachs on Human Rights in South Africa' (1990) 6 *SAJHR* 25
Budlender G 'The Right to Equitable Access to Land' (1992) 8 *SAJHR* 295
Budlender G 'Towards a Right to Housing' in van der Walt AJ (ed) *Land Reform and the Future of Landownership in South Africa* (Juta 1991) 45
Caldwell LK 'Rights of Ownership or Rights of Use? The Need for a New Conceptual Basis for Land Use Policy' 1975 *Environment LR* 409
Chaskalson M 'The Problem with Property: Thoughts on the Constitutional Protection of Property in the United States and the Commonwealth' (1993) 9 *SAJHR* 388
Chaskalson M 'The Property Clause: Section 28 of the Constitution' (1994) 10 *SAJHR* 131
Chiappinelli JA 'The Right to a Clean and Safe Environment: a Case for a Constitutional Amendment Recognizing Public Rights in Common Resources' (1992) 40 *Buffalo LR* 567
Christman J 'Can Ownership be Justified by Natural Rights?' 1986 (15) *Philosophy & Public Affairs* 156
Cohen GA 'Self-ownership, World-ownership, and Equality: Part II' (1986) 3/2 *Social Philosophy & Policy* 77
Cohen GA 'Self-ownership, World-ownership, and Equality' in Lucash FS (ed) *Justice and Equality Here and Now* (Cornell University Press 1986) 108
Corder H et al *A Charter for Social Justice: A Contribution to the South African Bill of Rights Debate* (Department of Public Law, University of Cape Town 1992)
Cross C 'An Alternate Legality: The Property Rights Question in Relation to South African Land Reform' (1992) 8 *SAJHR* 305
Davis DM 'The Case Against the Inclusion of Socio-economic Demands in a Bill of Rights Except as Directive principles' (1992) 8 *SAJHR* 475
De Villiers B 'Socio-economic Rights in a New Constitution: Critical Evaluation of the Recommendations of the South African Law Commission' 1992 *TSAR* 421
De Villiers B, Van Vuuren DJ and Wiechers M (eds) *Human Rights: Documents that Paved the Way* (Human Sciences Research Council 1992)
De Villiers B 'The Socio-economic Consequences of Directive Principles of State Policy: Limitations on Fundamental Rights'(1992) 8 *SAJHR* 188
Democratic Party *Freedom Under the Rule of Law: Advancing Liberty in the New South Africa: Draft Bill of Rights* (May 1993)
Domanski A 'Landownership and Natural Law' (1989) 52 *THRHR* 433
Du Plessis LM 'Glosses to the Working Paper of the South African Law Commission on Group and Human Rights (With Particular Refrence to the Issue of Group Rights)' (1989) 52 *THRHR* 421
Du Plessis W 'Regstellende Aksie met Betrekking tot Grond' (1991) 16 *TRW* 140
Dubischer R et al (eds) *Kommentar zum Bürgerlichen Gesetzbuch* vol 4 *Sachenrecht* (Luchterhand 1983)
Dugard J 'A Bill of Rights for South Africa?' (1990) 23 *Cornell Int LJ* 441

Ekey FL *Die Verminderung von Eigentümerrechten im Spannungsfeld zwischen Art. 14 I S. 1 GG und Art. 14 I S. 2 GG* (1988 dissertation München)
Ely JW *The Guardian of Every Other Right: a Constitutional History of Property Rights* (Oxford UP 1992)
Epstein 'No New Property' (1990) 56 *Brooklyn LR* 747
Epstein RA *Takings: Private Power and the Power of Eminent Domain* (Harvard UP 1985)
Exshaw EY 'The Right of Private Property' in Bridge JW et al (eds) *Fundamental Rights* (Sweet & Maxwell 1973) 73
Georgiades A *'Eigentumsbegriff und Eigentumsverhältnis'* in Baur F, Larenz K & Wieacker F (eds) *Beiträge zur europäischen Rechtsgeschichte und zum geltenden Zivilrecht: Festgabe für Johannes Sontis* (Beck 1977) 149
Glazewski J 'The Environment, Human Rights and a New South African Constitution' (1991) 7 *SAJHR* 167
Gray K 'Property in Thin Air' (1991) 50 *Cambridge LJ* 252
Grey TC 'The Disintegration of Property' in Pennock JR & Chapman JW (eds) *NOMOS XXII: Property* (New York UP 1980) 69
Grotius H *De Jure Belli ac Pacis* (1625) ed BJA Kanter van Hettinga-Tromp (Lugdunum Batavorum 1939)
Grotius H *De Iure Praedae* (1604–1605) ed HG Hamaker (Hagae Comitum 1868)
Grotius H *Inleidinge tot de Hollandsche Rechtsgeleerdheid* (1619–1621) ed F Dovring, HFWD Fischer and EM Meijers (Leiden 1952)
Häberle P *'Vielfalt der Property Rights und der verfassungsrechtliche Eigentumsbegriff'* 1984 *Archiv für das öffentliche Recht* 36
Haysom N 'Constitutionalism, Majoritarian Democracy and Socio-economic Rights' (1992) 8 *SAJHR* 451
Haysom N 'Democracy, Constitutionalism and the ANC's Bill of Rights for a New South Africa' (1991) 7 *SAJHR* 102
Hegel GWF *Grundlinien der Philosophie des Rechts* in Glockner H (ed) *Sämmtliche Werke* (Frommans Verlag 1952)
Honoré AM 'Ownership' in Guest AG (ed) *Oxford Essays in Jurisprudence* (Clarendon Press 1961) 107
Horwitz MJ 'The Transformation in the Conception of Property in American Law, 1780–1860' (1973) 40 *U Chicago LR* 248
Horwitz MJ *The Transformation of American Law 1780–1860* (Harvard UP 1977)
Hume D *Treatise of Human Nature* ed Selby-Bigge (Clarendon Press 1960)
Hund J 'A Bill of Rights for South Africa' (1989) 5 *Am J Jurisprudence* 23
Kant I *Sämmtliche Werke* ed G Hartenstein (Leopold Voss 1868)
Kimminich O *'Grenzen der Sozialbindung des Eigentums'* (1980) 10 *Agrarrecht* 177
Knowles D 'Hegel on Property and Personality' (1983) 33 *Philosophical Quarterly* 45
Kübler K ' *"Eigentum verpflichtet" — eine zivilrechtliche Generalklausel?*' (1960) 159 *Archiv für die civilistische Praxis* 236
Large DW 'This Land is Whose Land? Changing Concepts of Land as Property' 1973 *Wisconsin LR* 1039
Lewis C 'The Right to Private Property in a New Political Dispensation in South Africa' (1992) 8 *SAJHR* 389
Liver P *'Eigentumsbegriff und Eigentumsordnung'* in Faistenberger C & Mayrhofer H (eds) *Privatrechtliche Beiträge: Gedenkschrift Franz Gschnitzer* (Scientia Verlag 1969) 247
Locke J *Two Treatises of Government* (1698) ed P Laslett (New American Library 1960)
Macpherson CB 'Liberal-democracy and Property' in Macpherson CB (ed) *Property: Mainstream and Critical Positions* (Toronto UP 1978)
Marcus T 'Land Reform — Considering National, Class and Gender Issues' (1990) 6 *SAJHR* 178
Marx K *Das Kapital* ed Dietz (Verlag Berlin 1966), based upon the 4th ed by F Engels (1890)
Maunz T et al (eds) *Grundgesetz Kommentar* vol II (Beck 1990)
McCullough HB 'Parliamentary Supremacy and a Constitutional Grid: the Canadian Charter of Rights' (1992) 41 *ICLQ* 751
Meier-Hayoz A *'Vom Wesen des Eigentums'* in *Revolution des Technik — Evolutionen des Rechts: Festgabe für Karl Oftinger* (Schulthess 1969) 171
Michelman FI 'Property as a Constitutional Right' (1981) XXXVIII *Washington and Lee LR* 1097
Michelman FI 'Discretionary Interests — Takings, Motives and Unconstitutional Conditions: Commentary on Radin and Sullivan' (1992) 55 *Albany LR* 619
Michelman FI 'Takings, 1988' (1988) 88 *Columbia LR* 1600
Minogue KR 'The Concept of Property and its Contemporary Significance' in Pennock JR & Chapman JW (eds) *NOMOS XXII: Property* (New York UP 1980) 3
Monaghan HP 'Of "Liberty" and "Property" ' (1977) 62 *Cornell LR* 405

Munzer SR *A Theory of Property* (*Cambridge Studies in Philosophy and Law*) (Cambridge UP 1990)
Mureinik E 'Beyond a Charter of Luxuries: Economic Rights in the Constitution' (1992) 8 *SAJHR* 464
Murphy J 'A Note on the SA Law Commission's Interpretation of the Property Rights in Article 11 of the ANC Bill of Rights' (1992) 7 *SAPR/PL* 12
Murphy J 'Insulating Land Reform from Constitutional Impugnment: An Indian Case Study' (1992) XXXV *CILSA* 129; (1992) 8 *SAJHR* 362
Murphy J 'Property Rights in the New Constitution: An Analytical Framework for Constitutional Review' (1993) XXVI *CILSA* 211
Müller-Gatermann '*Soziales Mietrecht und Eigentumsgarantie*' (1985) 38 *NJW* 2628
Nawroth E '*Privateigentum als Problem der Raumordnungspolitik*' 1982 *Die neue Ordnung* 252
Nawroth E '*Das Bodeneigentum in einer sozialen Wirtschafts- und Gesellschaftsordnung*' in *Die Funktion des Grundeigentums in der Sozialordnung der 70er Jahre: Referate des 9. Deutschen Volksheimstättentages* (1970) 31
Nedelsky J *Private Property and the Limits of American Constitutionalism* (Chicago UP 1990)
Olivecrona K '*Die zwei Schichten im naturrechtlichen Denken*' (1977) 63 *ARSP* 79
Omar AM *The Role of the Bill of Rights for a Democratic South Africa: Key Issues* (Anti-Apartheidsfonds, University of Utrecht 1992)
Panichas GE 'Prolegomenon to a Political Theory of Ownership' (1978) 64/3 *ARSP* 333
Pathak RS 'Human Rights and the Development of the Environmental Law in India' (1988) 14 *Commonwealth Law Bulletin* 1171
Pawlowski HM '*Substanz- oder Funktionseigentum? Zum Eigentumsbegriff des geltenden Rechts*' 1965 *Archiv für die civilistische Praxis* 395
Pennock JR 'Thoughts on the Right to Private Property' in Pennock JR & Chapman JW (eds) *NOMOS XXII: Property* (New York UP 1980) 171
Pergande HG '*Die Kündigung von Wohnraum und die Sozialklausel im neuen Mietrecht*' (1964) 17 *NJW* 1925
Pestalozza C '*Eigentum verpflichtet*' (1982) 35 *NJW* 2169
Peterson AL 'The Takings Clause: In Search of Underlying Principles: Part I' (1989) 77 *California LR* 1301
Peterson AL 'The Takings Clause: In Search of Underlying Principles: Part II' (1990) 78 *California LR* 55
Radin MJ 'Property and Personhood' (1982) 34 *Stanford LR* 957
Radin MJ 'Evaluating Government Reasons for Changing Property Regimes' (1992) 55 *Albany LR* 597
Ramsauer U *Die faktischen Beeinträchtigungen des Eigentums* (Duncker & Humblot 1980)
Rawls J *A Theory of Justice* (Harvard UP 1971)
Reich CA 'The New Property' (1964) 73 *Yale LJ* 733
Renner K *The Institutions of Private Law and their Social Functions* ed O Kahn-Freund translated by Agnes Schwarzschild (Routledge & Kegan Paul 1949)
Rey H '*Dynamisiertes Eigentum*' 1977 *Zeitschrift für Schweizerisches Recht* 65
Riegel R '*Verfügungs- oder Nutzungseigentum? Einige Ueberlegungen zum Eigentumsbegriff*' 1975 *Bayerische Verwaltungsblätter* 412
Rittstieg H *Eigentum als Verfassungsproblem: zu Geschichte und Gegenwart des Bürgerlichen Verfassungsstaates* (Wissenschaftliche Buchgesellschaft 1976)
Robertson M 'Land and Human Rights in South Africa: (A Reply to Marcus and Skweyiya)' (1990) 6 *SAJHR* 215
Rose CM 'Property Rights, Regulatory Regimes and the New Takings Jurisprudence — An Evolutionary Approach' (1990) 57 *Tennessee LR* 577
Rycroft A 'Cases, Comments and New Developments: KwaZulu Natal Indaba Bill of Rights' 1986 *Natal U Law and Society R* 175
Rycroft A 'The Protection of Socio-economic Rights' 1985 *Natal U Law and Society R* 32
Sachs A 'Towards a Bill of Rights in a Democratic South Africa' (1990) 6 *SAJHR* 1
Sachs A *Protecting Human Rights in a New South Africa* (Oxford UP 1990)
Sax JL 'The Constitution, Property Rights and the Future of Water Law' (1991) 28 *Public Land and Resources Law Digest* 53
Schmitt-Kammler A '*Ungelöste Probleme der verfassungsrechtlichen Eigentumsdogmatik*' in *Festschrift der rechtswissenschaftlichen Fakultät zur 600-Jahr-Feier der Universität zu Köln* (1988) 821
Schoch F '*Die Eigentumsgarantie des Art. 14 GG*' 1988 *Jura* 113
Schut GHA '*Naar een meer Pluriforme Regeling van het Eigendomsrecht?*' 1981 *Rechtsgeleerd Magazijn Themis* 329
Schwartländer J & Willoweit D (eds) *Das Recht des Menschen auf Eigentum* (Engel 1983)
Sendler H '*Zum Funktionswandel des Eigentums in der planenden Gesellschaft*' 1975 *Gewerbe-Archiv* 353

Skweyiya Z 'Towards a Solution to the Land Question in Post-apartheid South Africa: Problems and Models' (1990) 6 *SAJHR* 195

Slagter WJ '*Eigendom en Pseudo-eigendom*' in *Quod Licet: Kleijn-bundel* (Kluwer 1992) 357

Slagter WJ '*Eigendom en Privaatrecht*' 1976 *Rechtsgeleerd Magazijn Themis* 276

Soell H '*Die Bedeutung der Sozialpflichtigkeit des Grundeigentums bei der Landschaftspflege und dem Naturschutz*' (1983) 98 *Deutsche Verwaltungsblätter* 241

Sonnenschein J '*Die Entwicklung des privaten Wohnraummietrechts 1986 bis 1988*' (1990) 43 *NJW* 17

Sontis JM '*Strukturelle Betrachtungen zum Eigentumsbegriff*' in Paulus G, Diederichsen U & Canaris CW *Festschrift für Karl Larenz zum 70. Genburtstag* (Beck 1973) 981

South Africa Government *Proposals on a Charter of Fundamental Rights* (Government Printer 1993)

South African Law Commission *Project 58: Group and Human Rights* Working Paper 25 (1989)

South African Law Commission *Project 58: Group and Human Rights* Interim Report (1991)

Stein E *Staatsrecht* 11 ed (Mohr 1988)

Stillman PG 'Property, Freedom and Individuality in Hegel's and Marx's Political Thought' in Pennock JR & Chapman JW (eds) *NOMOS XXII: Property* (New York UP 1980) 130

Sullivan KM 'Governmental Interests and Unconstitutional Conditions Law: a Case Study in Categorization and Balancing' (1992) 55 *Albany LR* 605

Swanson E 'A Land Claims Court for South Africa: Report on Work in Progress' (1992) 8 *SAJHR* 332

Tribe LH *American Constitutional Law* 2 ed (Foundation Press 1988)

Underkuffler LS 'The Perfidy of Property: Review of Nedelsky's *Private Property and the Limits of American Constitutionalism*' (1991) 70 *Texas LR* 293

Underkuffler LS 'On Property: an Essay' (1990) 100 *Yale LJ* 127

Van Alstyne W 'Cracks in "the New Property": Adjudicative Due Process in the Administrative State' (1977) 62 *Cornell LR* 445

Van den Bergh GCJJ *Eigendom — Grepen uit de Geschiedenis van een Omstreden Begrip (Rechtshistorische Cahiers* 1) 2nd print (Kluwer 1988)

Van der Merwe D 'Land Tenure in South Africa: A Brief History and some Reform Proposals' 1989 *TSAR* 663

Van der Merwe D 'Land Tenure in South Africa: Changing the Face of Property Law' (1990) 1 *Stellenbosch LR* 321

Van der Vyver JD 'Comments on the Constitutional Guidelines of the African National Congress' (1989) 5 *SAJHR* 133

Van der Vyver JD 'The Law Commission's Provisional Report on Group and Human Rights' (1989) 5 *SAJHR* vi

Van der Vyver JD 'The South African Law Commission's Provisional Report on Group and Human Rights' (1989) 106 *SALJ* 536

Van der Walt AJ 'Comparative Notes on the Constitutional Protection of Property Rights' (1993) 19 *Recht en Kritiek* 263

Van der Walt AJ 'Developments that may Change the Institution of Private Ownership so as to Meet the Needs of a Non-racial Society in South Africa' (1990) 1 *Stell LR* 26

Van der Walt AJ 'The Fragmentation of Land Rights' (1992) 8 *SAJHR* 431

Van der Walt AJ 'The Future of Common Law Landownership' in van der Walt AJ (ed) *Land Reform and the Future of Landownership in South Africa* (Juta 1991) 21

Van der Walt AJ 'The Impact of a Bill of Rights on Property Law' (1993) *SAPR/PL* 296

Van der Walt AJ 'Introduction' in van der Walt AJ (ed) *Land Reform and the Future of Landownership in South Africa* (Juta 1991) 1

Van der Walt AJ 'Notes on the Interpretation of the Property Clause in the New Constitution' (1994) 57 *THRHR* 181

Van der Walt AJ '*De Onrechtmatige Bezetting van Leegstaande Woningen en het Eigendomsbegrip: een Vergelijkende Analyse van het Conflict tussen de Privaat Eigendom van Onroerend Goed en Dakloosheid*' (1991) 17 *Recht en Kritiek* 329

Van der Walt AJ 'Squatting and the Right to Shelter' 1992 *TSAR* 40

Van der Walt AJ 'Towards the Development of Post-apartheid Land Law: an Exploratory Survey' 1990 *De Jure* 1

Vandevelde KJ 'The New Property of the Nineteenth Century: The Development of the Modern Concept of Property' (1980) 29 *Buffalo LR* 325

Van Goch T '*Naar een Gedifferentieerd Eigendomsbegrip*' (1982) 8 *Recht en Kritiek* 82

Van Neste F '*Eigendom Morgen*' 1983 *Tijdschrift voor Privaatrecht* 479

Van Wyk J 'The Namibian Land Conference — A First Step Towards Addressing a Burning Problem' (1992) 7 *SAPR/PL* 30

Verloren van Themaat A 'Property Rights, Workers' Rights and Economic Regfulation — Constitutional Protection for Property Rights in the United States of America and the Federal Republic of Germany: Possible Lessons for South Africa' (1990) XXIII *CILSA* 53

Von Savigny FC *Das Recht des Besitzes: eine civilistische Abhandlung* (1803) reprint (Darmstadt 1967) of 7th ed AF Rudorff (1864)
Wadley JB 'The Emerging "Social Function" Context for Land Use Planning in the United States: A Comparative Introduction to Recurring Issues' (1988) 28 *Washburn LJ* 22
Waldron J (ed) *Theories of Rights* (Oxford UP 1984)
Weber RH '*Eigentum als Rechtsinstitut: Beurteilungsstand und Entwicklungstendenzen*' 1978 *Zeitschrift für Schweizerisches Recht* 161
Wendt R *Eigentum und Gesetzgebung* (Heitmann 1985)
Weyreuther F '*Zum Grundrechtsschutz des Waldeigentums*' (1980) 2 *Natur und Recht* 137
Wheeler SC 'Natural Property Rights as Body Rights' (1980) 14 *Noûs* 171
Wiechers M ' 'n Monument in die Suid-Afrikaanse Regsontwikkeling: die Werkstuk van die Suid-Afrikaanse Regskommissie oor Groeps- en Minderheidsregte' (1989) 52 *THRHR* 311
Willemse RJ *The Property Clause in a Bill of Rights for South Africa* (1992 LLM Research Report University of the Witwatersrand)
Witzsch G 'The Right to a Healthy and Decent Environment in a New Lesotho Constitution?' (1990) 6 *Lesotho LJ* 167
Wolff M '*Reichsverfassung und Eigentum*' in *Festschrift für Wilhelm Kahl* (Mohr 1923) 3

## FAMILY RIGHTS

African National Congress 'Sexual Abuse and Aggression Against Women' Paper Lusaka 1989
African National Congress *Draft Bill of Rights: Preliminary Revised Version* (Centre for Development Studies, University of the Western Cape 1993)
Ashe M 'Conversation and Abortion' (1988) 82 *North Western U LR* 387
Australian Law Commission Discussion Paper 54 of 1993 *Equality before the Law*
Barton C 'Children: The International Perspective' (1989) 19 *J Family L* 369
Bedil S '*Christian League of Southern Africa v Rall* 1981 (2) SA 821 (O)' (1981) 98 *SALJ* 462
Bekker JC *Seymour's Customary Law in Southern Africa* 5 ed (Juta 1989)
Bekker JC & Maithufi IP 'The Dichotomy between "Official Customary Law" and "Non-official Customary Law" ' (1992) 17 *TRW* 47
Bennett B 'The Economics of Wifing Services: Law and Economics on the Family' (1991) 18 *J L and Society* 206
Bennett TW 'The Compatibility of African Customary Law and Human Rights' in Bennett TW et al (eds) *African Customary Law* (Juta 1991) 18 (also published as 1991 *Acta Juridica*)
Bennett TW 'The Conflict of Personal Laws: Wills and Intestate Succession' (1993) 56 *THRHR* 50
Bennett TW *A Sourcebook of African Customary Law for Southern Africa* (Juta 1991)
Blackstone W *The Commentaries on the Laws of England* 4 ed by R M Kerr (Blackstone Press 1876)
Boberg PQR *The Law of Persons and the Family* (Juta 1977)
Boberg PQR 'The Sins of the Fathers and the Law's Retribution' (1988) 18 *Businessman's Law* 35
Brinig MF & Carbone J 'The Reliance Interest in Marriage and Divorce' (1988) 62 *Tulane LR* 855
Bruch C 'One-Parent Families in the United States: Changing Law and Economics' in Meulders-Klein MT & Eekelaar J (eds) *Family, State and Individual Economic Security* vol I (Kluwer Law and Taxation 1988) 265
Burman S 'Capitalizing on African Strengths: Women, Welfare, and the Law' (1991) 7 *SAJHR* 215
Burman S 'The Category of Illegitimate Children in South Africa' in Burman S & Preston-Whyte E (eds) *Questionable Issue? Illegitimacy in South Africa* (Oxford UP 1992) 21
Burman S 'First-World Solutions for Third-World Problems' in Weitzman LJ & Maclean M (eds) *Economic Consequences of Divorce* (Clarendon Press 1992) 367
Burman S 'Maintaining the One-Parent Support in South Africa: Law and Reality' in Meulders-Klein MT & Eekelaar J (eds) *Family, State and Individual Economic Security* vol I (Kluwer Law and Taxation 1988) 507
Burman S 'Marriage Break-up in South Africa: Holding Want at Bay?' (1987) 1 *Int J L and the Family* 206
Burman S & Berger S 'When Family Support Fails: The Problems of Maintenance Payments in Apartheid South Africa' (1988) 4 *SAJHR* 194; 334
Cachalia F 'Citizenship, Muslim Family Law and a Future South African Constitution' (1993) 56 *THRHR* 392
Caine N 'Maternity Rights of Black Working Mothers' (1989) 5 *Responsa Meridiana* 444
Calhoun SW & Sexton AE 'Is It Possible to Take Both Fetal Life and Women Seriously? Professor Lawrence Tribe and his Reviewers' (1992) 49 *Washington and Lee LR* 437
Campanella J 'The Marital Rape Exemption Resurrected' (1994) 111 *SALJ* 31
Campbell AIL 'The Constitution and Abortion' (1990) 53 *Mod LR* 238
Chanock M 'Law, State and Culture: Thinking about "Customary Law" after Apartheid' in Bennett TW et al (eds) *African Customary Law* (Juta 1991) 52

Chapman JRT 'Violation Against Women as a Violation of Human Rights' (1991) 17 *Social Justice* 54
Church J 'Legal Aspects Relating to the Greater Participation of Women in the South African Economy and Concomitant Decrease in Population Growth' (1990) 31 *Codicillus* 26
Church J *'Secundum Ius et Aequitatem Naturalem*: A Note on the Recent Decision in *Van Erk v Holmer'* (1992) 33 *Codicillus* 32
Clark B 'Custody: The Best Interests of the Child' (1992) 109 *SALJ* 391
Clark B 'Should the Unmarried Father have an Inherent Right of Access to his Illegitimate Child?' (1992) 8 *SAJHR* 565
Clark B & van Heerden B 'The Legal Position of Children Born Out of Wedlock: A Comparative and Predictive Analysis' in Burman S & Preston-Whyte E (eds) *Questionable Issue? Illegitimacy in South Africa* (Oxford UP 1992) 36
Clark CM 'Race, Class, Gender, and Sexuality: On Angela Y Davis *Women, Culture, and Politics'* (1990) 17 *Social Justice* 195
Clive EM 'Reform of the Law on the Child in the Family' 1992 *Juridical R* 109
Collinge J-A 'Women Come out Fighting' *The Star* 23 February 1994
Cook RJ & Dickens BM 'Abortion Laws in African Commonwealth Countries' (1981) 25 *J African L* 60
Cretney SM and Masson JM *Principles of Family Law* 5 ed (Sweet & Maxwell 1990)
Daly K 'Reflections on Feminist Legal Thought' (1990) 17 *Social Justice* 7
Davel CJ *'Christian League of Southern Africa v Rall* 1981 (2) SA 821 (O)' (1981) 14 *De Jure* 361
Davis D 'Two Clauses that Mar the Bill of Rights' *Weekly Mail & Guardian* 15–21 October 1993
Davis SM 'Introduction: "Rethinking" American Family Law' (1985) 61 *North Dakota LR* 185
Democratic Party *Freedom Under the Rule of Law: Advancing Liberty in the New South Africa: Draft Bill of Rights* (May 1993)
Dewar J *Law and the Family* 2 ed (Butterworths 1992)
Dicker L 'The Prevention of Family Violence Act: Innovation or Violation' 1994 *De Rebus* 212
Dingwall R & Eekelaar J 'Rethinking Child Protection' in Freeman MDA (ed) *The State, the Law, and the Family* (Tavistock Publications 1984) 93
Dlamini CRM 'The Role of Customary Law in Meeting Social Needs' in Bennett TW et al (eds) *African Customary Law* (Juta 1991) 71
Douglas G 'The Family and the State Under the European Convention on Human Rights' (1988) 2 *Int J L and the Family* 76
Douglas G 'Individual Economic Security for the Elderly and the Divorced: A Consideration of the Position of England and Wales' in Meulders-Klein MT & Eekelaar J (eds) *Family, State and Individual Economic Security* vol I (Kluwer Law and Taxation 1988) 491
Dowd NE 'Work and Family: The Gender Paradox and the Limitations of Discrimination Analysis in Restructuring the Workplace' (1989) *Harvard Civil Rights–Civil Liberties LR* 79
Du Plessis LM 'Jurisprudential Reflections on the Status of Unborn Life' 1990 *TSAR* 44
Dworkin R 'The Concept of Unenumerated Rights' (1992) 59 *U Chicago LR* 381
Eckard B 'Toegangsresgte tot Buite-egtelike Kinders — Behoort die Wetgewer in te Gryp?' 1992 *TSAR* 122
Eekelaar J 'Equality and the Purpose of Maintenance' (1988) 15 *J of L and Society* 188
Eekelaar J 'Law Commission Reports on the Financial Consequences of Divorce' (1982) 45 *Modern LR* 420
Eekelaar J 'The Place of Divorce in Family Law's New Role' (1975) 38 *Modern LR* 241
Eekelaar J and Maclean M *Maintenance after Divorce* (Clarendon Press 1986)
Elliot FR 'The Family: Private Arena or Adjunct of the State' (1989) 16 *J of L and Society* 443
Ellman IM 'The Theory of Alimony' (1989) 77 *California LR* 1
English Law Commission Report No 103 *The Financial Consequences of Divorce* (October 1980)
English Law Commission Report No 112 *The Financial Consequences of Divorce* (December 1981)
English Law Commission Report No 170 *Facing the Future: A Discussion Paper on the Ground for Divorce* (May 1988)
Esseks JD 'Redefining the Family' (1990) 25 *Harvard Civil Rights–Civil Liberties LR* 183
Fineman ML 'Societal Factors Affecting the Creation of Legal Rules For Distribution of Property at Divorce' (1989) 23 *Family LQ* 279
Finley LM 'Transcending Equality Theory: A Way out of the Maternity and the Workplace Debate' (1986) 86 *Colorado LR* 1118
Forder C 'Constitutional Principle and the Establishment of the Legal Relationship between the Child and the Non-Marital Father: A Study of Germany, the Netherlands and England' (1993) 7 *Int J L and the Family* 40
Freeman MDA 'England: New Responses to Old Problems' (1987–8) 26 *J Family L* 69
Freeman MDA 'Introduction: Rethinking Family Law' in Freeman MDA (ed) *The State, the Law, and the Family* (Tavistock Publications 1984) 1

Freeman MDA 'Questioning the Delegalization Movement in Family Law: Do We Really Want a Family Court?' in Eekelaar JM & Katz SN *The Resolution of Family Conflict* (1984) 7
Freeman MDA 'Towards a Critical Theory of Family Law' (1985) 38 *Current Legal Problems* 153
Freeman MDA & Lyon CM *Cohabitation Without Marriage* (Gower 1983)
Gilligan C *In A Different Voice* (Harvard UP 1982)
Gimenez ME 'The Feminization of Poverty: Myth or Reality?' (1990) 17 *Social Justice* 43
Ginwala F, Mackintosh M & Massey M *Gender and Economic Policy in a Democratic South Africa* United Kingdom Open University Development Policy and Practice Working Paper No 21 (April 1991)
Glendon MA *Abortion and Divorce in Western Law* (Harvard UP 1987)
Glendon MA 'Modern Marriage Law and its Underlying Assumptions: The New Marriage and the New Property' (1980) 13 *Family LQ* 441
Glendon MA 'The *Morgentaler* Judgment: Constitutional Rights, Legislative Intention, and Institutional Design' (1992) 42 *U Toronto LJ* 22
Glendon MA *The New Family and the New Property* (Butterworths 1981)
Glendon MA '*Roe v Wade* in her Appraisal of the Canadian Position' (1989) 83 *North Western U LR* 569
Glendon MA *State, Law, and Family: Family Law in Transition in the United States and Western Europe* (North Holland 1977)
Glendon MA *The Transformation of Family Law: State, Law, and Family in the United States and Western Europe* (Chicago UP 1989)
Goldberg V 'The Right of Access of a Father of an Extramarital Child: Visited Again' (1993) 110 *SALJ* 261
Goodall K ' "Public and Private" in Legal Debate' (1990) 18 *Int J of the Sociology of L* 445
Gray KJ *The Reallocation of Property on Divorce* (Professional Books 1977)
Graycar R & Morgan J *The Hidden Gender of Law* (Federation Press 1990)
Greschner D 'Abortion and Democracy for Women: A Critique of *Tremblay v Daigle*' (1990) 35 *McGill LJ* 633
Hansson D & Russell D 'Made to Fail: The Mythical Option of Legal Abortion for Survivors of Rape and Incest' (1993) 9 *SAJHR* 500
Harris AP 'Race and Essentialism in Feminist Legal Theory' (1990) 42 *Stanford LR* 581
Heaton J 'Should the Consent of the Father of an Illegitimate Child be Required for the Child's Adoption?' (1989) XX *CILSA* 346
Heaton J 'Some General Remarks on the Concept "Best Interests of the Child" ' (1990) 53 *THRHR* 95
Hoffmann LH & Zeffertt DT *The South African Law of Evidence* 4 ed (Juta 1988)
Hoggett B 'Recent Reforms in Family Law: Progress or Backlash?' (1987) 11 *Dalhousie LJ* 5
Hutchings S 'Reg van Toegang vir die Vader van die Buite-egtelike Kind — Outomatiese Toegangsregte — Sal die Beste Belang van die Kind Altyd Seevier?' (1993) 56 *THRHR* 310
Hutchinson AC & Petter A 'Private Rights/Public Wrongs: The Liberal Lie of the Charter' (1988) 38 *U Toronto LJ* 278
Jacob H 'The Changing Landscape of Family Policy and Law' (1988) 21 *L and Society R* 743
Jacobson M 'Pregnancy and Employment: Three Approaches to Equal Opportunity' (1988) 68 *Boston U LR* 1019
Kaganas F & Murray C 'Law, Women and Family: The Question of Polygyny in a New South Africa' in Bennett TW et al (eds) *African Customary Law* (Juta 1991) 116
Katz SN 'Review of book by VC Fox and MH Quitt *Loving, Parenting and Dying: The Family Cycle in England and America, Past and Present* (1980)' (1983) 17 *Family LQ* 96
Keyser B 'Summary of provisions of Maintenance Amendment Act 2 of 1991' 1991 *Annual Survey of South African Law* 7
Kodilinye L 'Is Access the Right of the Parent or the Right of the Child? A Commonwealth View' (1992) 41 *ICLQ* 190
Kruger JM, Blackbeard M & de Jong M 'Die Vader van die Buite-egtelike Kind se Toegangsreg' (1993) 56 *THRHR* 696
Labuschagne JMT 'Persoonlikheidsgoedere van 'n Ander as Regsobjek: Opmerkinge oor die Ongehude Vader se Persoonlikheid- en Waardevormende Reg ten aansien van sy Buite-egtelike Kind' (1993) 56 *THRHR* 41
Labuschagne JMT 'Regsakkulturasie, Lobolo-funksies en die Oorsprong van die Huwelik' (1991) 54 *THRHR* 541
Langbein JH 'The Twentieth-Century Revolution in Family Wealth Transmission' (1988) 86 *Michigan LR* 722
Larson JE 'The Sexual Injustice of the Traditional Family' (1992) 77 *Cornell LR* 997
Law SA 'Women, Work, Welfare, and the Preservation of Patriarchy' (1983) 131 *U Pennsylvania LR* 1249

Le Roux T 'The Economically Active Married Woman and Dual Income Couples' in Steyn AF et al (eds) *Marriage and Family Life in South Africa: Research Priorities* (1987) 317
Levy RJ 'An Introduction to Divorce-Property Issues' (1989) 23 *Family LQ* 147
Leyshon DJ 'Abortion: In Search of a Constitutional Doctrine' (1991) 10 *Medicine and Law* 155 and 219
MacKinnon CA *Feminism Unmodified: Discourses on Life and Law* (Harvard UP 1987)
MacKinnon CA 'Reflections on Sex Equality under Law' (1991) 100 *Yale LJ* 1281
MacKinnon CA *Sexual Harassment of Working Women* (Yale UP 1979)
MacKinnon CA 'Unthinking ERA Thinking' (1987) 54 *U Chicago LR* 759
Meyerson D 'Sexual Equality and the Law' (1993) 9 *SAJHR* 237
Minow M 'Introduction: Finding our Paradoxes, Affirming Our Beyond' (1989) 24 *Harvard Civil Rights–Civil Liberties LR* 1
Mndaweni CB 'Limping Marriages in the New South Africa?' (1991) XXIV *CILSA* 215
Moosa E & Bosch S 'Muslim Family Law Must meet the Changes' Supplement to the *Weekly Mail & Guardian* December 1993.
Mureinik E 'Customary Law is Faring Well' *The Star* 15 October 1993
Murray C 'Democracy, the Family and the African Charter on Human Rights', paper published in the proceedings of the Fourth Annual Conference of the African Society of International and Comparative Law, Dakar, April 1992, 187.
Murray C & O'Regan C 'Putting Women into the Constitution' in Bazilli S (ed) *Putting Women on the Agenda* (1991) 33
Naffine N *Law and the Sexes: Explorations in Feminist Jurisprudence* (Allen & Unwin 1990)
Neave M 'Living Together — The Legal Effects of the Sexual Division of Labour in Four Common Law Countries' (1992) 17 *Monash U LR* 14
Nhlapo RT 'The African Family and Women's Rights: Friends or Foes?' in Bennett TW et al (eds) *African Customary Law* (Juta 1991) 137
Nhlapo RT 'International Protection of Human Rights and the Family: African Variations on a Common Theme' (1989) 3 *International J L and the Family* 1
Nhlapo RT 'Throwing the Baby out with the Bathwater' Supplement to the *Weekly Mail & Guardian* December 1993)
O'Donovan K *Sexual Divisions in Law* (Blackwell 1985)
Ohannessian T & Steyn M 'To See or not to See? — That is the Question' (1991) 54 *THRHR* 254
Oldham JT 'Is the Concept of Marital Property Outdated?' (1983–4) 22 *J Family L* 263
Olsen F 'The Family and the Market: A Study of Ideology and Legal Reform' (1983) 96 *Harvard LR* 1497
Organization of Women 'Cultural and Traditional Practices and how they Retard or Enhance Women's Emancipation and Participation in the Development of South Africa' paper presented by the Border Region of the Organization of Women at the 1990 Malibongwe Conference in Amsterdam
Organisation of Women 'The Nature of Women's Oppression', a paper presented by the Natal Organisation of Women at the Malibongwe Conference in Amsterdam in January 1990
Parker S 'Rights and Utility in Anglo-Australian Family Law' (1992) 55 *Mod LR* 311
Paterson T 'Is there still a Difference between a Common-law Marriage and a Customary Union?' (1992) 109 *SALJ* 18
Pearce D 'The Feminization of Poverty: Women, Work and Welfare' (1978) 11 *Urban and Social Change R* 28
Petersen H 'Perspectives of Women on Work and Law' (1989) 17 *Int J of the Sociology of L* 327
Place JL 'Women and Children in Southern Africa: An Introduction' in *Women and Children at Risk in Southern Africa* (Conference Proceedings Boston (1990)) 9
Rantao J 'The Forgotten Women' *Sunday Star* 5 December 1993
Reich C 'The New Property' (1964) 73 *Yale LJ* 733
Rheinstein M & König R 'Introduction' in *International Encyclopedia of Comparative Law* vol IV chapter 1 'Persons and Family' (Mohr 1974)
Rheinstein M & Glendon MA 'Interspousal Relations' in *International Encyclopedia of Comparative Law* vol IV ch 4 'Persons and Family' (Mohr 1980)
Rhode D *Justice and Gender: Sex Discrimination and the Law* (Harvard UP 1989)
Rhode D 'The "No-Problem" Problem: Feminist Challenges and Cultural Change' (1991) *Yale LJ* 1731
Robinson JA 'Die Ouer–Kind Verhouding in die Lig van 'n Menseregteakte — 'n Beknopte Oorsig oor die Posisie in Duitsland' 1992 *SAPR/PL* 228
Rose N 'Beyond the Public/Private Division: Law, Power and the Family' (1987) 14 *J L and Society* 61
Rutherford JA 'Beyond Individual Privacy: A New Theory of Family Rights' (1987) 39 *U Florida LR* 627
Sachs A *Protecting Human Rights in a New South Africa* (Oxford UP 1990)

Sachs A 'Towards a Bill of Rights in a Democratic South Africa' (1990) 6 *SAJHR* 1
Saldeen A '1986 Swedish Bill proposing a new Marriage Code' (1987–8) 26 *J Family L* 197
Sarkin-Hughes J 'A Perspective on Abortion Legislation in South Africa's Bill of Rights Era' (1993) 56 *THRHR* 83
Scales AC 'The Emergence of Feminist Jurisprudence: an Essay' (1986) 95 *Yale LJ* 1373
Schafer I 'Joint Custody' (1987) 104 *SALJ* 149
Schoeman M 'Gesamentlike Bewaring van Kinders' (1989) 52 *THRHR* 462
Scottish Law Commission Report No 135 *Family Law* (1992)
Sheehy E in Graycar R & Morgan J *The Hidden Gender of Law* (Federation Press 1990) 41
Sigcau S, as reported by Graham W 'Women's Struggle Still Far From Over' *The Star* 7 December 1993.
Sinclair J 'Divorce and Judicial Discretion — In Search of the Middle Ground' (1989) 106 *SALJ* 249
Sinclair J *An Introduction to the Matrimonial Property Act (1984)* (Juta 1984)
Sinclair J 'Maintenance Amendment Act 2 of 1991' (1992–3) 31 *J Family L* 461
Sinclair J 'Women's Rights and Family Law' in Lee R (ed) *Values Alive: A Tribute to Helen Suzman* (1990) 135
Smart C 'Feminism and Law: Some Problems of Analysis and Strategy' (1986) 14 *Int J Sociology of L* 109
Smart C 'Law's Power, the Sexed Body, and the Feminist Discourse' (1990) 17 *J L and Society* 194
Smart C 'Regulating Families or Legitimating Patriarchy? Family Law in Britain' (1982) 10 *Int J Sociology of L* 129
Sonnekus JC & van Westing A 'Faktore vir die Erkenning van 'n Sogenaamde Reg van Toegang vir die Vader van 'n Buite-egtelike Kind' 1992 *TSAR* 232
South African Government *Proposals on a Charter of Fundamental Rights for South Africa* (February 1993)
South African Law Commission *Project 58: Group and Human Rights* Interim Report (1991)
South African Law Commission *Family Law: Matrimonial Property Report* (1988)
South African Law Commission *Project 79: A Father's Rights in Respect of his Illegitimate Child* Working Paper 44 (nyp 1993)
South African Law Commission *Project 12: Review of the Law of Divorce* (1990)
South African Law Commission *Project 45: Women and Sexual Offences in South Africa* (1985)
South Africa Joint Committee of Parliament *Report on the Criminal Law and Criminal Procedure Act Amendment Bill, No 6 of 10 Feb 1989*
Sundberg JF *Family Law in Turmoil — The Norsemen on the Move* (1979)
Teitelbaum LE 'Family History and Family Law' (1985) 5 *Wisconsin LR* 1135
Thornton M 'The Public/Private Dichotomy: Gendered and Discriminatory' (1991) 18 *J L and Society* 448
Tribe LH *Abortion: The Clash of Absolutes* (Norton 1990)
Van der Vyver JD '*Christian League of Southern Africa v Rall* 1981 (2) SA 821 (O)' (1981) 44 *THRHR* 305
Van der Vyver JD & Joubert DJ *Persone- en Familiereg* 2 ed (Juta 1985)
Van Heerden F 'Onderhoudsverpligtinge Voortspruitend uit 'n Gebruiklike Huwelik' (1993) 56 *THRHR* 670
Van Niekerk A (ed) *The Status of Pre-Natal Life* (Lux Verbi 1991)
Van Niekerk SJ et al *Privilegies in die Bewysreg* (Butterworths 1984)
Van Onselen D 'TUFF — The Unmarried Fathers' Fight' 1991 *De Rebus* 499
Van Oosten FFW 'Inadequacies in the Promotion of Life Before Birth in South Africa' (1990) 9 *Medicine & L* 769
Van Wyk AH 'Safeguards for the Family: A South African Perspective' in *Constitutional Safeguards in Unitary and Federal States* (1990) 1 *Stell LR* 186
Van Zyl L 'Post-Divorce Support — Theory and Practice' (1989) 22 *De Jure* 71
Van Zyl L 'What do Women Want from the Law?' (1992) 109 *SALJ* 509
Wardle LD 'United States of America: All Quiet on the Federal Front' (1986–7) 25 *J Family L* 269
Weitzman L *The Divorce Revolution* (Free Press 1985)
Weitzman L 'Marital Property: Its Transformation and Division in the United States' in Weitzman LJ & Maclean M (eds) *Economic Consequences of Divorce* (1992) 85
Wintjen G 'Make Room for Daddy: A Putative Father's Rights to his Children' (1990) 24 *New England LR* 1059
Women and Law in Southern Africa Research Project *The Legal Situation of Women in Southern Africa* (1990)
Zimring FE 'Legal Perspectives on Family Violence' (1987) 75 *California LR* 521
Zuckerman AAS 'Formality and the Family — Reform and Status Quo' (1980) 96 *LQR* 248

## CULTURE, EDUCATION, AND RELIGION

Amankwa P 'Constitutions and Bills of Rights in Third World Nations: Issues of Form and Content' (1981) XIV *CILSA* 185
Beddard R (ed) *Economic, Social and Cultural Rights: Progress and Achievement* (MacMillan 1992)
Cardozo B *The Nature of the Judicial Process* (Oxford UP 1921)
Clarke DM 'Freedom of Thought and Educational Rights in the European Convention' (1987) 22 *The Irish Jurist* 28
Clements R 'Misconceptions of Culture: Native Peoples and Cultural Property under Canadian Law' (1991) 48 *U Toronto LR* 1
Davis D 'The Case Against the Inclusion of Socio-economic Demands in a Bill of Rights Except as Directive Principles' (1992) 8 *SAJHR* 475
Didcott JM 'Practical Workings of a Bill of Rights' in Van der Westhuizen J & Viljoen HP (eds) *A Bill of Rights for South Africa* (Butterworths 1988) 58
Erasmus MG ' 'n Akte van Menseregte vir Suid-Afrika' 1987 *SAPR/PL* 100
Forsyth CF & Schiller JE 'The Judicial Process, Positivism and Civil Liberty' (1981) 98 *SALJ* 218
Hahlo HR & Kahn E *The South African Legal System and Its Background* (Juta 1968)
Hart HLA *The Concept of Law* (Clarendon Press 1961)
Hart HLA 'Positivism and the Separation of Law and Morals' (1958) 71 *Harvard LR* 593
Haysom N 'Constitutionalism, Majoritarian Democracy and Socio-economic Rights' (1992) 8 *SAJHR* 451
Human Sciences Research Council *Report of Commission on Principles for the Provision of Education in South Africa* (De Lange Commission) (1981)
Kaplan W 'The Supreme Court of Canada and the Protection of Minority Dissent: The Case of the Jehovah's Witnesses' 1990 *New Brunswick LJ* 65
Khan AN 'Canadian Constitutional Guarantee of "Liberty" as it Affects Education and Children' 1993 *Journal of Law and Education* 335
Kmiec DW 'The Original Understanding of the Free Exercise Clause and Religious Diversity' 1991 *U Missouri LR* 591
Kumar A *Cultural and Educational Rights of the Minorities under the Indian Constitution* (Deep & Deep 1985)
Levin R 'People's Education and the Struggle for Democracy in South Africa' in Unterhalter E et al (eds) *Apartheid Education and Popular Struggles* (Ravan Press 1991) 117
MacFarlane LJ *The Theory and Practce of Human Rights* (Maurice Temple Smith 1985)
Mousin CB 'Confronting the Wall of Separation: A New Dialogue Between Law and Religion on the Meaning of the First Amendment' 1992 *Depaul LR* 1
Mureinik E 'Beyond a Charter of Luxuries: Economic Rights in the Constitution' (1992) 8 *SAJHR* 464
Naidu A *Fundamental Rights: A Bill of Rights for South Africa* (Transkei UP 1988)
Rains R 'Can Religious Practice be Given Meaningful Protection After *Employment Division v Smith*?' (1991) 62 *U Colorado LR* 687
Rhodes P 'We the People and the Struggle for a New World: The Constitution of the United States of America and International Human Rights' (1987) 30 *Howard LJ* 997
Robertson M *Human Rights for South Africans* (Oxford UP 1991)
Sachs A 'A Bill of Rights for South Africa: Areas of Agreement and Disagreement' (1989) 21 *Columbia Human Rights LR* 13
Sachs A *Protecting Human Rights in a New South Africa* (Oxford UP 1990)
Salomone RC *Equal Education Under Law* (St Martin's Press 1986)
Sanders AJGM *International Jurisprudence in African Context* (Butterworths 1979)
Sebidi L 'Towards the En-fleshment of a Dynamic Idea: The People's Education' in Mphahlele E (ed) *Education for Affirmation* (Skotaville 1987) 49
South African Law Commission *Project 58: Group and Human Rights* Interim Report (1991)
Stainsby J *'Plus ça change . . .*: Education and Equality Rights in the Supreme Court' (1988) 46 *U Toronto LR* 259
Teson FS 'International Human Rights and Cultural Relativism' (1984/85) 25 *Virginia J of Int L* 869
Van der Vyver JD '*Brown v Board of Education*: A Survey of the American Desegregation Programme' (1974) 91 *SALJ* 510
Van der Westhuizen J 'A Post-Apartheid Educational System: Constitutional Provisions' (1989) 21 *Columbia Human Rights LR* 113
Venter F 'Menseregte, Groepsregte en 'n Proses na Groter Geregtigheid' 1986 *SAPR/PL* 202
Woehrling J 'Minority Cultural and Linguistic Rights and Equality Rights in the Canadian Charter of Rights and Freedoms' 1985 31 *McGill LJ* 50

## SOCIAL AND ECONOMIC RIGHTS

Andreassen BA, Smith AG & Stokke H 'Compliance with Economic and Social Human Rights: Realistic Evaluations and Monitoring in the Light of Immediate Obligations' in Eide A & Hagtvet B *Human Rights in Perspective* (Blackwell 1992) 252

Asmal K 'Victims, Survivors and Citizens — Human Rights, Reparations and Reconciliation' (1992) 8 *SAJHR* 509

Bartholomeu W *The Irish Judiciary* (Notre Dame UP 1971)

Beinart B 'The Liberty of the Subject' (1953) 16 *THRHR* 30

Berenstein A 'Economic and Social Rights: Their Inclusion in the European Convention on Human Rights' 1981 *Human Rights LJ* 257

Berenstein A 'Reflections of Human Rights' 1988 *Human Rights LJ* 165

Beukes EP & Fourie FC van N 'Economic and Social Human Rights: An Exploratory Survey' 1988 *TRW* 18

Black 'Further Reflections on the Constitutional Justice of Livelihood' (1986) Rubin Lecture at The Columbia Law School, 20 March 1986, 5

Chowdhury SR & De Waart PJIM 'Significance of the Right to Development: An Introductory View' in Chowdhury SR, Denters EMG & De Waart PJIM *The Rights to Development in International Law* (Nijhoff 1992) 7

Chubb B *The Constitution and Constitutional Change in Ireland* (Dublin Institute of Public Administration 1978)

Claude RP & Weston BH (eds) *Human Rights in the World Community* (Pennsylvania UP 1989)

Dahl RA 'Democracy and Human Rights under Different Conditions of Development' in Eide A & Hagtvet B (eds) *Human Rights in Perspective* (Blackwell 1992) 235

Davis D 'The Case Against the Inclusion of Socio-Economic Rights in a Bill of Rights Except as Directive Principles' (1992) 8 *SAJHR* 475

Davis D 'Remaking the South African Legal Order' 1991 *Social Justice* 78

De Villiers B 'Directive Principles of State Policy and Fundamental Rights: The Indian Experience' (1992) 8 *SAJHR* 30

De Villiers B 'Socio-economic Rights in a New Constitution: Critical Evaluation of the Recommendations of the South African Law Commission' (1992) 3 *TSAR* 422

De Villiers B, Van Vuuren DJ & Wiechers M *Human Rights: Documents that Paved the Way* (HSRC 1992)

Dinstein Y 'Collective Human Rights of Peoples and Minorities' (1976) 25 *ICLQ* 102

Dlamini CRM 'Towards a Regional Protection of Human Rights in Africa: The African Charter on Human and Peoples' Rights' (1991) XXIV *CILSA* 199

Eide A 'Realization of Social and Economic Rights and the Minimum Threshold Approach' (1989) 10 *Human Rights LJ* 36

Epstein RA 'The Uncertain Quest for Welfare Rights' 1985 *Brigham Young U LR* 201

Fourie FC van N 'The Namibian Constitution and Economic Rights' (1992) 8 *SAJHR* 367

Freeden MT 'Human Rights and Welfare: A Communitarian View' 1990 *Ethics* 489

Ganji M *The Realization of Economic, Social and Cultural Rights: Problems, Policies, Progress United Nations* (1975) E/CN 4/1108 Rev 1

Ginsburg MI & Lesser L 'Current Developments in Economic and Social Rights: A United States Perspective' (1981) 2 *Human Rights LJ* 237

Glazewski J 'The Environment, Human Rights and a New South African Constitution' (1991) 7 *SAJHR* 182

Grimes RH & Horgan PT *Introduction to the Law in the Republic of Ireland* (Wolfhound Press 1981)

Hauserman 'Myth and Realities' in Davies P (ed) *Human Rights* (Routledge 1988) 152

Haysom N 'Constitutionalism, Majoritarian Democracy and Socio-Economic Rights' (1992) 8 *SAJHR* 457

Haysom N 'Democracy, Constitutionalism and the ANC's Bill of Rights for a New South Africa' 1991 *Social Justice* 45

Henkin L 'Economic-Social Rights as "Rights": A United States Perspective' (1981) 2 *Human Rights LJ* 229

Jaconelli J *Enacting a Bill of Rights* (Clarendon Press 1986)

Jain MP *Indian Constitutional Law* (Tripathi 1978)

Kagzi MCJ *The Constitution of India* (Metropolitan Book Co 1989)

Khushalani Y 'Human Rights Issues in Asia and Africa' (1986) 7 *Human Rights LJ* 403

Kiss AC 'The Peoples' Right to Self-Determination' (1986) 7 *Human Rights LJ* 165

Kooijmans PH 'Human Rights — Universal Panacea?' 1990 *Netherlands Int LR* 315

Lack D 'Human Rights and the Disadvantaged' (1989) 10 *Human Rights LJ* 53

Leuprecht P 'Reflections on Human Rights' (1988) 9 *Human Rights LJ* 163

Lippman M 'Human Rights Revisited: The Protection of Human Rights under the International Covenant on Civil and Political Rights' 1978 *Netherlands Int LR* 221
Lloyd D Lord *Introduction to Jurisprudence* 4 ed (Stevens 1979)
Locke J *Two Treatises of Government* (Cambridge UP 1960 critical ed)
Löcke J '*Soziale Grundrechte als Staatszielbestimmungen und Gesetzgebungsaufträge*' (1982) 107 *Archiv des öffentlichen Rechts* 15
M'Baye K 'The Organization of African Unity (OAU)' in Vasak K *The International Dimensions of Human Rights* (Greenwood Press 1982) 645
Maclachlan J *Human Rights in Retrospect and Reality* (Lindsey Press 1986)
Merten '*Über Staatsziele*' 1993 *Die öffentliche Verwaltung* 386
Morgan DG *Constitutional Law in Ireland* (Round Hall Press 1985)
Motshekga MS 'The African Charter on Human and People's Rights — Its Importance to Human Rights Thinking in South Africa' 1989 *Codicillus* 31
Müller JP 'Fundamental Rights in Democracy' (1983) 4 *Human Rights LJ* 131
Mureinik E 'Beyond a Charter of Luxuries: Economic Rights in the Constitution' (1992) 8 *SAJHR* 466
Murphy J 'Second Generation Rights and the Bill of Rights in South Africa' 1992 *SA Sociological Review* 31
Narain P 'Judicial Law Making and the Place of Directive Principles in the Indian Constitution' 1985 *J Indian Law Institute* 222
Partsch KJ 'Recent Developments in the Field of Peoples' Rights' 1986 7 *Human Rights* LJ 177
Peces-Barba G 'Reflections on Economic, Social and Cultural Rights' (1981) 2 *Human Rights LJ* 281
Pollack EH *Human Rights* (International Association for Philosophy of Law and Social Philosophy 1971)
Reddy KJ 'Fundamentalness of Fundamental Rights and Directive Principles in the Indian Constitution' 1980 *J Indian Law Institute* 403
Sabine GH *A History of Political Theory* 3 ed (Harrap 1964)
Sachs A 'Watch out — There's a Constitution About' 1992 *South Africa International* 188
Sachs A *Advancing Human Rights in South Africa* (Oxford UP 1992)
Sathe SP 'Constitutional Law' 1983 *Annual Survey of Indian Law* 178
Sharma SK *Directive Principles and Fundamental Rights* (Deep & Deep 1990)
Simsarian J 'Progress in Drafting Two Covenants on Human Rights in the United Nations' (1952) 46 *Am J Int L* 711
South African Law Commission *Project 58:Group and Human Rights* Interim Report (1991)
Starck C 'Europe's Fundamental Rights in the Newest Garb' (1982) 3 *Human Rights LJ* 103
Van Niekerk P 'Categories of Fundamental Rights and Constitutional Reform in South Africa' 1990 *SAPR/PL* 87
Vierdag K 'The Legal Nature of the Rights granted by the International Covenant on Economic, Social and Political Rights' 1978 *NYIL* 69
Walsh B 'Existence and Meaning of Fundamental Rights in the Field of Education in Ireland' (1981) 2 *Human Rights LJ* 323

## LIMITATION AND SUSPENSION

Badura P *Staatsrecht* (Beck 1986)
Basson DA & Viljoen HP *Suid-Afrikaanse Staatsreg* 2 ed (Juta 1988)
Boulle L, Harris B & Hoexter C *Constitutional and Administrative Law* (Juta 1989)
Burgos HS 'The Application of International Humanitarian Law as Compared to Human Rights Law in Situations Qualified as Internal Armed Conflict, Internal Disturbances and Tensions, or Public Emergency, with Special Reference to War Crimes and Political Crimes' in Kalshoven F & Sandoz Y (eds) *Implementation of International Humanitarian Law* (Nijhoff 1989) 1
Carpenter G *Introduction to South African Constitutional Law* (Butterworths 1987)
Chowdhury SR *Rule of Law in a State of Emergency: The Paris Minimum Standards of Human Rights Norms in a State of Emergency* (Printer Publishers 1989)
Colker R 'Section 1, Contextuality, and the Anti-Disadvantage Principle' (1993) 42 *U Toronto LJ* 77
Dugard J *Human Rights and the South African Legal Order* (Princeton UP 1978)
Dugard J *International Law — A South African Perspective* (Juta 1994)
Ellmann S 'A Constitution for All Seasons: Providing Against Emergencies in a Post-Apartheid Constitution' 1989 *Columbia Human Rights LR* 163
Erasmus MG 'Die Grondwet van Namibië' (1990) 1 *Stell LR* 277
Erasmus MG 'The International Relations Context of the Freedom Charter' in Steytler N (ed) *The Freedom Charter and Beyond — Founding Principles of a Democratic South African Legal Order* (Wyvern Publications 1991)
Gandhi PR 'The Human Rights Committee and Derogation in Public Emergencies' 1989 *German Yearbook of International Law* 323

Haysom N 'States of Emergency in a Post-Apartheid South Africa' (1989) 21 *Columbia Human Rights LR* 139
Henkin L 'Human Rights' in Bernhardt R (ed) *Encyclopedia of Public International Law* vol 28 (North Holland) 268
Henkin L 'International Law after the Cold War' *American Society of International Law Newsletter* (Nov–Dec 1993) 1
Higgins R 'Derogations under Human Rights Treaties' 1976/77 *BYIL* 281
Kirby M 'Human Rights — Emerging International Minimum Standards' (1993) 19 *Commonwealth Law Bulletin* 1252
Kiss AC 'Permissible Limitations on Rights' in Henkin L (ed) *The International Bill of Rights* (Columbia UP 1981)
Kommers DP *The Constitutional Jurisprudence of the Federal Republic of Germany* (Duke UP 1989)
Kriele M *Einführung in die Staatslehre — Die geschichtlichen Legitimitätsgrundlagen des demokratischen Verfassungsstaates* (Rowohlt 1975)
Mathews AS *Freedom, State Security and the Rule of Law* (Juta 1986)
Meron T *Human Rights in Internal Strife: Their International Protection* (Grotius Publications 1987)
Neethling J, Potgieter JM & Visser PJ *Law of Delict* (Butterworths 1993)
Oraa J *Human Rights in States of Emergency in International Law* (Clarendon Press 1992)
Rabie A 'Failure of the Brakes of Justice: *Omar v Minister of Law and Order*' (1987) 3 *SAJHR* 300
Riedel EH 'Assertion and Protection of Human Rights in International Treaties and their Impact in the Basic Law' in Starck C (ed) *Rights, Institutions and Impact of International Law According to the German Basic Law* (Nomos 1987) 197
Schabas W *International Human Rights Law and the Canadian Charter — A Manual for the Practitioner* (Carswell 1991)
Sieghart P *The International Law of Human Rights* (Clarendon Press 1983)
Tribe LH *Constitutional Choices* (Harvard UP 1985)
Van Wyk DH *Persoonlike Status in die Suid-Afrikaanse Publiekreg* (LLD thesis Unisa 1979)
Von Münch I *Grundgesetz Kommentar* (Beck 1985)
Wiechers M 'Namibia: The 1982 Constitutional Principles and their Legal Significance' 1989/90 *SAYIL* 1
Wilson R 'The Domestic Impact of International Human Rights Law' (1993) 19 *Commonwealth Law Bulletin* 1246
Woolman S 'Riding the Push-Me Pull-You: Constructing a Test that reconciles the Conflicting Interests which Animate the Limitation Clause'(1994) 10 *SAJHR* 60

APPENDIX

# CHAPTER 3
# FUNDAMENTAL RIGHTS

**7 Application**

(1) This Chapter shall bind all legislative and executive organs of state at all levels of government.

(2) This Chapter shall apply to all law in force and all administrative decisions taken and acts performed during the period of operation of this Constitution.

(3) Juristic persons shall be entitled to the rights contained in this Chapter where, and to the extent that, the nature of the rights permits.

(4) *(a)* When an infringement of or threat to any right entrenched in this Chapter is alleged, any person referred to in paragraph *(b)* shall be entitled to apply to a competent court of law for appropriate relief, which may include a declaration of rights.

*(b)* The relief referred to in paragraph *(a)* may be sought by —
(i) a person acting in his or her own interest;
(ii) an association acting in the interest of its members;
(iii) a person acting on behalf of another person who is not in a position to seek such relief in his or her own name;
(iv) a person acting as a member of or in the interest of a group or class of persons; or
(v) a person acting in the public interest.

**8 Equality**

(1) Every person shall have the right to equality before the law and to equal protection of the law.

(2) No person shall be unfairly discriminated against, directly or indirectly, and, without derogating from the generality of this provision, on one or more of the following grounds in particular: race, gender, sex, ethnic or social origin, colour, sexual orientation, age, disability, religion, conscience, belief, culture or language.

(3) *(a)* This section shall not preclude measures designed to achieve the adequate protection and advancement of persons or groups or categories of persons disadvantaged by unfair discrimination, in order to enable their full and equal enjoyment of all rights and freedoms.

*(b)* Every person or community dispossessed of rights in land before the commencement of this Constitution under any law which would have been inconsistent with subsection (2) had that subsection been in operation at the time of the dispossession, shall be entitled to claim restitution of such rights subject to and in accordance with sections 121, 122 and 123.

(4) *Prima facie* proof of discrimination on any of the grounds specified in subsection (2) shall be presumed to be sufficient proof of unfair discrimination as contemplated in that subsection, until the contrary is established.

**9 Life**

Every person shall have the right to life.

**10 Human dignity**

Every person shall have the right to respect for and protection of his or her dignity.

**11 Freedom and security of the person**

(1) Every person shall have the right to freedom and security of the person, which shall include the right not to be detained without trial.

(2) No person shall be subject to torture of any kind, whether physical, mental or emotional, nor shall any person be subject to cruel, inhuman or degrading treatment or punishment.

**12 Servitude and forced labour**

No person shall be subject to servitude or forced labour.

**13 Privacy**

Every person shall have the right to his or her personal privacy, which shall include the right not to be subject to searches of his or her person, home or property, the seizure of private possessions or the violation of private communications.

**14 Religion, belief and opinion**

(1) Every person shall have the right to freedom of conscience, religion, thought, belief and opinion, which shall include academic freedom in institutions of higher learning.

(2) Without derogating from the generality of subsection (1), religious observances may be conducted at state or state-aided institutions under rules established by an appropriate authority for that purpose, provided that such religious observances are conducted on an equitable basis and attendance at them is free and voluntary.

(3) Nothing in this Chapter shall preclude legislation recognising —
(a) a system of personal and family law adhered to by persons professing a particular religion; and
(b) the validity of marriages concluded under a system of religious law subject to specified procedures.

## 15 Freedom of expression

(1) Every person shall have the right to freedom of speech and expression, which shall include freedom of the press and other media, and the freedom of artistic creativity and scientific research.

(2) All media financed by or under the control of the state shall be regulated in a manner which ensures impartiality and the expression of a diversity of opinion.

## 16 Assembly, demonstration and petition

Every person shall have the right to assemble and demonstrate with others peacefully and unarmed, and to present petitions.

## 17 Freedom of association

Every person shall have the right to freedom of association.

## 18 Freedom of movement

Every person shall have the right to freedom of movement anywhere within the national territory.

## 19 Residence

Every person shall have the right freely to choose his or her place of residence anywhere in the national territory.

## 20 Citizens' rights

Every citizen shall have the right to enter, remain in and leave the Republic, and no citizen shall without justification be deprived of his or her citizenship.

## 21 Political rights

(1) Every citizen shall have the right —
(a) to form, to participate in the activities of and to recruit members for a political party;
(b) to campaign for a political party or cause; and
(c) freely to make political choices.

(2) Every citizen shall have the right to vote, to do so in secret and to stand for election to public office.

## 22 Access to court

Every person shall have the right to have justiciable disputes settled by a court of law or, where appropriate, another independent and impartial forum.

## 23 Access to information

Every person shall have the right of access to all information held by the state or any of its organs at any level of government in so far as such information is required for the exercise or protection of any of his or her rights.

## 24 Administrative justice

Every person shall have the right to —
(a) lawful administrative action where any of his or her rights or interests is affected or threatened;
(b) procedurally fair administrative action where any of his or her rights or legitimate expectations is affected or threatened;
(c) be furnished with reasons in writing for administrative action which affects any of his or her rights or interests unless the reasons for such action have been made public; and
(d) administrative action which is justifiable in relation to the reasons given for it where any of his or her rights is affected or threatened.

## 25 Detained, arrested and accused persons

(1) Every person who is detained, including every sentenced prisoner, shall have the right —
(a) to be informed promptly in a language which he or she understands of the reason for his or her detention;
(b) to be detained under conditions consonant with human dignity, which shall include at least the provision of adequate nutrition, reading material and medical treatment at state expense;
(c) to consult with a legal practitioner of his or her choice, to be informed of this right promptly and, where substantial injustice would otherwise result, to be provided with the services of a legal practitioner by the state;
(d) to be given the opportunity to communicate with, and to be visited by, his or her spouse or partner, next-of-kin, religious counsellor and a medical practitioner of his or her choice; and
(e) to challenge the lawfulness of his or her detention in person before a court of law and to be released if such detention is unlawful.

(2) Every person arrested for the alleged com-

mission of an offence shall, in addition to the rights which he or she has as a detained person, have the right —

(a) promptly to be informed, in a language which he or she understands, that he or she has the right to remain silent and to be warned of the consequences of making any statement;

(b) as soon as it is reasonably possible, but not later than 48 hours after the arrest or, if the said period of 48 hours expires outside ordinary court hours or on a day which is not a court day, the first court day after such expiry, to be brought before an ordinary court of law and to be charged or to be informed of the reason for his or her further detention, failing which he or she shall be entitled to be released;

(c) not to be compelled to make a confession or admission which could be used in evidence against him or her; and

(d) to be released from detention with or without bail, unless the interests of justice require otherwise.

(3) Every accused person shall have the right to a fair trial, which shall include the right —

(a) to a public trial before an ordinary court of law within a reasonable time after having been charged;

(b) to be informed with sufficient particularity of the charge;

(c) to be presumed innocent and to remain silent during plea proceedings or trial and not to testify during trial;

(d) to adduce and challenge evidence, and not to be a compellable witness against himself or herself;

(e) to be represented by a legal practitioner of his or her choice or, where substantial injustice would otherwise result, to be provided with legal representation at state expense, and to be informed of these rights;

(f) not to be convicted of an offence in respect of any act or omission which was not an offence at the time it was committed, and not to be sentenced to a more severe punishment than that which was applicable when the offence was committed;

(g) not to be tried again for any offence of which he or she has previously been convicted or acquitted;

(h) to have recourse by way of appeal or review to a higher court than the court of first instance;

(i) to be tried in a language which he or she understands or, failing this, to have the proceedings interpreted to him or her; and

(j) to be sentenced within a reasonable time after conviction.

## 26  Economic activity

(1) Every person shall have the right freely to engage in economic activity and to pursue a livelihood anywhere in the national territory.

(2) Subsection (1) shall not preclude measures designed to promote the protection or the improvement of the quality of life, economic growth, human development, social justice, basic conditions of employment, fair labour practices or equal opportunity for all, provided such measures are justifiable in an open and democratic society based on freedom and equality.

## 27  Labour relations

(1) Every person shall have the right to fair labour practices.

(2) Workers shall have the right to form and join trade unions, and employers shall have the right to form and join employers' organisations.

(3) Workers and employers shall have the right to organise and bargain collectively.

(4) Workers shall have the right to strike for the purpose of collective bargaining.

(5) Employers' recourse to the lock-out for the purpose of collective bargaining shall not be impaired, subject to section 33 (1).

## 28  Property

(1) Every person shall have the right to acquire and hold rights in property and, to the extent that the nature of the rights permits, to dispose of such rights.

(2) No deprivation of any rights in property shall be permitted otherwise than in accordance with a law.

(3) Where any rights in property are expropriated pursuant to a law referred to in subsection (2), such expropriation shall be permissible for public purposes only and shall be subject to the payment of agreed compensation or, failing agreement, to the payment of such compensation and within such period as may be determined by a court of law as just and equitable, taking into account all relevant factors, including, in the case of the determination of compensation, the use to which the property is being put, the history of its acquisition, its market value, the value of the investments in it by those affected and the interests of those affected.

## 29  Environment

Every person shall have the right to an environment which is not detrimental to his or her health or well-being.

## 30 Children

(1) Every child shall have the right —
*(a)* to a name and nationality as from birth;
*(b)* to parental care;
*(c)* to security, basic nutrition and basic health and social services;
*(d)* not to be subject to neglect or abuse; and
*(e)* not to be subject to exploitative labour practices nor to be required or permitted to perform work which is hazardous or harmful to his or her education, health or well-being.

(2) Every child who is in detention shall, in addition to the rights which he or she has in terms of section 25, have the right to be detained under conditions and to be treated in a manner that takes account of his or her age.

(3) For the purpose of this section a child shall mean a person under the age of 18 years and in all matters concerning such child his or her best interest shall be paramount.

## 31 Language and culture

Every person shall have the right to use the language and to participate in the cultural life of his or her choice.

## 32 Education

Every person shall have the right —
*(a)* to basic education and to equal access to educational institutions;
*(b)* to instruction in the language of his or her choice where this is reasonably practicable; and
*(c)* to establish, where practicable, educational institutions based on a common culture, language or religion, provided that there shall be no discrimination on the ground of race.

## 33 Limitation

(1) The rights entrenched in this Chapter may be limited by law of general application, provided that such limitation —
*(a)* shall be permissible only to the extent that it is —
  (i) reasonable; and
  (ii) justifiable in an open and democratic society based on freedom and equality; and
*(b)* shall not negate the essential content of the right in question,
and provided further that any limitation to —
*(aa)* a right entrenched in section 10, 11, 12, 14 (1), 21, 25 or 30 (1) *(d)* or *(e)* or (2); or
*(bb)* a right entrenched in section 15, 16, 17, 18, 23 or 24, in so far as such right relates to free and fair political activity,
shall, in addition to being reasonable as required in paragraph *(a)* (i), also be necessary.

(2) Save as provided for in subsection (1) or any other provision of this Constitution, no law, whether a rule of the common law, customary law or legislation, shall limit any right entrenched in this Chapter.

(3) The entrenchment of the rights in terms of this Chapter shall not be construed as denying the existence of any other rights or freedoms recognised or conferred by common law, customary law or legislation to the extent that they are not inconsistent with this Chapter.

(4) This Chapter shall not preclude measures designed to prohibit unfair discrimination by bodies and persons other than those bound in terms of section 7 (1).

(5) *(a)* The provisions of a law in force at the commencement of this Constitution promoting fair employment practices, orderly and equitable collective bargaining and the regulation of industrial action shall remain of full force and effect until repealed or amended by the legislature.

*(b)* If a proposed enactment amending or repealing a law referred to in paragraph *(a)* deals with a matter in respect of which the National Manpower Commission, referred to in section 2A of the Labour Relations Act, 1956 (Act 28 of 1956), or any other similar body which may replace the Commission, is competent in terms of a law then in force to consider and make recommendations, such proposed enactment shall not be introduced in Parliament unless the said Commission or such other body has been given an opportunity to consider the proposed enactment and to make recommendations with regard thereto.

## 34 State of emergency and suspension

(1) A state of emergency shall be proclaimed prospectively under an Act of Parliament, and shall be declared only where the security of the Republic is threatened by war, invasion, general insurrection or disorder or at a time of national disaster, and if the declaration of a state of emergency is necessary to restore peace or order.

(2) The declaration of a state of emergency and any action taken, including any regulation enacted, in consequence thereof, shall be of force for a period of not more than 21 days, unless it is extended for a period of not longer than three months, or consecutive periods of not longer than three months at a time, by resolution of the National Assembly adopted by a majority of at least two-thirds of all its members.

(3) Any superior court shall be competent to enquire into the validity of a declaration of a state of emergency, any extension thereof, and any action taken, including any regulation enacted,

under such declaration.

(4) The rights entrenched in this Chapter may be suspended only in consequence of the declaration of a state of emergency, and only to the extent necessary to restore peace or order.

(5) Neither any law which provides for the declaration of a state of emergency, nor any action taken, including any regulation enacted, in consequence thereof, shall permit or authorise —
*(a)* the creation of retrospective crimes;
*(b)* the indemnification of the state or of persons acting under its authority for unlawful actions during the state of emergency; or
*(c)* the suspension of this section, and sections 7, 8 (2), 9, 10, 11 (2), 12, 14, 27 (1) and (2), 30 (1) *(d)* and *(e)* and (2) and 33 (1) and (2).

(6) Where a person is detained under a state of emergency the detention shall be subject to the following conditions:
*(a)* An adult family member or friend of the detainee shall be notified of the detention as soon as is reasonably possible;
*(b)* the names of all detainees and a reference to the measures in terms of which they are being detained shall be published in the *Gazette* within five days of their detention;
*(c)* when rights entrenched in section 11 or 25 have been suspended —
 (i) the detention of a detainee shall, as soon as it is reasonably possible but not later than 10 days after his or her detention, be reviewed by a court of law, and the court shall order the release of the detainee if it is satisfied that the detention is not necessary to restore peace or order;
 (ii) a detainee shall at any stage after the expiry of a period of 10 days after a review in terms of subparagraph (i) be entitled to apply to a court of law for a further review of his or her detention, and the court shall order the release of the detainee if it is satisfied that the detention is no longer necessary to restore peace or order;
*(d)* the detainee shall be entitled to appear before the court in person, to be represented by legal counsel, and to make representations against his or her continued detention;
*(e)* the detainee shall be entitled at all reasonable times to have access to a legal representative of his or her choice;
*(f)* the detainee shall be entitled at all times to have access to a medical practitioner of his or her choice; and
*(g)* the state shall for the purpose of a review referred to in paragraph *(c)*(i) or (ii) submit written reasons to justify the detention or further detention of the detainee to the court, and shall furnish the detainee with such reasons not later than two days before the review.

(7) If a court of law, having found the grounds for a detainee's detention unjustified, orders his or her release, such a person shall not be detained again on the same grounds unless the state shows good cause to a court of law prior to such redetention.

## 35 Interpretation

(1) In interpreting the provisions of this Chapter a court of law shall promote the values which underlie an open and democratic society based on freedom and equality and shall, where applicable, have regard to public international law applicable to the protection of the rights entrenched in this Chapter, and may have regard to comparable foreign case law.

(2) No law which limits any of the rights entrenched in this Chapter, shall be constitutionally invalid solely by reason of the fact that the wording used *prima facie* exceeds the limits imposed in this Chapter, provided such a law is reasonably capable of a more restricted interpretation which does not exceed such limits, in which event such law shall be construed as having a meaning in accordance with the said more restricted interpretation.

(3) In the interpretation of any law and the application and development of the common law and customary law, a court shall have due regard to the spirit, purport and objects of this Chapter.

# INDEX

NOTE: The index covers text and footnotes

## A

ABORTION (*see also* BIRTH CONTROL; CONCEPTION AS INCEPTION OF LIFE; FETUS)
    discrimination and, 524–33
    fundamental rights and, 16n, 215, 216, 218, 220, 224, 227, 229–32, 233, 238–9
    limitation and, 244n, 253
    sex education and, 588
    state duty and, 96
    values and, 9n, 12
*ABSTRAKTE NORMENKONTROLLE*, 76–7
*ABWEHRRECHTE* (*see also* NEGATIVE RIGHTS), 86–7
ACADEMIC FREEDOM, 592
ACCESS TO — *see* CHILDREN; JUSTICE
ACCOUNTABILITY
    cabinet, 164
    executive, 376, 387–9
    judicial, 6, 7, 9, 12, 14
    parliamentary, 58
    political, 134
ACTIO POPULARIS, 421
ACTIVISM, JUDICIAL — *see* JUDICIAL ACTIVISM
ADMINISTRATIVE JUSTICE, 387–400
ADMINISTRATIVE LAW AND *GRUNDRECHTE*, 94–5
ADMISSION, 428–9
ADVERSARIAL/NON-ADVERSARIAL SYSTEMS/STYLES (*see also* INQUISITORIAL SYSTEMS; JUDICIAL FACT FINDING), 57, 119n, 402, 412, 427
ADVICE OF, ON THE, 147, 148n, 151n, 153n
AFFIRMATIVE ACTION, 8n, 24, 158, 179, 199, 207–10, 260, 379, 385, 462, 463, 497, 607n, 613
AFRICAN CHARTER ON HUMAN AND PEOPLES' RIGHTS, 127, 182, 188–9, 217, 225, 234, 238, 242, 254, 266, 521, 584, 607, 610
AFRICAN CUSTOMARY MARRIAGE — *see* CUSTOMARY MARRIAGE
AFTER-AMBLE (*see also* SCHEDULES, WEIGHT OF), 129, 204n, 207, 634
AIRWAVES, ACCESS TO AND REGULATION (*see also* INDEPENDENT BROADCASTING AUTHORITY), 289, 307
ALIENS, DISCRIMINATION AGAINST, 21
'ALL LAW IN FORCE', MEANING OF, 210, 522–3
ALTERNATIVE DISPUTE RESOLUTION, 57
AMERICAN CONVENTION ON HUMAN RIGHTS, 187, 217, 225, 229, 230, 234, 242, 254, 266, 464
ANGLOCENTRIC LEGAL TRADITIONS, SOUTH AFRICA AND, 1
APARTHEID (*see also* CRIME OF APARTHEID), 19, 133–4, 171, 174, 180–1, 505, 507n, 519, 548, 589–91
ARMED CONFLICT, 193n, 215
ARMS, 26, 321–3
ARREST, 401, 404, 407–9, 415
ARRESTED PERSONS, RIGHTS OF, 408–9
ARTS AND SCIENCE (*see also* SCIENCE), 286–7, 326
ASSEMBLY, FREEDOM OF, 22, 27, 175, 264, 292–337, 379
ASSOCIATION, FREEDOM OF (*see also* ASSOCIATIONS), 20, 27, 175, 264, 338–86, 441–2, 444, 445, 446, 448, 453, 586

ASSOCIATION, RIGHT OF — *see* ASSOCIATION, FREEDOM OF
ASSOCIATIONS (*see also* ASSOCIATION, FREEDOM OF), 99, 102, 338–86, 445
AUDITOR-GENERAL, 164, 169
*AUSGESTALTUNG* OF FUNDAMENTAL RIGHTS, 88n, 102
*AUT DEDERE AUT JUDICARE*, 181

## B

BALANCING OF INTERESTS (*see also* LIMITATION OF RIGHTS; PROPORTIONALITY), 27, 30, 70n, 72, 91–2, 97n, 106–7, 109, 110, 116n, 383, 471, 643, 645–6, 648, 650
BANJUL CHARTER — *see* AFRICAN CHARTER ON HUMAN AND PEOPLES' RIGHTS
BANNING (*see also* ASSOCIATIONS), 340–1, 368–70, 384
BARGAINING, COLLECTIVE — *see* COLLECTIVE BARGAINING
BELIEF, FREEDOM OF, 27, 235, 264
BINDING NATURE OF CHAPTER 3 (*see also* JUDICIARY, NOT BOUND BY CHAPTER 3), 211–12
BIRTH CONTROL (*see also* ABORTION), 7n, 20, 243, 244, 348, 532
BLACKS (AMERICAN) — *see* MINORITY
BLASPHEMY, 281–2
*BONI MORES*, 92, 367
BRANDEIS BRIEF, 56, 643
BROADCASTING, FUNDAMENTAL RIGHTS AND, 102, 103n
*BUNDESTREUE*, GERMANY, 114–15
*BUNDESVERFASSUNGSGERICHT*, 73–85, 111, 113–15, 117–21
*BUND–LÄNDER* RELATIONSHIP, GERMANY, 72n, 113–14
BUREAUCRACY AND CHANGE, 58–9, 101
BUSING, 585–6

## C

CABINET, SOUTH AFRICAN, 163–4
CAPITAL CRIMES, EXTRADITION FOR, 186–7
CAPITAL PUNISHMENT (*see also* CRUEL,INHUMAN OR DEGRADING TREATMENT OR PUNISHMENT; LIMITATION OF RIGHTS; PUNISHMENT), 3–4, 10n, 174, 184, 187, 195, 215, 216, 218, 220, 224–8, 241, 434, 437–8
CAUTIONARY RULE, 432
CENSORSHIP, 271–3, 282, 284
CHECKS AND BALANCES, 71n, 601
CHILDREN (*see also* GUARDIANSHIP; ILLEGITIMATE CHILDREN; LEGITIMATE CHILDREN; PARENTS)
  best interests of, 535, 537, 538, 556–7
  care, 514–15
  Convention on the Rights of, 180, 189, 195, 230
  custody of, 533, 556–8
  detention, 238
  education, 243, 581
  labour, 10, 52, 439
  pornography and, 285
  privilege and, 431
  protection of, 175
  rights of, 222, 230, 533–9, 617, 622
  source of wealth, 531n
  United Nations Declaration on the Rights of, 229–30
CHILLING EFFECT DOCTRINE (*see also* SPEECH, FREEDOM OF), 315, 329–30, 332
CHURCH AND STATE, 593, 594
CIVIL PROCEDURE, 417–23
CLASS ACTIONS, 422
CLAW BACK CLAUSES, 189
CLEAR AND PRESENT DANGER, 270n, 278–80, 287, 300n
CODESA, 137, 139–40
CO-DETERMINATION, 93–4, 97, 364–5
COLLECTIVE BARGAINING, 355–7, 441n, 442, 444–8, 606

COLLECTIVE RIGHTS — *see* GROUP RIGHTS
COLLISION OF RIGHTS, 108–9, 213–14, 218, 238, 258–9, 264, 326–7, 371, 379, 451, 527, 588, 596
COMMERCIAL TRANSACTIONS, CONSTITUTIONALITY OF, 16n
COMMISSION ON GENDER EQUALITY, 160, 164, 571–2
COMMISSION ON THE REMUNERATION OF REPRESENTATIVES, 165, 169
COMMISSION ON THE RESTITUTION OF LAND RIGHTS, 160, 164
COMMON INTEREST — *see* PUBLIC INTEREST
COMMON LAW, 210, 443, 452–3
COMMUNAL LAND, 493
COMMUNISM, 293, 377
COMPANY, 29, 55, 360–1, 362n, 365n, 451
COMPELLING GOVERNMENT INTEREST (*see also* LIMITATION OF RIGHTS), 24, 202, 243–4, 255, 300, 343–5, 348–9
COMPENSATION (*see also* EXPROPRIATION), 38, 495–7
COMPROMISE, 105, 119–20, 389, 397, 399, 533, 636
CONCEPTION AS INCEPTION OF LIFE, 187, 229, 230–1
CONCURRENCE OF RIGHTS — *see* COLLISION OF RIGHTS
CONCURRENT POWERS (*see also* GERMAN *LÄNDER*), 113, 166
CONFESSION, 428–9
CONFIDENCE, VOTE OF (*see also* ACCOUNTABILITY), 71n
CONFLICTING RIGHTS/INTERESTS — *see* COLLISION OF RIGHTS
CONFLICT (*see also* ARMED CONFLICT), 117–20, 162
CONSCIENCE, FREEDOM OF, 27, 175, 596
CONSCIENTIOUS OBJECTION — *see* MILITARY SERVICE
CONSENSUS (*see also* THEORIES) 105n, 140–1, 164
CONSERVATIVE ACTIVISM — *see* JUDICIAL ACTIVISM
CONSTITUTION, 1993 — *see* SOUTH AFRICAN CONSTITUTION
CONSTITUTIONAL ASSEMBLY, SOUTH AFRICAN, 160, 167, 170
CONSTITUTIONAL COURT (*see also* BUNDESVERFASSUNGSGERICHT), 159, 160, 168
CONSTITUTIONAL DEMOCRACY — *see* DEMOCRACY
CONSTITUTIONAL INTERPRETATION (*see also* INTERPRETATION), 3, 122–3, 126, 450
CONSTITUTIONALISM (*see also* DEMOCRACY), 1–6, 7, 8n, 11, 16n, 19, 23, 36, 38, 39, 87, 121, 264, 362n, 462, 526, 632, 634,
CONSTITUTIONALITY (*see also* CONSTITUTIONAL REVIEW; JUDICIAL REVIEW)
  affirmative action, 8n
  capital punishment, 3–4, 10n
  commercial transactions, 16n
  contraception, 7n
  death penalty, 226–7
  equality and, 81–3,
  judicial decisions, 77n
  legislation, 7, 76, 82–5
  national basis and, 16n
  polygyny, 564
  presumption of, 84, 127–8
  rent control, 8n
  rules of evidence and, 571
  unconstitutionality, effect of, 81–5
CONSTITUTIONAL JURISPRUDENCE, THEORIES OF (*see also* THEORIES), 11–19
CONSTITUTIONAL PRINCIPLES (*see also* SOUTH AFRICAN CONSTITUTION), 72n, 129, 158–60, 170, 634
CONSTITUTIONAL REVIEW (*see also* JUDICAL REVIEW), 5–26, 28, 63, 64, 203–4, 207, 209–10
CONSTITUTIONAL STATE (*see also* RECHTSSTAAT), 158, 635, 649
CONSTITUTIONAL THEORIES — *see* THEORIES
CONSTITUTIONAL VALUES — *see* VALUES
CONSULTATION, IN/AFTER, 147, 148n, 154, 162, 163

CONTENT, ESSENTIAL — *see* ESSENTIAL CONTENT OF RIGHT
CONTRACEPTION — *see* BIRTH CONTROL
CONTRACT CLAUSE, UNITED STATES, 8n
CONTRACT, FREEDOM OF, 618, 620
CONVENTION AGAINST TORTURE AND CRUEL, INHUMAN OR DEGRADING PUNISHMENT, 181, 239, 240
CONVENTION FOR A DEMOCRATIC SOUTH AFRICA — *see* CODESA
CONVENTION ON CONSENT TO MARRIAGE, MINIMUM AGE FOR MARRIAGE AND REGISTRATION OF MARRIAGES, 189
CONVENTION ON THE ELIMINATION OF DISCRIMINATION AGAINST WOMEN, 179–80, 189, 195
CONVENTION ON THE NATIONALITY OF MARRIED WOMEN, 189
CONVENTION ON THE POLITICAL RIGHTS OF WOMEN, 189
CONVENTION ON THE RIGHTS OF THE CHILD, 180, 189, 195, 230
CO-OPERATIVE FEDERALISM (*see also* FEDERALISM), 115
CORE ELEMENTS — *see* ESSENTIAL CONTENT OF RIGHT
CORPORAL PUNISHMENT (*see also* PUNISHMENT), 117n, 186, 194–5, 241–2
CORPORATION — *see* COMPANY
COUNTERMAJORITARIAN DIFFICULTY — *see* COUNTERMAJORITARIAN DILEMMA
COUNTERMAJORITARIAN DILEMMA (*see also* MAJORITARIANISM), 6–19, 29–30, 62, 64
COURT — *see* JUDICIARY
COVENANT, RESTRICTIVE, 92n, 211
CRIME OF APARTHEID (*see also* APARTHEID), 174, 180–1
CRIMES AGAINST HUMANITY, 174
CRIMINAL LAW, 95–6, 224, 233, 368–9
CRIMINAL PROCEDURE, 401–17
CROSS-EXAMINATION, HEARSAY AND, 431
CRUEL, INHUMAN OR DEGRADING TREATMENT OR PUNISHMENT (*see also* CORPORAL PUNISHMENT; PUNISHMENT)
  capital punishment, 434
  death penalty and, 3–4, 228
  fines, 437
  imprisonment, 435
  International Covenant on Civil and Political Rights, 174
  meaning of, 241–2
  security of the person and, 233, 234, 238
  torture, 173, 174, 233–4
  Universal Declaration of Human Rights, 173
  whipping, 434–5
CRUEL AND UNUSUAL PUNISHMENT — *see* CRUEL, INHUMAN OR DEGRADING TREATMENT OR PUNISHMENT
CULTURAL LIFE — *see* CULTURE, RIGHT TO
CULTURE, RIGHT TO (*see also* EDUCATION; RELIGION, FREEDOM OF), 379, 464–5, 573, 574–80, 603
CUSTODY OF CHILDREN — *see* CHILDREN
CUSTOMARY INTERNATIONAL LAW (*see also* INTERNATIONAL LAW), 173–4, 190–2, 216, 217, 638
CUSTOMARY LAW, 128, 210, 452–3, 520–3, 531–2, 559, 636
CUSTOMARY MARRIAGES (*see also* MARRIAGE), 544–5, 558–71

# D

DEATH PENALTY — *see* CAPITAL PUNISHMENT
DECLARATION ON THE ELIMINATION OF DISCRIMINATION AGAINST WOMEN, 127, 547
DEFAMATION, 288–9
DELEGATION, *RECHTSSTAAT* PRINCIPLE AND, 95n
DEMOCRACY (*see also* FIGHTING DEMOCRACY; *STREITBARE DEMOKRATIE*)
  assembly, 295n, 308n, 317n, 318–19
  association, 338

INDEX 705

DEMOCRACY *(cont)*
  concept of, 6, 26, 36, 42
  constitutional, 62–4
  constitutionalism and, 5–6, 526, 634
  economic, India, 618
  equality and, 647
  European Convention on Human Rights, 647
  expressive conduct, 315
  family law and, 504
  free expression and, 269–71, 273
  fundamental rights and, 28, 73n, 601–2
  interests and, 119n
  judicial/constitutional review and, 6, 8, 9, 28, 30, 41–5, 58, 79, 112, 121, 122, 647
  judicial paternalism and, 44
  judicial supremacy, 12,
  legislation and, 115n
  limitation of rights and, 646
  majoritarianism and, 2, 9,
  multi-party, 372
  political parties and, 383, 341
  property and, 462
  *Rechtsstaat* principle and, 111n
  representative government and, 17n
  republican, 73
  separation of powers and, 89n
  social, 58, 70, 582–3
  South African Constitution and, 5
  values and, 26
DEMOCRACY, FIGHTING — *see* FIGHTING DEMOCRACY
DEMOCRACY, MILITANT — *see* STREITBARE DEMOKRATIE
DEMONSTRATION (*see also* ASSEMBLY, FREEDOM OF), 264, 292, 295–9, 308n, 357n
DEROGATION (*see also* LIMITATION OF RIGHTS), 175, 186, 188, 217–18, 224, 629n, 658–62
DETAINEES, 263, 658, 660–1
DETENTION (*see also* ARREST; DETAINEES), 234, 237–8, 401, 404, 407–10
DEVELOPING COUNTRIES, 600n, 602
DEVELOPMENT
  African Charter on Human and Peoples' Rights, 610
  dignity and, 604n
  personal, 317n, 319, 584, 605n
  provincial government, system of, 167
  right to, 182, 188, 603
DF MALAN AGREEMENT, 138
DIE, RIGHT TO (*see also* EUTHANASIA), 232, 233
DIGNITY, 70n, 85, 88, 95, 124, 218–19, 245, 252, 264, 379, 604n, 636
DIRECTIVE PRINCIPLES, 45, 47–8, 54, 89n, 204, 221, 451, 474–5, 478, 612–21, 624–6, 628,
DIRECTIVE PRINCIPLES OF STATE POLICY — *see* DIRECTIVE PRINCIPLES
DISADVANTAGED GROUPS (*see also* AFFIRMATIVE ACTION; MINORITY), 16, 118, 354–5, 379
DISCRETION, 95, 405, 411, 432, 549–53
DISCRIMINATION (*see also* EQUALITY; SUSPECT CLASSIFICATION)
  aliens, 21
  anti-discrimination law, 201–6
  anti-union, 447
  apartheid, 180–1
  child, 21, 180
  creed, 20
  culture and, 352, 354, 355, 574–5, 577, 580
  equality and, 20, 200

DISCRIMINATION *(cont)*
  ethnic, 23
  irrational, 12, 13
  labour, 523
  language and, 175, 186
  membership, 344–5, 346, 357–8, 373, 383, 384, 385
  non-residents, 21
  poor, the, 212
  private, 6n, 210, 494, 503, 521, 523
  public accomodation and, 22n
  racial, 18, 20, 23–4, 175, 178–9, 205
  religion, 6, 175
  sex/gender, 20, 175, 285, 524–72
  state of emergency, 663
  unfair, 208–10, 241, 552
  women and, 11, 21, 90n, 179–80, 189, 195, 432, 449
DISSOCIATION *(see also* ASSOCIATION, FREEDOM OF*)*, 344, 442
DISSOLUTION OF MARRIAGE, INEQUALITY ON, 547–58, 568–70
DIVORCE — *see* DISSOLUTION OF MARRIAGE
DOMESTIC VIOLENCE, 284, 510n, 545–6
DOMICILE, 545
*DRITTWIRKUNG (see also DURCHSTRAHLUNG*; HORIZONTAL APPLICATION; RADIATING EFFECT*)*, 70n, 85, 88n, 89–96, 363n, 367
DUE PROCESS,
  arrest and detention, 409, 410
  civil proceedings, 418
  clause, 23, 26, 256, 594
  equal protection and, 23
  evidence and, 424, 425
  expropriation, 496
  fair trial and, 405, 412
  Germany, 77n
  innocence, presumption of and, 427
  international travel and, 256
  legal representation and, 95n
  liberty and, 3
  life and, 3, 215
  limitation and, 224, 228–9, 236
  procedural, 233, 401–2
  property and, 3, 462, 464, 466, 473, 487
  religion and, 594, 595
  security of the person and, 233, 235
  substantive, 46, 219, 233
  United States, 26, 46, 95n, 124–5, 219, 233, 405, 418, 425, 462, 464, 466, 595
*DURCHSTRAHLUNG (see also DRITTWIRKUNG)*, 85, 88n
DUTIES ON STATE — *see* STATE DUTIES

**E**

EDUCATION 101, 177, 243, 379, 574, 576, 577–8, 580–92, 606, 609, 610, 612n, 613, 621, 622, 627
*EIUSDEM GENERIS* INTERPRETATION, 251–2
ELECTRONIC MEDIA, ACCESS TO, 307n
EMERGENCY, STATE OF — *see* STATE OF EMERGENCY
EMINENT DOMAIN, 465, 467
EMPLOYMENT *(see also* FAIR EMPLOYMENT PRACTICES; LABOUR PRACTICES*)*, 359, 446, 606, 609, 613, 621
EMPOWERMENT, 354–5, 385, 387–8, 513
ENDURING VALUES — *see* VALUES

ENVIRONMENT, 50–1, 100n, 182, 188, 215, 222, 239, 463, 470, 477–8, 496, 497, 500–1, 603, 613, 623, 627
EPILOGUE — see AFTER-AMBLE
EQUALITY (see also DISCRIMINATION; EQUAL PROTECTION CLAUSE)
  abortion and, 524–6
  administrative justice and, 388
  assembly, 22
  association and, 340–1, 345n, 354–5, 379, 384
  Canada, 32–5, 197, 577
  constitutionality and, 83n
  constitutional principles and, 159
  culture and, 579, 580
  democracy and, 647
  discrimination and, 20, 175, 200
  divorce and, 557–8
  due process clause and, 23
  education and, 585–7, 587, 589–92
  evidence and, 424
  expression and, 264
  fair trial, 405, 432–3
  formal vs real, 515–18
  freedom and, 87n, 127, 128, 129, 235, 265, 273, 584, 586, 634, 647
  Gender Commission and, 571–2
  judicial review and, 116, 117, 120
  judiciary and, 22
  labour, 445
  liberty and, 196
  life, 221, 231
  limitation, 33–5, 235, 265–273
  marriage and, 540–7
  minority and, 202n, 578, 586
  opportunity and, 100n, 120, 372, 376, 582, 606
  parental, 540, 556–8
  political access and, 22–6
  private law and, 90–2
  property and, 455, 460
  race and, 20n
  religion and 592
  sex/gender and, 515, 518–72
  similarly situated test and, 197
  South Africa, 4, 22, 129, 159, 431–2, 579, 636, 647
  substantive, 20n, 124
  United States, 198-200
  untouchability and, 52n
  women, 197, 231, 503, 561, 567, 587, 634
EQUAL PROTECTION CLAUSE, 4, 11–12, 13, 20, 22n, 23, 90–2, 256
EQUAL PROTECTION OF THE LAWS (see also EQUALITY), 405
ESSENTIAL CONTENT OF RIGHT (see also LIMITATION OF RIGHTS), 223, 227, 228, 229, 235, 242, 328, 407, 438, 494, 637, 642, 645, 650, 659n
ETHNIC MINORITY — see MINORITY
EUROPEAN COMMISSION OF HUMAN RIGHTS, 185
EUROPEAN CONVENTION ON HUMAN RIGHTS, 127, 130n, 184–7, 191, 194, 195, 201, 225–6, 227, 228–9, 234, 237, 242, 254, 266, 443, 447–8, 463–4, 494, 584, 587–8, 595, 596, 607, 609, 645n, 652–3
EUROPEAN COURT OF HUMAN RIGHTS, 130n, 185, 638,
EUROPEAN SOCIAL CHARTER (see also EUROPEAN CONVENTION ON HUMAN RIGHTS), 184, 447, 609–10, 611, 623

EUROPEAN COMMUNITY TREATY, 448–9
EUTHANASIA (*see also* DIE, RIGHT TO), 215, 216, 232
EVIDENCE, 79–80, 239, 404, 423–32, 570–1, 643
EXECUTIVE DEPUTY PRESIDENT, 162, 163
EXHAUSTION OF AVAILABLE REMEDIES (*see also* SUBSIDIARITY), 175
EXPRESSION, FREEDOM OF (*see also* EXPRESSIVE CONDUCT), 27, 175, 235, 264–91, 308, 315, 345–7, 379, 443
EXPRESSIVE CONDUCT, 300, 302, 303, 304, 305, 306, 308–16, 331
EXPROPRIATION (*see also* COMPENSATION), 38, 462, 464, 466, 472, 473, 495–7, 487
EXTRADITION, 186–7
EXTRA-JUDICIAL PROTECTION, 419–20
EXTRA-TEXTUAL LIMITATION OF RIGHTS, 85, 97

## F

FAIR EMPLOYMENT PRACTICES (*see also* LABOUR PRACTICES), 191, 451–2, 453, 613
FAIR LABOUR PRACTICES — *see* LABOUR PRACTICES
FAIR TRIAL (*see also* PROCEDURAL FAIRNESS), 174, 186, 264, 403, 405, 412–13, 432–3, 604, 661
FAIRNESS (*see also* PROCEDURAL FAIRNESS), 388, 389, 401, 403
FAMILY
  assistance to, Europe, 613
  bill of rights and, 611
  definition of, 14
  democracy and, 504
  *Grundrechte* and, 101–2
  husband, head of, 544–5
  importance of in Germany, 116n
  labour and, 445
  privacy and, 243–4, 520
  private law and, 91
  privilege and, 430
  protection of, 175, 606, 608, 610, 613n
  size of, 253
  state and, 508–15
  welfare payments in United States, 612n
  women and, 502, 504, 505
FAMILY LAW, TRANSFORMATION OF, 503–8
FEDERAL CONSTITUTIONAL COURT — *see* BUNDESVERFASSUNGSGERICHT
FEDERALISM, 70, 72, 75n, 113–15, 187
FEMINIST WRITING, 510, 515
FETUS, 12n, 229–32, 526–8,
FIGHTING DEMOCRACY (*see also* STREITBARE DEMOKRATIE), 70, 340
FIGHTING WORDS (*see also* SPEECH, FREEDOM OF), 274, 284, 300n, 302
FINAL CONSTITUTION, 158, 159, 169–70
FINANCE (*see also* FISCAL MATTERS), 169, 373–5, 548–9
FINANCIAL AND FISCAL COMMISSION, 165, 169
FINES (*see also* PUNISHMENT), 437
FIRST-GENERATION RIGHTS (*see also* NEGATIVE RIGHTS; SECOND-GENERATION RIGHTS; THIRD-GENERATION RIGHTS), 172, 177, 574, 579, 602–4, 607, 611, 613, 623
FISCAL MATTERS, 166–7
FOETUS — *see* FETUS
FOOTNOTE 4 (*US v Carolene Products*), 16–17, 202n
FOREIGN CASE LAW (*see also* INTERPRETATION), 265, 638, 651,
FRANCHISE — *see* VOTE, RIGHT TO
FREE AND DEMOCRATIC ORDER — *see* FREE AND DEMOCRATIC SOCIETY
FREE AND DEMOCRATIC SOCIETY (*see also* LIMITATION OF RIGHTS), 27–8, 127–30, 223, 235, 242, 260, 265, 273, 328, 369n, 376, 406–7, 427, 634–5, 637, 642, 645–6, 649
FREE AND OPEN DEMOCRATIC SOCIETY — *see* FREE AND DEMOCRATIC SOCIETY

FREEDOM AND SECURITY OF THE PERSON — *see* PERSON, FREEDOM AND SECURITY OF THE
FREEDOM CHARTER, 135, 481, 483, 622

**G**

GENDER, 208, 518, 519, 571
GENEVA CONVENTIONS, 1949 AND 1977 PROTOCOLS, 660, 661
GENOCIDE CONVENTION, 181, 225
GERMAN *LÄNDER*, 72n, 113–14, 614
GOVERNMENT, LOCAL — *see* LOCAL GOVERNMENT
GOVERNMENT OF NATIONAL UNITY, 162–4, 647
GOVERNMENT, STRUCTURES OF 160–8
GROOTE SCHUUR MINUTE, 137–8
GROUP RIGHTS, 182, 450, 580, 586
GROUPS, DISADVANTAGED — *see* DISADVANTAGED GROUPS
*GRUNDRECHTE*, 70n, 71, 73n, 85–110
*GRUNDRECHTSFÄHIGKEIT*, 71n
*GRUNDRECHTSMÜNDIGKEIT*, 71n
GUARDIANSHIP (*see also* CHILDREN), 511n, 533–9, 545

**H**

HATE SPEECH (*see also* SPEECH, FREEDOM OF), 266n, 269n, 274–8, 284, 298n
HEALTH, 177, 204, 496, 607, 609–10, 613, 617, 623
HEARSAY, 431
HELSINKI ACCORD, 173
HOME, INVIOLABILITY OF, 244, 245, 250–1
HOMOSEXUALS, 10n, 186, 244, 348–9
HORIZONTAL APPLICATION (*see also* *DRITTWIRKUNG*; *DURCHSTRAHLUNG*; RADIATING EFFECT), 128, 210–11, 265–72, 452, 494–5
HOUSING, 14, 621
HUMANITARIAN LAW, 191, 638, 661
HUMAN REALIZATION (*see also* PERSONAL DEVELOPMENT), 608, 611
HUMAN RIGHTS COMMISSION, 160, 164, 193, 420, 571
HUNGER, FREEDOM FROM, 623

**I**

ILLEGITIMATE CHILDREN (*see also* CHILDREN), 21, 83n, 91–2, 503n, 535, 539, 540n, 588
ILLITERACY, 616, 622,
IMPRISONMENT, 96, 237, 242, 435–6
INDEPENDENT BROADCASTING AUTHORITY, 152–5, 289–90
INDEPENDENT ELECTORAL COMMISSION, 148–50
INDEPENDENT MEDIA COMMISSION, 151–2
INDIGENOUS LAW (*see also* CUSTOMARY LAW), 168
INFORMATION, 243–4, 251, 264, 390
INQUISITORIAL SYSTEMS, 402, 416–17
*INSTITUTIONSGARANTIE*, 101
*INSTITUTSGARANTIE*, 101
INTEGRATION, 87n, 105–6, 110, 118–19, 120
*INTEGRATIONSLEHRE* — *see* INTEGRATION
INTENTIONALISM, STRICT (*see also* THEORIES), 11–12
INTENTION, LEGISLATIVE, 82n, 104–5, 108, 122, 617, 633n
INTENT, ORIGINAL — *see* ORIGINAL INTENT
INTER-AMERICAN SYSTEM, HUMAN RIGHTS, 187–8
INTERNATIONAL BILL OF RIGHTS, 172, 638n
INTERNATIONAL CONVENTION ON THE ELIMINATION OF ALL FORMS OF RACIAL DISCRIMINATION, 178–9, 275, 463, 576
INTERNATIONAL CONVENTION ON THE SUPPRESSION AND PUNISHMENT OF THE CRIME OF APARTHEID, 180–1

INTERNATIONAL COVENANT ON CIVIL AND POLITICAL RIGHTS, 174–7, 189–91, 195, 201, 216–17, 224–5, 226–7, 229, 234, 237, 242, 254, 266, 275, 434, 447, 576, 578, 593, 607–8, 645, 653, 654n
INTERNATIONAL COVENANT ON ECONOMIC, SOCIAL AND CULTURAL RIGHTS, 177–8, 447, 575, 583–4, 606, 607–8
INTERNATIONAL HUMAN RIGHTS LAW, 178–89, 216–18, 638–9
INTERNATIONAL LABOUR CONVENTION, 609
INTERNATIONAL LABOUR ORGANIZATION CONVENTION ON INDIGENOUS AND TRIBAL POPULATIONS, 575–6
INTERNATIONAL LABOUR ORGANIZATION STANDARDS, INDUSTRIAL RELATIONS, 183, 191, 446–7, 660
INTERNATIONAL LAW (*see also* CUSTOMARY INTERNATIONAL LAW; INTERNATIONAL HUMAN RIGHTS LAW)
  association and, 368, 369n
  bill of rights interpretation and, 193, 194
  *Bundesverfassungsgericht* and, 75
  derogation and, 658
  directive principles and, 615
  emergency and, 651–2
  expression and, 265
  family law and, 521
  incorporation of, 637
  interpretation and, 265
  labour and, 446–9
  liberty and, 239
  life and, 214, 216, 222
  limitation and, 254, 265
  privacy and, 254
  property and, 463–4
  punishment and, 433
  second generation rights and, 606–11
  security of the person, 233–4
  sources, 195
  South Africa and, 127, 627, 637
INTERPRETATION
  after-amble/schedules, 204, 207
  clause, Canada 27, 578
  constitutional, 3, 84n, 122–3, 126, 243n, 441, 450, 480n, 499
  constitutional principles, 129
  context and, 30
  culture and, 579
  democratic-functional, 317n
  directive principles and, 617, 618, 619, 620
  *eiusdem generis*, 251–2
  equality and, 431–2
  expression, 264, 265
  functional method, 85
  fundamental rights and, 94n, 98n, 105, 192, 611, 617, 619, 620
  generous/broad/liberal approach, 30–1, 34–5, 47–51, 77, 78n, 243n, 251–2, 253, 261
  German Basic Law, 103–20
  history and, 13, 30–1
  institutional method, 85
  intention, 15
  International Covenant on Economic, Social and Cultural Rights, 584
  international law and, 193, 194, 637–9
  judicial role, 3, 17, 27, 260–2
  language and, 30

INTERPRETATION *(cont)*
  life and liberty, 48–50, 51
  literalism, 122, 126, 243n
  limitation clause, 640, 642–3
  minority rights and, 577
  movement and, 260–2
  narrow/restrictive approach, 6, 33–5, 78n, 111–5, 640, 642
  powers concurrent, 113
  preamble, 129
  property and, 480n, 490, 493, 499
  purposive, 30–1, 32–5, 124, 261, 431–2
  schedules/after-amble, 204, 207
  social charter and, 611
  social justice, 47–8, 60
  South Africa, 127–30, 204n, 207, 264, 265, 328–9, 453, 560, 579, 633–4
  standing and, 78n
  subjective choice, 26
  teleological, 80n
  textual, 4, 16n
  theories, 7, 14–5, 17n, 103–120, 127–30
INTERPRETATION CLAUSE, 27
INTERROGATION, 186, 401, 403, 404
INVERSE CONDEMNATION *(see also* PROPERTY), 499
*IUS IN BELLO*, 638

## J

JEHOVA'S WITNESSES, 595–6
JUDGES — *see* JUDICIARY
JUDICIAL ACTIVISM *(see also* JUDICIAL RESTRAINT), 7, 8, 17n, 29n, 30, 45–6
JUDICIAL DEFERENCE, 33, 58, 63
JUDICIAL FACT-FINDING, 78–9
JUDICIAL RESTRAINT *(see also* JUDICIAL ACTIVISM), 29n, 112n, 113n, 115
JUDICIAL REVIEW *(see also* CONSTITUTIONAL REVIEW)
  *abstrakte Normenkontrolle*, 76–7
  administrative justice and, 390, 399
  American experience, value for South Africa, 19, 26
  constitutionalism and, 121
  constitutional review distinguished, 64
  democracy and, 6, 8, 9, 26, 27, 28, 29, 30, 36, 41–5, 58, 79, 110n, 121, 122, 647
  detention and, 661
  emergency and, 656–8, 661
  functional/process approach to, 115–20
  German history of, 65, 67–9
  judges' own views 25, 26
  *konkrete Normenkontrolle*, 76
  legislation and, 5–6, 22
  majoritarianism and, 22
  political consensus and, 111
  political process theory of, 16–19
  public interest litigation as, 60
  reasonableness and, 29
  *Rechtsstaat* principle and, 83n
  social justice and, 58
  substantive, 64
JUDICIAL SCRUTINY — *see* SCRUTINY, DOCTRINE OF
JUDICIAL SERVICE COMMISSION, 168

JUDICIARY
   accountability, 6, 7, 9, 12, 14
   *Bundesverfassungsgericht*, 73–4
   constitutional interpretation and, 3
   constitutional principles and, 159
   countermajoritarian dilemma and, 8–9
   democratic role of, 16
   freedom and equality and, 22, 127, 128
   guardian of the constitution, 122, 283
   impartiality, 95
   independence of, 159, 376
   language and, 2
   majoritarianism and, 28
   omitted from s 7(1), 128n, 210
   other branches of government and, 8
   own views, 25, 26
   politicization of, 111
   promoting core values, 22
   public interest law/litigation and, 58–9
   second generation rights and, 606–7
   South Africa Constitution, 159, 168
   value preferences, 21
JUDICIARY, NOT BOUND BY CHAPTER 3 (*see also* BINDING NATURE OF CHAPTER 3), 128n, 210, 522
JURISDICTION DURING STATE OF EMERGENCY, 658
JURISTIC PERSONS, 71n, 243, 252–3, 291, 319n, 363n
*JUS COGENS*, 217–18, 240
JUSTICE (*see also* ADMINISTRATIVE JUSTICE; PROCEDURAL JUSTICE; SOCIAL JUSTICE), 55, 72n, 76n, 78n, 412, 415, 417–19, 432
JUSTICIABILITY (*see also* JUDICIAL REVIEW), 177, 606–7, 611, 623, 624
JUSTIFIABLE, REQUIREMENT FOR LIMITATION — *see* LIMITATION OF RIGHTS

### K

*KOALITIONSFREIHEIT*, 93, 359
*KOMPETENZ-KOMPETENZ*, 121
*KONKRETE NORMENKONTROLLE*, 76

### L

LABOUR PRACTICES, 191, 451–2, 523
LABOUR LAW/RIGHTS (*see also* ASSOCIATION, FREEDOM OF; ASSOCIATIONS), 10, 51–2, 93–4, 102, 355–7, 366n, 439–54, 456–7
LAND, 160, 164, 487–8, 497, 499–500, 636
LAND, COMMUNAL — *see* COMMUNAL LAND
LAND-USE PLANNING, 8n, 470, 497
LAND-USE REGULATION — *see* LAND-USE PLANNING
*LÄNDER*, GERMAN — *see* GERMAN *LÄNDER*
LANGUAGE, 2, 3, 30, 162, 186, 379, 576–9, 584–5, 591
LAW OF GENERAL APPLICATION (*see also* LIMITATION OF RIGHTS), 223, 224, 235, 242, 260, 265, 406, 408, 499, 642, 645
LEGALITY, 388
LEGAL REPRESENTATION, RIGHT TO, 49, 78, 95, 405, 414–15, 420, 604
LEGISLATION, 7, 20n, 82–5, 114, 116n, 128, 161–2, 236, 323–4, 340–1
LEGISLATIVE INTENTION — *see* INTENTION, LEGISLATIVE
LEGITIMACY, 45–6, 115, 122n
LEGITIMATE CHILDREN (*see also* CHILDREN), 83n, 534–5, 539, 545
LEGITIMATE EXPECTATION, 399
*LEISTUNGSRECHTE*, 100
LEVEL OF SCRUTINY — *see* SCRUTINY, DOCTRINE OF

INDEX 713

LIBERTY (*see also* LIFE; PROPERTY), 3, 48–51, 174, 196, 233, 236, 237n, 238–9, 243, 343, 457, 464, 466
LIFE (*see also* CONCEPTION AS INCEPTION OF LIFE; LIBERTY; PROPERTY), 3, 48–51, 174, 187, 204, 212–33, 240, 461–6, 526–8, 605, 660
LIFE OF THE NATION, EMERGENCY, 653,
LIMITATION OF RIGHTS (*see also* BALANCING OF INTERESTS; COMPELLING GOVERNMENT INTEREST; DEROGATION; ESSENTIAL CONTENT OF RIGHT; FREE AND DEMOCRATIC SOCIETY; LAW OF GENERAL APPLICATION; NECESSARY; PROPORTIONALITY; PUBLIC INTEREST; REASONABLE)
  administrative justice, 399
  assembly and, 301–3, 306, 309–10, 313, 315–16, 323–34, 329, 379n, 380, 381–6
  association, 356, 368–71
  Canada, 27, 30, 33–5, 70n, 126, 260, 309–10, 313, 315–16, 329, 356, 642, 643n
  contract and, 618
  democracy and, 646
  derogation distinguished, 640, 659
  differences, United States, Canada, Germany, 70n
  directive principles and, 617
  emergency and, 629
  equality and, 33–5, 209
  European Convention of Human Rights, 596
  expression and, 264, 265, 271–4, 285, 290n, 300n
  extra-textual, 25, 97
  freedom and security of the person, 235–6, 237
  Germany, 25, 70, 97, 102n, 107–8, 116, 250–1, 257, 323–7, 368–71
  immanent, Germany, 323n, 325, 368
  International Covenant on Civil and Political Rights, 175, 223
  Ireland, 618
  justifiable, demonstrably, 223, 645–6
  labour rights, 93, 451, 452–3
  life and, 218, 222–33
  military service and, 596
  movement, 254–5, 257, 259–60
  onus on state, 637, 643, 644
  privacy, 242, 243, 250–1, 253–4
  procedural rights, 406–7, 408, 437
  property, 72n, 471, 493–4, 497–9
  reasonableness and, 645–6, 648–9
  religion and, 596
  restrictively interpreted, 640, 642
  South Africa, 4, 126, 129–30, 209, 235–6, 242, 253–5, 259–60, 265, 271–4, 327–34, 406–7, 408, 437, 451, 452–3, 629–663
  speech and, 17
  sufficient importance, 28, 646
  suspension distinguished, 652
  United States, 24, 70n, 243, 255–6, 257, 290n, 300n, 301–3, 306, 641n
LINGUISTIC MINORITY — *see* MINORITY
*LOBOLO*, 565–6
LOCAL GOVERNMENT, 155–6, 167
LOCAL GOVERNMENT NEGOTIATING FORUM, 156
LOCK-OUT, 446, 453
*LOCUS STANDI IN IUDICIO* — *see* STANDING

# M

MAINTENANCE, 506n, 553–5, 570
MAJORITARIANISM (*see also* COUNTERMAJORITARIAN DILEMMA) 1, 7, 10, 19, 22, 28, 43
MAJORITY/MINORITY (*see also* MINORITY), 16, 112, 119, 339n, 376, 577–8
MARITAL POWER, 510n, 520n, 540–4

MARITAL PRIVACY (*see also* PRIVACY), 7n, 348
MARITAL RAPE, 510n, 545–6
MARITAL VIOLENCE (*see also* DOMESTIC VIOLENCE), 445–6
MARRIAGE (*see also* DISSOLUTION OF MARRIAGE), 101–2, 116n, 242-4, 253, 445, 506–8, 520, 540–7, 558–71
MARTIAL LAW, 630, 659
MEANING, ORIGINAL — *see* THEORIES
MEDIA, FREEDOM OF (*see also* PRESS, FREEDOM OF), 27, 287–90
MEMBERSHIP PRACTICES, ASSOCIATIONS, 340–1, 346–7, 357–8, 361, 364, 369, 373, 383–5
MILITANT DEMOCRACY — *see* STREITBARE DEMOKRATIE
MILITARY SERVICE, 596
MINISTERIAL RESPONSIBILITY (*see also* ACCOUNTABILITY), 71n
MINORITY (*see also* MAJORITY/MINORITY)
  assembly and, 318
  association and, 339n
  blacks, United States, 18
  Canada, 577–8
  culture and, 576, 577–8
  education, 578
  equality and, 202n, 578, 586
  ethnic, 17
  expression and, 274
  India, 577
  International Covenant on Civil and Political Rights, 175, 177
  legitimate power and, 13
  linguistic, 577–8, 586
  national, 16n
  majority and, 13, 16, 112, 118, 119, 120, 578
  private schools for, 578
  protection of, 16, 17, 18
  public schools for, 578
  racial, 16n, 17, 586
  religion, 16n, 17
  third generation rights and, 182n
  tribal, 43n
MORAL VALUES — *see* VALUES
MORALITY, 5–6, 15, 125, 282–6
MOTHER (*see also* WOMEN), 231, 243–4
MOVEMENT, FREEDOM OF, 22, 175, 222, 254–63, 326
MULTI-PARTY NEGOTIATING PROCESS, 5, 132, 137, 140–2, 219–20 478, 486–7
MUSLIM MARRIAGES (*see also* MARRIAGE, CUSTOMARY MARRIAGES), 544–5, 558–71

## N

*NASCITURUS* RULE, 526n
NATIONAL ASSEMBLY, 160–1
NATIONAL DEFENCE FORCE, 165
NATIONAL DEFENCE, STATE OF, 54, 660n
NATIONAL EXECUTIVE, SOUTH AFRICA, 162–4
NATIONAL PEACE ACCORD, 138, 294–5
NATIONAL UNITY AND RECONCILIATION, 129, 158, 634, 636
NATURAL JUSTICE (*see also* JUSTICE), 31, 272, 399
NATURAL LAW, 15, 19, 71, 87n
NECESSARY, REQUIREMENT FOR LIMITATION, 223, 235, 245, 255, 265, 301, 328, 332–3, 368, 381–2, 408, 437, 642, 644, 648–50
NEGATIVE RIGHTS (*see also* ABWEHRRECHTE), 85–7, 124–6, 177, 198, 257n, 462, 602, 604–5
NEGATIVE STATE ACTION/DUTY (*see also* STATE ACTION), 600, 605, 622, 627
NEW LEGAL ORDER, SOUTH AFRICAN, 631–3

NEW PROPERTY (*see also* PROPERTY), 457–8, 463, 465–6, 469, 480, 490–3, 548
NEW RIGHTS — *see* UNENUMERATED RIGHTS
NON-RESIDENTS, DISCRIMINATION, 21
*NULLA POENA SINE LEGE*, 95, 174, 225, 635

## O

*OBITER DICTA*, GERMANY, 85
OBSCENITY, 282–6
OMBUDSMAN, 57, 119, 390
ONUS OF PROOF, 27–8, 411, 427–8, 637, 643–4
OPEN AND DEMOCRATIC SOCIETY (*see also* FREE AND DEMOCRATIC SOCIETY), 127–9
OPINION, FREEDOM OF, 27, 235, 264, 317n
OPPOSITION, RIGHT TO FORM, 376
ORGANIZATION OF AMERICAN STATES, CHARTER OF, 187
ORGANIZE, RIGHT TO, 446
ORIGINAL INTENT (*see also* THEORIES), 3, 11–14, 31, 41–2, 123
ORIGINALISM — *see* ORIGINAL INTENT
OUSTER CLAUSES, 399
OWNERSHIP (*see also* PRIVATE PROPERTY), 468, 471, 492–3

## P

*PACTUM SUBJECTIONIS*, 601
*PACTUM UNIONIS*, 601
PARENTS (*see also* CHILDREN), 25, 92n, 533–40, 556–8, 581, 583, 587–8
PARIS MINIMUM STANDARDS OF HUMAN RIGHTS NORMS IN A STATE OF EMERGENCY (*see also* STATE OF EMERGENCY), 652
PARLIAMENTARY SYSTEM, SOUTH AFRICA, 160
PARTIES, POLITICAL — *see* POLITICAL PARTIES
PARTY STATE, 72
PATRIARCHY, 561
PEOPLES, MEANING OF, 188
PAY, EQUAL, 449, 607–8, 610–11, 622
PERSON, FREEDOM AND SECURITY OF THE, 174, 233–42, 263
PERSONAL DEVELOPMENT, 317n, 319, 584, 605n
PERSONAL RIGHTS, 212–63
PIRATE STATIONS, 290n
PLANNING LAWS, 259, 470, 496–7
PLURALISM, 110–11, 351, 504
POINTING-OUT, 429
POLICE POWER (*see also* EMINENT DOMAIN), 466–7, 497–8
POLITICAL OFFENCES, 137
POLITICAL PARTIES, 72–3, 101, 120, 326, 360, 371–6, 382–4
POLITICAL PROCESS THEORY (*see also* THEORIES), 16–19
POLITICAL QUESTION DOCTRINE, 112
POLYGAMY, 253, 593–4
POLYGYNY, 544, 558, 561–5
POOR, POSITION OF THE, 21, 600, 616
PORNOGRAPHY, 244, 269, 282–6
POSITIVE RIGHTS (*see also* NEGATIVE RIGHTS), 125n, 526, 605n,
POSITIVISM, 71n, 574
POST-AMBLE — *see* AFTER-AMBLE
POWER-SHARING, 590
PRACTICAL CONCORDANCE (*see also* INTERPRETATION), 106, 108–10
PREAMBLE, 47, 54, 129, 158, 612, 629–30
PRE-CONSTITUTIONAL RIGHTS, 71n, 86
PREROGATIVE POWERS, 163, 630, 632, 654, 656
PRESIDENT, THE, 162–3

PRESS, FREEDOM OF (*see also* MEDIA), 26–7, 102–3, 287–90
PRESSING AND SUBSTANTIAL CONCERNS, 130
PRETORIA MINUTE, 138
PRINCIPLES, CONSTITUTIONAL — *see* CONSTITUTIONAL PRINCIPLES
PRISONERS, 98, 183–4, 186, 435, 437–8, 595
PRIVACY, 7n, 20, 29, 175, 242–54, 264, 348–50, 379, 524
PRIVATE DISCRIMINATION (*see also* DISCRIMINATION), 210, 501, 521, 523, 594
PRIVATE LAW
   association and, 367, 374n
   *Drittwirkung* and, 90–2, 94n
   fundamental rights and, 52
   movement and, 259
   public interest law/litigation, 52–5
   public law distinction, 52, 502, 510
   right to life and, 231
PRIVATE PROPERTY (*see also* PROPERTY), 306–7, 455, 469
PRIVATE/PUBLIC DISTINCTION, 52, 502, 508–15
PRIVATE SCHOOLS, 101, 578
PRIVILEGE, 428–31, 571
PROCEDURAL FAIRNESS, 95, 399, 401, 403, 420–1, 633n
PROCEDURAL JUSTICE, 30–2
PROCEDURAL RIGHTS, 55, 78–80, 95–6, 224, 233, 369–70, 375, 401–38, 603
PROCLAMATION OF TEHERAN, 173
PROPERTY (*see also* LIFE; LIBERTY; NEW PROPERTY), 3, 26, 36–40, 45, 72n, 90, 93–4, 101, 175, 184, 187, 213, 259, 306–7, 360–1, 371, 379, 385, 401, 403, 455–500, 612
PROPORTIONALITY (*see also* LIMITATION OF RIGHTS), 27–8, 30, 70n, 79n, 92, 96, 108–9, 116, 118, 121, 223, 228, 250, 260, 299, 312n, 316n, 321, 323–4, 332, 356, 363, 368, 433, 648–9, 654, 657, 661–3, 654
PROPORTIONAL REPRESENTATION, 160
PROSECUTION, 402, 404–5, 411–12
PROVINCIAL GOVERNMENT, 165–7, 592
PROVINCIAL PUBLIC PROTECTORS, 160
PUBLIC FORUM DOCTRINE, 300–6, 309–10, 320, 329
PUBLIC FUNCTION DOCTRINE, 306
PUBLIC HOLIDAYS, PAID, 609
PUBLIC INDECENCY, 282–3
PUBLIC INTEREST LAW/LITIGATION, 35, 41, 45, 48–61
PUBLIC INTEREST, THE (*see also* LIMITATION OF RIGHTS), 46–7, 54–5, 102, 108, 119n, 468, 618
PUBLIC INTERNATIONAL LAW — *see* INTERNATIONAL LAW
PUBLIC/PRIVATE DISTINCTION — *see* PRIVATE/PUBLIC DISTINCTION
PUBLIC PROTECTOR, 160, 164, 390, 395–7, 399, 419–20
PUBLIC SAFETY/SECURITY, 324–5, 596
PUBLIC SERVANT, 98, 357n, 375n
PUBLIC SERVICE COMMISSION, 165
PUBLIC SERVICES, ACCESS TO, 613
PUBLIC VIOLENCE, 293
PUNISHMENT (*see also* CORPORAL PUNISHMENT; CRUEL, INHUMAN OR DEGRADING TREATMENT OR PUNISHMENT), 434–5
PURPOSIVE APPROACH/INTERPRETATION (*see also* INTERPRETATION), 24, 30–5, 63, 122–8, 261, 431–2, 633

# R

RACE/RACISM (*see also* DISCRIMINATION; EQUALITY), 16–17, 20n, 175, 179, 205, 268, 274–8, 293n, 573, 586
RADIATING EFFECT (*see also* DRITTWIRKUNG), 84n, 89–96
RAPE, 283–4, 537n, 539n,

INDEX 717

REASONABLE, REQUIREMENT FOR LIMITATION (*see also* LIMITATION OF RIGHTS), 27, 29, 223, 235, 242, 260, 265, 273, 328, 332–3, 381–2, 388–9, 406–7, 642, 645–6, 648–50
REASONABLENESS, 29, 388, 645–6, 648–50
REASONS, 399, 473
*RECHTSSTAAT*, 68n, 70, 72, 81n, 83n, 86, 89n, 95, 107, 116–17 121, 316n, 362, 365n, 635
RECONCILIATION — *see* NATIONAL UNITY AND RECONCILIATION; RECONSTRUCTION
RECONSTRUCTION, 129, 619–20
RECORD OF UNDERSTANDING, 140
REFUGEES, 215
RELATION TO OTHER RIGHTS — *see* COLLISION OF RIGHTS
RELIGION, FREEDOM OF, 6, 16–17, 26–7, 175, 235, 264, 281–2, 327n, 351, 359, 379, 384–5, 464–5, 573–4, 592–7
RELIGIOUS MINORITY — *see* MINORITY
REPRESENTATION, PROPORTIONAL — *see* PROPORTIONAL REPRESENTATION
REPRESENTATIVE DEMOCRACY — *see* DEMOCRACY
REPRODUCTIVE FREEDOM/RIGHT/AUTONOMY (*see also* WOMEN), 12n, 231, 524, 526, 528, 532, 546–7
RESERVE BANK, 164, 169
RESTITUTION, LAND, 487–8, 497, 636
RESTRAINT, JUDICIAL — *see* JUDICIAL RESTRAINT
RESTRUCTURING, 479, 636
REVIEW, JUDICIAL — *see* JUDICIAL REVIEW
RIGHT TO STRIKE — *see* STRIKE, RIGHT TO
RIGHTS, COLLISION OF — *see* COLLISION OF RIGHTS
RIGHTS, PRE-CONSTITUTIONAL — *see* PRE-CONSTITUTIONAL RIGHTS
RIGHTS, SUBSTANTIVE — *see* SUBSTANTIVE RIGHTS
RIGHTS, UNENUMERATED — *see* UNENUMERATED RIGHTS
RULE OF LAW, 1, 56, 134, 376

**S**

*SALUS REIPUBLICAE SUPREMA LEX*, 630, 651
SCHEDULES, WEIGHT OF, 128–9,
SCIENCE (*see also* ARTS AND SCIENCE), 103, 286–7, 575
SCRUTINY, DOCTRINE OF (*see also* SCRUTINY, LEVELS OF; SCRUTINY, STRICT), 23, 123
SCRUTINY, LEVELS OF, 23–4, 70n, 115–16, 203, 333n, 368, 381–2, 648
SCRUTINY, STRICT, 16n, 24, 120, 123, 202–3, 242, 243, 256n, 299, 435–6, 441n, 648
SEARCH, FREEDOM FROM, 26, 242, 250, 401, 403, 406–7
SECESSION, 189
SECOND-GENERATION RIGHTS, 72, 172, 177, 184, 187–8, 222, 270, 574, 599–628
SECURITY OF THE PERSON — *see* PERSON, FREEDOM AND SECURITY OF THE
SEIZURE (*see also* SEARCH, FREEDOM FROM), 26, 242, 403, 406–7
SELF-DETERMINATION, 159–60, 174, 182, 188, 364, 376, 379, 603
SELF-INCRIMINATION, 404, 428–30
SENATE, THE, 161
SEPARATE BUT EQUAL, 9n, 585, 589
SEPARATE DEVELOPMENT — *see* APARTHEID
SEPARATION OF POWERS, 49n, 58–61, 71, 79, 84n, 103–4, 159, 222, 224, 316n, 376, 601, 607, 613n, 617, 628, 631–2,
SERVITUDE, SLAVERY — *see* SLAVERY, SERVITUDE
SEX AND GENDER EQUALITY, 285, 515, 518–72
SEX EDUCATION, 588
SEX/GENDER, 518n, 519, 571
SEXUAL HARM, 283–4
SEXUALLY EXPLICIT MATERIAL, 285–6
SEXUALLY TRANSMITTED DISEASES, 588
SEXUAL ORIENTATION, 20
SHELTER, RIGHT TO, 623

SIGNIFICANT/SUBSTANTIAL GOVERNMENT INTEREST (*see also* COMPELLING STATE INTEREST), 24, 301
SILENCE, RIGHT TO, 404–5, 428–30
SIMILARLY SITUATED TEST, 32, 197
SIRACUSA PRINCIPLES, 644–5, 652, 654
SLAVERY, SERVITUDE, 164
SOCIAL AND ECONOMIC RIGHTS — *see* SECOND-GENERATION RIGHTS
SOCIAL AND POLITICAL JUSTICE — *see* SOCIAL JUSTICE
SOCIAL CHARTER, EUROPEAN — *see* EUROPEAN SOCIAL CHARTER
SOCIAL DEMOCRACY/STATE (*see also* RECHTSSTAAT), 47, 72, 93–4, 95n, 97, 99, 100n, 112n, 582–3
SOCIAL ENGINEERING, 36–7
SOCIAL JUSTICE, 46–8, 58, 60, 124, 460, 615,
SOCIAL RIGHTS (*see also* SECOND-GENERATION RIGHTS), 607n, 610
SOCIAL SECURITY, 177, 554, 556, 607–9
SOCIAL STATE — *see* SOCIAL DEMOCRACY/STATE
SOCIAL TRANSFORMATION, INDIA, 35–64
SODOMY, 10n, 253
SOLEMN PACT, 159
SOUTH AFRICAN POLICE SERVICE, 165
SOVEREIGNTY, 42, 376, 657
*SOZIALSTAATPRINZIP* (*see also* SOCIAL DEMOCRACY/STATE), 445
*SOZIALSTAAT* — *see* SOCIAL DEMOCRACY/STATE
SPECIAL RELATIONSHIPS, GERMANY, 98–9, 325
SPEECH, FREEDOM OF, 17, 22, 26, 108, 179, 264, 274–8, 284, 290–1, 299–300, 302n, 303, 308, 326, 345
STANDARD MINIMUM RULES FOR THE TREATMENT OF OFFENDERS (*see also* PRISONERS), 183–4, 191
STANDING, 20, 55–6, 76n, 78n, 389, 399, 421–3, 661
*STARE DECISIS*, 76n, 80
STATE — *see* GOVERNMENT
STATE ACTION, 46, 53n, 54, 346–7, 358, 605, 622, 627
STATE DUTIES, 175, 184–5, 600, 602, 606, 608, 624
STATE OF EMERGENCY, 40–1, 73, 175, 186, 215, 224, 235, 378, 410, 641, 650–60
STATE OF WAR, 654
STATE SECURITY, 278–80, 282, 653–4
STERILIZATION, 525, 547
*STREITBARE DEMOKRATIE*, 273, 276n, 375–6, 646
STRICT SCRUTINY — *see* SCRUTINY, DOCTRINE OF
STRIKE, RIGHT TO, 355, 442, 444–5, 448, 454
SUBSIDIARITY, 77n
SUBSTANTIVE RIGHTS, 603
SUFFICIENT IMPORTANCE — *see* LIMITATION OF RIGHTS
SUFFICIENT GOVERNMENT INTEREST (*see also* COMPELLING GOVERNMENT INTEREST; SIGNIFICANT/SUBSTANTIAL GOVERNMENT INTEREST; PROPORTIONALITY), 28n
SUSPECT CLASSIFICATION (*see also* DISCRIMINATION; SCRUTINY, DOCTRINE OF), 23–4, 202
SUSPENSION (*see also* DEROGATION), 224, 235, 237, 242, 255, 631, 652

## T

TAKING, TAKINGS (*see also* EXPROPRIATION), 8n, 26, 462, 466–7, 496, 499
TAX, 90n, 259, 375
*TEILHABERECHTE*, 100
THEORIES OF INTERPRETATION, 2, 7, 11–19, 24, 25, 103–20, 127–30
THEORIES, PROPERTY, 455–61
THEORY OF SOCIETY, 117–18
THIRD-GENERATION RIGHTS, 182, 188, 603
THOUGHT, FREEDOM OF, 27, 175
TORTURE, 173–4, 181–2, 189, 195, 222, 228, 233, 234, 238, 239-41

INDEX 719

TRADE UNIONS, 177, 326, 359, 362n, 442, 444–5, 613, 622
TRADITIONAL AUTHORITIES/LEADERS, 159, 165, 167–8, 559
TRANSACTIONS, COMMERCIAL — see COMMERCIAL TRANSACTIONS
TRANSITIONAL EXECUTIVE COUNCIL, 139n, 143–7
TRANSITIONAL PROVISIONS, 169
TRAVEL — see MOVEMENT, FREEDOM OF
TREATIES, 75, 192, 194

## U

UNCONSTITUTIONALITY — see CONSTITUTIONALITY
UNENUMERATED RIGHTS, 20, 125, 127, 612, 343, 617–18, 620
UNFAIR LABOUR PRACTICES — see LABOUR PRACTICES
UNITED NATIONS CHARTER, 171–2, 190
UNITED NATIONS COMMISSION ON HUMAN RIGHTS, 182
UNITY OF THE CONSTITUTION, GERMANY, 85, 105, 106, 110
UNIVERSAL DECLARATION OF HUMAN RIGHTS, 172–4, 190, 216, 233, 242, 254, 266, 447, 463, 575, 583, 593, 601, 607

## V

VAGUE NORMS/PROVISIONS, 20, 110, 112n, 117
VAGUENESS AND OVERBREADTH (see also CHILLING EFFECT DOCTRINE), 272n, 330
VALUES, 1–2, 4–6, 8, 9n, 12, 17–19, 21–2, 25–6, 30, 44, 63n, 64, 67n, 70, 74, 85, 87–9, 17, 120n, 121, 127, 272–3, 348, 427, 433, 610, 633–7
*VEREINIGUNGSFREIHEIT*, 93
*VERFASSUNGSBESCHWERDE*, 65–6, 77
*VERFASSUNGSDURCHBRECHUNG*, 68
*VERFASSUNGSKONFORME AUSLEGUNG*, 83–4
*VERFASSUNGSORGANTREUE*, 83
*VOLKSGEIST*, 9
VOLKSTAAT COUNCIL, 165, 168
VOTE, RIGHT TO, 19, 22, 155, 175, 604

## W

WAGE, 51, 177, 204, 439, 606, 607, 621–2
WAR CRIMES, 174
WAR PROPAGANDA, 266n
WAR, STATE OF — see STATE OF WAR
*WECHSELWIRKUNG*, 109–10
WELFARE, 72n, 450, 612n, 621
*WESENSGEHALT* (see also ESSENTIAL CONTENT OF RIGHT), 107
WESTMINSTER SYSTEM, 2, 22, 26–7, 126, 131
WHIPPING (see also PUNISHMENT), 242, 434–5, 438
WIFE, 566, 568
WOMEN (see also EQUALITY, MOTHER, SEX/GENDER, WIFE)
   affirmative action, 179
   capital punishment, 174, 225, 229
   discrimination/equality, 11, 21, 90n, 197, 205, 231, 432, 503, 524, 546–7, 561, 587, 634,
   divorce inequality, 568–9
   *Drittwirkung*, 91
   educational equality, 587
   empowerment, 354, 513
   international instruments and, 179–80, 189, 195
   labour, 440
   man/woman difference, 516–18
   objectivication of, 283–4, 565
   pay discrimination, 449
   pornography and, 283–5
   public/private dichotomy, 511–13

WOMEN *(cont)*
  reproductive freedom/right, 12n, 231
  role in society and family, 502, 504, 505
  special needs, 636
  special rights, 517–19
  subordination of, 231, 512–13, 515, 559–60
WORK, RIGHT TO, 93, 177, 439, 607–8, 610, 613
WORKERS, 55, 93–4, 439, 444–5, 447, 451, 621, 627
WORKING CONDITIONS, 177, 204, 595–6, 607–9

## Z

ZULU KING, 158n